Fodor's 04

MEXICO

D1509007

Where to Stay and Eat
for All Budgets

Must-See Sights
and Local Secrets

Ratings You Can Trust

Fodor's Travel Publications   New York, Toronto, London, Sydney, Auckland
www.fodors.com

FODOR'S MEXICO 2004

Editors: Laura Kidder, Jennifer Paull

Editorial Contributors: Rob Aikins, Patricia Alisau, Abigail Atha, Paige Bierma, Gary Chandler, Dave Downing, Satu Hummasti, Barbara Kastelein, Denise M. Leto, Maribeth Mellin, Jane Onstott, Mark Sullivan

Editorial Production: Tom Holton

Maps: David Lindroth, *cartographer;* Rebecca Baer and Robert Blake, *map editors*

Design: Fabrizio La Rocca, *creative director;* Guido Caroti, *art director;* Melanie Marin, *senior picture editor*

Production/Manufacturing: Lisa Montebello

Cover Photo (Abandoned amusement park [formerly Magical Mexico], Cancún): Joan Iaconetti

SPECIAL SALES

Fodor's Travel Publications are available at special discounts for bulk purchases for sales promotions or premiums. Special editions, including personalized covers, excerpts of existing guides, and corporate imprints, can be created in large quantities for special needs. For more information, contact your local bookseller or write to Special Markets, Fodor's Travel Publications, 1745 Broadway, New York, NY 10019. Inquiries from Canada should be directed to your local Canadian bookseller or sent to Random House of Canada, Ltd., Marketing Department, 2775 Matheson Boulevard East, Mississauga, Ontario L4W 4P7. Inquiries from the United Kingdom should be sent to Fodor's Travel Publications, 20 Vauxhall Bridge Road, London SW1V 2SA, England.

AN IMPORTANT TIP & AN INVITATION

Although all prices, opening times, and other details in this book are based on information supplied to us at press time, changes occur all the time in the travel world, and Fodor's cannot accept responsibility for facts that become outdated or for inadvertent errors or omissions. So **always confirm information when it matters,** especially if you're making a detour to visit a specific place. Your experiences—positive and negative—matter to us. If we have missed or misstated something, **please write to us.** We follow up on all suggestions. Contact the Mexico editor at editors@fodors.com or c/o Fodor's at 1745 Broadway, New York, New York 10019.

DESTINATION: MEXICO

Climbing a pyramid in the magnificent Maya ruins of Uxmal in the Yucatán. Descending into the formidable cleft of the Barrancas del Cobre. Strolling through the shady plaza of a colonial Heartland town in the heat and torpor of siesta time. Lolling on the beach in glittering Acapulco. Snorkeling in the Caribbean off Quintana Roo. Hitting a classic cantina in the capital. Gawking at the variety of chilies in an Oaxacan market. Any one of these experiences—not to mention dozens of others you may not have dreamed up yet—are quintessentially Mexican. An amazing diversity of cultures, people, and landscapes forms the core of this country's allure. Have a fabulous trip!

Karen Cure, Editorial Director

CONTENTS

Maps

CloseUps

ON THE ROAD WITH FODOR'S

A trip takes you out of yourself. Concerns of life at home completely disappear, driven away by more immediate thoughts—about, say, what new experience you'll have the next day, or where you'll have dinner. That's where Fodor's comes in. We make sure that you know all your options, so that you don't miss something that's around the next bend just because you didn't know it was there. Because the best memories of your trip might well have nothing to do with what you came to Mexico to see, we guide you to sights large and small all over the region. You might set out to hit the beach or climb a Maya pyramid, but back at home you find yourself unable to forget the sight of a gray whale or the sound of a marimba band in a village *zócalo*. With Fodor's at your side, serendipitous discoveries are never far away.

Our success in showing you every corner of Mexico is a credit to our extraordinary writers. Although there's no substitute for travel advice from a good friend who knows your style, our contributors are the next best thing—the kind of people you would poll for travel advice if you knew them.

San Diego-based writer Rob Aikins, who updated the Sonora chapter, developed a love for the people and culture of Mexico while traveling the Baja and Pacific coasts looking for surfing spots. He later complemented those experiences by attending the Universidad Nacional Autónoma de México (UNAM) in Mexico City and conducting research in various parts of the country. He recently filmed a documentary in Northern Baja California. He has been an editorial contributor to Fodor's *San Diego* and *Brazil* titles.

So drawn to the surrealism of Mexico that she turned a one-week vacation into a 20-year sojourn, Patricia Alisau has traveled just about every inch of the country on assignment for Mexican and U.S. journals. She has written for Mexico's *Vogue* magazine and, as a foreign correspondent, for the *New York Times*, the *Chicago Tribune*, and the Associated Press. This year, she updated the Acapulco chapter and sections of the Yucatán Peninsula chapter.

Heartland updater Abigail Atha spent eight years in Mexico, including six years in San Miguel de Allende. She has a degree in journalism and a culinary certificate from the Ritz Escoffier school in Paris, France.

Journalist Paige Bierma, who updated this edition's Smart Travel Tips and Understanding Mexico sections, lived in Mexico City for four years while reporting on Mexican politics and social issues for the Associated Press and various Texas- and California-based newspapers. She's now freelancing in San Francisco, though she left her heart in Mexico City.

Formerly based in San Francisco, journalist and travel writer Gary Chandler relocated to Guadalajara following his assignment there. Gary has also worked on Fodor's guides to Guatemala, El Salvador, and California. Special thanks go to Liza Prado for her help and insight.

Full-time Fodor's staffer Dave Downing left no gravestone unturned in researching El Día de los Muertos for a CloseUp feature. A fan of Mexican culture from siestas to fiestas, Dave has appeared on *The Travel Channel*; his travel articles have been published on the *The New York Times* Web site, among other places.

Barbara Kastelein made her way to Latin America from Holland via Great Britain, under whose gray skies she obtained a doctorate in literary studies. A freelance writer with special interests in travel, environment, and gastronomy, she has been living in Mexico's smoggy and sinful capital for eight years. She enjoys her colorful country of choice with her partner and two children, who can pronounce words like Popocatépetl and Tenochtitlán without a second thought. For this edition, Barbara updated the Mexico City chapter as well as parts of the Side Trips from Mexico City and Veracruz and the Northeast chapters.

Recipient of the prestigious Pluma de Plata award for writing on Mexico, Maribeth Mellin lives in San Diego near the Tijuana border in a home filled with folk art and photos from Latin America—including a snapshot of the 140-pound marlin she caught in the Sea of Cortez. She has authored travel books on Mexico, Costa Rica, Argentina, and Peru and is currently creating a fictional account of her adventures. Maribeth updated this year's Baja California chapter and half of the Yucatán Peninsula chapter.

Since earning a B.A. in Spanish language and literature, Jane Onstott has lived and traveled extensively in Latin America. She worked as director of communications and information for the Darwin Research Station in the Galapagos Islands, and studied painting in Oaxaca between 1995 and 1998. Since 1986 Jane has contributed to Fodor's guides to Mexico and South America; this year, she updated the Barrancas del Cobre, Pacific Coast Resorts, Oaxaca, and Chiapas and Tabasco chapters.

Losing his rent-controlled apartment in New York City convinced Mark Sullivan to hit the road. Over the course of six months he took more than 150 buses to travel from the Mexican border town of Nuevo Laredo to Panama. Along the way he contributed to the Side Trips from Mexico City and Veracruz and the Northeast chapters. In his past life as a Fodor's editor he oversaw the *South America, Central America,* and *UpClose Central America* guides.

ABOUT THIS BOOK

There's no doubt that the best source for travel advice is a like-minded friend who's just been where you're headed. But with or without that friend, you'll have a better trip with a Fodor's guide in hand. Once you've learned to find your way around its pages, you'll be in great shape to find your way around your destination.

SELECTION
Our goal is to cover the best properties, sights, and activities in all price ranges. In our dining sections, we make a point of including local food-lovers' hot spots as well as neighborhood options. You can go on the assumption that everything you read about in this book is recommended wholeheartedly by our writers and editors. Flip to On the Road with Fodor's to learn more about who they are. It goes without saying that no property mentioned in the book has paid to be included.

RATINGS
Orange stars ★ denote sights and properties that our editors and writers consider the very best in the area covered by the entire book. These, the best of the best, are listed in the Fodor's Choice section in the front of the book. Black stars ★ highlight the sights and properties we deem Highly Recommended, the don't-miss sights within any region. Fodor's Choice and Highly Recommended options in each region are usually listed on the title page of the chapter covering that region. Use the index to find complete descriptions. In cities, sights pinpointed with numbered map bullets ❶ in the margins tend to be more important than those without bullets.

SPECIAL SPOTS
Pleasures & Pastimes focuses on types of experiences that reveal the spirit of the destination. Watch for Off the Beaten Path sights. Some are out of the way, some are quirky, and all are worth your while. If the munchies hit while you're exploring, look for Need a Break? suggestions.

TIME IT RIGHT
Wondering when to go? Check On the Calendar up front and chapters' Timing sections for weather and crowd overviews and best days and times to visit.

SEE IT ALL
Use Fodor's exclusive Great Itineraries as a model for your trip. (For a good overview of the entire destination, follow those that begin the book, or mix regional itineraries from several chapters.) In cities, Good Walks guide you to important sights in each neighborhood; ► indicates the starting points of walks and itineraries in the text and on the map.

BUDGET WELL
Hotel and restaurant price categories from ¢ to $$$$ are defined in the opening pages of each chapter—expect to find a balanced selection for every budget. For attractions, we always give standard adult admission fees; reductions are usually available for children, students, and senior citizens. Look in Discounts & Deals in Smart Travel Tips for information on destination-wide ticket schemes.

BASIC INFO
Smart Travel Tips lists travel essentials for the entire area covered by the book; city- and region-specific basics end each chapter. We assume you'll check Web sites or call for particulars.

ON THE MAPS
Maps throughout the book show you what's where and help you find your way around. Black and orange numbered bullets ❶ ① in the text correlate to bullets on maps.

BACKGROUND	In general, we give background information within the chapters in the course of explaining sights as well as in CloseUp boxes and in Understanding Mexico at the end of the book. To get in the mood, review the suggestions in Books & Movies. The glossary can be invaluable.
FIND IT FAST	The chapters in this book begin with Mexico City, then shift up to Baja California and work south to the Yucatán Peninsula. All city chapters begin with exploring information, with a section for each neighborhood (each recommending a good tour and listing sights alphabetically). All regional chapters are divided into small areas, within which towns are covered in logical geographical order; attractive routes and interesting places between towns are flagged as En Route. Heads at the top of each page help you find what you need within a chapter.
DON'T FORGET	Restaurants are open for lunch and dinner daily unless we state otherwise; we mention dress only when there's a specific requirement and reservations only when they're essential or not accepted—it's always best to book ahead. Hotels have private baths, phone, TVs, and air-conditioning and operate on the European Plan (a.k.a. EP, meaning without meals) unless otherwise noted. We always list facilities but not whether you'll be charged extra to use them, so when pricing accommodations, find out what's included.
SYMBOLS	

Many Listings

- ★ Fodor's Choice
- ★ Highly recommended
- ⊠ Physical address
- ✛ Directions
- 🕮 Mailing address
- ☎ Telephone
- 🖶 Fax
- ⊕ On the Web
- 🖎 E-mail
- 💳 Admission fee
- 🕓 Open/closed times
- ► Start of walk/itinerary
- Ⓜ Metro stations
- ▭ Credit cards
- ⛟ Ruins

Outdoors

- 🏌 Golf
- ⛺ Camping

Hotels & Restaurants

- 🏨 Hotel
- 🛏 Number of rooms
- ☖ Facilities
- ⏍ Meal plans
- ✕ Restaurant
- ☖ Reservations
- 🏛 Dress code
- ⤩ Smoking
- ⌗ BYOB
- ✕🏨 Hotel with restaurant that warrants a visit

Other

- ☺ Family-friendly
- 🛈 Contact information
- ⇨ See also
- ⊠ Branch address
- ☞ Take note

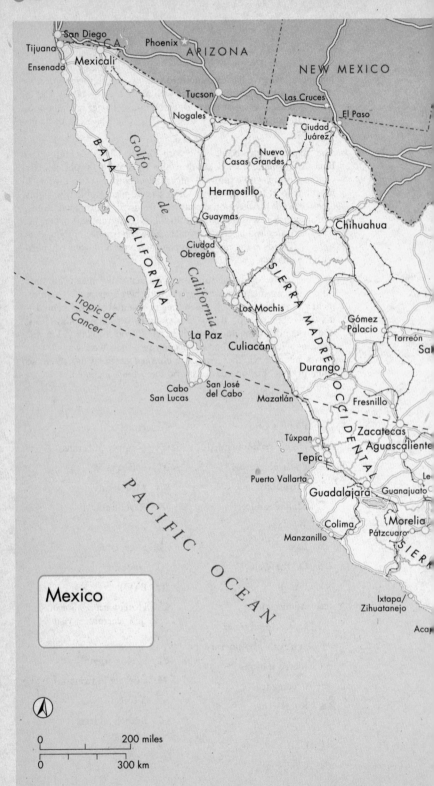

San Diego
Tijuana
Ensenada
Mexicali
CA
Phoenix
ARIZONA
NEW MEXICO
Tucson
Nogales
Las Cruces
El Paso
Ciudad
Juárez
Nuevo
Casas Grandes
BAJA
Golfo
de
CALIFORNIA
Hermosillo
Guaymas
Chihuahua
Ciudad
Obregón
CALIFORNIA
California
SIERRA
MADRE
Los Mochis
Tropic of
Cancer
La Paz
Culiacán
Gómez
Palacio
Torreón
Sa
Durango
OCCIDENTAL
Cabo
San Lucas
San José
del Cabo
Mazatlán
Fresnillo
Zacatecas
Aguascaliente
Túxpan
Tepic
Le
Puerto Vallarta
Guadalajara
Guanajuato
PACIFIC
Colima
Manzanillo
Morelia
Pátzcuaro
SIER

Mexico

Ixtapa/
Zihuatanejo
Aca

OCEAN

0   200 miles
0   300 km

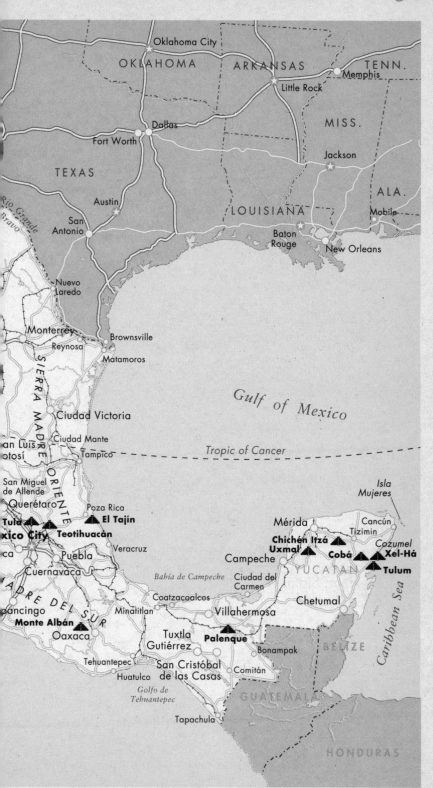

CALIFORNIA
Mexicali ★

Phoenix
ARIZONA   NEW MEXICO

BAJA
CALIFORNIA
Hermosillo ★
SONORA   CHIHUAHUA
Golfo de California
Chihuahua ★
BAJA
CALIFORNIA
SUR   COAHUIL

Tropic of
Cancer   SINALOA

La Paz ★   Culiacán ★   DURANGO   Saltille

Durango ★
ZACATECAS

Zacatecas ★

AGUASCALIENTES
Tepic ★
NAYARIT   Aguascalientes ★
Guanajuato ★
Guadalajara ★   GUANAJUATO
JALISCO

PACIFIC

Colima ★   Morelia ★   ME
COLIMA   MICHOACAN

GUERRERO

OCEAN

Mexican States
& Capitals

0   200 miles
0   300 km

WHAT'S WHERE

The geographical organization of the following paragraphs mirrors the organization of the book. Beginning with Mexico City, coverage then moves up to Baja California and works south to the Yucatán Peninsula.

(1) Mexico City

Two volcanoes and a pyramid complex flank Mexico's capital, once the center of Aztec civilization and now the country's cosmopolitan business, art, and culinary hub. From the Alameda, a leafy center of activity since Aztec times, to the Zona Rosa, a chic shopping neighborhood, and the marvelous Bosque de Chapultepec, with its many museums, gardens, and walking paths, Mexico City offers endless options for exploration.

(3) Baja California

Lively border traffic colors the culture of the upper reaches of the Baja California peninsula, where seaside towns absorb floods of weekenders. But you can't say you've really experienced the 1,000-mi-plus finger of land until you head south, off the beaten path. Boulder-strewn deserts, soaring mountain peaks, fishing villages, and pristine beaches can be found between the busy northern border and the highly developed Los Cabos resort at the southernmost tip.

(4) Sonora

Imagine Arizona a hundred years ago, when cowboys drove cattle across wide-open ranch land. Then add a coastline—a fringe of beach washed by a turquoise sea—and you've conjured up Sonora, Mexico's northernmost state. The sea may lure you for swimming, kayaking, and snorkeling, but the foothills of the Sierra Madre hold their own treasures, such as colonial Alamos, once a silver-mining center, and a sprinkling of adobe missions.

(5) Las Barrancas del Cobre

Some of the gorges in the Barrancas del Cobre system are deeper than the Grand Canyon in the United States. These canyons are home to the Tarahumara Indians, who are renowned for their running ability. You won't have to endure a marathon to enjoy the local trails though—you can set out for a short stroll or a daylong descent to the canyon floor. A train trip through this magnificent, largely uncharted region usually begins or ends in Chihuahua, a lively midsize city with a museum devoted to Pancho Villa.

(6) Guadalajara

Mexico's second-largest metropolis fully lives up to its reputation for being *señorial y moderna* (lordly and modern). The city retains a generous measure of colonial charm thanks to the landmarks of its historic center. Strolling through the quarter's squares, you'll likely encounter sombrero-topped bands of mariachis. Some of the country's best arts and crafts can be found at Tlaquepaque, on the city's outskirts, and Tonalá, about 10 minutes farther away. And at Tequila you can drink at the source of Mexico's famous firewater.

(7) The Heartland

Rich with the history of Mexico's revolution, the heartland is a treasury of colonial towns—Guanajuato, Zacatecas, Querétaro, Morelia, and Pátzcuaro, among others—whose residents lead quiet, largely traditional lives. Even in San Miguel de Allende, an expatriate art colony and home to a well-known language institute, women wash their clothes and gossip at the local *lavandaría* as they have for hundreds of years.

8 Pacific Coast Resorts

People call it the Mexican Riviera and Gold Coast, but the most apt way to refer to this jungle-backed coastline might be Tropical Paradise. Sun worshippers, water-sports lovers, cruise ships, and anglers all converge on the cove-scalloped Pacific coast. Ixtapa/Zihuatanejo is a two-for-one attraction, a laid-back fishing village adjoining a glitzy resort.

9 Acapulco

The beaches and nightlife of Acapulco have proved their staying power; for decades vacationers have planned their days around lying on their beach towels or hammocks and their nights around the buzzing restaurants and dance clubs. The cobblestone streets of nearby Taxco, the silver city, are lined with master jewelers.

10 Oaxaca

The prime appeal of Oaxaca state and its eponymous colonial capital is the old and the older. Baroque buildings from the Spanish conquest pass almost for new when compared with the magnificent, millennia-old remnants of the native Zapotec and Mixtec civilizations. Though less exotic than Oaxaca City, the state's coastal developments of Puerto Escondido and Bahías de Huatulco are beloved by surfers and beach bums.

11 Chiapas & Tabasco

The state of Chiapas has always been off the beaten path, best known for the colonial town of San Cristóbal and the jungle-covered ruins of the exquisite Maya city of Palenque, arguably the most fascinating ancient site in Mexico. If you're thinking of just passing through on the way to Guatemala, you might find that the region has plenty to make you linger.

12 Veracruz & the Northeast

Many Texans get their first taste of Mexico in the northeastern border towns of Nuevo Laredo, Reynosa, and Matamoros. Texan or otherwise, if you venture farther down to Monterrey, you'll find far more sophisticated dining, shopping, and cultural attractions of the country's third-largest city. The superb but little-explored pyramids of El Tajín and the raffish charm of Veracruz, the first European city established on the North American mainland, are among the many reasons to continue south.

13 The Yucatán Peninsula

Mexico's most-visited region will reward you with both spectacular beaches and evocative ruins—sometimes simultaneously, as at Tulum. After being mesmerized by the grace and power of sites such as Chichén Itzá and Uxmal, allow yourself to be taken in by the irresistible mix of sun, sand, and sea. Cancún was purpose-built for pleasure, while Isla Mujeres provides a more peaceful retreat. The world's second-largest barrier reef lies just off the island of Cozumel. Meanwhile, the coastline south of Cancún has been dubbed the Riviera Maya as an increasing number of luxe resorts stake their claim.

GREAT ITINERARIES

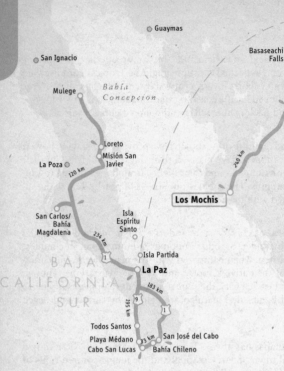

Canyons & Coasts
8 to 12 days

Natural wonders never cease in northern and western Mexico. From the heart-stopping views and hikes into the Barrancas del Cobre to Baja Sur's inland deserts, its annual migrations of whales, and the beaches of Los Cabos, opportunities for adventure and relaxation are everywhere.

Las Barrancas del Cobre *3 to 4 days.* Riding the Chihuahua al Pacífico rail line from west to east affords the most stunning views of the canyons. Start off in Los Mochis and make the mountain village of Cerocahui your first stop. From here, views of La Barranca de Urique are superb. Farther on, the 806-ft Basaseachi waterfalls are one of North America's highest cascades. If a dose of urban life feels like the appropriate tonic after taking in the canyons, spend the night in Chihuahua before catching a plane for La Paz.

La Paz *1 to 2 days.* Begin with a kayaking, snorkeling, or diving trip to Isla Espíritu Santo or Isla Partida in the Mar de Cortés—you're almost guaranteed to spot sea lions and whales. Spend the rest of the day in town; as sunset nears, head for the seaside malecón where couples and families stroll beside playgrounds on the sand. If you're here in the winter, join a tour to Bahía Magdalena, where migrating gray whales give birth.

Loreto *1 to 2 days.* Visitors to Loreto are largely intent on fishing in the rich waters off nearby islands, and even nonanglers enjoy a boat ride at dawn. Loreto's laid-back hotels are also the perfect base for exploring the nearby mountains and coast. Drive about two hours past cattle ranches and boulder-strewn hills to the well-preserved Misión San Javier, or drive a couple of hours north to the incomparably picturesque Bahía Concepción and the town of Mulegé, in an oasis by the sea.

Los Cabos *3 to 4 days.* Spend your first day in Los Cabos fishing for marlin or swimming and sunbathing at Playa Médano. Sample Cabo San Lucas's theme restaurants and trendy cafés that night. Begin Day 2 with breakfast at one of the Corridor's lavish resorts and snorkeling at Bahía Chileno. Stroll through San José del Cabo's plazas and galleries in the evening, and end the day dining on fresh fish. Spend the rest of your days exploring Baja's incomparable desert and sea scenery: head for the artsy enclave of Todos Santos, or to the East Cape for long drives on sandy desert roads beside the sea.

BY PUBLIC TRANSPORTATION
Distances here demand a fair amount of air travel: first from Mexico City to Los Mochis, then from Chihuahua to La Paz—which flies you over the canyons. The entire rail trip from Los Mochis to Chihuahua is a 15-hour proposition, but it's best to stop at towns along the way and reboard later in the day or the next day, or even the next. From La Paz, tour companies will take you to Bahía Magdalena to see whales. To get to Loreto (3 hours north of La Paz), the East Cape (1 hour south), and Los Cabos (2 hours south), rent a car so you can explore the quieter coastal stretches on your own. Buses also run throughout Baja Sur.

Colonial Mexico
7 to 10 days

Remarkably well preserved, these colonial cities are full of atmospheric haciendas and richly decorated cathedrals—along with intriguing juxtapositions of the colonial and the indigenous that are classic Mexico.

Querétaro *1 day.* This Heartland city has been called the cradle of independence. Its restored Plaza de la Independencia is filled with grand mansions once belonging to titled friends of the Crown. Amble around the square and nearby streets to see the Baroque Museo de Arte de Querétaro, housed in an 18th-century monastery; the Palacio del Gobierno del Estado; and the Jardín de la Corregidora.

San Miguel de Allende *1 to 2 days.* A cultural hub of the region, this friendly city is full of bookstores, art galleries, coffee shops, and American expats. Take time to visit some of the churches—the Gothic Revival Parroquia, the churrigueresque Iglesia de San Francisco, and the unique Oratorio de San Felipe Neri. Consider a side trip to the historic village of Dolores Hidalgo, home of the insurgent priest whose cry for independence started the 1810 war.

Guanajuato *2 to 3 days.* Splendid buildings rising above labyrinthine streets give Guanajuato its medieval appearance. Make your way to the main square and the impressive Teatro Juárez. El Museo Casa Diego Rivera, birthplace of the famed muralist, and the hulking Alhóndiga de Granaditas fortress are nearby. On Day 2, visit the Basílica Colegiata de Nuestra Señora de Guanajuato and La Valenciana—the former for its 8th-century statue of the Virgin, the latter for its elaborately carved pink facade and gilded altars.

San Cristóbal de las Casas *1 to 2 days.* San Cristóbal is a walking city, and on foot you encounter the same mix of colonial and indigenous cultures—from the iconic ocher-color cathedral to the mercado municipal bustling with Lacandon Maya merchants—that exists between the city and the surrounding Indian villages.

Mérida *2 days.* No city in Mexico has anything like Mérida's quirky self-confidence and cosmopolitan flair. At the same time the jaunty metropolis is just as Maya as San Cristóbal. Urbane streets like Paseo Montejo are offset by the chilies-to-crafts mercado. And the cathedral, built with stone from a Maya temple, contains a dark-skin Christ that was meant to reconcile people of Maya and Spanish descent. Mérida, the Yucatán's largest city, is at heart a typical Yucatecan town.

BY PUBLIC TRANSPORTATION

The easiest way to get to and between Querétaro, San Miguel de Allende, and Guanajuato is by luxury bus. From Mexico City the bus from the Observatorio or Northern bus terminals to Querétaro takes about 2 hours. From Querétaro it's another 2 hours to San Miguel. San Miguel to Guanajuato is a 2½-hour ride. Nearby León's airport has flights to Mexico City (1 hour), from which you can fly to Tuxtla Gutiérrez (2 hours), an hour west of San Cristóbal by bus. Then fly out of Tuxtla straight to Mérida (1 hour).

The Lost Cities of Ancient Mexico
9 to 11 days

Inhabited by numerous cultures in pre-Columbian days, Mexico has one of the world's most impressive collections of archaeological sites. The monumental Maya cities are at their finest on the Yucatán Peninsula and in jungly Tabasco and mountainous Chiapas.

Teotihuacán *1 day.* For the 14th- to 16th-century Aztecs, this was the birthplace of the gods. At its 8th-century peak Teotihuacán hummed with as many as 250,000 people, its massive, spellbinding pyramids symbolizing the ordered lives of people in the ancient Valley of Mexico. Just an hour outside of Mexico City by bus, these ruins are an essential first stop.

Villahermosa *2 to 3 days.* Villahermosa is roughly at the midpoint between ancient culture and modern develop-

ment. Head for the Parque Museo La Venta, with its enormous Olmec stone heads, for an in-depth look at a culture that preceded the Maya by several centuries. Later in the day, swing north out of town to Comalcalco, a Maya site with the only known brick temples in the Maya world. Save the best for last and make your way to Chiapas to see Palenque; its classicism is akin to that of Greek architecture.

Mérida *6 or 7 days.* A capital city of the Yucatán and the most Maya of all Yucatecan cities, Mérida is a perfect base for seeing the region's ruins. Take in the Museum of Anthropology to preview Maya art, and walk around the lively main square to view

its colonial mansions, cathedral, small churches, and shady plazas. On your second day, head to Chichén Itzá, an extensive site built by two different Maya empires. Spend all of Day 3 at beautiful Uxmal, the sterling example of the graceful Puuc architectural style. If time permits, you can spend a day at the smaller Puuc ruins of Kabah, Sayil, and Labná. Consider planning your trip around a local Maya festival to see the intriguing blend of pre-Hispanic beliefs and Catholic rituals.

BY PUBLIC TRANSPORTATION

In Villahermosa you can take a cab to the Parque Museo La Venta but you need to book an excursion to Comalcalco. Buses are unreliable. To get to Palenque you can catch a luxury bus from the ADO terminal; the trip takes about 2½ hours. There are also full-day excursions to Palenque from Villahermosa. From Tuxtla Gutiérrez there is a 1-hour flight to Mérida. You can take day trips to the major Yucatán sites from Mérida. Second-class buses do run to Chichén Itzá and Uxmal from Mérida's main bus terminal, but they have no air-conditioning and are a bit uncomfortable.

°C		°F
100		212
40		105
37		98.6
30		90
25		80
20		70
15		60
10		50
5		40
0		32
−5		20
−10		
−15		10
−20		0

Mexico is sufficiently large and geographically diverse enough that you can find a place to visit any time of year. October through May are generally the driest months; during the peak of the rainy season (June–September), it may rain for a few hours daily. But the sun often shines for the rest of the day, and the reduced off-season rates may well compensate for the reduced tanning time.

From December through the second week after Easter, the resorts—where most people go—are the most crowded and expensive. This also holds true for July and August, school-vacation months, when Mexican families fill hotels. To avoid the masses, the highest prices, and the worst rains, consider visiting Mexico during October, November, April, or May, just not during the traditional holiday periods. Rates at beach resorts can drop as much as 30% in the shoulder season, 50% in the off-season.

Mexicans travel during traditional holiday periods—Christmas through January 6, Three Kings Day, *Semana Santa* (Holy Week, the week before Easter), the week after Easter—and summertime school vacations as well as over extended national holiday weekends, called *puentes* (bridges). Festivals play a big role in Mexican national life. If you plan to travel during a major national event, reserve both lodgings and transportation well in advance.

Climate

Mexico's coasts and low-lying sections of the interior are often very hot if not actually tropical, with temperatures ranging from 17°C to 31°C (63°F to 88°F) in winter and well above 32°C (90°F) in summer. A more temperate area ranging from 16°C to 21°C (60°F to 70°F) is found at altitudes of 4,000 ft–6,000 ft. In general, the high central plateau on which Mexico City, Guadalajara, and many of the country's colonial cities are is springlike year-round.

⚑ Forecasts **Weather Channel Connection** ☎ 900/932–8437, 95¢ per minute from a Touch-Tone phone ⊕ www.weather.com.

ACAPULCO (PACIFIC COAST)

Jan.	88F	31C	May	90F	32C	Sept.	90F	32C
	72	22		75	24		75	24
Feb.	88F	31C	June	90F	32C	Oct.	90F	32C
	72	22		77	25		75	24
Mar.	88F	31C	July	90F	32C	Nov.	90F	32C
	72	22		77	25		73	23
Apr.	90F	32C	Aug.	91F	33C	Dec.	88F	31C
	73	23		77	25		71	22

COZUMEL (CARIBBEAN COAST)

Jan.	84F	29C	May	91F	33C	Sept.	89F	32C
	66	19		73	23		75	24
Feb.	84F	29C	June	89F	32C	Oct.	87F	31C
	66	19		75	24		73	23
Mar.	88F	31C	July	91F	33C	Nov.	86F	30C
	69	21		73	23		71	22
Apr.	89F	32C	Aug.	91F	33C	Dec.	84F	29C
	71	22		73	23		68	20

ENSENADA (BAJA CALIFORNIA NORTE)

Jan.	66F	19C	May	70F	21C	Sept.	79F	26C
	45	7		52	11		59	15
Feb.	68F	20C	June	73F	23C	Oct.	75F	24C
	45	7		54	12		54	12
Mar.	68F	20C	July	77F	25C	Nov.	72F	22C
	46	8		61	16		48	9
Apr.	69F	21C	Aug.	79F	26C	Dec.	68F	20C
	48	9		61	16		45	7

LA PAZ (BAJA CALIFORNIA SUR)

Jan.	73F	23C	May	91F	33C	Sept.	95F	35C
	54	12		59	15		73	23
Feb.	77F	25C	June	95F	35C	Oct.	91F	33C
	54	12		64	18		66	19
Mar.	80F	27C	July	97F	36C	Nov.	84F	29C
	54	12		71	22		61	16
Apr.	86F	30C	Aug.	97F	36C	Dec.	77F	25C
	55	13		73	23		54	12

MEXICO CITY (CENTRAL MEXICO)

Jan.	70F	21C	May	79F	26C	Sept.	72F	22C
	44	6		54	12		52	11
Feb.	73F	23C	June	77F	25C	Oct.	72F	22C
	45	7		54	12		50	10
Mar.	79F	26C	July	73F	23C	Nov.	72F	22C
	48	9		52	11		46	8
Apr.	81F	27C	Aug.	73F	23C	Dec.	70F	21C
	50	10		54	12		45	7

MONTERREY (NORTHEAST MEXICO)

Jan.	68F	20C	May	88F	31C	Sept.	88F	31C
	48	9		68	20		70	21
Feb.	73F	23C	June	91F	33C	Oct.	81F	27C
	52	11		72	22		63	17
Mar.	79F	26C	July	91F	34C	Nov.	73F	23C
	57	14		72	22		55	13
Apr.	86F	30C	Aug.	93F	34C	Dec.	70F	21C
	64	18		72	22		50	10

SAN MIGUEL DE ALLENDE (HEARTLAND)

Jan.	75F	24C	May	88F	31C	Sept.	79F	26C
	45	9		59	15		59	15
Feb.	79F	26C	June	88F	30C	Oct.	79F	26C
	48	9		59	15		54	12
Mar.	86F	30C	July	82F	28C	Nov.	75F	24C
	54	12		59	15		50	10
Apr.	88F	31C	Aug.	82F	28C	Dec.	75F	24C
	57	14		59	15		46	8

ON THE CALENDAR

Mexico is the land of festivals; if you reserve lodging well in advance, they're a golden opportunity to experience Mexico's culture. January is full of long, regional festivals. Notable are the Fiesta de la Inmaculada Concepción (Feast of the Immaculate Conception), which transforms the city of Morelia into a sea of lights and flowers for much of the month, and a series of folkloric dances in Chiapa de Corzo, Chiapas, that culminates in the Fiesta de San Sebastian, the third week in January.

Several cultural events take place at different times each year. Among these is Cancún's noteworthy Jazz Festival, which happens in the spring or fall and which draws a huge international crowd from the United States, South America, and Europe. The Isla Mujeres International Music Festival, during which the island fills with music and dancers from around the world, is another such event.

WINTER

Dec.	On the 12th, the Feast Day of the Virgin of Guadalupe, Mexico's patron saint is honored with processions and native folk dances, particularly at her shrine in Mexico City. In Puerto Vallarta, 12 days of processions and festivities lead up to the night of the 12th. Christmas and the days leading up to it (roughly the 16th through the 25th) see candlelight processions, holiday parties, and the breaking open of piñatas. Mexico City is brightly decorated, but don't expect any snow.
Dec. 23	The Night of the Radishes, a pre-Christmas tradition in Oaxaca, is one of the most colorful in Mexico: participants carve giant radishes into amusing shapes and display them in the city's main plaza.
Jan. 1	New Year's Day is a major celebration throughout the country. Agricultural and livestock fairs are held in the provinces.
Jan. 6	On the Feast of Epiphany the Three Kings bring gifts to Mexican children.
Jan. 17	The Feast of San Antonio Abad honors animals all over Mexico. Pets and livestock are decked out with flowers and ribbons and taken to church for a blessing.
Jan. 18	Taxco's patron saints are celebrated with the Feast of Santa Prisca and San Sebastián, including music and fireworks.
Feb.–Mar.	Día de la Candelaria, or Candlemas Day, means fiestas, parades, bullfights, and lantern-decorated streets. Festivities include a running of the bulls through the streets of Tlacotalpan, Veracruz. The pre-Lenten Carnaval season is celebrated throughout Mexico—most notably in Mazatlán and Veracruz, with parades of floats and bands.

SPRING

Mar. 21	Benito Juárez's Birthday, a national holiday, is most popular in Guelatao, Oaxaca, birthplace of the beloved 19th-century president of Mexico. This is also the day that Cuernavaca's Fiesta de la Primavera marks the beginning of spring.

Apr.	Semana Santa (Holy Week), the week leading to Easter Sunday (April 11), is observed with parades and passion plays.
Apr.–May	San Marcos National Fair, held in Aguascalientes, is one of the country's best fairs. It features Indian *matachnes* (dances performed by grotesque figures), mariachi bands, and bullfights. The 10-day Festival de las Artes (Arts Festival) brings music, theater, and dance troupes from all over Latin America to San Luis Potosí.
May	The first day of May is Labor Day, and workers parade through the streets.
May 5	Cinco de Mayo marks, with great fanfare countrywide, the anniversary of the French defeat by Mexican troops in Puebla in 1862.
May 15	The Feast of San Isidro Labrador is noted nationwide by the blessing of new seeds and animals. In Cuernavaca, a parade of oxen wreathed in flowers is followed by street parties and feasting.
SUMMER	
June 1	Navy Day is commemorated in all Mexican seaports and is especially colorful in Acapulco, Mazatlán, and Veracruz.
June 10	The Feast of Corpus Christi is celebrated in different ways. In Mexico City, children are dressed in native costumes and taken to the cathedral on the zócalo for a blessing. In Papantla, Veracruz, the Dance of the Flying Birdmen—a pre-Hispanic ritual to the sun—is held throughout the day.
June 24	On Saint John the Baptist Day, a popular national holiday, many Mexicans observe a tradition of tossing a "blessing" of water on most anyone within reach.
July	The Feria Nacional (National Fair) in Durango runs from the Day of Our Lady of Refuge (July 4) to the anniversary of the founding of Durango in 1563 (July 22). The old-time agricultural fair has become known across the country for its carnival rides, livestock shows, and music. The Guelaguetza Dance Festival, a pre-Columbian Oaxacan affair, usually falls on the first and third Monday of July. The Feast of Santiago in late July features *charreadas,* Mexican-style rodeos.
July 16	Our Lady of Mt. Carmel Day is celebrated with fairs, bullfights, fireworks, even a major fishing tournament.
Aug.	The Feast of St. Augustine brings a month of music, dance, and fireworks to Puebla. On the 26th (feast day) it's customary to prepare the famous *chiles en nogada.*
Aug. 15	Feast of the Assumption of the Blessed Virgin Mary is celebrated nationwide with religious processions. In Huamantla, Tlaxcala, the festivities include a running of the bulls and a carpet of flowers laid out in front of the church.
Aug. 25	The San Luis Potosí Patron Saint Fiesta honors the town patron, San Luis Rey, with traditional dance, music, and foods.

FALL	
Sept. 16	Independence Day (often celebrated for *two* days on the 15th and 16th) is marked throughout Mexico with fireworks and parties that outblast those on New Year's Eve. The biggest celebrations are in Mexico City.
Sept. 29	San Miguel Day honors St. Michael, the patron saint of all towns with San Miguel in their names—especially San Miguel de Allende—with bullfights, folk dances, concerts, and fireworks.
Oct.	October Festival means a month of cultural and sporting events in Guadalajara.
Oct. 4	The Feast of St. Francis of Assisi is a day for processions dedicated to St. Francis in parts of the country.
Oct. 12	The Día de la Raza (Day of the Race) is comparable to Columbus Day in the United States.
Oct.–Nov.	International Cervantes Festival in Guanajuato is a top cultural event that attracts dancers, singers, and actors from various countries.
Nov.	On All Souls' and All Saints' Days (November 1 and 2) Day of the Dead celebrations throughout the country reach their peak. Families welcome back the spirits of departed relatives to elaborate altars and refurbished grave sites. On the Monday following the Day of the Dead celebrations, the entire town of Taxco takes off to a nearby hill for the Fiesta de los Jumil. The *jumil* is a crawling insect, said to taste strongly of iodine, that's considered a great delicacy. Purists eat them alive; others prefer them stewed, fried, or combined with chili in a hot sauce.
Nov. 20	The Anniversary of the Mexican Revolution is a national holiday.
Nov.–Dec.	National Silver Fair, an annual Taxco event, is an occasion for even more silver selling than usual, the crowning of a Silver Queen, and jewelry and silver exhibitions.

PLEASURES & PASTIMES

Ancient Ruins Amateur archaeologists will find heaven in Mexico, where some of the greatest ancient civilizations—among them the Aztecs, the Olmecs, and the Maya—left their mark. Important discoveries in the past few years, such as those at Teotihuacán, have stoked the buzz of inquiry and speculation about these societies. Pick your period and your preference, whether for well-excavated sites or overgrown, out-of-the-way ruins barely touched by a scholar's shovel. The Yucatán is, hands down, the greatest source of ancient treasure, with such heavy hitters as Chichén Itzá and Uxmal, but you're unlikely to find any region in the country that doesn't have some interesting vestige of Mexico's pre-Columbian past. A visit to Mexico City's archaeological museum, one of the best in the world, could ignite the imagination of even those who thought they had no interest in antiquity, and help others focus on the places they'd most like to explore further.

Arts & Crafts Mexico is one of the best countries in the world to purchase *artesanías* (handicrafts), and many items are exempt from duty. Each region has a specialty, be it brightly colored textiles, expressive carved masks, or delicately wrought jewelry. There's an undeniable amount of inferior work for sale, but if you take the time to shop carefully and seek out legitimate artists, you can find exceptional, genuine works of folk art. *See* "Hecho a Mano" in Chapter 7 for more information. The folk art collections you'll find in many cities, including Morelia, San Cristóbal de las Casas, Puebla, and Zacatecas as well as the capital, can give you a deeper appreciation of the traditional forms.

The contemporary art scene is another hot spot on the cultural map. A wave of young experimental artists has drawn much international attention; they've propelled recent Mexican art exhibits in museums from New York to San Diego. To see the latest work at the source, check out the galleries in Mexico City or tap one of the country's impressive modern art museums, such as the Museo de Arte Contemporaneo in Monterrey.

Beaches A curve of golden sand may well be the first image that pops into your mind when you think of Mexico; the country's beaches are the lure for thousands upon thousands of travelers. Generally speaking, the Pacific is rougher and the waters less clear than the Caribbean, which is a better choice for snorkeling and scuba diving. Cancún, Cozumel, and Isla Mujeres, as well as what has come to be called the Riviera Maya, are among the best and most popular beach destinations on the Caribbean coast. All beach resorts offer a variety of water sports, including waterskiing, windsurfing, parasailing, and, if the water is clear enough, snorkeling and scuba diving. Surfers favor the beaches south of Rosarito, around Ensenada, and at Puerto Escondido, near Huatulco.

If you want to get in the water, do a little investigating before you plan your trip; the water in some areas is polluted, a side effect of fast, intense development. The Acapulco waters, though much improved by a cleanup effort, are still somewhat polluted. Tests done in 2002 showed that Zihuatanejo's bay was polluted as well, spurring local cleanup and conservation efforts.

Bullfighting

An import of the Spanish conquistadors, bullfighting was refined and popularized over the centuries, until every major city and most small towns had a bullring or some semblance of an arena. As in Spain, the last few decades have seen some decline of the popularity of the sport in Mexico, where it has been superseded by such modern games as soccer and has been the object of negative publicity by animal-rights activists. It remains a strong part of the Latin American culture, however, and can be thrilling to watch when performed by a skilled toreador. Ask at your hotel about arenas and schedules. Most fights are held on Sunday afternoon, and the most prestigious toreadors perform during the fall season.

Horseback Riding

The dry ranch lands of northern Mexico have countless stables and dude ranches, as do San Miguel de Allende and Querétaro in the heartland. Horses can be rented by the hour at most beaches, and horseback expeditions can be arranged to the Barrancas del Cobre in Chihuahua and the forest near San Cristóbal, Chiapas.

Music

From *norteño* to *mariachi* to *banda,* Mexico's varieties of music have at their core expressive power and verve that make their popularity instantly understandable.

Banda rose to fame in the 1990s. Brass bands small and large arrange tunes from other styles, including ranchera and cumbia. Among its premier practitioners is Banda del Recodo.

Cumbia has its roots in Colombia, where it is also a favorite. Immensely danceable, cumbia was *the* craze before banda came along.

Danzón is a European-influenced style, accompanying dignified dancing, that came originally to Veracruz from Cuba. The style's popularity there has waned, but not so in Mexico. The music has a special tie to Veracruz city, where people still dance to it in parks in the evenings.

Mariachi might seem to be Mexico's signature musical style, even though it is just one of many. It originated in the state of Jalisco, by some accounts at a garden party that dictator Porfirio Díaz threw for Americans in 1907. Mariachi bands play in plazas countrywide, their signature brass sounds backed up with guitars, most noticeably the huge, shoulder-strapped acoustic basses.

Nortec is an example of how traditional music forms are being used in a cutting-edge music scene; samples of *norteño* are mixed with electronica dance beats.

Norteño, characteristically sung without passion, is known for lyrics that pull no punches when it comes to the tragedies of life. It comes from northern Mexico—border country. Accordions are usually a part of norteño bands.

Ranchero is as passionate as Mexican music gets. Ranchero ("country") is often compared to American country music; its powerfully direct, relatively simple style was traditionally linked to the working class.

Modern Postcard 800/ 959-8365

Regional Cuisine

Mexico's food is as diverse and abundant as its geography. Distinct regional specialties typify each of the republic's 32 states and even the different provinces within the states. Fresh ingredients are bountiful, recipes are passed down through generations, and preparation requires much patience and loving care. (Mexican gastronomes are dismayed by foreigners' glaring misconceptions of Mexican food as essentially tacos, enchiladas, and burritos; they are bewildered by Tex-Mex and appalled by Taco Bell.)

The staples of rice, beans, chilies, and tortillas on which the poor subsist form the basis for creative variations of sophisticated national dishes but are by no means the only ingredients commonly used. As Mexican cooking continues to develop an international reputation, more people are recognizing its versatility. The increasing interest in *nueva cocina mexicana* (nouvelle Mexican cuisine) prompts chefs to take a fresh look at indigenous ingredients and cooking methods. Meanwhile, researchers such as Diana Kennedy continue to spread the word about traditional dishes.

You'll have a wealth of opportunities to try renowned dishes at the source and to sample flavors not readily available elsewhere. Curious about guayaba fruit, roasted kid, or the dozens of kinds of mole sauce? Now's your chance to taste them. Regional chapters describe local specialties; see also "La Cocina Mexicana" in Chapter 1 for more information.

Soccer

As in Europe, this is Mexico's national sport (known as *futból*). It is played almost year-round at the Estadio Azteca in Mexico City, as well as in other large cities.

Tennis & Golf

Most major resorts have lighted tennis courts, and there is an abundance of 18-hole golf courses, many designed by such noteworthies as Percy Clifford, Joe Finger, and Robert Trent Jones. At private golf and tennis clubs, you must be accompanied by a member to gain admission. Hotels that do not have their own facilities will often secure you access to ones in the vicinity.

FODOR'S CHOICE

The sights, restaurants, hotels, and other travel experiences on these pages are our editors' top picks—our Fodor's Choices. They're the best of their type in the area covered by the book—not to be missed and always worth your time. In the destination chapters that follow, you will find all the details.

LODGING

$$$$	**La Casa Que Canta,** Zihuatanejo. Instead of chocolate on your pillow, look for flower-petal mosaics. The folk art, infinity pool, and bay views are cool, too.
$$$$	**Fairmont Acapulco Princess.** A tony classic on Playa Revolcadero. Howard Hughes stayed here even before there was in-room wireless Internet access or aromatherapy treatments.
$$$$	**Four Seasons,** Mexico City. Modeled after an 18th-century palace, but equipped with the most up-to-date amenities.
$$$$	**Ikal del Mar,** Playa del Carmen. Poetic, sybaritic jungle lodge and spa. The luxury envelops you as readily as a piqué robe.
$$$$	**Presidente Inter-Continental Paraiso de la Bonita and Thalasso,** Puerto Morelos. Eclectic boutique hotel and killer spa. Fresh seaweed treatments in outdoor pools pamper you to the core.
$$$$	**Quinta Real,** Guadalajara. Brick, stone, and marble are used to good advantage in a hotel that's a blend of colonial and neocolonial. Objets d'art abound.
$$$$	**Las Ventanas al Paraíso,** Cabo San Lucas. Practically oozes luxury, from the sorbet offered poolside to the decadent spa treatments.
$$$–$$$$	**Casa de la Marquesa,** Querétaro. This 18th-century building may not have won over the woman it was supposedly built for, but it has charmed everyone since.
$$$–$$$$	**Quinta Real,** Zacatecas. Instead of crowds cheering a toreador, this space, once a bullring, fills with fans of the posh rooms and terrific restaurant.
$$–$$$$	**Las Mañanitas,** Cuernavaca. Artisanal work (hand-painted tiles, hand-carved bedsteads) make these rooms stand out.
$$$	**Camino Real,** Mexico City. A trifecta of excellence: a design by one of Mexico's best modern architects, renowned artwork, and a branch of Le Cirque.
$$$	**Hacienda de los Santos,** Alamos. The extensive grounds and gracious courtyards around these four linked colonial mansions practically demand a leisurely stroll.
$$$	**Hotel Emporio,** Veracruz. Elegance in spades, but also thoughtful amenities for kids.

BUDGET LODGING

$$	**Copper Canyon Sierra Lodge,** near Creel. Kerosene lamps instead of electric lights, the sounds of a waterfall instead of phones ringing—in short: delicious isolation.

$$	**Posada Coatepec,** Coatepec, near Jalapa. Caffeine fiends can live out their dreams in the 19th-century former home of a coffee plantation owner.
¢–$	**Casa San Juan,** Mérida. Cozy B&B near the main square. Firm mattresses and an affable Cuban hotelier are among the draws. Europeans love it.
¢	**Na Bolom,** San Cristóbal. Rustic rooms, beautiful gardens, and a scholarly air.

RESTAURANTS

$$$–$$$$	**Mi Cocina,** San José del Cabo. Torchlight casts a compelling glow on the dining terrace.
$$$–$$$$	**La Vela,** Acapulco. Ocean breezes, a sail-like roof, and fabulous red snapper.
$$–$$$	**Mariscos Villa Rica Mocambo,** Veracruz. An ostensibly casual beachside palapa with seriously good seafood.
$$$	**Casa la Aduana,** Aduana. One of Sonora's best restaurants takes a bit of scouting to find; it's down a dirt road in a tiny former mining town.
$–$$$	**Aguila y Sol,** Mexico City. Catch the wave of *nueva cocina mexicana,* with its creative new spins on indigenous dishes.
$–$$$	**La Pigua,** Campeche City. Lots of glass and greenery—not to mention local professionals who come for delicious seafood.
$–$$$	**L'Recif,** Manzanillo. Cliff-top palapa where divine shrimp in mango sauce is served up to the sound of crashing waves and (maybe) a glimpse of a whale.

BUDGET RESTAURANTS

$$	**Na Bolom,** San Cristóbal. Home-cooked meals shared with area Indians, resident intellectuals, and fellow travelers.
$–$$	**El Discreto Encanto de Comer,** Mexico City. Lunch in high Porfiriato style on Mexican-inflected French dishes.
$–$$	**El Gallo Centenario,** Mexico City. Opulent but young at heart. Kick off a meal of Mexican classics with a chrysanthemum-topped margarita.
$–$$	**Gran Café de la Parroquia,** Veracruz. Dramatically served *lechero* (coffee with milk) and unbeatable atmosphere.
$–$$	**El Naranjo,** Oaxaca City. Magnificent moles and chiles rellenos prepared with a contemporary spin. Cooking classes are a possibility.
$	**La Valentina,** Mexico City. A champion of traditional indigenous cuisine.
¢–$	**Bistrot Mosaico,** Mexico City. Perennial French favorites mean you'll have to vie with the locals for a table.

ARCHAEOLOGY

Chichén Itzá, Yucatán. The Maya site is unforgettable for its enormity, imperial structures, and classic imagery.

Palenque, Chiapas. Amazing temples and tombs—all bathed in beautiful light and surrounded by jungle. Once home to Pakal, a great 7th-century ruler.

El Tajín, Veracruz state. The extensive site includes the Pyramid of the Niches with its mesmerizing reliefs; unexcavated structures lurk in the surrounding jungle.

Templo Mayor, Mexico City. You won't have to trek into the jungle to see these Aztec ruins—they're right in the capital's historic center.

Teotihuacán, north of Mexico City. The history of this ancient site may still be mysterious, but its grandeur is unmistakable. It has one of the world's largest pyramids.

Tula, north of Mexico City. Once the capital of the Toltecs, Tula is marked by a statue-topped pyramid.

Tulum, Quintana Roo. Even the ancients wanted rooms with a view: Mexico's most-visited ruins overlook the blue-green Caribbean.

Uxmal, Yucatán. Uncluttered horizontal lines, ornate stone mosaics, soaring vaulted arches—it's all about understated elegance.

Yaxchilán, Chiapas. A watery glide along the Río Usumacinta—à la Indiana Jones—ends at temples with finely carved details and grand stairs.

BEACHES

Pie de la Cuesta, Acapulco. A wide beach with thatch-roof restaurants and straw palapas for shade. Come for the sunning, water-skiing, and boat rides; stay for the sunset.

Playa de Amor, Cabo San Lucas. At this secluded spot at the very tip of the Baja peninsula, the Pacific and the Sea of Cortez crash together.

Playa Norte, Isla Mujeres. To reach this beach with its calm, turquoise, waist-deep water just head north—you can't miss it.

Playa la Ropa, Zihuatanejo. A long stretch of soft sands, open-air restaurants, and hammocks beyond a rocky point.

Playa Zicatela, Puerto Escondido. Surf's up at this beach, where the Mexican Pipeline batters cream-color sand. November sees surfing competitions and bikini contests.

MUSEUMS

Museo de Antropología de Jalapa, Jalapa. The three main pre-Hispanic cultures of Veracruz state are illuminated through an amazing collection of artifacts: everything from delicate murals to whopping stone Olmec heads.

Museo de las Culturas, Oaxaca City. Themed galleries and salons surround the cloister of a former convent. Displays cover everything from artifacts to language to medicine. Save time for the botanical gardens.

Museo de Frida Kahlo, Mexico City. Kahlo's "Blue House" now guards the trappings of the artist's tumultuous life, from her sketches to her giant papier-mâché skeletons.

Museo Na Bolom, San Cristóbal. What happens when a Danish archaeologist marries a Swiss social activist and both end up in Mexico? You get an institute devoted to the study of ecology and of the Maya as well as this museum.

Museo Nacional de Antropología, Mexico City. One of the best archaeological collections in the world, hands down. Between the extraordinary artworks and the preserved ephemera of everyday life, you'll have a wonderful introduction to pre-Hispanic culture.

Museo de la Revolución Mexicana, Chihuahua City. The former home of Pancho Villa is filled with Revolution-era artifacts, including the car in which Villa was assassinated.

Parque Museo La Venta, Villahermosa. Hefty, Olmec stone heads line the aptly named Lake of Illusions. Theories about who (or what) the figures represent are as intriguing as the figures themselves.

PURE MEXICO

Calesa ride, Mérida. The well-preserved colonial buildings make any form of transportation other than horse-drawn carriage seem cheeky.

Cliff divers at La Quebrada, Acapulco. Daredevil *clavadistas* risk life and limb for your entertainment (and your tips). Arrive early and be generous.

Exploring Cuetzalan, a preserved colonial town. High in the lush Sierra Norte, you can absorb the sights and smells of the weekly market or wander through a nearby archaeological zone.

Scuba diving off the shores of Cozumel. If the waters here were good enough for Jacques Cousteau . . .

Sunsets in Puerta Vallarta. Big and fiery, the setting sun seems to spread like orange mercury over Bahía Banderas.

Whale-watching in Scammon's Lagoon, Baja Sur. Now a national park, this lagoon remains a perfect place to see gray whales up close.

SHOPPING

Emilia Castillo, Taxco (near Acapulco). Innovative silver designs in Mexico's premier "silver city."

Galleria Sergio Bustamante, Tlaquepaque (near Guadalajara). Shop here for Señor Bustamante's magical bronzes and ceramics or pay more abroad.

Mercado Artesanal La Ciudadela, Mexico City. This daily market packs the double punch of the best selection of crafts and the best bargains in the capital.

Mujeres Artesanas, Oaxaca City. Women artists unite—and the quality and selection of their crafts in this cooperative are fabulous.

WHERE ART COMES FIRST

Instituto Cultural Cabañas, Guadalajara. Theater spaces, art galleries, and flower-filled patios in a neoclassical structure. Large body of work by Mexican muralist José Clemente Orozco.

Museo de la Cerámica, Tlaquepaque (near Guadalajara). Award-winning pieces large and small in a museum that honors a great modern ceramist.

SMART TRAVEL TIPS

Finding out about your destination before you leave home means you won't squander time organizing everyday minutiae once you've arrived. You'll be more streetwise when you hit the ground as well, better prepared to explore the aspects of Mexico that drew you here in the first place. The organizations in this section can provide information to supplement this guide; contact them for up-to-the-minute details, and consult the A to Z sections that end each chapter for facts on the various topics as they relate to Mexico's many regions. Happy landings!

ADDRESSES

The Mexican method of naming streets can be exasperatingly arbitrary, so **be patient when searching for addresses.** Streets in the centers of many colonial cities are laid out in a grid surrounding the *zócalo* (main square) and often have different names on opposite sides of the square. Other streets simply acquire a new name after a certain number of blocks or when they cross a certain street. Numbered streets are usually designated *norte/sur* (north/south) or *oriente/poniente* (east/west) on either side of a central avenue.

Blocks are often labeled numerically, according to distance from a chosen starting point, as in "la Calle de Pachuca," "2a Calle de Pachuca," etc. Many Mexican addresses have "s/n" for *sin número* (no number) after the street name. This is common in small towns where there aren't many buildings on a block. Many addresses are cited as "Carretera a Querétaro, Km 30," which indicates that the property is at the 30th kilometer on the *carretera* (highway) to Querétaro.

Addresses are written with the street name first, followed by the street number (or "s/n"). A five-digit *código postal* (postal code) precedes, rather than follows, the name of the city: *Hacienda Paraíso, Calle Allende 211, 68000 Oaxaca.* Apdo. (*apartado*) means box; Apdo. Postal, or A.P., means post-office box number.

In Mexico City (and other cities), most addresses include their *colonia* (neighborhood), which is abbreviated as Col. Other abbreviations used in addresses include: Av. (*avenida,* or avenue); Calz. (*calzada,* or road); Fracc. (*fraccionamiento,* or housing estate); and Int. (interior).

Mexican states have postal abbreviations of two or more letters. To send mail to Mexico, you can use the following: Baja California: B.C.; Baja California Sur: B.C.S.; Campeche: Camp.; Chiapas: Chis.; Chihuahua: Chih.; Distrito Federal (Mexico City): D.F.; Guanajuato: Gto.; Guerrero: Gro.; Jalisco: Jal.; Estado de Mexico: Edo. de Mex.; Michoacán: Mich.; Morelos: Mor.; Nuevo Leon: N.I.; Oaxaca: Oax.; Querétaro: Qro.; Quintana Roo: Q. Roo; Sinaloa: Sin.; Sonora: Son.; Tabasco: Tab.; Veracruz: Ver.; Yucatán: Yuc.; Zacatecas: Zac.

AIR TRAVEL

BOOKING

When you book, look for nonstop flights and remember that "direct" flights stop at least once. Try to avoid connecting flights, which require a change of plane. Two airlines may operate a connecting flight jointly, so ask whether your airline operates every segment of the trip; you may find that the carrier you prefer flies you only part of the way. To find more booking tips and to check prices and make on-line flight reservations, log on to www.fodors.com.

CARRIERS

AeroCalifornia, Aeroméxico, America West, American, Continental, Delta, Mexicana, Northwest, and United all fly from the United States into Mexico City, the nation's main gateway. These airlines also have service to many of the coastal resorts (Acapulco, Cancún, Los Cabos, Mazatlán, Puerto Vallarta, etc.) as well as to such inland communities as Chihuahua City, Guadalajara, Hermosillo, and Monterrey. Alaska Airlines flies from the United States to Cancún, Ixtapa/Zihuatanejo, Los Cabos, Mazatlán, and Puerto Vallarta. US Airways has service to Cancún and Cozumel. British Airways flies nonstop from London to Mexico City.

Plane travel within Mexico costs about four times as much as bus travel, but it will save you considerable time. Aeroméxico and Mexicana serve most major cities. AeroCalifornia flies to Chihuahua, Guadalajara, Loreto, Mérida, Monterrey, Oaxaca, Puebla, Tepic, Tijuana, Veracruz, Villahermosa, and several other places. Aerocaribe (reserve through Mexicana) serves the Yucatán and the South. Aerolitoral serves the

nation's northeastern reaches, and Aeromar covers central Mexico; make reservations on either line through Mexicana or Aeroméxico. Aviacsa serves Cancún, Chetumal, Guadalajara, Mérida, and Tijuana.

From the U.S. AeroCalifornia ☎ 800/237-6225 in the U.S. Aeroméxico ☎ 800/237-6639 in the U.S. ⊕ www.aeromexico.com. Alaska Airlines ☎ 800/426-0333 in the U.S. ⊕ www.alaskaair.com. America West ☎ 800/235-9292 in the U.S. ⊕ www.americawest.com. American ☎ 800/433-7300 in the U.S. ⊕ www.aa.com. Continental ☎ 800/231-0856 in the U.S. ⊕ www.continental.com. Delta ☎ 800/241-4141 in the U.S. ⊕ www.delta.com. Mexicana ☎ 800/531-7921 in the U.S. ⊕ www.mexicana.com. Northwest ☎ 800/225-2525 in the U.S. ⊕ www.nwa.com. United ☎ 800/241-6522 in the U.S. ⊕ www.united.com. US Airways ☎ 800/428-4322 in the U.S. ⊕ www.usairways.com.

From the U.K. British Airways ☎ 0845/773-3377 ⊕ www.britishairways.com.

Within Mexico AeroCalifornia ☎ 55/5207-1392. Aeroméxico ☎ 55/5625-2622; 800/021-4010 in the U.S. ⊕ www.aeromexico.com. Aviacsa ☎ 961/612-8084 in Chiapas; 55/5448-8900 in Mexico City. Mexicana ☎ 55/5448-0990; 800/502-2000 in the U.S. ⊕ www.mexicana.com.

CHECK-IN & BOARDING

Always **ask your carrier about its check-in policy.** Plan to arrive at the airport about 2 hours before your scheduled departure time for domestic flights and 2½ to 3 hours before international flights. You may need to arrive earlier if you're flying from one of the busier airports or during peak air-traffic times. To avoid delays at airport-security checkpoints, try not to wear any metal. Jewelry, belt and other buckles, steel-toe shoes, barrettes, and under-wire bras are among the items that can set off detectors.

Assuming that not everyone with a ticket will show up, airlines routinely overbook planes. When everyone does, airlines ask for volunteers to give up their seats. In return, these volunteers usually get a several-hundred-dollar flight voucher, which can be used toward the purchase of another ticket, and are rebooked on the next flight out. If there are not enough volunteers, the airline must choose who will be denied boarding. The first to get bumped are passengers who checked in late and those flying on discounted tickets, so get to the gate and check in as early as possible, especially during peak periods.

Always **bring a government-issued photo ID to the airport;** even when it's not required, a passport is best.

CUTTING COSTS

The least expensive airfares to Mexico are priced for round-trip travel and must usually be purchased in advance. Airlines generally allow you to change your return date for a fee; most low-fare tickets, however, are nonrefundable. It's smart to call a number of airlines and check the Internet; when you are quoted a good price, book it on the spot—the same fare may not be available the next day, or even the next hour. Always check different routings and look into using alternate airports. Also, price off-peak flights, which may be significantly less expensive than others. Travel agents, especially low-fare specialists ($\Rightarrow$ Discounts and Deals), are helpful.

Consolidators are another good source. They buy tickets for scheduled flights at reduced rates from the airlines, then sell them at prices that beat the best fare available directly from the airlines. Sometimes you can even get your money back if you need to return the ticket. Carefully read the fine print detailing penalties for changes and cancellations, purchase the ticket with a credit card, and confirm your consolidator reservation with the airline.

🛈 Consolidators **AirlineConsolidator.com** ☎ 888/468-5385 ⊕ www.airlineconsolidator.com; for international tickets. **Best Fares** ☎ 800/576-8255 or 800/576-1600 in the U.S. ⊕ www.bestfares.com; $59.90 annual membership. **Cheap Tickets** ☎ 800/377-1000 or 888/922-8849 in the U.S. ⊕ www.cheaptickets.com. **Expedia** ☎ 404/728-8787; 800/397-3342 in the U.S. ⊕ www.expedia.com. **Hotwire** ☎ 866/468-9473 or 920/330-9418 ⊕ www.hotwire.com. **Now Voyager Travel** ⊠ 45 W. 21st St., 5th floor, New York, NY 10010 ☎ 212/459-1616 🖷 212/243-2711 ⊕ www.nowvoyagertravel.com. **Onetravel.com** ⊕ www.onetravel.com. **Orbitz** ☎ 888/656-4546 ⊕ www.orbitz.com. **Priceline.com** ⊕ www.priceline.com. **Travelocity** ☎ 888/709-5983; 877/282-2925 in Canada; 0870/876-3876 in the U.K. ⊕ www.travelocity.com.

ENJOYING THE FLIGHT

State your seat preference when purchasing your ticket, and then repeat it when you confirm and when you check in. For more legroom, you can request one of the few emergency-aisle seats at check-in, if you are capable of lifting at least 50 pounds—a Federal Aviation Administration requirement of passengers in these seats. Seats behind a bulkhead also offer more legroom, but they don't have underseat storage. Don't sit in the row in front of the emergency aisle or in front of a bulkhead, where seats may not recline.

Ask the airline whether a snack or meal is served on the flight. If you have dietary concerns, request special meals when booking. These can be vegetarian, low-cholesterol, or kosher, for example. It's a good idea to pack some healthful snacks and a small (plastic) bottle of water in your carry-on bag. On long flights, try to maintain a normal routine, to help fight jet lag. At night, get some sleep. By day, eat light meals, drink water (not alcohol), and **move around the cabin** to stretch your legs. For additional jet-lag tips consult *Fodor's FYI: Travel Fit & Healthy* (available at bookstores everywhere).

Smoking policies vary from carrier to carrier. Many airlines prohibit smoking on all of their flights; others allow smoking only on certain routes or certain departures. Ask your carrier about its policy.

FLYING TIMES

Mexico City is 4½ hours from New York, 4 hours from Chicago, and 3½ hours from Los Angeles. Cancún is 3½ hours from New York and from Chicago, 4½ hours from Los Angeles. Acapulco is 6 hours from New York, 4 hours from Chicago, and 3½ hours from Los Angeles. From London, Mexico City is a 12½-hour flight, Cancún 11¾ hours.

HOW TO COMPLAIN

If your baggage goes astray or your flight goes awry, complain right away. Most carriers require that you **file a claim immediately.** The Aviation Consumer Protection Division of the Department of Transportation publishes *Fly-Rights,* which discusses airlines and consumer issues and is available on-line. You can also find articles and information on mytravelrights.com, the Web site of the nonprofit Cosumer Travel Rights Center.

🛈 Airline Complaints **Aviation Consumer Protection Division** ⊠ U.S. Department of Transportation, C-75, Room 4107, 400 7th St. NW, Washington, DC 20590 ☎ 202/366-2220 ⊕ www.dot.gov/airconsumer. **Federal Aviation Administration Consumer Hotline** ⊠ for inquiries: FAA, 800 Independence Ave. SW, Room 810, Washington, DC 20591 ☎ 800/322-7873 in the U.S. ⊕ www.faa.gov.

RECONFIRMING

Check the status of your flight before you leave for the airport. You can do this on your carrier's Web site, by linking to a flight-status checker (many Web booking services offer these), or by calling your carrier or travel agent. Always confirm international flights at least 72 hours ahead of the scheduled departure time.

AIRPORTS

The main gateway to the country is Mexico City's Aeropuerto Internacional Benito Juárez (airport code: MEX), a large, modern airport. You can easily exchange money here as well as buy last-minute gifts (although at a higher price) on your way out of the country.

🔲 Airport Information **Aeropuerto Internacional Benito Juárez** ☎ 55/5571-3600.

BIKE TRAVEL

Bike travel in Mexico is a rough-and-ready proposition. Some roads have never seen a bicycle, and drivers aren't used to cyclists. Many roads lack shoulders and are often pitted. That said, cycling can be fun if you choose your destination with care. In the Yucatán, for example, bikes are a main form of transportation for locals, and bike-repair shops are common even in small towns. When planning your trip, consult an up-to-date AAA, Pemex, or Guía Roji map. You can find Pemex and Guía Roji maps in Mexico at most Sanborns restaurant-shops and such supermarket chains as Superama, Aurrera, and Commercial Mexicana for less than $10.

Be sure to carry plenty of water and everything you might need to repair your bike. Pack extra patch kits, as shards of glass often litter the roads. If you can take your bike apart and fold it up, buses will allow you to store it in the cargo space; likewise on trains in Las Barrancas del Cobre. *Bicycling Mexico* (Hunter Publishing Inc.), by Ericka Weisbroth and Eric Ellman, is the bicyclist's bible, complete with maps, color photos, historical information, and a kilometer-by-kilometer breakdown of every route possible. For a list of companies that run organized bike tours of Mexico, *see* Tours and Packages.

BIKES IN FLIGHT

Most airlines accommodate bikes as luggage, provided they're dismantled and boxed; check with individual airlines about packing requirements. Some airlines sell bike boxes, which are often free at bike shops, for about $15 (bike bags can be considerably more expensive). International travelers often can substitute a bike for a piece of checked luggage at no charge; otherwise, the cost is about $100. U.S. and Canadian airlines charge $40–$80 each way.

BUSINESS HOURS

BANKS & OFFICES

Banks are generally open weekdays 9–3. In larger cities, most are open until 5 or 7, and some of the larger banks keep a few branches open Saturday from 9 or 10 to 1 or 2:30 and Sunday 10–1:30; however, the extended hours are often for deposits or check cashing only. Banks will give you cash advances in pesos (for a fee) if you have a major credit card. Government offices are usually open to the public weekdays 8–3; along with banks and most private offices, they're closed on national holidays.

GAS STATIONS

Gas stations are normally open 7 AM–10 PM. Those near major thoroughfares in big cities stay open 24 hours, including most holidays.

MUSEUMS & SIGHTS

Along with theaters and most archaeological sights, museums are closed on Monday, with few exceptions. Hours are normally 9 to 5 or 6.

PHARMACIES

Pharmacies are usually open daily from 10 AM to 10 PM; in some small towns, they may close at 7 PM. Twenty-four-hour pharmacies are common in larger cities: look for the big-name 24-hour pharmacies such as Farmacia del Ahorro or Fenix.

SHOPS

Stores are generally open weekdays and Saturday from 9 or 10 AM to 7 or 8 PM; in resort areas, they may also be open on Sunday. In some resort areas and small towns, stores may close for a two-hour lunch break—about 2–4. Airport shops are open seven days a week.

BUS TRAVEL

Getting to Mexico by bus is no longer for just the adventurous or budget-conscious. In the past, bus travelers were required to change to Mexican vehicles at the border, and vice versa. Now, however, in an effort to bring more American visitors and their dollars to off-the-beaten-track markets and attractions, the Mexican government has removed this obstacle, and more transborder bus tours are available.

Gateway cities in Texas, such as El Paso, Del Rio, Laredo, McAllen, Brownsville, and San Antonio, along with Tijuana, are served by several small private lines as well as by Greyhound. If you'll be leaving Mexico by bus, you can buy tickets from the Greyhound representative in Mexico City.

The Mexican bus network is extensive. In large cities, bus stations are a good distance from the center of town. Though there's a trend toward consolidation, some towns have different stations for each bus line.

CLASSES

Mexican buses can be comfortable air-conditioned coaches with bathrooms, movies, reclining seats with seat belts, and refreshments (premier or deluxe) or they can be dilapidated "vintage" vehicles (second and third class) on which pigs and chickens travel and frequent stops are made. A lower-class bus ride can be interesting if you're not in a hurry and want to experience local culture; fares are up to 30% cheaper than those in the premium categories. Still, be prepared for cracked windows and litter in the aisles. Also bring something to eat in case you don't like the restaurant where the bus stops, and **carry toilet paper,** as rest rooms might not have any. For comfort's sake, if you're planning a long-distance haul, **buy tickets for first-class or better when traveling by bus within Mexico.** Smoking is prohibited on all first-class and deluxe buses.

There are several first-class bus lines. ADO and ADO GL (deluxe service) travel to Cancún, Chiapas, Oaxaca, Tampico, Veracruz, Villahermosa, and Yucatán from Mexico City. Cristóbal Colón goes to Chiapas, Oaxaca, Puebla, and the Guatemala border from Mexico City. Estrella Blanca goes from Mexico City to Manzanillo, Mazatlán, Monterrey, and Nuevo Laredo. ETN goes to Mexico City, Manzanillo,

Morelia, Puerto Vallarta, and Toluca. Estrella Blanca has first-class and deluxe service to all states but Yucatán, Quintana Roo, and Chiapas. You can take Estrella de Oro from Mexico City to Acapulco, Cuernavaca, Ixtapa, and Taxco.

PAYING

For the most part, plan to pay in pesos, although most of the deluxe bus services have started accepting credit cards such as Visa and MasterCard.

RESERVATIONS

Tickets for first-class or better—unlike tickets for the other classes—can and should be reserved in advance. You can make reservations for many, though not all, of the first-class bus lines, through the Ticketbus central reservations agency.
🚌 **Bus Information ADO** ☎ 55/5785-9659; 01800/702-8000 toll free in Mexico. **ADO GL** ☎ 55/5785-9659 ⊕ www.adogl.com.mx. **Cristóbal Colón** ☎ 55/5133-2444; 01800/849-6136 toll free in Mexico ⊕ www.cristobalcolon.com.mx. **Estrella Blanca** ☎ 55/5729-0707; 01800/507-5500 toll free in Mexico. **ETN** ☎ 55/5273-0251; 01800/800-3862 toll free in Mexico ⊕ www.etn.com.mx. **Estrella de Oro** ☎ 55/5549-8520 ⊕ www.autobus.com.mx. **Greyhound** ☎ 55/5669-0986; 01800/010-0600 toll free in Mexico; 800/231-2222 in the U.S. ⊕ www.greyhound.com. **Ticketbus** ☎ 55/5133-2424; 01800/702-8000 toll free in Mexico ⊕ www.ticketbus.com.mx.

CAMERAS & PHOTOGRAPHY

Mexico, with its majestic landscapes and varied cityscapes, is a photographer's dream. Mexicans seem amenable to having picture-taking visitors in their midst, but you should always **ask permission before taking pictures in churches or of individuals.** They may ask you for a *propina,* or tip, in which case a few pesos is customary. (Note that some indigenous peoples don't ever want to be photographed; taking pictures is also forbidden in some churches.) If you're bashful about approaching strangers, photograph people with whom you interact: your waiter, your desk clerk, the vendor selling you crafts. Even better, have a traveling companion or a passerby photograph you *with* them.

To avoid the blurriness caused by shaky hands, get a minitripod—they're available in sizes as small as 6 inches. (Although cameras are permitted at archaeological sites, many of them strictly prohibit the use of tripods.) Buy a small beanbag to support your camera on uneven surfaces. If you plan to take photos on some of the country's many beaches, bring a skylight (81B or 81C) or polarizing filter to minimize haze and light problems. If you're visiting forested areas, bring high-speed film to compensate for low light under the tree canopy and invest in a telephoto lens to photograph wildlife; standard zoom lenses in the 35–88 range won't capture enough detail.

Casual photographers should **consider using inexpensive disposable cameras** to reduce the risks inherent in traveling with sophisticated equipment. One-use cameras with panoramic or underwater functions are also nice supplements to a standard camera and its gear.

The *Kodak Guide to Shooting Great Travel Pictures* (available at bookstores everywhere) is loaded with tips.
Photo Help **Kodak Information Center** ☎ 800/ 242–2424 in the U.S. ⊕ www.kodak.com.

EQUIPMENT PRECAUTIONS

Don't pack film and equipment in checked luggage, where it is much more susceptible to damage. X-ray machines used to view checked luggage are extremely powerful and therefore are likely to ruin your film. Try to ask for hand inspection of film, which becomes clouded after repeated exposure to airport X-ray machines, and keep videotapes and computer disks away from metal detectors. Carry an extra supply of batteries, and be prepared to turn on your camera, camcorder, or laptop to prove to airport security personnel that the device is real.

Always **keep your film (and computer disks and videotapes) out of the sun** and on jungle trips keep your equipment in resealable plastic bags to protect it from dampness. As petty crime can be a problem, particularly in the cities, **keep a close eye on your gear.**

FILM & DEVELOPING

Film—especially Kodak and Fuji brands—is fairly easy to find in many parts of Mexico. If purchased in a major city, a roll of 36-exposure print film costs about the same as in the United States; the price is slightly higher in tourist spots and in more remote places. Advantix is available in Mexico, although developing may take one or two days. It's a good idea to pack more film than you think you'll need on your trip. One-hour and overnight film developing is fairly common.

VIDEOS

Videotapes are good quality and are easy to find in urban areas. Mexico uses VHS. The best places to buy tapes are Sanborns restaurant-shops (they're all over the place). A 120-minute tape costs about $3.

CAR RENTAL

When you think about renting a car, bear in mind that you may be sharing the road with bad local drivers—sometimes acquiring a driver's license in Mexico is more a question of paying someone off than of having tested skill. In addition, the highway system is very uneven: in some regions, modern, well-paved superhighways prevail; in others—particularly the mountains—potholes, untethered livestock, and dangerous, unrailed curves are the rule. Check on local road conditions before you rent.

Mexico manufactures Chrysler, Ford, General Motors, Honda, Nissan, and Volkswagen vehicles. With the exception of Volkswagen, you can get the same kind of midsize and luxury cars in Mexico that you can rent in the United States and Canada. Economy usually refers to a Volkswagen Beetle, which may or may not come with air-conditioning.

It can really pay to shop around: in Mexico City rates for a compact car with air-conditioning, manual transmission, and unlimited mileage range from $25 a day and $115 a week to $40 a day and $270 a week. In Acapulco and other resort areas, rates generally run $35 a day and $200 a week. None of these prices includes tax on car rentals, which is 15%, or insurance, which runs about $100 a week. While shopping for a good deal, avoid local agencies; **stick with the major companies** because they tend to be more reliable.

You can also hire a car with a driver through your hotel. The going rate is about $25 an hour within a given town. Limousine service runs about $55 an hour ($75 for a Mercedes-Benz), with a five-hour minimum. Rates for out-of-town trips are higher. **Negotiate a price before-hand** if you'll need the service for more than one day. If your hotel can't arrange limousine or car service, ask the concierge to refer you to a reliable *sitio* (cab stand); the rate will be lower.

Major Agencies Alamo ☎ 800/522-9696 in the U.S. ⊕ www.alamo.com. **Avis** ☎ 800/331-1084 in the U.S.; 800/879-2847 in Canada; 0870/606-0100 in the U.K.; 02/9353-9000 in Australia; 09/526-2847 in New Zealand ⊕ www.avis.com. **Budget** ☎ 800/527-0700 in the U.S.; 0870/156-5656 in the U.K. ⊕ www.budget.com. **Dollar** ☎ 800/800-6000 in the U.S.; 0124/622-0111 in the U.K., where it's affiliated with Sixt; 02/9223-1444 in Australia ⊕ www.dollar.com. **Hertz** ☎ 800/654-3001 in the U.S.; 800/263-0600 in Canada; 0870/844-8844 in the U.K.; 02/9669-2444 in Australia; 09/256-8690 in New Zealand ⊕ www.hertz.com. **National Car Rental** ☎ 800/227-7368 in the U.S.; 0870/600-6666 in the U.K. ⊕ www.nationalcar.com.

CUTTING COSTS

For a good deal, book through a travel agent who will shop around. Do look into wholesalers, companies that do not own fleets but rent in bulk from those that do and often offer better rates than traditional car-rental operations. Prices are best during off-peak periods. Rentals booked through wholesalers often must be paid for before you leave home.

Wholesalers Auto Europe ☎ 207/842-2000; 800/223-5555 in the U.S. 🖶 207/842-2222 ⊕ www.autoeurope.com.

INSURANCE

When driving a rented car you're responsible for any damage to or loss of the vehicle. You also may be liable for any property damage or personal injury that you may cause while driving. In Mexico, you're guilty until proven innocent, which means you could be jailed during investigations after an accident unless you have Mexican insurance.

REQUIREMENTS & RESTRICTIONS

In Mexico the minimum driving age is 18, but most rental car agencies require you to be between 21 and 25. Your own driver's license is acceptable, but an international driver's license is a good idea. It's available from the U.S. and Canadian automobile associations, and, in the United Kingdom, from the Automobile Association or Royal Automobile Club.

SURCHARGES

Before you pick up a car in one city and leave it in another, ask about drop-off charges or one-way service fees, which can be substantial. Note, too, that some rental agencies charge extra if you return the car before the time specified in your contract. To avoid a hefty refueling fee, **fill the tank just before you turn in the car,** but be aware that gas stations near the rental outlet may overcharge. It's almost never a deal to buy the tank of gas that's in the car when you rent it; the understanding is that you'll return it empty, but some fuel usually remains.

CAR TRAVEL

There are two absolutely essential points to remember about driving in Mexico. First and foremost is to **carry Mexican auto insurance.** If you injure anyone in an accident, you could well be jailed—whether it was your fault or not—unless you have insurance. Second, **if you enter Mexico with a car, you must leave with it.** In recent years, the high rate of U.S. vehicles being sold illegally in Mexico has caused the Mexican government to enact stringent regulations for bringing a car into the country.

You must cross the border with the following documents: title or registration for your vehicle; a birth certificate or passport; a credit card (AE, DC, MC, or V); a valid driver's license with a photo. The title holder, driver, and credit-card owner must be one and the same—that is, if your spouse's name is on the title of the car and yours isn't, you cannot be the one to bring the car into the country. For financed, leased, rental, or company cars, you must **bring a notarized letter of permission** from the bank, lien holder, rental agency, or company. When you submit your paperwork at the border and pay the $22 charge on your credit card, you'll receive a car permit and a sticker to put on your vehicle, all valid for up to six months. Be sure to **turn in the permit and the sticker** at the border prior to their expiration date; otherwise you could incur high fines.

One alternative to going through this hassle when you cross is to **have your paperwork done in advance** at a branch of Sanborn's Mexican Insurance; look in the Yellow Pages for an office in almost every town on the U.S.–Mexico border. You'll

still have to go through some of the procedures at the border, but all your paperwork will be in order, and Sanborn's
express window will ensure that you get
through relatively quickly. There's a $10
charge for this service. The fact that you
drove in with a car is stamped on your
tourist card, which you must give to immigration authorities at departure. If an
emergency arises and you must fly home,
there are complicated customs procedures
to face.

If you bring the car into the country you
must be in the vehicle at all times when it
is driven. You cannot lend it to another
person. Also, although a valid license from
home is good in Mexico, an international
driver's license isn't a bad idea. These permits are universally recognized, and having one in your wallet may save you a
problem with the local authorities.

EMERGENCY SERVICES

To help motorists on major highways, the
Mexican Tourism Ministry operates a fleet
of more than 350 pickup trucks, known as
the Angeles Verdes, or Green Angels. The
bilingual drivers provide mechanical help,
first aid, radio-telephone communication,
basic supplies and small parts, towing,
tourist information, and protection. Services are free, and spare parts, fuel, and lu-
bricants are provided at cost. Tips are
always appreciated (figure $5–$10 for big
jobs, $2–$3 for minor repairs). The Green
Angels patrol fixed sections of the major
highways twice daily 8–8 (later on holiday
weekends). If you break down, **pull off the
road as far as possible,** lift the hood of
your car, hail a passing vehicle, and ask
the driver to **notify the patrol.** Most bus
and truck drivers will be quite helpful. If
you witness an accident, do not stop to
help—inform the nearest official.

⛏ **Angeles Verdes, Mexico City** ☎ 55/5250-8221
or 55/5520-8555.

GASOLINE

Pemex (the government petroleum
monopoly) franchises all of Mexico's gas
stations, which you'll find at most junc-
tions and in cities and towns. Gas is mea-
sured in liters, and stations usually don't
accept U.S. or Canadian credit cards or
dollars. Fuel prices tend to be lower in
Mexico City and surroundings and near
the U.S. border, increasing the farther you
get from these areas. Overall, prices run

slightly to moderately higher than in the
United States. Premium unleaded gas
(called *magna premio*) and regular unleaded gas (*magna sin*) are available nationwide, but it's still best to **fill up
whenever you can.** Fuel quality is generally lower than that in the United States
and Europe. Vehicles with fuel-injected engines are likely to have problems after
driving extended distances.

Gas-station attendants pump the gas for
you and may also wash your windshield
and check your oil and tire air pressure. A
5- or 10-peso tip is customary, depending
on the number of services rendered. **Keep
a close eye on the gas meter** to make sure
the attendant is starting it at "0" and that
you're charged the correct price.

INSURANCE

You must **carry Mexican auto insurance,**
which you can purchase near border crossings on either the U.S. or Mexican side.
Guilty until proven innocent is part of the
country's Code Napoléon, so purchase
enough Mexican automobile insurance at
the border to cover your estimated trip.
It's sold by the day, and if your trip is
shorter than your original estimate, some
companies might issue a prorated refund
for the unused time upon application after
you exit the country.

⛏ **Instant Mexico Auto Insurance** ✉ 223 Via de
San Ysidro, San Ysidro, CA 92173 ☎ 619/428-3583;
800/345-4701 in the U.S. 🖶 619/690-6533 🌐 www.
instant-mex-auto-insur.com. **Oscar Padilla** ✉ 120
Willow Rd., San Ysidro, CA 92173 ☎ 619/428-4406;
800/258-8600 in the U.S. **Sanborn's Mexican Insurance** ✉ 2009 S. 10th St., McAllen, TX 78503
☎ 956/686-0711; 800/222-0158 in the U.S. 🌐 www.
sanbornsinsurance.com.

PARKING

A circle with a diagonal line superimposed
on the letter *E* (for *estacionamiento*) means
"no parking." Illegally parked cars are either towed or have wheel blocks placed on
the tires, which can require a trip to the
traffic-police headquarters for payment of
a fine. When in doubt, **park in a lot instead
of on the street;** your car will probably be
safer there anyway. Lots are plentiful, and
fees are reasonable—as little as $1 for a
whole day up to $1 an hour, depending on
where in the country you are. Sometimes
you park your own car; more often,
though, you hand the keys over to an attendant. There are a few (very few) parking

meters in larger cities; the cost is usually about 10 cents per 15 minutes.

ROAD CONDITIONS

There are several well-kept toll roads in Mexico—most of them four lanes wide. However, these *carreteras* (major highways) don't go too far out of the capital into the countryside. (*Cuota* means toll road; *libre* means no toll, and such roads are two lanes and usually not as smooth.) Some excellent roads have opened in the past decade or so, making car travel safer and faster. These include highways connecting Acapulco and Mexico City; Cancún and Mérida; Nogales and Mazatlán; León and Aguascalientes; Guadalajara and Tepic; Mexico City, Morelia, and Guadalajara; Mexico City, Puebla, Teotihuacán, and Oaxaca; Mexico City and Veracruz; and Nuevo Laredo and Monterrey. However, tolls as high as $40 one way can make using these thoroughfares prohibitively expensive.

In rural areas, roads are poor: **use caution, especially during the rainy season,** when rock slides and potholes are a problem. Be alert to animals, especially cattle and dogs. Note that driving in Mexico's central highlands may also necessitate adjustments to your carburetor. *Topes* (speed bumps) are common; slow down when approaching a village.

Generally, driving times are longer than for comparable distances in the United States. Common sense goes a long way, particularly if you have a lot of ground to cover. **Start early and fill up on gas;** don't let your tank get below half full. Allow extra time for unforeseen occurrences as well as for traffic, particularly truck traffic.

Approaches to most large cities are in good condition, but urban traffic can be horrendous. As you would in metropolitan areas anywhere, avoid rush hour (7–9 AM and 6–8 PM) and when schools let out (2–3 PM). Signage is not always adequate in Mexico, so **travel with a companion and a good map.** Always lock your car, and never leave valuable items in the body of the car (the trunk will suffice for daytime outings, but don't pack it in front of prying eyes).

ROAD MAPS

The Mexican government distributes free road maps from its tourism offices in Mexican consulates and embassies abroad. The Mexican Secretariat of Tourism will also mail maps on request, though it may take up to three months to receive them. Guía Roji and Pemex publish current city, regional, and national road maps, which are available in bookstores and big supermarket chains for under $10; gas stations generally don't sell maps.

RULES OF THE ROAD

When you sign up for Mexican car insurance, you should receive a booklet on Mexican rules of the road. It really is a good idea to read it to avoid breaking laws that differ from those of your country. If an oncoming vehicle flicks its lights at you in daytime, slow down: it could mean trouble ahead. When approaching a narrow bridge, the first vehicle to flash its lights has right of way. One-way streets are common. One-way traffic is indicated by an arrow; two-way, by a double-pointed arrow. Other road signs follow the widespread system of international symbols.

In Mexico City, **watch out for "Hoy no Circula" notices.** Because of pollution, all cars in the city without a Verification "0" rating (usually those built before 1994) are prohibited from driving one day a week (two days a week during high-alert periods). Posted signs show certain letters or numbers paired with each day of the week, indicating that vehicles with those letters or numbers in their license plates aren't allowed to drive on the corresponding day. Foreigners aren't exempt. Cars with license plate numbers ending in 5 or 6 are prohibited on Monday; 7 or 8 on Tuesday; 3 or 4 on Wednesday; 1 or 2 on Thursday; and 9 or 0 on Friday.

Mileage and speed limits are given in kilometers: 100 kph and 80 kph (62 mph and 50 mph, respectively) are the most common maximums. A few of the toll roads allow 110 kph (68 mph). In cities and small towns, observe the posted speed limits, which can be as low as 20 kph (12 mph). Seat belts are required by law throughout Mexico.

SAFETY ON THE ROAD

Never drive at night in remote and rural areas. *Banditos* are one concern, but so are potholes, free-roaming animals, cars with no working lights, road-hogging trucks, and difficulty in getting assistance. It's best to use toll roads whenever possible; although costly, they're much safer.

If you're driving from Manzanillo to Ixtapa/Zihuatanejo—about 8–10 hours with a meal stop—make the trip only during daylight hours, due to reports of carjackings around the area of Playa Azul. Military and police patrols have been increased on Carretera 200 and the number of incidents has dramatically decreased; still, exercise caution.

Some of the biggest hassles on the road might be from police who pull you over for supposedly breaking the law, or for being a good prospect for a scam. Remember to **be polite**—displays of anger will only make matters worse—and be aware that a police officer might be pulling you over for something you didn't do. Although efforts are being made to fight corruption, it's still a fact of life in Mexico, and the $5 it costs to get your license back is definitely supplementary income for the officer who pulled you over with no intention of taking you down to police headquarters.

If you're stopped for speeding, the officer is supposed to take your license and hold it until you pay the fine at the local police station. But the officer will always prefer a *mordida* (small bribe) to wasting his time at the station. If you decide to dispute a charge that seems preposterous, do so with a smile, and tell the officer that you would like to talk to the police captain when you get to the station. The officer usually will let you go rather than go to the station.

When crossing the streets by foot, **look both ways for oncoming traffic,** even with the light. Although pedestrians have the right of way by law, drivers disregard it. And more often than not, if a driver hits a pedestrian, he'll drive away as fast as he can without stopping, to avoid jail. Many Mexican drivers don't carry auto insurance, so you'll have to shoulder your own medical expenses.

CHILDREN IN MEXICO

Mexico has one of the strictest policies about children entering the country. All children, including infants, must have proof of citizenship (a birth certificate) for travel to Mexico. All children up to age 18 traveling with a single parent must also have a notarized letter from the other parent stating that the child has his or her permission to leave their home country. If the other parent is deceased or the child has only one legal parent, a notarized statement saying so must be obtained as proof. In addition, parents must now fill out a tourist card for each child over the age of 10 traveling with them.

If you're renting a car, don't forget to **arrange for a car seat** when you reserve. For general advice about traveling with children, consult *Fodor's FYI: Travel with Your Baby* (available in bookstores everywhere).

FLYING

If your children are two or older, ask about children's airfares. As a rule, infants under two not occupying a seat fly at greatly reduced fares or even for free. But if you want to guarantee a seat for an infant, you have to pay full fare. Consider flying during off-peak days and times; most airlines will grant an infant a seat without a ticket if there are available seats. When booking, **confirm carry-on allowances** if you're traveling with infants. In general, for babies charged 10% to 50% of the adult fare you are allowed one carry-on bag and a collapsible stroller; if the flight is full, the stroller may have to be checked or you may be limited to less.

Experts agree that it's a good idea to use safety seats aloft for children weighing less than 40 pounds. Airlines set their own policies: If you use a safety seat, U.S. carriers usually require that the child be ticketed, even if he or she is young enough to ride free, because the seats must be strapped into regular seats. And even if you pay the full adult fare for the seat, it may be worth it, especially on longer trips. Do **check your airline's policy about using safety seats during takeoff and landing.** Safety seats are not allowed everywhere in the plane, so get your seat assignments as early as possible.

When reserving, request children's meals or a freestanding bassinet (not available at all airlines) if you need them. But note that bulkhead seats, where you must sit to use the bassinet, may lack an overhead bin or storage space on the floor.

FOOD & SUPPLIES

Fresh milk isn't always readily available, though necessities such as disposable diapers can be found in almost every town.

LODGING

Most hotels in Mexico allow children under a certain age to stay in their parents' room at no extra charge, but others charge for them as extra adults; be sure to find out the cutoff age for children's discounts.

Many hotel chains in Mexico offer services that make it easier to travel with children. They include connecting family rooms, play areas such as kiddie pools and playgrounds, and kids' clubs with special activities and outings. Check with your hotel before booking to see if the services are included in the price or if there's an extra charge.

SIGHTS & ATTRACTIONS

Places that are especially appealing to children are indicated by a rubber-duckie icon (🐤) in the margin.

COMPUTERS ON THE ROAD

Internet cafés have sprung up all over Mexico, making e-mail by far the easiest way to get in touch with people back home. If you have a Toshiba or Macintosh laptop, bear in mind that having it serviced might be hopeless. Parts for these machines are hard to come by in Mexico.

Carry a spare battery because replacements are expensive and difficult to find. Always check with your hotel about surge protection, especially if the property isn't part of a major chain and/or is in an out-of-the-way place. Extreme electrical fluctuations and surges can damage or destroy your computer. Check with IBM for its pen-size modem tester that plugs into a phone and jack to test if the line is safe.

CONSUMER PROTECTION

Whether you're shopping for gifts or purchasing travel services, **pay with a major credit card** whenever possible, so you can cancel payment or get reimbursed if there's a problem (and you can provide documentation). If you're doing business with a particular company for the first time, contact your local Better Business Bureau and the attorney general's offices in your state and (for U.S. businesses) the company's home state as well. Have any complaints been filed? Finally, if you're buying a package or tour, always **consider travel insurance** that includes default coverage (⇨ Insurance).

🖪 BBBs **Council of Better Business Bureaus** ✉ 4200 Wilson Blvd., Suite 800, Arlington, VA 22203 ☎ 703/276-0100 ⊕ www.bbb.org.

CRUISE TRAVEL

Cozumel and Playa del Carmen have become increasingly popular ports for Caribbean cruises. Most lines—including Princess, Royal Caribbean International, Norwegian, Cunard, Holland America, and Royal Olympia—leave from Miami and/or other Florida ports such as Fort Lauderdale, Port Manatee, and Tampa. Texas passengers can take Royal Caribbean from Galveston and Royal Olympia or Norwegian from Houston to the Yucatán; Norwegian also has departures from Charleston, SC. Companies offering cruises down Mexico's Pacific coast (Baja California) include Princess, Norwegian, Royal Olympia, Royal Caribbean, and Holland America. Most depart from Los Angeles or San Diego and head to Los Cabos or Acapulco and points south; some trips originate in Vancouver or San Francisco. Carnival began cruises down Mexico's Pacific coast from a new terminal in Long Beach, CA, in spring 2003.

To learn how to plan, choose, and book a cruise-ship voyage, consult *Fodor's FYI: Plan & Enjoy Your Cruise* (available in bookstores everywhere).

🖪 Cruise Lines **Carnival** ☎ 888/227-6482 ⊕ www.carnival.com. **Cunard** ☎ 800/221-4770 ⊕ www.cunard.com. **Holland America** ☎ 800/426-0327 ⊕ www.hollandamerica.com. **Norwegian** ☎ 800/327-7030 ⊕ www.ncl.com. **Princess** ☎ 800/421-0522 ⊕ www.princess.com. **Regal** ☎ 800/270-7245 ⊕ www.regalcruises.com. **Royal Caribbean International** ☎ 800/327-6700 ⊕ www.royalcaribbean.com. **Royal Olympia** ☎ 800/872-6400 ⊕ www.epirotiki.com.

CUSTOMS & DUTIES

When shopping abroad, **keep receipts** for all purchases. Upon reentering the country, **be ready to show customs officials what you've bought.** Pack purchases together in an easily accessible place. If you think a duty is incorrect, appeal the assessment. If you object to the way your clearance was handled, note the inspector's badge number. In either case, first ask to see a supervisor. If the problem isn't resolved, write to the appropriate authorities, beginning with the port director at your point of entry.

IN MEXICO

Upon entering Mexico, you'll be given a baggage declaration form and asked to itemize what you're bringing into the country. You are allowed to bring in 3 liters of spirits or wine for personal use; 400 cigarettes, 25 cigars, or 200 grams of tobacco; a reasonable amount of perfume for personal use; one movie camera and one regular camera and 12 rolls of film for each; and gift items not to exceed a total of $300. If driving across the U.S. border, gift items must not exceed $50. You aren't allowed to bring firearms, meat, vegetables, plants, fruit, or flowers into the country. You can bring in one of each of the following items without paying taxes: a cell phone, a beeper, a radio or tape recorder, a musical instrument, a laptop computer, a portable copier or printer, and a typewriter. Compact discs are limited to 20 and DVDs to five.

Mexico also allows you to bring one cat, one dog, or up to four canaries into the country if you have two things: 1) a pet health certificate signed by a registered veterinarian in the United States and issued not more than 72 hours before the animal enters Mexico; and 2) a pet vaccination certificate showing that the animal has been treated for rabies, hepatitis, pip, and leptospirosis. Aduana Mexico (Mexican Customs) has a striking and informative Web site, though everything is in Spanish.
🗲 **Aduana Mexico** ⊕ www.aduanas.sat.gob.mx.

IN AUSTRALIA

Australian residents who are 18 or older may bring home A$400 worth of souvenirs and gifts (including jewelry), 250 cigarettes or 250 grams of cigars or other tobacco products, and 1,125 milliliters of alcohol (including wine, beer, and spirits). Residents under 18 may bring back A$200 worth of goods. Members of the same family traveling together may pool their allowances. Prohibited items include meat products. Seeds, plants, and fruits need to be declared upon arrival.
🗲 **Australian Customs Service** ⊕ Regional Director, Box 8, Sydney, NSW 2001 ☎ 02/9213-2000;

1300/363263; 02/9364-7222;1800/803-006 quarantine-inquiry line ⊕ www.customs.gov.au.

IN CANADA

Canadian residents who have been out of Canada for at least seven days may bring in C$750 worth of goods duty-free. If you've been away fewer than seven days but more than 48 hours, the duty-free allowance drops to C$200. If your trip lasts 24 to 48 hours, the allowance is C$50. You may not pool allowances with family members. Goods claimed under the C$750 exemption may follow you by mail; those claimed under the lesser exemptions must accompany you. Alcohol and tobacco products may be included in the seven-day and 48-hour exemptions but not in the 24-hour exemption. If you meet the age requirements of the province or territory through which you reenter Canada, you may bring in, duty-free, 1.5 liters of wine *or* 1.14 liters (40 imperial ounces) of liquor *or* 24 12-ounce cans or bottles of beer or ale. Also, if you meet the local age requirement for tobacco products, you may bring in, duty-free, 200 cigarettes and 50 cigars. Check ahead of time with the Canada Customs and Revenue Agency or the Department of Agriculture for policies regarding meat products, seeds, plants, and fruits.

You may send an unlimited number of gifts (only one gift per recipient, however) worth up to C$60 each duty-free to Canada. Label the package UNSOLICITED GIFT—VALUE UNDER $60. Alcohol and tobacco are excluded.
🗲 **Canada Customs and Revenue Agency** ⊠ 2265 St. Laurent Blvd., Ottawa, Ontario K1G 4K3 ☎ 204/983-3500 or 506/636-5064; 800/461-9999 in the U.S. ⊕ www.ccra.gc.ca.

IN NEW ZEALAND

All homeward-bound residents may bring back NZ$700 worth of souvenirs and gifts; passengers may not pool their allowances, and children can claim only the concession on goods intended for their own use. For those 17 or older, the duty-free allowance also includes 4.5 liters of wine or beer; one 1,125-milliliter bottle of spirits; and either 200 cigarettes, 250 grams of tobacco, 50 cigars, *or* a combination of the three up to 250 grams. Meat products, seeds, plants, and fruits must be declared upon arrival to the Agricultural Services Department.
🗲 **New Zealand Customs** ⊠ Head office: The Customhouse, 17-21 Whitmore St., Box 2218, Wellington

☎ 09/300-5399 or 0800/428-786 ⊕ www.customs.
govt.nz.

IN THE U.K.

If you are a U.K. resident and your journey was wholly within the European
Union, you probably won't have to pass
through customs when you return to the
United Kingdom. If you plan to bring back
large quantities of alcohol or tobacco,
check EU limits beforehand. In most cases,
if you bring back more than 200 cigars,
3,200 cigarettes, 10 liters of spirits, 110
liters of beer, and/or 90 liters of wine, you
have to declare the goods upon return.
🛈 HM Customs and Excise ⊠ Portcullis House, 21
Cowbridge Rd. E, Cardiff CF11 9SS ☎ 0845/010-
9000; 0208/929-0152; 0208/929-6731; 0208/910-
3602 complaints ⊕ www.hmce.gov.uk.

IN THE U.S.

U.S. residents who have been out of the
country for at least 48 hours may bring
home, for personal use, $800 worth of
foreign goods duty-free, as long as they
haven't used the $800 allowance or any
part of it in the past 30 days. This exemption may include 1 liter of alcohol (for
travelers 21 and older), 200 cigarettes,
and 100 non-Cuban cigars. Family members from the same household who are
traveling together may pool their $800
personal exemptions. For fewer than 48
hours, the duty-free allowance drops to
$200, which may include 50 cigarettes, 10
non-Cuban cigars, and 150 milliliters of
alcohol (or 150 milliliters of perfume containing alcohol). The $200 allowance can-
not be combined with other individuals'
exemptions, and if you exceed it, the full
value of all the goods will be taxed. Antiques, which the U.S. Bureau of Customs
and Border Protection defines as objects
more than 100 years old, enter duty-free,
as do original works of art done entirely
by hand, including paintings, drawings,
and sculptures. This doesn't apply to folk
art or handicrafts, which are in general
dutiable.

You may also send packages home duty-
free, with a limit of one parcel per ad-
dressee per day (except alcohol or tobacco
products or perfume worth more than
$5). You can mail up to $200 worth of
goods for personal use; label the package
PERSONAL USE and attach a list of its contents and their retail value. If the package
contains your used personal belongings,
mark it AMERICAN GOODS RETURNED to
avoid paying duties. You may send up to
$100 worth of goods as a gift; mark the
package UNSOLICITED GIFT. Mailed items
do not affect your duty-free allowance on
your return.

To avoid paying duty on foreign-made
high-ticket items you already own and will
take on your trip, register them with Customs before you leave the country. Consider filing a Certificate of Registration for
laptops, cameras, watches, and other digital devices identified with serial numbers
or other permanent markings; you can
keep the certificate for other trips. Otherwise, bring a sales receipt or insurance
form to show that you owned the item before you left the United States.
🛈 U.S. Bureau of Customs and Border Protection
⊠ for inquiries and equipment registration, 1300
Pennsylvania Ave. NW, Washington, DC 20229
☎ 202/354-1000 ⊕ www.customs.gov ⊠ for complaints, Customer Satisfaction Unit, 1300 Pennsylvania Ave. NW, Room 5.5D, Washington, DC 20229.

DINING

Mexican restaurants run the gamut from
humble hole-in-the-wall shacks, street
stands, *taquerías,* and American-style fast-
food joints to internationally acclaimed
gourmet restaurants. Prices, naturally, follow suit. To save money, **look for the
fixed-menu lunch** known as *comida corrida* or *menú del día,* which is served 1–4
almost everywhere in Mexico.

The restaurants we list are the cream of
the crop in each price category. Price categories are based on the least expensive en-
trée to the most expensive. For more
information on local foods throughout
Mexico, *see* "La Cocina Mexicana" in
Mexico City (Chapter 1) and the cuisine
sections that appear under Pleasures &
Pastimes in each chapter. Throughout this
guide, properties indicated by an ✕⊡ are
lodging establishments whose restaurant
warrants a special trip.

MEALTIMES

In Mexico, lunch is the big meal; dinner is
rarely served before 8 PM. Unless otherwise
noted, the restaurants listed in this guide
are open daily for lunch and dinner.

PAYING

Credit cards—especially American Express, MasterCard, and Visa—are widely

accepted at pricier restaurants. Bargains are usually cash only.

RESERVATIONS & DRESS

Reservations are always a good idea; we mention them only when they're essential or not accepted. Book as far ahead as you can, and reconfirm as soon as you arrive. (Large parties should always call ahead to check the reservations policy.) We mention dress only when men are required to wear a jacket or a jacket and tie.

WINE, BEER & SPIRITS

Mexican drinking establishments range from raucous cantinas, reserved for hard-drinking men, to low-key cafés. Be sure to sample some locally made tequila or mezcal (the one with the worm at the bottom). Both potent spirits are made from the agave plant, which is similar to but, in fact, not a cactus. Ask for a *reposado* (aged 2–12 months) or *aöejo* (aged 1–3 years) tequila for a smoother—and more expensive—taste. Locally brewed beers are mostly of the Corona category though the Negra Modelo and Indio brands are darker. Mexico's Baja California region has gained a reputation for its wines; ask your waiter to recommend a vintage.

DISABILITIES & ACCESSIBILITY

Mexico is poorly equipped for travelers with disabilities. There are no special discounts or passes, nor is public transportation, including the Mexico City Metro, wheelchair accessible. An exception is the city of Veracruz, where downtown street corners have ramps. Roads and sidewalks are often crowded—many have cobblestones—and people on the street won't assist you unless expressly asked. Further, you can't rent vehicles outfitted for travelers with disabilities.

Most hotels and restaurants have at least a few steps, and although rooms considered "wheelchair accessible" by hotel owners are usually on the ground floor, the doorways and bathroom may not be maneuverable. It's a good idea to call ahead to find out what a hotel or restaurant can offer. Despite these barriers, Mexicans with disabilities manage to negotiate places that most travelers outside Mexico would not consider accessible.

One Mexican travel agency that addresses the needs of people with disabilities is Varlo y Mar, which arranges trips to Puerto Vallarta. Plans to help travelers with disabilities visit Cancún, Cabo San Lucas, and other places are in the works.
Varlo y Mar ⊠ Oceana Indico 399, Col. Palmar de Aramara, Puerto Vallarta ☎ 322/224-1868 ⊕ www.accesiblemexico.com.

LODGING

The best choices of accessible lodging are found in major resort towns such as Acapulco, Cancún, and Mazatlán, and big cities such as Mexico City and Guadalajara.

RESERVATIONS

When discussing accessibility with an operator or reservations agent, **ask hard questions.** Are there any stairs, inside *or* out? Are there grab bars next to the toilet *and* in the shower/tub? How wide is the doorway to the room? To the bathroom? For the most extensive facilities meeting the latest legal specifications, **opt for newer accommodations.** If you reserve through a toll-free number, consider also calling the hotel's local number to confirm the information from the central reservations office. Get confirmation in writing when you can.
Complaints Aviation Consumer Protection Division (⇨ Air Travel) for airline-related problems. **Departmental Office of Civil Rights** ⊠ for general inquiries, U.S. Department of Transportation, S-30, 400 7th St. SW, Room 10215, Washington, DC 20590 ☎ 202/366-4648 ⊕ www.dot.gov/ost/docr/index.htm. **Disability Rights Section** ⊠ NYAV, U.S. Department of Justice, Civil Rights Division, 950 Pennsylvania Ave. NW, Washington, DC 20530 ☎ 202/514-0301 ADA information line; 800/514-0301 in the U.S.; 202/514-0383 TTY; 800/514-0383 TTY in the U.S. ⊕ www.ada.gov. **U.S. Department of Transportation Hotline** ☎ 800/778-4838 in the U.S.; 800/455-9880 TTY in the U.S. for disability-related air-travel problems.

TRAVEL AGENCIES

In the United States, the Americans with Disabilities Act requires that travel firms serve the needs of all travelers. Some agencies specialize in working with people with disabilities.
Travelers with Mobility Problems Access Adventures ⊠ 206 Chestnut Ridge Rd., Scottsville, NY 14624 ☎ 585/889-9096 ✉ dltravel@prodigy.net, run by a former physical-rehabilitation counselor.

CareVacations ✉ No. 5, 5110-50 Ave., Leduc, Alberta, Canada, T9E 6V4 ☎ 780/986-6404 or 877/478-7827 ⊕ www.carevacations.com, for group tours and cruise vacations. **Flying Wheels Travel** ✉ 143 W. Bridge St., Box 382, Owatonna, MN 55060 ☎ 507/451-5005 ⊕ www.flyingwheelstravel.com. **⚏ Travelers with Developmental Disabilities New Directions** ✉ 5276 Hollister Ave., Suite 207, Santa Barbara, CA 93111 ☎ 805/967-2841 or 888/967-2841 ⊕ www.newdirectionstravel.com.

DISCOUNTS & DEALS

Be a smart shopper and compare all your options before making decisions. A plane ticket bought with a promotional coupon from travel clubs, coupon books, and direct-mail offers or purchased on the Internet may not be cheaper than the least expensive fare from a discount ticket agency. And always keep in mind that what you get is just as important as what you save.

DISCOUNT RESERVATIONS

To save money, look into discount reservations services with Web sites and toll-free numbers, which use their buying power to get a better price on hotels, airline tickets, even car rentals. When booking a room, always call the hotel's local toll-free number (if one is available) rather than the central reservations number—you'll often get a better price. Always ask about special packages or corporate rates.

When shopping for the best deal on hotels and car rentals, **look for guaranteed exchange rates,** which protect you against a falling dollar. With your rate locked in, you won't pay more, even if the price goes up in the local currency. **⚏ Airline Tickets Air 4 Less** ☎ 800/AIR4LESS in the U.S.; low-fare specialist. **⚏ Hotel Rooms Accommodations Express** ☎ 800/444-7666 or 800/277-1064 in the U.S. ⊕ www.accommodationsexpress.com. **Hotels.com** ☎ 214/369-1246; 800/246-8357 in the U.S. ⊕ www.hotels.com. **Steigenberger Reservation Service** ☎ 800/223-5652 in the U.S. ⊕ www.srs-worldhotels.com. **Turbotrip.com** ☎ 800/473-7829 in the U.S. ⊕ www.turbotrip.com.

PACKAGE DEALS

Don't confuse packages and guided tours. When you buy a package, you travel on your own, just as though you had planned the trip yourself. Fly/drive packages, which combine airfare and car rental, are often a good deal. In cities, ask the local visitors bureau about hotel packages that include tickets to major museum exhibits or other special events.

ECOTOURISM

Ecoturismo is fast becoming a buzzword in the Mexican tourism industry, even though not all operators and establishments employ practices that are good for the environment. For example, in the so-called Riviera Maya, an area south of Cancún, hotel developments greatly threaten the ecosystem, including the region's coral reefs. Nevertheless, President Vicente Fox has pledged to support more ecotourism projects, and recent national conferences have focused on this theme.

Mexico has more than 18 million acres of preserves, national parks, and biosphere reserves. You can visit monarch butterfly sanctuaries, endangered sea-turtle nesting sites, saltwater lagoons where California gray whales breed, deep desert canyons, and volcanoes. To find out more about ecotourism opportunities and issues, contact the Asociación Méxicana de Turismo de Aventura y Ecoturismo (AMTAVE or Mexican Association of Adventure Travel and Ecotourism). Planeta.com is another great source for information on environmentally conscious travel in Mexico and throughout world; it even has a list of eco-friendly tour operators. **⚏ AMTAVE** ⊕ www.amtave.org. **Planeta.com** ⊕ www.planeta.com.

ELECTRICITY

For U.S. and Canadian travelers, electrical converters aren't necessary because Mexico operates on the 60-cycle, 120-volt system; however, many Mexican outlets have not been updated to accommodate three-prong and polarized plugs (those with one larger prong), so to be safe **bring an adapter.**

If your appliances are dual-voltage, you'll need only an adapter. Don't use 110-volt outlets marked FOR SHAVERS ONLY for high-wattage appliances such as blow-dryers. Most laptops operate equally well on 110 and 220 volts and so require only an adapter.

EMBASSIES

F Australia **Australian Embassy** ✉ Calle Rubén Darío 55, Col. Polanco, Mexico City ☎ 55/5531-5225 🌐 www.mexico.embassy.gov.au/quienes/mx/index.html.

F Canada **Canadian Embassy** ✉ Calle Schiller 529, Col. Polanco, Mexico City ☎ 55/5724-7900 🌐 www.canada.org.mx.

F New Zealand **New Zealand Embassy** ✉ Calle José Luis LaGrange 103, 10th fl., Col. Polanco, Mexico City ☎ 55/5283-9460.

F United Kingdom **British Embassy** ✉ Av. Río Lerma 71, Col. Cuauhtémoc, Mexico City ☎ 55/5207-2089 🌐 www.embajadabritanica.com.mx.

F United States **U.S. Embassy** ✉ Paseo de la Reforma 305, Col. Cuauhtémoc, Mexico City ☎ 55/5080-2000 🌐 www.usembassy-mexico.gov/emenu.html.

EMERGENCIES

The emergency number ☎ 060 works best in Mexico City and environs. In all other areas you're better off calling the local number for the police or other emergency services. For roadside assistance contact the Angeles Verdes. If you get into a scrape with the law, you can call the Citizens' Emergency Center in the United States. The Mexican Ministry of Tourism also has a 24-hour toll-free hot line, and local tourist boards may be able to help as well. Two medical emergency evacuation services are Air Ambulance Network and Global Life Flight.

F **Air Ambulance Network** ☎ 01800/010-0027 toll-free in Mexico; 800/327-1966 in the U.S. 🌐 www.airambulancenetwork.com. **Angeles Verdes, Mexico City** ☎ 55/5250-8221 or 55/5520-8555. **Citizens' Emergency Center** ☎ 202/647-5225 weekdays 8:15 AM–10 PM EST, Sat. 9 AM–3 PM; 202/634-3600 after hrs and Sun. **Global Life Flight** ☎ 01800/305-9400 or 01800/361-1600 toll-free in Mexico; 888/554-9729 in the U.S.; 877/817-6843 in Canada 🌐 www.globallifeflight.com. **Mexico Ministry of Tourism** ☎ 01800/903-9200 toll free in Mexico.

ENGLISH-LANGUAGE MEDIA

Some of Mexico's larger grocery stores have English-language magazines and books—albeit expensive ones. Expect to pay at least double what you'd pay back home. Several stores in Mexico City sell English-language publications, and you can probably find at least one place in other major cities and resorts to buy them. In most small towns you won't have much luck. At this writing, the *Miami Herald* and *El Universal* newspapers planned to publish an English-language newspaper called *The Herald* for distribution throughout Mexico. For English-language TV shows, cable channels on your hotel room's TV are your best bet.

ETIQUETTE & BEHAVIOR

In the United States and elsewhere in the world, being direct, efficient, and succinct is highly valued. But Mexican communication tends to be more subtle, and the American style is often perceived as curt and aggressive. Mexicans are extremely polite, so losing your temper over delays or complaining loudly will get you branded as rude and make people less inclined to help you. **Remember that things move at a slow pace** here and that there's no stigma attached to being late; be gracious about this and other local customs and attitudes. In restaurants, for example, a waiter would never consider bringing you your check before you ask for it; that would be rude. What's not considered rude, however, is dallying in bringing that check once you do ask for it. Learning basic phrases in Spanish such as *por favor* (please) and *gracias* (thank you) will make a big difference in how people respond to you.

BUSINESS ETIQUETTE

Personal relationships always come first here, so developing rapport and trust is essential. A handshake and personal greeting is appropriate along with a friendly inquiry about family, especially if you have met the family. In established business relationships, do not be surprised if you're greeted with a kiss on the cheek or a hug. Always be respectful toward colleagues in public and keep confrontations private. Meetings may or may not start on time, but you should be patient. When invited to dinner at the home of a client or associate, bring a gift and be sure to send a thank-you note afterward.

GAY & LESBIAN TRAVEL

Mexican same-sex couples keep a low profile, and foreign same-sex couples should do the same. Two people of the same gender can often have a hard time getting a *cama matrimonial* (double bed), especially in smaller hotels. This could be attributed to the influence of the Catholic church—

Mexico is a devoutly Catholic country. The same rule that applies all over the world holds in Mexico as well: alternative lifestyles in general are more accepted in cosmopolitan areas, such as Mexico City, Acapulco, Cancún, Cuernavaca, Guadalajara, Puerto Vallarta, San Miguel de Allende, and Veracruz City.

Gay- & Lesbian-Friendly Travel Agencies **Different Roads Travel** ⊠ 8383 Wilshire Blvd., Suite 520, Beverly Hills, CA 90211 ☎ 323/651-5557; 800/429-8747 in the U.S. (Ext. 14 for both) ✍ lgernert@tzell.com. **Kennedy Travel** ⊠ 130 W. 42nd St., Suite 401, New York, NY 10036 ☎ 212/840-8659; 800/237-7433 ☐ 212/730-2269 ⊕ www.kennedytravel.com. **Now, Voyager** ⊠ 4406 18th St., San Francisco, CA 94114 ☎ 415/626-1169; 800/255-6951 in the U.S. ⊕ www.nowvoyager.com. **Skylink Travel and Tour** ⊠ 1455 N. Dutton Ave., Suite A, Santa Rosa, CA 95401 ☎ 707/546-9888; 800/225-5759 in the U.S. ☐ 707/636-0951; serving lesbian travelers.

GUIDEBOOKS

Plan well and you won't be sorry. Guidebooks are excellent tools—and you can take them with you. You may want to check out color-photo-illustrated *Fodor's Exploring Mexico,* which is thorough on culture and history and is available at online retailers and bookstores everywhere.

HEALTH

AIR & WATER POLLUTION

Air pollution in Mexico City can pose a health risk. The sheer number of cars and industries in the capital, thermal inversions, and the inability to process sewage have all contributed to the high levels of lead, carbon monoxide, and other pollutants in Mexico City's atmosphere. Children, the elderly, and those with respiratory problems should avoid outdoor activities—including sightseeing—on days of high smog alerts. If you have heart problems, keep in mind that Mexico City is, at 7,556 ft, the highest metropolis on the North American continent. This compounded with the smog may pose a serious health risk, so check with your doctor before planning a trip.

In the last few years Mexico has had to make tough choices between much needed development and protecting the environment. In some places the rate of development has exceeded the government's ability to keep the environment safe. Stud-

ies released in early 2003 indicated that waters near 16 resort areas contained high levels of pollution from trash, sewage, or industrial waste. Of the resorts—which included Acapulco, Puerto Vallarta, Puerto Escondido, and Huatulco—Zihuatanejo was considered the most polluted. Two factors reportedly contributed to this: the waters off its shores are in a bay where pollution is more apt to accumluate than it would in open waters, and this area in particular was having difficulties properly treating its wastewater. Although the studies prompted some clean-up action, much more will need to be done. As swimming in polluted waters can cause gastrointestinal and other problems, ask locals about where it's best to swim.

DIVERS' ALERT

Do not fly within 24 hours of scuba diving.

FOOD & DRINK

In Mexico the major health risk, known as *turista,* or traveler's diarrhea, is caused by eating contaminated fruit or vegetables or drinking contaminated water. So **watch what you eat.** Stay away from ice, uncooked food, and unpasteurized milk and milk products, and **drink only bottled water** or water that has been boiled for at least 10 minutes (insist on this by saying *"quiero el agua hervida por diez minutos"*), even when you're brushing your teeth. Mild cases may respond to Imodium (known generically as loperamide or Lomotil) or Pepto-Bismol (not as strong), both of which you can buy over the counter; keep in mind, though, that these drugs can complicate more serious illnesses. Drink plenty of purified water or tea; chamomile tea (*te de manzanilla*) is a good folk remedy and it's readily available in restaurants throughout Mexico. In severe cases, rehydrate yourself with Gatorade or a salt-sugar solution (½ teaspoon salt and 4 tablespoons sugar per quart of water).

When ordering cold drinks at untouristed establishments, **skip the ice:** *sin hielo.* (You can usually identify ice made commercially from purified water by its uniform shape and the hole in the center.) Hotels with water-purification systems will post signs to that effect in the rooms. *Tacos al pastor*—thin pork slices grilled on a spit and garnished with the usual cilantro, onions, and chili peppers—are delicious but dangerous. It's also a good idea to pass up *ceviche,* raw fish cured in lemon juice—a favorite appetizer, especially at seaside resorts. The Mexican Department of Health warns that marinating in lemon juice does not constitute the "cooking" that would make the shellfish safe to eat. Also, be wary of hamburgers sold from street stands, because you can never be certain what meat they are made with (horse meat is common).

MEDICAL PLANS

No one plans to get sick while traveling, but it happens, so consider signing up with a medical-assistance company. Members get doctor referrals, emergency evacuation or repatriation, hot lines for medical consultation, cash for emergencies, and other assistance.

🔳 Medical-Assistance Companies **International SOS Assistance** ⊕ www.internationalsos.com ⊠ 8 Neshaminy Interplex, Suite 207, Trevose, PA 19053 ☎ 215/245-4707; 800/523-6586 in the U.S. ⊠ Landmark House, Hammersmith Bridge Rd., 6th fl., London W6 9DP ☎ 20/8762-8008 🖷 20/8748-7744 ⊠ 12 Chemin Riantbosson, 1217 Meyrin 1, Geneva, Switzerland ☎ 22/785-6464 ⊠ 331 N. Bridge Rd., 17-00, Odeon Towers, Singapore 188720 ☎ 6338-7800.

OVER-THE-COUNTER REMEDIES

Farmacias (pharmacies) are the most convenient place for such common medicines as *aspirina* (aspirin) or *jarabe para la tos* (cough syrup). You'll be able to find many U.S. brands (e.g., Tylenol, Pepto Bismol, etc.). There are pharmacies in all small towns and on practically every corner in larger cities. The Sanborns chain stores also have pharmacies.

PESTS & OTHER HAZARDS

Caution is advised when venturing out in the Mexican sun. Sunbathers lulled by a slightly overcast sky or the sea breezes can be burned badly in just 20 minutes. To avoid overexposure, **use strong sunscreens and avoid the peak sun hours** of noon to 2 PM. Sunscreen, including many American brands, can be found in pharmacies, supermarkets, and resort gift shops.

SHOTS & MEDICATIONS

According to the U.S. National Centers for Disease Control and Prevention (CDC), there's a limited risk of malaria and dengue fever in certain rural areas of Mex-

ico. In most urban or easily accessible areas you need not worry. However, if you plan to visit remote regions or stay for more than six weeks, **check with the CDC's International Travelers Hotline.** In areas where malaria and dengue, both of which are carried by mosquitoes, are prevalent, use mosquito nets, wear clothing that covers the body, apply repellent containing DEET, and use spray for flying insects in living and sleeping areas. Repellents (*repelentes contra moscos*) and sprays (*repelentes de sprie contra moscos*) can be purchased at pharmacies. In some places you see mosquito coils (*espirales contra moscos*) used; they can be purchased in hardware stores (*ferretería*) as well as in pharmacies. Also **consider taking antimalarial pills** if you are doing serious adventure activities in subtropical areas. There's no vaccine to combat dengue.

🔳 Health Warnings **National Centers for Disease Control and Prevention** (CDC) ⊠ National Center for Infectious Diseases, Division of Quarantine, Travelers' Health, 1600 Clifton Rd. NE, Atlanta, GA 30333 ☎ 877/394-8747 international travelers' health line; 800/311-3435 in the U.S. for other inquiries ⊕ www.cdc.gov/travel.

HOLIDAYS

Banks and government offices close on January 1, February 5 (Day of the Constitution), March 21 (Benito Juárez's birthday), May 1 (Labor Day), September 16 (Independence Day), November 20 (Day of the Revolution), and December 25. They may also close on unofficial holidays, such as Day of the Dead (November 1–2), and during Holy Week (the days leading to Easter Sunday). Government offices usually have reduced hours and staff from Christmas through New Year's Day.

INSURANCE

The most useful travel-insurance plan is a comprehensive policy that includes coverage for trip cancellation and interruption, default, trip delay, and medical expenses (with a waiver for preexisting conditions).

Without insurance you'll lose all or most of your money if you cancel your trip, regardless of the reason. Default insurance covers you if your tour operator, airline, or cruise line goes out of business. Trip-delay covers expenses that arise because of bad weather or mechanical delays. Study the fine print when comparing policies.

If you're traveling internationally, a key component of travel insurance is coverage for medical bills incurred if you get sick on the road. Such expenses aren't generally covered by Medicare or private policies. U.K. residents can buy a travel-insurance policy valid for most vacations taken during the year in which it's purchased (but check preexisting-condition coverage). British and Australian citizens need extra medical coverage when traveling overseas.

Always **buy travel policies directly from the insurance company**; if you buy them from a cruise line, airline, or tour operator that goes out of business you probably won't be covered for the agency or operator's default, a major risk. Before making any purchase, **review your existing health and home-owner's policies** to find what they cover away from home.

🛈 Travel Insurers In the United States: **Access America** ✉ 6600 W. Broad St., Richmond, VA 23230 ☎ 800/284-8300 in the U.S. ⊕ www.accessamerica.com. **Travel Guard International** ✉ 1145 Clark St., Stevens Point, WI 54481 ☎ 715/345-0505; 800/826-1300 in the U.S. ⊕ www.travelguard.com.

🛈 In the United Kingdom: **Association of British Insurers** ✉ 51 Gresham St., London EC2V 7HQ ☎ 020/7600-3333 ⊕ www.abi.org.uk. In Canada: **RBC Insurance** ✉ 6880 Financial Dr., Mississauga, Ontario L5N 7Y5 ☎ 800/565-3129 in the U.S. ⊕ www.rbcinsurance.com. In Australia: **Insurance Council of Australia** ✉ Insurance Enquiries and Complaints, Level 3, 56 Pitt St., Sydney, NSW 2000 ☎ 1300/363683 or 02/9251-4456 ⊕ www.iecltd.com.au. In New Zealand: **Insurance Council of New Zealand** ✉ Level 7, 111-115 Customhouse Quay, Box 474, Wellington ☎ 04/472-5230 ⊕ www.icnz.org.nz.

LANGUAGE

Spanish is the official language, although Indian languages are spoken by approximately 8% of the population and some of those people speak no Spanish at all. Basic English is widely understood by most people employed in tourism, less so in the less-developed areas. At the very least, shopkeepers will know the numbers for bargaining purposes.

As in most other foreign countries, knowing the mother tongue has a way of opening doors, so **learn some Spanish words and phrases.** Mexicans welcome even the most halting attempts to use the language.

Castilian Spanish—which is different from Latin American Spanish not only in pronunciation and grammar but also in vocabulary—is most widely taught outside Mexico. Words or phrases that are harmless or everyday in one country can offend in another. Unless you are lucky enough to be briefed on these nuances by a native coach, the only way to learn is by trial and error.

LANGUAGES FOR TRAVELERS

A phrase book and language-tape set can help get you started. *Fodor's Spanish for Travelers* (available at bookstores everywhere) is excellent.

LANGUAGE-STUDY PROGRAMS

Mexico has many language institutes, and attending one is an ideal way not only to learn Mexican Spanish but also to acquaint yourself with the customs and the people. For total immersion, most schools offer boarding with a family, but there's generally flexibility in terms of the type of lodgings and the length of your stay.

We recommend the places listed below for learning Spanish and living with a Mexican family. AmeriSpan Unlimited, based in the United States, can arrange for language study and homestays. Special programs include those at the Centro de Idiomas de la Universidad Autónoma Benito Juárez, which offers classes in Mixtec and Zapotec as well as Spanish, and at Cemanáuac, which has Latin American studies courses as well as language classes.

🛈 Language Institutes **Academia Falcon** ✉ Callejón de la Mora 158, 36000 Guanajuato ☎ 473/731-0745 ⊕ www.academiafalcon.com. **AmeriSpan Unlimited** ✆ Box 58129, Philadelphia, PA 19102 ☎ 800/879-6640 or 215/751-1100 ⊕ www.amerispan.com. **Cemanáuac** ✆ A.P. 5-21, CP 62051 Cuernavaca, Morelos ☎ 777/318-6407 ⊕ www.cemanahuac.com. **Centro de Idiomas de la Universidad Autónoma Benito Juárez** ✉ Calle Burgoa s/n, 68000 Oaxaca ☎☎ 951/516-5922. **Centro Internacional de Estudios para Extranjeros** ✉ Calle Tomás V. Gómez 125, 44600 Guadalajara, Jalisco ☎ 333/616-4399 ✉ Calle Libertad 42, Local 1, 48360 Puerto Vallarta, Jalisco ☎ 322/223-2082. **Iberoamerican University Programs for Foreign Students** ✉ Prolongación Paseo de la Reforma 880, 01210 Lomas de Santa Fe, Mexico, D.F. ☎ 55/5267-4243 ⊕ www.uia.mx/ibero/inter. **Instituto Allende** ✉ Ancha de San Antonio 20, 37700 San Miguel de Allende, Guanajuato ☎ 415/152-0190 or 415/152-0226 ⊕ www.instituto-allende.edu.mx.

Instituto de Lenguas Jovel, A.C. ☒ Calle Ma. Adelina Flores 21 San Cristóbal de las Casas ☎ (A.P. 62, 29200 San Cristóbal de las Casas, Chiapas) ☏☏ 967/678-4069 ⊕ www.institutojovel.com. **National Autonomous University of Mexico School for Foreign Students** ☒ Ex-Hacienda El Chorillo, Taxco ☎ (A.P. 70, 40200 Taxco, Guerrero) ☏☏ 762/622-0124. **SLI–Spanish Language Institute** ☒ Bajada de la Pradera 208, Col. Pradera 62170 Morelos ☎ 777/311-0063 ⊕ www.sli-spanish.com.mx or ☒ In the U.S. contact Language Link Inc., ☎ Box 3006, Peoria, IL 61612 ☎ 800/552-2051 in the U.S. ⊕ www.langlink.com.

LODGING

The price and quality of accommodations in Mexico vary from superluxurious, international-class hotels and all-inclusive resorts to modest budget properties, seedy places with shared bathrooms, *casas de huéspedes* (guest houses), youth hostels, and *cabañas* (beach huts). You may find appealing bargains while you're on the road, but if your comfort threshold is high, look for an English-speaking staff, guaranteed dollar rates, and toll-free reservation numbers.

The lodgings we list are the cream of the crop in each price category. Properties are assigned price categories based on the range from their least-expensive standard double room at high season (excluding holidays) to the most expensive. We always list the facilities that are available— but we don't specify whether they cost extra; when pricing accommodations, **always ask what's included and what costs extra.** Lodgings are denoted in the text with a house icon, ⌂ ; establishments with restaurants that warrant a special trip have ✕⌂ .

Assume that hotels operate on the European Plan (EP, with no meals) unless we specify that they use the Breakfast Plan (BP, with a full breakfast), the Continental Plan (CP, with a Continental breakfast), the Full American Plan (FP, all meals), or the Modified American Plan (MAP, with breakfast and dinner) or are all-inclusive (including all meals and most drinks and/or activities).

APARTMENT & VILLA RENTALS

If you want a home base that's roomy enough for a family and comes with cooking facilities, consider a furnished rental. These can save you money, especially if you're traveling with a group. Home-exchange directories sometimes list rentals as well as exchanges.

🖪 International Agents **At Home Abroad** ☒ 405 E. 56th St., Suite 6H, New York, NY 10022 ☎ 212/421-9165 ⊕ www.athomeabroadinc.com. **Hideaways International** ☒ 767 Islington St., Portsmouth, NH 03802 ☎ 603/430-4433; 800/843-4433 in the U.S. ⊕ www.hideaways.com membership $129. **Vacation Home Rentals Worldwide** ☒ 235 Kensington Ave., Norwood, NJ 07648 ☎ 201/767-9393; 800/633-3284 in the U.S. **Villanet** ☒ 1251 N.W. 116th St., Seattle, WA 98177 ☎ 206/417-3444; 800/964-1891 in the U.S. ⊕ www.rentavilla.com. **Villas and Apartments Abroad** ☒ 370 Lexington Ave., Suite 1401, New York, NY 10017 ☎ 212/897-5045; 800/433-3020 in the U.S. ⊕ www.ideal-villas.com. **Villas International** ☒ 4340 Redwood Hwy., Suite D309, San Rafael, CA 94903 ☎ 415/499-9490; 800/221-2260 in the U.S. ⊕ www.villasintl.com.

BED-AND-BREAKFASTS

The bed-and-breakfast craze hasn't missed Mexico, and the same delights that you find elsewhere in the world apply here, too—personable service, interesting local furnishings and decorative talent, and tasty morning meals. San Miguel de Allende and other Heartland cities have their share of charming places, as do Mexico City and parts of the Yucatán. If you arrive in Mexico City without a reservation, the Mexico City Hotel and Motel Association operates a booth at the airport that will assist you.

🖪 Reservation Services **Mexico City Hotel and Motel Association** ☎ 55/5571-3268 or 55/5571-3262

CAMPING

A host of camping opportunities exist in Mexico, but don't expect the typical U.S.-style campground. Mexico's are usually trailer parks with running water, cooking areas, and room to pitch tents; sites can cost $1–$10. To enjoy more rustic surroundings, you can set up camp off the road or on the beach in relative safety, and save loads of money. Usually, you can camp at an *ejido* (farming community) or on someone's land for free as long as you ask permission first; **ask locals about the safest and best spots.** The beaches at night aren't as safe as they once were; **be alert and don't camp alone.** And don't camp at archaeological sites.

Camping supplies are scarce in Mexico. Before you begin packing loads of camping gear, however, consider how much camping you'll actually do versus how much trouble it will be to haul around your tent, sleeping bag, stove, and accoutrements. Finding a place to store your gear can be difficult—lockers tend to be small.

In many towns along the Pacific and Caribbean coasts, beachside *palapas* (thatch-roof huts) are an excellent alternative to tent camping. All you'll need for a night in a palapa is a hammock (they don't cost much in Mexico), some mosquito netting, and a padlock for stashing your belongings in a locker.

HOME EXCHANGES

If you would like to exchange your home for someone else's, join a home-exchange organization, which will send you its updated listings of available exchanges for a year and will include your own listing in at least one of them. It's up to you to make specific arrangements.

🏠 Exchange Clubs **HomeLink International** ⌖ Box 47747, Tampa, FL 33647 ☎ 813/975-9825; 800/638-3841 in the U.S. ⊕ www.homelink.org; $110 yearly for a listing, on-line access, and catalog; $40 without catalog. **Intervac U.S.** ⌖ 30 Corte San Fernando, Tiburon, CA 94920 ☎ 800/756-4663 in the U.S. ⊕ www.intervacus.com; $105 yearly for a listing, on-line access, and a catalog; $50 without catalog.

HOSTELS

No matter what your age, you can save on lodging costs by staying at hostels. In Mexico, however, high-school and college students are more often the norm at hostels than older travelers. In some 4,500 locations in more than 70 countries around the world, Hostelling International (HI), the umbrella group for a number of national youth-hostel associations, offers single-sex, dorm-style beds and, at many hostels, rooms for couples and family accommodations. Membership in any HI national hostel association, open to travelers of all ages, allows you to stay in HI-affiliated hostels at member rates; one-year membership is about $28 for adults (C$35 for a two-year minimum membership in Canada, £13.50 in the United Kingdom, A$52 in Australia, and NZ$40 in New Zealand); hostels charge about $10–$30 per night. Members have priority if the

hostel is full; they're also eligible for discounts around the world, even on rail and bus travel in some countries.

🏠 Organizations **Hostelling International–USA** ⌖ 8401 Colesville Rd., Suite 600, Silver Spring, MD 20910 ☎ 301/495-1240 ⊕ www.hiayh.org. **Hostelling International–Canada** ⌖ 400-205 Catherine St., Ottawa, Ontario K2P 1C3 ☎ 613/237-7884; 800/663-5777 in the U.S. ⊕ www.hihostels.ca. **YHA Australia** ⌖ 422 Kent St., Sydney, NSW 2001 ☎ 02/9261-1111 ⊕ www.yha.com.au. **YHA England and Wales** ⌖ Trevelyan House, Dimple Rd., Matlock, Derbyshire DE4 3YH, U.K. ☎ 0870/870-8808 ⊕ www.yha.org.uk. **YHA New Zealand** ⌖ Level 3, 193 Cashel St., Box 436, Christchurch ☎ 03/379-9970 or 0800/278-299 ⊕ www.yha.org.nz.

HOTELS

It's essential to **reserve in advance** if you're traveling during high season or holiday periods. Overbooking is a common practice in some parts of Mexico, such as Cancún and Acapulco. Travelers to remote areas will encounter little difficulty in obtaining rooms on a walk-in basis unless it's during a holiday.

Hotel rates are subject to the 15% value-added tax (it's 10% in the states of Quintana Roo, Baja California, and Baja California Sur). In addition, many states charge a 2% hotel tax. Service charges and meals generally aren't included in the hotel rates.

The Mexican government categorizes hotels, based on qualitative evaluations, into *gran turismo* (superdeluxe, or five-star-plus, properties, of which there are only about 30 nationwide); five-star down to one-star; and economy class. Keep in mind that many hotels that might otherwise be rated higher have opted for a lower category to avoid higher interest rates on loans and financing.

High- versus low-season rates can vary significantly. Hotels in this guide have private bathrooms with showers, unless stated otherwise; bathtubs aren't common in inexpensive hotels and properties in smaller towns.

RESERVING A ROOM

If you're particularly sensitive to noise, you should call ahead to learn if your hotel of choice is on a busy street. Many of the most engaging accommodations in Mexico are on downtown intersections that experience heavy automobile and pedestrian traffic. And large hotels are known to have lobby bars with live music in the middle of an open-air atrium leading directly to rooms. When you book, request a room far from the bar.

Toll-Free Numbers Best Western ☎ 800/528-1234 in the U.S. ⊕ www.bestwestern.com. **Choice** ☎ 800/424-6423 in the U.S. ⊕ www.choicehotels.com. **Days Inn** ☎ 800/325-2525 in the U.S. ⊕ www.daysinn.com. **Doubletree Hotels** ☎ 800/222-8733 in the U.S. ⊕ www.doubletree.com. **Four Seasons** ☎ 800/332-3442 in the U.S. ⊕ www.fourseasons.com. **Hilton** ☎ 800/445-8667 in the U.S. ⊕ www.hilton.com. **Holiday Inn** ☎ 800/465-4329 in the U.S. ⊕ www.sixcontinentshotels.com. **Howard Johnson** ☎ 800/446-4656 ⊕ www.hojo.com. **Hyatt Hotels & Resorts** ☎ 800/233-1234 in the U.S. ⊕ www.hyatt.com. **Inter-Continental** ☎ 800/327-0200 in the U.S. ⊕ www.intercontinental.com. **Marriott** ☎ 800/228-9290 in the U.S. ⊕ www.marriott.com. **Le Meridien** ☎ 800/543-4300 in the U.S. ⊕ www.lemeridien-hotels.com. **Nikko Hotels International** ☎ 800/645-5687 in the U.S. ⊕ www.nikkohotels.com. **Omni** ☎ 800/843-6664 in the U.S. ⊕ www.omnihotels.com. **Radisson** ☎ 800/333-3333 in the U.S. ⊕ www.radisson.com. **Ritz-Carlton** ☎ 800/241-3333 in the U.S. ⊕ www.ritzcarlton.com. **Sheraton** ☎ 800/325-3535 in the U.S. ⊕ www.starwood.com/sheraton. **Westin Hotels & Resorts** ☎ 800/228-3000 in the U.S. ⊕ www.starwood.com/westin. **Wyndham Hotels & Resorts** ☎ 800/822-4200 in the U.S. ⊕ www.wyndham.com.

MAIL & SHIPPING

The Mexican postal system is notoriously slow and unreliable; **never send packages** or expect to receive them, as they may be stolen. (For emergencies, use a courier service or the express-mail service, with insurance). If you're an American Express cardholder, your best bet is to have packages sent to the nearest AmEx office.

Post offices (*oficinas de correos*) are found in even the smallest villages. International postal service is all airmail, but even so your letter will take anywhere from 10 days to six weeks to arrive. Service within Mexico can be equally slow.

PARCELS & OVERNIGHT SERVICES

Federal Express, DHL, and United Parcel Service are available in major cities and many resort areas, but Federal Express is the most widespread. These companies offer office or hotel pickup with 24-hour advance notice and are very reliable. From Mexico City to anywhere in the United States, the minimum charge is around $23 for a package weighing about one pound. Starting prices are higher for Australia, Canada, New Zealand, and the United Kingdom, and deliveries take longer. It's best to send all packages using one of these services.

Major Services DHL ⊕ www.dhl.com. **Federal Express** ⊕ www.federalexpress.com. **United Parcel Service** ⊕ www.ups.com.

POSTAL RATES

It costs 8.50 pesos (about 90¢) to send a postcard or letter weighing under 20 grams to the United States or Canada; it's 10.50 ($1) to Europe and 11.50 ($1.20) to Australia.

RECEIVING MAIL

To receive mail in Mexico, you can have it sent to your hotel or use *poste restante* at the post office. In the latter case, the address must include the words "a/c Lista de Correos" (general delivery), followed by the city, state, postal code, and country. To use this service, you must first register with the post office at which you wish to receive your mail. The post office posts and updates daily a list of names for whom mail has been received. Holders of American Express cards or traveler's checks can have mail sent to them in care of the local American Express office. For a list of offices worldwide, write for the *Traveler's Companion* from American Express.

American Express ✉ Box 678, Canal Street Station, New York, NY 10013 ⊕ www.americanexpress.com.

MONEY MATTERS

Prices in this book are quoted most often in U.S. dollars. We would prefer to list costs in pesos, but because the value of the currency fluctuates considerably, what costs 90 pesos today might cost 120 pesos in six months.

If you travel only by air or package tour, stay at international hotel-chain properties, and eat at tourist restaurants, you might not find Mexico such a bargain. If you want a closer look at the country and aren't wedded to standard creature comforts, you can spend as little as $25 a day on room, board, and local transportation. Speaking Spanish is also helpful in bargaining situations and when asking for dining recommendations.

Cancún, Puerto Vallarta, Mexico City, Monterrey, Acapulco, Ixtapa, Los Cabos, Manzanillo, and, to a lesser extent, Mazatlán and Huatulco are the most-expensive places to visit. All the beach towns, however, offer budget accommodations; lodgings are even less expensive in less accessible areas such as the Gulf coast and northern Yucatán, parts of Quintana Roo, some of the less-developed spots north and south of Puerto Vallarta in the states of Jalisco and Nayarit, Puerto Escondido, and the smaller Oaxacan coastal towns as well as those of Chiapas and Tabasco.

Average costs in major cities vary, although less than in the past because of an increase in business travelers. A stay in one of Mexico City's top hotels can cost more than $200 (as much or more than at the coastal resorts), but you can get away with a tab of $45 for two at what was once an expensive restaurant.

Probably the best value for your travel dollar is in smaller, inland towns, such as Mérida, Morelia, Guanajuato, and Oaxaca, where tourism is less developed. Although Oaxaca lodging can run more than $150 a night, simple colonial-style hotels with adequate accommodations for under $40 can be found, and tasty, filling meals are rarely more than $15.

Prices throughout this guide are given for adults. Substantially reduced fees are almost always available for children, students, and senior citizens. For information on taxes, *see* Taxes.

ATMS

ATMs (*cajeros automáticos*) are becoming more commonplace. Cirrus and Plus are the most frequently found networks. Before you leave home, **ask what the transaction fee will be** for withdrawing money in Mexico. (It's usually $3 a pop.)

Many Mexican ATMs cannot accept PINs (personal identification numbers) with more than four digits; if yours is longer, **ask your bank about changing your PIN (*número de clave*) before you leave home,** and keep in mind that processing such a change often takes a few weeks. If your PIN is fine yet your transaction still can't be completed—a regular occurrence—

chances are that the computer lines are busy or that the machine has run out of money or is being serviced.

For cash advances, plan to use Visa or MasterCard, as many Mexican ATMs don't accept American Express. The ATMs at Banamex, one of the oldest nationwide banks, tend to be the most reliable. Bancomer is another bank with many ATM locations, but they usually provide only cash advances. The newer Serfín banks have reliable ATMs that accept credit cards as well as Plus and Cirrus cards. (*See also* Safety, on avoiding ATM robberies.)

CREDIT CARDS

Credit cards are accepted in most tourist areas. Smaller, less expensive restaurants and shops, however, tend to take only cash. In general, credit cards aren't accepted in small towns and villages, except in hotels. Diners Club is usually accepted only in major chains; the most widely accepted cards are MasterCard and Visa. When shopping, you can usually get better prices if you **pay with cash.**

At the same time, when traveling internationally you'll **receive wholesale exchange rates** when you make purchases with credit cards. These exchange rates are usually better than those that banks give you for changing money. In Mexico the decision to pay cash or use a credit card might depend on whether the establishment in which you are making a purchase finds bargaining for prices acceptable. To avoid fraud, it's wise to **make sure that "pesos" is clearly marked on all credit-card receipts.**

Before you leave for Mexico, be sure to **find out your credit-card companies' toll-free card-replacement numbers** that work at home as well as in Mexico; they could be impossible to find once you get to Mexico, and the calls you place to cancel your cards can be long ones. **Carry these numbers separately from your wallet** so you'll have them if you need to call to report lost or stolen cards.

Throughout this guide, the following abbreviations are used: **AE**, American Express; **DC**, Diners Club; **MC**, MasterCard; and **V**, Visa.

🔲 Reporting Lost Cards **American Express** ☎ 800/528-2122 in the U.S. ⊕ www. americanexpress.com. **Diners Club** ☎ 702/797-

5532 ⊕ www.dinersclub.com. **MasterCard** ☎ 800/
307-7309 in the U.S. ⊕ www.mastercard.com. **Visa**
☎ 800/847-2911 in the U.S. ⊕ www.visa.com.

CURRENCY

At this writing, the peso was still "floating" after the devaluation enacted by the
Zedillo administration in late 1994. Although exchange rates have been as favorable as 10.6 pesos to US$1, 7.2 pesos to
C$1, 16.6 pesos to £1, 6.4 pesos to A$1,
and 5.8 pesos to NZ$1, the market and
prices continue to adjust. Check with your
bank or the financial pages of your local
newspaper for current exchange rates. For
quick estimates of how much something
costs in U.S. dollar terms, divide prices
given in pesos by 10. For example, 50
pesos would be about $5.

Mexican currency comes in denominations
of 10-, 20-, 50-, 100-, 200-, 500-, and
1,000-peso bills. Coins come in denominations of 1, 5, 10, and 20 pesos and 5, 10,
20, and 50 centavos. Many of the coins
and bills are very similar, so check carefully.

U.S. dollar bills (but not coins) are widely
accepted in border towns and in many
parts of the Yucatán, particularly in Cancún and Cozumel, where you'll often find
prices in shops quoted in dollars. However, you'll get your change in pesos.
Many tourist shops and market vendors as
well as virtually all hotel service personnel
also accept dollars.

CURRENCY EXCHANGE

ATM transaction fees may be higher
abroad than at home, but ATM currency-
exchange rates are the best of all because
they're based on wholesale rates offered
only by major banks. And if you take out
a fair amount of cash per withdrawal, the
transaction fee becomes less of a strike
against the exchange rate (in percentage
terms). However, most ATMs allow only
up to $300 a transaction. Banks and *casas
de cambio* (money-exchange houses) have
the second-best exchange rates. The difference from one place to another is usually
only a few centavos.

Most banks change money on weekdays
only until 1 (though they stay open until
5), although casas de cambio generally
stay open until 6 and often operate on
weekends. Bank rates are regulated by the
federal government and are therefore in-
variable, whereas casas de cambio have
slightly more variable rates. Some hotels
also exchange money, but for providing
you with this convenience they help themselves to a bigger commission than banks.

You can do well at most airport exchange
booths (except in Cancún). To avoid lines
at airport exchange booths, **get a bit of
local currency before you leave home.** You
won't necessarily do as well at rail and bus
stations, in hotels, in restaurants, or in
stores.

When changing money, count your bills
before leaving the bank or casa de cambio,
and don't accept any partially torn or
taped-together notes; they won't be accepted anywhere. Also, many shop and
restaurant owners are unable to make
change for large bills. Enough of these encounters may compel you to request *bil-
letes chicos* (small bills) when you
exchange money.

⚏ Exchange Services **International Currency Express** ⊠ 427 N. Camden Dr., Suite F, Beverly Hills,
CA 90210 ☎ 888/278-6628 orders 🖷 310/278-6410
⊕ www.foreignmoney.com. **Thomas Cook Currency
Services** ☎ 800/287-7362 in the U.S. for orders
and retail locations ⊕ www.us.thomascook.com.

TRAVELER'S CHECKS

Do you need traveler's checks? It depends
on where you're headed. If you're going to
rural areas and small towns, go with cash;
traveler's checks are best used in cities.
Lost or stolen checks can usually be replaced within 24 hours. To ensure a
speedy refund, buy your own traveler's
checks—don't let someone else pay for
them: irregularities like this can cause delays. The person who bought the checks
should make the call to request a refund.

OUTDOORS & SPORTS

Mexico is an outdoor and sports-enthusi-
ast's paradise. Besides hanging out on the
nation's beaches, all of which are public,
you can golf, surf, water-ski, fish, scuba
dive, snorkel, hike, and climb. Mexico
City, Guadalajara, Monterrey, and smaller
cities as well as beach resorts all have golf
facilities. Courses abound in Los Cabos,
an area that's been gearing up to become
Mexico's premier golf resort.

Surfers head up and down the peninsula of
Baja California and to Oaxaca, where the
waves of Puerto Escondido have been

drawing serious wave riders since the 1960s. Waterskiing is very popular at beach resorts, and the scuba diving and snorkeling in Cozumel, the Caribbean coast, and Cancún is excellent. Renting equipment isn't a problem in the larger resort areas.

Fishing is popular off both coasts, with most ocean-fishing enthusiasts heading for Baja California, Acapulco, and Oaxaca on the Pacific side, and Veracruz and the Yucatán on the Atlantic.

Las Barrancas del Cobre are favorite hiking and rock-climbing destinations, as are the volcanoes Popocatépetl and Iztaccíhuatl outside of Mexico City. River rafting is big in such states as Veracruz and Oaxaca.

PACKING

When traveling internationally, it's good to pack a change of clothes in your carry-on bag in case your other luggage is lost. Take at least a change of underwear, essential toiletries, and a shirt—add to that a bathing suit if you're heading to a beach resort. In your carry-on luggage, pack an extra pair of eyeglasses or contact lenses and enough of any medication you take to last a few days longer than the entire trip. You may also ask your doctor to write a spare prescription using the drug's generic name, since brand names may vary from country to country. In luggage to be checked, **never pack prescription drugs or valuables.** And don't forget to carry with you the addresses of offices that handle refunds of lost traveler's checks. Check *Fodor's How to Pack* (available in bookstores everywhere) for more tips.

To avoid customs and security delays, carry medications in their original packaging. Don't pack any sharp objects in your carry-on luggage, including knives of any size or material, scissors, manicure tools, and corkscrews, or anything else that might arouse suspicion. To avoid having your checked luggage chosen for hand inspection, don't cram bags full. The U.S. Transportation Security Administration suggests packing shoes on top and placing personal items you don't want touched in clear plastic bags.

For resorts, bring lightweight sportswear, bathing suits, and cover-ups for the beach. Bathing suits and immodest clothing are inappropriate for shopping and sightseeing, both in cities and beach resorts. Mexico City is a bit more formal than the resorts and, because of its high elevation, cooler. Men will want to bring lightweight suits or slacks and blazers for fancier restaurants; women should pack tailored dresses or pants suits. Many high-end Mexico City restaurants require jacket and tie; jeans are acceptable for shopping and sightseeing, but shorts are frowned upon for men and women. You'll need a lightweight topcoat for winter and an all-weather coat and umbrella in case of sudden summer rainstorms. Lately the rains have been appearing at other times of the year, so always **pack a small umbrella.**

Cancún and Acapulco are both casual and elegant; you'll see high-style sportswear, cotton slacks and walking shorts, and plenty of colorful sundresses. The sun can be fierce; **bring a sun hat and sunscreen** for the beach and for sightseeing. You'll need a sweater or jacket to cope with hotel and restaurant air-conditioning, which can be glacial, and for occasional cool spells. Few restaurants require a jacket and tie.

Luggage carts are free at the Mexico City airport, practically the only airport where you'll find them; bus and train stations don't have carts.

CHECKING LUGGAGE

You're allowed to carry aboard one bag and one personal article, such as a purse or a laptop computer. Make sure what you carry on fits under your seat or in the overhead bin. Get to the gate early, so you can board as soon as possible, before the overhead bins fill up.

Baggage allowances vary by carrier, destination, and ticket class. On international flights, you're usually allowed to check two bags weighing up to 70 pounds (32 kilograms) each, although a few airlines allow checked bags of up to 88 pounds (40 kilograms) in first class. Some international carriers don't allow more than 66 pounds (30 kilograms) per bag in business class and 44 pounds (20 kilograms) in economy. On domestic flights, the limit may be 50 pounds (23 kilograms) per bag. Most airlines won't accept bags that weigh more than 100 pounds (45 kilograms) on domestic or international flights. Check baggage restrictions with your carrier before you pack.

Airline liability for baggage is limited to $2,500 per person on flights within the United States. On international flights it amounts to $9.07 per pound or $20 per kilogram for checked baggage (roughly $640 per 70-pound bag) and $400 per passenger for unchecked baggage. You can buy additional coverage at check-in for about $10 per $1,000 of coverage, but it often excludes a rather extensive list of items, shown on your airline ticket.

Before departure, **itemize your bags' contents** and their worth, and label the bags with your name, address, and phone number. (If you use your home address, cover it so potential thieves can't see it readily.) Include a label inside each bag and **pack a copy of your itinerary**. At check-in, **make sure each bag is correctly tagged** with the destination airport's three-letter code. Because some checked bags will be opened for hand inspection, the U.S. Transportation Security Administration recommends that you leave luggage unlocked or use the plastic locks offered at check-in. TSA screeners place an inspection notice inside searched bags, which are resealed with a special lock.

If your bag has been searched and contents are missing or damaged, file a claim with the TSA Consumer Response Center as soon as possible. If your bags arrive damaged or fail to arrive at all, file a written report with the airline before leaving the airport.

Complaints **U.S. Transportation Security Administration Consumer Response Center** ☎ 866/289-9673 ⊕ www.tsa.gov.

PASSPORTS & VISAS

When traveling internationally, **carry your passport** even if you don't need one (it's always the best form of ID) and **make two photocopies of the data page** (one for someone at home and another for you, carried separately from your passport). If you lose your passport, promptly call the nearest embassy or consulate and the local police.

U.S. passport applications for children under age 14 require consent from both parents or legal guardians; both parents must appear together to sign the application. If only one parent appears, he or she must submit a written statement from the other parent authorizing passport issuance for the child. A parent with sole authority must present evidence of it when applying; acceptable documentation includes the child's certified birth certificate listing only the applying parent, a court order specifically permitting this parent's travel with the child, or a death certificate for the nonapplying parent. Application forms and instructions are available on the Web site of the U.S. State Department's Bureau of Consular Affairs (⊕ www.travel.state.gov).

ENTERING MEXICO

For stays of up to 180 days, Americans must prove citizenship through either a valid passport, certified copy of a birth certificate, or voter-registration card (the last two must be accompanied by a government-issue photo ID). Minors traveling with one parent need notarized permission from the absent parent. For stays of more than 180 days, all U.S. citizens, even infants, need a valid passport to enter Mexico. Minors also need parental permission.

Canadians need only proof of citizenship to enter Mexico for stays of up to six months. U.K. citizens need only a valid passport to enter Mexico for stays of up to three months.

Mexico has instituted a $17 visitor fee that applies to all visitors—except those entering by sea at Mexican ports who stay less than 72 hours, and those entering by land who do not stray past the 26–30-km (16–18-mi) checkpoint into the country's interior. For visitors arriving by air, the fee, which covers visits of more than 72 hours and up to 30 days, is usually tacked on to the airline-ticket price. You must pay the fee each time you extend your 30-day tourist visa.

You get the standard tourist visas on the plane without even asking for them. They're also available through travel agents and Mexican consulates and at the border if you're entering by land. The visas can be granted for up to 180 days, but this is at the discretion of the Mexican immigration officials. Although many officials will balk if you request more than 90 days, be sure to ask for extra time if you think you'll need it; going to a Mexican immigration office to renew a visa can easily take a whole day.

PASSPORT OFFICES

The best time to apply for a passport or to renew is in fall and winter. Before any trip, check your passport's expiration date, and, if necessary, renew it as soon as possible.

Australian Citizens **Passports Australia** ☎ 131-232 ⊕ www.passports.gov.au.

Canadian Citizens **Passport Office** ✉ to mail in applications: 200 Promenade du Portage, Hull, Québec J8X 4B7 ☎ 819/994-3500; 800/567-6868 in the U.S. ⊕ www.ppt.gc.ca.

New Zealand Citizens **New Zealand Passports Office** ☎ 04/474-8100 or 0800/225-050 ⊕ www.passports.govt.nz.

U.K. Citizens **U.K. Passport Service** ☎ 0870/521-0410 ⊕ www.passport.gov.uk.

U.S. Citizens **National Passport Information Center** ☎ 900/225-5674 or 900/225-7778 TTY [calls are 55¢ per minute for automated service or $1.50 per minute for operator service]; 888/362-8668 or 888/498-3648 TTY [calls are $5.50 each] ⊕ www.travel.state.gov.

REST ROOMS

Expect to find clean flushing toilets, toilet tissue, soap, and running water at public rest rooms in the major tourist destinations and at tourist attractions. Although many markets bus and train stations and the like have public facilities, you may have to pay a couple of pesos for the privilege of using a dirty toilet that lacks a seat, toilet paper (keep tissues with you at all times), and possibly even running water. You're better off popping into a restaurant, buying a little something, and using its rest room, which will probably be simple but clean and adequately equipped.

SAFETY

CRIME

The U.S. State Department has warned of "high" levels of crime against tourists in Mexico, especially in large cities, and noting an increase in the level of violence of the assaults and robberies committed. The largest increase in crime has taken place in Mexico City, where the age-old problem of pickpocketing has been overshadowed by robberies at gunpoint. Another development has been abductions and robberies in taxicabs hailed from the street (as opposed to hired from a hotel or taxi stand).

Reports indicate that uniformed police officers have, on occasion, perpetrated nonvio-

lent crimes. The patronage system is a well-entrenched part of Mexican politics and industry, and workers in the public sector—notably policemen and customs officials—are notoriously underpaid. Everyone has heard some horror story about highway assaults, pickpocketing, bribes, or foreigners languishing in Mexican jails. These reports apply in large part to Mexico City and more-remote areas of Oaxaca and Chiapas. So far, crime isn't such a problem in the heartland (cities like San Miguel de Allende), Puerto Vallarta, Cancún, and much of the rest of the country.

Use common sense everywhere, but **exercise particular caution in Mexico City.** In addition, **avoid remote, less-traveled areas of Oaxaca, Chiapas, and Guerrero,** as crime in these areas can be more life-threatening. **Don't wear any valuables, including watches,** and try not to act too much like a tourist. Keep your passport and all valuables in hotel safes, and carry your own baggage whenever possible.

Avoid driving on desolate streets, and don't travel at night, pick up hitchhikers, or hitchhike yourself. Use luxury buses (rather than second- or third-class vehicles), which take the safer toll roads. It's best to take only registered hotel taxis or have a hotel concierge call a *sitio* (stationed cab)—**avoid hailing taxis on the street. Avoid urges to get away from it all** on your own (even as a couple) to go hiking in remote national parks; women in particular shouldn't venture alone on to uncrowded beaches.

Use ATMs during the day and in big, enclosed commercial areas. Avoid the glass-enclosed street variety of banks where you may be more vulnerable to thieves who force you to withdraw money for them; abduction is also possible. This can't be stressed strongly enough.

Bear in mind that reporting a crime to the police is often a frustrating experience unless you speak excellent Spanish and have a great deal of patience. If you're victimized, contact your local consular agent or the consular section of your country's embassy in Mexico City.

WOMEN IN MEXICO

If you're on your own, consider using only your first initial and last name when registering at your hotel. **Don't wear a money**

belt or a waist pack, both of which peg you as a tourist. If you carry a purse, choose one with a zipper and a thick strap that you can drape across your body; adjust the length so that the purse sits in front of you at or above hip level. Store only enough money in the purse to cover casual spending. Distribute the rest of your cash and any valuables (including credit cards and your passport) between a deep front pocket, an inside jacket or vest pocket, and a hidden money pouch. Do not reach for the money pouch once in public.

If you're traveling alone or with other women rather than men, you may be subjected to *piropos* (catcalls). To avoid this, don't wear provocative clothes or enter street bars or cantinas alone; in some very conservative rural areas, even sleeveless shirts or Bermuda shorts may seem inappropriate to the locals. Your best strategy is to ignore the offender. Piropos are one thing, but more aggressive harassment is another. If the situation seems to be getting out of hand, don't hesitate to ask someone for help. If you express outrage, you should find no shortage of willing defenders. To save yourself some of this aggravation, look for the so-called ladies' bars. Such establishments are quieter and more comfortable for women without a male companion than the traditional cantinas, where the level of machismo can lead to unwelcome attention.

ZAPATISTA ACTIVITY

In February 2003, a pro-Zapatista group from the Nuevo Jerusalem community near Ocosingo in Chiapas State chased out the American owners of a guest ranch bordering the archaeological ruins of Toniná. The state government declined to intervene and downplayed the incident as an isolated event. Around the same time, however, Zapatista supporters pulled a group of French and Canadian kayakers out of the Río Jatate and detained them for a few hours. These events—combined with anti-tourism remarks made by Zapatista leader Subcomandante Marcos—have led the state department to strongly advise against travel to areas where there have traditionally been conflicts. Avoid rural areas to the east of Ocosingo and Chiapas's southeastern jungle areas.

SENIOR-CITIZEN TRAVEL

To qualify for age-related discounts, **mention your senior-citizen status up front** when booking hotel reservations (not when checking out) and before you're seated in restaurants (not when paying the bill). Be sure to have identification on hand. When renting a car, ask about promotional car-rental discounts, which can be cheaper than senior-citizen rates.

Mexican senior citizens must present a special government-issued credential to obtain discounts at any facility; foreign-issued credentials (such as those from AARP) aren't recognized in the country, and it's not enough to mention that you are a senior citizen.

🎓 Educational Programs **Elderhostel** ✉ 11 Ave. de Lafayette, Boston, MA 02111-1746 ☎ 877/426-8056; 978/323-4141 international callers; 877/426-2167 TTY ⊕ www.elderhostel.org. **Interhostel** ✉ University of New Hampshire, 6 Garrison Ave., Durham, NH 03824 ☎ 603/862-1147; 800/733-9753 in the U.S. ⊕ www.learn.unh.edu.

SHOPPING

At least three varieties of outlets sell Mexican crafts: indoor and outdoor municipal markets; shops run by Fonart (a government agency to promote Mexican crafts); and tourist boutiques in towns, malls, and hotels. Be sure to **take your time and inspect merchandise closely**: you'll find bargains, but quality can be inconsistent. Fonart shops are a good reference for quality and prices (the latter are fixed), and they accept credit cards. Boutiques also accept credit cards if not dollars. (You may be asked to pay up to 10% more on credit-card purchases; savvy shoppers with cash have greater bargaining clout.) A 10%–15% value added tax, locally called the *impuesto de valor agregado* or IVA, is charged on most purchases but is often included in the price; it may be disregarded entirely by eager or desperate market vendors.

Bargaining is widely accepted in markets, but you should understand that not all vendors will start out with outrageous prices. If you feel the price quoted is too high, start off by offering half the asking price and then slowly go up, usually to about 70% of the original price. Always **shop around.** In major shopping areas such as San Miguel, shops will wrap and send purchases back to the United States via a package-delivery company.

WATCH OUT

Items made from tortoiseshell (or any sea turtle products) and black coral aren't allowed into the United States. Neither are birds or wildlife curios such as stuffed iguanas or parrots. Both the U.S. and Mexican governments also have strict laws and guidelines about the import/export of antiquities. And don't plan to use your ceramic plates, bowls, and cups for anything other than decoration—most items have high levels of lead in them.

STUDENTS IN MEXICO

The ISIC student card or GO25 card can get you cut-rate plane tickets to Mexico at youth-oriented travel agencies. Within Mexico, many signs at tourist attractions will state that student discounts are only for Mexican students, but occasionally you'll get a discount by showing one of these cards. The Mundo Joven travel agency in Mexico City and other areas throughout the country sells ISIC and GO25 cards and offers good deals on plane tickets.

🛂 IDs & Services **STA Travel** ✉ 10 Downing St., New York, NY 10014 ☎ 212/627–3111; 800/777–0112 in the U.S. ⊕ www.sta.com. **Mundo Joven** ✉ Insurgentes Sur 510–D, Col. Crédito Constructor, Mexico City, D.F. 03940 ☎ 55/5661–3223 ⊕ wwwmundo-joven.com. **Travel Cuts** ✉ 187 College St., Toronto, Ontario M5T 1P7, Canada ☎ 416/979–2406; 800/592–2887 in the U.S.; 866/246–9762 in Canada ⊕ www.travelcuts.com.

TAXES

Mexico charges an airport departure tax of US$18 or the peso equivalent for international and domestic flights. This tax is usually included in the price of your ticket, but check to be certain. Traveler's checks and credit cards are not accepted at the airport as payment for this. Many states are charging a 2% tax on accommodations, the funds from which are being used for tourism promotion.

VALUE-ADDED TAX

Mexico has a value-added tax of 15% (10% in the states of Quintana Roo, Baja California, and Baja California Sur), called IVA (*impuesto de valor agregado*), which

is occasionally (and illegally) waived for cash purchases. Other taxes and charges apply for phone calls made from your hotel room.

TAXIS

Government-certified taxis have a license with a photo of the driver and a taxi number prominently displayed, a meter, and either an orange or green stripe at the bottom of the license plate. In many cities, taxis charge by zones. In this case, be sure to agree on a fare before setting off. For reasons of security, especially in Mexico City, it's always best to call a *sitio* (stationed) cab rather than to flag one on the street. Tipping isn't necessary unless the driver helps you with your bags, in which case a few pesos are appropriate.

AT THE AIRPORT

From the airport, it's best to **take the authorized taxi service.** Purchase the taxi vouchers sold at stands inside or just outside the terminal, which ensure that your fare is established beforehand. However, before you purchase your ticket, it's wise to locate the taxi originating and destination zones on a map and make sure your ticket is properly zoned; if you need a ticket only to Zone 3, don't pay for a ticket to Zone 4 or 5. Don't leave your luggage unattended while making transportation arrangements.

IN CITIES & BEACH RESORTS

In Mexican cities, **take a taxi rather than public transportation,** which, though inexpensive, is frequently slow and sometimes patrolled by pickpockets. (The exceptions are the air-conditioned buses in Acapulco, Cancún, and Mérida.) Always **establish the fare beforehand,** and count your change. In most of the beach resorts, there are inexpensive fixed-route fares, but if you don't ask, or your Spanish isn't great, you may get taken. In cities, especially the capital, be certain that the meter runs before getting in, and remember that there's usually an extra charge after 10 PM. For out-of-town and hourly services, negotiate a rate in advance; many drivers will start by asking how much you want to pay to get a sense of how street-smart you are. In all cases, if you are unsure of what a fare should be, ask your hotel's front-desk personnel or bell captain.

Hire taxis from hotels and taxi stands (*sitios*), or use those that you have summoned by phone. Street taxis might be the cheapest, but an alarming increase in abductions and violent crime involves street cabs—for safety's sake, avoid taking one. And never leave luggage unattended in a taxi.

In addition to private taxis, many cities have bargain-price collective taxi services using Volkswagen minibuses (called *combis*) and sedans. The service is called *colectivo* or *pesero*. Peseros run along fixed routes, and you hail them on the street and tell the driver where you are going. The fare—which you pay before you get out—is based on distance traveled. We recommend that you take only the *colectivos* (special airport taxis) that transport passengers from—and sometimes to—airports. In places like Cozumel you'll find that colectivos only are permitted to take passengers from airport terminals into town.

TELEPHONES

Most phones, especially in the better city hotels, have Touch-Tone (digital) circuitry. If you think you'll need to access an automated phone system or voice mail in the United States or elsewhere and you don't know what phone service will be available, it's a good idea to take along a Touch-Tone simulator (you can buy one for about $17 at most electronics stores).

AREA & COUNTRY CODES

The country code for Mexico is 52. When calling a Mexico number from abroad, dial the country code and then all of the numbers listed for the entry.

DIRECTORY & OPERATOR ASSISTANCE

Directory assistance is 040 nationwide. For international assistance, dial 00 first for an international operator and most likely you'll get one who speaks English; tell the operator in what city, state, and country you require directory assistance, and he or she will connect you.

INTERNATIONAL CALLS

To make an international call, dial 00 before the country code, area code, and number. The country code for the United States and Canada is 1, the United Kingdom 44, the United Kingdom 44, Australia 61, New Zealand 64, and South Africa 27.

LOCAL & LONG-DISTANCE CALLS

For local or long-distance calls, one option is to find a *caseta de larga distancia*, a telephone service usually operated out of a store such as a *papelería* (stationery store), pharmacy, restaurant, or other small business; look for the phone symbol on the door. Casetas may cost more to use than pay phones, but you have a better chance of immediate success. To make a direct long-distance call, tell the person on duty the number you'd like to call, and she or he will give you a rate and dial for you. Rates seem to vary widely, so shop around. Sometimes you can make collect calls from casetas, and sometimes you cannot, depending on the individual operator and possibly your degree of visible desperation. Casetas will generally charge 50¢–$1.50 to place a collect call (some charge by the minute); it's usually better to call *por cobrar* (collect) from a pay phone.

LONG-DISTANCE SERVICES

AT&T, MCI, and Sprint access codes make calling long-distance relatively convenient, but you may find the local access number blocked in many hotel rooms. First ask the hotel operator to connect you. If the hotel operator balks, ask for an international operator, or dial the international operator yourself. One way to improve your odds of getting connected to your long-distance carrier is to travel with more than one company's calling card (a hotel may block Sprint, for example, but not MCI). If all else fails, call from a pay phone.

F Access Codes **AT&T Direct** ☎ 01800/288-2872 or 01800/112-2020 toll free in Mexico. **MCI World-Phone** ☎ 01800/021-8000 or 01800/674-7000 toll free in Mexico. **Sprint** ☎ 01800/234-0000 or 01800/877-8000 toll free in Mexico.

PHONE CARDS

In most parts of the country, pay phones accept prepaid cards, called Ladatel cards, sold in 30-, 50- or 100-peso denominations at newsstands or pharmacies. Many pay phones accept only these cards; coin-only pay phones are usually broken. Still other phones have two unmarked slots, one for a Ladatel (a Spanish acronym for "long-distance direct dialing") card and the other for a credit card. These are primarily for Mexican bank cards, but some accept Visa or MasterCard, though *not* U. S. phone credit cards.

To use a Ladatel card, simply insert it in the appropriate slot, dial 001 (for calls to the States) or 01 (for calls in Mexico) and the area code and number you're trying to reach. Local calls may also be placed with the card. Credit is deleted from the card as you use it, and your balance is displayed on a small screen on the phone.

TOLL-FREE NUMBERS

Toll-free numbers in Mexico start with an 800 prefix. To reach them, you need to dial 01 before the number. In this guide, Mexico-only toll-free numbers appear as follows: 01800/123–4567. The 800 numbers listed simply 800/123–4567 work north of the border only.

TIME

Mexico has three time zones; most of the country falls in Central Standard Time, which includes Mexico City and is in line with Chicago. Baja California is on Pacific Standard Time—the same as California. Baja California Sur and parts of the northwest coast, including Sonora, are on Mountain Standard Time.

TIPPING

When tipping in Mexico, remember that the minimum wage is the equivalent of $3 a day and that most workers in the tourism industry live barely above the poverty line. There are also Mexicans who think in dollars and know, for example, that in the United States porters are tipped about $2 a bag. Many of them expect the peso equivalent from foreigners and may complain if they feel they deserve more— you and your conscience must decide.

What follows are some guidelines. Naturally, larger tips are always welcome: porters and bellhops, 10 pesos per bag at airports and moderate and inexpensive hotels and 20 pesos per person at expensive hotels; maids, 10 pesos per night (all hotels); waiters, 10%–15% of the bill, depending on service (make sure a service charge hasn't already been added, a practice that's particularly common in resorts); bartenders, 10%–15% of the bill, depending on service (and, perhaps, on how many drinks you've had); taxi drivers, 5–10

pesos is nice, but only if the driver helps you with your bags as tipping cabbies isn't necessary; tour guides and drivers, at least 50 pesos per half day; gas-station attendants, 3–5 pesos unless they check the oil, tires, etc., in which case tip more; parking attendants, 5–10 pesos, even if it's for valet parking at a theater or restaurant that charges for the service.

TOURS & PACKAGES

Because everything is prearranged on a prepackaged tour or independent vacation, you spend less time planning—and often get it all at a good price.

BOOKING WITH AN AGENT

Travel agents are excellent resources. But it's a good idea to collect brochures from several agencies, as some agents' suggestions may be influenced by relationships with tour and package firms that reward them for volume sales. If you have a special interest, **find an agent with expertise in that area**; the American Society of Travel Agents (ASTA; ⇨ Travel Agencies) has a database of specialists worldwide.

Make sure your travel agent knows the accommodations and other services of the place being recommended. Ask about the hotel's location, room size, beds, and whether it has a pool, room service, or programs for children, if you care about these. Has your agent been there in person or sent others whom you can contact?

Do some homework on your own, too: local tourism boards can provide information about lesser-known and small-niche operators, some of which may sell only direct.

BUYER BEWARE

Each year consumers are stranded or lose their money when tour operators—even large ones with excellent reputations—go out of business. So **check out the operator.** Ask several travel agents about its reputation, and try to **book with a company that has a consumer-protection program.** (Look for information in the company's brochure.) In the United States, members of the National Tour Association and the United States Tour Operators Association are required to set aside funds to cover payments and travel arrangements in the event that the company defaults. It's also a good idea to choose a company that participates in the American Society of Travel Agents' Tour Operator Program; ASTA will act as mediator in any disputes between you and your tour operator.

Remember that the more your package or tour includes, the better you can predict the ultimate cost of your vacation. Make sure you know exactly what is covered, and **beware of hidden costs.** Are taxes, tips, and transfers included? Entertainment and excursions? These can add up.

Tour-Operator Recommendations **American Society of Travel Agents** (⇨ Travel Agencies). **National Tour Association** (NTA) ✉ 546 E. Main St., Lexington, KY 40508 ☎ 859/226-4444; 800/682-8886 in the U.S. 🖨 859/226-4404 ⊕ www.ntaonline.com. **United States Tour Operators Association** (USTOA) ✉ 275 Madison Ave., Suite 2014, New York, NY 10016 ☎ 212/599-6599 ⊕ www.ustoa.com.

THEME TRIPS

Adventure Travel **Ceiba Adventures** ⌖ Box 2274, Flagstaff, AZ 86003 ☎ 928/527-0171 ⊕ www.ceibaadventures.com.

Art & Archaeology **Archaeological Conservancy** ✉ 5301 Central Ave. NE, #902, Albuquerque, NM 87108-9899 ☎ 505/266-1540 ⊕ www.americanarchaeology.com. **Crow Canyon Archaeological Center** ✉ 23390 Rd. K, Cortez, CO 81321 ☎ 970/565-8975; 800/422-8975 in the U.S. ⊕ www.crowcanyon.org. **Far Horizons Archaeological & Cultural Trips** ⌖ Box 91900, Albuquerque, NM 87199-1900 ☎ 505/343-9400; 800/552-4575 in the U.S. ⊕ www.farhorizons.com.

Bicycling **Backroads** ✉ 801 Cedar St., Berkeley, CA 94710-1800 ☎ 510/527-1555; 800/462-2848 in the U.S. ⊕ www.backroads.com. **Imagine Tours** ⌖ Box 475, Davis, CA 95617 ☎ 530/758-8782; 800/924-2453 in the U.S. ⊕ www.imaginetours.com.

Birding **Field Guides** ✉ 9433 Bee Cave Rd., Bldg. 1, Suite 150, Austin, TX 78733 ☎ 512/263-7295; 800/728-4953 in the U.S. ⊕ www.fieldguides.com. **Victor Emanuel Nature Tours** ✉ 2525 Wallingwood Dr., Suite 1003, Austin, TX 78746 ☎ 512/328-5221; 800/328-8368 in the U.S. ⊕ www.ventbird.com. **Wings** ✉ 1643 N. Alvernon Way, Suite 105, Tucson, AZ 85712 ☎ 888/293-6443 or 520/320-9868 ⊕ www.wingsbirds.com.

Butterfly Sanctuaries **Natural Habitat Adventures** ✉ 2945 Center Green Ct., Boulder, CO 80301 ☎ 303/449-3711; 800/543-8917 in the U.S. ⊕ www.nathab.com. **Rocamar Tours** ⌖ Box 201, Greely, Ontario, Canada K4P 1N5 ☎ 866/762-2627 ⊕ www.rocomar.com.mx.

Horseback Riding **Equitour FITS Equestrian** ⌖ Box 807, Dubois, WY 82513 ☎ 307/455-3363; 800/545-0019 in the U.S. ⊕ www.equitours.com.

Walking **Backroads** (⇨ Bicycling). **Butterfield & Robinson** ✉ 70 Bond St., Toronto, Ontario, Canada M5B 1X3 ☎ 416/864-1354; 800/678-1147 in the U.S. and Canada ⊕ www.butterfield.com.

Whale-Watching **American Cetacean Society** ⌖ Box 1391, San Pedro, CA 90733 ☎ 310/548-6279 ⊕ www.acsonline.org. **Baja Discovery** ⌖ Box 152527, San Diego, CA 92195 ☎ 619/262-0700; 800/829-2252 in the U.S. ⊕ www.bajadiscovery.com.

TRAIN TRAVEL

Mexico's only passenger train route is the spectacular, 16-hour ride through Las Barrancas del Cobre. The route—between Chihuahua City and Los Mochis on the Pacific coast—crosses dozens of picturesque mountain bridges and burrows through the native lands of the Tarahumara Indians. Known as the *Chepe*, this route was privatized in 1998 and remodeled cars went into service in 1999. There are no sleeping cars on these trains, but the first-class routes do have dining cars, a bar, reclining seats, and climate control. For more information, call the Ferrocarriles Mexicanos or the Mexican tourist board.

Ferrocarriles Mexicanos ☎ 888/484-1623 in the U.S.; 01800/122-4373 toll free in Mexico.

TRAVEL AGENCIES

A good travel agent puts your needs first. Look for an agency that has been in business at least five years, emphasizes customer service, and has someone on staff who specializes in your destination. In addition, **make sure the agency belongs to a professional trade organization.** The American Society of Travel Agents (ASTA)—the largest and most influential in the field with more than 20,000 members in some 140 countries—maintains and enforces a strict code of ethics and will step in to help mediate any agent-client disputes involving ASTA members if necessary. ASTA (whose motto is "Without a travel agent, you're on your own") also maintains a Web site that includes a directory of agents. (If a travel agency is also acting as your tour operator, *see* Buyer Beware *in* Tours and Packages.)

Local Agent Referrals **American Society of Travel Agents** (ASTA) ✉ 1101 King St., Suite 200, Alexandria, VA 22314 ☎ 703/739-2782; 800/965-2782 in the U.S. for 24-hr hot line ⊕ www.astanet.com. **Association of British Travel Agents** ✉ 68-71 Newman St., London W1T 3AH ☎ 020/

CONVERSIONS

DISTANCE

KILOMETERS/MILES

To change kilometers (km) to miles (mi), multiply km by .621. To change mi to km, multiply mi by 1.61.

km to mi		mi to km	
1 =	.62	1 =	1.6
2 =	1.2	2 =	3.2
3 =	1.9	3 =	4.8
4 =	2.5	4 =	6.4
5 =	3.1	5 =	8.1
6 =	3.7	6 =	9.7
7 =	4.3	7 =	11.3
8 =	5.0	8 =	12.9

METERS/FEET

To change meters (m) to feet (ft), multiply m by 3.28. To change ft to m, multiply ft by .305.

m to ft		ft to m	
1 =	3.3	1 =	.30
2 =	6.6	2 =	.61
3 =	9.8	3 =	.92
4 =	13.1	4 =	1.2
5 =	16.4	5 =	1.5
6 =	19.7	6 =	1.8
7 =	23.0	7 =	2.1
8 =	26.2	8 =	2.4

TEMPERATURE

METRIC CONVERSIONS

To change centigrade or Celsius (C) to Fahrenheit (F), multiply C by 1.8 and add 32. To change F to C, subtract 32 from F and multiply by .555.

°F	°C
0	-17.8
10	-12.2
20	-6.7
30	-1.1
32	0
40	+4.4
50	10.0
60	15.5
70	21.1
80	26.6
90	32.2
98.6	37.0
100	37.7

WEIGHT

KILOGRAMS/POUNDS

To change kilograms (kg) to pounds (lb), multiply kg by 2.20. To change lb to kg, multiply lb by .455.

kg to lb		lb to kg	
1 =	2.2	1 =	.45
2 =	4.4	2 =	.91
3 =	6.6	3 =	1.4
4 =	8.8	4 =	1.8
5 =	11.0	5 =	2.3
6 =	13.2	6 =	2.7
7 =	15.4	7 =	3.2
8 =	17.6	8 =	3.6

GRAMS/OUNCES

To change grams (g) to ounces (oz), multiply g by .035. To change oz to g, multiply oz by 28.4.

g to oz		oz to g	
1 =	.04	1 =	28
2 =	.07	2 =	57
3 =	.11	3 =	85
4 =	.14	4 =	114
5 =	.18	5 =	142
6 =	.21	6 =	170
7 =	.25	7 =	199
8 =	.28	8 =	227

LIQUID VOLUME

LITERS/U.S. GALLONS

To change liters (L) to U.S. gallons (gal), multiply L by .264. To change U.S. gal to L, multiply gal by 3.79.

L to gal		gal to L	
1 =	.26	1 =	3.8
2 =	.53	2 =	7.6
3 =	.79	3 =	11.4
4 =	1.1	4 =	15.2
5 =	1.3	5 =	19.0
6 =	1.6	6 =	22.7
7 =	1.8	7 =	26.5
8 =	2.1	8 =	30.3

CLOTHING SIZE

WOMEN'S CLOTHING

US	UK	EUR
4	6	34
6	8	36
8	10	38
10	12	40
12	14	42

WOMEN'S SHOES

US	UK	EUR
5	3	36
6	4	37
7	5	38
8	6	39
9	7	40

MEN'S SUITS

US	UK	EUR
34	34	44
36	36	46
38	38	48
40	40	50
42	42	52
44	44	54
46	46	56

MEN'S SHIRTS

US	UK	EUR
14½	14½	37
15	15	38
15½	15½	39
16	16	41
16½	16½	42
17	17	43
17½	17½	44

MEN'S SHOES

US	UK	EUR
7	6	39½
8	7	41
9	8	42
10	9	43
11	10	44½
12	11	46

7637-2444 ⊕ www.abtanet.com. **Association of Canadian Travel Agents** ✉ 130 Albert St., Suite 1705, Ottawa, Ontario K1P 5G4 🖷 613/237-3657 ⊕ www.acta.ca. **Australian Federation of Travel Agents** ✉ Level 3, 309 Pitt St., Sydney, NSW 2000 🖷 02/9264-3299 ⊕ www.afta.com.au. **Travel Agents' Association of New Zealand** ✉ Level 5, Tourism and Travel House, 79 Boulcott St., Box 1888, Wellington 6001 🖷 04/499-0104 ⊕ www. taanz.org.nz.

VISITOR INFORMATION

Learn more about foreign destinations by checking government-issued travel advisories and country information. For a broader picture, consider information from more than one country.

🚩 Mexico Tourism Board **United States** 🖷 800/446-3942 in the U.S. ⊕ www.visitmexico.com ✉ 21 E. 63rd St., 3rd fl., New York, NY 10021 🖷 212/821-0304 ✉ 300 N. Michigan Ave., 4th fl., Chicago, IL 60601 🖷 312/606-9252 ✉ 2401 W. 6th St., 5th fl., Los Angeles, CA 90057 🖷 213/351-2069 ✉ 4507 San Jacinto, Suite 308, Houston, TX 77004 🖷 713/772-2581 ✉ 5975 Sunset Dr., Suite 305, South Miami, FL 33143 🖷 786/621-2909.

Canada ✉ 1 Pl. Ville Marie, Suite 1931, Montréal, Québec H3B 2C3 🖷 514/871-1052 ✉ 2 Bloor St. W, Suite 1502, Toronto, Ontario M4W 3E2 🖷 416/925-0704 ✉ 999 W. Hastings St., Suite 1110, Vancouver, British Columbia V6C 2W2 🖷 604/669-2845.

United Kingdom ✉ Wakefield House, 41 Trinity Sq., London EC3N 4DJ 🖷 020/7488-9392.

🚩 Government Advisories **U.S. Department of State** ✉ Overseas Citizens Services Office, Room 4811, 2201 C St. NW, Washington, DC 20520 🖷 202/647-5225 interactive hot line; 888/407-4747 ⊕ www.travel.state.gov; enclose a cover letter with your request and a business-size SASE. **Consular Affairs Bureau of Canada** 🖷 613/944-6788; 800/267-6788 in the U.S. ⊕ www.voyage.gc.ca. **U.K. Foreign and Commonwealth Office** ✉ Travel Advice Unit, Consular Division, Old Admiralty Bldg., London SW1A 2PA 🖷 020/7008-0232 or 020/7008-0233 ⊕ www.fco.gov.uk/travel. **Australian Department of Foreign Affairs and Trade** 🖷 02/6261-1299 Consular Travel Advice Faxback Service ⊕ www.dfat.gov.au. **New Zealand Ministry of Foreign Affairs and Trade** 🖷 04/439-8000 ⊕ www. mft.govt.nz.

WEB SITES

Do check out the World Wide Web when planning your trip. You'll find everything from weather forecasts to virtual tours of famous cities. Be sure to **visit Fodors.com** (⊕ www.fodors.com), a complete travel-planning site. You can research prices and book plane tickets, hotel rooms, rental cars, vacation packages, and more. In addition, you can post your pressing questions in the Travel Talk section. Other planning tools include a currency converter and weather reports, and there are loads of links to travel resources.

Mexico's 32 states are beginning to post tourism sites, though few are in English. Two notables exceptions are: the Mexican Tourism Board's official page (⊕ www.visitmexico.com) with information about popular destinations, activities, and festivals; and the Mexico City Tourism Secretariat's site (⊕ www. mexicocity.gob.mx.eng/index.asp), which lists some of the capital's entertainment and tourist attractions.

The site of the Latin American Network Information Center at the University of Texas at Austin (⊕ http://lanic.utexas.edu/la/mexico) has one of the most complete set of links to all thing Mexican. Other excellent English-language sites for general history, travel information, facts, and news stories about Mexico are the United States' Library of Congress well-organized Mexico page (⊕ http://lcweb2.loc.gov/frd/cs/mxtoc.html), Mexico Online (⊕ www. mexonline.com), Mexico Web (⊕ http://mexico.web.com.mx/english), Mexico Connect (⊕ www.mexconnect. com), and the Mexico Channel (⊕ www. trace-sc.com).

For information on nature and the environment try Ron Mader's Planeta site (⊕ www.planeta.com/mexico.html), which has the latest news on ecotourism and ideas for hiking and adventure travel. If you're interested in visiting and/or climbing Mexico's volcanoes, the U.S. Geological Services and Cascades Volcano Observatory page (⊕ http://vulcan.wr.usgs. gov/Volcanoes/Mexico) is indispensable. For archaeology, two sites stand above others: Mesoweb (⊕ www.mesoweb.com), and the nonprofit site Ancient Mexico (⊕ www.ancientmexico.com).

MEXICO CITY

1

FODOR'S CHOICE

Aguila y Sol, for nueva cocina mexicana, Col. Polanco

Bistrot Mosaico, restaurant, Col. Condesa

Camino Real, hotel, Col. Polanco

El Discreto Encanto de Comer, restaurant, Col. Roma

Four Seasons, hotel, Col. Juárez

El Gallo Centenario, restaurant, Col. Centro

Mercado Artesanal La Ciudadela, crafts market, Col. Juárez

Museo de Frida Kahlo, Coyoacán

Museo Nacional de Antropología, Bosque de Chapultepec

The ruins of Templo Mayor, Col. Centro

La Valentina, restaurant, Col. Juárez

HIGHLY RECOMMENDED

EXPERIENCES A performance of the Ballet Folklórico de México at the Palacio de Bellas Artes, Alameda Central

Bazar Sábado, a crafts market, San Angel

Museo Dolores Olmedo Patino, Xochimilco

Museo Tamayo Arte Contemporáneo, Bosque de Chapultepec

Palacio de Bellas Artes, Alameda Central

Palacio Nacional, Col. Centro

Plaza San Jacinto, San Angel

El Nivel, the city's oldest cantina, Col. Centro

Bar León, a classic salsa bar, Col. Centro

So many wonderful hotels and restaurants can be found here that there's not enough space to list them all on this page. To see what Fodor's editors and contributors highly recommend, please look for the black stars as you leaf through this chapter.

Updated by
Barbara
Kastelein

MEXICO CITY IS A CITY OF SUPERLATIVES. It is both the oldest (founded in 1325) and the highest (7,350 ft) metropolis on the North American continent. And with nearly 24 million inhabitants, it's the most populous city in the world. At the southern edge of the Mesa Central region of the Plateau of Mexico, the city remains Mexico's industrial, financial, cultural, and political core. Fast, thrilling, and hard to get your head around, it seems permanently in the thrall of turbulent and exciting change—braving the 21st century while clinging to its deeply entrenched Aztec heritage.

As the gargantuan pyramids of Teotihuacán attest, the area around Mexico City was occupied from early times by a great civilization, probably Nahuatl in origin. The founding farther south of the Aztec capital, Tenochtitlán, did not occur until more than 600 years after Teotihuacán was abandoned, around AD 750. Between these periods, from 900 to 1200, the Toltec Empire controlled the valley of Mexico. As the story goes, the nomadic Aztecs were searching for a promised land in which to settle. Their prophecies announced that they would recognize the spot when they encountered an eagle, perched on a prickly pear cactus and holding a snake in its beak. In 1325, the disputed date of Tenochtitlán's founding, they discovered this eagle in the valley of Mexico. They settled on what was then an island in shallow Lake Texcoco and connected it to lakeshore satellite towns by a network of *calzadas* (canals and causeways, now freeways). Even then it was the largest city in the Western Hemisphere and, according to historians, one of the three largest cities on Earth. When he first laid eyes on Tenochtitlán in the early 16th century, Spanish conquistador Hernán Cortés was dazzled by the glistening lacustrine metropolis, which reminded him of Venice.

A combination of factors made the Spanish conquest possible. Aztec emperor Moctezuma II believed the white, bearded Cortés on horseback to be the mighty plumed serpent-god Quetzalcóatl, who, according to prophecy, was supposed to arrive from the east in the year 1519 to rule the land. Thus, Moctezuma welcomed the foreigner with gifts of gold and palatial accommodations. In return, Cortés initiated a massacre. He was backed by a huge army of Indians from other settlements such as Cholula and Tlaxcala, who saw a chance to end their submission to the Aztec empire. With these forces, the European tactical advantages of horses, firearms, and, inadvertently, the introduction of smallpox and the common cold, Cortés succeeded in erasing Tenochtitlán only two centuries after it was founded.

Cortés began building the capital of what he patriotically dubbed New Spain, the Spanish empire's colony that would spread north to cover what is now the southwestern United States, and south to Panama. *Mexico* comes from the word *Mexica* (pronounced *meh*-shee-ka), which was the Aztecs' name for themselves. (Aztec is the Spaniards' name for the Mexica.) At the site of Tenochtitlán's demolished ceremonial center— now the 10-acre Zócalo—Cortés started building a church (the precursor of the impressive Metropolitan Cathedral), mansions, and government buildings. He utilized the slave labor—and the artistry—of the vanquished native Mexicans. On top of the ruins of their city, and using rubble from it, they were forced to build what became the most European-style city in North America. But instead of having the random layout of contemporary medieval cities, it followed the grid pattern of the Aztecs. For much of the construction material the Spaniards quarried the local porous, volcanic reddish stone called *tezontle*. The Spaniards also drained the lakes, preferring wheels and horses (which they introduced to Mexico) over canals and canoes for transport. The land-filled lake

Numbers in the text correspond to numbers in the margin and on the Zócalo and Alameda Central; Zona Rosa, Bosque de Chapultepec, and Condesa; and San Angel and Coyoacán maps.

If you have 3 days

Start early with breakfast at the **Casa de los Azulejos** 13, which you can follow, if there is a clear sky, with a visit to the top of the **Torre Latinoamericana** 14 or with a stroll around the **Alameda Central** 18. Visit the **Palacio de Bellas Artes** 15 and then wind your way through the historic center on Calle Tacuba to have lunch in the historic Café de Tacuba; here, you are right on the corner of the **Zócalo** 1, with its cathedral, ruins, and museums. Be sure to visit the **Templo Mayor** 3, and then end your day overlooking it all from the bars in either the Hotel Majestic or the Holiday Inn Zócalo. Day 2, head for the **Museo Nacional de Antropología** 26 in the morning and enjoy lunch in one of the many swank eateries in the Polanco neighborhood. Then cab over to the **Mercado Artesanal La Ciudadela** to hit the crafts stalls. Consider an evening in the fashionable **Colonia Condesa** for cocktails and dinner. On Day 3, go to **San Angel**—start with the Bazar Sábado (if it's Saturday) or the **Museo Estudio Diego Rivera** 34. Head east to **Coyoacán,** with its lovely casa-museums, especially the **Museo de Frida Kahlo** 37 and **Museo de Leon Trotsky** 39. Visit downtown's Plaza Garibaldi for a rousing mariachi send-off, or go for a classy dinner and a few hours of dancing. If the Classic period site of **Teotihuacán** intrigues you, however, you could spend the third day there.

If you have 5 days

Follow the three-day itinerary, seeing San Angel and Coyoacán on the third day, then head to **Bosque de Chapultepec** 21 on Day 4 to stroll the green pathways and visit the museums and the **Zoológico** 27 to see the pandas. On Day 5 take a day trip to climb a pyramid at the ruins of **Teotihuacán.**

If you have 10 days

Take advantage of having more than a week by visiting more of the fascinating sights beyond the city center. (See also Chapter 2.) Follow the five-day outline and add a visit to the resort town of **Cuernavaca,** just over an hour's drive southeast of Mexico City. Spend the day in its museums and browsing its pretty main square, then overnight at one of the town's converted mansions. On Day 7 head back to Mexico City via Highway 95 and stop in **Xochimilco,** where you can ride through the floating gardens on a gondola-like boat. On Day 8 drive north to the ancient Toltec ruins at **Tula;** make an early start if you're traveling in warm weather so that you don't sizzle in the afternoon heat. Continue to the village of **Tepotzotlán,** which has a beautiful Jesuit church, returning to Mexico City for a relaxed dinner. The next day, head to **Puebla** for a three-hour tour, then pop over to the nearby town of **Cholula,** once a sacred ceremonial site, before returning to Puebla for the night. Alternatively, book an early trip with Puebla's tourist office to see the beautiful churches between Puebla and Cholula, and try to fit in the convent at Huejotzingo. En route back to Mexico City on the last day, drive to **Cacaxtla** to see some of the best-preserved Mesoamerican murals in Mexico.

bed turned out to be a soggy support for the immense buildings that have been slowly sinking into it since they were built.

The city flourished during the colonial period, filling what is now its historic center with architectural treasures. The Franciscans and Dominicans eagerly set about converting the Aztecs to Christianity, but some indigenous customs persisted. Street vending, for instance, is a city signature even today. It is said that the conquering soldiers looked out on them in 1520 and said they had never seen such a market, not even in Rome. In 1571 the Spaniards established the Inquisition in New Spain and burned heretics at its palace headquarters, now a museum in Plaza de Santo Domingo.

It took almost three centuries for Mexicans to rise up successfully against Spain. The historic downtown street 16 de Septiembre commemorates the "declaration" of Independence. On that date in 1810, Miguel Hidalgo, Father of the Catholic Church—and of a couple of illegitimate daughters—rang a church bell and cried out his history-making *grito* (shout): "Death to the *gachupines!* (wealthy Spaniards living in Mexico)! Long live the Virgin of Guadalupe!" Excommunicated and executed the following year, Hidalgo is one of many independence heroes who fostered a truly popular movement, culminating in Mexico's independence in 1821. The liberty bell that now hangs above the main entrance to the National Palace is rung on every eve of September 16 by the president of the republic, who then shouts a revised version of the patriot's cry: "¡Viva México!"

Flying in or out of Mexico City, you get an aerial view of the remaining part of Lake Texcoco on the eastern outskirts of the city. In daylight you can notice the sprawling flatness of the 1,480-square-km (570-square-mi) Meseta de Anáhuac (Valley of Mexico), completely surrounded by mountains. On its southeastern side, two usually snowcapped volcanoes, Popocatépetl and Iztaccíhuatl, are both well over 17,000 ft high. After a period of relative tranquility, Popocatépetl awoke and began spewing smoke, ash, and some lava in the mid-1990s; it has remained intermittently active since then.

Unfortunately, the single most widely known fact about Mexico City is that its air is polluted. There's no denying the smog and nightmarish traffic, but strict legislation in recent years has led to cleaner air and, especially after the summer rains, the city has some of the clearest, bluest skies anywhere. At 7,350 ft, the city often has mild daytime weather perfect for sightseeing and cool evenings.

If notoriety for smog brings Los Angeles to mind, so might the fault line that runs through the valley. In 1985 a major earthquake—8.1 on the Richter scale—took a tragic toll. The government reported 10,000 deaths, but locally it's said to be closer to 50,000. The last traces of that quake's damage are finally disappearing with the major renovation project in the capital's historic center, an overhaul which includes the application of the latest earthquake-resistant technology.

Glossy magazine ads usually tout Mexico's paradisiacal beach resorts and ancient ruins, but cosmopolitan, historic Mexico City—which goes by just "México" in Mexico—is a fascinating destination in itself. The city's vitality shows in the pace of its changes, such as the restoration of colonial buildings and the crop of new cafés. Other improvements, including new public lighting downtown and a police team specially trained for assisting tourists, make the capital an increasingly better place for an extended visit.

Cuisine Old & New The capital may be able to sate your cravings for blini or sushi, but some of the most intriguing dining experiences stem from Mexican chefs looking forward—or far backward. Some newcomers on the restaurant scene are experimenting with established Mexican favorites; others are bringing ancient dishes out of the archives and onto the table.

Until the 15th century, Europeans had never seen indigenous Mexican edibles such as corn, chilies of all varieties, tomatoes, potatoes, pumpkin, squash, avocado, turkey, cocoa, and vanilla. In turn, the colonization brought European gastronomic influence and ingredients—wheat, onions, garlic, olives, citrus fruit, cattle, sheep, goats, chickens, domesticated pigs (and lard for frying)—and ended up broadening the already complex pre-Hispanic cuisine into one of the most multifaceted and exquisite in the world: traditional Mexican.

The last decade has seen the evolution of *nueva cocina mexicana* (nouvelle Mexican cuisine) from a trend to an established and respected restaurant genre. The style emphasizes presentation and intriguing combinations of traditional ingredients and contemporary techniques. In the more serious or purist restaurants that aim to rescue recipes from the pre-Hispanic past, you can enjoy the delicate tastes of regional dishes gleaned from colonial reports, and indigenous cooking techniques such as steaming and baking. And, irrespective of fashion, market eateries offer pre-Hispanic seasonal delicacies such as crunchy fried grasshoppers and fried *maguey* larva.

Museums Mexico City is the cultural as well as political capital of the country, as evidenced by its 80-plus museums—some of the finest in Latin America. In buildings of architectural merit, you can see the stirring murals of such native sons as Diego Rivera, José Clemente Orozco, David Alfaro Siqueiros, and Juan O'Gorman; the haunting paintings of Frida Kahlo; stunning pre-Hispanic ceremonial pieces; and outstanding collections of religious art.

Nightlife & the Arts From high culture to down-and-dirty cantinas, Mexico City has it all. Its folklore ballet is justly renowned; the mariachi duels in Plaza Garibaldi epitomize the tradition of outdoor music. You'll also find trendy discos and steamy dance halls where salsa, merengue, and *danzón* (sensuous Cuban dance music) are headliners. Fine arts are having a moment too—during the past couple of years, the capital has been touted by the contemporary art world for its modern-art galleries and daring young painters, photographers, video artists, and sculptors.

EXPLORING MEXICO CITY

Most of Mexico City is aligned on two major intersecting thoroughfares: Paseo de la Reforma and Avenida Insurgentes—at 34 km (21 mi), the longest avenue in the city. Administratively, Mexico City is divided into 16 *delegaciones* (districts) and about 400 *colonias* (neighborhoods), many with street names fitting a given theme, such as a river, philosopher, or revolutionary hero. The same street can change names as it goes through different colonias. Hence, most street addresses include their colonia (abbreviated as Col.). Unless you're going to a landmark, it's important to tell your taxi driver the name of the colonia and, whenever possible, the cross street.

The principal sights of Mexico City fall into three areas. Allow a full day to cover each thoroughly, although you could race through them in four or five hours apiece. You can generally cover the first area—the Zócalo and Alameda Central—on foot. Getting around the Zona Rosa, Bosque de Chapultepec and Colonia Condesa will require a taxi ride or two, as will Coyoacán and San Angel in southern Mexico City.

The Zócalo & Alameda Central

The Zócalo, its surrounding Centro Histórico (historic center), and Alameda Central were the heart of both tremendous cities, Aztec and Spanish. There's a palpable European influence in this area, which is undergoing a major refurbishment. Seven hundred years of history lie beneath its jagged thoroughfares. The sidewalks hum with street vendors, hurried office workers, and tourists blinking in wonder. (Some streets have been converted into pedestrian-only zones.) Every block seems energized with perpetual noise and motion.

A Good Walk
Numbers in the text correspond to numbers in the margin and on The Zócalo and Alameda Central map.

An excellent point of departure for any tour of the city's center is the huge **Zócalo** ❶ ➤, the heart and soul of old downtown. From here you can literally see the layers of history in the buildings around you. A pair of buildings, the 1722 **Ayuntamiento**, or city hall, sit on the southern side of the square; on the west side you'll see colonial tiles of the arms of Cortés and other conquistadores. Walk up to the powerful **Catedral Metropolitana** ❷, crammed with religious art and icons. (A bit farther west of the cathedral is the National Pawn Shop in an 18th-century building, the Monte de Piedad, its large glass windows filled with jewelry and electronics.) Angle east across the square to the monumental **Palacio Nacional** ❸, covering two city blocks. Its interior is lined with Diego Rivera's profound mural of Mexican history. Head back north to see the **Templo Mayor** ❹, ruins from the Aztec capital, with its superb museum. Modern-art lovers should walk east on Calle Moneda to Academia to find the **Museo José Luis Cuevas** ❺. From there, backtrack on Calle Moneda one block, turn right to go north on Correo Mayor del Carmen for two blocks, make a left on Calle Justo Sierra, which becomes Donceles, for one block. At Republica de Argentina, turn right to the **Antiguo Colegio de San Ildefonso** ❻, now an art and history museum. Leaving the museum, walk a couple of blocks west on Republica de Cuba until you reach the historic **Plaza de Santo Domingo** ❼, studded with its Baroque church, a medical museum, and a gaggle of scribes. Follow Republica de Brasil south to Calle Tacuba; if you haven't had lunch yet, drop in at Café de Tacuba. Then stroll west to the **Museo Nacional de Arte** ❽ in the colonial Plaza Manuel Tolsá.

From Calle Tacuba, head two short blocks south to Calle Madero, one of the city's most architecturally varied streets. On the south side of Madero, between Bolivar and Gante, is the 1780 Baroque **Palacio de Iturbide** ❾. Go west along on the south side of Madero; less than a block past the palacio you'll come to the **Iglesia de San Francisco** ❿, with its beautifully painted walls. The stunning tilework of the **Casa de los Azulejos** ⑪ will draw your eye across Calle Madero.

The ultimate goals of the remainder of this walk are an antiques museum and a Diego Rivera mural museum. From Calle Madero, walk less than a half block west to Eje Central Lázaro Cárdenas, a wide four-lane avenue. At the corner and on your left, you can't miss the 1950s-style skyscraper, the **Torre Latinoamericana** ⑫, which has one of the best aerial views of the city as well as a sky-high aquarium. Cross the avenue and turn right (north) to explore the beautiful **Palacio de Bellas Artes** ⑬ opera house, the long side of which skirts Lázaro Cárdenas (its entrance is on Juárez). The 1908 post office building of **Dirección General de Correos** ⑭ is up Lázaro Cárdenas another 150 ft, across from Bellas Artes.

Pass the post office to Calle Tacuba and cross Lázaro Cárdenas one last time, where Calle Tacuba turns into Avenida Hidalgo. One block west, you'll come to the antiques-filled **Museo Franz Mayer** ⑮, which often hosts world-class art and photography exhibitions. (It's also a good place for a coffee break.) Across Avenida Hidalgo is the north end of the leafy park **Alameda Central** ⑯. To get to the **Museo Mural Diego Rivera** ⑰, take Juárez west to Calle Balderas. Turn right and walk a short block to Calle Colón to get back to the park. If you're interested in photography, make a detour to **Centro de la Imagen** ⑱; at the end of such a long day, it's best to take a cab.

TIMING　The Zócalo area will be quietest on Sunday, when bureaucrats have their day of rest. But Alameda Park will be jumping with children and their parents enjoying a Sunday outing. The park will be particularly festive during December, when dozens of "Santas" will appear with plastic reindeer to take wish lists. Although Mexicans celebrate on the night of December 24, the tradition of giving presents—especially to children—kicks in at dawn on January 6, the Day of the Three Kings, so for about a week beforehand the Three Wise Men of biblical lore replace the Santas in the Alameda. Gorgeous Christmas-light sculptures deck the Zócalo from end to end and stream up Calle Madero past Alameda Park to Paseo de la Reforma beyond the museums in Bosque de Chapultepec. Elaborate decorations also festoon the Zócalo in September for the Independence celebrations known as *Fiestas Patrias* (Patriotic Holidays); on September 16 a military parade marches through.

During the daytime, the downtown area is vibrant with activity. As in any capital, watch out for pickpockets, especially on crowded buses and subways, and avoid deserted streets at night.

The streets in the walking tour are fairly close to one another and can be covered in a day if you're short on time and don't linger over lunch; otherwise, a couple of days will make for a more leisurely tour. The Palacio Nacional, Templo Mayor and its museum, and the Museo Franz Mayer are each worth an hour of your time; you can cover the Palacio de Bellas Artes in a half hour unless you stumble upon one of its marvelous and epic temporary exhibitions. Remember that most museums close on Monday.

What to See

THE ZÓCALO　**Antiguo Colegio de San Ildefonso.** The college, a colonial building with
⑥　lovely patios, started out as a Jesuit school for the sons of wealthy Mexicans in the 18th century. It is now a splendid museum that showcases outstanding regional exhibitions. The interior contains murals by Diego Rivera, José Clemente Orozco, and Fernando Leal. ⊠ *Calle Justo Sierra 16, almost at the corner of República de Argentina, 2 blocks north*

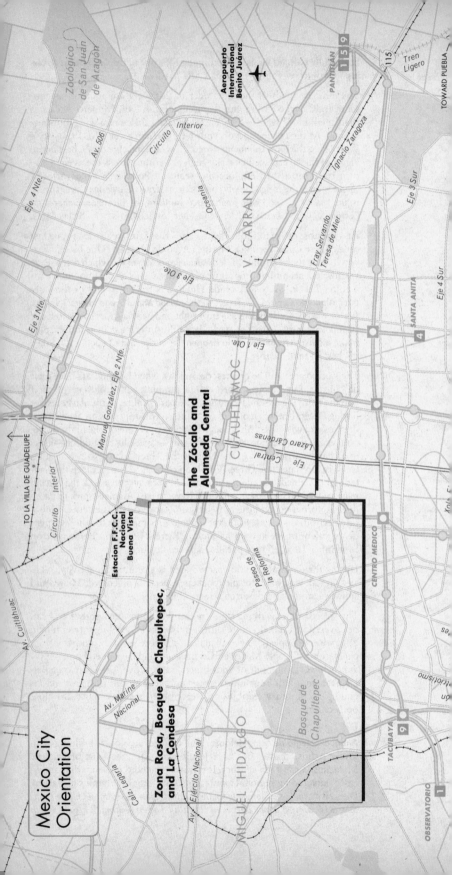

Mexico City Orientation

Zona Rosa, Bosque de Chapultepec, and La Condesa

The Zócalo and Alameda Central

San Angel and Coyoacán

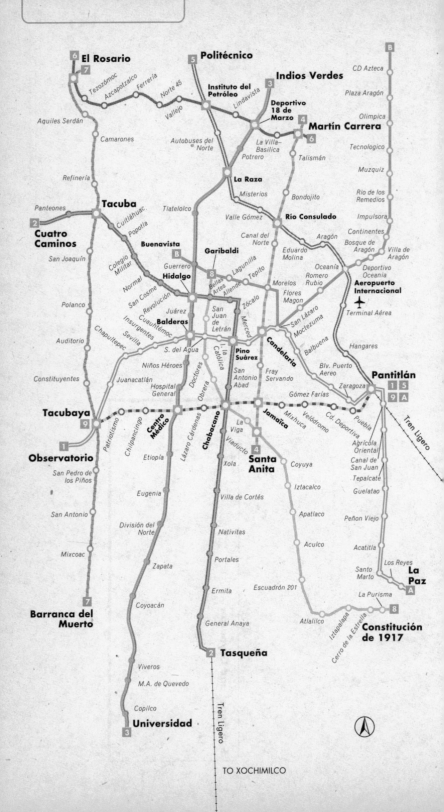

Mexico City Metro

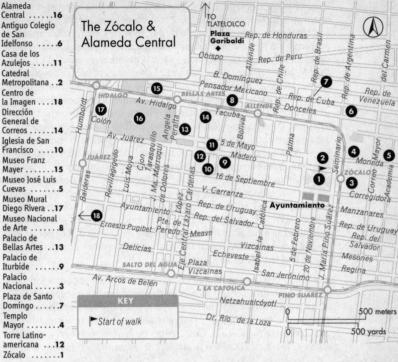

The Zócalo &
Alameda Central

KEY

► Start of walk

0 ——— 500 meters
0 ——— 500 yards

of the Zócalo, Col. Centro ☎ 55/5789–0485 ⊕ www.sanildefonso.
org.mx ✉ $3.50, free Tues. ⊙ Tues.–Sun. 10–6.

❷ Catedral Metropolitana. Construction on this oldest and largest cathedral
in Latin America began in the late 16th century and continued intermittently
throughout the next three centuries. The result is a medley of Baroque
and neoclassical touches. Inside are four identical domes, their airiness
grounded by rows of supportive columns. There are five altars and 14
chapels, mostly in the ornate churrigueresque style, named for Spanish
architect José Churriguera (died 1725). Like most Mexican churches, the
cathedral itself is all but overwhelmed by the innumerable paintings, altarpieces, and statues—in graphic color—of Christ and the saints. Over
the centuries, this cathedral began to sink into the spongy subsoil, but a
major engineering project to stabilize the structure was declared successful
in 2000. The older-looking church attached to the cathedral is the 18th-
century Sagrario chapel. ✉ Zócalo, Col. Centro ⊙ Daily 7–7.

❺ Museo José Luis Cuevas. Installed in a refurbished former convent, this
attractive museum displays international modern art as well as work by
Mexico's enfant terrible, José Luis Cuevas, one of the country's best-
known contemporary artists. The highlight is the sensational La Giganta
(The Giantess), Cuevas's 8-ton bronze sculpture in the central patio. Up-
and-coming Latin American artists appear in temporary exhibitions
throughout the year. ✉ Academia 13, at Calle Moneda, Col. Centro ☎ 55/
5522–0156 ✉ 90¢ ⊙ Tues.–Sun. 10–5:30.

★ ❸ Palacio Nacional. The grand national palace was initiated by Cortés on
the site of Moctezuma's home and remodeled by the viceroys. Its current form dates from 1693, although a third floor was added in 1926.
Now the seat of government, it has always served as a public-function
site. In fact, during colonial times, the first bullfight in New Spain took
place in the inner courtyard.

Diego Rivera's sweeping, epic murals on the second floor of the main courtyard exert a mesmeric pull. For more than 16 years (1929–45), Rivera and his assistants mounted scaffolds day and night, perfecting techniques adapted from Renaissance Italian fresco painting. The result, nearly 1,200 square ft of vividly painted wall space, is grandiosely entitled *Epica del Pueblo Mexicano en su Lucha por la Libertad y la Independencia* (*Epic of the Mexican People in Their Struggle for Freedom and Independence*). The paintings represent two millennia of Mexican history, filtered through Rivera's imagination. He painted pre-Hispanic times in innocent, almost sugary scenes of Tenochtitlán. Only a few vignettes— a man offering a human arm for sale, and the carnage of warriors—acknowledge the darker aspects of ancient life. As you walk around the floor, you'll pass images of the savagery of the conquest and the hypocrisy of the Spanish priests, the noble independence movement, and the bloody revolution. Marx appears amid scenes of class struggle, toiling workers, industrialization (which Rivera idealized), bourgeois decadence, and nuclear holocaust. These are among Rivera's finest work— as well as the most accessible and probably most visited. The palace also houses a minor museum that focuses on 19th-century president Benito Juárez and the Mexican Congress.

The liberty bell rung by Padre Hidalgo to proclaim independence in 1810 hangs high on the central facade. It chimes every eve of September 16, while from the balcony the president repeats the historic shout of independence to throngs of *chilangos* (Mexico City residents) below. ⊠ *East side of the Zócalo, Col. Centro* ☎ *No phone* ⊠ *Free; you'll be asked to leave an ID at the front desk* ☉ *Mon.–Sat. 9–6, Sun. 9–2.*

❼ Plaza de Santo Domingo. The Aztec emperor Cuauhtémoc built a palace here, where heretics were later burned at the stake in the Spanish Inquisition. The plaza was the intellectual hub of the city during the colonial era. Today, its most charming feature is the **Portal de los Evangelistas,** whose arcades are filled with scribes at old-fashioned typewriters who are filling in official forms, printing invitations, or composing letters for love-stricken swains.

The gloomy-looking **Palacio de la Escuela de Medicina Mexicana** (⊠ República de Brasil 33, at República de Venezuela, Col. Centro ☎ 55/5529–7543 ⊠ Free ☉ Daily 9–6), once the headquarters for the Inquisition, is catercorner to the lively portal. Founded by the Catholic Church in 1571 and closed by government decree in 1820, it was a medical school for many years. Now it serves as a fascinating museum portraying the history of medicine in this country.

The 18th-century Baroque **Santo Domingo church,** slightly north of the portal, is all that remains of the first Dominican convent in New Spain. The convent building was demolished in 1861 under the Reform laws that forced clerics to turn over all religious buildings not used for worship to the government. Today, you can still see white-robed Dominican nuns visiting the church. ⊠ *Between República de Cuba, República de Brasil, República de Venezuela, and Palma, Col. Centro* ☎ *No phone.*

❹ Templo Mayor. The ruins of the ancient hub of the Aztec empire were FodorśChoice unearthed accidentally in 1978 by telephone repairmen and have since ★ been turned into a vast archaeological site and museum. At this temple, dedicated to the Aztec cult of death, captives from rival tribes— as many as 10,000 at a time—were sacrificed to the bloodthirsty god of war, Huitzilopochtli. Seven rows of leering stone skulls adorn one side of the structure.

The adjacent **Museo del Templo Mayor** contains 3,000 pieces unearthed from the site and from other ruins in central Mexico; they include ceramic warriors, stone carvings and knives, skulls of sacrificial victims, a rare gold ingot, models and scale reproductions, and a room on the Spaniards' destruction of Tenochtitlán. The centerpiece is an 8-ton disk discovered at the Templo Mayor. It depicts the moon goddess Coyolxauhqui, who, according to myth, was decapitated and dismembered by her brother Huitzilopochtli. Call six weeks ahead to schedule free English-language tours by museum staff in the mornings. ⊠ *Seminario 8, at República de Guatemala; entrance on the plaza, near Catedral Metropolitana, Col. Centro* ☎ *55/5542–4784, 55/5542–4785, or 55/5542–4786* ⊕ *azteca.conaculta.gob.mx/templomayor* ⊠ *$3.50* ☉ *Tues.–Sun. 9–5.*

▶ ❶ **Zócalo.** Mexico City's historic plaza (formally called the Plaza de la Constitución) and the buildings around it were built by the Spaniards, using local slaves. This enormous paved square, the largest in the Western Hemisphere, occupies the site of the ceremonial center of Tenochtitlán, the capital of the Aztec empire, which once comprised 78 buildings. Throughout the 16th, 17th, and 18th centuries, elaborate churches and convents, elegant mansions, and stately public edifices were constructed around the square; many of these buildings have long since been converted to other uses. Clusters of small shops, eateries, cantinas, street stalls, and a few women in native Indian dress contribute to an inimitably Mexican flavor and exuberance.

Zócalo literally means "pedestal" or "base": in the mid-19th century, an independence monument was planned for the square, but it was never built. The term stuck, however, and now the word "zócalo" is applied to the main plazas of most Mexican cities. Mexico City's Zócalo (because it's the original, it's always capitalized) is used for government rallies, protests, sit-ins, and festive events. It's the focal point for Independence Day celebrations on the eve of September 16 and is a maze of lights, tinsel, and traders during the Christmas season. Flag-raising and -lowering ceremonies take place here in the early morning and late afternoon. ⊠ *Bounded on the south by 16 de Septiembre, north by Av. 5 de Mayo, east by Pino Suárez, and west by Monte de Piedad, Col. Centro.*

ALAMEDA CENTRAL ❶⑥ **Alameda Central.** Since Aztec times, when the Indians held their *tianguis* (market) on the site, this park has been one of the capital's oases of greenery and centers of activity. In the early days of the Viceroyalty, the Inquisition burned its victims at the stake here. Later, national leaders, from 18th-century viceroys to Emperor Maximilian and President Porfirio Díaz, envisioned the park as a symbol of civic pride and prosperity: over the centuries, it has been endowed with fountains, railings, a Moorish kiosk imported from Paris, and ash, willow, and poplar trees. The semicircular, white-marble monument, **Hemiciclo a Benito Juárez,** stands on the Avenida Juárez side of the park. It's a fine place for strolling, relaxing, and listening to live music on Sunday and holidays.

⓫ **Casa de los Azulejos.** Built as the palace of the counts of the Valle de Orizaba, an aristocratic family from the early period of Spanish rule, this 17th-century masterpiece acquired its name, the House of Tiles, from its elaborate tilework. The dazzling designs, along with the facade's iron grillwork balconies, make it one of the prettiest Baroque structures in the country. The interior is also worth seeing for its Moorish patio, monumental staircase, and a mural by Orozco. The building is currently occupied by Sanborns, a chain store and restaurant, and if you have plenty of time—service is slow—this is a good place to stop for a meal. ⊠ *Calle*

Madero 4, at Callejón de la Condesa, Alameda Central ☎ *55/5512–9820 Ext. 103* ☉ *Daily 7 AM–1 AM.*

⑱ Centro de la Imagen. This pioneering photography center stages the city's most important photography exhibitions, as well as occasional contemporary sculpture and other art or mixed media exhibitions. Photography by international artists is often grouped thematically, drawing parallels between various cultures. ⊠ *Plaza de la Ciudadela 2, at Balderas, Col. Centro* ☎ *55/5709–1510* ⊕ *www.conaculta.gob.mx/ cimagen* ⊠ *Free* ☉ *Tues.–Sun. 11–6.*

⑭ Dirección General de Correos. Mexico City's main post office building is a fine example of Renaissance revival architecture. Constructed of cream-color sandstone in 1908, it epitomizes the grand imitations of European architecture common in Mexico during the Porfiriato—the long dictatorship of Porfirio Díaz (1876–1911). Upstairs, the **Museo del Palacio Postal** shows Mexico's postal history. ⊠ *Calle Tacuba and Eje Central Lázaro Cárdenas, Alameda Central* ☎ *55/5510–2999 museum; 55/5521–7394 post office* ⊠ *Free* ☉ *Museum weekdays 9–4, weekends 10–2; post office weekdays 8–8, Sat. 9–1.*

⑩ Iglesia de San Francisco. On the site of Mexico's first convent (1524)— and supposedly the site of Moctezuma's zoo before that—this church's current 18th-century French Gothic incarnation reflects only one of the site's many incarnations. Its past includes use as a military barracks, hotel, circus, theater, and Methodist temple. On Independence Day in 1856 a conspiracy was uncovered here, leading to a decree to slice through the property with a road named Independencia, and the temporary banishment of the convent's religious folk. ⊠ *Calles Madero and 16 de Septiembre, Alameda Central* ☎ *No phone* ☉ *Daily 7 AM–8:30 PM.*

⑮ Museo Franz Mayer. Housed in the 16th-century Hospital de San Juan de Dios, this museum exhibits 16th- and 17th-century antiques, such as wooden chests inlaid with ivory, tortoiseshell, and ebony; tapestries, paintings, and lacquerware; rococo clocks, glassware, and architectural ornamentation; and an unusually large assortment of Talavera ceramics. The museum also has more than 700 editions of Cervantes's *Don Quixote.* The old hospital building is faithfully restored, with pieces of the original frescoes peeking through. ⊠ *Av. Hidalgo 45, at Plaza Santa Veracruz, Alameda Central* ☎ *55/5518–2267* ⊕ *www.franzmayer.org. mx* ⊠ *$2, free Tues.* ☉ *Tues. and Thurs.–Sun. 10–5, Wed. 10–7* ☞ *Call 1 wk ahead for an English-speaking guide.*

⑰ Museo Mural Diego Rivera. Diego Rivera's controversial mural, *Sueño de una Tarde Dominical en el Parque Alameda* (*Sunday Afternoon Dream in the Alameda Park*), originally was painted on a lobby wall of the Hotel Del Prado in 1947–48. Its controversy grew out of Rivera's Marxist inscription, "God does not exist," which the artist later replaced with the bland "Conference of San Juan de Letrán" to placate Mexico's dominant Catholic population. The 1985 earthquake destroyed the hotel but not the mural, and this museum was built across the street from the hotel's site to house it. ⊠ *Colón 7, at Calle Balderas, Alameda Central* ☎ *55/ 5510–2329* ⊠ *$1* ☉ *Tues.–Sun. 10–6.*

⑧ Museo Nacional de Arte (MUNAL). The collections of the national art museum, which fill a neoclassical building, span nearly every school of Mexican art, with a concentration on work made between 1810 and 1950. On display are Diego Rivera's portrait of Adolfo Best Maugard, José María Velasco's *Vista del Valle de México desde el Cerro de Santa Isabel* (*View of the Valley of Mexico from the Hill of Santa Isabel*), and Ramón Cano Manilla's *El Globo* (*The Balloon*). *El Caballito* (*The Lit-*

tle Horse), a statue of Spain's Carlos V on horseback, stands out front. ⊠ *Calle Tacuba 8, Col. Centro* ☎ *55/5130–3400* ⊕ *www.matemagica. com/munalo1.htm* ✉ *Free* ⊙ *Tues.–Sun. 10:30–5:30.*

★ ⑬ **Palacio de Bellas Artes.** Construction on this colossal white-marble opera house was begun in 1904 by Porfirio Díaz, who wanted to add yet another ornamental building to his accomplishments. He was ousted seven years later and the building wasn't finished until 1934. The striking structure is the work of Italian Adamo Boari, who also designed the post office; pre-Hispanic motifs trim the art deco facade. Inside the concert hall, a Tiffany stained-glass curtain depicts the two volcanoes outside Mexico City. Today the theater serves as a handsome venue for international and national artists, including the Ballet Folklórico de México. For an entrance fee you can see the interior, with its paintings by several celebrated Mexican artists, including Rufino Tamayo and Mexico's trio of muralists: Rivera, Orozco, and Siqueiros. There are interesting temporary art exhibitions as well, plus an elegant cafeteria. ⊠ *Eje Central Lázaro Cárdenas and Av. Juárez, Alameda Central* ☎ *55/5512–3633* ✉ *$3* ⊙ *Tues.–Sun. 10–5:50; cafeteria 11–6.*

off the beaten path

Tlatelolco. At Paseo de la Reforma's northern end, about 2 km (1 mi) north of the Palacio de Bellas Artes, the area known as Tlatelolco (pronounced tla-tel-*ohl*-coh) was the domain of Cuauhtémoc (pronounced kwa-oo-*teh*-mock)—the last Aztec emperor before the conquest—and the sister city of Tenochtitlán. In modern times its name continues to make residents shudder, as it was here that the Mexican army massacred several hundred protesting students in 1968. In addition, the 1985 earthquake destroyed several high-rise apartments in Tlatelolco, killing hundreds. The center of Tlatelolco is the Plaza de las Tres Culturas, so named because Mexico's three cultural eras—pre-Hispanic, colonial, and contemporary—are represented on the plaza in the form of the small ruins of a pre-Hispanic ceremonial center (visible from the roadway); the Iglesia de Santiago Tlatelolco (1609) and Colegio de la Santa Cruz de Tlatelolco (1535–36); and the modern Ministry of Foreign Affairs (1970). The *colegio* (college), founded by the Franciscans after the conquest, was once attended by the sons of the Aztec nobility. ⊠ *Plaza bounded on the north by Manuel González, on the west by Av. San Juan de Letrán Nte., and on the east by Paseo de la Reforma, between Glorietas de Peralvillo and Cuitláhuac, Tlatelolco.*

❾ **Palacio de Iturbide.** Built in 1780, this Baroque palace—note the imposing door and its carved-stone trimmings—became the residence of Agustín de Iturbide in 1822. One of the heroes of the independence movement, the misguided Iturbide proclaimed himself emperor of a country that had thrown off the imperial yoke of the Hapsburgs only a year before. His own empire, needless to say, was short-lived. Now his home is owned by Banamex (Banco Nacional de México), which sponsors cultural exhibitions in the atrium. ⊠ *Calle Madero 17, Col. Centro* ☎ *55/ 5225–0281* ✉ *Free* ⊙ *Inner atrium daily 10–7.*

☞ ⑫ **Torre Latinoamericana.** This 47-story skyscraper, the second-tallest building in the capital, was completed in 1956. On clear days the observation deck and café on the top floors give you terrific views of the city. The **Fantastic World of the Sea,** a sky-high aquarium, miraculously transported small sharks and crocodiles to the 38th floor. ⊠ *Eje Central Lázaro Cárdenas 2 at Calle Madero, Alameda Central* ☎ *55/5521–0844 observation deck; 55/5521–7455 aquarium* ⊕ *www.arts-history.mx/amex/*

rutapeatonal/torrelatino1.html ⊠ *Deck $4; aquarium $2.80* ⊙ *Deck daily 9:30 AM–11 PM; aquarium daily 9:30 AM–10 PM.*

Zona Rosa, Bosque de Chapultepec & the Colonias Condesa & Roma

Bosque de Chapultepec, named for the *chapulines* (grasshoppers) that populated it long ago, is the largest park in the city, a great green refuge from concrete, traffic, and dust. Housing five world-class museums, a castle, a lake, an amusement park, and the Mexican president's official residence, Chapultepec is a saving grace for visitors and locals. If you have time to visit only one of these museums, make it the Museo Nacional de Antropología—you won't find the likes of its exhibits anywhere else.

Stores, hotels, travel agencies, and restaurants line the avenues of the Zona Rosa, just east of the park—once a cultural center of Mexico City, it's now a first stop for shopping. Two nearby colonias, known simply as La Condesa and La Roma, are filled with fading 1920s and 30s architecture, shady parks, and inexpensive eateries that cater to the city's young and trendy. The capital's elite concentrated here at the turn of the 20th century before moving on to more fashionable fields in the 1940s. In the late 1990s a tide of artists, entrepreneurs, and foreigners brought a new wave of energy. La Condesa, the sprucer, hipper area of the two, centers around the large and leafy Parque México. Grittier La Roma is now home to a group of important art galleries as well as some of the city's best cantinas. A free magazine called *CP06140* (referring to La Condesa's zip code) comes out every two months with up-to-date listings of what to do and where to eat in these neighborhoods. You can pick up a copy in some local cafés and galleries.

A Good Walk

Numbers in the text correspond to numbers in the margin and on the Zona Rosa, Bosque de Chapultepec, and Condesa map.

Emperor Maximilian built the Paseo de la Reforma in 1865, modeling it after the Champs-Élysées in Paris. Its purpose was to connect the Palacio Nacional with his residence, the Castillo de Chapultepec. At the northeastern end of Reforma are Tlatelolco, the Lagunilla Market, and Plaza Garibaldi, where the mariachis cluster and strut. To the west, Reforma winds its leisurely way west into the wealthy neighborhoods of Lomas de Chapultepec, where posh houses and estates sit behind stone walls.

Start your exploration of the Zona Rosa at the junction of Reforma, Avenida Juárez, and Bucareli, just west of the Alameda Central ▶. Along the stretch of Reforma west of this intersection are a number of statues erected at the request of former Mexican president Porfirio Díaz to honor illustrious men, including Simón Bolívar, Columbus, Pasteur, and the Aztec emperor Cuauhtémoc. The best known, the **Monumento a la Independencia** ⑲, also known as El Angel, marks the western edge of the Zona Rosa. To get the best of the area's sights, walk along Hamburgo, Londres, and Copenhague streets—like others in the Zona, named for Continental cities. There's a crafts market, Mercado Insurgentes, also known as Mercado Zona Rosa, on Londres.

Four blocks southwest of the market, at Avenida Chapultepec, you'll come to the main entrance of **Bosque de Chapultepec** ⑳. Uphill from the park's entrance is the **Castillo de Chapultepec** ㉑ with its history museum. North of the Castillo on the near side of Paseo de la Reforma is the **Museo Nacional de Arte Moderno,** a modern art collection slated for a badly needed total renovation. Almost directly across Paseo de la Reforma on its north side and west of Calle Gandhi, you'll see the **Museo Tamayo Arte Contemporáneo** ㉒, in which you'll find Tamayo's paintings as well as those of other outstanding modern artists. West of the Museo Tamayo on the same side of Reforma is the **Museo Nacional de Antropología** ㉓, with its world-renowned collections of Mesoamerican art and artifacts. Cross Reforma again and you'll come to the entrance to the **Zoológico** ㉔.

Southeast of Bosque de Chapultepec are **Colonia Condesa** and **Colonia Roma,** whose attractive, tree-lined streets are peppered with art deco buildings in varying stages of renovation or picturesque decay. While it's possible to walk to Colonia Condesa from the Bosque de Chapultepec, you'd have to trek along busy, heavily trafficked roads; it's best to take a sitio taxi to the circular Avenida Amsterdam. Loop around Amsterdam until you reach Avenida Michoacán, where you can check out the boutiques and peek down the side streets. On Avenida Michoacán you'll find a sitio taxi stand—hop in for another short cab ride, this time to Colonia Roma's Plaza Río de Janeiro and more atmospheric strolling.

TIMING   You can easily spend an hour at each Bosque de Chapultepec museum, with the exception of the Museo Nacional de Antropología, which is huge compared with its sister institutions. You can have a quick go-through in two hours, but to really appreciate the fine exhibits, anywhere from a half day to two full days is more appropriate. Tuesday to Friday are good days to visit the museums and stroll around the park. On Sunday and Mexican holidays, they're often packed with families. A late-afternoon stroll in La Roma after the museum visits, with dinner in La Condesa, make an excellent way to wind down. Keep in mind that art galleries tend to close on Sunday. The colonias are a must-see in spring, when the jacarandas are in bloom.

What to See

BOSQUE DE   **Bosque de Chapultepec.** This 1,600-acre green space, literally the Woods
CHAPULTEPEC   of Chapultepec, draws hordes of families on weekend outings, cyclists,
⑳   joggers, and horseback riders into its three sections. Its museums rank among the finest in Mexico. This is one of the oldest parts of Mexico City, having been inhabited by the Mexica (Aztec) tribe as early as the 13th century. The Mexica poet-king Nezahualcoyotl had his palace here and ordered construction of the aqueduct that brought water to Tenochtitlán. Ahuehuete trees (Moctezuma cypress) still stand from that era, when the woods were used as hunting preserves.

At the park's principal entrance, one block west of the Chapultepec metro station, the **Monumento a los Niños Héroes** (Monument to the Boy Heroes) consists of six marble columns adorned with eaglets. Supposedly buried in the monument are the young cadets who, it is said, wrapped themselves in the Mexican flag and jumped to their deaths rather than surrender to the Americans during the U.S. invasion of 1847. To Mexicans, that war is still a troubling symbol of their neighbor's aggressive dominance: the war cost Mexico almost half of its national territory—the present states of Texas, California, Arizona, New Mexico, and Nevada.

Other sights in the first section of Bosque de Chapultepec include three small boating lakes, a botanical garden, and the Casa del Lago cultural center, which hosts free plays, cultural events, and live music on weekends. **Los Pinos,** the residential palace of the president of Mexico, is on a small highway called Avenida Constituyentes, which cuts through the park; it's heavily guarded and cannot be visited.

The less crowded second and third sections of Bosque de Chapultepec contain a fancy restaurant; **La Feria de Chapultepec; El Papalote, Museo**

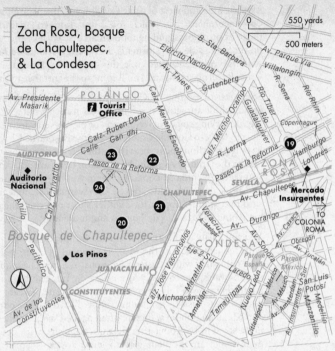

Zona Rosa, Bosque
de Chapultepec,
& La Condesa

del Niño (both described below); the national cemetery; and the Lienzo Charro (Mexican rodeos), held on Sunday afternoon.

㉑ **Castillo de Chapultepec.** The castle on Cerro del Chapulín (Grasshopper Hill) has borne witness to all the turbulence and grandeur of Mexican history. In its earliest permutations, it was an Aztec palace, where the Mexica made one of their last stands against the Spaniards. Later it was a Spanish hermitage, gunpowder plant, and military college. Emperor Maximilian used the castle, parts of which date from 1783, as his residence, and his example was followed by various presidents from 1872 to 1940, when Lázaro Cárdenas decreed that it be turned into the **Museo Nacional de Historia.**

Displays on the museum's ground floor cover Mexican history from the conquest to the revolution. The bathroom, bedroom, tea salon, and gardens were used by Maximilian and his wife, Carlotta, during their reign in the 1860s. The ground floor also contains works by 20th-century muralists O'Gorman, Orozco, and Siqueiros, and the upper floor is devoted to temporary exhibitions, Porfirio Díaz's malachite vases, and religious art. ⊠ *Section 1, Bosque de Chapultepec* ☎ *55/5286–0700* 💲 *$3* ☉ *Tues.–Sun. 9–4:30.*

㋡ **La Feria de Chapultepec.** This children's amusement park has various games and more than 50 rides, including a truly hair-raising haunted house and a *montaña rusa*—"Russian mountain," or roller coaster. Admission price varies, depending on which rides are covered and whether meals are included. ⊠ *Section 2, Bosque de Chapultepec* ☎ *55/5230–2121 or 55/5230–2112* 💲 *$6–$10* ☉ *Tues.–Fri. 10–6, weekends 10–8.*

㉓ **Museo Nacional de Antropología.** Architect Pedro Ramírez Vázquez's distinguished design showcases the national archaeological holdings, one of the finest such collections in the world. Each salon on the museum's two floors displays artifacts from a particular geographic region or culture. The collection is so extensive—covering some 100,000 square ft—that you could easily spend a day here, and that might be barely adequate. Explanatory labels have been updated, some with English translations, and free tours are available at set times between 3 and 6. You can also reserve a special tour with an English-speaking guide by calling the museum one week in advance, or opt for an English audio guide ($4) or English-language guidebooks for sale in the bookshop.

A good place to start is in the Orientation Room, where a film is shown in Spanish nearly every hour on the hour weekdays and every two hours on weekends. The film traces the course of Mexican prehistory and the pre-Hispanic cultures of Mesoamerica. The 12 ground-floor rooms treat pre-Hispanic cultures by region—such as Sala Teotihuacána, Sala Tolteca, Sala Oaxaca (Zapotec and Mixtec peoples), Sala Maya (Maya groups from many areas, including Guatemala), and so on. At this writing, the Sala Maya and the Sala Costa del Golfo were closed for renovation, due to reopen in 2004. Objects both precious and plebian, including statuary, jewelry, weapons, figurines, and pottery, evoke the intriguing, complex, and frequently bloodthirsty civilizations that peopled Mesoamerica for the 3,000 years that preceded the Spanish invasion. You will find the famous Aztec calendar stone—the original *Piedra del Sol* (Stone of the Sun)—in Room 7, the Sala Mexica, which describes Aztec life. A copy of the Aztec ruler Moctezuma's feathered headdress is displayed nearby in the same salon—strangely, the original headdress is in Vienna. An original stela from Tula, near Mexico City, massive Olmec heads from Veracruz, and vivid reproductions of Maya murals in a reconstructed temple are some of the other highlights. Be sure to see the magnificent tomb of 8th-century Maya ruler Pacal, which was discovered in the ruins of Palenque. The perfectly preserved skeletal remains lie in state in an immense stone chamber, and the stairwell walls leading to it are beautifully decorated with bas-relief scenes of the underworld. Pacal's jade death mask is also on display nearby.

The nine rooms on the upper floor contain faithful ethnographic displays of current indigenous peoples, using maps, photographs, household items, folk art, clothing, and religious articles. When leaving the museum, take a rest and watch the famous Voladores de Papantla (flyers of Papantla) as they swing by their feet down an incredibly high maypolelike structure. ⊠ *Paseo de la Reforma at Calle Gandhi, Section 1, Bosque de Chapultepec* ☎ *55/5286–2923 or 55/5553–6381; 55/5553–6386 for a guide* ⊕ *www.mna.inah.gob.mx* ⊠ *$3.50* ⊙ *Tues.–Sun. 9–7.*

★ ㉒ **Museo Tamayo Arte Contemporáneo** (Rufino Tamayo Contemporary Art Museum). Within its modernist shell, this sleek museum contains the paintings of the noted Mexican artist, works from his private collection, and temporary exhibitions on international contemporary artists. The selections from Tamayo's extensive personal collection demonstrate his unerring eye for great art; he owned works by Picasso, Joan Miró, René Magritte, Francis Bacon, and Henry Moore. ⊠ *Paseo de la Reforma at Calle Gandhi, Section 1, Bosque de Chapultepec* ☎ *55/5286–6519* ⊕ *www.museotamayo.org* ⊠ *$1.50* ⊙ *Tues.–Sun. 10–6.*

⟲ **El Papalote, Museo del Niño.** Five theme sections compose this excellent interactive children's museum: Our World; The Human Body; Con-Sci-encia, with exhibits relating to both consciousness and science; Communication, on topics ranging from language to computers; and Expression, which includes art, music, theater, and literature. There are also workshops, an IMAX theater, a store, and a restaurant. ⊠ *Av. Constituyentes 268, Section 2, Bosque de Chapultepec* ☎ *55/5237–1781 or 55/5237–1700* ⊕ *www.papalote.org.mx* ⊠ *$5* ⊙ *Weekdays 9–6, weekends 10–7.*

☺ ㉔ **Zoológico de Chapultepec.** During the early 16th century, Mexico City's zoo housed a small private collection of animals belonging to Moctezuma II; it became quasi-public when he allowed favored subjects to visit it. The current zoo opened in the 1920s and has the usual suspects as well as some superstar pandas. A gift from China, the original pair—Pepe and Ying Ying—produced the world's first panda baby born in captivity (much to competitive China's chagrin). In fact, the zoo has one of the world's best mating records for these endangered animals. The zoo includes the Moctezuma Aviary and is surrounded by a miniature train depot, botanical gardens, and lakes where you can go rowing. You'll see the entrance on Paseo de la Reforma, across from the Museo Nacional de Antropología. ⊠ *Section 1, Bosque de Chapultepec* ☎ *55/5553–6263 or 55/5256–4104* ⊕ *www.cnf.org.mx/zoologico/infozoo.html* ⊡ *Free* ♡ *Tues.–Sun. 9–4.*

COLONIA **Around Avenida Michoacán.** Restaurants, cafés, and hip boutiques radi-
CONDESA ate along and out from La Condesa's main drag, the Avenida Michoacán. It's a great place for a break from a sightseeing slog—just relax at a sidewalk table and watch the hip young world go by. You will be spoiled for choice, if you can find a seat, at the popular **Cafe La Selva** (⊠ Av. Vicente Suárez 38 C and D, off Av. Michoacán, Col. Condesa ☎ 55/5211–5170). Pick up a quick baguette or sandwich with your coffee at **Mantra** (⊠ Av. Tamaulipas 216, Col. Condesa ☎ 55/5516–0155).

A snack will fortify you for Avenida Michoacán's other main activity, shopping. The clothing stores often lean to the trendy; La Esquina, for instance, on Michoacán at the corner of Amatlán, dishes up the latest fads, as does Soho, on Avenida Vicente Suárez between avenidas Michoacán and Tamaulipas. Along the nearby streets you'll find a good mix of temptations—everything from Birkenstocks to risqué lingerie. As its name (The Open Closet) suggests, the bookstore **El Armario Abierto** (⊠ Agustín Melgar 25, at Pachuca, Col. Condesa ☎ 55/5286–0895) gives a rare glimpse of progressive Mexico; it specializes in sexuality-related books, videos, and other resources. **El Péndulo** (⊠ Av. Nuevo León 115, Col. Condesa ☎ 55/5286–9493 ⊕ www.pendulo.com), meanwhile, acts as a sort of cultural center. The store is stuffed with Spanish books and international CDs; classical guitarists and other musicians play on the weekends.

The designer shop Carmen Rion caps Michoacán where it meets the **Parque México,** which has a duck pond, plus one of the city's cheapest and best taxi stands. The park area used to be a racetrack, which explains the circular roads like the looping Avenida México and the occasional references to the Hipódromo (hippodrome) Condesa. From Michoacán you could also turn north on Tamaulipas and walk up a few blocks to visit a smaller park, the **Parque España** for a picnic or a stroll.

COLONIA ROMA Adventurous private art galleries, independent, artist-run spaces, and a rough-around-the-edges atmosphere are the hallmarks of La Roma. Like its western neighbor La Condesa, La Roma was once an aristocratic enclave with stately homes. Now it's known for its lively cantinas, pool halls, dance clubs, and night haunts of questionable repute. (See Nightlife for more details.) Gentrification creeps slowly but steadily onward, though, so enjoy this up-and-comer before it becomes too respectable.

Mexico City's first serious art galleries opened here in the 1980s. More recently, bookstores and cafés have helped transform the old neighborhood into the capital's full-blown arts district. The **Galería OMR** (⊠ Plaza Río de Janeiro 54, Col. Roma ☎ 55/5525–3095 or 55/5511–1179 ⊕ www.galeriaomr.com) is tucked away in a typical Colonia Roma house, with an early 20th-century stone facade and quirkily lopsided exhibition rooms. This active gallery has a strong presence in international art fairs and art magazines. It's open weekdays 10–3 and 4–7 and Saturday 10–2. A short walk from OMR, **Galería Nina Menocal** (⊠ Zacatecas 93, Col. Roma ☎ 55/5564–7443 ⊕ www.artnet.com/nmenocal.html) is directed by the enthusiastic, Cuban-born Nina Menocal. She radically influenced the art scene in Mexico by organizing exciting exhibitions with major Cuban artists. The gallery is open weekdays 10–7 and Saturday 10–2. The **Casa Lamm Cultural Center** (⊠ Av. Álvaro Obregón 99, Col. Roma ☎ 55/5525–0019 ⊕ www.nueve.com.mx/casalamm), a small mansion and national monument, nurtures artists and browsers with three exhibition spaces, a bookstore, a wide range of courses, and a superb restaurant. **Galería Pecanins** (⊠ Av. Durango 186 at Plaza Cibeles, Col. Roma ☎ 55/5514–0621) may be small but it's a significant local presence for art buyers. It's open weekdays 11–2:30 and 4–7.

ZONA ROSA   Thanks to a plethora of restaurants, cafés, art and antiques galleries, hotels, discos, and shops, the touristy Zona Rosa has been a favorite part of the city for years. The 29-square-block area is bounded by Paseo de la Reforma on the north, Niza on the east, Avenida Chapultepec on the south, and Varsovia on the west. With the mushrooming of fast-food spots and some tacky bars and stores, however, the area has lost some of its former appeal. Most of the buildings were built in the 1920s, as two- to three-story private homes for the well-to-do. All the streets are named after European cities; some, such as Génova, are garden-lined pedestrian malls accented with contemporary bronze statuary.

To enjoy the Zona Rosa, walk the lengths of Hamburgo and Londres and some of the side streets, especially Copenhague—a veritable restaurant row. The large crafts market on Londres is officially called **Mercado Insurgentes,** although most people refer to it as either Mercado Zona Rosa or Mercado Londres. Opposite the market's Londres entrance is Plaza del Angel, a small upscale shopping mall, the halls of which are crowded by antiques vendors on weekends.

⑲ Monumento a la Independencia. Known as El Angel, this Corinthian column topped by a gold-covered angel is the city's most uplifting monument, built to celebrate the 100th anniversary of Mexico's War of Independence. Beneath the pedestal lie the remains of the principal heroes of the independence movement; an eternal flame burns in their honor. ⊠ *Traffic circle between Calle Río Tiber, Paseo de la Reforma, and Calle Florencia, Zona Rosa.*

San Angel & Coyoacán

Originally separate colonial towns and then suburbs of Mexico City, San Angel and Coyoacán were both absorbed by the ever-growing capital. But in the process they've managed to retain their original pueblo charm and tranquility.

San Angel is a little colonial enclave of cobblestone streets, stone walls, pastel houses, rich foliage, and gardens drenched in bougainvillea. It became a haven for wealthy Spaniards during the Viceroyalty period, around the time of the construction of the Ex-Convento del Carmen. The elite were drawn to the area because of its rivers, pleasant climate, and rural ambience, and proceeded to build haciendas and mansions that, for many, were country homes. It is now sliced through by the busy Avenida Revolución; visitors usually focus on the area from the cobblestoned Avenida de la Paz, lined with some excellent eateries, to the

Ex-Convento on Avenida Revolución, and up to the Plaza San Jacinto and its famous Saturday market.

Coyoacán means "Place of the Coyotes." According to local legend, a coyote used to bring chickens to a friar who had saved the coyote from being strangled by a snake. Coyoacán was founded by Toltecs in the 10th century and later settled by the Aztecs, or Mexica. Bernal Díaz Castillo, a Spanish chronicler, wrote that there were 6,000 houses at the time of the conquest. Cortés set up headquarters in Coyoacán during his siege of Tenochtitlán and kept his famous Indian mistress La Malinche here. At one point he considered making Coyoacán his capital; many of the Spanish buildings left from the two-year period during which Mexico City was built still stand.

Coyoacán has had many illustrious residents from Mexico's rich and intellectual elite, including Miguel de la Madrid, president of Mexico from 1982 to 1988; artists Diego Rivera, Frida Kahlo, and José Clemente Orozco; Gabriel Figueroa, cinematographer for Luis Buñuel and John Huston; film star Dolores del Río; film director El Indio Fernández; and writers Carlos Monsiváis, Jorge Ibargüengoitia, and Nobel laureate Octavio Paz. It's also the neighborhood where the exiled Leon Trotsky met his violent death. Coyoacán's streets buzz with activity, and it has a popular food market, the Mercado Xicotencatl. On weekends families flock to its attractive *zócalo* (central square), second in importance and popularity only to the Zócalo downtown, to enjoy the neighborhood's famous ice creams.

A Good Tour

Numbers in the text correspond to numbers in the margin and on the San Angel and Coyoacán map.

Weekends are best for exploring the southern part of the city. Take a taxi or pesero down Avenida Insurgentes and get off at the **Monumento al General Alvaro Obregón** ▶, the somber gray granite monument marking the spot where the reformer Obregón was gunned down by a religious zealot in 1928. Cross Insurgentes to walk up the cobblestoned, restaurant-lined Avenida de la Paz. Next cross Avenida Revolución, and take the crooked street that leads upwards to the left of the little park until you come to San Angel's center, **Plaza San Jacinto** ㉕. Stroll to the **Centro Cultural Isidro Favela** ㉖ on the north side of the plaza and, if it's a Saturday, head farther north for arts and crafts at the **Bazar Sábado.**

Retrace your steps on Avenida de la Paz, to Avenida Revolución and Plaza del Carmen, which lies at the corner of Calle Monasterio. Inside is the colonial **Ex-Convento del Carmen** ㉗, interesting as an example of sacred architecture and for its religious artifacts. Then take Avenida Revolución one long block north past a flower market to see the modern Mexican and European works at the **Museo de Arte Carrillo Gil** ㉘ (known as the Carrillo Gil). Unless you have plenty of energy, get a taxi to take you up Avenida Altavista to the **Museo Estudio Diego Rivera** ㉙ (and to an elegant lunch in the San Angel Inn or Il Fornaio).

The next part of the tour goes to Coyoacán, which extends east of Avenida Insurgentes about 1 km (½ mi) from San Angel. You're best off taking a taxi to the **Plaza de Santa Catarina** on Avenida Francisco Sosa, about halfway into the center of Coyoacán, because the tour involves a lot of walking.

The pretty 16th-century Iglesia de Santa Catarina dominates this tiny plaza. It contains a bust of Mexican historian Francisco Sosa. Across the street is the **Casa de Jesús Reyes Heroles;** the former home of the

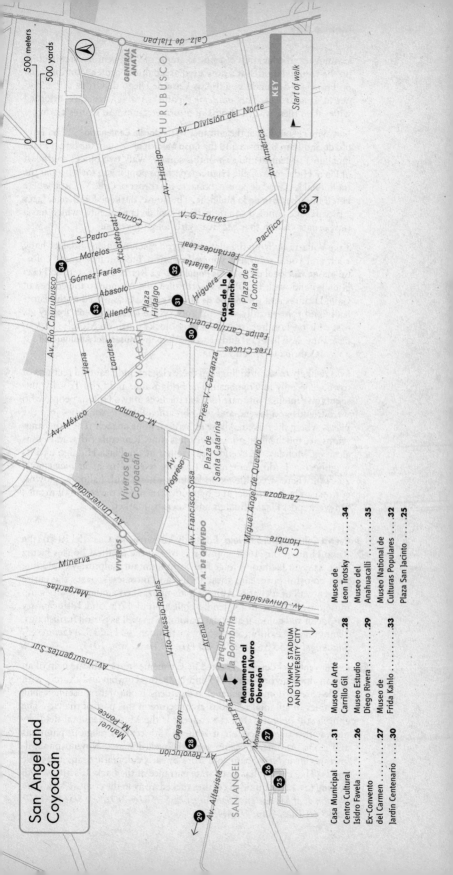

San Angel and Coyoacán

KEY

▲ Start of walk

500 meters
500 yards

CHURUBUSCO

Av. División del Norte

Av. Río Churubusco

COYOACÁN

Viveros de Coyoacán

Av. México

Av. Universidad

VIVEROS

M. A. DE QUEVEDO

SAN ANGEL

TO OLYMPIC STADIUM
AND UNIVERSITY CITY →

Casa de la Malinche

Monumento al General Alvaro Obregón

Parque de la Bombilla

GENERAL ANAYA

Calz. de Tlalpan

Av. América

Pacífico

V. G. Torres

Corina

Fernández Leal

Vallarta

S. Pedro
Morelos
Gómez Farías
Abasolo
Allende

Xicoténcatl

Plaza Hidalgo

Higuera

Plaza de la Conchita

Felipe Carrillo Puerto

Tres Cruces

Pres. V. Carranza

Plaza de Santa Catarina

Av. Progreso

Av. Ocampo

Viena
Londres

Av. Francisco Sosa

Miguel Angel de Quevedo

Zaragoza

C. Del Hombre

Minerva

Margaritas

Vito Alessio Robles

Arenal

Av. de la Paz

Monasterio

Ogazón

Av. Revolución

Av. Altavista

Manuel M. Ponce

Av. Insurgentes Sur

Av. Hidalgo

Casa Municipal **31**	Museo de Arte Carrillo Gil **28**	Museo de Leon Trotsky **34**	
Centro Cultural Isidro Favela **26**	Museo Estudio Diego Rivera **29**	Museo del Anahuacalli **35**	
Ex-Convento del Carmen **27**	Museo de Frida Kahlo **33**	Museo National de Culturas Populares **32**	
Jardín Centenario **30**		Plaza San Jacinto **25**	

ex-minister of education is a fine example of 20th-century architecture on the colonial model. It's now used as a cultural center. Continue east on Francisco Sosa and you'll pass **Casa de Diego de Ordaz** at the corner of Tres Cruces. This *mudéjar* (Spanish-Arabic) structure, adorned with inlaid tiles, was the home of a former captain in Cortés's army.

Now you're standing at the entrance of the **Jardín Centenario** ㉚. The Templo de San Juan Bautista and the **Casa Municipal** ㉛ sit in the larger **Plaza Hidalgo** adjacent to and east of this square. Walk two blocks southeast of Plaza Hidalgo on Calle Higuera, perhaps popping in for a beer at the traditional La Guadalupana cantina, to the corner of Calle Vallarta, where you'll find the **Casa de la Malinche.** The house, darkened with age, faces a picturesque cobbled square called Plaza de la Conchita, which has a tiny, ornate church that Mexican girls long to wed in.

Take Vallarta up from the plaza until you reach Avenida Hidalgo; hang a left and you'll soon find yourself opposite the entrance to the colorful **Museo Nacional de Culturas Populares** ㉜. Retrace your steps to Plaza Hidalgo and walk five blocks north on Calle Allende to the corner of Calle Londres and the **Museo de Frida Kahlo** ㉝. It's linked both historically and romantically with the fortresslike **Museo de Leon Trotsky** ㉞, east of it on Londres, then two long blocks north on Morelos. If you have time, hop in a taxi and head south to the **Museo del Anahuacalli** ㉟, a virtual shrine to Diego Rivera.

TIMING   You're likely to want to linger in these elegant and beautiful sections of town, especially in Coyoacán. The Frida Kahlo and Leon Trotsky museums give intense, intimate looks at the lives of two famous people who were friends and lovers, and who breathed their personalities into the places where they lived. Allow at least an hour at each. The other museums are much smaller and merit less time. Remember that museums close on Monday. Weekends are liveliest at the Plaza Hidalgo and its neighboring Jardín Centenario (usually referred to as *la plaza* or *el zócalo*), where street life explodes into a fiesta with balloons, clowns, cotton candy, live music, and hypnotic dancing to the sound of drums. On weekends, Plaza Hidalgo hosts a crafts market.

What to See

SAN ANGEL   **Centro Cultural Isidro Favela.** Formerly known as La Casa del Risco (the
㉖ Risco House), this 1681 mansion is one of the prettiest houses facing the Plaza San Jacinto. A huge free-form fountain sculpture—exploding with colorful porcelain, tiles, shells, and mosaics—covers the entire eastern wall of its patio. Although it's not ranked among the city's top museums, Favela left a splendid collection of 17th- and 18th-century European and colonial Mexican paintings, as well as period furnishings. Temporary art exhibitions also rotate through. ⊠ *Plaza San Jacinto 15, San Angel* ☎ *55/5616–2711* ⊠ *Free* ⊘ *Tues.–Sun. 10–5.*

㉗ **Ex-Convento del Carmen.** Erected by Carmelite friars with the help of an Indian chieftain between 1615 and 1628, this convent and church, with its tile-covered domes, fountains, and gardens, is one of the most interesting examples of colonial religious architecture in this part of the city. The church still operates, but the convent is the **Museo Regional del Carmen,** with a fine collection of 16th- to 18th-century religious paintings and icons. Another museum area, the well-designed **Novohispana,** illustrates life in New Spain with work by early colonial artisans and trade guilds. This exhibit has a separate entrance at the back. It's also worth visiting the 12 mummified corpses tucked away in the crypt. ⊠ *Av. Revolución 4, at Monasterio, San Angel* ☎ *55/5616–2816 or 55/5616–1177* ⊠ *$3* ⊘ *Tues.–Sun. 10–4:45.*

28 Museo de Arte Carrillo Gil. Considerably superior in terms of design and natural lighting to the city's Museo Nacional de Arte Moderno, this private collection contains early murals by Orozco, Rivera, and Siqueiros; works by modern European artists such as Klee and Picasso; and temporary exhibitions of young Mexican artists. ✉ *Av. Revolución 1608, at Av. Altavista, San Angel* ☎ *55/5550–1254* 💲 *$1.50* 🕐 *Tues.–Sun. 10–6.*

29 Museo Casa Estudio Diego Rivera. Some of Rivera's last paintings are still resting here on ready easels, and his denim jacket and shoes sit on a wicker chair, waiting. The museum that once was home to Diego Rivera and his artist wife, Frida Kahlo, appears as if the two could return at any moment to continue work. Architect Juan O'Gorman, who designed the 1931 building, was a close friend of Rivera. His work reflects his philosophy of progressive socialism and shows the influence of Le Corbusier and other European modernists; the house is now one of the city's architectural landmarks. ✉ *Calle Diego Rivera, at Av. Altavista, San Angel* ☎ *55/5616–0996* 💲 *$1* 🕐 *Tues.–Sun. 10–6.*

★ **25 Plaza San Jacinto.** This welcoming plaza with a grisly history constitutes the heart of San Angel. In 1847 about 50 Irish soldiers of St. Patrick's Battalion, who had sided with the Mexicans in the Mexican-American War, had their foreheads branded here with the letter *D*—for deserter—and were then hanged by the Americans. These men had been enticed to swim the Río Grande, deserting the ranks of U.S. General Zachary Taylor, by pleas to the historic and religious ties between Spain and Ireland. As settlers in Mexican Texas, they felt their allegiance lay with Catholic Mexico, and they were among the bravest fighters in the war. A memorial plaque (on a building on the plaza's west side) lists their names and expresses Mexico's gratitude for their help in the "unjust North American invasion." Off to one side of the plaza, the excellent arts and crafts market, **Bazar Sábado,** is held all day Saturday. ✉ *Between Miramon, Cda. Santisima, Dr. Galvez, and Calle Madero, San Angel.*

COYOACÁN **Casa de la Malinche.** This somber-looking residence was the home of La Malinche, Cortés's Indian mistress and interpreter, whom the Spaniards called Doña María and the Indians called Malintzín. La Malinche aided the conquest by enabling Cortés to communicate with the Nahuatl-speaking tribes he met en route to Tenochtitlán. Today she is a reviled Mexican symbol of a traitorous xenophile—hence the term *malinchista,* used to describe a Mexican who prefers things foreign. Legend says that Cortés's wife died in this house, poisoned by the conquistador. The house is not open to the public. ✉ *2 blocks east of Plaza Hidalgo on Calle Higuera at Vallarta, Coyoacán.*

31 Casa Municipal (Casa de Cortés). The place where the Aztec emperor Cuauhtémoc was held prisoner by Cortés is reputed to have been rebuilt in the 18th century from the stones of his original house by one of Cortés's descendants. Now a sandy color and topped by two coyote figures, it's used for municipal government offices; a small tourist bureau at the entrance offers maps and leaflets publicizing cultural events in the area. Usually you can wander through the wide arches to the pretty tile patio. ✉ *Plaza Hidalgo 1 between Calles Carillo Puerto and Allende, Coyoacán* ☎ *55/5658–0221* 🕐 *Daily 8–8.*

30 Jardín Centenario. The Centenary Gardens are barely separated from the **Plaza Hidalgo** by a narrow slow-moving road; both squares are referred to as Coyoacán's zócalo. The Jardín, with its shading trees, a fountain with two snarling coyotes, and a fringe of outdoor cafés, is the place to sit and people-watch. On weekends from 11 AM until about 10 PM it morphs into a lively, hippie-ish handicrafts market, complete with drum-

mers and palm readings. The larger Plaza Hidalgo hosts children's fun-
fairs, amateur musical and dance performances, clowns, bubble blow-
ers, cotton candy, and balloon sellers on weekends and national holidays.
It's studded with an ornate old bandstand and the impressive **Templo
de San Juan Bautista,** one of the first churches to be built in New Spain.
It was completed in 1582, and its door has a Baroque arch. During the
afternoon of September 15, before the crowds become suffocating at nightfall, this delightful neighborhood zócalo is probably the best place in
the capital to enjoy Independence Day celebrations. ⌧ *Between Calle
Centenario, Av. Hidalgo, and Caballo Calco, Coyoacán.*

33 **Museo de Frida Kahlo.** Kahlo has become a sort of cult figure, not only
because of her paintings—55 of 143 are self-portraits—but also because
of her bohemian lifestyle and flamboyant individualism. The "Blue
House" where she was born in 1907 (not 1910, as she wanted people
to believe) and died 47 years later, is both museum and shrine. Kahlo's
astounding vitality and originality are reflected in the house, from the
giant papier-mâché skeletons outside and the *retablos* (small religious
paintings on tin) on the staircase to the gloriously decorated kitchen and
the bric-a-brac in her bedroom. You can admire her early sketches, diary
entries, tiny outfits, wheelchair at the easel, plus her four-poster bed conveniently fitted with mirror above. Even if you know nothing about Kahlo,
a visit to the museum will leave you with a strong, visceral impression
of this pivotal feminist artist. ⌧ *Londres 247, at Calle Allende, Coyoacán*
☎ *55/5554–5999* ⌧ *$3* ☉ *Tues.–Sun. 10–5:45.*

34 **Museo de Leon Trotsky.** Resembling an anonymous and forbidding fortress,
with turrets for armed guards, this house is where Leon Trotsky lived
and was murdered. It's difficult to believe that it's the final resting place
for the ashes of one of the most important figures of the Russian Revolution, but that only adds to the allure of this austere dwelling, which
is owned by Trotsky's grandson. Anyone taller than 5 ft must stoop to
pass through doorways to Trotsky's bedroom—with bullet holes still
in the walls from the first assassination attempt, in which the muralist
Siqueiros was implicated—his wife's study, the dining room, and the study
where assassin Ramón Mercader—a man of many aliases—allegedly drove
a pickax into Trotsky's head. On his desk, cluttered with writing para-
phernalia and an article he was revising in Russian, the calendar is open
to that fateful day, August 20, 1940. All informative materials are in
Spanish only. ⌧ *Río Churubusco 410, Coyoacán* ☎ *55/5658–8732*
⌧ *$1* ☉ *Tues.–Sun. 10–5.*

35 **Museo del Anahuacalli.** Diego Rivera built his own museum for the thousands of pre-Columbian artifacts he collected over the years. The third-
floor studio that Rivera did not live long enough to use displays sketches
for some of his most controversial murals. The huge dark-gray building, constructed in the 1950s from volcanic rock, resembles an above-
ground tomb. If you visit between October and the end of December
you'll see one of the city's finest altars to the dead in honor of Rivera
himself. ⌧ *Calle del Museo 150, Coyoacán* ☎ *55/5617–4310 or 55/
5617–3797* ⌧ *$1* ☉ *Tues.–Sun. 10–6.*

32 **Museo Nacional de Culturas Populares.** A huge *arbol de la vida* (tree of
life) sculpture stands in the courtyard of this museum devoted to popular culture and regional arts and crafts. Its exhibitions and events are
nicely varied, including children's workshops, traditional musical concerts, and dance performances. On weekends the courtyard becomes a
small craft and sweets market. The museum shop stocks art books and
high-quality crafts. ⌧ *Av. Hidalgo 289 at Calle Allende, Coyoacán*

FRIDA KAHLO, A RIBBON AROUND A BOMB

O F COURSE, HE DOES PRETTY WELL for a little boy, but it is I who am the big artist."

Frida Kahlo's tongue-in-cheek comment about her husband to the Detroit News in 1933 seems less and less a joke as the years go by. This petite painter, who has gained international recognition since the 1980s for her colorful but pained self-portraits, has begun to overshadow the massive muralist Diego Rivera. Considered one of the 20th century's major artistic figures, Rivera created images—especially those rounded peasant women with braided hair, arms brim-full of creamy lilies—that have typified this country for more than a half century. The bizarre Beauty-and-the-Beast dynamics and sordid drama of the couple's relationship ensure the popularity of many of Mexico's museums and murals. But, if Diego dwarfed Frida in stature, he no longer does in fame.

Now, Kahlo's hauntingly beautiful face, broken body, and bright Tehuana costumes, along with a few exotic accessories such as monkeys, parrots, and hairless dogs, have become the trademark of Mexican femininity. Life-size cardboard cutouts with her bat-wing brows, moustache, and clunky ethnic earrings are as familiar here as Marilyn's pout and puffed-up white dress are in the United States.

In fact, Frida didn't even need to paint to make it into the history books. The controversy and scandal that surrounded her two marriages to Diego include his affair with her younger sister—the same year Frida suffered a third miscarriage and had toes removed from her right foot—and her affair with Communist exile Leon Trotsky. It's hard not to become mired in the tragic twists and turns of her life—from childhood polio to a tram accident that smashed her pelvis, a gangrenous foot that resulted in the amputation of a leg, as well as bouts of anorexia and alcoholism.

But she was also a groundbreaking artist who pioneered a new expressiveness, and her unique iconography of suffering transcended self-pity to create an existential art. Kahlo was the first Latin American woman to have a painting in the Louvre; her work caused a storm in Paris in 1939 (at an exhibition entitled Méxique), and the surrealists claimed it as supremely illustrative of their ideas. It was André Breton who described her art as "a ribbon around a bomb."

Frida, who was always frank about her start in painting—she did it to kill time in one of her many convalescences—had doubts that her paintings were surrealist, saying, "they are the most frank expression of myself." Later she expressed unease with her art for not being suitable to serve the aims of the Communist Party, of which she and Diego were avid supporters. Her gargantuan husband was more generous, emphasizing how the influence of the religious retablo (ex-voto) that Frida collected was transformed in her art to an exploration of the permanent miracle of life. "Frida . . . tore open her chest and heart to reveal the biological truth of her feelings," he wrote.

And Frida tried hard to be as much the comrade and revolutionary as the icon of long-suffering Mexican femininity. Her last public appearance was 11 days before her death, in a wheelchair at Diego's side, protesting the intervention of the United States in Guatemala.

— Barbara Kastelein

☎ *55/5554–8357* ⊕ *www.cnca.gob.mx/cnca/popul/mncp.htm* ✉ *Free* ⊙ *Tues.–Thurs. 10–6, Fri.–Sun. 10–8.*

off the beaten path

☢ **Six Flags of México.** This 100-acre theme park on the southern edge of the city comprises seven "villages": Mexican, French, Swiss, Polynesian, Moroccan, the Wild West, and Children's World. Shows include performances by trained dolphins. ⊠ *Southwest of Coyoacán on Carretera Picacho a Ajusco, Km 1.5* ☎ *55/5645–5434 or 55/ 5728–7200* ✉ *$20 includes entrance and all rides* ⊙ *Tues.–Thurs. 10–6, Fri.–Sun. 10–7.*

WHERE TO EAT

Mexico City has been a culinary capital ever since the time of Moctezuma. Chronicles tell of the extravagant banquets prepared for the Aztec emperor with more than 300 different dishes served for every meal.

Today's Mexico City is a gastronomic melting pot with some 15,000 restaurants. You'll find everything from simple family-style eateries and cantinas to five-star world-class restaurants. The number and range of international restaurants is growing and diversifying—although Spanish, Italian, and Argentine restaurants are dominant.

Mexico City restaurants open 7–11 AM for breakfast (*el desayuno*) and 1:30–5 for lunch (*la comida*)—although it's rare for Mexicans to eat lunch before 3 and you are likely to feel lonely if you arrive at a popular restaurant before 2. Lunch is an institution in this country, often lasting two hours, and until nightfall on Sundays. Consequently, evening meals may often be very light, consisting of sweet bread and coffee, a few tacos, or traditional *tamales* and *atole,* which can double up as breakfast.

When dining, most locals start out at 9 PM for dinner (*la cena*); restaurants stay open until 11:30 during the week and a little later on weekends. At deluxe restaurants, dress is generally formal (jacket at least), and reservations are almost always advised; see reviews for details. If you're short on time, you can always head to American-style coffee shops (VIPS, Denny's, and Sanborns) or recognizable fast-food chains that offer the tired but reliable fare of burgers, fried chicken, and pizzas all over the city; many are open 24 hours.

The popular *Cafe Chino* (Chinese cafés) all over town are a cheap and hearty option for a quick bite. Asian cuisine is still limited here, but you will find some good Japanese and a few real Chinese restaurants. Similarly, there are very few vegetarian restaurants, but you will have no trouble finding nonmeat dishes wherever you grab a bite. Vegans, however, may have a more difficult time finding desired ingredients.

Hygiene practices in food preparation are improving greatly as establishments learn about catering to foreign tourists with more vulnerable stomachs. If you want to avoid trouble, avoid sauces that have fresh cilantro or dishes garnished with lettuce shreds. The Distintivo H, a rigorous standard for disinfection and cleanliness, is an important step in the right direction. It is backed by the Tourism Ministry, and numerous upper-end restaurants are striving to meet its specifications.

Colonia Polanco, the upscale neighborhood on the edge of the Bosque de Chapultepec, has some of the best and most expensive dining (and lodging) in the city. Zona Rosa restaurants get filled pretty quickly on Saturday night, especially on Saturdays coinciding with most people's paydays: the 1st and 15th of each month. The same is true of San Angel,

LA COCINA MEXICANA

TO ENTERTAIN THE NOTION that Mexican food is little more than tacos, enchiladas, and burritos—or Tex-Mex or Taco Bell—would be culinary blasphemy to native gastronomes. Regional cooking is the heart and soul of Mexico, multiplied by the republic's 32 states and the provinces within them. Fresh ingredients abound, recipes are passed down through generations (think Like Water for Chocolate), and labor-intensive preparation requires much patience and loving care. With the staples—rice, beans, chilies, and corn—chefs are turning out ever more sophisticated variations on national dishes. But, of the Mexican chef's arsenal of ingredients, they're only the beginning.

Maize was sacred to the Indians, who have innumerable ways of preparing it—from faithful tortillas and tamales (cornmeal wrapped in banana leaves or corn husks) to tostadas (lightly fried, open tortillas topped with meat, lettuce, and the like) and tacos (tortillas briefly heated, filled, and wrapped into slim cylinders). Pozole (made with hominy) is a delicious pork-based soup. The sweet, corn-based drink atole, similar in consistency to hot chocolate, is a favorite breakfast or before-bed treat.

You'll find fish not just on the coasts but also in the lake regions around Guadalajara and in the state of Michoacán. Huachinango (red snapper), abalone, crab, and swordfish are all popular. And ceviche—raw mariscos (shellfish) marinated in lime juice then topped with chopped chilies, onions, and cilantro—is almost a national dish; just make sure it's fresh. Shrimp, lobster, and oysters can be huge and succulent; bear in mind the folk adage and eat oysters only in months with names that contain the letter r. Likewise avoid raw shellfish wherever cholera or water pollution might be a risk.

Mexicans love beef, pork, and barbacoa (barbecued lamb) with a variety of sauces. The complex, spicy mole is one of Mexico's proudest culinary inventions; its ingredients can number more than 100, including chilies, pumpkin seeds or nuts,

and in some cases, cacao. It is usually served over chicken or turkey.

Fresh fruits and vegetables are another Mexican pleasure. Jicama, papaya, mamey, avocado, mango, guayaba, squash, and tomatoes are just some of the produce native to Mexico. (All fresh produce should be washed in water with a commercial disinfectant—bacteria exist in Mexico that your stomach might not be happy with. For this reason, avoid eating at street stalls and beware of uncooked herbs such as cilantro).

Other Mexican specialties are less common abroad: antojitos or botanas (appetizers), chilaquiles (breakfast dishes made with tortilla strips scrambled with chilies, tomatoes, onions, cream, and cheese), and chiles en nogada (a large poblano chili stuffed with beef or cheese, raisins, onion, olives, and almonds and topped with a creamy walnut sauce and pomegranate seeds). Soups are hearty—particularly pozole, sopa azteca (avocado, chicken chunks, and tortilla in a broth), and don't forget to try the lighter sopa de flor de calabaza (zucchini-flower soup) or, if you get a chance, sopa de colorin, made from a bright red flower.

The astonishing assortment of breads, sweets, beers, wines (which are fast improving), and agave-based (cactus-related) liquors goes on and on. Sadly, shortage of the blue agave has caused tequila prices to soar, so watch out for cheap varieties that add sugarcane liquor or less digestible substances. Freshly squeezed fruit juices and fruit shakes (licuados) are safe to drink—if ordered in a restaurant with hygienic practices—and taste heavenly. And coffee ranges from americano (black) to organic varieties to sweet café de olla, which is laced with spices.

whereas the Condesa neighborhood buzzes with a younger crowd Thursday to Saturday.

	WHAT IT COSTS				
	$$$$	$$$	$$	$	¢
AT DINNER	over $25	$15–$25	$10–$15	$5–$10	under $5

Prices are per person for a main course, excluding tax and tip

Argentine

¢–$ ✕**Cambalache.** If you come with a few people to this ever-busy beef-lover's dream, try the Super Lomo Cambalache, a steak big enough for three or four people. Or try the Don Ignacio, a boneless chicken breast served in a mushroom sauce with pineapple and fresh sweet peppers. And why not sink your fork into the potato soufflé, a house specialty? ⊠ *Arquímedes 85, Col. Polanco* ☎ *55/5280–2080 or 55/5282–2922* ▭ *AE, MC, V.*

¢–$ ✕**Entrevero.** A Uruguayan may own this friendly eatery on the square of Coyoacán, but rest assured that all Argentine attractions appear on the menu—*provoleta* (grilled provolone cheese with oregano) among them. Entrevero is also one of the few restaurants in the capital where you will find good pizza, calzones, and gnocchi, and the *crema quemada* (a version of crème brûlée) is sinful. Fair prices and the excellent location guarantee it is always busy, so arrive a little early on weekends to get a table. ⊠ *Jardín Centenario 14-C, Col. Coyoacán* ☎ *55/5659–0066* ▭ *AE, MC, V* ☾ *No dinner Sun.*

¢–$ ✕**Rincón Argentino.** This established Argentine restaurant is known as much for its decor as for its exquisite cuts of beef. The ceiling is painted to resemble the sky, the bar is covered by a thatch roof, and the dining areas call to mind a stone-and-wood lodge. Most Argentines prefer their beef *bien cocida* (well done), but you can have it any way you like. ⊠ *Av. Presidente Masaryk 177, Col. Polanco* ☎ *55/5531–8617 or 55/ 5254–8775* ▭ *AE, MC, V.*

¢–$ ✕**La Taba.** Smart yet unpretentious, this restaurant in the south of the city is characterized by its generous portions of top-quality beef, done perfectly to your choice of five options—from blue to well done. The flavorful *chistorra* (a semicured chorizo-type sausage) stands out from the wide range of starters; vegetarians can choose from soups, pastas, and salads. The *bife de chorizo* (rump steak) is unforgettable, and big eaters might find room for one of the traditional Argentine desserts. ⊠ *Av. Revolución 1398, Col. Guadalupe Inn* ☎ *55/5662–3165 or 55/ 5662–2670* ▭ *AE, MC, V.*

Chinese

$–$$$ ✕**Mandarin House.** Standing proudly at the head of the eateries that line San Angel's cobbled Avenida de la Paz, this spacious restaurant offers predominantly Mandarin cuisine. The chef's specialties include *Pato Pekin* (duck with plum sauce and cucumber in crepes) and *Pollo Mo Su* (chicken with bamboo, cabbage, mushroom, and hoisin sauce). You may feel more comfortable in formal dress. ⊠ *Av. de la Paz 57, San Angel* ☎ *55/5616–4410 or 55/5616–4434* ⊠ *Cofre de Perote 205-B, Col. Lomas de Chapultepec* ☎ *55/5520–9870 or 55/5540–1683* ▭ *AE, MC, V* ☾ *No dinner Sun.*

$–$$ ✕**Chez Wok.** Above an elegant ladies' boutique on the corner of posh Polanco's Avenida Mazaryk and Tennyson, two Chinese chefs trained in Hong Kong prepare an extensive, excellent menu. Start with exotic frogs' legs Mandarin-style, served with lychees and shiitake mushrooms and steamed in lotus leaves. Three can share a hot pot of leg of venison with bamboo shoots in oyster sauce. A business crowd generates a lively lunchtime bustle. ⊠ *Tennyson 117, Col. Polanco* ☎ *55/5281–3410 or 55/5281–2921* ⊟ *AE, MC, V.*

French

★ **$–$$$** ✕ **Au Pied de Cochon.** Open round the clock on the ground floor inside the Hotel Presidente, this fashionable bistro continues to seduce well-heeled *chilangos* (people from the capital) with everything from oysters to oxtail. The roasted leg of pork with béarnaise sauce is the signature dish; the green-apple sorbet with Calvados is a delicate finish. The daily three-course set menu—which includes a glass of house wine—is only $16. ⊠ *Campos Elíseos 218, Col. Polanco* ☎ *55/5327–7756 or 55/5327–7700* ⌒ *Reservations essential* ⊟ *AE, MC, V.*

★ **$** ✕ **Le Bistro Littéraire.** At the far end of a French bookshop, La Bouquinerie, this gem is clearly run for love, not profit. Relish the aromatic escargots, couscous, duck, or moules marinières—but expect slow service. The wine list keeps in tune with the accessible prices of the cuisine. ⊠ *Camino al Desierto de los Leones 40, Prolongación Altavista, between Avs. Insurgentes and Revolución, San Angel* ☎ *55/5616–0632* ⊟ *AE, MC, V* ☉ *Closed Sun.*

¢–$ ✕ **Bistrot Mosaico.** You may have to wait for a table at this local-favorite restaurant, but the exquisite breads and chipotle mayonnaise that come to your table will signal the reward. Try the signature *terrine de berengenas* (eggplant) for a starter, or one of the salads, which are a cut above others in this neighborhood. The menu also lists quiche or sausage and lentils depending on whether it's sweltering or raining outside. ⊠ *Av. Michoacán 10, between Avs. Amsterdam and Insurgentes, Col. Condesa* ☎ *55/5584–2932* ⊠ *Guillermo González Camarena 800 Santa Fe* ☎ *55/5292–5326 or 5292–5156* ⊟ *AE, MC, V* ☉ *No dinner Sun.*

FodorsChoice ★

Greek

¢–$ ✕ **Agapi Mu.** Rambunctious Greek song and dance enliven this friendly Greek bistro Thursday through Saturday nights. Tucked away in a snug room of the converted Colonia Condesa home, you'll hum along as you partake of the atmosphere and the *paputsáka* (stuffed eggplant), *kalamárea* (fried squid Greek-style), and *dolmádes* (stuffed grape leaves). ⊠ *Alfonso Reyes 96, between Cuautla and Cuernavaca, Col. Condesa* ☎ *55/5286–1384* ⊟ *AE, MC, V* ☉ *No lunch Sun. and Mon.*

International

$–$$$$ ✕ **Bellini.** Revolving slowly on the 45th floor of the World Trade Center, Bellini maintains a formal, reserved atmosphere. Any effusiveness will likely be prompted by the spectacular views: romantically twinkling city lights at night and the volcanoes on a clear day. Despite the name, most dishes here aren't Italian but Mexican and international, with lobster as the house special. Finish in style with a flambéed dessert, such as strawberries jubilee or crêpes suzette. ⊠ *Av. de las Naciones 1, World Trade Center, 20 mins by car south of Zona Rosa, Col. Napoles* ☎ *55/5628–8305* ⊟ *AE, DC, MC, V.*

$–$$$ ✕ **Hacienda de los Morales.** This Mexican institution, set in a former hacienda that dates back to the 16th century, is grandly colonial in style, with dark-wood beams, huge terra-cotta expanses, and dramatic torches. You could start with the delicate walnut soup and follow with one of the chef's highlights, duck in raspberry sauce. Live trio music (three voices and guitars that play melodic traditional Mexican ballads) completes

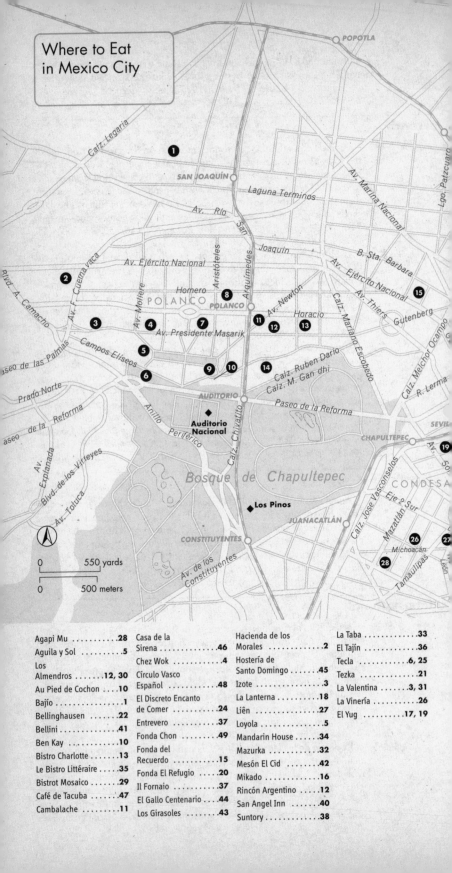

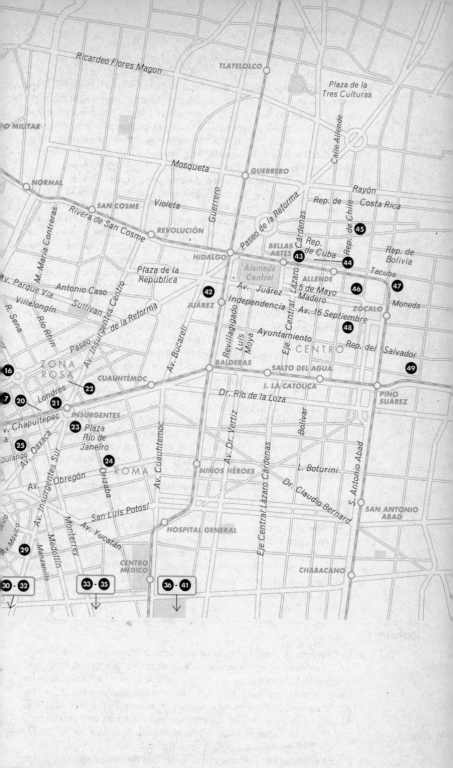

the atmosphere. ⊠ *Vázquez de Mella 525, Col. Bosque Polanco* ☎ *55/ 5096–3000 or 55/5096–3054* ⊟ *AE, DC, MC, V.*

$–$$ ✕ **Bellinghausen.** This cherished Zona Rosa lunch spot is one of the capital's classics. The partially covered hacienda-style courtyard at the back, set off by an ivy-laden wall, is a midday magnet for executives and tourists. A veritable army of waiters scurries back and forth serving such tried-and-true favorites as *sopa de hongos mexicana* (mushroom soup) and *filete chemita* (broiled steak with mashed potatoes). ⊠ *Londres 95, Zona Rosa* ☎ *55/5207–6149* ⊟ *AE, DC, MC, V* ⊘ *No lunch.*

$–$$ ✕ **El Discreto Encanto de Comer.** As the name implies, lunch certainly
Fodor'sChoice   achieves a discreet charm in this elegant upstairs restaurant. The 1910 house
★   exemplifies Porfiriato style with its striking stucco and stained glass. The cuisine is largely French with Mexican accents; menus are available in English but be sure to ask about daily specials. Outstanding dishes include foie gras *con salsa de pera* (with a delicate pear and pistachio sauce), Portobello carpaccio with artichoke, and a unique *camarones a tres pimientos* (shrimp stuffed with Gruyère and topped with a chili sauce touched with cinnamon). For dessert, look for strawberries sprinkled with black pepper or apricots steeped in cognac. ⊠ *Orizaba 76, Col. Roma* ☎ *55/ 5511–3860 or 55/5533–6074* ⊟ *AE, DC, MC, V* ⊘ *No dinner Sun.–Tues.*

★ $ ✕ **Bistro Charlotte.** You may get addicted to dining at Charlotte's intimate neighborhood bistro. At lunchtime regulars flock like clockwork to the quirky, chatty English chef for inspired culinary surprises. Most dishes are prepared with French and Mediterranean accents, yet Thai flourishes appear with increasing regularity. A small lament: there's only one Charlotte's. ⊠ *Lope de Vega 341, Col. Polanco* ☎ *55/ 5250–4180* ⊟ *MC, V* ⊘ *Closed weekends. No dinner.*

$ ✕ **Liên.** It's no wonder that in a city short on Asian food, an affordable, chic Vietnamese restaurant in a trendy part of town becomes a raging success. Liên strikes the right balance between Vietnamese and French cooking without being overly ambitious. Spring rolls are delicately flavored with mint and basil; the double-roasted duck with ginger sauce is so tender it falls off the bone. The place stays full until late, making it a hip spot for a wee-hours snack and drink. ⊠ *Av. Tamaulipas 48, at Calle Cadereyta, Col. Condesa* ☎ *55/5553–9901 or 55/5553–9918* ⊟ *AE, MC, V.*

★ ¢–$ ✕ **La Vinería.** A welcome addition to La Condesa, this dark, cozy restaurant and wine bar is ideal for a light meal and a sip. Try the *rollos de berenjena* (eggplant rolls) with goat cheese, nuts, and red pepper sauce, or the delicious *hojaldre con hongos* (mushroom pastry). Then indulge in a chablis, a tasty strudel, or a cigar. ⊠ *Av. Fernando Montes de Oca 52 - A, at Amatlán, Col. Condesa* ☎ *55/5211–9020* ⊟ *AE, MC, V* ⊘ *Closed Sun.*

Italian

$ ✕ **Il Fornaio.** A steady stream of well-heeled diners come here to taste *carpaccio di salmone* dressed with Belgian endive, grapefruit, cress, and a lightly citric vinegar, or enjoy an excellent *linguine ai sapori di mare* (linguine with seafood). The chef refuses to use anything but Italian ingredients; notice the authentic cheeses in dishes like the succulent veal in Gorgonzola sauce. The desserts, such as the sweet crepes (*crespelle al caffè*), are unforgettable. ⊠ *Av. Altavista 192, San Angel* ☎ *55/ 5616–5985* ⊟ *AE, DC, MC, V* ⊘ *No dinner Sun.*

$ ✕ **La Lanterna.** The Petterino family has run this two-story restaurant since 1966. The downstairs has the rustic feel of a northern Italian trattoria, with the cramped seating adding to the intimacy. All pastas are made on the premises; the Bolognese sauce is a favorite. Raw artichoke salad, *conejo en Salmi* (rabbit in a wine sauce), and *filete al burro nero* (steak in black butter) are all worthy dishes. ⊠ *Paseo de la Reforma 458, at Toledo, Col. Juárez* ☎ *55/5207–9969* 🖃 *AE, DC, MC, V* ⊗ *Closed Sun. and Dec. 25–Jan. 1.*

Japanese

$–$$$ ✕ **Ben Kay.** The silk-clad staff includes a sake sommelier in this prestigious restaurant in the Hotel Nikko. *Keiseki* is the specialty, a series of small, exquisite dishes. The menu is organized in helpful groupings that limit the anxiety of choice. Prices are high, but you're getting the best. ⊠ *Campos Elíseos 204, Col. Polanco* ☎ *55/5280–1111 Ext. 8600* 🖃 *AE, DC, MC, V.*

$–$$ ✕ **Mikado.** Strategically positioned between the Zona Rosa and the U. S. embassy, this notable spot can sate your sushi cravings at very fair prices. Immaculate hygiene, a fine sushi chef, an extensive menu, and a cheerful, bustling atmosphere downstairs make Mikado both welcoming and a real treat for the palate. ⊠ *Paseo de la Reforma 369, Col. Cuauhtémoc* ☎ *55/5525–3096* 🖃 *MC, V* ⊗ *No dinner Sun.*

$–$$ ✕ **Suntory.** This main branch of the Suntory restaurants in Mexico welcomes you with a Japanese garden at the entryway. You can choose between the teppanyaki room, the sushi bar, and the shabu-shabu room, with its copper pot of steaming vegetable broth for cooking wafer-thin slices of beef. It closes at 9 PM on Sunday. ⊠ *Torres Adalid 14, Col. del Valle* ☎ *55/5536–9432* 🖃 *AE, DC, MC, V* ⊗ *No dinner Sun.*

Mexican

★ **$–$$$$** ✕ **San Angel Inn.** During a meal in this magnificent old ex-convent, it may be hard not to fall into gluttony. Dark mahogany furniture, crisp white table linens, and beautiful blue-and-white Talavera place settings strike a note of restrained opulence. For a classic treat, have the *sopa de tortilla* (tortilla soup); note that the *puntas de filete* (sirloin tips) are liberally laced with chilies. Desserts—from light and crunchy meringues to pastries bulging with cream—can be rich to the point of surfeit. ⊠ *Calle Diego Rivera 50, at Av. Altavista, San Angel* ☎ *55/5616–0537 or 55/5616–2222* 🖃 *AE, DC, MC, V.*

$–$$$ ✕ **Aguila y Sol.** Chef/owner Marta Ortiz Chapa brings considerable experience to this exemplar of nueva cocina mexicana—she's the author of eight cookbooks on regional Mexican cuisine. The bright, modern dining room showcases her unbeatable creativity. Here's your chance to try indigenous produce with a new spin, such as an appetizer of *tortitas de huauzontle* (a green vegetable) with goat cheese, Parmesan, and a *chile pasilla* sauce or a main course of salmon in a maize crust with clams. Portions are not large, so you should have room for a luscious dessert, perhaps the mamey crème brûlée with a carnation-petal jelly. Also look for traditional drinks such as water flavored with *flor de jamaica* (hibiscus flower) or, in cold weather, *ponche de manzana* (apple punch). ⊠ *Av. Moliere 42, Col. Polanco* ☎ *55/5281–8354* 🖃 *AE, MC, V* ⊗ *No dinner Sun. and Mon.*

Fodor'sChoice
★

$–$$ ✕ **Fonda Chon.** This unpretentious family-style restaurant, deep in a downtown working-class neighborhood, is famed for its pre-Hispanic Mexican dishes. A knowledge of zoology, Spanish, and Nahuatl helps in making sense of a menu that takes in a gamut of ingredients from throughout the republic. *Escamoles de hormiga* (red-ant roe) is known as the "caviar of Mexico" for its costliness, but you may have to acquire a taste for it. Among the exotic dishes are armadillo in mango sauce and fillet of wild boar. ⊠ *Regina 160, near La Merced market, Col. Centro* ☎ *55/5542–0873* 🖃 *No credit cards* ⊗ *Closed Sun. No dinner.*

$–$$ ✕**Fonda El Refugio.** Since it opened in 1954, this restaurant has served dishes from each major region of the country. Along with a varied regular menu, there are tempting daily specials; you might find a mole made with pumpkin seeds or *huachinango a la veracruzana* (red snapper cooked in onions, tomatoes, and olives). Try the refreshing *aguas* (fresh-fruit and seed juices) with your meal and the *café de olla* (clove-flavor coffee sweetened with brown sugar) afterward. ⊠ *Liverpool 166, at Florencia, Zona Rosa* ☎ *55/5207–2732 or 55/5525–8128* ▤ *AE, DC, MC, V.*

$–$$ ✕**El Gallo Centenario.** Reopened after two years of restoration, this sublime restaurant near the Zócalo retains its opulence. The dining rooms have distinct characters; for an intimate space reserve the salon *de los anillos de compromiso* (of the engagement rings). For a laugh, ask for the salon *de las tiás* (of the aunts), decorated with black-and-white photos of severe-looking ladies. The chrysanthemum-topped margaritas are unequaled. Outstanding dishes include the beef fillet in *chichilo mole,* the least known of Oaxaca's famed seven moles. A classic dessert is *pastel de zapote* (a cake made with the sweet, black zapote fruit) but perhaps even more seductive is the *espuma de chocolate de metate,* a froth of chocolate and almond cookies. It's not a formal place, but you should try for a reservation. ⊠ *República de Cuba 79, between Chile and Palma, Col. Centro* ☎ *55/5512–6825 or 55/5512–6868* ▤ *AE, MC, V* ☾ *No dinner Sun.*

Fodor's Choice ★

$–$$ ✕**Hostería de Santo Domingo.** This genteel institution near downtown's Plaza Santo Domingo has been serving colonial dishes since the late 19th century in an atmospheric town house. Feast on tried-and-true favorites such as stuffed cactus paddles, thousand-flower soup, pot roast, and a stunning array of quesadillas. Among some of the best homemade Mexican desserts in town are the comforting flan and *arroz con leche* (rice pudding). The place is open for breakfast and is always full at lunch; it closes at 9 PM on Sunday. Get there early to avoid standing in line. ⊠ *Belisario Dominguez 72, Col. Centro* ☎ *55/5510–1434 or 55/5526–5276* ▤ *AE, DC, MC, V* ☾ *No dinner Sun.*

$ ✕**Los Almendros.** If you can't make it to the Yucatán, try the peninsula's unusual and lively food at one of this restaurant's two locations. The habañero chilies, red onions, and other native Yucatecan ingredients are a delightful surprise for those not yet in the know. Traditional dishes, such as a refreshing lime soup, share the menu with impossible-to-pronounce Maya cuisine. Especially worth trying is the *pescado tikinxic*—white fish in a mild red marinade of achiote seed and bitter orange juice. The branch in Colonia Guadalupe Inn does not serve dinner on Sunday. ⊠ *Campos Elíseos 164, Col. Polanco* ☎ *55/5531–6646* ⊠ *Av. Insurgentes Sur 1759, Col. Guadalupe Inn* ☎ *55/5663–5151* ▤ *AE, DC, MC, V.*

$ ✕**Casa de la Sirena.** The setting is the calling card here; the 16th-century mansión sits at the foot of the Templo Major ruins, stones from which were incorporated into the building. The atmospheric second-floor terrace is within sight and sound of numerous Indian dances honoring the spirits of the crumbling Aztec temples below. The cuisine pairs Cornish hen with a mango mole sauce and adds a spark to a plethora of meat and fish dishes. ⊠ *Guatemala 32, Col. Centro* ☎ *55/5704–3225 or 55/5704–3465* ▤ *AE, MC, V* ☾ *No dinner Sun.*

$ ✕**Los Girasoles.** Two prominent Mexico City society columnists own this downtown spot. Los Girasoles (which means sunflowers) is on a lovely old square in a restored three-story colonial home and serves light, tasty, and innovative nueva cocina mexicana. There are also pre-Hispanic delicacies such as *escamoles* (ant roe), *gusanos de maguey* (chilied worms), and *mini chapulines* (tiny crispy fried grasshoppers). It closes at 9 PM on

Sunday and Monday. ✉ *Plaza Manuel Tolsá on Xicoténcatl 1, Col. Centro* ☎ *55/5510–0630* ▤ *AE, MC, V* ☺ *No dinner Sun. or Mon.*

★ $ ✕ **Izote.** A reservation here is one of the hardest to get, as cookbook author Patricia Quintana won over the capital with her sophisticated take on pre-Hispanic flavors. Keep an eye out for the unique fish entrées, such as shark filet sautéed with chile pasilla, onion, garlic, and epazote, then steamed in chicken stock and *pulque* (a fermented cactus liquor). Tender lamb gets steamed as well, in maguey and banana leaves, after being quickly fried with chilies and a touch of cumin. ✉ *Av. Presidente Masaryk 513, at Socrates, Col. Polanco* ☎ *55/5280–1671* ♟ *Reservations essential* ▤ *AE, DC, MC, V* ☺ *No dinner Sun.*

$ ✕ **El Tajín.** Named after El Tajín Pyramid in Veracruz, this elegant lunch spot sizzles with pre-Hispanic influences. Innovative appetizers include *chilpachole*, a delicate crab and chili soup with epazote, while main dishes could include octopus cooked in its own ink. Prices are quite moderate for this caliber of cooking, and there's an impressive wine list to boot. Ancient Huastecan faces grinning from a splashing fountain add a bit of levity to the dining experience. ✉ *Centro Cultural Veracruzano, Miguel Angel de Quevedo 687, Coyoacán* ☎ *55/5659–4447 or 55/5659–5759* ▤ *AE, MC, V* ☺ *No dinner.*

$ ✕ **La Valentina.** The epitome of good taste in all things Mexican, La
FodorśChoice Valentina devotes itself to rescuing and promoting traditional native cui-
★ sine. It avoids gimmicks with balanced dishes that are soft on the palate, yet fragrant with blends of chilies, herbs, nuts, and flowers. Starters reflect specialties from across the country: from the far northern Chilorio tacos from Sinaloa to the famous *Panuchos Yucatecos* (fried tortillas with Yucatan-style spiced chicken or pork). The appetizing tamarind mole intensifies any poultry dish; the seductively titled "Symphony in Mexican Rose" bathes chicken in a walnut and chipotle sauce. ✉ *Av. Insurgentes Sur 1854B, Col. Florida, San Angel* ☎ *55/5662–0872 or 55/5662–0177* ✉ *Av. Presidente Masaryk 393, Col. Polanco* ☎ *55/5282–2297* ▤ *AE, DC, MC, V* ☺ *No dinner Sun.*

★ ¢–$ ✕ **Fonda del Recuerdo.** The popular *fonda* (modest restaurant) has made a name for itself with fish and seafood platters from the gulf state of Veracruz. Sharing their fame is the *torito*, a potent drink made from sugarcane liquor, and exotic tropical fruit juices. Every day from 1 to 10, five lively *jarocho* (Veracruz-style) and mariachi groups provide festive music. ✉ *Bahía de las Palmas 37, Col. Veronica Anzures* ☎ *55/5260–7339 or 55/5260–1292* ♟ *Reservations essential* ▤ *AE, DC, MC, V.*

★ ¢–$ ✕ **Tecla.** This see-and-be-seen eatery is a popular veteran of Mexico City's nueva cocina mexicana scene and the restaurants' locations and newsprint collage set a hip tone. The appetizers are especially intriguing, including squash flowers stuffed with goat cheese in a chipotle sauce and a spicy crab-stuffed chili. ✉ *Av. Moliere 56, Col. Polanco* ☎ *55/5282–0010* ✉ *Av. Durango 186A, Col. Roma* ☎ *55/5525–4920* ▤ *AE, MC, V* ☺ *No dinner Sun.*

¢ ✕ **Bajío.** Decorated in bright colors, Bajío attracts Mexican families and is run by vivacious Carmen "Titita" Ramírez—a culinary expert who has been featured in various food magazines. The labor-intensive 30-ingredient mole de Xico is a favorite; also excellent are *empanadas de plátano rellenos de frijol* (tortilla turnovers filled with bananas and beans) and *carnitas* (roast pork). You may have to go a little off the beaten track to get here, but it's worth it. ✉ *Cuitláhuac 2709, Col. Azcapotzalco, about a 20-min ride north of Zona Rosa* ☎ *55/5341–9889* ▤ *AE, MC, V* ☺ *No dinner.*

¢ ✕ **Café de Tacuba.** An essential breakfast, lunch, dinner, or snack stop downtown, this Mexican classic has been rewarding the hungry since it opened in 1912 in a section of an old convent. At the entrance to the atmospheric main dining room are huge 18th-century oil paintings depicting the invention of *mole poblano*, a complex sauce with a variety of chilies and chocolate that was created by the nuns in the Santa Rosa Convent of Puebla. A student group dressed in medieval capes and hats serenades Thursday–Sunday 3:30–11:30; mariachis play during dinner on other days. ⊠ *Calle Tacuba 28, at Allende, Col. Centro* ☎ *55/ 5518–4950* ⊟ *AE, MC, V.*

Polish

★ $–$$ ✕ **Mazurka.** The capital's first and only establishment to offer Polish food enjoys a glowing reputation among older Mexican families. Settle in with complimentary starters of blini with herring paste and cucumber, dill, and cream salad, as Chopin's polonaises trill and leap in the background. The "star of the house" is a crispy, oven-baked duck, stuffed with bitter apple and blueberries. Or try the juicy, sweet duck and pear with cassis. The generous "Pope's Menu" includes two sets of entrées and is only $23 a head. ⊠ *Nueva York 150, between calles Texas and Oklahoma Col. Napoles* ☎ *55/5543–4509 or 55/5523–8811* ⊟ *AE, MC, V* ⊘ *No dinner Sun.*

Spanish

$–$$$ ✕ **Tezka.** This Zona Rosa restaurant specializing in nueva cocina Basque was created by the acclaimed chef Arzac, who transposed many of his best dishes to Mexico from his restaurant in San Sebastían, Spain. Feast on yellow tuna in a sweet and spicy sauce, or liver prepared with beer, green pepper, and malt. The starters are exquisite, both to look at and taste; the *caldo de xipiron* (broth of baby squid) is the best in the city. A decent list of Spanish wines includes Cune, Vina Ardanza, and Reserva 904. ⊠ *Royal Hotel, Amberes 78, at Liverpool, Col. Juárez* ☎ *55/ 5228–9918 Ext. 5067* ⊟ *AE, DC, MC, V* ⊘ *Closed Sun. No dinner Sat.*

$–$$ ✕ **Círculo Vasco Español.** Dating from the 1890s, this huge, high-ceiling restaurant basks in the faded glamour of the days when dictator Porfirio Díaz dined here regularly. Its founders were Basque and though it has been run by Galicians for over 20 years, the signature dishes are still Basque—look for *rueda de robalo a la donostiarra* (sea bass cooked with parsley and white wine). Galician plates are no slouch either, and a hearty breakfast, like the omelette *de rajas con queso* (with poblano chilli and cheese), will set you up for serious sightseeing. ⊠ *Av. 16 de Septiembre 51, Col. Centro* ☎ *55/5518–2908* ⊟ *MC, V* ⊘ *No dinner.*

$–$$ ✕ **Loyola.** A Basque tour de force, the ample menu with unpronounceable but delicious items includes *kokotxas* (fish cheeks), tapas, black rice simmered in squid ink, oxtail, and many other such regional delicacies. Great salads and wines are another welcome feature. Courteous service, stained glass, Basque coats of arms, and the cozy hum of conversation from contented connoisseurs make this an excellent and authentic dining experience. ⊠ *Aristóteles 239, Col. Polanco* ☎ *55/5250–6756 or 55/5250–9097* ⊟ *AE, MC, V* ⊘ *No dinner.*

$ ✕ **Mesón El Cid.** This charming *mesón* (tavern) exudes an atmosphere of Old Spain. During the week, classic dishes such as paella, spring lamb, suckling baby pig, and Cornish hens with truffles keep customers happy, but on Saturday night this place comes into its own with a medieval banquet, including a procession of costumed waiters carrying huge trays of steaming hot viands. Further entertainment is provided by a student singing group dressed in medieval Spanish capes and hats. ⊠ *Humboldt 61, Col. Centro* ☎ *55/5512–7629* ⊟ *AE, MC, V* ⊘ *No dinner Sun.*

Vegetarian

¢–$ ✕ **El Yug.** Within the confines of an esoteric bookshop, this vegetarian spot offers delicious fare to the accompaniment of New Age music. Heaping salads, homemade soups, and main courses such as *chiles rellenos* (poblano chili stuffed with cheese) come with whole-grain bread. You can choose the daily *comida corrida* (fixed-price menu) for just over $4 or order à la carte. The sister restaurant in Colonia Juárez is open daily for breakfast, lunch, and dinner. ⊠ *Puebla 326-6, Col. Roma* ☎ *55/ 5553–3872* ⊠ *Varsovia 3, at Paseo de la Reforma Col. Juárez* ☎ *55/ 5525–5330* ⊟ *AE, MC, V* ⊗ *No dinner weekends.*

WHERE TO STAY

Although the city is huge and spread out, most hotels are clustered in a few neighborhoods. Colonia Polanco has a generous handful of business-oriented hotels; these tend to be familiar major chains. The Zona Rosa has plenty of big, contemporary properties; it's handy to have restaurants and other services right outside the door. La Condesa and La Roma don't have many places to stay, but at this writing the chic Hotel Condesa was in the works in its namesake neighborhood. The only pleasant tourist areas still poorly served for accommodation are Coyoacán and San Angel.

You can expect hotels in the $$$ and $$$$ categories to have purified water and extended (often 24-hour) room service as well as all the standard amenities.

Prices

Business travelers tend to fill up deluxe hotels during the week; some major hotels discount their weekend rates. Many smaller properties have taken the cue and offer similarly reduced rates as well. If you reserve through the toll-free reservations numbers, you may find rates as much as 50% off during special promotions.

	WHAT IT COSTS				
	$$$$	$$$	$$	$	¢
FOR 2 PEOPLE	over $250	$150–$250	$75–$150	$50–$75	under $50

Price categories are assigned based on the range between the least and most expensive standard double rooms in high season based on the European Plan (EP, with no meals) unless otherwise noted. Tax (17%) is extra.

Colonia Polanco & Bosque de Chapultepec

$$$$ ⊞ **Casa Vieja.** This sumptuously decorated mansion is simply stunning. Tastefully selected folk art, handsomely hand-carved furniture, and gilded wall trimmings complement patios and splashing fountains. Each suite has a full kitchen, CD player, hot tub, and picture window overlooking an inside garden. The hotel's Mexican restaurant is named after its huge floor-to-ceiling *Árbol de la Vida (Tree of Life)* sculpture. ⊠ *Eugenio Sue 45, Col. Polanco 11560* ☎ *55/5282–0067* 🖷 *55/5281–3780* ⊕ *www. casavieja.com* ↪ *10 suites* ♨ *Restaurant, in-room fax, in-room safes, kitchens, cable TV, bar, concierge, free parking* ⊟ *AE, MC, V* ⏍ *BP.*

$$$$ ⊞ **J. W. Marriott.** In keeping with its genteel neighborhood, this boutique hotel has personalized service and small, clubby public areas; nothing overwhelms here. Rooms are done with plenty of wood and warm colors but are otherwise unremarkable in decor. Each has a work desk with an outlet for a personal computer and modem. The hotel has a well-equipped

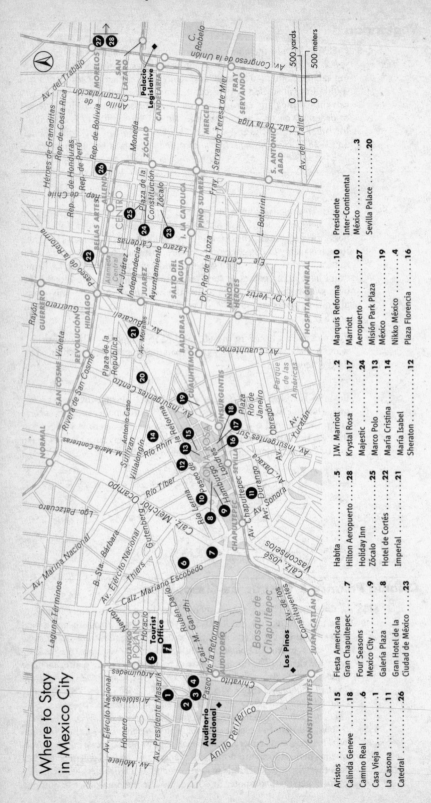

Where to Stay in Mexico City

500 yards
500 meters

24-hour business center. Attractive weekend rates range between $130 and $185. ⊠ *Andrés Bello 29, at Campos Elíseos, Col. Polanco 11560* ☎ *55/ 5999–0000* 🖷 *55/5999–0001* ⊕ *www.marriotthotels.com* ➹ *311 rooms* ⚬ *2 restaurants, coffee shop, in-room data ports, in-room safes, minibars, cable TV, pool, gym, bar, business services, meeting rooms, car rental, travel services* ▤ *AE, DC, MC, V.*

$$$$ 🏨 **Nikko México.** Part of the Nikko chain, this 42-floor high-rise occupies a prime Polanco position: adjacent to Bosque de Chapultepec, just a five-minute walk from the anthropology museum. With signage and menus in Japanese, English, and Spanish, it caters especially to business travelers and conferences. It's the second-largest hotel in the city and has marvelous views from the top-floor suites. Each room has at least three telephones with two lines; a pair of rooms are done in Japanese style, with tatami mats. Among the restaurants is the excellent Ben Kay (see Where to Eat). ⊠ *Campos Elíseos 204, Col. Polanco 11560* ☎ *55/ 5280–1111, 800/908–8800 in the U.S.* 🖷 *55/5280–9191* ⊕ *www. nikkohotels.com* ➹ *744 rooms, 24 suites* ⚬ *4 restaurants, in-room fax, in-room safes, minibars, cable TV, driving range, 4 tennis courts, indoor pool, gym, sauna, steam room, 2 bars, dance club, business services, meeting rooms, car rental, travel services, no-smoking rooms* ▤ *AE, DC, MC, V.*

$$$ 🏨 **Camino Real.** About the size of Teotihuacán's Pyramid of the Sun, this
Fodor$Choice   sleek, minimalist, bright pink and yellow, 8-acre city-within-a-city was
★   designed by Mexico's modern master, Legorreta. Impressive artworks embellishing the public spaces include Rufino Tamayo's mural *Man Facing Infinity* and a Calder sculpture. The fifth-floor executive level has 100 extra-large guest rooms with special amenities. El Centro Castellano restaurant offers free child care for long weekend lunchtimes, and Le Cirque, an upscale French restaurant, opened in 2003. ⊠ *Mariano Escobedo 700, Col. Polanco 11590* ☎ *55/5263–8888* 🖷 *55/5263–8898* ⊕ *www. caminoreal.com.mx* ➹ *625 rooms, 89 suites* ⚬ *3 restaurants, in-room safes, minibars, cable TV, 4 tennis courts, 2 pools (1 indoor), gym, 3 bars, concierge, business services, no-smoking floor* ▤ *AE, DC, MC, V.*

$$$ 🏨 **Fiesta Americana Gran Chapultepec.** Sleek and contemporary, this stylish hotel is located opposite the Bosque de Chapultepec, close to the city's main shopping area and five minutes from the Auditorio Nacional. Rooms are angled to maximize views; they're done in muted olives and browns. The spa, beauty salon, and barbershop guarantee you will be presentable for the ultramodern Asian bar, where you can hang out for sushi and cocktails. ⊠ *Mariano Escobedo 756, Col. Anzures 11590* ☎ *55/2581–1500* 🖷 *55/2581–1501* ⊕ *www.fiestaamericana.com* ➹ *189 rooms, 14 suites* ⚬ *Restaurant, in-room data ports, minibars, gym, spa, 2 bars, business services, meeting rooms, free parking* ▤ *AE, DC, MC, V.*

★ **$$$**   🏨 **Habita.** Characterized by pale colors and a spalike atmosphere, Mexico's first design hotel strikes a harmonious balance between style statements and minimalism. New-Age voices are piped into the rooms (you can turn them off, of course), and tasteful bowls of limes sit by state-of-the-art TV sets. Offering beautiful open-air views one floor above the pool and gym, the swanky tapas bar Área also draws Mexico City's chic nonguests Thursday to Saturday. ⊠ *Av. Presidente Masaryk 201, Col. Polanco 11560* ☎ *55/5282–3100* 🖷 *55/5282–3101* ⊕ *www.hotelhabita. com* ➹ *32 rooms, 4 suites* ⚬ *Restaurant, in-room data ports, in-room safes, minibars, gym, spa, bar, concierge, business services, meeting rooms, free parking* ▤ *AE, MC, V.*

$$$ 🏨 **Presidente Inter-Continental México.** This Inter-Continental has a dramatic five-story atrium lobby—a hollow pyramid of balconies—with music performed daily at the lively lobby bar. Rooms are spacious, and all have work areas. On clear days, the top two floors have views of the nearby snowcapped volcanoes. The executive floors have a lounge, concierge, and extra amenities. A number of smart stores and six eateries are on the premises, including Au Pied de Cochon. ⊠ *Campos Elíseos 218, Col. Polanco 11560* ☎ *55/5327–7700 or 800/447–6147 in the U. S.* ⊟ *55/5327–7730* ⊕ *www.interconti.com* ↷ *629 rooms, 30 suites* ⚱ *6 restaurants, coffee shop, minibars, cable TV, gym, lobby lounge, baby-sitting, concierge, business services, meeting rooms, car rental, travel services, parking (fee)* ⊟ *AE, DC, MC, V.*

Colonia Roma

$$$ ▥ **La Casona.** This charming hotel is an elegant, understated former mansion, registered as an artistic monument by Mexico's Institute of Fine Arts. From its sunny patios to its sitting rooms, the hotel's interior conveys the spirit of the Porfiriato. No two rooms are alike, but all have hair dryers, fluffy bathrobes and slippers, and good-size bathtubs. The two-story hotel building, with its salmon-color facade, looks out on a tree-lined street in Colonia Roma, about a 10-minute walk south of the Zona Rosa. ⊠ *Av. Durango 280, at Cozumel, Col. Roma, 06700* ☎ *55/ 5286–3001* ⊟ *55/5211–0871* ⊕ *www.hotellacasona.com.mx* ↷ *29 rooms* ⚱ *Restaurant, room service, in-room data ports, in-room safes, minibars, cable TV, gym, bar* ⊟ *AE, DC, MC, V* ⧖ *CP.*

Zona Rosa

$$$ ▥ **Galería Plaza.** Location gives this ultramodern hotel an edge; it's on a quiet street but plenty of shops, restaurants, and nightspots are nearby. Service and facilities are faultless; advantages include voice mail in all rooms, a heated rooftop pool with sundeck, a secure underground parking lot, and a 24-hour restaurant. ⊠ *Hamburgo 195, at Varsovia, Zona Rosa 06600* ☎ *55/5230–1717 or 888/559–4329* ⊟ *55/5207–5867* ⊕ *www.brisas.com.mx* ↷ *420 rooms, 19 suites* ⚱ *2 restaurants, room service, in-room safes, cable TV, pool, gym, lobby lounge, concierge, Internet, travel services, parking (fee)* ⊟ *AE, DC, MC, V* ⧖ *CP.*

$$$ ▥ **Krystal Rosa.** Part of the Mexican Krystal Hotel chain, this superbly run high-rise hotel is in the heart of the Zona Rosa and has an excellent view of the city from the rooftop pool terrace. There's a stylish lobby cocktail lounge, a bar with local entertainers, and a restaurant, Hacienda del Mortero, which serves excellent classic Mexican cuisine. Two club floors have VIP check-in and service, complimentary Continental buffet breakfast, and rooms with extra amenities. ⊠ *Liverpool 155, Zona Rosa 06600* ☎ *55/5228–9928* ⊟ *55/5511–3490* ⊕ *www.krystal.com. mx* ↷ *267 rooms, 35 suites* ⚱ *Restaurant, in-room safes, minibars, pool, bar, concierge, business services, parking (fee)* ⊟ *AE, DC, MC, V.*

★ **$$$** ▥ **Marco Polo.** Modern and intimate, the central Marco Polo has the amenities and personalized service often associated with a small European hotel. North-facing top-floor rooms have excellent views of Paseo de la Reforma and the Angel monument, and the U.S. Embassy is close by. Four penthouse suites have terraces, and are normally rented by the month. ⊠ *Amberes 27, Zona Rosa 06600* ☎ *55/5080–0063* ⊟ *55/5080–1446* ⊕ *www. marcopolo.com.mx* ↷ *59 rooms, 16 suites* ⚱ *Restaurant, in-room data ports, in-room safes, minibars, cable TV, gym, bar, Internet, business services, parking (fee)* ⊟ *AE, DC, MC, V* ⧖ *CP.*

$$ ▥ **Aristos.** On bustling Paseo de la Reforma, a few blocks east of the U. S. Embassy and near the Mexican Stock Exchange, this 15-story Zona Rosa–fringe hotel wears its age well. (It was one of the first luxury hotels in the area.) Rooms are warmly decorated in shades of peach and mauve, with brass and wood accents. The business center has a bilingual staff and a message service. ⊠ *Paseo de la Reforma 276, Zona Rosa*

06600 ☎ 55/5211–0112 🖷 55/5514–4473 🗳 320 *rooms, 25 suites* ☖ 3 *restaurants, cable TV, gym, hair salon, sauna, bar, business services, travel services, parking (fee)* ▭ *AE, DC, MC, V.*

$$ 🖼 **Calinda Geneve.** A Quality Inn, referred to locally as El Génova, this five-story 1906 hotel is fitted with traditional colonial-style carved-wood chairs and tables in the pleasant lobby; guest rooms are small but comfortable. The attractive Salón Jardín is part of the popular Sanborns restaurant chain. ✉ *Londres 130, Zona Rosa 06600* ☎ 55/5080–0800 🖷 *55/5080–0833* 🌐 *www.hotelescalinda.com.mx* 🗳 *300 rooms* ☖ *Restaurant, café, in-room safes, minibars, cable TV, room service, gym, bar, laundry facilities, business services* ▭ *AE, DC, MC, V.*

$$ 🖼 **Plaza Florencia.** The lobby of this hotel may be weighted with heavy furniture and dark colors, but the rooms upstairs are bright, modern, and soundproofed against the traffic noise of the busy avenue below. Higher floors have views of the Angel monument. Some large family suites are available. A business center offers fax, copy, computer, and Internet-access services. ✉ *Florencia 61, Zona Rosanot on Neighb list 06600* ☎ *55/5242–4700* 🖷 *55/5242–4785* 🌐 *www.plazaflorencia. com.mx* 🗳 *130 rooms, 12 suites* ☖ *2 restaurants, coffee shop, minibars, business services* ▭ *AE, DC, MC, V.*

$ 🖼 **Misión Park Plaza México.** A part of the Misión chain, this very comfortable hotel a few blocks from the Zona Rosa's eastern end is well placed for shopping and sightseeing. Mirrors, good light, and like-new bathrooms make the rooms pleasant; all have color TV with U.S. channels. Sixteen rooms have work areas, and you can use an Internet connection in an office off the lobby. The staff is friendly and accommodating. ✉ *Napoles 62, Zona Rosa 06600* ☎ *55/5533–0535* 🖷 *55/5533–1589* 🌐 *www.hotelesmision.com.mx* 🗳 *50 rooms* ☖ *Coffee shop, gym, lobby lounge, meeting rooms* ▭ *AE, MC, V* 🍽 *CP.*

Midtown & Along the Reforma

$$$$ 🖼 **Four Seasons Mexico City.** Ranking among the most luxurious hotels
Fodor'sChoice   in the capital, the Four Seasons repeatedly has won the AAA Five Dia-
★   mond Award. The eight-story building was modeled after the 18th-century Iturbide Palace downtown and surrounds a traditional courtyard with a fountain. Half the rooms overlook the lush inner courtyard garden. Geared to business travelers, rooms have Ethernet connections and the full-service business center houses a reference library. A well-stocked tequila bar off the lobby is a perfect predinner option. Excellent cultural tours of the city are offered free to guests on weekends. ✉ *Paseo de la Reforma 500, Col. Juárez 06600* ☎ *55/5230–1818; 01800/906–7500 toll-free in Mexico; 888/304–6755 in the U.S.* 🖷 *55/5230–1808* 🌐 *www. fourseasons.com* 🗳 *200 rooms, 40 suites* ☖ *2 restaurants, in-room data ports, minibars, cable TV, pool, gym, bar, dry cleaning, laundry service, business services, meeting rooms* ▭ *AE, DC, MC, V.*

$$$$ 🖼 **María Isabel Sheraton.** Don Antenor Patiño, the Bolivian "Tin King," inaugurated this Mexico City classic in 1969 and named it after his granddaughter, socialite Isabel Goldsmith. All guest and public rooms are impeccably maintained; penthouse suites in the 22-story tower are extra-spacious and exceptionally luxurious. The location—across from the Angel monument and the Zona Rosa, with Sanborns next door and the U.S. Embassy a half block away—is prime. ✉ *Paseo de la Reforma 325, Col. Cuauhtémoc 06500* ☎ *55/5242–5555* 🖷 *55/5207–0684* 🌐 *www.sheraton.com* 🗳 *681 rooms, 74 suites* ☖ *3 restaurants, room service, in-room data ports, in-room safes, minibars, cable TV, pool, gym, massage, sauna, 2 bars, concierge floor, business services, meeting rooms, parking (fee), no-smoking rooms* ▭ *AE, DC, MC, V.*

★ **$$$$** ⊞ **Marquis Reforma.** This plush, privately owned member of the Leading Hotels of the World is within walking distance of the Zona Rosa. Its striking art nouveau facade combines pink stone and curved glass, and the seventh-floor suites afford picture-perfect views of the Castillo de Chapultepec. An art deco theme defines the rooms. You can enjoy Mexican cuisine at La Jolla restaurant and take advantage of hard-to-find holistic, stress-busting massages at the health club. ⊠ *Paseo de la Reforma 465, Col. Cuauhtémoc 06500* ☎ *55/5229–1200; 800/235–2387 in the U.S.* 🖷 *55/5229–1212* ⊕ *www.marquisreformahl.com.mx* 🛏 *123 rooms, 85 suites* ♨ *2 restaurants, in-room data ports, in-room safes, minibars, gym, bar, business services, meeting rooms, no-smoking rooms* ⊟ *AE, DC, MC, V.*

$$ ⊞ **Imperial.** Suiting its name, this hotel occupies a stately, cupolaed, late 19th-century building right on the Reforma alongside the Columbus monument. Quiet elegance and personal service are keynotes of this privately owned property; rooms are done in pink and white. The hotel's Restaurant Gaudí has an understated, tony atmosphere and serves Continental cuisine with some classic Spanish selections. ⊠ *Paseo de la Reforma 64, Col. Juárez 06600* ☎ *55/5705–4911* 🖷 *55/5703–3122* ⊕ *www. hotelimperial.com.mx* 🛏 *50 rooms, 10 junior suites, 5 master suites* ♨ *Restaurant, café, in-room safes, minibars, cable TV, bar, business services, meeting rooms, travel services* ⊟ *AE, DC, MC, V.*

$$ ⊞ **Sevilla Palace.** Five panoramic elevators sweep through the 23 floors of this tower. The convention halls, meeting rooms, and computer facilities aim to cover the business bases, while a covered rooftop pool with hot tub, a health club, and a terraced rooftop lounge help the suits unwind. It's near the Columbus traffic circle and attracts lots of tourists from Spain. ⊠ *Paseo de la Reforma 105, Col. Revolución 06030* ☎ *55/ 5705–2800; 800/732–9488 in the U.S.* 🖷 *55/5703–1521* ⊕ *www. sevillapalace.com.mx* 🛏 *413 rooms* ♨ *2 restaurants, pool, gym, 3 bars, nightclub, meeting rooms* ⊟ *AE, MC, V.*

★ **$** ⊞ **María Cristina.** Brimming with old-world charm, this Spanish colonial-style gem is a Mexico City classic. Impeccably maintained since it was built in 1937, the building surrounds a delightful garden courtyard—the setting for its El Retiro bar. Three apartment-style master suites come complete with hot tubs. In a quiet residential setting near Parque Sullivan, the hotel is close to the Zona Rosa. ⊠ *Río Lerma 31, Col. Cuauhtémoc 06500* ☎ *55/5703–1212 or 55/5566–9688* 🖷 *55/5566–9194* 🛏 *140 rooms, 8 suites* ♨ *Room service, in-room safes, hair salon, bar, travel services* ⊟ *AE, MC, V.*

Downtown

$$ ⊞ **Gran Hotel de la Ciudad de México.** Ensconced in a former 19th-century department store, this hotel has rooms furnished in a modern style. Its distinctive Belle Epoque lobby—with a striking stained-glass Tiffany dome, chandeliers, gilded birdcages, and 19th-century wrought-iron elevators—is worth a visit in its own right. The Mirador breakfast restaurant overlooks the Zócalo. Run by Delmónicos, the Del Centro restaurant-bar is one of Mexico City's best. ⊠ *16 de Septiembre 82, at 5 de febrero Col. Centro 06000* ☎ *55/1083–7700* 🛏 *122 rooms* ♨ *2 restaurants, room service, cable TV, 2 bars, concierge, travel services, parking (fee)* ⊟ *AE, DC, MC, V.*

$$ ⊞ **Holiday Inn Zócalo.** This hotel couldn't have a better location—on the Zócalo and close to a gaggle of museums, restaurants, and historic buildings. The building may be historic, but the interior has the feel of a Holiday Inn. Although the glass-front lobby lacks personality, there's more flavor to the terrace restaurant, which is set with old-fashioned wrought-iron tables and has an amazing view of the Catedral Metropolitana and Palacio Nacional. Rooms are small but well equipped and all suites have data ports; five have Jacuzzi bathtubs. ⊠ *Av. 5 de Mayo at Zócalo, Col. Centro 06000* ☎ *55/5521–2121* 🖷 *55/5521–2122* ⊕ *www.holidayinnzocalo.com.mx* 🖵 *100 rooms, 10 suites* ⅃ *2 restaurants, room service, in-room safes, gym, bar, meeting rooms, travel services, parking (fee)* ▱ *AE, MC, V.*

★ $$ 🖽 **Hotel de Cortés.** This darling small hotel, managed by Best Western, is housed in a 1780 colonial building that's also a national monument. Rooms, in colonial style, are small and simply furnished; they open onto an enclosed central courtyard. Two comfortable soundproof suites overlook Alameda Park across the busy street. The Museo Franz Mayer is a block away, and it's an easy walk to Palacio de Bellas Artes. Loyal guests reserve many months in advance. ⊠ *Av. Hidalgo 85, Col. Guerrero 06000* ☎ *55/5518–2181; 800/908–1200 in the U.S.* 🖷 *55/5512–1863* ⊕ *www.hoteldecortes.com.mx* 🖵 *19 rooms, 10 suites* ⅃ *Restaurant, bar* ▱ *AE, DC, MC, V.*

$$ 🖽 **Majestic.** If you're interested in exploring the historic downtown, the atmospheric, colonial-style Majestic will give you a perfect location. It's also ideal for viewing the Independence Day (September 16) celebrations, for which many people reserve a room a year in advance. Although the front units have balconies and a delightful view, they can be noisy with car traffic until about 11 PM. ⊠ *Calle Madero 73, Col. Centro 06000* ☎ *55/5521–8600; 800/528–1234 in the U.S.* 🖷 *55/5512–6262* ⊕ *www.majestic.com.mx* 🖵 *85 rooms* ⅃ *Restaurant, coffee shop, bar, travel services* ▱ *AE, DC, MC, V.*

★ ¢ 🖽 **Catedral.** In the heart of historic downtown, this refurbished older hotel is a bargain, with many of the amenities of the more upscale hotels at less than half the price. Public areas sparkle with marble and glass. Guest rooms are done in a generic but cheerful contemporary fashion, and all have color TVs (local channels only) and phones. You can get a room with a view of the namesake Catedral, but keep in mind that its bells chime every 15 minutes, late into the night. El Retiro bar attracts a largely Mexican clientele to hear live Latin music. ⊠ *Donceles 95, Col. Centro 06000* ☎ *55/5512–8581* 🖷 *55/5512–4344* ⊕ *www.hotelcatedral.com.mx* 🖵 *116 rooms, 8 suites* ⅃ *Restaurant, coffee shop, room service, bar, nightclub, dry cleaning, laundry service, business services, travel services, free parking* ▱ *AE, MC, V.*

Airport

$$$ 🖽 **Hilton Aeropuerto.** Cool and compact—with a distinctive gray marble lobby and a bar with a wide-angle view of landing planes—the hotel feels like a private club, enhanced by an attentive but unobtrusive staff. Rooms come with full working gear for a traveling executive: two phone lines, modem connection, ergonomic chairs, and coffeemaker. Rooms have four different views—airstrip, street, atrium, or garden (bamboo plants set along a concrete ledge). ⊠ *Benito Juárez International Airport, at international terminal, 15620* ☎ *55/5133–0505; 800/774–1500 in the U.S.* 🖷 *55/5133–0500* ⊕ *www.hilton.com* 🖵 *129 rooms* ⅃ *Restaurant, in-room data ports, gym, bar, business services, meeting rooms, parking (fee)* ▱ *AE, DC, MC, V.*

$$$ 🖽 **Marriott Aeropuerto.** Over a short covered footbridge from the airport terminal, this deluxe hotel is quite sleek. A couple of services, including room service and the business center, run 24 hours, useful for travelers on odd-hours schedules. Even if you're only between flights and don't overnight, you can sit in one of the overstuffed chairs in the soothing lobby or catch a meal in the restaurant to get away from the

frantic energy of the airport. ✉ *Benito Juárez International Airport, 15520*
☎ *55/3003–0000; 800/228–9290 in the U.S.* 🖷 *55/3003–0001* ⊕ *www.*
marriott.com ⤳ *600 rooms, 8 suites* ♨ *Restaurant, coffee shop, in-room*
data ports, in-room safes, minibars, pool, gym, sauna, bar, meeting
rooms, car rental, free parking ⊟ *AE, DC, MC, V.*

NIGHTLIFE & THE ARTS

A good place to check for current events is *Tiempo Libre*, a weekly magazine listing activities and events in Spanish (⊕ www.tiempolibre.com.
mx). It's available at newsstands.

Citywide festivals with free music, dance, and theater performances by
local groups take place all year long but especially in July and August.
A three-week spring cultural and gastronomic festival with international headliners takes place in the Centro Histórico between March and
April. Check with the Mexico City Tourist Office for dates and details.
The **National Arts Council (CONACULTA)** also lists city festivals on
its Web site, ⊕ cartelera.conaculta.gob.mx, along with updates on
music, theater, film, and other cultural events of all stripes.

If you'd like to see a film, you can check movie listings by city and neighborhood on the Cinépolis Web site, ⊕ www.cinepolis.com.mx. Films
in English are generally subtitled.

The Arts

Dance

★ The world-renowned **Ballet Folklórico de México** (⊕ www.balletamalia.
com), of Amalia Hernández, is a visual feast of Mexican regional folk
dances in whirling colors. Lavish and professional, as you can see from
the Web site, it's one of the most popular shows in Mexico. Performances
Wednesday at 8:30 PM and Sunday at 9:30 AM and 8:30 PM are at the
beautiful Palacio de Bellas Artes (Palace of Fine Arts; Avenida Juárez at
Eje Central Lázaro Cárdenas)—it's a treat to see its Tiffany-glass curtain lowered. Call the Palacio de Bellas Artes box office (☎55/5512–3633)
or Ticketmaster (☎ 55/5325–9000) for information on prices and for
reservations. Hotels and travel agencies can also secure tickets.

The **National Dance Theater** (☎ 55/5280–8771) is a good forum for contemporary dance behind the Auditorio Nacional on Paseo de la Reforma.
The **Miguel Covarrubias Hall** (✉ National Autonomous University of
Mexico [UNAM], Av. Insurgentes Sur 3000, Ciudad Universitaria ☎ 55/
5665–6825), home of the university's dance department, frequently
sponsors modern-dance performances.

Music

Music thrums everywhere in the capital, from itinerant trumpeters and
drummers playing in the streets to marimba in the market places. Some
of the best street musicians can be found at popular lunchtime eateries,
especially in markets. It's customary to offer a tip of small change; at
least a few pesos will be appreciated. Free concerts spread through the
city's plazas on weekends when, again, donations are in order. Most Mexican music (salsa, *son, cumbia, danzón*) is for dancing and you will usually find a succession of great live bands in the dance halls and nightclubs.

The primary venue for classical music is the **Palacio de Bellas Artes**
(✉ Eje Central Lázaro Cárdenas and Av. Juárez, Col. Centro ☎ 55/
5512–3633), which has a main auditorium and the smaller Manuel Ponce
concert hall. The National Opera performs from February through

November at the palace. The National Symphony Orchestra stages classical and modern pieces at the palace in spring and fall.

Classical concerts (often free) are also held at the National Music Conservatory in the **Auditorio Silvestre Revueltas** (⊠ Av. Presidente Masaryk 582, Col. Polanco ☎ 55/5280–6347). Another good venue for classical music is in the south of the city, **Auditorio Blas Galindo** (⊠ Av. Río Churubusco, at Calz. de Tlalpan ☎ 55/5521–7960 or 5521–0686), in the Centro Nacional de las Artes (CNA, the National Arts Center).

For choral performances, look for one of the free performances of the Madrigalistas de Bellas Artes in the **Antiguo Palacio del Arzobispado** (⊠ Calle Moneda 4, Col. Centro ☎ 55/5228–1245).

The top concert hall, often touted as the best in Latin America, is **Ollin Yolitzli** (⊠ Periférico Sur 5141, Col. Isidro Favela ☎ 55/5606–0016 or 55/5606–8558); it hosts the Mexico City Philharmonic several times a year. The National Autonomous University of Mexico's Philharmonic orchestra performs at **Nezahualcoyotl Hall** (⊠ National Autonomous University of Mexico, Av. Insurgentes Sur 3000, Ciudad Universitaria ☎ 55/5622–7112 or 55/5606–8933).

For pop, rock, and Latin music stars such as Luis Miguel, Peter Gabriel, and Mercedes Sosa, check newspapers for attractions. The **Auditorio Nacional** (⊠ Paseo de la Reforma 50, across from Nikko México hotel, Col. San Miguel Chapultepec ☎ 55/5280–9250 or 55/5280–9979 ⊕ www.auditorio.com.mx) is smart and modern, with great acoustics. A choice venue, the **Hard Rock Cafe** (⊠ Campos Elíseos 278, Col. Chapultepec Polanco ☎ 55/5327–7120 or 5327–7171) is intimate with state-of-the-art sound. **Palacio de los Deportes** (⊠ Av. Río Churubusco and Calle Añil ☎ 55/5237–9999 Ext. 4264) has an open-air venue called the *Foro Sol* where you'll catch the glitzy shows of Madonna or the Rolling Stones. Though it's in need of an overhaul, the ambience is good at the **Teatro Metropolitano** (⊠ Independencia 90, Col. Centro ☎ 55/5510–1035 or 55/5510–1045).

Theater

Good live theater, whether in English or Spanish, is not Mexico City's strong suit. **Centro Cultural Heléico** (⊠ Av. Revolución 1500, Col. Guadalupe Inn ☎ 55/5662–8674) is one of the most reliable bets. The shows at the **Foro Antonio López Mancera** in the Centro Nacional de las Artes (⊠ CNA, Río Churubusco 79, at Calz. de Tlalpan ☎ 55/5481–4200 or 55/5481–4240) tend to be more hit-or-miss. **El Hábito** (⊠ Madrid 13, Coyoacán ☎ 55/5659–1139), run by the contentious satirist Jesusa Rodríguez, puts on lively music, cabaret, and political theater but you'll need proficient Spanish.

Nightlife

Night is the key word to understanding the timing of going out in Mexico City. People generally have cocktails at 7 or 8, take in dinner and a show at 10 or 11, head to discos at midnight, then find a spot for a nightcap or tacos somewhere around 3 AM. (Cantinas are the exception; people start hitting them in the late afternoon and most close by 11 PM.) The easiest way to do this if you don't speak Spanish is on a nightlife tour. If you set off on your own you should have no trouble getting around, but for personal safety absolutely avoid taking taxis off the street—take official hotel taxis or call a *sitio* (stationed) taxi.

Niza and Florencia streets in the Zona Rosa are practically lined with nightclubs, bars, and discos that are especially lively Friday and Saturday nights. Big hotels have bars and places to dance or be entertained, and they are frequented by locals. Outside the Zona Rosa, Paseo de la Reforma and Avenida Insurgentes Sur have the greatest concentration of nightspots. Remember that the capital's high altitude makes liquor extremely potent, even jolting. Imported booze is expensive, so you may want to stick with what the Mexicans order: tequila, *cerveza* (beer), and rum, usually as a *cuba libre* (with Coke).

Dancing

Dance emporiums in the capital run the gamut from cheek-to-cheek romantic to throbbing strobe lights and ear-splitting music. Most places have a cover charge, but it's rarely more than $10. Friday and Saturday are the busiest club nights, while Thursday's a good option if you'd like a bit of elbow room for dancing. The most popular clubs open Wednesday too. Some clubs require that reservations be made one to two days beforehand if you want a table.

★ **Bar León** (✉ República de Brasil 5, behind the Catedral Metropolitana in the Zócalo, Col. Centro ☎ 55/5510–2979) is a traditional salsa bar, dark, and low-ceilinged, with great live music and a rather small dance
★ floor. So popular you can barely move is the friendly **Mama Rumba** (✉ Querétaro 230, at Medellín, Col. Roma ☎ 55/5564–6920 ✉ Plaza San Jacinto 23, San Angel ☎ 55/5550–8099 or 55/5550–8090), a 10-minute cab ride from the Zona Rosa. A nondescript Cuban restaurant during the day, it turns on the heat Wednesday through Saturday nights. **Meneo** (✉ Nueva York 315, just off Av. Insurgentes Sur, Col. Napoles ☎ 55/5523–9448) is a modern dance hall for live salsa and merengue with two dance floors. **Salón Baraimas** (✉ Filomena Mata 7, between Av. 5 de Mayo and Calle Tacuba, Col. Centro ☎ 55/5510–4488) gives a serious setting for those who know how to salsa. To reserve a table you have to buy a bottle of rum or tequila. Dancing begins around 9 but live bands start at 11. So kitschy you won't know whether to laugh or groan, the noble old **Salón Colonia** (✉ Manuel M. Flores 33, at the Eje Central, Col. Obrera ☎ 55/5510–9915) is the capital's traditional dance hall for danzón and ballroom dancing. It's almost exclusively frequented by middle-aged or elderly Mexicans. **Salón Los Angeles** (✉ Lerdo 206, Col. Guerrero ☎ 55/5597–5181) takes you back in time to the 1930s, with decor straight out of a movie. The grand, open dance floor swings to the rhythms of danzón and salsa. When renowned Latin musicians such as Celia Cruz come to town, this is often where they perform. Local bands play danzón, cha-cha, and mambo upstairs in a converted factory at **Salón México** (✉ Pensador Mexicano, at San Juan de Dios Col. Centro ☎ 55/5510–9915), combining nostalgia with fresh energy. In recent years the huge **Salón 21** (✉ Moliere, at Andrómaco Col. Ampliación Granada, near Col. Polanco ☎ 55/5255–1496 or 55/5255–5658) has hosted the best international salsa and Afro-Caribbean bands to visit Mexico City; it's more of an event space than a dance hall, though.

If Latin music isn't your thing, two of the hippest discos in the city stand close to each other in the center. Founded by two Englishmen, the **Colmillo** (✉ Versailles 52, Col. Juárez ☎ 55/5592–6164) spins techno music downstairs and has an acid jazz bar upstairs. The **Pervert Lounge** (✉ Uruguay 70, between 5 de febrero and Isabel La Católica, Col. Centro ☎ 55/5518–0976) may not live up (or down?) to its name, but it's funky and fun.

In the south of town, **Alebrije** (✉ Altamirano 46, Loc. 2, in the Plaza Loreto, Col. San Angel ☎ 55/5616–5304) pulls in plenty of young dancers. For electronica lovers, **Box** (✉ Av. Moliere 425, at Andrómaco, Col. Polanco ☎ 55/5203–3365 or 55/5203–3356) is where it's happening.

In a high-ceilinged colonial mansion, the **Living Room** (⊠ Orizaba 146, Col. Roma ☎ 55/5203–3365 or 5203–3356) hosts one of the most popular gay clubs in town.

Bars

Nice bars to sit and have a few drinks in used to be hard to come by in Mexico City but the situation is improving. The rougher cantinas are usually noisy and sometimes seedy, with an early closing time (11 PM), but the better cantinas, full of character and local color, are well worth a visit. Bars are usually open Tuesday–Saturday 8 PM–3 AM and generally don't charge a cover, unless they are offering a good live band.

The most popular neighborhoods for barhopping include Col. Polanco, San Angel, Coyoacán, La Condesa, and, for cantinas, La Roma. The Zona Rosa is still quite busy, but it has lost ground to Polanco and La Condesa in the past couple of years. Drink prices fluctuate wildly according to area and establishment.

Bar Milán (⊠ Milán 18, at General Prim, Col. Juárez ☎ 55/5592–0031) is a local favorite with the young and hip; the music is good but very loud. Upon entering you need to change pesos into *milagros* (miracles), which are notes necessary to buy drinks throughout the night. The catch is to remember to change them back for pesos before last call. **La Bodeguita del Medio** (⊠ Cozumel 37, Col. Roma Norte ☎ 55/5553–0246 ⊠ Av. Insurgentes Sur 1798, Col. Florida ☎ 55/5661–4400) is a sit-down joint full of life, with every surface splashed with graffiti. Inspired by the original Havana establishment where Hemingway lapped up rum-and-mint mojitos, you can also try cheap Cuban food, but most people just drink.

A sophisticated crowd and mellow music set the scene at the **Camino Real** (⊠ Mariano Escobedo 700, Col. Nueva Anzures ☎ 55/5263–8888). The grand cantina **La Covadonga** (⊠ Puebla 121, at Córdoba, Col. Roma ☎ 55/5533–2922) has a beautiful antique bar, a good restaurant, and slaps happily with the sound of dominoes at night. The old rumba club **Gallos Centenario** (⊠ Rep. de Cuba 79, Col. Centro ☎ 55/5521–7886), now a decadently draped bar and restaurant, is a good spot for live music Friday and Saturday nights. **La Guadalupana** (⊠ Calle Higuera 14, Coyoacán ☎ 55/5554–6253), a famous cantina dating from 1932, is always packed and heavy on local color. The crowd is overwhelmingly male, so unaccompanied women will be showered with attention. Students and hip intellectuals of all ages pack **El Hijo del Cuervo** (⊠ Jardín Centenario 17, Coyoacán ☎ 55/5658–5306) for an interesting mix of rock and *nueva canción,* and the occasional theater show. Covers vary (up to $7), depending on the show. The bar of the restaurant **Ixchel** (⊠ Medellín 65, at Colima Col. Roma ☎ 55/5208–4055) is a great place for a relaxing sip; it's in a beautiful old building.

★ **El Nivel** (⊠ Calle Moneda, near the Templo Mayor, Col. Centro ☎ 55/5522–9755), Mexico City's first cantina, opened in 1855, is right off the Zócalo. It's a small traditional cantina where you can get a cheap beer or tequila and be served free appetizers like peanuts and *chicharrón* (crisp fried meat) as long as you keep ordering drinks. The bar is named after a water marker outside (called "el nivel") that warned the city about imminent floods during the 20th century. **La Nueva Ópera** (⊠ 5 de Mayo 10, at Filomeno Mata, Col. Centro ☎ 55/5512–8959) is one of the city's most elegant watering holes, and it's brought in top personalities since it opened in 1870. Don't forget to have your waiter point out the bullet hole allegedly left in the ceiling by Mexican revolutionary hero Pancho Villa. A fantastic old cantina, **El Portal de Cartagena**

(⌧ Chiapas 174, at Medellín, Col. Roma ☎ 55/5264–8714 or 55/5584–1113) is ideal for a long lunch and a few beers. With glass walls and three split-levels, **Rexo** (⌧ Saltillo 1, corner of Av. Vicente Suárez, Col. Condesa ☎ 55/5553–1300 or 55/5553–5337) becomes a roaring hive of activity.

Dinner Shows

The liveliest shows are in clubs downtown and in the Zona Rosa. **El Arroyo** (⌧ Av. Insurgentes Sur 4003, Tlalpan, a 40-min drive south of Zona Rosa ☎ 55/5573–4344), a huge complex complete with its own bull-ring, shows *novilleros* (novice toreros) trying out their skills from May to September. An open kitchen serves traditional Mexican specialties and drinks, such as the potent, cactus-derived pulque, from 8 to 8. On weekends, mariachi and jarocho musicians add to the buzz. The maze-like **La Bodega** (⌧ Popocatépetl 25, corner of Amsterdam, Col. Hipódromo ☎ 55/5525–2473) is a lively place for drinks and decent Mexican food. A quirky band of old chaps plays relaxed Latin and Caribbean dance music in the small front room, and the upstairs theater hosts visiting musicians. Try to catch Astrid Haddad, a wild feminist cabaret artiste. You won't get the jokes without excellent Spanish, but you'll be laughing at her act anyway. Admission starts at $4, not including the theater shows. At **Focolare** (⌧ Hamburgo 87, at Río Niza, Zona Rosa ☎ 55/5207–8257), you can watch a cockfight, mariachi singers, and traditional folk dancers Thursday through Saturday nights. The show costs $8.50; Mexican dinner and drinks are separate.

Mariachi Music

The traditional last stop for nocturnal Mexicans is **Plaza Garibaldi** (⌧ Col. Cuauhtémoc, east of Eje Central Lázaro Cárdenas, between República de Honduras and República de Perú), where exuberant and often inebriated mariachis gather to unwind after evening performances—by performing even more. There are roving mariachis, as well as *norteño* (country-style) music and white-clad *jarocho* bands (Veracruz-style), peddling songs in the outdoor plaza, where you can also buy beer and shots of tequila. Well-to-do Mexicans park themselves inside one of the cantinas or clubs surrounding the plaza and belt out their favorite songs with the hired musicians.

Tenampa (⌧ Plaza Garibaldi 12, Col. Cuauhtémoc ☎ 55/5526–6176) is one of the better cantinas, with some great paintings on the walls. Order a tequila and the musicians will be around shortly, offering to serenade you (a song costs about $5, though Mexicans typically haggle for a dozen), so the bar is rarely without the wailing mariachis for more than 10 minutes. These places stay open Sunday through Thursday until at least 2 AM, and even later Friday and Saturday.

Note: the square was spruced up in the early 1990s to improve its seedy image, but things still get rough late at night. Furthermore, leaving Plaza Garibaldi can be dangerous—be sure to arrange for transportation ahead of time. You may call a travel agency, drive your car and park in the well-lit ramp below the plaza, or call a safe sitio taxi.

A list of upcoming mariachi events and recommended locales can be obtained from the offices of the **Union Mexicana de Mariachis** (⌧ Mercados Altos, Plaza Garibaldi, Col. Cuauhtémoc ☎ 55/5526–6256).

SPORTS & THE OUTDOORS

Latin sports such as the *fiesta brava* (bullfighting)—brought to Mexico by the Spanish—have enjoyed popularity for more than four centuries in the capital, which attracts the country's best athletes. And although the roots of *fútbol* (soccer) are probably English, a weekend afternoon game at Mexico City's colossal Estadio Azteca leaves no question that this is the sport Mexicans are craziest about. Baseball and boxing have strong followings too, as does over-the-top *lucha libre* (wrestling). There are plenty of lovely parks for a safe jog or walk. For more challenging activities, seek out an ecotourism or adventure travel agency for a getaway such as white-water rafting in nearby Veracruz, volcano climbing in Puebla, or mountain biking in the Desierto de los Leones. Some city agencies leave much to be desired, though, so you may need to take extra initiative to find the right group.

Adventure Sports & Ecotourism

A number of adventure-travel agencies have sprouted up to entice both tourists and locals out of the smog and chaos of Mexico City for a weekend of white-water rafting, rappelling, or biking. One of the best is **México Verde Expeditions** (⊠ Homero 526, Int. 801, at Lamartine, Col. Polanco ☎ 55/5255–4400 or 55/5255–4465 ⊕ www.mexicoverde.com.mx), whose guides speak English and lead tours to the pristine areas of such nearby states as Veracruz and Morelos. Call a week in advance to make reservations and bring a sleeping bag and sunblock.

Marlene Ehrenberg Enriquez, a multilingual certified guide, is a pioneer ecotourism consultant. Her agency, **Marlene Ehrenberg Tours** (⊠ Av. Universidad 1953, edif.11-203, Universidad ☎ 55/5550–9080 ⊕ www.marlene366.tripod.com) offers specialized tours that focus on Mexico's ecology and culture. Mexico continues to develop both government offices and private industry groups to promote ecotourism, but these are still nascent. A good starting point for information is the **Asociación Mexicana de Turismo de Aventura y Ecoturismo** (⊠ AMTAVE; Homero 526, Int. 801, at Lamartine, Col. Polanco ☎ 55/5255–4400 or 55/5255–4465 ⊕ www.amtave.org), a group of ecotourism and adventure travel providers. The association produces an annual catalog and a bilingual (English-Spanish) Web site.

Bullfighting

The main season for bullfighting is the dry season, around November through March, when celebrated *matadores* appear at **Plaza México** (⊠ Calle Agusto Rodín 241, at Holbein, Col. Ciudad de los Deportes ☎ 55/5563–3959), the world's largest bullring (it seats 40,000). Tickets, about $3.50–$48, can be purchased at hotel travel desks or at the bullring's ticket booths weekends 9:30–2 and 3:30–7. The show goes on at 4 Sunday.

Soccer

Fútbol is the sport that Mexicans are most passionate about, which is evident in the size of their soccer stadium, **Estadio Azteca** (⊠ Calz. de Tlalpan 3465, Tlalpan ☎ 55/5617–8080), the second largest in Latin America. The World Cup Finals were held here in 1970 and 1986. You can buy tickets outside the stadium in the south of the city on the same day of any minor game. For more-important games, buy tickets a week in advance. The Pumas, a popular university-sponsored team, play at **Estadio Olímpica** (⊠ Av. Insurgentes Sur at Universidad Nacional Autónoma de México, Ciudad Universitaria).

Water Sports

The best place for swimming is your hotel pool. If you're desperate to row a boat, however, you can rent one in the lakes of Bosque de Chapultepec, near the Zoológico.

SHOPPING

The most-concentrated shopping area is the **Zona Rosa**, which stays chock-full of boutiques, jewelry stores, leather-goods shops, antiques stores, and art galleries.

Polanco, a choice residential neighborhood along the northeast perimeter of Bosque de Chapultepec, has blossomed into a more upscale shopping area. Select shops line the huge, ultramodern **Plaza Polanco** (✉ Jaime Balmes 11, Col. Polanco). You can also head to the **Plaza Masarik** (✉ Av. Presidente Masaryk and Anatole France, Col. Polanco). **Plaza Moliere** (✉ Moliere between Calles Horacio and Homero, Col. Polanco) is another upscale shopping area.

The **Colonia Condesa,** though better known for restaurants and cafés, is sprouting designer clothing boutiques, primarily for a younger crowd. Jewelers, shoe shops, and some hip housewares stores are squeezing in as well. Most cluster along avenidas Michoacán, Vicente Suárez, and Tamaulipas.

Hundreds of shops with more modest trappings and better prices are spread along the length of Avenida Insurgentes and Avenida Juárez.

Department Stores, Malls & Shopping Arcades

Department stores are generally open Monday, Tuesday, Thursday, and Friday 10–7, and Wednesday and Saturday 10–8.

Bazar del Centro (✉ Isabel la Católica 30, just below Calle Madero, Col. Centro), in a restored, late 17th-century mansion built around a garden courtyard, houses several chic boutiques and prestigious jewelers such as **Aplijsa** (☎ 55/5521–1923), known for its fine gold, silver, pearls, and gemstones, and **Ginza** (☎ 55/5518–6453), which has Japanese pearls, including the prized cultured variety. Other shops sell Taxco silver, Tonalá stoneware, and Mexican tequilas and liqueurs.

Liverpool (✉ Av. Insurgentes Sur 1310, Col. Guadalupe Inn ✉ Mariano Escobedo 425, Col. Polanco ✉ Plaza Satélite shopping center ✉ Perisur shopping center) is the largest retailer in Mexico City and often has bargains on clothes.

The upscale department store chain **El Palacio de Hierro** (✉ Av. Durango and Salamanca, Col. Condesa ✉ Plaza Moliere, Col. Polanco ✉ Plaza Coyoacán; Col. Xoco) is noted for items by well-known designers and seductive advertising campaigns.

Perisur shopping mall (✉ Periférico Sur, Perisur), on the southern edge of the city, near where the Periférico Expressway meets Avenida Insurgentes, is posh and pricey.

Plaza La Rosa (✉ between Amberes and Génova, Zona Rosa), a modern shopping arcade, has 72 prestigious shops and boutiques, including Aldo Conti and Diesel. It spans the depth of the block between Londres and Hamburgo, with entrances on both streets.

Portales de los Mercaderes (Merchants Arcade; ✉ extending the length of the west side of the Zócalo between Calles Madero and 16 de Septiembre, Col. Centro) has attracted merchants since 1524. It's lined with jewelry shops selling gold (often by the gram) and authentic Taxco silver at prices lower than those in Taxco itself, where the overhead is higher.

In the middle of the Portales de los Mercaderes is **Tardán** (✉ Plaza de la Constitución 7, Col. Centro ☎ 55/5512–2459), an unusual shop specializing in fashionable men's hats of every shape and style.

Sanborns is a chain of mini–department stores with some 65 branches in Mexico City. The most convenient are at Calle Madero 4 (its original store in the House of Tiles, downtown); several along Paseo de la Reforma (including one at the Angel monument and another four blocks west of the Diana Fountain); in San Angel (on Avenida de la Revolución and Avenida de la Paz); Coyoacán (at the Jardín Centenario); and in the Zona Rosa (one at the corner of Niza and Hamburgo and another at Londres 130 in the Hotel Calinda Geneve). They carry quality ceramics and crafts (and can ship anywhere), and most have restaurants or coffee shops, a pharmacy, ATMs, and periodical and book departments with English-language publications. They're great spots to meet a friend; if one of you runs late the other can have a coffee while waiting.

Santa Fe (✉ Salida a Toluca, Santa Fe) is the largest mall in Latin America, with 285 stores, a movie theater, an international exhibition center, hotels, and several restaurants. It's in the wealthy Santa Fe district, which in recent years has become the favored office real-estate property in the city. To get here, take the Periférico Expressway south to the exit marked CENTRO SANTA FE.

Markets

FodorsChoice ★ Open every day from about 10–5, the bustling **Mercado Artesanal La Ciudadela** (✉ Balderas, one block south of Parque José María Morelos, Col. Juárez) bursts with the widest range of wares and the best bargains in the capital. Browse through the crafts, from Talavera pottery, leather belts, guitars, tile-framed mirrors, hammocks, silverware, and papier-mâché skeletons to rugs, trays from Olinalá, and the ubiquitous sombrero. Prices are good but you can still haggle. A number of casual restaurants serve up hearty set-menu lunches for $3–$5. Covered stalls take up a whole square, a 10–15 minute walk from the Alameda.

★ A "must"—if you are in town on a Saturday—is a visit to the **Bazar Sábado** (Saturday Bazaar; ✉ Plaza San Jacinto, San Angel). Hundreds of vendors sell tons of crafts, silver, wood carvings, embroidered clothing, leather goods, wooden masks, beads, *amates* (bark paintings), and trinkets at stalls on the network of cobbled streets outside. Inside the bazaar building, a renovated two-story colonial mansion, are the better-quality—and higher-priced—goods, including *alebrijes* (painted wooden animals from Oaxaca), glassware, pottery, jewelry, and papier-mâché flowers. A patio buffet and an indoor restaurant will help you conquer hunger and thirst. The market is open daily 10–7.

Sunday 10–4, more than 100 artists exhibit and sell their painting and sculpture at the **Jardín del Arte** (Garden of Art; ✉ Río Nevada, between Sullivan and Manuel Villalongín, Parque Sullivan, northeast of the Reforma-Insurgentes intersection, Col. Cuauhtémoc). Along the west side of the park, a colorful weekend mercado with scores of food stands is also worth a visit.

The **Mercado Insurgentes** (also called Mercado Zona Rosa; ✉ between Florencia and Amberes, Zona Rosa) is an entire block deep, with entrances on both Londres and Liverpool. This typical neighborhood public market distinguishes itself from others in one noticeable way: most of the stalls (222 of them) sell crafts. You can find all kinds of handmade items—including serapes and ponchos, baskets, pottery, silver, pewter, fossils, and onyx, as well as regional Mexican clothing.

The enormous market **La Lagunilla** (⊠ Libertad, between República de Chile and Calle Allende, Col. Centro) has been a site for local trade and bartering for more than five centuries. The day to go is Sunday, when flea-market and antiques stands are set up outside. Dress down and watch out for pickpockets; it's known affectionately as the Thieves Market—local lore says you can buy back on Sunday what was stolen from your home Saturday.

Specialty Shops

Antiques

Antigüedades Coloniart (⊠ Estocolmo 37, at Hamburgo, Zona Rosa ☎ 55/5514–4799) has good-quality antique paintings, furniture, and sculpture. **Bazar de Antigüedades** (⊠ Between Londres and Hamburgo, opposite Mercado Insurgentes, Zona Rosa) is a line of antiques stores along a passageway, at its liveliest on a Saturday. **Galería Windsor** (⊠ Hamburgo 224, at Praga, Zona Rosa ☎ 55/5525–2881) specializes in 18th- and 19th-century antiques. **Rodrigo Rivera Lake** (⊠ Campos Elíseos 199-PH, Col. Polanco ☎ 55/5281–5505) collects high-quality antiques and decorative art. It's open by appointment only.

Art

The best group of modern galleries concentrates in Colonia Roma (see Exploring Mexico City). Collectors won't want to miss the best gallery in the south of the city, the **Galería Kin** (⊠ Altavista 92, Col. San Angel ☎ 55/5550–8641 or 55/5550–8910), which exhibits a wide variety of contemporary Mexican painting and sculpture. The **Juan Martín Gallery** (⊠ Dickens 33-B, Col. Polanco ☎ 55/5280–0277 ⊕ www.arte-mexico. com/juanmartin) shows avant-garde work. **Misrachi** (⊠ Av. Presidente Masaryk 523, Col. Polanco ☎ 55/5250–4105), a long-standing gallery, promotes well-known Mexican and international artists. The **Nina Menocal de Rocha Gallery** (⊠ Zacatecas 93, Col. Roma ☎ 55/5564–7209) specializes in up-and-coming Cuban painters. The **Oscar Roman Gallery** (⊠ Julio Verne 14, Col. Polanco ☎ 55/5280–0436 ⊕ www.arte-mexico. com/romanosc) is packed with work by good Mexican painters with a contemporary edge. The store and gallery of the renowned **Sergio Bustamante** (⊠ Nikko México hotel, Campos Elíseos 204, Col. Polanco ☎ 55/5282–2638 ⊠ Amberes 13, Zona Rosa ☎ 55/5525–9059 ⊠ Camino Real hotel, Mariano Escobedo 700, Col. Polanco ☎ 55/ 5254–7372) displays and sells the artist's wild sculpture, jewelry, and interior-design pieces.

Candy

Celaya (⊠ 5 de Mayo 39, Col. Centro ☎ 55/5521–1787), is a decades-old haven for those with a sweet tooth. It specializes in candied pineapple, guava, and other exotic fruit; almond paste; candied walnut rolls; and *cajeta,* a typical Mexican dessert of thick caramelized milk.

Designer Clothing

At first glance, the linen dresses in **Carmen Rion** (⊠ Av. Michoacán 30–A, at Parque México, Col. Condesa ☎ 55/5264–6179) may seem classic, but look closely and you'll find innovative ties and fastenings. The jewelry, often combining wood, silver and seed pods, is equally unique. The Little Black Dress has a D.F. outpost: **Chanel** (⊠ President Masaryk 450-2, Col. Polanco ☎ 55/5282–3121). **Frattina** (⊠ President Masaryk 420, at Calderón de la Barca and Edgar Allen Poe, Col. Polanco ☎ 55/ 5281–4036 ⊠ Altavista 52, San Angel ☎ 55/5550–6830) carries women-only work by international and top Mexican designers. If the exchange rate goes your way, a trip to **Hermès** (✉ President Masaryk 422A, between Calderón de la Barca and Edgar Allan Poe, Col. Polanco ☎ 55/5282–2118) may be in order for their legendary silk scarves and leather goods. Splashy, rock-star couture has a home at **Versace** (✉ President Masaryk 422B, between Calderón de la Barca and Edgar Allan Poe, Col. Polanco ☎ 55/5282–2454).

Jewelry

Taxco silver of exceptional style is sold at **Arte en Plata** (✉ Londres 162-A, Zona Rosa ☎ 55/5511–1422), with many designs inspired by pre-Columbian art. **Cartier** (✉ Amberes 9, Zona Rosa ☎ 55/5207–6109 ✉ Av. Presidente Masaryk 438, Col. Polanco ☎ 55/5281–5528) sells the sophisticated jewelry and clothes under the auspices of the French Cartier. The owner of **Los Castillo** (✉ Amberes 41, Zona Rosa ☎ 55/5511–8396) developed a unique method of melding silver, copper, and brass, and is considered by many to be Taxco's top silversmith. His daughter Emilia Castillo displays fine ceramic dishes with tiny inlaid silver figures, such as fish and birds. For unusual jewelry, mostly in silver, glass, and stone, look in at **Entenaya** (✉ Montes de Oca 47, Col. Condesa ☎ 55/5601–5414). **Pelletier** (✉ Torcuato Caso 237, Col. Polanco ☎ 55/5250–8600) sells fine jewelry and watches. **Tane** (✉ Amberes 70, Zona Rosa ☎ 55/5511–9429 ✉ Av. Presidente Masaryk 430, Col. Polanco ☎ 55/5281–4775 ✉ Santa Catarina 207, San Angel Inn ☎ 55/5616–0165) is a treasure trove of perhaps the best silver work in Mexico—jewelry, flatware, candelabra, museum-quality reproductions of archaeological finds, and bold new designs by young Mexican silversmiths.

Leather

Aries (✉ Florencia 14, Zona Rosa ☎ 55/5533–2509) is Mexico's finest purveyor of leather goods, with a superb selection of bags and accessories for men and women; prices are high. **Las Bolsas de Coyoacán** (✉ Carrillo Puerto 9, Coyoacán ☎ 55/5554–2010) specializes in high-quality leather goods. **Gaitán** (✉ Calle Sarasete 95-B, at Tetracini, Col. Peralvillo ☎ 55/5759–3393) carries an extensive array of leather coats, luggage, golf bags, and saddles. **Via Spiga** (✉ Hamburgo 136, Zona Rosa ☎ 55/5207–9997) has a fine selection of shoes, gloves, and handbags.

Mexican Crafts

Arte Popular en Miniatura (✉ Hamburgo 85, Col. Juárez ☎ 55/5525–8145) is a tiny shop filled with tiny things, from dollhouse furniture and lead soldiers to miniature Nativity scenes. Browse for folk art, sculpture, and furniture in the gallery **Artesanos de México** (✉ Londres 117, Zona Rosa ☎ 55/5514–7455). **Flamma** (✉ Hamburgo 167, Zona Rosa ☎ 55/5511–8499 or 55/5511–0266) is in a town house and sells beautiful handmade candles. Under the auspices of the National Council for Culture and Arts, **Fonart** (National Fund for Promoting Arts and Crafts; ✉ Juárez 89, Col. Juárez ☎ 55/5521–0171 ✉ main store–warehouse ✉ Av. Patriotismo 691, Col. Mixcoac ☎ 55/5563–4060) operates two stores in Mexico City, and others around the country. (See their Web site, www.fonart.gob.mx.) Prices are fixed and high, but the diverse, top-quality folk art and handcrafted furnishings from all over Mexico represent the best artisans. The best location is downtown, west of Alameda Park. Major sales at near wholesale prices are held from time to time at the main store–warehouse.

You can find handwoven wool rugs, tapestries, and fabrics with original and unusual designs at **Tamacani** (✉ Av. Insurgentes Sur 1748B, Col. Florida ☎ 55/5662–7133).

OUTSKIRTS OF MEXICO CITY

As the capital continues to expand, many attractions that used to be side trips are becoming more accessible. To the north of Mexico City stands the Basílica de Guadalupe, a church dedicated to Mexico's patron saint. It can be enjoyed in a half-day tour; if you get an early start, you could combine your visit with a jaunt to the pyramids of Teotihuacán in the afternoon. Xochimilco (pronounced kso-chee-*meel*-co), famous for its floating gardens, lies on the southern outskirts of the city. You can ride in gondola-like boats and get a fleeting sense of a pre-Hispanic Mexico City. The western extremes of the capital offer the popular Parque Nacional Desierto de los Leones—a forested national park with a Carmelite monastery in its center.

La Villa de Guadalupe
North of the Zócalo.

"La Villa"—the local moniker of the site of the two basilicas of the Virgin of Guadalupe—is Mexico's holiest shrine. Its importance derives from the miracle that the devout believe transpired here on December 12, 1531: an Aztec named Juan Diego received from the Virgin a cloak permanently imprinted with her image so he could prove to the priests that he had had a holy vision. The image has become a nationalist symbol of tremendous power and persistence. Although the story of the miracle and the cloak itself have been challenged for centuries, they are hotly defended by clergy and laity alike. As author Gary Wills observed, the story's "authority just grows as its authenticity diminishes." Every December 12, millions of pilgrims arrive, many crawling on their knees for the last few hundred yards, praying for cures and other divine favors. Outside the **Antigua Basílica** stands a statue of Juan Diego, who became the first indigenous saint in the Americas with his canonization in summer 2002. (This canonization was widely seen as a shrewd move on the part of the Catholic church as it tries to retain its position, particularly among Mexico's indigenous population.) The old basilica dates from 1536; various additions have been made since then. The altar was executed by sculptor Manuel Tolsá. The basilica now houses a museum of ex-votos (hand-painted depictions of miracles, dedicated to Mary or a saint in thanks) and popular religious art, paintings, sculpture, and decorative and applied arts from the 15th through 18th centuries.

Because the structure of the Antigua Basílica had weakened over the years and the building was no longer large enough or safe enough to accommodate all the worshipers, Pedro Ramírez Vázquez, the architect responsible for Mexico City's splendid Museo Nacional de Antropología, was commissioned to design a new shrine, consecrated in 1976. In this case, alas, the architect's inspiration failed him: the **Nueva Basílica** is a gigantic, circular mass of wood, steel, and polyethylene that feels like a stadium rather than a church. The famous image of the Virgin is encased high up in its altar at the back and can be viewed from a moving sidewalk that passes below. The holiday itself is a great time to visit if you don't mind crowds; it's celebrated with various kinds of music and dancers in feathered headdresses and shell anklets. Remember to bring some water with you; you'll need it in the crush. ⊠ *Paseo Zumarraga, Atrio de América, Col. Villa de Guadalupe* ☎ *55/5577–3654* ◷ *Daily 6 AM–9 PM.*

Xochimilco
21 km (13 mi) south of Mexico City center.

When the first nomadic settlers arrived in the Valley of Mexico, they found an enormous lake. As the years went by and their population grew, the land could no longer satisfy their agricultural needs. They solved the problem by devising a system of *chinampas* (floating gardens), rectangular structures akin to barges, which they filled with reeds, branches, and mud. They planted the barges with willows, whose roots anchored the floating gardens to the lake bed, making a labyrinth of small islands and canals on which vendors carried flowers and produce grown on the chinampas to market.

Today Xochimilco is the only place in Mexico where the gardens still exist. Go on a Saturday, when the *tianguis* (market stalls) are most active, or, though it's crowded, on a Sunday. On weekdays the place is practically deserted, so it loses some of its charm. Hire a *trajinera* (flower-painted boat); an arch over each spells out its name in flowers. As you sail through the canals, you'll pass mariachis and women selling tacos from other trajineras.

★ People also flock to Xochimilco for the **Museo Dolores Olmedo Patino**, which holds a superb collection of paintings by Frida Kahlo and the largest private collection of works by Kahlo's husband, the flamboyant muralist Diego Rivera. The museum was established by Olmedo, his lifelong model, patron, and onetime mistress. The lavish display of nearly 140 pieces from his cubist, post-cubist, and mural periods hangs in a magnificent 17th-century hacienda with beautiful gardens. Concerts and entertainment for children are held on weekends, while gaggles of geese and strutting peacocks add to the clamor. This is also the place to see the strange Mexican hairless dog: Ms. Olmedo shares Rivera's passion for these funny-looking creatures and keeps a few as pets on the grounds. The museum also has works by Rivera's common-law wife, Angelina Beloff. ⊠ *Av. México 5843* ☎ *55/5555–1016* 🎟 *$2.50* ☉ *Tues.–Sun. 10–6.*

Parque Nacional Desierto de los Leones
25 km (16 mi) west of Mexico City center.

The "Desert of Lions" owes its name to a quarrel in colonial days over land ownership by brothers called "León." Several walking trails crisscross this 5,000-acre national park's pine forest at 7,511 ft above sea level. Pack a lunch and enjoy it at one of the picnic tables. The park's focal point is the ruined 17th-century **ex-monastery of the Carmelites**, isolated amid an abundance of greenery; it's open Tuesday through Sunday from 9 to 5 and entrance costs 50 cents. The park played a significant role in the War of Independence: in late October 1810, at a spot called **Las Cruces**, Father Hidalgo's troops trounced the Spaniards but resolved not to go on to attack Mexico City, an error that cost the insurgents 10 more years of fighting.

Outskirts of Mexico City A to Z

BUS TRAVEL
Some tour companies offer combination visits to La Villa de Guadalupe and Teotihuacán. Ask at your hotel.

CAR TRAVEL
To get to **La Villa de Guadalupe,** take Paseo de la Reforma Norte until it forks into Calzada de Guadalupe, which leads directly to the shrine.

To get to **Xochimilco,** take Periférico Sur to the extension of División del Norte. The trip should take between 45 minutes and one hour, depending on traffic. (You may be better off taking a taxi, which may cost anywhere from $5 to $25, depending on the taxi company.)

For **Parque Nacional Desierto de los Leones,** follow Paseo de la Reforma all the way west. It eventually merges with the Carretera Libre at Toluca, and after 20 km (12 mi), you'll see signs for the turnoff; it's another 10 km (6 mi) to the park.

SUBWAY TRAVEL

You can reach **La Villa de Guadalupe** by taking the No. 3 metro line from downtown to Deportivo 18 de Marzo. Here, change to line No. 6 in the direction Martin Carrera, getting off at La Villa–Basílica stop.

For Xochimilco take metro line No. 2 to Taxqueña; here hop on the *tren ligero* ("light" train) that continues south to Xochimilco, or catch any bus marked Xochimilco.

MEXICO CITY A TO Z

To research prices, get advice from other travelers, and book travel arrangements, visit www.fodors.com.

AIR TRAVEL

AIRPORT   Mexico City's airport, Aeropuerto Internacional Benito Juárez (MEX), is the main gateway to the country.

The airport's newest wing has four banks and seven currency exchanges (*casas de cambio*); Cirrus and Plus ATMs that disburse pesos; places to rent cellular phones; an Internet room; and a food court, pharmacy, bookstore, and pricey shops. A multilevel parking garage charges $4 an hour for short-term parking.

Banks and currency exchanges rotate their schedules to provide 24-hour service. You can also use your ATM card to take pesos directly out of your U.S. account at ATMs (called *cajero automático* locally) here and throughout the city—and you'll get an even better exchange rate. Just remember that your home bank may charge $3 or more per transaction. Free carts are available in the baggage-retrieval areas but they do not fit through the grid once you have cleared customs so you must either hire a porter or carry your luggage yourself. The Mexico City Tourist Office, Mexican Ministry of Tourism (Sectur), and the Hotel Association have stands in the arrival areas that can provide information and find visitors a room for the night.

🛈 **Aeropuerto Internacional Benito Juárez** ☎ 55/5571-3600 and 55/5784-0471 for information ⊕ www.asa.gob.mx.

AIRPORT   If you're taking a taxi, be sure to purchase your ticket at an official air-
TRANSFERS   port taxi counter marked Transportación Terrestre (ground transportation), located just after the baggage area in national arrivals and in the concourse area (leaving customs to your left) in international arrivals. Under no circumstance take a *pirata* taxi (unofficial drivers offering their services). Government-controlled fares are based on which colonia you are going to and are usually $14–$16 (per car, not per person) to most hotels. A 10% tip is customary for airport drivers if they help with baggage. All major car-rental agencies have booths at both arrival areas.

Taxis are priced by zones; figure out your zone from the big map on the wall (if you're in the central part of the city, you'll probably need Zone

4 or 5, which will cost around $14). To get to the taxi rank, head left from the arrivals area and out of the building. Touts stand at the exit; if you don't have a ticket in your hand, they will attempt to charge you more for the same taxi ride. Do not hand your luggage to anyone offering to help, apart from your driver, unless you are prepared to pay them a tip. The yellow-and-white airport taxis are safe. Avoid the others.

Reaching the city center takes 20 minutes to an hour depending on the traffic. If you're leaving from the city center in the morning, going against traffic, you will reach the airport quickly. In the evening allow at least an hour, count on more time in the rainy season.

Going to the airport, your taxi driver will ask which terminal you want: "Nacional o Internacional?" This question refers to your airline, not your destination. Be careful: some flights have code-sharing between a Mexican and a foreign airline, and check-in could be in either terminal. (Note that you will not lose more than 10 minutes if you arrive at the wrong terminal, since both share the same building.)

Taking the metro between the airport and the city is an impractical option. Although there's a station relatively near the airport, it's in a dodgy neighborhood, and there's no transit service directly to the terminals. Also, heavy luggage is not allowed in the metro during rush hours.

CARRIERS Major North American carriers, including Air Canada, Alaska Airlines, American, America West, Canadian, Continental, Delta, Northwest, Trans World Airlines, United, and USAirways–Air France fly nonstop between Houston and Mexico City.

Mexicana has scheduled service from Chicago, Denver, Las Vegas, Los Angeles, Miami, New York, Orlando, San Antonio, San Francisco, and San Jose, as well as direct or connecting service at 30 locations throughout Mexico. Aeroméxico serves Mexico City daily from Atlanta, Dallas, Houston, Los Angeles, Miami, Orlando, New Orleans, New York, Phoenix, San Antonio, San Diego, and Tucson (as well as Tijuana). Aeroméxico serves some 35 cities within Mexico. Aerolitoral, a subsidiary of Aeroméxico based in Monterrey, serves north-central cities as well as San Antonio, Texas, via Monterrey from Mexico City. Aerocalifornia serves nearly 30 Mexican cities. Líneas Aéreas Azteca, which started up in 2001, connects the capital with a half-dozen other Mexican cities.
Aerocalifornia ☎ 55/5208-1457. **Aerolitoral** ☎ 55/5133-4010 ⊕ www.aerolitoral. com.mx. **Aeroméxico** ☎ 55/5133-4000 ⊕ www.aeromexico.com.mx. **Líneas Aéreas Azteca** ☎ 55/5716-8989. **Mexicana** ☎ 55/5448-0990 ⊕ www.mexicana.com.mx.

BUS TRAVEL TO & FROM MEXICO CITY
Greyhound buses make connections to major U.S. border cities, from which Mexican bus lines depart throughout the day. Reserved seating is available on first-class coaches, which are comfortable but not nearly as plush as the intercity buses. If you plan stopovers en route, make sure in advance that your ticket is written up accordingly. In Mexico, platform announcements are in Spanish only.

Within Mexico, buses are the most popular way to travel: you can board ultramodern, superdeluxe motor coaches that show U.S. movies and serve soft drinks, coffee, and sandwiches. ETN (Enlaces Terrestres Nacionales) serves cities to the west and northwest, such as Guadalajara, Morelia, Querétaro, Guanajuato, San Miguel de Allende, and Toluca. ADO buses depart southeast to such places as Puebla, Oaxaca, Veracruz, Mérida, and Cancún. Almost every route has reserved seating. Reserved-seat tickets for major bus lines can be purchased at Mexico City travel agencies, at bus stations, on the Internet, or by phone with a service called Ticketbus. Ticketbus sells tickets for the following lines: ADO, ADO-GL, AU, Cristobal Colon, Estrella de Oro, ETN, Greyhound, Linea 1, Plus, and Primera Plus.

Buses depart from four outlying stations (*terminales de autobuses*): Central de Autobuses del Norte, going north; Central de Autobuses del Sur, going south; Central de Autobuses del Oriente, going east; and Terminal de Autobuses del Poniente, going west. Around holidays, you'll need to book your ticket at least a week in advance.

Bus Depots Central de Autobuses del Norte ⊠ Av. Cien Metros 4907, Col. Magdalena de la Salina ☎ 55/5587-1552. **Central de Autobuses del Sur** ⊠ Tasqueña 1320 ☎ 55/5689-9745 or 55/5689-4987. **Terminal de Autobuses del Oriente** ⊠ Ignacio Zaragoza 200, Col. 7 de Julio ☎ 55/5762-5977. **Terminal de Autobuses del Poniente** (also known as "Observatorio") ⊠ Río Tacubaya and Sur 122, Col. Real del Monte ☎ 55/5271-4519. **Bus Lines ETN** ☎ 55/5577-6529, 55/5271-1262, or 55/5277-6529. **Greyhound** ☎ 55/5661-3135; 01800/010-0600 toll-free in Mexico ⊕ www.greyhound.com.mx. **Ticketbus** ☎ 55/5133-2424, 55/5133-2444, or 01800/702-8000 toll-free in Mexico ⊕ www.ticketbus.com.mx.

BUS TRAVEL WITHIN MEXICO CITY

The Mexico City bus system is used by millions of commuters because it's cheap and goes everywhere. Buses are packed during rush hours so, as in all big cities, you should be wary of pickpockets. One of the principal bus routes runs along Paseo de la Reforma, Avenida Juárez, and Calle Madero. This west–east route connects Bosque de Chapultepec with the Zócalo. A southbound bus may be taken along Avenida Insurgentes Sur to San Angel and University City, or northbound along Avenida Insurgentes Norte to the Guadalupe Basílica. Mexico City tourism offices provide free bus-route maps. The price is usually between 2 and 4 pesos (about 40¢), depending on your destination. Make sure you have some small change, at most a 10-peso coin, loose in your pocket. (Avoid showing a wallet on a bus.) Tell the driver your destination when boarding; he'll tell you the fare, which you pay directly. Some bus stops have shelters with the name of the stop written above, but more often you'll spot a stop by the line or cluster of people waiting. Buses run late but it's best to choose safer forms of transport after dark.

CAR TRAVEL

Major arteries into Mexico City include Highway 57 to the north, which starts at Laredo, Texas, and goes through Monterrey and Querétaro. Highway 95 comes in from Cuernavaca to the south, and Highway 190D from Puebla to the east. Highway 15 via Toluca is the main western route.

Millions of intrepid drivers brave Mexico City's streets every day and survive, but for out-of-towners the experience can be frazzling. One-way streets are confusing and rush-hour traffic is nightmarish. Rush hours generally include weekday mornings from 8 to 10 and again from 4:30 to 6:30 PM. Fridays are particularly clogged. You can hire a chauffeur for your car through a hotel concierge or travel service such as American Express.

Also, the strictly enforced law *Hoy No Circula* (Today This Car Can't Circulate) applies to all private vehicles, including your own. One of several successful efforts to reduce smog and traffic congestion, this law prohibits every privately owned vehicle (including out-of-state, foreign, and rental cars) from being used on one designated weekday. All cars in the city without a Verification "0" rating (usually those built before 1994) are prohibited from driving one day a week (two days a week during alert periods, which are usually in December and January). Cars in violation are inevitably impounded by the police. Expect a hefty fine as well.

The weekday you can't drive is specified by the last number or letter of the license plate: on a nonemergency week, 5–6 are prohibited on Monday; 7–8 on Tuesday; 3–4 on Wednesday; 1–2 on Thursday; and 9–0 on Friday. For further information, contact the Mexican Government Tourism Office nearest you, or log on to ⊕ www.mexicocity.com.mx/nocircula.html or the English-language ⊕ www.t1msn.imeca.com.mx/t1msn_valle_de_mexico/vehicula.asp and plan your schedule accordingly.

PARKING It's easiest to park in a staffed lot; these are especially common in the Centro. Street parking places can be hard to find. Police tow trucks haul away illegally parked vehicles, and the owner is heavily fined. Getting your car back is a tedious process. Locatel is an efficient 24-hour service for tracing vehicles that are towed, stolen, or lost (in case you forgot where you parked). There's a chance an operator on duty may speak English, but the service is primarily in Spanish.

🚹 **Locatel** ☎ 55/5658-1111.

EMBASSIES

The U.S. Embassy is open weekdays 9–5, but is closed for American and Mexican holidays; however, there's always a duty officer to take emergency calls on holidays and after closing hours. The embassy keeps a list of English-speaking local doctors on hand if you need to consult one. The Canadian Embassy is open weekdays 9–1 and 2–5 and is closed for Canadian and Mexican holidays. The British Embassy is open weekdays 8:30–3:30.

🚹 **British Embassy** ⊠ Río Lerma 71, Col. Cuauhtémoc ☎ 55/5207-2449 ⊕ www.embajadabritanica.com.mx. **Canadian Embassy** ⊠ Schiller 529, Col. Polanco ☎ 55/5724-7900 ⊕ www.canada.org.mx. **U.S. Embassy** ⊠ Paseo de la Reforma 305, Col. Juárez ☎ 55/5209-9100 ⊕ www.usembassy-mexico.gov.

EMERGENCIES

Dial 060, 065, or 080 for police, Red Cross, ambulance, fire, or other emergency situations. If you are not able to reach an English-speaking operator, call the Sectur hot line. For missing persons or cars call Locatel. You'll find English-speaking staff at both the American British Cowdray Hospital and Hospital Español. The Farmacias del Ahorro chain stays open until 10 PM; there are branches throughout the city.

🚹 Hospitals **American British Cowdray Hospital** ⊠ Calle Sur 136-116, corner of Observatorio, Col. las Américas ☎ 55/5230-8161 for emergencies; 55/5230-8000 switchboard ⊕ www.abchospital.com. **Hospital Español** ⊠ Ejército Nacional 613, Col. Granada ☎ 55/5203-3735 ⊕ www.hespanol.com. **Locatel** ☎ 55/5658-1111 **Sectur** ☎ 55/5212-0260.

ENGLISH-LANGUAGE MEDIA

The best place for English- and foreign-language newspapers and magazines is Casa de la Prensa, which has two locations in the Zona Rosa. Sanborns carries a few U.S. newspapers and an ample supply of magazines, paperbacks, and guidebooks. The American Book Store has an extensive selection of publications. Remember that most U.S. or foreign-published publications are about double the price you'd pay for them at home.

The Benjamin Franklin Library, actually a part of the U.S. Embassy, was instituted to create greater understanding and cultural exchange between the United States and Mexico. The library, open weekdays noon–7, has a substantial collection of English novels, a good reference section, and many U.S. periodicals. You must be at least 20 years old, fill out an application, and have a Mexican resident sign it in order to check out books, but anyone can browse through the stacks.

🚹 **American Book Store** ⊠ Bolivar 23, Col. del Valle ☎ 55/5575-2372 ⊠ Av. Insurgentes Sur 1188, Col. del Valle ☎ 55/5575-2372. **Benjamin Franklin Library** ⊠ Lon-

dres 16, Zona Rosa ☎ 55/5209–9100 Ext. 3482. **Casa de la Prensa** ⊠ Florencia 57, Col.
Juárez ⊠ Hamburgo 141, Zona Rosa ☎ 55/5208–1419.

INTERNET

Many hotels have complimentary e-mail service for guests. There's also
a proliferation of Internet cafés in areas such as the Colonia Condesa,
Coyoacán, and Zona Rosa. Charges can be as little as $3.50 an hour
for access. At Bits Café, you can have a cappuccino and cheesecake, or
a beer and a sandwich, while you catch up on your e-mail. It's open Monday–Saturday 10–11. Open from 8–11 on weekdays, 10–10 on weekends, JavaChat offers free bottomless coffee while you're on the computer.
🖳 Internet Cafés **Bits Café** ⊠ Hamburgo 165-C, at Florencia, 1 block south of the Angel
monument, Col. Juárez ☎ 55/5525–0144. **JavaChat** ⊠ Génova 44-K, next to McDonald's, Zona Rosa ☎ 55/5514–6856 or 55/5525–6853.

MONEY MATTERS

There are banks with 24-hour ATMs all over the city. Bital has the advantage of keeping longer hours than most other banks; for instance,
many of its branches are open on Saturday until 3 PM. Avoid going to
the banks around lunchtime when they're most crowded. The 15th and
of 30th or 1st of each month are also unbearably busy, as these are paydays. Banks generally have armed guards, so do not be alarmed by the
sight of uniforms and weapons. For safety reasons, it's best to use ATMs
in daylight, when other people are nearby.

Currency exchanges often have less favorable rates than the banks.
They're also harder to find, except in the Zona Rosa and the airport.

PESERO TRAVEL

Originally six-passenger sedans, now minibuses, peseros operate on a
number of fixed routes and charge a flat rate (a peso once upon a time,
hence the name). They're a good alternative to buses and taxis, but be
prepared for a jolting ride because many drivers like to turn their buses
into bucking broncos. Likely routes for tourists are along the city's
major west–east axis (Bosque de Chapultepec–Paseo de la
Reforma–Avenida Juárez–Zócalo) and north–south along Avenida Insurgentes, between the Guadalupe Basílica and San Angel–University City.
Peseros pick up passengers at bus stops and outside almost all metro
stations. Just stand on the curb, check the route sign on the oncoming
pesero's windshield, and hold out your hand. Tell the driver where to
stop, or press the button by the back door. If it's really crowded and
you can't reach the back door in time, just bang on the ceiling and yell,
"*Baja*," which means "getting down." Base fares are 2 pesos (about 20¢)
with the price going up to 3.50 pesos (about 35¢) according to how far
you travel. Exact change is appreciated by drivers and will save you a
lot of fuss. Avoid showing your wallet in a pesero; pickpockets have sharp
eyes and there's also the possibility of a hold-up. Peseros are also known
as "combis," "micros," and "rutas."

SIGHTSEEING TOURS

Various travel agencies run tourist-friendly, English-guided tours of
Mexico City and surrounding areas. The basic city tour ($39) lasts
eight hours and takes in the Zócalo, Palacio Nacional, Catedral Metropolitana, and Bosque de Chapultepec. A four-hour pyramid tour costs
around $23 and covers the Basílica de Nuestra Señora de Guadalupe
and the major ruins at Teotihuacán. Except for the Tren Turístico, the
tours described below can be booked through the agents listed in Travel
Agencies; most agencies offer some version of each tour.

BULLRING TOUR There are trips to the bullring on Sunday with a guide who will explain the finer points of this spectacle. This three-hour afternoon tour can usually be combined with the Ballet Folklórico–Xochimilco trip.

CULTURAL TOUR A seven-hour cultural tour is run Sunday morning only and usually includes a performance of the folkloric dances at the Palacio de Bellas Artes, a gondola ride in the canals of Xochimilco's floating gardens, and a visit to the modern campus of the National University.

NIGHTLIFE TOUR Nightlife tours are among the most popular tours of Mexico City. The best are scheduled to last five hours and include transfers by private car rather than bus; dinner at an elegant restaurant (frequently Bellini or at the Del Lago); a drink and a show at the Plaza Garibaldi, where mariachis play; and a nightcap at one of the cantinas around the square, which features Mexican folk dancers.

TROLLEY TOUR The Paseo por Coyoacán tourist trolleybus goes around the Coyoacán neighborhood, with a guide telling the history of the area in Spanish. It leaves from a stop opposite the Museo Nacional de Culturas Populares whenever there are enough people, so departures are not regular. It costs $3.50 and runs weekdays 10–5, weekends 10–6.

A good way to see the historic downtown—if you know some Spanish—is on Tren Turístico's charming replicas of 20-passenger trolleys from the 1920s. The 50-minute narrated tour ($3.50) includes the Zócalo, Colegio de San Ildefonso, Plaza de Santo Domingo, Plaza Manuel Tolsá (location of the Palacio de Minería and Museo Nacional de Arte), Plaza de la Santa Veracruz (Museo Franz Mayer), and the Palacio de Iturbide. Trolleys depart hourly 10–5 daily from the train's offices in front of Alameda Park.

🏢 **Paseo por Coyoacán** ✉ Av. Hidalgo, at Calle Allende Coyoacán ☎ 55/5662–8972. **Tren Turístico's** ✉ Av. Juárez 66, at Revillagigedo, Col. Centro ☎ 55/5512–1013.

SUBWAY TRAVEL

Transporting 5 million passengers daily, the metro, or STC (Collective Transportation System), is one of the world's best, busiest, and cheapest transportation systems—a ride costs 2 pesos (about 20¢). The clean marble-and-onyx stations are brightly lighted, and modern French-designed trains run quietly on rubber tires. Some stations, such as Insurgentes, are shopping centers. Even if you don't take a ride, visit the Zócalo station, which has large models of central Mexico City during three historic periods. Many stations have temporary cultural displays, from archaeological treasures to contemporary art; the Pino Suárez station has a small Aztec pyramid inside, a surprise discovery during construction.

There are 10 intersecting metro lines covering more than 160 km (100 mi). Segments of Lines 1 and 2 cover most points of interest to foreigners, including Zona Rosa, Bellas Artes, and Centro Histórico. At the southern edge of the city, the Tasqueña station (Line 2) connects with the electric train (*tren eléctrico*) that continues south to Xochimilco. To the southeast, the *tren ligero* ("light" train) from the Pantitlán station (Lines 1, 5, and 9) heads east to Chalco in the state of Mexico. The various lines also serve all four bus stations and the airport; however, only light baggage is allowed on board during rush hours. User-friendly, color-coded maps are sometimes available free at metro-station information desks (if there's an attendant) and at Mexico City tourism offices; color-keyed signs and maps are posted all around.

Trains run frequently (about two minutes apart) and are least crowded 10–4 and at night. To reduce incidences of harassment during crowded rush hours, regulations may require men to ride separate cars from women and children. The cars for women and children are marked "exclusivo para mujeres y niños." Hours vary somewhat according to the line, but service is essentially weekdays 5 AM–midnight, Saturday 6 AM–2 AM, Sunday and holidays 6 AM–1 AM.

🔳 STC (metro) ⊕ www.metro.df.gob.mx.

TAXIS

Mexico City taxis come in several colors and sizes. Unmarked, or *turismo*, sedans with hooded meters are usually stationed outside major hotels and in tourist areas; however, they are uneconomical for short trips. Their drivers are almost always English-speaking guides and can be hired for sightseeing on a daily or hourly basis (always negotiate the price in advance). Sitio (stationed) taxis operate out of stands, take radio calls, and are authorized to charge a small premium over the meter rate or will offer a set rate. Among these, Servi-Taxis, Radio-Taxi, and Taxi-Mex, which accepts American Express, offer 24-hour service. Most sitio companies offer hourly rates, some for as little as $10 per hour, for a minimum of two hours. Hiring a sitio for a few hours can be an easy way for you to spend a half day or more seeing sights that may be otherwise time-consuming to reach and/or that are of particular interest to you.

Unauthorized cab drivers (sometimes criminals who have stolen the cabs they drive) pose probably the single greatest danger to tourists in the capital. Although the situation has improved slightly, outsiders are especially vulnerable to their assaults, and many have been robbed or forced to withdraw money from ATMs. This danger is easily avoided; simply **do not hail taxis on the street** under any circumstances. If you need a cab but don't speak the Spanish necessary to call one yourself, your best bet is to have a hotel concierge or waiter call you a sitio. Be sure to establish the fare in advance if the sitio does not work with meter and premium. Otherwise, ask for a registered hotel taxi; even though it may be significantly overpriced, it's better than a street-cab rip-off.

Taxi drivers are authorized to charge 10% more at night, usually after 10. Tips are not expected unless you have luggage—then 10% is sufficient.

🔳 **Radio-Elite** ☎ 55/5660-1122. **Radio-Taxi** ☎ 55/5566-0077. **Servi-Taxis** ☎ 55/5271-2560. **Taxi-Mex** ☎ 55/5519-7690.

TELEPHONE CODES

A regional code for Mexico City—55—precedes eight-digit numbers dialed from within the city. To reach Mexico City from elsewhere in Mexico, dial 01 plus the 10-digit number; from abroad, dial 52 plus the 10-digit number. A Mexico City mobile phone normally begins with 044–55. If you call a Mexico City mobile phone (a *celular*) from outside the city, you merely dial 01–55 before the eight-digit number.

TRAIN TRAVEL

The train system in Mexico is in the process of being privatized and is depressingly moribund given its romantic history. Currently, trains are used almost exclusively for cargo, and there are no longer any passenger services to or from Mexico City that can be recommended to visitors.

TRAVEL AGENCIES

🔳 Local Agent Referrals **American Express** ⊠ Paseo de la Reforma 234, Col. Ciudad de los Deportes ☎ 55/5326-3521 ⊕ www.vacaciones.amex.com. **Grey Line Tours** ⊠ Londres 166, at Florencia Zona Rosa ☎ 55/5208-1163 ⊕ www.greyline.com.mx. **Mexico Travel Advisors (MTA)** ⊠ Génova 30, Col. Juárez ☎ 55/5525-7520 or 55/5525-7534.

VISITOR INFORMATION

The Mexico City Tourist Office (Departamento de Turismo del Distrito Federal, or DDF) maintains information booths at the domestic arrival area at the airport. In town, there are plenty of information booths in heavily trafficked areas such as the Zona Rosa, Chapultepec, the Centro and in the south. In addition to the central branches, there are smaller units without phones posted in Plaza San Jacinto, on Paseo de la on Reforma outside the Museo Nacional de Antropología, by the cathedral in the Centro, and at La Villa de Guadalupe.

The Secretariat of Tourism (Sectur) operates a 24-hour hot line called Infotur from 9 to 7 daily. Its multilingual operators have access to an extensive data bank with information on both Mexico City and the entire country. If lines are busy, keep trying. From outside Mexico City, call the Sectur Tourist Information Center in Colonia Polanco toll-free weekdays 8–8.

For more orientation info, check out the Web site www.mexicocity.com.mx.

🔲 **Infotur** ☎55/5250-0123. **Mexico City Tourist Office** ⊕www.mexicocity.gob.mx ✉Sala A1, Mexico City Airport, in National Arrivals ☎ 55/5786-9002 ✉ Amberes 54, at Londres, Zona Rosa ☎ 55/5525-9380 ✉ Entrada principal, Terminal de Autobuses del Norte, Av. Cien Metros 4907 ☎ 55/5719-1201 ✉ Casa Municipal, Plaza Hidalgo 1, ground floor, Coyoacán ☎ 55/5659-6009 ✉ Nuevo Embarcadero, Nativitas Barrio de Xaltocan, Xochimilco ☎ 55/5653-5209.**Secretariat of Tourism (Federal)** ✉ Av. Presidente Masaryk 172, Col. Polanco ☎ 55/5250-0493; 55/5250-0027; 01800/903-9200 toll-free in Mexico; 800/482-9832 in the U.S. ⊕ www.travelguidemexico.com or www.sectur.gob.mx. **Secretariat of Tourism (DF)** ✉ Av. Nuevo León 56, at Laredo Col. Condesa ☎ 55/5212-0260.

SIDE TRIPS FROM MEXICO CITY

2

FODOR'S CHOICE

Cuetzalan, colonial town southeast of Mexico City

Las Mañanitas, a hotel and restaurant, Cuernavaca

The ruins of Teotihuacán, north of Mexico City

The archaeological site of Tula, north of Mexico City

HIGHLY RECOMMENDED

RESTAURANTS Los Jarritos, Cuetzalan

Villa Rica, Puebla

HOTELS Camino Real, Puebla

Hacienda San Gabriel de las Palmas, Cuernavaca

EXPERIENCES Basilica de Ocotlán, church and pilgrimage site, Tlaxcala

Museo Amparo, a pre-Columbian and colonial art collection, Puebla

San Francisco Acatepec, Baroque church, Cholula

Santa María Tonantzintla, indigenous Baroque church, Cholula

The ruins of Cacaxtla

The ruins of Xochicalco

Updated by
Barbara
Kastelein and
Mark Sullivan

TO ESCAPE THE HUSTLE of Mexico City, simply strike out in any direction. You'll be pleasantly surprised to find that just outside its borders you can find villages and towns where the pace is decidedly slower. Most are graced with colonial-era cathedrals whose facades resemble a pastry chef's wildest fantasy. The city of Puebla, for instance, fairly bursts with Baroque flourishes and the colors of its famed Talavera tiles.

You could follow the example of the *chilangos* (Mexico City residents) and visit one of their favorite weekend getaways, such as balmy Cuernavaca or the lakeside community of Valle de Bravo. Or leave behind the modern world altogether and head to one of the ancient ruins found an hour or so outside the capital. Teotihuacán, to the north, is popular for its pair of pyramids dedicated to the sun and moon, but the ancient city is so vast that you'll have no trouble finding an unexplored corner. Or venture out to the Toltec capital of Tula, where an army of stone warriors stands guard, or east to Cacaxtla, renowned for brilliantly colored murals. Both are world-class archaeological sites that you just might have to yourself.

About the Restaurants

Many of the cities and towns surrounding the capital have delicious local specialties well worth seeking out. *Sopa Tlaxcala,* for example, is a flavorful soup named for the town east of Mexico City. It overflows with black beans, cheese, and tortillas, flavored with *chicharron* (pork fat). In Pachuca you'll find *pastes tradicional,* pastries stuffed with ground beef and potatoes that were favored by Cornish miners who came to work in the nearby silver mines. Puebla is famous for *mole poblano,* a spicy sauce combining the sweetness of chocolate and the heat of chilies.

Restaurants tend not to stay open as late as in the capital. In Amecameca and Cuetzalan, restaurants often close for dinner.

About the Hotels

Many of the interesting spots around Mexico City are less than two hours away, so in most cases a hotel won't be necessary. But for those that are a longer trip—or are simply irresistible—you'll generally have at least a few options to choose from. It could be your chance to stay in a 16th-century hacienda or wake up with a view of a volcano.

WHAT IT COSTS				
	$$$$	$$$	$$	$	¢
RESTAURANTS	over $25	$15–$25	$10–$15	$5–$10	under $5
HOTELS	over $250	$150–$250	$75–$150	$50–$75	under $50

Restaurant prices are for a main course excluding tax and tip. Hotel prices are for two people in a standard double room in high season, based on the European Plan (EP, with no meals) and excluding service and 17% tax.

NORTH OF MEXICO CITY

Little more than an hour north of Mexico City are two of the country's most celebrated ancient cities. The pyramids of Teotihuacán can be enjoyed in a day tour. The ruins of Tula, known for their battalion of basalt warriors, can be combined with a visit to the nearby colonial city of Tepotzotlán.

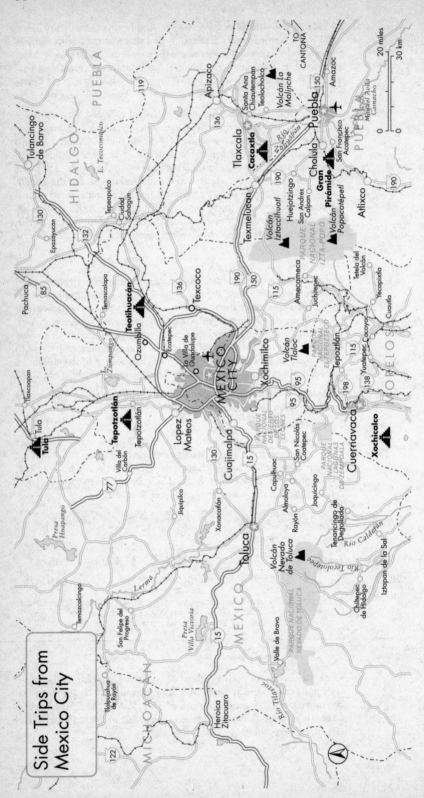

Side Trips from Mexico City

Teotihuacán

🔺 *50 km (31 mi) northeast of Mexico City center.*

There's no doubt about the monumental place Teotihuacán (*teh*-oh-tee-wa-*can*) holds in the region's history. At its height, somewhere around AD 600, it controlled much of central Mexico and traded with distant cities such as Tikal in Guatemala and Copán in Honduras. Archaeologists believe that more than 200,000 people called this sprawling metropolis their home, making it one of the world's biggest cities at the time.

But by AD 725, the city had been all but abandoned. The reason is unclear, but research indicates that it suffered a massive attack during which all the temples were toppled. Some of the destruction appears to have been at the hands of the city's residents, suggesting that there may have been a revolt caused by overcrowding, a drought-prompted famine, or the iron-fisted leadership.

Just who created this great city isn't known—even its original name has been lost. The Aztecs, who settled here centuries later, remembered how wondrous it had once been. They named it Teotihuacán, meaning "place where men became gods."

Most people enter near the **Cuidadela,** a massive citadel ringed by more than a dozen temples. The **Templo de Quetzalcóatl** (Temple of the Plumed Serpent) is the centerpiece. Here you'll find incredibly detailed carvings of the benevolent deity Quetzalcóatl, a serpent with its head ringed by feathers, jutting out of the facade.

One of the most impressive sights in Teotihuacán is the 4-km- (2½-mi-) long **Calzada de los Muertos,** the Avenue of the Dead. The Aztecs gave it this name because they mistook the temples lining either side for tombs. It leads all the way to the 126-ft-high **Pirámide de la Luna** (Pyramid of the Moon) which dominates the northern end of the city. Atop this structure, you can scan the entire city. Some of the most exciting recent discoveries, including a royal tomb, have been unearthed here. In late 2002, a discovery of jade objects gave important new evidence of a link between the Teotihuacán rulers and the Maya.

On the west side of the spacious plaza facing the Pyramid of the Moon is the **Palacio del Quetzalpápalotl** (Palace of the Plumed Butterfly); its beautifully reconstructed terrace has columns etched with images of various winged creatures. Nearby is the **Palacio de los Jaguares** (Palace of the Jaguars), a residence for priests. Spectacular bird and jaguar murals wind through its underground chambers.

The awe-inspiring **Pirámide del Sol** (Pyramid of the Sun) stands in the center of the city. With a base as broad as that of the pyramid of Cheops in Egypt, it is one of the largest pyramids ever built. Its size takes your breath away—often quite literally, during the climb up 242 steps on its west face. Deep within the pyramid archaeologists have discovered a clover-shape cave that they speculate may have been the basis for the city's religion, and perhaps the reason the city was built in the first place.

The best artifacts uncovered at Teotihuacán are on display at the Museo Nacional de Antropología in Mexico City. Still, the **Museo de la Sitio,** adjacent to the Pirámide del Sol, contains a few good pieces, such as the stone sculpture of the saucer-eyed Tlaloc, some black and green obsidian arrowheads, and the skeletons of human sacrifices arranged as they were when discovered.

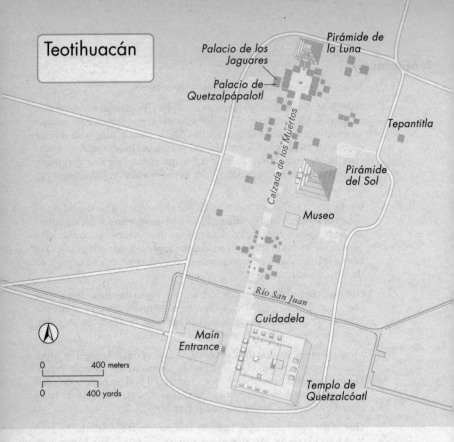

Teotihuacán

Palacio de los Jaguares
Pirámide de la Luna
Palacio de Quetzalpápalotl
Tepantitla
Calzada de los Muertos
Pirámide del Sol
Museo
Río San Juan
Cuidadela
Main Entrance
Templo de Quetzalcóatl

0   400 meters
0   400 yards

More than 4,000 one-story adobe and stone dwellings surround the Calzada de los Muertos; these were occupied by artisans, warriors, and tradesmen. The best example, a short walk east of the Pirámide del Sol, is called **Tepantitla.** Here you'll see murals depicting a watery realm ruled by the rain god Tlaloc. Human figures swim, dance, and even seem to play a game that resembles leapfrog. Restored in 2002, its reds, greens, and yellows are nearly as vivid as when they were painted more than 1,500 years ago.

There are five entrances to Teotihuacán, each near one of the major attractions. If you have a car, it's a good idea to drive from one entrance to another. Seeing the ruins will take several hours, especially if you head to the lesser-known areas. To help you find your way around, a good English-language guidebook is sold at the site. ☎ 594/956–0052 or 594/956–0276 ⊕ archaeology.la.asu.edu/teo ⊠ $3.50 ⊗ Daily 7–6.

Tepotzotlán

35 km (22 mi) north of Mexico City center.

In pre-Hispanic times, Tepotzotlán was an important stop along the trade route between Toluca and Texcoco. Tepotzotlán (pronounced teh-po-tzot-*lan*) is still a frequent stop for travelers headed to Tula and other nearby sights, and it has more than enough to keep you occupied for an afternoon.

In 1580 a group of Jesuit priests arrived in Tepotzotlán, intent on converting the locals. On the main square they built the **Iglesia de San Francisco Javier,** which ranks among the masterpieces of churrigueresque architecture. The unmitigated Baroque facade will catch your eye immediately; inside, handsome gilded altars stretch from floor to ceiling.

Look for the paintings of angels decorating the church—some are dark-skinned, a nod to the indigenous people forced to help in its construction. The Capilla de la Virgen de Loreto glows with gilding and mirrors.

The church is now part of the massive **Museo Nacional del Virreinato.** You're likely to be overwhelmed by the amount of colonial religious art brought here from churches all around the country. Look for the breathtaking 17th-century *Cristo del Arbol* (Christ of the Tree), carved from a single piece of wood. For a break, walk outside to the Claustro de los Naranjos, a lovely patio planted with tiny orange trees. ⊠ *Plaza Hidalgo 99* ☎ *55/5876-0332* ⊕ *www.inah.gob.mx* ☉ *Tues.–Sun. 9–6* ☎ *$2.*

Tepotzotlán is famous for its charming *pastorela,* which has been performed for more than three decades. The drama, which tells of the birth of Jesus Christ, includes a few professionals as well as loads of local extras playing shepherds and other bit parts. It is staged every year December 16–23 at the church.

Where to Eat

$–$$ ✕ **Casa Mago.** Across the square from the Museo Nacional del Virreinato you'll find a row of nearly identical outdoor cafés. This one, with a seemingly endless buffet on the weekends, serves up the best regional fare, such as locally caught trout *a la plancha* (from the grill). The staff will proudly tell you about the time in 1963 that Elizabeth Taylor stopped by for a beer. ⊠ *Plaza Virreynal 34* ☎ *55/5876-0229* ▤ *MC, V.*

Tula

 75 km (47 mi) north of Mexico City center.

Fodor'sChoice ★ The capital of the Toltecs, Tula is one of the most stunning archaeological sites in central Mexico. Much of the great city—known to its inhabitants as Tollán—was ransacked by the Aztecs. What remains, however, makes it worth the trip. From afar you can spot the stone sentinels standing guard atop its magnificent pyramid.

Tula rose to power about the same time as the fall of Teotihuacán. It is bordered on the north and west by carefully reconstructed ball courts. Between the courts sits the **Templo Quemado,** or Burned Palace. Its dozens of ruined columns delineate what was once an important governmental building. Directly to the east is the completely restored **Templo de Tlahuizcalpantecuhtli,** or Temple of the Morning Star. Climb up the uneven steps to reach the cresting row of 15-ft *atlantes,* or warriors. These awe-inspiring figures gaze southward over the main plaza. ☎ *773/732–1183* ⊕ *www.inah.gob.mx* ☎ *$3.50* ☉ *Tues.–Sun. 9–5.*

Pachuca

88 km (55 mi) north of Mexico City.

The mountains that rise above the busy city of Pachuca provide more than a stunning setting; they hold the silver mines that for centuries brought prosperity to the region. You get an idea of the vast amounts of money that once flowed through Pachuca when you see the **Reloj Monumento de Pachuca,** a neoclassical clock tower that dominates the Plaza de la Independencia. Built in 1910 to celebrate the country's centennial, it is an oddly formal flourish in this hardworking city. It now houses the tourist office.

Head up to the second floor of the former Covento de San Francisco to see the town's main draw, the **Museo de la Fotografia.** The small photography museum serves as a national archive for more than a million pictures. Only a fraction are displayed at any time, but they provide a good primer on how photography was used to document the revolution. Look for the lovely depictions of the country's churches by Guillermo Kahlo, a Jewish immigrant who was the father of Frida Kahlo. ⊠ *Calle de Arista* ☎ *771/713–6100* ⊠ *Free* ⊙ *Tues.–Sun. 10–6.*

Where to Eat

¢–$ ✕ **El Antiguo Huasteca.** Having faced the Plaza de la Independencia for more than 50 years, this casual cafeteria has stood the test of time. Waitresses in perfectly pressed pink uniforms serve up heaping portions of the *plato huasteca,* which could include *enchiladas de mole.* Convivial owner Armando Alamilla might just pull up a chair and tell you all about the region's history. The entrance is a bit hard to spot, as it's up some narrow steps. ⊠ *Metamoros 11* ☎ *No phone* ⊟ *No credit cards.*

¢–$ ✕ **Mi Antiguo Café.** A gleaming copper urn anchors this little café, the only place in town to get a good latte. The crepes make it a favorite place for breakfast. Grab a table by the huge glass doors and watch the activity in the main square. ⊠ *Metamoros 115* ☎ *No phone* ⊟ *No credit cards.*

North of Mexico City A to Z

To research prices, get advice from other travelers, and book travel arrangements, visit www.fodors.com.

BUS TRAVEL

To get to Teotihuacán, take one of the Línea Teotihuacán buses that depart every 15 minutes from the Central de Autobuses del Norte in Mexico City. (In the bus station, look for signs marked "piramides"; they don't say Teotihuacán.) The hour-long trip costs about $2.

Autotransportes Valle Mezquital, which also operates out of Central de Autobuses del Norte, runs buses to Tula and Tepotzotlán every 15 to 30 minutes. The ride to Tepotzotlán is just 45 minutes; it takes a couple of hours to get to Tula. Tickets are $2 to $4. Make reservations on line at www.ticketbus.com.mx.

ADO runs daily buses every half hour from Central de Autobuses del Norte to Pachuca. The 45-minute trip costs about $4.

🖪 Bus Companies **ADO** ☎ 55/5133–2424. **Autotransportes Valle Mezquital** ☎ 55/5567–9691. **Línea Teotihuacán** ☎ 55/5777–3573.

CAR TRAVEL

To get to Tepotzotlán from Mexico City, take Highway 57D toward Querétaro, where you'll come to the exit for Tepotzotlán. Tula is about 8 km (5 mi) north of Tepotzotlán on Highway 57D; its exit is clearly marked. To get to Teotihuacán, take Highway 85D.

Pachuca is a straight shot on the Mexico City–Pachuca Highway. Watch out for drunk drivers on the highways surrounding Mexico City, especially around local or national holidays. There's generally heavy traffic on the way back from Tepotzotlán and Tula after 4 PM on Sunday.

In general, the ruins have free parking but the parking areas are a short walk from the sites, so be sure not to leave any valuables in your car. Pachuca has guarded parking lots.

VISITOR INFORMATION

For information on the sights north of the capital, it's best to contact the main Mexico City tourism office.

SOUTH OF MEXICO CITY

Should the often dreary weather in Mexico City get the best of you, head to sunny Cuernavaca, as locals have for centuries. Now a thriving city, the capital of the state of Morelos has a handful of interesting museums and some excellent hotels. Tepoztlán can be visited either as a detour from Cuernavaca or a destination in its own right. The village has a pretty convent, a lively weekend market, and its own little pyramid perched high in the mountains.

Cuernavaca

85 km (53 mi) south of Mexico City center.

The road to Cuernavaca will likely heighten your anticipation—you'll catch your first glimpse of the city's lush surroundings from a mountain highway, through lacy pine branches. Cuernavaca basks in springlike temperatures for most of the year, making it perennially irresistible to Mexico City's elite. Aztec rulers, who called the place Cuauhnáhuac, relaxed in verdant botanical gardens. Cortés built a summer place—really a massive palace—on top of the ruins of the Aztec city he destroyed. Emperor Maximilian retreated here when the pressures of governing a country where he was despised grew too much to bear.

Cuernavaca lost some of its appeal over the years. Public gardens, such as Jardín Borda, only hint at the splendor of centuries past. Today, the best gardens grow behind the walls of private homes. But the city still has much to recommend it, and it makes a perfect base for exploring the region.

The city's most traditional square is **Plaza de Armas,** marked by a handsome, volcanic stone statue of revolutionary hero José María Morelos. On weekdays, the square itself fills with vendors from neighboring villages. On weekends it is crowded with stalls for crafts and silver and gold jewelry. To the north of the square is leafy **Jardín Juárez,** which hosts concerts at its bandstand.

North of the Plaza de Armas you'll find the **Museo Regional Cuauhnáhuac,** from the Aztec word for the valley. The fortresslike building was built in 1522 by Cortés as a stronghold, for the region had not been completely conquered. His palace sits atop the ruins of Aztec buildings, some of which have been partially excavated. There are plenty of stone carvings from the area on display, but the best way to digest all this history is by gazing at the murals Diego Rivera painted on the top floor between 1930 and 1932. They tell how Aztecs were brutally subjugated by the Spanish. ⊠ *Juárez and Hidalgo* ☎ *777/312–8171* ✍ *$3.50* ⊘ *Tues.–Sun. 9–6.*

Cortés ordered the construction of the **Catedral de la Asunción,** and like his palace, the cathedral doubled as a fortress. Cannons mounted above the flying buttresses helped bolster the city's defenses. The facade may give you a sense of foreboding, especially when you catch sight of the skull and crossbones over the door. The interior is much less ominous, though, thanks to the murals uncovered during renovations. The delicate brushwork recalls that of Japanese painted screens. ⊠ *Hidalgo and Av. Morelos* ⊘ *Daily 8 AM–6 PM.*

The lush **Jardín Borda** is one of the most popular sights in Cuernavaca. Designed in the late 18th century for a wealthy family, the Borda Gardens were so famous they attracted royalty. Maximilian and Carlotta visited frequently. Here the emperor dallied with the gardener's wife, called La India Bonita, who was immortalized in a famous portrait. Novelist Malcolm Lowry turned the formal gardens into a sinister symbol in his 1947 novel *Under the Volcano*. A pleasant café sits just inside the gates. ⊠ *Av. Morelos 103, at Hidalgo* ☎ *777/312–9237* ☞ *$1* ⊙ *Tues.–Sun. 10–5:30.*

On a quiet street south of the Plaza de Armas, the **Robert Brady Museum** shows the art and artifacts collected by the artist, antiquarian, and decorator from Fort Dodge, Iowa. Ceramics, antique furniture, sculptures, paintings, and tapestries fill the restored colonial mansion, all beautifully arranged in rooms painted with bright Mexican colors. ⊠ *Calle Netzahuacóyotl 4, between Hidalgo and Abasolo* ☎ *777/318–8554* ⊕ *www.geocities.com/bradymuseum* ☞ *$2* ⊙ *Tues.–Sun. 10–6.*

Where to Stay & Eat

When you need a break, there are plenty of little cafés surrounding the gently sloping Plazuela del Zacate, where Calle Fray Bartolomé de las Casas branches off from Hidalgo. Others face the Plaza de Armas.

$–$$ ✕ **Casa Hidalgo.** The marvelous view of the Palacio de Cortés helped make this restaurant a big hit among the foreigners in town. The menu mixes Mexican and international preparations; you might try *hojaldre de queso de cabra al tamarindo* (goat cheese pastry with tamarind sauce), followed by the *filetón hidalgo* (breaded veal stuffed with serrano ham and manchego cheese). Keep your eye out for the lively saxophonist in the jazz band that plays Thursday through Saturday night. ⊠ *Hidalgo 6, Col. Centro* ☎ *777/312–9605* ☐ *AE, DC, MC, V.*

¢–$$ ✕ **El Gallinero.** With a name meaning the Chicken Coop, it's no surprise this local favorite serves *pollo* done to perfection. Start with bananasteamed lamb or the fresh greens tossed with asparagus, pumpkin seeds, and goat cheese. Portions are not large, so you may have room for the flambéed wonders on the dessert menu. ⊠ *Francisco Leyva 94, Col. Centro* ☎ *777/312–7425* ☐ *AE, MC, V* ⊙ *Closed Mon. No dinner Sun.*

¢–$ ✕ **La Strada.** You can't go wrong with this old-time charmer, on a quiet street beside the Museo Regional Cuauhnáhuac. Choose from a range of specially prepared pastas after settling in on the candlelit terrace. A guitarist plays Wednesday and Friday nights. ⊠ *Salazar 38, around the corner from Palacio de Cortés* ☎ *777/318–6085* ☐ *AE, MC, V.*

$$–$$$$ ✕⌂ **Las Mañanitas.** An American expat opened this praised hotel in the Fodor'sChoice 1950s, outfitting the rooms with traditional fireplaces, hand-carved ★ bedsteads, hand-painted tiles in the bathrooms, and gilded crafts. The president and European princes stay here, and chilangos drive an hour on weekends just to dine at the restaurant ($–$$$), with its spectacular open-air terraces and garden inhabited by flamingos, peacocks, and African cranes. The *sopa de tortilla* is a classic, and don't miss the black-bottom (chocolate) pie. ⊠ *Ricardo Linares 107, 62000* ☎ *77/ 7314–1466; 01800/221–5299 toll-free in Mexico; 888/413–9199 in the U.S.* ☐ *77/7318–3672* ⊕ *www.lasmananitas.com.mx* ☞ *1 room, 21 suites* ♢ *Restaurant, room service, pool, bar; no room TVs* ☐ *AE.*

$$$ ⌂ **Camino Real Sumiya.** Woolworth heiress Barbara Hutton built this romantic hideaway amid formal Japanese gardens. The setting's theme carries into the main building, which includes an original Kabuki theater brought over from Kyoto. The rooms are set in the far part of the garden for privacy. ⊠ *Col. José Parres, Juitepec, 62550 Morelos, take Civac exit on Acapulco Hwy., about 15 mins south of town at Interior del Fracc. Sumiya* ☎ *777/329–9888* ☐ *77/7320–9142* ⊕ *www. caminoreal.com/sumiya* ☞ *157 rooms, 6 suites* ♢ *2 restaurants, 7 tennis courts, 2 pools, bar, concierge* ☐ *AE, DC, MC, V.*

★ **$$$** ⬚ **Hacienda San Gabriel de las Palmas.** A colorful history pervades the thick walls of this grand hacienda built under the orders of Cortés in 1529; many historic figures came here, from Zapata to de Iturbide. Now it's a haven of quiet, with birdcalls, the splashing of the waterfall, and the ringing of the chapel bell in the background. If you'd like to get even more blissed-out, visit the spa, which includes a temazcal. Antiques fill both the public areas and the guest rooms. Most rooms have a spacious private balcony and some have a private terrace as well. The hacienda's position outside Cuernavaca makes it easy to get to Taxco and other nearby sights. ⊠ *Carretera Federal Cuernavaca–Chilpancingo, Km 41.8, Amacuzac, 62642* ☎ *777/348–0636 in Cuernavaca; 55/5616–6032 in Mexico City; 01800/347–2642 toll-free in Mexico* 🖶 *55/5550–0657 in Mexico City* ⊕ *www.hacienda-sangabriel.com.mx* 🛏 *15 suites* ⟆ *Restaurant, tennis court, pool, spa, billiards, croquet, horseback riding, bar, meeting rooms* ▤ *AE, MC, V.*

$$ ⬚ **Hacienda de Cortés.** This 16th-century former sugar mill once belonged to the famed conquistador. Wandering around the gardens and discovering cascades, fountains, and sculptures is an enchanting experience, especially at dusk. Rooms are done with traditional Mexican furnishings and have lovely patios and gardens. Concerts of classical music are often held on weekends. ⊠ *Plaza Kennedy 90, Col. Atlacomulco, 62250* ☎ *77/7315–8844* 🖶 *77/7315–0035* 🛏 *22 rooms* ⟆ *Restaurant, pool, bar* ▤ *MC, V.*

Xochicalco

⛰ *23 km (14 mi) south of Cuernavaca.*

★ A trip to the wonderfully restored ruins of Xochicalco is one of the best reasons to visit Morelos state. Built by the Olmeca-Xicalanca people, the mighty hilltop city reached its peak between AD 700 and 900. It was abandoned a century later after being destroyed, perhaps by its own inhabitants.

With its several layers of fortifications, the city appears unassailable. The most eye-catching edifice is the **Pyrámide de Quetzalcóatl** (Temple of the Plumed Serpent). Carvings of vicious-looking snakes—all in the style typical of the Mayas to the south—wrap around the lower level, while figures in elaborate headdresses sit above. Be sure to seek out the **Observatorio** in a man-made cave reached through a tunnel on the northern side of the city. Through a narrow shaft in the ceiling the Xochicalco astronomers could observe the heavens. Twice a year—May 14 and 15 and July 28 and 29—the sun passes directly over the opening, filling the room with light.

There are dozens of other structures here, including three impressive ball courts. The site's solar-powered museum has six rooms of artifacts, including beautiful sculptures of Xochicalco deities found nearby. ⊠ *Hwy. 95D, southwest of Cuernavaca* ☎ *777/312–5955* 🎟 *$3.50* ⊙ *Tues.–Sun. 10–5.*

Tepoztlán

75 km (47 mi) south of Mexico City center.

Surrounded by sandstone monoliths that throw off a russet glow at sunset, Tepoztlán is a magical place. No wonder it attracts practitioners of astrology, meditation, yoga, and other New Age pursuits. But Tepoztlán keeps an eye on its traditions, so you'll still find barefoot women selling homegrown produce in the lively weekend market surrounding the main square.

CloseUp

TRADITIONAL MEDICINE MAKES A COMEBACK

HERBAL MEDICINE REMAINS an integral part of Mexican life, and still predominates in remote areas where modern medicines are hard to come by or too expensive for rural laborers. Even in the capital, most markets will have distinctive stalls piled with curative herbs and plants. Vendors will happily tell you how to prepare teas, poultices, and steam baths for inhalation.

The Aztecs were excellent botanists, and their extensive knowledge impressed the Spanish, who borrowed from Mexico's indigenous herbolarium and cataloged the intriguing new plants. Consequently, medicine remains one of the few examples of cultural practices and indigenous wisdom that has not been lost to history. Visitors to the capital can find a very informative display of medicinal plants used by the Aztecs in the Museum of Medicine, in the former Palace of the Inquisition, at the northwest corner of Plaza Santo Domingo.

A rich variety of herbs is harvested in the 300 rural communities of the fertile state of Morelos, where curanderos (natural healers) flock to the markets on weekends to offer advice and sell their concoctions. Armed with their wares and a good patter, they line the busier roads, and sometimes get a chance to hawk on buses. Stores in the state capital, Cuernavaca, sell natural antidotes for every ailment imaginable and potions for sexual prowess, lightening the skin, colic in babies, and IQ enhancement.

Chamanes (shamans) and healers abound at the weekend market in the main square of the picturesque mountain village of Tepoztlán. Long known for its brujos (witches), Tepoztlán continues to experience a boom in spiritual retreats and New Age shops. Visitors can benefit from the healing overload without getting hoodwinked by booking a session in one of the many good temazcales (Aztec sweat lodges) in town, such as the one in the elegant Posada del Tepozteco hotel on Calle del Paraíso, or at an excellent retreat, Hostal de la Luz on the road to Amatlán.

The temazcal is a "bath of cleansing" for body, mind, and spirit; a session consists of a ritual that lasts at least an hour, ideally (for first-timers) with a guide. Temazcales are igloo-shape clay buildings, round so as not to impede the flow of energy. They usually seat 6 to 12 people, who can participate either naked or in a bathing suit. Each guide develops his own style, under the tutelage of a shaman, so practices vary. In general, your aura (or energy field) is cleaned with a bunch of plants before you enter the temazcal, so that you start off as pure as possible. You will have a fistful of the same plants—usually rosemary, sweet basil, or eucalyptus—to slap or rub against your skin. You walk in a clockwise direction and take your place, and water is poured over red-hot stones in the middle to create the steam. Usually silence is maintained, although the guide may chant or pray, often in Nahuatl. The procedure ends with a warm shower followed by a cold one to close the pores.

The experience helps eliminate toxins, cure inflammations, ease pains in the joints, and relieve stress. Consequently, temazcales are growing in popularity, even drawing city executives from the capital on the weekends. You can find some of the most outstanding temazcales in Morelos's top spas, such as the Misión del Sol in Jiutepec and Hostería las Quintas in Cuernavaca. Less pricey are El Centro Mayahuel in Ahuacatitlán, or the temazcales of Teresa Contreras or Dr. Horacio Rojas in Cuernavaca. You could also try La Casa de los Arboles in Zacualpan de Amilpas.

— Barbara Kastelein

The town is famous for its tiny **Pirámide de Tepozteco.** Perched on a mountaintop, this temple dedicated to the Aztec diety Tepoztécatl attracts hikers not afraid of the somewhat arduous climb. The view over the valley is terrific. ⊠ *North end of Av. Tepoztlán* ☉ *Tues.–Sun. 9:30–5:30* 🎫 *$3.50.*

Rising above most of Tepoztlán's buildings is the buttressed **Ex-Convento Dominico de la Natividad.** The former convent, dating from 1559, has a facade adorned with icons dating from before the introduction of Christianity. Every year on September 8 the faithful assemble here to celebrate the town's patron saint. The evening before they climb the mountain for a rowdy celebration. ⊠ *Av. Revolución 1910* ☉ *Tues.–Sun. 10–5.*

Where to Stay & Eat

¢–$ ✕ **Los Colorines.** Hung with cheery red, white, and green *papeles picados* (paper cutouts), this family-friendly restaurant serves great bean soups, stuffed chilies, and grilled meats made in an attractive open kitchen. Special dishes include *huauzontles* (a fine, broccoli-like vegetable you scrape from the stalk with your teeth) and *sopa de colorín,* a soup made from the red blossom of the flower that gives the cheerful family restaurant its name. ⊠ *Av. del Tepozteco 13* ☎ *739/395–0198* ⊟ *No credit cards* ☉ *No dinner Sun.*

¢–$ ✕ **La Luna Mextli.** Across the road from the former convent, you can relax on the patio here with coffee and a newspaper. Fearsome masks and flying mermaids decorate the space, and local women patting tortillas leave no doubt that the food is fresh. ⊠ *Av. Revolución 16* ☎ *739/395– 1114* ⊟ *AE, MC, V* ☉ *No breakfast weekdays.*

¢ ✕ **Café Amor.** This second-story café overlooking the main street is a great place to stop for a cup of inky black coffee and a cheese or ham *torta* (sandwich). Nab one of the tiny tables on the balconies to watch the passing parade—quite literally when there's a festival in town. ⊠ *Av. del Tepozteco* ☎ *No phone* ⊟ *No credit cards* ☉ *No dinner.*

$$$ ▥ **Hostal de la Luz.** A new experiment in holistic tourism is making waves at the foot of the Quetzalcóatl mountains in the village of Amatlán.The whole complex is designed to blend with the environment and soothe its guests, from the traditional adobe to the use of feng shui. In addition to a temazcal, there's an ashram room and a bubbling flotation pool. The guest rooms have wicker meditation chairs set in bay window alcoves, the better to absorb the unparalleled views. All-inclusive weekend packages include concerts, workshops, and yoga. The resort is roughly a 15-minute drive from Tepoztlán. ⊠ *Carretera Tepoztlán-Amatlán, Km 4, Amatlán de Quetzalcóatl, 62520* ☎ *739/395–3374* 🖷 *739/395–0323* ⊕ *www.hostaldelaluz.com* 🛏 *13 rooms* ᓚ *Restaurant, pool, spa, meeting rooms* ⊟ *AE, MC, V* ⦿ *BP.*

$$ ▥ **Posada del Tepozteco.** Enjoy splendid views of both the village and the pyramid as you stroll through the bursts of purple and red bougainvillea in this hotel's terraced gardens. A honeymooner favorite, the inn is also a good place for children, with its trampoline, swings, and pair of pet rabbits. Most rooms have balconies and hot tubs. Make reservations for weekend stays two weeks in advance. ⊠ *Calle del Paraíso 3, 62520* ☎ *739/395–0010* 🖷 *739/395–0323* 🛏 *19 rooms* ᓚ *Restaurant, room service, tennis court, 2 pools, massage, steam room, bar, playground; no room TVs* ⊟ *AE, MC, V.*

¢ ▥ **Posada Ali.** With unobstructed views of the mountains from the rooms, this family-run inn draws many repeat customers. No two rooms are exactly alike, but all have charming hand-hewn furniture. There's a tiny pool in back. ⊠ *Natzahualcóyotl 2, 62520* ☎ *739/395–1971* 🛏 *8 rooms* ᓚ *Dining room, pool* ⊟ *MC, V.*

Cuautla

128 km (77 mi) south of Mexico City, 47 km (28 mi) east of Cuernavaca.

Cuautla's claim to fame is as the birthplace of Emiliano Zapata, one of the heroes of the Mexican Revolution, who rallied his troops with the phrase "Tierra y Libertad" (Land and Liberty). A statue of the moustachioed man stands in shady Plazuela de la Revolución del Sur.

On the south side of the main square you'll find the **Casa de Morelos** (⊠ Callejón del Castigo 3 ☎ 735/352–8331), a colonial-era home once occupied by José Maria Morelos, a priest who fought for the country's independence from Spain. Inside, relics tell the history of the region. It's open Tuesday–Sunday 10–5; admission costs $2.50. Three blocks off the main plaza is the **Museo José Maria Morelos y Pavón** (⊠ Galeana and Bollás sin Cabeza ☎ 735/353–9655), in what was once the town's train station. Here you'll find a hodgepodge of uniforms, flags, and other artifacts from the battle for independence. The most interesting item on display is a 1904 steam engine once ridden by Zapata. It's kept in working order, and on weekends at 5 PM you can take a ride in the pair of antique wooden carriages that trail behind. The museum is open Tuesday–Sunday 10–5; admission is 50¢.

One of the region's oldest archaeological sites, **Chalcatzingo** was abandoned in 500 BC, centuries before cities like Teotihuacán and Tula were founded. Built by the Olmecs, the site is best known for its unusual rock carvings. Here you can spot a depiction of a female ruler with an elaborate headdress seated in the mouth of a menacing-looking cave. ⊠ *20 km (12 mi) east of Cuautla on Hwy. 160* ☎ *No phone* 🖃 *$2* ⊙ *Tues.–Wed. 10–5, Thurs.–Sun. 9–6.*

Where to Eat

¢–$ ✕ **Las Golondrinas.** On an unpromising street north of the main square, this courtyard restaurant in a colonial-era mansion is a pleasant surprise. Caged songbirds trill while the bow-tied waiters fill you in on the local specialties. Don't pass up the *sopa de calabaza flor* (squash flower soup) or the *arrachara norteña* (grilled steak). ⊠ *Nicolás Catalán 19* ☎ *735/ 354–1350* 🖃 *MC, V.*

South of Mexico City A to Z

To research prices, get advice from other travelers, and book travel arrangements, visit www.fodors.com.

BUS TRAVEL

Buses run daily every 10 minutes to Cuernavaca and every 15 minutes to Tepoztlán and Cuautla from Mexico City's Central de Autobuses del Sur, at the Taxqueña Metro station. It takes about an hour and a half to reach Cuernavaca, and two hours to get to Tepoztlán and Cuautla. The most reliable company is Grupo Pullman de Morelos, which has the most frequent service.

🚍 Bus Company **Grupo Pullman de Morelos** ☎ 55/5549-3505 in Mexico City; 777/ 318-4638 in Cuernavaca

CAR TRAVEL

To head toward Cuernavaca from the capital, take Periférico Sur and turn south on Viaducto Tlalpán. The *cuota* (toll road, Route 95D) costs about $10 but only takes about 1½ hours. The *carretera libre* (free road, Route 95) takes much longer.

Tepoztlán is 26 km (16 mi) east of Cuernavaca via Route 95D. Cuautla is about 30 km (18 mi) south of Tepoztlán on the same road.

It's easy to find street parking in these towns.

VISITOR INFORMATION

The Cuernavaca Tourist Office is a few blocks north of the Jardín Borda; it's open weekdays 9 to 3 and 5:30 to 7. There are information kiosks in most of Cuernavaca's bus stations, but they open late in the day. The extremely helpful Cuautla Tourism Office is near the entrance of the Museo José Maria Morelos y Pavón. It's open daily 9 to 8.

🖪 **Cuernavaca Tourist Office** ⊠ Av. Morelos 278, Col. Centro ☎ 777/318-7561. **Cuautla Tourism Office** ⊠ Galeana and Bollás sin Cabeza ☎ 735/352-5221.

SOUTHEAST OF MEXICO CITY

As you travel east of Mexico City, size up Popocatépetl (poh-poh-kah-*teh*-pettle) and Iztaccíhuatl (ees-tah-*see*-wattle), the twin volcanoes that tower over the valley. The main magnet in this direction is Puebla, a well-preserved colonial town that is capital of the state of the same name. It's the source of some of Mexico's proudest culinary signatures. You could be drawn onwards by nearby Cholula, with its dozens of churches, or Tlaxcala, with a pair of shady plazas perfect for spending a lazy afternoon. Farther north in Puebla state you'll find the mountain town of Cuetzalan, with its wonderful Sunday market. No matter where you end up, the ruins of an ancient city are likely to be quite close.

The Volcanoes & Amecameca

Leaving Mexico City on Route 150D (known as the Carretera to Puebla or the Puebla Highway), you'll see Mexico's second- and third-highest peaks, **Popocatépetl** and **Iztaccíhuatl,** to your right—if the clouds and climate allow. "Popo," 17,887 ft high, is the pointed volcano farther away, sometimes graced with a plume of smoke; "Izta" is the larger, rugged one covered with snow. Popo saw a renewed period of activity since the mid-1990s, which seemed to be coming to an end at the beginning of 2003.

As legend has it, the Aztec warrior Popocatépetl was sent by the emperor—father of his beloved Iztaccíhuatl—to bring back the head of a feared enemy in order to win Iztaccíhuatl's hand. He returned triumphantly only to find that Iztaccíhuatl had killed herself, believing him dead. The grief-stricken Popo laid out her body on a small knoll and lit an eternal torch that he watches over, kneeling. Each of Iztaccíhuatl's four peaks is named for a different part of her body, and its silhouette conjures up its nickname, "Sleeping Woman."

Popo is strictly off-limits for climbing but Izta can be explored—as long as you are accompanied by recommended guides and are fully equipped—along several of its rugged peaks. You'll be rewarded with sublime views of Popo and other volcanoes, with the Pico de Orizaba (or Citlaltepetl) to the east and the Nevada de Toluca to the west. The **Parque Nacional Iztaccíhuatl–Popocatépetl,** or Parque Nacional Izta-Popo for short, has been setting up new paths and picnic areas in its pine forests.

The town of **Amecameca** is the most convenient base for mountaineers and hikers. Its tourism infrastructure is no-frills but adequate, and the offices of the national park and CONANP (the national commission for protected areas) are both here.

What to See

☺ **La Hacienda de Panoaya,** also known as Parque de los Venados Acariciables (pettable deer), has plenty of animals for curious kids, with ostriches, emus, and llamas as well as deer. But the menagerie is only part of the game; there are also two museums. The **Museo Internacional de los Volcanes** has some interesting information on volcanoes, but it's primarily a big thrill for kids, who love to scream at the recorded sound of an eruption. Meanwhile, the **Museo Sor Juana Inés de la Cruz** honors its namesake, a nun, scholar, and author who learned to read here and went on to produce some of the most significant poetry and prose of the 17th century. De la Cruz's intellectual appetite and accomplishments were truly exceptional in her time, the more so because of her fervent defense of women's right to greater freedoms, particularly the freedom to study. The restaurant on the grounds is quite good, with vegetarian choices alongside the (surprise) venison dishes. The hacienda is a 15-minute walk out of town along the boulevard Iztaccíhuatl. ☒ *Carretera México-Cuautla, Km 58 Amecameca* ☏ *597/978–2670 or 597/978–2813* 🖅 *$2; $2 for animal park* ☉ *Zoo daily 9–5; museums weekends 9–5.*

A cobbled road lined with olive trees and cedars leads to the hilltop **Santuario del Sacromonte,** a church and active seminary known for the *Cristo de Sacromonte*. The black Christ figure, made of sugarcane, is said to date to 1527; it's kept in a cavelike space behind the altar. On clear days, this perch is one of the best spots for breathtaking views over Amecameca towards the volcanoes. Take a bumpy track even higher up to reach the little Guadalupita chapel. ☒ *Cerro del Sacromonte* ☏ *No phone* ☉ *Daily 9–5.*

Puebla

120 km (75 mi) east of Mexico City center.

Puebla, the fourth-largest city in Mexico, overflows with religious structures; it probably has more ex-convents and monasteries, chapels, and churches per square mile than anywhere else in the country. In fact, the valley of Puebla, which includes Cholula, was said to have 224 churches and 10 convents and monasteries in its heyday in the 17th century. The city retains a strong conservative religious element.

Spain chose the town's location with strategy in mind: it was near major indigenous cities and it was crossed by two major trade routes. The battle of May 5, 1862—resulting in a short-lived victory against French invaders—took place north of town. On Cinco de Mayo, the national holiday, the celebrations include a spectacular procession, and throughout May, bullfights are held in the city's intimate bullring.

Though much of Puebla was destroyed by a French siege in 1863, it was quickly rebuilt and its colonial architecture remains particularly splendid, winning the city's status as a United Nations Patrimony of Humanities site. The idiosyncratic Baroque structures, built with red bricks, gray stone, and white stucco, are decorated with the famously beautiful Talavera tiles produced from local clay. With a population approaching 2 million, it remains a prosperous town, with textiles, ceramics, and a Volkswagen plant bolstering the local economy.

The city center generally follows a tidy grid pattern. The streets are either avenidas or calles, and most are numbered. Avenidas run east (*oriente*) and west (*poniente*), while calles run north (*norte*) and south (*sur*). Odd-numbered avenidas start south of the *zócalo* (town square) and even-numbered avenidas start from the square's north side. Odd-numbered calles begin on the west of the zócalo, even-numbered calles to the east.

A Good Walk

Practically every street in Puebla's historic center has something interesting to see—just remember to look up, as that's where you'll see the outstanding gargoyles and mortar- and tile-work. Start with the pre-Columbian and colonial art at the excellent **Museo Amparo** ⑩ ▶. (The modern works of the **Museo-Taller Erasto Cortés** ⑪ are just around the corner.) Make a right on leaving the Museo Amparo and walk up to Avenida 5 Poniente; hang a left and walk to the end of the next block to look in at the **Catedral** ⑧. Take a stroll around the square, then head up Avenida 5 de Mayo a couple of blocks to the **Iglesia de Santo Domingo** ⑤ to admire its opulently gilded chapel.

Hop in a cab to the intersection of Avenida 4 Poniente and Calle 11 Norte to catch a tour of **Uriarte Talavera** ②. (If you've got a passion for steam engines, detour from here a few blocks up Calle 11 Norte to the park to the **Museo Nacional de los Ferrocarriles** ①.) If Talavera pottery isn't your cup of tea, walk one block west from Santo Domingo on Avenida 4 Oriente, turn right, and go a few blocks north on Calle 3 Norte to the wonderful **Centro Cultural Santa Rosa** ③; don't forget to see the kitchen where Puebla's mole sauce was invented. From the cultural center, turn east on Avenida 14 Poniente and make a left on Avenida 5 de Mayo—passing yet another fantastically decorated chapel, on the left side of the street—to reach the mysterious and lurid **Ex-Convento Secreto de Santa Mónica** ④. After this it's high time for lunch; jump in a cab to the busy Villa Rica seafood restaurant on Calle 14 Sur.

After lunch, devote the afternoon to shopping, strolling, and slipping into any chapels or churches that catch your eye. Start at **La Calle de las Dulces** ⑥ where you can pick up specially shaped candies for souvenirs as well as some cookies for a snack. Then head east along Avenida 6 Oriente to the **Barrio del Artista** ⑦ to spy on the painters. Less than two blocks south you will come to the **Mercado de Artesanías El Parián** ⑨, a real feast for shoppers. If you're not too loaded down with purchases yet, walk three blocks farther south to the **Callejón de los Sapos** ⑫, for more shopping and cold drink in a café.

TIMING The length of this walk depends on how much time you spend exploring the streets and shops and peeking into the smaller churches, of which there are far too many to list. Before starting out, call the Uriarte Talavera to find out what times their tours are given; they're only held three times a day on weekdays, so if you'd like to take one, plan accordingly. The art and crafts collections in the Museo Amparo, Centro Cultural Santa Rosa could each soak up at least an hour and a half. Note that most museums are closed Monday, but the Museo Amparo is closed Tuesday.

Some of the blocks are very long so if you get tired or need to save time, hail a taxi. They're safe and should cost no more than $4 for a ride in the city center—just remember to fix the price before you set off. It can get quite warm around midday, so bring some water and sunblock.

What to See

⑦ **Barrio del Artista.** You can watch painters and sculptors working in the galleries here daily; weekends are the busiest time. You may also purchase pieces, or continue walking down Calle 8 Norte and buy Talavera pottery, cheaper copies of Talavera, and other local crafts and souvenirs from the dozens of small stores and street vendors along the way. ⊠ *Calle 8 Norte and Av. 6 Oriente* ☉ *Daily 10–6.*

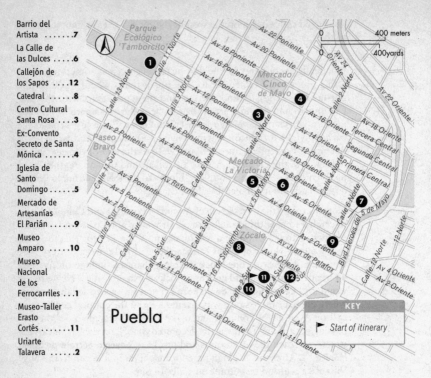

Puebla

6 La Calle de las Dulces. Puebla is famous for *camote,* a candy made from sweet potatoes and fruit. Sweets Street, also known as Calle de Santa Clara, is lined with shops competing to sell a wide variety of freshly made camote and many other sugary treats in the shape of sombreros, guitars, sacred hearts, and pistols. Packed in pretty baskets, these make good presents. Don't fail to try the cookies—they're even more delicious than they look. ⊠ *Av. 6 Oriente between Av. 5 de Mayo and Calle 4 Norte* ⊙ *Daily 9–8.*

12 Callejón de los Sapos. Toad Alley cuts diagonally behind the cathedral, and the attached square, Plazuela de los Sapos, is the up-and-coming antiques market and café area for the trendy. It brims with bright young things on Sunday and is a good place to hang out for a beer and live music on Friday and Saturday nights. ⊠ *Av. 5 Oriente and Calle 6 Sur* ⊙ *Daily 10–7.*

8 Catedral. The cathedral was partially financed by Puebla's most famous son, Bishop Juan de Palafox y Mendoza, who donated his personal fortune to build its famous tower, the second-largest church tower in the country. Palafox was the illegitimate son of a Spanish nobleman who grew up poor but inherited his father's wealth. Onyx, marble, and gold adorn the cathedral's high altar, designed by Mexico's most illustrious colonial architect, Manuel Tolsá. ⊠ *Calle 2 Sur, south of the zócalo* ⊙ *Daily 10–6.*

3 Centro Cultural Santa Rosa. The colonial former convent houses a museum of crafts from the state's seven regions; wandering through the well-designed rooms will give you a good introduction to traditional Mexican arts. The museum also contains the intricately tiled kitchen where Puebla's renowned chocolate mole sauce is believed to have been invented by the nuns, as a surprise for their demanding gourmet bishop. ⊠ *Av.*

14 Poniente between Calles 3 and 5 Norte ☎ *222/232–9242 or 222/ 232–7792* 🎟 *$1* ⊙ *Tues.–Sun. 10–5.*

❹ **Ex-Convento Secreto de Santa Mónica.** Quirky and large, the ex-convent originally opened in 1688 as a spiritual refuge for women whose husbands were away on business. Despite the Reform Laws of the 1850s, it functioned as a convent until 1934, requiring that the nuns withdraw completely from the outside world. You can see the peepholes through which the nuns watched mass in the church next door and tour the crypt where they are buried. Curiosities include the gruesome display of the preserved heart of the convent's founder, and the velvet paintings in the *Sala de los Terciopelos* in which the feet and faces seem to change position as you view them from different angles. ✉ *Av. 18 Poniente 103, near Av. 5 de Mayo* ☎ *222/232–0178* 🎟 *$2* ⊙ *Tues.–Sun. 9–6.*

❺ **Iglesia de Santo Domingo** (Santo Domingo Church). The beautiful church is especially famous for its overwhelming **Capilla del Rosario,** where almost every inch of the walls, ceilings, and altar is covered with gilded carvings and sculpture. Dominican friars arrived in Puebla as early as 1534, only 13 years after the conquest, and the chapel of La Tercera Orden (The Third Order) was originally called "the chapel of the dark-skinned," so designated for the mixed-race population that shortly ensued. ✉ *Av. 5 de Mayo at Av. 4 Poniente* ⊙ *Daily 10–6.*

❾ **Mercado de Artesanías El Parián.** Browse among these stalls and shops for regional craftwork, such as onyx, Talavera, silverware, basketwork, clothing, papier-mâché figurines, candles, and sweets. The market is also a good place to get a bite to eat. ✉ *Av. 4 Oriente and Calle 6 Norte* ⊙ *Daily 10–7:30.*

★ ▶ ❿ **Museo Amparo.** Home to the private collection of pre-Columbian and colonial art of Mexican banker and philanthropist Manuel Espinoza Yglesias, the museum was a pioneer in interactive information systems. Accessible (in four different languages) and modern, it exhibits unforgettable pieces from diverse regions of the country. Displays are organized clearly and artfully, with evocative videos and ancient poems. Temporary exhibitions often showcase current international work, as well as the museum's own collection of contemporary and modern pieces. The museum also functions as a cultural center and library, hosting events and conferences. One of the most beautiful museums in Mexico, it does full justice to its philosophy that art is a "language through which humanity has endeavored to represent and understand the world." ✉ *Calle 2 Sur at Av. 9 Oriente* ☎ *222/246–4646* ⊕ *www.museoamparo.com* 🎟 *$2.50, free Mon.* ⊙ *Wed.–Mon. 10–6.*

❶ **Museo Nacional de los Ferrocarriles.** Fittingly occupying the shell of a 19th-century train station, the national railway museum offers a nostalgic treat. Period engines sit on the disused platforms. ✉ *Calle 11 Norte at Av. 12 Poniente* ☎ *222/232–4988* 🎟 *Free* ⊙ *Tues.–Sun. 10–5.*

⑪ **Museo-Taller Erasto Cortés.** Erasto Cortés Juárez was Puebla's most important 20th-century artist. This museum of modern art opened its doors in 2000 as a real contribution to the Mexican scene: temporary exhibitions showcase up-and-coming international artists, and the permanent display of Cortés' vibrant engravings and bold portraits is a pleasure. ✉ *Av. 5 Oriente at Calle 4 Sur* ☎ *222/232–1277 or 222/232–4647* 🎟 *Free; temporary exhibitions $1.20* ⊙ *Tues.–Sun. 10–5.*

❷ **Uriarte Talavera.** This pottery factory was founded in 1824 and is one of the few authentic Talavera workshops left today. To be authentic, the pieces must be hand-painted in intricate designs with natural dyes derived from minerals, which is why only five colors are used: blue, black, yellow, green, and a reddish pink. There's a shop on-site, and free tours in English of the factory are given weekdays at 11, noon, and 1. If you miss the tour, you can only see the shop and the patio. ⊠ *Av. 4 Poniente 911, at Calle 11 Norte* ☎ *222/232–1598* ⊕ *www.uriartetalavera.com* ⊙ *Weekdays 9–6:30, Sat. 10–6:30, Sun. 11–6.*

Where to Stay & Eat

Puebla is noted for its regional cuisine. Two of Mexico's most popular dishes were supposedly created here to celebrate special occasions—and in both cases, nuns get the credit. One specialty is mole, a sauce made with as many as 100 ingredients, the best-known mole being one with bitter chocolate. The other local specialty is *chiles en nogada,* green poblano chilies filled with ground meats, fruits, and nuts, then covered with a sauce of chopped walnuts and cream, and topped with red pomegranate seeds; the colors represent the red, green, and white of the Mexican flag.

For after-dinner drinks, head to Avenida Juárez. Mariachis keep the songs coming at **La Cantina de los Remedios** (Av. Juárez 2504, Col. la Paz, ☎222/ 249–0843).

★ **$–$$** ✕ **Villa Rica.** This buzzing eatery evokes its sister restaurant in Veracruz, one of the best seafood restaurants in the country. The wooden decor and a grand thatched roof create the seaside palapa ambience, and live music makes it a firm lunchtime favorite. Specialties such as *chilpachole* (crabmeat soup flavored with epazote) and conch fillet are done with notably fresh ingredients. It's a good place to bring children since in addition to kids' menus there's a game area, plus free weekend nanny service from 2 to 6. ⊠ *Calle 14 Sur 3509* ☎ *222/211–2060 or 222/211– 2061* ⊟ *AE, DC, MC, V.*

$ ✕ **Fonda de Santa Clara.** Founded in 1965, this popular spot is a classic, with two branches in Puebla (other branches are in Acapulco and Mexico City). Both of the Puebla locales have great settings and regional dishes. The original, near the zócalo, has a cozier, home-style atmosphere, but the larger newcomer at Paseo Bravo still manages a nice colonial feel. ⊠ *Calle 3 Poniente 307* ☎ *222/242–2659* ⊠ *Paseo Bravo, Calle 3 Poniente 920* ☎ *222/246–1919* ⊟ *MC, V.*

$ ✕ **Las Bodegas del Molino.** This restaurant's setting—an elegant 16th-century hacienda at the edge of town—is matched by its fine cuisine. If you're not sure about mole, give it a try here: the same woman has been making it since 1982, and her seductive, fruity blend will probably win you over. Make time to request a tour (Matthijs de Kool speaks excellent English) of the fabulous premises, which are being renovated with admirable care. Romantics should book a private dinner in the French Room. ⊠ *Molino de San José del Puente* ☎ *222/249–0483 or 222/249–0399* ⊟ *AE, MC, V.*

¢–$ ✕ **La Piccola Italia.** The business lunch crowd jostles with local notable families in this prestigious restaurant. A display of the house specialty, homemade pasta, greets you in the entranceway. ⊠ *Teziutlán Norte 1, Col. La Paz* ☎ *222/231–3220* ⊟ *AE, V.*

¢ ✕ **La Tecla.** Modish, spacious design, and decently priced nouvelle Mexican cuisine has made this branch of the Mexico City restaurant a hit in Puebla. Try the duck tacos in green sauce, or fillet of veal bathed in corn fungus and Roquefort. ⊠ *Ave. Juárez 1909, between Calles 19 and 21 Sur* ☎ *222/246–2616* ⊟ *AE, MC, V.*

★ **$$$** ▥ **Camino Real.** Formerly a convent, this 16th-century building radiates historic character, from its luminous restored frescos to the wooden shutters. Each room's decor is based on its original look, which varied depending on each nun's donation to the order. The junior suite was once the convent's chapel, and the presidential suite has original 16th-century gilded furnishings and carpeting. The entire property has been sensitively restored, and the staff is warm and professional. ⊠ *Av. 7 Poniente 105, 72000* ☎ *222/229–0909 or 222/229–0910* 🖷 *222/232–9251* ⊕ *www.caminoreal.com/puebla* ⟿ *75 rooms, 9 suites* ⌂ *2 restaurants, in-room data ports, bar, business services* ⊟ *AE, DC, MC, V.*

$$$ 🏨 **Mesón Sacristía de Capuchinas.** Though this 17th-century building is in the center of Puebla, it's very quiet, thanks to its thick walls. Each room has a slightly different, somewhat austere, decor. Many have beamed ceilings; some have wrought-iron bedsteads or religious icons. The suites are decorated in a contemporary style. ⊠ *Av. 9 Oriente 16, 72000* ☎ *222/232–8088 or 222/246–6084* ⊕ *www.mesones-sacristia.com* ⟿ *7 suites* ⌂ *Restaurant, bar* ⊟ *AE, MC, V.*

$$ 🏨 **Mesón Sacristía de la Compañia.** Each individually decorated room in this converted colonial mansion is outfitted with antiques that are also for sale. Warming touches are both literal and figurative; you'll be welcomed with a plate of cookies, and if it gets chilly heaters are brought to your room. The rich colors of folk art pervade the cozy but stylish Confessional bar (aptly named, as tongues loosen after a few libations), and the patio is a feast for the eyes. The attractive restaurant serves tasty regional dishes. ⊠ *Calle 6 Sur 304, at Callejón de los Sapos, 72000* ☎*222/242–3554* 🖷 *222/232–4513* ⊕ *www.mesones-sacristia.com* ⟿ *8 rooms* ⌂ *Restaurant, room service, cable TV, bar, free parking* ⊟ *AE, MC, V* ⦿*BP.*

$$ 🏨 **El Mesón del Ángel.** At the city's entrance—a bit far from the attractions—is this quiet and cheery hotel with spacious, colorful gardens. The executive area is designed for business travelers; it consists of a separate building with 70 rooms and its own pool, restaurant, and business area. ⊠ *Av. Hermanos Serdan 807, 72100* ☎ *222/223–8300* 🖷 *222/223–8301* ⊕ *www.mesondelangel.com.mx* ⟿ *192 rooms* ⌂ *Restaurant, room service, in-room safes, 2 pools, bar, business services, meeting rooms* ⊟ *AE, DC, MC, V* ⦿ *BP.*

$ 🏨 **Hotel Royal.** Small and well maintained, this hotel on the main square is one of the less expensive choices in Puebla. The best rooms are the junior suites, which overlook the zócalo and get plenty of light. Overnight parking (9 PM–8 AM) is free. ⊠ *Portal Hidalgo 8, 72000* ☎ *222/242–4740* 🖷 *222/242–4743* ⊕ *www.hotelr.com* ⟿ *45 rooms* ⌂ *Restaurant, cable TV, bar* ⊟ *AE, MC, V* ⦿ *BP.*

off the beaten path

⟳ **Africam Safari.** A 25-minute drive from the city brings you to vampire bats, Bengal tigers, zebras, and chimps, as well as a well-kept botanical garden. Check dates for the occasional night safaris that give visitors a chance to see the big cats and other nocturnal creatures at their most perky. ⊠ *Km 16.5 on the road to Valsequillo, Puebla* ☎ *222/236–1212; 55/5575–2731 in Mexico City* ⌑ *$7.50* ⊙ *Daily 10–5.*

Cholula & the Colonial Treasures of Puebla State

Before the Spanish Conquest, Cholula, 8 km (5 mi) west of Puebla, reportedly had hundreds of temples and rivaled Teotihuacán as a cultural and ceremonial center. The *mercado santuario* (market sanctuary) system was developed here in AD 1200, whereby satellite cities of Cholula exchanged cultural ideas and began trading with the Gulf region and Oaxaca. On his arrival, Cortés ordered every temple destroyed, and a church built in its place. The town fathers claim that Cholula has 365 church cupolas, one for every day in the year. Work is taking place to preserve the region's heritage and a number of the 39 churches in

Cholula—and the 128 in the surrounding area—have been painstakingly restored.

These days, weekends are the liveliest time to visit Cholula, when you can catch the Sunday market and some live music with dinner. Even busier are the town's many festivals, especially the *feria de San Pedro,* during first two weeks of September. This celebration includes *la bajada de la Virgen,* when the Virgin of Remedies is carried down from her church atop the Gran Pirámide and stays a night in each of the town's neighborhoods.

Thanks in part to the student presence at the respected Universidad de las Americas, some pleasant eateries have popped up under the *portales* (the arches along one side of the zócalo) and on Avenida Hidalgo. The town is divided into three municipalities; most of the major sites of interest are divided between San Pedro Cholula and San Andres Cholula. While Cholula is only a 15-minute taxi ride ($6–$8) from Puebla, it's worth staying a night or two to savor the town's slower, friendlier pace.

The **Gran Pirámide** (Great Pyramid) was the hub of Olmec, Toltec, and Aztec religious centers and is, by volume, the largest pyramid in the world. It consists of seven superimposed structures connected by tunnels and stairways. Ignacio Márquina, the architect in charge of the initial explorations in 1931, decided to excavate two tunnels partly to prove that *el cerrito* (the hill), as many still call it, was an archaeological trove. When seeing the **Zona Arqueológica** you'll walk through these tunnels to a vast 43-acre temple complex, once dedicated to Quetzalcóatl. On top of the pyramid stands the Spanish chapel **Nuestra Señora de los Remedios** (Our Lady of the Remedies). Almost toppled by a quake in 1999, it has been beautifully restored. From the top of the pyramid you'll have a clear view of other nearby churches, color-coded by period: oxidized red was used in the 16th century, yellow in the 17th and 18th, and pastel colors in the 19th. You can obtain an English-language guide for $6. ✉ *Calz. San Andrés at Calle 2 Norte* ☎ *222/247–9081* 🎟 *$3 includes museum* 🕐 *Daily 9–6.*

The huge, impressive **Ex-Convento de San Gabriel** includes a trio of churches. The most unusual is the Moorish-style **Capilla Real,** with 49 domes. It was built in 1540 and originally was open on one side, to facilitate conversion of huge masses of people. About 20 Franciscan monks still live in one part of the premises, so be respectful of their privacy. ✉ *2 Norte s/n, east of Cholula Zócalo* ☎ *No phone* 🕐 *Daily 10–12:30 and 4:30–6.*

★ The exterior of the 16th-century church of **Santa María Tonantzintla** may be relatively simple, but inside waits an explosion of color. To facilitate the conversion of the native population, Franciscan monks incorporated elements recalling the local cult of Tonantzin in the ornamentation of the chapel. The result is a jewel of the indigenous Baroque. The polychrome wood-and-stucco carvings—inset columns, altarpieces, and the main archway—were completed in the late 17th century and are the essence of churrigueresque. The carvings, set off by ornate gold-leaf figures of plant forms, angels, and saints, were made by local craftspeople. Flash photography is not allowed. ✉ *Av. Reforma, 5 km (3 mi) south of Cholula* ☎ *No phone* 🕐 *Daily 9–6.*

★ The stunning, well-preserved church of **San Francisco Acatepec** has been likened to "a temple of porcelain, worthy of being kept beneath a crystal dome." Construction began in 1590, with the elaborate Spanish Baroque decorations added between 1650 and 1750. Multicolored Talavera tiles cover the exceptionally ornate facade. The interior blazes with polychrome plasterwork and gilding; a sun radiates overhead. Unlike the nearby Santa María Tonantzintla, the ornamentation hews to the standard representations of the Incarnation, the Evangelists, and the Holy Trinity. Look for St. Francis, to whom the church is dedicated, between the altarpiece's spiraling columns. ⊠ *6½ km (4 mi) south of Cholula* ⊙ *Daily 9–6* ☎ *No phone.*

Huejotzingo is a must for lovers of religious art and history. The sleepy town, which offers pristine views of Iztaccíhuatl, is known for its cider but is truly swamped with visitors only at carnival time (on the Saturday before Ash Wednesday and on Shrove Tuesday). The battle against the French is reenacted on May 5; the concomitant masked dance comes closer to recalling the festivities of the agricultural year of Tlaloc (the Aztec rain god). The town also hosts a Festival of Cider from September 22 to October 2.

The town's 16th-century Franciscan monastery, the **Ex-Convento de Huejotzingo,** is known for its marvelously decorated corner chapels, each depicting angels. Diffuse light filters through the original onyx windows; the preserved gilded altarpiece is a rarity. The museum on the side documents Spanish missions in the area, but information is poor and not available in English. ⊠ *Plazuela de San Francisco de Asís s/n, 15 km (9 mi) northwest of Cholula on Hwy. 150* ☎ *No phone* 🎫 *$2* ⊙ *Monastery daily 8–7; museum Tues.–Sun. 10–4:30.*

Where to Stay & Eat

¢–$ ✕ **La Lunita.** A stone's throw from the Gran Pirámide, this little eatery has bumped up its prices a bit, but it's still a good place for a cold drink after a sweltering afternoon in the archaeological zone. It's welcoming and cluttered with bric-a-brac; their specialty is *acamayas,* a kind of crayfish. ⊠ *Av. Morelos at 6 Norte* ☎ *222/247–0011* ▭ *No credit cards.*

¢ ✕ **Las Mañanitas.** The nicest restaurant under the portales has a handsome bar and a tidily rustic look. The service is friendly and the portions generous, even for a small *pozole* (hominy soup with pork). Check the board outside for the daily specials, or go for a classic regional dish like mole poblano. ⊠ *Portal de Guerrero 17* ☎ *222/261–2537* ▭ *No credit cards* ⊙ *Closed Tues.*

¢ ▥ **Hotel Posada Señorial (Centro Histórico).** This place claims the distinction of being the only hotel on the zócalo; look for the small entrance under the arches by a busy coffee shop. The rooms are comfortable and done in pastels, but some are depressingly dark, so ask to see a selection. ⊠ *Portal de Guerrero 5* ☎☎ *222/247–0341 or 222/247–7719* ⤸ *27 rooms* ⚊ *Cable TV* ▭ *MC, V.*

Tlaxcala

30 km (19 mi) north of Puebla, 120 km (75 mi) east of Mexico City.

Tlaxcala (pronounced tlas-*ca*-la) is a place where you may well find yourself lingering longer than you had planned, lulled by a few hours spent on the Plaza Xicohténcatl or at a café in one of the colonnades near the zócalo. The distinctive terra-cotta roofs gave the state capital the name *Ciudad Roja,* or the Red City. Climb up to one of the hilltop churches and a sea of ruddy roofs will stretch out around you.

Bordered by Calle Camargo and Avenida Juárez, the **zócalo** has a beautifully tiled bandstand shaded by graceful trees. Young couples hang out on the benches surrounding a quartet of fountains. Adjoining the zócalo at its southeast corner is another square, **Plaza Xicohténcatl.** Souvenir shops line its eastern edge. To the north of the zócalo is the **Palacio de Gobierno** (⊠ Between Av. Lira y Ortega and Av. Juárez). Inside the eastern entrance

are murals by local painter Desiderio Hernández Xochitiotzin depicting Tlaxcala's pivotal role in the Spanish conquest. The city aligned itself with Cortés against the Aztecs, thus swelling the conqueror's ranks
significantly. The palace is open daily 8–8. To the west of the Palacio
de Gobierno is the **Parroquia de San José** (⊠ Av. Lira y Ortega and Calle
Lardizábal), cheerfully decorated in vivid shades of yellow and green.
Don't miss the pair of fonts near the entrance that depict Tlaxcalan, a
god of war. The church is open daily 9–6.

To the west of Plaza Xicohténcatl is the fascinating **Museo de la Memo-
ria,** with a colonial-era facade but a strikingly modern interior. By focusing on the folklore and festivals of various indigenous cultures, the
Museum of Memory recounts the region's past and present. ⊠ *Av. Independencia 3* ☎ *246/466–0791* ☉ *Tues.–Sun. 10–5* 🎟 *$1.*

The **Catedral de Nuestra Señora de la Asunción** stands atop a hill one block
south of Plaza Xicohténcatl. The cathedral's most unusual feature is its
Moorish-style wood ceiling beams, carved and gilded with gold studs.
There are only a few churches of this kind in Mexico, as mudéjar flourishes were popular here only during the very early years after the Spanish conquest. Don't miss the view of the city's bullring from the churchyard.
The cathedral's austere monastery, now home to the **Museo Regional de
Tlaxcala,** displays 16th- to 18th-century religious paintings as well as a
small collection of pre-Columbian pieces. A beautiful outdoor chapel near
the monastery has notable Moorish and Gothic traces. ⊠ *Calz. de San
Francisco* ☎ *246/462–0952* ☉ *Daily 9–6* 🎟 *Museum $3.50.*

★ On a hill about 1 km (½ mi) northwest of the center of Tlaxcala stands
the ornate **Basílica de Ocotlán.** You can see its churrigueresque facade,
topped with twin towers adorned with the apostles, from just about everywhere in the city. The church is most notable as a pilgrimage site. In
1541 the Virgin Mary appeared to a poor peasant, telling him to cure
an epidemic with water from a stream that had suddenly appeared. Franciscan monks, eager to find the source of the miracle, ventured into the
forest. There they discovered raging flames that didn't harm one particular pine (*ocotlán*). When they split the tree open, they discovered
the wooden image of the Virgen de Ocotlán, which they installed in a
gilded altar. Many miracles have been attributed to the statue, which
wears the braids popular for indigenous women at the time. Behind the
altar is the brilliantly painted *Camarín de la Virgen* (Dressing Room of
the Virgin) that tells the story. At the base of the hill is the charming
Capilla del Pocito de Agua Santa, an octagonal chapel decorated with
images of the Virgen de Ocotlán. The faithful come to draw holy water
from its seven fountains. ⊠ *Calle Guridi y Alcocer* ☎ *246/465–0960*
☉ *Daily 9–6.*

Where to Eat

$ ✕ **Fonda del Convento.** In a low stone building on a tree-lined street, this
unassuming café is overlooked by most travelers but is always packed
with locals. The series of small dining rooms means it won't be hard to
find a quiet table. The delicious traditional fare includes such dishes as
chicken broth with creamy avocados and strips of cactus flambéed with
bits of onion and chilies. ⊠ *Calz. de San Francisco 1* ☎ *246/462–0765*
🖃 *AE, DC, MC, V.*

Cacaxtla

🔺 *100 km (63 mi) east of Mexico City center.*

★ At the archaeological site of Cacaxtla you'll see some of Mexico's most
vividly colored murals. Accidentally discovered in 1975 by a farmer, the

main temple at Cacaxtla contains breathtaking murals depicting scenes of a surprisingly vicious battle between two bands of warriors. The nearly life-size figures wearing jaguar skins clearly have the upper hand against their foes in lofty feathered headdresses.

The site, dating from AD 650 to AD 900, is thought to be the work of the Olmeca-Xicalanca people. Other stunning paintings adorn smaller structures. The newly restored Templo Rojo, or Red Temple, is decorated with stalks of corn with cartoonlike human faces. Perhaps the most delightful is in the Templo de Venus, or Temple of Venus. Here you see two figures dancing in the moonlight, their bodies a striking blue.

On a hill about 1½ km (1 mi) north of Cacaxtla is the site of **Xochité-catl**, with four Classic period pyramids. You can see both sites with the same admission ticket. To reach Cacaxtla and Xochitécatl, head south from Mexico City toward Peubla on Carretera Federal 119. Veer off to the right toward the town of Nativitas. Both sites are near the village of San Miguel del Milagro. ⊠ *About 19 km (12 mi) southwest of Tlaxcala on Carretera Federal 119* ☎ *246/416–0477* ⊕ *www.cnca.gob.mx/cnca/inah/zonarq/cacaxtla.html* ☜ *$3.50* ☉ *Tues.–Sun. 10–4:30.*

Cuetzalan

320 km (198 mi) north east of Mexico City, 182 km (113 mi) north of Puebla city.

Fodor'sChoice The colonial town of Cuetzalan in the Sierra Norte region is one of the
★ most precious and unspoiled attractions in the state of Puebla. The Sierra Norte has been referred to as the *Sierra Mágica* (magical mountain range) for the mystic beliefs held by the pre-Hispanic peoples who inhabited this lush, dramatic swath of land. Cuetzalan's breathtaking landscape is etched with canyons, rushing rivers, and caves, and swaddled in dense, outsize vegetation. Because of its elevation the town is often enveloped in clouds. It's a long trip but a worthwhile one—you'll need to be patient, as the winding mountain roads slow things down. Wear sturdy walking shoes and be prepared for cool and damp weather.

The Totonacs first established Cuetzalan as a settlement. The Nahuas then invaded the territory, followed by the Spaniards in 1531. Today the town and its surroundings are still home to a large variety of ethnic groups, who make up over half the local population. These indigenous groups retain many of their traditions, from language and dress to agriculture and social customs.

At the weekly Sunday market, or *tianguis,* in the town center, local farmers come to sell and trade corn, coffee, beans, spices, and citrus fruits. Most people wear indigenous dress and chatter in Nahuatl, sizing up the cinnamon or bargaining for guavas. The atmosphere, color, and fragrant smells of this lively event are not to be missed.

On the town's **zócalo** you'll find the Renaissance-style church, La Parroquia de San Francisco, as well as the Palacio Municipal. The bandstand and the municipal clock tower were both built in the early 20th century.

The church of **El Santuario de Guadalupe** shows a gothic strain in its needle-slim tower and the pointed arch of the main door. Its common name, La Iglesia de los Jarritos (church of the little pitchers) refers to its landmark spire, prettily adorned by 80 clay vessels. ⊠ *Calz. de Guadalupe* ☉ *Daily 9–6.*

Originally a coffee processing plant, the **Casa de la Cultura** has been revamped to combine a public library, the town archives, and an interesting ethnographic museum, which is well worth visiting though information is available only in Spanish. Opposite the building across Avenida Miguel Alvarado is Cuetzalan's daily crafts market. ⊠ *Av. Miguel Alvarado 18* ☎ *No phone* ⊘ *Daily 10–6* 🎫 *Free.*

About 8 km (5 mi) outside Cuetzalan lies the splendid archaeological zone of **Yohualichan,** founded by Totonacs around AD 400. Partly obscured from the road by an austere stone church, Yohualichan (which means the House of Night) consists of a beautiful hilltop grouping of administrative and ceremonial buildings, houses, plazas, and a long ball court. ⊠ *Carretera a Santiago* ☎ *No phone* ⊘ *Tues.–Sun. 9–5* 🎫 *$3.*

off the
beaten
path

☝ **Las Grutas.** Under Cuetzalan's limestone slopes winds an extensive cave system, with over 100 km (62 mi) of passages. Access is limited, but you can arrange for a guide to show you a few caverns bristling with stalactites and stalagmites. Ask at the tourism office for guide recommendations; the entrances are 20 to 30 minutes from town.

Where to Stay & Eat

★ ¢ ✕ **Los Jarritos.** This cavelike restaurant is an unforgettable trove of regional cuisine. Even simple items like the salsas and *frijoles* (small black beans) are intensely flavored. There's an exquisite *sopa de setas* (soup of succulent oyster mushrooms) or you could try the signature dish, *enchiladas de picadillo con mole de olla* (ground beef and raisin enchiladas with a savory local mole). On Saturday night there are live music and dance performances, including Los Voladores (flyers). ⊠ *Plazuela Lopez Mateo 7* ☎ *233/331–0558* 🖃 *MC, V* ⊘ *Closed Mon.–Thurs. No dinner Sun.*

¢ ✕ **La Terraza.** Though it's known for its good seafood—like the tasty *pulpos enchipotlados* (octopus in hot chipotle sauce)—this simple spot caters to various cravings with pasta, hamburgers, even hotcakes for breakfast. ⊠ *Calle Hidalgo 33* ☎ *233/331–0262* 🖃 *No credit cards.*

¢ 🏨 **Hotel Casa de Piedra.** While still a work in progress, this hotel tops the rest. Guest rooms have wooden furniture and small balconies, giving you a view over the town or the flourishing, overgrown yard cackling with turkeys. The split-level family rooms sleep at least four people. More rooms, a bar, another restaurant, and meeting rooms are in the works. It's less than two blocks from the zócalo. ⊠ *Calle Lic. Carlos García 11 73560* ☎ *233/331–0030; 222/249–4089 in Puebla* ⊕ *www. lacasadepiedra.com* 🛏 *11 rooms* ♨ *Restaurant, free parking; no room phones, no room TVs* 🖃 *AE, MC, V.*

¢ 🏨 **Hotel Posada Cuetzalan.** Centrally located and well established, this cheerful hotel has colorful rooms, a pair of pretty patio gardens, and a busy restaurant. The staff can help organize cave tours. ⊠ *Zaragoza 12 73560* ☎ *233/331–0154* 🛏 *37 rooms* ♨ *Restaurant, cable TV, mountain bikes, laundry service, free parking* 🖃 *MC, V.*

Entertainment

On Saturday nights, Los Jarritos restaurant hosts a spectacular show of Los Voladores, or flyers. Five men brightly dressed as the *hombre pájaro* (bird man) conduct the ritual. They climb a tall pole, then let themselves down twirling on ropes. There's no set fee, but a donation of at least 20 pesos is standard. ⊠ *Plazuela Lopez Mateo 7* ☎ *233/331–0558.*

Southeast of Mexico City A to Z

To research prices, get advice from other travelers, and book travel arrangements, visit www.fodors.com.

BUS TRAVEL

Buses with the line Los Volcanes, part of the bus company Cristobal Colon, leave for Amecameca from Mexico City's Terminal del Oriente (TAPO) every 20 minutes daily. The trip takes approximately 1¼ hours and costs cost less than $2. The buses returning to the capital from Amecameca run just as frequently up to 9:30 PM; they leave from a small bus station behind the old flour factory on the northwest side of the zócalo.

Buses from different lines run daily every 20 minutes to Puebla's CAPU bus station from the TAPO. It's a two-hour ride and it costs about $8. ADO is the cleanest and most reliable bus line; you can book in advance with the service Ticketbus.

Autobuses Unidos buses run between Cholula and Mexico City's TAPO station several times daily. The ride costs $5 and takes just under an hour. It's "servicio economico," so the buses don't have bathrooms. It's easiest take a bus from Mexico City to Puebla, then take a taxi ride to Cholula.

Autotransportes ATAH buses to Tlaxcala make several daily trips from the TAPO in Mexico City. The ride takes just under two hours and costs about $8. To get to Cacaxtla you can take the Zacatelo–San Martín bus from Puebla bus station.

Texcoco/Primera Plus bus lines makes the six-hour trip to Cuetzalan from the TAPO, on weekends only. They generally do two trips each day, but service fluctuates; the ride costs about $10. Via/ADO has more frequent trips to Cuetzalan from Puebla; the trip takes four hours and costs $6.

🚏 Bus Depots **Puebla** ✉ CAPU, Blvd. Norte 4222 **Tlaxcala** ✉ Estación de Autobuses Tlaxcala, Camino Tepeinte s/n.

🚏 Bus Lines **ADO** ☎ 55/5133-2424 in Mexico City; 233/331-0411 in Cuetzalan. **Autobuses Unidos** ☎ 55/5133-1100 ext. 54 in Mexico City. **Autotransportes ATAH** ☎ 55/5571-3422, 55/5542-8907, or 55/5542-2007 in Mexico City. **Texcoco/Primera Plus** ☎ 233/331-0498 in Cuetzalan. **Ticketbus** ☎ 01800/702-8000 toll-free in Mexico ⊕ www.ticketbus.com.mx. **Los Volcanes** ☎ 55/5133-2433 in Mexico City; 01800/849-6136 toll-free in Mexico ⊕ www.cristobalcolon.mx.

CAR TRAVEL

From Mexico City, head east on the Viaducto Miguel Aleman toward the airport and exit right onto Calzada Zaragoza, the last wide boulevard before arriving at the airport; this becomes the Puebla Highway at the tollbooth. Route 150D is the toll road straight to Puebla; Route 190 is the scenic—and bumpy—free road. The trip takes about 1½ hours on Route 150D, three hours on Route 190. To go directly to Cholula, take the exit at San Martín Texmelucan and follow the signs; the drive takes roughly an hour and a half.

You'll need to go to Puebla to get to Tlaxcala; from there, take Highway 119 north. To reach Cuetzalan from Puebla, take federal highway 129 to Zaragoza. From there, roads are reasonably well surfaced to Cuetzalan town. Be careful; there are dangerous curves and some of the other vehicles on the road should have been consigned to the scrap yard long ago. To get to Amecameca, take the Puebla Highway and after about 40 minutes, look for an Amecameca signpost on the right.

Puebla has several safe parking lots; it's easy to find spaces in Cholula too. There's plenty of parking around the ruins of Cholula and Cuetzalan.

EMERGENCIES

The Brigada del Rescate del Socorro Alpino de México handles emergencies in the Parque Nacional Izta-Popo. You can find pharmacies open until 10 PM in each town, even remote Cuetzalan.

▣ Hospitals Cuetzalan ⊠ Miguel Alvarado 85, Centro ☎ 233/331-0127. **Puebla** ☎ 222/219-3300.

▣ Hot Line Brigada del Rescate del Socorro Alpino de México ☎ 55/5392-9299, 044-55-2698-7557, 044-55-3118-1426.

▣ Pharmacies Amecameca ⊠ Farmacia Popular, Plaza de la Constitución 7 ☎ 597/978-1026. **Cholula** ⊠ Farmacia Nuestra Señora del Sagrado Corazon, Av. Hidalgo 103 B ☎ 222/247-0398. **Cuetzalan** ⊠ Farmacia San Francisco, Av. Miguel Alvarado 7, at Privada Miguel Alvarado ☎ 233/331-0122 or 233/331-0104. **Puebla** ☎ 222/220-5254.

MONEY MATTERS

Puebla has plenty of banks in the city center, including some on Avenida 5 de Mayo. In Cholula, branches of several major banks border the zócalo; all have automatic teller machines. In Cuetzalan, there's a Banamex with an ATM on Avenida Miguel Alvarado at Calle Francisco Madero.

VISITOR INFORMATION

The CONANP bureau in Amecameca, near the church on the zócalo, is a rich source of information on the volcanoes. It also makes guiding arrangements for climbing Izta.

The Puebla Municipal Tourist Office is open weekdays 9–5, Sunday 9–3. Be sure to get the state and city map "Puebla Destinos a tu alcance." Ask for Rene Paredes if you'd like to set up a tour in English (perhaps not perfectly fluent but understandable) to churches in the countryside, Cholula, and Huejotzingo.

Cholula has a bureau apiece in the San Pedro and San Andrés areas. Alfredo Torres of the San Pedro office speaks English; that location is open from 9 to 7 daily. The San Andrés office is open only on weekdays from 10 to 5; if you speak fluent Spanish, ask for Refugio Gallegos, whose knowledge and enthusiasm for the area are remarkable.

The Tlaxcala Tourist Office, in the rear of the Palacio de Gobierno, is open weekdays 9–6; on weekends a stand is open downstairs 9–6.

Cuetzalan's tourism information office is pretty bare-bones and chances are slim that anyone will speak English, but you can pick up a list of hotels and restaurants, leaflets on local attractions, and transit info. It's open daily from 10 to 6.

▣ CONANP ⊠ Plaza de la Constitución 10-B, Amecameca ☎ 597/978-3829 or 597/978-3830 ⊕ www.iztapopo.gob.mx. **Cuetzalan** ⊠ Dirección Municipal de Turismo, Hidalgo 29 ☎ 233/331-0004 ⊕ www.puebla.gob.mx/cultura/ciudades/cuetzalan.html. **Puebla Municipal Tourist Office** ⊠ Portal Hidalgo 14, Centro Histórico ☎ 222/246-1890 or 222/246-1580 ☐ 222/242-4980 ⊕ www.ayuntamiento.pue.gob.mx. **Puebla State Tourism Office** ⊠ Av. 5 Oriente 3, Centro Histórico, 72000 Puebla ☎ 222/246-2044 ☐ 222/242-3161 ⊕ www.puebla.gob.mx and www.turismopuebla.com.mx. **San Andrés Cholula** ⊠ Av. 16 de Septiembre 102 ☎ 222/247-8606 Ext. 205. **San Pedro Cholula Tourist Office** ⊠ 12 Oriente at 4 Norte ☎ 222/261-2393 ☐ 222/247-1969. **Tlaxcala tourist office** ⊠ Av. Juárez 18, at Lardizábal ☎ 246/465-0960 ⊕ www.tlaxcala.gob/turismo.com.

WEST OF MEXICO CITY

Heading west from Mexico City into the state of Mexico, you'll find a string of good day-trip sights, such as the long-extinct volcano, Nevado de Toluca. For a longer excursion, push on to Valle de Bravo, a lovely lakeside colonial village popular with vacationing chilangos.

Parque Nacional Nevado de Toluca

65 km (40 mi) west of Mexico City center

At 15,090 ft, the Nevado de Toluca, an extinct volcano, is Mexico's fourth-tallest mountain; if you drive to the crater or brave a climb on a clear day, you'll be rewarded with a great valley view. The volcano's crater (at 11,800 ft) is studded with two lakes, known as *El Sol* (the sun) and *La Luna* (the moon). There are two park entrances, a lower and a higher. If you plan to hike, save some energy by going to higher one (*la segunda pluma*). There are several hiking trails; the most popular takes you from the second entrance up to the crater's edge, then down to the lakes inside. If you're hungry for more you can tackle the tough climb up the far side of the crater to the summit. The trails are quite clear, but if you like you can hire a guide at the park entrance. Note that the driving road is sometimes blocked by snow. ⊠ *La Comisión Estatal de Parques Naturales (State Commission of National Parks) José Vicente Villava 212 Toluca* ☎ *722/213–0375 or 722/214–9919* ⊕ *www.edomexico.gob.mx/portalgem/se/anp/nevado.htm (in Spanish)* ☉ *Daily 10–5* ⌦ *25¢.*

Valle de Bravo

75 km (47 mi) west of Mexico City center.

A few hours here explains why "Valle" is often billed as Mexico's best-kept secret. The pines, clear air, and sparkling Lago Valle de Bravo make it very different from most people's idea—and experience—of Mexico.

This colonial lakeside treasure is peppered with white stucco houses trimmed with wrought-iron balconies, red-tile roofs, and red-potted succulents. Connected to Mexico City mostly via a two-lane, winding, mountainous road, the town is visited almost exclusively by other Mexicans, particularly weekenders from the capital. The town and its suburb of Avándaro are enclaves for established artists and the extremely wealthy; the posh homes of presidents of the largest companies in Mexico fringe the lakefront.

Valle was founded in 1530 but has no significant historical sights to speak of other than the St. Francis of Assisi cathedral on the town square and the church of Santa Maria, with a huge crucified black Christ on its altar. Rather than sightsee, saunter the streets and check out the bazaars, boutiques, galleries, and markets. Valle is famous for its lacelike fabrics called *deshilados* and earthenware and hand-glazed ceramics. The lake spurs plenty of water sports, and the more daring can look into hang gliding or parasailing. In winter, the monarch butterflies come through the area during their migration to Michoacán.

While Valle de Bravo has a verdant European feel, it is an enclave, and therefore lacks a substantial, independent character. (In fact, the town caters to weekenders so intently that by Monday full-time residents are sometimes without water, all having gone to the hotels and restaurants.) The town attracts plenty of visitors without making an effort; a side effect of this sit-back attitude is that the tourist center near the lake isn't very useful. If you plan to come on a weekend, make sure you make hotel reservations well in advance. To avoid the crowds from the capital and nab lower hotel rates, visit during the week. The disadvantage to this strategy is that some restaurants and shops close at least one weekday.

Where to Stay & Eat

¢ ✕ **La Balsa Flotante de Avándaro.** You may feel a little wobbly on this floating restaurant, but it's the place to eat and be seen. As you might suspect, it specializes in fish and seafood; bands play during weekend lunchtimes. ⊠ *Embarcadero Municipal s/n* ☎ *726/262–5523* ▭ *MC, V* ⊘ *Closed Mon.*

¢ ✕ **La Michoacana.** You can gaze over Valle's red-tile rooftops here as you nibble on a free appetizer of roasted chipotle peppers. The restaurant's pride is the *Cecina Michoacana* (grilled salt beef), and it also serves tasty tortilla soup, enchiladas, and other traditional standbys. ⊠ *Calle de la Cruz 100* ☎ *726/262–1625* ▭ *AE, MC, V.*

¢ ✕ **El Torito Willi's.** This hearty restaurant offers tacos and grilled meat in a friendly family atmosphere. Specialties are charcoal-grilled and barbecued beef and the famous *taco Mar y Tierra* (the equivalent of surf and turf, in a taco). It opens full-time only during Easter and summer holidays. ⊠ *Francisco González Bocanegra 200* ☎ *726/262–2781* ▭ *AE, MC, V* ⊘ *Closed weekdays Sept.–Easter.*

$$$ ▦ **Avandaro Golf & Spa Resort.** This former country club morphed into the most upscale resort in Valle. All guest rooms have fireplaces and great views of the pine forest. If the 18-hole par-72 golf course doesn't tempt you, perhaps a massage, facial, or yoga class at the high-tech spa will. An extra restaurant joins the ranks on weekends. The property is about 10 minutes from Valle de Bravo, so if you didn't come by car you'll need to take taxis into town. ⊠ *Vega del Río, Fracc. Avándaro, 51200* ☎ *726/266–0366; 55/5280–1532 in Mexico City* ▦ *726/266–0905* ⊕ *www.grupoavandaro.com.mx* ⟿ *60 rooms* ⌂ *Restaurant, room service, cable TV, 18-hole golf course, 7 tennis courts, 2 pools, health club, sauna, spa, bar* ▭ *AE, MC, V.*

$$ ▦ **Hotel los Arcos.** Four blocks north of the zócalo, this hotel encircles a swimming pool. The guest rooms are cinnamon-colored and many have fireplaces; if you visit in winter, make sure your fireplace works as they're the only heat source. Others have balconies with views of the mountains and village. The restaurant is open weekends only. ⊠ *Francisco González Bocanegra 310, 51200* ☎ *726/262–0042 or 726/262–1363* ▦ *726/266–0905* ⟿ *24 rooms* ⌂ *Restaurant, pool* ▭ *AE, MC, V* ⎀ *BP.*

West of Mexico City A to Z

To research prices, get advice from other travelers, and book travel arrangements, visit www.fodors.com.

BUS TRAVEL

Zinacantepec buses depart for Valle de Bravo every 20 minutes daily between 5 AM and 7:30 PM from Mexico City's Terminal Poniente (West Terminal, commonly referred to as Observatorio). The journey takes about three hours, and a round-trip ticket costs about $8.

🚍 Bus Line **Ticketbus** ☎ 55/5133-2424 in Mexico City; 01800/702-8000 toll-free in Mexico ⊕ www.ticketbus.com.mx. **Zinacantepec** ☎ 55/5271-0344 in Mexico City.

CAR TRAVEL

By car from Mexico City, follow Paseo de la Reforma all the way west. It eventually merges with the Carretera Libre at Toluca. Alternatively, you can take the toll highway, Highway 15 ($9, but worth it) to Toluca. For the Parque Nacional Nevado de Toluca, make a 44-km (27-mi) detour south on Route 130. The drive takes about an hour. Valle de Bravo is an additional hour and a half away; from Toluca take the Federal 134, otherwise known as the Temascatepc highway. Avoid this drive on Friday and Sunday evenings, when the weekenders are in a frenzied rush.

Try to avoid the drive at night, period, as highway 134 is very windy and has no lighting.

VISITOR INFORMATION
The Mexico State Tourist Office in Toluca is open weekdays 9–6. The municipal tourism office for Valle de Bravo is unfortunately not very helpful.

Mexico State Tourist Office ⊠ Urawa 100, Gate 110, Toluca ☎ 722/219–5190 or 722/219–6158 ⊕ www.gem.uaemex.mx/turismo. **Valle de Bravo Turismo Municipal** ⊠ 5 de febrero 100 ☎ 726/262–1678 ⊕ www.valledebravo.com.mx.

BAJA CALIFORNIA

3

So many wonderful hotels and restaurants can be found in this area that there's not enough space to list them all on this page. To see what Fodor's editors and contributors highly recommend, please look for the black stars as you leaf through this chapter.

By Maribeth
Mellin

BAJA (MEANING LOWER) CALIFORNIA is an arid stretch of land dipping southward from the international boundary that divides California and Mexico. The Mar de Cortés—also called the Golfo de California—separates Baja from the Mexican mainland.

Although only 21 km (13 mi) across at one point and 193 km (120 mi) at its widest, Baja has one of the most varied and beautiful terrains on the planet. The peninsula's two coasts are separated by great mountain ranges, with one peak soaring more than 10,000 ft high. Countless bays and coves with pristine beaches indent both shores, and islands big and small—many inhabited only by sea lions—dot the 3,364 km (2,086 mi) of coastline. You'll find stretches of desert as dry as the Sahara, as well as cultivated farmlands, vineyards, and resorts lush with swaying palm trees.

Varied, too, is the demographic makeup of Baja. The border strip of northern Baja is densely populated. Tijuana is home to more than 2 million people, making it more populous than the entire remainder of the peninsula. La Paz, with about 250,000 residents, is the only city of any size south of Ensenada. The two towns at Los Cabos (The Capes) are among the fastest-growing regions in the country.

Baja is divided politically into two states—Baja California (also called Baja Norte, meaning North Baja) and Baja California Sur (South)—at the 28th parallel, about 710 km (440 mi) south of the border. Near the tip of the peninsula, a monument marks the spot where the Tropic of Cancer crosses the Carretera Transpeninsular (Transpeninsular Highway, or Mexico Highway 1).

Baja travelers have traditionally been adventurous, and the peninsula is a cult destination. Back in the days of Prohibition, the Hollywood crowd learned the joy of having a nearby international border. John Steinbeck brought attention to La Paz when he made it a setting for his novella *The Pearl*. Bing Crosby is said to have put up some of the money for the first resort hotel in San José del Cabo when the only way to get there was aboard a yacht or private plane.

Today you'll fly in on commercial jets and check into thoroughly modern hotels. The rich and famous still find Baja, particularly the southern tip, an ideal escape, and you can see them in secluded hotels along Los Cabos Corridor. But Baja is no longer the exclusive turf of adventurers. Caravans of motor homes and pickups occasionally clog the Carretera Transpeninsular, and flights into Loreto, La Paz, and Los Cabos are often packed with first-time visitors. Plans are afoot for a series of marinas along the mainland and peninsula coasts of the Mar de Cortés, a development aimed to attract even more visitors. The plan, called the Escalera Nautica (Nautical Ladder), has been strongly opposed by environmental groups and local communities. Such developments have made Baja's resort towns more mainstream, but you can still find adventure and sublime solitude at the peninsula's hidden beaches and bays.

Exploring Baja California

Of the two states in the Baja Peninsula, the northern half, Baja California, contains the largest cities and highest population. Tijuana, Tecate, and Mexicali—the peninsula's border cities—have close ties to the Southwestern United States. San Felipe, the northernmost Baja town on the Mar de Cortés, is a popular weekend escape for Arizonans and southern Californians. Similarly, Rosarito and Ensenada, on Baja's northern Pacific coast, are practically extensions of the southern California coast.

South of Ensenada the natural side of Baja appears in desolate mountain ranges and fields of cacti and boulders.

Baja California Sur is more remote, in spite of its strong American influences. The most populated areas lie on the gulf coast. The Pacific side is more popular with migrating gray whales, who travel by the thousands every winter from the Bering Strait to isolated coves and lagoons along this coast. For those few months, people come from around the world to Guerrero Negro and a few bays and lagoons farther south. Loreto, on the Mar de Cortés, is beloved by sportfishers who find seclusion in this small, developing town. La Paz is the capital of Baja California Sur, the region's major port, and a busy center of commerce and government. Los Cabos, made up of the two towns of Cabo San Lucas and San José del Cabo, has become one of the fastest-growing and most expensive resort areas in Mexico. Despite all the development and steep prices, it remains a mysteriously natural hideaway.

If you plan to drive the peninsula, you must have Mexican auto insurance (the cost depends on the type of car and coverage purchased). Always carry water, and make sure your vehicle is in good condition. Keep your gas tank at least half full at all times—remote gas stations may be out of gas just when you need it. For the most part, the Transpeninsular Highway is well maintained, although some areas are marred by potholes or gravel and rocks. In addition, it often has only two lanes, and sharing them with semis and speeding buses can be somewhat unnerving.

About the Restaurants

Restaurants as a rule are low-key, except in Tijuana, Ensenada, and Los Cabos, where dining options range from *taquerías* (taco stands) to upscale Continental dining rooms. Dress is accordingly casual at nearly all Baja restaurants, and reservations are not required unless otherwise noted. Moderate prices prevail even in city restaurants—except in Los Cabos, which can be extraordinarily expensive. Some places add a 15% service charge to the bill.

About the Hotels

Baja lodging is mostly low-key—except in world-class Los Cabos. Until the 1980s, fishing lodges prevailed along the southern tip of Baja. Now Los Cabos draws golfers, anglers, and sybarites to deluxe hotels that front championship courses and incomparable water views. In the rest of Baja, you can find great deals at small, one-of-a-kind hostelries.

Reservations are a must on holiday weekends for most of Baja's coastal towns; some hotels require a minimum two-night stay for a confirmed reservation. Some resorts have minimum night requirements throughout the high season. Several hotels in Baja have toll-free numbers that connect directly to the hotel; although the operator may answer in Spanish, there is usually someone who speaks English in the office. Some hotels don't keep their fax machines on nonstop, so you may have to call to ask them to connect it. If making a reservation on the Web, ask for a confirmation and print it out before you leave. A few of the out-of-the-way and budget-price hotels do not accept credit cards; some of the more lavish places add a 10%–20% service charge to your bill. Most properties also raise their rates for the December–April high season (and raise them even higher for the days around Christmas). Rates here are based on high-season standards. Expect to pay 25% less during the off-season. Many hotels offer midweek discounts of 30%–50% off the weekend rates; always ask about special promotions.

Baja aficionados will tell you that you haven't really explored the peninsula unless you've driven its entire length, stopping at small towns and secluded beaches along the way. That's a major journey, requiring at least a week of travel time—one way. Keep in mind that regulars who boast of making the drive in two or three days are actually racing down the highway, stopping only to eat and sleep. With less than a week, focus on the area around where you enter Baja. If you have five days, you can see the most interesting towns in one state and still linger a bit. With three days you're best off staying within the immediate vicinity of your entry point.

3

Numbers in the text correspond to numbers in the margin and on the Tijuana, Ensenada, La Paz, Los Cabos Coast, San José del Cabo, and Cabo San Lucas maps.

If you have 3 days

In northern Baja, you can explore Tijuana, Rosarito, and Ensenada. Start in **Tijuana** ❶–⓫ ☞, then head south before nightfall to a hotel in ▣ **Rosarito** or **Puerto Nuevo.** Tour **Ensenada** ⓬–⓳ the next day, and spend the third day in Rosarito before heading back to the border.

In Baja Sur, you're best off staying in ▣ **Los Cabos** ☞ for golf, sportfishing, and snorkeling.

If you have 5 days

You can do a thorough tour of northern Baja, starting with a full day and overnight in ▣ **Tijuana** ❶–⓫ ☞. From there head to the small town of **Tecate,** then on to **Mexicali** and ▣ **San Felipe.** Overnight in San Felipe, and spend Day 3 checking out the beaches before driving the backcountry to ▣ **Ensenada** ⓬–⓳. Devote Day 4 to exploring La Bufadora and downtown Ensenada; then head up the coast for a lobster feast at **Puerto Nuevo.** On Day 5, head back to Tijuana and the border.

If you'd rather tour Baja Sur, begin in ▣ **Los Cabos** ☞, spending the night there and starting out early the next day for ▣ **La Paz** ⓴–㉘. Spend Day 2 exploring downtown La Paz and on Day 3, head up the coast to ▣ **Loreto.** Spend Days 4 and 5 making your way back to Los Cabos at a leisurely pace.

If you have 7 days

If you want to cover great distances—and spend much time in the car—you could drive the length of the peninsula in a week, especially if you arrange to begin in the north and drop off your car in the south. Most rental-car agencies will charge you a whopping drop-off fee, however, and the terrain covered isn't always awe-inspiring. (A leisurely round-trip takes about 14 days, especially as many of Baja's treasures take some extra time and effort to reach.) Start in **Tijuana** ❶–⓫ ☞ on Day 1. Head south before nightfall to a hotel in ▣ **Rosarito** or **Puerto Nuevo.** On Day 2, move on to **Ensenada** ⓬–⓳ for a brief tour of the city; then head south to **San Quintín** and ▣ **Guerrero Negro.** If you're traveling between January and March, arrange for a whale-watching tour for the next day. If not, overnight in Guerrero Negro and then move on for a full day's trip to ▣ **Mulegé** on the Mar de Cortés. The drive between the two coasts, through stark desert scenery, is one of the most beautiful and desolate in Baja. Spend Night 3 or 4 in Mulegé. Move on to ⬚ **Loreto** and spend the next night there. If you didn't stay in Guerrero Negro for whale-watching, spend an extra night in Loreto and arrange a boat tour of the Mar de Cortés. Devote Day 6 of the drive to **La Paz** ㉒– ㉘. On Day 7, continue on to **Los Cabos**.

Several agencies in the United States book reservations at Baja hotels, condos, and time-share resorts, which may actually cost less than hotel rooms if you are traveling with a group of four or more.

WHAT IT COSTS				
$$$$	**$$$**	**$$**	**$**	**¢**
RESTAURANTS over $25	$15–$25	$10–$15	$5–$10	under $5
HOTELS over $250	$150–$250	$75–$150	$50–$75	under $50

Restaurant prices are for a main course excluding tax and tip. Hotel prices are for two people in a standard double room in high season, based on the European Plan (EP, with no meals) and excluding service and 17% tax.

Timing

Baja's climate is extreme, thanks to its desert locale. Temperatures in Tijuana, Ensenada, and Rosarito are similar to those in southern California. Mexicali gets extremely hot in the summer. Northern Baja's resort cities are crowded on holiday weekends, and advance reservations are a must.

Baja Sur's winters are mild, but not warm; Loreto, La Paz, and Los Cabos can get downright chilly in the evening. Sportfishing aficionados prefer the summer months: although the temperatures are high, the fish are abundant. Loreto and La Paz tend to be crowded only on holiday weekends, but Los Cabos is crowded through much of the year, except at the height of the summer heat.

BAJA CALIFORNIA NORTE

The most populous state of the peninsula is fittingly capped with Tijuana, Baja's largest city, just 29 km (18 mi) south of San Diego. Its promoters like to call it "the most visited city in the world," and the border crossing to Tijuana is the busiest in the United States.

By comparison, the state's capital, Mexicali, has a population of only 900,000 residents and attracts few tourists; travelers who pass through it are usually en route to coastal San Felipe.

On Baja's Pacific coast, travelers stream down the Carretera Transpeninsular (Highway 1) to the beach communities of Rosarito and Ensenada. English is spoken as freely as Spanish here, and the dollar is as readily accepted as the peso. Between Baja's towns, the landscape is unlike any other, with cacti growing beside the sea, and stark mountains and plateaus rising against clear blue skies.

Highway 3 runs east from Ensenada to San Felipe through the foothills of the Sierra San Pedro Martir. The same highway runs north from Ensenada to Tecate through the Guadalupe Valley, where you'll find many of the area's vineyards and wineries. If you're traveling south, Ensenada is the last major city on the northern section of Mexico Highway 1. San Quintín, 184 km (114 mi) south of Ensenada, is an agricultural community said to be the windiest spot in Baja. Sportfishing is particularly good here. Farther south are turnoffs for a dirt road to San Felipe and a paved road to Bahía de los Angeles, a remote bay beloved by fishermen and naturalists. A new marina is in the works in Bahía de los Angeles and the highway to the bay is being widened to accommodate trailers with large boats. Both developments are part of a larger plan to construct a chain of marinas along the Mar de Cortés.

At the end of the northern section of Baja, 595 km (369 mi) from Ensenada, stands a steel monument in the form of an eagle, 138 ft high. It marks the border between the states of Baja California and Baja California Sur, and the time changes from Pacific to Mountain as you cross that 28th parallel. Guerrero Negro, Baja Sur's northernmost town, with hotels and gas stations, is 2 km (1 mi) south.

Tijuana

▶ *29 km (18 mi) south of San Diego.*

Tijuana is the only part of Mexico many people see—a distorted view of the country's many cultures. Before the city became a gigantic recreation center for southern Californians, it was a ranch populated by a few hundred Mexicans. In 1911 a group of Americans invaded the area and attempted to set up an independent republic; they were quickly driven out by Mexican soldiers. When Prohibition hit the United States in the 1920s and the Agua Caliente Racetrack and Casino opened (1929), Tijuana boomed. Americans seeking alcohol and gambling flocked across the border, spending freely and fueling the region's growth. Tijuana became the entry port for what some termed a "sinful, steamy playground" frequented by Hollywood stars.

Then Prohibition was repealed, Mexico outlawed gambling, and Tijuana's fortunes declined. Although the flow of travelers from the north slowed to a trickle, Tijuana still captivated those in search of the sort of fun not allowed back home. Drivers heading into Baja's wilderness passed through downtown Tijuana, stopping along Avenida Revolución and its side streets for supplies and souvenirs.

When the toll highway to Ensenada was finished in 1967, travelers bypassed the city. But Tijuana began attracting residents from throughout Latin America at the same time, and the population mushroomed from a mere 300,000 in 1970 to more than 2 million today. As the government struggles to keep up with the growth and demand for services, thousands live without electricity, running water, or adequate housing in squatters' villages along the border. Petty crime is a significant problem; moreover, the area has become headquarters for serious drug cartels, and violent crime—reaching the highest levels of law enforcement and business—is booming. You're unlikely to witness a shooting or some other frightening situation, but be mindful of your surroundings, stay in the tourist areas, and guard your belongings.

City leaders, realizing that tourism creates jobs and bolsters Tijuana's fragile economy, are working hard to attract visitors. Avenida Revolución, the main street, is lined with tourist-oriented shopping arcades, restaurants, and bars. The city has an international airport; a fine cultural center that presents international music, dance, and theater groups; and deluxe high-rise hotels. The demand for business-class services has increased with the growth of *maquiladoras* (foreign manufacturing plants). There's even a nascent opera company. Although it's no longer considered just a bawdy border town, the city remains best known as a place for an intense, somewhat exotic daylong adventure.

And then, of course, there's shopping. From the moment you cross the border, people will approach you or call out and insist that you look at their wares. If you drive, workers will run out from auto-body shops to place bids on new paint or upholstery for your car. All along Avenida Revolución and its side streets, shops sell everything from tequila to Tiffany-style lamps. If you intend to buy food in Mexico, get the U.S. customs list of articles that are illegal to bring back so that your purchases won't be confiscated.

② **Avenida Revolución.** This infamous strip, lined with an array of shops and restaurants that cater to uninhibited travelers, has long been Tijuana's main tourism zone. Shopkeepers call out from their doorways, offering low prices for an assortment of garish souvenirs and genuine folk art treasures. Many shopping arcades open onto Avenida Revolución; inside the front doors are mazes of stands with low-priced pottery and other crafts.

⑧ **Centro Cultural (CECUT).** The cultural center was designed by architects Manuel Rosen and Pedro Ramírez Vásquez, who also created Mexico City's famous Museo Nacional de Antropología. The stark, low-slung tan buildings fronted by the globe-like Omnimax Theater have become a beloved local landmark. The center's Museo de las Californias provides an excellent overview of the history, geography, and flora and fauna of Baja. The Omnimax shows films on a rotating schedule; some are in English. Exhibitions on art and culture change frequently, and the center's stage hosts performances by international groups. ⊠ *Paseo de los Héroes and Av. Mina, Zona Río* ☎ *664/687–9600* ⊕ *www.cnca.gob. mx* ☜ *Museum $2, museum and Omnimax Theater $3.50* ☉ *Daily 10–6.*

④ **L.A. Cetto Winery.** Most of Baja's legendary wineries are in the Ensenada region, but Tijuana does have this branch of one of Mexico's finest wineries. You can tour the bottling plant and sample the excellent wines while watching a video on the winery's operations in the Guadalupe Valley. The wine shop's prices are far lower than those in regular liquor stores. ⊠ *Cañon Johnson 2108, at Av. Constitución Sur, Centro* ☎ *664/685–3031 or 664/685–1644* ☜ *$2 for tour and wine tasting* ☉ *Mon.–Sat. 10–5.*

ⓒ ⑤ **Mundo Divertido.** This popular amusement park in the Río zone includes a miniature golf course, batting cages, bumper boats, go-carts, a roller coaster, and a video-game parlor. Admission is free, and the rides cost just a few pesos. ⊠ *Calle Velasco 2578 at Paseo de los Heroes, Zona Río* ☎ *664/634–3213 or 664/634–3214* ☉ *Weekdays noon–9, weekends 11–10.*

③ **El Palacio Frontón.** For many years, the magnificent Moorish-style Jai Alai Palace hosted fast-paced jai alai games. The sport has declined in popularity, however, and the Palacio is now occasionally used for boxing contests and concerts. ⊠ *Av. Revolución at Calle 7, Centro* ☎ *664/634– 3213* ☉ *Weekdays noon–9, weekends noon–9:30.*

⑩ **Playas Tijuana.** Along the oceanfront is this mix of modest and expensive residential neighborhoods, with a few restaurants and hotels. The isolated beaches are visited mostly by residents.

⑪ **Plaza de Toros Monumental.** The "Bullring by the Sea" sits at the northwest corner of the beach area near the U.S. border. The bullring is occasionally used for summer concerts. ☎ *664/688–0125.*

⑦ **Plaza Río Tijuana.** The area's largest shopping complex has good restaurants, department stores, hundreds of shops, and the Cineopolis, a multiplex theater where several English-language films are usually shown. Shade trees and flowers line the sidewalks that lead from the shopping

Fishing

Baja is considered one of the world's great sportfishing destinations. The fishing is best in the south, with large fishing fleets in Loreto, La Paz, and Los Cabos. Although summer brings the most fish, anglers are sure to catch something year-round. Fishing from Ensenada and San Quintín is best in summer and early fall.

Food & Wine

Baja's cuisine highlights all kinds of seafood. Fresh fish, lobster, shrimp, and abalone are particularly good. Beef, pork, and local quail are also excellent. Keep an eye out for two dishes that originated in Baja: *langosta Puerto Nuevo* (lobster grilled or boiled in oil and served with beans, rice, and tortillas) that comes from the fishing settlement of the same name near Tijuana, and *tacos de pescado* (chunks of deep-fried fish wrapped with condiments in a corn tortilla), which are said to have begun in the northern Baja town of San Felipe. In both Baja states, you'll find scores of restaurants serving great authentic Mexican dishes, as well as those that combine U.S. and Mexican flavors in burritos, burgers, and pizza.

Mexico's best domestic wines are nurtured in the vineyards in the Santo Tomás and Guadalupe valleys outside Ensenada, and one of the country's most popular beers, Tecate, comes from the Baja Norte town of the same name.

Golf

With well-established courses in most major cities, Baja is growing in popularity among golfers. Los Cabos has experienced a particular boom, with several excellent, championship-level courses open and others in development stages.

Kayaking

Both the Pacific Ocean and the Mar de Cortés have isolated bays and coves ideal for kayaking. Some hotels and outfitters in Ensenada, Loreto, La Paz, and Los Cabos offer kayak rentals and excursions, and some U.S. companies offer kayaking trips to the Mar de Cortés.

Whale-Watching

Gray whales migrate to the Pacific coast of Baja from January through March. numerous whale species winter in the Mar de Cortés as well. Whale-watching expeditions are available in Ensenada, Guerrero Negro, San Ignacio, Loreto, La Paz, and Los Cabos.

---

complex to the Centro Cultural. ⊠ *Paseo de los Héroes, across from the Centro Cultural, Zona Río* ☎ 664/684–0402.

⑨ Pueblo Amigo. This entertainment center resembles a colonial Mexican village, with stucco facades and tree-lined paths leading to a domed gazebo. The complex includes a hotel, several restaurants and clubs, a huge grocery store, and a large branch of the Caliente Race Book, where gambling on televised races and sporting events is legal. Things get more lively at night. ⊠ *Paseo de Tijuana between Puente Mexico and Av. Independencia, Zona Río.*

❶ San Ysidro Border Crossing. Locals and tourists jostle each other along the pedestrian walkway through the Viva Tijuana dining and shopping center and into the center of town. Artisans' stands line the walkway and adjoining streets, offering a quick overview of the wares to be found all over town.

6 Zona Río. The section that runs along Avenida Paseo de los Héroes, parallel to the dry Tia Juana River, is one of the city's main thoroughfares, with large statues of historic figures, including Abraham Lincoln. With its impressive **Centro Cultural,** several shopping complexes, fine restaurants, and fashionable discos, this part of town rivals Avenida Revolución for tourists' as well as locals' attention. A massive 10-story-high cathedral dedicated to the Virgin of Guadalupe is under construction in this neighborhood. It's due to be finished early in 2004; it will surely be a city landmark. ⊠ *Paseo de los Héroes between Blvd. Sanchez Taboada and the border, Zona Río.*

Where to Stay & Eat

$$–$$$ ✕ **El Faro de Mazatlán.** Fresh fish prepared simply is the hallmark of one of Tijuana's best seafood restaurants. This is the place to try ceviche, abalone, squid, and lobster without spending a fortune. Frequented by professionals, the dining room is a peaceful spot for a long, leisurely lunch. Appetizers and soup are included in the price of the meal. ⊠ *Blvd. Sanchez Taboada 9542, Zona Río* ☎ *664/684–8883* ▭ *MC, V.*

$$–$$$ ✕ **Señor Frog's.** Kitschy license plates, posters, and Mexican crafts cover the walls of this wildly popular restaurant where waiters encourage patrons to eat, drink, and sing along with the blaring music. Known for its barbecued ribs and chicken, the kitchen also prepares good Mexican standards such as tacos and *carne asada* (grilled strips of marinated meat). ⊠ *Pueblo Amigo, Paseo Tijuana 60, Zona Río* ☎ *664/682–4962* ▭ *AE, MC, V.*

$–$$$ ✕ **Cien Años.** In this gracious Spanish colonial–style restaurant, dishes include crepes filled with *huitlacoche* (fungus that grows on corn), shrimp with nopal cactus, and tender beef with avocado and cheese. Each has an unusual blend of flavors—tamarind, Mexican oregano, mango, poblano chilies—that distinguishes the taste of even the *queso fundido* (melted cheese wrapped in tortillas). ⊠ *Av. José María Velasco 1407, Zona Río* ☎ *664/634–7262* ▭ *MC, V.*

$–$$ ✕ **Chiki Jai.** The Monje family moved to Tijuana from Madrid in 1947, bringing Basque and Spanish cuisine to a tiny restaurant by El Palacio Frontón. They specialize in paella, but they also have a special way with calamari. Meals start with hot homemade bread and Roquefort cheese—the perfect accompaniment to a jug of sangria. ⊠ *Av. Revolución 1388, Centro* ☎ *664/685–4955* ▭ *No credit cards.*

$–$$ ✕ **La Fonda de Roberto.** Traditional dishes from all over the country share the menu here. Try the *chiles en nogada* (chilies stuffed with raisins and meat and topped with cream and pomegranate seeds), meats with spicy *achiote* sauce, and many varieties of mole. Portions are small, so order liberally and share samples. ⊠ *La Sierra Motel, Blvd. Cuauhtémoc Suroeste 2800, also called Old Ensenada Hwy., near Blvd. Agua Caliente Zona Río* ☎ *664/686–4687* ▭ *MC, V* ☉ *Closed Mon.*

¢–$$ ✕ **Carnitas Uruapan.** You'll need to take a cab to this festive restaurant, where patrons mingle at picnic tables and toast one another to live mariachi music. The main attraction here is *carnitas* (marinated pork roasted over an open pit), sold by weight and served with homemade tortillas, salsa, cilantro, guacamole, and onions. ⊠ *Blvd. Diaz Ordaz 12650 at Fracc. El Prado Otay Mesa* ☎ *664/681–6181* ▭ *No credit cards.*

★ ¢–$ ✕ **La Especial.** At the foot of the stairs leading to an underground shopping arcade you'll find the best place in the tourist zone for home-style Mexican cooking. The gruff, efficient waiters shuttle platters of carne asada, enchiladas, and burritos, all with a distinctive flavor found only

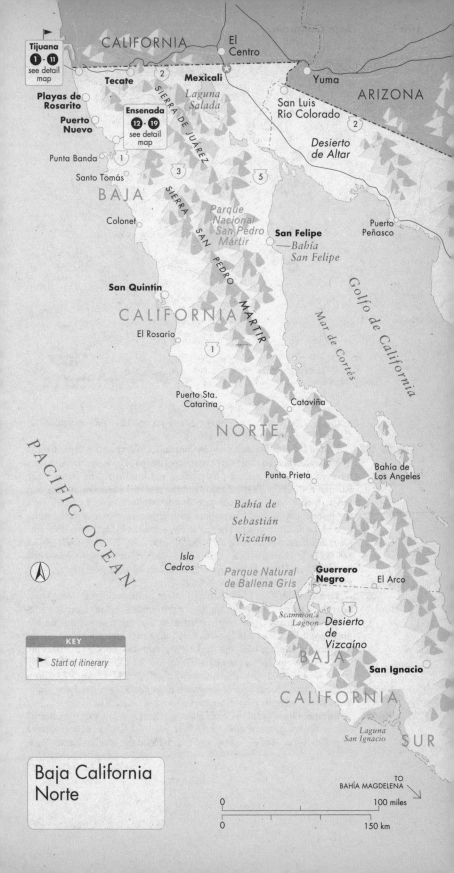

Baja California
Norte

at this busy, cavernous basement dining room. ⊠ *Av. Revolución 718, Centro* ☎ 664/685–6654 ☰ *MC, V.*

★ **$$–$$$** ✕⛯ **Real Del Mar Residence Inn by Marriott.** Golfers and escapists relish this all-suites hotel a short drive south of Tijuana. The suites' living rooms have vaulted brick ceilings, fireplaces, and kitchens. The Rincón San Román restaurant on the grounds of the resort is excellent and attracts diners from Tijuana and Rosarito. It nods to both France and Mexico; for instance, you could have beef with either an escargot garlic sauce or a chipotle chile sauce. The full-service spa provides ample diversion for nongolfers. ⊠ *Ensenada toll road, Km 19.5, 22710* ☎ *661/631–3670; 800/331–3131 in the U.S.* ⛬ *661/631–3677* ⊕ *www.realdelmar.com. mx* ⇆ *75 suites* ⟁ *2 restaurants, snack bar, 18-hole golf course, pool, gym, spa, bar* ☰ *AE, MC, V* |⊙| *CP.*

$$$ ⛯ **Camino Real.** This fashionable, modern purple-and-yellow high-rise near the Centro Cultural is the most prestigious hotel in town. It's a favorite of business types, but tourists also snap up reservations for the plush rooms decorated in browns and gold and the excellent restaurant. The location can't be beat, but the lack of a swimming pool is a detraction. ⊠ *Paseo de los Héroes 10305, Zona Río 22320* ☎ *664/633–4000* ⛬ *664/633–4001* ⊕ *www.tjcamino.com* ⇆ *235 rooms, 15 suites* ⟁ *Restaurant, room service, in-room data ports, in-room safes, minibar, cable TV, gym, 2 bars, laundry service* ☰ *AE, MC, V.*

$$–$$$ ⛯ **Lucerna.** Once one of the most charming hotels in Tijuana, the Lucerna is now showing its age. Still, the lovely gardens, large pool surrounded by palms, touches of tile work, and folk art lend the hotel a distinct Mexican character. ⊠ *Paseo de los Héroes 10902, at Av. Rodríguez, Zona Río 22320* ☎ *664/633–3900; 800/582–3762 in the U.S.* 🖷 *664/634–2400* ⊕ *www.hotel-lucerna.com.mx* ⊅ *156 rooms, 9 suites* ⚘ *Restaurant, coffee shop, room service, cable TV, pool, gym, nightclub, Internet, travel services* ⊟ *AE, MC, V.*

$$ ▦ **Grand Hotel.** The twin, mirrored towers of the hotel and a high-rise office building are Tijuana's most ostentatious landmarks. The rooms could use modernization, but are large; ask for one with good views of the city. It's an ideal spot for business travelers and anyone looking for a touch of luxury. The hotel mall has an Internet café. ⊠ *Blvd. Agua Caliente 4558, Zona Río 22420* ☎ *664/681–7000* 🖷 *664/681–7016* ⊕ *www.grandhoteltij.com.mx* ⊅ *422 rooms* ⚘ *Restaurant, minibars, 2 tennis courts, pool, gym, nightclub, shops, travel services* ⊟ *AE, MC, V.*

$$ ▦ **Fiesta Inn.** This quirky hotel sits between two boulevards on a landscaped island, next to the thermal spring for the 1920s-era Agua Caliente Spa. Today's rooms are modern and comfortable. The Vita Spa includes individual and couples' hot tubs fed from the healing spring and spa treatments at reasonable prices. ⊠ *Paseo de los Héroes 18818, Zona Río 22320* ☎ *664/634–6901; 800/343–7821 in the U.S.* 🖷 *664/634–6912* ⊕ *www.fiestainn.com* ⊅ *122 rooms, 5 suites* ⚘ *Restaurant, coffee shop, in-room data ports, in-room fax, cable TV, pool, gym, spa, laundry service, Internet, free parking* ⊟ *AE, MC, V.*

¢ ▦ **Hotel Nelson.** Were it better cared for, the Nelson's pale pink, five-story corner building might be considered a historic landmark. It feels like an older downtown inn, with a barbershop, somewhat noisy bar, and coffee shop on the ground floor. The rooms are serviceable and clean; the best have air-conditioning, heat, and cable TV. ⊠ *Av. Revolución 721, Centro 22000* ☎ *664/685–4302* 🖷 *664/685–4304* ⊅ *92 rooms* ⚘ *Restaurant, bar, parking (fee); no a/c in some rooms, no TV in some rooms* ⊟ *MC, V.*

¢ ▦ **La Villa de Zaragoza.** This brown stucco motel's strong suit is location; it's near El Palacio Frontón and around the corner from Avenida Revolución. The neighborhood can be noisy, though, so it's best to choose a room at the back. Some rooms have kitchenettes; the guarded parking lot is a major plus. The motel is used by tour groups, so book ahead for holidays and weekends. ⊠ *Av. Madero 1120, Centro 22000* ☎ *664/685–1832* 🖷 *664/685–1837* ⊕ *www.hotellavilla.biz* ⊅ *66 rooms* ⚘ *Restaurant, cable TV, free parking* ⊟ *MC, V.*

Nightlife & the Arts

Tijuana has toned down its Sin City image, but there are still plenty of boisterous bars on Avenida Revolución. Locals, however, prefer the classier nightclubs in the Zona Río. Tijuana's discos usually have strict dress codes—no T-shirts, jeans, or sandals allowed.

Baby Rock (⊠ Calle Diego Rivera 1482, Zona Río ☎ 664/634–2405), an offshoot of a popular Acapulco disco, attracts a young, hip crowd.

The **Hard Rock Cafe** (⊠ Av. Revolución 520, between Calles 1 and 2, Centro ☎ 664/685–0206) has the same menu and decor as other branches of the ubiquitous club.

Businessmen (there's a definite shortage of women here) favor **María Bonita** (⊠ Camino Real hotel, Paseo de los Héroes 10305, Zona Río ☎ 664/633–4000). Designed after the famed L'Opera bar in Mexico City, this small clublike tavern serves several brands of fine tequila along with beer and mixed drinks, and patrons are encouraged to play dominoes, chess, and card games at the tables.

Tijuana has its own brand name beer, thanks to the Czech brew master at **Tijuana Brewery Company/La Cervecería** (⊠ Blvd. Fundadores 2951, Centro ☎ 664/638–8662). The European-style pub serves Tijuana Claro and Tijuana Oscura, the light and dark beers brewed in the glassed-in brewery beside the bar. *Botanes,* or appetizers, include *chiles rellenos* (cheese-stuffed chilies deep-fried in batter) and smoked tuna; bands play some nights.

Sports & the Outdoors

BULLFIGHTING   Skilled matadors from throughout Mexico and Spain face down bulls in Tijuana. Admission to bullfights varies, depending on the fame of the matador and the location of your seat—try for one in the shade. Fights are held at **El Toreo de Tijuana** (⊠ Blvd. Agua Caliente, Zona Río ☎ 664/686–1510) Sunday at 4:30, May through October. In July and August you can see bullfights at the **Plaza de Toros Monumental** (⊠ Playas Tijuana area, Ensenada Hwy., Playas Tijuana ☎ 664/686–1219) Sunday at 4:30.

Shopping

The Avenida Revolución shopping area spreads across Calle 2 to the pedestrian walkway leading from the border. Begin by checking out the stands along the border-crossing walkway. You may find that the best bargains are closer to the border; you can pick up your piñatas and serapes on your way out of town. The traditional shopping strip is Avenida Revolución between Calles 1 and 8; it's lined with shops and arcades that display a wide range of crafts and curios. Bargaining is expected on the streets and in the arcades, but not in the finer shops.

Importaciones Sara (⊠ Av. Revolución 635, Centro ☎ 664/688–0488) has a wide selection of imported perfumes and fine clothing at attractive prices. High-quality furnishings and art are tastefully displayed at **Mallorca** (⊠ Calle 4 at Av. Revolución, Centro ☎ 664/688–3502). **La Piel** (⊠ Av. Revolución between Calles 4 and 5, Centro ☎ 664/634–1651) has dependable quality in its leather jackets, backpacks, and luggage. The shops in **Plaza Revolución** (⊠ Calle 1 at Av. Revolución, Centro) sell quality crafts.

You can find great buys on fashionable clothing and shoes at the **Plaza Río Tijuana** (⊠ Paseo de los Héroes 96 and 98, Zona Río ☎ 664/684–0402) center. **Sanborns** (⊠ Av. Revolución at Calle 8, Centro ☎ 664/688–1462) has beautiful crafts from throughout Mexico, an excellent bakery, and chocolates from Mexico City. The **Tijuana Tourist Terminal** (⊠ Av. Revolución between Calles 6 and 7, Centro ☎ 664/683–5681) is a one-stop center with clean rest rooms. The nicest folk-art store, **Tolán** (⊠ Av. Revolución 1471, between Calles 7 and 8, Centro ☎ 664/688–3637), carries everything from antique, carved wooden doors to tiny, ceramic miniature village scenes.

MARKET   The **Mercado Hidalgo** (⊠ Av. Independencia at Av. Sanchez Taboada, 5 blocks east of Revolución, Zona Río) is Tijuana's municipal market, with rows of fresh produce, some souvenirs, and the best selection of piñatas in Baja.

Playas de Rosarito

29 km (18 mi) south of Tijuana.

For better or worse, Rosarito has seen a transformation during the past few decades. Once a suburb, it has grown into a self-governed municipality separate from Tijuana. The region attracted considerable attention when 20th Century Fox built a permanent movie-production studio on the coastline south of town to film the mega-success *Titanic*. Today, the complex doubles as a theme park and a working studio.

Meanwhile, Rosarito's population, now about 100,000, has been growing steadily. The city's main drag, alternately known as the Old Ensenada Highway and Boulevard Benito Juárez, reflects the unrestrained growth and speculation that have both helped and harmed Rosarito. The street is packed with restaurants, bars, and shops in a jarring juxtaposition of building styles. Fortunately, the building boom has slowed and the town's boosters are attempting to beautify the boulevard.

Southern Californians use Rosarito as a weekend getaway, and the crowd is far from subdued—the town's on the spring break circuit. The police do their best to control the revelers, but spring and summer weekend nights can be outrageously noisy. But hedonism shares the bill with healthier pursuits. Surfers, swimmers, and sunbathers come here to enjoy the beach, which stretches from the power plant at the north end of town to about 8 km (5 mi) south. Horseback riding, jogging, and strolling are popular along this uninterrupted strand, where whales swim within viewing distance on their winter migration. Americans and Canadians continue to swell the ranks in vacation developments and gated retirement communities.

Rosarito has few historic or cultural attractions, beaches and bars being the main draws. Sightseeing consists of strolling along the beach or down **Boulevard Benito Juárez**'s collection of shopping arcades, restaurants, and motels.

Nearly everyone stops at the Rosarito Beach Hotel, the town's landmark historic hotel. Built during Prohibition, it has huge ballrooms, tiled fountains and stairways, murals, and a glassed-in pool deck overlooking the sea. A wooden pier stretches over the ocean; on calm days, there's no better place to watch the sunset than from the café tables along its glassed-in edges.

Museo Wa-Kuatay. Rosarito's history is illustrated in exhibits on the Kumiai Indians, the early missions, and ranching in the region at this small museum. ⊠ *Blvd. Juárez next to the Rosarito Beach Hotel* ☏ *No phone* 🎫 *Free* ⊘ *Open Tues.–Sun. 9–5.*

☾ **Foxploration.** Fox Studios has expanded its operation to include a film-oriented theme park. Guests learn how films are made by visiting a set resembling a New York street scene, and another filled with props from *Titanic*. Exhibits on filming, sound and light effects, and animation are both educational and entertaining, and Fox's most famous films are shown in the large state-of-the-art theater. The park includes a children's playroom where kids can shoot thousands of foam balls out of air cannons, a food court with U.S. franchises, and a large retail area. ⊠ *Old Ensenada Hwy., Km 32.8, Popotla* ☏ *661/614–9499* ⊕ *www.foxploration. com* 🎫 *$9–$12* ⊘ *Mon., Thurs., Fri. 9–5:30; weekends 10–6:30.*

Galería Giorgio Santini. Baja's finest painters and sculptors display their work in this architecturally stunning gallery. Stop by for a glass of wine or an espresso in the coffee shop, and learn something about Baja's vibrant art scene. ⊠ *Old Ensenada Hwy., Km 40* ☏ *661/614–1459* ⊕ *www.giorgiosantini.com* 🎫 *Free* ⊘ *Thurs.–Tues. 11–8.*

Where to Stay & Eat

★ **$$–$$$** ✕ **La Leña.** The cornerstone restaurant of the Quinta Plaza shopping center, La Leña is spacious and impeccably clean, with tables spread far enough apart for privacy. Try any of the beef dishes, especially the tender carne asada with tortillas and guacamole or the steak and lobster combo. ⊠ *Quinta Plaza, Blvd. Juárez 2500* ☎ *661/612–0826* ▱ *MC, V.*

$–$$$ ✕ **El Nido.** A dark, wood-paneled restaurant with leather booths and a large central fireplace, this is one of the oldest eateries in Rosarito. Diners unimpressed with newer, fancier places come here for mesquite-grilled steaks and for grilled quail from the owner's farm in the Baja wine country. ⊠ *Blvd. Juárez 67* ☎ *661/612–1430* ▱ *No credit cards.*

$–$$$ ✕ **El Patio.** Calm amid the bustle of the Festival Plaza complex, this tasteful, colonial-style restaurant is the best spot for a relaxed, authentic Mexican meal. The aromas of chilies, mole, and grilled meats spark the appetite. The menu favors dishes like grilled quail, shrimp crepes, and chicken with poblano sauce. The bar is peaceful as well—a good place to enjoy a cocktail away from the street-side crowds. ⊠ *Festival Plaza, Blvd. Juárez* ☎ *661/612–2950* ▱ *MC, V.*

¢–$ ✕ **La Flor de Michoacán.** Michoacán-style carnitas, served with homemade tortillas, guacamole, and salsa, are the hallmark of this rustic Rosarito landmark, established in 1950. The tacos, *tortas* (sandwiches), and tostadas are great. Takeout is available. ⊠ *Blvd. Juárez 291* ☎ *661/612–1858* ▱ *No credit cards* ⊘ *Closed Wed.*

¢ ✕ **Tacos El Yaqui.** For true down-home Mexican cooking, nothing beats this taco stand. Carne asada tacos with fresh corn tortillas are superb and the perfect fix for late-night munchies. The stand is clean and the cooks use purified water. ⊠ *Calle de la Palma off Blvd. Juárez, across from the Rosarito Beach Hotel* ☎ *No phone* ▱ *No credit cards.*

$$–$$$ ▨ **Rosarito Beach Hotel and Spa.** Charm rather than comfort is the main reason for staying here. The rooms in the oldest section have hand-painted wooden beams and heavy dark furnishings. Those in the tower have air-conditioning and a more modern pastel look. Reduced midweek rates and special packages are often available. ⊠ *Blvd. Juárez, south end of town* ⏃ *(Box 430145, San Diego, CA 22710)* ☎ *661/612–0144; 800/343–8582 in the U.S.* ⊕ *www.rosaritobeachhotel.com* ⤶ *180 rooms, 100 suites* ♨ *2 restaurants, in-room safes, tennis court, 2 pools, gym, spa, beach, bar, playground; no a/c in some rooms* ▱ *MC, V.*

$$ ▨ **Las Rocas.** This white hotel with blue-tile domes would be the most romantic in the area if the rooms were renovated. The least expensive ones are small; others are larger and have fireplaces and microwaves. All have ocean views; even the pool and whirlpool seem to spill into the Pacific. An excellent full spa offers state-of-the-art treatments at reasonable prices. ⊠ *Old Ensenada Hwy., Km 38.5, 22710* ☎ *661/614–0357; 888/527–7622 in the U.S.* ▤ *661/614–0360* ⊕ *www.lasrocas.com* ⤶ *40 rooms, 34 suites* ♨ *3 restaurants, cable TV, some kitchenettes, 2 pools, hot tub, spa, beach, 2 bars* ▱ *MC, V.*

$–$$ ▨ **Brisas del Mar.** This roadside motel is especially good for families—the large pastel rooms comfortably accommodate four people. A few of the suites on the second story have hot tubs and ocean views. The motel is on the inland side of Boulevard Juárez, and traffic noise can be a problem. ⊠ *Blvd. Juárez 22, 22710* ☎☎ *661/612–2547; 888/871–3605 in the U.S.* ⊕ *www.hotelbrisas.com* ⤶ *69 rooms, 2 suites* ♨ *Restaurant, pool, bar* ▱ *MC, V.*

$–$$ ▨ **Festival Plaza.** Designed with unrestrained fun in mind, the motel-like rooms are in an eight-story building beside the road and bars. The casitas close to the beach are the quietest accommodations and have small hot tubs, living rooms with fold-out couches, but no kitchen facilities. The 13 villas just south of Rosarito have full kitchens. The central courtyard serves as a concert stage, playground, and party headquarters. Discounted room rates are often available, especially in winter. ⊠ *Blvd. Juárez 1207, 22710* ☎ *661/612–2950; 800/453–8606 in the U.S.* ▤ *661/612–0124* ⊕ *www.festivalplaza.com* ⤶ *203 rooms,*

5 suites, 7 casitas, 13 villas ☖ *6 restaurants, pool, 7 bars, dance club* ▱ *MC, V.*

$–$$ ⌨ **Los Pelicanos Hotel.** Guests return annually to their favorite rooms in this small hotel by the beach. Those without ocean views are inexpensive; rates are higher for rooms on the top floors. Some rooms have little outside light. The restaurant is a local favorite for sunset cocktails. ⊠ *Calle Ebano 113, 22710* ☎ *661/612–0445 or 661/612–1757* ⊕ *www.los-pelicanos.com* ⤴ *39 rooms* ☖ *Restaurant, bar* ▱ *AE, MC, V.*

Nightlife & the Arts

Rosarito's many restaurants keep customers entertained with live music, piano bars, or *folklórico* (folk music and dance) shows, and the bar scene is hopping as well. Drinking-and-driving laws are stiff; the police will fine you no matter how little you've had. If you drink, take a cab or assign a designated driver. The police also enforce laws that prohibit drinking in the streets; confine your revelry to the bars.

The **Festival Plaza** (⊠ Blvd. Juárez 1207 ☎ 661/612–2950) has become party central for Rosarito's younger crowd and presents live concerts on the hotel's courtyard stage most weekends. In the hotel complex are **El Museo Cantina Tequila** (☎ 661/612–2950), dedicated to the art of imbibing tequila and stocked with more than 130 brands of the fiery drink. Also at Festival Plaza, **Rock & Roll Taco** is a taco stand and the largest (and probably the most rambunctious) dancing and drinking hangout in town.

Papas and Beer (⊠ On the beach off Blvd. Juárez near Rosarito Beach Hotel ☎ 661/612–0444) draws a young, energetic crowd for drinking and dancing on the beach and small stages.

Rene's Sports Bar (⊠ Carretera Transpeninsular, Km 28 ☎ 661/612–1061) draws a somewhat quieter, older crowd; the restaurant isn't great, but a few pool tables, TVs broadcasting sporting events, and a convivial gaggle of gringos make the bar a great hangout.

There's a lot going on at night at the **Rosarito Beach Hotel** (⊠ Blvd. Juárez ☎ 661/612–0144): live music at the ocean-view **Beach Comber Bar**; a Mexican Fiesta on Friday and Saturday nights; and occasional live bands and dances in the cavernous ballroom.

Sports & the Outdoors

GOLF   The **Real del Mar Golf Club** (⊠ 18 km [11 mi] south of the border on Ensenada toll road ☎ 661/631–3670) has 18 holes overlooking the ocean. Golf packages are available at some Rosarito Beach hotels.

HORSEBACK   You can hire horses at the north and south ends of Boulevard Juárez
RIDING   and on the beach south of the Rosarito Beach Hotel for $10 per hour. If you're a dedicated equestrian, ask about tours into the countryside, which can be arranged with the individual owners.

SURFING   Surfers head south of Rosarito to long beaches where there are good beach breaks. The most popular are just known by the kilometer marking on the Old Ensenada Highway, and include **Popotla** (Km 33), **Calafía** (Km 35.5), and **Costa Baja** (Km 36). The water is chilly most of the year, but reaches the mid 70s in August and September. The **Inner Reef Surf Shop** (⊠ Old Ensenada Highway, Km 34.5 ☎ 661/613–2065) rents surfboards, boogie boards, and wet suits.

Shopping

Shopping is far better in Rosarito than in most Baja cities, especially for pottery, wood furniture, and high-end household items favored by condo owners in nearby expat clusters. Curio stands and open-air artisans' markets line Boulevard Juárez both north and south of town. Major hotels have shopping arcades with decent crafts stores.

Apisa (⊠ Blvd. Juárez 2400 ☎ 661/612–0125) is said to be the finest home-decor shop in town, and sells contemporary furnishings and iron sculptures from Guadalajara. **Casa la Carreta** (⊠ Old Ensenada Hwy., Km 29 ☎661/612–0502), one of Rosarito's best furniture shops, is worth a visit just to see the wood-carvers shaping elaborate desks, dining tables, and armoires. **Casa Torres** (⊠ Rosarito Beach Hotel Shopping Center, Blvd. Juárez ☎ 661/612–1008) carries a wide array of imported perfumes. There are several shops in this center by the hotel's parking lot, along with an Internet café. The **Mercado de Artesanías** (⊠Blvd. Juárez 306 ☎ no phone) has the largest selection of manufactured souvenirs, with everything from sombreros to serapes. Resembling a colonial church with its facade of hand-painted tiles, **La Misión del Viejo** (⊠ Blvd. Juárez 139 ☎ 661/612–1576) displays hand-carved chairs, tin lamps shaped like stars, and glazed pottery.

Puerto Nuevo (Newport)

Old Ensenada Hwy., Km 44, 12 km (7½ mi) south of Rosarito.

Southern Californians regularly cross the border to indulge in the classic Puerto Nuevo meal: grilled lobster, refried beans, rice, homemade tortillas, salsa, and lime. At least 30 restaurants are packed into this village; nearly all offer the identical menu. The perennial attraction has become so popular that the town holds a wine and lobster festival in October. An artisans' market sits at the entrance to the restaurant row, and stands selling pottery, serapes, and T-shirts line the highway. Several longtime favorite inns and restaurants hug the road south to Ensenada. A marina is under construction at Puerto Salina south of Puerto Nuevo; when completed (there's no finish date in sight), it will allow private boaters to anchor and refuel before reaching Ensenada.

Where to Stay & Eat

Don't expect much variety in the food at any of the Puerto Nuevo restaurants: people come here for the classic lobster meal. Some places have full bars; others serve only wine and beer. **La Casa de la Langosta** (⊠ Tiguron at Anzuelo ☎ 661/664–4102) serves grilled fish along with lobster and shrimp. **Ortega's** (⊠ Chinchorro 12 ☎ 661/664–1411 ⊠ Anzuelo and Arpon ☎ 661/664–1079) branches are the most crowded spots. **Ponderosa** (⊠ Chinchorro 8 ☎ 661/644–1026) is on the smaller and quieter side and is run by a gracious family. **Puerto Nuevo II** (⊠ Av. Renteria 2 ☎ 661/644–1454) offers unusual preparations of scallops and abalone (when it's available). Lobsters in most places are priced as small, medium, and large—medium is about $15. Some of the lobster comes from the waters off Baja's shores, and is frozen when not in season (October through March). Many places import frozen lobster from the mainland; most are open for lunch and dinner on a first-come, first-served basis. Some take credit cards.

$$–$$$ ☒ **Hacienda Bajamar.** On the grounds of the Bajamar golf resort, south of Puerto Nuevo and about halfway between Rosarito and Ensenada, this hacienda-style hotel surrounds a central courtyard. Rooms have hand-carved furnishings and French doors leading to landscaped patios. Private condos (some for rent) edge the golf course and the cliffs overlooking the ocean. ⊠ *Old Ensenada Hwy., Km 77.5, 22800 Ensenada* ☎ *661/ 155–0184; 619/472–8522 in the U.S.* 🖷*661/155–0186* ⊕*www.bajamar. com* ⤶ *81 rooms* ⚭ *Restaurant, snack bar, room service, cable TV, driving range, golf course, 2 tennis courts, pool, spa, bar* 🖃 *AE, MC, V.*

$$ ⊞ **La Fonda.** Landmark La Fonda has well-worn rooms decorated with carved-wood furniture, old bullfighting posters, and local folk art; most have ocean views. There are no phones or televisions, just the beach to keep you entertained. The bar is packed on weekend nights. Ask for a room as close to the surf as possible. The hotel is south of Puerto Nuevo in La Misión. ⊠ *Old Ensenada Hwy., Km 59, 22710* ⊕ *(Box 430268, San Ysidro, CA 92143)* ☎ *646/155–0307* ⇥ *26 rooms* ⌂ *Beach, bar; no room phones, no room TVs* ⊟ *No credit cards.*

$$ ⊞ **New Port Beach Hotel.** The closest accommodations to the lobster restaurants are in this sand-color complex with ocean views. Rooms have heaters for chilly winter nights, along with cable TV, small balconies, and simple blue-gray and white furnishings. The hotel has dance bands in the upstairs lounge, marimba music on the weekend in the lobby bar, and classical music on Sunday. ⊠ *Old Ensenada Hwy., Km 45, 22712* ☎ *661/614–1166; 800/582–1018 in the U.S.* ⎙ *661/614–1174* ⊕ *www. newportbeachhotel.com* ⇥ *147 rooms* ⌂ *Restaurant, in-room safes, cable TV, 2 tennis courts, pool, gym, bar, no-smoking rooms* ⊟ *MC, V.*

Sports & the Outdoors

GOLF **Bajamar** (⊠ Old Ensenada Hwy., Km 77.5 ☎ 661/155–0184; 646/155–0161 for tee times) has 18 holes of championship-level golf on the cliffs above the ocean and another nine holes near the beach.

en route Open views of pounding surf and jagged cliffs are interspersed with one-of-a-kind hotels and restaurants along the coastline between Rosarito and Ensenada. The paved highway (Mexico Highway 1) between the two cities often cuts a path between low mountains and high oceanside cliffs. Exits lead to rural roads, oceanfront campgrounds, and an ever-increasing number of resort communities. The small fishing villages of **San Miguel** and **El Sauzal** sit off the highway to the north of Ensenada, and you can see the **Coronado Islands** clearly off the coast.

Ensenada

104 km (65 mi) south of Tijuana, 75 km (47 mi) south of Rosarito.

In 1542 Juan Rodríguez Cabrillo first discovered the seaport that Sebastián Vizcaíno named Ensenada-Bahía de Todos Santos (All Saints' Bay) in 1602. Since then the town has drawn a steady stream of explorers and developers. First ranchers made their homes on large plots along the coast and into the mountains. Gold miners followed in the late 1800s. After mine stocks were depleted, the area settled back into a pastoral state, but the harbor gradually grew into a major port for shipping agricultural goods. Today, the third-largest city in Baja with a population of some 369,000, it's one of Mexico's largest seaports and has a thriving fishing fleet and fish-processing industry.

There are no beaches in Ensenada proper, but beaches north and south of town are satisfactory for swimming, sunning, surfing, and camping. On summer and holiday weekends the population swells, but the town rarely feels overcrowded. Ensenada tends to draw those who want to explore a more traditional Mexican city.

Many cruise ships stop for at least a few hours in Ensenada to clear Mexican customs; thus, Ensenada is called Baja's largest cruise-ship port. Both the waterfront and downtown's main street are pleasant places to stroll. If you are driving, be sure to take the Centro exit from the highway, since it bypasses the commercial port area.

⑬ Las Bodegas de Santo Tomás. One of Baja's oldest wineries gives tours and tastings at its downtown winery and bottling plant. The local restaurant, La Embotelladora Vieja, is one of Baja's finest. The winery also operates La Esquina de Bodegas, a café, shop, and gallery in a bright-blue building across Avenida Miramar. ⊠ *Av. Miramar 666, Centro* ☎ *646/174–0836 or 646/174–0829* ✆ *$2* ☉ *Tours, tastings daily at 11, 1, and 3.*

⑲ Catedral Nuestra Señora de Guadalupe. The city's largest cathedral is named for the country's patron saint, and is the center of celebrations on December 12, the feast of the Virgin of Guadalupe. Though modest in comparison to cathedrals on the mainland, the church does have impressive stained-glass windows. ⊠ *Av. Floresta at Av. Juárez, Centro.*

⑭ Mercado de Mariscos. At the northernmost point of Boulevard Costero, the main street along the waterfront, is an indoor-outdoor fish market where row after row of counters display piles of shrimp, tuna, dorado, and other fish caught off Baja's coasts. Outside, stands sell grilled or smoked fish, seafood cocktails, and fish tacos. Browsers can pick up some standard souvenirs, eat well for very little money, and take some great photographs. The original fish taco stands line the dirt path to the fish market. If your stomach is on the delicate side, try the fish tacos at the cleaner, quieter **Plaza de Mariscos** in the shadow of the giant beige **Plaza de Marina** that blocks the view of the traditional fish market from the street.

⑮ Muelle de Pescador. Fishing and whale-watching boats depart from the pier. The area around the pier has been remodeled, and a broad *malecón* (seaside walkway) with park benches and palms runs along the waterfront. ⊠ *Blvd. Costero at Av. Alvarado, Centro.*

⑫ **Parque Revolución.** Revolution Park is the most traditional plaza in Ensenada, with a bandstand, playground, and plenty of benches in the shade. The plaza takes on a festive feeling weekend evenings, when neighbors congregate on the benches and children chase seagulls. ⊠ *Av. Obregón between Calles 6 and 7, Centro.*

⑰ **Paseo Calle Primera.** The renamed Avenida López Mateos is the center of Ensenada's traditional tourist zone. High-rise hotels, souvenir shops, restaurants, and bars line the avenue for eight blocks, from its beginning at the foot of the Chapultepec Hills to the dry channel of the Arroyo de Ensenada. Tourist promoters have sponsored a beautification project along the avenue, which now has sidewalks, outdoor cafés, and restored storefronts. Businesses use one or both street names for their addresses, though most stick with López Mateos. Locals shop for furniture, clothing, and other necessities a few blocks inland on **Avenida Juárez,** in Ensenada's downtown area.

⑯ **Plaza Cívica.** This block-long concrete park with sculptures of Mexican heroes Benito Juárez, Miguel Hidalgo, and Venustiano Carranza feels more like a monument than a gathering spot, but there are benches and horse-drawn carriages at the ready. ⊠ *Blvd. Costero at Av. Riveroll, Centro.*

⑱ **Riviera del Pacífico.** Officially called the Centro Social, Cívico y Cultural de Ensenada, the Riviera is a rambling white, hacienda-style mansion built in the 1920s. An enormous gambling palace, hotel, restaurant, and bar, the glamorous Riviera was frequented by wealthy U.S. citizens and Mexicans, particularly during Prohibition. When gambling was outlawed in Mexico and Prohibition ended in the United States, the palace lost its raison d'être. You can tour some of the elegant ballrooms and halls, which occasionally host art shows and civic events. Many of the rooms are locked; check at the main office to see if someone is available to show you around. The gardens alone are worth visiting, and the building houses the **Museo de Historia de Ensenada,** a museum on Baja's history. ⊠ *Blvd. Costero at Av. Riviera, Centro* ☎ *646/177–0594* ⊠ *Building and gardens free, museum donations requested* ☉ *Daily 9:30–2 and 3–5.*

---

off the beaten path

La Bufadora. Seawater splashes up to 75 ft in the air, spraying sightseers standing near this impressive tidal blowhole (*la bufadora* means the buffalo snort) in the coastal cliffs at Punta Banda. Legend has it that the blowhole was created by a whale or sea serpent trapped in an undersea cave; both these stories, and the less romantic scientific facts, are posted on a roadside plaque here. The road to La Bufadora along Punta Banda, an isolated, mountainous point that juts into the sea, is lined with stands selling olives, tamales, strands of chilies and garlic, and terra-cotta planters. The drive gives short-term visitors a sampling of Baja's wilderness and is well worth a half-day excursion. Public rest rooms are available, and there are a few restaurants including the extremely popular Gordo's, which is open Friday through Sunday. There's a small fee to park near the blowhole. A public bus runs from the downtown Ensenada bus station to Maneadero, the nearest town on the highway to La Bufadora. There, you can catch a minibus labeled Punta Banda that goes to La Bufadora. ⊠ *Hwy. 23, 31 km (19 mi) south of Ensenada, Punta Banda.*

Beaches

The waterfront in Ensenada proper is taken up by fishing boats, repair yards, and commercial shipping. The best swimming beaches are south of town. **Estero Beach** is long and clean, with mild waves; the Estero Beach Hotel takes up much of the oceanfront, but the beach is public. Surfers populate the beaches off Highway 1 north and south of Ensenada, particularly **San Miguel, Tres Marías,** and **Salsipuedes;** scuba divers prefer **Punta Banda,** by La Bufadora. Lifeguards are rare, so swimmers should be cautious. The tourist office in Ensenada has a map that shows safe diving and surfing beaches.

Where to Stay & Eat

★ $$–$$$$ ✕ **El Rey Sol.** From its chateaubriand *bouquetière* (garnished with a bouquet of vegetables) to the savory chicken chipotle, this family-owned French restaurant sets the standard for fine dining in Baja. Louis XIV–style furnishings and an attentive staff make it both comfortable and elegant. The sidewalk tables are a perfect place to dine and enjoy people-watching. The small café in the front sells pastries, all made on the premises, to go. ⊠ *Av. López Mateos 1000, Centro* ☎ 646/178–1733 ▤ *AE, MC, V.*

$–$$$ ✕ **La Embotelladora Vieja.** Ensenada's most elegant restaurant was once a wine-aging room at the Santo Tomás winery. The Baja French menu could include smoked tuna, grilled lobster in cabernet sauvignon sauce, or quail with sauvignon blanc sauce. Some dishes are available without alcohol-enhanced sauces. ⊠ *Av. Miramar 666, Centro* ☎ 646/178–1660 ▤ *AE, MC, V* ◷ *Closed Mon.*

★ $–$$$ ✕ **Mariscos de Bahía de Ensenada.** Red lights flicker around the front door, making this popular seafood house just off the main drag easy to spot. The place is packed on weekends. Clams, shrimp, lobster, red snapper, squid, and other fresh seafood are fried, baked, broiled, or grilled, and served with a basic iceberg-lettuce salad, white rice, and tortillas made fresh at the window-front tortillería. A few canopied sidewalk tables allow for outdoor dining. ⊠ *Av. Riveroll 109, Centro* ☎ 646/178–1015 ▤ *AE, MC, V.*

★ $–$$ ✕ **Hacienda Del Charro.** Hungry patrons hover over platters of chiles rellenos, enchiladas, and fresh chips and guacamole at heavy wooden picnic tables. Plump chickens slowly turn over a wood fire by the front window, and the aroma of simmering beans fills the air. ⊠ *Av. López Mateos 454, Centro* ☎ 646/178–2114 ▤ *No credit cards.*

$–$$ ✕ **Oxidos Café.** Baja meets L.A. at this new-wave café where the metal sculptures and other original art are as interesting as the food. The menu aims to satisfy hungry diners with hearty burgers, ribs, and pasta. The bar is a gathering spot for local artists—you're sure to get into some interesting conversations if you hang out here. ⊠ *Av. Ruíz 108, Centro* ☎ 646/178–8827 ▤ *No credit cards.*

¢–$ ✕ **Bronco's Steak House.** A great find near the Riviera del Pacífico, Bronco's serves exceptional steaks and Mexican specialties. Try the *puntas de filete al chipotle,* tender beef tips with smoke-flavored chipotle chilies. Tripe appears frequently on the menu, satisfying the cravings of the local diners gathered at many of the wood tables. Brick walls, wood-plank floors, and hanging spurs and chaps give the place a Wild West feel, but the mood is subdued and relaxed. Locals rave about the weekend breakfast buffet. ⊠ *Av. López Mateos 1525, Centro* ☎ 646/172–4892 ▤ *AE, MC, V.*

$$ ▥ **Estero Beach Resort.** Families love this long-standing resort on Ensenada's best beach. The best rooms (some with kitchenettes) are by the sand; the worst are by the parking lot. Nonguests should check out the outstanding collection of folk art and artifacts in the resort's small museum. Midweek winter rates are a real bargain. ⊠ *Mexico Hwy. 1, 10 km (6 mi) south of Ensenada, Estero Beach* ⌂ *(482 W. San Ysidro Blvd., San Ysidro, CA 92173)* ☎ 646/176–6230 or 646/176–6255 ⎙ 646/176–

6925 ⊕ *www.hotelesterobeach.com* ⇦ *94 rooms, 2 suites, RV park* ⟁ *Restaurant, kitchenettes, 4 tennis courts, pool, horseback riding, volleyball, bar, shops, playground* ☰ MC, V.

★ $$ ⊞ **Hotel Coral & Marina.** The largest resort on the Baja Norte coast features a marina with slips for 600 boats and customs-clearing facilities. All rooms here are suites. Those in the two eight-story towers are decorated in burgundy and dark green; most have waterfront balconies, seating areas, and international phone service. The full-service spa, tennis courts, and water-sports center are added attractions that keep the hotel full during boat races and holidays. The rates are often lower on winter weekdays. ⊠ *Mexico Hwy. 1, Km 103, Zona Playitas 22860* ☎ 646/175–0000; 800/862–9020 *in the U.S.* ≅ 646/175–0005 ⊕ *www.hotelcoral.com* ⇦ *147 suites* ⟁ *Restaurant, room service, minibars, cable TV, 2 tennis courts, 3 pools (1 indoor), gym, hot tub, spa, boating, fishing, free parking* ☰ MC, V.

★ $$ ⊞ **Punta Morro.** Just five minutes from Ensenada, this secluded all-suites hotel is a great place to relax. The restaurant, perched above the crashing waves, has an excellent combination of Continental cuisine and fresh seafood. All rooms have seaside terraces and fireplaces. Studios with kitchens are the least expensive units; two- and three-bedroom suites are available for groups and families. ⊠ *Mexico Hwy. 1, Km 106, Zona Playitas* ✆ *(Box 434263 San Diego CA 92143)* ☎ 646/178–3507; 800/526–6676 *in the U.S.* ≅ 646/174–4490 ⊕ *www.punta-morro.com* ⇦ *24 suites* ⟁ *Restaurant, in-room data ports, refrigerators, pool, hot tub, beach, bar* ☰ AE, MC, V ⦿I CP.

$$ ⊞ **Las Rosas.** All guest rooms in this intimate hotel north of Ensenada face the ocean and pool; some have fireplaces and hot tubs, and even the least expensive are lovely. The atrium lobby has marble floors, mint-green-and-pink couches that look out at the sea, and a glass ceiling that glows at night. Make reservations far in advance. ⊠ *Mexico Hwy. 1, north of Ensenada, Zona Playitas* ✆ *374 E. H St. Chula Vista CA 91910* ☎ 646/174–4320 or 646/174–4360 ≅ 646/174–4595 ⊕ *www.lasrosas.com* ⇦ *48 rooms* ⟁ *Restaurant, pool, hot tub, bar* ☰ AE, MC, V.

¢ ⊞ **Hotel del Valle.** Fishermen and budget travelers frequent the clean, basic rooms in this small hotel on a relatively quiet side street. Although the rooms lack air-conditioning, they're well maintained and have fans and phones. Guests have use of a coffeemaker in the lobby and parking spaces in front of the rooms. Ask about rate discounts—those posted behind the front desk are about 40% higher than guests in the know normally pay. ⊠ *Av. Riveroll 367, Centro 22800* ☎ 646/178–2224 ≅ 646/174–0466 ⇦ *43 rooms* ⟁ *Cable TV; no a/c* ☰ MC, V.

¢ ⊞ **Joker Hotel.** A bizarre, colorful mishmash of styles makes it hard to miss the Joker, which is conveniently located for those traveling south of Ensenada. The spacious rooms have private balconies. Traffic noise from the highway and from guests leaving at the crack of dawn can be a problem; try to stay away from the road and the busiest parts of the parking lot. ⊠ *Mexico Hwy. 1, Km 12.5, Ejido Chapultepec 22800* ☎ 646/176–7201 ≅ 646/177–4460 ⇦ *40 rooms* ⟁ *Restaurant, cable TV, pool, hot tub, bar, nightclub* ☰ MC, V.

Nightlife & the Arts

Ensenada is a party town for college students, surfers, and other young tourists, though it's also possible to enjoy a mellow evening out. **La Capilla** (⊠ Hotel El Cid, Paseo Calle Primera 997, Centro ☎ 646/178–2401 Ext. 104) is better suited to an older crowd who enjoy live Cuban music and romantic ballads in a relaxed setting. **Hussong's Cantina** (⊠ Av. Ruíz 113, Centro ☎ 646/178–3210) has been an Ensenada landmark since 1892 and has changed little since then. A security guard stands by the front door to handle the often rowdy crowd—a mix of locals and tourists of all ages over 18. The noise is usually deafening, pierced by mariachi and ranchera musicians and the whoops and hollers of the pie-eyed. **Papas and Beer** (⌧ Av. Ruíz 102, Centro ☎ 646/174–0145) attracts a collegiate crowd.

Sports & the Outdoors

FISHING   Boats leave the Ensenada **sportfishing pier** regularly. The best angling is from April through November, with bottom fishing good in winter. Charter vessels and party boats are available from several outfitters along Avenida López Mateos and Boulevard Costero and off the sportfishing pier. Trips on group boats cost about $45 for a half day or $100 for a full day. Mexican fishing licenses for the day or year are available at the tourist office or from charter companies.

You can book sportfishing packages including transportation, accommodations, and fishing through **Baja California Tours** (⌧ 7734 Herschel Ave. Suite O La Jolla CA 92037 ☎ 858/454–7166; 800/336–5454 in the U.S. 🖷 858/454–2703 ⊕ www.bajaspecials.com). **Ensenada Clipper Fleet** (⌧ Sportfishing Pier, Blvd. Costero at Av. Alvarado, Centro ☎ 646/178–2185) has charter and group boats. **Sergio's Sportfishing** (⌧ Sportfishing Pier, Blvd. Costero at Av. Alvarado, Centro ☎ 646/178–2185 ⊕ www.sergios-sportfishing.com), one of the best sportfishing companies in Ensenada, has charter and group boats, and slips for guests' boats.

GOLF   The **Baja Country Club** (⌧ Mexico Hwy. 1 south of Ensenada, Maneadero ☎ 646/177–5523) has a secluded 18-hole course in a resort development.

WATER SPORTS   Estero Beach and Punta Banda (en route to La Bufadora south of Ensenada) are both good kayaking areas, although facilities are limited. **Expediciones de Turismo Ecológico y Aventura** (⌧ Blvd. Costero 1094-14, Centro ☎ 646/178–3704 ⊕ www.mexonline.com/ecotur.htm) runs kayaking trips and other adventure tours in the region.

Dale's La Bufadora Shop (⌧ Rancho La Bufadora, Punta Banda ☎ 646/154–2092) offers scuba diving trips (with all gear available for rent) to seamounts and walls off Punta Banda. They also have whale-watching trips in the winter.

Some of the best surf on the coast is found off Islas de Todos Santos, two islands about 19 km (12 mi) west of Ensenada. Only the best and boldest surfers challenge the waves here, which can reach 30 ft in winter. Surfers must hire a boat to take them to the waves. Calmer, but still exciting, waves crash on the beaches at San Miguel, Tres Marías, and Salsipuedes. **San Miguel Surf Shop** (⌧ Av. López Mateos at Calle Ruíz, Centro ☎ 646/178–1007) is the unofficial local surfing headquarters. They can guide you toward the best areas and to gear rental.

WHALE-   Boats leave the Ensenada **sportfishing pier** for whale-watching trips from
WATCHING   December through February. The gray whales migrating from the north to bays and lagoons in southern Baja pass through Todos Santos Bay, often close to shore. Binoculars and telephoto camera lenses come in handy. The trips last about three hours. Vessels and tour boats are available from several outfitters at the sportfishing pier. You can book whale-watching packages, which include transportation, accommodations, and the boat trips, through the American company **Baja California Tours** (☎ 858/454–7166 or 800/336–5454 in the U.S. 🖷 858/454–2703 ⊕ www.bajaspecials.com).

Shopping

Most of the tourist shops are located along Avenida López Mateos beside the hotels and restaurants. There are several two-story shopping arcades, many with empty shops. Dozens of curio shops line the street, all selling similar selections of pottery, serapes, and more.

Artes Don Quijote (⊠ Av. López Mateos 503, Centro ☎ 646/174–4082) has an impressive array of carved wood doors, huge terra-cotta pots, and crafts from Oaxaca. It's closed on Tuesday. **Bazar Casa Ramirez** (⊠ Av. López Mateos 510, Centro ☎ 646/178–8209) sells high-quality Talavera pottery and other ceramics, wrought-iron items, and papier-mâché figurines. Be sure to check out the displays upstairs. At **Los Castillo** (⊠ Av. López Mateos 1076, Centro ☎ 646/178–2335), the display of silver jewelry from Taxco is limited but of excellent quality. The **Centro Artesenal de Ensenada** has a smattering of galleries and shops. By far, the best shop there is **Galería de Pérez Meillón** (⊠ Blvd. Costero 1094–39, Centro ☎ 646/174–0394), with its museum-quality Casas Grandes pottery and varied folk art by indigenous northern Mexican peoples.

La Esquina de Bodegas (⊠ Av. Miramar at Calle 6, Centro ☎ 646/178–3557) is an innovative gallery, shop, and café in a century-old winery building. Bargain hunters are delighted with **Los Globos** (⊠ Calle 9, 3 blocks east of Reforma, Centro ☎ no phone), a daily open-air swap meet. Vendors and shoppers are most abundant on weekends. **Mario's Silver** (⊠ Calle Primera 1090-6, Centro ☎ 646/178–2451) has several branches along the main street tempting shoppers with displays of silver and gold jewelry. **La Mina de Salomón** (⊠ Av. López Mateos 1000, Centro ☎ 646/178–1733) carries elaborate jewelry in a tiny gallery next to El Rey Sol restaurant.

Side Trip to the Valle de Guadalupe

Most of Baja's wineries are in the Valle de Guadalupe northeast of Ensenada on Highway 3 to Tecate. The valley, originally settled by Russian immigrants, is one of the loveliest parts of the state, with vast vineyards and rambling hacienda-style estates. The area settled by the Russians is now called Colonia Rusa; it's about 32 km (20 mi) from Ensenada. A few of the wineries in the valley are open to the public; some require appointments. **Chateau Camou** (☎ 646/177–3303 ⊕ www. chateau-camou.com.mx) is a good example of the new wave of valley wineries; it offers tours by appointment. **Domecq** (⊠ Hwy. 3, Km 73 ☎ 646/165–2249) offers wine tastings and tours on weekdays 10–4 and Saturday 10–1:30. **L.A. Cetto** (⊠ Hwy. 3, Km 73.5 ☎ 646/155–2264) has wine tastings and tours daily 10–4. Serious oenophiles should call ahead to visit **Monte Xanic** (☎ 646/174–6155 ⊕ www.montexanic.com. mx), one of the finest wineries in Mexico. Their wines were served at President Vicente Fox's inaugural dinner.

Baja California Tours (☎ 858/454–7166 or 800/336–5454 in the U.S. ☎ 858/454–2703 ⊕ www.bajaspecials.com) frequently offers winery tours, which include visits to several wineries, a historical overview of the valley, transportation from the border, and lunch.

The **Museo Comunitario del Valle de Guadalupe** (⊠ Hwy. 3, Km 70 ☎ 646/ 155–2030), open Tuesday–Sunday 9–5, contains a display of Russian household items from the local indigenous settlements in a 1905 Russian home. If it's not open, ask around for the caretaker.

Fiesta Farms Organic Herb & Flower Ranch (⊠ Hwy. 3, Km 90.5 ☎ 760/ 451–0912 in the U.S.) offers guided tours on Saturday at 11 AM. The fields are prettiest after the spring rains in April and May, when the desert flowers and herbs bloom. The farm is open weekdays 8–3 and Saturday 8–noon.

★ **$$** ✕ **Laja.** One sign that the Valle de Guadalupe has its sights on Napa is this extraordinary restaurant. The ambitious prix fixe menu changes frequently, but may include *escabeche* (pickled) mussel salad, ling cod with crab sauce, and braised apples with vanilla and honey ice cream, all served with excellent regional wines. Polished woods and windows overlooking the valley make the dining room as sleek as the menu. A meal here is well worth the drive. ⊠ *Hwy. 3, Km 83* ☎ *646/155–2556* ⌂ *Reservations essential* ⊟ *No credit cards* ⊘ *Closed Mon.–Wed. No dinner Thurs. or Sun.*

Tecate

32 km (20 mi) east of Tijuana, 112 km (69 mi) northeast of Ensenada.

Tecate is a quiet border community with a population of about 100,000 and the pleasant ambience of a small Mexican town. Visitors stop by on day trips from Tijuana, Ensenada, or San Diego to shop and to have lunch at modest cafés facing the pleasant Parque Hidalgo. Tecate's most famous attraction is the Rancho la Puerta spa. Downtown Tecate is centered on the **Parque Hidalgo.** A few cabdrivers, shoe-shine boys, schoolchildren, and snuggling couples hang out around the small gazebo. On summer evenings, dance and band concerts are held in **Parque López Mateos,** on Highway 3 south of town.

One of the most popular beers in Mexico comes from the **Tecate Brewery** (⊠ Av. Hidalgo at Calle Carranza ☎ 665/654–9478). Now part of the huge Cervecería Cuauhtémoc-Moctezuma corporation, the brewery has been updated and produces several brews, including the famed red cans of Tecate beer. Tours of the brewery are available only for groups and must be arranged in advance, but you can visit the beer gardens and quaff two free beers. It's open weekdays 10–5, weekends 10–2.

Home owners from both sides of the border shop for floor tiles, garden fountains, and flower pots at **Baja-Mex-Tile** (⊠ Blvd. Juárez 9150 ☎ 665/654–0204).

Where to Stay & Eat

¢–$ ✕ **El Jardín.** Nearly everyone who wanders through town on a day trip ends up stopping here. The setting is plain and the food simple Mexican fare, but the café tables outside have a nice view of the children playing in the plaza. Musicians stop by in the evening, offering to play for a few pesos. ⊠ *Callejón Libertad 274* ☎ *665/654–3453* ⊟ *No credit cards.*

¢ ✕ **Panadería de Tecate.** Open 24 hours every day except Christmas and New Year's, this simple bakery is famed throughout the region. The kitchen whips up more than 100 types of cookies, doughnuts, *pan dulce* (sweet bread), crunchy *bolillos* (rolls), and cakes. ⊠ *Av. Juárez 331* ☎ *665/654–0040* ⊟ *No credit cards.*

$$$$ 🏨 **Rancho la Puerta.** Spanish-style buildings and modern glass-and-wood structures spread throughout the sprawling ranch at this isolated spa. Guests stay in luxurious private cottages and check in for at least a week to indulge in the perfect blend of exercise, diet, and pampering. Advance reservations are essential. Transportation is available to and from the San Diego airport. ⊠ *Hwy. 2, 5 km (3 mi) west of Tecate, 21275* ☎ *665/654–9155; 760/744–4222 or 800/443–7565 in the U.S.* 🖶 *760/744–5007 in the U.S.* ⊕ *www.rancholapuerta.com* ⇱ *80 rooms* ⌂ *Restaurant, refrigerators, 4 tennis courts, pool, 2 health clubs, hair salon, spa; no smoking* ⊟ *MC, V* ⍾ *FAP.*

$ 🏨 **Rancho Tecate Resort.** The long, low buildings of this handsome resort cluster in the hills outside Tecate. The lobby is is filled with antiques (the original owner was an avid collector) and the guest rooms are carpeted and comfortable. Diversions include a 3-hole golf course, a man-made lake, and hiking trails. ⊠ *Hwy. 3, Km 10, 10½ km (6½ mi) south of Tecate, 21275* ☎ *665/654–0011* 🖷 *665/654–0241* ⊕ *www.ranchotecateresort.com* ⇆ *45 rooms* ⚷ *Restaurant, 3-hole golf course, tennis court, pool, hot tub* 🚃 *MC, V.*

Mexicali

136 km (84 mi) east of Tijuana.

Mexicali, with a population of about 850,000, shares the Imperial Valley farmland and the border crossing with Calexico, a small California city. As the capital of Baja California, Mexicali sees a great deal of government activity and a steady growth of maquiladoras. Most visitors come to town on business, and the city's sights are few and far between. A tourist-oriented strip of curio shops, restaurants, and bars is along Avenida Francisco Madero, a block south of the border.

Where to Stay & Eat

$–$$$ ✕ **La Misión Dragon.** Chinese laborers came to Mexicali in the early 20th century to work on irrigation and railroad projects. As a result, the city has one of the largest Chinese populations (and some of the best Chinese restaurants) in Mexico. The most famous restaurant is renowned for its crispy special duck and suckling pig in plum sauce. ⊠ *Blvd. Lázaro Cárdenas 555* ☎ *686/566–4400* 🚃 *MC, V.*

$$ 🏨 **La Lucerna.** The prettiest hotel in Mexicali, the colonial-style Lucerna has plenty of palms and fountains around the pools and carved-wood furnishings in the dark, somber rooms. A newer section has suites with separate seating areas and modern furnishings. Conventions and business meetings sometimes fill the hotel; advance reservations are advised. ⊠ *Av. Benito Juárez 2151, 21270* ☎ *686/564–7000; 800/582–3762 in the U.S.* 🖷 *686/566–4706* ⊕ *www.hotel-lucerna.com.mx* ⇆ *175 rooms, 28 cabins, 4 suites* ⚷ *2 restaurants, 2 pools, bar* 🚃 *MC, V.*

en route | **Parque Nacional San Pedro Mártir.** Baja's interior mountain ranges are filled with hidden caves and mountain hideaways. This park is more accessible than most, and even a short drive or hike up its rough trails offers a different perspective on Baja. As long as it hasn't been raining, a regular car can handle the dirt road into the park. ⊠ *140 km (87 mi) south of Ensenada, turn off Hwy. 1 south of Colonet and drive 98 km (61 mi) east to the park* ☎ *no phone.*

San Quintín

191 km (118 mi) south of Ensenada.

Agricultural fields line the highway as you enter San Quintín, the largest producer of tomatoes in Baja. The Oaxacan migrant workers who plant and pick the fertile valley's produce live in squalid camps out of the view of travelers. **Bahía de San Quintín,** which fronts a few small hotels, is among northern Baja's best fishing grounds, along with **Bahía Falsa** and **Bahía Santa Maria,** and the area's few hostelries tend to cater to anglers. Roadside stands sell the local delicacy, Pismo clams, fresh and cooked. Travelers often stop here for essentials en route farther south; this is the last major outpost until Guerrero Negro (a drive of about six hours).

Where to Stay

¢–$ 🏨 **Old Mill.** Anglers ease their boats into the sheltered bay at this long-time favorite hideaway and set up housekeeping in a variety of rooms, some with kitchens. The lodge-style bar with its huge fireplace is filled with locals and travelers on weekend nights. ⊠ *South of San Quintín on a dirt road leading to the bay* ⬡ *Box 2631 Spring Valley CA 91979* ☎ *800/479–7962 in the U.S.; 01800/025–5141 toll free in Mexico* 🖷 *616/165–3376* ⊕ *www.oldmillbaja.com* ⟿ *28 rooms, 2 suites* ⬦ *Restaurant, bar* ⊟ *No credit cards.*

¢   🏠 **Don Eddie's Landing.** Catering mainly to fishermen, Don Eddie's has all the right amenities; its clean, no-frills rooms have TVs, fans, and heaters. Most importantly, it's got a launching ramp for boats and can arrange charters. Naturally, conversation in the restaurant and bar is rather one-dimensional. ⊠ *Off Hwy. 1 on the bay, 22930; follow the signs for the turnoff and drive 5 km (3 mi) to reach the hotel* ☎ *616/162–2722 or 616/162–3143* ⊕ *www.doneddies.com* ⟿ *17 rooms* ⬦ *Restaurant, pool, fishing, bar* ⊟ *No credit cards.*

San Felipe

198 km (123 mi) south of Mexicali, 244 km (151 mi) southeast of Ensenada.

San Felipe (population 25,000) is the quintessential fishing village with one main street (two if you count the highway into town). It sits at the edge of the northern Mar de Cortés, which is protected as an ecological reserve in this region. The *malecón* (seaside walkway) runs along a broad beach with a swimming area. Taco stands, bars, and restaurants are clustered at the south end of the beach.

In 1948 the first paved road from Mexicali was extended into town, at which point San Felipe became significant. Prior to that time only a few fishermen and their families lived along the coast; now there are impressive shrimping fleets.

A getaway spot for years, San Felipe has several campgrounds and modest hotels, which fill up quickly during winter and spring holidays. Snowbirds arrive in recreational vehicles in winter, setting up huge vacation communities in local trailer parks. On holiday weekends San Felipe can be boisterous—dune buggies, motorcycles, and off-road vehicles abound—but most of the time it's a quiet, relaxing place. The town also appeals to sportfishers, especially in spring. Launches, bait, and supplies are readily available.

The **Bahía San Felipe** has dramatic changes in its tides. They crest at 20 ft, and because the beach is so broad, the waterline can move in and out up to 1 km (about ½ mi).

The main landmark in San Felipe is the **shrine of the Cerro de la Virgen** (Virgin of Guadalupe), at the north end of the malecón on a hill overlooking the sea. A steep stairway leads to the shrine; fishermen traditionally light a candle to the Virgin here before heading out to sea. From the hilltop you'll have an awesome view of the bay and beach.

Where to Stay & Eat

$$–$$$ ✕ **Red Lobster.** A Mexican combo plate with grilled chicken rather than the ubiquitous carne asada is a good choice here, as are all the shrimp dishes. Ask what the fishermen have brought in that day—it could be anything from clams to *huachinango* (red snapper). ⊠ *Av. Mar de Cortés at Chetumal* ☎ *686/577–0483* ⊟ *MC, V.*

$–$$$ ✕ **El Nido.** One in a chain of reliable steak houses, this comfy restaurant is known for its good burgers, steaks, and seafood platters. The Mexican specialties are toned down for tourists' palates. You can order imported whiskey or scotch to go with your beef, but beware of high prices. ⊠ *Av. Mar de Cortés 348* ☎ *686/577–1660* ⊟ *MC, V* ☉ *Closed Mon.*

¢–$ ╳ **Rice and Beans.** The name nearly says it all—the word "fish" should precede it. This is the place to try *mantaraya* (stingray) tacos and fish soup, along with San Felipe's famous shrimp. It's a casual hangout for the expat-retiree gang. ✉ *Malecón at Av. Chetumal* ☎ 686/577–1770 🖃 *No credit cards.*

$$ ⊞ **El Cortez.** Easily the most popular hotel in San Felipe, El Cortez has several types of setups, including moderate-price bungalows and modern hotel rooms. The hotel's beachfront and second-story bars are both enduringly beloved, and the restaurant is the nicest water-view dining spot in town. The hotel is a five-minute walk from the malecón. ✉ *Av. Mar de Cortés s/n, 21850* ✉ *(Box 1227, Calexico, CA 92232)* ☎ *686/577–1055* 🖶 *686/577–1752* ⟿ *77 rooms, 4 suites, 24 bungalows* ♣ *Restaurant, room service, cable TV, pool, 2 bars, gift shop* 🖃 *MC, V.*

$$ ⊞ **San Felipe Marina Resort.** Most rooms at this low-slung terra-cotta building facing the sea have kitchens, woven rugs on white-tile floors, folk-art decorations, and sea views. The least expensive rooms lack kitchens and good views. The pool sits above the beach next to a *palapa* (thatch-roof) bar; a second, indoor pool is a delight on cold winter days. The resort is a five-minute drive south of town and has an RV campground next door. ✉ *Carretera San Felipe Aeropuerto, Km 4.5, 21850* ☎ *686/577–1568; 800/291–5397 in the U.S.* 🖶 *686/577–1569* ⟿ *60 rooms, 123 RV spaces* ♣ *Restaurant, 2 tennis courts, 2 pools (1 indoor), gym, bar, shops* 🖃 *AE, MC, V.*

Sports & the Outdoors

FISHING The northern part of the Mar de Cortés offers plentiful sea bass, snapper, corbina, halibut, and other game fish. Clamming is good here as well. **Alex Sportfishing** (☎ 686/577–1442), runs day trips on small skiffs. **Casey's Baja Tours** (☎ 686/577–2739) runs tours to Puertocitos, a small community with natural hot springs south of San Felipe, along with other desert and sea activities. **Tony Reyes Sportfishing** (☎ 714/538–9300 in the U.S. 🖶 714/538–1368 in the U.S.) is one of the most reputable companies offering multiday trips, and uses a U.S.-based company to organize trips.

BAJA NORTE A TO Z

To research prices, get advice from other travelers, and book travel arrangements, visit www.fodors.com.

AIR TRAVEL

There are few international flights into Baja Norte; most travelers access the area from the border at San Diego. Several airlines offer flights between mainland Mexico and Tijuana or Mexicali, which currently have the only commercial flights in the region.

AIRPORTS Tijuana's Aeropuerto Alberado Rodriguez (TIJ) is on the eastern edge of the city, near the Otay Mesa border crossing. Mexicali's international airport, Aeropuerto Internacional General Rodolfo Sánchez Taboada (MXL), is about 11 km (7 mi) east of the city. Both airports have all the key facilities, such as currency exchange booths and restaurants, but they can be confusing for first-timers. You must show your ticket before reaching the airline counter. Don't rely on electronic tickets, since their computers sometimes don't function.

🇫 **Aeropuerto Alberado Rodriguez** ☎ 664/684-2876. **Aeropuerto Internacional General Rodolfo Sánchez Taboada** ☎ 686/553-5071.

AIRPORT Private taxis and *colectivos* (shared vans) are available at both airports.
TRANSFERS Buy your tickets from the taxi counters, where fares are posted. Colectivos to most hotels in the cities cost about $5, taxis about double that.

CARRIERS Mexicana flies from Tijuana to Mexico City, Guadalajara, and Zacatecas connecting with other national and international flights. Aeroméxico flies to Los Cabos, La Paz, and Mexicali on the Baja Peninsula and to several cities in mainland Mexico. AeroCalifornia flies between Tijuana and La Paz.

AeroCalifornia ☎ 664/682-8754; 664/684-2876 in Tijuana. **Aeroméxico** ☎ 664/685-2230 in Tijuana; 686/557-2551 in Mexicali ⊕ www.aeromexico.com. **Mexicana** ☎ 664/634-6596 in Tijuana; 686/552-9391 in Mexicali ⊕ www.mexicana.com.

BUS TRAVEL

Greyhound buses head to Tijuana from downtown San Diego several times daily. Buses to San Diego and Los Angeles depart from the Greyhound terminal in Tijuana 14 times a day. Fares are $5 each way. Mexicoach runs buses from the trolley depot in San Ysidro and the large parking lot on the U.S. side of the border to the Tijuana Tourist Terminal at Avenida Revolución between Calle 6 and 7. These shuttles make the circuit every 15 minutes between 8 AM and 9 PM; the fare is $1.50.

Buses connect all the towns in Baja Norte and are easy to use; stations are in Ensenada, Mexicali, San Felipe, Tecate, and Tijuana. There are usually three buses a day. Buses traveling to Rosarito stop at a small terminal on Boulevard Juárez across from the Rosarito Beach Hotel. There is no official bus station here; check at the hotels for bus-schedule information.

Buses to destinations in Baja and mainland Mexico depart from Tijuana's Central de Autobuses. Autotransportes de Baja California covers the entire Baja route and connects in Mexicali with buses to Guadalajara and Mexico City. Elite has first-class service to mainland Mexico. Transportes del Pacífico goes to Mexico City and other points on the mainland from Mexicali.

Tijuana's Camionera de la Línea station is located just inside the border and has bus service to Rosarito and Ensenada along with city buses to downtown. The downtown station for buses within the city is at Calle 1a and Avenida Madero. To catch the bus back to the border from downtown, go to Calle Benito Juárez (also called Calle 2a) between Avenidas Revolución and Constitución.

Colectivos (small, often striped zans) cover neighborhood routes in most Baja cities and towns. The destination is usually painted on the windshield; look for them on main streets.

Bus Lines **Autotransportes de Baja California** ☎ 664/686-9010. **Elite** ☎ 664/688-1979. **Greyhound** ☎ 664/686-0697 or 664/688-0165 in Tijuana; 800/231-2222 in the U.S. ⊕ www.greyhound.com. **Mexicoach** ☎ 664/685-1440; 619/428-9517 in the U.S. ⊕ www.mexicoach.com. **Transportes del Pacífico** ☎ 664/621-2983.

Bus Stations **Ensenada bus station** ⊠ Av. Riveroll 1075, between Calles 10 and 11, Ensenada ☎ 646/178-6680. **Mexicali bus station** ⊠ Centro Cívico, Av. Independencia, Mexicali ☎ 686/557-2410. **San Diego** ⊠ 120 W. Broadway ☎ 619/239-2366. **San Felipe bus station** ⊠ Av. Mar Caribe at Av. Manzanillo, San Felipe ☎ 686/577-1516. **Tecate bus station** ⊠ Av. Benito Juárez at Calle Abelardo Rodríguez, Tecate ☎ 665/654-1221. **Tijuana city bus station** ⊠ Calle 1a at Av. Madero ☎ 664/688-0752. **Tijuana Camionera de la Línea** ⊠ Centro Comercial Viva Tijuana, Vía de la Juventud Oriente 8800. **Tijuana Central de Autobuses** ⊠ Calz. Lázaro Cárdenas at Blvd. Arroyo Alamar, Tijuana ☎ 664/621-2982 or 664/621-7640.

CAR RENTAL

Many U.S. car-rental companies do not allow you to drive their cars into Mexico. Avis permits its cars to go from San Diego into Baja as far as 724 km (450 mi) south of the border. Cars must be returned by the renter to San Diego, and you must declare your intention to take the car into Mexico and purchase Mexican auto insurance. Southwest Car Rentals allows its cars as far as Ensenada. California Baja Rent-A-Car rents four-wheel-drive vehicles, convertibles, and sedans for use throughout Mexico (the only company to do this). If you plan to rent your car in Tijuana or San Diego and drop it in Los Cabos, be prepared to pay a hefty sum (up to $900) on top of the rental price.

Fiesta Rent-a-Car and Hertz have offices in Ensenada. The larger U.S. rental agencies have offices at the Tijuana International Airport (Aeropuerto Alberado Rodriguez), and Avis and Budget have offices in downtown Tijuana.

 Avis ⊠ Blvd. Cuauhtémoc 1705, Tijuana ☎ 664/683-0605 ⊕ www.avis.com. **Budget** ⊠ Paseo de los Héroes 77, Tijuana ☎ 664/634-3303 ⊕ rent.drivebudget.com. **California Baja Rent-A-Car** ⊠ 9245 Jamacha Blvd., Spring Valley, CA 91977 ☎ 619/470-7368; 888/470-7368 in the U.S. ⊕ www.cabaja.com. **Fiesta Rent-a-Car** ⊠ Hotel Corona at Blvd. Costero, Ensenada ☎ 646/176-3344. **Hertz** ⊠ Av. Blancarte between Calles 1 and 2, Ensenada ☎ 646/178-2982 ⊕ www.hertz.com. **Southwest Car Rentals** ⊠ 2975 Pacific Hwy. ☎ 619/497-4811; 800/476-8849 in the U.S. ⊕ www. southwestcarrental.net.

CAR TRAVEL

The best way to thoroughly tour Baja Norte is by car, although the driving can be complicated. If you're just visiting Tijuana, Tecate, or Mexicali, it's easiest to park on the U.S. side of the border and walk across.

From San Diego, U.S. 5 and I–805 end at the San Ysidro border crossing; Highway 905 leads from I–5 and I–805 to the Tijuana border crossing at Otay Mesa. U.S. 94 from San Diego connects with U.S. 188 to the border at Tecate, 57 km (35 mi) east of San Diego. I–8 from San Diego connects with U.S. 111 at Calexico—203 km (126 mi) east—and the border crossing to Mexicali. San Felipe lies on the coast, 200 km (124 mi) south of Mexicali via Highway 5.

To head south into Baja from Tijuana, follow the signs for Ensenada Cuota, the toll road (also called Highway 1 and, on newer signs, the Scenic Highway) that runs south along the coast. There are two clearly marked exits for Rosarito, and one each for Puerto Nuevo, Bajamar, and Ensenada. The road is excellent, although it has some hair-raising curves atop the cliffs and is best driven in daylight (the stretch from Rosarito to Ensenada is one of the most scenic drives in Baja). Tollbooths accept U.S. and Mexican currency; tolls are about $3. Rest rooms are available near toll stations. The alternative free road—Highway 1D or Ensenada Libre—has been vastly improved, but it's difficult for the first-timer to navigate. (The entry to the 1D is on a side street in a congested area of downtown Tijuana, and the highway is quite windy.) Highway 1 continues south of Ensenada through San Quintín to Guerrero Negro, at the border between Baja California and Baja Sur, and on to the southernmost tip of Baja; there are no tolls past Ensenada.

Mexico Highway 2 runs east from Tijuana to Tecate and Mexicali. There are toll roads between Tijuana and Tecate and between Tecate and Mexicali. The 134-km (83-mi) journey from Tecate east to Mexicali on La Rumorosa, as the road is known, is as exciting as a roller-coaster ride, with the highway twisting and turning down steep mountain grades and over flat, barren desert.

If you're traveling only as far as Ensenada or San Felipe, you do not need a tourist card, unless you stay longer than 72 hours. If you know you'll be traveling south of Ensenada, you can get the form at the Mexican Customs Office. You must have Mexican auto insurance, available at agencies near the border.

The combination of overpopulation, lack of infrastructure, and heavy winter rains makes many of Tijuana's streets difficult to navigate by automobile. It's always best to stick to the main thoroughfares. Most of Rosarito proper can be explored on foot, which is a good idea on weekends, when Boulevard Juárez has bumper-to-bumper traffic. To reach Puerto Nuevo and other points south, continue on Boulevard Juárez (also called Old Ensenada Highway and Ensenada Libre) through town. At this writing, however, Boulevard Juárez was being widened to four lanes between Rosarito and Puerto Nuevo, creating massive traffic snarls; construction may last into fall 2003. Most of Ensenada's attractions are within five blocks of the waterfront; it's easy to take a long walking tour of the city. A car is necessary to reach La Bufadora and most of the beaches.

When driving farther south to San Quintín, Guerrero Negro, and Baja Sur, be sure to fill up your gas tank when it's half full. Few towns appear on the highway, and you quickly have the feeling you are headed into the unknown (unless you're following a caravan of RVs). Don't drive at night, and watch your speed. You never know when a pothole or arroyo will challenge your driving skills. Also, the cattle on the ranches abutting the highway tend to wander onto the road, an especially dangerous situation at night when they're nearly impossible to spot.

PARKING Large parking lots stretch on both sides of Interstate 5 at San Ysidro, close to the border. The lots charge $8 to $12 per day; though most have an attendant, they aren't actually guarded, so you shouldn't leave any valuables in your car.

In Tijuana, there are parking lots along Avenida Revolución and at most major attractions. There's plenty of waterfront parking along Avenida Costera in Ensenada. Parking is less accessible in Rosarito; try the large lot on Avenida Juárez by the Commercial Mexicana grocery store.

🔳 **Mexican Customs Office** ⊠ inside San Ysidro border crossing ☎ 664/682-3439 or 664/684-7790.

EMBASSIES
🔳 **U.S. Consulate** ⊠ Tapachula 96, Tijuana ☎ 664/622-7400.

EMERGENCIES
In an emergency anywhere in Baja Norte, dial **066**. The operators speak at least a bit of English.

The Tijuana government publishes a small guide to crime for tourists, available at information desks. It lists the agencies to contact if you've been involved in a crime, and lists the crimes that tourists most often commit (carrying weapons, purchasing illegal drugs, public drunkenness). Crime victims should contact the State District Attorney's Office or the U.S. Consulate General.

🔳 **State District Attorney** ☎ 664/638-5209. **U.S. Consulate General** ⊠ Tapachula 96, Tijuana ☎ 664/622-7400.

LANGUAGE
A great way to get to know Ensenada is to attend weekend or weeklong classes at one of the schools catering to those who wish to improve their Spanish language skills.

🔳 Spanish Classes **Baja California Language College** ☎ 646/174-5688; 877/444-2252 in the U.S. 🌐 www.bajacal.com offers several language programs including weekend classes and homestays. **International Spanish Institute of Ensenada** ☎ 646/176-0109 is well established and popular with San Diegans taking weekend classes.

LODGING

RESERVING A
ROOM

Several companies specialize in arranging hotel reservations in northern Baja. Baja Information is one of the oldest and best agencies working with Baja hotels and tourism departments. Baja California Tours books hotel rooms in the cities and outlying areas. Mexico Condo Reservations books hotel and condo accommodations and represents La Pinta Hotels, a chain with several hotels on the peninsula.

Baja California Tours ✉ 7734 Herschel Ave., Suite O, La Jolla, CA 92037 ☎ 858/454-7166; 800/336-5454 ⊠ 858/454-2703 ⊕ www.bajaspecials.com. **Baja Information** ✉ 6855 Friars Rd., Suite 26, San Diego, CA 92108 ☎ 619/298-4105; 800/522-1516 in CA, NV, AZ; 800/225-2786 elsewhere in the U.S. ⊠ 619/294-7366. **Mexico Condo Reservations** ✉ 4420 Hotel Circle Ct., Suite 230, San Diego, CA 92108 ☎ 619/275-4500; 800/262-9632 ⊠ 619/456-1350 ⊕ www.mexicocondores.com.

MONEY MATTERS

Dollars are as prevalent as pesos in Baja Norte, and many visitors don't bother changing money. If you wish to deal in pesos, change money at your hotel or a currency exchange point. Be sure to keep some cash on you if you're traveling south, since some places do not accept credit cards and ATMs are nearly nonexistent.

TOURS & PACKAGES

Baja California Tours has comfortable, informative bus trips throughout northern Baja. Seasonal day and overnight trips focus on whale-watching, fishing, shopping, wineries, sports, dude ranches, and art and cultural events in Tijuana, Rosarito, Ensenada, and San Felipe.

Baja California Tours ✉ 7734 Herschel Ave., Suite O, La Jolla, CA 92037 ☎ 858/454-7166; 800/336-5454 ⊠ 858/454-2703 ⊕ www.bajaspecials.com.

TROLLEY TRAVEL

The San Diego Trolley travels from the Santa Fe Depot in San Diego, at Kettner Boulevard and Broadway, to within 100 ft of the border every 15 minutes from 5 AM to midnight. The 45-minute trip costs $2.50.

San Diego Trolley ☎ 619/233-2004.

VISITOR INFORMATION

Baja tours, Mexican auto insurance, a monthly newsletter, and workshops are available through Discover Baja, which is a membership club for Baja travelers.

Baja's largest cities have several tourism offices operated by different agencies. These regional tourist offices are usually open weekdays 9–7 (although some may close in early afternoon for lunch) and weekends 9–1. Some of the smaller areas do not have offices. The excellent Baja California State Secretary of Tourism distributes information on the entire state.

Of Ensenada's two tourist bureaus, the most comprehensive is on Boulevard Costero. Mexicali has both a Convention and Tourism Bureau and a State Secretary of Tourism office, as does Tijuana. Tijuana Convention and Tourism Bureau has two offices, one within the San Ysidro border crossing, and one on Avenida Revolución. The Tijuana Tourist Trust operates an office in the Zona Río. Rosarito, San Felipe, and Tecate also each have a tourist office. The best Web sites for different cities are often private ones that are casually linked to the tourism bureau.

Baja California State Secretary of Tourism ✉ Paseo de los Héroes 10289, Tijuana ☎ 664/634-6330 ⊠ 664/634-7157 ⊕ www.turismobc.gob.mx. **Discover Baja** ✉ 3089 Clairemont Dr., San Diego, CA 92117 ☎ 619/275-4225; 800/727-2252 ⊠ 619/275-1836 ⊕ www.discoverbaja.com. **Ensenada Tourism** ✉ Blvd. Costero 1477, Ensenada ☎ 646/172-3022 ⊕ www.ensenada-tourism.com. **Ensenada Tourist Board** ✉ Blvd. Cárdenas

609, Ensenada 🖼 646/178-8578 ⊕ www.enjoyensenada.com. **Mexicali Convention and Tourism Bureau** ⊠ Calz. López Mateos at Calle Compresora, Mexicali 🖼 686/552-2376 🖼 686/557-2561 ⊕ www.mexicaliturismo.com. **Mexicali State Secretary of Tourism Office** ⊠ Calle Calafia at Calz. Independencia, Mexicali 🖼 686/566-1277. **Rosarito Tourist Board** ⊠ Blvd. Juárez 907, Oceana Plaza Shopping Center, Rosarito 🖼 624/612-0396; 800/962-2252 in the U.S. ⊕ www.rosaritobch.com. **San Felipe Tourist Information Office** ⊠ Av. Mar de Cortés, San Felipe 🖼 686/577-1155, 686/577-1865, or 686/577-1155 ⊕ www.sanfelipe.com.mx. **Tecate Tourist Information** ⊠ Callejón Libertad, Tecate 🖼 665/654-1095. **Tijuana Convention and Tourism Bureau** ⊠ inside the San Ysidro border crossing, Tijuana 🖼 664/683-1405 ⊠ Av. Revolución between Calles 3 and 4, Tijuana 🖼 664/684-0481 or 664/688-0555 ⊕ www.tijuanaonline.org. **Tijuana Tourist Trust** ⊠ Paseo de los Héroes 9365-201, Zona Río, Tijuana 🖼 664/684-0537; 888/775-2417 in the U.S. ⊕ www.seetijuana.com.

BAJA CALIFORNIA SUR

With the completion in 1973 of the Carretera Transpeninsular (Mexico Highway 1), travelers gradually started finding their way down the 1,708-km (1,059-mi) road, drawn by the wild terrain and the pristine beaches of both coastlines. Baja California Sur became Mexico's 30th state in 1974, and the population and tourism have been growing ever since. Still, Baja Sur remains a rugged and largely undeveloped land. Many people opt to fly to the region rather than brave Highway 1. The road is in fairly good repair, but there are potholes in some stretches, and services (gas, rest rooms) may not be available. Those venturing on the Carretera Transpeninsular should be well prepared with water and other provisions for a long drive in desolate but beautiful country.

Whale-watching in Scammon's Lagoon, San Ignacio Lagoon, Magdalena Bay, and throughout the Mar de Cortés is a main attraction in winter. History buffs enjoy Loreto, where the first mission in the Californias was established. La Paz, today a busy governmental center and sportfishing city, was the first Spanish settlement in Baja. At the southernmost tip of the peninsula, fishing aficionados, golfers, and sun worshippers gather in Los Cabos, one of Mexico's most popular and most expensive coastal resorts.

Guerrero Negro & Scammon's Lagoon

720 km (446 mi) south of Tijuana, 771 km (478 mi) north of La Paz.

Every December through March, thousands of gray whales swim 8,000 km (5,000 mi) south from Alaska's Bering Strait to the tip of the Baja Peninsula. Up to 6,000 whales swim past and stop close to the shore at several spots along the Baja coast—including Scammon's Lagoon near Guerrero Negro—to give birth to their calves. These newborns each weigh about half a ton and consume nearly 50 gallons of milk a day. In the past, Guerrero Negro was the headquarters for whale-watching trips, but many operators have moved farther south, to Laguna San Ignacio and Bahía Magdalena. If you're driving, though, it's still easiest to arrange for a boat in Guerrero Negro.

If it weren't for the whales and the Transpeninsular Highway, which passes near town, few would venture to Guerrero Negro, a town of 10,000. Those traveling south can easily bypass the town. The name Guerrero Negro, which means Black Warrior, was derived from a whaling ship that ran aground in Scammon's Lagoon in 1858. Near the Desierto de Vizcaíno (Vizcaíno Desert), on the Pacific Ocean, the area is best known for its salt pans, which provide work for much of the town's population and produce one-third of the world's salt supply. Salt water collects in some

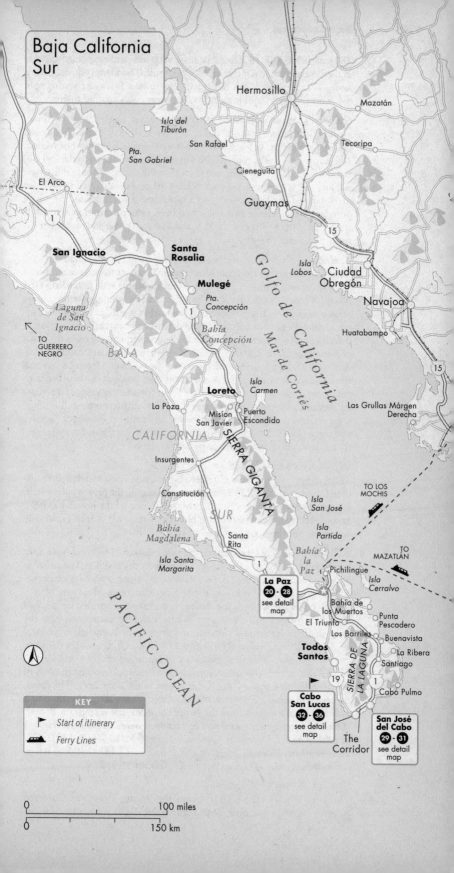

Baja California Sur

Hermosillo

Mazatán

Isla del Tiburón

San Rafael

Tecoripa

Pta. San Gabriel

Cieneguita

El Arco

Guaymas

15

San Ignacio

Santa Rosalia

Isla Lobos

Ciudad Obregón

Golfo de California

Mulegé

Navajoa

Pta. Concepción

Laguna de San Ignacio

1

Bahía Concepción

Mar de Cortés

Huatabampo

TO GUERRERO NEGRO

BAJA

15

Loreto

Isla Carmen

La Poza

Misión San Javier

Puerto Escondido

Las Grullas Márgen Derecha

CALIFORNIA

SIERRA GIGANTA

Insurgentes

TO LOS MOCHIS

Constitución

SUR

Isla San José

Bahía Magdalena

Santa Rita

Isla Partida

Bahía la Paz

TO MAZATLÁN

Isla Santa Margarita

1

Pichilingue

Isla Cerralvo

La Paz
20 · **28**
see detail map

Bahía de los Muertos

El Triunfo

Punta Pescadero

PACIFIC OCEAN

Los Barriles

Buenavista

La Ribera

Todos Santos

SIERRA DE LA LAGUNA

Santiago

Cabo Pulmo

19

Cabo San Lucas
32 · **36**
see detail map

1

San José del Cabo
29 · **31**
see detail map

The Corridor

KEY

⚑ *Start of itinerary*

� *Ferry Lines*

0   100 miles

0   150 km

780 square km (300 square mi) of sea-level ponds and evaporates quickly in the desert heat, leaving great blocks of salt. The town is dusty, windy, and generally unpleasant, but it happens to be a favored roosting spot for osprey, which build huge nests on power poles around town.

Scammon's Lagoon is about 27 km (17 mi) south of Guerrero Negro, down a rough but passable sand road that crosses the salt flats. The lagoon got its name from U.S. explorer Charles Melville Scammon of Maine, who came here in the mid-1800s. On his first expedition to the lagoon, Scammon and his crew collected more than 700 barrels of valuable whale oil, and the whale rush was on. Within 10 years, nearly all the whales in the lagoon had been killed, and it took almost a century for the whale population to increase to what it had been before Scammon arrived. It wasn't until the 1940s that the U.S. and Mexican governments took measures to protect the whales.

These days, whale-watching boats—most of them *pangas* (small skiffs)—must get permission from the Mexican government to enter Scammon's Lagoon, now a national park called **Parque Natural de la Ballena Gris** (Gray Whale Natural Park). The other major whale-watching spots (also protected by the government) are farther south, at Laguna San Ignacio and Bahía and Laguna Magdalena, both on the Pacific coast. If traveling on your own, you can reach Laguna San Ignacio from the town of San Ignacio or Loreto. Bahía Magdalena—regulars call it "Mag Bay"—is about a four-hour drive across the peninsula from La Paz and two hours from Loreto. Fishermen will take you out in their boats to get closer to the whales at both places. But for a better view, and an easier stay in this rugged country, travel with an outfitter who will arrange your transportation, accommodations, and time on the water. Whales will come close to your boat, rising majestically from the water, and sometimes swim close enough to be patted on the back.

Where to Stay & Eat

There are several hotels in Guerrero Negro, none of which is worth visiting for its own sake. Rates tend to increase during the peak whale-watching season from January through March. None of the hotels has heat, and winter nights can be downright frigid. Credit cards aren't normally accepted, but the hotels do take traveler's checks.

$ ✕⊞ **Malarrimo.** This trailer park–cum–Mexican and seafood restaurant has motel rooms and cabañas with private baths and TV. The cabañas are more comfortable and have sleeping lofts along with a regular beds. It fills up quickly and is one of the best deals in town. Maps and photos of Baja cover the walls in the dining room; give their grilled or steamed fresh fish, lobster, and clams a try. Whale-watching excursions from the hotel are also immensely popular and are run by knowledgeable local guides. ⊠ *Blvd. Zapata, 23940* ☎ *615/157–0250* ⊕ *www.malarrimo. com* ⇨ *10 motel rooms, 6 cabañas* ⚑ *Restaurant* ⊟ *No credit cards.*

$ ⊞ **La Pinta.** A few kilometers outside of town, looking like an oasis of palms in the desert, La Pinta is the largest hotel in the area. The clean, functional rooms are dependable, the setting more attractive than that of other local lodgings, and the American-Mexican restaurant decent. Whale-watching excursions can be arranged here. ⊠ *La Pinta Hwy. 1 at 28th parallel, Domicilio Conocido, 23940* ☎ *615/157–1301; 619/275–4500 or 800/800–9632 in the U.S.* ⊟ *615/157–1306* ⊕ *www. lapintahotels.com* ⇨ *28 rooms* ⚑ *Restaurant* ⊟ *MC, V.*

Sports & the Outdoors

WHALE-
WATCHING The gray whales that migrate from the Bering Strait are Guerrero Negro's biggest attraction. With a sturdy vehicle, you can drive the 24-

THE BOOJUM TREES OF BAJA

Mexico's boojum trees, shaped like upside-down carrots, seem like something out of a Dr. Seuss book. These odd trees only grow in a tiny section of the Baja California desert, near Highway 1, one hour south of Guerrero Negro. You can't miss them, since boojum trees can grow to be 90 ft tall and tower awkwardly over other desert flora such as datillos, elephant trees, and even giant cardón cacti.

The boojum's common name, "cirio," was given by Spanish missionaries who thought its hanging yellow flowers resembled the slender candles (cirios) used in churches. Naturalist Godfrey Sykes gave the trees their English common name in the 1920s; the story goes that when he first saw one he exclaimed, "it must be a boojum!," referring to an ominous creature in Lewis Carroll's poem "The Hunting of the Snark."

km (15-mi) washboard dirt and sand road to Scammon's Lagoon and arrange a trip with the boat captains who await passengers there. Trips usually cost $25–$40 per person depending on the type of boat and length of tour. Start early to take advantage of the calmest water and best viewing conditions. Whale-watching from the shores of the lagoon can be disappointing without binoculars, but it is still an impressive sight to see the huge mammals spouting water high into the air.

Eco-Tours Malarrimo (⊠ Blvd. Zapata, 23940 ☎ 615/157–0100 ⊕ www. malarrimo.com) is the best tour operator in the area. It offers four-hour trips with bus transportation to and from the lagoon (about 75% of the trip is spent in small skiffs among the whales with English-speaking guides) and lunch for $45 per person. Reserve several months in advance, especially for February, a peak whale-spotting time.

San Ignacio

227 km (141 mi) southeast of Guerrero Negro.

San Ignacio is an oasis amid the Desierto de Vizcaíno. Date palms, planted by Jesuit missionaries in the late 1700s, sway gently, in sync with the town's laid-back air. San Ignacio is primarily a place to organize whale-watching and cave-painting tours or to stop and cool off in the shady *zócalo* (town square).

Where to Stay

$ 🏨 **La Pinta.** This simple, functional hotel is a pleasant place to stay on your transpeninsular journey—although you may wish for a bit more for the money. White arches frame the courtyard and pool, and the rooms are decorated with folk art and wood furnishings. Both the river and town are within walking distance. The hotel staff can set up whale-watching trips with local guides. ⊠ *2 km (1 mi) west of Hwy. 1 on an unnamed road into town 23920* ☎ *624/154–0300; 619/275–4500 or 800/ 800–9632 in the U.S.* ⊕ *www.lapintahotels.com* 🛏 *28 rooms* ⚐ *Restaurant, pool, bar* ⊟ *MC, V.*

Sports & the Outdoors

WHALE-
WATCHING San Ignacio is the base for trips to Laguna San Ignacio, 59 km (35 mi) from San Ignacio on the Pacific coast. The lagoon is one of the best places to watch the gray-whale migration, and local boat captains will usually take you close enough to pet the new baby whales. Tours arranged through **Baja Discovery** (⌂ Box 152527, San Diego, CA 92195 ☎ 619/262–0700;

800/829–2252 ⊕ www.bajadiscovery.com) include round-trip transport from San Diego to San Ignacio Lagoon, by van to Ensenada and
private plane to the lagoon. The company operates a comfortable camp
at the lagoon with solar-heated showers and private tents facing the water.
Baja Expeditions (⊠ 2625 Garnet Ave., San Diego, CA 92109 ☎ 858/
581–3311; 800/843–6967 🖷 858/581–6542 ⊕ www.bajaex.com) operates a camp at the lagoon and offers tours including air transportation from San Diego. **Ecoturísticos Kuyima** (⊠ Av. Morelos 23 ☎ 615/
154–0070 ⊕ www.kuyima.com) in San Ignacio offers transport between the town and the lagoon, operates a campground at an isolated
area of the lagoon, and has adventure tours to cave paintings including
overnights in San Ignacio and at the lagoon.

Santa Rosalia

77 km (48 mi) southeast of San Ignacio.

You'll find a fascinating mix of French, Mexican, and American Old
West–style architecture in this dusty mining town. Santa Rosalia is
known for its **Iglesia Santa Barbara** (Av. Obregón at Calle Altamirano),
a prefabricated iron church designed by Alexandre-Gustave Eiffel, creator of the Eiffel Tower. The dull iron panels of the little church are brightened by a few stained-glass windows. Be sure to stop by **El Boleo** (⊠ Av.
Obregón at Calle 4), where fresh breads tempt customers weekday
mornings at 10. A fire demolished many of the old wooden houses in
the center of town in 2001; fortunately, it was extinguished before
reaching the church and businesses by the sea.

Where to Stay

¢ 🏨 **Hotel Frances.** The former glory of this 1886 French mansion shines
through despite its modest furnishings. The Frances sits on a steep hill,
and many of its refurbished rooms open onto a second-story porch with
views of town and the sea. There's a small pool and classy restaurant
in the courtyard. ⊠ Av. 11 de Julio at Calle Jean M. Cousteau, 23920
☎☎ 615/152–2052 ➲ 17 rooms ⌂ Restaurant, pool ⊟ No credit
cards.

¢ 🏨 **El Morro.** Santa Rosalia's version of a resort hotel is on the waterfront a bit south of town. Rooms, in a series of one-story buildings connected by rock arches and tile mosaics, are large and comfortable; some
have terraces and tile bathrooms. The rooms are a bit worn, but the reasonable price and the proximity of the sea even the score. The restaurant serves excellent Mexican dishes and seafood with French sauces.
⊠ 1½ km (1 mi) south of Santa Rosalia on Hwy. 1, 23900 ☎☎ 615/
152–0414 ➲ 40 rooms ⌂ Restaurant, pool, bar ⊟ No credit cards.

Mulegé

64 km (40 mi) south of Santa Rosalia.

Mulegé has become a popular base for exploring the nearby **Sierra de
Guadalupe** mountains, the site of several prehistoric rock paintings of
human and animal figures. Access to the paintings is good, though you
must have a permit and go with a licensed guide. The paintings are a
UNESCO World Heritage Site. Tours typically involve a bumpy ride followed by an even bumpier climb on *burros* (donkeys). Kayaking in **Bahía
Concepción,** the largest protected bay in Baja, is spectacular. Once a mission settlement, this charming tropical town of some 3,500 residents swells
in winter, when Americans and Canadians fleeing the cold arrive in motor
homes. There are several campgrounds outside town.

Where to Stay

★ **$–$$** ⊡ **Hotel Serenidad.** A Mulegé mainstay for Baja aficionados since the late 1960s, the Serenidad is owned by the Johnson family, longtime Baja residents. The hotel is a delightful escape, with simple rooms in brick and stucco buildings scattered under bougainvillea vines and fruit trees. Some rooms have fireplaces and/or air-conditioning and separate bedrooms. The Saturday-night pig roast is a Baja tradition. ⊠ *2½ km (1½ mi) north of Mulegé, Hwy. 1, 23900* ☎ *615/153–0530* 🖷 *615/153–0311* ⊕ *www.hotelserenidad.com* ⇩ *48 rooms* ⚭ *Restaurant, cable TV, pool, bar, airstrip; no a/c in some rooms* ⊟ *MC, V.*

¢ ⊡ **Hacienda.** Guests read and lounge in rocking chairs by the pool or along the bar at this modest hotel steps from the town plaza. Kayak trips and tours to cave paintings in the mountains can be arranged. Rooms are spartan but work fine for a night or two. ⊠ *Calle Madero 3, 23900* ☎ *615/153–0021* 🖷 *615/153–0377* ⇩ *24 rooms* ⚭ *Restaurant, pool, bar, travel services* ⊟ *No credit cards.*

Sports & the Outdoors

DIVING **Cortez Explorers** (⊠ Calle Moctezuma 75A, 23900 ☎ 615/153–0500 🖷 615/153–0500 ⊕ www.cortez-explorer.com) conducts dive trips to the rocky reefs off the Santa Inez Islands in the Mar de Cortés. They rent dive equipment, mountain bikes, and ATVs, and offer resort courses and snorkeling trips.

KAYAKING **EcoMundo/Baja Tropicales** (⊠ Hwy. 1 Km 111, Bahía Concepción, Apdo. 60, 23900 ☎ 615/153–0320) rents kayaks, wet suits, and other gear and has several types of kayaking tours, including day and overnight trips in the area of Mulegé. Whale-watching trips on the Pacific coast are also available. Their EcoMundo center on Bahía Concepción includes a learning center, cafeteria, and a center for participants in the tours.

Mountain Trips (⊠ Hotel Las Casitas, Av. Madero 50 ☎ 615/153–0232) is run by Salvador Castro Drew, a Mulegé native who leads tours to the cave paintings and working ranches in the mountains.

Loreto

134 km (83 mi) south of Mulegé.

Loreto's setting on the Mar de Cortés is truly spectacular: the gold and green hills of the Sierra de la Giganta seem to tumble into the cobalt water. According to local promoters, the skies are clear 360 days of the year, and the desert climate harbors few bothersome insects.

The Kikiwa, Cochimi, Cucapa, and Kumiai Indian tribes first inhabited the barren lands of Baja. Jesuit priest Juan María Salvatierra founded the first California mission at Loreto in 1697, and not long after, the indigenous populations were nearly obliterated by disease and war. Seventy-two years later, a Franciscan monk from Mallorca, Spain—Father Junípero Serra—set out from here to establish a chain of missions from San Diego to San Francisco, in the land then known as Alta California.

In 1821 Mexico achieved independence from Spain, which ordered all missionaries home. Loreto's mission was abandoned and fell into disrepair. Then in 1829, a hurricane virtually destroyed the settlement, capital of the Californias at the time. The capital was moved to La Paz, and Loreto languished for a century. In the late 1970s, when oil revenue filled government coffers, the area was tapped for development. An international airport was built and a luxury hotel and tennis center opened, followed a few years later by a seaside 18-hole golf course. The infrastructure for a resort area south of town at Nopoló was set in place. But the pace of development slowed as the money dried up.

Loreto is once again flush with developments, thanks to an influx of money from FONATUR, the federal government's tourism development fund. A new hotel opened in 2002 by the golf course, and downtown Loreto's waterfront now has a pristine waterfront seawall and sidewalk *malecón* with park benches. Entrepreneurs are opening small hotels and restaurants, and investors are buying up land. Some say little Loreto will someday be another Los Cabos.

For now, Loreto has a population of around 13,000 full-time residents and an increasing number of part-timers who winter at hotels, homes, and trailer parks. It's still a good place to escape the crowds, relax, and go fishing or whale-watching. The Parque Marítimo Nacional Bahía de Loreto protects much of the Mar de Cortés in this area, but there are a few cruise ships that use Loreto as a port of call and the marina at Puerto Escondido is central to the government's plans for a series of marina. With any luck, new developments will be contained in the Nopoló area.

The **malecón** along Calle de la Playa is a pleasant place to walk, jog, or sit watching the sunset. A small marina shelters yachts and the panga fleet; the adjoining beach is a popular gathering spot for locals, especially on Sunday afternoon, when kids hit the playground.

Loreto's main historic sight is **La Misión de Nuestra Señora de Loreto.** The stone church's bell tower is the town's main landmark, rising above the main plaza and reconstructed pedestrian walkway along Salvatierra. ⊠ *Calle Salvatierra at Calle Misioneros.*

El Museo de los Misiones, also called the Museo de Historia y Antropologia, contains religious relics, tooled leather saddles used in the 19th century, and displays of Baja's history. ⊠ *Calle Salvatierra s/n, next door to La Misión de Nuestra Señora de Loreto* ☎ *613/135–0441* ☞ *$2.70* ☉ *Tues.–Sun. 9–1 and 2–6.*

Nopoló, the targeted resort area, is about 8 km (5 mi) south of Loreto. The nine-court tennis complex and 18-hole golf course have been spiffed up and the classy Camino Real hotel attracts many first-time visitors to the area. Condo complexes and private homes continue to rise on the lots laid out back in the 1970s, and plans for a major resort area are progressing.

Puerto Escondido, 16 km (10 mi) down Highway 1 from Nopoló, has an RV park, **Tripui** (☎ 613/133–0818 ☎ 613/133–0828), with a good restaurant, a few motel rooms, a snack shop, bar, stores, showers, laundry, a pool, and tennis courts. There's a boat ramp at the Puerto Escondido marina close to Tripui; to pay the fee required to launch here, pay the attendant at the parking lot. The **port captain's office** (☎ 613/135–0656 ☎ 613/135–0465) is just south of the ramp, but it's rarely open.

Isla Danzante, 5 km (3 mi) southeast of Puerto Escondido, has good reefs and diving opportunities. Picnic trips to **Coronado Island,** inhabited only by sea lions, may be arranged in Loreto, Nopoló, or Puerto Escondido. The snorkeling and scuba diving on the island are excellent. Danzante and other islands off Loreto are now part of the Parque Marítimo Nacional Bahía de Loreto. Commercial fishing boats are not allowed within the 60-square-km (23-square-mi) park.

A trip to **Misión San Javier,** 32 km (20 mi) southwest of Loreto, is one of the best ways to see Baja at its most picturesque. A high-clearance vehicle is useful for the three-hour drive to the mission—don't try getting here if the dirt and gravel road is muddy. The road climbs past small ranches, palm groves, and the steep cliffs of the Cerro de la Giganta. Unmarked trails lead off the road to caves and remnants of **Indian cave paintings.** The mission village is a remote community of some 300 residents, many of whom come outdoors when visitors arrive. The church, built in 1699, is impressive and well preserved, set amid fruit orchards. It's often locked; ask anyone hanging about to find the person with the keys, and you'll be allowed to go inside to look at the stained-glass windows and ornate altar. Slip a few pesos into the contribution box as a courtesy to the village's inhabitants, who need all the help they can get to keep the church well maintained. Loreto residents make pilgrimages to the mission for the patron saint's festival, celebrated December 1–3. Although you can drive to San Javier on your own, it helps to have a guide along to lead you to the caves and Indian paintings. Most hotels, or the tour companies listed below *in* Sports & the Outdoors, can arrange tours. You can spend the night in a small bungalow at **Casa de Ana** (☎ 613/135–1552 in Loreto) and get a rare view into a small Baja community.

Where to Stay & Eat

$–$$$ ✕ **El Nido.** If you're hungry for steak, chicken, and hearty Mexican combo plates, then this is your place. As close as you'll get to a steak house in these parts, El Nido caters to a meat-and-potatoes crowd. The brass and woodwork and courteous waiters make up for prices that seem outrageously high for the neighborhood. ⊠ *Calle Salvatierra 154* ☎ *613/135–0027* ▤ *No credit cards.*

¢–$ ✕ **Café Olé.** Locals and gringos hang out here for terrific breakfasts of scarmbled eggs with *chorizo* (sausage) and huevos rancheros. It also serves good burgers, ice cream, and french fries. ⊠ *Calle Francisco Madero* ☎ *613/135–0496* ▤ *No credit cards.*

★ **¢–$** ✕ **Pachamama.** The owners (she's from Argentina, he's from Mexico City) of this gem have combined their cultures and cuisines to create a place worth repeated visits. Sit at one of the wooden tables in front of the small plaza and nibble on regional cheeses or empanadas, then move on to a salad of goat cheese and sliced homegrown tomatoes or a marinated *arrachera* (skirt) steak. Sandwiches are made on homemade bread—makes you wish the place were open for lunch. ⊠ *Calle Davis 13 at Calle Salvatierra* ☎ *613/135–1655* ▤ *No credit cards* ☉ *Closed Sept. No lunch.*

★ **$$$$** ▦ **Danzante Resort.** This all-inclusive hilltop resort facing Isla Danzante is architecturally stunning and ecologically sensitive. Owners Michael and Lauren Farley are Baja experts, writers, and underwater photographers; they work closely with the local community. Guest rooms have bent-twig furnishings, wrought-iron bedsteads, patios with hammocks, and thoughtful items like binoculars and books. Phones and TVs are nonexistent, except for sporadic cellular phone access. There are plenty of activities to pursue, including hikes, kayaking, and bird-watching. ⊠ *32 km (20 mi) south of Loreto off Hwy. 1, 23800* ☎ *144/613/104–4005; 408/354–0042 in the U.S.* ◳ *408/354–3268 in the U.S.* ⊕ *www.danzante.com* ⇆ *9 suites* ⚐ *Restaurant, pool, massage, beach, dive shop, horseback riding, hiking; no room phones, no TV, no kids under 8, no-smoking rooms* ▤ *MC, V* ¶◎¶ *FAP.*

$$–$$$ ▦ **Hotel Posada de los Flores.** The rose-color walls of this surprisingly chic hotel rise beside downtown's plaza. The public areas are its forte. A glass-bottom pool doubles as a skylight above the atrium lobby, and the rooftop sundeck and restaurant are delightfully decorated with huge planters of bougainvillea. Exposed beams and locally crafted tile decorate the lobby and hallways. The guest rooms, however, are less inviting, and can be very dark and noisy. ⊠ *Calle Salvatierra at Calle Francisco Madero, 23880* ☎ *613/135–1162; 877/245–2860 in the U.S.* ⊕ *www.posadadelasflores.com* ↭ *10 rooms, 5 junior suites* ⚇ *2 restaurants, in-room safes, minibars, pool, 2 bars, laundry service, car rental; no kids, no smoking* ⊟ *MC, V* ◯ *BP.*

★ **\$\$** ▥ **Camino Real.** Loreto's fanciest resort perches on the waterfront, at the edge of Nopoló's golf course. A battalion of water toys awaits at the pool area. The bright guest rooms have double sinks in the bathrooms and large closets, but confoundingly small balconies. The rooftop suites, however, have terraces complete with hot tubs. The restaurants are good and reasonably priced—a welcome fact since there are no other dining choices within walking distance. ⊠ *Blvd. Misión de Loreto s/n, Nopoló 23880* ☎ *613/133–0010; 800/873–7484 in the U.S.* ⊟ *613/133–0020* ⊕ *www.loretobaja.com* ↭ *149 rooms, 6 suites* ⚇ *2 restaurants, room service, minibars, cable TV, pool, beach, 2 bars, shop, car rental* ⊟ *AE, MC, V.*

\$\$ ▥ **Hotel Oasis.** One of the original in-town hostelries, the Oasis remains an ideal base for those who want to be in town and spend plenty of time on the water. Rooms vary greatly in size and comfort; the best have a view of the water and hammocks on the front terraces. Guests gather in the large bar in the evening to exchange fishing tales and wish each other luck over breakfast. (A couple of meal-plan options are available.) The hotel has its own fleet of skiffs. The owners also operate Casa de Ana in San Javier. ⊠ *Calle de la Playa, Apdo. 17, 23880* ☎ *613/135–0112; 800/497–3923 in the U.S.* ⊟ *613/135–0795* ⊕ *www.hoteloasis.com* ↭ *39 rooms* ⚇ *Restaurant, pool, boating, fishing, bar* ⊟ *MC, V.*

\$\$ ▥ **Villas de Loreto.** You'd be hard pressed to miss a TV in this hideaway. There are plenty of activities, from biking to kayaking to lolling in a hammock with a book. Fishing tours can be arranged, and there's a PADI dive shop on premises. Rooms have brightly colored quilts and porches; the beach house has a fireplace (as do five other rooms) and full kitchen. ⊠ *Antonio Mijares at beach, Colonia Zaragoza 23880* ☎ *613/135–0586* ⊟ *613/135–1355* ⊕ *www.villasdeloreto.com* ↭ *12 rooms and 1 beach house* ⚇ *Refrigerators, pool, beach, dive shop, bicycles, laundry service, Internet, pets allowed; no room phones, no room TVs, no smoking* ⊟ *MC, V* ◯ *CP.*

\$ ▥ **Motel el Dorado.** All the necessary amenities plus ceiling fans and a congenial bar are available at this spanking clean motel. All that's missing is a pool, but the waterfront is a block away. ⊠ *Paseo Hidalgo at Calle Pipila, 23880* ☎ *613/135–1500* ⊟ *613/135–1700* ⊕ *www.moteleldorado.com* ↭ *11 rooms* ⚇ *Bar, fishing* ⊟ *MC, V.*

Sports & the Outdoors

FISHING Fishing put Loreto on the map, especially for American enthusiasts. Cabrilla and snapper are caught year-round; yellowtail in spring; and dorado, marlin, and sailfish in summer. If you're a serious angler bring tackle. Some sportfishing fleets do update their equipment regularly. All Loreto-area hotels can arrange fishing, and many own skiffs. Local anglers congregate with their small boats on the beach at the north and south ends of town. **Arturo's Fishing Fleet** (⊠ Paseo Hidalgo between the plaza and marina ☎ 613/135–0766 ⊟ 613/135–0022 ⊕ www.arturosport.com) has several types of boats and fishing packages and operates the water-sports concession at the Camino Real hotel. **The Baja Big Fish Company** (⊠ Paseo Hidalgo 19, by the plaza ☎ 613/104–0781 ⊕ www.bajabigfish.com), which specializes in light tackle and fly-fishing, has full fishing packages from the United States and fishing trips from Loreto. It's closed September through May.

GOLF   The 18-hole **Loreto Campo de Golf** (☎ 613/135–0788 or 613/133–0554) is along Nopoló Bay. Several hotels in Loreto have golf packages and reduced or free greens fees.

TENNIS   The **Loreto Tennis Center** (✉ Blvd. Misión de Loreto s/n ☎ 613/135–0408), 8 km (5 mi) south of town, has nine courts open, for a fee, to the public.

WATER SPORTS   **Arturo's Fishing Fleet** (✉ Calle Hidalgo between the plaza and marina ☎ 613/135–0409 ⊟ 613/135–0022 ⊕ www.arturosport.com) offers dive services. Kayaking, whale-watching, scuba certification courses, dive trips to the islands, and hiking tours can be arranged through the **Baja Outpost** (✉ Blvd. Mateos near the Oasis Hotel ☎ 613/135–1134; 888/649–5951 in the U.S. ⊕ www.bajaoutpost.com). Extremely knowledgeable guides from the **Danzante Resort** (☎ 408/354–0042 in the U.S. ⊟ 408/354–3268 in the U.S. ⊕ www.danzante.com) take dedicated divers to explore the Loreto Marine Sanctuary. Loreto outdoor specialists **Las Parras Tours** (✉ Calle Salvatierra at Calle Francisco Madero ☎ 613/135–1010 ⊟ 613/135–0900) provides experienced local guides for kayaking, as well as for whale-watching, scuba diving and certification, visiting San Javier, and hiking to cave paintings in the mountains. The U.S.-based company **Sea Quest** (☎ 360/378–5767 ⊕ sea-quest-kayak.com) offers several trips that begin in Loreto. Options include kayaking with gray whales in Magdalena Bay or San Ignacio Lagoon.

Shopping

Loreto's shopping district is located along the pedestrian zone on Calle Salvatierra, where there are several souvenir shops and stands, plus the town's only supermarket. **El Alacrán** (✉ Calle Salvatierra 47 ☎ 613/135–0029) has remarkable folk art, jewelry, and sportswear.

La Paz

354 km (220 mi) south of Loreto.

In the slowest part of the off-season, during the oppressive late summer heat, you can easily see how La Paz received its name: "The Peace." It's the most traditional city on the peninsula, even as it has grown to a population of 250,000, with a large contingent of retirees from the United States and Canada. Travelers use La Paz as both a destination in itself and a stopping-off point en route to Los Cabos. There's always excellent scuba diving and sportfishing in the Mar de Cortés—La Paz is the stop off for divers and fishermen headed for **Cerralvo**, **La Partida,** and the **Espíritu Santo** islands, where parrot fish, manta rays, neons, and angels blur the clear waters by the shore, and marlin, dorado, and yellowtail leap from the sea.

Hernán Cortés and his soldiers were drawn to La Paz in 1535 by stories of magnificent pearls found in local oysters. In 1720, missionaries arrived to deliver salvation to the indigenous Pericú people. Instead, they introduced smallpox, which decimated the local populace within 30 years. La Paz became the capital of the Californias in 1829. In 1853 a group of U.S. Southerners, led by William Walker, tried to make La Paz a slave state, but Mexicans quickly banished them. In 1940 disease wiped out the oyster beds, and with the pearls gone, La Paz no longer attracted prospectors.

La Paz officially became the capital of Baja California Sur in 1974 and is now the state's largest settlement. It is the site of the governor's house and the state's bureaucracy, jail, and power plant, as well as the ferry port to Mazatlán.

What to See

㉓ Biblioteca de las Californias. Specializing in the history of Baja California, the library houses the best collection of historical documents on the peninsula. Unfortunately, it has been relegated to a small section of this building, which has been turned into a children's cultural center. ⊠ *Av. Madero at Calle 5 de Mayo, Centro* ☎ *612/122–0162* ☉ *Weekdays 9–6.*

㉔ La Catedral de Nuestra Señora de la Paz. Downtown's church was built in 1860 near the site of La Paz's first mission, which was established that same year by Jesuit Jaime Bravo. The simple stone building has a modest gilded altar. ⊠ *Calle Juárez* ☎ *no phone.*

㉗ Ferry Terminal. The busy warehouselike spot in Pichilingue has a large parking lot. Roadside stands serving oysters and grilled fish line the highway across the street.

㉒ Fidepaz Marina. At La Paz's west end is the construction zone for the 500-acre marina, a long-term development that has yet to reach completion. FONATUR, the government's tourism trust, has taken over the project, which may bring further development to the area. There is a resort hotel by the waterfront.

㉑ Malecón. La Paz's seawall, tourist zone, and main drag are all rolled into one. It runs along Paseo Alvaro Obregón, and was renovated in 2003 with a new sidewalk and several park areas with benches.

㉒ Malecón Plaza. A two-story white gazebo is the focus at this small concrete square where musicians sometimes appear on weekend nights. Across the street, Calle 16 de Septiembre leads inland to the city center.

Marina La Paz. At the southwest end of the malecón, this ever-growing development is home to condominiums, vacation homes, and a pleasant walkway lined with casual cafés.

㉖ Museo de Antropología. La Paz's culture and heritage is well represented at its anthropology museum, with re-creations of Comondu and Las Palmas Indian villages, photos of cave paintings found in Baja, and copies of Cortés's writings on first sighting La Paz. Many exhibit descriptions are written only in Spanish, but the museum's staff will help you translate. ⊠ *Calle Altamirano at Calle 5 de Mayo, Centro* ☎ *612/122–0162* 🖼 *Donation requested* ☉ *Daily 9–6.*

㉘ Pichilingue. Since the time of Spanish invaders, Pichilingue was known for its preponderance of oysters bearing black pearls. In 1940 a disease killed them off, leaving the beach deserted. Today Pichilingue is a pleasant place for sunbathing and watching sportfishing boats bring in their hauls. Palapa restaurants on the beach serve oysters *diablo* (raw oysters steeped in a fiery-hot sauce) and inexpensive grilled fish. The road to Pichilingue curves northeast along the bay about 16 km (10 mi) to the terminals where the ferries from Mazatlán and Topolobampo arrive and many of the sportfishing boats depart.

㉕ Plaza Constitución. The true center of La Paz is this traditional zócalo, which also goes by the name Jardín Velazco. Concerts are held in the park gazebo and locals gather here for art shows and fairs.

Beaches

Off a dirt road just past Pichilingue, **Playa Tecolote** and **Playa Coyote** are adjacent crystal-blue coves with clean beaches. Both have restaurants, water-sports equipment rentals, and palapas for shade. Camping is allowed in the parking lots. **Playa Balandra,** on a side road between Pichilingue and Tecolote, is a peaceful cove favored by kayak and snorkeling operations from town.

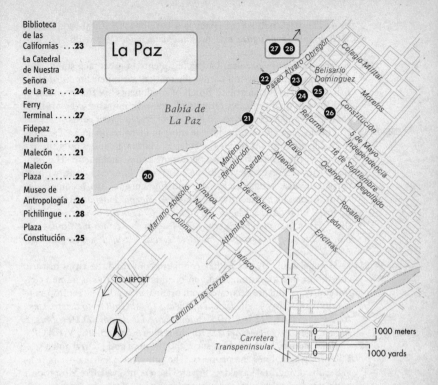

La Paz

Bahía de
La Paz

Paseo Álvaro Obregón

Belisario Dominguez

Colegio Militar

Morelos

Constitución

5 de Mayo

Independencia

16 de Septiembre

Degollado

Rosales

León

Encinas

Reforma

Bravo

Allende

Ocampo

Madero

Revolución

Serdán

5 de Febrero

Altamirano

Jalisco

Mariano Abasolo

Sinaloa

Nayarit

Colima

TO AIRPORT

Camino a las Garzas

Carretera
Transpeninsular

0   1000 meters
0   1000 yards

Where to Stay & Eat

$–$$$ ✕ **El Bismark II.** You've got to go a bit out of your way for a local home-style Mexican restaurant. Tuck into seafood cocktails, enormous grilled lobsters, or carne asada served with beans, guacamole, and homemade tortillas. Families settle down for hours at long wood tables, while waitresses divide their attention between patrons and soap operas on the TV above the bar. The desultory service is a drawback. A smaller Bismark is located on the malecón. ✉ *Degollado and Calle Altamirano, Centro* ☎ *612/122–4854* ▤ *MC, V.*

★ **$–$$$** ✕ **La Mar y Peña.** The freshest, tastiest seafood cocktails, ceviches, and clam tacos imaginable are served in this nautical restaurant crowded with locals. If you can come with friends, go for the *mariscada,* a huge platter of shellfish and fish for four. ✉ *Calle 16 de Septiembre between Isabel de la Catolica and Albañez, Centro* ☎ *612/122–9949* ▤ *AE, MC, V.*

$–$$ ✕ **El Cangrejo Loco.** A few sidewalk tables sit outside this tiny family-run café; seats are hard to come by at lunchtime. A long list of seafood cocktails offers shrimp, crab, and clams with lime, chilies, or soy sauce. Entrées include a great quesadilla with cheese and crab, manta ray tacos, and stuffed crab. ✉ *Obregón between Bravo and Ocampo, Malecón* ☎ *612/122–1359* ▤ *No credit cards.*

$–$$ ✕ **La Pazta.** Locals who crave international fare rave about this trattoria with sleek black-and-white decor and excellent homemade pasta and pizzas. Imported cheeses and wines, and bracing espresso and cappuccino are all welcome changes from the local seafood and taco fare. ✉ *Allende 36, Centro* ☎ *612/125–1195* ▤ *MC, V.*

¢–$ ✕ **El Quinto Sol Restaurante Vegetariano.** El Quinto's brightly painted exterior is covered with snake symbols and smiling suns. The all-vegetarian menu includes fresh juices and herbal elixirs. The four-course prix-fixe *comida corrida* (daily special) is a bargain; it's served from noon to 4. The back half of the space is a bare-bones natural-foods store. ⊠ *Belisario Domínguez and Av. Independencia, Centro* ☎ 612/122–1692 ⊟ *No credit cards.*

★ ¢ ✕ **Taco Hermanos Gonzalez.** La Paz has plenty of great taco stands, but the Gonzalez brothers still corner the market with their hunks of fresh fish wrapped in corn tortillas. Bowls of condiments line the small stand, and the top quality draws crowds of sidewalk munchers. ⊠ *Mutualismo and Esquerro, Centro* ☎ *No phone* ⊟ *No credit cards.*

$$$–$$$$ 🛏 **Crowne Plaza Resort.** By far the most modern resort in La Paz, this hacienda-style inn sits beside the Fidepaz Marina. Its suites range in size and style; the largest have two bedrooms and a kitchenette. The pool flows through several levels in the courtyard. The restaurant, with its cordial service, serene ambience, and fine cuisine, has become a favorite among local executives. ⊠ *Lote A, Marina Fidepaz, Apdo. 482, Centro 23000* ☎ *612/124–0830; 800/227–6963 in the U.S.* 🖷 *612/124–0837* ⊕ *www.crowneplaza.com* ⬦ *54 suites* ⚭ *Restaurant, pool, gym, bar, nightclub, playground, business services, travel services* ⊟ *AE, MC, V.*

★ **$$** 🛏 **El Angel Azul.** Owner Esther Ammann converted the city's historic courthouse into a charming bed-and-breakfast whose rooms frame a central courtyard and are decorated with original artwork. The rooftop suite overlooks the city. ⊠ *Av. Independencia 518, at Guillermo Prieto, Centro 23000* ☎ *612/125–5130* ⊕ *www.elangelazul.com* ⬦ *10 rooms, 1 suite* ⚭ *Bar; no kids under 12, no-smoking rooms* ⊟ *MC, V* ⦿ *CP.*

$$ 🛏 **Hotel Marina.** Lush gardens surround the pool and Jacuzzi and a seaside promenade lines the property. The full-service marina offers fishing, scuba diving, and kayaking. Private charters are available. Most rooms have terraces with water views and are airy, clean, and functional. ⊠ *Carretera a Pichilingue, Km 2.5, 23000* ☎ *612/121–6254; 800/826–1138 in the U.S.* 🖷 *612/121–6177* ⊕ *www.hotelmarina.com.mx* ⬦ *86 rooms, 5 suites* ⚭ *Restaurant, tennis court, pool, hot tub, marina, bar* ⊟ *AE, MC, V.*

$$ 🛏 **Howard Johnson La Concha Beach Resort.** It's hard to tell if Howard Johnson will stick with this venerable resort, which the company is trying to rename La Paz Plaza. The pluses include the beach, complete watersports center, and a notably good restaurant. At this writing, the somewhat dreary rooms are scheduled to be remodeled. A separate building, with its own pool, houses condos. There's a shuttle to town. ⊠ *Carretera a Pichilingue, Km 5, between downtown and Pichilingue, 23010* ☎ *612/121–6344 or 612/121–6161; 800/999–2252 in the U.S.* 🖷 *612/121–6218* ⊕ *www.laconcha.com* ⬦ *107 rooms* ⚭ *Restaurant, minibars, pool, dive shop, 3 bars, shops, car rental, travel services* ⊟ *AE, MC, V.*

$–$$ 🛏 **Los Arcos.** This colonial-style 1950s hotel is a La Paz landmark. The lobby leads to the central courtyard, where the rush of water in the fountain drowns out the noise from the street. Most rooms have balconies, some facing the bay. The Cabañas de los Arcos next door consists of several small brick cottages surrounded by gardens and a small hotel with a pool. ⊠ *Obregón 498, between Rosales and Allende, Malecón 23000* ☎ *612/122–2744; 520/529–4529 or 800/347–2252 in the U.S.* 🖷 *612/125–4313; 520/529–4549 in the U.S.* ⊕ *www.losarcos.com* ⬦ *93 rooms and 18 suites at hotel, 20 bungalows and 23 rooms at Cabañas* ⚭ *Restaurant, coffee shop, minibars, cable TV, 2 pools, sauna, bar* ⊟ *MC, V.*

$–$$ 🛏 **La Perla.** This brown low-rise hotel is a La Paz fixture. Rooms have white walls and light-wood furnishings; some have king-size beds. The pool is on a second-story sundeck away from main street traffic. Noise is a factor in the oceanfront rooms; the trade-off is wonderful sunset

views over the malecón. ✉ *Paseo Obregón 1570, Malecón 23010*
☎ *612/122–0777* 🖶 *612/125–5363* 🛏 *116 rooms* 🍴 *Restaurant, pool,*
bar, shops 🗐 *AE, MC, V.*

$ 🏨 **Hotel Suites Club El Moro.** A vacation-ownership resort with suite
rentals on a nightly and weekly basis, El Moro has a garden of lush palms
and a densely landscaped pool area. You can recognize the building by
its stark-white turrets and domes. Rooms are Mediterranean style, with
arched windows, Mexican tiles, and private balconies. Some rooms
have kitchens and can sleep up to five people. A small café serves light
fare. ✉ *Carretera a Pichilingue, Km 2, between downtown and Pichilingue*
23010 ☎🖶 *612/122–4084 or 612/125–2828* ⊕ *www.clubelmoro.com*
🛏 *21 suites* 🍴 *Café, pool, bar* 🗐 *AE, MC, V.*

¢ 🏨 **Pensión California.** You can nab a bed here for less than $20; though
the hacienda is run-down, the blue-and-white rooms have baths and are
clean. The courtyard has picnic tables and a TV. ✉ *Av. Degollado 209,*
Centro 23000 ☎ *612/122–2896* 🛏 *25 rooms* 🍴 *Picnic area; no room*
TVs 🗐 *No credit cards.*

Nightlife & the Arts

El Teatro de la Ciudad (✉ Av. Navarro 700, Centro ☎ 612/125–0004) is
La Paz's cultural center. The theater seats 1,500 and stages shows by visiting performers and local ensembles. **La Terraza** (✉ La Perla hotel, Paseo
Obregón 1570, Malecón ☎ 612/122–0777) is the best spot for both sun-
set- and people-watching along the malecón. The hotel also has a disco
on weekend nights. **Las Varitas** (✉ Calle Independencia 11, Centro ☎ 612/
125–2025), a lively Mexican rock club, heats up after midnight.

Sports & the Outdoors

BOATING & The considerable fleet of private boats in La Paz now has room for dock-
FISHING ing at three marinas: **Fidepaz Marina** at the north end of town, and the
Marina Palmira and **Marina La Paz** south of town. Most hotels can arrange sportfishing trips. Tournaments are held in August and November. The **Jack Velez Fleet** (✉ Apdo. 402, Centro 23000 ☎ 612/128–
7518) has cabin cruisers; charters start around $100 per person. The
company also offers whale-watching, snorkeling, and scuba trips.

KAYAKING The calm waters off La Paz are perfect for kayaking, and novice and
experienced kayakers enjoy multiday trips along the coast to Loreto or
out to the nearby islands. **Baja Expeditions** (✉ 2625 Garnet Ave., San Diego,
CA 92109 ☎ 858/581–3311 or 800/843–6967 🖶 858/581–6542
⊕ www.bajaex.com), one of the oldest outfitters working in Baja, offers several options for kayaking tours, including multinight trips between Loreto and La Paz. A support boat carries all gear, including
ingredients for great meals. **Baja Quest** (✉ Sonora 174, Centro ☎ 612/
123–5320 🖶 612/123–5321) has day and overnight trips. **Fun Baja**
(✉ Carretera a Pichilingue, Km 2 ☎ 612/121–5884 🖶 612/121–5592
⊕ www.funbaja.com) offers kayak trips around the islands along with
scuba and snorkel trips and land tours. **Nichols Expeditions** (✉ 497 N.
Main, Moab, UT 84532 ☎ 435/259–3999 or 800/648–8488 🖶 435/
259–2312 ⊕ www.nicholsexpeditions.com) offers kayaking tours to
Isla Espíritu Santo and between Loreto and La Paz, with camping along
the way.

SCUBA DIVING & Popular diving and snorkeling spots include the coral banks off Isla Es-
SNORKELING píritu Santo, the sea lion colony off Isla Partida, and the seamount 14
km (9 mi) farther north (best for serious divers). **Baja Diving & Service**
(✉ Paseo Obregón 1665-2, Malecón ☎ 612/122–1826 🖶 612/122–8644)
rents equipment, has a small hotel for divers, and operates diving and
snorkeling tours. **Baja Expeditions** (✉ 2625 Garnet Ave., San Diego, CA
92109 ☎ 858/581–3311 or 800/843–6967 🖶 858/581–6542) runs

multiday live-aboard dive trips. The **Cortez Club** (✉ La Concha Beach Resort, Carretera a Pichilingue, Km 5, between downtown and Pichilingue ☎ 612/121–6344 or 612/121–6161) is a full-scale water-sports center with a bar, equipment rental, and scuba, snorkeling, kayaking, and sportfishing tours. **Fun Baja** (✉ Carretera a Pichilingue, Km 2 ☎ 612/121–5884 🖷 612/121–5592 ⊕ www.funbaja.com) offers scuba and snorkel trips with the sea lions.

WHALE-
WATCHING

La Paz has become a center for whale-watching expeditions to Bahía Magdalena on the Pacific coast. Most hotels can make all the arrangements, but keep in mind that any whaling trip will entail about six hours' transportation from La Paz and back for two–three hours on the water. Serious whale fans with extra time can stay overnight in San Carlos, the small town by the bay. You can do the trip on your own by taking a public bus from La Paz to San Carlos and then hiring a boat captain to take you into the bay. Check with the tourist office before starting your trip for hotel arrangements. **Baja Expeditions** (✉ 2625 Garnet Ave., San Diego, CA 92109 ☎ 858/581–3311 or 800/843–6967 🖷 858/581–6542) runs whale-watching trips to the bay. You can also arrange a trip through **Baja Quest** (✉ Sonora 174, Centro ☎ 612/123–5320 🖷 612/123–5321). The water-sports center **Cortez Club** (✉ La Concha Beach Resort, Carretera a Pichilingue, Km 5, between downtown and Pichilingue ☎612/121–6344 or 612/121–6161) runs extremely popular whale-watching trips in winter.

Shopping

Artesanías la Antigua California (✉ Obregón 220, Malecón ☎ 612/125–5230) has the nicest selection of Mexican folk art in La Paz, including wooden masks and lacquered boxes from Guerrero Negro, along with a good supply of English-language books on Baja. **Artesanía Cuauhtémoc** (✉ Av. Abasolo between Calles Nayarit and Oaxaca, south of downtown, Centro ☎ 612/122–4575) is the workshop of weaver Fortunado Silva, who creates and sells cotton place mats, rugs, and tapestries. Julio Ibarra oversees the potters and painters at **Ibarra's Pottery** (✉ Calle Prieto 625, Centro ☎ 612/122–0404). His geometric designs and glazing technique result in gorgeous mirrors, bowls, platters, and cups. Unusual pottery can be found at **Mexican Designs** (✉ Calle Arreola 41 at Av. Zaragoza, Centro ☎ 612/123–2231). The pottery boxes with cactus designs are good souvenirs. **La Tiendita** (✉ Malecón ☎612/125–2744) has embroidered guayabera shirts and dresses, tin ornaments and picture frames, and some black pottery from Oaxaca.

Los Barriles & the East Cape

105 km (65 mi) south of La Paz.

The Mar de Cortés coast north of Los Cabos has long been a favored hideaway for anglers and adventurers. The area known as the East Cape consists of a string of settlements and fishing villages between La Paz and San José del Cabo—including Los Barriles, Buena Vista, and La Ribera, all accessible from Highway 1. From Punta Pescadero in the north to Cabo Pulmo in the south, the cape is renowned for its rich fishing grounds, top-notch diving, and, when the wind kicks up, excellent windsurfing. Food and lodging tend to be modest affairs; most hotels have meal plans—a good idea since fine dining is scarce.

There's an outback feel to the East Cape, with a robust group of American "settlers" making their presence known. Many of the communities are accessible via paved road from Los Cabos. For the intrepid traveler, a three-hour drive on a dirt washboard takes you along the coast to La

Ribera, Punta Colorado, and Cabo Pulmo—the latter a superb dive site within a national marine reserve. (This route is *not* recommended for those bothered by dust or long stretches of precipitous driving conditions.)

The village of Cabo Pulmo is home to 100 or so residents, depending on the season. Power comes from solar panels, and drinking water is trucked in over dirt roads. Near the beach, solar-powered cottages are for rent at the **Cabo Pulmo Beach Resort** (⊠ Cabo Pulmo ☎ 624/141–0244 ⊟ 624/143–0371 ⊕ www.cabopulmo.com), which also has a full-service PADI dive facility. Cabo Pulmo is a magnet for serious divers, kayakers, and windsurfers, and remains one of southern Baja's natural treasures.

Windsurfers take over the East Cape in winter, when stiff breezes provide ideal conditions. **VelaWindsurf** (☎ 800/223–5443 in the U.S. ⊕ www. velawindsurf.com) offers windsurfing and kite boarding lessons and trips to the East Cape from November to March. Water-sports equipment and boat trips are available through area hotels, although regulars tend to bring their own gear and rent cars for getting to isolated spots. The nearest airport is at San José del Cabo, about a two-hour drive from the farthest East Cape hotels; several car-rental agencies have desks at the airport. Expensive shuttle service can be arranged through most hotels, and there are plenty of cabs in the area.

Where to Stay & Eat

$–$$ ✕ **Otra Vez.** Whether you're in the mood for some simple grilled seafood, an omelet, or lobster New Orleans, this great little California-style café is sure to please. This may be the only time you see sprouts in Baja, so stock up. The clientele largely consists of expat retirees and tourists who gossip freely while listening to the Beach Boys. *⊠ Calle 20 de Noviembre, Los Barriles* ☎ *624/141–0249* ⊟ *MC, V* ☾ *Closed Aug.–Sept.*

$$ ▥ **Hotel Buena Vista Beach Resort.** Sixty tile-roof bungalows sit along flower-lined paths next to pools and lawns. Some rooms have private terraces. The fishing fleet is excellent, as are other diversions, such as diving, snorkeling, kayaking, horseback riding, and trips to natural springs. A European plan without meals is available from November through March, which cuts the rate in half. *⊠ Hwy. 1, Km 105, 23500 Buena Vista* ☎ *624/141–0033; 619/429–8079 or 800/752–3555 in the U.S.* ⊟ *624/141–0133* ⊕ *www.hotelbuenavista.com* ➱ *60 rooms* ⚐ *Restaurant, tennis court, 2 pools, hot tub, massage, beach, fishing, horseback riding; no room TVs* ⊟ *MC, V* ⏏◯⏐ *FAP.*

★ **$$** ▥ **Hotel Palmas de Cortés.** Formerly low-key, the Palmas has become a full-blown resort. Often featured on sportfishing shows, the hotel is near the famed Cortez banks and has its own fleet. Its enormous swimming pool has a swim-up bar. Some guest rooms have fireplaces and/or kitchens. *⊠ On the beach; take the road north through Los Barriles and continue to the beach, Los Barriles* ⚲ *Box 9016 Calabasas CA 91372* ☎ *624/141–0214; 800/368–4334 in the U.S.* ⊟ *624/141–0046* ⊕ *www.bajaresorts. com* ➱ *20 rooms, 15 suites, 10 condos* ⚐ *Restaurant, tennis court, pool, gym, fishing, playground, Internet, airstrip* ⊟ *MC, V* ⏏◯⏐ *FAP.*

$$ ▥ **Hotel Punta Pescadero.** This secluded resort is one of the most peaceful spots in Baja. Rooms have private waterfront terraces and are reserved far in advance by regulars who enjoy the sense of complete escape—miles of windswept beach and calm coves with superb snorkeling. The hotel can arrange for tours to local sights. *⊠ Camino de Los Barriles a El Cardonal, 23000 Punta Pescadero, 12 km (7 mi) north of Los Barriles* ☎ *624/121–0101; 800/426–2252 in the U.S.* ⊟ *624/126–1771* ⊕ *www. puntapescadero.com* ➱ *21 rooms* ⚐ *Restaurant, refrigerators, in-room VCRs, pool, beach, dive shop, fishing, airstrip* ⊟ *MC, V.*

The **Plaza Del Pueblo** (✉ Hwy. 1, Los Barriles) is the area's most complete shopping opportunity. The small shopping center includes an Internet café, a tackle store, an ice cream parlor, and a bakery.

Los Cabos

195 km (121 mi) south of La Paz.

At the southern tip of the Baja California peninsula, the land ends in a rocky point called El Arco (The Arch), a place of stark beauty. The desert ends in sandy coves, with cactus standing at their entrances like sentries under the soaring palm trees, and the warm waters of the Mar de Cortés swirl into the Pacific Ocean's rugged surf.

The conquistadors focused their attention on La Paz during expeditions from mainland Mexico in the mid-1500s. Well aware of the loot to be had, pirates found the tip of the Baja peninsula ideal for spotting Spanish galleons traveling from the Philippines to Spain's empire in central Mexico. In their turn, missionaries came to convert the few thousand local Indians who lived in mountain villages. The Jesuits established the mission of San José del Cabo in the mid-18th century, but their settlements didn't last long. The missionaries (and other Europeans) brought syphilis and smallpox along with their preachings, and, like elsewhere on the peninsula, the susceptible indigenous population was nearly wiped out after a few decades.

Anglers rediscovered this remote region in the 20th century. When pilots flew over Baja during World War II, they spotted the swirling waters and fertile fishing grounds from the air, and word soon spread. Wealthy adventurers with private planes and boats created a demand for fishing lodges, airstrips, and other services, and the region became a cult destination. By the 1960s a half dozen exclusive resorts were thriving on the cliffs and shores amid the barren landscape.

Connected by a 32-km (20-mi) stretch of highway called the **Corridor,** the two towns of Cabo San Lucas and San José del Cabo were distinct until the late 1970s, when the Mexican government's office of tourism development (FONATUR) targeted the southern tip of Baja as a major resort and dubbed the area Los Cabos. The destination now consists of three major areas: San José del Cabo, Cabo San Lucas, and the Corridor.

Los Cabos has become one of Mexico's most popular and most expensive coastal getaways, with deluxe hotels, championship golf courses, and some of the best sportfishing in the world. Hotels in this area have some of the highest room rates in the country. A few elegant spots command $500 or more a night for enormous suites; more mainstream accommodations run $200 or more per night. Budget rooms are extremely difficult to find. Expect to pay $60 for the most basic lodgings.

The population growth rate here is among the fastest in Mexico. The area's infrastructure received much-needed improvements when APEC (the Asian Pacific Economic Conference) brought world leaders to town for a conference in 2002. For instance, a toll road was built from the airport to the Corridor, reducing driving time (though local cab drivers don't feel it's worth the $3 toll). But despite all the development that has taken place, and the steep prices that have come along with it, the area remains a natural hideaway.

The best way to see the sights of Los Cabos is on foot. Downtown San José and Cabo San Lucas are compact, with the plaza, church, shops, and restaurants within a few blocks of one another. Bus service runs be-

tween the towns, with stops along the Corridor. If you plan to dine at the Corridor hotels or travel frequently between the two towns, it's a good idea to rent a car for a few days. As for the beaches, remember that red flags warn of unsafe swimming conditions, yellow flags indicate that you should use caution, and green flags show safe swimming areas. There are no lifeguards on area beaches.

San José del Cabo

San José del Cabo is the municipal headquarters for Los Cabos. The hotel zone, including several new all-inclusive properties, faces a long stretch of waterfront on the Mar de Cortés. The downtown area with its adobe houses and jacaranda trees is the loveliest part of Los Cabos. Entrepreneurs have converted old homes into stylish restaurants and shops, and the government has enlarged and beautified the main plaza. A 9-hole golf course and private residential community are south of the town center. Unfortunately, bumper-to-bumper traffic often clogs the streets during weekday business hours. Despite the development, San José remains the more peaceful of the two towns—the one to come to for a quiet escape. If you are in search of an exciting nightlife and a rowdy beach scene, you may be better off staying in Cabo San Lucas.

30 **Boulevard Mijares.** The main street in town runs roughly perpendicular to the sea. Its north end abuts Avenida Zaragoza, a spot marked by a long fountain; here you'll find the modest yellow city hall, the **Palacio Municipal.** The boulevard's south end has been designated a tourist zone, with Los Cabos Club de Golf as its centerpiece. A few reasonably priced hotels are situated perpendicular to the boulevard (about a 10-minute walk from shops and restaurants) on a beautiful long beach where the surf, unfortunately, is too dangerous for swimming.

29 **Estero de San José.** The spot where the freshwater Río San José flows into the sea is at the end of the tourist strip, on Paseo San José by the Presidente Inter-Continental Los Cabos. The estuary is a natural preserve and more than 200 species of birds can be spotted here. If you plan to spend time here, be sure to douse yourself with insect repellent. A new marina is supposed to be built east of the estuary as part of the Nautical Ladder project.

31 **Plaza Mijares.** Locals and travelers mingle at the large central plaza, which has a white wrought-iron gazebo and green benches set in the shade. Small concerts and art shows are sometimes held here. The town's church, **Iglesia San José,** looms above the plaza. Be sure to walk up to the front and see the tile mural of a captured priest being dragged toward a fire by Indians.

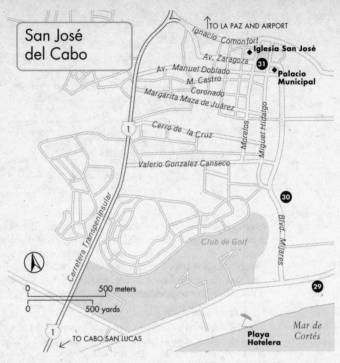

San José
del Cabo

BEACHES **Playa Hotelera** is the stretch of beach where most of San José's hotels are located. It's beautiful, but the current is dangerously rough, and swimming is not advised. The best swimming beach near San José is **Playa Palmilla,** which is protected by a rocky point south of town. The northern part of the beach is cluttered with boats and shacks, but if you walk south you'll reach the Hotel Palmilla beach, a long stretch of tan sand and calm sea.

WHERE TO STAY & ✕ **Mi Cocina.** Torches glow on the dining terrace here, and the tables are
EAT spaced enough so that you won't have to share your sweet nothings with
$$$–$$$$ a neighbor. You could start with a tequila martini and a tequila-cured
Fodor'sChoice salmon appetizer. Main courses, such as filet mignon with a potato-leek
★ galette (flat cake), look beyond Mexico. If you don't want to splash out on dinner, stop by the tapas bar. ⊠ *Casa Natalia, Blvd. Mijares 4, Centro* ☎ *624/142–5100* ▤ *AE, MC, V.*

$–$$$$ ✕ **Tropicana Bar and Grill.** Start the day with coffee and French toast at this enduringly popular restaurant. The back patio quickly fills for every meal with a loyal clientele who enjoy the garden setting. The menu includes U.S. cuts of beef and imported seafood along with fajitas, chiles rellenos, and lobster, always in demand. ⊠ *Blvd. Mijares 30, Centro* ☎ *624/142–1580* ▤ *AE, MC, V.*

$$–$$$ ✕ **Tequila Restaurante.** An old adobe home serves as the setting for this classy restaurant. The lengthy tequila list gives you a chance to savor the finer brands of Mexico's national drink, and the menu challenges you to decide between excellent Mexican dishes and innovative Pacific Rim spring rolls, salads, and seafood with tequila sauces. ⊠ *Manuel Doblado s/n, Centro* ☎ *624/142–1155* ▤ *No credit cards.*

★ **$–$$$** ✕ **Baan Thai.** The aromas alone are enough to lead you through the door; once inside you'll be greeted with visual and culinary delights. The formal dining room is decorated with Asian antiques, and a fountain mur-

murs on a patio. The chef blends Asian spices with aplomb, creating sublime pad thai, brandy and garlic lamb chops with peanut sauce, and the catch of the day with lemon black bean sauce. Prices are very reasonable for such memorable food. ⊠ *Morelos and Obregón, across from El Encanto Inn, Centro* ☎ *624/142–3344* ▤ *MC, V* ☯ *Closed Sun.*

$–$$$ ✕**Damiana.** For a special night out, come to this small hacienda tucked beside the plaza, past the center of town. Bougainvilleas wrap around the tall pines shading the wrought-iron tables, and the pink adobe walls glow in the candlelight. Start with fiery oysters diablo, then move on to the tender chateaubriand, charbroiled lobster, or the restaurant's signature shrimp steak, made with ground shrimp. ⊠ *Blvd. Mijares 8* ☎ *624/142–0499* ▤ *AE, MC, V.*

$$ ✕**Fandango.** This quirky restaurant has an excellent reputation among longtime residents, and its eclectic menu should please almost everyone. Try the sweet-potato fritters, Greek salad, or baby green beans with chilies and toasted almonds. A festive mural, Chinese umbrellas, and a candlelit patio bespeak Fandango's carefree style. ⊠ *Obregón 19 at Av. Morelos, Centro* ☎ *624/142–2226* ▤ *MC, V* ☯ *Closed Sun.*

$ ✕**Baja Natural.** Tucked down a flight of steps away from the busy streets, this low-key kid-pleaser is a good place to cool off with fresh-fruit smoothies, juices, shakes, or power drinks. Hamburgers, hot dogs, and veggie burgers round out the options. ⊠ *Manuel Doblado between Morelos and Hidalgo, Centro* ☎ *624/142–3105* ▤ *No credit cards* ☯ *Closed Sun. No dinner.*

★ **$$$$** ▦**Casa Natalia.** Standing gracefully on San José's most charming street is this beautiful boutique hotel. The rooms are decorated in regional Mexican motifs and have king-size beds, remote-control air-conditioning, and private patios. The suites have hot tubs and hammocks on the large terraces. The welcoming, personalized service is reinforced by the owners's living on the premises. The restaurant, Mi Cocina, is worth seeking out. ⊠ *Blvd. Mijares 4, Centro 23400* ☎ *624/142–5100; 888/277–3814 in the U.S.* ▤ *624/142–5110* ⊕ *www.casanatalia.com* ⌕ *14 rooms, 2 suites* ⚫ *Restaurant, in-room safes, pool, massage, bar* ▤ *AE, MC, V* ¶◯| *CP.*

$$$$ ▦**Presidente Inter-Continental Los Cabos.** The all-inclusive hotel sits amid cactus gardens next to the estuary and has three sections centered by pools and lounging areas. The best rooms are on the ground floor and have terraces. All rooms have showers instead of tubs. You can choose between gourmet restaurants and themed buffets at dinner, order 24-hour room service, or opt for fast-food nachos, hot dogs, and fries at several food carts. ⊠ *Paseo San José, at the end of the hotel zone, 23400* ☎ *624/142–0211; 800/327–0200 in the U.S.* ▤ *624/142–0232* ⊕ *hotels.loscabos.interconti.com* ⌕ *395 rooms, 4 suites* ⚫ *3 restaurants, room service, in-room data ports, in-room safes, 3 tennis courts, 3 pools, beach, fishing, horseback riding, children's programs (ages 5–12), no-smoking rooms* ▤ *AE, MC, V* ¶◯| *FAP.*

$$ ▦**Tropicana Inn.** This small hotel is a great option if you aren't desperate to be on the beach. The stucco buildings decorated with tile murals of Diego Rivera paintings frame a pool and palapa bar in a quiet enclave behind San José's main boulevard. Rooms are maintained to look brand-new. ⊠ *Blvd. Mijares 30, Centro 23400* ☎ *624/142–0907* ▤ *624/142–1590* ⊕ *www.tropicanacabo.com* ⌕ *39 rooms, 2 suites* ⚫ *Restaurant, room service, cable TV, minibars, pool, bar, free parking* ▤ *AE, MC, V.*

$ ▦**Posada Terranova.** San José's best inexpensive hotel is a friendly place where guests return so frequently they're almost part of the family. The large rooms have two double beds and tile bathrooms. You can congregate at the front patio tables or in the restaurant and it still feels like a private home. ⊠ *Calle Degollado at Av. Zaragoza, Centro 23400* ☎ *624/*

142–0534 ☎ *624/142–0902* ⊕ *www.hterranova.com.mx* ⬎ *20 rooms*
♨ *Restaurant, room service, cable TV, bar* ⊟ *AE, MC, V.*

¢–$ ▣ **Posada Señor Mañana.** Accommodations at this quirky place run the
gamut from small, no-frills rooms to larger rooms with air-conditioning, fans, cable TV, coffeemakers, and refrigerators. Hammocks hang
on an upstairs deck, and you can store food and prepare meals in the
communal kitchen. The owners also have inexpensive cabañas by the
beach. ⊠ *Obregón by the Casa de la Cultura, Centro 23400* ☎ *624/*
142–0462 ☎ *624/142–1199* ⊕ *www.srmanana.net* ⬎ *11 rooms* ♨ *No*
a/c in some rooms ⊟ *MC, V.*

NIGHTLIFE & THE
ARTS San José's nightlife is subdued; there are no bars like the raucous joints
in San Lucas. At **Havanas** (⊠ Hwy. 1, Km 29 ☎ no phone), the excellent jazz band of owner-singer Sheila Mihevic plays in the hip club
Wednesday through Friday. Local guides who work with kayaking and
adventure-tourism companies hang out at **Rawhide** (⊠ Obregón at Guerrero ☎ 624/142–3626). Tropicana Inn guests, other tourists, and locals
mingle at the **Tropicana Bar and Grill** (⊠ Blvd. Mijares 30 ☎ 624/142–
1580), an old standby.

SPORTS & THE
OUTDOORS **Ecotours.** Baja Wild (⊠ Obregón at Guerrero, San José ☎ 624/148–2222
or 624/142–5300 ⊕ www.bajawild.com) offers a good selection of
tours, including hikes to canyons, hot springs, a fossil-rich area, and caves
with rock paintings. It also runs diving, whale-watching, rock-climbing
and rappelling trips.

Fishing. Most hotels in San José can arrange fishing trips. There's no marina in town, so you'll board your boat at the marina in Cabo San Lucas.
The boats at **Gordo Banks Pangas** (⊠ La Playa, near San José del Cabo
☎ 624/142–1147; 800/408–1199 in the U.S. ⊕ www.gordobanks.com)
are near some of the hottest fishing spots in the Mar de Cortés, the famed
outer and Inner Gordo Banks.

Kayaking. Kayak tours and rentals are available through **Los Lobos del
Mar** (⊠ Brisas del Mar RV park, on the south side of San José ☎ 624/
142–2983). The tours paddle along the Corridor's peaceful bays and
are especially fun in winter when gray whales pass by offshore. **Baja Wild**
(⊠ Obregón at Guerrero, San José ☎ 624/148–2222 or 624/142–5300
⊕ www.bajawild.com) has kayak tours at Cabo Pulmo.

Surfing. For good surfing tips, rentals, and lessons, head to **Costa Azul
Surf Shop** (⊠ Hwy. 1, Km 28, along the Corridor ☎ 624/142–2771
⊕ www.costa-azul.com.mx).

SHOPPING San José's shops and galleries carry a gorgeous array of high-quality folk
art, jewelry, and housewares. In fact, serious shoppers staying elsewhere should plan on splurging here. **ADD** (⊠ Av. Zaragoza at Hidalgo
☎ 624/143–2055), an interior-design shop, sells lovely hand-painted dishes
from Guanajuato and carved wood furniture from Michoacán. Across
from City Hall is **Almacenes Goncanseco** (⊠ Blvd. Mijares 18 ☎ no
phone), where you can get film, postcards, groceries, and liquor. **Amigos Smokeshop and Cigar Bar** (⊠ Calle Doblado at Av. Morelos ☎ 624/
142–1138) is a classy shop and cigar bar selling fine Cuban and Mexican cigars and Casa Noble tequila. Look for visiting celebs here. **Los
Castillo** (⊠ Av. Zaragoza at Hidalgo ☎ 624/142–4717) carries original
jewelry pieces from the famed Taxco designers.

Copal (⊠ Plaza Mijares ☎ 624/142–3070) has an array of carved animals from Oaxaca, masks from Guerrero Negro, and heavy wooden furnishings. For fresh produce, flowers, meat, fish, and a sampling of local
life in San José, visit the **Mercado Municipal,** off Calle Doblado. **Veryka**

(✉ Blvd. Mijares 6B ☎ 624/142–0575) is associated with galleries in San Miguel de Allende and Oaxaca, two of the finest art centers in Mexico. This shop's selection of huipiles, masks, tapestries, and pottery is coveted by collectors.

The Corridor

Many of the legendary fishing lodges and exclusive resorts built before the government stepped in were located along the wild cliffs between San José del Cabo and Cabo San Lucas. Since the mid-1980s the area has developed as a destination unto itself. It has several private communities, large-scale resorts, and championship golf courses. Much of the development is centered at either Cabo Real or Cabo del Sol. The venerable 1950s Palmilla hotel is emblematic of recent changes; it will reopen in 2004 with a new spa, restaurant, and villas. The highway along the Corridor has four lanes and well-marked turnoffs for the hotels.

BEACHES **Costa Azul,** east of Cabo Real, is the most popular surfing beach in Los Cabos. A few small campgrounds and casual restaurants line the beach. **Playa Palmilla** is one of the Corridor's best swimming beaches.

Two bays, **Bahía Chileno** and **Bahía Santa María,** are terrific for diving and snorkeling.

WHERE TO STAY & ✕ **Pitahayas.** This elegant restaurant occupies a lovely niche above the
EAT beach at Cabo del Sol. The Pacific Rim menu blends Thai, Polynesian,
$$–$$$$ and Chinese influences in unusual recipes. Lobster might have a vanilla bean sauce, octopus turns up in a spicy salad, and the catch of the day comes with a refreshing mango relish. Dress to impress. ✉ *Sheraton Hacienda del Mar, Hwy. 1, Km 10* ☎ *624/145–8010* ⊟ *AE, MC, V.*

$ ✕ **Zippers.** Home to the surfing crowd and those who don't mind a bit of sand in their burgers, this casual palapa-roof restaurant sits on Costa Azul beach just south of San José. It's the place to be to watch sporting events on TV. ✉ *Hwy. 1, Km 18.5* ☎ *No phone* ⊟ *No credit cards.*

$$$$ ⊞ **Casa Del Mar.** This hacienda-style hotel is all about luxurious privacy. A hand-carved door leads into the courtyard-lobby, and stairways curve up to the rooms, spa, and library. Rooms have bathrooms with whirlpool bathtubs set a few steps above the main bedroom. A series of flowing streams, fountains, and gardens leads around the pool to a wide stretch of beach. The restaurant is excellent. ✉ *Hwy. 1, Km 19.5, 23410 Cabo San Lucas* ☎ *624/144–0030; 888/227–9621 in the U.S.* 🖷 *624/144–0034* ⊕ *www.casadelmargolfandspa.com* ⊷ *25 rooms, 31 suites* ⚑ *Restaurant, room service, in-room data ports, in-room safes, pool, spa, beach* ⊟ *AE, MC, V.*

★ $$$$ ⊞ **Esperanza.** Created by the prestigious Auberge Resorts, this luxurious inn is utterly polished. The guest rooms have handcrafted furnishings, Frette linens, and dual-head showers; villas take the luxe even further with private pools and butler service. French and Mexican recipes get a Baja twist in the restaurant. At the spa you can relax with a stone massage or bask in a steam cave; it's open to nonguests by appointment. ✉ *Hwy. 1, Km 3.5, 23410* ☎ *624/145–8641; 866/311–2226 in the U. S.* 🖷 *624/145–8651* ⊕ *www.esperanzaresort.com* ⊷ *50 suites, 6 villas* ⚑ *Restaurant, in-room data ports, in-room safes, minibars, in-room DVD players, pool, gym, spa, beach, shops* ⊟ *AE, MC, V.*

$$$$ ⊞ **Hotel Cabo San Lucas.** Looking like a mountain lodge nearly buried in palms, this long-standing Corridor hotel is a favorite of Baja devotees. Rooms are furnished with cheery yellow and blue fabrics and light-wood pieces; suites and villas are more luxurious with large terraces. The hacienda-style buildings are right above Chileno Beach, one of the best diving spots in Los Cabos. ✉*Hwy. 1, Km 14.5, 23410 Cabo San Lucas* ☎*624/144–0014 or 866/733–2226 in the U.S.* 🖷 *624/144–0015; 323/655–*

3243 in the U.S. ⊕ *www.hotelcabo.com* ⇌ *89 rooms, 7 villas* ⚐ *Restaurant, in-room safes, pool, beach, dive shop, fishing* ⊟ *AE, MC, V.*

$$$$ ⊡ **Las Ventanas al Paraíso.** The service is sublime in this den of luxury.
Fodor'sChoice All suites have hot tubs, fireplaces, and telescopes for viewing whales
★   at sea and stars at night. The hotel is filled with handcrafted lamps and
doors, sculpture, and paintings. The restaurants are outstanding and
the spa offers the latest luxurious treatments; nonguests must make advance reservations. There's even a luxury program for pets. ⊠ *Hwy.
1, Km 19.5, 23400 Cabo San Lucas* ☎ *624/144–0300; 888/767–3966
in the U.S.* 🖷 *624/144–0301* ⊕ *www.lasventanas.com* ⇌ *61 suites* ⚐ *2
restaurants, in-room data ports, in-room safes, cable TV, 2 tennis
courts, 2 pools, hot tub, spa, beach, fishing, 2 bars; some pets allowed*
⊟ *AE, MC, V.*

$$ ⊡ **Casa Terra Cotta.** In the hills above Playa Costa Azul, this tiny bed-
and-breakfast offers four secluded minivillas amid lush gardens. All have
arched brick roofs, terra-cotta tile floors, and verandas ideal for whale-
watching. The enormous breakfasts, made entirely with homegrown or
organic ingredients, are legendary. Reserve at least six weeks in advance.
⊠ *Hwy. 1, Km 28.5, ½ km [¼ mi] up hill, 23410* ☎ *624/142–4250*
⊕ *www.terracotta-mex.com* ⇌ *3 rooms, 1 suite* ⚐ *Massage, bar* ⊟ *No
credit cards* ⦿❘ *BP.*

SPORTS & THE   **ATV Tours. Desert Park** (⊠ Cabo Real, across from the Meliá Cabo Real
OUTDOORS   hotel, Corridor ☎ 624/144–0127) leads ATV (all-terrain vehicle) tours
through the desert arroyos and canyons on the inland side of the Cabo
Real development. Fees start at $50 per person.

Diving and Snorkeling. Bahía Chileno, a white-sand cove protected by
towering brown cliffs, has superb snorkeling. There's a concession stand
on the beach with snorkeling-gear rental run by Cabo Acuadeportes;
you can also rent gear at their Cabo San Lucas shop.

Fishing. Most Corridor hotels have excellent fishing fleets, with the
boats anchored at the marina in Cabo San Lucas. Hotels can set up the
trips and provide transportation to the marina and box lunches. **Victor's Sport Fishing** (☎ 624/142–1092 🖷 624/142–1093) has a fleet of
pangas on the Palmilla resort's beach. **Jig Stop Tours** (☎ 800/521–2281
in the U.S.) books fishing trips for several Los Cabos fleets.

Golf. Los Cabos is a hot spot for golf, hosting tournaments, including
the PGA Senior Grand Slam. The courses that have brought so much
attention this way are all in the Corridor and serve as the centerpieces
for mega-resort developments. Expect to pay exorbitant greens fees—
nearly $200 in winter, and $140 in summer. **Cabo del Sol** (☎ 624/145–
8200; 800/386–2405 in the U.S.) a resort development, has an 18-hole
Jack Nicklaus course and an 18-hole Tom Weiskopf course. The Robert
Trent Jones II–designed **Cabo Real Golf Club** (⊠ Meliá Cabo Real hotel
☎ 624/144–0040; 800/393–0400 in the U.S.) has 18 holes. The **El Dorado** (☎ 624/144–5451; 800/393–0400 in the U.S.), an 18-hole Jack Nick-
laus course, covers rough seaside terrain in Cabo Real. Among the most
spectacular golf courses is the 27-hole Jack Nicklaus–designed course
at the **Palmilla Golf Club** (⊠ Palmilla resort, Hwy. 1, Km 1 ☎ 624/144–
5250; 800/637–2226 in the U.S.).

Horseback Riding. The **Cuadra San Francisco Equestrian Center** (⊠ on
Corridor hwy. across from Cabo Real development ☎ 624/144–0260)
is a professional center with training and trail rides. The ride through
back canyons is more interesting than that at the beach, and the horses
and guides are both excellent. Make advance reservations.

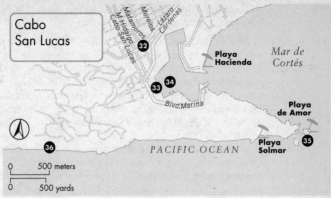

Cabo San Lucas

Cabo San Lucas, once an unsightly fishing town with dusty streets and smelly canneries, has become Los Cabos's center of tourism activity. The sportfishing fleet is headquartered here, and cruise ships anchor off the marina. Trendy restaurants and bars line the streets, and massive hotels have risen on every available plot of waterfront turf—alas, a five-story condo-hotel complex along the bay blocks the view from the town's side streets. Cabo San Lucas is decidedly *in*—for its rowdy nightlife, its slew of restaurants, and its shopping. Most of the shops, services, and restaurants are found between Avenida Cárdenas and the waterfront. The area around the Cárdenas stoplight leading into town by the Puerto Paraíso mall is also a busy hub.

★ ③⑤ **El Arco.** The most spectacular sight in Cabo San Lucas, this natural rock arch is visible from the marina and from some of the hotels but is more impressive from the water. You should take at least a short boat ride out to the arch and Playa de Amor, the beach underneath, to fully appreciate Cabo.

③④ **Bahía de Cabo San Lucas.** The sportfishing fleet is docked in this bay, and glass-bottom boats are available at the water's edge.

③⑥ **El Faro de Cabo Falso.** The Lighthouse of the False Cape, built in 1890 and set amid sand dunes, is on the cliffs above the Pacific coast. You need a four-wheel-drive vehicle to reach the lighthouse by land; most hotels can arrange off-road-vehicle tours.

③③ **Mercado de Artesanías.** Paved walkways run from the busy Boulevard Marina—formerly a dusty main drag—to the hotels and beaches on the east end of town and west to this market at the marina.

③② **Plaza Amelia Wilkes.** The main downtown street, Avenida Lázaro Cárdenas, passes this pretty square with its white wrought-iron gazebo. Buildings around the plaza house galleries and restaurants.

BEACHES
Fodor'sChoice
★

Playa de Amor consists of a secluded cove at the very end of the peninsula, with the Mar de Cortés on one side and the Pacific Ocean on the other. The contrast between the peaceful azure cove on the Mar de Cortés and the pounding white surf of the Pacific is dramatic. **Playa Hacienda,** in the inner harbor by the Hacienda Hotel, has the calmest waters of any beach in town and there's good snorkeling around the rocky point. **Playa Médano,** just north of Cabo San Lucas, is the most popular stretch in Los Cabos (and possibly in all Baja) for sunbathing and people-watching. The 3-km (2-mi) span of white sand is always crowded, especially on weekends. **Playa Solmar,** on the fringe of the Solmar Hotel, is a beautiful wide beach but it has dangerous surf with a swift under-tow. Stick to sunbathing here.

✕ **Edith's Café.** The Caesar salad and flambéed crepes are served table-side at this small café, where dinners are accompanied by Mexican trios or soft jazz. Even the simplest quesadilla is enhanced by Oaxacan cheese and homemade tortillas, and the meat and fish dishes are creative, with unusual chili or tropical fruit sauces. The place sometimes bustles with families in early evening, so dine later if you're looking for romance. ⊠ *Paseo del Pescador near Playa Médano, Centro* ☎ *624/143–0801* ⊟ *MC, V.*

$–$$$$ ✕ **Mocambo.** Veracruz (known for its regional seafood preparations) meets Los Cabos in an enormous dining room packed with locals. The menu features hard-to-find regional dishes such as octopus ceviche, shrimp empanadas, and a heaping mixed seafood platter that includes sea snails, clams, and octopus, with lobster and shrimp. Musicians stroll among the tables and the chatter is somewhat cacophonous, but you're sure to have a great dining experience here. ⊠ *Leona Vicario at Calle 20 de Noviembre, Centro* ☎ *624/143–2122* ⊟ *AE, MC, V.*

$–$$$$ ✕ **Pancho's.** This festive restaurant, a favorite among locals, has an enormous collection of tequilas (almost 500 labels); take advantage of owner John Bragg's encyclopedic knowledge of tequila and sample a few. Oaxacan tablecloths, murals, painted chairs, and streamers add to the fun atmosphere. Try regional specialties like tortilla soup or chiles rellenos. The breakfast and lunch specials are a bargain. ⊠ *Hidalgo between Zapata and Serdan, Centro* ☎ *624/143–2891* ⊟ *AE, MC, V.*

★ $–$$$$ ✕ **Sancho Panza.** The sophisticated menu, decor, and live jazz make this small bistro an excellent spot for a lingering dinner. Try the steamed mussels, flank steak stuffed with goat cheese, and sublime wahoo in a savory broth. The menu changes constantly, as does the art in the Daliésque bar and the extraordinary selection of imported wines in the wine warehouse. Wine and tequila tastings are held frequently. ⊠ *Blvd. Marina, behind KFC and Plaza Las Glorias, Centro* ☎ *624/143–3212* ⊟ *AE, MC, V* ☉ *Closed Sun.*

$$–$$$ ✕ **Capo San Giovannis.** Owner Gianfranco Zappata and his master pastry chef–wife, Antonella, perform a culinary concert that keeps you coming back for encores. Try their green salad with lobster chunks, salmon with champagne and leek sauce and *mela,* an apple and nut pastry topped with caramel. For a romantic touch, dine on the starlit back patio. There's a 10% discount for cash. ⊠ *Av. Guerrero at Cárdenas, Centro* ☎ *624/143–0593* ⊟ *MC, V* ☉ *Closed Mon.*

$$–$$$ ✕ **Mi Casa.** One of Cabo's best restaurants is in a cobalt-blue building painted with a mural of a burro, near the main plaza. Mexican cuisine shines with fresh tuna and dorado served with tomatillo salsa or Yucatecan achiote, or with sophisticated dishes such as chiles en nogada. The large back courtyard is especially nice at night, when it's illuminated by candlelight. ⊠ *Av. Cabo San Lucas, Centro* ☎ *624/143–1933* ⊟ *MC, V.*

★ $–$$ ✕ **Marisquería Mazatlán.** The crowds of locals lunching at this simple seafood restaurant are a good sign—as are the huge glasses packed with shrimp, ceviche, and other seafood cocktails. You can dine inexpensively on wonderful seafood soup, or spend a bit more for tender *pulpo ajillo* (marinated octopus with garlic, chilies, onion, and celery). ⊠ *Mendoza at Calle 16 de Septiembre, Centro* ☎ *624/143–8565* ⊟ *MC, V.*

$–$$ ✕ **The Office.** Playa Médano is lined with cafés on the sand, some with lounge chairs, others with more formal settings. All serve the same basics—cold beer, snacks, fish tacos, french fries—and most accompany the meal with loud American rock. The Office, which has provided perfect vacation photo opportunities for more than a decade, is the best. ⊠ *Playa Médano, Centro* ☎ *624/143–3464* ⊟ *MC, V.*

¢–$ ✕ **Señor Greenberg's Mexicatessen.** Pastrami, chopped liver, knishes, bagels, lox, cheesecake—you can find them all behind the glass counters of this decent Mexican incarnation of a New York deli. It's open 24 hours; the air-conditioning, stacks of newspapers, and soft music might pull you back more than once. ⊠ *Plaza Nautica on Blvd. Marina, Centro* ☎ *624/143–5630* ▤ *MC, V.*

★ $$$$ 🏨 **Hotel Hacienda.** Sitting at the edge of the bay, the Hacienda resembles a Spanish colonial inn with white arches and bell towers, stone fountains, and statues of Indian gods set amid hibiscus and bougainvillea. The white rooms have red-tile floors, tile baths, and folk art. The watersports center has any gear you might need. Though tiny, the Wellness Center offers excellent massages and holistic healing treatments. ⊠ *Playa Médano, Centro 23410* ☎ *624/143–0665 or 624/143–0666; 800/733–2226 in the U.S.* 🖷 *624/143–0666* ⊕ *www.haciendacabo.com* ⤳ *60 rooms, 12 suites, 30 beachfront cabañas* ⚑ *Restaurant, in-room safes, some kitchenettes, pool, massage, beach, bar* ▤ *AE, MC, V.*

$$$$ 🏨 **Meliá San Lucas.** The most popular beach in Los Cabos is where you'll find the Meliá and its huge, ever-packed pool areas, a hot tub under the palms, and all the equipment you could need for playing on and in the water. Rooms have easygoing light-wood furnishings and heavy drapes to block out the midday sun. Early reservations are essential. ⊠ *Playa Médano, Centro 23410* ☎ *624/143–4444; 800/336–3542 in the U.S.* 🖷 *624/143–0418* ⊕ *www.solmelia.com* ⤳ *144 rooms, 6 suites* ⚑ *3 restaurants, in-room safes, minibars, 2 pools, hot tub, beach* ▤ *AE, MC, V.*

$$$ 🏨 **Pueblo Bonito Rosé.** Mediterranean-style buildings curve around the elegant grounds at this Playa Médano resort. Flemish tapestries decorate the spacious lobby; statues reminiscent of Roman busts guard reflecting pools. The spacious suites have private balconies overlooking the grounds; some have kitchenettes. The spa is the best in San Lucas, and the facilities are open to the public for a fee. Many of the suites are used as time-share units, with guests booking in for a week. ⊠ *Playa Médano, Centro 23410* ☎ *624/143–5500; 800/990–8250 in the U.S.* 🖷 *624/143–5979* ⊕ *www.pueblobonito.com* ⤳ *260 suites* ⚑ *2 restaurants, in-room safes, minibars, cable TV, pool, beach, spa* ▤ *MC, V.*

$$$ 🏨 **Pueblo Bonito Sunset Beach.** A whole new neighborhood has opened up in Los Cabos, thanks to the developer of this resort. On the Pacific side of Baja's tip a series of earth-tone villas spread down a hillside to a sprawling pool and a long beach. (Limit your swimming to the pool, as the surf is too rough.) All suites face the ocean and are filled with dark-wood furnishings. You can take the winding paths wind around the property or hop in an electric cart. The food is excellent, which is a good thing since there are no other restaurants around and a cab to San Lucas costs $10 each way. The hotel runs a shuttle to its Rosé property. ⊠ *Predio Paraíso Escondido s/n, Centro 23410* ☎ *624/142–9999; 800/990–8250 in the U.S.* 🖷 *624/142–9957* ⊕ *www.pueblobonito. com* ⤳ *118 suites* ⚑ *2 restaurants, in-room safes, minibars, cable TV, 2 tennis courts, pool, beach, gym* ▤ *MC, V.*

★ $$$ 🏨 **Solmar Suites.** The Solmar sits against cliffs at the tip of Land's End, facing the Pacific. The rooms are decorated in Mexico–Santa Fe style, with tile baths. The adjacent time-share and condo units have kitchenettes and a private pool area. The surf here is far too dangerous for swimming, but don't miss a stroll along the wide strip of beach. The Solmar's sportfishing fleet is first-rate. The good restaurant hosts a Saturday-night Mexican fiesta and buffet dinner. ⊠ *Av. Solmar at Blvd. Marina, Apdo. 8, Centro 23410* ☎ *624/143–3535; 310/459–9861 or 800/344–3349 in the U.S.* 🖷 *624/143–0410; 310/454–1686 in the U.S.* ⊕ *www.solmar.com* ⤳ *82 junior suites, 14 studios, 27 deluxe suites* ⚑ *Restaurant, in-room safes, minibars, cable TV, 3 pools, beach, fishing, bar* ▤ *AE, MC, V.*

$$ ⬚ **The Bungalows Breakfast Inn.** If solitude and a reasonable room rate are more important than being in the center of the action, this is your place, 10 blocks from the beach. Several two-story buildings frame a small, heated pool. Rooms are beautifully decorated with Mexican textiles and art. ⊠ *Calle Constitución, 5 blocks from main plaza, Centro 23410* ☎ *624/143–5035* ⊕ *www.cabobungalows.com* ⇗ *16 suites* ⌂ *Pool; no smoking* ⊟ *No credit cards* ⬚| *CP.*

$$ ⬚ **Finisterra.** An eight-story-high palapa covers this beachfront hotel's restaurant and bar next to two free-form swimming pools. Suites with oceanfront balconies are by far the nicest, though the standard rooms in the beachfront tower are bright, cheery, and spacious. The Whale Watcher bar atop a high cliff has the best view in town. ⊠ *Blvd. Marina, Centro 23410* ☎ *624/143–3333; 520/529–4529 or 800/347–2252 in the U.S.* ☎ *624/143–0590* ⊕ *www.finisterra.com* ⇗ *280 rooms, 125 junior suites* ⌂ *2 restaurants, in-room safes, some kitchenettes, cable TV, 3 pools, gym, spa, 2 bars, travel services* ⊟ *AE, MC, V.*

$ ⬚ **Cabo Inn.** What this small palapa-roof hotel lacks in luxury, it makes up for in character. The small, comfortable rooms have tangerine and cobalt sponge-painted walls and stained-glass windows above the headboards. The eight rooms on the lower level have refrigerators; a kitchen, barbecue and picnic area, and a television round out the communal amenities. ⊠ *Calle 20 de Noviembre and Vicario, Centro 23410* ☎ *624/ 143–0819* ⊕ *www.mexonline.com/caboinn.htm* ⇗ *21 rooms* ⌂ *Picnic area, refrigerators* ⊟ *No credit cards.*

$ ⬚ **Chile Pepper Inn.** Upon entering the pretty garden patio, you'll be greeted with a warm *hola* from the friendly staff. A few blocks off the town center, this tiny inn offers delightful rooms at unbeatable prices. Each is named for a type of chili and features handmade wooden furniture and chili-decorated tiles around the doorway and in the bathroom. Internet access and local calls are toll free. Reserve a few months in advance; the inn fills quickly. ⊠ *Calle 16 de Septiembre and Calle Abasolo, Centro 23410* ☎ *624/143–8611; 877/708–1918 in the U.S.* ☎ *624/143–0510* ⊕ *www.chilepepperinn.com* ⇗ *9 rooms, 1 suite* ⌂ *No-smoking rooms* ⊟ *MC, V.*

$ ⬚ **Siesta Suites.** This oasis of calm off the main drag scene offers you a lot for the money. There's no pool, but the suites have full-size refrigerators, and between the two double beds and wide padded couches that make excellent beds even for grown-ups, you'll have room to sleep quite a crew. The three-story hotel sits two blocks from the marina, and the proprietors keep a close eye on the place and offer great budget tips. ⊠ *Calle Zapata, Apdo. 310, Centro 23410* ☎ *624/143–6494; 866/ 271–0952 in the U.S.* ⊕ *www.cabosiestasuites.com* ⇗ *5 rooms, 15 suites* ⌂ *Kitchenettes* ⊟ *AE, MC, V.*

NIGHTLIFE & THE ARTS Some travelers choose Cabo San Lucas for its nightlife, which consists mainly of noisy bars with blaring music and plenty of dancing, flirting, and imbibing. The latest U.S. rock plays over an excellent sound system at **Cabo Wabo** (⊠ Calle Guerrero ☎ 624/143–1198), but the impromptu jam sessions with appearances by Sammy Hagar—an owner—and his many music-business friends are the real highlight. **Edith's** (⊠ Paseo del Pescador at Playa Médano ☎ 624/143–0801) presents live jazz in a tasteful garden setting. **El Galeón** (⊠ Blvd. Marina ☎ 624/143–0443) is a welcome refuge for the quieter crowd, who sip brandy by the piano bar. **Giggling Marlin** (⊠ Blvd. Marina ☎ 624/143–1182) seems to have been around forever as the favorite watering hole for anglers. **Sancho Panza Wine Bistro** (⊠ Blvd. Marina in the Plaza Las Glorias Hotel ☎ 624/143–3212) is the place to sip imported wines served by the glass while listening to live soft jazz. **Squid Roe** (⊠ Av. Cárdenas ☎ 624/143–0655) is the rowdiest spot in town, packed with young foreigners who work in the local tourist industry and know how to party. **La Varitas** (✉ Calle Gomez behind Puerto Paraíso ☎ 624/143–9999) is a branch of La Paz rock club favored by young Mexicans who love to dance.

SPORTS & THE
OUTDOORS

Diving. El Arco is a prime diving and snorkeling area, as are several rocky points off the coast. Divers consider the sandfalls, an underwater cascade of sand that flows from 90 ft to 1,200 ft below sea level, an essential experience; many also undertake the two-hour boat trip to the coral reefs off Cabo Pulmo, off the East Cape. Most hotels can arrange diving trips and equipment rental. **The Activity Center** (✉ Playa Médano ☎ 624/143–0309) has every type of water and land-sports equipment, including diving gear, wave runners, Windsurfers, and parasails. The oldest and most complete dive shop in the area is **Amigos del Mar** (✉ Blvd. Marina across from sportfishing docks at the marina ☎ 624/143–0505; 800/344–3349 in the U.S.). **Cabo Acuadeportes** (✉ Hotel Hacienda, Playa Médano ☎ 624/143–0117) offers diving trips along with all other imaginable water sports, and rents snorkel gear at Chileno Bay.

Ecotours. Capeland Tours & Expeditions (✉ Playa Médano beside Billygans bar ☎ 624/143–0775) offers ecotours to Caduaño, a small community near the Sierra de la Laguna mountains. The tour includes a ride in a four-wheel-drive vehicle to a region rich in fossils. Other tours include visits to the woodworkers and leather factories in Miraflores and the waterfalls and lakes in the mountains. Trips include a great barbecue lunch at a small ranch.

Fishing. More than 800 species of fish teem in the waters off Los Cabos. Most hotels will arrange fishing charters, which include a captain and mate, tackle, bait, licenses, and drinks. Prices start at about $300 per day for a 25-ft cruiser. Some charters provide lunch, and most can arrange to have your catch mounted, frozen, or smoked. Most of the boats leave from the sportfishing docks in the Cabo San Lucas marina. Usually there are a fair number of pangas for rent at about $30 per hour with a five-hour minimum. **The Gaviota Fleet** (✉ Bahía Condo Hotel, Playa Médano ☎ 624/143–0430; 800/932–5599 in the U.S. ⊕ www.grupobahia.com) has held the record for the largest marlin caught in Cabo's waters, a claim all companies try to achieve. The company has charter cruisers and pangas. Minerva and John Smith oversee **Minerva's** (✉ Av. Madero between Blvd. Marina and Guerrero ☎ 624/143–1282 ⊕www.minervas.com), the renowned tackle store in San Lucas. The Minerva fleet has three charter fishing boats. Some of the Corridor's priciest hotels choose the **Pisces Sportfishing Fleet** (✉ Cabo Maritime Center on Blvd. Marina ☎ 624/143–1288 ⊕ www.piscessportfishing.com) for their guests. The fleet includes the usual 31-ft Bertrams and extraordinary 50- to 70-ft Hatteras cruisers with tuna towers and staterooms. The **Solmar Fleet** (✉ Blvd. Marina, across from the sportfishing dock ☎624/143–0646 or 624/143–4542; 800/344–3349 in the U.S. ☎ 624/143–0410; 310/454–1686 in the U.S. ⊕ www.solmar.com) is one of the oldest and most reputable companies in the area. The boats and tackle are always in good shape, and regulars wouldn't fish with anyone else.

Horseback Riding. Cantering down an isolated beach or up a desert trail is one of the great pleasures of Baja (as long as the sun isn't beating down on your head). Horses are available for rent in front of the Playa Médano hotels; contact **Rancho Collins Horses** (☎624/143–3652). **Red Rose Riding Stables** (✉ Hwy. 1, Km 4 ☎ 624/143–4826) has healthy horses for all levels of riders and an impressive array of tack.

Whale-Watching. The gray-whale migration doesn't end at Baja's Pacific lagoons. Plenty of whales of all sizes make it down to the warmer waters off Los Cabos and into the Mar de Cortés. To watch whales from shore, go to the beach at the Solmar Suites or any Corridor hotel, or the lookout points along the Corridor highway. Several companies run whale-watching trips from Cabo San Lucas. Check with **Cabo Acuadeportes** (⊠ Hotel Hacienda, Playa Médano ☎ 624/143–0117) for excursions. **Cabo Expeditions** (⊠ Plaza Las Glorias hotel, Blvd. Marina ☎ 624/143–2700) offers snorkeling and whale-watching tours in rubber boats. The tour boats that run snorkeling and sunset cruises also offer whale-watching tours in winter.

SHOPPING   Boulevard Marina and the side streets between the waterfront and the main plaza are filled with an ever-changing parade of small shops.

El Callejón (⊠ Guerrero between Cárdenas and Av. Madero ☎ 624/143–1139) has multiple showrooms with gorgeous furniture, lamps, dishes, and pottery. **Cartes** (⊠ Plaza Bonita, Blvd. Marina ☎ 624/143–1770) is the best of Los Cabos's many home-furnishing stores, with an irresistible array of hand-painted pottery and tableware, pewter frames, handblown glass, and carved furniture. **Dos Lunas** (⊠ Plaza Bonita, Blvd. Marina ☎ 624/143–1969) has a trendy selection of colorful sportswear and straw hats.

Galería Gatemelatta (⊠ on dirt road to Hotel Hacienda ☎ 624/143–1166) specializes in colonial furniture and antiques. Need a new bathing suit? Check out the selection at **H2O de los Cabos** (⊠ Av. Madero at Guerrero ☎ 624/143–1219), where you can choose between skimpy thongs and modest one-piece suits. **J&J Habanos** (⊠ Av. Madero between Blvd. Marina and Guerrero ☎ 624/143–6160) is a cigar aficionado's heaven, with a walk-in humidor stocked with pricey cigars. The shop also sells expensive tequilas. **Magic of the Moon** (⊠ Hidalgo near Blvd. Marina ☎ 624/143–3161 ⊕ www.magicofthemoon.com) is the place to shop for handmade women's sundresses, skirts, and lingerie in fashionable fabrics and styles. **Mama Eli's** (⊠ Av. San Lucas ☎ 624/143–1616) is a three-story gallery with fine furnishings, ceramics, appliquéd clothing, and children's toys. **Necri** (⊠ Blvd. Marina between Av. Madero and Ocampo ☎ 624/143–0283) has a mainstream selection of folk art and furnishings.

The palatial entrance of **Puerto Paraíso** (⊠ Av. Cárdenas at the entrance to town, Cabo San Lucas) leads into a three-story marble and glass enclosed mall. You'll find a few U.S. chains (Häagen-Dazs, a Johnny Rockets diner, a Ruth's Chris steak house) and the promise of name-brand stores, but at this writing many of the storefronts were empty. One of the oldest folk-art shops in the area, **Zen Mar** (⊠ Cárdenas beside the Mar de Cortés hotel, ☎ 624/143–0661) displays an excellent selection of masks from Oaxaca and Guerrero.

At the **crafts market** in the marina, you can pose for a photo with an iguana, plan a ride in a glass-bottom boat, or browse to your heart's content through stalls packed with blankets, sombreros, and pottery.

Todos Santos

72 km (45 mi) north of Cabo San Lucas.

The Pacific side of the tip of Baja is gradually being developed. The small agricultural town of Todos Santos has become a haven for artists, architects, and speculators contributing to a rapid rise in real estate prices. The town sits a bit inland from the rugged coast and is classically charming with its 19th-century brick-and-stucco buildings and small central plaza. Most of the older adobe buildings are on calles Centenario, Legaspi, and Topete around the main square. It's an ideal haven if you deplore the overdevelopment of Baja's tip, since both Los Cabos and La Paz are within easy driving distance (for shopping, dining, and taking care of business). Entrepreneurs have turned some of the plaza-front buildings into galleries and cafés, and there's always a new spot to check out. Business hours are erratic, especially in September and October.

Los Cabos regulars typically drive up the coast to Todos Santos on day trips, stopping to watch surfers at Playa Migriño, Playa Los Cerritos, and Punta Gaspareo. El Pescadero, the largest settlement before Todos Santos, is populated by ranchers and farmers who grow herbs and vegetables for the restaurants in Los Cabos. Seasonal produce is sold at small stands by the side of the road. Dirt roads intersect the highway at several points along the way to Todos Santos, but you should attempt these roads only with four-wheel-drive vehicles—sands on the beach or in the desert may stop conventional vehicles in their tracks.

During high season, you may find tour buses clogging the streets around the plaza in Todos Santos; it's a pit stop on tours between Cabo San Lucas and La Paz. When the buses leave, the town is a pleasant and peaceful place to wander through shops and galleries. If you drive to Todos Santos on your own, head back to Cabo before dark; Highway 19 between the two towns is unlighted and is prone to high winds and flooding. When you get to town, be sure to pick up *El Calendario de Todos Santos,* a free guide (published eight times a year, in English) with the most current events and developments. It's available at many hotels, shops, and restaurants.

Where to Stay & Eat

$$–$$$ ✕ **Cafe Santa Fe.** The setting, with tables amid herb gardens in an overgrown courtyard, is part of the appeal, but the main highlight is the food—salads and soups made from homegrown organic vegetables and herbs, homemade pastas, and fresh fish with light herbal sauces. Many Cabo residents lunch here weekly. ⊠ *Calle Centenario* ☎ *612/145–0340* 🚫 *No credit cards* ⊘ *Closed Tues. and parts of Sept. and Oct.*

$–$$$ ✕ **Los Adobes.** Locals swear by the fried, cilantro-studded local cheese and pork loin stuffed with huitlacoche at this pleasant outdoor restaurant. The menu is a bit overambitious, but it does offer several vegetarian options, something of a rarity in these parts. At night, the place sparkles with star-shaped lights. The Internet café within the restaurant has high-speed access and reasonable rates. ⊠ *Calle Hidalgo s/n* ☎ *612/145–0203* 🚫 *MC, V* ⊘ *No dinner Sun.*

$–$$ ✕ **Caffé Todos Santos.** Omelets, bagels, granola, and delicious whole-grain breads delight the breakfast crowd at this small café; deli sandwiches, fresh salads, and an array of tamales, *flautas* (tortillas rolled around savory fillings), and combo plates are lunch and dinner highlights. Check for fresh seafood on the daily specials board, and pick up a loaf of bread for the road. ⊠ *Calle Centenario 33* ☎ *612/145–0300* 🚫 *MC, V.*

$–$$ ✕ **Mi Costa.** Locals crave the shrimp with garlic and oil served at this concrete-floor, palapa-covered café. On Sunday, families fill the dining area, feasting on peeled shrimp, fish tacos, and grilled fish fillets. The ambience is Mexican casual—feel free to fetch your own napkins and condiments. ⊠ *Militar at Ocampo* ☎ *No phone* 🚫 *No credit cards.*

$$ ✕🏠 **Posada La Poza.** Looking for a civilized, self-contained retreat? The Swiss owners here aim to please with their chic posada beside a bird-filled lagoon and the open sea. The suites are handsomely decorated with rust-tone walls, modern furniture, and Swiss linens; you'll have a CD player

and binoculars on hand, but no TVs or phones to distract you. There's a palm-fringed pool and a terrific restaurant—even if you're not staying, come by for fettuccine with white truffle sauce and organic salads. The restaurant is closed Thursday. ⊠ *Follow the signs on Hwy. 19 and on Av. Juárez to the beach, 23300* ☎ *612/145-0400* 📠 *612/145-0453* ⊕ *www.lapoza.com* ➥ *7 rooms* ⚕ *Restaurant, in-room safes, minibars, pool, massage, bar, Internet; no room phones, no room TVs* ⊟ *MC, V* ❙⊙❙ *BP.*

$$–$$$ ⊞ **Hotel California.** New owners transformed this hotel with a famous name from a run-down shell to a sophisticated inn. The previous owners encouraged the rumor that the Eagles song originated here, but the myth was debunked. The handsome, well-kept place should now draw guests on its own merit. A deep blue and ocher color scheme runs throughout, and the rooms have eclectic mixes of antiques and folk art. Some rooms have an ocean view. The bar has become a local hot spot. ⊠ *Calle Juárez at Morelos 23300* ☎ *612/145-0522* 📠 *612/145-0288* ➥ *11 rooms* ⚕ *Restaurant, pool, bar* ⊟ *MC, V.*

★ $$ ⊞ **Todos Santos Inn.** The four guest rooms in this converted 19th-century house are unparalleled in design and comfort. Gorgeous antiques are set against stone walls under brick ceilings. Ceiling fans and the shade from garden trees keep the rooms cool and breezy. The absence of telephones and TVs makes a perfect foil for the conceits of Los Cabos. The inn's wine bar and restaurant are open in the evening, and good restaurants are within easy walking distance. ⊠ *Calle Legaspi, 23300* ☎📠 *612/145-0040* ➥ *6 rooms* ⚕ *Restaurant, bar; no room phones, no room TVs* ⊟ *No credit cards.*

¢–$ ⊞ **Hostería Las Casitas.** If Los Cabos has got you feeling like turning down the volume (and the cash flow), this B&B in a lush garden setting might give you the quiet you're looking for—and great breakfasts. A couple of rooms share a shower but have their own toilets and sinks; the other two rooms share all facilities. The buildings' traditional Mexican architecture makes for cool accommodations. Owner Wendy Faith's art-glass studio is also on-site. ⊠ *Calle Rangel at Obregón and Hidalgo, Apdo. 73, 23300* ☎📠 *612/145-0255* ⊕ *www.mexonline.com/lascasitas. htm* ➥ *4 rooms, 2 suites with bath* ⊟ *No credit cards* ❙⊙❙ *CP.*

BAJA SUR A TO Z

To research prices, get advice from other travelers, and travel arrangements, visit *www.fodors.com.*

AIR TRAVEL

Baja Sur has airports in La Paz, Los Cabos, and Loreto, all serviced by many domestic and international airlines.

AIRPORTS La Paz airport (LAP) is about 16 km (10 mi) north of town. Loreto's airport (LTO) is 7 km (4½ mi) southwest of town. Los Cabos International Airport (SJD) is about 11 km (7 mi) north of San José del Cabo and about 48 km (30 mi) from Cabo San Lucas. At Los Cabos, time-share hustlers assault visitors with offers of free transportation, which implies a commitment to tour their properties. To avoid the sales pitch, go directly to the transportation desk by the exit from the airport to arrange a ride into town.

🛈 **Los Cabos International Airport** ☎ 624/146-5013. **Loreto Airport** ☎ 613/135-0565. **La Paz Airport** ☎ 612/112-0082.

AIRPORT Taxis between the La Paz and Loreto airports and their respective towns
TRANSFERS are inexpensive and convenient. In Los Cabos, cabs to and from the airport are outrageously expensive. Expect to pay at least $25, but a ride

can cost over $50 depending on the distance. Some Los Cabos hotels offer airport transfers for a fee, which is usually less than a cab. Ask about the availability of such a service when you make your reservation. Some hotels have sign-up sheets with which you can arrange to share the expense of a cab with other travelers.

CARRIERS AeroCalifornia serves La Paz airport from Tijuana, Tucson, and Los Angeles, has daily flights from Los Angeles to Loreto's airport, and flies to Los Cabos from Los Angeles and Tijuana. Aeroméxico flies to La Paz from Los Angeles, Tucson, Tijuana, Mexico City, and other cities within Mexico; it flies to Los Cabos and Loreto from San Diego and Mexico City. Mexicana has flights to Los Cabos airport from Guadalajara, Mexico City, and Los Angeles. Alaska Airlines operates its own terminal at Los Cabos airport and has flights from Anchorage, Fairbanks, Portland, Phoenix, San Francisco, San Diego, Los Angeles, and Seattle. America West flies into Los Cabos from Phoenix, Continental from Houston and Newark. Delta and American have seasonal nonstop flights, but they don't have offices in Los Cabos. Other international airlines may have service in winter. Many of the U.S. carriers do not have offices or customer phone numbers in Los Cabos. Ask the hotel's concierge or tour desk to reconfirm your flight.

▸ **AeroCalifornia** ☎ 612/125-1023 in La Paz; 624/143-3700 in Los Cabos; 613/135-0500 in Loreto; 800/237-6225 in the U.S. **Aeroméxico** ☎ 612/122-0091 in La Paz; 624/142-0398 in Los Cabos; 800/237-6639 in the U.S. ⊕ www.aeromexico.com. **Alaska Airlines** ☎ 624/142-2362 in Los Cabos ⊕ www.alaskaair.com. **America West** ☎ 01800/363-2597 toll free in Mexico ⊕ www.americawest.com. **Continental** ☎ 624/142-3840 in Los Cabos; 800/525-0280 in the U.S. ⊕ www.continental.com. **Mexicana** ☎ 624/142-0230 in Los Cabos; 800/531-7921 in the U.S. ⊕ www.mexicana.com.

BOAT & FERRY TRAVEL

The ferry system connecting Baja to mainland Mexico constantly undergoes rate and schedule changes. Sematur ferries connect La Paz and Mazatlán every day except Saturday; it's an 18-hour trip. Ferries also head from La Paz to Topolobampo, the port at Los Mochis, every day except Sunday; this is a 17-hour trip. Tickets for both ferry routes are available at La Paz Terminal at the dock on the road to Pichilingue and also at the Sematur Office. The Sematur Web site *should* have the most up-to-date information, but isn't always accurate. Purchase your ticket in advance—it's probably best to use a Mexican travel agent—and expect confusion. Continuous changes in Sematur procedure and pricing make it difficult for even ferry personnel to keep up with the latest policy. One-way fares range from about $60 to $100, depending on whether you spring for a berth with a bathroom or not. Baja Speed operates a high-speed trimaran ferry from La Paz to Topolobampo once a day; the trip takes four hours. Its schedule is generally more stable than Sematur's, and tickets cost roughly $50.

If you plan to take a car or a motor home on the ferry to the mainland, you must obtain a vehicle permit before boarding the ferry and must have Mexican auto-insurance papers; everyone crossing to the mainland also needs a tourist card. Tourism officials in La Paz strongly suggest that you obtain the vehicle permit when crossing the U.S. border into Baja; although permits are not needed in Baja, offices at the border are better equipped to handle the paperwork than those in La Paz. Tourist cards also are available at the border. It's wise to take copies of the following, in triplicate, plus the original: passport, tourist card, birth certificate, and vehicle registration. Also, you'll need make a reservation for vehicle transportation on a ferry at least a few weeks in advance.

Ferry service between Santa Rosalia and Guaymas on the mainland Pacific coast has been discontinued.

🚢 **Baja Speed** ✉ Calle 5 de Mayo at Obregón, La Paz ☎ 612/123-1313. **La Paz Terminal** ☎ 612/125-4440. **Santa Rosalia ferry terminal** ☎ 615/152-0014. **Sematur Office** ✉ Calle 5 de Mayo 502 ☎ 612/125-2366 ☎ 612/125-6588 🌐 www.ferrysematur.com.mx.

BUS TRAVEL TO & FROM BAJA SUR

The Autotransportes de Baja California bus line runs from Tijuana to La Paz, stopping at towns en route; the peninsula-long trip takes 22 hours. It also has a route from La Paz to Guerrero Negro (the bus stops at the highway entrance to town). This trip takes anywhere from six to nine hours. Loreto is serviced by both Autotransportes de Baja California and the local Aguila bus line. The Loreto bus terminal sits at the entrance to town. The buses run several times daily and overall they're clean, safe, and comfortable. You don't need to make advance reservations.

🚌 **Aguila** ☎ 612/122-4270 or 612/122-3063. **Autotransportes de Baja California** ☎ 612/122-6476 or 612/122-7094. **Loreto bus terminal** ✉ Calle Salvatierra at Calle Tamaral ☎ 613/135-0767.

BUS TRAVEL WITHIN BAJA SUR

The Aguila bus line runs from Todos Santos and La Paz to Los Cabos.

In La Paz it's fairly easy to get around by bus: city buses run along the malecón and into downtown. Buses run between Cabo San Lucas and San José del Cabo, and will stop along the Corridor if you ask the driver. There are covered bus stops with benches (but no signs) along Highway 1 in the Corridor. The easiest place to catch a bus in San José is at the stoplight at the intersection of Calle Doblado and Highway 1. In San Lucas, you can catch one at the stoplight on Highway 1 in front of the Puerto Paraíso mall. A ride costs $2.

🚌 **Aguila** ☎ 612/122-4270 or 612/122-3063.

CAR RENTAL

California Baja Rent-A-Car rents four-wheel-drive vehicles, convertibles, and sedans for use throughout Mexico; you can pick up a car in San Diego and drop it off in Los Cabos, but expect to pay a hefty additional charge.

Thrifty has an office south of Loreto in Nopoló. They'll deliver your car to town. Budget in Loreto has a few four-wheel-drive vehicles available. Avis and Hertz have desks at La Paz airport. Hertz has an additional office on Avenida Obregón in town. Avis, Hertz, and Thrifty all have 4-wheel-drive vehicles, but they need to be reserved well in advance.

Several car-rental agencies have desks at Los Cabos airport and in San José or Cabo San Lucas. Reserve a car in advance during high season, especially if you want a van, four-wheel-drive, or air-conditioning. Most agencies rent VW bugs and topless VW bugs, which seem like fun until you're under the blazing sun for several hours.

🚗 **Avis** ☎ 612/124-6312; 612/122-2651 in La Paz; 624/146-0388 at Los Cabos airport 🌐 www.avis.com. **Budget** ✉ Paseo Hidalgo near the malecón, Loreto ☎ 613/135-1090 ✉ Paseo Obregón at Hidalgo, La Paz ☎ 612/122-1919 or 612/122-7655 🌐 www.budget.com. **California Baja Rent-A-Car** ✉ 9245 Jamacha Blvd., Spring Valley, CA 91977 ☎ 619/470-8368 or 888/470-7368 in the U.S. 🌐 www.cabaja.com. **Dollar** ☎ 624/142-0100; 624/143-1250 in Los Cabos 🌐 www.dollar.com. **Hertz** ☎ 612/124-6330 at La Paz airport; 624/142-0375 at Los Cabos airport ✉ Av. Obregón 2130, La Paz ☎ 612/122-5300; 612/122-0919 at La Paz airport 🌐 www.hertz.com. **Thrifty** ✉ Loreto airport ☎ 613/133-0612 🌐 www.thrifty.com.

CAR TRAVEL

Mexico Highway 1, also known as the Carretera Transpeninsular, runs 1,700 km (1,060 mi) from Tijuana to Cabo San Lucas. The highway's condition varies depending on the weather and intervals between road repairs. Don't drive it at high speeds or at night—it's not lighted. There are exits for all the principal towns in Baja Sur.

The road between San José del Cabo and Cabo San Lucas was widened to four lanes and reinforced; elevated bridges have eliminated the flooding problems that long plagued the road.

PARKING It's easy to find street parking in La Paz. In the resort hotspots, though, it's a different story. In San José del Cabo, congested streets make parking difficult; park outside the town center rather than trying to navigate narrow one-way streets. It can also be tricky to find parking in Cabo San Lucas, but there's a large, free lot by the marina.

CRUISE TRAVEL

Several cruise lines use Cabo San Lucas as a port of call. Carnival makes a short stop during its cruise between Los Angeles and Mexico's mainland Pacific coast. Princess has cruises to Los Cabos and the Mexican Riviera from Los Angeles and San Francisco. Royal Caribbean stops off during its Panama Canal and Mexican Riviera cruises. **Cruise West, Lindblad Expeditions,** and **Clipper Cruise Line** run cruises in the Mar de Cortés, focusing on nature, and combine the Mar de Cortés ports of La Paz and Loreto with the Barrancas del Cobre on the mainland. **Baja Expeditions** has live-aboard ships for diving and whale-watching trips.

Baja Expeditions ⊠ 2625 Garnet Ave., San Diego, CA 92109 ☎ 858/581-3311; 800/843-6967 🖷 858/581-6542 ⊕ www.bajaex.com. **Carnival** ☎ 800/327-9501 in the U. S. **Clipper Cruise Line** ☎ 800/325-0010 in the U.S. **Cruise West** ☎ 800/888-9378 in the U.S. **Lindblad Expeditions** ☎ 212/765-7740 or 800/397-3348 in the U.S. ⊕ www. expeditions.com. **Princess** ☎ 800/421-0522 in the U.S. **Royal Caribbean** ☎ 800/327-6700 in the U.S.

EMERGENCIES

The state of Baja California Sur has instituted an **emergency number** for police, fire, and medical problems: **060.** The number can be used throughout the state and there are English-speaking operators.

Fire ☎ 612/122-7474 in La Paz. **Hospital** ☎ 612/122-7377 in La Paz; 624/143-1594 in Cabo San Lucas; 624/142-0013 in San José del Cabo. **Police** ☎ 612/122-122-0054 in La Paz; 624/143-3977 in Cabo San Lucas; 624/142-2835 in San José del Cabo. **Red Cross** ☎ 612/122-1111 in La Paz; 624/143-3300 in Cabo San Lucas; 624/142-0316 in San José del Cabo.

INTERNET

Galería Don Tomás in La Paz has Internet access in artful surroundings. Baja Net in La Paz has ports for laptops along with many computer terminals. Both charge about $10 an hour. Dr. Z's Internet Café and Bar in Cabo San Lucas has a full bar and casual menu, and charges $9 an hour for Internet access. Cabocafe in San José del Cabo offers access for $9 an hour.

Internet Cafés Baja Net ⊠ Av. Madero 430, La Paz ☎ 612/125-9380. **Cabocafe** ⊠ Plaza José Green, Suite 3, Blvd. Mijares, San José del Cabo ☎ 624/142-5250. **Dr. Z's Internet Café and Bar** ⊠ Blvd. Cárdenas Cabo San Lucas ☎ 624/143-5390. **Galería Don Tomás** ⊠ Av. Obregón 229, La Paz ☎ 612/128-5508.

MONEY MATTERS

As in Baja Norte, finding ATMs in heavily touristed areas isn't a problem, and some places use dollars as well as pesos. If you're going to a less developed area, though, go equipped with cash.

TAXIS

In Loreto, taxis are in good supply and fares are inexpensive; it costs $5 or less to get anywhere in town. Taxi fares in Los Cabos, however, are outrageous. It costs at least $38 to take a taxi between the two towns. Try to share a cab whenever possible. In La Paz, taxis are readily available and inexpensive. A ride within town costs under $5; a trip to Pichilingue costs between $7 and $10. If you'd like to explore the remote beaches, however, *see* Car Rental. Illegitimate taxis are not a problem in this region. The cars are often Volkswagen bugs, except in Los Cabos, where vans are commonly used.

TOURS

For whale-watching tours, *see* Guerrero Negro and San Ignacio.

For kayaking and diving in the marine park off of Loreto, or for inland trips to Misión San Javier, *see* Loreto.

With the water as the main attraction in Los Cabos, most tours involve getting into a boat and diving or fishing. It's a must to take a ride to El Arco, the natural rock arches at Land's End, and Playa de Amor, where the Mar de Cortés merges with the Pacific. Nearly all hotels have frequent boat trips to these destinations; the fare depends on how far your hotel is from the point. Tour boats dock by the arts-and-crafts market in the Cabo San Lucas marina, and the sidewalk along the water is lined with salespeople offering boat rides. Check out the boat before you pay, and make sure there are life jackets on board.

Contactours has land and sea tours of Los Cabos for groups, and booking agents at several hotels. TourCabos runs boat trips, offers horseback riding, and can provide information on water sports. Nomadas de Baja offers hiking, snorkeling, and kayaking tours of Los Cabos with an ecological bent. Pez Gato, on the marina near Plaza Las Glorias hotel in Los Cabos, has sailing and sunset cruises on a 46-ft catamaran, with live music as well as snorkeling and sailing tours. All trips depart from the marina in Cabo San Lucas; call or stop by the booth at the marina for further information. Discover Baja Travel Club is a great source of info for travel throughout the peninsula.

🚩 Tour Operator Recommendations **Contactours** ✉ Blvd. Marina, Los Cabos ☎ 624/143-3333 or 624/143-2439 🌐 www.contactincentives.com. **Discover Baja Travel Club** ✉ 3089 Clairemont Dr., San Diego, CA 92117 ☎ 619/275-4225; 800/727-2252 🖶 619/275-1836 🌐 www.discoverbaja.com. **Nomadas de Baja** ☎ 624/148-1468 in Los Cabos 🖶 624/142-4388 🌐 www.nomadasdebaja.com. . **Pez Gato** ☎ 624/143-3797 in Los Cabos. **TourCabos** ✉ Plaza Los Cabos, Paseo San José ☎ 624/142-4040 in Los Cabos 🖶 624/142-0782.

VISITOR INFORMATION

The Baja California Sur State Tourist Office is in La Paz near the Fidepaz Marina. It's open weekdays 9–5. There's also an information stand on the malecón across from Los Arcos hotel, which stays open daily 9–5. The booth is a more convenient spot, and it can give you info on Scammon's Lagoon, Santa Rosalia, and other smaller towns.

The Loreto Tourist Information Office is in the Palacio Municipal on the main plaza. It's open weekdays 9–5.

There are no official tourist-information offices in Los Cabos; hotel tour desks are the best sources of information. Avoid tour stands on the streets; they are usually associated with time-share operations. The Web site of the *Gringo Gazette* (www.gringogazette.com) can be helpful or at least interesting.

In Todos Santos, pick up a copy of *El Calendario de Todos Santos* for information on local events. Local residents maintain a Web site, www.todossantos-baja.com.

🖪 **Baja California Sur State Tourist Office** ✉ Mariano Abasolo s/n, La Paz ☎ 612/124-0100, 612/122-5939, or 612/124-0100 🖷 612/124-0722 ⊕ www.bajacalifornia.gob.mx. **Loreto Tourist Information Office** ✉ Municipal Building on Plaza Principal, Loreto ☎ 613/135-0411 ⊕ www.gotoloreto.com. **La Paz Hotel Association** ✉ Obregón at Calle 16 de Septiembre, La Paz ☎ 612/125-6844; 866/733-5272 in the U.S. ⊕ www.vivalapaz.com.

SONORA

4

FODOR'S CHOICE
Casa la Aduana, restaurant in Aduana
Hacienda de los Santos, hotel in Alamos

HIGHLY RECOMMENDED

RESTAURANTS   Las Palmeras, Alamos
Restaurant Marlyn, Bahía Kino
La Roca, Nogales

EXPERIENCES   Alamos, a preserved colonial town

Updated by
Rob Aikins

SONORA, Mexico's second-largest state, is also its second richest. Ranch lands feed Mexico's finest beef cattle, and rivers flowing west from the Sierra Madre are diverted by giant dams to irrigate a low-rainfall area. Among Sonora's many crops are wheat and other grains, cotton, vegetables, nuts, and fruit—especially citrus, peaches, and apples. Hermosillo, Sonora's capital, bustles with agricultural commerce in the midst of the fertile lands that turn dry again toward the coast.

In the more rural areas, this stretch of the Mexican northwest is reminiscent of the American Wild West: *rancheras,* ballads of love and deception, blare from saloons and truck radios, and tiny *ranchitos* (small ranches) dot the cactus-strewn countryside.

The Sonoran desert dominates the landscape through northern Sonora and into southern Arizona. Long stretches of flat scrub are punctuated by brown hills and mountains, towering saguaros, and organ-pipe cacti. This arid landscape, especially at the sea, is a vacation and retirement paradise for neighbors in Arizona, for whom the beaches of Sonora are closer, cheaper, and more interesting than those of southern California. In fact, good highways south of Nogales, Mexico, make the beaches of Puerto Peñasco (Rocky Point) and San Carlos–Guaymas as accessible to Tucson natives as those of Los Angeles or San Diego, California.

Highway 15 begins at the border town of Nogales, Sonora, adjacent to the U.S. town of Nogales, Arizona. It continues south through Hermosillo and reaches the Mar de Cortés (officially called the Golfo de California) at Guaymas, 418 km (259 mi) from the Arizona border. South of Guaymas, the harsh Sonoran desert is left behind, and the landscape begins to take on a more tropical character as it enters the state of Sinaloa just north of the city of Los Mochis. Except in the mountains, the entire region is hot between May and late September, with afternoon temperatures in midsummer sometimes exceeding 120°F (49°C).

In 1540 Francisco Vázquez de Coronado, governor of the provinces to the south, became the first Spanish leader to visit the plains of Sonora. More than a century later, Father Francisco Kino led a missionary expedition to Sonora and what is now southern Arizona—an area referred to as the Pimería Alta for the band of Pima Indians still living there. The Italian-born padre and his fellow friars founded half a dozen missions there. Although Alamos, in the south of Sonora, boomed with silver-mining wealth in the late 17th century, no one paid much attention to the northern part of the region. When the United States annexed a giant chunk of Mexico's territory after the Mexican-American War (1846–48), northern Sonora suddenly became a border area—and a haven for Arizona outlaws. International squabbles bloomed and faded over the next decades as officials argued over issues such as the right to pursue criminals across the border. Porfirio Díaz, dictator of Mexico for most of the years between 1876 and 1911, finally moved to secure the state by settling it.

Settlers from Sonora, however, proved a hardy and independent bunch ill-suited to accepting the dictums of politicos in faraway Mexico City. Sonorans and their neighbors, the Chihuahenses, were major players in the Mexican Revolution, and the republic was ruled by three Sonorans: Plutarco Elías Calles, Adolfo de la Huerta, and Abelardo Rodríguez. Despite the enormous cost and destruction to railroads and other infrastructure, the Mexican Revolution brought prosperity to Sonora. With irrigation from the state's dams, inhabitants have been able to grow enough wheat and vegetables not only for Mexico but also for export.

Exploring Sonora

Sonoran landscapes are as varied as the state is vast. From the seemingly endless tracts of desert that tumble into the Gulf of California to the mountains of the Sierra Madre and the fields and valleys that nurture its produce and livestock, Sonora is a place of dramatic contrasts.

Mexico Highway 2 enters Sonora's far northwest from Baja California, paralleling the U.S. border. There are several crossing points, but most people entering Sonora from the United States do so at Nogales, south of Tucson, Arizona. Thanks to the Only Sonora program, you needn't post a bond when driving into the state of Sonora via Nogales, and you are also exempt from a tourist tax (technically, if spending 72 hours or less). Don't neglect to get Mexican auto insurance, though.

About the Restaurants

Restaurants in this neck of the woods are often laid-back; you'll find family-run establishments virtually everywhere. Casual dress (but not beachwear) is always acceptable, and reservations are rarely needed.

About the Hotels

In Sonora you might find yourself sleeping in a converted mansion or convent in fashionable Alamos, growing a Hemingway beard in a beach bungalow at Bahía Kino, or luxuriating in a posh resort in San Carlos. Lodging in Sonora is no longer the bargain it once was, and winter prices are similar to those of comparable accommodations in other parts of Mexico. Hotels rates sometimes include the 17% tax; so be sure to check this when you're quoted a price.

WHAT IT COSTS				
$$$$	**$$$**	**$$**	**$**	**¢**
RESTAURANTS over $25	$15–$25	$10–$15	$5–$10	under $5
HOTELS over $250	$150–$250	$75–$150	$50–$75	under $50

Restaurant prices are for a main course excluding tax and tip. Hotel prices are for two people in a standard double room in high season, based on the European Plan (EP, with no meals) and excluding service and 17% tax.

Timing

Summer temperatures in Sonora are as high as they are in southern Arizona, so unless you're prepared to broil, plan your trip for sometime between October and May. Even in winter, daytime temperatures can rise above 80°F (27°C), but at night the temperature drops considerably.

Nogales

▶ ❶ *100 km (62 mi) south of Tucson via Hwy. 19, on the Arizona-Mexico border.*

Bustling Nogales can become fairly rowdy on weekend evenings, when underage Tucsonans head south of the border to drink. It has some good restaurants, however, and visitors can find fine-quality crafts in addition to the usual souvenirs. If you're just coming for the day, it's best to park on the Arizona side of the border—you'll see many guarded lots that cost about $8 for the day—and walk across. Most of the good shopping is within easy strolling distance of the border.

The shopping area centers mainly on Avenida Obregón, which begins a few blocks west of the border entrance and runs north–south; just follow the crowds. Most of the good restaurants are also on Obregón. Take

Because it is so large and spread out, the state of Sonora demands eight days or more to really do it justice. With less time, you'll do best to choose one area and concentrate on exploring it. Most visitors to Sonora choose the sea, where desert landscapes collide with the shimmering blue Gulf of California.

Numbers in the text correspond to numbers in the margin and on the Sonora map.

4

If you have 3 days

Take Highway 15 south from Nogales to the state capital, ⊡ **Hermosillo** ④ ☞, where you will find a variety of good hotels and restaurants. Overnight here and spend the next morning touring the city or browsing through the Centro Ecológico, which is of special interest to children. After lunch, drive west on Highway 16 to ⊡ **Bahía Kino** ⑤, a perfect beach for a one- or two-night retreat. The drive back to the Arizona border from Bahía Kino is about six hours.

An alternative three-day itinerary is to cross the U.S. border at Lukeville-Sonoyta and head straight for the beaches of ⊡ **Puerto Peñasco** ③ ☞ for the rest of the first day. The next day you can continue to lounge, lunch overlooking the beach, and tap your feet to live jazz in the evening, or spend the day exploring the lunarlike regions of the **El Pinacate** ②. On your last day, admire the formidable desert scenery as you loop east to **Nogales** ①. Spend an afternoon shopping there before you cross the U.S. border.

If you have 5 days

Take Highway 15 from **Nogales** ① ☞ to **Guaymas** ⑦; the drive will take six or seven hours. Exploring the town of Guaymas and the adjacent resort area of ⊡ **San Carlos** ⑧ will give you plenty to do for two days and nights. Continue south and then east for 3½ hours to charming colonial ⊡ **Alamos** ⑨, in the foothills of the Sierra Madre. After one or two nights in Alamos, head back north. You might consider spending the night along the tranquil shores of **Bahía Kino** ⑤ on your way home.

If you have 8 days

Combine the second of the three-day itineraries with the five-day itinerary, but stop off at ⊡ **Hermosillo** ④ on the way down to **Guaymas** ⑦. If you have extra time, you might want to take a short side trip from Alamos to **Aduana** ⑩, former site of a thriving silver mine and current location of a thriving restaurant.

Obregón as far south as you like; you'll know you have entered workaday Mexico when the shops are no longer fronted by English-speaking hustlers trying to lure you in the door.

Where to Eat

$–$$$ ✕ **El Cid.** For more than 20 years, this clean, festive restaurant has earned its reputation for good food and service. Menu staples include burgers, fresh seafood, and traditional Mexican specialties like *camarones ajo* (grilled garlic shrimp) and carne asada. A few more exotic items such as frog's legs and quail add to the mix. ⊠ *Av. Obregón 124, Centro* ☎ *631/312–1500* ☰ *MC, V.*

★ $–$$$ ✕ **La Roca.** You'll find this elegant restaurant within walking distance of the border. The old stone house, built against a cliff, has several dining rooms, some with fireplaces; a balcony overlooks a patio with a fountain and magnolia trees. Look for the excellent seafood dishes and the *queso la Roca* (seasoned potato slices covered with melted cheese) appetizer. Reservations are suggested weekend nights. ⊠ *Calle Elias 91, Centro* ☎ *631/312–0891* ⊟ *MC, V.*

$$ ✕ **Elvira.** The dining room of this long-established restaurant bursts with color and bristles with stamped tin stars. Choose from half a dozen different moles, from the rich, exotic, and dark *mole poblano*, made with nuts, seeds, tortillas, chocolate, and chilies, to the *manchamanteles*, a sweet stew built around pineapple, banana, and apple. A free shot of tequila comes with each meal. ⊠ *Av. Obregón 1, Centro* ☎ *631/312–4773* ⊟ *MC, V.*

Shopping

Nogales's wide selection of crafts, furnishings, and jewelry makes for some of Sonora's best shopping. At more informal shops, bargaining is not only acceptable but expected. The following shops tend to have fixed prices. East of the railroad tracks, **El Changarro** (⊠ Calle Elias 93, below Restaurant La Roca, Centro ☎ 631/312–0545) carries high-quality furniture, including both antiques and rustic-style modern pieces, blown glass, stone carvings, and ceramics. **Mickey** (⊠ Av. Obregón 128–130, Centro ☎ 631/312–2299) has two floors of handcrafted Mexican treasures, *equipale* (pigskin) furniture, Talavera ceramic dishes, pottery, and glassware. **El Sarape** (⊠ Av. Obregón 161, Centro ☎ 631/312–0309) specializes in sterling-silver jewelry from Taxco and pewter housewares and crafts from all over Mexico.

El Pinacate

❷ *50 km (31 mi) west of Lukeville-Sonoyta.*

Midway between the Arizona border and the beach town of Puerto Peñasco, this reserve is best known for its volcanic rock formations and craters so moonlike that they were used for training the Apollo astronauts. (Its official name is La Reserva de El Pinacate y El Gran Desierto de Altar but it's generally called El Pinacate.) The diversity of the lava flows makes Pinacate unique, as does the striking combination of Sonoran desert and volcanic field. Highlights of the area include **Santa Clara peak,** a little more than 4,000 ft high and 2.5 million years old, and **El Elegante crater,** 1½ km (1 mi) across and 750 ft deep, created by a giant steam eruption 150,000 years ago. Don't try recreating the moon walk, though—going into the craters damages them.

There are no facilities of any kind at Pinacate. You'll need to bring your own water—take plenty of it—food, and extra gasoline, as well as a good map, which you can get at Si Como No bookstore in Ajo, Arizona, Tucson's Map and Flag Center, or at the Intercultural Center for the Study of Desert and Oceans (CEDO) in Puerto Peñasco, Mexico. A high-clearance vehicle is strongly advised, and four-wheel-drive is recommended. Keep in mind that the desert is no stranger to drug traffickers and illegal border crossings, so use common sense and don't risk getting stranded. Primitive camping is allowed with a permit obtainable from the ranger station at the entrance on Highway 8 (no phone). You must register at the park entrance. For current park information, contact the International Sonoran Desert Alliance in Ajo, Arizona, at 520/387–6823.

Summer temperatures can be blistering. The best time to visit is between November and March, when daytime temperatures range between 60°F

4

Beaches

Lively hotels and restaurants line the coastal areas around San Carlos, Guaymas, and Puerto Peñasco, but if you are willing to take more time for travel and forgo facilities, you'll find miles and miles of more-secluded beaches along the Mar de Cortés. Most of Sonora's main beaches have paved access roads, but some of the best—like pristine Playa San Nicolás just south of Bahía Kino (Kino Bay)—await the adventurous at the end of rutted, washed-out dirt tracks.

Local Specialties

Sonoran cuisine has all the makings for stellar surf and turf: it's distinguished by its terrific steaks and, on the coast especially, its fresh fish and seafood. Sonora is also the home of the giant flour tortilla, *machaca* (air-dried beef), and some of the best *carne asada* (thin, grilled, marinated meat) in Mexico. Seafood lovers will find shrimp, scallops, octopus, clams, and fish, both freshwater and ocean species. Traditional-Mexican food lovers can relish the abundance of dishes such as enchiladas, tacos, and tamales. Indeed, the style of Mexican cooking with which most Americans are familiar derives from this region.

(16°C) and 90°F (32°C). Tours can be arranged through the tourism office in Puerto Peñasco. An excellent naturalist-led day tour in English from Ajo is available from **Ajo Stage Lines** (⊠ 321 Taladro, Ajo, AZ 85321 ☎ 520/387–6559; 800/942–1981 in the U.S. ⊕ www.ajostageline. com) for about $85. ⊠ *Highway 8 at Km. 51, near Ejido Nayarit* ☎ *no phone* ⊠ *Donation requested* ⊙ *Daily 8–5.*

Puerto Peñasco

▶ ❸ *104 km (65 mi) south of the Arizona border at Lukeville on Mexico Hwy. 8.*

Puerto Peñasco was dubbed Rocky Point by British explorers in the 18th century, and that's the name most Americans know it by today. The town itself was established about 1927, after Mexican fishermen found abundant shrimp beds in the area and American John Stone built the first hotel. Al Capone was a frequent visitor during the Prohibition era, when he was hiding from U.S. law.

The real appeal of Puerto Peñasco, at the north end of the Mar de Cortés, is the miles of sandy beaches punctuated by stretches of black, volcanic rock. A remarkably high tide change—as much as 23 ft—makes for great exploring among countless tide pools.

To the beaches add low prices for accommodations, food, and drink, and you've got a popular wintering spot for American RVers and retirees and a favorite weekend getaway for Arizonans. Although Rocky Point is rather faceless, the "old town" has a number of interesting shopping stalls, fish markets, and restaurants.

This coastline is rapidly changing, however. A number of major projects have been developed—including a complex with a shopping center, a luxury hotel, condos and villas, a yacht club, a golf course, and a marina—all designed to attract an upscale clientele. Even more dramatic changes to the landscape may result from the "Escalera Náutica" (Nautical Ladder), a series of high-end marinas up and down the Baja Peninsula and

Sonora and Sinaloa coasts, being pushed by President Fox's administration. Only time will tell whether these plans will reach fruition, and if they do, what their impact on ecology and the local economy will be.

The northern Gulf area forms an impressive desert-coast ecosystem, and scientists from both the United States and Mexico conduct research programs at the **Intercultural Center for the Study of Desert and Oceans** (known as CEDO, its acronym in Spanish), about 3 km (2 mi) east of town on Fremont Boulevard, Fraccionamiento Las Conchas. You can take an English-language tour of the facility to learn about the ecology of the area and its history, or just pick up a tide calendar (useful if you're planning beach activities) or field guide from the gift shop. Talks and nature outings—including tide-pool walks, Pinacate excursions, and kayaking expeditions of area estuaries—are offered sporadically. ⊠ *Turn east at municipal building and follow signs for Caborca Rd., where there will be signs for Las Conchas Beach and CEDO* ☎ *638/382–0113* ⊕ *www. cedointercultural.org* ☒ *Free, donation for tours* ☉ *Mon.–Sat. 9–5, Sun. 10–2; tours Tues. at 2, Sat. at 4.*

Not far from CEDO you'll find the **Acuario Cet–Mar,** which focuses on the Mar de Cortés ecosystem and the local intertidal zone. The tanks, filled with many kinds of fish, sharks, and turtles, have information in both Spanish and English. You can buy a bag of squid to feed the fish. ⊠ *Las Conchas* ☎ *638/382–0010* ⊕ *www.cedointercultural.org* ☒ *$2* ☉ *Weekdays 10–2:30, weekends 10–5.*

Where to Stay & Eat

$$–$$$ ✕ **La Casa del Capitán.** Perched atop Puerto Peñasco's tallest point, this restaurant has the best views over the bay and the town below. There's inside dining, but the long outdoor porch overlooking the sea is the place to be. A wide-ranging menu includes everything from nachos and quesadillas to flaming brandied jumbo shrimp. ⊠ *Av. del Agua 1, Cerro de la Ballena* ☎ *638/383–5698* ☐ *MC, V.*

$–$$ ✕ **La Curva.** This friendly family restaurant with great Mexican food is easy to spot if you look for the mermaid on the sign. The menu lists 20 different shrimp dishes, such as Hawaiian-style shrimp wrapped in bacon and served in a sweet sauce. ⊠ *Blvd. Kino and Comonfort, Centro* ☎ *638/383–3470* ☐ *MC, V.*

$–$$ ✕ **Friendly Dolphin.** This bright blue-and-pink palace feels like a home, with nicely stuccoed ceilings, hand-painted tiles, and an upstairs porch with a harbor view. Unique family recipes include foil-wrapped shrimp or fish prepared *estilo delfín*—steamed in orange juice, herbs, and spices. Gaston, the operatic owner, can easily be coaxed to sing traditional ranchera songs in a baritone as rich and robust as the food. ⊠ *Av. Alcantar 44, Col. Puerto* ☎ *638/383–2608* ☐ *MC, V.*

$–$$ ✕ **Lily's.** You can either gaze at the gulf or people-watch from this popular split-level restaurant on the *malecón* (waterfront). The menu has a handful of American dishes but favors seafood, such as the *pescado relleno*, a huge fillet of flounder stuffed with shrimp and covered in cheese. ⊠ *Blvd. Kino at Calle Zaragoza, Col. Puerto* ☎ *638/383–2510* ☐ *AE, MC, V.*

$$ ✕⊞ **Playa Bonita.** One of the first three hotels in Puerto Peñasco, Playa Bonita has clean, comfortable rooms, although it's beginning to show its age. Ask for a room facing the hotel's broad, sandy beach. This place is very popular with Americans. An RV park offers 300 hookups at $17–$20 a day. As the name of the Puesta del Sol restaurant ("setting of the sun") implies, this is a perfect place to see the sun set, with plenty of beachfront patio seating. Seafood gets a Euro spin in dishes such as fish Florentine (with a white wine sauce and spinach) and shrimp crepes. Don't miss the divine margaritas. ⊠ *Paseo Balboa 100, Playa Hermosa,*

CloseUp

THE MAQUILA'S MARCH TO MODERNITY

WHEN MEXICO BEGAN ITS Border Industrialization Program in 1965, few could have imagined the social and environmental ills that open markets and prosperous free-trade deals would spawn three decades later. Mexico's maquiladoras (also known as maquilas) are foreign-owned assembly plants that produce cars, electronics, and garments for export to the First World; the passage of the North American Free Trade Agreement (NAFTA), which relaxed tariffs on goods moving across North American borders, made the maquila a profitable tool in getting cheap products to the United States. Even prior to NAFTA, repeated recessions and peso devaluations in the 1980s, combined with drought and chronic poverty in many of the northern and central agricultural states, brought both multinational companies and desperate migrant workers to Tijuana and Ensenada in Baja California, Nogales in Sonora, Matamoros in Tamaulipas, and above all, Ciudad Juárez in the state of Chihuahua.

Shantytowns sprang up, most of which are still lacking in clean water, sanitation, schools, electricity, and other basic infrastructure; companies and city governments have had no legal obligation, no financial incentive, and in the case of the local governments, no tax revenue, to provide for inhabitants. With time, the living conditions have improved marginally in some areas, but even with the meager allowances for housing or health care, workers here are still exploited by American labor standards. And because NAFTA has only an impotent Commission on Environmental Cooperation (CEC) to evaluate, but not enforce, the safe environmental procedures outlined in the agreement, hundreds of maquilas regularly dump hazardous waste along the border. It's estimated that less than half of American maquilas follow Mexican law and return their toxic waste to the United States. Many maquila workers live with contaminated water as a result.

But the maquila industry also created hundreds of thousands of jobs, gave impetus to Mexico's economy, and effectively threw a grenade in the midst of rural Mexico's family mores and values— for better and worse. Academic studies chart devastating social disintegration and the heartbreaking effect on young children; but Mexican women—who for the first time earn a wage and decide what to do with it—are viewed by many to have finally found liberation from rural, macho servitude.

Ciudad Juárez sits above anonymous swathes of the huge state of Chihuahua, just over the Río Bravo (or Rio Grande) from El Paso, Texas. Over the last three decades more than a million souls have come to toil in the maquilas, assembling televisions, clothes, car parts, calculators, telephones, and other appliances for the wealthiest market in the world. Juárez became a magnet for young women, lured from the interior of the country by plentiful jobs. As it turned out, though, not only was their labor cheap, but so were their lives. Since 1993, there have been over 270 officially recognized murders of young women, their bodies dumped in the desert or side streets around town. Hundreds of others have disappeared and are presumed dead. The maquila murders in Juárez have become a scandal of international proportions, and although most cases remain unsolved, local, state, and even international protest is beginning to mount. The documentary film Señorita Extraviada (2001) plumbs the horrific situation.

The maquila zone poses profound questions with no easy answers, but it still looks a long way from resolution, as a quick drive into the hills reveals the squalor in which people live. Hopeful young men and women are carted in from their rank little huts every day to make gadgets for others, before they can make a life for themselves.

— Barbara Kastelein

85550 ☎ 638/383–2586; 888/232–8142 in the U.S. ⊕ www. playabonitaresort.com ⇨ 120 rooms, 6 suites ⚭ Restaurant, pool, hot tub, beach, bar ☰ MC, V.

$　✕⊡ **Costa Brava.** All the rooms in this small, clean downtown hotel overlook the Gulf and have balconies. It's just down the street from the old town area. The restaurant (1$–2$) serves up substantial seafood plates (shrimp, prawns). ⊠ *Malecón Kino and Paseo Estrella, Col. Puerto, 83550 ☎ 638/383–4100 or 638/383–3130 ≞ 638/383–3621 ⇨ 25 rooms ⚭ Restaurant, cable TV, bar, free parking ☰ MC, V.*

$$　⊡ **Viña del Mar.** With an old-town location and sweeping ocean views, this tidy hotel gives you an opportunity to sample most of Puerto Peñasco's pleasures without venturing too far from your room. You'll be right by the beach and the shops and restaurants of the malecón—a terrific location for bargain prices. Rooms are bright white: milky walls, white-tile floors. ⊠ *Av. Primer de Junio, Col. Puerto 83550 ☎ 638/383–3601 or 638/383–3603 ≞ 638/383–3714 ⇨ 110 rooms ⚭ Restaurant, cable TV, pool, hot tub, beach, dance club, 3 bars, meeting room ☰ MC, V.*

$–$$　⊡ **Plaza Las Glorias.** Sitting like a sand-color fortress overlooking the beach, Plaza Las Glorias was the first large chain hotel to hit town. Its open lobby with towering quadrangular ceiling and bamboo-covered skylights draws gasps of admiration from the busloads of tourists who flock here. Rooms are standard; for just a bit more money, junior suites offer refrigerator, microwave, and ocean view. ⊠ *Paseo Las Glorias 1, Playa Hermosa 83550 ☎ 638/383–6010; 800/342–2644 or 800/515–4321 in the U.S. ≞ 638/383–6015 ⇨ 258 rooms, 52 suites ⚭ 2 restaurants, cable TV, pool, hot tub, beach, snorkeling, 2 bars ☰ MC, V.*

Nightlife

Puerto Peñasco's nightlife centers around drinking—and we don't mean Shirley Temples. The sports bar **Latitude 31** (⊠ Blvd. Benito Juárez, en route to Col. Puerto ☎ 638/388–4311) has a great view of the harbor. **The Lighthouse** (⊠ Lote 2, Fracc. el Cerro ☎ 638/383–2389), a pretty restaurant-bar overlooking the harbor, appeals to a more sophisticated crowd. The owners are jazz musicians, and you can dance to live music between 6 and 10 every night except Monday. Popular among the young and those who don't want to put too much distance between the water's edge and their next margarita is **Manny's Beach Club** (⊠ Avs. Coahuila and Primera, El Mirador ☎ 638/383–3605). Recorded music blares constantly in this local landmark.

Sports & the Outdoors

WATER SPORTS　At **Sun and Fun Dive and Tackle** (⊠ Blvd. Benito Juárez s/n at Calle 2, entrance to old port ☎ 638/383–5450) you can rent fishing, diving, or snorkeling equipment or receive PADI and NAUI scuba instruction. Sunset cruises, fishing charters, and snorkeling trips can all be booked here.

Hermosillo

▶ ➍ *185 km (115 mi) south of Magdalena on Hwy. 15.*

Hermosillo (population 850,000) is the capital of Sonora, a status it has held on and off since 1831. It's the seat of the state university and benefits from that institution's cultural activities. If you know a bit of Spanish, you might think the city's name means "little beauty." In fact, it honors José María González Hermosillo, one of the leaders in Mexico's War of Independence.

Settled in 1742 by Captain Augustín de Vildosola and a contingent of 50 soldiers, Hermosillo was originally called Pitic, the Pima Indian name for "the place where two rivers meet." The city's most prestigious neighborhood—home to the governor and U.S. consul, among other prominent citizens—still bears the name Pitic. Located immediately north of the highway into town and behind the Hotel Bugambilia, the area is worth an hour's stroll to view the creative handling of concrete, tile, and other materials in the homes of Hermosillo's affluent residents.

As the state's business center, Hermosillo is largely modern, but some lovely plazas and parks hark back to a more graceful past. Although Hermosillo is usually just considered a jumping-off point for Bahía Kino or Guaymas, it has a number of attractions in its own right, as well as the best accommodations and restaurants until you reach Guaymas or San Carlos.

At the center of town, look for charming **Plaza Zaragoza,** a town square shaded by orange trees and towering figs. Edging the plaza are the town hall and a lovely Moorish-style wrought-iron gazebo. On the plaza's south side stands the **Catedral de Nuestra Señora de la Asunción.** The church was built over the site of an adobe chapel between 1877 and 1912; during the extended construction time, its neoclassic style was somewhat diluted.

Atop the Cerro la Campana (Hill of Bells), which offers the best viewpoint in the city, stands a former penitentiary, now the **Museo de Sonora.** The cells now hold 18 permanent exhibits on astronomy, anthropology, history, geology, geography, and culture, all with a Sonoran slant. The bulk of the exhibits are graphic displays, including charts and maps of trade routes and native populations. Each display has a short summary in English. ⊠ *Jesús García Final s/n, Col. La Matanza* ☎ *662/217–2714* ⊠ *$3* ☉ *Tues.–Sat. 10–5, Sun. 9–4.*

On the highway south of town sits the **Centro Ecológico,** an environmental and ecological park with more than 500 species of plants and animals, both native to Sonora as well as exotic. The outdoor park is best visited November through March because of the heat and lack of shade the rest of the year. The zoo section has a wide variety of animals, but they're sadly cramped in small cages. An observatory holds shows on weekends. ⊠ *Carretera a Guaymas, Km 2.5, 5 km (3 mi) south of Hermosillo* ☎ *662/250–1225* ⊕ *www.centroecologico.com.mx* ⊠ *$2* ☉ *Daily 8–5.*

Where to Stay & Eat

$$ ✕ **Xochimilco.** If you want to try regional specialties and are willing to go with the set meal, come to this large, institutional-looking place on a narrow side street near town center. Popular with locals and regulars from across the border, Xochimilco's meals are designed for two or more, and include carne asada, ribs, tripe, vegetable salad, beans, and fresh flour tortillas. ⊠ *Av. Obregón 51, at Gutiérrez, Col. Villa de Seris* ☎ *622/250–4089* ⊟ *MC, V.*

$–$$ ✕ **Sonora Steak.** Come to this sophisticated, understated old house to slice into the finest cuts of the famous Sonoran beef at reasonable prices. The specialty, rib-eye steak, is aged 10–18 days at 12–18°C (64°F). Vegetarians can graze on watercress salad, or opt for cream of green chili soup or penne with fresh tomato and basil. The restaurant is a good spot for a late-night meal—it's open until 2 AM. ⊠ *Blvd. Kino 914, Zona Hotelera* ☎ *662/210–0313* ⊟ *MC, V.*

$$$ ▣ **Fiesta Americana.** Hermosillo's premier hotel, this full-service property is the largest in town and popular among business travelers. The guest rooms stick to a safely tasteful beige-and-forest-green decor. The adjacent disco is one of the most popular in town. ⊠ *Blvd. Kino 369, Col. Lomas Pitic 83010* ☎ *622/259–6000; 800/343–7821 in the U.S.* ⊟ *622/*

259–6062 ⊕*www.fiestaamericana.com* ⟋*221 rooms* ⟋*Restaurant, cafe-teria, cable TV, tennis court, pool, gym, bar, dance club, shop, business services, meeting rooms, car rental, travel services* ⊟ *AE, MC, V.*

$$–$$$ ▦ **Holiday Inn Hermosillo.** Two-thirds of the attractive rooms in this contemporary, two-story hotel surround a large green lawn and a good-size pool. Rooms have comfortable molded plastic bathtubs as well as coffeemakers and radio alarm clocks. Free transfer from the airport is included in the room price. ⊠ *Blvd. Kino and Ramón Corral 1110, Zona Hotelera 83010* ☎ *662/289–1700; 800/623–3300 in the U.S.* ⎙ *662/214–6473* ⊕ *www.sixcontinentshotels.com* ⟋ *132 rooms, 10 suites* ⟋ *Restaurant, cable TV, pool, gym, bar, meeting rooms, business ser-vices, travel services, free parking* ⊟ *AE, MC, V.*

$ ▦ **Hotel Bugambilia.** This pleasant small property has a trio of top as-sets: comfortable rooms, a convenient location in the hotel zone, and a good restaurant. The bougainvillea-drenched bungalows facing the parking spaces are most popular; other rooms surround the pool. Guests can use the facilities at the Holiday Inn, across the street. ⊠ *Blvd. Kino 712, Zona Hotelera 83010* ☎ *662/214–5050* ⎙ *662/214–5252* ⟋ *104 rooms* ⟋ *Restaurant, room service, cable TV, pool, free parking* ⊟ *AE, MC, V* ⏏*BP.*

Nightlife & the Arts

Hermosillo is home to several lively nightspots. **Bar Freedom** (⊠ Blvd. Kino 1012, Zona Hotelera ☎ 662/215–0640) is a popular upscale joint for the youngish set. The **Joyce** disco (⊠ Fiesta Americana, Blvd. Kino 369, Zona Hotelera ☎ 622/259–6000) pulls in an affluent clientele; it's open Thursday–Saturday only. **Marco n' Charlie's** (⊠ Blvd. Rodríguez at Calle San Luis Potosí, Zona Hotelera ☎ 662/215–3061) is a watering hole for the town's upper crust. **La Trova Arte–Bar** (⊠ Calle Guerrero and Tamaulipas, Zona Hotelera ☎ 662/214–2861) has musicians playing romantic music for dancing Wednesday through Saturday.

Shopping

In the downtown markets of Hermosillo, particularly along Avenidas Serdán and Monterrey, you can buy anything from blankets and can-dles to wedding attire, as well as a selection of cowboy boots. The va-riety of goods concentrated in this area equals what you'll find in Nogales, and the prices are better. Local sweets, called *coyotas* (pie crust surrounding brown sugar or a treacle-like sweet), can be purchased in the Villa de Seris neighborhood, near restaurant Xochimilco. At **Ehui!** (⊠ Av. Serdán at Pino Suárez, Centro ☎ 662/212–4010) the friendly Mex-ican and American owners will tell you the history behind *torote* grass baskets, beautifully carved rain sticks, reproductions of Yaqui testaments, and more typical souvenirs.

Ruta de Río Sonora

300 km (180 mi) between Hermosillo and Cananea.

The state highways that follow the state's namesake river are a terrific, adventurous way to see a less-touristy side of Sonora. Between Hermosillo and Cananea, the riverbanks are speckled with small towns, each with its own charm. This was the region's first inhabited area; it was settled by the Pima and Opata groups. The *ruta* (route) is also linked to the ar-rival of the Europeans; the Spanish explorer Alvar Núñez Cabeza de Vaca followed the Río Sonora during his travels between central Mexico and what is now the United States in the mid-16th century. The towns of Ures and Banámichi are two of the largest and oldest towns on the route, both offering a glimpse of traditional Sonoran life. As is typical of the area, each has a colonial church and a heart-of-town square. When people come into town from the surrounding ranches, they end up in the squares for both business and pleasure—you'll see plenty of cowboy boots and hats. It's easiest to drive up the valley from Hermosillo; driving part of the route makes a great day trip, especially in autumn when the trees along the river turn golden. It's also possible to drive south from Cananea, but you'd have to go over mountain roads, which are particularly difficult in bad weather. *To follow the route from Hermosillo, take Sonora 14 east to Mazocahui, passing through Ures and continue north on Sonora 118.*

Bahía Kino

⑤ *107 km (64 mi) west of Hermosillo on Sonora highway 100.*

On the eastern shore of the Mar de Cortés lies Bahía Kino, home to some of the prettiest beaches in northwest Mexico. For many years, Bahía Kino was undiscovered except by RV owners and other aficionados of the unspoiled. In the past decade or so, great change has come at the hands of North Americans who have been building condos and beach houses here. The moniker "Bahía Kino" actually refers to twin towns: Kino Viejo (Old Kino, the Mexican village) and Kino Nuevo (New Kino), where facing a long strand of creamy beach you'll find private homes, condos, RV sites, and other tourist facilities.

There's little to do in Bahía Kino, so after hanging around a few days, you might consider taking a run across the narrow channel to **Isla del Tiburón** (Shark Island), designated an ecological preserve in 1963. Permission to visit Tiburón may be obtained from the Seri Indian government; they can also provide a reliable boatman-guide. Only the Seri Indians, for whom Isla del Tiburón is a traditional fishing ground, are permitted to ferry travelers across and guide them around the island. The trip, which is of most interest to anglers and bird-watchers, costs about $250 per boatload of one to four passengers. ⊠ *Seri Indian government: main street, across from the Pemex station, Kino Viejo* ☎ *662/242–0557 or 662/242–0590.*

For a crash ethnography lesson, poke around the interesting if hodgepodge collection of photographs, musical instruments, and dioramas in the **Museo de los Seris.** ⊠ *Blvd. Mar de Cortés at Calle Progreso* ☎ *No phone* 🖭 *60¢* ☉ *Wed.–Sun. 8–6.*

If you'll be in town a week or more, it's worthwhile to obtain a temporary membership to the **Club Deportivo.** For $15 a month, you'll be introduced to most of the town's temporary residents and some locals as well. The club offers everything from quilting and Spanish classes to dances and other social activities. There's also a golf course; for a $5 fee even duffers can use the 9-hole sand course with artificial greens. ⊠ *Calle Cadiz s/n at Plaza del Mar RV Park* ☎ *662/242–0321.*

Where to Stay & Eat

$–$$$ ✕ **El Pargo Rojo.** Fishnets and realistic reproductions of the fish you'll be eating decorate this restaurant, whose name means "red snapper." The catch of the day varies, but you can depend on consistent quality. Classics like a brimming shrimp cocktail could be followed by fish stuffed with shrimp, clams, squid, and octopus. Depending on your luck, you'll be serenaded either by Mexican musicians or by the ceaseless wailing of recorded, polkalike *norteña* music on Mexican MTV. ⊠ *Blvd. Mar de Cortés 1426, Kino Nuevo* ☎ *662/242–0205* ▭ *MC, V.*

★ $–$$$ ✕ **Restaurant Marlyn.** Though this place may be a bit hard to find at first, you may well find yourself returning, drawn by the clean, unpretentious atmosphere and congenial service—not to mention margaritas as big as fishbowls. Superb seafood dishes include *sopa de siete mares* (soup of the seven seas) and *jaiba a la diabla* (a spicy hot crab dish). ⊠ *Calles Tastiota and Guaymas, Kino Viejo* ☎ *662/242–0111* ⊟ *MC, V* ⊘ *Closed Mon.*

$–$$ ✕ **Jorge's Restaurant.** This clean, comfortable family restaurant overlooks the bay: a perfect spot for morning coffee, pancakes, and pelican viewing. At other meals portions tend to be small, but the food is quite good, and the owner and his daughters play the guitar and sing in the evening. ⊠ *Near the end of Blvd. Mar de Cortés at Alecantres, Kino Nuevo* ☎*662/242–0049* ⊟ *No credit cards.*

$–$$ ✕ **La Palapa.** This thatch-roof spot may be plain, but the food's delicious. The shrimp brochette with green chilies and the breaded oysters are memorable; this is also the place for a great, juicy cheeseburger. ⊠*Blvd. Mar de Cortés and Wellington, on the way into Kino Nuevo* ☎ *662/242–0210* ⊟ *MC, V.*

$ ▦ **Posada Las Aves.** There's a lot to love about these one- and two-bedroom apartments. It's a great deal: the two largest units—which sleep five or six comfortably in two bedrooms—have a fireplace in the living room, full kitchen and dining room, and cost just $115 a night. All of the units are spacious, with sturdy wood cabinets, clunky wood and vinyl couches, and sparkling tile bathrooms. ⊠ *Calle Veracruz between Calles Nautla and Tecolutla, Kino Nuevo 83340* ☎ *662/242–0242* ⤏ *11 apartments* ⚘ *Picnic area, kitchens, cable TV, pool, playground, free parking* ⊟ *No credit cards.*

¢ ▦ **Posada del Mar.** A beachfront location is the bright spot here; you can see the sea from the wide second-story balcony. Rooms, on the other hand, are dark and could use some sprucing up. On the grounds, cacti and stone walkways surround a central fountain. You can commandeer a grill in the picnic area for a barbecue. ⊠ *Blvd. Mar de Cortés and Calle Creta, Kino Nuevo 83340* ☎☎ *662/242–0155* ⤏ *42 rooms, 2 suites, 2 bungalows* ⚘ *Picnic area, pool; no room TVs* ⊟ *MC, V.*

Shopping

Kino has little in the way of crafts or even souvenirs, but **Alcatraz** (⊠ Calle Tastiota 12, Kino Nuevo ☎ 662/242–0570), which is Mexican Spanish for calla lily, offers Talavera-style plates, mounted deer heads, shell ornaments, and plenty of gift items and housewares from all over Mexico.

Punta Chueca

➏ *27 km (17 mi) north of Bahía Kino.*

This rustic Seri fishing village perches at the end of a long, bumpy, winding dirt road. (You'll need a sturdy high-clearance vehicle to make this scenic drive.) You'll pass exquisite vistas of the bay, distant empty beaches, and rolling mountains. The inhabitants of this community live a subsistence lifestyle, relying on the sea and desert much as they have for hundreds of years.

With fewer than 700 remaining members, the Seri tribe represents an ancient culture on the verge of dying out. The Seris' love for their natural surroundings is evident in the necklaces that they have traditionally worn and now create to sell. Pretty little shells are wound into the shape of flowers and strung with wild desert seeds and tiny bleached snake vertebrae to result in delicate necklaces. Seri women weave elaborate *canastas* (baskets) of torote grass, which have become highly prized and expensive.

As you get out of your car anywhere in town, be prepared to encounter an entourage of Seri women dressed in colorful ankle-length skirts, their heads covered with scarves and their arms laden with necklaces for sale. The Seri are best known, however, for the carved ironwood figurines that represent the animal world around them, including dolphins, turtles, and pelicans. Many Mexican merchants have taken to machine-making large figures out of ironwood for the tourist trade, thereby seriously depleting the supply of the lilac-blossomed tree that grows only in the Sonoran desert. (If the bottom of the statuette is clean cut, it was cut with an electric saw and not made by the Seri.) For this reason, the Seri now carve figures out of several types of stone, including soapstone.

Guaymas

❼ *128 km (79 mi) south of Hermosillo.*

The buzz and bustle of Guaymas—Mexico's seventh-largest port—has a pleasant backdrop of rusty red, saguaro-speckled mountains that nudge the deep-blue waters of a sprawling bay on the Mar de Cortés. The Spanish arrived in this "port of ports" by the mid-16th century. In 1701, two Jesuit priests, Father Kino and his colleague Juan María Salvatierra, erected a mission base here intended to convert the native Guaimas, Seri, and Yaqui Indians.

Guaymas was declared a commercial port in 1814 and became an important center of trade with Europe as well as within Mexico. In 1847, during the Mexican-American War, U.S. naval forces attacked and occupied the town for a year. Bumbling filibuster William Walker also managed to take Guaymas for a short time in 1853, and in 1866, during Maximilian's brief reign, the French took control. Today's foreign invaders are mostly travelers passing through on their way somewhere else. Given its proximity to the beaches of San Carlos and Mazatlán, modern Guaymas is more a stepping-stone than a destination. That said, it's a congenial seaside town that some folks prefer to more tourist-oriented, spread-out San Carlos.

No visit to a Mexican town is complete without a trip to the *mercado,* or municipal market, bursting with colors and smells and a glimpse at daily life. After the throngs, you'll find quiet at the 19th-century church **Parroquia de San Fernando.** Or you might relax across the street at **Plaza 13 de Julio,** a typical Mexican park with a Moorish-style bandstand and matching benches.

Where to Stay & Eat

$–$$ ✕ **Los Barcos.** Across the street from the harbor, Los Barcos offers a predictable seafood-and-steak menu. The main room is large and somewhat sterile, with an enormous bar along the back wall. The fan-cooled, thatch-roof adjoining room is more relaxed, with its jukebox and walls painted with smiling dolphins and octopi. The crab tostadas are especially recommended. ✉ *Calle 22 and Malecón, Centro* ☎ *622/222–7650* ▭ *MC, V.*

$–$$ ✕▥ **Hotel Armida.** On the edge of town but still close to downtown, this sand-color hotel has a large, well-kept pool, and a good coffee shop where locals gather for power breakfasts. At the excellent steak house, El Oeste ("The West," $$–$$$), the stuffed and mounted heads of mountain goats, cougars, and bison gaze down at diners. Large, bright accommodations are plain but serviceable, with comfortable beds; many have balconies overlooking the pool. The economy rooms at the back are a great bargain. ✉ *Carretera Internacional, Salida Norte 85400* ☎ *622/222–5220* ▤ *622/224–0448* ⊕ *www.hotelarmida.com* ⇗ *125* rooms ⚷ 2 restaurants, coffee shop, room service, cable TV, pool, bar, meeting rooms, free parking ▤ MC, V.

$$ 🖭 **Playa de Cortés.** This fine, sprawling old hotel overlooking Bahía de Bacochibampo has a traditional, hospitable main lobby with towering wooden beam ceilings and a fireplace. Some rooms are furnished with hand-carved antiques; many have fireplaces and balconies. Private casitas are less attractively furnished, but are closest to the beach. ⊠ *Bahía de Bacochibampo, Col. Miramar 85450* ☎ *622/221–0135; 800/623–4400 or 800/782–7608 in the U.S.* 🖷 *622/221–0135* 🛏 *89 rooms, 22 suites, 9 bungalows* ⚷ *Restaurant, room service, cable TV, tennis court, pool, beach, bar* ▤ *AE, MC, V.*

Nightlife

The younger set heads to **Charles Baby** (⊠ Av. Serdán and Calle 25, Centro ☎ no phone), open Friday–Sunday. Also open on the weekends is **Xanadu** (⊠ Malecón at Malpica, Centro ☎ no phone).

San Carlos

❽ *20 km (12 mi) northwest of Guaymas.*

Long considered an extension of Guaymas, and still occasionally referred to as San Carlos, Nuevo Guaymas, this resort town—on the other side of the rocky peninsula that separates Bahía de Bacochibampo from Bahía de San Carlos—has a personality of its own. Whitewashed houses with red-tile roofs snuggle together along the water where countless yachts and motorboats are docked. The town is a laid-back favorite among professional anglers, North American tourists, and the time-share crowd, as well as wealthy Mexican families from Guaymas. There's a growing assortment of hotels and condominiums, as well as two marinas and a country club with an 18-hole golf course.

The overlapping of desert and semitropical flora and fauna has created a fascinating diversity of species along this coast. Among marine life, more than 650 species of fish exist here; red snapper, marlin, corbina, yellowtail, sea bass, and flounder are commonly caught. Whales have occasionally been spotted in Bahía de San Carlos, but more common are dolphins and pelicans. The water is calm and warm enough for swimming through October. Scuba, snorkeling, fishing, and boat excursions are popular, too.

The quiet 5-km (3-mi) stretch of sandy beach at **Los Algodones,** where the San Carlos Plaza Hotel and Club Med are now, was in the 1960s a location site for the film *Catch 22.* (In fact, it's still called the Catch 22 beach on many maps.) San Carlos lies in the shadow of the jagged twin-peak **Tetakawi mountain,** a sacred site where native warriors once gathered to gain spiritual strength. The **Mirador Escénico,** or scenic lookout, is the best place in San Carlos to view the Mar de Cortés. Take the steep road up here for a great photo op or just to get an idea of the lay of the land. Just north of the Mirador is Zorro Cove, a great place to snorkel. An interesting day trip can be made by boat out to the pristine **Isla de San Pedro Nolasco,** an ecological reserve where sea lions claim the rocks.

San Carlos itself has no real city center; instead, it stretches for miles along the four-lane **Corredor Escénico** (Scenic Corridor), which is officially called Boulevard Beltrones, after a former governor of Sonora.

Where to Stay & Eat

$–$$ ✕**Rosa's Cantina.** Bearing little resemblance to the saloon in Marty Robbins's song "El Paso," this cozy, pink, laid-back restaurant has two large dining rooms filled with picnic tables. Ask anyone in town and they'll tell you Rosa's ample breakfasts are the best way to start the day. Try the machaca (dried beef) with eggs and yummy salsa; the tortilla soup is great for lunch or dinner. Gringos who miss being pampered will appreciate the nonsmoking section, decaf coffee, and salad bar. ⊠ *Calle Aurora 297, Creston* ☎ *622/226–1000* ☰ *MC, V.*

$$$ ✕⊡ **Plaza Las Glorias.** This condo-hotel complex overlooks the San Carlos marina. Pastels soften the rooms, and most accommodations have a tiny kitchenette. Some corner rooms have hot tubs on outdoor patios; if one's available, you can book it for no extra cost. A shuttle takes guests to the hotel beach club, with its pool and beach toys. El Embarcadero restaurant ($–$$) is a good place to try hearty, traditional Mexican soups, like the *caldo Xochitl,* a steaming chicken consommé with white rice, avocado, chili, and lemon. ⊠ *Calle Gabriel Estrada s/n, Sector La Herradura 85506* ☎ *622/226–1021; 800/342–2644 in the U.S.* ☏ *622/226–1035* ⊕ *www.sidek.com.mx* ⊠ *87 rooms, 18 suites* ⚵ *Restaurant, snack bar, refrigerators, cable TV, 2 pools, baby-sitting, car rental, travel services* ☰ *AE, MC, V.*

$$$ ⊡ **San Carlos Plaza Hotel and Resort.** Rising from Bahía de San Carlos, this huge, striking pink edifice is the most luxurious hotel in Sonora. The arresting atrium lobby opens onto a large pool and beach. Attractive rooms—all with an ocean view—have contemporary furnishings, and rooms on the first two floors have balconies overlooking the sea. Children love the swimming-pool slide and horseback riding on beautiful Algodones beach. ⊠ *Paseo Mar Barmejo Norte 4, Los Algodones 85506* ☎ *622/227–0077; 800/854–2320 in the U.S.* ☏ *622/227–0098* ⊕ *www.guaymassancarlos.net* ⊠ *132 rooms, 41 suites* ⚵ *3 restaurants, snack bar, in-room safes, cable TV, minibars, 2 tennis courts, 2 pools, gym, hot tub, beach, 2 bars, meeting rooms* ☰ *AE, MC, V.*

$ ⊡ **Fiesta San Carlos.** Every room in this small, beachfront, family-run hotel soaks up views of the gulf. The minimally decorated rooms are clean and comfortable. Some rooms with kitchens are available. ⊠ *Blvd. Beltrones, Km 8.5, Carretera Escénico 85506* ☎ *622/226–0229 or 662/226–1318* ⊕ *fiestasancarlos.com* ⊠ *33 rooms* ⚵ *Restaurant, pool, bar, free parking; no room phones, no room TVs* ☰ *MC, V* ⊠⊙ *BP.*

$ ⊡ **Hacienda Tetakawi.** This hotel and trailer park across from the beach on the main street of town is a Best Western. Rooms are generic but clean, and each has a balcony, a few with a view of the sea. ⊠ *Blvd. Beltrones, Km 10, San Carlos 85000* ☎ *622/226–0248* ⊠ *22 rooms* ⚵ *Restaurant, pool, bar* ☰ *MC, V.*

Nightlife & the Arts

For two floors of paintings and sculpture by a variety of Mexican and foreign artists, stop by the **Galería Bellas Artes** (⊠ Villa Hermosa 111, Sector Villahermosa ☎622/226–0073), where their work is for sale. It's open Monday–Saturday 9:30–5. Every Tuesday the **San Carlos Plaza Hotel** (☎622/226–0545) hosts an evening of folkloric dancing and singing along with dinner buffet and open bar ($18). Reservations are encouraged, and the hotel will provide transportation from some hotels.

For conversation and exotic drinks, try **Mai-Tai Bar** (⊠ Plaza Las Glorias ☎ 622/226–1021). **Ranas Ranas** (⊠ Carretera San Carlos, Km 9.5, Carretera Escénico ☎ 622/226–0610) is a party-down bar with a beach view. During the filming of *Mask of Zorro,* Antonio Banderas hung out at **Tequilas Bar** (⊠ Calle Almirante s/n, La Marina ☎ 622/226–0545), still a popular nightspot.

Sports & the Outdoors

GOLF Anyone can get a tee time at the 18-hole golf course at the **Club de Golf San Carlos** (⊠ Av. de los Yaquis between Loma Bonita and Solimar

622/226–1102); the $52 greens fee includes a cart. People staying in area hotels usually get lower greens fees. There are also a baker's dozen tennis courts, some of which are lighted.

WATER SPORTS **Gary's Dive Shop** (✉ Blvd. Beltrones, Km 10 ☎ 622/226–0049; 622/226–0024 after hours ⊕ www.garysdivemexico.com) runs fishing, snorkeling, and PADI-certified diving excursions. You can also book sunset cruises, and whale-watching and customized expeditions.

Shopping

Kiamy's Gift Shop (✉ Blvd. Beltrones, Km 10 ☎ 622/226–0400) is like a bazaar, with something for everyone: silver jewelry, earrings, leather bags, ceramics, Yaqui Indian masks, T-shirts, and caps, as well as a variety of souvenirs. **Sagitario's Gift Shop** (✉ Blvd. Beltrones 132 ☎ 622/226–0090), across from the entrance to the San Carlos Country Club, features clothing and a variety of crafts, including wood carvings, baskets, high-quality rugs, and Talavera tile.

Alamos

★ ❾ *257 km (160 mi) southeast of Guaymas.*

With its cobblestone streets, charming central plaza, 250-year-old Baroque church, and thoughtfully restored haciendas, Alamos is the most authentically restored colonial town in Sonora. In the ecologically rich zone where the Sonoran desert meets a dry tropical forest (also called the semitropical thorn forest) in the foothills of the Sierra Madre, the entire town is designated a national historic monument.

Coronado camped here in 1540, and a Jesuit mission (later destroyed in an Indian rebellion) was established in 1630, but the town really boomed when silver was discovered in the area during the 1680s. Wealth from the mines financed Spanish expeditions to the north—as far as Los Angeles and San Francisco during the 1770s and '80s—and the town became the capital of the state of Occidente, which combined the provinces of Sinaloa and Sonora, from 1827 to 1832. A government mint was established here in 1864. The mines closed by the end of the 19th century, and the town went into decline.

These days, Alamos has reinvented itself as a tourist spot. Leading the movement are a relatively large number of expats who have bought and restored sprawling haciendas near the center of town, turning some into luxurious private homes, others into hotels. So far, the foreigners' efforts to keep the town producing magical, postcard moments seem to be successful.

Points of interest include the impressive **Parroquia de Nuestra Señora de la Concepción,** constructed on the site of a 17th-century adobe church destroyed in an Indian uprising. Fronting the parish church is the beautiful central square, the **Plaza las Armas;** its ornate Moorish-style wrought-iron gazebo was brought from Mazatlán in 1904. To the west of the square, on the Cerro de Guadalupe, the old Alamos **jail** is still in use. You can purchase belts and other accessories made by the prisoners.

If possible, time your trip to Alamos to include a Saturday **house and garden tour** of some of the superbly restored mansions and their interior patios and gardens. You can get information on the tour schedule from the tourist office or any of the local hotels; the suggestion donation for the tour is $8.

Don't miss the **Museo Costumbrista de Sonora** for an excellent overview of the cultural history of the state of Sonora. The numerous well-marked (some in English) displays include artifacts from the nearby silver mines and coins from the mints of Alamos and Hermosillo, as well as typical examples of the clothing and furnishings of prominent local families. ⊠ *Calle Guadalupe Victoria 1, on Plaza las Armas* ☎ *647/428–0053* ☜ *$1* ⊙ *Wed.–Sun. 9–6.*

Fishing is a popular pastime in this area. Not far from Alamos, Presa (Reservoir) Adolfo Ruíz Cortines—as well as the smaller Presa Tatjiosa and Presa El Veranito—are full of black bass, catfish, and other freshwater species. For information on fishing trips, call the tourism office.

Where to Stay & Eat

★ $ ✕ **Las Palmeras.** This Mexican family restaurant is crammed onto the sidewalk across the street from the Museo Costumbrista de Sonora and right on the main square. Here you might get homemade *rosca* bread (a sweet, round loaf) with your coffee and an assortment of daily specials. The corn tamales are hard to beat; other specialties include the *chiles relleno* (cheese-stuffed chile peppers) and the *carne milanesa* (similar to chicken-fried steak). ⊠ *Lázaro Cárdenas 9* ☎ *647/428–0065* ⚑ *Reservations not accepted* ▤ *No credit cards.*

$ ✕ **Polo's.** Locals, gringos, and expats all converge here; the owner can generally be found roaming the restaurant chatting it up with everyone. The food is simple but very good: sandwiches, shish kebab, and Sonoran steaks. ⊠ *Calle Zaragoza 4* ☎ *647/428–0001* ⚑ *Reservations not accepted* ▤ *No credit cards.*

$ ✕ **Los Sabinos.** This small, unpretentious family home–turned–mini café has seating indoors and out, and an extensive menu. House specials include beef tips and ranch-style shrimp, along with fried fillet of sole in garlic butter and lots of kid-favorites like quesadillas and burgers. No alcoholic beverages are sold here. ⊠ *Calle 2 de Abril Poniente 15* ☎ *647/428–0598* ⚑ *Reservations not accepted* ▤ *No credit cards.*

$$$ ▥ **Hacienda de los Santos.** Alamos's most opulent hotel rambles across
FodorśChoice the lushly landscaped grounds of four restored and linked colonial man-
★ sions. In gracious courtyards and lining long porticos are centuries-old pieces of religious art, hand-carved antique furniture, and inviting leather sofas, all collected by the American owners. The spacious bedrooms also have antiques, as well as fireplaces. A spa offers massage and beauty treatments; park your plane for free in the hotel's private hangar. ⊠ *Calle Molina 8, 85763* ☎ *647/428–0222* 🖷 *647/428–0367* ⊕ *www.haciendadelossantos.com* ⇌ *8 rooms, 5 suites* ⚑ *Restaurant, cable TV, 3 pools, gym, spa, bar; no kids under 16, no smoking* ▤ *AE, MC, V* ❑❑ *BP.*

$$ ▥ **Casa Encantada.** Just off the main square, this lovely converted 18th-century mansion was once owned by one of Alamos's wealthy Spanish mine owners. Rooms retain a colonial character, with high-beamed ceilings, fireplaces, and carved-wood furnishings; all have tile baths and good lighting. ⊠ *Calle Juárez 20, 85760* ☎ *647/428–0482* 🖷 *647/428–0400* ⇌ *10 rooms* ⚑ *Pool; no room phones, no room TVs* ▤ *V* ❑❑ *BP.*

$$ ▥ **Casa de los Tesoros.** This hotel, the House of Treasures, is a picturesque and romantic converted 18th-century convent. The rooms were once nuns' cells, but now they're no longer austere—they've got fireplaces, tile baths, antique furnishings, and striking local art. The restaurant is excellent. ⊠ *Av. Obregón 10, 85763* ☎ *647/428–0010* 🖷 *647/428–0400* ⊕ *www.tesoros-hotel.com* ⇌ *13 rooms, 2 suites* ⚑ *Restaurant, pool, bar* ▤ *MC, V* ❑❑ *BP.*

Shopping

It's worth a peek into the three crowded rooms of **El Nicho Curios** (✉ Calle Juárez 15 ☎ 647/428–0213), filled with treasures ranging from Mexican religious paintings to old jewelry and regional pottery. Small stores lining **Plaza Alameda** (northwest of the central plaza) sell Mexican sweets, fabrics, belts, and hats, among other items. *Tianguis* (market stalls) line **Plaza las Armas** every day, but Sunday brings artisans and vendors from the surrounding area.

Aduana

⑩ *10 km (6 mi) west of Alamos.*

Tucked a couple of miles down a dirt road off the main road to Alamos, Aduana was once the site of one of the richest mines in the district. The village lacks the revitalized charm of Alamos, but it's nonetheless worth a visit—especially for a meal at one of Sonora's best restaurants.

On the main plaza is the **Iglesia de Nuestra Señora de Balvanera.** A cactus that grows out of one of the church's walls is said to mark the spot where the Virgin appeared to the Yaqui Indians in the late 17th century, an event that is celebrated by a procession every November 21 and festivities that bring tens of thousands of the faithful in the preceding week.

Where to Eat

$$$ ✕ **Casa la Aduana.** This may be an unlikely place for a restaurant of this
Fodor'sChoice   caliber, but the four dining rooms are regularly filled with visitors. For-
★   mer Californians Samuel and Donna Beardsley see to it that the four-course, prix-fixe meals are exceptional; entrée selections might include chicken in apple-chipotle cream or grilled Norwegian salmon. Everything is made on the premises, including the breads and the sublime desserts. Though reservations aren't mandatory, they're recommended. ✉ *Domicilio Conocido* ☎ *647/482–2525* ▭ *MC, V.*

SONORA A TO Z

To research prices, get advice from other travelers, and book travel arrangements, visit www.fodors.com.

AIR TRAVEL

AIRPORTS   Both Hermosillo and Guaymas have international airports: General Ignacio L. Pesqueira International Airport (HMO) and General José M. Yanez International Airport (GYM), respectively.

🛈 **General José M. Yanez International Airport** ✉ Domicilio Conocido, Carretera a San José de Guaymas Guaymas ☎ 622/221-0634. **General Ignacio L. Pesqueira International Airport** ✉ Km. 9.5, Carretera Hermosillo a Bahía Kino Hermosillo ☎ 662/261-0000.

AIRPORT   To get between the airports and their respective towns, you'll need to
TRANSFERS   take a taxi. Take only the licensed taxis available at the airport taxi stands—avoid unlicensed, unmarked taxis. A ride from Hermosillo's airport to the town center takes about 15 minutes and should cost about $6. A trip from the Guaymas airport to Guaymas's center should cost $5 and take about 10 minutes. To get to San Carlos from the Guaymas airport should take 20 minutes and cost $10. Local hotels sometimes offer shuttles; ask about these in advance.

CARRIERS   AeroCalifornia offers daily nonstop jet service from Los Angeles and Tucson to Hermosillo. Aeroméxico and its subsidiary Aerolitoral have daily flights to Hermosillo from Tucson, and flights from Los Angeles to Hermosillo. Aeroméxico has direct flights to Hermosillo from many cities in Mexico—including Mexico City, Tijuana, Chihuahua, and Guadalajara, with connections to Guaymas. Mexicana offers domestic service between Hermosillo and other major Mexican cities as well. America West Express has daily flights to Hermosillo and Guaymas from Phoenix.

AeroCalifornia ☎ 662/260-2555; 800/237-6225 in the U.S. **Aeroméxico** ☎ 01800/021-4050 toll free in Mexico; 800/237-6639 in the U.S. ⊕ www.aeromexico.com. **America West Express** ☎ 800/235-9292 or 800/235-9292 in the U.S. ⊕ www.americawest.com. **Mexicana** ☎ 662/261-0112; 01800/849-1529 toll free in Mexico ⊕ www.mexicana.com.

BUS TRAVEL

Frequent buses travel to Hermosillo and Guaymas from Nogales, Tijuana, and Mexicali via Grupo Estrella Blanca. Transportes Baldomero Corral (TBC) offers direct service from Tucson to Nogales, Hermosillo, Guaymas, and Alamos. TUFESA has frequent service between Hermosillo and Guaymas, Nogales, and other destinations within Sonora and northern Mexico. Transportes del Pacifico (TAP) connects Hermosillo to other Sonoran cities as well as to Mazatlán, Guadalajara, Tepic, and Tijuana.

A bus trip from Nogales to Hermosillo takes approximately five hours. The trip to Guaymas from Nogales is about six hours, and the ride from Nogales to Alamos will take roughly nine hours. Tickets for these long-range trips start around $20. If you're crossing the border and don't already have a tourist visa, ask if the bus driver will make a stop at the Km 21 checkpoint to allow you to acquire one.

Bus Information Grupo Estrella Blanca ☎ 662/213-4050. **Transportes Baldomero Corral (TBC)** ☎ 520/903-2801. **Transportes del Pacifico (TAP)** ☎ 662/212-6870. **TUFESA** ☎ 662/213-0442.

CAR RENTAL

In Guaymas, the agencies to contact are Budget and Hertz, both on the main highway. Budget and Hertz are also in Hermosillo, with branches at the airport.

Budget ✉ Garmendia 46, at Tamaulipas, Col. San Benito, Hermosillo ☎ 662/222-1430 ✉ General Ignacio L. Pesqueira International Airport, Hermosillo ☎ 662/261-0141 ✉ Blvd. Augustín García López s/n, Col. Delicias, Guaymas ☎ 662/222-1450 or 622/222-5500 ⊕ www.budget.com. **Hertz** ✉ General Ignacio L. Pesqueira International Airport, Hermosillo ☎ 662/261-0110 ✉ Calz. Agustin Garcia Lopez 625 Norte, Col. Las Villas, Guaymas ☎ 622/222-1000 ⊕ www.hertz.com.

CAR TRAVEL

Many visitors to Sonora travel by car from Tucson via I–19 to the border in Nogales, Arizona. Mexico's Highway 15, a divided four-lane toll road, begins in Nogales, Sonora. This highway is the fastest way to get to Hermosillo and Guaymas–San Carlos, but expect to pay approximately $15 in tolls. The alternative "Libre" (free) routes are generally slower and not as well maintained, though by no means problematic.

There are two points of entry into Nogales. Most drivers take I–19 to the end and then follow the signs to the border crossing. This route, however, will take you through the busiest streets of Nogales, Mexico. It's better to take the Mariposa exit west from I–19, which leads to the international truck crossing and joins a small periphery highway that connects with Highway 15 after skirting the worst traffic.

The official checkpoint for entering Mexico is 21 km (13 mi) south of Nogales. It's here that you have to buy insurance and complete paperwork to bring in your car if you haven't already done so in Tucson at either Sanborn's Mexico Insurance or the Arizona Automobile Association.

As a result of the Only Sonora program, tourists driving into Mexico through Nogales and not intending to leave the state need not make a deposit for the vehicle (though insurance is still required). Fill out necessary paperwork at the Sonora Only booth at the Km 21 checkpoint. Bring a valid driver's license and vehicle registration. A six-month tourist visa ($20) is required of anyone planning to stay longer than three days; this is also available at the Km 21 checkpoint. Keep the receipt if you'll be making more than one foray into Sonora over a period of six months.

Driving in Sonora is best on the toll roads; these are well maintained and have gas stations at regular intervals. Highways between major destinations are in generally good condition, and towns and turn-offs are usually clearly marked. Roads in remote areas range from smooth pavement to dirt track. Avoid driving at night since roads (even toll roads) are not well-lit and often lack shoulders.

⚑ Arizona Automobile Association ⊠ 8204 E. Broadway, Tucson, AZ ☎ 520/296-7461 ⊠ 6950 N. Oracle Rd., Phoenix, AZ ☎ 520/885-0694 or 800/352-5382. **Sanborn's Mexico Insurance** ⊠ 105 W. Grant, Tucson, AZ ☎ 520/882-5000.

CONSULATES

There is a U.S. Consulate in Hermosillo, in back of the Telcel office building near downtown.

⚑ United States U.S. Consulate ⊠ Calle Monterrey 141 ☎ 662/217-2375.

EMERGENCIES

For emergency fire, police, or medical attention call 060.

The Green Angels in Hermosillo is a very helpful state-run roadside assistance service for travelers in distress.

⚑ Green Angels ☎ 662/212-3253 in Hermosillo; 01800/903-9200 toll free in Mexico. **Hospitals** ☎ 662/259-0900 in Hermosillo; 622/222-0122 in Guaymas. **Red Cross** ☎ 662/214-0010 in Hermosillo; 622/222-5555 in San Carlos; 638/383-2266 in Puerto Peñasco.

MONEY MATTERS

In the border towns, including Nogales and Puerto Peñasco, American dollars are readily accepted and usually preferred. Elsewhere, you can change money at local banks and at some larger hotels. ATMs are easy to find in most towns, with the exception of remote villages like Aduana.

TOURS

Arizona Coach Tours runs mostly senior-citizen package tours to Alamos, San Carlos, Puerto Peñasco, and the Copper Canyon. Mexico Tours offers escorted and unescorted bus tours, hotel and condo reservations, and general advice about Pacific coast destinations.

⚑ Tour Operator Recommendations Arizona Coach Tours ⊠ 200 E. 35th St., Tucson, AZ ☎ 520/791-0210 ⊕ www.azcoachtours.com. **Mexico Tours** ⊠ 1604 E. Seneca, Tucson, AZ ☎ 520/325-3284; 800/347-4731 in the U.S. ⊕ www.mexi-tours.com.

TRANSPORTATION AROUND SONORA

By far the easiest way to get around is by car—San Carlos and Bahía Kino are particularly spread out, and Bahía Kino has no taxi service of any kind. Most hotels have car-rental agencies. Buses between towns are frequent and inexpensive.

VISITOR INFORMATION

In addition to the tourism offices listed below, the Sonora Department of Tourism, in Hermosillo, will send you mounds of information and a helpful, full-color magazine. The tourism folks at Hermosillo, Bahía Kino, and San Carlos speak great English and take their jobs seriously. The Hermosillo and San Carlos bureaus are open weekdays 9–5. The Bahía

Kino office is open weekdays 9–3. The office in Guaymas is ostensibly open weekdays 8–4 but often closes for no apparent reason. The Alamos tourism office is open weekdays 8–5, and the Puerto Peñasco office stays open weekdays 9–4.

🚩 **Alamos** ✉ Main Plaza, Calle Juárez 6, Alamos ☎ 647/428-0450. **Bahía Kino** ✉ Calle Mar de Cortez at Calle Catalina, Kino Nuevo, Bahía Kino ☎ 662/242-0447. **Guaymas** ✉ Calle 19 and Av. 6, Guaymas ☎ 622/226-0313. **Hermosillo** ✉ Paseo del Canal at Comonfort, Edificio Sonora, 3rd floor, Hermosillo ☎ 662/217-0076; 800/476-6672 in the U.S. ⊕ www.sonoraturismo.gob.mx. **Puerto Peñasco** ✉ Blvd. Juárez 320-B at V. Estrella, Puerto Peñasco ☎ 638/383-6122 or 638/383-5010; 888/850-8122 in the U.S. **San Carlos** ✉ Blvd. Beltrones, Edificio Hacienda Plaza, San Carlos ☎ 622/226-0202.

LAS BARRANCAS DEL COBRE

FROM LOS MOCHIS TO CHIHUAHUA CITY

5

FODOR'S CHOICE

Museo de la Revolución Mexicana in Chihuahua City

Copper Canyon Sierra Lodge, near Creel

HIGHLY RECOMMENDED

RESTAURANTS La Casa de los Milagros, Chihuahua City

Tungar, Creel

HOTELS El Fuerte Lodge, El Fuerte

Holiday Inn Hotel & Suites, Chihuahua City

Hotel Mansión Tarahumara, Posada Barrancas

Hotel Posada Barrancas Mirador, Posada Barrancas

Hotel San Francisco, Chihuahua City

Margarita's, Creel

EXPERIENCES The ascent by train from El Fuerte to Bahuichivo

Urique, a small town at the bottom of the deepest canyon

Revised by
Jane Onstott

THE MAGNIFICENT series of gorges known collectively as Las Barrancas del Cobre (the Copper Canyon) is the real treasure of the Sierra Madre. Inaccessible to the casual visitor until the early 1960s and still largely uncharted, the canyons may now be explored by taking one of the most breathtaking rides in North America. The Chihuahua al Pacífico railroad passes through 87 tunnels and crosses 39 bridges on its journey through country as rich in history and culture as it is in physical beauty.

The *barrancas* (canyons) of the Sierra Tarahumara, as this portion of the Sierra Madre Occidental is known, form part of the Pacific "Ring of Fire," a belt of seismic and volcanic activity ringing the globe. As a result of its massive geologic movement, a large quantity of the earth's buried mineral wealth was shoved toward the surface. The canyons were then carved over eons by the Urique, Septentrión, Batopilas, and Chínipas rivers and further defined by wind erosion. Totaling more than 1,452 km (900 mi) in length and roughly four times the area of the Arizona Grand Canyon, the gorges are nearly a mile deep and wide in places. The average height of the peaks is 8,000 ft, and some rise to more than 12,000 ft. Four of the major canyons—Cobre, Urique, Sinforosa, and Batopilas—descend deeper than the Grand Canyon, Urique by nearly 1,500 ft. The area's name refers to the color of the lichen on the canyon walls.

The idea of building a rail line to cross this region was first conceived in 1872 by Albert Kinsey Owen, an idealistic American socialist. Owen met with some success initially. More than 1,500 people came from the States to join him in Topolobampo, his utopian colony on the Mexican west coast, and in 1881 he obtained a concession from Mexican president General Manuel Gonzales to build the railroad. Construction on the flat stretches near Los Mochis and Chihuahua presented no difficulties, but eventually the huge mountains of the Sierra Madre got in the way of Owen's dream, along with the twin scourges of typhoid and disillusionment within the community.

Owen abandoned the project in 1893, but it was taken up in 1900 by American railroad magnate and spiritualist Edward Arthur Stilwell. One of Stilwell's contractors in western Chihuahua was Pancho Villa, who ended up tearing up his own work during the Mexican Revolution in order to impede the movement of government troops. By 1910, when the revolution began, the Mexican government had taken charge of building the railroad line. Progress was painfully slow until 1940, when surveying the difficult Sierra Madre stretch finally began in earnest. Some 90 years and more than $100 million after it was started, the Ferrocarril Chihuahua al Pacífico was dedicated on November 23, 1961.

The railroad no longer starts at Topolobampo but at nearby Los Mochis, and Chihuahua City—capital of the eponymous state—is at the other end of the line. Chihuahua was established in 1709, after the Spanish discovered silver in the area around 1649. Chihuahua still derives some of its wealth from mining, as well as from ranching, agriculture, and lumber.

Mexico's largest state was once heavily populated by the Tarahumara, close relatives of the Pima Indians of southern Arizona. They are renowned for their running ability and endurance—Tarahumara is a Spanish corruption of their word Rarámuri, which means "running people." Today winners of international marathon races, the Tarahumara in earlier times hunted deer by chasing them to the point of collapse. Like other native groups, the Tarahumara's way of life was totally disrupted by the arrival of the Europeans. The Spanish forced them to labor in the mines,

5

You'll see some beautiful scenery even if you only ride the railroad—including a look into the canyons during a 15-minute stop at Divisadero—but you'll take in only a fraction of what the canyons have to offer if you don't get off the train.

Most people make their way into the Barrancas del Cobre via Los Mochis, which is the easiest route if you're coming from California or Arizona. More important, the most dramatic canyon scenery is at the western end of the ride, and you're likely to miss it if you approach Los Mochis in the evening. Train delays of three hours or more are not unusual, so even during the extended daylight hours of summer, you can't count on reaching the scenic end of the route before dark.

Even if you drive down to either Los Mochis or Chihuahua, your itinerary will largely be dependent on the schedule of the Chihuahua al Pacífico train: it runs in each direction only once a day, so you must plan the time spent in each stop accordingly. (Alternatively, you can drive or take a bus as far as Creel from Chihuahua, and arrange hikes or ride the train from there through some of the canyon's best scenery.) The following itineraries assume you will add on a day's train ride to return to your starting point—unless you catch one of the daily Aerolitoral flights between Los Mochis and Chihuahua. The small turboprops fly low over the mountains and canyons, providing magnificent views.

Note: The Sinaloa-Chihuahua state border divides two time zones: Mountain Time to the west and Central Time to the east.

Numbers in the text correspond to numbers in the margin and on the Barrancas del Cobre map.

If you have
3 days

Departing from **Los Mochis** ❶ (or better yet, **El Fuerte** ❷ ►), take the morning Chihuahua al Pacífico train and get off at Bahuichivo, where you can explore the 18th-century church at 🏨 **Cerocahui** ❸ and the overlook into the Barranca de Urique. The next day, continue to 🏨 **Divisadero** ❹, where it's practically impossible not to get a room with a view. Spend your last day exploring **Creel** ❺ and taking a short hike to the falls near Cusárare. If you begin the trip in **Chihuahua City** ❽, make Cerocahui your final stop.

If you have
5 days

Starting in the west, spend a day and night in the old colonial town of 🏨 **El Fuerte** ❷ ►, catching the train the next morning. Follow the three-day itinerary above, and use the last day and night to extend your time in 🏨 **Creel** ❺, with a visit to the mission church of San Ignacio or a drive and hike to the Cascada de Basaseachi. If you start in the east, you might take the extra day to explore **Chihuahua City** ❽.

If you have
8 or more days

Spend a day each in 🏨 **El Fuerte** ❷ ►, 🏨 **Cerocahui** ❸, and 🏨 **Divisadero** ❹, then extend your stay in 🏨 **Creel** ❺ to include a trip down to the former silver-mining town of **Batopilas** ❻. It's six to eight hours each way by car (preferably four-wheel-drive) or bus, so you'll want to spend two nights to make the trip worthwhile. (Alternately, extend your stay in

Cerocahui to allow an overnight visit to the small town of Urique, in the canyon of the same name.) You'll be ready for modern conveniences after that, so plan to enjoy the restaurants and museums of ▣ **Chihuahua City** ⑧ for an additional day. Another option would be to visit the Mennonite museum near **Cuauhtémoc** ⑦ and tour one of the surrounding farms before going on to Chihuahua.

---

and later both Mexicans and Americans put them to work on the railroads. The threat of slavery and the series of wars that began in the 1600s and continued until the 20th century forced them to retreat deeper into the canyons, where they are still at the mercy of outsiders: nowadays, it's loggers and drug lords. Some families are still seminomadic, moving to the high plateaus of the Sierra Madre in summer and down to the warmer canyon floor in winter. Their population, diminished over the years by disease, drought, and poverty, is estimated today at 50,000 to 60,000. Note that the Tarahumara can be uncomfortable having their picture taken; always ask politely first.

Exploring the Barrancas del Cobre

Imagine visiting the Grand Canyon in the days before it was tamed by tourist facilities and you'll have some sense of what a trip through the Barrancas del Cobre will be like—for better and for worse. That is, with the opportunity to encounter a relatively untouched natural site come some of the discomforts of the rustic experience. But if you are careful in your choice of time to visit and are properly prepared, the trip's myriad rewards should far outstrip any inconveniences.

About the Restaurants

Outside small Barrancas del Cobre villages such as Creel and Batopilas, there are few eateries except those connected with lodges: at Cerocahui, Divisadero, and Posada Barrancas hearty meals are generally included in room rates. There are a few more dining options in Creel, where, in addition to hotel dining rooms, you'll find small cafés along the town's main street, Avenida López Mateos.

You'll have the greatest choice of restaurants in Chihuahua City. The state is a large producer of beef, so steak houses and informal eateries serving *carne asada* (thin, charbroiled or grilled slices of marinated beef) abound, but seafood flown in from the coast is also available. Some of Chihuahua's best-known restaurants are in the Zona Dorada, on Avenida Juárez starting at its intersection with Calle Colón. In Los Mochis your best bet is seafood.

Dress is casual everywhere except at some of Chihuahua's pricier restaurants. Unless otherwise indicated, reservations aren't necessary.

About the Hotels

The hotels in Chihuahua City, including several international chains, cater to both tourists and business travelers. In Cerocahui, Divisadero, Posada Barrancas (*posada* means "inn"), and Creel, most hotels are pine-log types heated by gas furnaces or wood-burning stoves. The lodges send buses or cars to meet the train, and for this reason, reservations are recommended. In summer, October, and around Christmas and Easter, it's important to book in advance. Where indicated, rates for hotels include meals.

WHAT IT COSTS					
	$$$$	**$$$**	**$$**	**$**	**¢**
RESTAURANTS	over $25	$15–$25	$10–$15	$5–$10	under $5
HOTELS	over $250	$150–$250	$75–$150	$50–$75	under $50

Restaurant prices are for a main course excluding tax and tip. Hotel prices are for two people in a standard double room in high season, based on the European Plan (EP, with no meals) and excluding service and 17% tax.

Timing

Unless you're planning to head deep into the barrancas, winter—December through February—is not the best time to come. Although the scenery can be breathtaking in the snow, some of the hotels in the region are inadequately prepared for the cold. The warmest months are May, June, and July. The rainy season, late June through September, brings precipitation for a short period every day, but this normally won't impede plans to hike or sightsee. It's temperate in the highlands in summer. If you're planning to hike down into the canyons, however, summer temperatures at the bottom can be broiling. Overall, the best months to visit are September and October, when the weather is still warm and rains have brought out all the colors in the Sierra Tarahumara.

Many people come during Easter and Christmas, specifically to see the Tarahumaras' colorful take on church holidays. On these and other religious feast days, many Tarahumara communities dance throughout the night, and villages challenge one another in races that can go for days. The men run in small groups, upward of 161 km (100 mi) or more, all the while kicking a wooden ball. It's not *just* fun and games—each village places a huge communal wager for this winner-take-all event.

Los Mochis

❶ *763 km (473 mi) south of Nogales on the Arizona-Mexico border.*

At the western end of the rail line, Los Mochis (population 331,000) is an agricultural boomtown. The rail terminus and the city's location about 19 km (12 mi) from the harbor at Topolobampo make it the export center of the state of Sinaloa. As such it is not terribly attractive, and most visitors are here for business or an overnight before boarding the train first thing in the morning.

The **Museo Regional del Valle del Fuerte** rotates work by local, regional, national, and international artists, and has a didactic exhibit on the area's history. A replica of a railroad steam engine is on permanent display. Labels are in Spanish only. ✉ *Blvd. Rosales s/n at Av. Obregón, Centro* ☎ *668/812–4692* 💲 *50¢* 🕐 *Tues.–Sat. 9–1 and 4–7, Sun. 10–1.*

Cottonwood trees and bougainvillea line the highway from Los Mochis to **Topolobampo.** Fields en route are planted with crops ranging from sugarcane to marigolds and mangoes. Once the site of Albert Owen's utopian colony and the center of the railroad-building activity in the area, it is now a suburb of Los Mochis. **Isla El Farallón,** off the coast, is a breeding ground for the sea lions that gave the town its name: in the language of the Mayo Indians who once dominated the area, *Topolobampo* means "watering place of the sea lions."

Where to Stay & Eat

$–$$ ✕ **El Farallón.** Nautical decor and murals set the tone for the excellent fish served at this simple downtown restaurant. The taquitos of marlin or shrimp are excellent, and you'll also find nigiri sushi and sashimi—

rare in Mexico despite an abundance of seafood. For dessert sample some *pitalla* (cactus fruit) ice cream. ⊠ *Av. Obregón 593, at Calle Angel Flores* ☎ *668/812–1428 or 668/812–1273* ⊟ *AE, MC, V.*

$–$$ ✕ **Restaurante España.** This slightly upscale restaurant in downtown Los Mochis pulls in the local business crowd. The house specialty is paella with seafood, pork, and chicken; it serves at least two people. The $7 breakfast buffet, served until noon, lines up hearty Mexican favorites such as *pozole* (hominy soup) and *chilaquiles* (tortilla strips cooked with cheese, mild chilies, and chicken) along with the usual suspects (omelets). ⊠ *Av. Obregón 525 Poniente* ☎ *668/812–2221 or 668/812–2335* ⊟ *AE, MC, V.*

$ ✕ **Las Fuentes.** This unpretentious, colonial-style restaurant specializes in Sinaloan and U.S. beef cuts. Try the local favorite, *cabrería*, a thinly cut, tender fillet. Yummy *queso fundido* (cheese fondue) is made with fresh flour tortillas. Corn tortillas are made on the premises throughout the day. ⊠ *Blvd. López Mateos 1070 Norte, at Jiquilpan* ☎ *668/812–4770* ⊘ *Closed Good Friday–Easter* ⊟ *AE, MC, V.*

$$ ▦ **Hotel Plaza Inn.** Los Mochis's only five-star hotel caters to businesspeople and tourists with pluses like hair dryers and coffeemakers; suites have bathtubs. However, rooms suffer from a disconcerting color palette combining various hues of pink, coral, and sea-foam green. Duck hunters and fishermen are lured with sporting packages. ⊠ *Av. Leyva at Cárdenas, 81200* ☎ *668/816–0800; 800/862–9026 in the U.S.* 🖷 *668/818–1590* ⊕ *www.plazainnhotel.net* ⬔ *100 rooms, 27 suites* ♨ *2 restaurants, in-room safes, pool, bar, nightclub, meeting rooms, travel services* ⊟ *AE, MC, V.*

$$ ▦ **Hotel Santa Anita.** The central reservations link of the Balderrama chain, this downtown hotel will book tours in its sister hotels in El Fuerte, Cerocahui, and Divisadero. Built in 1959, the four-story property has midsize, dim rooms fitted with comfortable modern furniture; most have air-conditioning. ⊠ *Av. Leyva at Hidalgo, 81200* ☎ *668/818–7046; 800/896–8196 in the U.S.* 🖷 *668/812–0046* ⊕ *www.mexicoscoppercanyon. com* ⬔ *125 rooms, 5 suites* ♨ *Restaurant, cable TV, bar, business services, meeting rooms, travel services, free parking* ⊟ *AE, MC, V.*

$ ▦ **Corintios Hotel.** Rooms here are plain and looking a bit long in the tooth, but this modern-style hotel with a dark-glass facade is centrally located and offers services often not available in this price range, including remote-control cable TV and room service. Junior suites differ only from regular rooms in that they have a king-size bed, but the master suite has a king-size bed, sofa-sleeper, and Jacuzzi tub. The three-story hotel has no elevator. ⊠ *Av. Obregón 580 Poniente, 82000* ☎🖷 *668/818–2300* ⬔ *34 rooms, 5 suites* ♨ *Restaurant, cable TV, gym, hot tub, bar* ⊟ *AE, MC, V.*

¢ ▦ **Taj Majal.** The younger sister to the aging Corintios offers free Internet access on a common computer, comfortable beds, room service, and coffeemakers. Despite the graceful affect of the pointed arches of the building's facade and interior hallways, the rooms turn out to be small and standard. ⊠ *Av. Obregón 400 Oriente, 81200* ☎ *668/818–6095* 🖷 *668/818–6095* ⬔ *23 rooms, 3 suites* ♨ *Restaurant, Internet* ⊟ *AE, MC, V.*

Nightlife

Friends (⊠ Hotel Plaza Inn Av. Leyva at Cárdenas ☎ 668/818–7046), the most popular bar and disco in town, is open Thursday through Saturday nights only. Music, often live, varies from techno to rock en español. **Yesterday** (⊠ Av. Obregón 579 at Guerrero ☎ 668/815–3810) is a convivial nightclub. Live bands play different types of music—but predominantly oldies—Wednesday–Sunday 9 PM–2 AM (often later on Saturday nights).

5

Hiking

Hiking in the Barrancas del Cobre is fantastic if you take the proper precautions. *Mexico's Copper Canyon Country*, by M. John Fayhee, is a good source of information. But even the most experienced trekkers should enlist the help of local guides, who can be contacted through area hotels or through travel agents in Los Mochis, El Fuerte, and Chihuahua. Few adequate maps are available, and many of the better-worn routes into the canyon are made by the Tarahumara, whose prime concern is getting from one place to another rather than getting to the canyon floor. Also, the presence of well-guarded marijuana plantations throughout the canyon makes it safer to travel with a local guide who knows which areas to avoid.

La Barranca de Urique is most easily reached—by horse, bus, truck, or on foot—from Cerocahui. Hotels in Creel, Divisadero, and Posada Barrancas offer tours ranging from easy rim walks to a 27-km (17-mi) descent to the bottom. If you're in Cusárare, a gentle and rewarding hike is the 6-km (4-mi) walk from the Copper Canyon Lodge to 100-ft-high Cusárare Falls. More challenging but also more impressive is a full-day trek to the base of the Cascada de Basaseachi. The descent to Batopilas—not for acrophobes—requires an overnight stay.

Horseback Riding

Hotels throughout the canyons can arrange for local guides and reasonably gentle horses; however, these trips aren't for couch potatoes. The trails into the canyon are narrow and rocky as well as slippery if the weather is icy or wet. At rough spots you might be asked to dismount and walk part of the way. A fairly easy and inexpensive ride is to Wicochic Falls at Cerocahui, about two hours round-trip, including a half-hour hike at the end, where the trail is too narrow for the horses. From Divisadero, horses can be hired to the tiny settlement of Wacajipare, deep within the canyon. The vistas are stunning, but again, it's not for the fainthearted.

Local Crafts

A main source of cash income for the Tarahumara is their crafts, including simple handwoven baskets made from sotol (an agave-like plant) or pine needles, carved wooden dolls, rustic pottery, brightly colored woven belts and sashes made on back-strap looms, and wooden fiddles from which the men produce haunting music. The Tarahumara women, who are generally shy about talking with tourists, sell their wares throughout the canyon area, especially at train stops and tourist lodges. Despite their reticence, they are persistent; in fact, wherever a tourist sets foot, women or children seem to materialize with a few items for sale. Their prices are fair, so bargaining is unnecessary. Chihuahua is known for affordable cowboy boots, and *bota* (boot) shops proliferate downtown.

Shopping

If you're headed to Divisadero, Creel, or beyond, snacks and reading material can help pass the long train journey. **La Cava Deli** (⊠ Periférico Ortíz Mena 2000 ☎ 614/410–9940) sells American and Mexican beers, a good selection of wines and liquors, Cuban cigars, and snack foods. **Librería Los Mochis** (⊠ Calle Madero 402 Poniente, at Av. Leyva) has a

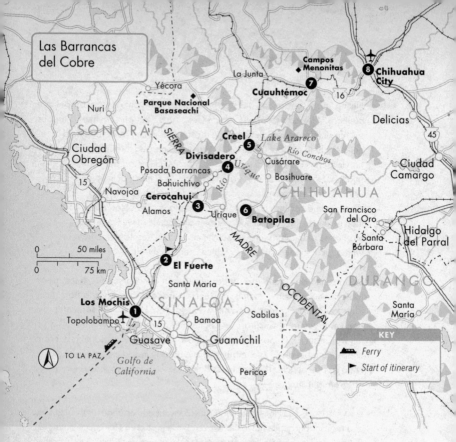

Las Barrancas
del Cobre

limited selection of English-language magazines and plenty of Spanish-language daily newspapers.

El Fuerte

▶ ❷ *80 km (50 mi) northeast of Los Mochis.*

If you prefer a peaceful, laid-back small town to the bustle and traffic of commercial Los Mochis, take a bus to El Fuerte, stay the night, and sleep in an hour longer before grabbing the 7:30 train to points east.

Originally named for Saint John the Baptist, this small colonial town is known today as El Fuerte for its 17th-century fort, built by the Spaniards to protect against attacks by the local Mayo, Sinaloa, Zuaque, and Tehueco Indians. Conquistador Don Francisco de Ibarra and a small group of soldiers founded it as San Juan Bautista de Carapoa in 1564. Located along El Camino Real (literally, the "Royal Road"), El Fuerte was one of the frontier outposts from which the Spanish set out to explore and settle New Mexico and California. For three centuries, it was a major trading post for gold and silver miners from the nearby Sierras and the most important commercial and farming center of the area. It was chosen as Sinaloa's capital in 1824 and remained so for several years.

Now a rather sleepy town of some 45,000 residents, El Fuerte has intact colonial mansions, two of the most accessible being the Posada del Hidalgo and El Fuerte Lodge. Most of the historic houses are set off the cobblestone streets leading from the central plaza. Tour operators use El Fuerte as a base for hiking, fishing, or tubing excursions. Some area hotels get in on the action by organizing float trips on the river outside town. You'll see heron and egrets as well as magpies, kingfishers, and many other birds as you float downstream past willow trees, cacti, and lilac bushes that grow along shore.

Where to Stay & Eat

$–$$ ✕ **El Mesón del General.** Just a block off the main plaza, this sparely decorated restaurant is the best bet in town for black bass (*lobina*) from the nearby reservoirs or, in summer, crayfish (*cauque*) from nearby rivers. If someone in your party craves Chinese instead of Mexican food, you can order it from the restaurant at the back, run by the same owners. ✉ *Benito Juárez 202* ☎ *698/893–0260.* ▤ *MC, V.*

★ **$$** ▥ **El Fuerte Lodge.** Years ago, hunting guide Robert Brand married a local woman and revived this 380-year-old mansion as an inn. His widow now tends the lodge, its charm heightened by furnishings like an antique grandfather clock and hand-stenciled furniture. *Artesanías* (folk art) decorate the high-ceiling guest rooms; the beds have beautifully carved and painted headboards. Clusters of chairs and tables on wide verandas invite socializing. ✉ *Montesclaro 37, 81820* ☎ *698/893–0226* 🖷 *698/ 893–1246* ⤶ *31 rooms* ⚭ *Restaurant, bar* ▤ *MC, V.*

$$ ▥ **Posada del Hidalgo.** With its gardens and cobblestone paths, this restored 1895 hacienda harks back to a more gracious era. It's difficult to choose between the larger rooms with balconies and the slightly more modern rooms that open onto the flower-filled gardens. All are decorated with rough-hewn handcrafted furniture. ✉ *Hidalgo 101* 🖷🖷 *698/893–1194* 🖉 *Reservations: Hotel Santa Anita, Av. Leyva and Hidalgo, Apdo. 159, 81200 Los Mochis* ☎ *800/896–8196 in the U.S.* 🖷 *668/812–0046* ⊕ *www.mexicoscoppercanyon.com* ⤶ *48 rooms, 3 suites* ⚭ *Restaurant, pool, bar, dance club; no room phones, no room TVs* ▤ *AE, MC, V.*

¢ ▥ **Río Vista Lodge.** On the Cerro de las Pilas, the highest spot in El Fuerte, perches this small, adobe-and-wood posada owned by local birding guide Eleazar Gamez. Rooms are rustic but creatively decorated with family heirlooms and antiques donated by friends in town. Great river views, low prices, and a relaxed, family-friendly feel make this a favorite. ✉ *Cerro de las Pilas 81820* ☎ *698/893–0413* ⤶ *11 rooms* ⚭ *Restaurant* ▤ *No credit cards.*

en route ★ As the train ascends almost 5,906 ft from El Fuerte to Bahuichivo, it passes through or over the majority of the rail line's tunnels and bridges, including the longest and highest of both. The scenery shifts from Sinaloan thorn forest, with cactus and scrublike vegetation, to the pools, cascades, and tropical trees of the Río Septentrión canyon. Past Temoris, where a plaque marks the 1961 dedication of the railroad by President López Mateos, the setting shifts to the oak and pine forest that characterizes the higher elevations.

Cerocahui

❸ *160 km (100 mi) northeast of El Fuerte.*

The quiet mountain village of Cerocahui, just inside the Sinaloa state border, is a good place to get a sense of how people live in the canyon area. Across the dirt street from the Hotel Misión is **Misión San Francisco Javier,** a graceful little temple established by the Jesuits. Although the order arrived in the area in 1680, Tarahumara Indian uprisings and other difficulties delayed construction of the church until 1741. It is said that this was the favorite church of the founder, Father Juan María de Salvatierra, because the Tarahumara were the most difficult Indians to convert. Nearby is a boarding school for Tarahumara children, which tour groups sometimes visit. Both of the town's hotels provide transportation to and from the train station at Bahuichivo, about a 40-minute drive along a bumpy, mostly unpaved road.

The prime reason to come to Cerocahui is its accessibility to **La Barranca de Urique.** It's a lovely ride to the **Cerro del Gallego lookout,** one of the best spots for magnificent views. From there you can make out the slim thread of the Río Urique and the old mining town of Urique, a dot on the distant canyon bottom. A public bus makes the trip from Cerocahui daily after the late arrival of the second-class train, but many people opt for the local hotels' full-day or overnight tours.

> off the
> beaten
> path

★ **Urique.** A journey to the small town of Urique offers a fascinating glimpse into canyon life. At the bottom of the system's deepest canyon—1,640 ft above sea level—Urique enjoys an excellent, semitropical climate. Residents plant orchards of citrus and guava trees, and sycamore and fig trees dot the area. The Río Urique, which carved the great canyon, slides lazily along in the dry season but races briskly after the summer rains. Browse in the old general store, El Central, and the town church, and then munch on a lunch at the town's best restaurant, La Plaza, on the main square. Rafting expeditions can be arranged through Paraíso del Oso, in Cerocahui.

In the surrounding countryside, the Tarahumara eschew town life, preferring to live in separate family enclaves throughout the valley or in small communities such as Guadalupe, 7 km (4½ mi) from Urique. The most direct path to this town is across a 400-ft-long suspension bridge that rocks and sways above the river. It's not for the faint-of-heart, although the tiny town can also be accessed by car.

You can visit Urique as a day trip from Cerocahui, two to three hours each way by car, or ride horses or hike down into the canyon. Tours are offered through Cerocahui hotels Paraíso del Oso and Misión. The best lodgings in Urique are Hotel Estrella del Río, which has large rooms, hot water, and impossibly hefty pillows ($35 double).

Where to Stay

$$$$ **Hotel Misión.** Part of the Balderrama chain, this is one of just two lodges in Cerocahui. The main house, which looks like a cross between a ski lodge and a hacienda, contains the hotel's office, small shop, and a combined dining room, bar, and lounge surrounding two large fireplaces. The plain, whitewashed rooms have beamed ceilings, Spanish colonial–style furnishings, and wood-burning stoves. Wide verandas draw guests outside to sit in leather rocking chairs, perhaps to sip a glass of wine from the hacienda's own vineyard. ⊠ *Cerocahui* ☏ *Reservations: Hotel Santa Anita, Av. Leyva and Hidalgo, Apdo. 159, 81200 Los Mochis* ☎ *668/818–7046 Ext. 432; 800/896–8196 in the U.S.* 🖷 *668/812–0046* ⊕ *www.mexicoscoppercanyon.com* 🛏 *38 rooms* ♿ *Restaurant, bar, lounge, shop* ☰ *AE, MC, V* ¶❚¶ *FAP.*

$$$ **Paraíso del Oso Lodge.** Doug "Diego" Rhodes runs this down-to-earth lodge, which is perfectly situated for bird-watching, walks in the woods, or a horseback ride into the canyons. Ranch-style rooms with handmade wooden furniture and wood-burning stoves face a grassy courtyard. A generator provides electricity for guest rooms; a fireplace in the bar and kerosene lamps in the restaurant-lounge give the common areas a glow. Doug, a loquacious U.S. transplant, gives tours and rafting trips. His stable's horses have plenty of zip. ⊠ *5 km (3 mi) outside of Cerocahui* ☏ *Reservations: Box 31089, El Paso, TX 79931* ☎ *800/884–3107 in the U.S.* 🖷 *915/585–7027* ⊕ *www.mexicohorse.com* 🛏 *21 rooms* ♿ *Dining room, horseback riding, free parking* ☰ *MC, V* ¶❚¶ *FAP.*

Divisadero & Posada Barrancas

❹ *80 km (50 mi) northeast of Cerocahui, in the state of Chihuahua.*

There's little to do in Divisadero and Posada Barrancas, two whistle-stops five minutes apart on the Continental Divide. Nonetheless, the canyon scenery and refreshing lack of man-made distractions provide a breath of fresh air, and it's impossible to be unmoved by their Barrancas del Cobre vistas—especially marvelous at sunset. A popular excursion that takes about seven to eight hours round-trip on foot is to Wacajipare, a Tarahumara village in the canyon. The Hotel Divisadero Barrancas offers its guests a few other guided tours as well.

Where to Stay

★ $$$$ **Hotel Posada Barrancas Mirador.** This beautiful pink hotel—another link in the Balderrama chain—perches on the edge of the Barrancas del Cobre. The dining room and all the guest rooms have spectacular views; balconies seem to hang right over the abyss. Accommodations are bright and comfortable, although on the small side, with lovely tile floors, old-fashioned chunky chimneys and a small terrace with table and two chairs for enjoying canyon views. ⊠ *Posada Barrancas train station* ⌂ *Reservations: Hotel Santa Anita, Av. Leyva and Hidalgo 81200 Los Mochis* ☎ *635/578–3020; 800/862–9026 in the U.S.* 🖷 *668/812–0046* ⊕ *www.mexicoscoppercanyon.com* ↝ *51 rooms* ⚘ *Restaurant, bar, meeting room* ☐ *AE, MC, V* ⭘ *FAP.*

$$$ **Hotel Divisadero Barrancas.** The dining room and Rooms 1–10 in the old section and 35–52 in the newer section of this canyon-rim hotel have panoramic views. There's a reading room and a café with many types of coffee and tea; the view from the second-story dining room and lounge is magnificent; and the food is good. Rooms are also top-notch, with beautiful comforters on the beds. Rates include several walking tours; for an extra fee you could tackle a seven-hour guided descent into the canyon (October–March only). ⊠ *Divisadero train station* ⌂ *Reservations: Av. Mirador 4516 31000 Chihuahua City, Chihuahua* ☎ *614/415–1199* 🖷 *614/415–6575* ⊕ *www.hoteldivisadero.com.mx* ↝ *52 rooms* ⚘ *Restaurant, bar, meeting room* ☐ *AE, MC, V* ⭘ *FAP.*

★ $$ **Hotel Mansión Tarahumara.** It's a bit disconcerting to come across a red-turreted castle out in canyon country, but somehow this whimsical fancy works. All rooms (15 in separate cabins) have Spanish contemporary–style light-pine furniture and individual heaters, with walls of stone and pine paneling and exposed beam ceilings. The staff is typically helpful and courteous. ⊠ *Posada Barrancas train station* ⌂ *Reservations: Av. Juárez 1602-A, Col. Centro, 31000 Chihuahua City, Chihuahua* ☎ *614/415–4721* 🖷 *614/416–5444* ↝ *57 rooms, 1 suite* ⚘ *Restaurant, indoor pool, lake, sauna, steam room, bar, dance club, meeting room, travel services* ☐ *MC, V* ⭘ *FAP.*

$ **Rancho Posada Mirador.** This is a good base from which to explore the Barrancas del Cobre. Rooms have ocher stucco walls, ceramic-tile floors, and colonial-style, hand-painted furniture; some have cozy fireplaces. The lobby–dining room has a massive stone fireplace, beamed ceiling, and wood furniture. ⊠ *Posada Barrancas train station* ⌂ *Reservations: Hotel Santa Anita, Apdo. 159, 81200 Los Mochis* ☎ *668/818–7046 Ext. 432; 800/896–8196 in the U.S.* 🖷 *668/812–0046* ⊕ *www.mexicoscoppercanyon.com* ↝ *38 rooms* ⚘ *Restaurant, bar* ☐ *AE, MC, V* ⭘ *BP, FAP.*

Creel

⑤ *60 km (37 mi) northeast of Divisadero.*

Surrounded by pine-covered mountains, Creel is a mining, ranching, and logging town that grew up around the railroad station. The largest settlement in the area, it's also a gathering place for Tarahumara seeking supplies and markets for their crafts. It's easy to imagine American frontier towns at the turn of the 20th century looking like Creel—without, of course, the international backpacking contingent that makes this town its base. For the number of lodgings and restaurants, the availability of nearby excursions, and the existence of simple yet sound infrastructure for overnight guided trips into the canyon, Creel is the most convenient base for visitors to the Sierra Tarahumara.

Right in the middle of the town plaza, a cooperative group of tour guides specializes in day trips to areas of interest around Creel. One of the most common day tours is a visit to **Lake Arakeko,** a nearby mission church, a Tarahumara cave dwelling, and rock formations in a variety of weird shapes. The lake visit is little more than a "stop and look," with a chance to buy Tarahumara crafts. The better parts of the two- to three-hour tour are visits to **Valle de los Hongos** (Valley of the Mushrooms), where rocks perch atop each other precariously, and the nearby **Valle de los Monjes** (Valley of the Monks), where monolithic rocks resemble towering figures. The Tarahumara call this the Valley of the Erect Penises, but tourism pundits have changed the name. Before you reach this spot you'll stop at **Valle de las Ranas** (Valley of the Frogs), where a few of the formations do look quite froglike. Each stop provides great photo-ops.

Many half-day tours also include a visit to **Cusárare,** whose Tarahumara name means "eagle's nest." Located 26 km (16 mi) from Creel, it's the site of a Jesuit mission, built in 1741, that still serves as a center for religious and community affairs for the Tarahumara who live in the area. Inside the simple whitewashed structure, men and women stand for the Sunday service, women on one side, men on the other. The main reason to visit, however, is to take the easy 6-km (4-mi) hike through a lovely piñon forest to see the **Cusárare waterfall,** most impressive during or just after the rainy months.

A popular way to spend the day is to hike to **Recohuata hot springs,** which involves climbing down from the canyon rim into the Barranca de Tararecua. Some tour guides leave their clients at the rim to be guided down to a series of pools by youngsters stationed at the trailhead for this purpose. This tour can be combined with a trip to the magnificent canyon lookout point at **Divisadero,** some 43 km (27 mi) away on a windy road.

Several other worthwhile day trips along the way to the colonial town of Batopilas are **Basihuare,** where wide horizontal bands of color cross huge vertical outcroppings of rock; the **Barranca de Urique overlook,** a perspective that differs from the one at Divisadero; and **La Bufa,** site of a former Spanish silver mine. Seventy-three kilometers (45 miles) northwest of Creel, along an unpaved, winding road, the 806-ft **Cascada de Basaseachi** are among the highest cascades in North America.

Where to Stay & Eat

★ ¢–$ ✕ **Tungar.** "The Hangover Hospital," as it is nicknamed, is a home-style, no-smoking, counter-only café with probably the best, most authentic Mexican food in town. The menu includes such traditional morning pick-me-ups—and hangover cures—as *menudo* (tripe soup) or the more palatable pozole (hominy soup with chunks of pork, which when doctored with lime and chili, produces a powerful sweat). For lunch consider a few delicious stingray tostadas or a *burro montado*, flour tortillas with melted cheese, beans, and beef stew. ⊠ *Calle Francisco Villa s/n, next to train depot* ☎ *No phone* 🚫 *No credit cards* ⊘ *No dinner. No lunch Sun.*

¢–$ ✕ **Veronica's.** This clean, simple eatery on the main street may take its time with service, but remains popular nonetheless. Order up one of the *comidas corridas* (set meals with soup and main course), or à la carte staples like the *discada* (mixed grilled meats and veggies served with hot tortillas) or vegetable soup. ⊠ *Av. López Mateos 34* ☎ *635/456–0631* 🚫 *No credit cards.*

$$ ▦ **Best Western: The Lodge at Creel.** This simple lodge has several wings of log cabin–like rooms with pine floors and walls. Gas-log heaters controlled by wall thermostats are disguised as wood-burning stoves, giving cheer to otherwise plain accommodations. Bathrooms are small and cramped. The cozy bar was expanded in 2002; there's also a large dining room, which can be chilly in winter. ⊠ *Av. López Mateos 61, 33200* ☎ *635/456–0071; 800/879–4071 in the U.S.* 📠 *635/456–0082* ⊕ *www.thelodgeatcreel.com* 🛏 *28 rooms, 1 suite* ⌂ *Restaurant, bar, travel services, free parking* 🚫 *AE, MC, V.*

$$ ▦ **Copper Canyon Sierra Lodge.** In a peaceful piñon forest near the Cusárare falls and an old mission church, this natural beauty has no electricity: no TV or ringing phones here. The pine-panel and white stucco rooms have red tile floors and area rugs; bathrooms are romantically equipped with kerosene lamps and woodstoves. The excellent meals are served in a beautiful yet simple dining room. This spot is best for those with wheels or who want a night or two of isolation; it's 26 km (16 mi) from Creel. ⊠ *Cusárare* 📠 *635/456–0036* ⌖ *Copper Canyon Lodges, Box 85, Leonard, MI 48367* ☎ *800/776–3942 in the U.S.* 📠 *248/236–0960* ⊕ *www.sierratrail.com* 🛏 *22 rooms* ⌂ *Restaurant, bar, travel services, free parking; no room phones, no in-room TVs* 🚫 *No credit cards* ⍩ *FAP.*

Fodor'sChoice
★

$$ ▦ **Sierra Bonita.** Perched on a hill just outside Creel, this spot is quite self-contained, with a restaurant, bar, and even a disco open on the weekends. Rooms and suites have less of a rustic look than most in the canyon area, with polyester bedspreads, tile floors, and no real attempt to "go Western." Vans make the five-minute jaunt to Creel on demand. ⊠ *Carretera Gran Visión s/n, 33200* 📠📠 *635/456–0615* 🛏 *8 rooms, 10 cabins, 2 suites* ⌂ *Restaurant, room service, cable TV, bar, dance club, shop, travel services, free parking* 🚫 *MC, V.*

$ ▦ **Cabañas Pueblo Viejo.** This funky complex has cabins individually designed to resemble an old Mexican village. Owner-manager don Francisco swears newlyweds love the squeaky, steel-bed-framed bed in the "jail" room. Despite the whimsy, rooms are comfortable and have TVs and heaters; each small breakfast area has a toaster, coffeemaker, and sink. Some family-size suites have separate sleeping quarters and multiple beds. ⊠ *Behind KOA Hotel 33200* ☎ *614/411–3706 reservations in Chihuahua City* 📠 *614/418–2516* 🛏 *15 rooms, 5 suites* ⌂ *Restaurant, bar, travel services, free parking* 🚫 *MC, V* ⍩ *BP, FAP.*

★ ¢ ▦ **Margarita's.** Tiny touts at the train station will guide you to one of the best deals in town. Catercorner from the town plaza, this backpackers' haven has a single, coed dorm room (about $7 gets you a bunk, breakfast, and dinner) as well as private rooms with bath. The rooms—with wrought-iron lamps and light-wood furnishings—are as pleasant as anything at three times the price. A second-story addition, to be completed in 2003, will house a restaurant and Internet café. ⊠ *Av. López Mateos 11, 33200* ☎ *635/456–0045* 🛏 *17 rooms, 1 dorm* ⌂ *Restaurant, bicycles, travel services* 🚫 *No credit cards* ⍩ *MAP.*

¢ ▨ **Margarita's Plaza Mexicana.** This pretty, two-story hotel is one of the town bargains. Each room has a heater and a different wall mural. One disadvantage is that the tequila-and-mariachi parties, often hosted for tour groups in the central courtyard, can get quite noisy. The restaurant always bustles with tour groups, travelers, and a smattering of locals. ⊠ *Calle Elfido Bautista s/n, off Av. López Mateos, 33200* ☎☎ *635/ 456–0245* ↝ *26 rooms* ♢ *Restaurant, bar, travel services; no TV in some rooms* ⊟ *No credit cards* ⵔⵔ *MAP.*

Nightlife

Most people hang out in the hotels where they are staying, as there are only a few other options. When the sun goes down on weekend evenings, **Laylo's Lounge** (⊠ Av. López Mateos 25, next to El Caballo Bayo restaurant, ☎ 635/456–0136) has music and sometimes other types of performers; it can get rowdy at times. The hotel **Sierra Bonita** (⊠ Carretera Gran Visión s/n ☎ 635/456–0615), on a hill west of town, has a disco Friday through Sunday that sometimes hosts live bands playing *norteño* (northern Mexican) tunes or Caribbean *cumbia*. When the music is canned, you might get some pop or rock thrown in.

Shopping

At the west end of Avenida López Mateos, **Artesanías Victoria** (☎ 635/ 456–0030) sells huge Tarahumara pots and other artifacts, some from elsewhere. On the plaza, **Casa de las Artesanías** (☎ 635/456–0080) is a museum focusing on traditional Tarahumara life, including a beautiful exhibit of black-and-white photographs. The gift shop has Tarahumara crafts and dolls. Be sure to pay a visit to **Misión Tarahumara** (☎ 635/456– 0097), on the east side of the plaza. The shop sells only Tarahumara handiwork, including violins, woven belts, and simple pots of pine needles or unglazed clay. Here you'll also find English-language books on the culture. Proceeds benefit the mission hospital.

Batopilas

❻ *80 km (50 mi) southeast of Creel.*

Veins of silver—mined on and off from the time of the conquistadors— made this remote village of fewer than 800 people one of the wealthiest towns in colonial Mexico. At one time it was the only place in the country besides Mexico City that had electricity. The hair-raising, 80-km (50-mi) ride down a narrow, unpaved road to the languid town at the bottom of the Barranca de Batopilas takes five or six hours by pickup truck from Creel (closer to seven hours on the local bus, which runs back and forth every day except Sunday). Sights in this relatively lush oasis, in the middle of the semitropical thorn forest, include the ruined **hacienda of Alexander Shepherd,** built in the late 1800s by one of the town's wealthiest mine owners; the original **aqueduct,** which still serves the town; and the triple-dome 17th-century **Satevó mission church,** mysteriously isolated in the Satevó Valley on a scenic 16-km (10-mi) round-trip hike from town. Because it takes most of the day to get down to Batopilas, you'll need to spend at least one night at one of the town's modest posadas. Allow more time to explore the canyon's depths, and be sure to take a local guide, as local drug traffic makes wandering the area alone unwise.

Where to Stay

¢ ▨ **Real de Minas.** Owner Martín Alcaraz earned his stripes during his years as a hotel manager before opening his own small place. It's a charming spot, and more accessible than before as it now has a phone. Each room has decent beds and rustic furnishings but no TV or telephone, which is as it should be—guests come here to experience nature with few distractions. ⊠ *Donato Guerra at Pablo Ochoa* ☎☎ *649/456–9045* ➷ *8 rooms* ⚏ *No room phones, no room TVs* ⊟ *No credit cards.*

Cuauhtémoc

❼ *128 km (79 mi) northeast of Creel, 105 km (65 mi) southwest of Chihuahua.*

A rather anomalous experience in Mexico is a visit to the **Campos Menonitas,** individual family farms of a large Mennonite community surrounding Cuauhtémoc. Some 20,000 Mennonites came to the San Antonio Valley in 1922 at the invitation of President Alvaro Obregón, who gave them the right to live freely and autonomously in return for farming the land. Set up a tour in Chihuahua City through **Divitur Chihuahua** (⊠ Rio de Janeiro 310-1, Col. Panamericana ☎☎ 614/414–6046).

Also worth a visit is the **Mennonite Museum and Cultural Center** (⊠ Carretera a Rubio, Km. 2.5 ☎ 625/582–1382). So far this museum shows a typical Mennonite house from the first pioneers, combining living quarters, kitchen, and stable under one roof.

Where to Stay & Eat

$–$$ ✕ **Rancho Viejo.** People from Chihuahua City make regular trips to Cuauhtémoc just to dine at this simple country restaurant in the town center. Steaks are the specialty—rib eye, T-bone, or New York cuts—but seafood and Mexican *antojitos* (enchiladas, tacos, and the like) are also served. Roving musicians sing ballads during dinner, and although the kitchen closes at midnight the bar stays open until at least 2 AM. ⊠ *Av. Vicente Guerrero at Calle Tercera 303* ☎ *625/582–4360* ⊟ *MC, V.*

¢ ▥ **Motel Tarahumara Inn.** You'll find most of the creature comforts you need at this two-story motel just a few blocks from the main plaza. Rooms have heat; suites have sofa beds and kitchenettes with refrigerator and stove. The friendly front desk staff will lend guests dishes and pots and pans as needed. ⊠ *Av. Allende 373* ☎☎ *625/581–1919* ➷ *55 rooms, 4 suites* ⚏ *Restaurant, kitchenettes, cable TV, gym, bar, meeting room, free parking* ⊟ *AE, MC, V.*

Chihuahua City

❽ *375 km (233 mi) south of El Paso–Ciudad Juárez border, 1,440 km (893 mi) northwest of Mexico City.*

If you're arriving from the peaceful Barranca del Cobre, the sprawling city of Chihuahua—with more than 670,000 inhabitants—might come as a bit of a jolt. But then, the city is known for its revolutionary nature: two of Mexico's most famous war heroes are closely tied to Chihuahua. The father of Mexican independence, Father Miguel Hidalgo, and his coconspirators were executed here by the Spanish in 1811. And Chihuahua was home to General Pancho Villa. His revolutionary army, the División del Norte (Northern Army Division), helped overthrow dictator Porfirio Díaz in 1910 and was extremely active in the ensuing civil war. A half century earlier, Benito Juárez, known as the Abraham Lincoln of Mexico, made Chihuahua his base when the French invaded the country in 1865.

FodorśChoice ★ Whatever you do, don't miss the **Museo de la Revolución Mexicana,** better known as La Casa de Pancho Villa. Villa lived in this 1909 mansion, also called the "Quinta Luz" (*quinta* means "manor," or "country house"), with his wife, Luz Corral. Although Villa married dozens of women, Corral was considered his only legitimate wife, as the couple was married in both civil and church ceremonies. She lived in this house until her death on June 6, 1981, willing the residence to the government. The 50 small rooms that used to board Villa's bodyguards now house a vast array of artifacts of Chihuahua's cultural and revolutionary history. Parked in the museum's courtyard is the bullet-ridden 1919 Dodge in which Villa was assassinated in 1923 at the age of 45. ⊠ *Calle Décima 3010, near Calle Terrazas, Col. Santa Rosa* ☎ *614/416–2958* ✉ *$1* ⊗ *Tues.–Sat. 9–1 and 3–7, Sun. 10–5.*

Known as the **Parroquia del Sagrado,** the cathedral is also worth a visit. Construction on this stately Baroque structure on the Plaza de Armas was begun by the Jesuits in 1726 and—because of local Chichimeca Indian uprisings and the expulsion of the Jesuits—not completed until 1825. The opulent church has Carrara marble altarpieces and a ceiling studded with 24-karat gold ornaments; the huge German-made pipe organ from the late 18th century is still used on special occasions. In the basement, the small **Museo de Arte Sacro** displays 18th-century paintings, primarily those in the Mexican Baroque tradition. ⊠ *Plaza de Armas, Centro* ☎ *No phone* ✉ *Museum $1.80* ⊗ *Weekdays 10–2 and 4–6.*

The **Palacio de Gobierno** was built by the Jesuits as a monastery in 1882. Converted into government offices in 1891, it was destroyed by a fire in the early 1940s and rebuilt in 1947. Murals around the state capitol's patio depict famous episodes from the history of the state of Chihuahua, and a plaque commemorates the spot where Father Hidalgo was executed on the morning of July 30, 1811. ⊠ *Calle Aldama at Plaza Hidalgo, Centro* ☎ *614/410–1077* ✉ *Free* ⊗ *Daily 8–8.*

The **Palacio Federal** houses the city's main post office and telegraph office, as well as the *calabozo,* or dungeon, where Hidalgo was imprisoned by the Spanish prior to his execution. His pistols, traveler's trunk, crucifix, and reproductions of his letters are on display. ⊠ *Av. Juárez between Calles Neri Santos and Carranza, Centro* ☎ *614/429–3300 Ext. 1056* ✉ *50¢* ⊗ *Tues.–Sun. 9–7.*

Consecrated in 1721, the **Iglesia de San Francisco** is the oldest church in Chihuahua. Father Hidalgo's decapitated body was interred in the chapel here from 1811 until 1827, when it was sent to Mexico City. (His head was publicly displayed for 10 years by Spanish Royalists in Guanajuato on the Alhóndiga de Granaditas.) Although the church's facade is relatively sober, its Baroque altarpieces, decorated with 18th-century paintings, are worth perusal. ⊠ *Av. Libertad at Calle 15, Centro* ☎ *No phone* ✉ *Free* ⊗ *Daily 7–2 and 5–7.*

Slightly outside the center of town but worth a visit is the cultural center of the Universidad de Chihuahua, known as **Quinta Gameros.** This hybrid French Second Empire–art nouveau mansion, with stained-glass windows, ornate wooden staircases, rococo plaster wall panels, and lavish ironwork, was begun in 1907 by architect Julio Corredor Latorre, a Colombian architect, for Manuel Gameros, a wealthy mining engineer. On the ground floor are changing archaeological or fine-arts exhibits; on the second floor, the mismatched and rather amateurish contemporary paintings belonging to the state university. ⊠ *Calle Bolívar 401, at Calle de la Llave, Centro* ☎ *614/416–6684* ✉ *$2.50* ⊗ *Tues.–Sun. 11–2 and 4–7.*

A restoration project has made the site of the town's original settlement, **Santa Eulalia,** particularly appealing. The 30-minute drive southeast of town, about $40 one-way by taxi (significantly less by bus), is repaid by the colonial architecture and cobblestone streets of this village, which was founded in 1652. The religious artwork in the 18th-century cathedral is noteworthy.

Opened in 2001, the **Nombre de Dios caverns** are just outside the northeast side of the city, about 30 minutes from the city center. An illuminated, 1.6-km (1-mi) path takes you past rock formations and stalactites and stalagmites, which have been given names such as Christ, the Waterfall, and the Altar. ⊠ *H. Colegio Militar s/n, Sector Nombre de Dios* ☎ *614/400–7059* 🖃 *Weekdays $2.50, weekends $3* ☉ *Tues.–Fri. 9–4, weekends 10–5.*

off the beaten path

Casas Grandes. Some 300 km (186 mi) northwest of Chihuahua, the twin towns of Nuevo Casas Grandes and Casas Grandes are the gateways to the ancient area known as Paquimé, declared a UNESCO World Heritage site in 1998. Nuevo Casas Grandes, a two-horse town with wide, dusty streets and cowboys in regalia, has the hotels, craft shops, and most of the local restaurants. An archaeological site and museum are in sleepy Casas Grandes, a one-horse town 8 km (5 mi) away.

Near the aspen-lined Casas Grandes River, sheltered by the burnt-sienna peaks of the Sierra Madre Occidental, Paquimé was inhabited by peoples of the Oasis America culture between AD 700 and 1500. The trading and ceremonial city was poised between the Pueblo cultures of today's Southwestern United States (to whom they were related) to the north and their Mesoamerican neighbors to the south. Architecture and cultural traditions were borrowed from each. Paquimé was a cosmopolitan commercial center whose residents manufactured jewelry and raised fowl and macaws imported from the tropics. Evidence of their engineering and architectural savvy still stands, in the form of heat-shielding walls, T-shape doorways for defense, and intricate indoor plumbing systems. The high-tech museum on-site shows Paquimé artifacts and ceramics and has bilingual (English and Spanish) videos, displays, and interactive computers describing local cultural, religious, and economic practices and Mexican history until the Revolution of 1910. ☎ *636/692–4140* 🖃 *Museum $3.50* ☉ *Tues.–Sun. 10–5.*

In Nuevo Casas Grandes, Restaurante Constantino (⊠ Minerva 112, across from Hotel Paquimé ☎ 636/694–1005) makes great enchiladas and has a full breakfast menu. Family-style Hotel Piñon (⊠ Av. Juárez 605, Nuevo Casas Grandes ☎ 636/694–0655) has a swimming pool (closed in winter), a restaurant, bar, and a private collection of ancient *ollas* (clay pots) from Paquimé. Hotel Hacienda (⊠ Av. Juárez 2603 Norte, Nuevo Casas Grandes ☎ 636/694–1046), with a restaurant, bar, and swimming pool, is one of the best places to stay in town.

Omnibus de México makes the five-hour trip from Chihuahua to Nuevas Casas Grandes (about $20). To get to the ruins, it's easiest to hail a taxi from the bus station in Nuevas Casas Grandes. Once there, head for the *zócalo* (main square). Paquimé is a 10-minute walk from town—follow the PAQUIMÉ sign on Avenida Constitución.

Where to Stay & Eat

$$–$$$$ ✕ **La Calesa.** A large, dim, and rather elegant room with wood paneling and red tablecloths and curtains, this looks like the classic steak house it is. The filet mignon and rib-eye steaks are particularly recommended; try the former cooked with mushrooms. Live piano music adds a dash of panache. ⊠ *Av. Juárez 3300 Centro* ☎ *614/410–1038* 🖃 *AE, MC, V.*

$–$$ ✕ **Café del Paseo.** Two doors down from Quinta Gameros, this casual, friendly evening hot spot is known for good service. Original art decorates walls painted Santa Fe pinks, peaches, and ochers, and a *trova* group sings popular ballads Wednesday to Sunday after 8:30 PM. The specialty is *arrachera a la borracha,* tenderized beef marinated in beer and grilled with mushrooms and onions. The restaurant opens daily at 4 PM. ⊠ *Bolivár 411* ☎ *614/410–3200* ▭ *AE, MC, V* ☻ *No lunch.*

$–$$ ✕ **Rincón Mexicano.** Chihuahua residents return repeatedly to this traditional eatery for dependable Mexican food and a perennially cheerful atmosphere. Mariachis serenade patrons in both the bright blue-and-yellow restaurant and the adjacent bar. Popular dishes include T-bone and rib-eye steaks, carne asada, and northern Mexico staples such as cactus salad and sizzling platters of fajitas. ⊠ *Av. Cuauhtémoc 2224, Col. Cuauhtémoc* ☎ *614/411–1510* ▭ *AE, MC, V.*

¢–$ ✕ **Ah Chiles.** If you like it hot, this is the spot. A block from Plaza Hidalgo, this branch of the informal Chihuahua chain serves norteño (northern Mexican) food. Order at the counter, then choose your salsa—green or red, hot or mild. ⊠ *Calle Aldama 712, at Av. Vicente Guerrero, Centro* ☎ *614/437–0977* ▭ *No credit cards.*

¢–$ ✕ **Café Mandala.** If you need your palm read, or just want to sit back and smell the incense, head for this informal New Age eatery at a lookout above Chihuahua. (It's best to call ahead to make an appointment for Spanish card, palm, or coffee-ground readings.) The tables on the outdoor terrace fill quickly on summer evenings, when the city lights provide a romantic backdrop. The food—tacos, tostadas, and other Mexican fare—has a healthful and sometimes vegetarian slant. Try the nontraditional tacos, with a mix of grilled green peppers, tomatoes, mushrooms, and cheese. ⊠ *Mirador de la Calle 11* ☎ *614/416–0266* ⌲ *Reservations not accepted* ▭ *No credit cards* ☻ *No lunch.*

★ **¢–$** ✕ **La Casa de los Milagros.** According to legend, the owner of this Revolution-era house fell in love with one of Pancho Villa's "girls." His wife prayed to Saint Anthony, and when her husband returned, the house was dubbed "House of Miracles." Today it's *the* place for light snacks, coffee, drinks, and, Thursday through Sunday after 8 or 8:30 PM, live *música de trova* (romantic ballads). Although most come for just a bite, you can also get soup or a steak. The high-ceilinged rooms are often hung with paintings or photos by local talent. ⊠ *Victoria 812, near Ocampo, Centro* ☎ *614/437–0693* ▭ *No credit cards* ☻ *No lunch.*

★ **$$$** ▥ **Holiday Inn Hotel & Suites.** This appealing property combines comfort and convenience; it's 10 minutes from the downtown sights. Each guest room has a kitchen with stove, refrigerator, dishwasher, and coffeemaker, and a long counter where you can eat or work. A TV with VCR swivels between the living area and the bedroom. The English-speaking staff is friendly and helpful. ⊠ *Calle Escudero 702, Fracc. San Felipe 31000* ☎ *614/439–0000; 800/465–4329 in the U.S.* ⊟ *614/414–3313* ⊕ *www.sixcontinentshotels.com* ⇄ *74 suites* ⌂ *Restaurant, kitchens, cable TV, in-room VCRs, pool, gym, sauna, basketball, free parking; no-smoking rooms* ▭ *AE, DC, MC, V* ⎮⚬⎮ *CP.*

$$$ ▥ **Westin Soberano Chihuahua.** Atop a rise that has magnificent views of the city and surrounding mountains, Chihuahua's most elegant hotel sparkles with fountains and marble. Designed around an atrium with a cascading waterfall, the hotel is a distinct contrast to the rustic accommodations of the canyons. Rooms are plush yet understated, with richly patterned textiles, TVs in tall chests, and baths with both tub and shower. ⊠ *Barranca del Cobre 3211, Fracc. Barrancas 31125* ☎ *614/429–2929; 888/625–5144 in the U.S.* ⊟ *614/429–2900* ⊕ *www.starwood.com/westin* ⇄ *194 rooms, 10 suites* ⌂ *2 restaurants, cable*

TV, tennis court, pool, gym, steam room, racquetball, 2 bars, business services, meeting rooms, free parking; no-smoking rooms ☱ *AE, DC, MC, V.*

★ **$–$$** ▣ **Hotel San Francisco.** A favorite of Mexican business travelers, this modern five-story hotel has a prime location behind the Plaza de Armas. Clean and comfortable rooms—which in 2002 were thoroughly renovated—have firm mattresses, large TVs, bathtubs, and desks. The lobby is dotted with classic-style statues and urns, and massive floral arrangements. Local calls are free, as are Internet access and some secretarial services. As this is a business-oriented hotel, weekend rates are almost half the weekday rate. ⊠ *Victoria 409, Centro 31000* ☎ *614/416–7550; 800/ 847–2546 in the U.S.* 🖷 *614/415–3538* ⊕ *www.hotelsanfrancisco. com.mx* ➫ *111 rooms, 20 suites* ⌂ *Restaurant, in-room data ports, cable TV, bar, business services, Internet, meeting rooms, free parking; no-smoking rooms* ☱ *AE, MC, V.*

$$ ▣ **Palacio del Sol.** The high-rise downtown hotel looks faded from the outside, but inside, rooms and public spaces are redecorated on a regular basis. At this writing, rooms on the seventh floor and up had been redecorated. From the revolving front door to the stained-glass "sun" mural in the lobby bar, the public spaces seem permanently stuck in an earlier, less sophisticated era. ⊠ *Independencia 116, Centro 31000* ☎ *614/416–6000; 800/852–4049 in the U.S.* 🖷 *614/416–9947* ⊕ *www. hotelpalaciodelsol.com* ➫ *174 rooms, 26 suites* ⌂ *2 restaurants, in-room data ports, cable TV, gym, bar, shop, laundry service, meeting rooms, car rental, travel services, free parking* ☱ *AE, MC, V.*

$ ▣ **Posada Tierra Blanca.** Across the street from the Palacio del Sol but considerably less expensive, this modern motel-style property is convenient to downtown sights. Rooms in wings surrounding the gated swimming pool have firm mattresses, pseudo-antique furnishings, and large TVs. ⊠ *Niños Héroes 102, Centro 31000* ☎ *614/415–0000* 🖷 *614/ 416–0063* ➫ *90 rooms, 3 suites* ⌂ *Restaurant, cable TV, pool, piano bar, free parking* ☱ *MC, V.*

Nightlife & the Arts

This large city is more sedate than one might expect; and its hardworking residents generally wait for the weekends to kick up their heels. **La Casa de los Milagros** (⊠ Victoria 812, Centro ☎ 614/437–0693) starts to groove after 8:30 PM. At the glass-encased, neon-laced restaurant and bar **Cervecería La Taberna** (⊠ Av. Juárez 3331, Centro ☎ 614/415–8380) you can play pool or, on Friday and Saturday nights, dance to a DJ. At **Hotel Sicomoro** (⊠ Blvd. Ortiz Mena 411, Col. Unidad Presidentes ☎ 614/413–5445) artists play romantic and folk music Wednesday–Saturday in the lobby bar.

Shopping

In addition to selling gems and geodes from the area, **Artesanías y Gemas de Chihuahua** (⊠ Calle Décima 3015, across from the Museo de la Revolución Mexicana, Col. Santa Rosa ☎ 614/415–2882) carries exceptional silver jewelry and a variety of other crafts. It's closed Monday. Across the street from the *calabozo* (jail) where Father Hidalgo was held, the **Casa de las Artesanías del Estado de Chihuahua** (⊠ Av. Juárez 705, Centro ☎ 614/437–1292) carries the best selection of Tarahumara and regional crafts in the city. **Mercado de Artesanías** (⊠ Calle Victoria 506 [another entrance on Calle Aldama 511], between Calles Quinta and Guerrero, Centro ☎ 614/416–2716), a block wide with two entrances, sells everything from inexpensive jewelry, candy, and T-shirts to mass-produced crafts from all over the region.

LAS BARRANCAS DEL COBRE A TO Z

To research prices, get advice from other travelers, and book travel arrangements, visit www.fodors.com.

AIR TRAVEL

You can fly into either Chihuahua or Los Mochis from Los Angeles, Tucson, Mexico City, or other major U.S. and Mexican cities.

AIRPORTS   The Chihuahua airport (CUU) is a roughly 10-minute drive from the city center. The Los Mochis–Topolobambo airport (LMM) is about 30 minutes outside Los Mochis on the road to Topolobambo.
🏠 **Aeropuerto de Chihuahua** ✉ Blvd. Juan Pablo II, Km 14 ☎ 614/420-5104. **Aeropuerto Los Mochis Topolobampo** ✉ Carretera Los Mochis Topolobampo, Km 12.5 ☎ 668/815-3070.

AIRPORT   The trip from the Chihuahua airport into town costs $10 in a shared
TRANSFERS   van taxi and $16 for a private taxi. The cost of a taxi between Los Mochis airport and the city is about $14.

CARRIERS   Aeroméxico and its feeder airline, Aerolitoral, have daily flights to Chihuahua from Los Angeles, Phoenix, Las Vegas, and El Paso. Within Mexico, the airlines have daily flights from Mexico City, Monterrey, Guadalajara, and Tijuana. AeroCalifornia has daily flights to Los Mochis from Los Angeles, Tucson, Tijuana, Mexico City, and Guadalajara.
🏠 **AeroCalifornia** ✉ Av. Leyva 99 Norte, Centro, Los Mochis ☎ 668/818-1616 ✉ Lateral Periférico Ortíz Mena 1809, Col. Campestre Virreyes, Chihuahua ☎ 614/437-1022.
Aeroméxico ✉ Paseo Bolívar 405, next to Quinta Gameros, Centro, Chihuahua ☎ 614/415-6303 in Chihuahua; 668/815-2570 in Los Mochis ⊕ www.aeromexico.com.

BOAT & FERRY TRAVEL

The Topolobampo–La Paz passenger ferry has been replaced with a swift Baja Speed catamaran which makes the journey four times per week, weather permitting. The 4-hour sailing costs $45 for tourist-class seats and $55 for a seat on the upper deck, including box lunch and two drinks. At this writing, boats leave Los Mochis at 3 PM Tuesday, Thursday, Saturday, and Sunday and arrive in La Paz around 7 PM. (Boats depart the same day from La Paz at 8 AM for Topolobampo.) The schedule is changeable, though, so be sure to contact Agencia de Viajes Vahome ahead of time for information and reservations. Cars are still crossed on the cargo ferry, which takes 8–10 hours and departs daily except Saturday at 9 PM. Cost varies by vehicle, but those up to 5 m (16 ft) in length cost $175 and include the driver's fare and dinner. As this ferry is used principally by commercial truck drivers, the company discourages—but does not prohibit—women and children from using it.
🏠 **Agencia de Viajes Vahome** ✉ Av. Leyva 121 Sur, Centro Los Mochis ☎ 668/815-6120.

BUS TRAVEL

The Omnibus de México lines run clean, air-conditioned first-class buses from Ciudad Juárez to Chihuahua. These leave every few hours from 4 AM to about 8 PM. Ask for one that makes at most one or two stops. The cost of the 4½-hour trip is approximately $27. This line also links these and other northern Mexico cities to Guadalajara, Mexico City, San Miguel de Allende, and others in the central region.

Grupo Estrella Blanca (which includes Chihuahuense, Elite, and other lines) buses connect the border cities to Puerto Peñasco, Chihuahua, and Creel, and as far south as Huatulco, in Oaxaca state.

You can take a bus from Los Mochis inland to El Fuerte; the 89 km trip takes about an hour and a half. Local buses depart from the corner of calles Zaragoza and Cuauhtemoc, in downtown Los Mochis.

Bus Depots Chihuahua City ✉ Terminal Central de Autobuses de Chihuahua, Carretera al Aeropuerto, Km 2.5 ☎ 614/420-5398. **El Fuerte** ✉ Mercado Independencia, Avs. Independencia and Degollado. **Los Mochis** ✉ Rosendo G. Castro at Calle Constitución ☎ 668/815-0062 **Bus Information Grupo Estrella Blanca** ☎ 614/429-0242 in Chihuahua; 668/812-1757 in Los Mochis. **Omnibus de México** ☎ 614/420-1580 in Chihuahua.

CAR RENTAL

Avis, Budget, and Hertz all have offices at the airport in Chihuahua. Car-rental companies at the airport in Los Mochis and in town include Budget and Hertz.

Avis ✉ Av. Agustín Melgar 1909, Chihuahua ☎ 614/414-1999 ⊕ www.avis.com. **Budget** ✉ Ortíz Mena 3322, Col. Magesterial, Chihuahua ☎ 614/414-2171 ✉ Guillermo Prieto 850 Norte, Los Mochis ☎ 668/815-8300 ⊕ www.budget.com. **Hertz** ✉ Av. Revolución 514, at Josue Neri Santos, Centro, Chihuahua ☎ 614/416-6473 ✉ Av. Leyva 167 Norte, Los Mochis ☎ 668/812-1122 ⊕ www.hertz.com.

CAR TRAVEL

Most U.S. and Canadian visitors drive to Chihuahua via Mexico Highway 45 from El Paso–Ciudad Juárez border, a distance of 375 km (233 mi). The four-lane toll road, Carretera 15, between Nogales on the Arizona border and Los Mochis is 763 km (473 mi).

Paved roads connect Chihuahua City to Creel and Divisadero: take Mexico Highway 16 west to San Pedro, then State Highway 127 south to Creel. The 300-km (186-mi) trip takes 3½–4 hours in good weather. This drive, through the pine forests of the Sierra Madre foothills, is more scenic than the railroad route via the plains area. Driving is a good option if you have a four-wheel-drive vehicle, because there are many worthwhile, if difficult, excursions into the canyons from Creel. From Divisadero to Bahuichivo, the dirt road is full of potholes and is especially dangerous in rain or snow.

EMERGENCIES

To contact the police, fire department, or an ambulance in Chihuahua or Los Mochis dial 060.

Chihuahua has an abundance of pharmacies with late-night service in the city center, including Farmacia del Ahorro. In Los Mochis, Farmacia Internacional will deliver for a fee.

Red Cross ☎ 668/815-0808 in Los Mochis; 614/411-1619 in Chihuahua.

Hospitals Hospital Central del Estado ✉ Calle 33 and Rosales, Col. Obrera, Chihuahua ☎ 614/415-9000. **Hospital Santa Rita** ✉ Calle Angel Flores 266 Sur, Los Mochis ☎ 668/815-4800.

Pharmacies Farmacia del Ahorro ✉ Calle Aldama at Calle 13, Centro, Chihuahua ☎ 614/410-9017. **Farmacia Internacional** ✉ Av. Leyva at Rendón, Los Mochis ☎ 668/812-5556.

INTERNET

Internet access in this region can be slow, but it is inexpensive, at less than $2 per hour. You can find Internet cafés in the area's larger towns.

Internet Cafes Café Internet Club ✉ Calle Degollado 737 Sur, Los Mochis ☎ 668/821-8960. **Papelería de Todo** ✉ Calle López Mateos 30, Creel ☎ 635/456-0122. **Quik Acces** ✉ Calle Aldama 109 Chihuahua City ☎ 614/415-3377.

MONEY MATTERS

Be sure to change money before you get into the Barrancas del Cobre: there are no banks in Cerocahui, Divisadero, or Posada Barrancas, and no guarantee that the hotels in those places will have enough cash to accommodate you. All of the banks listed below have ATMs. In Creel, the Banco Serfín is open weekdays 9–4. In Los Mochis, business hours for major banks such as Banamex are generally weekdays between 8:30 and 4:30; some banks are open Saturday morning and some change traveler's checks until 1 or 2 PM only. In Chihuahua, most banks are open weekdays 9–1:30 and 3:30–7:30, and Saturday 9–1:30. Banco Bital in downtown Chihuahua is open Monday–Saturday 8–7. In El Fuerte, Bancomer is open weekdays 8:30–4. Hotels have slightly lower exchange rates but normally you won't have to wait in line.

🏧 **Banamex** ✉ Av. Guillermo Prieto at Calle Hidalgo, Los Mochis ☎ 668/812-0116. **Banco Bital** ✉ Av. Libertad 1922, Centro, Chihuahua ☎ 614/416-0880. **Bancomer** ✉ Av. Constitución at Av. Juárez, El Fuerte ☎ 698/893-1145. **Banco Serfín** ✉ Av. López Mateos 17, Centro Creel ☎ 635/456-0060.

TAXIS

In Chihuahua and Los Mochis, taxis are easy to find and can be engaged at hotels or hailed on the street. Always agree on a price before getting into the cab. In smaller towns and at lodges throughout the Barrancas del Cobre, it's best to make taxi arrangements through your hotel.

TOURS

Most large hotels in Los Mochis and Chihuahua have in-house travel agencies that arrange tours of the Barrancas del Cobre area, as well as hiking, hunting, and fishing expeditions. In Los Mochis, tours arranged by Hotel Santa Anita will book you almost exclusively into their own line of hotels throughout the canyon region. In El Fuerte, contact Copper Canyon Adventures, which offers individualized and group tours from sedate to adventurous. In Chihuahua, Rojo y Casavantes and Turismo Al Mar offer plane and train tickets as well as city tours, Mennonite Camps, and canyon sojourns. Divitur offers booking services as well as kayaking, mountain biking, and hiking. Doug Rhodes, of Paraíso del Oso Hotel in Cerocahui, leads horseback tours into the Barranca de Urique. He also offers day rentals of mountain bikes and, between July and September, rafting trips. (Communications to Cerocahui are spotty, so contact him with plenty of lead time.)

From the United States, the oldest operator in the area is Pan American Tours. Prices for tours between Los Mochis and Chihuahua range from about $410 to $875 per person (three to seven nights); custom tours can be arranged. Synergy Tours runs individual and group trips about 10 times a year, including off-the-beaten-path treks. The California Native runs independent and small-group escorted trips through the barrancas. Four- to 11-day trips for individuals start around $650; group trips last one to two weeks and begin at $1,870. Adventure Bike Tours does seven-day guided mountain bike descents to Batopilas.

🚴 **Adventure Bike Tours** ✉ 220 E. Palmdale St., Tucson, AZ 85714 ☎ 520/807-0706; 800/926-1140 in the U.S. ⊕ www.adventurebiketours.com. **The California Native** ✉ 6701 W. 87th Pl., Los Angeles, CA 90045 ☎ 800/926-1140 in the U.S. ⊕ www.calnative.com. **Copper Canyon Adventures** 🖨 698/893-0915; 800/530-8828 in the U.S. ⊕ www.coppercanyonadventures.com. **Divitur** ✉ Rio de Janeiro 310-1, Col. Panamericana Chihuahua 🖨 614/414-6046 ⊕ www.divitur.com.mx. **Pan American Tours** 📠 5959 Gateway W. 160-B, El Paso, TX 79925 ☎ 800/876-3942 in the U.S. ⊕ www.panamericantours.com. **Paraíso del Oso** 📠 Box 31089, El Paso, TX 79931 ☎ 800/884-3107 in the U.S. 🖨 915/585-7027 ⊕ www.mexicohorse.com. **Rojo y Casavantes** ✉ Av. Vincente Guerrero 1207, Centro, Chihuahua ☎ 614/439-5858 or 614/415-5787 ⊕ www.

rycsa.com.mx. **Synergy Tours** ✉ 7335 E. Indian Plaza, Suite 120, Scottsdale, AZ 85251 ☎ 800/569-1797 in the U.S. 🖷 480/994-4439 ⊕ www.synergytours.com. **Turismo Al Mar** ✉ Calle Verna 2202, Col. Mirador, Chihuahua 🖷🖷 614/416-6589 🖷 614/416-5950.

TRAIN TOURS Sierra Madre Express of Tucson runs its own deluxe trains (with dome-dining and Pullman cars) to the Barrancas del Cobre from Tucson via Nogales on eight-day, seven-night trips about six times a year. Its trips combine the charm of sleeping on the train with first-class accommodations, starting at $2,795 per person. The company's slogan is "soft adventure of a lifetime"; the trips are geared toward older folks and those who want to view the canyon scenery and experience Tarahumara culture without roughing it.

The American Orient Express II began tours through the Barrancas del Cobre in early 2003. The experience evokes the days of more glamorous train travel; travelers dress for dinner. The eight-day trip begins in Tuscon, Arizona, and makes stops in Nogales, San Carlos, and Alamos (Sonora), and El Fuerte before entering the canyon proper, where it stops at Divisadero and Creel. Rates begin at $2,890.

🚩**American Orient Express** ⌖ 5100 Main St., Suite 300 Downers Grove, IL 60515 ☎ 800/320-4206 in the U.S. ⊕ www.americanorientexpress.com. **Sierra Madre Express of Tucson** ⌖ Box 26381, Tucson, AZ 85726 ☎ 520/747-0346; 800/666-0346 in the U.S. ⊕ www.sierramadreexpress.com.

TRAIN TRAVEL

Other than the private train cars of the Sierra Madre Express and the American Orient Express, there is no passenger service from any U.S. border city to either Los Mochis or Chihuahua.

The Ferrocarril Chihuahua al Pacífico line (CHEPE) runs a first-class and a second-class train daily in each direction from Chihuahua and Los Mochis through the Barrancas del Cobre. The first-class train departs from Los Mochis at 6 AM (sit on the right side of the train for the best views) and arrives in Chihuahua about 15 hours later. You can bypass Los Mochis and depart 1½ hours later from El Fuerte, a smaller town nestled in the foothills. Delays of several hours are not unusual, as the cargo trains with which CHEPE shares the rails tend to break down often. Westbound, the passenger train departs from Chihuahua at 6 AM and arrives in Los Mochis around 9 PM. The price of a first-class ticket is about $102 each way; you should arrange stopovers when you buy tickets.

State police with automatic weapons travel aboard to discourage would-be thieves. Food and drink in the dining car and bar are predictably expensive, and although it is technically forbidden to bring your own food and drink, conductors generally ignore this bending of rules.

Make reservations a week or more in advance during the busy months of July, August, and October, and around Christmas and Easter. Some find it most convenient to book through a hotel, tour company, or travel agency, although you can also buy tickets at the train station or major hotels in Los Mochis or Chihuahua.

The second-class train leaves an hour later from each terminus but makes many stops and is scheduled to arrive 3½ hours later in both directions than the first-class train. It is rarely crowded and quite comfortable; the train's cars were on the first-class route a few years ago, until the first-class dining and passenger cars were upgraded. Instead of a sit-down restaurant there is a snack car selling burritos, sandwiches, and soft drinks. No reservations are needed; tickets are $51 each way.

If you're driving down to Los Mochis, you're better off leaving your car there and taking the train round-trip. El Fuerte is a more charming starting point than Los Mochis, and if you board there, you'll get another hour's sleep on departure day. If you want to avoid taking the train both directions, you could hop a flight between Chihuahua City and Los Mochis. The most dramatic scenery is found between El Fuerte and Creel, so it's best to take the trip from west to east. If you decide to begin your trip in the east, consider driving to Creel or Divisadero and doing a round-trip from there. The scenery between Chihuahua City and Creel is mainly farmland.

Ferrocarril Chihuahua al Pacífico ☎ 614/439-7210 or 439-7212 in Chihuahua; 668/824-1167 in Los Mochis; 01800/367-3900 toll free in Mexico ⊕ www.ferromex.com.mx.

VISITOR INFORMATION

The government tourist office in Chihuahua is open weekdays 9–4. A smaller office at the Palacio de Gobierno, on Plaza Hidalgo, is open weekdays 8:30–6, weekends 10–5. At the former, Sonia Estrada, who speaks fluent English, will answer questions and help visitors (in person or over the phone) make travel arrangements all over the state.

The Oficina de Turismo in Los Mochis, on the first floor of the Unidad Administrativa del Gobierno del Estado building, is generally lacking in information.

Government Tourist Office ✉ Av. Libertad and Calle 13, 2nd floor, Centro, Chihuahua ☎ 614/429-3421 or 614/429-3300 Ext. 4511 or 4512 ✉ Palacio de Gobierno, Calle Aldama between Avs. Vicente Guerrero and Carranza, Centro, Chihuahua ☎ 614/429-3596 or 614/429-3300 Ext. 4515 ⊕ www.coppercanyon-mexico.com. **Oficina de Turismo** ✉ Av. Allende at Calle Ordoñez, Los Mochis ☎ 668/815-1090; 01800/508-0111 toll free in Mexico.

GUADALAJARA

6

FODOR'S CHOICE
Galería Sergio Bustamante, Tlaquepaque shop
Instituto Cultural Cabañas, Guadalajara cultural center
Museo de la Cerámica, Tlaquepaque
Quinta Real, Guadalajara hotel

HIGHLY RECOMMENDED
HOTELS   Fiesta Americana, Guadalajara
Hotel de Mendoza, Guadalajara
Lake Chapala Inn, Chapala
La Nueva Posada, Ajijic

RESTAURANTS   Ajijic Grill, Ajijic
La Destilería, Guadalajara
La Feria, Guadalajara
La Pianola, Guadalajara
La Trattoria, Guadalajara
Pierrot, Guadalajara
Santo Coyote, Guadalajara
Tacos Providencia, Guadalajara

EXPERIENCES   Catedral, Guadalajara
La Fuente, Guadalajara bar
Museo Regional, Guadalajara
Teatro Degollado, Guadalajara

Updated by
Gary Chandler

TRADITIONS ARE PRESERVED AND CUSTOMS PERPETUATED in Guadalajara; it's a place where the fiesta is an art form and the siesta is an institution—as are mariachi bands, tequila, and the Mexican hat dance. Still, the nation's second-largest city and the capital of the state of Jalisco is engaged in a struggle to retain its provincial ambience and colonial charm as its population surpasses 7 million. Émigrés who left Mexico City after the devastating 1985 earthquake and staggering numbers of the rural poor seeking employment created a population explosion that continues to strain public services and increase pollution. Despite these problems, you can still enjoy stately churrigueresque architecture and tree-lined boulevards, parks, and plazas

Guadalajara has always been one of Mexico's most socially traditional and politically conservative cities. It has also been a seat of Christian fundamentalism and was one of the strategic areas of the *cristeros,* a movement of Catholic zealots in western Mexico in the 1920s. Tapatíos, as the city's residents are called (the name may come from *tlapatiotl,* three units or purses of cacao or other commodities used as currency by the Indians of the area), even seem to take a certain amount of pride in their rather straight and narrow outlook.

Still, Tapatíos are historically accustomed to challenge and change. Within 10 years of its founding in 1531, Guadalajara's location shifted three times. In 1542 the city council followed the advice of Doña Beatriz Hernández to build the community in the center of the Atemajac Valley, where it could expand. It was thus placed on a mile-high plain of the Sierra Madre, bounded on three sides by rugged cliffs and on the fourth by the spectacular Barranca de Oblatos (Oblatos Canyon). Geographically removed from the rest of the republic during the nearly 300 years of Spanish rule, the city cultivated and maintained a political and cultural autonomy.

By the end of the 16th century, money was flowing into Guadalajara from the region's rich farms and silver mines, creating the first millionaires of what was then known as New Galicia. Under orders from Spain, much of the wealth was lavished on magnificent churches, residences, and monuments. Many of these reminders of the golden era still stand in downtown Guadalajara.

The suburbs of Tlaquepaque (pronounced tla-kay-*pah*-kay) and Tonalá (pronounced toe-na-*la*) produce some of Mexico's finest and most popular traditional crafts and folk art. Lago de Chapala (Lake Chapala)—Mexico's largest body of fresh water—and the nearby towns of Chapala and Ajijic have lured retirees from the United States and Canada, who enjoy most of the amenities they were accustomed to north of the border.

EXPLORING GUADALAJARA

Beginning around 1960, 20th-century architecture started to threaten the aesthetic of this provincial state capital. During the 1980s the city declared 30 blocks in the heart of downtown a cultural sanctuary. The result is the Centro Histórico, a restored area whose 16th-century buildings are connected by a series of large Spanish-style plazas where children chase balloons, young lovers coo on tree-shaded park benches, and grandparents stroll past vendors and marble fountains. At the nearby Plaza de los Mariachis, sombreroed troubadours stroll about, strumming their guitars and singing traditional songs.

Most sights and large hotels are in three areas: the Zona Centro, which includes the Centro Histórico and which extends west to Calle Feder-

If you have 3 days

Spend your first day in the Centro Histórico. The next day, spend the morning and have lunch in Tlaquepaque, and visit Tonalá in the afternoon. These two towns are the best places in Guadalajara to shop. On your third day, see some of the city sights outside the Centro Histórico and take in a show.

If you have 5 days

Tour the Centro Histórico on your first day, and then devote a day to Tlaquepaque and another to Tonalá. Visit Lago de Chapala on Day 4. Spend your final day back in Guadalajara, perhaps visiting the Basílica de la Virgen de Zapopan, for which you'll need several hours, or the Zoológico Guadalajara. Plan an afternoon of strolling past the mansions that were built by Guadalajara's upper classes in the glorious twilight before the 1910 revolution; the best area is in a six-block radius around Avenida Vallarta west of Avenida Chapultepec. If you'd like to get your feet on the ground in more natural surroundings, hike in the nearby Barranca de Oblatos.

If you have 7 days

Spend a day in Guadalajara's Centro Histórico and two days exploring and shopping in Tlaquepaque and Tonalá. On Day 4 head to Chapala, a village on the lake of the same name. Head west to Ajijic and make it your base for further lake region explorations. Spend Day 5 in San Juan Cosalá, with its thermal spas, and Day 6 in Tequila. Return to Guadalajara to spend your last day taking in some sights outside the Centro Histórico.

6

alismo and east to Calzada Independencia; the Zona Minerva, which surrounds the Minerva Fountain and Los Arcos monument; and the Zona Plaza del Sol, near the Plaza del Sol shopping mall and ExpoGuadalajara convention center. Guadalajara also has three autonomous municipalities—Zapopan, Tlaquepaque, and Tonolá—within its borders. An hour away are the tranquil villages on Lago de Chapala's receding shores, and Tequila, home of Mexico's most famous liquor.

Timing

A near-perfect semitropical climate and proximity to the Pacific Ocean—240 km (149 mi) away—ensure warm, sunny days and cool, clear nights. The rainy season is from July to September; afternoon downpours can be fierce, but they usually last no more than an hour.

Although sights are open and prices remain fairly constant year-round, Guadalajara's high season is officially from September to February. The great weather and a good number of events attract national and international visitors. In early September Guadalajara hosts the international mariachi and tequila festival, bringing traditional troubadours from as far away as Japan and running daily train trips to Tequila. (Tequila has its own festival in late November.) In October the city puts on the Fiestas de Octubre, a monthlong country fair-like event that's sprinkled with top-flight international entertainment. Note that most museums and some other sights are closed on Monday—always check ahead.

Centro Histórico

A Good Walk

Numbers in the text correspond to numbers in the margin and on the Guadalajara Centro Histórico map.

Guadalajara's 17th-century **Catedral** ➊ ☞, on the north side of the Plaza de Armas, is the place to start exploring downtown. After you've marveled at the interior, exit through the main doors and cross Avenida Alcalde to Plaza de la Ciudad de Guadalajara, with its large fountain, café, and benches scattered beneath laurel trees. To your right (with your back toward the cathedral) across Avenida Hidalgo is the **Palacio Municipal** ➋, whose second-floor Salón Guadalajara often features cultural exhibits.

From the corner of Avenidas Alcalde and Hidalgo, head one block east to Calle Liceo, where you'll see the **Museo Regional de Guadalajara** ➌. You'll pass the Rotunda de los Hombres Ilustres de Jalisco, a tree-shaded square whose central colonnaded rotunda covers a mausoleum containing the remains of 17 of the state of Jalisco's most eminent people. After you leave the museum, turn right and walk three blocks on Calle Liceo to the small **Casa-Museo López Portillo** ➍ and then the **Museo del Periodismo y de las Artes Gráficas** ➎ on Avenida Alcalde.

Backtrack to the Museo Regional, make a left, and head east along Avenida Hidalgo, past the Palacio Legislativo—a former customhouse, tobacco warehouse, and inn that today houses Jalisco's state legislature—and the Palacio de Justicia, which was built in 1588 as part of Guadalajara's first convent and now is the state courthouse. Across Avenida Hidalgo on your right sprawls the Plaza de la Liberación, at the east end of which rises the **Teatro Degollado** ➏. Behind it is the start of the Plaza Tapatía, a five-block-long pedestrian mall lined with shops, trees, and sculpture. At the end, visit the **Instituto Cultural Cabañas** ➐. Then proceed back west to the modernistic Quetzalcóatl Fountain in the center of the plaza outside the institute. (Too heavy for its base, the statue's 5-ton serpent head lies in one of the institute's patios.) Turn left and walk down the stairs to the sprawling Mercado Libertad. Turn left again when you leave the market to reach the **Plaza de los Mariachis** ➑.

Return to Plaza Tapatía, then cut down a block to Calle Morelos, where you'll pass numerous bridal shops. Continue west to the **Templo de San Agustín** ➒. As you leave the church, walk west on Calle Morelos and then turn left onto Avenida Corona. A half block south is the main entrance of the **Palacio de Gobierno** ➓, with its interesting murals. Exit the palacio back onto Avenida Corona and cross the street to the Plaza de Armas, where you can rest on a wrought-iron bench, imagining yourself in the Porfiriato—Mexico's Victorian period—when wealthy *dons* and *doñas* strolled amid the trees and flower beds around the ornately sculpted kiosk, a gift from France in 1910. With the cathedral to your right, you've come full circle back to the north side of the plaza.

What to See

➍ **Casa-Museo López Portillo.** Guadalajara's López Portillo family included prominent writers and politicians, such as an early 20th-century Jalisco governor and his Mexico City–born grandson, José López Portillo, president of Mexico from 1976 to 1982. A series of French Baroque–style rooms in what was once their home display antique furniture and household items, though none from the famous family, oddly enough. There's a spacious interior patio, and a small art gallery in the rear. ⊠ *Calle Liceo 177, at Calle San Felipe, Centro Histórico* ☎ *33/3613–2411 or 33/3613–2435* 🖅 *Free* ☉ *Tues.–Sun. 10–6.*

Arts & Architecture

You can find all kinds of Mexican and international arts in Guadalajara—from the traditional Ballet Folklórico at the Teatro Degollado to rock groups at the Instituto Cultural Cabañas. Galleries and museums around town also offer the best of modern and traditional work. Numerous 16th-century colonial buildings fill the downtown area, connected by a series of large, Spanish-style plazas. There also seems to be a church every block or two—there are 15 in the downtown area alone, all dating from the colonial era. Some have elaborately carved facades, and others conceal ornate Baroque altars and priceless oil paintings behind sober stone exteriors.

Shopping

Blown glass, hand-carved wood furniture, fine leather work, and hand-glazed pottery are local traditions. Two of the most common ceramic techniques are *barro bruñido*, in which the pieces are hand-burnished to a soft sheen, and *petatillo*, in which glaze is applied to earthenware in a fine crosshatch pattern. Guadalajara is also home to a thriving shoe industry. At sprawling markets you can bargain for anything from embroidered shirts to *huaraches* (woven leather sandals), and sleek shopping malls have full-service department stores and trendy boutiques.

Sports

Highly stylized *charreadas*, traditional equestrian events with teams of elegantly clad women and men, are presented weekly, and bullfights are held in October and November. Late August through May, soccer fans crowd Estadio Jalisco (Jalisco Stadium).

★ ▶ ❶ **Catedral.** Begun in 1561 and consecrated in 1618, this focal point of downtown is an intriguing mélange of Baroque, Gothic, and other styles. Its emblematic twin towers replaced the originals, which fell in the earthquake of 1818. Ten of the silver-and-gold altars were gifts from King Fernando VII, donated in appreciation of Guadalajara's financial support of Spain during the Napoleonic Wars. Some of the world's most beautiful *retablos* (altarpieces) hang on the cathedral walls; above the sacristy (often closed to the public) is the priceless 17th-century painting by Bartolomé Esteban Murillo, *The Assumption of the Virgin*. In a loft high above the main entrance is a magnificent late 19th-century French organ, which is played during the afternoon mass on the third Sunday of the month and in May's organ festival. ⊠ *Av. Alcalde between Av. Hidalgo and Calle Morelos, Centro Histórico* ☎ *No phone* ☒ *Free* ⊙ *Daily 8–7.*

❼ **Instituto Cultural Cabañas.** This landmark neoclassical-style cultural center was designed by the famous Spanish architect-sculptor Manuel Tolsá. It was originally used as a shelter for widows, the elderly, and orphans; later it was a home for indigent children. Today its 106 rooms and 23 flower-filled patios house permanent and revolving art exhibitions (ask for an English-speaking guide at the front desk). The central dome and walls of the main chapel display a series of murals painted by José Clemente Orozco in 1938–39, including *The Man of Fire*, widely considered his finest work. In all, there are 57 murals by Orozco, plus many of his smaller paintings, cartoons, and drawings. ⊠ *Calle Cabañas*

FodorsChoice ★

8 *Centro Histórico* ☎ *33/3668–1640* ✉ *$1, free Sun.* ☉ *Tues.–Sat. 10:15–5:45, Sun. 10:15–2:30.*

❺ **Museo del Periodismo y de las Artes Gráficas.** Guadalajara's first printing press was set up on this site in 1792; in 1810, the press was used to print the first 2,000 copies of "El Despertador Americano," which urged would-be Mexicans to join the War of Independence. Today you can see displays of historic newspapers, printing presses, and recording equipment in this fine old mansion, known as the Casa de los Perros because of the two wrought-iron *perros* (dogs) guarding its roof. ⊠ *Av. Alcalde 225, between Calle Reforma and Calle San Felipe, Centro Histórico* ☎ *33/3613–9285 or 33/3613–9286* ✉ *80¢* ☉ *Tues.–Sat. 10–6, Sun. 10:30–3.*

★ ❸ **Museo Regional de Guadalajara.** Constructed as a seminary and public library in 1701, this distinguished building has been home to the Guadalajara Regional Museum since 1918. The first-floor galleries contain artifacts and memorabilia that trace the history of western Mexico from prehistoric times through the Spanish conquest; the center courtyard is often the site of revolving exhibitions. On the second-floor balcony are five 19th-century carriages, including one used by General Porfirio Díaz. The galleries here have an impressive collection of paintings by European and Mexican artists, including Bartolomé Esteban Murillo. Unfortunately the museum has no English-language materials. ⊠ *Calle Liceo 60, Centro Histórico* ☎ *33/3614–9957* ✉ *$3, free Sun.* ☉ *Tues.–Sat. 9–5:45, Sun. 9–5.*

❿ **Palacio de Gobierno.** The initial adobe structure of 1643 was replaced with this churrigueresque and neoclassical stone structure in the 18th century. Within are Jalisco's state government offices and two of José Clemente Orozco's most passionate murals. The one just past the entrance, in the stairwell to the right, depicts a gigantic Father Miguel Hidalgo looming amid shadowy figures—including the pope, Hitler, and Mussolini—representing oppression and slavery. The other mural, in the former state-legislature quarters on the upper level (look for a door marked CONGRESO), portrays Hidalgo, Juárez, and other figures of the 1850s Reform era. ⊠ *Av. Corona between Calle Morelos and Pedro Moreno, Centro Histórico* ☎ *No phone* ☉ *Daily 9–8:45.*

❷ **Palacio Municipal.** City Hall was designed and built in 1952 with an arched facade and interior patios to fit in with neighboring buildings. Inside are colorful murals of the city's founding, painted by Guadalajara native Gabriel Flores. Free walking tours of the Centro Histórico begin here every Saturday morning at 10 (in Spanish only). ⊠ *Av. Hidalgo at Av. Alcalde, Centro Histórico* ☎ *No phone* ☉ *Weekdays 9–8.*

❽ **Plaza de los Mariachis.** This small, triangular plaza just south of the Mercado Libertad was once the perfect place to tip up a beer and experience the most Mexican of music. The beer and music are still here—all night, in fact—but the once picturesque spot is boxed in by a busy street and market on two sides and a run-down neighborhood on the third. It's safest to visit in the day or early evening; mariachi serenades start at about $8 a song. Use the pedestrian overpass from the south side of Plaza Tapatía to avoid heavy traffic. ⊠ *Calz. Independencia Sur, Centro Histórico.*

★ ❻ **Teatro Degollado.** Inaugurated in 1866, this magnificent theater was modeled after Milan's La Scala. Above the Corinthian columns gracing the entrance is a relief depicting Apollo and the nine Muses. Inside, the refurbished theater has kept the traditional red-and-gold color scheme, and the balconies ascend to a multitier dome adorned with Ger-

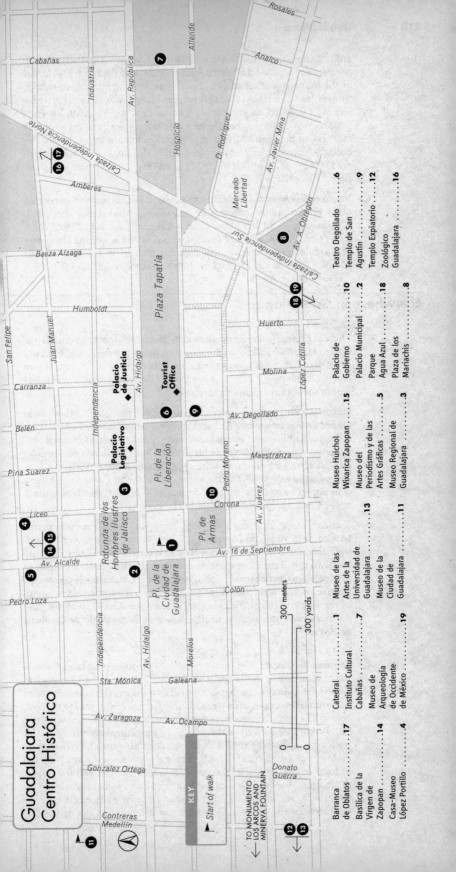

Guadalajara
Centro Histórico

KEY

→ Start of walk

TO MONUMENTO
LOS ARCOS AND
MINERVA FOUNTAIN

300 meters

300 yards

ardo Suárez's depiction of Dante's *Divine Comedy*. The theater is the permanent home for the Jalisco Philharmonic and the Ballet Folklórico of the University of Guadalajara and hosts visiting orchestras, theater troupes, and numerous other companies. According to legend, Guadalajara was founded on the site of what is now the Plaza de los Fundadores, which flanks the theater's east side. A sculpted frieze on the rear wall of the Teatro Degollado depicts the historic event. ⊠ *Av. Degollado between Av. Hidalgo and Calle Morelos, Centro Histórico* ☎ *33/3614–4773 or 33/3613–1115* ⊠ *Free; ticket prices for show vary* ☉ *Weekdays 10–2.*

❾ Templo de San Agustín. One of the city's oldest churches has been remodeled many times since its consecration in 1573, but the sacristy is original. The building to the left of the church, originally an Augustinian cloister, is now the Escuela de Música (School of Music) of the University of Guadalajara. Free recitals and concerts are held on its patio. ⊠ *Calle Morelos 188, at Av. Degollado, Centro Histórico* ☎ *33/3614–5365* ☉ *Daily 8–1 and 5–8.*

Elsewhere in Guadalajara

A Good Tour

There are several noteworthy museums and other sights just outside the Centro Histórico and beyond. Pick a day, pick a direction, and head out exploring. Although you can walk to or between some places, you're better off hopping a cab or a bus as you'll need to walk a great deal within some of the sights themselves.

Heading west from the Catedral, you'll come first to the **Museo de la Ciudad de Guadalajara** ⓫ ▶. Farther west, across Avenida Federalismo, is the beautiful Gothic **Templo Expiatorio** ⓬, and a fine collection of contemporary art in the **Museo de las Artes de la Universidade de Guadalajara** ⓭, across the street. Continue west along Avenida Vallarta to the Monumento Los Arcos and the impressive Minerva Fountain. All these sites are on or near the route of Trolley 400 or 500, which head back to the Centro Histórico on Avenida Hidalgo.

You can easily fill a day exploring Zapopan, including visits to the **Basílica de la Virgen de Zapopan** ⓮, 7 km (4½ mi) northwest of downtown, and the neighboring **Museo Huichol Wixarica de Zapopan** ⓯. If you prefer to spend the day exploring the natural world, head northeast to the **Zoológico Guadalajara** ⓰, a huge zoo, and the **Barranca de Oblatos** ⓱, a canyon with waterfalls, hiking trails, and scenic lookouts. Head south of the Centro Histórico to see the **Parque Agua Azul** ⓲, with its paleontology museum, and the nearby **Museo de Arqueología de Occidente de Mexico** ⓳.

What to See

❿ Barranca de Oblatos. The multipronged 2,000-ft-deep Oblatos Canyon has several hiking trails and the narrow Cola de Caballo waterfall, named for its horse-tail shape. A portion of the canyon complex called Barranca de Huetitán has a steep, winding, 5-km (3-mi) trail to the river below. The trails are less strenuous at Barranca de Oblatos (the name of this entrance as well as the whole canyon); there are no maps, but routes are wide and paved with stones. Both areas can be crowded on mornings and weekends. To get here take a northbound electric bus from in front of the Mercado Libertad; continue to the end and the stop at the Parque Mirador Indepencia if you're only interested in the view; alternatively, get off at the Periférico stop and catch any eastbound bus for Huetitán and Oblatos. Although you can see the Cola de Caballo from the Zoológico Guadalajara, for a closer look catch an Ixcantan-tus-bound bus from Glorieta La Normal, a traffic circle 10 blocks north of the cathedral, and ask to be let off at the *mirador de la cascada* (waterfall viewpoint).

⑭ Basílica de la Virgen de Zapopan. This vast church, with an ornate plateresque facade and *mudéjar* (Moorish) tile dome, was consecrated in 1730. It's known throughout Mexico as the home of La Zapopanita, Our Lady of Zapopan. The 10-inch-high statue is venerated as the source of many miracles in and around Guadalajara. Every October 12, more than a million people crowd the streets leading to the basilica, to which the Virgin is returned after a five-month tour of parish churches throughout the state. Take a taxi here, or take the light rail to Avila Camacho (Line 1), cross the street, and catch Bus 631. ✉ *Av. Hidalgo at Calle Morelos, Zona Zapopan Norte* ☎ *33/3633–0141 or 33/3633–6614* ☉ *Daily 10–8.*

⑲ Museo de Arqueología de Occidente de México. The Archaeological Museum of Western Mexico houses mostly pottery and clay figures made by the ancient peoples of what are now the states of Colima, Jalisco, and Nayarit. A collection of urns in the shape of dogs is especially notable, though the overall presentation at this tiny museum is lacking. Combine a stop here with a visit to Parque Agua Azul, just across the street. ✉ *Av. 16 de Septiembre 889, south of Zona Centro* ☎ *33/3619–0104* 💲 *30¢* ☉ *Tues.–Sun. 9–noon and 5–7:30.*

⑬ Museo de las Artes de la Universidad de Guadalajara. The University of Guadalajara's impressive contemporary art museum is in an exquisite early 20th-century building. The permanent collection of 20th-century drawings and paintings includes several murals by Orozco, done when he returned to Guadalajara at age 53. Revolving exhibitions have contemporary works from Latin America, Europe, and the United States. When leaving, be sure to visit the Templo Expiatorio, across the way. ✉ *Av. López Cotilla 930, at Av. Díaz de Leon, west of Zona Centro* ☎ *33/3134–2222 Ext. 1680* 💲 *Free* ☉ *Tues.–Sun. 10–6.*

▶ ⑪ Museo de la Ciudad de Guadalajara. In a series of rooms surrounding a tranquil interior patio of a spacious, two-story, colonial mansion, you'll find informative artwork, artifacts, and reproductions of documents about the city's development from pre-Hispanic times through the 20th century. Ask about English-language materials at the entrance or in the library upstairs. ✉ *Calle Independencia 684, Zona Centro* ☎ *33/3658–2531 or 33/3658–3706* 💲 *45¢, free Sun.* ☉ *Tues.–Sat. 10–5:30, Sun. 10–2:30.*

★ ⑮ Museo Huichol Wixarica de Zapopan. The Huichol Indians of northern Jalisco and neighboring states of Zacatecas and Nayarit are famous for their fierce independence and their exquisite mosaics made of beads and yarn. This small but well-designed museum next to the Basílica de la Virgen de Zapopan displays many excellent examples of Huichol artworks. Placards in English and Spanish explain tribal history as well as the art. There's a small gift shop at the exit. ✉ *Av. Hidalgo at Calle Morelos, Zona Zapopan Norte* ☎ *33/3636–4430* 💲 *50¢* ☉ *Mon.–Sat. 9:30–1 and 3–5:45, Sun. 10–2.*

⑱ Parque Agua Azul. This popular park has playgrounds, tropical birds in cages, an orchid house, and acres of trees and grass crisscrossed by walking paths. There aren't many butterflies in the huge, geodesic *mariposario* (butterfly sanctuary), but the semitropical garden inside is still quite pleasant. The **Museo de la Paleontología** (✉ Av. Dr. R. Michel 520, south of Zona Centro ☎ 33/3619–7043 💲 40¢ ☉ Tues.–Sun. 10–6), on the park's east side, has plant and animal fossils (including a mammoth skeleton)

THE STRUGGLE OF THE HUICHOL

THE HUICHOL (WEE-CHOL) INDIANS' **TRUE NAME** is the Wirraritari, or "people who populate places of thorny plants." It's a fitting name for this hardy and reclusive group, whose independence has helped them preserve their traditions better than many of Mexico's native communities. Most notable among those traditions in the use of peyote, a hallucinogenic cactus fruit, in complex spiritual ceremonies. Huichol artists also create magical and remarkable "paintings," by pressing colorful beads or yarn onto wood molds smeared with sap.

The Huicholes fiercely resisted Spanish— and later Mexican—intrusion; nowadays, most live in northern Jalisco, southern Nayarit, and Zacatecas, in a remote 592,800-acre reservation established in 1953. In recent years, however, the ownership and boundaries of some Huichol lands, much of it rented out to farmers and cattle breeders, have come under dispute. The conflict has not been peaceful, with allegations of human rights violations perpetrated by Nayarit police as well as by the current "tenants." In the mid-1990s, after a long investigation, Mexico's Human Rights Commission (CEDH) corroborated many of the Huichol allegations, and a recent constitutional amendment affirmed the autonomy of the Huichol and other indigenous communities within Mexico. But problems continue— there remains intense pressure to develop some Huichol lands, and the Mexican Army, in its highly visible war on drugs, has arrested Huicholes coming back from religious pilgrimages in the San Luis Potosi desert, where they collect peyote.

as well as exhibits—some hands-on for kids—on the origin of the planet. Free guided Spanish-language tours are offered at 11, 12:30, and 4:30. (Note that there's no museum entrance from inside Agua Azul; you must walk out and around to the park's north side to get in.) ✉ *Calz. Independencia Sur between González Gallo and Las Palmas, south of Zona Centro* ☎ *33/3619–0332* 🖾 *40¢* ☉ *Tues.–Sun. 10–6.*

⑫ Templo Expiatorio. The striking, Gothic Church of Atonement is perhaps Guadalajara's most beautiful church. Modeled after the Orvieto Cathedral in Italy, it has remarkable stained-glass windows and a lovely rose window above the choir and pipe organ. It's fronted by a large plaza and backed by the outstanding Museo de las Artes de la Universidad de Guadalajara. ✉ *Calle Díaz de León 930, at Av. López Cotilla, west of Zona Centro* ☎ *33/3825–3410* ☉ *Daily 7 AM–10 PM.*

🖐 ⑯ Zoológico Guadalajara. On the edge of the jagged Barranca de Huetitán (Huetitán Canyon), the city's impressive zoo has more than 1,500 animals representing some 360 species. There's a kids' zoo, two aviaries, and a herpetarium with 130 species of reptiles, amphibians, and fish. For 50¢ you can take a guided train tour around part of the grounds. The adjacent Selva Mágica (Magic Jungle) amusement park, has carnival rides and attractions; admission is $1.30. The complex is 6 km (nearly 4 mi) northeast of downtown. ✉ *Paseo del Zoológico 600, off Calz. Independencia, north of Zona Centro* ☎ *33/3674–4488 or 33/3674–3976* 🖾 *$3.15* ☉ *Wed.–Sun. 10–6.*

WHERE TO EAT

You'll find a good deal of variety in Guadalajara: Chinese dishes, Continental delicacies, Argentine-style steaks, fresh seafood. There's a growing contemporary food scene, led mostly by expats and U.S.-trained Mexican chefs, but tradition dies hard here. Look for such savory regional specialties—often served in simple places—as *tortas ahogadas,* literally "drowned tortas," sandwiches doused in warm tomato sauce; *birria,* a spicy stew prepared with goat, lamb, or beef in a light tomato broth; *pozole,* a thick pork and hominy soup; and *carne en su jugo,* consisting of steak bits in a clear spicy broth with bacon, beans, and cilantro, usually served with a side of tiny, grilled, whole onions.

Eateries here tend to be very affordable, and most stay open fairly late and have reliable service. It's advisable to dress well for meals in the more expensive restaurants.

WHAT IT COSTS				
	$$$$	**$$$**	**$$**	**$**	**¢**
AT DINNER	over $25	$15–$25	$10–$15	$5–$10	under $5

Prices are per person for a main course, excluding tax and tip

★ **$$–$$$** ✗ **Pierrot.** Wall-mounted lamps, fresh flowers on each table, and an extensive wine list are among the gracious touches in this quiet French dining room. To start, try one of the mouthwatering pâtés, followed by the trout almandine or the pâté-stuffed chicken breast in tarragon sauce; the menu has beef dishes, too. For dessert consider the mousse or the crêpes suzette. ⊠ *Calle Justo Sierra 2355, Zona Minerva* ☎ *33/3630–2087 or 33/3615–4758* ▤ *MC, V* ⊘ *Closed Sun.*

$–$$$ ✗ **El Farallón de Tepic.** At this open-air establishment beneath a bright-blue awning, you can order fresh *pescado*—usually red snapper or an equally mild fish—grilled with garlic or butter, in classic tomato sauce, breaded, or stuffed with seafood and cheese. The pescado *sarandeado* (Jalisco-style whole barbecued fish stuffed with vegetables) is worth every second of the 30-minute wait. Try the homemade flan for dessert. ⊠ *Av. Niño Obrero 560, Zona Zapopan Sur* ☎ *33/3121–2616 or 33/3121–9616* ▤ *AE, MC, V* ⊘ *No dinner.*

$$ ✗ **La Estancia Gaucha.** In a town that loves Argentine cuisine, this no-nonsense steak house is widely considered the cream of the crop. Among the best cuts here are the *churrasco estancia* (rib eye) and the *bife de chorizo* (essentially New York strip steak). The empanadas are delicious, and there's homemade ravioli for lunch on Sunday. Piano music accompanies dinner Wednesday through Saturday. ⊠ *Av. Niños Héroes 2860, Zona Minerva* ☎ *33/3122–6565 or 33/3122–9985* ▤ *AE, MC, V* ⊘ *No dinner Sun.*

$$ ✗ **Formosa Gardens.** Guadalajara's Asian residents visit Formosa Gardens, which has sister restaurants in Beijing and Taiwan, for the tastes of home: the menu has Chinese, Japanese, and Thai dishes. The Peking duck is crisp and tasty, and the deep-fried orange beef is sweet and tangy. The restaurant is in a beautiful mansion that has several dining rooms with muted orange and yellow color schemes as well as a pleasant garden area. ⊠ *Av. Union 322, Zona Centro* ☎ *33/3615–7415* ▤ *AE, DC, MC, V* ⊘ *No dinner Sun.*

★ **$$** ✗ **Santo Coyote.** With faux waterfalls and walls crammed with folk art, you may feel like you're in Disney World rather than a popular Guadalajara restaurant. (There's even a gift shop.) But this haven of new Mexican cuisine is a favorite among the city's jet-setters. Try the wood-fired roast or grilled *cabrito* (goat) or consider the baby back ribs topped with a tamarind and pepper sauce. Service and presentation are good. ☒ *Calle Lerdo de Tejada 2379, Zona Minerva* ☎ 33/3616–6978 ☰ MC, V.

$–$$ ✕ **Casa Bariachi.** This grand restaurant is a favorite among locals, a place to celebrate with friends and enjoy mariachi bands. Expect waiters as well as diners to sing along. The menu highlights steaks, and the fiesta continues until 3 AM. A bar by the same name and catercorner to the restaurant is also open late. ☒ *Av. Vallarta 2221, between Zona Centro and Zona Minerva* ☎ 33/3615–0029 ☰ AE, MC, V ☉ *Closed Sun.*

★ **$–$$** ✕ **La Destilería.** If you can't make it to the village of Tequila, here's the next best thing: a friendly restaurant–cum–tequila museum that serves decent Mexican fare and 240 varieties of the fiery liquor. Antique photos of tequila distilleries and bilingual plaques explaining the history of tequila line the brick walls. ☒ *Av. México 2916, Zona Minerva* ☎ 33/3640–3110 ☰ AE, MC, V ☉ *No dinner Sun.*

★ **$–$$** ✕ **La Feria.** Mariachis, Mexican folkloric dancing, and dance contests among diners make La Feria festive. Come for a late lunch or appetizers to catch the 3:30 show, or for a late-night dinner to catch the 10 o'-clock show (9 on Sunday). The shrimp tacos are scrumptious, as are the *parilladas* (various grilled meats) for two. After the show, play *lotería* (a type of bingo) for a bottle of tequila or have a parakeet choose your fortune. ☒ *Av. Corona 291, Zona Centro* ☎ 33/3613–1812 or 33/3613–7150 ☰ AE, MC, V.

★ **$–$$** ✕ **Tacos Providencia del Centro.** The tacos here are as tasty as they are unique, but it's much more than a taco joint. In fact, most people come for the excellent steak and the extensive beer and tequila offerings. Better known as La Rinconada for the corner building it occupies, this grand old restaurant has appeared in numerous Mexican movies and TV comedies. Its dining area has arched pillars, high vaulted ceilings, and a giant central fountain. ☒ *Calle Morelos 86, at Plaza Tapatía, Centro Histórico* ☎ 33/3613–9914 or 33/3613–9925 ☰ AE, MC, V.

★ **$–$$** ✕ **La Trattoria.** Guadalajara's top Italian restaurant has a well-deserved reputation as a family place. The menu's best options include spaghetti *frutti di mare* (with seafood) and *scaloppine alla Marsala* (beef medallions with Marsala and mushrooms). The fresh garlic bread is delicious, and all meals include the salad bar. Even with a large dining room and closely spaced tables, lines aren't uncommon; arrive before 8 PM to beat the crowd. ☒ *Av. Niños Héroes 3051, Zona Minerva* ☎ 33/3122–1817 ☰ AE, MC, V.

$ ✕ **La Chata.** Black-and-white photos of old Guadalajara and exquisitely glazed plates adorn the walls of this bustling, casual eatery. Savor the zesty *chiles rellenos* (stuffed peppers), or try one of the spicy roasted meat dishes. Wash it down with a tangy *jugo de lima,* the distinctive lime juice popular throughout Jalisco. La Chata can be especially crowded on weekends, but the line moves quickly. Breakfast is served as well. ☒ *Av. Corona 126, between Av. López Cotilla and Av. Juárez, Zona Centro* ☎ 33/3613–0588 ☰ AE, MC, V.

$ ✕ **Karne Garibaldi.** In the *1996 Guinness Book of World Records,* this Tapatío institution holds the record for the fastest service in the world: 13.5 seconds for a table of six. This lightning service is possible because there's only one thing on the menu: carne en su jugo, that tasty combination of finely diced beef and bacon simmered in a rich beef broth. Served with grilled onions, tortillas, and refried beans mixed with corn, it's a great down-home meal. Don't be put off by the somewhat gritty area surrounding the restaurant. ☒ *Calle Garibaldi 1306, west of Zona Centro* ☎ 33/3826–1286 ☰ AE, MC, V.

★ **$** ✕ **La Pianola.** Enter this restaurant through the left entrance, otherwise you'll end up in the kitchen. The front dining area has good avenue views, the back one is in a large, airy courtyard. Specialties from the varied Mexican menu include pozole and chiles *en nogada*, spicy stuffed chili peppers in a walnut cream sauce. The signature player-piano music accompanies the meal. ⊠ *Av. México 3220, Zona Minerva* ☎ *33/ 3813–1385 or 33/3813–2412* ⊟ *AE, MC, V.*

¢–$ ✕ **Antigüedades Café Bazar del Carmen.** This café's tables are in a corner of the small, peaceful Plaza del Carmen. Not only can you order coffee, tea, and a range of pastries and light lunch items, but you can also browse in the small on-site antiques store. Enjoy *trensas de champignon* (braided bread stuffed with mushrooms), which is served with a small salad. Follow it with cappuccino and a slice of chocolate cake. ⊠ *Calle Jacobo Galvez 45-B, off Av. Juárez, Zona Centro* ☎ *33/ 3658–2266* ⊟ *No credit cards.*

WHERE TO STAY

Hotels run the gamut from older establishments in the Centro Histórico to representatives of the large chains, most of which are on or near Avenida López Mateos Sur, a 16-km (10-mi) strip extending from the Minerva Fountain to the Plaza del Sol shopping center. Several hotels are close to the ExpoGuadalajara convention center.

Call ahead if you're apprehensive about noise levels outside your hotel room; many places are on busy intersections, in which case rooms higher up or in the back tend to be less noisy. If fresh air is important to you, ask if there are balconies, as many hotels have windows that won't open. Also, you can expect hotels in the $$$ and $$$$ categories to have purified-water systems and English-language TV channels among other amenities.

WHAT IT COSTS				
$$$$	**$$$**	**$$**	**$**	**¢**
FOR 2 PEOPLE over $250	$150–$250	$75–$150	$50–$75	under $50

Price categories are assigned based on the range between the least and most expensive standard double rooms in high season based on the European Plan (EP, with no meals) unless otherwise noted. Tax (17%) is extra.

$$$$ 🏨 **Quinta Real.** Stone and brick walls, colonial arches, and objets d'art Fodor's Choice fill public areas of this luxury hotel. Suites are plush, if a bit small, with ★ select neocolonial furnishings, including glass-top writing tables and faux-fireplaces with marble mantelpieces. Bathrooms have marble sinks and bronze fixtures; some suites have sunken hot tubs. Note that junior suites are actually larger (and slightly more expensive) than master suites. The hotel provides free passes to nearby Gold's Gym. ⊠ *Av. México 2727, at Av. López Mateos Norte, Zona Minerva 44680* ☎ *33/3669–0600; 01800/362–1500 toll-free in Mexico* 🖷*33/3669–0601* ⊕*www.quintareal. com* ⇄ *76 suites* ⌂ *Restaurant, in-room data ports, pool, bar, babysitting, concierge, business services, meeting rooms, travel services, nosmoking rooms* ⊟ *AE, DC, MC, V.*

$$$–$$$$ 🏨 **Camino Real.** A 15-minute cab ride from downtown will bring you to the first of Guadalajara's luxury hotels. Guest rooms are large and reasonably well decorated; the glass and marble bathrooms are luxurious. Many rooms and suites surround the pools and gardens, where trios serenade during the excellent Sunday-morning buffet brunch. Rooms in the rear face noisy Avenida Vallarta. ⊠ *Av. Vallarta 5005, Zona Minerva 45040* ☎*33/3134–2424; 01800/903–2100 toll-free in Mexico; 800/ 722–6466 in the U.S.* 🖷 *33/3134–2404* ⊕ *www.caminoreal.com/ guadalajara* ⇄ *195 rooms, 10 suites* ⌂ *2 restaurants, golf privileges,*

Where to Stay & Eat in Guadalajara

Galería de Calzado

Av. Golfo de Cortés

Monumento Los Arcos and Tourist Office

Gran Plaza Guadalajara

Av. Vallarta

Av. Vallarta

Minerva Fountain

Homero
Fideos
Arias
Av. López Mateos Norte
Gómez
V.S. Álvarez
Azuela
S. Díaz
Rivas
Quevedo

San Martín de Porres

P.P. Velázquez

Calz. Lázaro Cárdenas

San Francisco

Circunvalación

San Ernesto
San Juan Bosco
La Reyna
San Agustín
Sta. Beatriz
San Enrique

Av. López Mateos Sur

Av. Guadalupe

Av. Niños Héroes

La Luna
Noche
Nebulosa
Hercules
Atmósfera
Día
Firmamento
Sol

Del Parque

Av. La Aurora

Juan Epeyac

de Zumárraga

Valeriano

Av. Chapalita

Merced

Eclipse
Hayo
Cosmos

San Vicente de Paul el Carmen

Ubilete
Av. del Árbol
12 de Diciembre
Av. de las Rosas

Plaza del Angel

Parque de las Estrellas

Calz. Láz.

Cuauhtémoc
Tonallan
Aztlán
Tlahuac
Av. Xochitl
Tezozomoc

Av. del Niño Obrero

Plancarte

Tizoc

Av. Plaza del Sol

Av. López Mateos Sur

Av. Mariano Otero

Expo Guadalajara

Av. de las Rosas

La Pradera

Las Estrellas

Av. Arboleda

Elote

Betab
Calaba
Piñ

Moctezuma

Mixcoatl

Plaza del Sol

Turquesa

Club Hípico

Av. Topacio

Diamante

0   600 meters
0   600 yards

Av. C

putting green, tennis court, 4 pools, gym, bar, baby-sitting, playground, concierge, no-smoking rooms = *AE, DC, MC, V.*

$$$ 🏨 **Hilton.** Adjacent to the ExpoGuadalajara convention center, the Hilton is a premier business destination. Although it lacks character, it has modern furnishings and many business services, including a multilingual staff, a well-equipped business center, and an executive floor (a stay here gets you free breakfast in a private dining area). There are also excellent spa facilities. ⊠ *Av. de las Rosas 2933, Zona Cruz del Sur 44540* 🕿 *33/ 3678–0505; 01800/003–1400 toll-free in Mexico; 800/445–8667 in the U.S.* 🖷 *33/3678–0511* ⊕ *www.guadalajarahilton.com* ➲ *402 rooms, 20 suites* ⌕ *2 restaurants, in-room data ports, golf privileges, pool, gym, hair salon, massage, spa, bar, concierge floor, business services, meeting rooms, no-smoking rooms* = *AE, DC, MC, V.*

$$$ 🏨 **Presidente Inter-Continental.** A busy hotel with a mirrored facade and a 12-story atrium lobby, the Inter-Continental attracts sophisticated business clientele. For the best city view, request a room on an upper floor facing the Plaza del Sol shopping center. A Tane silver shop is one of the many on-site stores, and the health club is one of the city's best. ⊠ *Av. López Mateos Sur 3515, Zona Plaza del Sol 45050* 🕿 *33/ 3678–1234; 01800/904–4400 or 01800/327–0200 toll-free in Mexico* 🖷 *33/3678–1222* ⊕ *www.interconti.com* ➲ *379 rooms, 30 suites* ⌕ *2 restaurants, coffee shop, in-room data ports, golf privileges, pool, health club, massage, sauna, spa, steam room, bar, shops, baby-sitting, concierge floor, business services, meeting rooms, airport shuttle, car rental* = *AE, DC, MC, V.*

$$–$$$ 🏨 **Crowne Plaza Guadalajara.** Well-tended gardens surround a large, inviting pool, bringing a bit of nature to this hotel near Plaza del Sol. Public areas have a tasteful mix of antiques and reproductions. Rooms have marble baths and lots of natural light; those in the tower have city views, and those in the low-rise wing surround the pool and gardens. (Note that this hotel caters to families, so rooms near the playground area can be loud.) Plaza Club rooms include a buffet breakfast in their rates. The excellent top-floor restaurant is the only one in Guadalajara with a panoramic view. ⊠ *Av. López Mateos Sur 2500, Zona Plaza del Sol 45050* 🕿 *33/3634–1034; 01800/365–5500 toll-free in Mexico* 🖷 *33/3631–9393* ⊕ *www.crownegdl.com.mx* ➲ *290 rooms, 4 suites* ⌕ *3 restaurants, in-room data ports, golf privileges, 2 tennis courts, pool, gym, hair salon, bar, shops, baby-sitting, playground, concierge floor, business services, car rental, kennel, no-smoking floor* = *AE, DC, MC, V.*

★ $$–$$$ 🏨 **Fiesta Americana.** The dramatic glass facade of this high-rise faces the Minerva Fountain and Los Arcos monument, on the city's west side. Four glass-enclosed elevators ascend dizzyingly above the 14-story atrium lobby to the enormous guest rooms, which have modern furnishings, marble bathrooms, and great views. The lobby bar has live music every night but Sunday. The business center is extraordinarily well equipped. ⊠ *Av. Aurelio Aceves 225, Zona Minerva 44100* 🕿 *33/ 3825–3434; 01800/504–5000 toll-free in Mexico* 🖷 *33/3630–3725* ⊕ *www.fiestamericana.com* ➲ *352 rooms, 39 suites* ⌕ *Restaurant, in-room data ports, 2 tennis courts, pool, gym, hair salon, bar, shops, baby-sitting, concierge, business services, meeting rooms, car rental, no-smoking floor* = *AE, DC, MC, V.*

★ $$ 🏨 **Hotel de Mendoza.** This refined downtown hotel is convenient—on a quiet side street a block from the Teatro Degollado—and elegant, with its impressive postcolonial architecture. Low, beamed ceilings, hand-carved furniture and doors, and wrought-iron railings decorate public areas and the clean, comfortable rooms. Standards are a bit small, so suites are worth the extra money. Some rooms and suites have balconies overlooking the small but inviting courtyard pool, beside the hotel's acclaimed international restaurant. ✉ *Calle Venustiano Carranza 16, Zona Centro 44100* ☎ *33/3613–4646; 01800/361–2600 toll-free in Mexico* 🖷 *33/3613–7310* ⊕ *www.demendoza.com.mx* ↪ *87 rooms, 17 suites* ♨ *Restaurant, pool, meeting rooms* ⊟ *AE, DC, MC, V.*

$$ 🏨 **Hotel Plaza Diana.** Mexican and European travelers favor this hotel two blocks from the Minerva Fountain. The white stucco lobby adjoins a small lounge and busy restaurant. Standard-size rooms have white walls and ceilings and bright, patterned fabrics; the quietest rooms are on the upper floors in the rear. Some suites have saunas. ✉ *Circunvalación Agustín Yáñez 2760, Zona Minerva 44100* ☎ *33/3540–9700; 01800/024–1001 toll-free in Mexico* 🖷 *33/3540–9715* ⊕ *www.hoteldiana.com.mx* ↪ *136 rooms, 15 suites* ♨ *Restaurant, bar, airport shuttle, travel services* ⊟ *AE, DC, MC, V.*

$$ 🏨 **Santiago de Compostela.** A converted 19th-century building across from the Parque San Francisco has simple, modern accommodations. More expensive rooms face the park and have tall, narrow windows with iron balconies. Suites have Jacuzzis. The open-air pool overlooks Guadalajara's south side from a fifth-floor terrace. ✉ *Av. Colón 272, Centro Histórico 44100* ☎ *33/3613–8880; 01800/365–5300 toll-free in Mexico* 🖷 *33/3658–1925* ↪ *89 rooms, 5 suites* ♨ *Restaurant, pool, bar, shop* ⊟ *AE, DC, MC, V.*

$–$$ 🏨 **Hotel Francés.** Guadalajara's oldest hotel, dating from 1610, is also a national monument. Stone columns and colonial arches surround a pleasant three-story atrium lobby and dining area, with a polished marble fountain and an old-time gated elevator. The charm, however, stops outside the doors to the guest rooms, where threadbare linens, dingy bathrooms, and drafts are serious drawbacks. Rooms facing Calle Maestranza have tiny 17th-century balconies, but they also have street noise. ✉ *Calle Maestranza 35, Centro Histórico 44100* ☎ *33/3613–1190; 33/3613–0936; 01800/718–5309 toll-free in Mexico* 🖷 *33/3658–2831* ⊕ *www.hotelfrances.com* ↪ *50 rooms, 10 suites* ♨ *Restaurant, fans, bar, dance club, car rental* ⊟ *AE, MC, V.*

$ 🏨 **Hotel Cervantes.** Marbles floors and tinted windows add touches of the modern to the lobby. Upstairs, however, the comfortable, carpeted rooms are adorned with old-time photos and bright Mexican-style linens—a nod to the traditional. All rooms have sofa beds; suites also have terraces. There are several pastry shops and bookstores nearby, and the Centro Histórico is just a short walk away. ✉ *Calle Priciliano Sánchez 442, Zona Centro* ☎ *33/3613–6686 or 33/3613–6816* ⊕ *www.hotelcervantes.com.mx* ↪ *95 rooms, 5 suites* ♨ *Restaurant, bar, pool, laundry service, parking, meeting rooms* ⊟ *AE, DC, MC, V.*

$ 🏨 **Hotel Posada Guadalajara.** Don't confuse this colonial-style hotel with the Hotel Guadalajara Plaza just down the street. The clean, comfortable rooms here have carved-wood furniture and open onto breezy walkways with wrought-iron rails; ask for a room upstairs and away from the street. A courtyard has a small pool with a stone fountain in the middle, and a rooftop patio has lawn chairs and a nice view. The posada occasionally welcomes visiting sports teams, so evenings here can be raucous. ✉ *Av. López Mateos Sur 1280, between Zona Minerva and Zona Plaza del Sol 45040* ☎ *33/3121–2022 or 33/3121–2424* 🖷 *33/3122–1834* ⊕ *www.posadaguadalajara.com.mx* ↪ *152 rooms, 18 suites* ♨ *Restaurant, pool, bar* ⊟ *AE, MC, V.*

¢–$ 🏨 **San Francisco Plaza.** On a quiet side street, this attractive two-story colonial-style hotel faces a small triangular plaza. Potted palms and geraniums surround a gurgling stone fountain in the pleasant courtyard sitting area. High ceilings and arches, and friendly service, make up for the somewhat worn furnishings. Some rooms have terraces looking on to a courtyard. ✉ *Calle Degollado 267, Centro Histórico 44100* ☎ *33/*

3613–8954 or 33/3613–8971 📠 33/3613–3257 ⇖ 74 rooms, 2 suites
⌂ Restaurant, laundry service ⊟ AE, MC, V.

NIGHTLIFE & THE ARTS

A string of nightspots generally geared to the under-30 crowd lines Avenida Vallarta. The whole Centro area has a lot of nightlife. Numerous modern, multiscreen movie theaters play current Hollywood films—most in English with Spanish subtitles—plus a sprinkling of Mexican, Latin American, and European movies. Tickets are generally $4–$5 (half that price on Wednesday). The major malls—Magno Centro, Gran Plaza, and Plaza del Sol—all have theaters.

Guadalajara is an active cultural and performing-arts center, with excellent local talent and well-known artists and entertainers from abroad. The U.S. and Canadian communities around Lago de Chapala maintain a schedule of English-language cultural events. Pick up the free publications *Ocio* and *InformArte* at any tourist office for listings.

Nightlife

BARS ★ Don't miss **La Fuente** (✉ Calle Pino Suarez, Zona Centro ☎ no phone), perhaps the most charming and unpretentious cantina in town. Opened in 1921 and moved to its present site in 1950, the bar attracts business types, intellectuals, and blue-collar workers, all of whom come for the cheap drinks, animated conversation, and live traditional music. Above the bar, look for an old bicycle caked in dust. It's been here since 1957, when, legend has it, one of a long list of famous people (most say it was the father of local newspaper baron Jesus Alvarez del Castillo) arrived without any money, and left the bike to pay for his drinks.

Live tropical tunes Wednesday through Saturday after 10 draw crowds to **Cubilete** (✉ General Río Seco 9, Centro Histórico ☎ 33/3613–2096). A hot spot in town is the **Hard Rock Cafe** (✉ Centro Magno mall, Av. Vallarta 2425, 1st floor, Zona Minerva ☎ 33/3616–4560). Live bands play acoustic music Wednesday through Saturday from 8:30 PM to 10 PM, and then play rock, naturally, from 10 PM until 2 AM. The Fiesta Americana hotel's sleek **Lobby Bar** (✉ Av. Aurelio Aceves 225, Zona Minerva ☎ 33/3825–3434) has live, low-key entertainment—usually jazz—Monday through Saturday after 8.

For some local color, stop at **La Maestranza** (✉ Calle Maestranza 179, Zona Centro ☎ 33/3613–5878), a renovated 1940s cantina full of bullfighting memorabilia. After 9 Tuesday through Sunday, patrons cluster around the small stage at **La Peña Cuicacalli** (✉ Av. Niños Héroes 1988, at Suarez traffic circle, Zona Centro ☎ 33/3825–4690). There's *rock en español* on Tuesday and folk music from Mexico, Latin America, and Spain most other nights.

Dance Clubs

Maxim's (✉ Hotel Francés, Calle Maestranza 35, Zona Centro ☎ 33/3613–1190 or 33/3613–0936) is open until the wee hours and is one of the better downtown discos. Well-dressed professional types 25 and older go one floor up to **El Mito** (✉ Centro Magno mall, Av. Vallarta 2425, 2nd floor, Zona Minerva ☎ 33/3615–7246), where there's '70s and '80s music Wednesday, Friday, and Saturday from 10 PM to 4 AM. Wednesday is ladies night, with free entry for women, a $17 entry for men, and an open bar for everyone.

Salón Veracruz (✉ Calle Manzano 486, behind the Hotel Carlton, Zona Centro ☎ 33/3613–4422) is a spartan, old-style dance hall where a 15-

piece band keeps hundreds of hoofers moving to Colombian *cumbia;* Dominican merengue; and *danzón,* a waltzlike dance invented in Cuba and favored in Veracruz. It's open Wednesday to Sunday 10 PM to 3:30 AM. You can dance most of the night to popular Latin and European music at the multilevel **Tropigala** (✉ Av. López Mateos Sur 2188, Zona Minerva ☎ 33/3122–5553 or 33/3122–7903), which is across from the Plaza del Sol mall.

The Arts

Dance

Ballet Folklórico of the University of Guadalajara. The university's internationally acclaimed troupe offers traditional Mexican folkloric dances and music in the Teatro Degollado every Thursday at 8:30 PM and Sunday at 10 AM. ☎ 33/3614–4773 ✉ *$2.50–$11.*

Performance Venues

Ex-Convento del Carmen. Classical music performances are held in the former convent Tuesday at 8:30 PM; Wednesday is dedicated to book presentations or poetry readings. Friday and Saturday at 8:30 PM and Sunday at 6 PM see theatrical presentations. There's also a spacious art gallery and bookshop. ✉ *Av. Juárez 638, Centro Histórico* ☎ *33/ 3614–7184.*

Instituto Cultural Cabañas. Large-scale theater, dance, and musical performances take place on a patio here. The Tolsá Chapel hosts more intimate events, and subtitled English-language films are often shown in the theater. Exhibitions of both Mexican and foreign art are on display, and there are free art classes. ✉ *Calle Cabañas 8, Zona Centro* ☎ *33/ 3668–1640.*

Plaza de Armas. The State Band of Jalisco, the Municipal Band, and sometimes even the Philharmonic play at the bandstand on Tuesday, Thursday, and Sunday evenings around 6:30. ✉ *Av. Corona between Calle Morelos and Pedro Moreno, across from Palacio de Gobierno, Zona Centro.*

Teatro Degollado. Nationally and internationally famous artists perform here year-round. The refurbished velvet seats are comfortable, the acoustics are excellent, and the central air-conditioning can be a treat. ✉ *Calle Degollado between Av. Hidalgo and Calle Morelos, Zona Centro* ☎ *33/ 3614–4773 or 33/3613–1115.*

Symphony

Orquesta Filarmónica de Jalisco. Conducted by Maestro Guillermo Salvador, performances take place Sunday at 12:30 PM and Friday night at 8:30 at the Teatro Degollado. ☎ *33/3658–3812 or 33/3658–3819* ✉ *$2–$12.*

SPORTS & THE OUTDOORS

Bullfighting

Corridas (bullfights) are held on Sunday at 4:30 from October to December at **Plaza Nuevo Progreso** (✉ Calle M. Pirineos 1930 and Calz. Independencia Nte., north of Zona Centro, across from Estadio Jalisco, which is 5 km (3 mi) northeast ☎ 33/3637–9982 or 33/3651–8506) will get you there). Tickets are sold for the *sol* (sunny) or *sombra* (shady) side of the bullring, and prices are $9–$60. You can buy tickets at the bullring or at the bullring's booth in Plaza México. *Novilleros* (apprentice matadors) work the cape many mornings between 7 AM and 1 PM, and it doesn't cost anything to watch them practice.

Charreadas

Charreadas take place year-round at the **Lienzo Charros de Jalisco** (✉ Av. Dr. R. Michel 577, south of Zona Centro ☎ 33/3619–0315 or 33/3619–3232), next to Parque Agua Azul, Sunday at noon. The competitors participate in 10 equestrian and roping events, mariachis or *bandas* (brass bands) perform during breaks, and food and drinks are available. Admission is about $2.

Golf

Guadalajara's top golf clubs—El Palomar and Santa Anita—are for members only. Hotels such as the Hilton, Camino Real, Crowne Plaza, and Inter-Presidente have arrangements that allow guests to play. If you've got an afternoon flight, perhaps you can get in a round at the **Atlas Chapalita Golf Club** (✉ Carretera Guadalajara-Chapala, Km 6.5, El Salto ☎ 33/3689–2620 or 33/3689–2752), an 18-hole, par-72 course designed by Joe Finger that's on the way to the airport. The greens fee is $47. Tuesday and Thursday are the least-crowded days at **Las Cañadas Country Club** (✉ Av. Bosques San Isidro 777, Zapopan ☎ 33/3685–0285 or 33/3685–0412), a rolling, 18-hole course in an exclusive area of the Zapopan district. Greens fees are $50–$55.

Guadalajara's premier golf course is at the private **El Palomar Country Club** (✉ Paseo del la Cima 437 ☎ 33/3684–4434 or 33/3684–4436). On a hill outside town, this 18-hole, par-72 course designed by Victor Langham is blissfully removed from the city's din and has several challenging holes and water features. To play you'll need guest passes; check with your hotel. Just down the hill from El Palomar is the **Club de Golf Santa Anita** (✉ Carretera a Morelia, Km 6.5 ☎ 33/3686–0321), a private club with an excellent, 18-hole, 6,800-yard course—the region's longest. See if your concierge can arrange guest passes for you to play here.

Health Clubs

There are three convenient locations of **Gold's Gym** (✉ Av. Vallarta 1791, between Zona Centro and Zona Minerva ☎ 33/3630–2221 ✉ Av. Xóchitl 4203, Zona Plaza del Sol ☎ 33/3647–0420 ✉ Av. Niños Héroes 2851, southwest of Zona Centro ☎ 33/3647–4960). Although each has weights, machines, and classes, the Vallarta location is closest to the Zona Centro and has the best hours (weekdays 6 AM–11 PM, Saturday 8–5, and Sunday 8–3), and the Xóchitl branch is the best equipped, with a pool, a climbing wall, and a basketball court, among other things. The smaller Niños Héroes location is for women only. Guest passes cost about $8 a day. The health club at the **Presidente Inter-Continental** (✉ Av. López Mateos Sur 3515, Zona Plaza del Sol ☎ 33/3678–1227) hotel allows nonguests to use its facilities for about $12 a day. It has exercise equipment, a heated pool, and a spa, and it's open daily 5:30 AM–11 PM.

Soccer

Two professional teams and a university team play at **Estadio Jalisco** (✉ Calle Siete Colinas 1772 at Calz. Independencia Nte., Zona Huentitán ☎ 33/3637–0301 or 33/3637–0299) including one of Mexico's favorite teams, Las Chivas (The She-Goats) de Guadalajara, who generally play on Sunday. The two regular seasons run January through April or May and July through December. Tickets cost $1.50–$26.

Tennis

Nonguests are allowed to use courts at various top hotels for a small fee. Most places have some equipment for rent, but it's best to bring your own. The court at the **Camino Real** (⊠ Av. Vallarta 5005, Zona Minerva ☎ 33/3134–2424) hotel is open daily 7 AM–10 PM. You can play on the two courts at the **Crowne Plaza Guadalajara** (⊠ Av. López Mateos Sur 2500, Zona Minerva ☎ 33/3634–1034) daily from 7 AM until it gets dark. The **Fiesta Americana** (⊠ Av. Aurelio Aceves 225, Zona Minerva ☎ 33/3825–3434) has two courts.

Water Parks

Approximately 50 km (31 mi) southwest of Guadalajara are two water parks with thermal pools and lots of entertainment for adults and children. You can readily reach them by taxi, although buses also run from the old or new bus terminals to the village of Villa Corona. **Agua Caliente** (⊠ Carretera a Barra de Navidad, Km 56, Villa Corona ☎ 33/3778–0022 or 33/3778–0784) has a large wave pool and water slides, thermal pools, gardens, and restaurants. All of the facilities are open on weekends; some are closed midweek. Admission is $2. The entrance fee to the intimate **Chimulco** (⊠ Camino Real, Km ½, Villa Corona ☎ 33/3778–0014) is $4. It has a thermal pool, water slides, boat rides, and a large children's play area.

SHOPPING

Store hours tend to be Monday through Saturday 9 or 10 until 8, and Sunday 10–2; some shops close during lunch, usually 2–4 or 2–5, and others close all day on Sunday. Guadalajara now has more than 50 malls; their stores generally stay open during lunch and on weekends. *Tianguis* (street markets) take place every day throughout the city. If you're interested in high-quality arts and crafts as well as home furnishings be sure to head for the satellite communities of Tlaquepaque and Tonalá.

Serious art-, crafts-, and antiques-lovers may want to consult with Roberto Alvarado of **El Antiquario** (⊠ Calle Argentina 73, ½ block off Av. Vallarta, Zona Minerva ☎ 33/3827–1990 ⊕ www.elantiquario. com). Alvarado has devoted decades of his life to the art and antiques business, and he runs personalized buying tours for around $100 a day. One week's advance notice is requested, although he can sometimes accommodate requests made on shorter notice.

The state-government-run **Instituto de Artesanía Jalisciense** (⊠ Calz. González Gallo 20 at Calz. Independencia Sur, south of Zona Centro ☎ 33/3619–4664), on the northeast side of Parque Agua Azul, has a wide selection of the exquisite blown glass and hand-glazed pottery typical of Jalisco artisans. You'll also find leather goods, wood furniture, silver, and Huichol art. Note that prices here are fixed.

Malls

Centro Magno. A number of upscale boutiques and bistros, along with a large cineplex, a dance club, and a Hard Rock Cafe, make this center a trendy shopping and dining spot. It's a few blocks east of the Minerva Fountain. ⊠ *Av. Vallarta 2425, Zona Minerva* ☎ *33/3630–1113 or 33/3630–1776.*

Galería del Calzado. The 60 stores in this west-side complex all sell high-quality shoes and accessories. Prices are often lower prices than those in the States. ⊠ *Av. México 3225, Zona Minerva* ☎ *33/3647–6422.*

La Gran Plaza. This sleek glass-and-steel structure contains 334 commercial spaces, 14-theater cineplex, and a large food court. It's just east of the Camino Real hotel. ✉ *Av. Vallarta 3959, Zona Minerva* ☎ *33/3122–3004.*

Plaza del Sol. One of the city's largest malls sprawls like a park, with 270 commercial spaces, outdoor patios, trees and garden areas, and parking for 2,100 cars. It's across from the Presidente Inter-Continental hotel. ✉ *Av. López Mateos Sur 2375, at Mariano Otero, Zona Minerva* ☎ *33/3121–5950.*

Markets

El Baratillo. This flea market encompasses 30 city blocks lined with stalls, tents, and blankets, all piled high with new, used, and antique merchandise. It operates on Sunday from 7 to 5. ✉ *On and around Calle Esteban Loera, some 15 blocks east of Mercado Libertad, east of Zona Centro.*

Mercado Libertad. What's commonly known as the Mercado San Juan de Dios covers three square blocks and is one of Latin America's largest enclosed markets. Don't be intimidated by its grubby brick exterior; the inside is well lit and enjoyable, albeit a bit cramped. Browse through more than 1,000 stalls selling everything from clothing and crafts to live animals and gold watches. It's a particularly good place to shop for leather shoes and sandals as well as typical silver jewelry. The hours are daily 10 to 8. ✉ *Calz. Independencia Sur, use pedestrian bridge from south side of Plaza Tapatía, Zona Centro.*

SIDE TRIPS FROM GUADALAJARA

As interesting and enjoyable as Guadalajara can be, getting out is just as fun. You can shop for crafts in Tlaquepaque and Tonalá, explore the Lago de Chapala region, or unlock the secrets of Mexican firewater in Tequila.

Tlaquepaque & Tonalá

For inveterate shoppers, a combined visit to the crafts meccas of Tlaquepaque and Tonalá makes a perfect day trip from Guadalajara. If you really want to shop till you drop, there are at least two good bed-and-breakfasts in Tlaquepaque, a charming town that's reminiscent of but less congested and more picturesque than Guadalajara. If you prefer a more tranquil base of operations, consider staying in Tlaquepaque and taking one or more day trips into Guadalajara, only 15–20 minutes away by cab.

Tlaquepaque

7 km (4½ mi) southeast of downtown Guadalajara.

Tlaquepaque is known throughout Mexico as an arts-and-crafts center. Among its offerings are intricate blown-glass miniatures; exquisite pottery; jewelry, silver, and copper ware; leather and hand-carved wood furniture; and handwoven clothing. More than 300 shops—many of which are run by families with centuries-old traditions of workmanship—line pedestrian malls and plazas in this charming town.

The community's craft heritage began with the distinctive decorated pottery fashioned by the Tonaltecan Indians, who lived in the area in the mid-16th century. After local authorities met here to sign a regional proclamation of independence from Spain in 1821, the village emerged from obscurity as wealthy Guadalajara residents began to build palatial summer houses—many of which have been restored and now house shops and restaurants. As more people came to purchase the pottery and intricate glass creations (glassblowing was introduced from Europe in 1870), weavers, jewelers, and wood-carvers also arrived and built workshops.

In 1973 downtown Tlaquepaque underwent a major renovation, the highlight of which was the creation of a wide pedestrian mall, Calle Independencia. More shops line Calle Juárez, a block south, as well as many side streets.

A GOOD WALK   Begin your tour near the west end of pedestrian-only Calle Independencia, at the **Museo Regional de la Cerámica** ⟨20⟩ ▶, with its modest but worthwhile collection of regional pottery. Walk east on Calle Independencia for three blocks. Along the way you can admire the contemporary ceramics at Galería Sergio Bustamante or the Baroque-style statues and wood-and-gilt altarpieces at Agustín Parra Diseño Novohispano. A block farther along is the lively main plaza; after visiting the modest **Templo Parroquial de San Pedro Apóstal** ⟨21⟩, walk north on Calle Priciliano Sánchez to the excellent **Museo del Premio Nacional de la Cerámica Pantaleon Pandura** ⟨22⟩. You'll pass Folklor Gastronómico on the way to the museum; stop in for a delicious comida corrida, or return to the plaza for a more festive meal and a drink at El Parián.

WHAT TO SEE

⟨22⟩

FodorśChoice
★

Museo del Premio Nacional de la Cerámica Pantaleon Pandura. The name of this museum honors Pantaleon Pandura, the father of modern ceramics in Jalisco. Winning pieces from Tlaquepaque's national ceramics competition, held every June, are displayed here. The items fill several rooms surrounding an interior courtyard and are truly remarkable—from huge, intricately painted urns to tediously constructed nativity scenes. The museum offers guided tours in English or Spanish and can arrange a sculpting workshop (with free clay) if you give the staff a day's notice. ⊠ *Calle Priciliano Sánchez at Calle Flórida* ☎ *33/3639–5646, 33/3635–1089, or 33/3659–2858 Ext. 217* ✆ *Free* ⊙ *Tues.–Sat. 10–6.*

▶ ⟨20⟩ **Museo Regional de la Cerámica.** Exhibits at this museum, which is in a colonial mansion, explain the evolution of ceramic wares in the Atemajac Valley during the 20th century. Although the presentation isn't always strong, the displays do enlighten you (in English and Spanish) about the six most common processes used by local ceramics artisans, including bruñido, which involves polishing large urns with smoothed chunks of *pirita* (a mineral). ⊠ *Calle Independencia 237* ☎ *33/3635–5404* 🖾 *Free* ◷ *Mon.–Sat. 10–6, Sun. 10–3.*

㉑ **Templo Parroquial de San Pedro Apóstal.** The Franciscan friars who founded this tiny parish church during the Spanish Conquest named it after the apostle San Pedro de Analco. In keeping with the Mexican custom of adding to the town's name the name of its patron saint, Tlaquepaque was officially changed to San Pedro Tlaquepaque in 1915. The altars of Our Lady of Guadalupe and the Sacred Heart of Jesus are intricately carved in silver and gold. ⊠ *Calle Guillermo Prieto at Calle Morelos, bordering main plaza* ☎ *33/3635–1001* ◷ *Daily 7 AM–9 PM.*

need a break?   El Parián. When you're ready for lunch or a drink, head to this enormous, partly covered cantina diagonal from the main plaza. It's in a onetime marketplace that dates from 1883; for a few dollars the local mariachis will treat you to a song or two as you sip a margarita or *cazuela*, a traditional drink made of fruit and tequila and served in a ceramic pot. ⊠ *Jardín Hidalgo* ☎ *33/3659–2362.*

WHERE TO EAT   ✕ **Casa Fuerte.** Dine on such delicious Mexican dishes as chicken stuffed
$–$$ with *huitlacoche* (a corn fungus that's Mexico's answer to the truffle) and shrimp in tamarind sauce. There are tables on the sidewalk or on a patio with palms and a fountain. ⊠ *Calle Independencia 224* ☎ *33/ 3639–6481* 🖾 *AE, MC, V.*

$ ✕ **El Abajeño.** Quality Mexican specialties are served on the tree-shaded patio of this converted hacienda. Good bets include *carnitas* (shredded pork) or *filete tapado* (cheese-topped fillet of beef) for two. Mariachi music starts at 3:30 most days, and there are Mexican dance performances beginning at 4:30 on weekends. ⊠ *Calle Juárez 231* ☎ *33/3635–9015 or 33/3635–9097* 🖾 *MC, V.*

¢   ✕ **Folklor Gastronómico.** Only open on weekday afternoons, this excellent little restaurant serves homemade *comida corridas* (lunch specials) in a peaceful courtyard. The menu changes daily but always includes soup or rice, a main dish, a dessert, and an *agua fresca*. Proceeds support a local ballet folklórico group, which practices in the back—hence the name and the short hours—and whose members help out with the service. ⊠ *Calle Priciliano Sánchez 113* ☎ *33/3635–3314* 🖾 *No credit cards.*

WHERE TO STAY   🛏 **Quinta Don José.** This B&B is a labor of love for the young Ameri-
$ can couple that owns, operates, and continues to improve it. The location is ideal, just blocks from the main plaza and shopping area. Rooms vary in size and in the amount of natural light they have—look at a few before you decide. Suites face the pool, and are spacious if a bit dark. The master suite has wonderful tile work and a whirlpool bath. The hearty breakfasts are served in an inner courtyard. ⊠ *Av. Reforma 139, 45500* ☎ *33/3635–7522; 01800/777–2468 toll-free in Mexico; 800/537–9567 in the U.S. or Canada* 🖨 *33/3659–9315* ⊕ *www.quintadonjose.com* 🛏 *6 rooms, 5 suites* ⚡ *Pool, bar, laundry service* 🖾 *AE, MC, V* ⫶O⫶ *BP.*

$ 🛏 **La Villa del Ensueño.** Though it's a 10-minute walk from the center of Tlaquepaque, this intimate B&B is still near the town's fabulous shopping. The restored 19th-century hacienda has thick white adobe walls, exposed beam ceilings, and plants in huge unglazed pots. Smokers should request a room with private balcony, as smoking isn't allowed inside. ⊠ *Florida 305, 45500* ☎ *33/3635–8792* 🖨 *33/3659–6152* ⊕ *www.*

mexonline.com/ensueno.htm ⋈ *14 rooms, 4 suites* ⟁ *2 pools, bar, no-smoking rooms* ⊟ *AE, MC, V* ⓄⒾ *BP.*

SHOPPING Behind the doors of **Agustín Parra Diseño Novohispano** (⊠ Calle Independencia 158 ☎ 33/3657–8530 or 33/3657–0316) is a mystical gallery and shop of carved wooden pieces and ceramic figurines. Influenced by the unique Baroque style of 17th-century New Spain, artist Agustín Parra creates everything from ornate tables and doors to religious icons. **Bazar Hecht** (⊠ Calle Juárez 162 ☎ 33/3659–0205) is one of several excellent stores on Juárez, one of the less-trafficked side streets with great shops and restaurants. The Hecht family is known throughout Mexico for its high-quality, ornately sculpted tables, armoires, and chairs.

Color seems to explode at **La Casa Canela** (⊠ Calle Independencia 258 ☎ 33/3635–3717 or 33/3657–1343). Each of its more than 24 rooms is filled with vivid papier-mâché flowers, finely glazed pottery, and elegant furniture. All the rooms surround a courtyard filled with tropical blooms and life-size statues. Free tequila and snacks are served on Saturday. Sergio Bustamante's work is found in galleries throughout the world, but you can purchase his magical sculptures or silver- and gold-plated jewelry for less at **Galería Sergio Bustamante** (⊠ Calle Independencia 238 ☎ 33/3639–5519; 33/3659–7110; 33/3657–8354; or 01800/024–2727 toll-free in Mexico). The window displays don't do justice to this artist's creations, especially the large ceramic and bronze figures.

FodorśChoice
★

Tonalá
8 km (5 mi) east of Tlaquepaque.

One of the region's oldest pueblos, quiet but prosperous Tonalá is a place of dusty cobblestone streets and stucco-covered adobe houses. The village was both the pre-Hispanic capital of the Atemajac Valley Indians and the capital of New Spain when Captain Juan de Oñate moved Guadalajara here in 1532. Within three years, however, Indians and a lack of water forced the Spaniards out.

Although it's been swallowed by ever-expanding Guadalajara, Tonalá remains homey, independent, and industrious. Municipal officials estimate that more than 6,000 artisans live and work here. Indeed, much of the ceramics and pottery sold in Tlaquepaque (and in many other parts of the world) are made in Tonalá. More than 20 distinct moulding and firing techniques—many of them centuries old—are used to create the intricately painted flatware and whimsical figures found here.

On Thursday and Sunday, Tonalá merchandise is sold at bargain prices at a terrific street market, with block after block packed with vendors from 8 AM to 4 PM. Except for a concentration of shops on Avenida de los Tonaltecas, the main drag into town, most of Tonalá's shops and factories are spread out; the town also has unusually long blocks, so wear your most comfortable walking shoes. Many stores are open daily 10–2 and 4–7. Some no longer close for a siesta; some are closed on Monday.

A GOOD WALK Begin your tour at the many different workshops that make up **La Casa de los Artesanos** ㉓ ▶, on Avenida de los Tonaltecas between Calle 16 de Septiembre and Calle Matamoros. From here you'll pass scores of stores and workshops as you cruise north along the broad, busy avenue. Turn right onto Av. Juárez and enter downtown where the town church, the **Santuario** ㉔, and the Palacio Municipal face the Plaza Principal. Walk north on Av. Morelos to **Artesanías Erandi** ㉕ and **Galería José Bernabe** ㉖, both specializing in local ceramics. Continue north on Morelos several long blocks, turning east (right) on Calle La Paz and left onto Av. Alvaro Obregón to see handmade wooden masks at **El 7** ㉗. Return the way you came, this time turning west (right) onto Avenida López Cotilla. Not far past Avenida de los Tonaltecas is **La Casa de Salvador Vásquez Carmona** ㉘, where the owner sells his fanciful ceramic pottery.

WHAT TO SEE
㉕ **Artesanías Erandi.** One of Tonalá's largest exporters of hand-painted ceramics abroad has its exhibition center in founder Jorge Wilmot's former workshop. To see artisans in action, stop by their factory three blocks away. ✉ *Calle Morelos 86* ☎ *33/3683–0101* ☉ *Mon.–Sat. 9–6* ✉ *Factory* ✉ *Av. López Cotilla 118* ☎ *33/3683–0253* ☉ *Weekdays 9:30–6, Sat. 9:30–2.*

▶ ㉓ **La Casa de los Artesanos.** This virtual department store of Mexican folk art and crafts displays an excellent selection of pieces by Tonalá's best artisans. The work of generations is here, including items made of wood, glass, wrought iron, brass, and of course clay. Prices are reasonable, and the staff can direct you to local artisans' studios. ✉ *Av. de los Tonaltecas Sur 140* ☎ *33/3284–3066 or 33/3284–3068* ☉ *Weekdays 9–8, weekends 9–3.*

㉘ **La Casa de Salvador Vásquez Carmona.** On a small patio behind his home, Carmona molds enormous ceramic pots and glazes them with intricate designs. Numerous award certificates hang in his living room. Call before visiting. ✉ *Av. de los Maestros 328, west of Av. de los Tonaltecas* ☎ *33/3683–2896.*

㉖ **Galería José Bernabe.** The Bernabe family has made exquisite petatillo ceramics and simpler stoneware for generations. The sprawling workshop in back of the gallery is open to visitors. ✉ *Av. Hidalgo 83, between Zapata and Constitución* ☎ *33/3683–0040 or 33/3683–0877* ☉ *Weekdays 10–3 and 4–7, weekends 10–3* ☉ *Workshop closed Sun.*

㉔ **Santuario.** In the parish church, Moorish arches form the nave and paintings of the Stations of the Cross fill the walls. Next door is the simple Palacio Municipal (City Hall), and the Plaza Principal is across the street. ✉ *Av. Juárez at Av. Hidalgo.*

㉗ **El 7.** Tonalá native J. Cruz Coldívar Lucano, who signs his work and named his shop El 7 (*el siete*), makes striking hand-painted masks, as well as decorative plates and other wall hangings. He has exhibited throughout North and South America as well as in Europe. The Spanish Crown owns a number of his works. Note that his studio is several long blocks from the plaza on Privado Alvaro Obregón, off the main avenue of the same name. ✉ *Privado Alvaro Obregón 28* ☎ *33/3683–1122* ☉ *Weekdays 9–6, Sat. 9–2.*

WHERE TO EAT
✕ **Restaurant Jalapeños.** Steaks are the specialty in this small but clean
$ restaurant whose walls are adorned with brightly painted ceramic vegetables. Come for a late breakfast or dinner, or enjoy the daily lunch special, with soup, main dish, drink, and dessert for less than $5. ✉ *Av. Madero 23, ½ block south of Plaza Principal* ☎ *33/3683–0344* ☐ *MC, V* ☉ *Closed Tues.*

$ ✕ **El Rincón del Sol.** A peaceful covered patio invites you to sip margaritas while listening to live guitar music that begins around 3 every day but Monday. Try one of the steak or chicken dishes or the chilies *en nogada,* a classic dish with the three colors of the Mexican flag: a spicy *poblano* chili (green), stuffed with a mixture of ground meat and fruit, covered in a sweet cream sauce (white) and topped with pomegranate seeds (red). ✉ *Av. 16 de Septiembre 61* ☎ *33/3683–1989 or 33/3683–1940* ☐ *MC, V.*

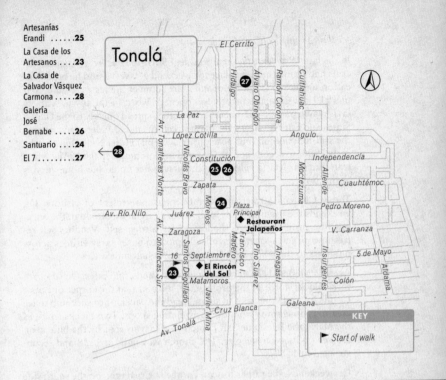

Tonalá

La Paz
López Cotilla
Nicolás Bravo
Constitución
Zapata
Juárez
Morelos
Zaragoza
16
Septiembre
Santos Degollado
Matamoros
Javier Mina
Cruz Blanca

Av. Tonaltecas Norte
Av. Tonaltecas Sur
Av. Río Nilo
Av. Tonalá

El Cerrito
Hidalgo
Álvaro Obregón
Ramón Corona
Cuitlahuac
Angulo
Independencia
Moctezuma
Allende
Cuauhtémoc
Pedro Moreno
V. Carranza
5 de Mayo
Insurgentes
Colón
Galeana
Aldama

Plaza
Principal
Restaurant
Jalapeños

El Rincón
del Sol

Francisco I.
Madero
Pino Suárez
Aneagasti

KEY

▶ Start of walk

Around Lago de Chapala

Jagged mountains and tranquil towns ring Lago de Chapala, Mexico's largest inland lake. Sunsets here are spectacular, and there's just enough humidity to keep the abundant bougainvillea thriving. Spanish settlement in the area dates from 1538, when Franciscan friar Miguel de Bolonio arrived to convert the Taltica Indians to Christianity. Their chief was named Chapalac, from which the name Chapala may have originated.

In the 1960s, Mexico's favorable rate of exchange and the springlike climate around Lago de Chapala began to attract U.S. and Canadian retirees to the area. More than 40,000 expats now call this region home at least part of the year. In the 1990s, however, upstream water was diverted to serve Mexico City, Guadalajara, and elsewhere, and the lake, which was never very deep anyway, began to shrink. It has retreated as much as a half mile in places, leaving what was once premier waterfront property facing muddy marshland. In addition, fertilizers have washed into the lake from nearby farms, speeding the growth of water hyacinth, an already fast-growing surface plant. The plants blanket the shoreline, blocking boat access and killing fish by reducing oxygen levels in the water. Governors of Jalisco and presidents of the republic have promised to save this lake, and yet it continues to shrink.

The town of Chapala is the area's largest settlement; Ajijic, 8 km (5 mi) to the west, is somewhat less developed and has a community of expat artists and writers. The towns and villages along the lake are linked by one highway with multiple names (e.g., Carretera Chapala-Ajijic or Carretera Ajijic-Jocotepec).

Chapala

45 km (28 mi) south of Guadalajara.

In the late 19th century, then-president Porfirio Díaz heard that aristo-crats had found the ideal place for weekend getaways, and he began va-cationing here in 1904. More and more summer homes were built, and in 1910 the Chapala Yacht Club opened. Word of the town, with its lavish lawn parties and magnificent estates, spread quickly to the United States and Europe. Along the main street, Avenida Madero, you can see the still-functioning (but now rather decrepit) Hotel Nido, built in the early 1900s to accommodate Díaz and his entourage. In the 1940s, Mex-ican film star María Félix spent the first of her numerous honeymoons at this hotel.

Today Chapala attracts a less influential assortment of visitors. On weekends the town still fills with Mexican families, although the once-bustling promenade is a shadow of its former self. Vendors sell re-freshments and souvenirs, while dilapidated buses carry visitors across mudflats to the lake's edge—now nearly a half mile away.

Avenida Madero is lined with restaurants, shops, and cafés. On Madero, three blocks north of the promenade, the plaza, at the corner of López Cotilla, is a relaxing spot to sit and read the paper, or to succumb to ice cream or doughnuts from the surrounding shops. Two blocks south of the plaza, the Iglesia de San Francisco is easy to spot by the blue neon crosses on its twin steeples. The church was built in 1528 and recon-structed in 1580.

On weekends, the rather forlorn Parque la Cristianía, on the south side of the *malecón* (boardwalk), fills with Tapatíos taking a respite from the city and browsing the remaining souvenir booths. Boys compete in energetic games of volleyball, while kids play on jungle gyms and swings. Indoor/outdoor cafés at the end of the promenade serve up seafood (but—because of the shrinking lake—no longer the native whitefish, *pescado blanco*).

WHERE TO STAY & EAT

$-$$ ✕ **Mariscos Guicho's.** The best of the waterfront seafood joints, Guicho's serves savory caviar tostadas, frogs' legs, garlic shrimp, and spicy seafood soup. The bright orange walls and checkerboard tablecloths lend the place an authentic Mexican charm. ⊠ *Paseo Ramón Corona 20* ☎ *376/765–3232* ▭ *No credit cards* ☾ *Closed Tues.*

$ ✕ **Cozumel.** Ajijic residents regularly drive over to Chapala for the Wednesday chicken cordon bleu special, which includes wine or a mar-garita in addition to an opening cocktail and nachos. Other days choose from seafood and international dishes (you still get the free drink), and listen to a mariachi band on Wednesday and Friday. Reservations are essential for Wednesday night. ⊠ *Paseo Corona 22-A* ☎ *376/765–4606* ▭ *MC, V* ☾ *Closed Mon.*

$ ✕ **Restaurant Cazadores.** This grandly turreted brick building was once the summer home of the Braniff family, owners of the now-defunct air-line. On the menu are seafood and beef dishes, which are a bit over-priced. But the lovely patio overlooking the boardwalk is pleasant, especially in the evening. ⊠ *Paseo Ramón Corona 8, northeast corner* ☎ *376/765–2162* ▭ *AE, MC, V* ☾ *Closed Mon.*

¢-$ ✕ **El Arbol del Café.** Expatriates cherish this modest café for its roasted-on-the-premises coffee, imported teas, and homemade cakes. Sip a de-caffeinated cappuccino (hard to find in Mexico) and peruse the day's English-language papers. The bulletin board at the door has rental, for-sale, and other listings. ⊠ *Av. Hidalgo 236* ☎ *376/765–3908* ▭ *No credit cards* ☾ *Closed Sun.*

¢ 🏨 **Hotel Villa Montecarlo.** The simple, clean rooms here are in three-story contiguous units, all with patios or terraces. The grounds are enormous and well maintained, with several eating and play areas. One of the two swimming pools (the biggest in the area) is filled with natural thermal water. Popular with Mexican families, the hotel offers frequent discounts and packages. ⊠ *Av. Hidalgo 296, about 1 km (½ mi) west of Av. Madero, 45900* 🕾🕾 *376/765–2216, 376/765–2120, or 376/765–2025* 🗭 *46 rooms, 2 suites* ⌔ *Restaurant, 2 tennis courts, 2 pools, bar, laundry service, free parking* 🖃 *AE, MC, V.*

★ ¢ 🏨 **Lake Chapala Inn.** It's a pity this charming European-style inn was built just about the time the lake began to recede. Three of the four rooms in this renovated mansion face the distant lake; all have high ceilings and whitewashed oak furniture. An English-style breakfast is included in the rate (with a Continental breakfast on Sunday). Owner-operator Alicia McNiff is a delight. ⊠ *Paseo Ramón Corona 23, 45900* 🕾 *376/765–4786* 🖷 *376/765–5174* 🌐 *www.mexconnect.com/amex/chapalainn-index.html* 🗭 *4 rooms* ⌔ *Dining room, pool, library, laundry service* 🖃 *No credit cards* ⊠|⊙| *BP.*

Ajijic
8 km (5 mi) west of Chapala.

Ajijic is defined by its narrow cobblestone streets, pastel buildings, and gentle pace. Still, the foreign influence is unmistakable: galleries and crafts shops abound, English is spoken almost as widely here as Spanish, and license plates run the gamut from British Columbia to Texas. Although Lago de Chapala has receded here also, the change is less dramatic and desultory than in nearby Chapala, and the arts scene gives Ajijic its very own raison d'être.

The Plaza Principal (also called the Plaza de Armas or El Jardín) is a tree- and flower-filled central square at the corner of Avenida Colón and Avenida Hidalgo. The Iglesia de San Andrés (Church of St. Andrew) sits on the plaza's north side, shaded by laurel and tulip trees and brightened with roses, lilies, and hibiscus bushes in the courtyard. In late November the plaza fills for the saint's nine-day fiesta.

Walk down Calle Morelos (the continuation of Avenida Colón) toward the lake and you'll find boutiques that sell everything from designer fashions to traditional arts and crafts. Turn left onto Avenida 16 de Septiembre or Avenida Constitución, to find about a dozen art galleries and studios.

Northeast of the plaza, along the highway, activity centers surround the soccer field, which doubles as a venue for bullfights and concerts. Locals and visitors frequent the movie theater, cybercafé, athletic club, and Salvador's restaurant—a local institution.

WHERE TO STAY & EAT

★ $–$$ ✕ **Ajijic Grill.** The yakitori and tempura in this Japanese restaurant are better than average, though the sushi leaves much to be desired. The large patio in the center is prettiest at night, when it's softly lighted by tiny white lights. ⊠ *Calle Morelos 5* 🕾 *376/766–2458* 🖃 *MC, V* ⊙ *Closed Tues.*

$–$$ ✕ **La Bodega de Ajijic.** A covered patio overlooking a grassy lawn and a small pool serves as the dining area for this low-key restaurant. The menu has a mix of Italian and Mexican dishes, which are a bit small and overpriced. Still, the service is friendly, and there's live music—usually guitar or harp—most nights. ⊠ *Av. 16 de Septiembre 124* 🕾 *376/766–1002* 🖃 *MC, V* ⊙ *Closed Mon.*

$–$$ ✕ **Johanna's.** If you tire of Mexican or Continental cuisine, come to this intimate bit of Bavaria on the lake. The authentic German cuisine includes excellent sausages and homemade goose or duck pâté. Main dishes come with soup or salad as well as applesauce and cooked red cabbage. For dessert indulge in plum strudel or blackberry-topped torte. ⊠ *Carretera Chapala-Jocotepec, Km 6.5* ☎ *33/3766–0437* ⊟ *No credit cards* ⊘ *Closed Mon.*

¢–$ ✕ **Salvador's.** An old mainstay that's showing its years, this cafeteria-like eatery is a popular expat hangout. There's a well-kept salad bar and specialties from both south and north of the border. A pianist performs during the fabulous Sunday brunch as well as during lunch on Wednesday. On Friday people come in droves for the beloved fish-and-chips lunch special. ⊠ *Carretera Chapala-Jocotepec Ote. 58* ☎ *33/3766–2301* ⊟ *No credit cards.*

★ $ ✕🏨 **La Nueva Posada.** Well-kept gardens framed in bougainvillea define this charming inn. Rooms are spacious, with carpet, high ceilings, and local crafts. Villas share a private courtyard and have tile kitchenettes. The bar has brick domed ceilings and leather chairs surrounding custom-made tables; there's jazz or Caribbean music most evenings. Out in the garden restaurant ($), strands of tiny white lights set the mood for an evening meal, where anything from chef Lorraine Russo's eclectic menu is recommended. ⊠ *Calle Donato Guerra 9* ⊡ *(A.P. 30, 45920)* ☎ *376/766–1344* 🖷 *376/766–1444* ⊕ *www.mexconnect.com/ MEX/rest/nueva/posada.htm* 🛏 *19 rooms, 4 villas* ⚵ *Restaurant, fans, pool, bar, laundry service* ⊟ *MC, V* ⏍ *BP.*

$ 🏨 **Los Artistas.** Surrounded by an acre of splendid gardens, this spacious yet intimate inn has rooms with white textured walls and red tile floors. Each is uniquely decorated with colorful handwoven Mexican bedspreads, wrought-iron or carved-wood bed frames, and fresh-cut flowers. Four rooms have fireplaces, and most rooms have patios shaded by bowers of blooming things. There are no televisions or radios to spoil the tranquility. The owners, transplants from Alaska, often join guests at breakfast. ⊠ *Calle Constitución 105, 45920* ☎ *33/3766–1027* 🖷 *33/ 3766–1762* ✉ *artistas@laguna.com.mx* 🛏 *6 rooms* ⚵ *Pool* ⊟ *No credit cards* ⏍ *BP.*

$ 🏨 **Swan Inn.** Don't be deterred by the somewhat sterile foyer and dining room of this small B&B. Rooms at the back face a Japanese garden and have sloping ceilings, modern furnishings, and paintings by the late founder. Casitas, which have kitchenettes, open onto the small, well-maintained pool. The inn is centrally located, next to the nonprofit Lake Chapala Society's tree-filled grounds and close to several art galleries. ⊠ *Av. 16 de Septiembre 18, 45920* ☎ *376/766–0917 or 376/766–2354* ⊕ *www. mexconnect.com/amex/swan* 🛏 *6 rooms, 2 casitas* ⚵ *Some kitchenettes, pool, laundry service* ⊟ *No credit cards* ⏍ *BP.*

NIGHTLIFE & THE ARTS

There's live music most nights at **La Bodega** (⊠ Calle 16 de Septiembre 124 ☎376/766–1002). The rambling, hacienda-style **Posada Ajijic** (⊠Calle Morelos ☎33/3766–0744 or 33/3766–0430) is a restaurant, bar, and popular weekend dance place with an unobstructed view of the lake bed.

Several art galleries offer painting and sculpture lessons. Many are on Avenida 16 de Septiembre and Calle Constitución. Luisa Julian shows her work and offers classes at **Estudio Arte Galaría** (⊠ Calle Ramon Corona 11, at Av. 16 de Septiembre ☎ 376/766–1292).

SHOPPING

Ajijic's main shopping strip is on Calle Morelos, but there are also many excellent galleries and shops east of Morelos, on Avenida 16 de Septiembre and Calle Constitución. **Artesanía Huichol** (⊠ End of Calle Donato Guerra ☎ no phone) sells remarkable, high-quality Huichol artwork from surrounding towns. There's a large crafts shop at the local branch of the state-run **Instituto de Artesanía Jalisciense** (⊠ Carretera Chapala-Jocotepec, Km 6.5 ☎ 33/3766–0548). The **Mi México** (✉ Calle Morelos 8 ☎ 33/3766–0133) boutique sells women's clothing and jewelry as well as pottery, blown glass, and other crafts.

Five kilometers (3 miles) west of Ajijic on the main highway, a **cactus vivero** (nursery) has some 300 types of cactus for sale. Although a potted cactus may not make a very practical souvenir, entrance to the garden and nursery is free, and the variety and beauty of these hardy plants is remarkable. It's open daily 8–2 and 3–5:30.

SPORTS & THE OUTDOORS The **Rojas family** (✉ Paseo Del Lago and Camino Real, 4 blocks east of Los Artistas B&B ☎ 376/766–4261) has been leading horseback trips for more than 30 years. A ride along the lakeshore or in the surrounding hills costs around $7 an hour.

San Juan Cosalá
2 km (1 mi) west of Ajijic.

San Juan Cosalá is known for its natural thermal-water spas on the shores of Lago de Chapala, with the mountains rising to the north. The **Hotel Balneario San Juan Cosalá** (✉ Calle La Paz Ote. 420 at Carretera Chapala-Jocotepec, Km 13 ☎☎ 376/761–0222 or 376/761–0302) welcomes day-trippers to its four large swimming pools and two wading pools; admission is $7. Note that weekends can be crowded and loud.

WHERE TO STAY

$$ 🏨 **Villas Buenaventura Cosalá.** You can relax for free in the hotel's outdoor thermal pools or rent some time in one of two private hot tubs or two private pools. The one- and two-bedroom suites here are large and clean, if a bit sterile. The outbuildings are brightly painted, and the grounds are dotted with sculpture. On many weekends during high season the hotel requires a two- or three-night minimum stay. ✉ *Carretera Chapala-Jocotepec, Km 13.5, 45920* ☎ *376/761–0202* 🖶 *376/761–0364* ➥ *19 suites* 🍴 *Restaurant, some kitchenettes, 5 pools, hot tub, massage, sauna* ☰ *MC, V.*

$ 🏨 **Hotel Villa Bordeaux.** This hotel is adjacent to and operated by the same people as the Hotel Balneario. Rooms are small but attractive, with brick walls and high ceilings. The pools are reserved for guests and are quiet. A stay here gets you access to the Hotel Balneario facilities as well. ✉ *Calle La Paz Ote. 420 at Carretera Chapala-Jocotepec, Km 13, 45900* ☎ *376/761–0494* ➥ *11 rooms* 🍴 *Restaurant, pool, massage, sauna* ☰ *MC, V.*

Jocotepec
15 km (10 mi) west of Ajijic

At the western end of Lago de Chapala, small Jocotepec is a world away from its tourist-impacted neighbors, Ajijic and Chapala. The town has long been famous for its white serapes; unfortunately the delicately made shawls are increasingly hard to find. It remains a refreshingly traditional Mexican town, though. An example of this is the Sunday *paseo*, where adolescent boys and girls circle the main plaza in opposite directions, flirting under the supervision of older relatives sitting in the middle or along the edges.

WHERE TO STAY

$–$$ 🏨 **Los Dos Bed & Breakfast.** On a hillside overlooking Jocotepec and the lake, Los Dos has a well-kept garden and a pleasant terrace where breakfast is served. The suites—one is a tri-level cottage—are spacious and filled with artwork by the owner-operators, Phyliss Rauch and her husband, the noted Austrian painter Georg Rauch. Georg's studio is on-site; be sure to ask for a tour. ✉ *Calle Rico 191, 45800 Nestipac* ☎🖶 *376/763–0657* ⊕ *www.mexconnect.com/MEX/losdos* ➥ *3 suites* 🍴 *Pool, kitchenettes, some pets allowed* ☰ *No credit cards* 🍴 *BP.*

Tequila

56 km (35 mi) northwest of Guadalajara.

For a close look at how Mexico's most famous liquor is made from the spiny blue agave plant that grows in the fields alongside the highway, spend part or all of a day in this tidy village, about 59 km (37 mi) from outside the city of Guadalajara. It's said that centuries ago, the Tiquilas, a small Nahuatl-speaking tribe, discovered that the heart of the agave produced a juice that could be fermented to make intoxicating drinks. When distilled (an innovation introduced after the arrival of the Spanish in the 16th century), the fermented liquid turns into the heady liquor, which in this and only a few other regions can be rightfully labeled tequila.

Museo National del Tequila (✉ Calle Ramon Corona 34 ☎ 374/742–2410) has antique distilling equipment and displays that trace the development of tequila. The museum is open Tuesday through Sunday 10 to 5; admission is $1.50. The **Sauza Museum** (✉ Calle Albino Rojas 22 ☎ 374/742–0247) has memorabilia of the Sauza family, a tequila-making dynasty second only to the Cuervos. Admission to the museum, which is open Tuesday through Sunday 10 to 4, is $1.

Opened in 1795, the **José Cuervo Distillery** (✉ Calle José Cuervo 73 ☎ 374/742–2442) is the world's oldest tequila distillery. Every day, 50 tons of agave hearts are processed into 74,000 liters of tequila here. Hard-hat tours are offered Monday through Saturday every hour on the hour, from 10 AM to 2 PM; the tours at 10 and noon are in English. Admission is $3.

GUADALAJARA A TO Z

To research prices, get advice from other travelers, and book travel arrangements, visit www.fodors.com.

AIR TRAVEL

AIRPORT The Aeropuerto Internacional Libertador Miguel Hidalgo is 16½ km (10 mi) south of Guadalajara, en route to Chapala.
🛈 **Aeropuerto Internacional Libertador Miguel Hidalgo** ✉ Av. Solidaridad Iberoamericana, Km 17.5, Tlaquepaque ☎ 33/3688–5248 or 33/3688–5127.

AIRPORT The Carretara Guadalajara–Chapala (Guadalajara–Chapala Highway)
TRANSFERS stretches north from the airport to the city and south to the Lago de Chapala. It's 30 minutes to Guadalajara and 45 minutes to Chapala, but the trip can be delayed in either direction by slow-moving caravans of trucks and weekend recreational traffic.

Autotransportaciones Aeropuerto is a 24-hour airport shuttle service that goes anywhere in the Guadalajara area in *combis* (VW buses). Fares, based on distance, range from $8 to $12 for up to three people going to the same part of the city. A private taxi to Guadalajara costs $12 to $15; it's $20 to $25 to Lago de Chapala. At the airport, buy tickets for a shuttle or taxi from booths outside the terminal exit. To the airport, hotel taxis have set rates, as do regular city taxis.
🛈 Taxi & Shuttles **Autotransportaciones Aeropuerto** ☎ 33/3812–4278.

CARRIERS AeroCalifornia serves Tucson and Los Angeles as well as many Mexican cities. Aeroméxico has nonstop service to Guadalajara from Los Angeles and extensive internal flights. Mexicana has direct flights from Chicago, Los Angeles, San Francisco, and San José. Through Dallas, American Airlines provides service to Guadalajara from all cities in its system. Flights on Continental are routed through the Houston hub. Delta Air Lines flies direct from Los Angeles and Atlanta.

☎AeroCalifornia ☎ 33/3616-2525. Aeroméxico ☎ 33/3669-0202. American Airlines ☎ 33/3616-4402.Continental ☎ 33/3647-4251. Delta Air Lines ☎ 33/3630-3530. Mexicana ☎ 33/3613-5097.

BUS TRAVEL TO & FROM GUADALAJARA

First-class, air-conditioned buses with rest rooms run daily to Guadalajara from most major cities on the border. Greyhound has schedule and fare information for service into Mexico, although you'll have to change to a Mexican carrier at the border. Guadalajara's Nueva Central Camionera (New Central Bus Station) is 10 km (6 mi) southeast of downtown. Elite has first-class service to Mexico City and many other destinations. ETN is the most upscale line, and its prices match its service. Primera Plus has first- and second-class buses serving mainly central and western Mexico. Omnibus de México serves the U.S. border and intermediate destinations.

Buses to and from such nearby destinations as Chapala, Ajijic, and Tequila depart from the Antigua Central Camionera (Old Central Bus Station), northeast of the Parque Agua Azul on Avenida Dr. R. Michel, between Calle Los Angeles and Calle 5 de Febrero. Autotransportes Guadalajara Chapala has service to lakeside towns for $3. It's about 45 minutes to Chapala and another 15 minutes to Ajijic; there are departures every half hour from 6 AM to 9:30 PM. Make sure you ask for the *directo* (direct) as opposed to *clase segunda* (second class), which stops at every little pueblo en route. Most buses continue on to Jocotepec; otherwise, catch a local line from either Chapala or Ajijic.

☎Autotransportes Guadalajara Chapala ☎ 33/3619-5675. Elite ☎ 33/3679-0404. ETN ☎ 33/3600-0477 or 01800/360-4200 toll-free in Mexico. Greyhound ☎ 01800/ 712-8819 toll-free in Mexico; 800/231-2222 in the U.S. Omnibus de México ☎ 33/ 3600-0469. Primera Plus ☎ 33/3600-0398.

BUS TRAVEL WITHIN GUADALAJARA

Buses run every few minutes between 6 AM and 11 PM to all local attractions, including those in Tlaquepaque, Tonalá, and Zapopan; most buses pass through or near the Zona Centro. Unlike many Mexican cities, Guadalajara has actual bus stops, or *paradas,* marked by signs or sheltered benches. Fares are roughly 35¢, making buses the preferred mode of transportation for Guadalajara natives; expect to stand during the day. For Zapopan, Tlaquepaque, and Tonalá, large mint-green Tur buses (Greyhound-like buses) cost aound 70¢ and are generally faster, less crowded, and more comfortable than other buses. Signs in their windows indicate the destinations. Tur buses take a limited number of passengers; if one doesn't stop, it's either full or you're not at a proper stop.

Main destinations that you can reach from the Zona Centro include: Zapopan (northbound Tur bus from Avenida Alcalde and Calle Juan Manuel or Avenida 16 de Septiembre and Calle Madero); Tonolá and Tlaquepaque (green southbound Tur bus from Avenida Alcalde and Calle Juan Manuel or Avenida 16 de Septiembre and Calle Madero); Zona Minerva (electric, westbound Par Vial buses numbered 400 or 500 from Calle Independencia); Zona Plaza del Sol (westbound Bus 258 from Alcalde and Calle San Felipe); Zoológico, Barranca de Oblatos, Parque Mirador Independencia, and the soccer and bullfighting stadiums (electric, northbound Par Vial Bus 600 from Calzada Independencia in front of Mercado Libertad or Bus 60, which goes as far as the zoo); Parque Agua Azul (southbound Bus 62-A or C from Calzada Independencia).

CAR RENTAL

Major Agencies Alamo ⊠ Av. Niños Héroes 982 South of Zona Centro, Guadalajara ☎ 33/3613-5531 or 33/3613-5560. **Avis** ⊠ Hilton, Av. de las Rosas 2933, Zona Cruz del Sur, Guadalajara ☎ 33/3671-3422; 33/3688-5528 to the airport. **Budget** ⊠ Av. Niños Héroes 934, at Av. 16 de Septiembre, Zona Centro, Guadalajara ☎ 33/3613-0027 or 33/3613-0287. **Dollar** ⊠ Av. Federalismo Sur 580, at Av. de la Paz, Zona Centro, Guadalajara ☎ 33/3826-7959. **Express Rent a Car** ⊠ Calle Manzano 444, Zona Centro, Guadalajara ☎ 33/3614-1465 or 33/3614-1865. **Hertz** ⊠ Av. 16 de Septiembre 738-B, Zona Centro, Guadalajara ☎ 33/3688-6080; 33/3688-5633 to the airport.

CAR TRAVEL

Major routes include Ruta 54 (Route 54), which leads south to Colima (220 km [136 mi]) and north to Zacatecas (320 km [198 mi]). Ruta 15 hugs the southern shore of Lago de Chapala before continuing southeast to Morelia (255 km [58 mi]) and Mexico City (209 km [130 mi]). Ruta 15D is the toll road to Mexico City. Heading northwest from Guadalajara, both 15 and 15D pass through some of the most beautiful country in Jalisco and neighboring Nayarit state.

To reach Tlaquepaque, take Avenida Revolución southwest. At the Plaza de la Bandera, turn right onto Calzada del Ejército and cross the plaza to the first light. Turn left onto Boulevard General Marcelino García Barragán (also known as Boulevard Tlaquepaque). Follow the *glorieta* (traffic circle) around to Avenida Niños Héroes. The first intersection is Calle Independencia, the pedestrian mall in Tlaquepaque. From the Plaza del Sol area, take Calzada Lázaro Cárdenas southeast toward the airport and pick up the Carretera Guadalajara–Chapala. (*Note:* bypass the airport/highway exit and take the next one, to the Alamo glorieta). Fork off to the north onto Avenida Niños Héroes. Either trip should take about 25 minutes. To travel from Tlaquepaque to Tonalá, take Avenida Río Nilo southeast directly into town and the intersection of Avenida de los Tonaltecas (5 minutes).

In Guadalajara, beware of heavy traffic and *topes* (speed bumps). Traffic circles are common at many busy intersections. Parking in the city center can be scarce, so take a taxi or bus if you're not staying nearby; otherwise, try the underground lots across from the Palacio Municipal (Avenida Hidalgo and Calle Pedro Loza) and below the Plaza de la Liberación (Avenida Hidalgo and Calle Belén, in front of the Teatro Degollado). If you park illegally, the police may tow your vehicle: you'll have to go to the municipal transit office to pay a fine and then to one of the *correlones* (holding areas) to pay the tow charge (around $15) and retrieve your car.

CONSULATES

British Consulate ⊠ Calle Jesus de Rojas 20, Zona Zapopan, Guadalajara ☎ 33/3343-2296. **Canadian Consulate** ⊠ Fiesta Americana, Av. Aurelio Aceves 225, Zona Centro, Guadalajara ☎ 33/3616-5642; 33/3615-6215; 01800/706-2900 toll-free in Mexico for after-hours emergencies. **U.S. Consulate** ⊠ Calle Progreso 175, between Av. López Cotilla and Av. Libertad, Zona Centro, Guadalajara ☎ 33/3825-2700; 33/3825-1717; 33/3826-5553 after-hours emergencies.

EMERGENCIES

Emergency Services Cruz Verde (Green Cross municipal emergency medical service) ☎ 33/3812-5143 or 33/3614-5252. **Federal Highway Patrol** ☎ 33/3629-5082 or 33/3629-5085. **General Emergencies** ☎ 080. **Guadalajara City Police** ☎ 33/3668-0800 or 33/3617-0770. **Red Cross** ☎ 33/3614-5600 or 33/3614-2707. **State Police** ☎ 33/3675-3060. **Tourist Police** ☎ 01800/903-9200 toll-free in Mexico.

Hospitals Hospital del Carmen ⊠ Calle Tarascos 3435, Zona Minerva, Guadalajara ☎ 33/3813-1224 or 33/3813-0025. **Hospital México-Americano** ⊠ Calle Colomos 2110,

Zona Centro, Guadalajara ☎ 33/3641-3141. **Hospital San Javier** ✉ Av. Pablo Casals 640, Col. Providencia, Zona Minerva, Guadalajara ☎ 33/3669-0222.

🗐 Late-Night Pharmacies **Benavides** ✉ Calle Morelos 468, near el Palacio Municipal, Zona Centro, Guadalajara ☎ 33/3614-7676 ✉ Av. Hidalgo 307-A, Zona Centro, Guadalajara ☎ 33/3637-7280. **Farmacias Guadalajara** ✉ Av. Javier Mina 221, between Calle Cabañas and Vicente Guerrero, Zona Centro, Guadalajara ☎ 33/3618-3767.

ENGLISH-LANGUAGE MEDIA

The *Guadalajara Reporter,* a weekly newspaper sold for 90¢ at newsstands and hotels, is light on news but has excellent community and cultural listings. You can also get the paper off the Web at ⊕ www.guadalajarareporter.com. The monthly newspapers *Ojo del Lago* and *Lake Chapala Review* cover the Lago de Chapala area. Many top-end hotels have CNN in English.

🗐 Bookstores **Libros de Chapala** ✉ Av. Madero 230, Chapala 🕾 no phone. **Sanborn's** ✉ Av. 16 de Septiembre 127, Centro Histórico, Guadalajara ☎ 33/3613-6693 ✉ Av. López Mateos 2718, Plaza del Sol mall, Zona Cruz del Sur, Guadalajara ☎ 33/3647-2510.

MAIL, INTERNET & SHIPPING

The main *correos* (post office) is open weekdays 8–7. American Express cardholders can receive mail at the AmEx office in Zona Minerva. It has hours weekdays 9 to 6 and Saturday 9 to 1. Note that the Mexican postal system is notoriously slow and unreliable; for important letters or packages, use a courier service such as Federal Express or DHL.

There are several decent Internet cafés in the heart of the Zona Centro. The cost is usually $1.20 to $1.50 per hour, and most places charge in 15-minute increments. Alteck has fast Internet connections as well as national and international fax and phone service. It's open weekdays 9 to 8 and Saturday 9 to 7. Compu-Flash, another place with fast Internet connections, is one block east of the Hotel Cervántes. Its hours are weekdays 9:30 AM–10 PM and Saturday 9–8.

🗐 Courier Services **Federal Express** ✉ Av. Washington 1129, Zona Centro, Guadalajara 🕾 01800/900-1100 toll-free in Mexico. **DHL** ✉ Av. Chapultepec Sur 590, Plaza Chapultepec, Local 4-D West of Zona Centro, Guadalajara ☎ 33/3585-8963.

🗐 Cybercafés **Alteck** ✉ Calle Pedro Mereno 702 Zona Centro, Guadalajara ☎ 33/3613-1198 🖴 33/3614-4934. **Compu-Flash** ✉ Calle Priciliano Sánchez 402, Zona Centro, Guadalajara 🕾 33/3614-7165 🖴 33/3124-1072.

🗐 Postal Information **American Express** ✉ Av. Vallarta 2440, Zona Minerva, Guadalajara 🕾 33/3818-2323 🖴 33/3616-7665. **Correos** ✉ Av. Alcalde 500, Zona Centro, Guadalajara ☎ 33/3614-4770.

MONEY MATTERS

ATMs are the most convenient way to get cash, and offer the best exchange rates. (Be sure your PIN has only four digits.) You can also change foreign cash and traveler's checks at a *casa de cambio,*; there are dozens on Calle López Cotilla, east of Avenida 16 de Septiembre, and are generally open weekdays 9–7 and Saturday 9–1.

SUBWAY TRAVEL

Guadalajara's underground *tren ligero* (light train) system is clean, safe, and efficient. Line 1 runs north–south along Avenida Federalismo from the Periférico (city beltway) Sur to Periférico Norte, near the Benito Juárez Auditorium. Line 2 runs east–west along Juárez from Tetlán in eastern Guadalajara to Avenida Federalismo, with stops at Avenida 16 de Septiembre (Plaza Universitario) and Mercado Libertad. Lines 1 and 2 form a "T," meeting at the Juárez station at Parque Revolución, at the corner of Avenida Federalismo and Avenida Juárez. Trains run about every 15 minutes from 6 AM to 11 PM; a token for one trip costs about 35¢.

TAXIS

In Guadalajara taxis are safe, readily available, and reasonably priced. All cabs are supposed to use meters, but it's common to agree on a fixed price at the outset. Schedules listing fares to downtown and all major attractions are posted in most hotel lobbies, and cab drivers should produce a copy upon request. *Sitios* (cab stands) are near all hotels and attractions. Fares go up about 25% after 10 PM. The cabs that you can hail away from the hotels might be slightly more expensive than those you can get at the hotels.

The fare from downtown Guadalajara to Tlaquepaque comes to about $6, a bit more to Tonalá. A cab from Tlaquepaque to Tonalá runs about $4.

TOURS

The city tourism office conducts a free, two-hour, guided walking tour every Saturday, starting at 10 AM at the Palacio Municipal Palace (Spanish only). The Tourist Board of Zapopan offers free guided trolley tours of Zapopan weekends at 10 AM; call ahead to arrange an English-speaking guide. You can hire a *calandria* (horse-drawn carriage) in front of the Museo Regional, the Mercado Libertad, or Parque San Francisco. The charge is about $15 for an hour-long tour for up to five passengers; it's $10 with a coupon available at the tourist office. Few drivers speak English, though.

Panoramex offers bus tours of Guadalajara and Tlaquepaque, and excursions to Lago de Chapala and Tequila ($13–$20 per person). The bilingual guides of Ajijic's Charter Club Tours lead tours of Guadalajara, shopping and factory trips in Tlaquepaque and Tonalá, and treks to lesser known yet scenic towns throughout the state of Jalisco. Sonrisa Tours is another established, reliable tour operator. With a day's notice, you can visit many home studios on free tours offered by the Tonalá municipal tourist office, beginning from the Casa de Artesanos.

Each Saturday the *Tequila Express*—the only train to travel to or from the city—leaves Guadalajara on a 10-hour trip (from 10:30 AM to 8:30 PM) that includes a tour of the Hacienda San José del Refugio distillery in Amatitlán (not Tequila), a satisfying lunch, a mariachi and ballet folklórico performance, and an unlimited supply of Mexico's most famous liquor. Tickets are $55 and are available through the Guadalajara's Cámera de Comercio (Chamber of Commerce) or Ticketmaster. **Cámera de Comercio** ⊠ Av. Vallarta 4095, Zona Minerva, Guadalajara ☎ 33/3122-7920 or 33/3880-9099. **Charter Club Tours** ⊠ Carretera Chapala-Jocotepec, Plaza Montaña mall, Ajijic ☎ 376/766-1777. **Panoramex** ⊠ Av. Federalismo Sur 944, Zona Centro, Guadalajara ☎☎ 33/3810-5057 or 33/3810-5005 ⊕ www.panoramex.com.mx. **Sonrisa Tours** ⊠ Paseo del Hospicio 63, Plaza Tapatía, Zona Centro, Guadalajara ☎ 33/3618-9601, 33/3617-2511, or 33/3617-2590. **Ticketmaster** ☎ 33/3818-3800.

TRAVEL AGENCIES

Local Agent Referrals American Express ⊠ Av. Vallarta 2440, Zona Minerva, Guadalajara ☎ 33/3818-2323. **Copenhagen Tours** ⊠ Av. J. Manuel Clouthier 156, Col. Prados Vallarta, Zona Minerva, Guadalajara ☎ 33/3629-7957 or 33/3629-4758.

VISITOR INFORMATION

The Guadalajara branches of the Jalisco state tourist office have information about the city and other parts of Mexico; there's also has a branch in Chapala. All branches are open on weekdays and weekends, though hours vary in each location. Guadalajara's municipal tourist office is in front of the Palacio Municipal; it also has kiosks downtown in the Plaza Guadalajara, near Los Arcos monument on Avenida Vallarta east of the Minerva Fountain, in Parque San Francisco, in front of the Instituto Cultural Cabañas, in front of Mercado Libertad, at Calle Vicente Guerrero 233 (open weekdays only), and at the airport. Hours are generally Monday–Saturday 9–7.

The Tourist Board of Zapopan (open weekdays 9 to 7:30) provides information and maps about metropolitan Guadalajara, including Zapopan, Tonalá, and Tlaquepaque. Both the Tlaquepaque (weekdays 9 to 7) and Tonalá (weekdays 9 to 3) tourist offices will cheerfully dispense maps and whatever brochures are available. At least one of the attendants usually speaks some English. In Ajijic, the nonprofit Lake Chapala Society, open Monday–Saturday 10–2, provides information about the area.

🛈 **Guadalajara Municipal Tourist Office** ✉ Monumento Los Arcos, Av. Vallarta 2641, 1 block east of Minerva Fountain, Zona Minerva, Guadalajara ☎ 33/3616-9150 or 33/3615-1182 ⊕ www.vive.guadalajara.gob.mx. **Jalisco state tourist offices** ✉ Calle Morelos 102, in Plaza Tapatía, Centro Histórico, Guadalajara ☎ 33/3668-1600; 01800/363-2200 toll-free in Mexico ⊕ http://visita.jalisco.gob.mx ✉ Palacio de Gobierno, Centro Histórico, Guadalajara ☎ no phone ✉ Calle Madero 407-A, 2nd floor, Chapala ☎☎ 376/765-3141. **Lake Chapala Society** ✉ Av. 16 de Septiembre 16, Ajijic ☎ 376/766-1582 ⊕ www.mexconnect/MEX/lcsindex.html. **Tlaquepaque Municipal Tourist Office** ✉ Calle Morelos 288, Tlaquepaque ☎ 33/3635-5756 or 33/3657-3846. **Tonalá Municipal Tourist Office** ✉ Av. de los Tonaltecas Sur 140, in La Casa de los Artesanos, Tonalá ☎ 33/3683-0067. **Tourist Board of Zapopan** ✉ Av. Vallarta 6503, Ciudad Granja, Zona Zapopan, Guadalajara ☎ 33/3110-0754 or 33/3110-0755 ⊕ www.zapopan.gob.mx.

THE HEARTLAND

7

FODOR'S CHOICE
Casa de la Marquesa, hotel, Querétaro
Quinta Real, hotel, Zacatecas

HIGHLY RECOMMENDED

HOTELS La Casa de Espiritus Alegres B&B, Guanajuato
Casa Luna, San Miguel de Allende
Casa Quetzal, San Miguel de Allende
Hacienda Mariposas, Pátzcuaro
Mansión Iturbe, Pátzcuaro
Villa Montaña, Morelia

RESTAURANTS La Casona Del Cielo, Guanajuato
Chez Nicole, Guanajuato
La Cuija, Zacatecas
Harry Bissett's, San Miguel de Allende

EXPERIENCES El Museo Casa Diego Rivera, Guanajuato
La Valenciana, an ornate colonial church, Guanajuato
Museo Pedro Coronel, Zacatecas
Museo Rafael Coronel, Zacatecas
Santuario de Mariposas el Rosario, near Morelia

Updated by
Abigail Atha

MEXICO'S HEARTLAND, so named for its central position in the country, is known for its well-preserved colonial architecture, its fertile farmland and surrounding mountains, and its leading role in Mexican history, particularly during the War of Independence (1810–21). The Bajío (ba-*hee*-o), as it is also called, corresponds roughly to the states of Guanajuato and parts of Querétaro and Michoacán. In the hills surrounding the cities of Guanajuato, Zacatecas, Querétaro, and San Miguel de Allende, the Spanish found silver in the 1500s, leading them to colonize the area heavily.

Three centuries later, wealthy Creoles (Mexicans of Spanish descent) in Querétaro and San Miguel took the first audacious steps toward independence from Spain. When their clandestine efforts were discovered, two of the early insurgents, Ignacio Allende and Father Miguel Hidalgo, began in earnest the War of Independence.

When Allende and Hidalgo were executed in 1811, another native son, José María Morelos, picked up the independence banner. This mestizo (mixed race) mule skinner–turned–priest–turned–soldier, with his army of 9,000, came close to gaining control of the land before he was killed in 1815. Thirteen years later, the city of Valladolid was renamed Morelia in his honor.

Long after the War of Independence ended in 1821, the cities of the Bajío continued to play a prominent role in Mexico's history. Three major events took place in Querétaro alone: in 1848 the Mexican-American War ended with the signing of the Treaty of Guadalupe Hidalgo; in 1867 Austrian Maximilian of Hapsburg, crowned Emperor of Mexico by Napoleon III of France, was executed in the hills north of town; and in 1917 the Mexican Constitution was signed here.

The heartland honors the events and people that helped shape modern Mexico. In ornate cathedrals or bucolic plazas, down narrow alleyways or atop high hillsides, you'll find monuments—and remnants—of a heroic past. During numerous fiestas, you can savor the region's historic spirit. On a night filled with fireworks, off-key music, and tireless celebrants, it's hard not to be caught up in the vital expression of national pride.

Tourism is welcomed in the heartland, especially in these hard economic times, and, for the most part, it doesn't disrupt the normal routines of residents. Families visit parks for Sunday picnics, youngsters tussle in school courtyards, old men chat in shaded plazas, and Purépecha women in traditional garb sell their wares in crowded *mercados* (markets). Unlike areas where attractions have been specifically designed for tourism, the Bajío relies on its historic ties and the architectural integrity of its cities to appeal to travelers.

Exploring the Heartland

Many travelers barrel past the heartland to points north or west of Mexico City, but there are plenty of reasons to stop here: browsing in the shops of San Miguel or Guanajuato for bargains in silver and other local crafts, or heading to the state of Michoacán, renowned for its folklore and folk crafts, especially ceramics and lacquerware. Stay longer to linger over the wealth of architectural styles that each of the colonial cities has to offer. Although it may be most convenient to tour by car, there is frequent inexpensive bus service from one city to the next throughout the Bajío.

About the Restaurants

Restaurants in this neck of the woods don't stay open quite as late as they do in the capital. Locals usually have lunch anywhere between 1 and 5 PM and dinner between 7 and 10 PM. Dress is casual; the line is generally drawn at shorts.

About the Hotels

In many of the heartland's colonial cities, restored haciendas of the fabulously rich residents of centuries past make the best lodgings. Often near the center of town, sometimes facing directly onto plazas, some of these mansions date from the 16th century. There are also deluxe modern high-rises and functional, low-cost hotels. Except for five-star hotels, most properties in the region aren't heated; you may want to bring warm, comfortable clothes for indoor wear, or to inquire in advance if heating is important to you. In restored colonial properties, rooms often vary dramatically as to size and furnishings, so if you aren't satisfied with the one you are shown, ask to see another. High season, for the most part, is limited to specific dates surrounding Christmas, Easter, and regional festivals. Most moderate and inexpensive hotels quote prices with 15% value-added tax already included.

WHAT IT COSTS				
$$$$	**$$$**	**$$**	**$**	**¢**
RESTAURANTS over $25	$15–$25	$10–$15	$5–$10	under $5
HOTELS over $250	$150–$250	$75–$150	$50–$75	under $50

Restaurant prices are for a main course excluding tax and tip. Hotel prices are for two people in a standard double room in high season, based on the European Plan (EP, with no meals) and excluding service and 17% tax.

Timing

One of the most pleasing aspects of the heartland is its superb climate— it rarely gets overly hot, even in the middle of summer, and although winter days can get nippy, especially in northern Zacatecas, they are generally temperate. Average temperatures in the southern city of Morelia range from 20°C (68°F) in May to just under 10°C (49°F) in January. Zacatecas is more extreme, with winter temperatures as low as 0°C (32°F) and snow flurries every several years, and summer highs of 28°C–30°C (81°F–85°F). Nights are cool all year in most of the region's cities. The rainy season across the heartland hits between June and October and is generally strongest in July and August.

Consider going to the heartland for cultural festivals or religious events: in October Guanajuato's three-week-long International Cervantes Festival, which brings actors, musicians, painters, and hundreds of thousands of visitors to town; in late November San Miguel's Jazz Festival International; and November 1–2 on the island of Janítzio, where local Purépecha (also called Tarascan) Indians hold a Day of the Dead in honor of their ancestors. Millions of monarch butterflies arrive near Morelia between early November and early March.

SAN MIGUEL DE ALLENDE

San Miguel de Allende first began luring foreigners in the late 1930s when American Stirling Dickinson and prominent local residents founded an art school in this mountainous settlement. The school, now called the Instituto Allende, has grown in stature over the years—as has the city's reputation as a writers' and artists' colony. Walk down any cobblestone

If you have only a couple of days to spare, stop in any of several colonial cities for a taste of life in the heartland—each one has its own particular flavor. If you happen to fall under the heartland's peaceful, friendly spell, you'll want a week to 10 days to give yourself time to drink in the atmosphere of two or three of the region's cities.

Numbers in the text correspond to numbers in the margin and on the San Miguel de Allende, Guanajuato, Zacatecas, Querétaro, Morelia, and Pátzcuaro maps.

7

If you have 3 days

Head to 🏛 **Guanajuato** ⑫–㉒ ⌐, the most architecturally dramatic of the heartland cities. Make a day trip from here to the picturesque town of **San Miguel de Allende** ①–⑪ to shop for crafts.

Another option is to go from Mexico City to the Michoacán capital of 🏛 **Morelia** ㊵–㊾ ⌐ and spend a day taking in its stately architecture and café-lined plaza. The next day, drive on to **Pátzcuaro** ㊿–㊶, set among volcanoes in the center of Purépecha Indian country. Spend the morning in the bustling market or strolling in the surrounding countryside before making a late-afternoon return to Mexico City.

If you have 5 days

Make 🏛 **Guanajuato** ⑫–㉒ ⌐ your base and allow an extra day to see its churches and museums—perhaps even the gruesome Mummy Museum. Stop off at the town of Dolores Hidalgo, home of Mexican independence, on your way to a day of shopping in 🏛 **San Miguel de Allende** ①–⑪. Overnight in San Miguel and the next morning head for 🏛 **Querétaro** ㉜–㊴. This quiet colonial city is considered the capital of the Bajío. After a night in a downtown hotel, return to Mexico City or to the airport outside Guanajuato (2½ hours).

If you decide to spend several days in Michoacán, you can easily fill your time exploring the state's colonial towns and enjoying the lush, mountainous countryside. After three days in 🏛 **Morelia** ㊵–㊾ ⌐ and 🏛 **Pátzcuaro** ㊿–㊶, take a day trip to explore the crater on an extinct volcano in **San Juan Parangaricútiro** or the ruins of an ancient Purépecha Indian capital, **Tzintzuntzan** (both are easy day trips from Pátzcuaro), before returning on the final day to Morelia and Mexico City.

If you have 7 days

From your base in 🏛 **Guanajuato** ⑫–㉒ ⌐, consider adding to the first of the five-day itineraries a round-trip flight from León's Guanajuato International Airport to 🏛 **Zacatecas** ㉓–㉛. This would give you a day and a half to explore the northern colonial mining city. Because it lies off the main tourist track, Zacatecas has a refreshingly unself-conscious attitude. Another possibility for a week in the heartland would be to make a loop from Mexico City that includes both 🏛 **Morelia** ⌐ and 🏛 **Guanajuato.** You'd have time for leisurely side trips to **Pátzcuaro** ㊿–㊶ and 🏛 **San Miguel de Allende** ①–⑪ and a stop in 🏛 **Querétaro** ㉜–㊴. When in Pátzcuaro, be sure to take a boat out to the island town of Janítzio on nearby Lake Pátzcuaro, home of Mexico's most famous Day of the Dead festival (lasting up to two days), or to the island of Yunuen, which isn't as yet besieged by tourists.

street and you're likely to see residents of a variety of national origins. Some come to study at the Instituto Allende or the Academia Hispano-Americana, some to escape the harsh northern winters, and still others to retire.

Cultural offerings in this town of about 110,000 reflect its large American and Canadian community. There are literary readings, art shows, a yearly jazz festival, psychic fairs, aerobics and past-life regression classes, and a lending library. International influence notwithstanding, San Miguel, declared a national monument in 1926, retains its Mexican characteristics. Wandering down streets lined with 18th-century mansions, you'll also discover fountains, monuments, and churches—all reminders of the city's illustrious, and sometimes notorious, past. The onetime headquarters of the Spanish Inquisition in New Spain, for example, is at the corner of Calles Hernández Macías and Pila Seca. The former Inquisition jail stands across the way. Independence Day is celebrated with exceptional fervor in San Miguel, with fireworks, dances, and parades September 15 and 16, and bullfights and cultural events for the remainder of the month, including the running of the bulls.

Exploring San Miguel de Allende

You'll find most of San Miguel's sights in a cluster downtown, which you can visit in a couple of hours.

Begin at the main plaza, otherwise known as **El Jardín** ① ⌐. After you get a feel for the square, stop into **La Parroquia** ②, the sandstone church on its south side. Three blocks northeast of La Parroquia (make a right Calle San Francisco, on the north side of El Jardín, to Calle Juárez) is the **Iglesia de San Francisco** ③, with a heavily ornamented facade. Take a few steps north on Calle Juárez to Calle Mesones, then east to Calle Colegio, where the colorful **Mercado Ignacio Ramírez** occupies a cavernous structure off the west side of the street. The dome of the **Oratorio de San Felipe Neri** ④ is visible just before the market.

A block west of the church on Calle Insurgentes, **La Biblioteca Pública** ⑤ is a great place to catch up on town events. Continue west from the library two blocks to Calle Hernández Macías, then head south to the **Bellas Artes** ⑥ cultural center at No. 75 and the ornate **Iglesia de la Concepción** ⑦ behind it. Take Hernández Macías south for a block and turn left on Calle Umarán to reach the **Casa de Ignacio Allende** ⑧, birthplace of the Mexican national hero. You've circled back to the southwest corner of El Jardín.

After making your way around the center of town, consider a leisurely stroll to sights a bit farther afield. From the south side of the plaza (by La Parroquia), head west four blocks on Calle Umarán until you reach Calle Zacateros. Turn south on this narrow cobblestone street for some of the town's most interesting crafts shops—stocked with everything from silver jewelry to Mexican ceremonial masks.

Past the shops, Calle Zacateros becomes Ancha de San Antonio. On your left at No. 20 is the renowned **Instituto Allende** ⑨, where many of San Miguel's foreign visitors come to study. From the institute, continue a bit farther south on Ancha de San Antonio, then turn left onto Callejón del Cardo. Continue past St. Paul's Episcopal Church, an expat house of worship, until you arrive at the cobblestone Calle Aldama on your left. Head downhill and walk briefly through a neighborhood of whitewashed houses before reaching the north entrance to the 5-acre Parque Benito Juárez, an oasis of evergreens, palm trees, and gardens.

Let us take you there...

The traditions of MEXICO await you.

Enjoy convenient flight times and onward connections to Mexico's fabulous beaches or fascinating colonial cities. Discover all the wonders that Mexico has to offer and let Mexicana take you there.

Find America *with a Compass*

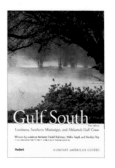

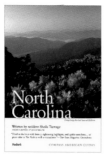
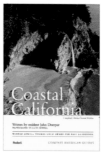

Written by local authors and illustrated throughout
with spectacular color images, Compass American
Guides reveal the character and culture of more than
40 of America's most fascinating destinations. Perfect
for residents who want to explore their own backyards
and for visitors who want an insider's perspective
on the history, heritage, and all there is to see and do.

7

Architecture

Financed largely by the region's fabulously wealthy silver mines, the cities of the heartland are architectural masterpieces full of buildings richly worked with curvaceous lines, human, animal, plant, and geometric motifs, and sculptural depth that accents the play of light and shadow. From the stately, almost European grandeur of Morelia to the steep, labyrinthine allure of Guanajuato and the sandstone pink splendor of Zacatecas, no two towns are alike. San Miguel de Allende's Gothic-style parish church puts a Gallic touch on an otherwise very Mexican skyline. And in Pátzcuaro and Querétaro, the ornate 16th-century colonial mansions surrounding the city squares have been converted into hotels and government offices, making their interior patios accessible to the public.

Cuisine

It's no surprise that culinary tastes vary widely in the heartland, which spans a large area across central Mexico. In the state of Michoacán, Purépecha Indian influences predominate. The tomato-based *sopa tarasca* (a soup with cheese, cream, and tortillas) is one of the best-known regional specialties. Because of the numerous lakes and rivers in the state, several types of freshwater fish are often served in Michoacán restaurants.

At the northern end of the heartland, in Zacatecas, the hearty, meat-eating tastes of the *norteños* (northerners) rule the dinner table. Although beef is the favored dish, other specialties include *asado de boda* (wedding barbecue), pork in a spicy but semisweet sauce. The region is also known for its cheese and wine. And because of San Miguel's expatriate community, the city has a wealth of worthy eateries.

Hiking & Walking

With its rolling farmland, lofty volcanoes, lakes, and Indian villages, Michoacán is a perfect area for day hikes. Trails near Pátzcuaro wind up to nearby hilltops for great views across town and the surrounding countryside, and in Uruapan—64 km (40 mi) away and 2,000 ft lower in elevation—you can walk along a lush river valley. And no tour of the heartland would be complete without a few days of leisurely strolling on the avenues and backstreets of colonial cities and towns.

From the north edge of the park, follow Calle Diezmo Viejo to the terracotta–color mansion known as La Huerta Santa Elena. From here turn left and walk one block uphill on Calle Recreo to the **Lavaderos Publicos** ⑩, San Miguel's outdoor laundry and a favorite gathering spot for local women. Calle Recreo, above the *lavandería*, heads north back toward the plaza, passing the town's bullfighting ring. If you'd like a view of the entire city, turn right off Calle Recreo onto Calle Hospicio, follow Hospicio three blocks to Calle Pedro Vargas, turn right, and head uphill to **El Mirador's** ⑪ overlook. Otherwise, follow Recreo until reaching Calle Correo, turn left, and walk three blocks to return to El Jardín.

TIMING   A walk through San Miguel will take a two to three hours—or more, should you linger over coffee or a meal. Keep in mind that the public library and the Instituto Allende are closed Sunday, and the Casa de Ignacio Allende is closed Monday.

6 Bellas Artes. This impressive cloister across the street from the U.S. Consulate was once the Royal Convent of the Conception. Since 1938 it has been an institute for the study of music, dance, and the visual arts. There are rotating exhibits and a cafeteria on the patio. A bulletin board at the entrance lists cultural events. ✉ *Calle Hernández Macías 75, El Centro* ☎ *415/152–0289* ✉ *Free* ⊙ *Mon.–Sat. 9–8, Sun. 10–2.*

5 La Biblioteca Pública. Notices—about such things as literary readings and yoga and aerobics classes—are posted on the bulletin board in the entranceway to the library. There's a lovely courtyard café inside, as well as the offices of the English-language newspaper *Atención San Miguel* and reading rooms with back issues of popular publications and books in English. On Sundays at noon a two-hour house-and-garden tour (about $15) of San Miguel leaves from the library. ✉ *Calle Insurgentes 25, El Centro* ☎ *415/152–0293* ⊙ *Weekdays 10–2 and 4–7, Sat. 10–2.*

8 Casa de Ignacio Allende. A host of statues will leave no doubt as to this building's former resident: this is the birthplace of Ignacio Allende, one of Mexico's great independence heroes. Allende was a Creole aristocrat who, along with Father Miguel Hidalgo, plotted in the early 1800s to overthrow the Spanish regime. At clandestine meetings held in San Miguel and nearby Querétaro, the two discussed strategies, organized an army, gathered weapons, and enlisted the support of clerics for the struggle ahead.

Spanish Royalists learned of their plot and began arresting conspirators in Querétaro on September 13, 1810. Allende and Hidalgo received word of these actions and hastened their plans. At dawn on September 16, they rang out the cry for independence, and the fighting began. Allende was captured and executed by the Royalists the following year. As a tribute to his brave efforts, San Miguel El Grande was renamed San Miguel de Allende in the 20th century. ✉ *Calle Cuna de Allende 1, El Centro* ☎ *415/152–2499* ✉ *$3* ⊙ *Tues.–Sun. 10–4.*

El Charco del Ingenio. Northeast of the city center, San Miguel's botanical garden is an enjoyable place to walk or cycle, particularly in the early morning or late afternoon. Its five-odd miles of pathways wind past more than 1,500 species of cacti and succulents. ✉ *1½ km (1 mi) northeast of El Jardín; signs point the way off Cuesta de San Jose* ☎ *No phone* ✉ *$1* ⊙ *Sunrise–sunset.*

7 Iglesia de la Concepción. Just behind the Bellas Artes cultural center, this church has one of the largest domes in Mexico. The two-story dome (completed in 1891) and the elegant Corinthian columns and pilasters gracing its drum are said to have been inspired by the dome of the Hôtel des Invalides in Paris. Ceferino Gutiérrez (of La Parroquia fame) is credited with its design. ✉ *Calle Canal between Calles Hernández Macías and Zacateros, El Centro* ☎ *No phone.*

3 Iglesia de San Francisco. This church has one of the finest churrigueresque facades in the state of Guanajuato. This term for the style refers to José Churriguera, a 17th-century (Baroque) Spanish architect, noted for his extravagant surface decoration. Built in the late 18th century, the church was financed by donations from wealthy patrons and by revenue from bullfights. Topping the elaborately carved exterior is the image of Saint Francis of Assisi. Below, along with a crucifix, are sculptures of Saint John and Our Lady of Sorrows. ✉ *Calle Juárez between Calles San Francisco and Mesones, El Centro* ☎ *No phone.*

9 Instituto Allende. The school is in the former country estate of the Count of Canal. Since its founding in 1951, thousands of students from around

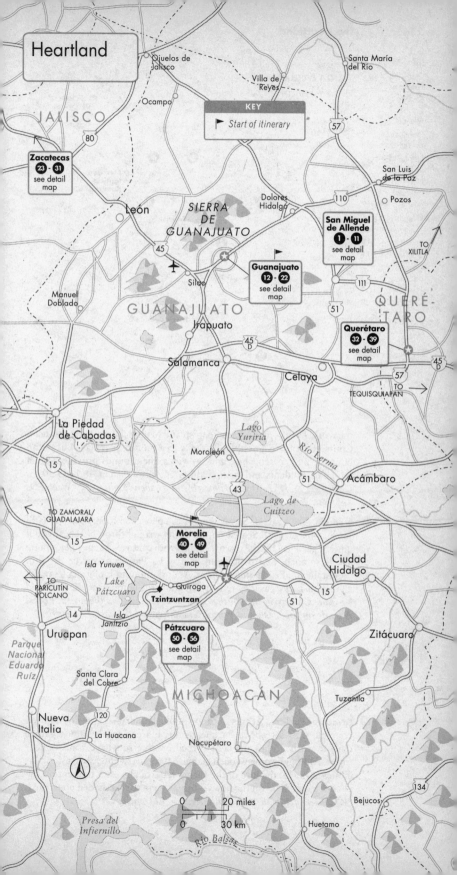

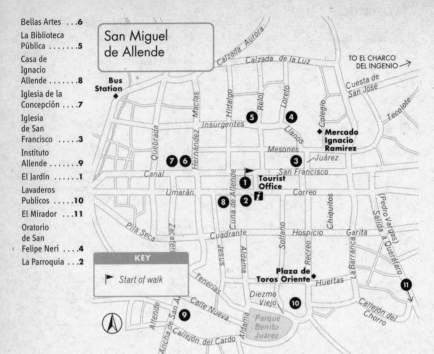

the world have come to learn Spanish and to take classes in the arts here. Courses last from a couple of weeks to a month or longer. Lush with bougainvillea, rosebushes, and ivy vines, the grounds provide a quiet refuge for students and visitors alike. ⊠ *Ancha de San Antonio 20, El Centro* ☎ *415/152–0190* ⊕ *www.instituto-allende.edu.mx* ⊘ *Weekdays 8–6, Sat. 9–1.*

▶ **①** **El Jardín.** The heart of San Miguel is the plaza commonly known as El Jardín (the garden). Seated on one of its wrought-iron benches, you'll quickly get a feel for the town: old men with canes exchange tales, young lovers smooch, and bells from nearby La Parroquia pierce the thin mountain air at each quarter hour. At dusk thousands of grackles make a fantastic ruckus as they return to roost in the laurel trees. ⊠ *Bounded by Calle Correo on the south, Calle San Francisco on the north, Portal Allende on the west, and Portal Guadalupe on the east, El Centro.*

need a break? On the southwest corner of the main plaza is **Café del Jardín** (⊠ Portal Allende 2, El Centro ☎ 415/152–5006). This unassuming little café has excellent coffee, cappuccino, hot chocolate, and, in the evening, pizza. Breakfasts are tasty and inexpensive, and the service is friendly.

⑩ **Lavaderos Publicos.** At this outdoor public laundry—a collection of red concrete tubs set above Parque Benito Juárez—local women gather daily to wash clothes and chat as their predecessors have done for centuries. Although some women claim to have more-efficient washing facilities at home, the lure of the spring-fed troughs—not to mention the chance to catch up on the news—brings them to this shaded courtyard. ⊠ *Calle Diezmo Viejo at Calle Recreo, El Centro.*

⓫ **El Mirador.** Climb El Mirador (The Lookout) for a panorama of the city, mountains, and reservoir below. The vista is great at sunset, and chances are you won't be alone. Locals and tourists like to join Pedro Vargas, whose bronze image commands this spot. ⊠ *Calle Pedro Vargas, El Centro.*

❹ **Oratorio de San Felipe Neri.** Built by local Indians in 1712, the original chapel can still be glimpsed in the eastern facade, made of pink stone and adorned with a figure of Our Lady of Solitude. The newer, southern front was built in an ornate Baroque style. In 1734 the wealthy Count of Canal paid for an addition to the Oratorio. His **Templo de Santa Casa de Loreto,** dedicated to the Virgin of Loreto, is just behind the Oratorio. Its main entrance, now blocked by a grille, is on the Oratorio's left rear side. Peer through the grille to see the heavily gilded altars and effigies of the count and his wife, under which they are buried. ⊠ *Calles Insurgentes and Loreto, El Centro* ☎ *No phone.*

❷ **La Parroquia.** This towering Gothic Revival parish church, made of local *cantera* sandstone, was designed in the late 19th century by self-trained mason Ceferino Gutiérrez, who sketched his designs in the sand with a stick. Gutiérrez was purportedly inspired by postcards of European Gothic cathedrals. Since the postcards gave no hint of what the back of those cathedrals looked like, the posterior of La Parroquia was done in quintessential Mexican style.

La Parroquia still functions as a house of worship, although its interior has been changed over the years. Gilded wood altars, for example, were replaced with neoclassical stone altars. The original bell, cast in 1732, still calls parishioners to mass several times daily. ⊠ *South side of El Jardín on Calle Correo, El Centro* ☎ *No phone.*

Where to Eat

For its size, San Miguel has a surprisingly large number of international restaurants. The steady influx of American and Canadian visitors supports a variety of Tex-Mex and health-food places. A European influence has contributed to variations on French, Italian, and Spanish themes.

$$–$$$ ✕ **El Market Bistro.** You can choose among dining spaces here: either a lush, stone-paved garden with a piano or a private dining room with a glowing fireplace. The French menu includes classics such as *tournedos rossini,* a marinated sirloin smothered in foie gras, red wine sauce, and mushrooms. The leek and potato soup and goat cheese salad are delectable. ⊠ *Calle Hernández Macías 95, El Centro* ☎ *415/152–3229* ▭ *AE, MC, V.*

$$ ✕ **Bella Italia.** Two pieces of advice for a meal at this family-owned restaurant: ask about the daily specials, and leave room for the tiramisu. Lunch is served on the patio, dinner indoors. The staff takes care to recommend a bottle from the rotating list of Italian wines to match the homemade pastas or fish brought from the Sea of Cortez. ⊠ *Calle Hernández Macías 59, El Centro* ☎ *415/152–4989* ▭ *AE, MC, V.*

$$ ✕ **Bugambilia.** Founded in 1945, Mercedes Arteaga Tovar's restaurant has a well-earned reputation for serving fine traditional Mexican cuisine. Try such classic specialties as *pollo en mole poblano* (chicken coated in a traditional mole sauce) and *sopa azteca* (classic tortilla soup served with a variety of toppings). The candlelit, tree-filled colonial courtyard and live classical guitarist make for a romantic setting. ⊠ *Calle Hidalgo 42, El Centro* ☎ *415/152–0127* ▭ *AE, MC, V.*

$$ ✕ **La Capilla.** Nab a table in the plant-filled courtyard for a nouvelle spin, with choices such as wild mushroom ravioli and carefully crafted desserts. ⊠ *Calle Cuna de Allende 10, El Centro* ☎ *415/152–0698* 🖃 *AE, MC, V* 🕙 *Closed Tues.*

★ $ ✕ **Harry Bissett's.** This New Orleans–style café and oyster bar reels in the local crowd. The menu is always extensive but weekend brunches stand out. Look for the duck gumbo, crab cakes Benedict, and the chocolate truffle cake. ⊠ *Calle Hidalgo 12, El Centro* ☎ *415/152–2645* 🖃 *AE, MC, V.*

¢ ✕ **La Buena Vida.** Don't miss this fabulous bakery and tiny coffee shop and its mouthwatering orange scones, chocolate-chip cookies, lemon bread, and breakfast specials. If the few patio tables are full, take your treats to the Jardín. ⊠ *Calle Hernández Macías 72–5, El Centro* ☎ *415/152–2211* 🖃 *No credit cards* 🕙 *No dinner.*

¢ ✕ **La Palapa.** Hit this increasingly popular outdoor spot for the best fish tacos in San Miguel—especially the mahimahi tacos. ⊠ *Calle Nueva 8, El Centro* 🖃 *No credit cards* 🕙 *Closed Sun.*

Where to Stay

San Miguel's hotels fill up quickly in summer and winter, when northern tourists migrate here in droves. Make reservations several months in advance if you plan to visit at these times or during the September Independence Day festivities.

$$$–$$$$ 🏨 **Casa de Sierra Nevada.** Built in 1580 as the residence of the archbishop of Guanajuato, this elegant country-style inn still attracts ambassadors, diplomats, film stars, and other luminaries; however, the formerly attentive service has declined. Lace curtains, handwoven rugs, and chandeliers adorn some rooms; fireplaces, cozy terraces, and skylights enhance others. The hotel runs the separate **Casa de Sierra Nevada en el Parque,** an exquisitely restored 18th-century ex-hacienda with just five guest rooms. Its restaurant serves refined versions of traditional Mexican dishes and has a wonderful view of Parque Benito Juárez. ⊠ *Calle Hospicio 46, El Centro 37700* ☎ *415/152–7040* 🖷 *415/152–1436* ⟿ *17 rooms, 16 suites* ⌂ *2 restaurants, cable TV, pool, massage, spa, horseback riding, bar; no kids under 16* 🖃 *AE, MC, V* ⊠ *Casa de Sierra Nevada en el Parque* ⊠ *Santa Elena 2, El Centro.*

$$$–$$$$ 🏨 **Casa Rosada.** This hotel has the best location in San Miguel, just half a block from the main square. The colonial building dates from 1792 when it was the Hospital de Naturales de la Purisima Concepcion. Guest rooms have a soothingly calm cream-color decor. Two of the suites have balconies with views of the countryside. ⊠ *Calle Cuna de Allende 12, El Centro 37700* ☎ *415/152–0382* 🖷 *415/152–0382* ⊕ *www. casarosadahotel.com* ⟿ *13 rooms, 4 suites* ⌂ *In-room safes, cable TV, bar* 🖃 *AE, MC, V.*

★ $$$ 🏨 **Casa Quetzal.** Three blocks from the main square, this boutique hotel offers unique suites, each with its own characteristic style. A Guatemalan mask or a Chiapan rug might decorate the wall of your guest room. ⊠ *Calle Hospicio 34, El Centro 37700* ☎ *415/152–0501* 🖷 *415/152–4961* ⊕ *www.casaquetzalhotel.com* ⟿ *6 suites* ⌂ *Minibars, cable TV, airport shuttle* 🖃 *AE, MC, V* 🍽 *BP.*

★ $$ 🏨 **Casa Luna.** Each room in this restored 300-year-old Spanish colonial house has a special antique or bright folk art, such as painted gourd masks or a carved wooden headboard. Some have vaulted ceilings, others have private patios. The rooftop honor bar is spectacular at night, lighted by some two dozen miniature tin star lights. Cooking classes are frequently available on-site. A three-night minimum stay is required; children are allowed only when the entire house is rented to one party. ⊠ *Calle Pila Seca 11, El Centro 37700* ☎ *415/152–1117* ⊕ *www.casaluna.com* ⟿ *8 rooms, 1 suite* ⌂ *Dining room, massage, shop* 🖃 *MC, V* 🍽 *BP.*

$$–$$$ ▦ **Casa Schuck.** The work of American expatriates, Casa Schuck is the reincarnation of a 19th-century villa. All rooms open onto a gorgeous jacaranda-filled courtyard; from the choicest suite, "The Royal," you'll also have a view of the town's prestigious church. The B&B is just a few blocks off the town's main square. ⊠ *Bajada de Garita 3, El Centro, 37700* ☎ *415/152–0657* ⊕ *www.casaschuck.com* ⊟ *MC, V* ⧉|*BP.*

$$ ▦ **Villa Scorpio al Puente.** This cozy B&B boasts a stunning rooftop-patio view of San Miguel and the surrounding countryside. A well-stocked library, three gardens, and an elegant salon provide comfortable places to visit with friends or enjoy a quiet afternoon. The guest rooms's down bedding and gas fireplaces help ward off the evening chill. The 250-year-old house was connected to an underground tunnel system used during the revolution. ⊠ *Calle Quebrada 93, El Centro 37700* ☎☎ *415/152–7575* ⊕ *www.villascorpio.com* ↝ *5 rooms* ♿ *Dining room, spa, bar, library* ⊟ *No credit cards* ⧉| *BP.*

¢   ▦ **Posada de las Monjas.** This 19th-century inn has been operating as a hotel for more than 50 years. Rooms are simply furnished in a colonial style. Some in the old wing are uncomfortably dark and cramped. Head up to the rooftop public terrace for great city views; the building is near the hulking dome of the Iglesia de la Concepción. Some rooms have fireplaces, and there's a communal TV in the lobby, which looks like a formal Mexican living room. ⊠ *Calle Canal 37, El Centro 37700* ☎ *415/152–0171* ▱ *415/152–6227* ⊕ *www.posadalasmonjas.com* ↝ *65 rooms* ♿ *Restaurant, bar, laundry service, free parking; no room TVs* ⊟ *MC, V.*

Nightlife & the Arts

The Arts

San Miguel, long known as an artists' colony, continues to nurture that image today. Galleries, museums, and arty shops line the streets near El Jardín; most close weekdays between 2 and 4 and are open weekends 10 or 11 to 2 or 3. Two government-run salons—at **Bellas Artes** and **Instituto Allende**—feature the work of Mexican artists. The **Galería de Arte Contemporáneo** (⊠ Plaza Principal 14, El Centro ☎ 415/152–0454) sells works by contemporary Mexican artists. The two collectors behind the regional and international talent of **Galería Atenea** (⊠ Calle Jesús 2, El Centro ☎ 415/152–0785) have a flair for attractive watercolors and Bustamante jewelry. The rambling rooms of **Galería Duo Duo** (⊠ Calle Pila Seca 3, El Centro ☎ 415/152–6211) are filled with all kinds of items in all price ranges, from handmade scarves to iconographic pillows. **Galería del Pueblo** (⊠ Calle Correo 12A, El Centro ☎ 415/152–1448) shows an extensive collection of Huitchol beadwork and yarn paintings. For a taste of contemporary Mexican art stop by **Galería San Miguel** (⊠ Plaza Principal 14, El Centro ☎ 415/152–0454). **Kligerman Gallery** (⊠ Calle San Francisco 11, El Centro ☎ 415/152–0951) has contemporary Mexican and American art.

For more than 20 years, San Miguel has played host to the world-class **Festival de Musica de Camara** in August, a feast of classical chamber music that in past years has included the illustrious Tokyo String Quartet. The **Jazz Festival International** takes place around the last week in November. Tickets for the concerts, workshops, and after-hour jam sessions may be purchased individually or for the series. Call the tourist office for dates and details.

Nightlife

On most evenings in San Miguel you can readily satisfy a whim for a literary reading, an American movie, a theatrical production, or a turn on a dance floor. The most up-to-date listings of events can be found in the English-language paper *Atención San Miguel,* published every Sunday. The bulletin board at the Biblioteca Pública is also a good source of current events.

Agave Azul (⊠ Calle Mesones 99, El Centro ☎ 415/152–1958) draws a crowd for live music, dancing and of course, tequila. **Mama Mia** (⊠ Calle Umarán 8, El Centro ☎ 415/152–2063) presents everything from Peruvian folk music, classical guitar, and flamenco to salsa and rock. The rotating art exhibitions and comfortable leather chairs at **El Petit Bar** (⊠ Calle Hernández Macías 95, El Centro ☎ 415/152–3229) attract an eclectic mix of locals and tourists.

Sports & the Outdoors

The **Club de Golf Malanquin** (⊠ Celaya Hwy., Km 3 ☎ 415/152–0516) has a heated pool, steam baths, tennis courts, and 9 holes of golf, all of which are open to the public for a guest fee of $45 on weekdays or $70 on weekends; it's closed Monday. The exclusive **Hotel Hacienda Taboada** (⊠ Dolores Hidalgo Hwy., Km 8 ☎ 415/152–0888) has several geothermal pools, manicured grounds, and tennis courts. It's open to the public for about $15, which includes lunch; it's closed Wednesday. **Taboada** (⊠ Dolores Hidalgo Hwy., Km 8) has three outdoor geothermally heated pools, one of which is Olympic-size and good for doing laps. They are open to the public for $3.50; it's closed Tuesday.

Ballooning

Gone with the Wind Balloon Adventures (⊠ Calle Recreo 68, El Centro ☎ 415/152–6735) offers hot-air balloon rides over town and the surrounding countryside with licensed-certified pilots from Napa Valley, California. The one-hour flights depart at 6 or 7 AM, depending on the season. The $150 cost includes breakfast upon landing.

Bullfights

To witness the pageantry of a traditional Mexican bullfight, go to the **Plaza de Toros Oriente** (⊠ off Calle Recreo, El Centro), which has events several times a year. The most important contest takes place in the last week of September during *la fiesta de San Miguel.* Tickets cost about $3 for a seat in the sun and $10 for a seat in the shade. Call the tourist office for more information.

Horseback Riding

Aventuras San Miguel (⊠ Calle Recreo 10, El Centro ☎ 415/152–6406) rents horses at reasonable rates. The equestrian center of the hotel **Casa de Sierra Nevada** offers riding lessons, carriage rides, and horse rental at its 500-acre ranch for about $50 per hour.

Shopping

For centuries San Miguel's artisans have been creating crafts ranging from straw products to metalwork. Although some boutiques in town may be a bit pricey, you can find good buys on silver, brass, tin, woven-cotton goods, and folk art. Store hours tend to be erratic, but most stores open daily at around 9, shut their doors for the traditional afternoon siesta (2 to 4 or 5), then reopen in the afternoon until 7 or 8, and open for just a half day on Sunday. Most San Miguel shops accept MasterCard and Visa.

Markets

Spilling out for several blocks behind the Mercado Ignacio Ramírez, the **Mercado de Artesanías** (artisans' market) is where you'll find vendors of

HECHO A MANO

HANDMADE IN MEXICO: *some of the world's finest artesanías (crafts) come from this country. Artisanal work is varied, original, colorful, and inexpensive, and it supports millions of families who are carrying on ancient and more recent traditions. Although cheap, shoddy items masquerading as "native crafts" are certainly common, careful shoppers who take their time can come away with real works of folk art. Also keep in mind that many items are exempt from duty.*

The crafts to look for are ceramics, woodwork, lacquerware, leather, weaving and textiles, and silver, gold, and semiprecious-stone jewelry. Each region has its specialty. Cities that are noted for the quality of their crafts are Puebla (Chapter 2); Nogales in Sonora (Chapter 4); Guadalajara, Tlaquepaque, and Tonalá in Jalisco (Chapter 6); San Miguel de Allende, Guanajuato, and Pátzcuaro in the heartland (Chapter 7); Taxco in Morelos (Chapter 9); Oaxaca City in Oaxaca (Chapter 10); San Cristóbal de las Casas in Chiapas (Chapter 11); and Mérida in Yucatán (Chapter 13).

Ceramics. Talavera-style tiles (blue majolica) and other ceramic ware are at their best in Puebla. Oaxaca state is known for its unglazed, burnished black pottery. Inventive masks and figurines come from Valle de Bravo, Pátzcuaro in the state of Michoacán, Tonalá outside of Guadalajara, Taxco, and Chiapas.

Jewelry. Silver is best in Taxco, San Miguel de Allende, and Oaxaca; be sure purchases are stamped "925," which means 92.5% pure silver. You can find gold filigree in Guanajuato and Oaxaca. Oaxaca and Chiapas are also known for their amber, but be aware that much of what is sold as amber is in fact glass or plastic. Good rules of thumb: don't buy amber off the street; and if it seems like a great bargain, it's probably fake. For semiprecious stones, go to jewelers' shops in Puebla and Querétaro. Coral jewelry is sold in the Yucatán and other coastal areas, but because of the massive ecological damage caused by coral

harvesting, the practice around it is environmentally unsound.

Leather. The key places to find quality leatherwork are Guadalajara, Oaxaca (for sandals), Chiapas (for belts and purses), and the Yucatán (for bags).

Metalwork. Look for copper in Santa Clara del Cobre in Michoacán, and tin in San Miguel de Allende and Oaxaca.

Weavings and Textiles. Fabric work is quite varied: you'll find rebozos (shawls) and blankets around Oaxaca, Guadalajara, Jalapa, and Pátzcuaro; huipiles (heavily embroidered tunics worn by Indian women) and other embroidered clothing in Michoacán, Oaxaca state, Chiapas, and the Yucatán; masterfully woven rugs, some colored with natural dyes, in Oaxaca; hammocks and baskets in Oaxaca and the Yucatán; lace in the colonial cities of the heartland area; guayaberas (comfortable, embroidered or pleated men's dress shirts, now usually mass-produced) along the Gulf coast; and reed mats in Oaxaca and Valle de Bravo. The Mezquital region east of Querétaro can also be rewarding, as can shopping for Huichol Indian yarn paintings and embroidery near Puerto Vallarta.

Woodwork. Look for masks in Mexico City; alebrijes (painted wooden animals) in Oaxaca; furniture in Cuernavaca, Guadalajara, San Miguel de Allende, Querétaro, Tequisquiapan, and Pátzcuaro; lacquerware in Uruapan and Pátzcuaro in Michoacán, Chiapa de Corzo in Chiapas, and Puerto Vallarta for pieces from Olinalá in Guerrero state; and guitars in Paracho, Michoacán.

local work—glass, tin, and papier-mâché—as well as some of the best prices on silver jewelry in town. **Mercado Ignacio Ramírez,** a traditional Mexican covered market off Calle Colegio, one block north of Calle Mesones, is a colorful jumble of fresh fruits and vegetables, flowers, bloody butchers' counters, inexpensive plastic toys, taco stands, and Mexican-made cassettes. Both markets are open daily from around 8 AM until 7.

Specialty Shops

FOLK ART **Artes de México** (⊠ Calz. Aurora 47, at Dolores Hidalgo exit, Col. Guadalupe ☎ 415/152–0764) has been producing and selling traditional crafts, including furniture, metalwork, and ceramics, for more than 40 years. **La Calaca** (⊠ Calle Mesones 93, El Centro ☎ 415/152–3954) focuses on quality antique and contemporary Latin American folk and ceremonial art. Although the inventory at the **Casa Maxwell** (⊠ Calle Canal 14, El Centro ☎ 415/152–0247) has slipped in quality, there's still a reasonable selection of folk art. **La Guadalupana** (⊠ Calle Jesús 25-A, inside Jasmine Day Spa, El Centro ☎ 415/152–7973) sells all manner of items adorned with images of Mexico's beloved Virgin of Guadalupe—from temporary tattoos to coffee mugs. **Talisman Boutique 2** (⊠ Calle San Francisco 7, El Centro ☎ 415/152–0438) sells beautiful embroidered *huipiles* (tunics or blouses) from southern Mexico and Guatemala. **Zócalo** (⊠ Calle Hernández Macías 110, El Centro ☎ 415/152–0663) sells vibrant artwork and furniture at fair prices. It's closed on Sunday.

HOUSEWARES **Casa Canal** (⊠ Calle Canal 3, El Centro ☎ 415/152–0479), in a beautiful old hacienda, sells new furniture, much of it in traditional styles. **Casa María Luisa** (⊠ Calle Canal 40, El Centro ☎ 415/152–0130) focuses on a wild combination of contemporary Mexican furniture, household items, and art. **Casa Vieja** (⊠ Calle Mesones 83, El Centro ☎ 415/152–1284) has tons of glassware and ceramics, housewares, picture frames, furniture, and more. **CLAN destino** (⊠ Calle Zacateros 19, El Centro ☎☎ 415/152–1623) features an eclectic international mix of antiques, contemporary art, and jewelry. **México Lindo** (⊠ Calle Mesones 85, El Centro ☎ 415/152–0730) sells a good selection of hand-painted tiles and ceramics from Dolores Hidalgo. **La Zandunga** (⊠ Calle Hernández Macías 129, El Centro ☎ 415/152–4608) sells high-quality, 100% wool rugs from Oaxaca.

JEWELRY Established in 1963, **Joyería David** (⊠ Calle Zacateros 53, El Centro ☎ 415/152–0056) has an extensive selection of gold, silver, copper, and brass jewelry, all made on the premises. A number of pieces contain Mexican opals, amethysts, topaz, malachite, and turquoise. **Platería Cerro Blanco** (⊠ Calle Canal 17, El Centro ☎ 415/152–0502) creates and crafts its own silver and gold jewelry and will arrange a visit to its *taller* (workshop) on request. The reputable **7th Heaven** (⊠ Sollano 31, El Centro ☎ 415/154–4677) designs and creates its own silver, gold, and carved amber pieces.

Side Trips from San Miguel de Allende

Dolores Hidalgo

50 km (31 mi) north of San Miguel via Rte. 51.

Dolores Hidalgo played an important role in the fight for independence. It was here, before dawn on September 16, 1810, that local priest Father Miguel Hidalgo gave an impassioned sermon to his clergy that ended with the *grito* (cry), "Death to bad government!" At 11 PM on September 15, politicians throughout the land repeat a revised version of the grito—"Viva Mexico! Viva Mexico! Viva Mexico!"—signaling the start of Independence Day celebrations. On September 16 (and only on this day), the bell in Hidalgo's parish church is rung.

Casa Hidalgo, the house where Father Hidalgo lived, is now a museum. It contains copies of important letters Hidalgo sent or received, and other independence memorabilia. ⊠ *Calle Morelos 1* ☎ *418/182–0171* ▨ *About $3* ⊙ *Tues.–Sat. 10–5:45, Sun. 10–4:45.*

Dolores Hidalgo is famous for its lovely hand-glazed Talavera-style ceramics, most notably tiles and tableware. There are good prices at the town's many stores and factories. After shopping, head for the plaza for some of the most exotic ice creams you'll taste—flavors such as mole, avocado, beer, and corn. The town is an easy one-hour bus ride from San Miguel de Allende's Central de Autobuses.

Pozos
35 km (21 mi) northeast of San Miguel de Allende

The captivating, high-desert town of Pozos was a silver-mining center in the late 19th century. Now it's almost a ghost town; you can peek at abandoned buildings or the simple, echoing chapel. Rarely will you see another tourist. The Casa Montana hotel is the hub of information and activity; the owner can arrange a tour of the old mines. It also has a collection of photos of Pozos and the surrounding area.

The town is a forty-five minute drive from San Miguel; look for a road marked "Dr. Mora."

WHERE TO STAY
$$
Casa Montana. You can steep yourself in the town's colonial atmosphere with an overnight on its main square. Guest rooms have local artwork, fireplaces, and wonderful deep tubs. Have a meal on the bouganvillea-filled terraces and if you get the chance, have a margarita with the owner and hear her stories about coming to Pozos. There's shuttle service for both the Guanajuato and Mexico City airports. ⊠ *Jardín Juarez Plaza 37910* ☎ *442/293–0032 or 442/293–0034* ⊕ *www.casamontanahotel. com* ➵ *5 rooms* ⊘ *Restaurant, airport shuttle* ⊟ *MC, V.*

San Miguel de Allende A to Z

To research prices, get advice from other travelers, and book travel arrangements, visit www.fodors.com.

AIR TRAVEL
AIRPORT
León's Guanajuato International Airport (BJX) is roughly a 1½-hour drive from San Miguel. It's a small airport, so the check-in desks can have long lines.

AIRPORT TRANSFERS
Taxis from Guanajuato International Airport to downtown San Miguel cost about $60.

CARRIERS
Aeroméxico flies from Los Angeles. American travels from Dallas–Fort Worth. Continental has service from Houston. Mexicana comes from Chicago.

🔢 **Aeroméxico** ☎ 477/714-7156 or 477/716-6226 ⊕ www.aeromexico.com. **American** ☎ 477/714-0483 or 477/716-5551 ⊕ www.aa.com. **Continental** ☎ 477/718-5254 or 477/718-5199 ⊕ www.continental.com. **Mexicana** ☎ 477/716-3697 or 477/714-9500 ⊕ www.mexicana.com.

BUS TRAVEL
Daily buses run direct from Mexico City's Central del Norte to the Central de Autobuses in San Miguel. Several major lines have frequent service; tickets cost about $24. They include ETN, Flecha Amarilla,

Primera Plus, Herradura de Plata, and Pegasso Plus. Travel time is about four hours.

🚌 ETN ☎ 415/154-5135 or 415/152-6407. **Flecha Amarilla** ☎ 415/152-7323. **Herradura de Plata** ☎ 415/152-0725. **Pegasso Plus** ☎ 415/152-0725. **Primera Plus** ☎ 415/152-0084.

CAR RENTAL

Hola Rent a Car has a limited selection of manual-transmission compacts available.

🚗 **Hola Rent a Car** ✉ Plaza Principal 2, Int. 5, El Centro ☎ 415/152-0198.

CAR TRAVEL

Driving time from Mexico City to San Miguel is roughly 4 hours via Highway 57 (to Querétaro) then Highway 111. Traveling on Highway 45 from Mexico City, a road connecting to Highway 57 and 111 bypasses Querétaro, saving a half hour. Guanajuato is 100 km (62 mi), about 1½ hours, west of San Miguel.

Driving in San Miguel can be frustrating, especially during rush hours; try to avoid the crowded streets in the morning and evening.

EMBASSIES

The U.S. Consulate is open weekdays 9–1.

🏛 **U.S. Consulate** ✉ Calle Hernández Macías 72, El Centro ☎ 415/152-2357 during office hours; 415/152-0653 for emergencies.

EMERGENCIES

The staff at Hospital de la Fé can refer you to an English-speaking doctor.

San Miguel has many pharmacies. American residents recommend Botica Agundis, where English speakers are often on hand. It's open daily 10:30 AM–11 PM.

🚑 Emergency Contacts **Ambulance–Red Cross** ☎ 415/152-4121 or 415/152-4225. **Fire Department** ☎ 415/152-2888. **Police** ☎ 415/152-0022. **Traffic Police** ☎ 415/152-0538. 🏥 Hospital **Hospital de la Fé** ✉ El Libramiento at Dolores Hidalgo 43, Mesa el Malanquin ☎ 415/152-2233 or 415/152-2320. 💊 Pharmacy **Botica Agundis** ✉ Calle Canal 26, El Centro ☎ 415/152-1198.

ENGLISH-LANGUAGE MEDIA

El Colibrí has a good selection of paperback novels, magazines, and a few art supplies. Libros el Tecolote has a great selection of new and used books on Mexican art, history, literature, and cooking.

📖 **El Colibrí** ✉ Sollano 30, El Centro ☎ 415/152-0751. **Libros el Tecolote** ✉ Calle Jesús 11, El Centro ☎🖨 415/152-7395.

MAIL, INTERNET & SHIPPING

Border Crossings offers 24-hour answering and fax service, a Mexico address for receiving mail, packing and shipping, e-mail, a gift shop and art gallery, and other services. Internet service costs about $1.50 an hour. Internet San Miguel charges $5 an hour for the fastest Internet access in town. Coffee, beer, and fresh juices are available.

✉ **Border Crossings** ✉ Correo 19, Int. 2, El Centro ☎ 415/152-2497 🖨 415/152-3672. **Internet San Miguel** ✉ Calle Mesones 57, side entrance at Relox, El Centro ☎ 415/154-4634 ⊕ www.internetsanmiguel.com.

MONEY MATTERS

A better bet for money exchange than the slow-moving bank lines is Intercam, open weekdays 9–6, Saturday 9–2.

💱 **Intercam** ✉ Calles San Francisco 4, Correo 15, or Juárez 27, El Centro ☎ 415/154-6660.

TAXIS

You can easily hail a taxi on the street or find one at taxi stands—such as Sitio Allende in the main plaza. Flat rates to the bus terminal, train station, and other parts of the city apply.

Sitio Allende ☎ 415/152-0192.

TOURS

Aventuras San Miguel has off-the-beaten-track mountain-bike treks, "ghost town" trips, even nighttime full-moon excursions. Colonial México Tours runs historical tours to Guanajuato, Querétaro, and Dolores Hidalgo. Recommended for local tours is PMC (Promotion of Mexican Culture).

Tour Operator Recommendations Aventuras San Miguel ⊠ Calle Recreo 10, El Centro ☎ 415/152-6406 🖶 415/152-6153. **Colonial México Tours** ⊠ Plaza Portal Allende 4, 2nd fl., El Centro ☎☎ 415/152-5794. **PMC** ⊠ Calle Cuna de Allende 11, El Centro ☎ 415/152-1630 🖶 415/152-0121.

TRANSPORTATION AROUND SAN MIGUEL DE ALLENDE

San Miguel de Allende is best covered on foot, keeping in mind two pieces of advice. The city is more than a mile above sea level, so you might tire quickly during your first few days here if you aren't accustomed to high altitudes. Streets are paved with rugged cobblestones, and some have no sidewalks. Wear sturdy footwear, such as athletic or other rubber-sole walking shoes.

TRAVEL AGENCIES

Viajes Vértiz is the American Express representative in San Miguel.

Local Agent Referral Viajes Vértiz ⊠ Calle Hidalgo 1A, El Centro ☎ 415/152-1856 or 415/152-1695 🖶 415/152-0499.

VISITOR INFORMATION

Delegación de Turismo, on the southeast corner of El Jardín, in a glassed-in office next to la Terraza restaurant, is open weekdays 10–5, Saturday 10–2. Although the tourism board doesn't have a Web site, www.portalsanmiguel.com is a helpful Internet resource, with info on local galleries, restaurants, community events and services, real estate, and so on. For information on Pozos, check www.mineraldepozos.com.

Delegación de Turismo ☎ 415/152-6565.

GUANAJUATO

▶ *100 km (62 mi) west of San Miguel de Allende, 365 km (226 mi) northwest of Mexico City.*

Once Mexico's most prominent silver-mining city, Guanajuato is a colonial gem, tucked into the mountains at 6,700 ft. This provincial state capital is distinguished by twisting cobblestone alleyways, colorful houses, 15 shaded plazas, and a vast subterranean roadway where a rushing river once coursed. In the center of town is **Alhóndiga de Granaditas,** an 18th-century grain-storage facility that was the site of Mexico's first major victory in its War of Independence from Spain.

The city fills to overflowing in mid-October with the Festival Internacional Cervantino (International Cervantes Festival), a three-week celebration of the arts. During the rest of the year, things keep a steady, lively pace. Students rush to class with books tucked under their arms, women eye fresh produce at the Mercado Hidalgo, and old men greet each other from behind whitewashed doorways. On weekend nights, *estudiantinas* (student minstrels dressed as medieval troubadours) serenade the public in the city squares.

Exploring Guanajuato

Although Guanajuato's many plazas and labyrinthine streets may seem confusing at first, this is not a bad city in which to get lost. The center is small, and there are wonderful surprises around every corner. Remember that the top of the Alhóndiga (which you can see from many spots in town) points north, and the spires of the Basílica Colegiata Nuestra Señora de Guanajuato, at Plaza de lá Paz, point south. Because of the underground roads, you can walk around the city center without the usual hassles of traffic.

a good walk

The tourist office, at Plaza de la Paz 14 ☞, is a good place to begin a walking tour. Turn right and walk up Obregón to reach **Jardín Unión** ⑫, Guanajuato's central square. The ornate **Teatro Juárez** ⑬ is just past the Jardín to your right on Calle Sopeña. The hardy might want to make a detour and take a half-hour climb to **El Pípila** ⑭, a monument to a hero of the War of Independence of 1810 that looms over the center of the city. If you're interested, bear right on Calle Sopeña just past Teatro Juárez. A sign marked EL PÍPILA will direct you onto Callejón de Calvario, which eventually leads to the hillside memorial.

Head back into town on Calle Cantarranas, a main street that winds down the hill and around the Jardín Unión. Just before Calle Cantarranas changes its name to Calle Pozitos, you'll see the **Universidad de Guanajuato** ⑮. A short way down from where Calle Cantarranas becomes Calle Pozitos is **El Museo Casa Diego Rivera** ⑯, birthplace of Mexico's famous muralist. Calle Pozitos weaves past more residences and eventually becomes Calle 28 de Septiembre. On the left, just past the junction with Mendizabal, is the **Alhóndiga de Granaditas** ⑰, a former fortress converted into a state museum. Head one block south to return to Avenida Juárez and the glassed-in **Mercado Hidalgo** ⑱.

Turn right on Juárez as you leave the market and continue until the road splits near the Jardín Reforma. Bear left and cut down Calle Reforma, a short alley lined with shops. Keep right at the end of the street and you'll come to two pleasant courtyards: Plaza de San Roque, which hosts outdoor performances during the Cervantes Festival, and Plaza de San Fernando, a shady square where many book fairs are held. After the Plaza de San Roque continue southeast and this short detour will return you to Avenida Juárez, where it's a slight climb up to Plaza de la Paz, a 19th-century square surrounded by some of the city's finest colonial buildings, including the 18th-century **Mansión del Conde de Rul** ⑲. The bright-yellow 17th-century Baroque **Basílica Colegiata de Nuestra Señora de Guanajuato** ⑳ dominates the plaza. If you continue up Avenida Juárez about a half block past the plaza, you'll pass the tourist office again and arrive back at the Jardín Unión. If you'd like to take a gander at the colonial church **La Valenciana** ㉑ you can catch a bus there from the city center. If you've a taste for the macabre instead of gilding, get a taxi to go up Avenida Juárez to **Museo de las Momias** ㉒.

TIMING   A walk around the center of town will take a couple of hours. Remember that most museums and the theater are closed Monday.

What to See

⑰ **Alhóndiga de Granaditas.** A massive stone structure with horizontal slit windows, this 18th-century grain-storage facility served as a jail under Emperor Maximilian and as a fortress during the War of Independence, where El Pípila helped the revolutionaries overcome the royalists. It's now a state museum with exhibits on local history, archaeology, and crafts. The hooks on which the Spanish Royalists hung the severed heads of

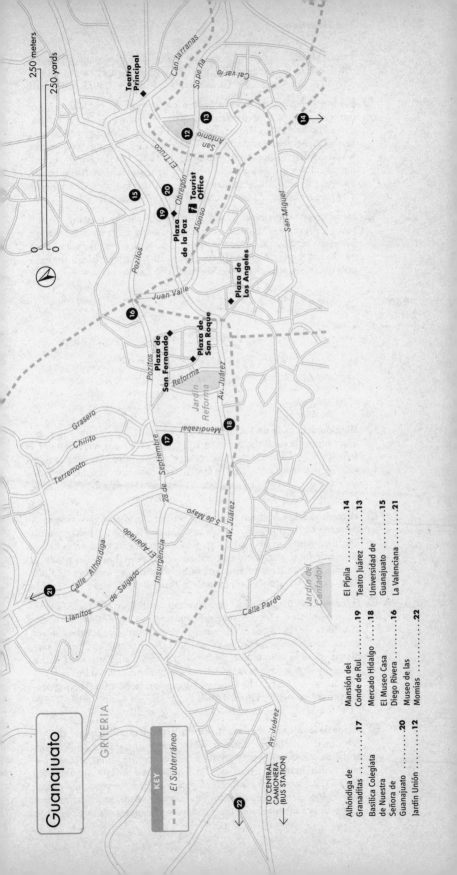

Guanajuato

KEY

- - - El Subterráneo

Teatro Principal

Tourist Office

Plaza de la Paz

Plaza de Los Angeles

Plaza de San Fernando

Plaza de San Roque

Jardín Reforma

Jardín del Cantador

TO CENTRAL CAMIONERA (BUS STATION)

250 meters

250 yards

Street names

Cantarranas, Sopeña, Calvario, San Antonio, El Truco, Obregón, Alonso, Pozitos, Juan Valle, San Miguel, Reforma, Av. Juárez, Mendizabal, 28 de Septiembre, 5 de Mayo, Grasero, Chilito, Terremoto, Insurgencia, El Apartado, Calle Alhóndiga, de Salgado, Llanitos, Calle Pardo, GRITERIA, Av. Juárez

Father Hidalgo, Ignacio Allende, and two other independence leaders still dangle on the exterior. ⊠ *Calle 28 de Septiembre 6, El Centro* ☎ *473/732–1112* ☎ *About $3* ⊙ *Tues.–Sat. 10–1:30 and 4–5:30, Sun. 10–2:30.*

㉔ Basílica Colegiata de Nuestra Señora de Guanajuato. A 17th-century Baroque church painted a striking shade of yellow, the Basílica dominates Plaza de la Paz. Inside is the oldest Christian statue in Mexico, a bejeweled 8th-century statue of the Virgin. The highly venerated figure was a gift from King Philip II of Spain in 1557. On the Friday preceding Good Friday, miners, accompanied by floats and mariachi bands, parade to the Basílica to pay homage to the Lady of Guanajuato. ⊠ *Plaza de la Paz, El Centro* ☎ *No phone* ⊙ *Daily 9–8.*

⑫ Jardín Unión. This tree-lined, wedge-shape plaza is Guanajuato's central square. All three sides of the wedge are pedestrian walkways. Tuesday, Thursday, and Sunday evenings, musical performances take place in the band shell here; at other times, groups of musicians break into impromptu song along the plaza's shaded tile walkways.

> **need a break?** For alfresco dining at the Jardín, try the terrace at the **Hotel Museo Posada Santa Fé** (⊠ Jardín Unión 12, El Centro ☎ 473/732–0084). Try the *pozole estilo Guanajuato* (hominy soup into which you spoon, or squeeze, onions, radishes, lettuce, lime, and chili peppers).
>
> **El Cafe** (⊠ Calle Sopeña 10, El Centro ☎ 473/732–2566) has indoor and outdoor tables next to Teatro Juárez and serves good soups and sandwiches, as well as an interesting assortment of spiked specialty coffees—among them *cafe diable* (coffee, rum, and lemon juice).

⑲ Mansión del Conde de Rul. This 18th-century residence, now a government office, housed the count of Rul and Valenciana, who owned La Valenciana, which was then the country's richest silver mine. The two-story structure was designed by famed Mexican architect Eduardo Tresguerras. ⊠ *Plaza de la Paz at Av. Juárez and Callejón del Estudiante, El Centro* ☎ *No phone* ☎ *Free* ⊙ *Weekdays 8–6.*

⑱ Mercado Hidalgo. You can't miss this 1910 cast-iron-and-glass structure, designed by the one-and-only Gustave Eiffel. Though the balcony stalls are filled with T-shirts and cheap plastic toys, the lower level is full of authentic local wares and colorful basketry, as well as fresh produce, peanuts, and honey-drenched nut candies shaped like mummies. ⊠ *Calle Juárez near Mendizabal, El Centro* ⊙ *Daily 8–8.*

★ ⑯ El Museo Casa Diego Rivera. This museum, birthplace of Mexico's best-known muralist, Diego Rivera, contains family portraits and furniture as well as works by the master, among them his studies for the controversial mural commissioned for New York City's Rockefeller Center. Completed in 1933, the mural contained a portrait of Lenin and had a decidedly Communist bent, which caused it to be destroyed immediately after it was displayed. The museum's upper galleries show revolving contemporary art exhibitions. ⊠ *Calle Pozitos 47, El Centro* ☎ *473/732–1197* ☎ *$2* ⊙ *Tues.–Sat. 10–6:30, Sun. 10–2:30.*

㉒ Museo de las Momias. For a macabre thrill, check out this unique though run-down museum at the municipal cemetery off Calzada del Panteón, at the west end of town. In the museum, mummified human corpses—once buried in the cemetery—are on display. Until the law was amended in 1858, if a grave site hadn't been paid for after five years, the corpse was removed to make room for new arrivals. Because of the mineral properties of the local soil, these cadavers (the oldest is more than 130 years old) were in astonishingly good condition upon exhumation. Some of them are exhibited in glass cases. You'll need to catch a cab to get here; it's atop a steep hill. ⊠ *Panteón Municipal* ☎ *473/732–0639* ▦ *$3* ⊙ *Daily 9–6.*

⑭ El Pípila. A half-hour climb from downtown is the monument to Juan José de los Reyes Martínez, a young miner and hero of the War of Independence of 1810. Nicknamed El Pípila, De los Reyes crept into the Alhóndiga de Granaditas, where Spanish Royalists were hiding. With a stone shield strapped to his back, he set the front door ablaze. The Spanish troops were captured by Father Hidalgo's army in this early battle, giving the independence forces their first major military victory. There's a splendid view of the city from the monument. It's easiest to take a taxi or a bus (marked PÍPILA) from the Jardín. ⊠ *Carretera Panorámica, on bluff above south side of Jardín Unión, El Centro.*

⑬ Teatro Juárez. Adorned with bronze lion sculptures and a line of large Greek muses overlooking the Jardín Unión from the roof, the theater was inaugurated by Mexican dictator Porfirio Díaz in 1903 with a performance of *Aïda*. It now serves as the principal venue of the annual International Cervantes Festival. You can take a brief tour of the art deco interior. ⊠ *Calle Sopeña s/n, El Centro* ☎ *473/732–0183* ▦ *$1.20* ⊙ *Tues.–Sun. 9–1:45 and 5–7:45.*

⑮ Universidad de Guanajuato. Founded in 1732, the university was formerly a Jesuit seminary. The original churrigueresque church, **La Compañía,** still stands next door. The facade of the university building, built in 1955, was designed to blend in with the town's architecture. If you do wander inside, check out the bulletin boards for notices of cultural events in town. ⊠ *Calle Lascurain de Retana 5, ½ block north of Plaza de la Paz, El Centro* ☎ *473/732–0006* ⊙ *Weekdays 8–3:30.*

★ ㉑ La Valenciana. Officially called La Iglesia de San Cayetano, this is one of the best-known colonial churches in all of Mexico. The mid- to late 18th-century pink stone facade is brilliantly ornate. Inside are three altars, each hand-carved in wood and gilded, in different styles: plateresque, churrigueresque, and Baroque. There are also fine examples of religious painting from the viceregal period.

The silver mine near the church, Mina y Bocamina Valenciana, was discovered in 1529 and continued to produce until the early 1800s. An excellent guided tour of the mine (in Spanish only) includes the history of the mine, miners, and the creation of the 1,650-ft-deep mine shaft. The mine and the church are also included in any guided tour of Guanajuato, and buses (marked LA VALENCIANA) frequently make the trip from the city center. ⊠ *Carretera Guanajuato–Dolores Hidalgo, Km 2* ☎ *No phone* ⊙ *Daily 9–6* ▦ *Mine tour $3.*

Where to Eat

Guanajuato's better restaurants are in hotels near the Jardín Unión and on the highway to Dolores Hidalgo. For simpler fare, private eateries around town offer a good variety of Mexican and international dishes. Dress tends to be casual.

★ $$ ✕ **Chez Nicole.** The service and food at this lovely French restaurant are equally excellent; try for a table in the garden. One favorite is a sole served with white asparagus spears and mashed *camote* (sweet potato). The chocolate crepes with kiwis and plums are a must for dessert. ⊠ *Calle Arcos de Guadalupe 3, Marfil* ☎ *473/733–1013* ▤ *AE, MC, V* ⊙ *Closed Mon.*

$–$$ ✕ **Casa del Conde de la Valenciana.** Come to this refurbished 18th-century home across the street from La Valenciana for superbly prepared traditional Mexican and international fare. Fresh gazpacho comes in a bowl made of ice, and the tender *lomo en salsa de ciruela pasa* (pork shoulder in prune sauce) and *pollo a la flor de calabaza* (chicken with poblano chili slices and squash-blossom sauce) are delicious. Round out the meal with luscious mango ice cream served in the rind. ✉ *Carretera Guanajuato–Dolores Hidalgo, Km 5, La Valenciana* ☎ *473/732–2550* 🍽 *MC, V* ☉ *Closed Sun. No dinner.*

$–$$ ✕ **El Comedor Real.** Indulge in the chef's special here—the *Filete Domenech* (named after the chef), a tender fillet of beef served over a potato pancake and wrapped in a woven pasta basket. Troubadours perform every Friday and Saturday at 10:30 PM at La Cava, the bar next door. ✉ *Camino a la Valenciana s/n, Km 1, La Valenciana* ☎ *473/732–0485* 🍽 *AE, MC, V.*

★ $ ✕ **La Casona Del Cielo.** The creative menu attracts a crowd eager to try adventurous flavors like *huitlacoche* (a corn fungus delicacy) and crocodile meat. There are tamer choices too, such as tender beef and homemade ice cream. ✉ *Calle Pastita 76, Presa* ☎ *473/731–2000* 🍽 *AE, MC, V.*

$ ✕ **El Gallo Pitagórico.** Prevail over the 100-plus steps that lead to the threshold of El Gallo Pitagórico and bask in the exceptional view of downtown Guanajuato. You'll be further rewarded by a plate of the house specialty, *Filetto Claudio,* (fillet marinated in olive oil, capers, parsley, and garlic). Make room for dessert—a velvety tiramisu. If the weather is fair, ask to have your aperitif in the top-story bar, which offers a view surpassing that of the restaurant. ✉ *Constancia 10, behind the Teatro Juárez, El Centro* ☎ *473/732–9489* 🍽 *MC, V.*

¢ ✕ **El Unicorno Azul.** If you're growing weary of heavy meat dishes, stop by this food counter just behind Jardín Unión: it serves fruit, yogurt, and vegetarian burgers and sandwiches. The owner will cheerfully recommend other health-food places and yoga classes. ✉ *Plaza del Baratillo 2, El Centro* ☎ *473/732–0700* 🍽 *No credit cards* ☉ *Closed Sun.*

Where to Stay

Guanajuato's less expensive hotels are along Avenida Juárez and Calle de la Alhóndiga. Moderately priced and upscale properties are near the Jardín Unión and on the outskirts of town. It's best to secure reservations at least six months in advance if you plan to attend the Cervantes Festival, which usually runs from mid- to late October.

★ $$ 🏠 **La Casa de Espíritus Alegres Bed and Breakfast.** A paradise for folk-art lovers, this "house of good spirits" is filled with extraordinary crafts from every state in Mexico. Owned by a California artist, the lovingly restored hacienda (circa 1700) has thick stone walls and serene grounds lush with bougainvillea, banana trees, and calla lilies. All rooms have hand-glazed tile baths, fireplaces, and private terraces. Marfil is about a 15-minute drive from the center of town—frequent bus service is available. ✉ *La Ex-Hacienda La Trinidad 1, 36250 Marfil* ☎ *473/733–1013* ⊕ *www.casaspirit.com* ➬ *5 rooms, 2 suites* ♦ *Bar, library, shop, laundry service, free parking; no kids under 13* 🍽 *No credit cards* ⦿ *BP.*

$$ 🏠 **Parador San Javier.** This immaculately restored hacienda was converted into a hotel in 1971. A safe from the Hacienda San Javier and old wood trunks still decorate the large, plant-filled lobby. Rooms are clean and spacious with inviting blue-and-white-tile baths. A few of the 16 colonial-style rooms reached via a stone archway have fireplaces. Newer rooms in the adjoining high-rise have satellite TVs. A word of caution: large convention groups sometimes crowd the facility. ⊠ *Plaza Aldama 92, El Centro 36020* ☎ *473/732–0626* 🖷 *473/732–3114* 🛏 *100 rooms, 12 suites* ♨ *2 restaurants, café, pool, bar, dance club, free parking* ▤ *AE, MC, V.*

$$ 🎫 **Hostería del Frayle.** A half block off Jardín Unión, this quiet four-story lodging was once the Casa de Moneda, where ore was taken to be refined after it was brought out of the mines. Built in 1673 and turned into a hotel in the mid-1960s, it has whitewashed plaster and wood-beam rooms (which nonetheless are somewhat dark), arranged around a small maze of stairways, landings, and courtyards. Some rooms have excellent views of the Pípila, Teatro Juárez, and Jardín Unión. The staff is extremely friendly and helpful. ⊠ *Calle Sopeña 3, El Centro 36000* 🖷 *473/732–1179* 🛏 *32 rooms, 5 suites* ♨ *Restaurant, cable TV, bar, laundry service* ▤ *MC, V.*

$$ 🎫 **Hotel Museo Posada Santa Fé.** This colonial-style inn, at the Jardín Unión, has been in operation since 1862. Large historic paintings by local artist Don Manuel Leal hang in the wood-paneled lobby. Rooms facing the plaza can be noisy; quieter rooms face narrow alleyways. ⊠ *Plaza Principal at Jardín Unión 12, El Centro 36000* ☎ *473/732–0084* 🖷 *473/732–4653* 🛏 *47 rooms, 9 suites* ♨ *Restaurant, cable TV, bar, laundry service, free parking* ▤ *AE, MC, V.*

¢ 🎫 **Hotel Socavón.** Don't be put off by the gloomy, tunnel-like entrance of this modest five-story property: open-air walkways, with views of surrounding mountains, lead to guest quarters. Each small room—simply furnished with a bed, desk, and tiny TV—has a wood-beam ceiling and a modern bath. Fourth-floor corner rooms have some good views. ⊠ *Calle de la Alhóndiga 41A, El Centro 36000* ☎ *473/732–6666* 🖷 *473/732–7344* 🛏 *40 rooms* ♨ *Restaurant, bar* ▤ *AE, MC, V.*

Nightlife & the Arts

Guanajuato, on most nights a somnolent provincial capital, awakens each fall for the **International Cervantes Festival** (⊠ Plaza de San Francisquito 1, El Centro ☎ 473/731–1150 or 473/731–1161; 532/325–9000 Ticketmaster 🖷 473/732–6775). For three weeks in October world-renowned actors, musicians, and dance troupes perform nightly at the Teatro Juárez and other venues in town. Plaza San Roque, a small square near the Jardín Reforma, hosts a series of *Entremeses Cervantinos*—swashbuckling one-act farces by classical Spanish writers. Grandstand seats require advance tickets, but crowds often gather by the edge of the plaza and watch for free. Hundreds of thousands of people attend the festivities each year. If you plan to be in Guanajuato for the festival, contact the Festival Internacional Cervantino office at least six months in advance for top-billed events.

At other times of the year, nightlife in Guanajuato consists of dramatic, dance, and musical performances at **Teatro Juárez** (⊠ Calle Sopeña s/n, El Centro ☎ 473/732–0183). Friday and Saturday at 8 PM, *callejoneadas* (mobile musical parties) begin in front of Teatro Juárez and meander through town (don't forget to tip the musicians). You'll find several nightclubs in or near the downtown area, including **El Bar** (⊠ Calle Sopeña 10, El Centro ☎ 473/732–2566), where students gather for drinks and salsa dancing. The **Castillo Santa Cecilia** (⊠ Camino a la Valenciana s/n, Km 1, La Valenciana ☎ 473/732–0485) offers live music on Friday and Saturday nights. For an evening of hopping music and lively dancing visit **La Dama de las Camelias** (⊠ Calle Sopeña 32, El Centro).

Shopping

Artesanías Vázques (✉ Calle Cantarranas 8 ☎☎ 473/732–5231) carries Talavera ceramics from Dolores Hidalgo. You'll find painterly, old-style majolica ceramics at **Capelo** (✉ Cerro de la Cruz s/n, a dirt road off the Guanajuato–Dolores Hidalgo Hwy, past La Valenciana ☎ 473/732–8964). **Casa del Conde de la Valencia** (✉ Carretera Guanaju-ato–Dolores Hidalgo, Km 5, La Valencia ☎ 473/732–2550) special-izes in brass, tin, ceramic, and wrought-iron home decorations from Mexico and Africa. The **Gorky González Workshop** (✉ Pastita Ex-huerta de Montenegro s/n, past the baseball stadium ☎ 473/731–0389) offers high-quality ceramics (at a higher price). Some jewelry and regional knick-knacks are sold at the **Mercado Hidalgo.** Other shops around Plaza de la Paz and Jardín Unión sell ceramics and woolen shawls and sweaters. Silver is available from street vendors and shops clustered near La Va-lenciana and La Valencia.

Side Trip to León

56 km (35 mi) northwest of Guanajuato.

Best known as the shoe-making capital of Mexico, León is also an im-portant center for industry and commerce. With more than 1 million people, it is the state's most populous urban area.

If you know footwear and have the time (and patience) to browse through the downtown shops, you might find some good buys in León. First try the **Plaza del Zapato,** a mall with 70 stores on Boulevard Adolfo López Mateos, roughly one block from the bus station. From here take a taxi west (about a 10-minute ride) to the **Zona Peatonal,** a pedestrian zone with several shoe stores. On **Calle Praxedis Guerrero,** various artisans' stands sell leather goods.

Guanajuato A to Z

AIR TRAVEL

AIRPORT León's Guanajuato International Airport (BJX) is 40 km (25 mi) west of the city of Guanajuato.

AIRPORT TRANSFERS A taxi ride from the airport to Guanajuato costs about $30 and takes around 30–45 minutes.

CARRIERS Aeroméxico flies from Los Angeles. American travels from Dallas–Fort Worth. Continental has service from Houston. Mexicana comes from Chicago.

🖪 **Aeroméxico** ☎ 477/714-7156 or 477/716-6226 ⊕ www.aeromexico.com. **American** ☎ 477/714-0483 or 477/716-5551 ⊕ www.aa.com. **Continental** ☎ 477/718-5254 or 477/718-5199 ⊕ www.continental.com. **Mexicana** ☎ 477/716-3697 or 477/714-9500 ⊕ www.mexicana.com.

BUS TRAVEL

Direct bus service is available between the Central del Norte in Mex-ico City and Guanajuato's Central Camionera. Flecha Amarilla offers hourly service daily. For frequent first-class service use Estrella Blanca. Travel time is about five hours; tickets cost $28. Deluxe buses, includ-ing those of Primera Plus (Flecha Amarilla's first-class service) and ETN, connect Guanajuato to Mexico City, San Miguel, and Guadala-jara. There are several departures daily. The trip between Guanajuato and San Miguel takes a little over an hour; the ride between Guanaju-ato and Guadalajara lasts four hours. Taxis to downtown Guanajuato from the Camionera cost $2–$3.

Flecha Amarilla buses leave Guanajuato's Central Camionera every 15 minutes daily for León; the ride takes about 45 minutes and costs less than $1.

🚌 **Estrella Blanca** ☎ 473/733-1344. **ETN** ☎ 473/733-1579. **Flecha Amarilla** ☎ 473/733-1332 or 473/733-1333. **Primera Plus** ☎ 473/733-1332 or 473/733-1333.

CAR RENTAL

Avis will drop a car at your hotel in Guanajuato.

🚗 **Avis** ✉ Hotel Fiesta Americana, Los Gabilanes, León ☎ 471/713-6040 🌐 www.avis.com.

CAR TRAVEL

Guanajuato is 365 km (226 mi), about five hours, northwest of Mexico City via Highway 57 (to Querétaro), then via Highway 45. It's about an hour and a half away from San Miguel de Allende.

You won't need a car in central Guanajuato. Many of the attractions are within strolling distance of one another and located between Avenida Juárez and Calle Pozitos, the city's two major north–south arteries. The twisting subterranean roadway—El Subterráneo—also has a primarily north–south orientation.

You can take Highway 45 directly to León; the drive takes a little more than half an hour.

EMERGENCIES

Few people in Guanajuato have a good command of English, so in an emergency it's best to contact your hotel manager or the tourist office.

El Fénix (pharmacy) is open Monday–Saturday 8 AM–9:45 PM, Sunday 9–9.

🚑 **Ambulance-Red Cross** ☎ 473/732-0487. **El Fénix** ✉ Av. Juárez 104, El Centro ☎ 473/732-6140. **Hospital General** ☎ 473/733-1577. **Police** ☎ 473/732-0266.

INTERNET

Redes Internet, open weekdays 9:30–8 and Saturday 10–3, charges $3 an hour for Internet access.

🖥 Internet Café **Redes Internet** ✉ Alonso 70, El Centro ☎ 473/732-0611.

MONEY MATTERS

There are several currency exchange points and banks with ATMs in Guanajuato's center.

TAXIS

You can find taxis at *sitios* (taxi stands) near the Jardín Unión, Plaza de la Paz, and Mercado Hidalgo.

Taxis between León and Guanajuato cost about $17 one way.

TOURS

The following tour operators give half- and full-day tours with English-speaking guides. These tours typically include the Museo de las Momias, the church and mines of La Valenciana, the monument to Pípila, the Panoramic Highway, subterranean streets, and residential neighborhoods. Night tours often begin at El Pípila for a view of the city lights and end at a dance club. Estudiantinas usually perform during the weekend tours.

🚌 Tour Operator Recommendations **Transporte Exclusivo de Turismo** ✉ Av. Juárez at Calle 5 de Mayo, El Centro ☎ 473/732-5968. **Transporte Turísticos de Guanajuato** ✉ Plaza de la Paz 2, by Basílica de Guanajuato, El Centro ☎ 473/732-2134 or 473/732-2838.

TRAVEL AGENCIES

Viajes Georama is the local American Express representative. Viajes Frausto is reliable for hotel and airline reservations.

🖥 **Local Agent Referrals Viajes Frausto** ⊠ Calle González Obregón 10, El Centro ☎ 473/732-3580 🖶 473/732-6620. **Viajes Georama** ⊠ Plaza de la Paz 34, El Centro ☎ 473/732-5909 🖶 473/732-1954.

VISITOR INFORMATION

The Guanajuato tourist office is open daily 9–7. You can pick up a map of León there. The local government Web site, www.guanajuato.gob.mx, has some basic information in English on the area's historical background, culture, and architecture.

🖥 **Guanajuato tourist office** ⊠ Plaza de la Paz 14, El Centro ☎ 473/732-1574 or 473/732-1982 Ext. 107 🖶 473/732-4251.

ZACATECAS

603 km (375 mi) northwest of Mexico City.

In colonial days Zacatecas was the largest silver-producing city in the world, sending great treasures of the precious metal to the king of Spain. Still a large silver-mining center, with factories producing silver jewelry and trade schools training apprentices in the fine art of handmade silver craft, Zacatecas is relatively undiscovered by foreigners. Although it is a state capital with a population of some 300,000, it has the feel of a much smaller place; for instance, it's kept spotlessly clean. This city is also known for its historic role as the scene of one of Pancho Villa's most spectacular battles and for its 18th-century colonial architecture.

One of the town's unique charms is the *tambora*, a musical walk up and down the streets and alleyways led by a *tamborazo*, a typical local band that shatters the evening quiet with merriment. Also known as a *callejoneada* (*callejón* means "alley"), the tambora is a popular free-for-all, in which everyone along the way either joins in the procession or leans from balconies and doorways to cheer the group. During the December *feria* (festival), the tamborazos play night and day as they serenade the Virgin of Zacatecas.

Exploring Zacatecas

Most of Zacatecas's colonial sights are near the city center, making it an easy place to explore on foot—and there's rarely much traffic in town. You may need time to acclimate to the high altitude, though.

a good walk

Start your tour at the Plaza de Armas, in the center of the city. Here you'll find the stunning **Catedral de Zacatecas** 🐵 ▶ and the **Palacio del Gobierno** 🐵. Across the street from the plaza are two beautiful colonial buildings worth exploring; one is known as the **Palacio de la Mala Noche** 🐵 because of a local legend. Go to the Plaza Santo Domingo, two blocks west of the cathedral, to see the art in the **Museo Pedro Coronel** 🐵 and the Baroque **Templo de Santo Domingo** 🐵 right next door. To visit the museum of the other Coronel brother—both were equally fanatical art collectors—return to the cathedral, turn left on Avenida Hidalgo, and walk about 1 km (½ mi) north of the plaza to the **Museo Rafael Coronel** 🐵.

For a longer walk (or, if you're feeling winded, a quick taxi ride), head south on Avenida Hidalgo until you come to Juárez, then go right (roughly west) up the hill, passing the several-block-long Alameda park and the Social Security Hospital to get to **La Mina Eden** 🐵. After tour-

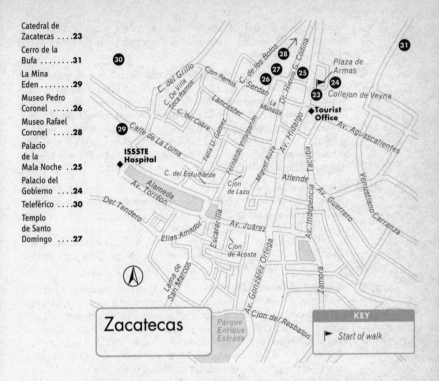

Zacatecas

Parque
Enrique
Estrada

KEY

▶ *Start of walk*

ing the mine, you can take an elevator up to Cerro del Grillo (Cricket Hill) and catch the **Teleférico** ㉚ cable car across the city to **Cerro de la Bufa** ㉛, the site of Pancho Villa's famous battle.

TIMING   You can walk through the town center in under two hours, but leave another couple of hours to go through the museums. Check the museum hours, as all close at least one day a week; the Museo Pedro Coronel is closed Thursday, for instance, while the Museo Rafael Coronel is closed Wednesday.

What to See

㉓ **Catedral de Zacatecas.** This is one of Mexico's finest interpretations of Baroque style. Each of the facades tells a different legend. According to one of them, an anticlerical governor of the state used the cathedral's silver cross and baptismal font to mint Zacatecas's first silver coins. ✉ *South side of Plaza de Armas on Av. Hidalgo* ☎ *No phone* ☉ *Daily 8–2 and 4–6.*

㉛ **Cerro de la Bufa.** The city trademark, this rugged hill is the site of Pancho Villa's definitive battle against dictator Victoriano Huerta in June 1914. The spacious **Plaza de la Revolución**, paved with the three shades of pink Zacatecan stone, is crowned with three huge equestrian statues of Villa and two other heroes, Felipe Angeles and Panfilo Natera. Also on-site are the **Sanctuario de la Virgen de Patrocinio** a chapel dedicated to the patron of the city, and the **Museo de la Toma de Zacatecas** (☎ 492/922–8066 ✆ $1), which has nine rooms filled with historic objects such as guns, newspapers, furniture, and clothing from the days of Pancho Villa. It's open Tuesday–Sunday 10–4:30. ✛ *If driving, follow Av. Hidalgo north from town to Av. Juan de Tolosa; turn right and continue until you come to a fountain; take 1st immediate right off re-*

torno (crossover) onto Calle Mexicapan, which leads to Carretera Panorámica. Turn right to signposted Carretera La Bufa, which leads to the top of the hill.

㉙ La Mina Eden. Now a tourist attraction, the Eden Mine supplied most of Zacatecas's silver from 1586 until 1960. An open mine train runs down into the underground tunnels. The tour is in Spanish, but you'll have no trouble imagining what the life of the miners was like. Be sure to wear sturdy shoes and bring a sweater. Farther down the train track is another stop at, of all places, a discotheque. There's a small gift shop at the entrance. ⊠ *Entrance on Antonio Dovali off Av. Torréon beyond Alameda García de la Cadena* ☎ 492/922–3002 ☑ $2 ☉ *Daily 10–6.*

★ **㉖ Museo Pedro Coronel.** Originally a Jesuit monastery, this building was used as a jail in the 18th century. The museum houses the work of Zacatecan artist and sculptor Pedro Coronel and his extensive collection of works by Picasso, Dalí, Miró, Braque, and Chagall, among others, as well as art from Africa, China, Japan, India, Tibet, Greece, and Egypt. ⊠ *Av. Fernando Villalpando at Plaza Santo Domingo* ☎ 492/ 922–8021 ☑ *About $2* ☉ *Fri.–Wed. 10–5.*

★ **㉘ Museo Rafael Coronel.** The mellowed pink 18th-century facade of the Ex-Convento de San Francisco conceals a rambling structure of open, arched corridors, all leading through garden patios to rooms that contain an amazing collection of some 4,500 *máscaras* (masks). These images of saints and devils, wise men and fools, animals and humans were used in regional festivals all over Mexico. There's also an outstanding display of puppets. The museum is northeast of the town center toward Lomas del Calvario. ⊠ *Off Vergel Nuevo between Chaveño and Garcia Salinas* ☎ 492/922–8116 ☑ *About $2* ☉ *Thurs.–Tues. 10–5.*

㉕ Palacio de la Mala Noche. A pair of beautiful 18th-century colonial buildings stands across from the downtown plaza. Both declared national monuments, they are built from native pink stone and have lacy ironwork balconies. One, a municipal building, is known as The Palace of the Bad Night. Legend has it that this was the home of a silver-mine owner who was called upon so often to help the needy that he built a hidden door from which he could enter and leave the palace undisturbed. Up the hill along the side of the palace, you can find the so-called hidden door. The other building now houses the Continental Plaza hotel. ⊠ *Av. Hidalgo 639* ☑ *Free* ☉ *Weekdays 8:30–3 and 5–8, weekends 10–2.*

㉔ Palacio del Gobierno. The Governor's Palace is an 18th-century mansion with flower-filled courtyards and, on the main staircase, a powerful mural painted in 1970 by António Pintor Rodríguez that depicts the history of Zacatecas. ⊠ *East side of Plaza de Armas* ☑ *Free* ☉ *Daily 9–2 and 5–8.*

> **need a break?**
>
> El Teatro Caffé (⊠ Av. Hidalgo 501, inside Teatro Caldreon ☎ 492/ 922–8620), in a restored 100-year-old theater adorned in celestial murals, is a hopping coffee shop where students swap ideas over a cappuccino or a *Neive Opera* (vanilla ice cream topped with chocolate syrup, espresso, and cream).

㉚ Teleférico. The only cable car in the world that crosses an entire city, the Teleférico runs from **Cerro del Grillo** (Cricket Hill) above the Mina Eden to Cerro de la Bufa. True, it crosses at the narrowest point, but it presents a magnificent panoramic view of the city and its many Baroque church domes and spires. It's also well worth the cost to get the ride up to Cerro de la Bufa, which is quite a climb otherwise. Cerro del Grillo station: ✉ *Off Paseo Díaz Ordaz, a steep walk from Plaza de Armas* ☎ *492/922–5694* ✉ *About $2* ☉ *Daily 10–6, except when there are high winds.*

㉗ **Templo de Santo Domingo.** This 18th-century Jesuit church has an ornamented facade and a rich interior that includes gold-leaf religious paintings. The sacristy also contains an impressive collection of religious art. ✉ *Av. Fernando Villalpando at Plaza Santo Domingo* ☎ *No phone* ☉ *Daily 7:30–3 and 5:30–8:30.*

Where to Stay & Eat

Several of Zacatecas's better restaurants are in hotels, and many of the best lodgings are in beautiful, well-preserved 18th- and 19th-century buildings. Other popular restaurants are on Avenida Juárez, which intersects Avenida Hidalgo.

★ **$–$$** ✕ **La Cuija.** Regional food is the strength of this large restaurant, whose name means "the gecko." Start off with an appetizer of three quesadillas: one each of squash blossoms, cheese, and huitlacoche. Also recommended are the *crema de labor* (a cream soup with corn and squash blossoms) and asado de boda (pork in a semisweet and spicy sauce). The wine comes from the owner's Cachola Vineyards in Valle de las Arsinas. A traditional Mexican trio plays Thursday–Sunday afternoons. ✉ *Centro Commercial El Mercado, bottom level* ☎ *492/922–8275* 🗀 *AE, V.*

¢–$ ✕ **Café y Nevería Acrópolis.** This quaint diner is trimmed with paintings and sketches given to the owner by some of the famous people who have eaten here, including a small acrylic by Rafael Coronel. Enjoy a strong Turkish coffee and watch the locals flood in for breakfast. The *chilaquiles verdes* (strips of fried tortilla smothered in a tangy green sauce and white cheese) is served with an alluring basket of pastries and bread. Traditional café fare like hamburgers, sandwiches, and fruity shakes are available for lunch. ✉ *Av. Hidalgo at Plazuela Candelario Huizar, alongside the cathedral* ☎ *492/922–1284* 🗀 *MC, V.*

¢–$ ✕ **El Paraiso.** The fashionable cantina for the Zacatecano elite more than 100 years ago, El Paraiso is still a town favorite today. It's an ideal opportunity to sample various traditional dishes such as *enchiladas de ayer* (yesterday's enchiladas). These may sound like leftovers, but the friendly waiters promise that the flavor is enhanced by the second day. ✉ *Av. Hidalgo at Plaza Goitia* ☎ *492/922–6164* 🗀 *AE, MC, V.*

¢ ✕ **El Recoveco.** Choose from 25 different steaming plates of traditional Mexican dishes at this rustic, full-buffet diner. At lunch you'll likely find Spanish rice, beans, *pollo en mole* (chicken in a mole sauce), an array of fresh salads, and fruit water. The staff is friendly and the price is right at just $4 for an all-you-can-eat lunch, $3.50 for breakfast. ✉ *Av. Torréon 513, in front of the Alameda* ☎ *492/924–2013* 🗀 *No credit cards.*

$$$–$$$$ ✕🏨 **Quinta Real.** This hotel must be one of the most unusual in the world: FodorsChoice it's built around Mexico's oldest bullring, the second one constructed ★ in the Western Hemisphere. The plush rooms are large and bright; their pastel fabrics complement the dark traditional furniture. The bar occupies some of the former bull pens, and an outdoor café takes up two levels of the spectator area. Fine Continental cuisine is served in the elaborate, formal restaurant ($$), with an awesome view of the *plaza de toro* (bullring) and the aqueduct beyond. ✉ *Av. Gonzales Ortega s/n, to the side of the aqueduct, 98000* ☎ *492/922–9104* 🖷 *492/922–8440* ⊕ *www.quintareal.com* 🛏 *49 suites* ⚐ *Restaurant, minibars, cable TV, bar, shops, laundry service, free parking* 🗀 *AE, MC, V.*

$$–$$$ 🏨 **Mesón de Jobito.** This early 19th-century apartment building stood for well over a hundred years before its conversion to a four-star hotel.

The two levels of guest rooms are done in tasteful modern decor, with wall-to-wall carpet and striped drapes. The restful atmosphere is enhanced by the Mesón's perfect location on a blissfully quiet little plaza a few blocks from the cathedral. ⊠ *Jardín Juárez 143, 98000* 🏠 *492/924–1722* ⊕ *www.mesondejobito.com.mx* 🛏 *53 rooms, 6 suites* 🍴 *2 restaurants, cable TV, bar, laundry service, parking (fee)* 🟰 *AE, MC, V.*

$$ 🔲 **Continental Plaza.** This beautiful old colonial building faces the Plaza de Armas and the cathedral in the heart of the city. The pink-stone facade dates from the 18th century; unfortunately the modern interior is rather stark and charmless. Rooms facing the plaza are within earshot of late-night and early morning tamborazo music during festivals. That said, you'll get a great view of the goings-on from your small balcony. ⊠ *Av. Hidalgo 703, 98000* 🏠 *492/922–6183* 🖨 *492/922–6245* 🛏 *86 rooms, 13 suites* 🍴 *Restaurant, bar, laundry service, convention center, free parking* 🟰 *AE, MC, V.*

$ 🔲 **Hostal del Vasco.** For a truly Zacatecano hotel, consider this clean, quiet place. The spacious brown-carpeted suites have dark antiques and marble bathrooms; some are equipped with a small kitchen (but no cookware). Sprawling plants and singing birds—Pepe the parrot leads the choir—enliven the two-story interior courtyard. ⊠ *Alameda and Velasco 1, 98000* 🏠 *492/922–0428* ⊕ *www.hostaldelvasco.com* 🛏 *18 suites* 🍴 *Some kitchenettes, cable TV, hair salon, laundry service, free parking* 🟰 *AE, MC, V.*

¢ 🔲 **Posada de la Moneda.** This very Mexican hotel in the middle of downtown is tidily polished, if a bit threadbare. The rooms are clean and have pint-size balconies. ⊠ *Av. Hidalgo 413, 98000* 🏠 *492/922–0881* 🛏 *34 rooms, 2 suites* 🍴 *Restaurant, cable TV, bar* 🟰 *AE, MC, V.*

Nightlife & the Arts

A must-see if only for its uniqueness, **El Malacate** (⊠ La Mina Eden 🏠 492/922–3002), the discotheque in the Eden mine, is more than 1,000 ft underground. It's best to make reservations at this popular place, which is both crowded and noisy. It's open Thursday–Saturday nights; the cover charge is about $7. Bands play nightly at the **Quinta Real** (⊠ Av. Gonzales Ortega s/n, 🏠 492/922–9104) in a romantic bar located to one side of the old bullring.

Shopping

Don't expect to find quality crafts in Zacatecas; souvenirs are more along the line of tacky knickknacks than handmade crafts. There's some decent silver jewelry, although not as much as you would expect.

Opposite the east end of Plaza de Armas is **La Cazzorra** (⊠ Av. Hidalgo 713 🏠 492/924–0484), a collectibles shop with authentic antiques, books about Zacatecas, Huichol art, *rebozos* (a traditional woven wrap still widely used for warmth), and a fine selection of jewelry from the local silver factory. The owners are a good source of information about the city. The **Centro Comercial El Mercado** (⊠ Calle Hidalgo, next to cathedral) has a few shops with silver goods. **Centro Platero Zacatecas** (🏠 492/923–1007) sells silver jewelry with regional designs, made in its factory in nearby Guadalupe. **Sa Pe Ca** (🏠 492/922–0273) sells a large selection of silver jewelry and accessories for women and men. **Güichito** (⊠ Av. Hidalgo 126 🏠 492/922–1907) specializes in handmade traditional candies from the region.

Side Trips from Zacatecas

Guadalupe

7 km (4½ mi) southeast of Zacatecas.

If you're interested in colonial art and architecture, don't miss this small town. Its centerpiece is the **Ex-Convento de Guadalupe,** founded by Franciscan monks in 1707. It currently houses the **Museo de Arte Virreinal** (*virreinal* means "viceregal," or "colonial"), run by the Instituto Nacional de Antropología e Historia. The convent is itself a work of art, with its Baroque **Templo de Guadalupe** and the **Capilla de Nápoles,** but even more impressive is the stunning collection of religious art under its roof. Its displays include works by Miguel Cabrera, Nicolás Rodríguez Juárez, Cristóbal de Villalpando, and Andrés López. ⊠ *Jardín Juárez s/n* ☎ *492/923–2386* 🖾 *$3* ⏰ *Daily 10–4:30.*

In the 18th-century mansion of don Ignacio de Bernárdez, the **Centro Platero Zacatecas** is a school and factory for handmade silver jewelry and other items. Stop in to watch student silversmiths master this fine tradition. ⊠ *Casco de la Ex-Hacienda Bernárdez* ☎ *492/923–1007* ⏰ *Weekdays 10–6, Sat. 10–2.*

Zona Arqueológica La Quemada

50 km (31 mi) southwest of Zacatecas on Hwy. 54, 3 km (2 mi) off highway.

This ancient city was already a ruin before the Spaniards arrived in the 16th century. The site's original name, "Chicomostoc," means "place of the seven tribes." Although it was once believed that seven different Native American cultures built here, one community atop the other, this theory is currently under scrutiny. The remaining edifices appear to be constructed of thin slabs of stone wedged into place. The principal draw is a group of rose-color ruins containing 11 large, round columns built entirely of the same small slabs of rock seen in the rest of the ruins. An impressive site museum has a scale model of the ruins and some interesting artifacts. To get here, take a bus toward Villanueva, get off at the entrance to La Quemada, and walk 3 km (2 mi). The bus ride takes about an hour. Alternatively, take a taxi or guided tour. ☎ *No phone* 🖾 *$3* ⏰ *Site and museum daily 10–4:30.*

Zacatecas A to Z

To research prices, get advice from other travelers, and book travel arrangements, visit www.fodors.com.

AIR TRAVEL

AIRPORT The Zacatecas La Calera airport (ZCL) is 29 km (18 mi) north of town.

AIRPORT TRANSFERS Aerotransportes shuttles make the trip between Zacatecas and the airport for about $5; private taxis cost about $15.
📑 **Aerotransportes** ☎ 492/922-5946.

CARRIERS Mexicana has direct service to Zacatecas from Chicago and Los Angeles. It also offers plenty of nonstop flights from other cities in Mexico, including Mexico City, Guadalajara, and Cancún.
📑 **Mexicana** ⊠ Av. Hidalgo 406 ☎ 492/922-7470 or 492/922-3248 ⊕ www.mexicana.com.

BUS TRAVEL

Major bus lines run several first- and second-class buses daily from Mexico City's Central de Autobuses del Norte to Zacatecas. The Zacatecas bus depot is a couple of miles southwest of the town center. Estrella Blanca is the first-class service offered by Futura. The trip takes eight to nine hours and costs about $53.

🚹 **Estrella Blanca** ☎ 492/922-0042. **Futura** ☎ 492/922-0042.

CAR TRAVEL

Zacatecas is about 7½–8 hours by car from Mexico City via Highway 57 (to Querétaro and San Luis Potosí) and Highway 49.

EMERGENCIES

English is not generally spoken in Zacatecas, so it's best to contact your hotel manager or the tourist office in case of an emergency. The emergency line for fire, police, or medical attention is 066.

Pharmacies are abundant; try Farmacia Isstezac, open daily 8 AM–10 PM.

🚹 **Farmacia Isstezac** ✉ Tacuba 153 ☎ 492/924-0690. **Hospital General** ☎ 492/923-3004. **Police** ☎ 492/922-0180. **Red Cross** ☎ 492/922-3005.

INTERNET

Cronos, open Monday–Saturday 9–8 and Sunday 10:30–8, charges $2 an hour for Internet access.

🚹 Internet Café **Cronos** ✉ Av. Rayon 212 ☎ 492/922-1548.

MONEY MATTERS

There are several currency exchanges and banks with ATMs in downtown Zacatecas.

TOURS

Viajes Mazzoco, a well-established travel agency and the local American Express representative, gives a four-hour tour of the city center, the Mina Eden, the Teleférico, and La Bufa for about $12 a person. There are also tours to La Quemada ruins and environs ($16). Ask in advance for an English-speaking guide.

Operadora Zacatecas is recommended by the tourism office, and offers tours of the city center and elsewhere in the area. Juan Dela O of DelaOTours offers a lively introduction to the sights of Zacatecas.

🚹 Tour Operator Recommendations **DelaOTours** ✉ 2 da. de Matamoros 153-C ☎☎ 492/922-3464. **Operadora Zacatecas** ✉ Av. Hidalgo 630 ☎ 492/922-2552. **Viajes Mazzoco** ✉ Calle Fatima 115 ☎☎ 492/922-0859.

TRANSPORTATION AROUND ZACATECAS

You can get to most of the town-center attractions on foot, although you might want to hire a taxi if you want to want to visit the farther-flung sights like the Cerro de la Bufa. The city has an excellent and inexpensive bus system; rides cost only 30¢ and buses are clearly marked.

VISITOR INFORMATION

The tourist information office is open weekdays 9–8, weekends 9–7.

🚹 Tourist information office ✉ Av. Hidalgo 403, 2nd fl. ☎ 492/924-4047 or 492/924-0552.

QUERÉTARO

63 km (39 mi) southeast of San Miguel de Allende, 220 km (136 mi) northwest of Mexico City.

In 1810 the first plans for independence were hatched at the Querétaro home of Josefa Ortiz de Domínguez—known as La Corregidora, wife of El Corregidor, Querétaro's mayor of the time. She was a heroine of the independence movement. In 1848 the Mexican-American War was concluded in this city with the signing of the Treaty of Guadalupe Hidalgo. Emperor Maximilian made his last stand here in 1867 and was executed by firing squad on the Cerro de las Campanas (Hill of the Church Bells), north of town. A small memorial chapel, built by the Austrian government, marks the spot. A gigantic statue of Benito Juárez crowns a park on the crest of the hill just above it. Also, in 1917, the Mexican Constitution, which is still in force, was signed here. Now Querétaro is a state capital and an industrial center of more than 1 million people.

Throughout Querétaro are markers, museums, churches, and monuments that commemorate the city's heroes and historic moments. A prevailing sense of civic pride is evident in the impeccably renovated mansions, the flower-draped cobblestone pedestrian walkways, and the plazas, which are softly lighted at night. On Sunday evening couples dance to live *danzón* music in the main plaza, or simply chat with their friends. The people are among the most congenial in central Mexico and are quick to share their favorite sites and tales with travelers.

Querétaro is also renowned for opals—red, green, honey, and fire stones. Caveat emptor: some street vendors sell opals so full of water that they crumble shortly after purchase. Buy from reputable dealers.

Exploring Querétaro

Although Querétaro sprawls, the historic district is relatively compact.

a good walk

Most sights are near the **Plaza de la Independencia** ㉜ ⌐. The **Palacio del Gobierno del Estado** ㉝ is on the plaza's northwest corner. If you walk around the square counterclockwise, you'll come to the Palacio de Justicia, originally built as a mansion for the wealthy Domingo Iglesia and, beside it, the **Casa de Ecala** ㉞. Just past the Casa de Ecala is Avenida Libertad Oriente, one of the city's bougainvillea-draped pedestrian walkways. Turn west here and walk two blocks to reach Calle Corregidora. Bear right again, and in the middle of a long block you'll find the entrance to the **Museo Regional de Querétaro** ㉟. Cross the street to Avenida Madero, another "pedway," this one lined with shops. The city's main square, Jardín Obregón, will be on your right.

One block past Avenida Juárez on the corner of Calle Allende Sur and Avenida Madero you'll see the former **Casa de la Marquesa** ㊱, an 18th-century mansion converted into a hotel. Across Calle Allende, next to the Templo de Santa Clara, is the neoclassical **Fuente de Neptuno** ㊲. From the fountain, head south on Calle Allende and walk almost a block to a fine example of Baroque architecture, the **Museo de Arte de Querétaro** ㊳. Retrace your steps to Calle Corregidora. Make a left and walk one block to Avenida 16 de Septiembre. Across the street is the **Jardín de la Corregidora** ㊴.

TIMING It takes about two hours to walk through Querétaro's compact center. The museums are closed Monday.

What to See

㉞ **Casa de Ecala.** Currently housing the offices of DIF, a family-services organization, this Mexican Baroque palace has its original facade. As the story goes, its 18th-century owner adorned his home elaborately to outdo his neighbor, starting a remodeling war in which the Casa de Ecala eventually triumphed. Visitors are welcome to walk around the courtyard when the offices are open. ⊠ *Pasteur Sur 6, at Plaza de la Independencia* ☉ *Daily 9–2 and 4–6.*

㊱ **Casa de la Marquesa.** Today a five-star hotel, this beautifully restored 18th-century house was built by the second Marqués de la Villa del Villar del Aguila. Most of the legends about the house's construction sug-

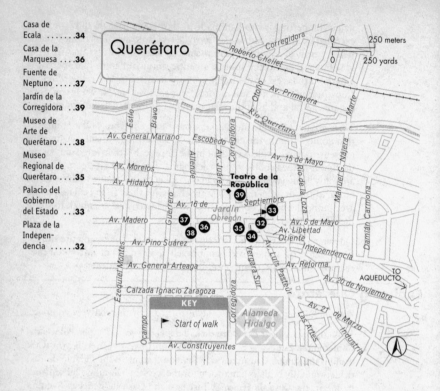

gest that it was built to impress a nun with whom the marquis was terribly smitten. But he didn't live to see the casa completed in 1756, and
its first resident was his widow, who had a penchant for things Arabic.
The interior is *mudéjar* (Moorish) style, with lovely tile work. Stop in
for a drink and the elegant atmosphere of **Don Porfirio's Bar.** ⊠ *Av.
Madero 41, El Centro.*

**need a
break?**

Cafeteria El Naranjo (⊠ Av. Madero 48 ☎ 421/224–0136 Ext. 109)
has a wide selection of specialty coffee, including the Sexy Coffee
(coffee, rum, Kahlúa, and whole cream).

③⑦ Fuente de Neptuno. Built in 1797 by Eduardo Tresguerras, the renowned
Mexican architect and a native of the Bajío, the fountain originally stood
in the orchard of the San Antonio monastery. According to one story,
when the monks faced serious economic problems, they sold part of their
land and the fountain along with it. It now stands next to the Templo
de Santa Clara. ⊠ *Calle Allende at Av. Madero.*

③⑨ Jardín de la Corregidora. This plaza is prominently marked by a statue
of the War of Independence heroine—Josefa Ortiz de Domínguez—whose
moniker it bears. Behind the monument stands the **Arbol de la Amis-
tad** (Tree of Friendship). Planted in 1977 in a mixture of soils from around
the world, the tree symbolizes Querétaro's hospitality to all travelers.
This is the calmest square in town, with plenty of choices for patio dining. ⊠ *Calle Corregidora at Av. 16 de Septiembre.*

③⑧ Museo de Arte de Querétaro. A fine example of Baroque architecture, the
museum is housed in an 18th-century Augustinian monastery. Its collection focuses on European and Mexican paintings from the 17th
through 19th centuries, and there are rotating exhibits of 20th-century

art. Note the elegant and fascinating Baroque patio, and ask for an explanation of the symbolism of its columns and the figures in the conch shells at the top of each arch. ⊠ *Calle Allende 14 Sur* ☎ *421/212–2357* ⊕ *www.queretaro-mexico.com.mx/museo-arte* ⊠ *About $1.50, free Tues.* ☉ *Tues.–Sun. 10–6.*

㉟ Museo Regional de Querétaro. This bright-yellow, 17th-century Franciscan monastery displays the works of colonial and European artists in addition to historic memorabilia, including early copies of the Mexican Constitution and the table on which the Treaty of Guadalupe Hidalgo was signed. ⊠ *Calle Corregidora 3, at Av. Libertad Ote.* ☎ *421/212–2031* ⊠ *About $3* ☉ *Tues.–Sun. 10–7.*

㉝ Palacio del Gobierno del Estado. Also known as La Casa de la Corregidora, in 1810 this was the home of Querétaro's mayor-magistrate (El Corregidor) and his wife, Josefa Ortiz de Domínguez (La Corregidora). On many evenings, conspirators—including Ignacio Allende and Father Miguel Hidalgo—came here under the guise of participating in La Corregidora's literary salon. When El Corregidor learned that they were actually plotting the course for independence, he imprisoned his wife in her room. La Corregidora managed to whisper a warning to a coconspirator, who notified Allende and Hidalgo. A few days later, on September 16, Father Hidalgo tolled the bell of his church to signal the beginning of the fight for freedom. A replica of the bell can be seen atop the building. Now the Palacio houses municipal government offices. ⊠ *Northwest corner of Plaza de la Independencia* ⊠ *Free* ☉ *Weekdays 8 AM–9 PM, Sat. 8–3.*

▶ ㉜ Plaza de la Independencia. Bordered by carefully restored colonial mansions, this immaculate square, also known as Plaza de Armas, is especially lovely at night, when the central fountain is lighted. Built in 1842, the fountain is dedicated to the Marqués de la Villa del Villar, who constructed Querétaro's elegant aqueduct and provided the city with drinking water. The old stone aqueduct with its 74 towering arches still stands at the east end of town. ⊠ *Bounded by Av. 5 de Mayo on the north, Av. Libertad Ote. on the south, Pasteur on the east, and Vergara Sur on the west.*

Where to Eat

Many of Querétaro's dining spots are near the main plaza (Jardín Obregón), along Calle Corregidora, near the Teatro de la República, and particularly in the Jardín de la Corregidora. There are fancier restaurants in hotels on the Plaza de la Independencia and off Highway 57, north of the city.

$$–$$$ ✕ **Restaurante Josecho.** Bullfight aficionados and other sports fans frequent this highway road stop next to the bullring at the southwest end of town as much for the lively atmosphere as for the food. Wood-paneled walls are hung with hunting trophies, including peacocks, elk, bears, and lions; waiters celebrate patrons' birthdays by singing and blasting a red siren. In the evenings a classical guitarist or pianist performs. House specialties include *filete Josecho* (steak with cheese and mushrooms) and *filete Chemita* (steak sautéed in butter with onions). Save room for the creamy coconut ice cream. ⊠ *Dalia 1, next to Plaza de Toros Santa María* ☎ *421/216–0229 or 421/216–0201* ⊟ *AE, MC, V.*

$–$$ ✕ **El Mesón de Chucho el Roto.** Named after Querétaro's version of Robin Hood, this restaurant is on the quiet Plaza de Armas. It's a good place to try regional dishes, like tacos of either steamed goat, shrimp with nopal cactus, or squash blossoms. ⊠ *Plaza de Armas* ☎ *421/212–4295* ⊟ *AE, MC, V.*

¢–$$ ✕ **La Nueva Fonda del Refugio.** In the Jardín de la Corregidora, this restaurant offers intimate indoor and outdoor dining. Inside, the tables are topped with fresh flowers outside, comfortable *equipaje* chairs face the surrounding gardens. For a delicious regional twist order the *filete de huitlacoche,* a steak fillet smothered in a corn fungus sauce. At night, you'll be serenaded by guitar-playing trios. ⊠ *Jardín de la Corregidora 26* ☏ *421/212–0755* ▭ *AE, MC, V.*

¢–$ ✕ **Bisquets Bisquets.** Mexican families flock to this friendly spot after church for—you guessed it—biscuits, made fresh on the premises. Pick a traditional topping like butter and jelly or go for something more unusual like mole or tuna. There are also good enchiladas *Queretanas,* with cheese, potatoes, carrots, and cream, and *huevos al albañil* (eggs with red sauce and beans). ⊠ *Av. Pino Suarez 7* ☏ *421/214–1481* ▭ *No credit cards.*

¢–$ ✕ **La Mariposa.** This spot is easily recognized by the wrought-iron butterfly (*mariposa*) over the entrance. It's the place for coffee and cake or a light Mexican lunch: tacos, tamales, and *tortas* (sandwiches). It's a favorite among locals despite its very plain, cafeteria-like appearance. ⊠ *Angela Peralta 7* ☏ *421/212–1166 or 421/212–4849* ▭ *No credit cards.*

Where to Stay

Querétaro offers a variety of elegant and unique restored properties. Lower-price hotels are near the main plaza and thus tend to be noisy; restored colonial mansions are on or near the city's many plazas in the heart of town; and deluxe properties are on the outskirts of town.

$$$–$$$$ ☒ **Casa de la Marquesa.** This handsomely restored property, originally
Fodor'sChoice an 18th-century private home, is in the heart of Querétaro. Each large
★ guest room is furnished in antiques, tasteful art, parquet floors, and area rugs. Rooms in the main building are more elegant and expensive than those in La Casa Azul (children under 12 are not admitted in the main building). The property's award-winning restaurant, Comedor de la Marquesa, is elegant and a bit austere. It specializes in such regional rarities as boar, venison, and *escamole* (ant eggs) in season, as well as more-traditional international cookery. ⊠ *Av. Madero 41, 76000* ☏ *421/ 212–0092* 🖷 *421/212–0098* ⇘ *25 suites* ⚐ *2 restaurants, room service, bar, shop* ▭ *AE, MC, V.*

$$$ ☒ **Hacienda Jurica.** A favorite getaway for Mexico City families, this sprawling 16th-century ex-hacienda has nearly 30 acres of grassy sports fields, topiary gardens, a horse stable, and golf at a nearby course. Antique horse-drawn carriages dot the grounds and courtyards, and the spacious earth-tone rooms have substantial dark-wood furniture. The hacienda is in Jurica, an upscale residential neighborhood 13 km (8 mi) northwest of the city off Highway 57 and is easiest to reach by car. ⌖ *Carretera Mexico–San Luis Potosí, Km 229, Apdo. 338, 76100* ☏ *421/218– 0022* 🖷 *421/218–0136* ⊕ *www.hoteljurica.com.mx* ⇘ *176 rooms, 6 suites* ⚐ *Restaurant, minibars, 2 tennis courts, pool, billiards, horseback riding, bar, laundry service, free parking* ▭ *AE, MC, V.*

$$$ ☒ **Mesón de Santa Rosa.** On the quiet Plaza de la Independencia, this elegant property was used almost 300 years ago as a stopover for travelers to the north. Rooms are clustered around a quiet courtyard; lace-hung glass doors and wood-beam ceilings maintain the colonial charm. ⊠ *Pasteur Sur 17, 76000* ☏ *421/224–2623* 🖷 *421/212–5522* ⇘ *5 rooms, 16 suites* ⚐ *Restaurant, minibars, cable TV, pool, bar* ▭ *AE, MC, V.*

$$ ☒ **Holiday Inn Querétaro.** This gracious, well-run establishment has a lot more charm than others in the chain. Located 3 km (about 2 mi) west of the historic district off Highway 57, the contemporary building incorporates many colonial touches such as stone archways and domed *boveda* (vaulted) ceilings. Sunny, ample rooms are comfortably ap-

pointed with rustic Mexican furnishings and cheery pastel bedspreads. ⊠ *Av. 5 de Febrero 110, 76000* ☎ *421/216–0202* ⊟ *421/216–8902* ⊕ *www.holidayinn.com.mx* ⤳ *171 rooms, 4 suites* ⚲ *2 restaurants, minibars, cable TV, pool, gym, piano bar, baby-sitting, travel services, free parking, no-smoking rooms* ⊟ *AE, MC, V.*

$ 🖭 **Hotel Mirabel.** A favorite among business travelers and convention-eers, this modern high-rise at the bottom of its price range hums with activity. Its carpeted rooms are insulated and quiet and have wooden desks. Some double rooms have views of the Alameda Hidalgo park; some singles overlook a soccer stadium. ⊠ *Av. Constituyentes Ote. 2, 76000* ☎ *421/214–3099 or 421/214–3444* ⊟ *421/214–3585* ⊕ *www.hotelmirabel.com.mx* ⤳ *170 rooms, 10 suites* ⚲ *Restaurant, cable TV, bar, meeting room, free parking* ⊟ *AE, MC, V.*

Nightlife & the Arts

Band concerts are held in the **Jardín Obregón,** Querétaro's main square, every Sunday evening at 6. A monthly publication called *Tesoro Turístico* (all in Spanish), available at the tourist office, provides information about current festivals, concerts, and other cultural events.

Shopping

A number of stores around town sell opals (not milky white, like Australian opals, but beautiful nonetheless) and other locally mined gems. If you're in the market for loose stones or opal jewelry, do some comparison shopping, as you're apt to find better prices here than in the United States. **Lapidaria Querétaro** (⊠ Corregidora 149 Nte. ☎ 421/212–0030) is a reputable dealer of loose stones and opals. **Villalone y Artesanos** (⊠ Av. Libertad 24-A ☎ 421/212–8414) offers friendly service and authentic stones.

El Globo (⊠ Corregidora 41, at Independencia ☎ 421/212–1019 or 421/212–8883), boasting more than 100 hundred years of service in Querétaro, offers a variety of extravagant cookies, chocolates, freshly baked breads, cakes, and pies.

Side Trips from Querétaro

Tequisquiapan
70 km (43 mi) southeast of Querétaro, off Rte. 120.

This tranquil, pretty spot drenched in sun and bougainvillea and flowering trees was long famous for its restorative thermal waters. In recent years, though, Tequis (as the locals call it) has suffered a dearth of hot water, reportedly due to the extraordinary water consumption of a paper mill in the area. Many spas struggle on as simple swimming pools–recreation areas, but as the main tourist draw has receded with the once-warm waters, most are deserted midweek. Things do liven up on hot weekends, however. Check with the tourist office for directions to the spas, most of which are outside of town.

The town's main plaza is punctuated with the **Templo de Santa María de la Asunción,** begun in 1874 in the neoclassical style but not completed until the beginning of the 20th century. In late May or early June, the city hosts a weeklong wine and cheese festival.

Tequis's reputation for high-quality wicker and other crafts holds strong, so you may wish to head to the **Mercado de Artesanías** (⊠ Calz. de los Misterios s/n ☎ no phone), where woven goods, jewelry, and locally made furniture are sold.

Xilitla

Approximately 320 km (198 mi) northeast of Querétaro.

Feel the ordinary world fade away with a trip to the decidedly off-the-beaten-path **Las Pozas** (The Pools), the extraordinary sculpture garden of the late, eccentric English millionaire Edward James (1907–84). Friend of artists Dalí and Picasso and rumored to be the illegitimate son of King Edward VII, James spent 20 years building 36 surrealist concrete structures deep in the waterfall-filled Xilitla jungle. These amazing structures are half-finished fantasy castles, gradually falling to ruin as the rain forest slithers in to claim them. It's like the ultimate child's fort. The castles don't have walls—just vine-entwined pillars, secret passageways, and operatic staircases leading nowhere.

It's a 6- to 7-hour thrilling but exhausting mountainous drive to Xilitla, with hairpin turns and spectacular desert, forest, and jungle vistas. Plan on staying at least two nights, as you'll want time to soak up the jungle magic. If you choose not to drive, you can take a bus to Ciudad Valles (1½-hour drive from Xilitla) or fly to Tampico (3½-hour drive from Xilitla), and arrange ahead for the staff of Posada El Castillo to pick you up. ✢ *From Querétaro, head north on Hwy. 57 (Carretera Mexico–San Luis Potosí). Take the* PEÑA DE BERNAL *turnoff, marked on a bridge overpass and also on a smaller sign at the Cadareyta exit. Continue north through Bernal, after which the road will join Rte. 120. Take 120 through Jalpan and then on to Xilitla, just across the border in the state of San Luis Potosí. The turnoff to Las Pozas is just beyond Xilitla on the left after passing a small bridge* ▨ *$1.50* ☉ *Daily dawn–dusk.*

WHERE TO STAY

$$ ▨ **Posada El Castillo.** When he wasn't living in his jungle hut, Edward James stayed in town (a 10-minute drive away) in a whimsical house that feels like an extension of the garden structures at Las Pozas—except that it has walls. That house, El Castillo (the castle), is now a quirky inn run by Lenore and Avery Danziger, who have made an award-winning documentary film about James that they happily screen for guests. Rooms are adorned with simple wooden furnishings; the best rooms have huge Gothic windows and panoramic mountain views. You can arrange to have meals here; otherwise there are few dining options in the area. ⊠ *Ocampo 105, 79900 Xilitla, San Luis Potosí* ☎ *136/365–0038* 🖷 *136/365–0055* ⊕ *www.junglegossip.com* ⇶ *8 rooms* ⌂ *Pool* ▭ *No credit cards.*

Querétaro A to Z

To research prices, get advice from other travelers, and book travel arrangements, visit www.fodors.com.

BUS TRAVEL

Daily buses run direct between Mexico City's Central del Norte (North Bus Station) and Querétaro's Central de Autobuses, which is a couple of miles southeast of the town center. Major lines have frequent service; travel time is about three hours and tickets cost about $20. Buses also leave several times a day for Guanajuato, San Miguel de Allende, and Morelia.

🖪 **ETN** ☎ 421/229–0078 or 421/229–0019. **Flecha Amarilla** ☎ 421/211–4001. **Futura** ☎ 421/229–0022. **Omnibus de México** ☎ 421/229–0029.

CAR RENTAL

Budget has an office in downtown Querétaro.

🖪 **Budget** ⊠ Av. Constituyentes Ote. 73 ☎🖷 421/213–4498 ⊕ www.budget.com.

CAR TRAVEL

It takes about three hours to get to Querétaro from Mexico City by car via Highway 57. From Querétaro, another hour's drive will get you to Tequisquiapan; take Highway 57 to Route 120. Xilitla is at least six hours away.

EMERGENCIES

Dial 066 for medical, fire, and theft emergencies.

Ambulance-Red Cross ☎ 421/229-0545 or 421/229-0665. **Emergency** ☎ 066. **Fire Department** ☎ 421/212-3939 or 421/212-0627. **Police** ☎ 421/220-8303 or 421/220-9191. **Sanatorio Alcocer Pozo (Hospital)** ✉ Calle Reforma 23 ☎ 421/212-0149 or 421/212-1787. **Traffic Police** ☎ 421/213-8424.

INTERNET

Web Café, open Monday–Saturday 10–10 and Sunday 4–10, charges $3 an hour for Internet access.

Internet Café **Web Café** ✉ Ezequiel Montes Sur 67 ☎ 421/216-0250 or 421/216-7272.

MONEY MATTERS

Casa de Cambio Acueducto is open weekdays 9–2 and 4–6 and Saturday 9–1.

Casa de Cambio Acueducto ✉ Av. Juárez Sur 58 ☎ 421/212-9304.

TOURS

The tourist office conducts hour-long trolley tours of the city's historic landmarks at 9, 10, and 11 AM and at 4, 5, and 6 PM Tuesday–Sunday; all commentary is in Spanish. To arrange a city tour in English, call the office—one day in advance if possible. The cost is about $1.50.

TRANSPORTATION AROUND QUERÉTARO

Most of Querétaro's historic sites are within walking distance of one another in the downtown district and can be reached by a series of walkways that are closed to car traffic most of the day. If you want to venture farther afield, you will find that taxis run frequently along the main streets and are inexpensive.

TRAVEL AGENCIES

Turismo Beverly offers full travel services; they should have an English-speaking agent.

Local Agent Referral **Turismo Beverly** ✉ Av. Tecnologia 118 ☎ 421/216-1500 or 421/216-1260 🖷 421/216-8524.

VISITOR INFORMATION

Querétaro's Dirección de Turismo del Estado is open weekdays 8–8, weekends 9–8.

Tequisquiapan's Oficina de Turismo is open daily 9–7; its Web site, www.tequisquiapan.com.mx, has a bit of descriptive information in English.

Dirección de Turismo del Estado ✉ Plaza de Armas ☎ 421/212-1412 or 421/212-0907 🖷 421/212-1094. **Oficina de Turismo de Tequisquiapan** ✉ Andador Independencia 1, Plaza Miguel Hidalgo ☎ 427/273-0295.

MORELIA

▶ *302 km (187 mi) west of Mexico City.*

With its long, wide boulevards and earth-tone colonial mansions, Morelia is the gracious capital of the state of Michoacán—as well as a UNESCO World Heritage Site. Founded in 1541 as Valladolid (after the Spanish city), it changed its name in 1828 to honor José María Morelos, the town's most famous son. The legendary mule skinner–turned–priest took up the battle for independence after its early leaders were executed in 1811.

Morelos began with an ill-equipped army of 25 but soon organized a contingent of 9,000 that nearly gained control of the country. Although he was defeated and executed in 1815, he left behind a long-standing reformist legacy that called for universal suffrage, racial equality, and the demise of the hacienda system. The city today still pays tribute to Morelos—his former home has been turned into a museum, and his birthplace is now a library.

Morelianos love music, and several annual festivals are designed to indulge their taste. Each May the city celebrates the International Organ Festival in the cathedral, giving voice to its outstanding 4,600-pipe organ. The last two weeks in July are given to the Festival International de Música, featuring Baroque and chamber music, with orchestras participating from throughout Mexico.

Morelia has the delicious distinction of being the candy capital of Mexico. So strong is the sweet-eating tradition that the city has an entire market devoted to sweets.

Exploring Morelia

To explore Morelia and its surrounding hillside neighborhoods thoroughly would take some time. However, a stroll through the historic plazas will give you a feel for the city's vitality. Although the vehicle and sidewalk traffic can get a little heavy at times, Morelia is a pedestrian-friendly place; it also tries to hold back the tide of street vendors that floods most cities.

a good walk

Begin your walk in Morelia's tree-lined downtown **Plaza de Armas** ④⓪ ▶, on the east side of which is the city's famed **Catedral** ④①. As you leave the cathedral, cross Avenida Madero Oriente to the **Palacio de Gobierno** ④②, a former seminary. From the palace it's four blocks east along Avenida Madero Oriente to Calle de Belisario Domínguez. Make a right and walk one block south to the Templo de San Francisco. To the rear of the church, in the former convent of San Francisco, is the entrance to the **Casa de las Artesanías del Estado de Michoacán** ④③, a virtual cornucopia of crafts from around the state.

From the crafts museum, go west to join Calle Vasco de Quiroga, a street lined with vendors, and walk two blocks south until you come to Calle del Soto Saldaña. Head west another two blocks to Avenida Morelos Sur. The corner building on the right is the **Casa Museo de Morelos** ④④, which displays memorabilia of the independence leader. It's one block north from the museum to Calle Antonio Alzate and then one block west (where the street name changes to Calle Corregidora) to Calle García Obeso. On this corner stands the **Museo Casa Natal de Morelos** ④⑤, Morelos's birthplace. Continue west on Calle Corregidora until you reach Calle Abasolo. On Calle Allende, one block to the north, you'll find the **Museo Regional Michoacano** ④⑥.

After leaving the museum take Calle Abasolo back to the plaza; 2½ blocks to the north, you'll see the **Museo del Estado** ④⑦ on the right side of the street (which changes to Calle Guillermo Prieto at Avenida Madero Oriente). Return to Avenida Madero Oriente and then go 2 blocks to the right to the corner of Avenida Valentín Gómez Farías, to the **Mercado de Dulces** ④⑧.

For a longer stroll, take Avenida Madero Oriente east a dozen blocks or so to where it forks. Stay to the right; you'll see the **Fuente de las**

Tarascas on a traffic island to your left. Just past the fountain, More-lia's mile-long **aqueduct** begins. This 1875 structure, which consists of 253 arches, once carried the city's main source of drinking water. It's particularly beautiful at night when its arches—some rising to 30 ft—are illuminated. Two blocks farther along (Madero is now called Avenida Acueducto) is the entrance to **Bosque Cuauhtémoc,** Morelia's largest park. If you happen by during the week, you may encounter university students studying (or lounging) beneath the palms and evergreens. On weekends, especially Sunday, families on outings take over. Two blocks past the park entrance, you'll see the **Museo de Arte Contemporáneo** 49, also on the right side of the street.

TIMING A tour through Morelia's center will take roughly two hours, not including the time spent in the museums. Remember that most museums, except the Casa de las Artesanías del Estado de Michoacán, close on Monday.

What to See

43 **Casa de las Artesanías del Estado de Michoacán.** In the 16th century, Vasco de Quiroga, the bishop of Michoacán, helped the Purépecha Indians develop artistic specialties so they could be self-supporting. At this two-story museum and store, you can see the work that the Purépechas still produce: copper goods from Santa Clara del Cobre, lacquerware from Uruapan, straw items and pottery from Pátzcuaro, guitars from Paracho, fanciful ceramic devil figures from Ocumicho. At the **Museo Michoacana de las Artesanías** in the two main floors around the court-yard, some of these items are showcased behind glass while artists demonstrate how they are made. ⊠ *Calle Fray Juan de San Miguel 129* 🕾 *443/312–2486 museum; 443/312–1248 store* 🖾 *Free* 🕐 *Mon.–Sat. 10–3 and 5–8, Sun. 10–4:30.*

㊹ Casa Museo de Morelos. What is now a two-story museum was acquired in 1801 by José María Morelos and was home to generations of the Mexican independence leader's family until 1934. Owned by the Mexican government, it contains family portraits, various artifacts from the independence movement (such as a camp bed used by Ignacio Allende), and the blindfold Morelos wore for his execution. The excellent free tour is in Spanish only. ⊠ *Av. Morelos Sur 323* ☎ *443/313–2651* ⊠ *About $2* ☉ *Daily 9–7.*

㊶ Catedral. Morelia's cathedral is a majestic structure built between 1640 and 1744. It is known throughout Mexico for its 200-ft Baroque towers, among the tallest in the land, and for its 4,600-pipe organ, one of the finest in the world. The organ is the vehicle for the international organ festival held here each May. ⊠ *Av. Madero between Plaza de Armas and Av. Morelos* ☎ *No phone.*

㊽ Mercado de Dulces. If you have a sweet tooth, don't miss Morelia's candy market. All sorts of local sweets are for sale, such as *ate* (a candied fruit) and *cajeta* (heavenly caramel sauce made from goat's milk). ⊠ *Av. Madero Pte. at Av. Valentín Gómez Farías* ☉ *Daily 10–9.*

㊾ Museo de Arte Contemporáneo. The works of contemporary Mexican and international artists are on view at this well-lighted museum near the Bosque Cuauhtémoc. ⊠ *Av. Acueducto 18* ☎ *443/312–5404* ⊠ *Free* ☉ *Tues.–Sun. 10–2 and 4–8.*

㊺ Museo Casa Natal de Morelos. José María Morelos's birthplace is now a library and national monument housing mostly literature and history books (as well as two murals by Moreliano Alfredo Zalce). Be sure to visit the courtyard in back where a marker and an eternal flame honor the fallen hero in this tranquil square. ⊠ *Calle Corregidora 113* ☎ *443/ 312–2793* ⊠ *Free* ☉ *Daily 9–7.*

㊼ Museo del Estado. Across from a small plaza with statues of Bishop Vasco de Quiroga and Spanish writer Miguel de Cervantes, this history museum is in a stately mansion that was once the home of the wife of Agustín de Iturbide, Mexico's only native-born emperor. A highlight of the collection is a complete Morelia pharmacy dating from 1868. ⊠ *Calle Guillermo Prieto 176* ☎ *443/313–0629* ⊠ *Free* ☉ *Tues.–Sun. 10–2 and 4–8.*

㊻ Museo Regional Michoacano. An 18th-century former palace, the museum traces the history of Mexico from its pre-Hispanic days through the Cardenista period, which ended in 1940. President Lázaro Cárdenas, a native of Michoacán, was one of Mexico's most popular leaders because of his nationalization of the oil industry and his support of other populist reforms. The ground floor contains an art gallery, plus archaeological exhibits from Michoacán. Upstairs is an assortment of colonial objects, including furniture, weapons, and religious paintings. ⊠ *Calle Allende 305* ☎ *443/312–0407* ⊠ *About $3* ☉ *Tues.–Sat. 9–7, Sun. 9–4.*

need a break? When you've finished your tour of the Muséo Regional Michoacano, walk across the street to the colonial stone *portales* (arcades). The portales on one side of the square contain popular sidewalk cafés. For a sandwich, an order of guacamole with chips, or a good selection of juices, coffees, and teas, try **Hotel Casino** (⊠ Portal Hidalgo 229 ☎ 443/313–1328).

㊷ Palacio de Gobierno. This former Tridentine seminary, built in 1770, has had such notable graduates as independence hero José María Morelos, social reformer Melchor Ocampo, and the first emperor of Mexico, Agustín de Iturbide. Striking murals decorate the stairway and second floor. Painted by local artist Alfredo Zalce in the early 1960s, they depict dramatic, often bloody scenes from Mexico's history. Zalce is the last of the great modern muralists still living. ⊠ *Av. Madero 63* ☎ *443/312–8598* 🖾 *Free* ⊘ *Weekdays 8 AM–10 PM.*

▶ ④ **Plaza de Armas.** During the War of Independence, several rebel priests were brutally murdered on this site, and the plaza, known as Plaza de los Mártires, is named after them. Today, however, the square belies its violent past: sweethearts stroll along the tree-lined walks and friends chat under the colossal silver-domed gazebo. ⊠ *Bounded on the north by Av. Madero, on the south by Calle Allende, on the west by Calle Abasolo, and on the east by the cathedral.*

Where to Eat

Some of Michoacán's tastiest dishes—tomato-based sopa tarasca, corn products such as *huchepos* (sweet tamales) and *corundas* (savory triangular tamales), and game (rabbit and quail)—are served at Morelia restaurants. As a rule, more-upscale restaurants are in hotels near the plaza and on the outskirts of town.

$–$$$ ✕ **Fonda Las Mercedes.** This delightful restaurant's arty, modern furnishings somehow fit perfectly in the plant-filled stone patio of this restored colonial mansion. The inside dining room, which is equally pleasant, may be cozier on chilly days or evenings. Offerings from the eclectic menu include lots of soups and six kinds of crepes. If you dare, try the sinfully rich pasta with pistachios and pine nuts in cream sauce. ⊠ *Calle León Guzmán 47* ☎ *443/312–6113* ⊟ *AE, MC, V* ⊘ *No dinner Sun.*

$–$$ ✕ **Boca del Río.** The fresh seafood for this cheerful yet cafeteria-like restaurant is trucked in daily from Sinaloa and Veracruz. There are light snacks like the popular *coctel de camarones* (shrimp cocktail), along with heartier fare, such as the *jaiba rellena* (mushroom-and-cheese-stuffed crabs liberally seasoned with garlic). For dessert, head across the street to the sprawling Mercado de Dulces. ⊠ *Av. Valentín Gómez Farías 185* ☎ *443/312–9974* ⊟ *MC, V.*

$–$$ ✕ **Casa de la Calzada.** In a restored weekend home a block and a half from the aqueducts, this elegant restaurant offers tables in a fountain-studded courtyard and in richly painted dining rooms hung with contemporary art. Look for contemporary Mexican dishes like the taste-bud fiesta of *pollo del jardín de los naranjos*, chicken stuffed with Mexican sausage and shrimp and coated in a citrus sauce. ⊠ *Calz. Fray Antonio de San Miguel 344* ☎ *443/313–5319* ⊟ *AE, MC, V.*

$ ✕ **La Casa del Portal.** Overlooking the Plaza de Armas and quartered in four distinctly decorated dining rooms, this venerable restaurant hones in on local dishes. Served in a succulent red sauce, the corundas are topped with chopped pork, sour cream, and chili poblano strips. Don't miss the *arrachera Valladolid,* a succulent slice of skirt steak served with *nopales* (sliced and steamed cactus), guacamole, and beans. ⊠ *Calle Guillermo Prieto 30* ☎ *443/317–4217 or 443/313–4899* ⊟ *AE, MC, V.*

¢ ✕ **Taquería Pioneros.** There's a reason the tables are full at lunch at this positively plain taco shop: it has delicious grilled meats, served Michoacán style with salsas and mountains of fresh, hot tortillas made on-site. The *pionero* (beef, ham, bacon, onions, and cheese, all grilled) is the only style served in a half portion, which is plenty for most appetites. ⊠ *Calle Aquiles Serdan 7, at Calle Ocampo* ☎ *443/313–4938* ⚲ *Reservations not accepted* ⊟ *No credit cards.*

Where to Stay

Morelia offers a number of pleasant colonial-style hotels both in the downtown and outlying areas. Generally, the cheapest properties are near the bus station, moderately priced selections are clustered around the plaza (or on nearby side streets), and deluxe resort hotels are in or near the Santa María hills.

★ $$$ ▦ **Villa Montaña.** French count Philippe de Reiset has fitted this villa with all the trappings of a wealthy Mexican estate. High above Morelia in the Santa María hills, its five impeccably groomed acres are dotted with stone sculptures. Each individually decorated unit has at least one piece of antique furniture, and most have a fireplace and private patio. The hotel's renowned restaurant serves North American, French, and Mexican cuisine from its huge windows you'll have a marvelous view of Morelia, especially at night. Children under age eight are discouraged from dining in the restaurant. ⊠ *Calle Patzimba 201, 58000* ☎ *443/314–0231 or 443/314–0179* 🖶 *443/315–1423* ⊕ *www.villamontana.com.mx* ⌨ *15 rooms, 25 suites* ⚘ *Restaurant, in-room safes, tennis court, pool, piano bar, baby-sitting, laundry service, business services, meeting rooms, free parking* ⊟ *AE, MC, V.*

$$–$$$ ▦ **Hotel Virrey de Mendoza.** Built in 1565 to house a Spanish nobleman, this downtown hotel still radiates plenty of old-world atmosphere. The elegant lobby lounge is fitted with an enormous stone fireplace and cushy black leather couches. Guest rooms have dark colonial-style furnishings, lace curtains, soaring ceilings, and creaking hardwood floors, and the bathrooms have porcelain tubs. ⊠ *Av. Madero Pte. 310, 58000* ☎ *443/ 312–0633 or 443/312–4940* 🖶 *443/312–6719* ⊕ *www.hotelvirrey.com* ⌨ *40 rooms, 15 suites* ⚘ *Restaurant, coffee shop, cable TV, bar, laundry service, Internet, free parking* ⊟ *AE, MC, V.*

$$ ▦ **Hotel Posada de la Soledad.** In a restored private mansion built in the late 17th century, this charming hotel is one block from the Plaza de Armas. Rooms vary in size, decoration, amenities, and price. The rooms in the original section surround an elegant patio with a large fountain and massive bougainvilleas. Rooms in a newer section are smaller and plain but quiet; rooms on Calle Ocampo get loud traffic noise from the street. If you're not impressed with the room you are shown, ask to see another. ⊠ *Ignacio Zaragoza 90, 58000* ☎ *443/312–1888 or 443/ 312–8990* 🖶 *443/312–2111* ⊕ *www.hsoledad.com* ⌨ *48 rooms, 9 suites* ⚘ *Restaurant, cable TV, bar* ⊟ *AE, MC, V.*

$ ▦ **Hotel Mansión Acueducto.** An elaborate wood and wrought-iron staircase leads from the elegant lobby to more-modest quarters upstairs. Rooms have dark, colonial-style furniture; older units overlook the aqueduct and nearby park. Rooms in the motel-like wing have views of the garden, pool, and surrounding city. At times, student groups book the entire property. ⊠ *Av. Acueducto 25, 58230* ☎ *443/312–3301* 🖶 *443/ 312–2020* ⊕ *www.hotelmansionacueducto.com* ⌨ *36 rooms, 1 suite* ⚘ *Restaurant, cable TV, pool, bar, free parking, no-smoking rooms* ⊟ *MC, V.*

¢   ▦ **Hotel Valladolid.** Right on the Plaza de Armas, this property has plain but clean rooms with brick floors and striped bedspreads. The price includes coffee and juice. Although the accommodations are far from deluxe, this location offers easy access to downtown, and the staff is friendly. ⊠ *Portal Hidalgo 245, 58000* ☎ *443/312–0027* 🖶 *443/312–4663* ⌨ *25 rooms* ⚘ *Restaurant; no room phones* ⊟ *AE, MC, V.*

Nightlife & the Arts

Morelia has two lively folk-music clubs, both in beautiful locations downtown. **Colibri** (⊠ Galeana 36 ☎ 443/312–2261) has folk music from throughout Latin America every night from 9:30 PM to 1 AM. **La Porfiriana** (⊠ Calle Corregidora 694 ☎ 443/312–2663) presents spirited salsa music Tuesday–Saturday 7 PM–3 AM.

Side Trip to Santuario de Mariposas el Rosario

Approximately 115 km (71 mi) east of Morelia.

★ Every year 100 million monarch butterflies migrate from the United States and Canada to winter in the easternmost part of Michoacán, near the border of México state. A visit to the **Santuario de Mariposas el Rosario** between early November and early March is an awesome sensory experience. Caked with orange-and-black butterflies, the sanctuary's pine forest looks like it's on fire. Listen closely and you'll hear the rustle of millions of wings beating. The hike to the groves is a steep climb, and the high altitude (10,400 ft) will require that you take it slowly.

This day trip takes about 10 hours, but it's well worth the effort. If you choose not to drive the rough roads, catch a guided tour in Morelia. ⊠ *Hwy. 15 east to Zitácuaro, then take marked but unnumbered road north to Angangueo, and on to sanctuary entrance* ☎ *No phone* ⊠ *$2 (plus tip for guide)* ☉ *Daily 10–5.*

Morelia A to Z

To research prices, get advice from other travelers, and book travel arrangements, visit www.fodors.com.

AIR TRAVEL

AIRPORT Aeropuerto Internacional Francisco Mujica (MLM) is 24 km (15 mi) north of Morelia.

AIRPORT TRANSFERS A taxi ride between the town center and the airport will cost about $12.

CARRIERS Aeroméxico flies daily to Morelia from Mexico City's international airport.
🔳 **Aeroméxico** ☎ 800/021-4000 in the U.S. ⊕ www.aeromexico.com.

BUS TRAVEL

Direct bus service is available daily between the Terminal Poniente (commonly referred to as the Observatorio) in Mexico City and Morelia's Central de Autobuses. Several bus lines have frequent service; the most direct trip ($18) takes four hours on ETN. Herradura de Plata is another bus line. Buses leave every hour or two around the clock.
🔳 **Central de Autobuses** ⊠ Eduardo Ruiz, between Av. Valentín Gómez Farías and Guzmán ☎ 443/312-5664. **ETN** ☎ 443/313-7440 or 443/313-4137. **Herradura de Plata** ☎ 443/312-2988.

CAR RENTAL

Budget has an office at the Francisco Mujica airport. National's office is beside the airport.
🔳 **Budget** ⊠ Aeropuerto Internacional Francisco Mujica ☎ 443/313-3399 ⊕ www.budget.com.

CAR TRAVEL

The drive from Mexico City to Morelia on the toll road, Highway 15, through Toluca, Atlacamulco, Contepec, and Maravatio takes about four hours.

EMERGENCIES

Dial 070 for medical, fire, and theft emergencies.

🛈 Ambulance–Red Cross ☎ 443/314-5151. **Consumer Protection Office** ☎ 443/315-6202. **Fire Department** ☎ 443/320-1780. **Hospital de la Cruz Roja** ☎ 443/314-5073. **Hospital Memorial** ☎ 443/315-1047 or 443/315-1099. **Police** ☎ 443/326-8522.

INTERNET

Chat Room Cyber Café, open Monday–Saturday 9 AM–10 PM and Sunday noon–9, charges $2 an hour for Internet access.

🛈 Internet Café **Chat Room Cyber Café** ✉ Calle Nigromante 132-A ☎ 443/312-9222.

MONEY MATTERS

Consultoría Internacional Casa de Cambio is open Monday–Saturday 9:30–5:30.

🛈 **Consultoría Internacional Casa de Cambio** ✉ Calle Guillermo Prieto 48 ☎ 443/313-8308.

TOURS

Several worthy operators conduct tours of Morelia and the butterfly sanctuary. Contact Ayangupani through David Saucedo Ortega at the Villa Montaña front desk.

🛈 Tour Operator Recommendations **Ayangupani** ✉ Calle Patzimba 201 ☎🖷 443/315-4045. **Explora Viajes** ✉ Av. Madero Ote. 493B ☎ 443/312-7766 🖷 443/312-7660. **Morelia Operadores de Viajes** ✉ Isidro Huarte 481 ☎ 443/312-8723 or 443/312-8747 🖷 443/312-9591.

TRANSPORTATION AROUND MORELIA

As in many heartland cities, Morelia's major sights are near the center of town and easy to get to on foot. Street names in Morelia change frequently, especially on either side of Avenida Madero, the city's main east–west artery. Taxis can be hailed on the street or found near the main plaza. Buses run the length of Avenida Madero.

TRAVEL AGENCIES

Gran Turismo is the American Express representative.

🛈 **Gran Turismo** ✉ Edificio Ejecutivo Camelinas, Av. Camelinas 3233, Int. 102-103 ☎ 443/324-0484 🖷 443/324-0495.

VISITOR INFORMATION

Secretaría Estatal de Turismo is open weekdays 9–8, Saturday 9–7, and Sunday 9–3.

🛈 Tourist Information **Secretaría Estatal de Turismo** ✉ Palacio Clavijero, Calle Nigromante 79 ☎ 443/317-2371 🖷 443/312-9816.

PÁTZCUARO

58 km (36 mi) southwest of Morelia

Pátzcuaro, the 16th-century capital of Michoacán, exists in a time warp. This beautiful lakeside community at 7,250 ft in the Sierra Madre is home to the Purépecha Indians, who fish, farm, and ply their crafts as they have for centuries. Women wrapped tightly in their striped wool *rebozos* (shawls) hurry to market in the chilly morning air. Men in traditional straw hats wheel overburdened carts down crooked, dusty backstreets.

The architecture, too, has remained largely unchanged over the years. In the 16th century, under kindly Bishop Vasco de Quiroga, Pátzcuaro underwent a building boom. After he died in 1565, the state capital was moved to Morelia, and the town became a cultural (and architectural) backwater for hundreds of years. These days 16th-century mansions surround the downtown plazas; one-story whitewashed houses with sloping red tile roofs line the side streets and hills.

Despite the altitude, the weather in Pátzcuaro is temperate year-round. (Autumn and winter nights, however, are cold; sweaters and jackets are a must.) On November 1 the town is inundated with tourists en route to Janítzio, an island in Lake Pátzcuaro, where one of the most elaborate Day of the Dead graveyard ceremonies in all of Mexico takes place. At numerous small towns around the lake you can buy craft items from their makers, in the process absorbing a bit of small-town rural Mexico.

Exploring Pátzcuaro

You can zip through Pátzcuaro's historic center, but the town and outlying areas deserve to be explored at a leisurely pace. There can be some traffic in the Plaza Bocanegra and on the main road coming into town, but elsewhere it is blissfully quiet.

a good walk

Start your walk at the tourist office on the **Plaza Vasco de Quiroga** 50 ▶. Cross to the east side of the square and turn right on Calle Dr. José María Coss; in less than a block you'll see a long cobblestone walkway leading to **La Casa de los 11 Patios** 51, a former convent now housing a number of crafts shops. As you leave the complex, continue up a stone walkway to Calle Lerín. To the north (past Calle Portugal) is the **Templo de la Compañía** 52, the state's first cathedral. After visiting the church, continue another half block north to the **Museo de Artes Populares** 53 on your right.

Directly down Enseñanza Arciga and across a cobblestone courtyard is **La Basílica de Nuestra Señora de la Salud** 54. Walk downhill from the basilica (take Buena Vista to Calle Libertad and turn left) to reach the **Biblioteca Pública Gertrudis Bocanegra** 55. For a nice detour from the library, continue for a half block to the large outdoor mercado sprawled along Calle Libertad and its side streets. At times the road is so crowded with people and their wares—fruit, vegetables, beans, rice, herbs, and other necessities of daily life—that it's difficult to walk. If you press on for about a block, you'll see an indoor market to your left, filled with more produce, large hanging slabs of meat, hot food, and a variety of cheap trinkets. When you're finished with your market tour, retrace your steps down Calle Libertad. Across the street from the library, you can rest at **Plaza Bocanegra** 56, one block north of your starting point, Plaza Vasco de Quiroga.

TIMING   A brisk walk through town will take just a couple of hours; allow more time for the craft museum (closed Monday) and for a break in a café.

What to See

54 **La Basílica de Nuestra Señora de la Salud.** The church was begun in 1554 by Vasco de Quiroga, and throughout the centuries others—undaunted by earthquakes and fires—took up the cause and constructed the church in honor of the Virgin of Health. Near the main altar is a statue of the Virgin made of derivatives of cornstalks and orchids. Several masses are still held here daily; the earliest begins shortly after dawn. Out front, Purépecha women sell hot tortillas, herbal mixtures for teas, and religious objects. You can glimpse Lake Pátzcuaro in the distance. ⊠ *Enseñanza Arciga, near Calle Benigno Serrato* ☎ *No phone.*

55 **Biblioteca Pública Gertrudis Bocanegra.** In the back of this library, a vast mural painted by Juan O'Gorman in 1942 depicts in great detail the history of the region and of the Purépecha people. In the bottom right of the mural, you can see Gertrudis Bocanegra, a local heroine who was shot in 1814 for refusing to divulge the revolutionaries' secrets to the Spaniards. ⊠ *North side of Plaza Bocanegra* ☉ *Weekdays 9–7, Sat. 10–2.*

51 **La Casa de los 11 Patios.** An 18th-century convent, 11 Patios houses a number of high-quality shops featuring Purépecha handiwork. As you meander through the shops and courtyards, you'll encounter weavers producing large bolts of cloth, artists trimming black lacquerware with gold, and seamstresses embroidering blouses. If you plan to shop in Pátzcuaro, this is a good place to start. ⊠ *Calle Madrigal de las Altas Torres s/n* ☉ *Daily 10–2 and 4–8.*

53 **Museo de Artes Populares.** Home to the Colegio de San Nicolás Obispo in the 16th century, the building today houses displays of colonial and contemporary crafts, such as ceramics, masks, lacquerware, paintings, and ex-votos in its many rooms. Behind this building is a *troje* (traditional Purépecha wooden house) braced atop a stone platform. ⊠ *Enseñanza Arciga* ☎ *434/342–1029* ⌨ *About $3* ☉ *Tues.–Sat. 9–7, Sun. 9–2:30.*

56 **Plaza Bocanegra.** The smaller of the city's two squares (it's also called Plaza Chica), this is the center of Pátzcuaro's commercial life. Bootblacks, pushcart vendors, and bus and taxi stands are all in the plaza, which is embellished by a statue of the local heroine, Gertrudis Bocanegra. ⊠ *Bounded by Av. Libertad on the north, Portal Regules on the south, Benito Mendoza on the west, and Iturbe on the east.*

▶ **50** **Plaza Vasco de Quiroga.** A tranquil courtyard surrounded by ash and pine trees and 16th-century mansions (since converted into hotels and shops), the larger of the two downtown plazas commemorates the bishop who restored dignity to the Purépecha people. During the Spanish conquest, Nuño de Guzmán, a lieutenant in Hernán Cortéz's army, committed atrocities against the local population in his efforts to conquer western Mexico. He was eventually arrested by the Spanish authorities, and in 1537 Vasco de Quiroga was appointed bishop of Michoacán. Attempting to regain the trust of the indigenous people, he established a number of model villages in the area and promoted the development of *artesanía* (crafts) commerce among the Purépechas. Quiroga died in 1565, and his remains were consecrated in the **Basílica de Nuestra Señora de la Salud.** ⊠ *Bounded by Calle Quiroga on the north, Av. Ponce de León on the south, Portal Hidalgo on the west, and Calle Dr. José María Coss on the east.*

need a break? Before heading to Lake Pátzcuaro, sit in **Plaza Vasco de Quiroga** for a moment and enjoy a rich Michoacán ice cream you can buy under the portals on the west side of the plaza. Or sip a warming Doña Paca cappuccino spiked with *rompope* (egg liqueur) at the sidewalk café in front of Mansión Iturbe.

52 Templo de la Compañía. Michoacán's first cathedral was begun in 1540 by order of Vasco de Quiroga and completed in 1546. When the state capital was moved to Morelia some 20 years later, the church was taken over by the Jesuits. Today it remains much as it was in the 16th century. Moss has grown over the crumbling stone steps outside; the dank interior is planked with thick wood floors and lined with bare wood benches. ⊠ *Calle Lerín s/n near Calle Alcantaría* ☎ *No phone.*

off the beaten path **Lake Pátzcuaro.** A 10-minute taxi ride from downtown are the tranquil shores of Lake Pátzcuaro. A few lakeside restaurants here serve fresh whitefish and other local catches. Amble along the dock or peek into the waterfront crafts shops. Try to make time for a boat trip to Janítzio (the largest of Lake Pátzcuaro's five islands) or to tiny Yunuen, which offers a clear-eyed view of island life. Wooden launches, with room for 25 people, depart for Janítzio and the other islands daily 9–6. Purchase round-trip tickets for $3 at a dockside office (prices are controlled by the tourist department). The ride to Janítzio takes about 30 minutes and is particularly beautiful in late afternoon, when the sun is low in the sky. Once you're out on the lake, fishermen with butterfly nets may approach your boat. The nets are no longer used for fishing, but for a small donation these locals will let you take their picture.

On most days (November 1 being the exception), Janítzio is a quiet albeit touristy island inhabited by Purépecha Indians. It's crowned by a huge statue of independence hero José María Morelos, which is accessible by a cobblestone stairway. Although the road twists past many souvenir stands as it ascends, don't be discouraged. The view from the summit—of the lake, the town, and the surrounding hills— is well worth the climb. Inside the statue are some remarkable murals that spiral up from the base to the tip of the monument.

Although Janítzio has succumbed to tourism, the small island of Yunuen is just beginning to attract visitors. This tranquil town has just a few families, and provides a more accurate picture of island life than does Janítzio. You can get a boat to here from the ferry landing, or arrange to stay overnight in simple yet clean cabins available for visitors. The office of tourism can provide information.

Where to Eat

Many restaurants in Pátzcuaro specialize in seafood. In addition to whitefish, look for *trucha* (trout) and *charales* and *boquerones* (two small, locally caught fish served as appetizers). Finding a satisfying meal in Pátzcuaro can be a challenge; focusing on local Purépecha dishes, such as sopa tarasca, may prove most rewarding. As a rule, restaurants are around the two plazas and in hotels. Since the large meal is served at midday, many dining establishments are shuttered by 9.

$–$$ ✕ **El Primer Piso.** This second-floor restaurant overlooks Plaza Vasco de Quiroga, and on warm nights you can watch the comings and goings from a balcony table. There's plenty to look at inside as well; the restaurant doubles as an art gallery. The eclectic menu provides a break from the rather monotonous Pátzcuaro fare: try the pear salad with goat cheese, walnuts, and watercress, or the white-chocolate mousse with blackberries and melon cream. ⊠ *Plaza Vasco de Quiroga 29* ☎ *434/342–0122* ▤ *AE, MC* ⊘ *Closed Tues.*

¢–$ ✕ **Doña Paca.** At this terrific family-run restaurant you'll find some of the best examples of local cuisine. Look for the fish specials and the tamale-like corundas with cream sauce. ⊠ *Hotel Mansión Iturbe, Portal Morelos 59* ☎ *434/342–0268* ▤ *AE, MC, V.*

¢–$ ✕ **El Patio.** Although this low-key restaurant serves mouthwatering whitefish platters (including salsa, vegetables, and french fries), it's possible to duck in at midday for just a strong cappuccino or glass of Mexican wine. For a late-afternoon snack, go for a plate of quesadillas with a side order of guacamole or the sopa tarasca. ⊠ *Plaza Vasco de Quiroga 19* ☎ *434/342–0484* ▤ *MC, V.*

¢–$ ✕ **El Viejo Gaucho.** Join the crowd for a festive night of live music from North, Central, and South America performed in front of a mural, repainted each season. Try the *Churrasco Argentino* (seasoned steak) and don't forget to top it with *chimichurri* (an Argentine sauce made with fresh herbs and olive oil). Most entrées are pseudo-Argentinian, but pizza, hamburgers, and American-style french fries are also available. ⊠ *Iturbe 10* ☎ *434/342–3627* ▤ *AE, MC, V* ⊘ *No lunch.*

Where to Stay

Although Pátzcuaro has no deluxe hotels, there is an ample number of clean, moderately priced properties. Most are on or within a few blocks of the Plaza Vasco de Quiroga. Several more-expensive hotels are on Avenida Lázaro Cárdenas, the road to Lake Pátzcuaro. If you're planning to be in town on or near November 1–2, the Day of the Dead, make hotel reservations at least six months in advance.

★ $$–$$$ ▥ **Hacienda Mariposas.** The amenities of this getaway are exceptional, from the friendly bilingual staff to the terrific restaurant. The distractions are low-tech: live music during dinner, horseback riding trips, birdsong from the surrounding pine forest. Guest rooms have fireplaces (as well as central heating) and beds topped with down comforters, plus CD players with a selection of music. The property is a few minutes' drive from town; transportation to and from Pátzcuaro is included. ⊠ *Santa Clara del Cobre Hwy., Km 3, 61600* ☎ *434/342–4738 or 443/ 333–0762; 800/573–2386 in the U.S.* 🖷 *707/575–1166* ⊕ *www. haciendamariposas.com* ⇆ *12 rooms* ⚴ *Restaurant, spa, horseback riding; no room TVs* ▤ *AE, MC, V* ⊙ *BP.*

$$–$$$ ▥ **Hotel Posada La Basílica.** On some mornings, strains from mass at the neighboring Basílica de Nuestra Señora de la Salud filter softly into this inn. The 17th-century building has comfortable, individually decorated

rooms, some with fireplaces. Thick wood shutters cover floor-to-ceiling windows, and walls are trimmed in hand-painted colonial designs. ⊠ *Enseñanza Arciga 6, 61600* ☎ *434/342–1108* 🖶 *434/342–0659* ⬙ *12 rooms* ⚲ *Restaurant, free parking* ⊟ *AE, MC, V.*

★ **$$** 🏨 **Mansión Iturbe.** Housed in a 17th-century mansion, this hotel still retains much of its colonial charm. Stone archways ring plant-filled courtyards. Rooms, with large wood-and-glass doors, are partially carpeted. Bicycles are lent to guests for a few hours per stay, and every fourth night is free. The owners are an excellent source of information regarding Pátzcuaro and the surrounding areas. ⊠ *Portal Morelos 59, 61600* ☎ *434/342–0368 or 434/342–3628* 🖶 *443/313–4593 in Morelia* ⊕ *www.mexonline.com/iturbe.htm* ⬙ *10 rooms, 4 suites* ⚲ *3 restaurants, bicycles, travel services, no-smoking rooms* ⊟ *AE, MC, V* ⦿*BP.*

¢ 🏨 **Cabañas Yunuen.** This complex was built on the island of Yunuen in collaboration with the Department of Tourism to promote visits to some of the area's more authentic communities. There are six cabins in all: two each for 2, 4, and 16 people; each has a kitchenette with small refrigerator. Breakfast or dinner and round-trip transportation by boat is included in the price. Be sure to call ahead for reservations. ⊠ *Domicilio Conocido, Isla de Yunuen* ☎ *434/342–4473* ⬙ *6 cabins* ⚲ *Dining room, kitchenettes, billiards, Ping-Pong* ⊟ *No credit cards.*

¢ 🏨 **Los Escudos.** Today a cozy hotel, this property was originally a 16th-century home. Its courtyards bloom with potted plants, and guest rooms contain small murals. Ten rooms situated in back and shielded from street noise open onto an outdoor patio; five rooms have fireplaces. ⊠ *Portal Hidalgo 73, 61600* ☎ *434/342–0138 or 434/342–1290* 🖶 *434/342–0649* ⬙ *31 rooms, 2 suites* ⚲ *Restaurant, free parking* ⊟ *MC, V.*

Nightlife & the Arts

The **Danza de los Viejitos** (Dance of the Old Men), a widely known regional dance, is performed during Saturday dinner at Hotel Posada de Don Vasco (⊠ Av. Las Americas 450) for approximately $12 (includes dinner). The dance is also performed Saturday night at 9 PM at Los Escudos, on Plaza Vasco de Quiroga.

Shopping

Pátzcuaro has some of Mexico's finest folk-art shopping. **Artesanías El Naranjo** (⊠ Plaza Vasco de Quiroga 29-2), an intimate group of stores, offers a variety of ceramics, clothing, and folk art. **Bordados Santa Cruz** (⊠ Calle Dr. José María Coss 3 ☎ 433/338–1425) is a women's embroidery collective. For fresh-ground local coffee appealingly packaged in burlap bags, visit **El Café Uruapan** (⊠ Benito Mendoza 3 ☎ 434/342–5061). Since 1898, the family-run **Chocolate Casero Joaquinita** (⊠ Enseñanza Arciga 38 ☎ 434/342–4514) has been concocting delectable homemade cinnamon-spiced hot-chocolate tablets. Don't miss the stands in front of the basilica and at the daily mercado west of Plaza Chica for an array of inexpensive local crafts. **Mantas Tipicas** (⊠ Calle Dr. José María Coss 5 ☎ 434/342–1324) sells hand-loomed tablecloths and more. Visit the doorway of Jesús García Zavala at **Platería García** (⊠ Enseñanza Arciga 28 ☎ 434/342–2036) for hand-worked silver Purépecha jewelry in the pre-Columbian tradition. **Santa Teresa Velas y Cirios** (⊠ Calle Portugal 1 ☎ 434/342–0918) sells handsome handmade candles.

Side Trips from Pátzcuaro

Tzintzuntzan

🔺 *17 km (10½ mi) northeast of Pátzcuaro.*

When the Spanish came to colonize the region in the 16th century, some 40,000 Purépechas lived and worshiped in this lakeshore village, which they called "place of the hummingbirds." The ruins of the pyramid-shape temples, or *yacatas,* found in the ancient capital of the Purépecha kingdom, still stand today and are open to the public for $2. There are also vestiges of a 16th-century Franciscan monastery where Spanish friars attempted to convert the Indians to Christianity. Although Tzintzuntzan lost some prominence when Bishop Vasco de Quiroga moved the seat of his diocese to Pátzcuaro in 1540, the village is still well known for the straw and ceramic crafts made by the Purépecha Indians and sold in numerous shops along the main street of town. The bus marked QUIROGA takes a half hour to get from Pátzcuaro's Central Camionera to Tzintzuntzan.

Santa Clara del Cobre

20 km (12½ mi) south of Pátzcuaro.

Since before the conquest, Santa Clara del Cobre has been a center for copper arts. Now the local copper mines are empty, but the artisans still make gorgeous vessels, plates, napkin rings, and jewelry using the traditional method of pounding out each piece of metal by hand. For an introduction to quality and range of styles available, visit the **Museo del Cobre** (✉ Calles Morelos and Pino Suárez, near the plaza), open Tuesday–Sunday 10–3 and 5–7. Admission is 50¢. Then explore the 50-some little shops and factories in town. The friendly owners speak English at **Arte y Cobre** (✉ Calle Pino Suárez 53 ☎ no phone). Although the selection isn't as extensive as other shops along the square, the prices are often less expensive. The bus to Santa Clara del Cobre from Pátzcuaro's Central Camionera takes 40 minutes.

Uruapan

64 km (40 mi) west of Pátzcuaro.

The subtropical town of Uruapan is distinctly different from its lakeside neighbor: some 2,000 ft lower than Pátzcuaro, although still at an elevation of 5,300 ft, it's a populous commercial center with a warm climate and lush vegetation. The town's name is derived from the Purépecha word *urupan,* meaning "where the flowers bloom." Uruapan celebrates Palm Sunday with a lively procession through the streets, brass bands, and a spectacular, bargain-filled crafts market in the central plaza—one of the best in all of Mexico.

You can get to Uruapan from Pátzcuaro by car or bus. Highway 14 and the toll road are the most direct routes between the two cities. There's also frequent bus service on the Flecha Amarilla and other major lines; travel time is about 70 minutes.

You can see several points of interest within a few hours. The **Mercado de Antojitos,** an immense, sprawling market, begins in back of the Museo Regional de Arte Popular and extends quite a distance north along Calle Constitución. Along the road, Purépecha Indians sell large mounds of produce, fresh fish, beans, homemade cheese, and a variety of cheap manufactured goods. If you travel south along Calle Constitución, you'll come to a courtyard where vendors sell hot food.

The **Museo Regional de Arte Popular,** opposite the north side of Uruapan's Plaza Principal, was a 16th-century hospital before its conversion. It houses a collection of crafts from the state of Michoacán, including an excellent display of lacquerware made in Uruapan. ☎ 452/524–3434 ☞ *Free* ♡ *Tues.–Sun. 9:30–1:30 and 3:30–6.*

Parque Nacional Eduardo Ruiz (about six long blocks from the Plaza Principal off Calle Independencia) is a gem of an urban park. Its paved paths meander through verdant tropical acreage past abundant waterfalls, fountains, and springs to the source of the Río Cupatitzio. A trout farm and a popular playground also are here.

Eleven kilometers (7 mi) south along the Río Cupatitzio is the magnificent waterfall at **Tzaráracua.** At this point the river plunges 150 ft off a sheer rock cliff into a riverbed below; a rainbow seems to hang perpetually over the site. Buses marked TZARÁRACUA leave sporadically from the Plaza Principal in Uruapan. You can also take a taxi for about $3, or drive there via Avenida Lázaro Cárdenas.

Farther afield, about 32 km (20 mi) north of Uruapan, lies the dormant **Paricutín volcano.** Its initial burst of lava and ashes wiped out the nearby village of San Juan Parangaricútiro in 1943. Today travelers can visit this buried site by hiring gentle mountain ponies and a Purépecha guide in the town of Angahuan. To reach Angahuan, take Los Reyes bus from Uruapan's Central Camionera or go by car via the Uruapan-Carapan highway.

Pátzcuaro A to Z

To research prices, get advice from other travelers, and book travel arrangements, visit www.fodors.com.

BUS TRAVEL

Buses run daily between the Terminal Poniente (commonly referred to as the Observatorio) in Mexico City and Pátzcuaro's Central Camionera on the southwestern outskirts of town. Several lines offer frequent service; the most direct trip, which takes five hours, is on either Herradura de Plata, Pegasso Plus, or ETN. Transportation coming from most heartland cities goes to Morelia; buses leave about every 15 minutes from there on the 45-minute trip to Pátzcuaro.

🚍 Bus Depot **Central Camionera** ⊠ El Libramiento ☎ No phone.
🚍 Bus Information **ETN** ☎ 434/342–1060; 443/313–7440 in Morelia. **Herradura de Plata and Pegasso Plus** ☎ 434/342–1045.

CAR TRAVEL

The Mexico City–Guadalajara tollway cuts driving time to Pátzcuaro to 4½ or 5 hours, and the trip on to Guadalajara to 4 hours by car. From Morelia, the excellent free road to Pátzcuaro takes just over an hour. You'll have to rent a car in Mexico City or Morelia, as there are no rental outlets in Pátzcuaro.

EMERGENCIES

Pharmacies are plentiful; Farmacia Gems is popular with residents. Pátzcuaro offers medical services through Hospital Civil.

🏥 **Farmacia Gems** ⊠ Benito Mendoza 21 ☎ 434/342–0332. **Hospital Civil** ⊠ Romero 10 ☎ 434/342–0285. **Police** ☎ 434/342–0004. **Traffic Police** ☎ 434/342–0565.

INTERNET

Informatica Integral de Pátzcuaro, open daily 9–9, charges $1.50 an hour for Internet access.

🌐 Internet Café **Informatica Integral de Pátzcuaro** ⊠ Plaza Vasco de Quiroga 64 ☎ no phone.

MONEY MATTERS

Bancomer–BBVA has a 24-hour ATM. Banamex has an ATM for use during business hours.

🔻 **Banamex** ✉ Portal Juárez 32 ☎ 434/342–1550 or 434/342–1031. **Bancomer–BBVA** ✉ Benito Mendoza 23 ☎ 434/342–0901.

TOURS

Guide Francisco Castilleja is highly knowledgeable about pre-Hispanic philosophy, history, archaeology, and medicinal herbs. He speaks fluent English, German, French, and Spanish.

🔻 Tour Operator Recommendations **Francisco Castilleja** ✉ Centro Eronga, Profr. Urueta 105 ☎ 434/344–0167.

TRANSPORTATION AROUND PÁTZCUARO

Many of Pátzcuaro's principal sights are near the Plaza Vasco de Quiroga and Plaza Bocanegra in the center of town. Taxis and buses to the lake can also be found at the latter square. If you want to visit surrounding villages, taxi drivers will drive you for a reasonable rate. Be sure to agree on a fee before setting out.

VISITOR INFORMATION

Delegación de Turismo is the official tourism office, and although you may not find anyone here who speaks English, they will do their best to provide information regarding excursions outside Pátzcuaro. It's open Monday–Saturday 9–2 and 4–7, Sunday 9–2.

Dirección de Orientación y Fomento al Turismo offers maps and can answer basic questions about tourist facilities in Pátzcuaro. It's open daily 9–3 and 5–7.

🔻 **Delegación de Turismo** ✉ Plaza Vasco de Quiroga 50A ☎☎ 434/342–1214. **Dirección de Orientación y Fomento al Turismo** ✉ Portal Hidalgo 1, on Plaza de Quiroga ☎ 434/342–0215 or 434/342–0216 ☎ 434/342–0967.

PACIFIC COAST RESORTS

8

FODOR'S CHOICE

La Casa Que Canta, Zihuatanejo hotel

Playa la Ropa, Zihuatanejo

L'Recif, Manzanillo restaurant

Sunsets in Puerta Vallarta

HIGHLY RECOMMENDED

SHOPPING Galería Rosas Blancas, Puerto Vallarta

Galería Uno, Puerto Vallarta

Gallery Michael, Mazatlán

Mercado de Artesanía Turístico, Zihuatanejo

Nidart, Mazatlán

EXPERIENCES Acuario Mazatlán, an aquarium

Bandidos, Zihuatanejo bar

La Bodeguita del Medio, Puerto Vallarta bar-restaurant

Isla Navidad, Manzanillo golf course

Ixtapa Aqua Paradise, dive operator

Mexican Fiesta, dinner show in Mazatlán

Playa Isla de los Venados, Mazatlán

Playa las Gatas, Zihuatanejo

Vista Vallarta, Puerto Vallarta golf course

*So many wonderful hotels and restaurants can be found in this area
that there's not enough space to list them all on this page. To see what
Fodor's editors and contributors highly recommend, please look for the
black stars as you leaf through this chapter.*

Updated by
Jane Onstott

SOUTHERN CALIFORNIANS MAY CONSIDER Baja their backyard, and party animals from southern Arizona have all but colonized Punto Peñasco, Sonora, but Mazatlán is still the major Mexican resort closest to the United States. Some 1,200 km (745 mi) south of the Arizona border, it marks the beginning of the so-called Gold Coast, what cruise-ship operators now call the Mexican Riviera, with ports-of-call at Mazatlán, Puerto Vallarta, Manzanillo, and Ixtapa/Zihuatanejo. The region's resort towns are in four different states: coast-hugging Sinaloa; Jalisco, home of tequila and mariachis; tiny Colima; and finally Guerrero, where Acapulco has long been the vacation king. The 1,400-km (870-mi) stretch of coast is Mexico's tropical paradise, where it's all about sun, sand, agreeably warm water, and hospitable people.

Thanks to its excellent port and the fertility of the surrounding countryside, Mazatlán is a busy commercial and shipping center. More than 600,000 acres of area farmland produce tomatoes, melons, cantaloupes, wheat, and cotton. Many of these products—along with tens of thousands of tons of shrimp, tuna, and sardines hauled in annually—are processed and frozen for American and Japanese markets.

Proximity to the United States, excellent sportfishing, and decent surfing account for Mazatlán's popularity as a resort. The port sits at the juncture of the Pacific and the Sea of Cortez, forming what has been called the world's greatest natural fish trap. Accommodations are about half the cost of those in Cancún or Los Cabos. In addition, downtown Mazatlán has several charming plazas and some beautifully restored late 19th- and turn-of-the-20th-century buildings.

Late film director and sometime resident John Huston put Puerto Vallarta, some 323 km (200 mi) south of Mazatlán, on the map when he filmed Tennessee Williams's *The Night of the Iguana* on the outskirts of town in 1963. Elizabeth Taylor accompanied Richard Burton during the filming, and the gossip about their romance (both were married at the time, but not to each other) brought this quaint Mexican fishing village to the public's attention. Before long, travel agents were deluged with queries about it. Puerto Vallarta is still picturesque even though its fabled cobblestone streets can become clogged with traffic. But for a truer sense of the Eden that once was, visit one of the gorgeous natural coves south of town, or travel north to Punta de Mita on the tip of the Bahía de Banderas (Bay of Flags).

Conquistador Hernán Cortés envisioned Manzanillo as a gateway to the Orient: from these shores, Spanish galleons brought in the riches of Cathay to be trekked across the continent to Veracruz, where they would fill vessels headed for Spain. Manzanillo never gained the stature that Cortés envisioned, but that didn't stop pirates from staking it out during the colonial era. Chests of loot are rumored to be buried beneath the sands.

With the coming of the railroads, Manzanillo became a major port of entry. It's now Mexico's second-busiest port, and you can see the lights of freighters at anchor along the southern beaches. Fifty years ago, a few seaside hotels opened up on the outskirts of town, which vacationers reached by train. The jet age, however, seemed to doom the port as a sunny vacation spot. Then Bolivian tin magnate Antenor Patiño built Las Hadas (The Fairies), a lavish Moorish-style resort inaugurated in 1974. It attracted the beautiful people, and for a while Las Hadas was better known than Manzanillo itself.

The Mexican government has steadily worked to develop for tourism the pristine coast between Manzanillo and Puerto Vallarta, dubbing it

8

Beaches

Mexico's Pacific Coast doubtless has some of North America's most inviting beaches, with deliciously warm waters and spectacular sunsets. And there are beaches for every taste—from the lively to the isolated. In Mazatlán, long stretches of soft beige sand hug the hotel and condo zones north of downtown; runners love the long boardwalk fronting downtown's less showy beaches, which are also frequented by fishermen setting out to sea and surfers catching waves nearer the shore. Puerto Vallarta's in-town crescents of golden sand are often fringed with palms; endless stretches of gloriously unpopulated shores run to the north, and soft, creamy sands line craggy coves to the south. In Manzanillo every day is a beach day, and Sundays are downright festive, with half the town gathered to play onshore. The volcanic sand is a mix of black, brown, and beige; the southernmost beaches are the darkest and sometimes flecked with gold. Farther south, Ixtapa has a long, narrow beach fronting the hotel zone. The beaches on the deep bay of neighboring Zihuatanejo are protected from the surf.

Horseback Riding

Horseback riding along the shore is popular, and you can rent horses by the hour at major beaches. A more pleasant experience, however, is to ride inland on a trek of several hours, a half day, or even overnight to waterfalls, hot springs, or colonial villages in the Sierra Madre. The horses that make these trips seem better cared for, and generally happier, than those standing under palm trees or under the hot sun of a shadeless beach, waiting for riders.

Shopping

You can spend as much time shopping in Puerto Vallarta as you can lazing in the sun. Stores that sell crafts from around the country vie with upscale art galleries and clothing and jewelry boutiques for your attention, especially downtown. Mazatlán and Ixtapa/Zihuatanejo have colorful markets and folk-art shops. In the former, look for shell art and carved wood; in the latter, masks from Jalisco and Guerrero states and beaded bowls and statuettes made by the Huichol Indians.

Water Sports

Sportfishing is good off Puerto Vallarta most of the year, particularly for billfish, rooster fish, mahimahi, yellowtail, and bonito. Manzanillo claims to be the world's sailfish capital; the season runs from mid-October through March. Blue marlin and dorado are also abundant. Ixtapa/Zihuatanejo is one of Mexico's most popular sportfishing destinations. Anglers revel in the profusion of sailfish (November through March), black and blue marlin (May through January), yellowfin tuna (November through June), and mahimahi (November through January). Light-tackle fishing in the lagoons and just off the beach in *pangas* (skiffs) for *huachinango* (red snapper) is also popular. In November, Mazatlán, Puerto Vallarta, and Manzanillo host international fishing tournaments.

Parasailing, swimming, windsurfing, sailing, kayaking, and waterskiing are popular at Pacific Coast resorts. Manzanillo, Mazatlán, and San Blas have some of the finest surfing in Mexico, and the best diving spots in this area are found around the islands off Puerto Vallarta and Ixtapa. Puerto Vallarta hosts Mexico's annual boat show each November, as well as various sailing regattas in winter.

"La Costa Alegre," or happy coast. A four-lane toll road now cuts the driving time between Manzanillo and Guadalajara, Mexico's second-largest city, to three hours. About an hour north of Manzanillo, at the Jalisco state line across from Barra de Navidad, the Grand Bay hotel is but one example of the newer luxury resorts. The complex spreads over some 1,200 acres on a peninsula between the Pacific Ocean and the Navidad Lagoon, 20 minutes west of the Manzanillo airport.

Of the Gold Coast resorts, Ixtapa/Zihuatanejo, some 500 km (300 mi) south of Manzanillo, is the destination whose popularity is growing the fastest. Like Cancún, Ixtapa was the brainchild of the Mexican government in the early 1970s. With an offshore island and many beautiful beaches, this resort comprises two distinct destinations only 7 km (4½ mi) from each other. Ixtapa is the glitzier of the two, with international chain hotels lining its hotel zone, but it's far smaller and more low-key than resorts such as Puerto Vallarta, Cancún, and even Mazatlán. Its development put neighbor Zihuatanejo, a sleepy fishing village on a gorgeous bay, on the tourist map. In Zihuatanejo, La Casa Que Canta is one of the world's finest small hotels.

Exploring the Pacific Coast Resorts

As you travel down the Pacific Coast, there's one element you won't be able to ignore: the ocean. Aquamarine swells provide a scenic backdrop to beachside *palapas* (thatch-roof huts) and lanky palm trees. Rolling waves are a boundless playground for boogie boarders, jet-skiers, and surfers. And the salt water yields a dazzling variety of fresh seafood that is sliced, diced, and spiced into tasty regional dishes.

Although Mexico's Pacific Coast cultures were in some ways as fascinating as that of the better known Aztecs, they left behind no major monuments, and so have been largely ignored by archaeological research teams. This isn't the place to explore ruins, museums, and cathedrals. Rather it's a place to pick a spot to settle, immersing yourself in the simultaneously bustling and restful resort lifestyle of great dining, shopping, sunbathing, and almost any sort of water sport.

About the Restaurants

Shrimp, octopus, oysters, and fresh fish are the highlights; be sure to have a seafood cocktail along the beach. You can savor traditional *pescado sarandeado* (whole fish rubbed with salt and spices and grilled over hot coals) as well as elaborate dishes devised by imported European chefs. Mazatlán has many casual, lively restaurants that serve surf-and-turf and Mexican favorites. Puerto Vallarta has the widest array of restaurants, some with spectacular views, others hidden in the small, romantic patios of former homes, and still others as popular for people-watching as they are for great seafood. Manzanillo's restaurants lack the sophistication of those in Puerto Vallarta, but most serve fresh, reasonably priced seafood. In Ixtapa/Zihuatanejo, restaurants range from open-air palapas on the beach to deluxe establishments with international chefs.

Some hotel restaurants add 15% IVA (value-added tax) as well as a service charge to your tab. Many more humble establishments charge neither, so check your bill and tip accordingly.

About the Hotels

Mazatlán has its share of comfortable beachfront hotels as well as large concentrations of trailer parks. In Puerto Vallarta, accommodations range from tiny inns to luxury waterfront hotels and spectacular resorts on secluded coves. Big beachfront properties are the norm in Ixtapa; Zihuatanejo has budget hotels and several of Mexico's most exclusive small hotels.

Hotels raise their rates for the high season (December 15 through Easter week); rates are also on the high side during July and August, when Mexican families swarm the beaches for their summer vacations. In Manzanillo high season corresponds only to specific holidays, especially Christmas, Easter, and summer vacation (July–August). For the best prices, visit in May, June, September, or October. Note, however, that hurricanes may crop up between late September and early November. Price categories are based on high-season rack rates; expect to pay less by asking for "package rates," which include breakfast, or other specials. Prices should be at least 25% less during the off-season.

WHAT IT COSTS					
	$$$$	**$$$**	**$$**	**$**	**¢**
RESTAURANTS	over $25	$15–$25	$10–$15	$5–$10	under $5
HOTELS	over $250	$150–$250	$75–$150	$50–$75	under $50

Restaurant prices are for a main course excluding tax and tip. Hotel prices are for two people in a standard double room in high season, based on the European Plan (EP, with no meals) and excluding service and 17% tax.

When to Go

Resorts on this coastal stretch are at their best in winter, with temperatures of 20–30°C (70–80°F) and a bit higher in Ixtapa and Zihuatanejo. The off-season brings humidity, mosquitoes, and higher temperatures (northernmost Mazatlán remains coolest), but also emptier beaches, warmer water (about 20°C/70°F), and less-crowded streets—plus 25%–35% lower room rates and cheaper rental-car costs. During and right after the rainy season (June–October), the countryside, the Sierra Madre Occidental, and the Sierra Madre del Sur turn a brilliant green.

MAZATLÁN

Mazatlán is the Nahuatl (Aztec) word for "place of the deer," and long ago it did, indeed, shelter many of these creatures. Duck, quail, pheasant, and other wildfowl fed in the lagoons, and mountain lions, rabbits, and coyotes roamed the surrounding hills. Today there's a dearth of deer, and although hunting is still practiced, deep-sea fishing is the main lure: Mazatlán has one of Mexico's largest sportfishing fleets, and anglers haul in some of the coast's biggest catches, both in size and number. Approximately 12,000 billfish are caught and released each year, including some of gargantuan proportions.

More numerous than the visitors who come to fish are those who come to sun, surf, and sail. And although the Zona Dorada—lined with hotels, shops, and tourist-oriented restaurants—certainly has the feel of a tourist town, Mazatlán's post-colonial downtown reminds you that this city of nearly 700,000 souls is also a dignified port with an interest in arts and culture.

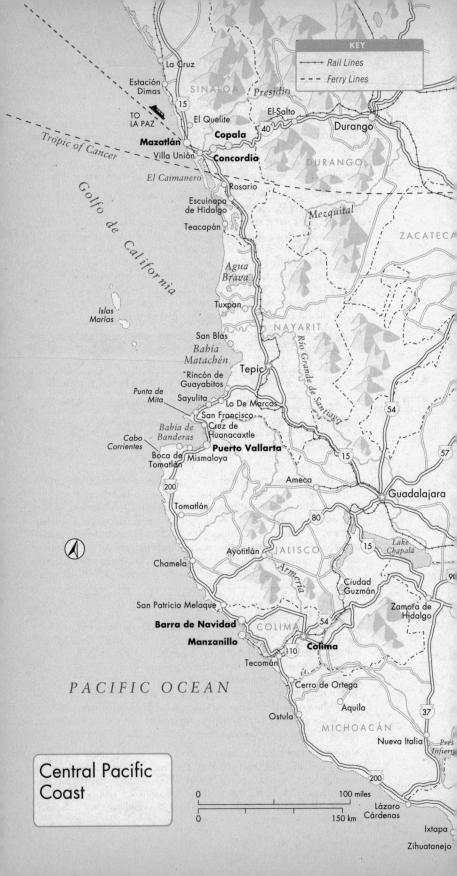

Central Pacific
Coast

The Spanish first visited the Mazatlán region in 1531, and later the colonial government built a small fort and watchtowers to protect Spanish galleons from English and French pirates. The settlement was just a smudge on the map until the mid-19th century, when it became northwestern Mexico's most important city and port. As such, it drew the attention of outsiders seeking to challenge the Mexican government in this sparsely settled part of the country. In 1847, during the Mexican–American War, U.S. forces marched down from the border, occupying the city and closing the port. In 1864, French ships bombarded the city and then controlled it for several years. The British occupied the port for a short period in 1871. Mexico's own internal warring factions took over from time to time. And after the Civil War in the United States, a group of Southerners tried to turn Mazatlán into a slave city.

Exploring Mazatlán

Though many visitors never leave the Zona Dorada (Golden Zone)—a broad avenue lined with hotels, shops, and party-down restaurants—downtown Mazatlán is a fun place to explore. Mazatlán's historic district consists of distinctive late 19th- and early 20th-century edifices and Italianate mansions built by shipping magnates. Downtown's mainly three-story buildings have fanciful wrought ironwork, wooden shutters, and thick walls painted a variety of pastel colors. The city's newest resort area, aptly dubbed Nuevo Mazatlán, is north of the Zona Dorada, around Punta Cerritos on a long—and so far lonely—stretch of beachfront property called Emerald Bay.

Numbers in the text correspond to numbers in the margin and on the Mazatlán map.

a good tour

Start in the **Zona Dorada** ① ► at Punta Camarón. North along Avenida Camarón Sábalo is the stuff resorts are made of: bars and restaurants, shell and souvenir shops, beachfront hotels. This route affords a good view of Mazatlán's three Pacific islands—Isla de los Pájaros, Isla del Venado, and Isla de los Lobos (also referred to as Isla de Chivos). Just past the Faro Mazatlán resort, Avenida Camarón Sábalo becomes Avenida Sábalo Cerritos and crosses over the Estero del Sábalo lagoon. The area north of here is slowly being developed as "Nuevo Mazatlán" (New Mazatlán), an exclusive area slated to be filled with high-end resorts.

South of the Zona Dorada, the main road changes names frequently. Mazatlán's main seaside highway begins at Punta Camarón and is here called Avenida del Mar. About halfway between Punta Camarón and downtown and a few blocks inland is the city's highly recommended aquarium, **Acuario Mazatlán** ②, on Avenida de los Deportes. Avenida del Mar continues past beaches popular with residents and travelers staying at the budget hotels across the street. You're sure to notice the avenue's main landmark, the Monumento al Pescador: an enormous statue of a voluptuous, nude woman reclining on an anchor, her hand extended toward a fisherman dragging his nets.

Soon after the monument, Avenida del Mar becomes Paseo Claussen (named for one of the German originators of Pacífico beer). Calles Juárez and Cinco de Mayo lead from the coast-hugging road to Mazatlán's busy downtown. The heart of the city is **Plaza Revolución** ③, also called *el zócalo* (main square) or Plazuela República. On the square's north side is the twin-spired **Catedral de Mazatlán** ④; on facing streets are the City Hall, banks, and a post office. About three blocks south of the zócalo is the Teatro Angela Peralta, built between 1860 and 1874. Beautifully restored, the theater is now an official historic monument. Stop for a drink or a bite at any one of the establishments around the nearby Plaza Machado, known for its lively neighborhood fiestas. Three blocks west, the unassuming Casa de la Cultura houses the **Museo de Arte de Mazatlán** ➎. Just a few doors away, the **Museo Arqueológico de Mazatlán** ➏ has archaeological pieces from early Pacific coast tribes.

Back along the waterfront, Paseo Claussen continues past El Fuerte Carranza, an old Spanish fort built to defend the city against the French. Next you'll come to Playa Olas Altas, where, at High-Divers Park, young men plunge into the sea, Acapulco-style, from a small white platform. It's spectacular at night, when the divers leap carrying flaming torches. Continuing south you'll see La Mazatleca, a bronze nymph, and across the street, a small bronze deer, the symbol of Mazatlán. Just down the road is the Monumento a la Continuidad de la Vida (Monument to the Continuity of Life), a large fountain with a handsome couple atop a large conch shell and a school of leaping porpoises. Above the Olas Altas area is **Cerro del Vigía** ➐, a hill with terrific vistas.

What to See

★ ☺ ➋ **Acuario Mazatlán.** A perfect child-pleaser, Mazatlán's aquarium has tanks of sharks, sea horses, and multicolor salt- and freshwater fish. Be sure to take in the skating macaw and penny-pinching parrot at bird shows held several times daily. There's also a sea-lion show as well as botanical gardens, a large playground, an aviary, a gift shop, and snack bars. ✉ *Av. de los Deportes 111 Olas Altas* ☎ *669/981–7815* 🖃 *$4.50* ☽ *Daily 9:30–6.*

➐ **Cerro del Vigía** (Lookout Hill). The view from this windy hill above Olas Altas is fantastic: you can see both sides of Mazatlán, the harbor, and the Pacific. The steep road up is better suited for a private car or taxi than for walking. At the top of the hill you'll find a rusty cannon and the Centenario Pérgola, built in 1848 to celebrate the end of the U.S. invasion. The restaurant here may be unexceptional, but it's a great pit stop for a beer or soft drink.

➍ **Catedral de Mazatlán.** The bright yellow spires of the downtown cathedral are a city landmark. Begun in 1855, the church wasn't completed until the end of that century, and embraces a variety of architectural styles. Made a basilica in 1935, it has a gilded and ornate triple altar, with murals of angels overhead and many small altars along the sides. ✉ *Calles Juárez and 21 de Marzo, Centro* ☎ *No phone.*

➏ **Museo Arqueológico de Mazatlán.** The town's archaeological museum has a small, marginally interesting collection of regional artifacts. Among these are black-and-red pottery of the Totorames, an indigenous tribe that inhabited the area up until 200 years before the Spanish arrived. ✉ *Calle Sixto Osuna 76, at Av. Venustiano Carranza, Centro* ☎ *669/981–1455* 🖃 *Free* ☽ *Tues.–Sun. 8–3.*

need a break?
The sidewalk tables at **Copa de Leche and Fonda Santa Clara** (✉ Paseo Olas Altas, near Calle Sixto Osuna, Centro ☎ No phone) are perfect for watching sunsets.

➎ **Museo de Arte de Mazatlán.** This small museum shows the work of local, regional, and national artists, including Gerardo Santamarino, José Luis Cuevas, and Armando Nava. Varied cultural events in the upstairs gallery draw locals and a smattering of savvy foreigners Thursday evening; look for posters or flyers here or around town. ✉ *Calle Sixto Osuna and Av. Venustiano Carranza, Centro* ☎ *669/985–3502* 🖃 *$1* ☽ *Tues.–Fri. 10–2 and 4–7, Sat. 10–2.*

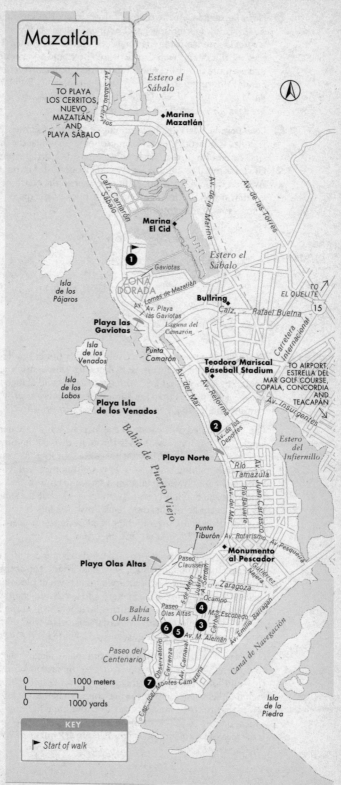

Mazatlán

❸ Plaza Revolución. At the center of downtown, this city square hosts one of the most fascinating gazebos in Mexico—below the traditional, wrought-iron bandstand is what looks like a '50s diner. The multicolor tiles on floors and walls, ancient jukebox, and soda fountain couldn't make a more surprising sight. Tourists and locals surround the bandstand Sunday afternoon to hear local musicians play. ✉ *Bounded by Calle 21 de Marzo to the north, Calle Flores to the south, Av. Benito Juárez to the east, and Av. Nelson to the west Centro.*

▶ ❶ Zona Dorada. Marking the beginning of Mazatlán's touristy Golden Zone is Punta Camarón, the rocky outcropping on which the disco Valentino sits, resembling a Moorish palace. To the north, Avenida Playa las Gaviotas (until recently called Avenida Rodolfo T. Loaiza) splits off from Avenida Camarón Sábalo, running closer to the beach before rejoining Camarón Sábalo. In this four-block pocket are many hotels, shops, restaurants, and nightclubs.

> **need a break?**
>
> There are several colorful places to cool your heels while exploring the city's old downtown. **Royal Dutch Café** (✉ Av. Constitución and Av. Benito Juárez, Centro ☎ No phone) proffers coffee and cakes in a relaxed interior courtyard setting. **El Café Gourmet Memorial** (✉ Calle Carnaval 1209, Centro ☎ No phone) is a good place to stop for coffee and pastries near the Angela Peralta Theater. **El Túnel** (✉ Calle Carnaval 1207, Centro ☎ No phone) is a Mazatlán institution for informal regional snacks.

AROUND MAZATLÁN

Concordia. A pleasant yet relatively unexceptional small town, Concordia is known for its furniture makers, its 18th-century church, and its unglazed clay pottery. Lined with organ cactus and mango trees, the drive is especially pretty after the summer rains cover nearby hills and distant mountains in green. *48 km (30 mi) east of Mazatlán.*

Copala. Huddled at the foot of the Sierra Madre Occidental, Copala's single cobblestone street winds through town to the tiny town square and 18th-century church, which is above a gorge. As you amble about this former mining town, you'll pass old homes with colorful facades enlivened with flowering vines and trees and embellished with ironwork balconies and window coverings. Refresh yourself at a simple yet charming restaurant before heading back down the hill. If you really want to get away from it all, several of the small restaurants near the square rent rooms. *25 km (15 mi) east of Concordia.*

Teacapán. A serene drive into cattle and coconut country makes a great day trip. Tour companies such as Marlin Tours stop at the town of Teacapán en route to the 17th-century mining town of El Rosario; trips often include stops at a Spanish cemetery and lovely old church and a visit to nearby thermal springs. Some trips include a stop at the lovely old hacienda of Antonio Haas, a Mazatlán historian who takes pride in his extensive and immaculate gardens. *131 km (81 mi) south of Mazatlán.*

El Quelite. The 2,000 inhabitants of this quiet village dedicate themselves to farming and raising cattle. Tours to the area take in a tortilla factory and local bakery and include a typical country lunch; some also include a demonstration of the pre-conquest ball game known as *ulama*. (Note that tours to the area also stop at a huge fighting-cock breeding ranch; be sure to ask the tour operator if this facility is on the itinerary if the idea of visiting it upsets you.) *29 km (18 mi) northeast of Mazatlán off Carretera 15.*

Beaches

Playa los Cerritos. A long stretch of sand running for several miles from the Marina Mazatlán to Punta Cerritos, Playa los Cerritos is just north of the Zona Dorada. Still relatively unpopulated (although the construction of condos may change that), it's great for long, uninterrupted walks; a steep drop-off and undertow make it less than ideal for swimming. Around Punta Cerritos are thatch-roof eateries frequented by surfers.

Playa Isla de la Piedra. Sixteen kilometers (10 miles) of unspoiled beach allows enough room for everyone to spread out. This is also the place to rent a horse for a good long ride on the beach. On Sunday, the beach looks like a small village, with families listening to boom boxes and enjoying all-day picnics. Many of the small palapas along the north end of the beach serve a tasty smoked marlin and other seafood treats. You can access the beach in one of the water taxis that cross the navigation canal dividing downtown from Isla de la Piedra; taxis depart from a pier just behind the Pacifica Brewery.

★ **Playa Isla de los Venados.** An amphibious sort of tank, a relic from WWII, makes regularly scheduled departures from El Cid hotel, in the Zona Dorada, to Deer Island—a 20-minute ride. (You can also get here on snorkeling and day cruises arranged through area tour operators.) The beach is pretty, uncluttered, and clean, and you can hike to small, secluded coves covered with shells.

Playa Norte. This strip of dark-brown sand runs parallel to the stretch of waterfront road that's known as Avenida del Mar. It's popular with those staying at hotels across the avenue. Palapas selling cold drinks (including whole chilled coconuts), tacos, and fresh fish line the beach. Fishermen land their skiffs at the sheltered cove at the south end, a section sometimes referred to as Los Pinos (the pines).

Playa Olas Altas. High Waves Beach, Mazatlán's first tourist beach, borders Paseo Claussen south of Playa Norte. Surfers congregate here in summer months, when the waves are at their highest. Men dive into the shallow sea when a paying crowd gathers at High Divers Park; nearby is the Monumento a la Continuidad de la Vida, a bronze statue of a pair of happy humans joined by a team of playful dolphins.

Playa Sábalo and Playa las Gaviotas. Mazatlán's two most popular beaches parallel the Zona Dorada. Both are crowded with vendors who sell pottery, lace tablecloths, and silver jewelry or rent boats, Windsurfers, and other toys. The beach is protected from heavy surf by Isla de los Pájaros (Island of Birds), Isla del Venado (Deer Island), and Isla de Lobos (Sea Lion Island), regularly called Isla de Chivos (Goat Island) by the locals. When you tire of sand and sun, repair to one of the many beachfront hotel restaurants willing to accommodate sandy, skimpily clad customers.

Where to Eat

★ $$$-$$$$ ✕ **Angelo's.** With its fresh flowers, cream-and-beige color scheme, gentle piano music, and soft candlelight, Angelo's is by far Mazatlán's most elegant restaurant. The Italian cuisine is outstanding—try the veal scallopini with mushrooms or shrimp marinara on pasta—and the service is impeccable. ⊠ *Pueblo Bonito hotel, Av. Camarón Sábalo 2121, Zona Dorada* ☎ *669/914–3700* ▭ *AE, MC, V* ⊙ *No lunch.*

★ $$$-$$$$ ✕ **Sr. Peppers.** Elegant yet unpretentious, with ceiling fans, plants, and candlelit tables, Sr. Peppers serves choice, mesquite-grilled steaks and lobsters. This is the place locals go for a fancy night out, and to enjoy the dance floor and live music. The Mexico City–born owner fell in love with Mazatlán on a vacation years ago and opened this instantly popular restaurant by luring gringos off the beach with flyers promising free margaritas and Angus beef delivered fresh from the United States. Service and attention to detail are still hallmarks. ⊠ *Av. Camarón Sábalo across from Faro Mazatlán hotel, Zona Dorada* ☎ *669/914–0101* ▤ *AE, MC, V* ☽ *No lunch.*

$–$$$ ✕ **La Casa Country.** This boisterous, faux-rustic-Western restaurant across from the Holiday Inn serves steaks and Mexican dishes to a crowd of·locals and visitors. Steaks are grilled over charcoal or firewood—the *arrachera* (skirt steak) served with kettle beans and guacamole is a good bet, as is the rib eye with baked potato. Fresh-fruit margaritas and piña coladas are served by the pitcher; at night, country-music fans are brought to their feet for dancin' and carousin' until 2 AM. ⊠ *Av. Camarón Sábalo s/n, Zona Dorada* ☎ *669/916–5300* ▤ *AE, MC, V.*

★ $–$$$ ✕ **La Concha.** One of Mazatlán's prettiest waterside dining spots is a large enclosed palapa with three levels of seating and tables by the sand. Adventurous types might attempt the stingray with black butter or calamari in its ink; the more conservative can try a thick filet mignon. In winter there's live music in the evenings, and the spacious dance floor is adorned with twinkling lights. La Concha is open for breakfast as well as lunch and dinner. ⊠ *El Cid Moro, Av. Camarón Sábalo s/n, Zona Dorada* ☎ *669/913–3333* ▤ *AE, MC, V.*

$–$$$ ✕ **Pedro & Lola.** Authentic Mexican seafood is served in this 19th-century building that's filled with contemporary art. Try the *papillot*, the day's fresh catch cooked in foil with white wine, shrimp, and mushrooms. Named after Mexican *ranchera* singers Pedro Infante and Lola Beltrán, the restaurant has excellent live music (often oldies rock) on weekend evenings. Reservations are recommended Thursday through Saturday. ⊠ *Calle Carnaval 1303, at Plazuela Machado, Centro* ☎ *669/982–2589* ▤ *AE, MC, V* ☽ *No lunch.*

$–$$$ ✕ **Restaurante Pancho's.** You can dine upstairs or down, inside or out at this hopping seaside restaurant, where seafood is the specialty. Choose from enormous platters to share, soups, and ceviche. You can also order filet mignon smothered in mushrooms and served with rice, steamed veggies, baked potato, and thick Texas-style toast. Portions are generous, and the food is so good that you'll most likely clean your plate. More great news: it's open from 7 AM to 11 PM. ⊠ *Av. Playa las Gaviotas 408, Centro Comercial las Cabanas, Local 11-B, Zona Dorada* ☎ *669/914– 0911* ▤ *MC, V.*

$–$$$ ✕ **El Shrimp Bucket.** In Old Mazatlán, across from the water, this patio restaurant is the "in" spot for social mavens at breakfast (from 6 AM) and businessmen for lunch and dinner; there's also live music at night. The specialty is jumbo shrimp stuffed with cheese, wrapped in bacon, sautéed, and served with white rice and steamed veggies. The fried shrimp served in a clay bucket and the barbecued ribs are also good bets; portions are large. ⊠ *Hotel Siesta, Paseo Olas Altas 11–126 Sur, Olas Altas* ☎ *669/981–6350* ▤ *AE, MC, V.*

★ $–$$ ✕ **Panamá Restaurant y Pastelería.** Low prices, large portions, and lots of choices—for breakfast, lunch, and dinner—make this bustling coffee shop a standout. For kids and not-so-adventurous eaters there are burgers and fries, sandwiches, and pancakes (any time of day). The soups are yummy, the salads are healthful, and the cakes and pastries are baked fresh throughout the day. ⊠ *Camarón Sábalo 400, Zona Dorada* ☎ *669/ 913–6977* ▤ *AE, MC, V.*

Where to Stay

$$$–$$$$ ▦ **Pueblo Bonito Emerald Bay.** The first (and so far, only) major resort property in Nuevo Mazatlán offers seclusion and exclusivity for those who eschew the busy Zona Dorada. Suites are in freestanding villas whose neoclassical design elements bring to mind luxurious European palaces. The grounds have lakes, fishponds, tropical birds, and gardens; in late summer, sea turtles lay their eggs on the property's long beach. ✉ *Av. Ernesto Coppel Campaña 201, Nuevo Mazatlán 82110* ☎ *669/989– 0525; 800/990–8250 in the U.S.* 🖷 *669/988–0718 or 669/989–0525* ⊕ *www.pueblobonito.com* ⤳ *258 suites* ⌂ *Restaurant, room service, in-room safes, kitchenettes, cable TV, 2 pools, gym, hair salon, massage, sauna, beach, bar, children's programs (ages 6–12), laundry service, concierge, airport shuttle, car rental, travel services, free parking* ▤ *AE, MC, V.*

$$$ 🏨 **Pueblo Bonito.** One of Mazatlán's comeliest properties, this all-suites hotel and time-share resort has an enormous lobby with chandeliers and beveled-glass doors; terra-cotta-color rooms have domed ceilings. Pink flamingos stroll manicured lawns, golden koi swim in small ponds, and bronzed sunbathers repose on padded white lounge chairs by the crystal-blue pool. Angelo's is a dining must—as elegant as Mazatlán gets. ✉ *Av. Camarón Sábalo 2121, Zona Dorada 82110* ☎ *669/914–3700; 800/990–8250 in the U.S.* 🖷 *669/914–1723* ⊕ *www.pueblobonito. com* ⤳ *250 suites* ⌂ *3 restaurants, room service, in-room safes, kitchenette, cable TV, 2 pools, gym, massage, sauna, beach, bar, children's programs (ages 6–12), laundry service, concierge, Internet, car rental, travel services, free parking* ▤ *AE, MC, V.*

$$$ 🏨 **Royal Villas Resort.** Panoramic elevators transport you from the cool marble atrium lobby of this pyramid-shaped, 12-story structure to the upper floors. More ample and functional than elegant, one- and two-bedroom suites have ocean views and balconies. Access to the inviting pool is by a bridge that crosses over a fish-filled pond. ✉ *Av. Camarón Sábalo 500, Zona Dorada 82110* ☎ *669/916–6161; 800/898–3564 in the U.S.* 🖷 *669/914–0777* ⊕ *www.royalvillas.com.mx* ⤳ *125 suites* ⌂ *2 restaurants, kitchenettes, room service, cable TV, pool, gym, hot tub, beach, bar, laundry service, business services, meeting rooms, travel services, free parking, no-smoking rooms* ▤ *AE, MC, V.*

$$–$$$ 🏨 **El Cid Megaresort.** Mazatlán's largest resort has four properties, three of which are together in the Zona Dorada. A free shuttle connects these to the upscale Marina El Cid Hotel and Yacht Club, at the north end of town overlooking the 100-slip marina. A stay at any El Cid property allows you to use the full-service spa and fitness center, the golf school and course, and the aquatics center. ✉ *Av. Camarón Sábalo s/n, Zona Dorada 82110* ☎ *669/913–3333; 800/525–1925 in the U.S.* 🖷 *669/914– 1311* ⊕ *www.elcid.com* ⤳ *1,320 rooms, suites, and studios* ⌂ *8 restaurants, cable TV, 27-hole golf course, 11 tennis courts, 8 pools, gym, spa, beach, marina, 3 bars, dance club, shops, children's programs (ages 4–12), laundry service, business services, meeting rooms, car rental, travel services, no-smoking rooms* ▤ *AE, MC, V* ⦿ *All-inclusive, EP.*

★ $$ 🏨 **Casa Contenta.** A colonial-style building on the beach houses seven one-bedroom apartments filled with Mexican furniture and fittings. There's also a separate house with three bedrooms, three baths, a living and dining room, and even servants' quarters; it accommodates as many as eight people. The bargain prices bring many repeat clients, so book this one well in advance. ✉ *Av. Playa las Gaviotas 224, Zona Dorada 82110* ☎ *669/913–4976* 🖷 *669/913–9986* ⊕ *www.casacontenta. com.mx* ⤳ *8 units* ⌂ *Kitchens, cable TV, pool, free parking; no room phones* ▤ *MC, V.*

$$ 🏨 **Holiday Inn Sunspree Resort.** The Holiday Inn attracts tour and convention groups that fill the rooms and create a party mood by the pool and on the beach. The Kid's Spree program provides activities for children; adults can attend tennis clinics and borrow snorkel equipment or boogie boards. Rooms are done in whites and pastels, with large slid-

ing doors that open to views of the islands. ✉ *Av. Camarón Sábalo 696, Zona Dorada 82110* ☎ *669/913–2222; 800/465–4329 in the U.S.* 🖷 *669/914–1287* ⊕ *www.holiday-inn.com* ➥ *160 rooms, 23 suites* ♿ *3 restaurants, refrigerators, cable TV, pool, gym, beach, volleyball, bar, shop, children's programs (ages 5–12), business services, meeting rooms, no-smoking rooms* ▱ *AE, MC, V.*

$$ 🏨 **Hotel Plaza Marina.** Near the Fisherman's Monument downtown, this hotel has standard rooms that overlook the pool and ocean view suites with kitchenettes. The clientele is mainly Mexican, and the restaurant and bar are sometimes clouded with lots of cigarette smoke. The gym is tiny and poorly equipped; most guests aren't here to work out. The staff is professional and friendly. ✉ *Av. del Mar 73, Playa Norte 82110* ☎ *669/982–3622; 01800/711–9465 toll-free in Mexico* 🖷 *669/ 982–3499* ➥ *56 rooms, 43 suites* ♿ *Restaurant, some kitchenettes, pool, bar, meeting rooms, free parking* ▱ *AE, MC, V.*

★ $$ 🏨 **Playa Mazatlán.** Families and laid-back singles favor this Gaviota Beach hotel for its reliable guest quarters and consistently good service. Each sunny, no-frills room has comfy beds with tile headboards, a tile table and chairs by a sliding-glass window, and a terrace or balcony. Palapas for shade line the beach just beyond the first-floor rooms; at night, candles flicker in the breeze at the open-air restaurant. The popular Mexican Fiesta dinner show is offered year-round. ✉ *Av. Playa las Gaviotas 202, Zona Dorada 82110* ☎ *669/989–0555; 800/762–5816 in the U.S.* 🖷 *669/914–0366* ⊕ *www. playamazatlan.com.mx* ➥ *413 rooms* ♿ *2 restaurants, room service, cable TV, 3 pools, gym, hair salon, 2 hot tubs, beach, 2 bars, shops, dry cleaning, laundry service, concierge, convention center, meeting rooms, car rental, free parking* ▱ *AE, MC, V.*

★ $$ 🏨 **Los Sábalos.** This white high-rise is smack in the center of the Zona Dorada and on a long clean beach. Rooms are boldly decorated in bright blue and stark white and have such perks as coffeemakers and hair dryers. For the price it's one of the town's best lodging bets. You'll be in the thick of the action here, and it's the home of Joe's Oyster Bar, an informal dance club popular with the younger set. ✉ *Av. Playa las Gaviotas 100, Zona Dorada 82110* ☎ *669/983–5333; 800/528–8760 in the U.S.; 877/756–7532 in Canada* 🖷 *669/983–8156* ⊕ *www. lossabalos.com* ➥ *85 rooms, 100 suites* ♿ *4 restaurants, room service, in-room safes, cable TV, pool, spa, beach, 2 bars, dance club, shops, babysitting, concierge, meeting rooms* ▱ *AE, MC, V.*

$–$$ 🏨 **El Quijote Inn.** This tranquil five-story inn is on the beach in the middle of the Zona Dorada. Room sizes and configurations vary; most are one- and two-bedroom suites with full kitchens. All units have tile floors and rattan furnishings; most have a patio or a balcony. The outdoor bar and restaurant overlook both the beach and the nicely landscaped pool area with its large hot tub. ✉ *Avs. Camarón Sábalo and Tiburón, Zona Dorada 82110* ☎ *669/914–1134* 🖷 *669/914–3344* ➥ *18 rooms, 52 suites* ♿ *Restaurant, some kitchens, pool, hot tub, beach, bar, meeting room* ▱ *AE, MC, V.*

¢–$ 🏨 **Azteca Inn.** Rooms in this three-story low-rise have disconcerting bright-red curtains and plaid bedspreads; beyond that, they're spartan, but it's hard to complain as this is just about the only budget hotel in the Zona Dorada. The courtyard pool has a hot tub, and the bar feels like a cross between a terrarium and an American dive. The staff couldn't be friendlier. ✉ *Av. Playa las Gaviotas 307, Zona Dorada 82110* ☎ *669/913–4655* 🖷 *669/913–7476* ⊕ *www.aztecainn.com.mx* ➥ *74 rooms* ♿ *Cafeteria, cable TV, pool, hot tub, bar* ▱ *AE, MC, V.*

¢ 🏨 **Hotel Siesta.** The beach across the street is rocky, but this hotel's rates are a bargain and its Olas Altas location invites you to truly explore downtown Mazatlán. Rooms are plainly furnished but comfortable. Request a room that doesn't overlook the interior courtyard as these quarters also face the Shrimp Bucket restaurant, where live music is played nightly until 11. ⊠ *Paseo Olas Altas 11 Sur, Playa Olas Altas 82110* ☎ *669/981–2640* 🖷 *669/982–2633* ⊕ *www.lasiesta.com.mx* 📞 *58 rooms* ⟁ *Restaurant, room service, bar, dry cleaning, laundry service, car rental, travel services* 🖃 *AE, MC, V.*

Nightlife

Marking the southern edge of the Zona Dorada, Valentino, Bora Bora, Pepe's & Joe, and Sheik are all part of the complex known as **Fiesta Land** (⊠ Av. Camarón Sábalo at Calz. Rafael Buelna, Zona Dorada ☎ 669/984–1666). Valentino, with its decorative white towers rising above Punta Camarón, has two dance clubs—one geared toward a younger crowd, the other with more tranquil, romantic music—as well as a karaoke salon. Bora Bora is a palapa restaurant and bar renowned for its raucous disco music and table-dancing; like Valentino, it opens after 9 PM. Pepe's & Joe is a microbrewery with American-style burgers and dogs. The extravagant Sheik restaurant delights diners with waterfalls, ocean views, Moorish-inspired stained-glass windows, marble floors, and a central domed skylight.

El Caracol Disco Club (⊠ Av. Camarón Sábalo s/n, Zona Dorada ☎ 669/913–3333), at El Cid Castilla, has a high-tech disco, billiards, board and arcade games, and different theme nights throughout the week. A $20 cover includes all drinks and games. **Joe's Oyster Bar** (⊠ Los Sábalos hotel, Av. Playa las Gaviotas 100, Zona Dorada ☎ 669/983–5333) is a popular beachfront spot where young people gather to dance and listen to music.

★ The **Mexican Fiesta** (⊠ Av. Playa las Gaviotas 202, Zona Dorada ☎ 669/989–0555), a dinner show that's held Tuesday and Saturday (as well as Thursday in high season) from 7 to 10:30 at the Playa Mazatlán hotel, is a good entertainment bet. The $28 entrance fee covers an all-you-can-eat Mexican buffet, an open bar, entertainment, and dancing. A favorite with young revelers bent on belting down tequila shooters and generally whooping it up is **Señor Frog's** (⊠ Av. del Mar s/n, Zona Costera ☎ 669/982–1925). It's also a restaurant that serves good barbecued ribs and chicken with corn on the cob. Bandidos carry tequila bottles and shot glasses in their *bandoliers,* Revolution-era ammunition belts.

Sports & the Outdoors

Baseball

The people of Mazatlán loyally support their team, **Los Venados** (☎ 669/981–1710 ⊠ Blvd. Justo Sierra, Zona Estadio), a Pacific League Triple A team. Regular season games are played at the Teodoro Mariscal Baseball Stadium October through December, longer if the team makes the play-offs. Purchase tickets at the stadium box office after 1 PM on game day; prices range from $2 for nosebleed seats to $6 for assigned seats.

Bullfights & Charreadas

Bullfights are held most Sunday afternoons at 3:30 from December through April at the bullring—Plaza de Toros Monumental—on Calzada Rafael Buelna near Calle de la Marina. *Charreadas* (rodeos) take place year-round, also on Sunday. Tickets (about $10–$20 for charreadas; $20–$35 for bullfights) are available at the bullring, through most hotels and travel agencies, and from **Valentino** (☎ 669/984–1666) nightclub.

Fishing

Sportfishing fleets operate from the docks south of the lighthouse, in Marina Vallarta, and in Marina Mazatlán, near the Faro Mazatlán hotel. Hotels can arrange charters, or you can contact the companies directly. Deep-sea fishing charters include a full day of fishing, bait, and tackle and usually an ice chest with ice. Prices range from $80 to $100 per person on a party boat, or from $240 to $380 to charter a boat for 1 to 6 passengers. Super pangas are usually 25-ft skiffs geared for bottom fishing closer to shore; rates run about $60 for a shared boat or $240 for a charter.

For bass fishing in El Salto Reservoir, a lake several hours northeast of Mazatlán off Carretera 40, contact **Amazing Outdoors Tours** (✉ El Patio Restaurant, Camarón Sábalo 2601, Zona Dorada ☎ 669/984–3151 ⊕ www.basselsalto.com). The reputable **Aries Fleet** (☎ 669/916–3468) is connected with El Cid Hotel and operates from Marina El Cid. The company offers bottom fishing in pangas (one to four passengers; $35 per hour, four-hour minimum) as well as shared or charter boats for big-game fishing. **Bill Heimpel's Star Fleet** (☎ 669/982–2665 ⊕ www.starfleet. com.mx), which has fast twin-engine boats, is well regarded. **Escualo Fleet** (✉ Marina Mazatlán, Zona Dorada ☎ 669/913–0303 ⊕ www. escualosportfishing.com) has shared boats and individual charters.

Golf

It may be older and dowdier than other area courses, but the 9-hole course at **Club Campestre de Mazatlán** (✉ Carretera Internacional Sur ☎ 669/ 980–1570) is also substantially cheaper (and therefore good for duffers). Greens fees are $18 for 9 holes; caddies ($5 but tip generously) and a limited number of carts ($10) are available. The last 9 holes of the spectacular 27-hole course at **El Cid Golf and Country Club** (☎ 669/913–3333 Ext. 3261) were designed by Lee Trevino. There's a putting green and driving range, and fees include caddy. Green fees are $73, plus $40 for a cart and $17 for a caddy. Hotel guests pay significantly less. At the **Estrella del Mar Golf Club** (☎ 669/982–3300), just south of Mazatlán proper on Isla de la Piedra (Stone Island), you'll find a championship, 18-hole Robert Trent Jones Jr. course. Clinics are offered, as is free transportation from some of Mazatlán's major hotels. There's a pro shop, driving range, and putting green. Carts and transportation to and from the course are included in the $110 greens fee.

Tennis

Many of the hotels have courts, some of which are open to the public, and there are a few public courts not connected to the hotels. Call in advance for reservations at **El Cid Megaresort** (✉ Av. Camarón Sábalo s/ n, Zona Dorada ☎ 669/913–3333), which has nine courts. The **Racquet Club las Gaviotas** (✉ Av. Ibis s/n, at Av. Río Bravo, ☎ 669/913–5939) has seven courts for rent by the hour. **Club de Tenis San Juan** (✉ Av. Camarón Sábalo s/n, across from Hotel Costa de Oro, Zona Dorada ☎ 669/913–5344), has courts for rent by the hour.

Water Sports

You can rent Jet Skis, Hobie Cats (two-person catamarans), kayaks, and Windsurfers at most beachfront hotels. Parasailing is popular along the Zona Dorada, and scuba diving and snorkeling are catching on. There aren't, however, any extraordinary dive spots; the best snorkeling is around Isla de los Venados.

Centro Acuático El Cid (✉ Av. Camarón Sábalo s/n, next to Hotel La Puesta del Sol, Zona Dorada ☎ 669/913–3333 Ext. 3341) has parasailing and rents Wave Runners, kayaks, boogie boards, sailboats, and banana boats. Staff members here can also arrange half-day boat trips to Isla de los Venados and sunset cruises aboard the trimaran *Kolonahe*, docked at El Cid Marina.

🌣 The 4-acre **Parque Acuático Mazagua** (✉ Av. Sábalo Cerritos and Entronque Habal Cerritos, Nuevo Mazatlán ☎ 669/988–0152) has 20 water activities—including water slides, wading pools, and a pool with man-made waves—as well as picnic facilities that have barbecue grills. Entrance is about $8 per person; the park is open 10 AM–6 PM Tuesday through Sunday for most of the year and daily in July, August, and during school holidays.

Shopping

Mazatlán has a range of souvenirs and folk art from around the country. Some of the best shops are in the Zona Dorada, particularly along Avenidas Camarón Sábalo and Playa las Gaviotas, where you can buy everything from piñatas to silver jewelry. Bargaining isn't the norm in shops, but it's expected in markets. The gigantic **Mercado Central,** downtown between Calles Juárez, Ocampo, Serdán, and Leandro Valle, is open daily and filled with produce, pungent meat and fish, and a sprinkling of handicrafts. Although the latter are more along the lines of souvenirs than folk art, it's fun to search for great buys.

Crafts

★ Mazatlán's most beautiful shop may well be **Gallery Michael** (✉ Av. Camarón Sábalo 19, Zona Dorada ☎ 669/916–7816 ✉), with several rooms of tastefully chosen folk art, religious icons, and jewelry. The **Mazatlán Arts and Crafts Center** (✉ Av. Playa las Gaviotas 417, Zona Dorada ☎ 669/913–2120) was once a place to view artisans at work. Today the center, which is open weekdays 9–9 and Saturday 9–3, is a good place to browse for onyx chess sets, straw sombreros, leather jackets, sandals, coconut masks, and colorful piñatas.

★ The gallery and workshop **Nidart** (✉ Calle Libertad 45 and Calle Carnaval, Centro ☎ 669/981–0002) sells handcrafted leather masks, ceramic figurines and sculptures, contemporary black-and-white photos, and other Mexican arts and crafts in a beautiful setting. Artisans can occasionally be seen producing these wares in open workshops. Its hours are Monday–Saturday 10–2; it's sometimes open later in high season, but don't count on it. If floor-to-ceiling shells that have been glued, strung, and molded into every imaginable form—from necklaces to kitschy statuettes—interest you, you'll love **Sea Shell City** (✉ Av. Playa las Gaviotas 407, Zona Dorada ☎ 669/913–1301).

Jewelry

Madonna (✉ Av. de las Garzas 1, in Inn at Mazatlán, Zona Dorada ☎ 669/914–2389) has an extensive collection of silver and gold jewelry as well as handicrafts. **Rubio Jewelers** (✉ Costa de Oro hotel, Av. Camarón Sábalo L-1, Zona Dorada ☎ 669/914–3167) carries fine gold, silver, and platinum jewelry. It's also Mazatlán's exclusive distributor of Sergio Bustamante's whimsical ceramic and bronze sculptures.

Mazatlán A to Z

To research prices, get advice from other travelers, and book travel arrangements, visit www.fodors.com.

AIR TRAVEL

AIRPORT Aeropuerto Internacional Rafael Buelna is about 25 km (18 mi) south of town—a good 40-minute drive.
🎫 **Aeropuerto Internacional Rafael Buelna** ☎ 669/982–2177.

AIRPORT TRANSFERS To get to the airport you must take a private taxi, which will cost between $20 and $30. Autotransportes Aeropuerto Volkswagen van shuttles provide service to downtown Mazatlán, the hotel zones, and elsewhere for about $5 per person. The company also has private cabs (for one to four passengers) that cost $20.

🚐 Shuttles **Autotransportes Aeropuerto** ☎ 669/981-5554.

CARRIERS Aeroméxico has daily flights from multiple U.S. and Mexican cities, and nonstop service from San Diego (twice weekly). Alaska Airlines flies nonstop from Los Angeles, although not every day. Continental flies daily nonstop from Houston, and from other major U.S. airports to Mexico City. AeroCalifornia has direct flights from Los Angeles; La Paz, in Baja California; and Mexico City. It sometimes has nonstop Los Angeles–Mazatlán flights in high season. Mexicana flies in nonstop daily from Mexico City, and daily direct from Los Angeles. America West links Mazatlán to Phoenix with daily, nonstop flights.

✈ **AeroCalifornia** ☎ 669/913-2042; 800/237-6225 in the U.S. **Aeroméxico** ☎ 669/982-3444; 01800/021-4000 toll-free in Mexico; 800/237-6639 in the U.S. **Alaska Airlines** ☎ 669/985-2730; 800/225-2752 in the U.S. **America West** ☎ 669/981-1184; 800/235-9292 in the U.S. **Continental** ☎ 800/523-3273 in the U.S. **Mexicana** ☎ 669/982-2888; 800/531-7921 in the U.S.

BOAT & FERRY TRAVEL

The car-and-passenger ferry between La Paz in Baja California Sur and Mazatlán takes about 18 hours and is fairly reliable. One-way fares are about $60 for tourist-class passage, $76 for a tiny cabin (bath down the hall), and $97 for berth with bath. Cost for transporting vehicles varies by size, beginning at about $430. Check the schedule and purchase tickets in advance, as prices and times change frequently. Royal Caribbean, Holland America, and Princess, among other cruise lines, include Mazatlán on their seven-day Mexican Riviera cruises.

⛴ **Ferry service** ✉ Prolongación de Calle Carnaval s/n, Fracc. Playa Sur ☎ 669/985-2228 ⊕ www.viajesahome.com.

BUS TRAVEL

The Mazatlán bus terminal is at Carretera Internacional 1203, three blocks behind the Sands Hotel. Elite, one of the area's best bus lines, has service to the U.S. border and south to Guadalajara, Mexico City, and the southern coast. Estrellas del Pacífico serves western Mexico.

Buses and minibuses run frequently along all main avenues. Fares start at about 40¢ and increase slightly, depending on the destination. Look for the bright green buses, which cost just a little more and are new and air-conditioned.

🚌 **Elite** ☎ 669/981-3811. **Estrellas del Pacífico** ☎ 669/984-2817.

CAR RENTAL

🚗 Major Agencies **Budget** ✉ Av. Camarón Sábalo 402, Zona Dorada ☎ 669/913-2000. **Hertz** ✉ Av. Camarón Sábalo 314, Zona Dorada ☎ 669/913-4955; 669/985-0845 to the airport. **National** ✉ Av. Camarón Sábalo 7000, Zona Dorada ☎ 669/913-6000 ✉ CineMax shopping center, Av. Camarón Sábalo s/n, Zona Dorada ☎ 669/986-4560 ✉ cruise ship terminal ☎ 669/913-6000.

CAR TRAVEL

Mazatlán is 1,212 km (751 mi) from the border city of Nogales, Arizona, on the good but quite expensive toll road 15-D, or on the federal highway 15. One overnight stop is recommended. Within the city, it's fairly easy to navigate the coast-hugging roads (one or two lanes in each direction). Parking can be difficult downtown, but most hotels and restaurants in the Zona Dorada have lots.

CONSULATES

Canadian Consulate ✉ Av. Playa las Gaviotas 202, Zona Dorada ☎ 669/913-7320.
U.S. Consul ✉ Av. Playa las Gaviotas, across from Hotel Playa Mazatlán, Zona Dorada
☎ 669/916-5889.

EMERGENCIES

Balboa Hospital & Walk-In Clinic ☎ 669/916-7933. **General Emergency Number**
☎ 060. **Toll-Free Medical Advice** ☎ 01800/903-9200 in Mexico.

ENGLISH-LANGUAGE MEDIA

The best place for English-language books and maps is Mazatlán Book
and Coffee Company, across from the Costa de Oro Hotel in Plaza Galería.
Posted hours are daily 9–7, although it's not terribly loyal to the schedule in low season. Mazatlán's English-language monthly magazine, *Pacific Pearl,* has ads and articles of interest to locals and visitors.
Bookstore Mazatlán Book and Coffee Company ☎ 669/916-7899.

MAIL, INTERNET & SHIPPING

The main post office is downtown, across from the main plaza and offers MexPost shipping, with rates slightly cheaper than the international
shipping companies. Many of the major hotels offer at least one computer for checking e-mail. As cybercafés open and close with regular-
ity, ask your concierge to suggest one.
Mail Services Post office ✉ Av. Juárez at 21 de Marzo, Centro ☎ 669/981-2121.

MONEY MATTERS

Credit cards are widely accepted at hotels and restaurants; small, family-run establishments prefer cash. Although many hotels will change
your dollars to pesos without charging a commission, they don't offer
as good a rate as do banks, most of which have ATM machines and are
open weekdays 8:30–4:30. One exchange office is Casa de Cambio
Puebla, which is open weekdays 9–6 and Saturday 9–2.
Banks Banamex ✉ Calle Flores at Av. Juárez, Centro ☎ 669/982-7733.
Exchange House Casa de Cambio Puebla ✉ Calle García Vigil 106 Centro ☎ 951/
514-5103.

TAXIS

Taxis cruise the Zona Dorada strip, which is about 3 km (2 mi) north
of downtown, regularly. You can hail them on the street. Fares start at
$3; discuss the fare and conduct any negotiations before setting out.
A fun way to get around is in a *pulmonía* (topless VW Beetle), so you
can sunbathe and take pictures as you cruise along—just beware of the
bus fumes. The fare, for up to three passengers, starts at about $3 for
a short trip.

TOURS

Centro Aquático El Cid offers unguided trips to Isla de los Venados, including lunch, snorkeling, and kayaking ($35). Boats depart from the
beach in front of El Cid at 10, noon, and 2, and return at noon, 2, and
4. King David Tours runs a bay tour that stops on Isla de la Piedra and
includes lunch and open bar. The price is $20–$25 with two activities;
choose from snorkeling, horseback riding, or banana-boat rides.

Mazatleco Tours leads kayaking tours to Isla de los Venados, where you
can then hike or snorkel (four hours, $34). The price includes hotel pickup,
transportation, and a box lunch. The company also leads kayaking
trips (best in winter) to bird-watch among the mangroves south of town
($45, includes lunch). Marlin Tours runs a city tour, colonial tour (Co-
pala and Concordia), and a tequila factory tour as well as an eight-hour
excursion (about $37) ending in Teacapán, near the Nayarit border. The

van tour makes stops in towns, ranches, and sometimes a thermal spring, and includes Continental breakfast and drinks. Lunch at a seaside restaurant and an optional boat ride aren't included in the price.

Olé Tours specializes in custom tours to El Quelite, Concordia, and Copala. Pronatours, in El Cid complex, offers a variety of tours, including jaunts by trimaran to Isla de los Venados ($42, includes lunch and open bar, daily except Monday) for snorkeling, kayaking, and banana boat rides. Robert Hudson, an American who has lived in Mazatlán for decades, conducts customized tours, historic-district tours, and spearfishing, snorkeling, and hiking trips; he also gives surfing classes.
🏢 **Centro Acuático El Cid** ☎ 669/913–3333 Ext. 3341 in Mazatlán. **King David Tours** ☎ 669/914–1444. **Marlin Tours** ✉ Camarón Sábalo 1504, Zona Dorada ☎ 669/913–5301. **Mazatleco Tours** ✉ Paseo de la Isla 3, Isla Mazatlán ☎ 669/916–5933. **Olé Tours** ✉ Av. Camarón Sábalo 7000, Centro ☎ 669/916–6288 ⊕ www.oletours.com. **Pronatours** ✉ Av. Camarón Sábalo s/n, Centro Comercial El Cid, Local 2627, Zona Dorada ☎ 669/916–7720. **Robert Hudson** ☎ 669/913–1764 ⊕ www.hudsontours.com.

TRAVEL AGENCIES
🏢 Local Agent Referrals **American Express** ✉ Av. Camarón Sábalo 1500, Locales 15 and 16, Zona Dorada ☎ 669/913–0600.

VISITOR INFORMATION
The Sinaloa State Tourism Office is open weekdays 9–5.
🏢 **Sinaloa State Tourism Office** ✉ Av. Camarón Sábalo s/n, Banrural Bldg., 4th floor, Zona Dorada ☎ 669/916–5160 through 669/916–5165.

PUERTO VALLARTA

One of Mexico's most popular vacation spots, Puerto Vallarta is on the edge of the Sierra Madre range and has been attracting outsiders since the 16th century. Its Bahía de Banderas drew pirates and explorers as early as the 1500s; it was used as a stopover on long trips as a place for the crew to relax (or maybe plunder and pillage). Sir Francis Drake apparently stopped here. In the mid-1850s, Don Guadalupe Sánchez Carrillo developed the bay as a port for the silver mines by the Río Cuale. Then it was known as Puerto de Peñas (Rocky Port) and had about 1,500 inhabitants. In 1918 it was made a municipality and renamed for Ignacio L. Vallarta, a governor of Jalisco.

In the 1950s Puerto Vallarta was essentially a pretty hideaway for those in the know—the wealthy and some hardy escapists. When it first entered the general public's consciousness, with John Huston's 1964 movie *The Night of the Iguana,* it was a quiet fishing and farming community. After the movie was released, tourism boomed, and today PV (as it's now called) is a city with some 250,000 residents. Airports, hotels, and highways have supplanted palm groves and fishing shacks. About 3 million people visit each year, and from November through April cobblestone streets are clogged with pedestrians and cars. There are now nearly 18,000 hotel rooms in Puerto Vallarta, with another 4,000 in Nuevo Vallarta, on the bay's northern edge in Nayarit State.

Hurricane Kenna, a Category 5 storm, hit the Pacific coast on October 25, 2002. Small homes and businesses from north of Manzanillo to around San Blas, Nayarit, were devastated; simple structures of palm were blown away by winds or washed away by huge tidal surges. The hotel zone in PV, as well as the malecón and nearby streets, were devastated by five-story waves. Shopkeepers, restaurant owners, and hoteliers were quick to put the town back together. Though most places were repaired within weeks, it took months to restore several businesses, including the Sheraton hotel.

A more profound and lasting effect on the landscape is the result of the city's vast popularity and resulting growth. But while PV has spread north and south over the years, every attempt has been made to keep intact the character and image of downtown. City ordinances require houses there to be painted white with red-tile roofs, limit the number of floors, and dictate other architectural details. Pack mules still occasionally clop down the streets and, in the background, velvety green hills look so close they seem to spring from the sea. Steep mountain roads curve and twist through jungles of pines and palms, and rivers rush down to meet fine sand beaches and rocky coves.

Exploring Puerto Vallarta

Central Puerto Vallarta has several major components. The Zona Hotelera (Hotel Zone), with most of PV's deluxe resorts, is north of town. Still farther north is the Marina Vallarta, a public marina that's practically a town unto itself with more resorts as well as restaurants, minimalls, condos, an 18-hole golf course, a 355-slip marina, a cruise-ship pier, and the Royal Pacific Yacht Club. Farther north is Nuevo Vallarta, just over the state line in Nayarit, at the mouth of the Río Ameca. This beautiful community with beachfront houses and condos on canals with direct access to the bay is home to several all-inclusive resorts.

Downtown, a.k.a. Viejo Vallarta, is the heart of the city, where many two- and three-story houses have been converted to shops, galleries, and restaurants. Dividing downtown in two is the Río Cuale. This river—which ranges from ebullient to anemic, depending on the rains—embraces a sliver of an island with cultural center, museum, restaurants, and shops. South of downtown and the Río Cuale, Olas Altas and Los Muertos are two beaches backed by lively outdoor restaurants and modest hotels. If you head farther south still, en route to Manzanillo, the coast is sprinkled with some of the Mexican Riviera's most exclusive resorts. You won't see them from Carretera 200 (Highway 200); most are on the beach, down manicured but unpaved roads.

A rental car is helpful to fully explore the Zona Hotelera, marina area, Nuevo Vallarta, and the many beaches and small towns north to Punta de Mita. That said, at a minimum of $50 per day for car rental, many visitors will save money using taxis and city buses, and thus avoid hassles with parking (not to mention drinking and driving). Taxis cruise up and down the main drags, and buses fly along—most at a terrifying speed. A car is a serious hindrance downtown and in the Río Cuale area. You can see most of the interesting sights on foot—just be sure you wear comfortable shoes for the cobblestone streets.

Numbers in the text correspond to numbers in the margin and on the Puerto Vallarta map.

a good walk

When you start seeing cobblestone streets, you're in the downtown area, also known as Viejo Vallarta. Start your walk at the northern end of the **malecón** ❽ ➤, which runs parallel to Paseo Díaz Ordáz beginning at Avenida 31 de Octubre. Nine blocks south, Díaz Ordáz merges with Calle Morelos at the old lighthouse tower. Two blocks farther south is the town's main square, Plaza de Armas. On the northern side of this busy, tree-shaded plaza you'll see the **Palacio Municipal** ❾ (City Hall), and one block east, **La Iglesia de Nuestra Señora de Guadalupe** ❿, which is topped by a distinctive crown. Across the street from the plaza on the malecón, Los Arcos, the distinctive arches leading to the town's much-loved outdoor amphitheater, were destroyed by Hurricane Kenna. The distinctive limestone arches have since been rebuilt, and the venue continues to host evening concerts and crafts shows.

Head south a few blocks and turn left on Calle A. Rodríguez. After a few blocks you'll come to the busy Mercado Municipal at the foot of the upper bridge over the Río Cuale. The steep hillside above, dotted with vine-drenched villas, is called Gringo Gulch, which you can reach by climbing the steps on Calle Zaragoza. The most famous attraction in this neighborhood, named after the hundreds of U.S. expats who settled here in the 1950s and '60s, is Elizabeth Taylor's former home, **Casa Kimberley** ⑪. In the middle of the Río Cuale lies the **Isla Río Cuale** ⑫, which is accessible by bridges for both pedestrians and autos and is a great place to stroll, shop, and eat.

What to See

⑪ **Casa Kimberley.** Elizabeth Taylor's former home is connected to Richard Burton's former home across the street by the pink-and-white "love bridge" he had constructed. Part of the house has been converted into an unattractive bed-and-breakfast, but you can tour other areas of it daily 9–6. Burton bought the 24,000-square-ft home for Taylor's 32nd birthday after their much-publicized romance during his filming of *The Night of the Iguana* with Ava Gardner, Deborah Kerr, and Sue Lyon. Taylor owned the house for 26 years, and left most of her possessions behind (all on display) when she sold it. ⊠ *Calle Zaragoza 445, Centro* 🖶🖶 *322/222–1336* 🖃 *$8.*

⑩ **La Iglesia de Nuestra Señora de Guadalupe.** The Church of Our Lady of Guadalupe is topped by an ornate crown that replicates the one worn by Carlota, the empress of Mexico in the late 1860s. The crown toppled during an earthquake that shook this area of the Pacific Coast in October 1995, but was quickly replaced with a fiberglass version in time for the celebration of the Feast of the Virgin of Guadalupe (December 12). ⊠ *Calle Hidalgo, 1 block east of zócalo, Centro* 🕐 *7:30 AM–8 PM.*

⑫ **Isla Río Cuale.** Surrounded by the Río Cuale, this island effectively slices the downtown area in two. It has an outdoor marketplace as well as trendy restaurants and inexpensive cafés. A bronze statue of film director John Huston dominates the central plaza. Just beyond the statue, at the island's east end, the **Casa de la Cultura** (🖶 *322/223–2500*) sells the work of local artists, offers art and dance classes, and hosts cultural events.

The **Museo Arqueológico** (⊠ *Western tip of island, Centro* 🖶 *No phone*) has a small collection of pre-Columbian figures and Indian artifacts. The museum is open daily 10–6. Admission is free, but a donation is requested. To reach Isla Río Cuale from the town's north side, cross the bridge at Encino and Juárez or at Libertad and Miramar. From the south, cross at Ignacio L. Vallarta and Aquiles Serdán, or at Insurgentes and Aquiles Serdán.

▶ ❽ **Malecón.** The malecón is downtown's main drag, a nice place to rest on a wrought-iron bench. A seawall and sidewalk run along the bay, and restaurants, cafés, and shops are across the street. You'll see some interesting sculpture along the walkway—among other pieces, the bronze sea horse that has become Puerto Vallarta's trademark, and *La Nostalgia,* a bronze statue of a seated couple, inspired by the love life of author Ramiz Barquet. The latest sculptural addition is *Rotunda del Mar,* a collection of whimsical statues by artist Alejandro Colunga, which survived the 2002 tsunami caused by Hurricane Kenna. ⊠ *Parallel to Paseo Díaz Ordáz, extending about 16 blocks from Río Cuale northeast to 31 de Octubre, Centro.*

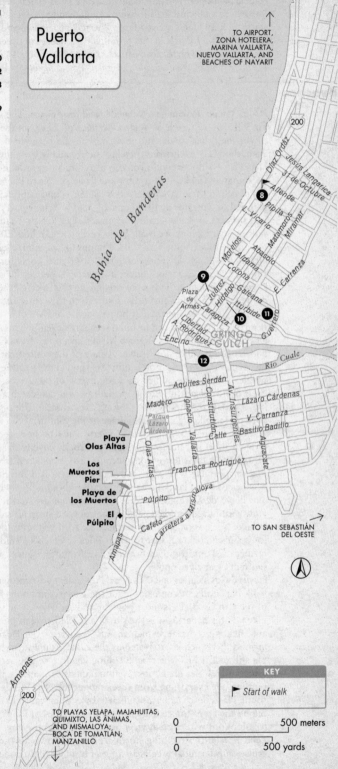

Puerto Vallarta

↑
TO AIRPORT,
ZONA HOTELERA,
MARINA VALLARTA,
NUEVO VALLARTA, AND
BEACHES OF NAYARIT

200

Bahía de Banderas

Díaz Ordaz
Jesús Langarica
31 de Octubre
Allende
Pipila
L. Vicario
Matamoros
Miramar
Morelos
Aldama
Abasolo
Corona
E. Carranza
Juárez
Hidalgo
Galeana
Plaza
de
Armas
Zaragoza
Iturbide
Libertad
A. Rodríguez
GRINGO
GULCH
Guerrero
Encino

8
9
10
11
12

Río Cuale

Aquiles Serdán

Madero
Av. Insurgentes
Lázaro Cárdenas
V. Carranza
Basilio Badillo
Parque
Lázaro
Cárdenas
Ignacio Vallarta
Constitución
Calle
Aguacate

**Playa
Olas Altas**

Olas Altas

Francisca Rodríguez

**Los
Muertos
Pier**

**Playa de
los Muertos**

Púlpito

**El
Púlpito**

Cafeto
Carretera a Mismaloya

Amapas

TO SAN SEBASTIÁN
DEL OESTE
↗

Amapas

200

TO PLAYAS YELAPA, MAJAHUITAS,
QUIMIXTO, LAS ÁNIMAS,
AND MISMALOYA;
BOCA DE TOMATLÁN;
MANZANILLO

KEY

▶ *Start of walk*

0 ———————— 500 meters

0 ———————— 500 yards

⑨ **Palacio Municipal.** The late Manuel Lepe's 1981 mural depicting Puerto Vallarta as a fanciful seaside fishing and farming village hangs above the stairs on City Hall's second floor. Puerto Vallarta's most famous artist, Lepe is known for his blissful, primitive-style scenes of the city, filled with smiling angels. The tourism office is on the first floor. ✉ *Av. Juárez, on Plaza de Armas, the main plaza, Centro* ☎ *No phone* ☉ *Weekdays 9–5.*

Beaches

Playas Yelapa, Majahuitas, Quimixto, and Las Ánimas. The secluded fishing village and beach of Yelapa is about an hour southeast of downtown; the other towns and their beaches lie between it and Boca de Tomatlán. Day excursions travel to the area daily from the Marina Vallarta cruise-ship terminal; you can also hire a motor launch from Boca de Tomatlán ($43 round-trip for one to six people to Playa Las Ánimas; about $86 to Yelapa). Water taxis ($6.50 round-trip) depart from the pier at Los Muertos at 10:30 and 11 AM for Yelapa and return to pick you up at 3 or 4 PM. Seafood shanties edge Yelapa's sands and parasailors float high above it all. From here, you can hike 20 minutes into the jungle to see some waterfalls. Quimixto has calm, clear waters that attract boatloads of snorkelers. You can rent a horse for a 15-minute ride to a large, clear pool under a waterfall—perfect for a dip.

Playa de Mismaloya. This once pristine cove is where "the movie" was made. The 13-km (8-mi) drive south from the center of town on Carretera 200 passes spectacular houses, some of PV's oldest and quietest resorts, and a slew of condo and time-share developments. You can take a taxi or one of the bright green Mismaloya buses from Calles Vallarta and Basilio Badillo, downtown. Although the construction of La Jolla de Mismaloya (a huge hotel complex) spoiled the pristine nature of the jungle-fringed cove, it affords a good view of Los Arcos, and the cove itself is still beautiful. From Mismaloya you can catch a cab inland 2 km (1 mi) on the dirt road to the jungle restaurants Chino's and El Eden.

Boca de Tomatlán. This small village at the mouth of the Río Tomatlán is about 17 km (10½ mi) south of Puerto Vallarta. Just off the coast road down a short but bumpy dirt drive is a rocky cove with several restaurants. Water taxis leave from Boca to Los Arcos, an offshore rock formation popular with skin and scuba divers, and the more secluded beaches of Playa las Ánimas and Yelapa. About halfway between Boca and Playa de Mismaloya, Chee Chee's, a massive, terraced restaurant and swimming-pool complex, spreads down a steep hillside like a small village. Next door, similarly terraced Le Kliff restaurant is a great spot for a sunset cocktail. Just south of Boca is Chico's Paradise, and a bit farther on, Las Orquidias. Both are riverfront restaurants where you can swim in clear river pools.

Playas de los Muertos and Olas Altas. Proximity to downtown's lively sidewalk bars and cafés here has made these two contiguous beaches south of the Río Cuale PV's most popular and crowded beaches. Long ago, Playa de los Muertos was the site of a battle between pirates and Indians, hence the name, which means "Beach of the Dead." The area around the beach is promoted as the Zona Romántica, but most people still call it Los Muertos. Strolling vendors selling lace tablecloths, kites, and jewelry are almost as abundant as sunbathers. Beach toys for rent include everything from rubber inner tubes to Windsurfers. To the south, Playa de los Muertos ends at a rocky point called El Púlpito. Walking up the steps (more than 100) at the east end of Púlpito street leads to a lookout with a great view of the beach and the bay.

Zona Hotelera. Stretching north from downtown to the marina and cruise-ship terminal area is a string of beaches often collectively called the Zona Hotelera or Hotel Zone. The beach changes a bit with the character of each resort it fronts, but it is particularly nice by the Fiesta Americana and the Krystal hotels.

Nuevo Vallarta and Nayarit. When PV swells with tourists, local families head out of town to the unpopulated beaches at the north end of Bahía de Banderas, in the state of Nayarit. Twelve kilometers (7 miles) north of Nuevo Vallarta, on yet another beautiful beach, is the simple town of Bucerías, where a loyal flock of snowbirds has encouraged the growth of small hotels and restaurants. Beyond Bucerías are long stretches of deserted beach around Cruz de Huanacaxtle and La Manzanilla, where kids play in the shallow waters while their parents sip beer or soft drinks. Destiladeras is a long, semirocky beach with good surf. The coast road continues to the popular beach at El Anclote, with simple restaurants. Just beyond is Punta de Mita, home of the posh Four Seasons, the boutique resort Casa Las Brisas, and a blue bay that's nice for swimming; around the bend are waves for surfing. This is a prime spot for viewing a sunset; in winter, whales come here to mate and give birth. Scuba divers like the fairly clear waters and abundance of tropical fish and coral on the bay side of the Isla Marietas, about a half hour offshore. A dirt road leads from Punta de Mita to Sayulita (you can also reach it in about 45 minutes from Puerto Vallarta on Carretera 200 past Bucerías). In addition to hotels and restaurants, Sayulita has excellent surfing and beautiful beaches. Some say it's like PV was 40 years ago. Fifteen minutes north of Sayulita is San Francisco, unofficially known as San Pancho, with modest rental bungalows and eateries, a 1½-km-long (1-mi-long) barely developed stretch of sand, and more great surfing spots. A half hour beyond San Francisco, the pretty beach at Lo de Marco is also popular with surfers.

Where to Eat

★ **$$$–$$$$** ✕ **Café des Artistes.** PV's most sophisticated dining spot has a beautiful garden with a breathtaking view of the Pacific. Owner/chef Thierry Blouet blends Mexican ingredients with European techniques to produce such interesting combinations as cream of prawn and pumpkin soup, mussels in a scallop mousse, and roast duck with soy and honey. Special menus allow the chef to combine some of his signature dishes with appropriate wines and, of course, dessert. A piano and flute provide musical accompaniment. ✉ *Av. Guadalupe Sánchez 740, Centro* ☎ 322/222–3228 ⚲ *Reservations essential* ▤ *AE, MC, V* ☽ *No lunch.*

$$$–$$$$ ✕ **Felipe's.** Felipe Palacio's gracious family home has the charm of old Vallarta and spectacular views of the bay and town from its multilevel terraces. Try the grilled seafood or the superbly prepared steaks served with baked potato and veggies. The upper terrace is a good spot to stargaze and order a drink and an appetizer. ✉ *Prolongación Av. Insurgentes 466, Col. Alta Vista* ☎ 322/222–3820 ▤ *AE, MC, V* ☽ *No lunch.*

$$$ ✕ **Daiquiri Dick's.** The beachside patio dining room of this longtime local favorite frames a view of the bay at Playa de los Muertos. "Brunch" lasts all day (9 to 5) and consists of a long menu full of soups, salads, pizza, crab cakes, and ceviche—don't expect traditional American breakfast favorites. The Caesar salad explodes with flavor, and the medallions of beef tenderloin demi-glacé and the lobster tacos are superb. Finish off with a hazelnut daiquiri. ✉ *Av. Olas Altas 314, downtown* ☎ 322/222–0566 ▤ *MC, V* ☽ *Closed Wed. May–Aug.; and month of Sept.*

$$$ ✕ **River Cafe.** Candles flicker at romantic tables lining the riverbank, and tiny white lights wrap the palm trees surrounding the multilevel terrace. Attentive waiters serve such international dishes as steak, lobster, and pasta to a well-dressed crowd. Each plate is a visual as well as a culinary treat. If you're not into a romantic dinner, stop in for breakfast, or belly up to the intimate bar for a drink and—Thursday through Sunday evenings—a listen to the live jazz. ⊠ *Isla Río Cuale, Local 4, Isla Río Cuale* ☎ *322/223–0788* ▤ *AE, MC, V.*

★ **$$$** ✕ **Trio.** Founding German chef Bernhard Guth is now joined by Uls Henrickson to continue the restaurant's tradition of serving avant-garde Mediterranean creations. Try the orange-crusted sea bass with a sweet puree of garbanzo, dates, olives, and cider or the rack of lamb and ravioli with lamb ragout. The artsy crowd and professional staff make for a wonderful dining experience. The kitchen often stays open until just shy of midnight, and there's a rooftop terrace on which to dine or have drinks. ⊠ *Calle Guerrero 264, Centro* ☎ *322/222–2196* ▤ *AE, MC, V.*

$$–$$$$ ✕ **Blue Shrimp.** Although the crustaceans are rosy pink, not azure, the lighting is on the blue side, making you feel as if you're underwater. Choose your shrimp by size and weight, and the kitchen then prepares it to order. Most dishes are accompanied by rice and steamed veggies. And if your favorite recipe isn't on the menu, you can even bring your own. Lobster and a variety of fish plates are also available, or dive into the salad bar for just a buck. ⊠ *Calle Morelos 779, Centro* ☎ *322/222–4246* ▤ *AE, MC, V.*

$$–$$$ ✕ **Café Maximilian.** The efficient, genuinely friendly staff make this a top Olas Altas dining spot. Viennese and other European entrées dominate the menu, which is modified each year when the restaurant participates in PV's culinary festival. Recent innovations include the herb-crusted rack of lamb served with horseradish and pureed vegetables au gratin and the venison medallions with chestnut sauce served with braised white cabbage and steamed vegetables. You can also order these dishes at the coffeehouse next door; it specializes in sandwiches and desserts. Try the warm apple tart with cinnamon ice cream and caramel sauce. ⊠ *Av. Olas Altas 380, Olas Altas* ☎ *322/223–0760* ▤ *AE, MC, V* ☯ *Closed Sun.*

★ **$–$$$$** ✕ **La Palapa.** Hurricane Kenna swept everything but the kitchen away from this thatch-roof restaurant on the beach at Los Muertos. But its fans couldn't live for long without its panfried goat cheese appetizers, tortilla soup, Angus beef, and fresh seafood prepared in interesting ways. The resilient owners get things running before you can say "Bon appétit," and the musicians serenade patrons at dinner. For a romantic evening, reserve a table for two under the stars, choose from one of several set menus, and finish up with marshmallows toasted on your own private bonfire. Reservations are recommended. ⊠ *Calle Pulpito 103 Los Muertos* ☎ *322/222–5225* ▤ *MC, V.*

★ **$–$$$** ✕ **Adobe Café.** Minimalist decor in shades of white and earth tones, stark tree branches, and fresh flowers make for a delightful dining experience. Specialties include black bean soup, pork tenderloin in rum, and one of the best desserts in town: a sinfully rich chocolate mousse between two layers of chocolate cake and chocolate icing. ⊠ *Calle Basilio Badillo 252, Col. E. Zapata* ☎ *322/222–6720* ▤ *MC, V* ☯ *Closed Tues. and June–Sept. No lunch.*

$–$$$ ✕ **Archie's Wok.** Although the lumpia can be limp and the salads are sometimes overdressed, the Asian-fusion cuisine here is a great break from Continental and Mexican food. International music at a discreet level permits conversation, and ceiling fans rustle the lacy limbs of potted ferns and palms. There are plenty of choices for noncarnivores, including stir-fry pastas with green veggies and mushrooms, Chinese sesame cucumber salad, and Vietnamese fish in banana leaves. ⊠ *Calle Francisca Rodriguez 130, Los Muertos* ☎ *322/222–0411* ▤ *MC, V* ☯ *Closed Sun.*

★ **$–$$$** ✕ **Cafe de Olla.** A large tree extends from the dining-room floor through the roof, local artwork adorns the walls, and salsa music often plays in the background. This is the place for cheap, down-to-earth Mexican food—enchiladas, *carne asada* (grilled strips of marinated meat), and *chiles rellenos* (stuffed, batter-fried chili peppers). The restaurant is hugely popular; you may need to wait a short while for a table, especially for breakfast, which begins at 9 AM. Service is excellent. ⊠ *Calle Basilio Badillo 168-A, Los Muertos* ☎ *322/223–1626* ▭ *No credit cards* ⊘ *Closed Tues.*

★ **$–$$$** ✕ **Chico's Paradise.** It's easy to while away hours—or even the day—under the huge, multilevel palapa, taking a dip in the river or watching tortillas being made by hand. Seafood, including fresh jumbo shrimp and stuffed crab, is a specialty, but chiles rellenos and chicken burritos are also popular. Or just come for the huge tropical drinks. In the off-season, Chico's closes just after sunset. ⊠ *Carretera a Manzanillo, Km 20, just south of Boca de Tomatlán* ☎ *322/222–0747* ▭ *No credit cards.*

★ **$–$$$** ✕ **Don Pedro's.** Everything is a treat at this giant beachfront palapa in Sayulita, a half hour north of the airport, where European-trained chef and co-owner Nicholas Parrillo serves an array of fish, seafood, and poultry sprinkled with herbs and grilled over mesquite. From the crusty herbed breads and pizzas baked in wood-fire ovens to the rich mango ice cream, everything is as fresh as can be. ⊠ *Calle Marlin 2, midway along Sayulita town beach, 35 km (22 mi) north of Puerto Vallarta airport, Sayulita* ☎ *329/291–3090* ▭ *AE, MC, V* ⊘ *Closed Aug.–Oct.*

$–$$ ✕ **Andale.** Although many long-timers have been drinking, rather than eating, at this Olas Altas hangout for years, the restaurant serves great burgers, herb-garlic bread, black-bean soup, and jumbo shrimp as well as nightly drink specials at the chummy bar. The interior is cool, dark, and informal; two rows of tables line the narrow outdoor patio. ⊠ *Av. Olas Altas 425, Olas Altas* ☎ *322/222–1054* ▭ *MC, V.*

$–$$ ✕ **La Bodeguita del Medio.** Near the malecón's north end, this attractive restaurant-bar has a sea view from its second-floor dining room. The menu varies by season, but, if possible, try the roast pork, the paella, or the pork loin in tamarind sauce; order rice, salad, or fried plantains separately. Like its Havana namesake, La Bodeguita sells Cuban rum and cigars, and the music—like the cuisine—is pure Caribbean. A Cuban sextet performs every night but Monday from 9 PM to 2 AM. ⊠ *Paseo Díaz Ordáz 858, Centro* ☎ *322/223–1585* ▭ *AE, MC, V.*

Where to Stay

★ **$$$$** ⊞ **Las Alamandas.** Personal service and exclusivity lure movie stars and royalty to this low-key resort that's surrounded by a nature preserve. Among the outdoor activities are boat rides along the Río San Nicolás. Although the villas are painted hot pink, they remain hidden by all the trees and plants. Each villa houses suites that are filled with folk art. In-door-outdoor living rooms have modern furnishings with deliciously nubby fabrics in bright, bold colors and Guatemalan-cloth throw pillows. You can fly in via the small airstrip or take the hotel's limo from either the airport at Puerto Vallarta or Manzanillo—each about 1½ hours away. There's a two-night minimum. ⊠ *Carretera 200, Km 85* ⌖ *(Apartado postal 201, San Patricio Melaque 48980)* ☎ *322/285–5500 or 888/882–9616* ⊠ *322/285–5027* ⊕ *www.alamandas.com* ⊅ *14 suites* ⌂ *2 restaurants, room service, tennis court, pool, gym, beach, snorkeling, fishing, mountain bikes, croquet, horseback riding, Ping-Pong, volleyball, 2 bars, shops, laundry service, concierge, meeting room* ▭ *AE, MC, V* ⊮ *EP, FAP.*

$$$$ ⊞ **The Careyes.** Resembling a boldly painted village, this resort is on a gorgeous bay along Mexico's so-called Turtle Coast, 98 km (60 mi) north of Manzanillo airport and 172 km (107 mi) south of Puerto Vallarta. Freshly painted rooms and suites are done in rich tones of yellow ocher, coral, and sapphire blue. The full-service spa has European beauty and body treatments; a deli sells fine wines, prosciutto, and other necessities of the good life. A full range of water-sports equipment awaits you at the beach. ⊠ *Carretera a Barra de Navidad, Km 53.5, 48970 Costa Careyes, Jalisco* ☎ *315/351–0000; 800/325–3589 in the U.S.* 🖷 *315/351–0100* ⊕ *www.luxurycollection.com* ↩ *48 rooms, 4 suites* ᕴ *Restaurant, 2 tennis courts, pool, gym, spa, beach, snorkeling, boating, fishing, bar, shops, meeting rooms* ⊟ *AE, MC, V.*

$$$$ 🏨 **Four Seasons Resort.** At the northern end of Bahía de Banderas, a 40-minute drive northwest of the PV airport, this hotel was designed for exclusivity. Spacious rooms are in red-tile-roof Mexican-style casitas of one, two, and three stories and fitted with traditional Four Seasons amenities. Each has elegant yet earthy furnishings and a private terrace or balcony—many with a sweeping sea view. The Jack Nicklaus–designed championship golf course has a challenging, optional 19th island hole. A good variety of sporting and beach equipment is on hand for you to use, and golf and spa packages are available. ⊠ *Punta de Mita, Bahía de Banderas, 63734 Nayarit* ☎ *329/291–6000; 800/819–5053 in the U.S.* 🖷 *329/291–6015* ⊕ *www.fourseasons.com* ↩ *113 rooms, 27 suites* ᕴ *3 restaurants, room service, in-room data ports, in-room safes, minibars, cable TV, 19-hole golf course, 4 tennis courts, pool, wading pool, gym, spa, beach, horseback riding, 2 bars, baby-sitting, children's programs (ages 5–12), dry cleaning, laundry service, concierge, meeting rooms, car rental* ⊟ *AE, DC, MC, V.*

$$$$ 🏨 **Hotelito Desconocido.** This isolated hotel on a long stretch of beach is an idyllic escape for those willing to pay dearly for simple pleasures. Rooms and suites are in casitas that incorporate local building styles and materials, including plank floors, reed mats, bamboo walls, and palm-frond roofs; rustic-style bathrooms have tile floors. Solar power runs essential equipment, but rooms are cooled only by battery-powered fans and lit by lanterns and candles; there's no TV or telephone. In the morning, signal for coffee and croissants by running the flag up the flagpole. Meals plans are available, though they don't include drinks; it also costs extra to use the kayaks and bikes or to go horseback riding. ⊠ *Playón de Mismaloya s/n, Cruz de Loreto Tomatlán* ✑ *(Carretera a Mismaloya 479-102, Edificio Scala, 48380)* ☎ *322/222–2526; 800/851–1143 in the U. S.* 🖷 *322/223–0293* ⊕ *www.hotelito.com* ↩ *16 rooms, 13 suites* ᕴ *2 restaurants, pool, massage, spa, beach, boating, bicycles, billiards* ⊟ *AE, MC, V* ⍾ *FAP.*

$$$$ 🏨 **Hotel Sierra Nuevo Vallarta.** On a long, wide expanse of creamy sand beach in Nuevo Vallarta, the Sierra is a deluxe property. Rooms are light and airy, with tile floors, light-wood and wicker furniture, and pastel bedspreads. Activities are nonstop: jungle and city tours, cookouts, beach parties, Mexican fiestas, disco blasts, theme nights, musicals, and karaoke. A golf course is minutes away. ⊠ *Paseo de los Cocoteros 19, 63732 Nuevo Vallarta* ☎ *322/297–1300; 800/448–5028 in the U.S.* 🖷 *322/297–0267* ⊕ *www.sidek.com.mx* ↩ *345 rooms and suites* ᕴ *3 restaurants, in-room safes, minibars, cable TV, 2 tennis courts, 4 pools, fitness classes, beach, windsurfing, boating, bicycles, billiards, horseback riding, volleyball, 3 bars, concierge, meeting rooms* ⊟ *MC, V* ⍾ *All-inclusive.*

★ $$$$ 🏨 **El Tamarindo.** This magical resort is on 16 km (10 mi) of private coast surrounded by more than 2,000 acres of ecological reserve and jungle. The architecture embodies the Careyes style that first appeared in the 1960s, rendering simple design elements (with a Mediterranean flavor) in local building materials. Many of the villas have private plunge pools and outdoor living rooms; all have nubby fabrics, oiled wood, and other classy elements. At night, the gracious staff lights more than 1,500 candles around the villas to create a truly enchanting setting. ⊠ *Car-*

retera Melaque–Puerto Vallarta, Km 7.5, 48970 Cihuatlán, Jalisco ☎ *315/351–5032; 800/325–3589 in the U.S.* 📠 *315/351–5070* 🌐 *www. luxurycollection.com* ⇄ *29 villas* ⚘ *Restaurant, 18-hole golf course, 2 tennis courts, pool, beach, dive shop, snorkeling, bar* ▤ *AE, MC, V.*

$$$–$$$$ 🏨 **Meliá Puerto Vallarta.** On the beach in Marina Vallarta, this sprawling, top-of-the-line hotel is close to the 18-hole golf course. The lobby is an odd blend of cool marble and tile, industrial-strength rust-and-marine-blue paint with lilac accents, and wicker furniture. The large rooms are softer, with natural tones of blue, cream, and sand; all have balconies with chairs. Amenities include a huge pool, an outdoor theater, and nightly shows—you can even take dance or Spanish classes or practice your aim on the shooting range. ✉ *Paseo de la Marina Sur 7, Marina Vallarta 48354* ☎ *322/221–0200; 800/336–3542 in the U.S.* 📠 *322/221–0118* 🌐 *www.solmelia.com* ⇄ *356 rooms, 4 suites* ⚘ *3 restaurants, in-room safes, cable TV, 2 tennis courts, pool, 2 hot tubs, gym, beach, 3 bars, shops, children's programs (ages 4–12), laundry service, concierge, meeting rooms* ▤ *AE, DC, MC, V* 🍴 *All-inclusive.*

★ **$$$** 🏨 **Camino Real.** One of PV's first hotels is on a small bay south of town. Fragrant white jasmine and other tropical plants grace the grounds. Rooms have marble floors with white furniture and bright pink, yellow, and purple highlights against stark white walls; plush robes are classy touches. La Brisa restaurant serves superb seafood lunches; elegant, upscale La Perla has excellent international food and inspired desserts. An 11-story tower houses the Camino Real Club, where guests receive upgraded amenities and breakfast on a terrace overlooking the sea. ✉ *Playa las Estacas, Km 3.5, 48300* ☎ *322/221–5000; 800/722–6466 in the U.S.* 📠 *322/221–6000* 🌐 *www.caminoreal.com* ⇄ *326 rooms, 11 suites* ⚘ *4 restaurants, 24-hour room service, in-room safes, minibars, cable TV, 2 tennis courts, 2 pools, wading pool, health club, beach, 2 bars, babysitting, children's programs (ages 5–10), laundry service, concierge, meeting rooms, travel services* ▤ *AE, DC, MC, V* 🍴 *CP, EP.*

$$$ 🏨 **Fiesta Americana.** The dramatically designed terra-cotta building rises above a deep-blue pool that flows under bridges and palm oases; a seven-story palapa covers the lobby and a large round bar. The ocean-view rooms have a modern pink and terra-cotta color scheme, and each has beige marble floors, a balcony, and a tile bath with a powerful shower. The beach bustles with activity and equipment rentals. It's about halfway between the Marina Vallarta complex and downtown. ✉ *Blvd. Francisco Medina Ascencio, Km 2.5, Zona Hotelera 48300* ☎ *322/224–2010; 800/343–7821 in the U.S.* 📠 *322/224–2108* 🌐 *www.fiestaamericana. com.mx* ⇄ *255 rooms, 36 suites* ⚘ *3 restaurants, pool, beach, 3 bars, concierge, meeting rooms, car rental, travel services* ▤ *AE, MC, V.*

$$$ 🏨 **La Jolla de Mismaloya.** Although it seems a pity to have plopped such a huge hotel on lovely Mismaloya Bay, its guests—who consistently give this hotel high marks—have half the bay to themselves as well as fabulous views. Huge, brightly decorated one- and two-bedroom suites have terraces and well-equipped kitchens, and there are many activities for children. ✉ *Zona Hotelera Sur, Km 11.5, Mismaloya 48300* ☎ *322/228–0660; 800/322–2343 in the U.S.* 📠 *322/228–0853* 🌐 *www. lajollademismaloya.com* ⇄ *303 suites* ⚘ *5 restaurants, room service, in-room data ports, minibars, cable TV, tennis court, 4 pools, gym, hot tub, spa, beach, dive shop, snorkeling, 3 bars, shops, baby-sitting, children's programs (ages 5–11), laundry service, concierge, business services, convention center, car rental, travel services* ▤ *AE, MC, V* 🍴 *All-inclusive, EP.*

$$$ 🏨 **Marriott Casa Magna.** One of PV's largest and most glamorous hotels is on the beach in the marina area. The vast, plant-filled marble lobby is hung with wrought-iron chandeliers, the adjacent bar is wide open to the sea air, and the huge infinity pool is right on the beach. Rooms have polished and unpolished marble, blond woods, and floral-print fabrics. And if the water sports, kid's club, and other hotel amenities aren't enough, you also have access to the facilities of the Marina Vallarta complex, including a huge shopping center, a yacht club, and restaurants. ✉ *Paseo de la Marina 5, Marina Vallarta 48354* ☎ *322/226–0000; 800/ 228–9290 in the U.S.* 🖷 *322/226–0060* ⊕ *www.marriott.com* ➳ *404 rooms, 29 suites* ⚬ *4 restaurants, room service, in-room data ports, in-room safes, minibars, cable TV, 3 tennis courts, pool, gym, hot tub, beach, 3 bars, baby-sitting, children's programs (ages 5–12), laundry service, concierge, business services, meeting rooms, car rental, no-smoking rooms* ⊟ *AE, DC, MC, V.*

$$$ 🏨 **Paradise Village.** Built like an Aztec pyramid, this Nuevo Vallarta hotel and time-share property has its own marina and hosts an international sailing regatta each March. All suites have balconies with either marina or ocean views; the smallest, a junior suite, is 700 square ft. Furnishings are functional: there are sofa beds and well-equipped kitchens. Locals like to visit the spa, which is noted for its massages and facials. ✉ *Paseo de los Cocoteros 18, 63732 Nuevo Vallarta* ☎ *322/226–6770; 800/995–5714 Ext. 111 in the U.S.* 🖷 *322/226–6752* ⊕ *www.paradisevillage.com* ➳ *490 suites* ⚬ *3 restaurants, 2 snack bars, 18-hole golf course, room service, kitchens, cable TV, 4 tennis courts, 3 pools, gym, spa, beach, windsurfing, jet skiing, basketball, volleyball, 4 bars, dance club, shops, convention center, car rental, travel services* ⊟ *AE, MC, V.*

★ $$–$$$ 🏨 **Westin Regina.** This elegant yet spare and modern high-rise is on a choice 21-acre site in Marina Vallarta. In addition to four pools, a long stretch of beach, and a full range of facilities and activities, the Westin has spacious balconied rooms with marble bathrooms and brightly colored, handwoven spreads and drapes. Rooms above the sixth floor have ocean views; those below face the 600 palm trees surrounding the beautiful pools. Concrete-and-stone floors massage bare feet, and top-of-the-line mattresses with whisper-soft duvets make for heavenly siestas. Most suites have Jacuzzis. ✉ *Paseo de la Marina Sur 205, Marina Vallarta 48354* ☎ *322/226–1100; 800/228–3000 in the U.S.* 🖷 *322/ 226–1131* ⊕ *www.westinpv.com* ➳ *266 rooms, 14 suites* ⚬ *2 restaurants, 2 snack bars, room service, in-room safes, kitchenettes, cable TV, 3 tennis courts, 4 pools, gym, 2 hot tubs, spa, beach, 2 bars, baby-sitting, children's programs (ages infant–12), laundry service, concierge, car rental, no-smoking rooms* ⊟ *AE, DC, MC, V.*

★ $$ 🏨 **Buenaventura.** A good value, this hotel has an ideal location on the northern edge of downtown, about 10 blocks from the malecón and, in the opposite direction, the shops, hotels, and restaurants on the airport highway. The bright, cheerful rooms have beam ceilings and pale-wood furnishings. The property suffered damage during Hurricane Kenna, and the pool, beach club, lobby, and other public areas were subsequently renovated and upgraded. ✉ *Av. México 1301, Centro 48350* ☎ *322/226–7000 or 888/859–9439* 🖷 *322/222–3546* ➳ *232 rooms, 4 suites* ⚬ *2 restaurants, room service, cable TV, 2 pools, hot tub, massage, beach, snorkeling, jet skiing, volleyball, 3 bars, baby-sitting, laundry service, car rental, travel services* ⊟ *AE, MC, V* ⭐ *All-inclusive, EP.*

$$ 🏨 **Krystal Vallarta.** This full-service resort and time-share property resembles a small village, with stone pathways and gardens leading to the pool area, shops, and accommodations. All guest quarters exude Mexican character, with tile floors and Spanish colonial-style furnishings. Rooms and suites are pretty and bright, but not all have a balcony. Master villas have separate dining and living rooms as well as private pools. The beach is commodious and secluded. ✉ *Av. de las Garzas s/n Zona*

Hotelera 48300 ☎ *322/224–0202; 800/231–9860 in the U.S.* 🖷 *322/224–0222* ⊕ *www.krystal.com.mx* ⇗ *102 rooms, 54 suites, 99 villas* ⚭ *6 restaurants, in-room safes, minibars, cable TV, 2 tennis courts, 3 pools, 3 wading pools, gym, massage, beach, racquetball, 2 bars, dance club, baby-sitting, dry cleaning, laundry service, concierge, car rental, travel services, no-smoking rooms* ☰ *AE, MC, V.*

★ **$–$$** 🏨 **Casa Dulce Vida.** Four blocks off the busy malecón this hidden villa has seven suites of various sizes filled with Mexican art and comfortable furniture. All have well-equipped kitchens and most have ocean-view terraces; the largest has two bedrooms, two baths, and a separate dining room. There's a red-tile pool and tropical gardens. In high season, the property only accepts weeklong bookings. ⊠ *Calle Aldama 295, Centro 48300* ☎ *322/222–1008; 800/600–6026 in the U.S.* 🖷 *322/222–5815* ⊕ *www.dulcevida.com* ⇗ *7 suites* ⚭ *Kitchens, pool* ☰ *V* ⦿ *CP.*

$–$$ 🏨 **Villa Amor.** What began as a home on top of a hill was transformed into luxury palapa suites among the trees, with more outdoor than indoor living and beautiful views of Sayulita's coast. Accommodations range from a basic room for two (with a hot plate and a small fridge) to two-bedroom suites for four with a terrace and a plunge pool. The restaurant is good and has live music on weekends. The staff is friendly, and a beautiful beach is just a short walk away. You can borrow bikes, surfboards, and fishing and snorkeling equipment. ⊠ *Playa Sayulita 63842 Sayulita, Nayarit* ☎ *329/291–3010* 🖷 *329/275–0263* ⊕ *www.villaamor.com* ⇗ *21 villas* ⚭ *Restaurant, kitchenettes, tennis court, massage, snorkeling, fishing, bicycles, laundry service, concierge* ☰ *No credit cards.*

$ 🏨 **Casa Andrea.** One- and two-bedroom apartments in this spiffy property are truly homey. Each is different, but all have ceiling fans, comfortable furniture, and dark-wood beams that contrast with bright white ceilings and walls. Use the hotel's computer to check your e-mail, or curl up with a book or watch a video in the library. Coffee and pastries are served each morning on the garden patio. The location, just a few blocks from Los Arcos and the boardwalk, is a real plus. The management prefers that you book this property by the week, although exceptions are sometimes made. ⊠ *Calle Francisca Rodriguez 174, Centro 48380* 🖷🖷 *322/222–1213* ⊕ *www.casa-andrea.com* ⇗ *11 apartments* ⚭ *Kitchens, pool, hot tub, bar, library, Internet* ☰ *No credit cards* ⦿ *CP.*

$ 🏨 **Playa Los Arcos.** By far the most popular hotel on the beach near the Río Cuale, the Los Arcos has a friendly, casual air and an open central courtyard with pool. A glass elevator rises to the simple yet comfortable rooms, which are fitted with rustic light-wood and pastel furnishings and have small balconies. There's live music nightly until 11:30, and a Mexican fiesta on Saturday evenings. ⊠ *Av. Olas Altas 380, Olas Altas 48380* ☎ *322/222–1583* 🖷 *322/222–2418* ⇗ *170 rooms, 5 suites* ⚭ *Restaurant, cable TV, pools, beach, bar* ☰ *AE, MC, V.*

¢ 🏨 **Posada de Roger.** If you hang around the pool, it's not hard to get to know the other guests—most of them savvy budget travelers from Europe and Canada. The spare, simple rooms have phones, TVs, and air-conditioning; the showers are hot, the beds comfortable—if you like a very firm mattress. The location a few blocks from Los Muertos beach and in an area known for its restaurants is a real boon The on-site indoor-outdoor bar and restaurant (the latter serving breakfast only) are very popular with locals as well as visitors. ⊠ *Calle Basilio Badillo 237, Col. E. Zapata 48380* ☎ *322/222–0836 or 322/222–0639* 🖷 *322/223–0482* ⊕ *www.puerto-vallarta.com/posada* ⇗ *48 rooms* ⚭ *Restaurant, pool, bar, Internet* ☰ *AE, MC, V.*

Nightlife

Puerto Vallarta is a party town, where the discos open at 10 PM and stay open until 3 or 4 AM. A $12 cover charge is the norm (at least for men) in the popular discos, many of which are at hotels. Mexican fiestas are popular and can be lavish affairs with buffet dinners, folk dances, and even fireworks. Make reservations with the hotels that host them or with a travel agency.

Fodor'sChoice
★
La Bodeguita del Medio (⊠ Paseo Díaz Ordáz 858 Centro ☎ 322/223–1585) is a wonderful Cuban bar whose friendly vibe makes meeting new friends easy. The **Camino Real** (⊠ Carretera a Barra, Km 3.5, Playa Las Estacas ☎ 322/221–5000) hosts cultural events, such as music concerts and folkloric dances, on the first Thursday of every month at 9 PM. The Krystal Vallarta hotel has **Christine** (⊠ Av. de las Garzas s/n Zona Hotelera ☎ 322/224–0202), which has spectacular light shows set to music—from disco to techno.

Club Roxy (⊠ Av. Ignacio L. Vallarta 217, Col. E. Zapata ☎ 322/223–2424) has live rock and R&B, with an occasional reggae set, usually beginning by 8 PM. As its name implies, **Collage** (☎ 322/221–0505), on the highway at the Marina Vallarta complex, has a mishmash of establishments: several restaurants, a bowling alley, billiards, two bars, shuffleboard, a video arcade, and a disco. **El Faro** (⊠ Royal Pacific Yacht Club, Marina Vallarta ☎ 322/221–0541) is a romantic spot from which to admire the bay and marina from atop a 110-ft lighthouse. There's often live guitar music between 11 PM and midnight.

The dance club **Jabalú** (⊠ Av. Ignacio L. Vallarta 399, Los Muertos ☎ 322/222–0491) attracts a youngish, relatively well-dressed crowd. **J.&B.** (⊠ Blvd. Francisco Medina Ascencio 2043, Zona Hotelera ☎ 322/224–4616), pronounced "Jota Bay," is popular for dancing to live salsa. The techno music at **The Zoo** (⊠ Paseo Díaz Ordáz 630, Centro ☎ 322/222–4945), facing the boardwalk near Olas Altas, attracts a twentysomething crowd.

Sports & the Outdoors

Biking

Bike Mex (⊠ Calle Guerrero 361, Centro ☎ 322/223–1834) provides the gear (24-speed mountain bikes, gloves, and helmets) and snacks for several different bike tours, which can be tailored to your experience and fitness level. The most popular excursion is a four-hour trip inland to bathe in an impressive waterfall. More ambitious options include all-day rides to Punta de Mita or Yelapa, as well as a four-day, three-night excursion for advanced riders. Bike Mex also offers hiking and surfing packages.

Fishing

The billfish tournament in November draws dedicated fishermen from all over the world. **Pacific Fishing, Inc.** (☎ 322/221–2616 or 888/237–7358) is operated by third-generation sportsman Tat Tatterson, who promotes catch-and-release fishing. High-season prices for an eight-hour trip—including lunch, gear, and bait—are $600 for a cabin cruiser and $450 for a super panga; there's a discount in low season (late spring through early fall).

Golf

Puerto Vallarta has several impressive courses with first-class services including driving range and putting greens, lessons, pro shop, and clubhouse. The Four Seasons has an 18-hole course at its Punta de Mita property, as does El Tamarindo, on Carretera 200 south of Puerto Vallarta. Both are wonderful courses, but if you're not a guest, you'll find tee times hard to come by.

At the Paradise Village hotel and condo complex is **El Tigre** (✉ Paseo de los Cocoteros 18, Nuevo Vallarta ☎ 322/226–6739), an 18-hole course with 12 water features. The greens fee of $156 include a shared cart, practice balls, and tax. Puerta Vallarta's original course is the 18-hole one at **Los Flamingos Country Club** (✉ 12 km [8 mi] north of airport, Nuevo Vallarta ☎ 329/296–5006), designed by Percy Clifford. The greens fee is $115, including a shared cart and a bucket of balls. Joe Finger designed the 18-hole course at **Marina Vallarta** (☎ 322/221–0545 or 322/221–0073); the $99 greens fee includes a shared cart and tax.

The 18-hole course at **Mayan Palace** (✉ Paseo de las Moras 1, Nuevo Vallarta ☎ 322/226–1543) includes a golf cart for each player in its greens fees of $110. The **Vista Vallarta** (✉ Circuito Universidad 653, Col. San Nicolás ☎ 322/290–0030 or 322/290–0040) course has 18 holes designed by Jack Nicklaus and another 18 by Tom Weiskopf. It costs $130 to play either course.

Horseback Riding

You arrange for hour-long horseback rides along the shore at area beaches. **Rancho Charro** (✉ Playa Grande ☎ 322/224–0114 ⊕ www.ranchoelcharro.com) provides transportation to and from your hotel for three- to eight-hour rides to area rivers and waterfalls. **Rancho El Ojo de Agua** (✉ Cerrada de Cardenal 227, Fracc. Aralias ☎ 322/224–0607) conducts sunset and half-day horseback rides, some including lunch and time for a swim in a mountain stream. The staff can also arrange excursions of up to five nights to colonial villages in the Sierra Madre.

Scuba Diving & Snorkeling

An underwater preserve surrounding Los Arcos, a granite rock formation off Playa Mismaloya, is a popular spot for diving and snorkeling. The rocky bay at Quimixto, about 32 km (20 mi) south of PV and accessible only by boat, is a good spot for both snorkeling and diving. Punta de Mita, about 80 km (50 mi) north, has Las Marietas Islands, with lava tubes and caves to be explored. In winter, humpback whales are spotted; the rest of the year, divers look for manta ray, sea turtles, and schools of brightly colored fish. A bit beyond, big fish lurk around the underwater pinnacles and caves around El Morro islands—areas for experienced divers only.

Many of the larger resort hotels rent snorkeling and diving equipment and offer introductory dive courses at their pools. For PADI-certification courses, daylong dive trips, and equipment rentals, contact **Chico's Dive Shop** (✉ Paseo Díaz Ordáz 772, Centro ☎ 322/222–1895). Trips to Los Arcos accommodate kids and snorkelers as well as those who want a 2-tank dive ($80). The PADI dive masters at **Pacific Scuba** (✉ Francisco Medina Ascencio 2486, Centro ☎ 322/209–0364) teach courses, rent equipment, and arrange trips. Two-tank dives cost around $225; packages that include accommodations are also available.

Tennis

Most of the larger hotels have tennis courts for their guests' use. **Los Flamingos Country Club** (✉ 12 km [8 mi] north of airport, Nuevo Vallarta ☎ 329/298–0280) has courts. At **Los Tules Tennis Club** (✉ Condominios Los Tules, Carretera al Aeropuerto, Km. 2.5, across from Gigante supermarket, Zona Hotelera ☎ 322/226–1030) you can take lessons or join organized tournaments in addition to renting court time.

Children love **Splash** (⊠ Carretera a Tepic, Km 155, Nuevo Vallarta ☎ 322/297–0723), where they can plummet down enormous water slides, swim, and play on playground equipment and carnival rides. There are restaurants and bars as well as sea lion and dolphin shows. The park is open daily 10–6; admission is $12.

Shopping

Puerto Vallarta has been described as a shopper's paradise punctuated with hotels and beaches. There are plenty of malls, small specialty shops, and fine-art galleries. This is a great place to shop for handicrafts, from the region and throughout Mexico. Masks, pottery, lacquerware, carved-wood animals, hand-dyed woven rugs, and embroidered clothing are just some of what's available in shops and markets. If possible comparison shop; quality varies. There's also a good selection of Mexican silver in PV, but watch out for *chapa,* a combination of alloys. Real silver carries the 0.925 stamp required by the government.

In the Mercado Municipal, at Avenida Miramar and Libertad, flowers, piñatas, produce, and plastics are all shoved together in indoor and outdoor stands that cover a full city block. The strip of shops along Isla Río Cuale is an outdoor market of sorts, with souvenir stands and exclusive boutiques interspersed with eateries. Most of the brand-name clothing stores are along the malecón and down its side streets.

The highway on the north side of town is lined with small arcades and large shopping centers. The best selections are at the huge Paradise Plaza, next to Paradise Village Resort in Nuevo Vallarta, where you'll find boutiques as well as a bank, a hair salon, a video arcade, and cafés. Other centers include Gigante Plaza, by the Fiesta Americana hotel; Plaza Malecón, at the beginning of Paseo Díaz Ordáz; Plaza Marina, on the highway at Marina Vallarta; and Villa Vallarta, by the Plaza las Glorias hotel.

Prices in the shops are fixed, and U.S. dollars and credit cards are accepted. Bargaining is expected in the markets and by the vendors on the beach, who also freely accept American money. Most stores are open daily 10–8. A few close for siesta at 1 or 2, then reopen at 4.

Art

In Marina Vallarta **Arte de las Américas** (⊠ Edificio de las Palmas, Marina Vallarta ☎ 322/221–1985) shows a good number of wonderful contemporary painters, many from Oaxaca. The gallery is owned by the same people as Galería Uno. **Galería Arte Latinoamericano** (⊠ Calle Josefa Ortiz Domínguez 155, Centro ☎ 322/222–4406) has contemporary art, sculptures, and lithographs. **Galería Dante** (⊠ Calle Basilio Badillo 269, Col. E. Zapata ☎ 322/222–2477) is a 6,000-square-ft gallery and sculpture garden with classical, contemporary, and abstract works from more than 50 Latin American artists. Contemporary paintings and sculpture are displayed at **Galería Pacífico** (⊠ Calle Aldama 174, Centro ☎ 322/222–1982), a pioneer gallery nearly 20 years old. You'll find ★ wonderful, varied art in many media at **Galería Uno** (⊠ Calle Morelos 561, Centro ☎ 322/222–0908). Owners Jan Lavender and Martina Goldberg love to showcase local talent, especially emerging artists. Internationally known Sergio Bustamante—the creator of life-size brass, copper, and ceramic animals—has several galleries: **Sergio Bustamante** (⊠ Av. Juárez 275, Centro ☎ 322/222–1129 ⊠ Paseo Díaz Ordáz 716, Centro ☎ 322/223–1407 ⊠ Paseo Díaz Ordáz 542, Centro ☎ 322/222–5480).

Clothing

La Bohemia (⊠ Calle Constitución at Calle Basilio Badillo, Col. E. Zapata ☎ 322/222–3164 ⊠ Plaza Neptuno Interior, Marina Vallarta ☎ 322/221–2160) sells contemporary resort wear, designer art wear, unique jewelry, and accessories. **Express–Guess** (⊠ Paseo Díaz Ordáz 660, Centro ☎ 322/222–6470) carries its own line of quality sportswear for men and women. **Güeros** (⊠ Calle Zaragoza 160, Centro ☎ 322/222–0633) sells contemporary clothing with Huichol designs for men, women, and children, as well as shoes, handbags, straw, leather, and home furnishings.

María de Guadalajara (⊠ Puesta del Sol condominiums, Marina Vallarta ☎ 322/221–2566 ⊠ Calle Morelos 550, Centro ☎ 322/222–2387) carries comfortable women's clothing in gauzy fabrics and luscious colors. You'll find tropical-print dresses, cotton blouses and pants, hand-painted clothing, jewelry, and shoes at **Sucesos Boutique** (⊠ Calle Libertad and Av. Hidalgo, Centro ☎ 322/222–1002).

Folk Art

Galería de Ollas (⊠ Calle Morelos 101, Local 3-D, Centro ☎ 322/223–1045 ⊠ Paradise Plaza, Nuevo Vallarta ☎ 329/297–1200) is the only place you can buy the wondrous pottery from the village of Mata Ortiz. **Galería Rosas Blancas** (⊠ Av. Juárez 523, Centro ☎ 322/222–1168) has a large stock of excellent folk art. You'll find highly prized beaded masks and statuettes, yarn art, and other folk crafts at the **Huichol Collection Gallery** (⊠ Calle Morelos 490, Centro ☎ 322/222–0182). **Mundo de Azulejos** (⊠ Av. Venustiano Carranza 374, Col. E. Zapata ☎ 322/222–2675) sells decorative tiles. The shop's artisans will also re-create your favorite scene or work of art in a series of tiles in 24 to 48 hours.

Glassblowers at the **Mundo de Cristal** (⊠ Av. Insurgentes 333, at Calle Basilio Badillo, Col. E. Zapata ☎ 322/222–4157) factory create both avant-garde and classic designs. **Olinalá** (⊠ Av. Lázaro Cárdenas 274, Centro ☎ 322/222–4995) specializes in painted ceremonial masks from throughout Mexico. It also sells contemporary paintings. **Puerco Azul** (⊠ Condominios Marina las Palmas II Marina Vallarta ☎ 322/221–0594) carries one-of-a-kind items for the home, including furniture, ceramics, antiques, and glassware. **Querubines** (⊠ Av. Juárez 501–A, Centro ☎ 322/222–2988) has utilitarian and decorative folk art, especially woven goods. Look for painted gourds from Michoacán, Talavera pottery, Oaxacan rugs, vintage posters, and more. **Talavera Etc.** (⊠ Av. Ignacio L. Vallarta 266, Col. E. Zapata ☎ 322/222–4100) has a small but well-edited selection of majolica ceramics and hand-crafted jewelry.

Jewelry

Joyerí Viva (⊠ Calle Basilio Badillo 274, Col. E. Zapata ☎ 322/222–4078) represents jewelers from around world, and has a large inventory of jewelry in silver, gold, and gemstones, as well as shoes and purses. **Joyas Finas Suneson** (⊠ Calle Morelos 593, Centro ☎ 322/222–5715) specializes in silver jewelry and objets d'art by some of Mexico's finest designers.

At **Ric Taxco** (⊠ Centro Comercial Las Glorias, Local C8, Zona Hotelera ☎ 322/224–4598), much of the sterling silver and gold jewelry is inspired by pre-Hispanic designs.

Puerto Vallarta A to Z

To research prices, get advice from other travelers, and book travel arrangements, visit www.fodors.com.

AIR TRAVEL

AIRPORT Puerto Vallarta's Aeropuerto Internacional Gustavo Díaz Ordáz is 7½ km (4.5 mi) north of town, not far from the resorts at Marina Vallarta.

🛈 **Aeropuerto Internacional Gustavo Díaz Ordáz** ⊠ Carretera a Tepic, Km 7.5, Zona Aeropuerto ☎ 322/221-1298 or 322/221-1325.

AIRPORT TRANSFERS Volkswagen vans provide economical transportation from the airport to PV hotels. Taxis or vans to the exclusive resorts between PV and Manzanillo can run well over $100.

CARRIERS Mexicana has direct service from Chicago and Mexico City. Aeroméxico has flights from multiple U.S. and Mexican cities. Alaska Airlines serves the western United States, with direct flights from Los Angeles, San Francisco, and Seattle. American has daily nonstop flights from Dallas/Fort Worth and on Saturday and Sunday from Chicago O'Hare. Continental flies nonstop daily from Houston. America West has nonstop daily flights from Phoenix.

🛈 **Aeroméxico** ☎ 322/224-2777; 01800/021-4000 toll-free in Mexico; 800/237-6639 in the U.S. **Alaska Airlines** ☎ 01800/252-7522 toll-free in Mexico; 800/252-7522 in the U.S. **America West** ☎ 322/221-1333; 800/235-9292 in the U.S. **American** ☎ 01800/904-6000 toll-free in Mexico; 800/433-7300 in the U.S. **Continental** ☎ 322/221-2213; 800/523-3273 in the U.S. **Mexicana** ☎ 322/221-1266 or 322/224-8900; 800/531-7921 in the U.S.

BUS TRAVEL

One kilometer (½ mile) north of the airport is PV's Central Camionero, or central bus station. ETN has the most luxurious service to Guadalajara, Mexico City, and many other destinations, with roomy, reclining seats. Transportes del Pacífico serves the Pacific Coast region. Elite/Futura has first-class service to Acapulco, Mexico City, the U.S. border, and other destinations. Primera Plus serves destinations throughout Mexico. Southern Jalisco towns such as Barra de Navidad are best reached on Transportes Cihuatlán.

City buses serve downtown, Zona Hotelera, and the southern beaches. Bus stops—marked by blue-and-white signs—are every two or three blocks along the highway (Carretera Aeropuerto) and in town. Buses to Playa Mismaloya and Boca de Tomatlán run about every 15 minutes from the corner of Avenida Insurgentes and Basilio Badillo downtown.

🛈 **Central Camionero** ⊠ Puerto Vallarta-Tepic Hwy. Km 9, Las Mojoneras ☎ 322/221-0739. **Elite/Futura** ☎ 322/221-0848 or 322/221-0850. **ETN** ☎ 322/290-0119. **Primera Plus** ☎ 322/290-0715. **Transportes Cihuatlán** ☎ 322/221-0021. **Transportes del Pacífico** ☎ 322/290-0993.

CAR RENTAL

🛈 Major Agencies **Budget** ⊠ Blvd. Francisco Medina Ascencio 1680, Centro ☎ 322/222-3355. **Dollar** ⊠ Av. Paseo de las Palmas 1728, Zona Hotelera ☎ 322/223-1354; 322/221-1001 to the airport. **National** ⊠ Marriott hotel, Av. Paseo la Marina 5, Marina Vallarta ☎ 322/221-0004; 322/221-1226 at the airport.

CAR TRAVEL

Puerto Vallarta is about 1,900 km (1,200 mi) south of Nogales, Arizona, at the U.S.–Mexico border, 354 km (220 mi) from Guadalajara, and 167 km (104 mi) from Tepic. As in any crowded city, driving in PV can be unnerving. From December through April—peak tourist season—traffic clogs the small cobblestone streets downtown. During the rainy season, from July through October, the streets may become flooded and the city's steep hills muddy and slippery. Parking is a also a challenge, so unless you're planning extensive exploring outside the city center or are truly married to your vehicle, consider using taxis and city buses.

CONSULATES

Canadian Consulate ⊠ Calle Zaragoza 160, Centro ☎ 322/222-5398. **U.S. Consulate** ⊠ Calle Zaragoza 160, 2nd floor, Centro ☎ 322/222-0069.

EMERGENCIES

Ambulance/Red Cross ☎ 322/222-1533. **Ameri Med Hospital** ⊠ Plaza Neptuno, Marina Vallarta ☎ 322/221-0023. **General Emergency Number** ☎ 060. **Police** ⊠ City Hall, Calle Morelos and Calle Iturbide, Centro ☎ 322/221-2587.

ENGLISH-LANGUAGE MEDIA

There's no shortage of printed English-language information in PV. In addition to lots of slick (and truly helpful) map guides, check out the ad-driven but informative *PV Tribune*. The *Vallarta Voice* is a monthly English-language paper.

MAIL, INTERNET & SHIPPING

For sending and receiving mail and packages, go to Mail Boxes Etc., which also offers fax and e-mail services. The Net House is open from dawn to the wee hours seven days a week, and has computers with English-language keyboards. It's air-conditioned and serves coffee.

Internet Café The Net House ⊠ Av. Ignacio L. Vallarta 232, Col. E. Zapata ☎ 322/222-6953.

Mail Service Mail Boxes Etc. ⊠ Blvd. Francisco Medina Ascencio, Edificio Andrea Mar Local 7, Marina Vallarta ☎ 322/224-9434.

MONEY MATTERS

Credit cards are widely accepted at hotels and restaurants; expect to pay in cash at small, family-run places. For the best exchange rate go to the bank (most have ATM machines). Most hotels offer a significantly lower exchange rate although they don't charge commissions.

Banks Bancomer ⊠ Plaza Marina ☎ 322/221-0662. **Banmex** ⊠ Calle Juárez, at Calle Zaragoza, Centro ☎ 322/226-6110.

TAXIS

The ride from the Nuevo Vallarta hotels to downtown costs about $10; from Marina Vallarta to downtown, about $5. The minimum fare, for example from one downtown destination to another, is between $2.50 and $3 (depending on your negotiating skills). Be sure to agree on a fare before embarking. Cabs are plentiful, and you can easily hail one on the street. They aren't metered, though, so be sure to agree on a fare before embarking.

TOURS

The five-hour city tour runs from Marina Vallarta and Gringo Gulch to the Río Cuale and Playa Mismaloya. Daytime bay cruises go to Los Arcos, Yelapa, Quimixto, or Playa las Ánimas, and to Isla Marietas for whale-watching (in winter), snorkeling, swimming, and lunch. Most depart from the Terminal Marítima at around 9 AM.

Local fishermen at Punta de Mita have formed the Sociedad Cooperativa Corral de Risco, which offers fishing, whale-watching, diving, and snorkeling trips around the Marieta islands at reasonable rates. The guides may not speak English as well as the more polished PV operators, but they know the local waters and the fees go directly to them and their families. Vallarta Adventure arranges many types of tours. One takes you to San Sebastian del Oeste, an interesting old mining town high in the Sierra Madre, 62 km (38 mi) from Puerto Vallarta; or you can arrange to go on shopping or tequila-tasting expeditions outside Guadalajara. Harris Tours offers city tours and expeditions to three jungle locations south of PV proper. Each lasts approximately six hours and costs about $25 (large group).

Natura Tours offers numerous types of nature-oriented excursions, including bass and deep-sea fishing, scuba diving, hiking, horseback riding and biking. Villa tours arranged by the International Friendship Club will get you inside the garden walls of some of Puerto Vallarta's prettiest homes. Tours depart promptly at 11 AM (arrive by 10:30) from the Hotel Molina del Agua on Wednesday and Thursday November through April. The $25 fee benefits worthy charities.

🚩 **Harris Tours** ☎ 322/223-2972. **International Friendship Club** (c/o Hotel Molina del Agua, ✉ Av. Ignacio L. Vallarta 130, Col. E. Zapata ☎ 322/222-1957. **Natura Tours** ✉ Carretera Aeropuerto, Km 5.5, Zona Hotelera ☎☎ 322/224-0410. **Sociedad Cooperativa Corral de Risco** ✉ Av. El Anclote, Manzana 17, No. 1, Corral de Risco, Punta de Mita ☎ 329/291-6298. **Vallarta Adventure** ✉ Av. de las Palmas 39, Nuevo Vallarta ☎ 329/297-1212 ✉ Edificio Marina Golf, Local 13-C, Calle Mástil, Marina Vallarta ☎ 322/221-0836.

TRAVEL AGENCIES
🚩 Local Agent Referrals **American Express** ✉ Calle Morelos 660, Centro ☎ 322/223-2955.

VISITOR INFORMATION
The municipal tourist office, open weekdays 8–4, is on the Plaza Principal. The Jalisco State Tourism Office is open weekdays 9–5.
🚩 **Jalisco State Tourism Office** ✉ Plaza Marina shopping center, Local 144 & 146, Marina Vallarta ☎ 322/221-2676. **Municipal Tourist Office** ✉ Av. Independencia 123, Centro ☎ 322/223-2500.

MANZANILLO

Crystal-blue waters lap the black-and-gold volcanic sand on Manzanillo's twin *bahías* (bays), Manzanillo and Santiago. Each is home to a town of the same name, both of which lack polish and have a dearth of shops, museums, and other attractions. It's the very lack of sophistication combined with inviting beaches and some great resorts that attract a certain type of tourist—or rather, traveler. In the July–September rainy season, rivers and lagoons swell, forming waterfalls and ponds.

Manzanillo's fanciest resorts are on and above La Península de Santiago, a spit of land separating Bahía de Santiago and Bahía de Manzanillo. Although less imposing now that it's surrounded by competing hotels, Las Hadas resort is a fanciful collection of white domes and peaks that radiate pink in the midday heat. When Bolivian tin magnate Antenor Patiño conceived of this dazzling palace in the early 1960s, Manzanillo was easier to reach by air or sea than by land; it was a rugged, primitive port that attracted hardy sailors and beachcombers. When Patiño's retreat was completed in 1974, the international social set began to visit Manzanillo, and yet it remained essentially a port city with few attractions.

A government project to beautify downtown promises a huge garden and pedestrian walkway and an upgrade of the surrounding area. But frankly, despite the mega-statue of a leaping turquoise sailfish by Chihuahua sculptor Sebastián, the downtown waterfront area is just about as desultory as ever. What services and restaurants there are, are strung along the boulevard with little sense of connection or community. Many shops and hotel desks close for afternoon siesta; on Sunday most businesses (including restaurants) shut down, and everyone heads for the beach.

North of Manzanillo proper, the Gold Coast continues to be developed. Out of a wild peninsula just across from the small town of Barra de Navidad, big-time investors created Isla Navidad, a 1,230-acre resort complex. About 20 minutes north of Manzanillo's airport, the exclusive property looms like a mirage to the surfer transplants and simple shopkeepers across the channel in Barra de Navidad. Public areas are all plush and classy; outside, multiple swimming pools flow from one to another via falls and slides, all surrounded by lush landscaping.

Travelers on a tight budget usually head to Barra de Navidad and Melaque, about an hour north. As with the rest of the Pacific Coast, Manzanillo is in the midst of a building boom, mainly condominiums, to accommodate the growing number of Canadian snowbirds and Guadalajara residents buying vacation homes here. The resorts are spread out along the coast road that connects the towns of Manzanillo and Santiago.

Exploring Manzanillo

The Santiago area, on Bahía de Santiago between the Santiago and Juluapán peninsulas, offers little indication that it's a tourist destination save the string of hotels and restaurants on several pretty beaches. Playa la Audiencia, home to the Hotel la Sierra, is a nice little cove with dark sand, a restaurant on the beach, and water-sports outfitters. On the far side of the bay, Playa La Boquita is a sheltered cove popular with families.

Directly east of Bahía de Santiago is Bahía Manzanillo, where Las Hadas and Karmina Palace hotels nestle in a sheltered cove and less expensive hotels line such quiet beaches as Playa Azul. Playa las Brisas, in the so-called Zona Hotelera, is less popular than it once was, but it's still great for long walks on the beach. Las Brisas is backed by the Laguna de San Pedrito (San Pedrito Lagoon). On the far side, the highway continues away from the water toward *el centro* (downtown), a busy, jam-packed seaport with little of interest.

Just north of downtown, the **Museo Universitario Arqueológico** displays 5,000 of its more than 18,000 artifacts, which come from the immediate region, the state of Colima, and elsewhere in Mesoamerica. Chamber music, folkloric dance, and other cultural events are sometimes presented Friday evening. ✉ *San Pedrito traffic circle, Centro* ☎ *314/ 332–2256* ✉ *$1* ☉ *Tues.–Sat. 10–2 and 5–8, Sun. 10–1.*

At the beginning of the harbor, Carretera 200 jogs around downtown and intersects with Carretera 110 to Colima. Avenida Morelos leads past the shipyards and into town. The zócalo, known as **Jardín de Alvaro Obregón**, is right on the main road by the waterfront. It's sunstruck and shadeless during the day, but can be quite lively in the cool of the evening. Streets leading away from the plaza have ice cream and lingerie stores and shops selling postcards, T-shirts, etched shot glasses, and funky shell art.

Beaches

Playa la Boquita. At the east end of Bahía de Santiago, the popular La Boquita has palm-leaf palapas for shade, informal restaurants, and outfitters that rent water toys. The calm, waveless water is perfect for swimming and snorkeling. The beach in front of Club Santiago, once the favored hangout for locals, is now accessible only by walking north

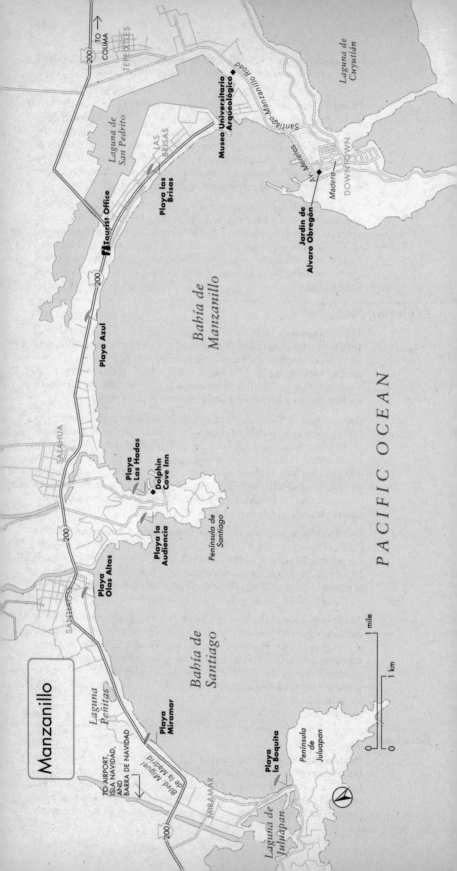

along the beach from the highway or through the club gates. There's no fee to enter; just stop and let the guard write down your car's license number if you're driving.

Playa Miramar. Miramar means "look at the sea." There are restaurants, water sports outfitters, and horses for hire. Vendors sell jewelry and beachwear from stalls across from the Hotel Maeva. On weekends, families camp out for the day, renting shade umbrellas and lounge chairs from the hotel. Although the waves are a little stronger than at Playa la Boquita, this is still a good spot for swimming.

Playa Olas Altas. This beach's name means "high waves." (It's also known as Playa de Oro.) The surfers who come here don't mind the lack of services found at more popular stretches.

Playa la Audiencia. On the east side of the Peninsula de Santiago, below the Hotel la Sierra and between two rock outcroppings, Playa la Audiencia is small but inviting, with calm water, shade umbrellas, and water sports equipment for rent. The local Indians supposedly granted Cortés an audience here—thus the name. It's a good spot for snorkeling.

Playa las Hadas. Across the Peninsula de Santiago from the Playa la Audiencia, this small, secluded, rocky beach is a good snorkeling spot. It's favored by guests from the Hotel las Hadas and the adjoining Karmina Palace. Expensive restaurants at both hotels serve drinks, snacks, and full meals. A water-sports concession rents jet skis, small sailboats, and kayaks; it also arranges dive and snorkel trips.

Playas Azul and Playa las Brisas. Playa Azul, also called Playa Santiago, runs along the Bahía de Manzanillo to Playa las Brisas. The surf gets rough along Azul; swimming is better toward las Brisas, although neither is in vogue. Restaurants and hotels at intervals along the beach are good places to rest and eat when you tire of walking or playing in the surf.

Where to Eat

★ **$$$–$$$$** ✕**Legazpi.** Maroon-and-white striped cushions adorn dark-wood chairs and banquets, brass lamps hold thick white candles, and wide windows afford dramatic bay views. The menu is Italian with an emphasis on Mediterranean dishes. Be sure to check out the cozy bar, where there's a mural depicting the history of Manzanillo. ⊠ *Las Hadas Hotel, Av. De los Riscos and Av. Vista Hermosa, Fracc. Península de Santiago* 🕾*314/ 334–0101 Ext. 3512* ▤ *AE, MC, V* ☉ *Closed Sun. No lunch.*

$–$$$ ✕ **El Bigotes.** Waitresses in funky, meter maid–style uniforms serve good seafood to the tune of canned music and the rhythm of crashing waves at this unpretentious restaurant. The specialty is the Jalisco favorite *pescado sarandeado* (whole fish rubbed with salt and spices and grilled over hot coals). Also recommended are the gigantic portions of ceviche (shrimp or fish) and the *camerón mustache* (butterfly shrimp breaded in shredded coconut and sautéed). ⊠ *Blvd. Miguel de la Madrid 3157, Zona Hotelera* 🕾 *314/334–0831* ▤ *MC, V.*

$–$$$ ✕**L'Recif.** Waves crash on the rocks below this huge cliff-top palapa, a
Fodor'sChoice 15-minute drive from Manzanillo's Zona Hotelera toward La Boquita
★ beach. If you're visiting in March, try to be here at 5 PM, when you might catch a glimpse of a whale. There's a little of everything on the menu—seafood, pasta, chicken, beef—but the signature dish is the camerón L'Recif (shrimp stuffed with cheese, wrapped in bacon, and broiled); it's served with mango sauce and sides of mashed potatoes and sautéed corn, zucchini, and carrots. ⊠ *Cerro del Cenicero s/n, El Naranjo, Condominio Vida del Mar, Península de Juluapán* 🕾 *314/335–0900* ▤ *MC, V* ☉ *Closed May–Oct. No lunch.*

$–$$$ ✕**Toscana.** When the popular Willy's restaurant closed due to hurricane damage, the owners transferred its most beloved dishes to this, their other restaurant. Specialties include seafood shish kebab served with rice and steamed vegetables, a "three lettuce" salad with goat cheese, and a Caesar salad. For dessert, try the tiramisu. Most of the tables sit on the simple outdoor terrace overlooking the beach. There's also a dance floor where electric-guitar music is played nightly after 8:30 PM. ⊠ *Blvd. Costero Miguel de la Madrid 3177, Zona Hotelera* ☎ *314/333–2515* ▤ *MC, V* ⊗ *No lunch.*

$ ✕ **Limbo.** A palapa roof covers a wraparound, street-side terrace at this easygoing restaurant near the entrance to Las Hadas and the Karmina Palace. Rock music plays at a level that permits conversation, and subdued lighting mitigates the brightly painted walls and their amateurish murals. Portions are generous, and the *arrachera norteña*—thin beef fillets served with french fries, guacamole, beans, and a basket of tortillas— is quite tender. Breakfast offerings include yogurt, eggs, and *chilaquiles* (fried tortillas in a mild chili sauce). ⊠ *Av. Audiencia s/n, in Plaza Pacífico, across from Mantarraya Golf Course, near entrance to Fraccionamiento Península de Santiago* ☎ *314/334–1562* ▤ *MC, V.*

¢–$ ✕ **Juanito's.** Owned by an American who settled in Manzanillo in 1976, Juanito's is the spot to watch U.S. football and other sporting events in good company. It's the most popular place in town for breakfast, and it also has burgers, milk shakes, fries, barbecued ribs, and fried chicken. Decoration is minimal, but the service is quick and the coffee strong and hot. Check your e-mail or surf the Web on one of two on-site computers. ⊠ *Blvd. Costero, Km 14, Olas Altas* ☎ *314/333–1388* ⚐ *Reservations not accepted* ▤ *AE, MC, V.*

Where to Stay

$$$$ ▥ **Sierra.** This white-stucco giant on pretty La Audiencia beach fills up with families and conventioneers. Rooms have light woods, tile floors, and turquoise fabrics; junior suites are carpeted. All guest quarters have private balconies, but poor design blocks the view on many—ask for a room in the low-rise section. There's a large free-form pool, a spa, and several bars and restaurants on the property. ⊠ *Av. Audiencia 1, Playa la Audiencia 28200* ☎ *314/333–2000; 800/448–5028 in the U.S.* 🖨 *314/333–2272* ⤳ *328 rooms, 11 suites* ⚐ *3 restaurants, cable TV, 4 tennis courts, pool, gym, beach, boating, 4 bars, shops, children's programs (ages 4–12), meeting rooms* ▤ *AE, MC, V* ⭗ *All-inclusive.*

$$$–$$$$ ▥ **Las Hadas.** Las Hadas delights with its exotic, Moorish-style buildings on 15 acres of flower-and-vine-covered grounds. Cream-on-white room decoration is elegant and understated; polished marble, fine sheets, and plush towels are the norm. Amenities include a golf course, a marina, and Legazpi restaurant—one of the city's best. ⊠ *Av. De los Riscos and Av. Vista Hermosa Fracc. Península de Santiago 28867* ☎ *314/331–0101 or 888/559–4329* 🖨 *314/331–0125* ⊕ *www.brisas.com.mx* ⤳ *184 rooms, 36 suites* ⚐ *3 restaurants, room service, in-room safes, cable TV, 18-hole golf course, 10 tennis courts, pool, gym, hair salon, massage, beach, marina, 3 bars, shops, baby-sitting, concierge, travel services* ▤ *AE, DC, MC, V.*

$$$–$$$$ ▥ **Karmina Palace.** Manzanillo's newest all-inclusive, all-suites hotel is a short walk from neighboring Las Hadas resort. Punctuating the rambling grounds are cascades, fountains, multitier lagoon pools, and a beautiful palapa restaurant at the ocean's edge. Each junior suite has marble floors, a balcony or terrace, a sofa bed, and a large tub with separate shower facilities. Corner suites have two bedrooms, each with a bath, a kitchen, and a dining room as well as a balcony with a plunge pool. ⊠ *Av. Vista Hermosa 13, Fracc. Península de Santiago, 28200* ☎ *314/334–1313 or 877/527–6462* 🖨 *314/334–1915* ⊕ *www.karminapalace.*

com ☞ *325 suites* ♨ *3 restaurants, room service, in-room safes, some kitchens, refrigerators, cable TV, 8 pools, gym, spa, beach, shops, children's programs (ages 4–12), laundry service, concierge, free parking* ⊟ *AE, V* ⧯ *All-inclusive.*

$$ ⊞ **Dolphin Cove Inn.** The good news is that the rooms and one-bedroom suites are bright, clean, and private, with pretty views from their balconies or terraces. There are also great beaches nearby, and breakfast is included in the rate. The bad news? The property has endless stairs: leading to the pool, the restaurant, office, sundries store, and neighboring properties. ⊠ *Av. Vista Hermosa s/n, Fracc. Península de Santiago 28860* ☎ *314/334–1692 or 888/497–4138* 🖷 *314/334–1689* ⊕ *www. dolphincoveinn.com* ☞ *27 rooms, 11 suites* ♨ *Restaurant, kitchenettes, pool, beach, free parking* ⊟ *MC, V* ⧯ *BP.*

$–$$ ⊞ **Marina Puerto Dorado.** There are excellent views of the bay and harbor from this low-rise, which looks a lot like a condo complex. Each suite has a kitchen, dining bar, and living room; furnishings in some suites, however, are showing their age. Mix with other guests at the pool, in the whirlpool, or on the shaded or exposed lounge chairs overlooking the beach. ⊠ *Av. Lázaro Cárdenas 101, Fracc. las Brisas Playa Azul 28200* 🖷🖷 *314/334–1480* ☞ *27 suites* ♨ *Restaurant, pool, beach, bar, shop, free parking* ⊟ *MC, V* ⧯ *CP.*

★ $ ⊞ **La Posada.** This bright pink hotel has been a favorite with North Americans since 1957. With only 23 rooms, most guests get to know each other well, mingling in the *sala*, a large, open-air living-dining area with a communal coffeepot. Rooms are comfortable enough though not fancy (there's only one on the beach), and old iron keys work their antique locks. There's honor-system beer- and soft-drink service. ⊠ *Av. Lázaro Cardenas 201 Fracc. las Brisas–Playa Azul 28200* 🖷🖷 *314/333–1899* ☞ *23 rooms* ♨ *Snack bar, pool, beach, bar* ⊟ *MC, V* ⧯ *BP.*

¢ ⊞ **Marbella.** This is one of the few budget accommodations on the beach, which faces the open ocean, not the bay. Rooms have tile floors and tiny, palm-shaded balconies; the best rooms look out onto the sand. There's a good Spanish/seafood restaurant, El Marinero, and a buffet restaurant. ⊠ *Coast rd. between Manzanillo and Santiago Zona Hotelera 28869* ☎ *314/333–1103* 🖷 *314/333–1222* ✉ *hotmarbella@prodigy. net.mx* ☞ *92 rooms* ♨ *2 restaurants, pool, beach, bar* ⊟ *AE, MC, V.*

¢ ⊞ **María Cristina.** A clean but drab two-story motel in the Santiago area, the María Cristina is just four blocks from the beach. All rooms have cable TV, but only three—they call them "bungalows"—are air-conditioned; cheaper rooms have ceiling fans. ⊠ *Calle 28 de Agosto 36, Santiago 28860* ☎ *314/333–0966* 🖷 *314/334–1430* ☞ *21 rooms* ♨ *Cable TV, pool, shop, free parking; no a/c in some rooms* ⊟ *MC, V.*

Nightlife

Bar de Félix (⊠ Blvd. Miguel de la Madrid 805, Zona Hotelera ☎ 314/ 333–9277), adjacent to the club VOG, is a large bar with crimson faux-velvet settees, a dance floor, and a giant-screen TV. For a lively drinking and dancing scene, head for **Colima Bay Café** (⊠ Blvd. Costero 921, Zona Hotelera ☎ 314/333–0168), *the* in spot. **Hacienda San Germán** (⊠ Blvd. Miguel de la Madrid 11280, Fracc. Península de Santiago, Santiago ☎ 314/333–9440), a large club close to the hotels around Las Hadas, often has variety shows on weekend evenings, and sometimes has mariachis or crooners midweek during lunch (4–6 PM) or dinner (9–11 PM). **VOG** (⊠ Blvd. Miguel de la Madrid 805, Zona Hotelera ☎ 314/333– 1875) plays disco music Thursday through Saturday.

Sports & the Outdoors

Fishing

Billed the "Sailfish Capital of the World," Manzanillo has fleets that regularly hook marlin, dorado, roosters, and tuna. Sportfishing boats are available at major hotels and through tour agencies. Contact **Ocean Pacific Adventures** (📠 314/335–0605) to charter a 26-ft boat (1 to 5 people) for $225, or a 40-ft cruiser (1 to 10 people) for $275. Both tours last five hours and include fishing license and a case each of beer and soda as well as the usual ice, bait, and tackle.

Golf

The 9-hole course at **Club Santiago** (✉ Av. Camarón 1-A, Club Santiago Santiago ☎ 314/335–0410), designed by Larry Hughes, has the usual amenities, including carts, caddies, pro shop, and snack shop. The greens fee is $45; carts cost an additional $38. Robert Von Hagge
★ mapped out the impressive 27-hole **Isla Navidad** (☎ 314/355–6439) course in the Grand Bay resort complex. The expansive clubhouse has steam, sauna, and whirlpool as well as restaurant-bar. Greens fees are $130 (9 holes) to $160 (27 holes). Caddies charge $25, and a shared cart is $30. **La Mantarraya** (✉ Av. De los Riscos and Av. Vista Hermosa Fracc. Península de Santiago ☎ 314/331–0101), the 18-hole golf course designed by Roy Dye at Las Hadas hotel, has been rated among the world's 100 best courses by *Golf Digest*. The greens fee is about $100; a cart costs another $50.

Water Sports

You can rent kayaks, paddleboats, Windsurfers, and snorkel and scuba gear at many beachside hotels and outfitters. The rocky points off Manzanillo's peninsulas and coves make for good snorkeling and scuba diving. **Pacific Watersports** (✉ Las Hadas hotel, Av. De los Riscos and Av. Vista Hermosa Fracc. Península de Santiago ☎ 314/333–1848) organizes guided diving and snorkel tours.

Shopping

Shopping in Manzanillo is poor. Most hotels offer a small selection of folk art and beachwear, and there are souvenir shops around the main square and in Plaza Manzanillo, a shopping center on the coast road between Santiago and Manzanillo. The newest center is Plaza Salagua, with a Soriana department store and other shops. It's across from the VOG disco on Boulevard Miguel de la Madrid. Most of the shops are closed 2–4; many are open Sunday 10–2. The **Centro Artesenal las Primaveras** (✉ Av. Juárez 40, Santiago ☎ 314/333–1699) has a large but disappointing assortment of handicrafts of so-so quality.

Side Trips

Barra de Navidad

55 km (34 mi) northwest of Manzanillo.

Barra, as it's usually called, is a laid-back little surfers' town that's beginning to attract outside attention. Since the luxurious Grand Bay hotel was built in the late 1990s, a well-heeled crowd of yachties has taken to shopping along one of the two main streets. In fact, shopping here is much better than in Manzanillo, and although most of the family-owned stores sell much the same things—carved wooden bowls and ceramic plates from Guerrero, sarongs from Indonesia, and snow globes with mermaid and sea-life themes—it's fun to compare bric-a-brac and prices. Interspersed with the shops are informal restaurants that specialize in fresh fish. The brown-sand beaches are also lined with open-air restaurants, perfect retreats from the strong coastal sun. At low tide you can walk along the beach from Barra to San Patricio Melaque, a distance of about 6 km (4 mi).

WHERE TO STAY
& EAT
$–$$

✗ **Nacho.** People come to this beachfront family restaurant for delicious seafood and strong, wonderful *cafe de olla* (Mexican coffee). The specialty is charcoal-grilled fish, but also try the *campechana,* an appetizer of clams, shrimp, and fish, or one of several seafood salads or soups. Service is on the slow side. ⊠ *Calle Legazpi 100* ☎ *315/355–5138* ▭ *No credit cards.*

★ $$$–$$$$

🏨 **Grand Bay.** On a 1,200-acre peninsula between the Pacific and the Navidad Lagoon, 30 minutes north of Manzanillo airport, this no-holds-barred resort cascades down to a private, though not terribly scenic, beach. More enticing are the complex's Spanish arches, shady patios, cool fountains, and lush gardens—not to mention the tiered pools connected by slides and waterfalls. Rooms have imported-marble baths, original art, deluxe amenities, and balconies with mountain or sea views. You can play the adjacent Robert Von Hagge–designed golf course, and there's boat service to the town of Barra de Navidad, just across the bay. ⊠ *Isla Navidad 48987* ☎ *314/331–0500; 800/996–3426 in the U.S.* 🖶 *315/355–6071* ⊕ *www.islaresort.com.mx* ⇥ *158 rooms, 41 suites* ⟁ *3 restaurants, in-room safes, minibars, cable TV, 27-hole golf course, 3 tennis courts, 3 pools, gym, beach, dive shop, snorkeling, jet skiing, marina, waterskiing, fishing, volleyball, 3 bars, shops, baby-sitting, children's programs (ages 4–12), concierge* ▭ *AE, MC, V.*

¢–$

🏨 **El Marquez.** Although it's far from fancy, the friendly staff (it's a family operation) and clean rooms make El Marquez a good alternative to some of the pricier accommodations on the beach. It's a few blocks from the center of town and the beach, and it has a small pool. Choose a room with a ceiling fan or air-conditioning. ⊠ *Calle Filipinas s/n 48987* ☎ *335/355–5304* 🖶 *315/355–6300* ⇥ *30 rooms* ⟁ *Some fans, pool, free parking; no a/c in some rooms* ▭ *MC, V.*

Colima

98 km (61 mi) northeast of Manzanillo.

Colima, the capital of the eponymous state, is about an hour from Manzanillo via an excellent toll road that continues on to Guadalajara. An easygoing provincial city, Colima is most famous for the pre-Hispanic "Colima dog" figurines, which originated in this region and are on display—along with other archaeological pieces—at the **Museo de las Culturas del Occidente** (Museum of Western Cultures; ⊠ Casa de la Cultura, Calz. Galván and Av. Manuel Gallardo ☎ 312/313–0608) It's open Tuesday–Sunday 9–7, and admission is $1.50.

The **Museo Universitario de Culturas Populares** (University Museum of Popular Culture; ⊠ Calle Gabino Barreda and Manuel Gallardo ☎ 312/ 312–6869) has a large collection of pre-Hispanic and contemporary Indian costumes, masks, instruments, and other artifacts. Entry to the museum, which is open Tuesday–Sunday 10–2 and 5–8, is free. The town of **Comala,** a 15-minute ride north of Colima, is noted for hand-carved furniture and ironwork, and for the charming cafés to which Colima residents flock on holidays and weekends.

WHERE TO STAY
★ $$$$

🏨 **Mahakua Hacienda de San Antonio.** Ahhh, the Mahakua. This stunning hacienda was originally built as the home of 19th-century German immigrant Arnold Vogel on his 5,000-acre coffee plantation. It was completely refurbished in the 1970s and is now leased to Aman Resorts, famous for its ultra-luxurious (and *ultra-expensive*) properties around the world.

Rooms have 15-ft beamed ceilings and blend European and American appointments with Mexican handicrafts. Have lunch by the enormous pool, drinks around the fire in the convivial library, and dinner in the courtyard or the dining room. The staff is warm and attentive. ⊠ *San Antonio 28450* ☎ *312/313–4411 or 888/802–9127* 🖷 *312/314–3727* ⊕ *www.amanresorts.com* 🖎 *22 rooms, 3 suites* ⚒ *Restaurant, pool, massage, horseback riding, bar, library, travel services* ▭ *AE, MC, V.*

Manzanillo A to Z

To research prices, get advice from other travelers, and book travel arrangements, visit www.fodors.com.

AIR TRAVEL

AIRPORT   Manzanillo's Aeropuerto Internacional Playa de Oro is 32 km (20 mi) north of town, on the way to Barra de Navidad.
🗊 **Aeropuerto Internacional Playa de Oro** ☎ 314/333-2525.

AIRPORT   Volkswagen vans transport passengers from the airport to major resorts;
TRANSFERS   these shuttles are less expensive than taxis.

CARRIERS   Aeroméxico has daily flights from Houston, Los Angeles, and Atlanta, with a plane change in Mexico City. Mexicana serves the region via Mexico City. Alaska Airlines flies nonstop from Los Angeles. America West has twice-weekly flights from Phoenix, and AeroCalifornia flies in from Mexico City and Los Angeles daily.
🗊 **AeroCalifornia** ☎ 314/334-1414; 800/237-6225 in the U.S. **Aeroméxico** ☎ 314/333-015; 01800/021-4000 toll-free in Mexico; 800/237-6639 in the U.S. **Alaska Airlines** ☎ 01800/252-7522 toll-free in Mexico; 800/252-7522 in the U.S. **America West** ☎ 314/334-1140; 800/235-9292 in the U.S. **Mexicana** ☎ 314/333-2323; 800/531-7921 in the U.S.

BUS TRAVEL

The resorts in the Manzanillo area are several miles from the main bus station on Boulevard Costero Miguel de la Madrid, which is no more than a parking lot full of buses. Elite and Estrella Blanca connect Manzanillo with other Pacific coast cities and Mexico City; the former has a longer list of destinations. Primera Plus serves Puerto Vallarta, Guadalajara, Tijuana, Mexico City, Acapulco, and smaller coastal towns. ETN has comfortable buses—with wide, almost totally reclining seats—to Guadalajara, Colima, Morelia, and Mexico City.
🗊 **Elite/Estrella Blanca** ☎ 314/332-0432. **ETN** ☎ 314/334-1050. **Primera Plus** ☎ 314/332-0515.

CAR RENTAL

🗊 Major Agencies **Dollar** ⊠ Hotel Karmina Palace, Av. Vista Hermosa 13, Fracc. Península de Santiago ☎ 314/334-1313. **Hertz** ⊠ Blvd. Costero Miguel de la Madrid 1246-B, Zona Hotelera ☎ 314/333-3141. **National** ⊠ Blvd. Costero Miguel de la Madrid 1070, Zona Hotelera ☎ 314/333-1140; 314/334-0124 to the airport.

CAR TRAVEL

The trip south from the Arizona border to Manzanillo is about 2,419 km (1,500 mi); from Guadalajara, it is 332 km (206 mi) over mostly well-kept highways; from Puerto Vallarta, 242 km (150 mi) on Carretera 200, which winds through the mountains beginning in Tepic, in the state of Nayarit. Streets in downtown Manzanillo are congested, but parking is rarely a problem and having a car is a plus to reach the farther flung beaches and restaurants.

EMERGENCIES

☎ **Fire Department** ☎ 314/312-5858. **Hospital de Manzanillo** ☎ 314/336-7272. **Police** ☎ 314/334-0557 or 314/336-7300. **Public Security** ☎ 314/332-1004. **Red Cross** ☎ 314/336-5770.

MAIL, INTERNET & SHIPPING

The correos is about five blocks south of the main plaza in downtown. It's open weekdays 8 –7and Saturday 9–1. Juanito's restaurant in Santiago has several computers at which you can access the Internet and e-mail.

☎ Internet **Juanito's** ✉ Blvd. Costero, Km 14, Olas Altas ☎ 314/333-1388.
☎ Mail **Correos** ✉ Calle Galindo 30, Centro.

MONEY MATTERS

There are plenty of banks in downtown Manzanillo and Santiago, most with ATMs. Many visitors prefer to change money at the front desk of their hotel, where the poorer exchange rate is offset by the convenience and the absence of a bank fee for an international ATM transaction.

☎ Bank **Banamex** ✉ Calle México 136, Centro ☎ 314/332-0115.

TAXIS

Cabs are unmetered and are easy to hail on the streets. Agree on a price beforehand. The minimum fare will be $1.50, though cabs departing from hotels often charge nearly twice as much. For sightseeing, rates run about $13 per hour or $50–$80 per day, depending on your destination.

TOURS

Manzanillo is spread out; consider a guided orientation tour. More appealing, though, than the city tours are the sportfishing trips, sunset cruises, horseback outings, and excursions to the state capital, Colima, as well as to Comala and the dormant and active volcanoes near the capital. Currently North America's most active volcano, Volcán de Fuego (a.k.a. Volcán de Colima), must be viewed from a distance, but if you're lucky you'll witness large tongues of fire and streams of lava leaping and flowing from the crater. The spectacle is most impressive after sunset.

Agencia de Viajes Bahías Gemelas offers city, walking, fishing, and horseback-riding tours. Viajes Héctours offers the same tours as Bahías Gemelas, plus shopping, bay cruises, tours on four-wheelers, and day excursions to the beach or area banana plantations.

☎ **Agencia de Viajes Bahías Gemelas** ✉ Blvd. Costero Miguel de la Madrid 1556, Zona Hotelera ☎ 314/333-1000. **Viajes Héctours** ✉ Blvd. Costero Miguel de la Madrid 3147, Zona Hotelera ☎ 314/333-1707.

VISITOR INFORMATION

The Colima State Tourism Office is open weekdays 9–3 and 5–7, Saturday 10–2. The municipal tourism office is open weekdays 8–2.

☎ **Colima State Tourism Office** ✉ Blvd. Costero Miguel de la Madrid 1033, Zona Hotelera ☎ 314/333-2277. **Municipal Tourism Office** ✉ Av. Juárez 100, Centro ☎ 314/332-6238.

IXTAPA & ZIHUATANEJO

The towns of Ixtapa and Zihuatanejo offer a taste of Mexico present and past. Ixtapa (eesh-*tah*-pa), where most Americans stay, is young and glitzy. Exclusively a vacation resort, it was created in the 1970s by Mexico's National Fund for Tourism Development, which also dreamed up Cancún and Huatulco and developed Los Cabos. Thirty-odd years ago Zihuatanejo (see-wa-ta-*nay*-ho), only 7 km (4 mi) southeast along the coast from Ixtapa, was a fishing village, the exclusive domain of locals and adventurers willing to forgo running water, electricity, and paved streets for the chance to live in—or just visit—paradise. It's still charming even though it has gained more admirers, its streets have been paved, its infrastructure has been brought up to date, and some of its fishermen have become entrepreneurs.

Long before Columbus sailed to America, Zihuatanejo was a retreat for indigenous nobility. Figurines, ceramics, stone carvings, and stelae verify the presence of civilizations dating as far back as the Olmecs (3000 BC). Weaving was likely the dominant industry, as evidenced by pre-Hispanic figurines, bobbins, and other related artifacts found in the area. The original Nahuatl name, Cihuatlán, means "place of women."

In 1527, Spanish conquistadors launched a trade route from Zihuatanejo Bay to the Orient. Galleons returned with silks, spices, and, according to some historians, the Americas' first coconut palms, brought from the Philippines. But the Spaniards did little colonizing here. A scout sent by Cortés reported back to the conquistador that the place was nothing great, tagging the name Cihuatlán with the diminutive and less-than-flattering suffix "ejo"—hence "Zihuatanejo."

Ixtapa and Zihuatanejo have few sights, but they're both pleasant places to stroll—the former especially if you enjoy a modern beach ambience and shops, the latter if you prefer local color.

Exploring Ixtapa & Zihuatanejo

Ixtapa

The Zona Hotelera extends along a 3-km (2-mi) strip of wide, sandy beach called Playa del Palmar, on the Pacific. It's fun to walk along the shore to check out the various hotel scenes and water-sports activities, though the strong surf sometimes discourages swimming. You can also walk the length of the zone on Paseo Ixtapa, a landscaped thoroughfare lined with village-style shopping malls. At the Zona Hotelera's southeast end is the 18-hole Palma Real Golf Club; at the zone's northwest end is the Marina Ixtapa development, with a 600-slip yacht marina, the 18-hole Marina Golf Course, and an enclave of restaurants and shops. Take a taxi 15 minutes up the coast from Ixtapa's Zona Hotelera to Playa Linda. From here it's a 10-minute boat ride to **Isla Ixtapa** (Ixtapa Island), where you can spend the day eating, sunning, and swimming.

Zihuatanejo

Zihuatanejo is near the back of a deep, enclosed bay with calm beaches. To tour the town, start by taking a taxi to the municipal *muelle* (pier), from which skiffs regularly depart for the 10-minute ride to Playa las Gatas, most easily accessible by water. The sportfishing boats depart from this pier, too, and it's the beginning of the Paseo del Pescador (Fisherman's Walk), or malecón, which runs along the main beach, the most picturesque part of the town itself. Follow the brick-paved seaside path, which is only ½ km (⅓ mi) long and is fronted by small restaurants and shops. Along the way you'll pass a basketball court that doubles as the town square. Most of the budget accommodations are in downtown Zihuatanejo; the glamorous hotels are on or overlooking La Ropa beach. For true seclusion, venture to the growing beach town of Troncones, a 20-minute drive northwest of Zihuatanejo.

The malecón ends at the **Museo Arqueológico de la Costa Grande** (⊠ Off Paseo del Pescador ☎ 755/554–7552), where pre-Hispanic murals, maps, and archaeological pieces describing the Olmec, Tarascan, and Aztec cultures are on permanent display. It's open Tuesday–Sunday 9–6; admission is 60¢. Beyond the museum, a footpath cut into the rocks leads to Playa la Madera.

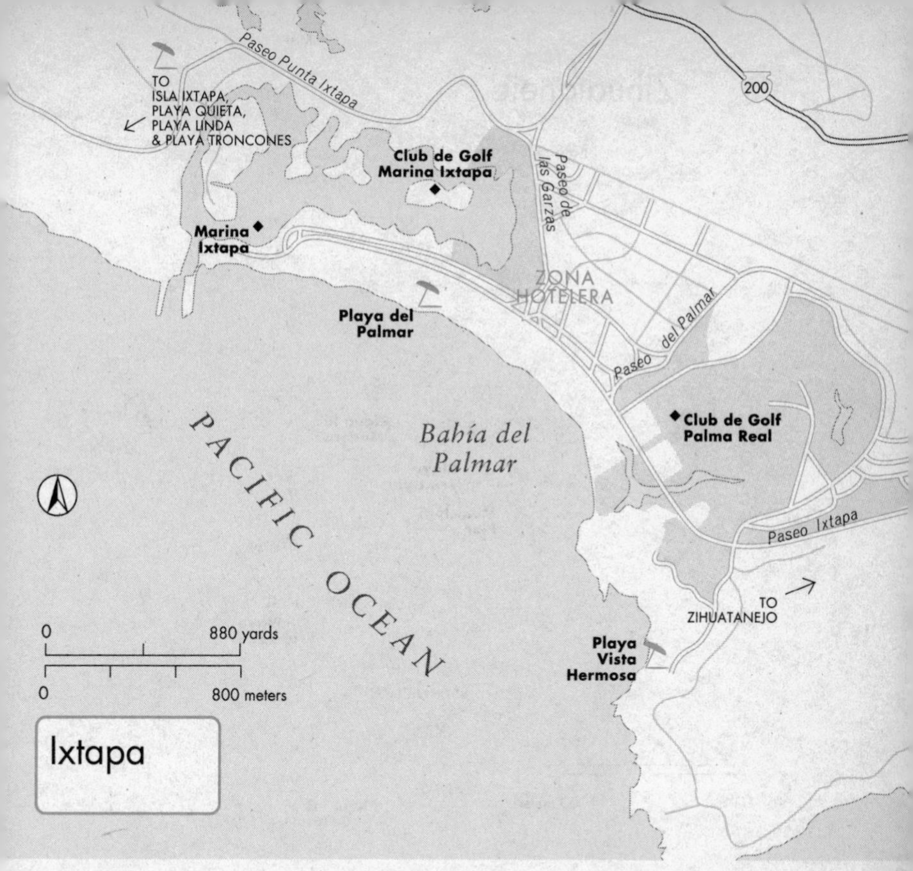
Paseo Punta Ixtapa
TO
ISLA IXTAPA,
PLAYA QUIETA,
PLAYA LINDA
& PLAYA TRONCONES
200
Club de Golf
Marina Ixtapa
Paseo de
las Garzas
Marina
Ixtapa
ZONA
HOTELERA
Playa del
Palmar
Paseo del Palmar
Club de Golf
Palma Real
PACIFIC OCEAN
Bahía del
Palmar
Paseo Ixtapa
TO
ZIHUATANEJO
Playa
Vista
Hermosa
0
880 yards
0
800 meters
Ixtapa

Beaches

Ixtapa

Isla Ixtapa. The most popular beach on Isla Ixtapa (and the one closest to the boat dock) is Playa Cuachalalate, named for a local tree whose bark has been used as a remedy for kidney ailments since ancient times. This beach is lined with seafood eateries and water equipment concessions and is excellent for swimming. A short walk across to the other side of the island is gorgeous Playa Varadero, another beach with informal eateries and water-sports outfitters. Just behind the restaurants is Playa Coral, with crystal-clear water that's ideal for snorkeling. Playa Carey, toward the island's south end, is small. Pangas run between the boat landings at both Cuachalalate and Varadero beaches and Playa Linda on the mainland.

Playa Quieta and Playa Linda. About 10 minutes north of Ixtapa's Zona Hotelera, thatch-roof restaurants dispense beer, sodas, and the catch of the day at Playa Quieta. It's bordered at one end by an estuary with birds and gators. You can rent horses, and a warren of vendors sell souvenirs and handcrafts. The beach is protected by Isla Ixtapa offshore, as is nearby Playa Linda, where you'll find several high-rise hotels and the ferry ($3.50 round-trip) to Isla Ixtapa.

Playa del Palmar. Ixtapa's main beach, this 3-km-long (2-mi-long) broad sandy stretch runs along the Zona Hotelera. Here many hotel concessions rent water-sports equipment to guests and nonguests. Since this is essentially open sea, the surf can be strong.

Playa Vista Hermosa. Although you can only access this beach, which is just south of Playa del Palmar, by boat or through the Hotel las Brisas, it isn't private (no Mexican beaches are). The hotel seems to cling to the cliffs; you reach the sand via walkways and an elevator. Aside from

the hotel's beachfront restaurant, which is open to all, there aren't any facilities or services here.

Zihuatanejo

Playa la Madera. You can reach tiny Playa la Madera, which is across the Zihuatanejo Bay, via a seaside footpath cut into the rocks or by car. This pancake-flat, dark-sand beach has a sprinkling of small, inexpensive hotels and restaurants. It was named *madera,* or "wood," beach because it was a Spanish port for shipping oak, pine, cedar, and mahogany cut from the nearby Sierra Madre del Sur.

Fodor'sChoice
★
Playa la Ropa. The area's most beautiful beach is beyond a rocky point across the bay and a 20-minute walk from Playa la Madera and a 5-minute taxi ride from town. Along this 1-km (½-mi) stretch of soft sand are open-air restaurants—with hammocks for post-meal siestas—a few hotels, and water-sports outfitters. It got its name ("clothing beach") when a cargo of Oriental silks and garments washed on to it from a Spanish galleon shipwrecked offshore.

Fodor'sChoice
★
Playa las Gatas. Named for the *gatas* (nurse sharks) that once lingered here, this beach is bordered by a long row of hewn rocks that create a breakwater. Legend has it that a Tarascan king built the breakwater so that this stretch of sand would be sheltered for his daughter's use. The clear waters are ideal for swimming, snorkeling, and diving, and summer swells create small but very surfable waves. The beach is lined with simple seafood eateries that provide lounge chairs for sunning. You can walk here, scrambling over some rocks on a point, in about 20 minutes from Playa la Ropa. You can also take one of the skiffs, which run from the municipal pier every 10 or 15 minutes between 8 and 5. Buy your round-trip ticket (about $3.50) at the office on the pier, and keep the stub for your return trip.

Playa Principal. At the edge of town, the picturesque main beach (a.k.a. Playa Municipal) is rimmed by the Paseo del Pescador. Here local fishermen keep their skiffs and gear, used for nightly fishing journeys. They return here in the early morning to sell their catches.

Where to Eat

Ixtapa

★ **$$$–$$$$** ✕ **Beccofino.** This marina-side restaurant is always crowded. You can eat inside, where dark, polished woods contrast with bright white linens, or outside on the canopy-sheltered deck. Among the best dishes on the Northern Italian menu are minestrone soup, *caprese* salad (with tomatoes, basil, and mozzarella), fish fillet (usually red snapper or mahimahi) with a champagne sauce, and chicken cacciatore. Many of the pastas are made in-house, and breakfast is available after 9:30 AM. ✉ *Plaza Marina Ixtapa* ☎ *755/553–1770* ⬧ *Reservations essential* ▭ *AE, MC, V.*

$$$–$$$$ ✕ **Bogart's.** Tables are separated by palm trees, and a Moorish fountain and piano music create a background of gentle sound. The international menu includes onion soup with a "turban" of crusty bread, pepper-crusted filet mignon, and *suprema Casablanca* (breaded chicken breasts stuffed with lobster). For dessert consider bananas—flambéed dramatically at your table—or one of the sorbets. Reservations are a good idea here. ✉ *Krystal Ixtapa, Blvd. Ixtapa s/n* ☎ *755/553–0333 Ext. 47* ▭ *MC, V* ☉ *No lunch.*

$$–$$$ ✕ **El Galeón.** People-watchers like to settle in at the rope- and rigging-adorned bar of this Marina Ixtapa restaurant. You can eat on the terrace or in a reproduction galleon right on the water. The fresh tuna steak is outstanding, as are the pastas; upscale Mexican and international fare are also available. The signature dish is *pollo galleón*, medallions of chicken breast stuffed with lobster and bathed in a three-cheese sauce, served with mashed potatoes and steamed vegetables. ✉ *Plaza Marina Ixtapa* ☎ *755/553–2150* ▭ *AE, MC, V.*

¢–$$ ✕ **Casa Morelos.** The wooden bar, ocher walls, and handmade furnishings make this tiny restaurant seem like a true cantina; there are also tables on the patio. The *chiles rellenos de camaró* (egg-battered peppers stuffed with shrimp), fajitas, and tuna steak topped with three kinds of chilies are all filling and delicious. After dinner, have a margarita and head next door to Señor Frogs for some dancing. Or come really early for a generous breakfast; the restaurant opens at 7:30 AM. ✉ *La Puerta shopping center, Blvd. Ixtapa s/n* ☎ *755/553–0578* ▭ *MC, V.*

¢–$ ✕ **Nueva Zelanda.** Although it's open all day, this sparkling little coffee shop is best known for its tasty breakfasts. This branch opened after the success of the original eatery in downtown Zihuatanejo. Both kitchens have fresh fruit juices and salads as well as a variety of *tortas* (sandwiches on large, crusty rolls). ✉ *Los Patios shopping center, behind bandstand, Blvd. Ixtapa s/n* ☎ *755/553–0632* ✉ *Calle Cuauhtémoc 23, Zihuatanejo* ☎ *755/554–2340* ⬧ *Reservations not accepted* ▭ *No credit cards.*

¢–$ ✕ **Ruben's.** For more than two decades, Ruben's has served consistently good food and received local praise. The charcoal-grilled burgers are made of top sirloin paddies, and the french fries, deep-fried zucchini, and baked potatoes will delight those who crave American treats. For dessert try the baked or grilled bananas glazed with cinnamon and sugar and served with a dollop of fresh cream. ✉ *Centro Comercial Flamboyant, next to Bancomer bank, Blvd. Ixtapa s/n* ☎ *755/553–0055* ▭ *No credit cards.*

Zihuatanejo

$$$ ✗ **Paul's.** The taciturn Swiss owner—whose name is, indeed, Paul—may well greet you dressed in shorts and an unbuttoned Hawaiian shirt. His fashion choices may be tropical and carefree, but his dishes are international and carefully prepared. Start with a fresh artichoke or escargot appetizer or the lentil soup; follow it with quail, pork chops, or poached mahimahi served with a dill sauce. There's also a sushi bar that's popular for takeout or dine-in. ⊠ *Av. Benito Juárez s/n* ☏ *755/554–6528* ⊟ *MC, V* ⊘ *Closed May. No lunch.*

★ **$$–$$$$** ✗ **Kau-Kan.** Owner-chef Ricardo Rodriguez, who studied in Paris before returning to Mexico and the upscale kitchen of La Casa Que Canta hotel, serves imaginative, exquisitely prepared seafood. On the menu you'll find whatever's freshest: perhaps melt-in-your-mouth abalone or grilled mahimahi under a sweet, spicy pineapple sauce. The shrimp-stuffed potatoes and the lobster with fresh basil and a garlic sauce are legendary. A few large oil paintings adorn the walls, but the main visual attraction is the gorgeous view of Zihuatanejo Bay. Reservations are truly a good idea. ⊠ *Carretera Escénica, Lote 7 en route to Playa La Ropa* ☏ *755/554–8446* ⊟ *AE, MC, V* ⊘ *Closed 2 wks in Sept. No lunch.*

$–$$$ ✗ **Coconuts.** Its name is a nod to the region's previous status as a coconut plantation, and under the direction of chef Patricia Cummings, it has become one of Zihuatanejo's top restaurants. Try the roast pork loin, the sweet and zesty coconut shrimp, or one of the vegetarian items. Five different dessert coffees are prepared flaming at your table. ⊠ *Av. Agustín Ramírez 1* ☏ *755/554–2518* ⊟ *AE, DC, MC, V* ⊘ *Closed Aug.–early Oct.*

$–$$$ ✗ **Rossy.** This affable beachfront restaurant serves Mexican-style seafood on a roof terrace or right on the sand. Dishes include a popular mixed platter—grilled crayfish, lobster, fish fillet, shrimp, a small salad, rice, french fries—and the local specialty *huachinango a la talla* (red snapper seasoned with herbs and barbecued). Musicians of one sort or another—usually a lone keyboard player—serenade diners on weekends. ⊠ *South end of Playa la Ropa* ☏ *755/554–4004* ⊟ *MC, V.*

$–$$$ ✗ **La Perla.** Eat (or just drink) indoors at the dark, old-fashioned bar, where the TV is often tuned to a sporting event. Or head for one of many white plastic tables on the large, informal, palm-shaded patio overlooking Playa la Ropa. Among the seafood specialties are *filete La Perla* (fish fillet baked with cheese) and *langosta a la diabla,* a spicy lobster dish served with rice and either raw or steamed veggies. ⊠ *Playa la Ropa* ☏ *755/554–2700* ⊟ *AE, MC, V.*

¢–$$$ ✗ **La Sirena Gorda.** Oil paintings and a bronze statue depict the namesake "fat mermaid" at this small, friendly restaurant near the pier and the fish market. Specialties include the seafood tacos and the octopus kebab. The setting is casual, with a lively bar and a wraparound patio opening onto the town's lazy street scene. ⊠ *Paseo del Pescador 90* ☏ *755/554–2687* ⌂ *Reservations not accepted* ⊟ *MC, V* ⊘ *Closed Wed.*

¢–$$ ✗ **Casa Elvira.** Named for the aging owner and onetime chef, this local institution is near the downtown pier and Paseo del Pescador. It's not fancy, but the staff is helpful and low key, and the food is habitually good. The fare consists of Mexican dishes and such simple seafood plates as fish steamed in foil and served with rice and french fries; lobster is a specialty, though it will push your tab into the $$$ category. The restaurant is open for breakfast December through Easter. ⊠ *Paseo del Pescador 32* ☏ *755/554–2061* ⊟ *MC, V.*

¢–$ ✗ **La Mordida.** Although in Mexico *mordida* usually refers to a bribe or a payoff, at this simple eatery, the word retains a more literal meaning: "a bite." Join the throngs after 5 PM for pizza and charcoal-broiled burgers at one of the few, small, street-side tables. Takeout is also an option.

✉ *Paseo de la Boquita 20* ☎ *755/554–8216* ⚑ *Reservations not accepted* ▤ *No credit cards* ⊙ *No lunch.*

Where to Stay

Ixtapa

★ **$$$** ▨ **Las Brisas Ixtapa.** This immense, pyramid-shape wonder slopes down a hill to its own cove and beach. Although rooms are small and have low ceilings, they're comfortable and modern, with red tile floors, blue tile headboards, and firm but plump mattresses. Each room has a balcony with a hammock, a chaise lounge, and a table; junior suite balconies also have hot tubs. Guests and nonguests enjoy the hotel's excellent Portofino and El Mexicano restaurants, which are open for dinner only (in low season only one or the other is open each night). The staff is friendly and professional. ✉ *Playa Vista Hermosa, 40880* ☎ *755/553–2121 or 888/559–4329* ⎙ *755/553–0751* ⊕ *www.brisas. com.mx* ⇝ *404 rooms, 19 suites* ⚲ *5 restaurants, room service, in-room safes, cable TV, 4 lighted tennis courts, 3 pools, wading pool, gym, hair salon, 4 bars, shops, children's programs (ages 4–12), laundry service, business services, meeting rooms, car rental, travel services, no-smoking rooms* ▤ *AE, DC, MC, V.*

$$$ ▨ **Krystal Ixtapa.** This beachfront hotel is shaped like a boat with its bow pointing seaward. What it lacks in charm it makes up for in amenities. The contemporary rooms have comfortable beds made up with fine sheets and blue and yellow comforters. Club Krystalito has children's activities, the excellent meeting facilities attract many conventions, Bogart's restaurant serves stellar international cuisine, and the Christine disco is Ixtapa's most popular. ✉ *Blvd. Ixtapa s/n, 40880* ☎ *755/553–0333; 800/231–9860 in the U.S.* ⎙ *755/553–0336* ⊕ *www.krystal.com.mx* ⇝ *254 rooms, 20 suites* ⚲ *4 restaurants, coffee shop, in-room safes, cable TV, 2 tennis courts, pool, gym, hair salon, dance club, children's programs (ages 3–10), concierge, meeting rooms, car rental, travel services, no-smoking rooms* ▤ *AE, DC, MC, V.*

$$$ ▨ **Riviera Beach Resort.** Furnishings are an adroit mix of rustic and modern in this 11-story resort. Rooms are done in cheerful blue and yellow color schemes with framed acrylic paintings. Junior suites have views from both the living room and the bedroom. Neither rooms nor suites have balconies, but windows do open to the sea breezes. A children's pool with a slide lures kids away from the free-form main pool, which has a swim-up bar. El Ancla restaurant serves a dynamite breakfast buffet for $13; El Arrecife, open for dinner only, specializes in steak and fresh seafood. ✉ *Blvd. Ixtapa s/n, 40880* ☎ *755/553–1066 or 888/809–6133* ⎙ *755/ 553–1991* ⊕ *www.riviera.com.mx* ⇝ *150 rooms, 23 suites* ⚲ *2 restaurants, in-room safes, minibars, cable TV, 2 lighted tennis courts, pool, wading pool, gym, hot tub, massage, sauna, spa, steam room, 3 bars, meeting rooms, travel services, no-smoking rooms* ▤ *AE, MC, V.*

$$–$$$ ▨ **Best Western Posada Real.** Casual and charming, the four-story Posada Real is more intimate than most Ixtapa hotels. Shell-shape lamps above the headboards invite you to read in the firm bed; air-conditioning units are quiet and efficient. The pool has a swim-up bar and water that's heated when necessary. The grounds also have a putting green. ✉ *Blvd. Ixtapa s/n, 40880* ☎ *755/553–1745; 800/528–1234 in the U.S.* ⎙ *755/553– 1805* ⊕ *www.bestwestern.com* ⇝ *110 rooms* ⚲ *Restaurant, cable TV, putting green, pool, hot tub, volleyball, 2 bars, shop, laundry service, car rental, travel services, no-smoking rooms* ▤ *AE, MC, V.*

$$ ▨ **Barceló.** Attractively landscaped grounds and a veranda restaurant surround the large, geometric pool at this modern high-rise. Rooms are done in rust and navy blue and have tiny, triangular terraces. Thoughtful touches include coffeemakers and makeup mirrors. ⊠ *Blvd. Ixtapa s/n, 40880* ☎ *755/555–2000* 🖷 *755/553–0808* ⊕ *www.barcelo.com* ⇌ *228 rooms, 5 suites* ⚏ *4 restaurants, room service, in-room safes, minibars, 4 tennis courts, pool, gym, 3 bars, children's programs (ages 6–12), laundry service, meeting rooms, travel services, no-smoking rooms* ▤ *MC, V* ❘○❘ *All-inclusive, EP.*

Troncones

$$ ▣ **El Burro Borracho.** Six comfortable stone cottages sit right on the 5-km-long (3-mi-long) beach. Relax in a hammock on your private patio, or go beachcombing, boogie-boarding, hiking, or caving. Afterward, retreat to the congenial bar-restaurant, with menu options ranging from cheeseburgers to fresh lobster. ⊠ *Playa Troncones* ⌂ *(A.P. 277 40880 Zihuatanejo, 40880)* ☎ *755/553–2800* 🖷 *755/553–2807* ⇌ *6 bungalows* ⚏ *Restaurant, beach, hiking* ▤ *No credit cards.* ·

$–$$ ▣ **Casa Ki.** Each bungalow at this homey haven in the wilds of Troncones has a tiny refrigerator and a patio with hammocks. There's also a house (for $165 a night), with a full kitchen, a small living room, two bedrooms, two en suite bathrooms, and a long porch looking right onto the sand and waves. All guests have access to a communal kitchen and dining room, as well as barbecue facilities, at the center of the property; there's also a meditation room. ⊠ *Playa Troncones* ⌂ *(A.P. 405 40880 Zihuatanejo, 40880)* ☎ *755/553–2815* ⊕ *www.casa-ki.com* ⇌ *3 bungalows, 1 house* ⚏ *Dining room, refrigerators, beach, free parking* ▤ *No credit cards* ❘○❘ *CP* ☉ *Closed mid-Sept.–mid-Oct.*

Zihuatanejo

$$$$ ▣ **Casa Cuitlateca.** Zihuatanejo's smallest boutique hotel affords spectacular bay views. In the guest rooms, inlaid stone floors and whitewashed stucco walls show handmade furnishings, folk art, and such details as tree-trunk lintels to their best advantage. There's a beautiful infinity pool and a rooftop, cool-water whirlpool. The staff will arrange nearly any excursion you can think of, and the patio restaurant, open to the public for dinner only, serves a multicourse, prix-fixe meal. Children under 16 aren't encouraged because of a few dangerous areas without railings. ⊠ *Calle Playa la Ropa, 40880* ☎ *755/554–2448 or 877/541–1234* 🖷 *755/554–7394* ⊕ *www.casacuitlateca.com* ⇌ *3 rooms, 1 suite* ⚏ *Restaurant, pool, hot tub; no room TVs* ▤ *AE, MC, V.*

$$$$ ▣ **La Casa Que Canta.** The "House That Sings" clings to a cliff above
Fodor'sChoice   Playa la Ropa. All guest quarters have lovely furnishings and folk art;
★   suites have bay views from outdoor living areas. Bathrooms are luxurious, as are such touches as flower petals arranged in intricate mosaics on your bed each day. The infinity pool seems to be airborne; below it, a saltwater pool has a waterfall and Jacuzzi. The restaurant serves guests breakfast and lunch; dinners here are more formal and are open to the public (reservations required). The location isn't good for children; those under 16 aren't allowed. ⊠ *Camino Escénico a Playa la Ropa, 40880* ☎ *755/554–6529 or 888/523–7030* 🖷 *755/554–7900* ⊕ *www. lacasaquecanta.com* ⇌ *21 suites, 3 apartments* ⚏ *Restaurant, in-room safes, minibars, pool, saltwater pool, gym, hot tub, spa; no room TVs, no kids* ▤ *AE, DC, MC, V.*

★ $$$$ ▣ **Villa del Sol.** Paths meander through gardens, passing coconut palms and fountains en route to Playa la Ropa. Rooms are artistically and individually designed, with bright but not overpowering, textiles and folk-art furnishings; all have terraces or balconies. Meals at the Villa del Sol restaurant are elegant; the Cantina Bar and Grill is more casual. MAP is required in high season, and only a few suites accommodate children under 14. ⊠ *Playa la Ropa, 40880* ☎ *755/554–2239 or 888/ 389–3239* 🖷 *755/554–2758* ⊕ *www.hotelvilladelsol.com* ⇌ *70 rooms* *and suites* ⚥ *2 restaurants, in-room safes, cable TV, 2 tennis courts, 4 pools, gym, massage, beach, 3 bars, travel services, no-smoking rooms* ▤ *AE, MC, V* ⦿❘ *EP, MAP.*

$$ ▣ **Ávila.** Although institutional in character, this hotel is well situated in the center of town facing the beach at Paseo del Pescador. Rooms are large and clean but are showing signs of age and have hard beds and noisy air-conditioning. Rooms 11 through 13 are the best; they share a wide, furnished patio overlooking the beach. Only sea-view rooms have cable TV. In March this place fills up with fishing-tournament participants. ⊠ *Calle Juan N. Alvarez 8, 40880* ☎ *755/554–2010* 📠 *755/554–8592* ⤳ *27 rooms* ⚥ *Beach, fans, some cable TV* ▤ *MC, V.*

$$ ▣ **Bungalows Pacíficos.** On three terraces above Playa la Madera, this property has bungalows that are spacious but basic. You can enjoy the breezes and take in the view from a veranda with a hammock, a table, and chairs. Walk to Zihuatanejo's restaurants, just 10 minutes away, or cook in the bungalow's fully equipped kitchen. The owner, who speaks Spanish, English, and German, enjoys sharing her knowledge of prime birding sites. ⊠ *Cerro de la Madera s/n 40880* ☎📠 *755/554–2112* ⦿ *www.zihuatanejo.net/bungalowspacificos* ⤳ *6 units* ⚥ *Kitchens; no a/c, no room TVs* ▤ *No credit cards.*

$$ ▣ **Solimar Inn Suites.** On a quiet plaza four blocks from the main beach, this family-owned hotel has suites with thick white walls, tile floors, and bright accent colors. Living/dining rooms have kitchenettes and built-in couches that double as beds. Long-term guests receive discounts; some rent a blender, microwave, and a coffeepot and stay for weeks. ⊠ *Plaza los Faroles, 40880* ☎📠 *755/554–3692* ⤳ *12 suites* ⚥ *Fans, kitchenettes, pool, bar, travel services* ▤ *MC, V.*

$–$$ ▣ **Irma.** One of Zihuatanejo's originals, this simple but comely colonial-style hotel is on a bluff overlooking Playa la Madera, which is accessible via a stairway. Rooms have tile floors, and plastered-cement wall units for storing clothing. Request an ocean-view room; most of these are better furnished, fresher, and more up to date than rooms without views. There's a patio overlooking the sea and twin, dark-blue pools surrounded by tables and lounge chairs. ⊠ *Playa la Madera, 40880* ☎ *755/554–2105* 📠 *755/554–3738* ⤳ *73 rooms* ⚥ *Restaurant, 2 pools, bar* ▤ *MC, V.*

$–$$ ▣ **Sotavento Beach Resort.** This multilevel oldie-but-goodie is on a cliff overlooking the bay. Below, accessible by more than 200 stairs, are Playa la Ropa and the hotel's beach bar and lounge chairs. Guest quarters are old but well maintained, with ceiling fans and white cement closet and shelving units. The cheapest rooms are on the first floor and have no view, but most rooms are large and airy and have terraces with hammocks and chaise lounges. Mattresses are a bit thin; the sound of the waves may help soothe you to sleep. ⊠ *Playa la Ropa, 40880* ☎ *755/554–2032; 877/ 699–6685 in the U.S.; 877/667–3702 in Canada* 📠 *755/554–2975* ⦿ *www.beachresortsotavento.com* ⤳ *70 rooms, 30 suites* ⚥ *2 restaurants, fans, pool, beach, 4 bars, travel services; no a/c* ▤ *AE, MC, V.*

Nightlife

A good way to start an evening is a happy hour at one of the hotel bars. Most bars are informal, but discos have a dress code; you may be turned away if you're wearing shorts, tank tops, or tennis shoes. A number of hotels have Mexican fiesta nights with buffets and folkloric dance performances.

★ There's live piano music nightly at **Bandidos** (⊠ Calle Pedro Ascencio 2, at Calle Cinco de Mayo, Zihuatanejo ☎ 755/553–8072), which serves drinks, snacks, and full meals at the interior bar and outdoor patio, and usually offers more lively strains of live music after 9. Next to the Best Western Posada Real, **Carlos 'n' Charlie's** (✉ Blvd. Ixtapa s/n, Ixtapa ☎ 755/553–0085) has late-night dancing on a raised platform by the beach. **Christine** (✉ Krystal Ixtapa hotel, Blvd. Ixtapa s/n, Ixtapa ☎ 755/553–0333), the town's most popular (and most expensive) disco, has varied music and high-tech light shows. You'll get a gorgeous nighttime view from atop the 85-ft-high faux-lighthouse tower of **El Faro** (✉ Plaza Marina Ixtapa, Ixtapa ☎ 755/555–2510), attached to El Galeón restaurant.

El Infierno y la Gloria (✉ La Puerta shopping center, Blvd. Ixtapa s/n, Ixtapa ☎ 755/553–0304) serves decent food but is better known as the place to stop for a drink, either in the intimate cantina (with karaoke some nights) or in the restaurant, where TVs bolted high on the walls are a constant diversion. Tops for sunset viewing (with live music in high season) is the beachfront **Lobby Bar** (✉ Las Brisas Ixtapa hotel, Playa Vista Hermosa, Ixtapa ☎ 755/553–2121). **Señor Frog's** (✉ La Puerta shopping center, Blvd. Ixtapa s/n, Ixtapa ☎ 755/553–0692), across from the Riviera Beach Resort, is the place to go for tequila shots and dancing.

Sports & the Outdoors

Fishing

The area is best known for its feisty sailfish, hooked year-round. Seasonally you'll find yellowfin tuna, dorado, blue and black marlin, mackerel, barracuda, bonito, and others. Before you leave home, you can get information and make bookings through **Ixtapa Sportfishing Charters** (✉ 19 Depue La., Stroudsburg, PA 18360 ☎ 570/688–9466 📠 570/688–9554 ● ixtapasportfishing.com). Cost ranges from $190 for one–two people aboard a 25-ft super panga to $900 for a 46-ft yacht accommodating eight fisherpersons.

Cooperativo de Pescadores (✉ Paseo del Pescador 81, Zihuatanejo ☎ 755/554–2056) charges $150 for up to four passengers in small, fast skiffs and $200–$250 for larger, more comfortable, albeit somewhat slower craft. **Cooperativo Triángulo del Sol** (✉ Paseo del Pescador 20, Zihuatanejo ☎ 755/554–3758 or 755/554–2056) offers day trips in boats from 26 to 36 ft. Prices range from $120 for up to three people for close-to-shore fishing in a motor launch to $150 per person for deep-sea fishing.

Golf

Part of the Marina Ixtapa complex, the challenging 18-hole, par-72 course at the **Club de Golf Marina Ixtapa** (✉ Ixtapa ☎ 755/553–1410) was designed by Robert Von Hagge. Greens fees are $75 (including cart). Caddies charge $20, and you can rent clubs. The **Palma Real Golf Club** (✉ Blvd. Ixtapa s/n, Ixtapa ☎ 755/553–1062) has an 18-hole, par-72 championship course designed by Robert Trent Jones Jr. It abuts a wildlife preserve that runs from a coconut plantation to the beach; you may glimpse a gator while you play. A round costs $65 mid-December through mid-April and $50 the rest of the year.

Horseback Riding

Many area tour operators can arrange guided horseback excursions. Costs are high (around $40 for a ride of less than 1½ hours), but they include transportation and usually a soft drink or beer after the ride. You can rent horses with guides for $20 an hour at **Rancho Playa Linda** (☎ 755/554–3085) just up the coast from Ixtapa. Excursions generally leave in the morning and again in the afternoon after the heat has abated, about 4 or 5 PM.

Tennis

At the **Club de Golf Marina Ixtapa** (✉ Ixtapa ☎ 755/553–1410) fees are $10–$12, and you can rent equipment. Fees are $4 per hour ($8 at night) to play on one of the four courts at the **Palma Real Golf Club** (✉ Blvd. Ixtapa s/n, Ixtapa ☎ 755/553–1030 or 755/553–1163). In Zihuatanejo, **Villa del Sol** (✉ Playa la Ropa, Zihuatanejo ☎ 755/554–2239) has courts available to nonguests, although they pay double what guests pay ($20 per hour, $30 at night) and guests receive priority.

Water Sports

Outfitters line Ixtapa's Playa del Palmar. Parasailing costs about $22 for an 8-minute ride or $32 for 15 minutes; waterskiing runs about $38 per half hour; banana-boat rides are about $5.50 per person for a 20-minute trip. On Playa la Ropa, next to La Perla restaurant in Zihuatanejo, Hobie Cats rent for about $27 an hour depending on boat size, and classes are $25 per half hour. Windsurfers—when you can find them—rent for $20 an hour; classes, which include six hours over four days, cost $40.

SCUBA DIVING   More than 30 dive sites in the area range from deep canyons to shallow reefs. The waters here are teeming with sea life, and visibility is generally excellent. On Isla Ixtapa, **Centro de Buceo Oliverio** (✉ Playa de Cuachalalate, Ixtapa ☎ 755/554–3992) provides rental equipment, instruction, and guided dives ($50 per tank). Experienced PADI dive masters run trips and teach courses at ★ **Ixtapa Aqua Paradise** (✉ Centro Comercial Los Patios, Local 137, Ixtapa ☎ 755/553–1510). Owned and operated by NAUI master diver and marine biologist Juan Barnard, the **Zihuatanejo Scuba Center** (✉ Centro Hotel Paraíso Real, Playa La Ropa, Zihuatanejo ☎ 755/554–3873) runs one- and two-tank dives as well as five-day certification courses.

WATER PARK   **Magic World** (✉ Blvd. de las Garzas s/n, Ixtapa ☎ 755/553–1359), next to the Ixtapa Palace Hotel, has such amusements as wave pools and water slides as well as several restaurants. It's open Tuesday–Sunday 10:30–5:30 and admission is $6.50.

Shopping

Ixtapa

As you enter Ixtapa from the airport or from Zihuatanejo, you'll see a large handicrafts market, **Mercado de Artesanía Turístico,** on the right side of Boulevard Ixtapa. The result of an ordinance banning vendors from the beach, this market is open weekdays 10–10 and has some 150 stands, selling handicrafts, T-shirts, and kitschy souvenirs. Across the street from the Zona Hotelera, the shopping area is loosely divided into *centros comerciales,* or malls, with boutiques, restaurants, pharmacies, and grocery stores.

Zihuatanejo

Downtown Zihuatanejo has a fascinating **mercado municipal** with a labyrinth of small stands on the east side of the town center, on Avenida Benito Juárez between Avenida Nava and Avenida González. On Zihuatanejo's western edge is the ★ **Mercado de Artesanía Turístico** (✉ Calle Cinco de Mayo between Paseo del Pescador and Av. Morelos), with some 250 stands selling jewelry of shell, beads, and quality silver as well as hand-painted bowls and plates, hammocks, gauzy blouses, T-shirts, and souvenirs. Near the main plaza, **Casa Marina** (✉ Paseo del Pescador 9 ☎ 755/554–2373) is a two-story building with individual boutiques selling folk art, hammocks, and hand-loomed rugs. It's generally closed Sunday except when the cruise ships call.

In addition to these shops, the tiny three-block nucleus of central Zihuatanejo has several worthwhile shops; most are closed Sunday. Shop for silver and gold jewelry at **Alberto's** (✉ Calle Cuauhtémoc 15, across from Cine Paraíso ☎ 755/554–2161). **Arte Mexicano Nopal** (✉ Av. Cinco de Mayo 56 ☎ 755/554–7530) sells Mexican handicrafts, reproductions of ancient art, and natural pine furniture that can be finished according to the client's tastes. **Coco Cabaña** (✉ Av. Agustín Ramírez 1 ☎ 755/554–2518) is a fascinating folk-art shop at Coconuts restaurant.

In the Villa del Sol hotel, **Gala Art** (✉ Playa la Ropa ☎ 755/554–7774) exhibits and sells paintings, jewelry, and bronze, wood, and marble sculptures crafted by artists from throughout Mexico. **Galería Maya** (✉ Calle Nicolás Bravo 58 ☎ 755/554–4606) is very browseable for its folk art and glad rags from Oaxaca and Chiapas as well as from Guatemala. **Lupita's** (✉ Calle Juan N. Alvarez 5 ☎ 755/554–2238) has been selling colorful women's apparel—including handmade items from Oaxaca, Yucatán, Chiapas, and Guatemala—for more than 20 years.

Ixtapa & Zihuatanejo A to Z

To research prices, get advice from other travelers, and book travel arrangements, visit www.fodors.com.

AIR TRAVEL

AIRPORT You can fly to Aeropuerto de Zihuatanejo, 12 km (8 mi) southeast of Zihuatanejo, from Houston, Los Angeles, and other major U.S. cities.
🛈 **Aeropuerto de Zihuatanejo** ☎ 755/554-2070.

AIRPORT
TRANSFERS From the airport, the taxi fare to Ixtapa's Zona Hotelera is about $23; the trip takes about 20 minutes. To Zihuatanejo, the 15-minute trip costs about $18.

CARRIERS Mexicana has daily flights from U.S. and Mexican cities. Aeroméxico flies from multiple U.S. and Mexican cities. Alaska Airlines has direct flights three times a week from Los Angeles. America West has twice-weekly direct service from Phoenix. Houston is the hub for Continental, which offers daily direct flights.
🛈 **Aeroméxico** ☎ 01800/021-4000 toll-free in Mexico; 800/237-6639 in the U.S. **Alaska Airlines** ☎ 01800/252-7522 toll-free in Mexico; 800/426-0333 in the U.S. **America West** ☎ 755/554-8634; 800/235-9292 in the U.S. **Continental** ☎ 755/554-4219; 800/525-0280 in the U.S. **Mexicana** ☎ 01800/502-2000 toll-free in Mexico; 800/531-7921 in the U.S.

BOAT TRAVEL

Several cruise lines, including Holland America, Princess, and Royal Cruise Lines, sail to Ixtapa and Zihuatanejo as part of their seven-day Riviera Mexicana trips.

BUS TRAVEL

The Estrella de Oro bus company has deluxe service to Acapulco, Cuernavaca, Taxco, and Mexico City. Estrella Blanca offers first-class service to the same destinations as well as to Querétaro, Aguascalientes, León, Puerto Escondido, and the U.S. border. The two bus companies have terminals near each other at the southern edge of Zihuatanejo on Carretera 200; both also have ticket offices in Ixtapa's Plaza Ixpamar.
🛈 **Estrella Blanca** ☎ 755/554-3476 in Zihuatanejo; 755/553-0465 in Ixtapa. **Estrella de Oro** ☎ 755/554-2175.

CAR RENTAL

Major Agencies Budget ✉ Blvd. Ixtapa s/n, Ixtapa ☎ 755/553-0397; 755/553-0517; 755/554-4837 at the airport. **Hertz** ✉ Calle Nicolás Bravo 13, Local 10, Zihuatanejo ☎ 755/554-2255; 755/554-2590 at the airport.

CAR TRAVEL

The Autopista del Sol connects Ixtapa and Zihuatanejo to Mexico City, passing Acapulco en route; tolls on the 6-hour trip total around $55. Otherwise, the trip from Mexico City takes about 8 hours. Acapulco is a 3½-hour drive on Carretera 200, which passes through small towns and coconut groves and has spectacular ocean views. The drive from Manzanillo takes about 7 hours. A highway that's slated to be finished in mid- to late 2003 will connect Ixtapa/Zihuatanejo to Morelia, Michoacán (5 hours) and on to Mexico City (another 2½ hours.)

Driving in Ixtapa and Zihuatanejo is a breeze: neither city is congested and no one is any particular hurry. On-street parking is plentiful, and although security isn't really a problem, there are also inexpensive guarded lots.

CONSULATE

United States Consulate ✉ Paseo Ixtapa, Plaza Ambiente, Local 9, Ixtapa ☎ 755/553-2100.

EMERGENCIES

Hospital General de Zihuatanejo ✉ Av. Morelos s/n at Mar Egeo, Zihuatanejo ☎ 755/554-3965. **Police** ☎ 755/554-2040. **Red Cross** ☎ 755/554-2009. **Tourist Protection** ☎ 755/554-4455.

INTERNET

Many hotels in Ixtapa have business centers with Internet access. In Zihua, access is more limited. One of the least expensive is Eme's Computación, which is near the center of town. Hours are limited: Monday–Saturday 9 AM–2 PM.

Internet Cafés Eme's Computación ✉ Calle Benito Juárez Local 2, near Calle Juan N. Alvarez, Zihuatanejo ☎ 755/554-0661.

MONEY MATTERS

Although many businesses accept credit cards or U.S. traveler's checks in small denomination, many prefer cash. Change cash or traveler's checks at banks, money exchange booths, or—at a slightly lower rate—hotels. Most area banks have ATMs.

Banks Banco Bital ✉ Blvd. Ixtapa s/n, Ixtapa ☎ 755/553-0642. **Bancomer** ✉ Av. Benito Juárez at Calle Nicolás Bravo, Zihuatanejo ☎ 755/554-7490.

TAXIS & MINIBUSES

Unless you plan to travel great distances or visit remote beaches, taxis and buses are the best way to get around. Taxis are plentiful, and you can call for one or hail one on the street; fares are reasonable and fixed. The fare from Ixtapa's Zona Hotelera to Zihuatanejo is $4. You can call APAAZ or UTAAZ for a cab; both companies offer 24-hour service. Minibuses run every 10–15 minutes between the Ixtapa hotels and downtown Zihuatanejo until 10 PM; the fare is about 40¢.

Taxi Companies APAAZ ☎ 755/554-3680. **UTAAZ** ☎ 755/554-4583.

TOURS

The tour company VIPSA offers several popular cruises, including 2½-hour sunset cruises ($45) and 4-hour swim and snorkel cruises aboard the 44-ft *Noyoltzi*, with a maximum of 25 passengers. Both include open bar (domestic drinks); the snorkel cruise includes a snack. In addition, VIPSA offers horseback-riding excursions, as does TIP, which also has tours that take in town or country. Intermar Ixtapa organizes all types of tours in both the town and the country.

To see pink flamingos and other wading birds, head for Barra de Potosí (15 minutes past the airport), where a beautiful *laguna* (lake) is an unofficial bird sanctuary. You can go on a tour, hire a local fisherman, or take a bus or taxi—you'll pay less for the latter, you'll be able to linger at one of the casual restaurants lining the beach. You can hire a fisherman's boat from Zihuatanejo's municipal pier for a trip to the scenic, remote Playa Manzanillo, which is great for snorkeling.

Intermar Ixtapa ⊠ Paseo Ixtapa s/n, Centro Commercial Los Patios, Local 105, Ixtapa ☎ 755/553-2666. **TIP** ⊠ Calle Juan N. Alvarez and Calle Benito Juárez, Local 2, Zihuatanejo ☎ 775/554-7511. **VIPSA** ⊠ Hotel Barceló, Blvd. Ixtapa s/n, Ixtapa ☎ 755/553-2480 ⊠ Las Brisas Ixtapa hotel, Playa Vista Hermosa ☎ 755/553-2214.

TRAVEL AGENCIES

Local Agent Referrals American Express ⊠ Hotel Krystal Ixtapa, Blvd. Ixtapa, Ixtapa ☎ 755/553-0853 ⊜ 755/553-1206. **TIP** ⊠ Calle Juan N. Alvarez and Calle Benito Juárez, Local 2, Zihuatanejo ☎ 755/554-7511.

VISITOR INFORMATION

The Guerrero State Tourism Office is open weekdays 8–9 and Saturday 8–3. Ixtapa's Oficina de Convenciones y Visitantes (Convention and Visitors' Bureau) is helpful with hotel and tour operator recommendations. It's open weekdays 9–2 and 4–7.

Guerrero State Tourism Office ⊠ La Puerta shopping center, Blvd. Ixtapa s/n, Ixtapa ☎ 755/553-1967. **Oficina de Convenciones y Visitantes** ⊠ Paseo de las Gaviotas 12, Ixtapa ☎ 755/553-1144 ⊕ www.ixtapa-zihuatanejo.org.

ACAPULCO

9

FODOR'S CHOICE

The divers at La Quebrada

Emilia Castillo, Taxco shop

Fairmont Acapulco Princess, hotel

Pie de la Cuesta, beach

La Vela, Acapulco restaurant

HIGHLY RECOMMENDED

HOTELS   Camino Real Acapulco Diamante

Elcano

Fairmont Pierre Marqués

Los Flamingos

Posada de la Misión, Taxco

Villas Ukae Kim

RESTAURANTS   Baikal

El Mural, Taxco

Hacienda

Hostería el Adobe, Taxco

Pipo's

Zorrito's

SHOPPING   Spratling Ranch, Taxco

EXPERIENCES   Enigma, nightclub

El Fuerte de San Diego, fort

Palladium, nightclub

Iglesia de San Sebastián, Taxco church

Zucca, nightclub

Updated by
Patricia Alisau

MEXICAN MURALIST DIEGO RIVERA IS SAID TO HAVE BEEN SO AWESTRUCK by Acapulco's sunsets that he re-created them on canvas. In the 1950s, this vibrant port city, which has one of the world's most beautiful bays, attracted Hollywood celebrities. This is also where John and Jackie Kennedy spent their honeymoon. Likewise, Henry and Nancy Kissinger, Liz Taylor and Michael Todd, and Bill and Hillary Clinton. Three Rambo flicks starring Sylvester Stallone were filmed here, as was *Blow* with Johnny Depp and Penélope Cruz. Singers such as Julio Iglesias and a host of others maintain residences here, carrying on the Hollywood tradition that started long ago.

The natural harbor of Bahía de Acapulco (Acapulco Bay) is the city's centerpiece. By day this stretch of the Pacific, 433 km (268 mi) south of Mexico City, is a deep tempting blue; at night the water flashes and sparkles with city lights. Thanks to warm waters, almost constant sunshine, and balmy year-round temperatures most people plan their day around the beach—whether it's to lounge in a hammock or to snorkel, parasail, fish, or water-ski. Still, a few things have been known to lure people away from the sands: championship golf courses, tennis courts, food and crafts markets, fabulous restaurants.

At night Acapulco rouses itself from the day's torpor and prepares for the long hours ahead. Eating out is one of the city's great pleasures. In addition to the showy places, there are plenty of good no-frills, down-home joints that take you to the real Mexico. Acapulco's nightlife is also legendary, with new and ever more spectacular dance clubs constantly opening. Perpetually crowded, the discos are grouped in twos and threes, and most people hit several places in a night.

Acapulco has managed to age gracefully over the years even as it's grown into a town of a million inhabitants. Care is lavished on its upkeep. The city fathers initiated a multimillion-dollar beautification program some time ago, which is renewed annually to keep the bay, beaches, and streets landscaped and clean.

EXPLORING ACAPULCO

Old Acapulco is on the bay's western edge. Its streets run inland, forming a grid that's easy to explore on foot. Since the late 1940s, Acapulco has expanded eastward. Former President Miguel Alemán Valdés bought up miles of the coast just before the road and airport were built, as his namesake Avenida Costera Miguel Alemán testifies. Today this wide, coastal boulevard—whose poshest stretch is simply called the "Costera"—and the areas just off it are home to many major hotels, restaurants, and malls. You'll need a car to explore it as well as Acapulco Diamante, still farther east. Running from Las Brisas to Barra Vieja beach, this 3,000-acre expanse encompasses exclusive Punta Diamante and Playa Diamante, with its upscale hotels and residential developments, private clubs, and pounding surf.

To the west, Pie de la Cuesta is known for its fabulous sunsets—a good reason to venture here late in the afternoon. Grab a beach chair, sip a drink, and gaze at the stream of colors moving across the sky. Although Pie de la Cuesta's main road has been paved and it now has an all-inclusive resort (popular with Canadians), the tiny area has seen little development.

You can get a feel for Acapulco during a short stay if you take in some downtown sights along with your beach activities. With more time, you can enjoy excursions to isolated beaches as well as to Taxco, a colonial

9

If you have 3 days Spend the first day parasailing, waterskiing, or simply sunning. That evening take a sunset cruise that includes a ringside view of Acapulco's daredevil *clavadistas* (divers) at La Quebrada. The following day pay an early visit to the Mercado Municipal, the waterfront, and the *zócalo* (town square). Head to the beach for some rays and take in some late-afternoon shopping in the boutiques and handicrafts markets along Avenida Costera Miguel Alemán. Come nightfall, "shake off the dust" (as they say in Mexico) at one of the city's glitzy discos. The next day return to the beach or head out fishing. Later, take in the Mexican Fiesta at the Acapulco International Center, and toast Acapulco during a late candlelit dinner.

If you have 5 days Follow the three-day itinerary. On the fourth day visit El Fuerte de San Diego, built in the 18th century to protect Acapulco from pirates and today home of the history museum. Then swing down the street to the Casa de Mascaras, with its collection of Guerrero masks. For a taste of the 1950s Acapulco of John Wayne and Johnny Weissmuller, hire a taxi to take you into the hills above Caleta and Caletilla; make it a point to drop into Los Flamingos hotel, which Weissmuller once owned with others from the Hollywood gang. Head out to Pie de la Cuesta, a beach west of town, for a late lunch and boat ride or waterskiing on Laguna Coyuca (Coyuca Lagoon), and then cross the road and park your body under an umbrella to watch the sun set. Set the next morning aside for the thrilling Shotover Jet boat ride on the Río Papagayo (Papagayo River). Devote a few hours to Mágico Mundo Marino or the ruins at Palma Sola.

If you have 7 days Follow the five-day itinerary and, on the sixth day, rent a car or arrange for a tour to Taxco, a colonial treasure of twisting cobblestone streets and some 2,000 silver shops, a three-hour drive north of Acapulco; plan to spend the night. In addition to shopping for silver, visit the Iglesia de San Sebastián y Santa Prisca, the town's most important landmark, on Plaza Borda, and the Casa Humboldt, which houses a museum. Try to get a front-row seat at one of the bars or restaurants on the square and spend an hour watching the activity: weddings, funerals, baptisms, and vendors selling baskets and animal figurines. The following day, tour the Grutas de Cacahuamilpa, an expanse of subterranean chambers.

town a delightful three-hour drive north of Acapulco, where the Baroque towers of Santa Prisca church overlook cobblestone streets lined with silversmiths.

Timing

Temperatures hover at the 30°C (80°F) mark just about year-round, and sunshine is virtually a given. Winter sees its share of snowbirds from the United States and Canada, but the busiest times are Christmas week, Easter week, and during the July–August school vacation. Most hotels are booked solid during these times, so plan to make reservations months in advance. Prices during Christmas week rise 30%–60% above those in low season.

Costera

Avenida Costera Miguel Alemán hugs the Bahía de Acapulco from the Carretera Escénica (Scenic Highway) in the east to Playa Caleta (Caleta Beach) in the southwest—a distance of about 8 km (5 mi). Most of the major beaches, shopping malls, and hotels are along or off this avenue, and locals refer to its most exclusive stretch—from El Presidente hotel to Las Brisas—simply as "Costera." Because many an address is listed only as "Costera Miguel Alemán" and streets off this avenue have no logical pattern, addresses are rarely used; directions are usually given from a major landmark.

Numbers in the text correspond to numbers in the margin and on the Acapulco map.

a good tour

Take a drive or taxi ride along the Costera Miguel Alemán, starting on its eastern edge at La Base, the Mexican naval base south of Playa Icacos. When you come to Playa Icacos, you'll see the **Casa de la Cultura** ❶ ▶ cultural complex on the beach side (just past the Hyatt Regency hotel); a little farther down is **CiCi** ❷, a children's amusement park. About 1 km (½ mi) past it, on the right side of the Costera, lies the Acapulco International Center (often called simply the convention center); you might return here in the evening to attend a Mexican Fiesta. Continue along through the commercial heart of the Costera until you reach **Parque Papagayo** ❸, one of the country's top municipal parks.

What to See

▶ ❶ **Casa de la Cultura.** This cultural complex includes a small archaeological museum, first-class regional and Mexican handicrafts for sale, and the Ixcateopan art gallery. ⊠ *Av. Costera Miguel Alemán 4834, Costera* ☎ *744/484–4004* ☜ *Free* ☉ *Weekdays 9–2 and 5–8, Sat. 9–2.*

❷ **CiCi.** A water-oriented theme park for children, the Centro Internacional para Convivencia Infantil, fondly known as CiCi, has dolphin and seal shows, a freshwater pool with wave-making apparatus, a water slide, miniaquarium, and other attractions. Swim with the dolphins for $90 an hour or $51 for a half hour, including entrance to the park and transportation from your hotel (it's easy to catch a cab for the return trip). ⊠ *Av. Costera Miguel Alemán, across from Hard Rock Cafe, Costera* ☎ *744/484–8210* ☜ *$3* ☉ *Daily 10–6.*

❸ **Parque Papagayo.** Named for the hotel that formerly occupied the grounds, this park is on 52 acres of prime Costera real estate, just after the underpass that begins at Playa Hornos. Youngsters enjoy the life-size model of a Spanish galleon, made to look like the ones that sailed into Acapulco when it was Mexico's capital of trade with the Orient. There's an aviary, a roller-skating rink, a racetrack with mite-size race cars, a space shuttle replica, bumper boats in a lagoon, and other rides. ⊠ *Av. Costera Miguel Alemán, Costera* ☎ *744/485–9623* ☜ *No entrance fee; rides 45¢ each; $5 and $8 ride packages available* ☉ *Park: daily 10–8. Rides section: nightly 4–11.*

Old Acapulco

Old Acapulco, one of the areas that you can easily tour on foot, is where the locals go to dine, enjoy a town festival, run errands, and worship. Also known as El Centro, it's where you'll find the zócalo, the church, and El Fuerte de San Diego. Just up the hill from Old Acapulco is La Quebrada and its famous divers.

9

Nightlife

The minute the sun slips over the horizon, the Costera comes alive with people milling around window-shopping, deciding where to dine, and generally biding their time until the disco hour. Acapulco's nightclubs are open 365 days a year from about 10:30 PM until they empty out. There's little in the way of theater here, but Placido Domingo gives the occasional benefit concert, and the Acapulco Symphonic Orchestra is one of Mexico's best. International pop-music fests and several film events such as black- and French-cinema festivals are gaining popularity.

Shopping

The abundance of air-conditioned shopping malls and boutiques and open-air flea markets makes picking up souvenirs a snap. Look for handicrafts and silver jewelry. The state of Guerrero is especially known for hand-painted ceramics, items made from *palo de rosa* wood, primitive bark paintings depicting scenes of village life and local flora and fauna, and embroidered textiles. The colonial town of Taxco is one of world's silver capitals.

Sun, Sand & Surf

Golfers can tee off at the 9-hole municipal course or at one of four 18-hole championship courses in Acapulco Diamante. Most hotels have pools, and many have tennis clubs as well. The lure of Acapulco's sands is irresistible, though. You can eat in a beach restaurant, dance, and sleep in a *hamaca* (hammock)—all without leaving the water's edge. There are also plenty of quiet and even isolated beaches within reach.

The water teems with sailfish, marlin, shark, and mahimahi, making fishing as popular as waterskiing, windsurfing, kayaking, and bronco riding (one-person Jet Skis). Although visibility isn't as good here as in the Caribbean, scuba diving is also an option. It's best in December through February, when the water is the most transparent. A Canadian warship was scuttled to make diving more appealing.

Old Acapulco's southern peninsula has remnants of the first version of Acapulco. This primarily residential area was prey to dilapidation and abandonment for many years, but efforts were made to revitalize it—such as reopening the Caleta Hotel and opening the aquarium at Playa Caleta. Although its prime is definitely past, it's still a popular area for budget travelers and those seeking a retro experience. The Plaza de Toros, where bullfights are held on Sunday from the first week of January to Easter, is in the center of the peninsula.

a good tour

A few blocks inland from the intersection of Avenida Costera Miguel Alemán and Calle Diego Hurtado de Mendoza, is the sprawling **Mercado Municipal** ④ ▶, a good starting point. You'll want to take the bus marked MERCADO or have a taxi drop you off; it's best to navigate El Centro on foot. A few blocks west, **El Fuerte de San Diego** ⑤ is on the hill overlooking the harbor next to the army barracks. At the fort, you can hire a guide for a trip to the **Palma Sola** archaeological site, just northwest of Old Acapulco. Alternatively you can continue your walking tour by leaving the fort and wandering along the **malecón** ⑦, with its series of docks. Adjoining it is the **zócalo** ⑧, Old Acapulco's center. A 15-minute walk up the hill from the zócalo brings you to **La Quebrada** ⑨, where the famous cliff divers perform their daredevil stunts daily. From here or from the zócalo you can grab a cab to the **Mágico Mundo Marina** ⑩ to visit the aquarium.

What to See

⑤ **Casa de Mascaras.** A private home has been turned into a gallery for a stunning collection of 550 handmade ceremonial masks, most from the state of Guerrero. Some are representative of those still used in such traditional ritualistic dances as "Moors and the Christians" and "Battle of the Tigers." ⊠ *Calle Morelos s/n, ex-zona militar B, a half block from Fuerte de San Diego, Old Acapulco* ☎ *744/486–5577* ⊠ *Free (donation suggested)* ☉ *Mon.–Sat. 10–6.*

★ ⑥ **El Fuerte de San Diego.** Under the Spaniards, Acapulco became a very lucrative port for trade with the Philippines. The original fortress, built in 1616 to protect the rich city from pirates, was destroyed by an earthquake in 1776; the current, pentagonal one went up in the 18th century. Today the fort houses the **Museo Historico de Acapulco** (Acapulco History Museum), the state's top cultural attraction. Bilingual videos and text explain exhibits tracing the city's history from the first pre-Hispanic settlements 3,000 years ago, to the exploits of such pirates as Sir Francis Drake, through the era of the missionaries, and up to Mexico's independence from Spain in 1821. There are also displays of precious silks, Talavera tiles, exquisitely hand-tooled wooden furniture, and delicate china. A good multimedia show in Spanish (for English a minimum of 15 persons is needed) on the history of Acapulco is staged outside the museum grounds on Thursday, Friday, and Saturday at 8 PM for $10 a person. ⊠ *Calle Hornitos and Calle Morelos, Old Acapulco* ☎ *744/482–3828* ⊠ *$3.25* ☉ *Tues.–Fri. 10–5, Sat. 10–5 and 7–9:30, Sun. 10–5.*

☺ ⑩ **Mágico Mundo Marino.** In addition to an aquarium, Magic Marine World has a free sea lion show and swimming pools—not to mention clean rest rooms. You can also rent Jet Skis, inner tubes, kayaks, and other equipment here for use on Playa Caleta, a beach connected to this park via a pedestrian bridge. From Playa Caleta you can take the glass-bottom boat to Isla la Roqueta—about 10 minutes each way—to snorkel. ⊠ *Playa Caleta, Old Acapulco* ☎ *744/483–1215* ⊠ *$2. Round-trip boat ride to Isla la Roqueta: $3* ☉ *Daily 9–6.*

⑦ **Malecón.** A stroll by the docks will remind you that Acapulco is still a lively commercial port and fishing center. The cruise ships anchor here, and at night Mexicans bring their children to play on the small tree-lined promenade. Farther west, by the zócalo, are the docks for the sight-seeing yachts and smaller fishing boats, a good spot for people-watching. ⊠ *Av. Costera Miguel Alemán, between Calle Escudero on the west and El Fuerte de San Diego on the east, Old Acapulco.*

▶ ④ **Mercado Municipal.** Locals come to this sprawling municipal market to buy their everyday needs, from fresh vegetables and candles to plastic buckets and love potions. In addition, you can buy baskets, pottery, hammocks—there's even a stand offering charms, amulets, and talismans. The stalls within the mercado are densely packed together and there's no air-conditioning, but things stay relatively cool. Come as early as possible to avoid the crowds. ⊠ *Calle Diego Hurtado de Mendoza and Av. Constituyentes, a few blocks west of Costera, Old Acapulco* ☉ *Daily 5 AM–7 PM.*

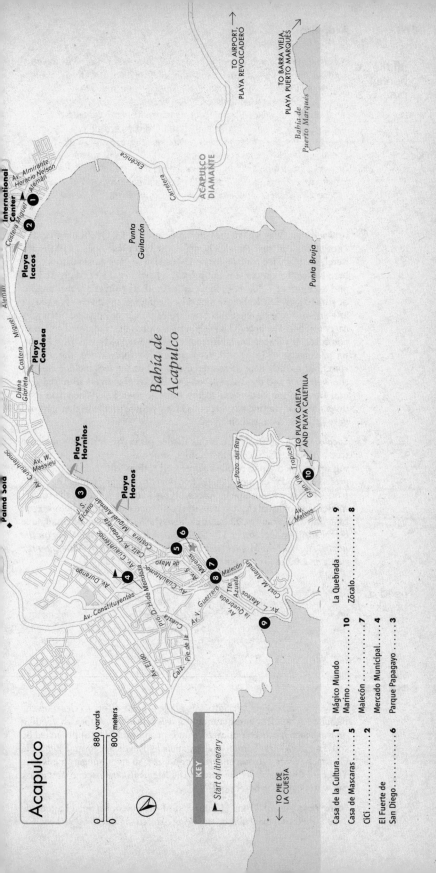

Acapulco

880 yards
800 meters

KEY

▲ Start of itinerary

TO PIE DE
LA CUESTA →

Av. Almirante
Horacio Nelson
Alemán

International
Center

Costera Miguel

Av. Cuauhtémoc

Playa
Icacos

Palma Sola ◆

Alemán

Miguel

Costera

Av. W.
Massieu

Diana
Glorieta

Playa
Condesa

Playa Hornitos

Playa
Hornos

S.
Elcano

Av. Durango

Av. Cuauhtémoc

Costera M. Alemán

Calz. Av. Cuauhtémoc

Av. 5
de Mayo

Av. Constituyentes

Pro. D. H.de Mendoza

Cuesta

Av. Guerrero

la Quebrada

Calz. Pie de la

Av. E.Judeo

Morelos

Malecón

Tte.
Azueta

Av. L. Mateos

Costa M. Alemán

Av. Pozo del Rey

Gran Vía Tropical

Av.
L. Mateos

TO PLAYA CALETA
AND PLAYA CALETILLA →

Bahía de
Acapulco

Punta
Guitarrón

Punta Bruja

Carretera

Escénica

ACAPULCO
DIAMANTE

TO AIRPORT,
PLAYA REVOLCADERO →

TO BARRA VIEJA,
PLAYA PUERTO MARQUÉS →

Bahía de
Puerto Marqués

off the
beaten
path

Palma Sola. Taking the name of the neighborhood closest to it, this archaeological site juts up a mountainside northeast of Old Acapulco. The area is blanketed in petroglyphs dating from more than 2,000 years ago and executed by the Yopes, Acapulco's earliest known inhabitants. Stone steps with intermittent plazas for viewing the ancient art are set along a path through virgin vegetation. A cave used as a ceremonial center is atop the mountain, more than 1,000 ft above sea level. The site is still being studied by staff members of the National Institute of Archaeology and History, which built the small information center at the entrance. You need a guide and driver to get here; make arrangements at El Fuerte de San Diego. ☎ 744/482–3828 for tours ☲ Free ☾ Daily 9–5.

❾ **La Quebrada.** Way above downtown Acapulco, La Quebrada (literally "gorge"; in this case cliffs) is home to the Plaza las Glorias El Mirador hotel, *the* place for tourists in the 1940s. These days most visitors come here to see the clavadistas jump from a height of 130 ft daily at 1 PM and evenings at 7:30, 8:30, 9:30, and 10:30. The dives are thrilling, so be sure to arrive early. Before they take the plunge, the divers say a prayer at a small shrine on the cliffs. Sometimes they dive in pairs; often they carry torches. The hotel's La Perla supper club is the traditional and most comfortable viewing spot, but you'll be obligated to buy a drink or buffet package for $25 or $40, respectively. (Be forewarned: the tequila, rum, and brandy here are watered down, but the fees include tips for the wait staff and the divers.) You can also see the divers from the general observation deck next to the hotel (about $2). When you exit, divers may be waiting to greet you. Many people tip them; they get paid very little for risking their lives.

FodorsChoice
★

❽ **Zócalo.** Old Acapulco's hub is this shaded plaza, overgrown with dense trees. All day it's filled with vendors, shoe-shine men, and people lining up to use the pay phones. After siesta, they drift here to meet and greet. On Sunday evening there's often music in the bandstand. The zócalo fronts **Nuestra Señora de la Soledad** (Our Lady of Solitude) the town's modern but unusual church, with its stark-white exterior and bulb-shaped blue-and-yellow spires. The church hosts the festive Virgin of Guadalupe celebration on December 12. ⊠ *Bounded by Calle Felipe Valle on the north, Av. Costera Miguel Alemán on the south, Calle J. Azueta on the west, and Calle J. Carranza on the east, Old Acapulco.*

need a
break?

Just off the zócalo is **Sanborns,** a store that sells books, souvenirs, and sundries and has a restaurant. Locals and visitors often linger for hours over a newspaper and a cup of coffee here. **Cafetería Astoria** is a little outdoor café on the zócalo where businesspeople stop for breakfast before work or meet mid-morning for a cappuccino and a sweet roll.

Beaches

In the past few years, city officials made a great effort to clean up the Bahía de Acapulco, and maintaining it is a priority. Although vending on the beach has been outlawed, you'll probably still be approached by souvenir hawkers. Some beaches, such as Revolcadero and Pie de la Cuesta, have very strong undertows and surf, so swimming isn't advised. You can always follow the lead of the Mexican cognoscenti and enjoy the waters at your hotel pool.

Barra Vieja. About 27 km (17 mi) east of Acapulco, between Laguna de Tres Palos and the Pacific, this long stretch of uncrowded beach is

THREE DAYS ON THE CHEAP

A VACATION IN ACAPULCO needn't drain your wallet dry. Some of the best things to do are inexpensive, if not entirely free. And choosing your lodging with care will save still more money. The cliff-side Los Flamingos in Old Acapulco is a good bet; not only do the affordable rates include transportation to the beach and downtown, but a stay here means that you're following in the footsteps of such Hollywood celebrities as Fred MacMurray and Johnny Weissmuller. One of Acapulco's best deals, however, is the charming Boca Chica: it's next to Playa Caleta, and its rates include a full (and substantial) breakfast.

Day One: Spend the morning sunning on Playa Caleta. Have lunch at La Cabaña, a beachside seafood place with a bit of history. Early in the afternoon, take the bus into Old Acapulco and tour the Fuerte de San Diego; exhibits in its museum recount Acapulco's history. The neighboring Casa de Mascaras has displays of hand-carved indigenous ceremonial masks. Have dinner at La Casa de Tere, a real local joint.

Day Two: Hit Old Acapulco's Mercado Municipal late in the morning. Remember to bargain as you browse through its stalls of crafts, cotton blouses, and leather belts.

Drop into one of the zócalo's cafés for a late-afternoon bite. Afterward have a seat on a bench and watch the world go by, before wandering to the waterfront. Splurge on a $20 ticket for a sunset cruise—with drinks and dancing—on the Bonanza or economize and head to the viewing platform at the Plaza las Glorias El Mirador hotel to watch the divers at La Quebrada. Afterward take a cab to Zorrito's for dinner.

Day Three: Late in the morning or early in the afternoon, take a bus to Pie de la Cuesta, a strip of beach west of downtown. Spend the day here sunbathing and snacking. Hang around for what is arguably Acapulco's most brilliant sunset or take a cab or bus to the Playa Condesa and the Fiesta Americana Condesa hotel—its bar is always fun, particularly during happy hours when drinks are really cheap. Affordable restaurants nearby include Beto's and Carlos 'n' Charlie's.

---

somewhat more inviting than Pie de la Cuesta because the drive out is much more pleasant. Most people make the trip out here for the solitude and to feast on *pescado à la talla* (red snapper marinated in spices and grilled over hot coals).

Playa Caleta and Playa Caletilla. On the southern peninsula in Old Acapulco, these two beaches rivaled La Quebrada as the main tourist area in Acapulco's heyday. Now they attract families. Boats to Isla la Roqueta leave from here.

Playa Condesa. Referred to as "the strip," this stretch of sand facing the middle of Bahía de Acapulco has more than its share of visitors, especially singles. The restaurants that line it are lively joints.

Playa Hornos and Playa Hornitos. Running from the Plaza las Glorias Paraíso to Las Hamacas hotel, these beaches are packed shoulder to shoulder on weekends with locals and visitors who know a good thing: graceful palms shade the sand, and there are scads of casual eateries within walking distance.

Playa Icacos. Stretching from the naval base to El Presidente hotel, away from the famous strip, this beach is less populated than others on the Costera. The morning waves are especially calm.

FodorśChoice **Pie de la Cuesta.** You'll need a car or cab to reach this relatively unpopulated
★ spot, about a 25-minute drive west of downtown. A string of simple, thatched-roof restaurants and new, rustic inns border the wide beach, and straw palapas provide shade. What attracts people to Pie de la Cuesta, besides the long expanse of beach and spectacular sunsets, is beautiful Laguna Coyuca, a favorite spot for waterskiing, freshwater fishing, and boat rides. The boats will ferry you to La Laguna restaurant, where, some people claim, the pescado à la talla is even better than at Barra Vieja.

Playa Puerto Marqués. Tucked below the airport highway, this strand is popular with Mexican tourists, so it tends to get crowded on weekends.

Playa Revolcadero. A wide, sprawling beach fronting the Fairmont Pierre Marqués and Fairmont Acapulco Princess hotels, its water is shallow and its waves are fairly rough. People come here to surf and ride horses.

WHERE TO EAT

Every night the restaurants fill up, and every night you can sample a different cuisine, whether you opt to head for a greasy spoon serving regional favorites to an eatery with the finest international dishes. On the Costera Miguel Alemán are dozens of beachside eateries with *palapa* (palm frond) roofs, as well as wildly decorated rib and hamburger joints popular with visitors under 30—not necessarily in age, but definitely in spirit.

Loud music blares from many restaurants along the Costera, especially those facing Playa Condesa, and proprietors will aggressively try to hustle you inside with offers of drink specials. If you're looking for a hassle-free evening, avoid this area or decide in advance precisely where you want to dine. Most establishments that cater to visitors purify their drinking and cooking water.

At the best places in town, a main dish of meat or fish can run up to $60, and the atmosphere and views are fantastic. Ties and jackets are out of place, but so are shorts or jeans. Unless stated otherwise, all restaurants are open daily for lunch and dinner; dinner-only places open around 6:30 or 7.

WHAT IT COSTS				
$$$$	$$$	$$	$	¢
DINING over $25	$15–$25	$10–$15	$5–$10	under $5

Prices are per person for a main course at dinner, excluding tax and tip.

Acapulco Diamante

Italian

$$$–$$$$ ✕ **Casa Nova.** Casa Nova is carved out of a cliff that rises from Bahía de Acapulco. The views, both from the terrace and the air-conditioned dining room, are spectacular, the service is impeccable, and the Italian cuisine is divine. You can choose the fixed-price *menu turístico* or order à la carte. Favorites include lobster tail, linguine *alle vongole* (with clams, tomato, and garlic), and *costoletta di vitello* (veal chops with mushrooms). ⊠ *Carretera Escénica 5256, Las Brisas* ☎ *744/446–6237* ⚒ *Reservations essential* 🖃 *AE, MC, V* ☯ *No lunch.*

Mexican

★ $$-$$$$ ✕**Hacienda.** Personable, efficient waiters dress as classy *charros* (Mexican cowboys with silver-studded outfits) and mariachis entertain at this restaurant in a colonial hacienda, once a millionaire's estate. The menu has such dishes as sautéed oysters from Loreto (Baja California) served with chile-poblano mousseline. Besides seafood, chateaubriand made with Black Angus tenderloin is a specialty. Sunday sees a champagne brunch for $28. ✉ *Fairmont Acapulco Princess hotel, Playa Revolcadero Revolcadero* ☎ 744/469–1000 ▤ *AE, DC, MC, V* ⊘ *No lunch.*

Seafood

$$$-$$$$ ✕**La Vela.** On a wharf that juts out into Bahía de Puerto Marqués, this
Fodor'sChoice casual, open-air dining spot has wooden floors and a dramatic roof that
★ simulates a huge white sail. It's very atmospheric after dark, when the lights of Puerto Marqués flicker in the distance. A variety of fish and shellfish dishes are on the menu, but the specialty is the red snapper *à la talla* (basted with chili and other spices and broiled over hot coals). ✉ *Camino Real Acapulco Diamante, Carretera Escénica, Km 14, Acapulco Diamante* ☎ 744/466–1010 ▤ *AE, DC, MC, V.*

Costera

American

$$-$$$ ✕**Carlos 'n' Charlie's.** Although it's part of a large chain, this is an Acapulco landmark. It cultivates an atmosphere of controlled craziness: prankster waiters, a jokester menu, and eclectic decorations. The crowd is mostly young and relaxed, and the menu straddles the border, with ribs, stuffed shrimp, and oysters among the best offerings. ✉ *Av. Costera Miguel Alemán 112, Costera* ☎ 744/484–1285 or 744/484–0039 ▤ *AE,MC, V.*

$-$$$ ✕**Hard Rock Cafe.** This link in the international Hard Rock chain is one of Acapulco's most popular spots, and with good reason. The famous New York–cut steaks, hamburgers, and brownies, as well as the Southern-style fried chicken and ribs, are well prepared, and the portions are ample. The taped rock music begins at noon, and a live group starts playing at 11 PM (except Tuesday). ✉ *Av. Costera Miguel Alemán 37, Costera* ☎ 744/484–6680 ▤ *AE, MC, V.*

Contemporary

★ $$-$$$$ ✕**Baikal.** Modern, ultrachic Baikal is *the* place to see and be seen. The dining room has a white-on-white color scheme and 12-ft-high windows that frame the sparkling bay; sea-theme short films are shown from time to time on drop-down movie screens. The menu is small but select, with dishes that fuse French, Asian, and Mexican preparations and ingredients. Try the cold cream of cucumber soup spiced with mint and mild jalapeño; the sliced abalone with a *chipotle* (dried, smoked chilies) vinaigrette is also a good bet. Soft bossa nova and jazz play in the background. ✉ *Carretera Escénica 22, Costera* ☎ 744/446–6867 ⌚ *Reservations essential* ▤ *AE, DC, MC, V* ⊘ *Closed Mon. May–Nov. No lunch.*

Continental

$$$$ ✕**Madeiras.** At this local favorite, the bar-reception area has dramatic coffee tables whose glass tops rest on carved wooden animals; the dishes and flatware were created by Taxco silversmiths; and all tables have views of Bahía de Acapulco. Dinner is a four-course, prix-fixe meal. Specialties include tasty chilled soups and a delicious red snapper baked in sea salt (a Spanish dish); there are also steak choices. Seatings are every 30 minutes from 7 PM to 10:30 PM. Reserve well in advance on weekends and for Christmas and Easter week. ✉ *Carretera Escénica 33-B, just*

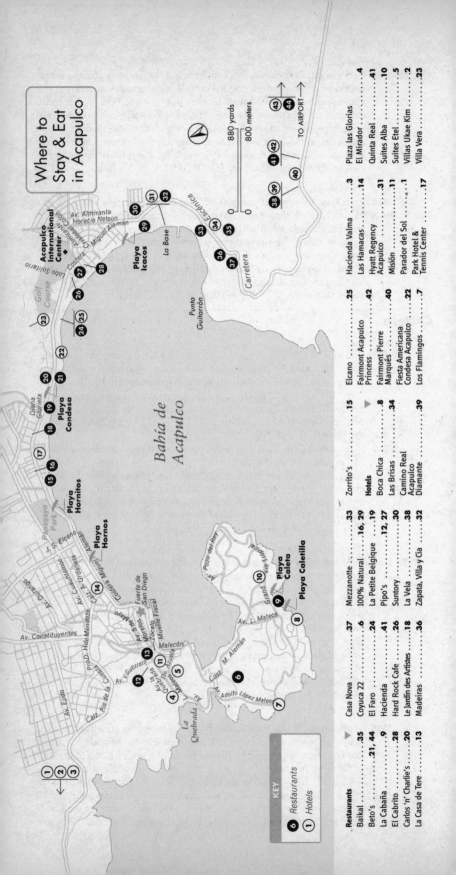

Where to Stay & Eat in Acapulco

KEY

6 *Restaurants*

1 *Hotels*

Restaurants

Baikal	35
Beto's	.....21, 44
La Cabaña	9
El Cabrito	28
Carlos 'n' Charlie's	20
La Casa de Tere	13
Casa Nova	37
Coyuca 22	6
El Faro	24
Hacienda	41
Hard Rock Cafe	26
Le Jardín des Artistes	18
Madeiras	36
Mezzanotte	33
100% Natural	...16, 29
La Petite Belgique	19
Pipo's	.....12, 27
Suntory	30
La Vela	38
Zapata, Villa y Gia	32
Zorrito's	15

Hotels

Boca Chica	8
Las Brisas	34
Camino Real Acapulco	...22
Los Flamingos	7
Elcano	25
Fairmont Acapulco Princess	...42
Fairmont Pierre Marqués	...40
Fiesta Americana Condesa Acapulco	...22
Diamante	39
Hacienda Valma	3
Las Hamacas	14
Hyatt Regency Acapulco	...31
Misión	11
Parador del Sol	1
Park Hotel & Tennis Center	...17
Plaza las Glorias	4
El Mirador	41
Quinta Real	10
Suites Alba	5
Suites Etel	2
Villas Ukae Kim	2
Villa Vera	23

880 yards

800 meters

TO AIRPORT

past La Vista shopping center, Costera ☎ 744/446–5636 ⌒ *Reservations essential* ▤ *AE, MC, V* ⊘ *No lunch.*

$$–$$$$ ✕ **La Petite Belgique.** Mexican-born Yolanda Brassart, who spent years in Europe studying the culinary arts, reigns in the kitchen of this small bistro. You're greeted by the enticing aromas of goose-liver pâté, home-baked breads, and apple strudel. The menu changes every three months but usually includes boned duck stuffed with almonds and mushrooms and served with a white wine and mushroom sauce. ⊠ *Plaza Marbella, Costera* ☎ 744/484–7725 ▤ *AE, MC, V.*

French

$$$–$$$$ ✕ **Le Jardín des Artistes.** Tables at this thoroughly French garden hideaway have fresh flowers and Tiffany lamps, and discreet waiters deliver dishes made rich by classic cream and butter sauces. The Swiss chef has gained a local following thanks to his delicious escargots in garlic butter, red-snapper fillet with savory mustard sauce, and smoked trout soufflé. After dinner, stroll through the snazzy art gallery. ⊠ *Calle Vicente Yañez Pinzón 11, Costera* ☎ 744/484–8344 ⌒ *Reservations essential* ▤ *AE,MC, V* ⊘ *Closed Sun.–Wed. in Sept. and Oct. No lunch.*

Health Food

¢–$ ✕ **100% Natural.** Along the Costera Miguel Alemán are several of these 24-hour restaurants that specialize in quick service and light, healthful food: sandwiches made with whole-wheat bread, soy burgers, chicken dishes, yogurt shakes, fruit salads. You'll recognize these eateries by their green signs with white lettering. The original—and best—is across from the Acapulco Plaza hotel. ⊠ *Av. Costera Miguel Alemán 200, near Acapulco Plaza, Costera* ☎ 744/485–3982 ⊠ *Av. Costera Miguel Alemán 3111, next to Oceanic 2000, Costera* ☎ 744/484–8440 ▤ *MC, V.*

Italian

$$–$$$$ ✕ **Mezzanotte.** You may end up dancing with your waiter—perhaps atop a table—on a Friday or Saturday evening; you'll definitely end up mixing with the who's who of Acapulco just about any night of the week. The stylish interior has a large sunken dining area, original sculptures, and huge bay windows looking out to sea. Clients rave about the fettuccine with smoked salmon in avocado sauce and the charcoal-grilled sea bass with shrimp and artichokes in a citrus sauce. For a light ending to the meal, there's gelato. ⊠ *Carretera Escénica 28–1, in La Vista shopping center, Costera* ☎ 744/446–5727 ▤ *AE,MC, V.*

Japanese

$$$$ ✕ **Suntory.** You can dine either in a blessedly air-conditioned room or in the delightful Asian-style garden. It's one of Acapulco's few Japanese restaurants and one of the few deluxe places that's open for lunch. Most diners opt for the *teppanyaki* (thin slices of beef and vegetables seared on a hot grill), prepared at your table by skilled chefs. ⊠ *Av. Costera Miguel Alemán 36, across from La Palapa hotel, Costera* ☎ 744/484–8088 ▤ *AE, MC, V.*

Mexican

$–$$$$ ✕ **Zapata, Villa y Cia.** The music and the food are strictly local, and the memorabilia recalls the Mexican Revolution—guns, hats, and photographs of Pancho Villa. The highlight of an evening is a visit from a sombrero-wearing baby burro, so be sure to bring your camera. (If per chance the burro is missing, it's likely that the search is on for a younger one.) The menu has the ever popular fajitas, tacos, and grilled meats. ⊠ *Hyatt Regency Acapulco, Av. Costera Miguel Alemán 1, Costera* ☎ 744/469–1234 ▤ *AE, DC, MC, V* ⊘ *No lunch.*

$–$$$ ✕ **El Cabrito.** As the name implies, goat is a specialty of this restaurant—here it's served charcoal-grilled. You can also choose from among such truly Mexican dishes as chicken in *mole* (spicy chocolate-chili sauce); shrimp in tequila; and jerky with egg, fish, and seafood. ⊠ *Av. Costera Miguel Alemán, between CiCi and Centro Internacional, Costera* ☎ 744/484–7711 ⊟ *MC, V.*

★ **$–$$$** ✕ **Zorrito's.** When Julio Iglesias is in town, he heads to this open-air, street-side eatery after the discos close. It's open almost all the time, serving Acapulco's famous green-and-white *pozole* (pork and hominy soup) as well as such steak dishes as *filete tampiqueña* (a strip of tender grilled beef), which comes with tacos, enchiladas, guacamole, and beans. ⊠ *Av. Costera Miguel Alemán and Calle Anton de Alaminos, next to Banamex, Costera* ☎ 744/485–3735 ⊟ *MC, V* ⊙ *Closed 7 AM–9 AM Mon. and Wed.–Sun and 7 AM–2 PM Tues.*

Seafood

$$–$$$$ ✕ **El Faro.** Classy El Faro resembles a lighthouse, right down to its nautical interior, with portholes and gleaming sculptures that evoke anchors and waves. Spanish chef Jorge Pereira adds Basque and Mediterranean touches to his original creations. For starters, there's a lettuce salad with goat cheese, dried wild fruits, and herb-infused olive oil. Favorite main dishes are haddock with clams and seared tuna medallions with baby onions. A pianist tickles the ivories Tuesday–Sunday, 9 PM–midnight. ⊠ *Elcano hotel, Av. Costera Miguel Alemán 75, Costera* ☎ 744/484–3100 ⊟ *AE, MC, V.*

$–$$$$ ✕ **Beto's.** By day you can eat right on the beach and enjoy live music; by night this palapa-roof restaurant is transformed into a romantic dining area lighted by candles and paper lanterns. Whole red snapper, lobster, and ceviche are recommended. At the Barra Vieja beach branch, the specialty is pescado à la talla. ⊠ *Av. Costera Miguel Alemán at Playa Condesa, Costera* ☎ 744/484–0473 ⊠ *Barra Vieja* ☎ 744/444–6071 ⊟ *AE, MC, V.*

★ **$–$$$$** ✕ **Pipo's.** On a rather quiet stretch of the Costera, this old, family-run restaurant doesn't have an especially interesting view, but locals come here for the fresh fish, good service, and reasonable prices for most dishes. Try the *huachinango veracruzano* (red snapper baked with tomatoes, peppers, onion, and olives) or the fillet of fish in *mojo de ajo* (garlic butter). The original location downtown is also popular with locals. ⊠ *Av. Costera Miguel Alemán and Nao Victoria, across from Acapulco International Center, Costera* ☎ 744/484–0165 ⊠ *Calle Almirante Bretón 3, Old Acapulco* ☎ 744/482–2237 ⊟ *AE, MC, V.*

Old Acapulco

Continental

$$$–$$$$ ✕ **Coyuca 22.** More celebrities have eaten at Acapulco's most beautiful restaurant than you can shake a stick at. You sit gazing down on Doric pillars, statuary, an enormous illuminated obelisk, a small pool, and the bay beyond; it's like eating in a partially restored Greek ruin. Choose from two fixed menus or order à la carte; all dishes are artful. Seafood and prime rib are specialties. ⊠ *Av. Coyuca 22 (10-min taxi ride from the zócalo), Old Acapulco* ☎ 744/482–3468 or 744/483–5030 ⊛ *Reservations essential* ⊟ *AE, MC, V* ⊙ *Closed Apr. 30–Nov. 1.*

Mexican

$–$$$ ✕ **La Casa de Tere.** Hidden in a commercial district downtown (signs point the way), this spotless, open-air eatery is in a league of its own—expect beer-hall tables and chairs, colorful Mexican decorations, and photos of Acapulco of yore. The varied menu includes outstanding *sopa* *de tortilla* (tortilla soup), chicken mole, and flan. The fixed-price lunch is only $6.50. ⊠ *Calle Alonso Martín 1721, 2 blocks from Av. Costera Miguel Alemán, Old Acapulco* ☎ *744/485–7735* ▤ *No credit cards* ⊘ *Closed Mon.*

Seafood

$–$$$ ✕ **La Cabaña.** In the 1950s, this local favorite, which is run by the Alvarez family, was a bohemian hangout that attracted renowned bullfighters as well as Mexican songwriter Agustín Lara and his lady love, María Félix. You can see their photo over the bar and sample the same dishes that made the place famous then: baby-shark tamales, seafood casserole, or shrimp prepared with sea salt, curry, or garlic. The restaurant is smack in the middle of Playa Caleta, and there are free lockers for diners who want to take a swim. ⊠ *Playa Caleta Lado Ote. s/n, Fracc. las Playas (a 5-min taxi ride east of town square), Old Acapulco* ☎ *744/ 482–5007* ▤ *AE, MC, V.*

WHERE TO STAY

Accommodations run the gamut from sprawling, big-name complexes with endless amenities to small, family-run inns where hot water is a luxury. Wherever you stay, prices will be reasonable compared with those in the United States. Service is generally good as well: Acapulqueños have been catering to visitors for more than half a century.

Acapulco Diamante is home to some of Mexico's most luxurious hotels—so lush and well equipped that most guests don't budge from the minute they arrive. Its beach, Playa Revolcadero, is too rough for swimming, though, and the heart of Acapulco is a 25-minute, $8–$14 taxi ride away.

There's much more activity on Avenida Costera Miguel Alemán, with its many discos, shops, restaurants. All the Costera properties have freshwater pools and sundecks, and most have restaurants and/or bars overlooking or on the beach. Hotels across the street are almost always less expensive than those directly on the beach; because there are no private beaches in Acapulco, all you have to do is cross the road to enjoy the sand.

Downtown Acapulco's beaches and restaurants are popular with Mexican vacationers. The hotels attract Canadian and European bargain-hunters. To the west, Pie de la Cuesta is peppered with nondescript inns and rustic lodges, where a beachside location might just be more a common characteristic than hot running water. For nightlife or shopping, you'll have to go into Acapulco proper.

WHAT IT COSTS				
$$$$	**$$$**	**$$**	**$**	**¢**
LODGING over $250	$150–$250	$75–$150	$50–$75	under $50

Price categories are assigned based on the range between the least and most expensive standard double rooms in high season based on the European Plan (EP, with no meals) unless otherwise noted. Tax (17%) is extra.

Acapulco Diamante

★ **$$$$** ▦ **Camino Real Acapulco Diamante.** This stunning hotel is at the foot of a lush hill on exclusive Playa Pichilingue, far from the madding crowd. All rooms are done in pastels and have tile floors, luxurious baths, and such up-to-date amenities as laptop-size safes outfitted with chargers;

all rooms also have balconies or terraces with a view of peaceful Puerto Marqués bay. Eleven extra-spacious club rooms have their own concierge and extra amenities. ⊠ *Calle Baja Catita (off Carretera Escénica at Km 14), Acapulco Diamante, 39867* ☎ *744/466–1010; 800/722–6466 in the U.S.* 🖷 *744/466–1111* ⊕ *www.caminoreal.com/acapulco* ⇨ *145 rooms, 11 suites* ♿ *3 restaurants, room service, in-room safes, minibars, cable TV, golf privileges, tennis court, 3 pools, gym, spa, beach, snorkeling, boating, waterskiing, fishing, 2 bars, baby-sitting, children's programs (ages 5–15), laundry service, concierge, meeting room, car rental, travel services, no-smoking rooms* ☰ *AE, DC, MC, V* ⦿ *BP, EP.*

$$$$

Fodor's Choice

★

🏨 **Fairmont Acapulco Princess.** The Princess is one of those places that seems to lure the rich and famous (Howard Hughes once hid away in a suite here). Near the reception desk, fantastic ponds with waterfalls and a slatted bridge hint at the luxury throughout. Large, airy rooms have cane furniture, marble floors, and such high-tech features as wireless Internet access. You can dine in seven excellent restaurants, and get in a match at the tennis center, which hosts international tournaments. The Spa Willow Stream, open to guests and nonguests, has aromatherapy, thalassotherapy, body wraps, and other treatments as well as a fitness center, hair salon, Jacuzzi, sauna, and Swiss showers. ⊠ *Playa Revolcadero Revolcadero* ☎ *(A.P. 1351, 39300)* ☎ *744/469–1000; 800/441–1414 in the U.S.* 🖷 *744/469–1016* ⊕ *www.fairmont.com* ⇨ *927 rooms, 92 suites* ♿ *6 restaurants, café, room service, in-room safes, cable TV, 18-hole golf course, 11 tennis courts, 5 pools, health club, hair salon, spa, beach, snorkeling, boating, waterskiing, fishing, basketball, 3 bars, dance club, shops, baby-sitting, children's programs (ages 3–12), laundry service, concierge, business services, meeting room, car rental, travel services* ☰ *AE, DC, MC, V* ⦿ *EP, MAP.*

★ **$$$$**

🏨 **Fairmont Pierre Marqués.** You're doubly blessed if you stay at this hotel, which was built as a beach hideaway for J. Paul Getty in 1958: you have access to all the Fairmont Acapulco Princess's facilities *and* peace and quiet. There's a hint of hacienda here, with the red-tile roofs, natural wood furniture, and ceiling fans. Choose from standard rooms, executive premier (with small refrigerators) rooms, suites, villas, and duplex bungalows (with private patios). ⊠ *Playa Revolcadero, Revolcadero* ☎ *(A.P. 1351, 39907)* ☎ *744/466–1000; 800/441–1414in the U.S.* 🖷 *744/466–1046* ⊕ *www.fairmont.com* ⇨ *220 rooms, 74 executive premier rooms, 25 suites, 10 villas* ♿ *2 restaurants, room service, in-room safes, minibars, some refrigerators, cable TV, 18-hole golf course, 5 tennis courts, 3 pools, beach, bar, shops, baby-sitting, children's programs (ages 3–12), playground, laundry service, concierge, meeting room, car rental, travel services* ☰ *AE, DC, MC, V.*

$$$$

🏨 **Quinta Real.** A member of Mexico's most prestigious hotel chain, this low-slung hillside resort overlooks the sea in the posh Punta Diamante area, about a 15-minute drive from downtown Acapulco. The 74 suites have balconies, marble floors, Mexican-made hardwood furniture, earth-tone rugs and fabrics, and closet door handles shaped like iguanas—a signature motif. The beach here is lovely and seemingly endless. ⊠ *Paseo de la Quinta Lote 6, Desarrollo Turmstico Real Diamante, Acapulco Diamante 39907* ☎ *744/469–1500; 800/457–4000 in the U.S.* 🖷 *744/469–1515* ⊕ *www.quintareal.com* ⇨ *74 suites* ♿ *Restaurant, room service, cable TV, 4 pools, gym, spa, beach, snorkeling, boating, fishing, bar, baby-sitting, laundry service, concierge, Internet, car rental* ☰ *AE, DC, MC, V.*

$$$–$$$$

🏨 **Las Brisas.** Las Brisas is a hilltop haven that's particularly popular with honeymooners. The complex has a variety of quarters—from one-bedroom units to deluxe private casitas complete with small private pools—that all have beautiful bay views. As the facilities are very spread out, transportation is by white-and-pink Jeep; you can rent one for $75 a day or wait for a staffer to pick you up, though the wait can be up to 20 minutes. A stylish Continental breakfast is delivered to your room each morning. There's a Fiesta Mexicana show every Saturday from December to April. ✉ *Carretera Escénica 5255, Las Brisas, 39868* ☎ *744/ 469–6900; 888/559–4329 in the U.S. and Canada* 🖷 *744/484–2269* ⊕ *www.brisas.com.mx* ⇋ *300 units* ♿ *2 restaurants, in-room data ports, 5 tennis courts, 3 pools, exercise equipment, hair salon, hot tub, sauna, snorkeling, boating, fishing, 2 bars, dry cleaning, laundry service, concierge, meeting room, car rental, travel services* ▤ *AE, DC, MC, V* ⊗ *CP.*

The Costera

$$$$ 🏨 **Hyatt Regency Acapulco.** The Hyatt is popular with business travelers, conventioneers, and—thanks to its bold Caribbean color schemes and striking design—television producers, who have opted to use it as the setting for many a Mexican soap opera. It has everything you need and more, including four outstanding eateries (one of them a kosher restaurant), a spa, and a deluxe shopping area. It's also the only hotel in Latin America with an on-site synagogue, supervised by the orthodox rabbinate of Mexico City. The west side of the property insulates you from the noise of the maneuvers of the nearby naval base. ✉ *Av. Costera Miguel Alemán 1, Costera 39869* ☎ *744/469–1234; 800/633–7313 in the U.S. and Canada* 🖷 *744/484–3087* ⊕ *www.hyatt.com* ⇋ *607 rooms, 17 suites* ♿ *4 restaurants, snack bar, room service, in-room safes, minibars, cable TV, 5 tennis courts, 2 pools, gym, spa, beach, 3 bars, shops, baby-sitting, children's programs (ages 8–12) in high season only, laundry service, meeting room, business center, car rental, travel services, free parking* ▤ *AE, MC, V.*

★ $$$ 🏨 **Elcano.** Restored so that it has its original 1950s glamour, this perennial favorite is sparkling and fresh. Rooms are snappy in white and navy blue, with white-tile floors and modern bathrooms. There's a beachside restaurant with an outstanding breakfast buffet, a more elegant indoor restaurant, and a gorgeous pool that not only seems to float above the bay, but also has whirlpools built into its corners. ✉ *Av. Costera Miguel Alemán 75, Costera 39690* ☎ *744/484–1950; 800/972–2162 in the U.S.* 🖷 *744/484–2230* ⊕ *www.hotel-elcano.com* ⇋ *163 rooms, 17 suites* ♿ *2 restaurants, room service, minibars, cable TV, golf privileges, pool, gym, beach, snorkeling, boating, waterskiing, fishing, 2 bars, baby-sitting, laundry service, concierge, travel services* ▤ *AE, MC, V.*

$$$ 🏨 **Villa Vera.** A five-minute drive north of the Costera leads to the place where Elizabeth Taylor married Mike Todd and where Lana Turner settled for three years. That said, the glamour of what was once a very exclusive hotel is all in its history. Although some villas were once private homes and have their own pools, most accommodations are unremarkable. There's no beach, so the main pool with its swim-up bar is the hub. The Villa Vera Spa and Fitness Center, open to guests and nonguests, has exercise machines, free weights, milk baths, herbal wraps, algae treatments, and several types of massages. ✉ *Lomas del Mar 35, Costera* ⊡ *(A.P. 560, 39690)* ☎ *744/484–0333 or 888/554–2361* 🖷 *744/484–7479* ⊕ *www.clubregina.com* ⇋ *24 rooms, 25 suites, 6 villas* ♿ *Restaurant, minibars, cable TV, in-room VCRs, 4 tennis courts, 15 pools, fitness classes, gym, spa, bar, shop, laundry service, concierge, meeting room, car rental, travel services* ▤ *AE, MC, V.*

$$ 🏨 **Fiesta Americana Condesa Acapulco.** As it's right in the thick of the main shopping and restaurant district, the Condesa is ever popular with tour groups. It also has one of the liveliest lobby bars and is on one of

the best beaches in town, Playa Condesa. Rooms are done in pastel tones and have light-wood furniture and tile floors. ⊠ *Av. Costera Miguel Alemán 97, Costera 39690* ☎ *744/484–2828; 800/343–7821 in the U.S.* 🖶 *744/484–1828* ⊕ *www.fiestaamericana.com* ⤴ *492 rooms, 8 suites* ⅋ *2 restaurants, room service, minibars, cable TV, 2 pools, beach, parasailing, waterskiing, bar, shop, baby-sitting, children's programs (ages 4–12), dry cleaning, laundry service, concierge, business services, meeting room, car rental, travel services* ▤ *AE,MC, V* ⦿❘ *BP, EP.*

$$ 🏨 **Las Hamacas.** Rooms at this friendly, 1950s Acapulco hotel surround a large inner courtyard. It's across the street from the beach, a three-minute drive from downtown, and it has a lovely garden of coconut palms from its former days as a plantation. The spacious, light-filled rooms have contemporary wood furniture; those facing the leafy courtyard are tranquil. Junior suites sleep two adults and two children. A stay here gets you access to a beach club. ⊠ *Av. Costera Miguel Alemán, Costera 39670* ☎ *744/483–7006* 🖶 *744/483–0575* ⊕ *www.hamacas.com.mx* ⤴ *100 rooms, 20 suites* ⅋ *Restaurant, room service, cable TV, golf privileges, 2 pools, hair salon, paddle tennis, Ping-Pong, bar, shop, meeting room, travel services, free parking* ▤ *MC, V.*

$$ 🏨 **Park Hotel & Tennis Center.** A helpful staff, a savvy Bulgarian manager, and a prime location make this an appealing place to stay. Rooms, which have colonial-style furnishings are around a garden with a good-size pool. Some have kitchenettes and balconies; all are spotlessly clean and well priced. The Park has an excellent tennis center, and it's only a block to the beach. ⊠ *Av. Costera Miguel Alemán 127, Costera* 🖉*(A.P. 269, 39670)* ☎ *744/485–5992* 🖶 *744/485–5489* ⤴ *88 rooms* ⅋ *Cable TV, 3 tennis courts, pool, bar, shops, car rental, free parking* ▤ *MC, V.*

Old Acapulco

$$ 🏨 **Boca Chica.** German visitors love this Old Acapulco mainstay, right down to its antique switchboard. It's a few steps from a swimming cove, and the open-air lobby has lovely views of Bahía de Caletilla. Rooms are small—with old-fashioned slats on the door, little balconies, and nondescript furnishings—but they're very clean and fresh. The pretty palapa restaurant serves 20 varieties of sushi; there's also a landscaped jungle garden and a pool. The Mexican breakfasts are ample. ⊠ *Playa Caletilla, across the bay from Isla la Roqueta and Mágico Mundo Marino, Old Acapulco 39390* ☎ *744/483–7641; 800/346–3942 in the U.S.* 🖶 *744/483–9513* ⊕ *http://acapulco-bocachica.com* ⤴ *42 rooms, 3 suites* ⅋ *Restaurant, pool, beach, dive shop, snorkeling, fishing, bar, shops, laundry service, car rental, free parking* ▤ *MC, V* ⦿❘ *BP.*

★ $$ 🏨 **Los Flamingos.** Almost a historical monument, this hot-pink, cliff-side hotel was the favored hangout of John Wayne, Johnny ("Tarzan") Weissmuller, and the rest of the gang from Hollywood back in the 1950s. Today it draws Europeans for its fine views and its *coco locos,* (rum drinks served in a green coconut, Acapulco's signature concoctions), which barman Esteban Castañeda will tell you were invented here in the 1960s. Rooms have bright pink walls and spartan, shower-only baths. Weissmuller liked to stay in the circular two-bedroom master suite. The hotel provides free transportation to the beach and downtown. ⊠ *Av. López Mateos, Fracc. las Playas, Old Acapulco 39390* ☎ *744/482–0690* 🖶 *744/483–9806* ⊕ *www.acapulco-cvb.org/losflamingos* ⤴ *46 rooms, 2 suites* ⅋ *Restaurant, pool, bar, laundry service, free parking* ▤ *MC, V.*

$ 🏨 **Plaza las Glorias El Mirador.** With its white walls, red-tile roofs, and hand-carved Mexican furnishings, El Mirador exudes nostalgia. It's on a hill with a knockout view of Bahía de Acapulco and La Quebrada, where the cliff divers perform. Many suites have refrigerators, hot tubs, and stunning ocean vistas. Note that rates here almost triple in mid-December and early January; if you're on a tight budget stay here some other time. ⊠ *Quebrada 74, Old Acapulco 39300* ☎ *744/483–1155; in 800/342–2644 the U.S.* ☏ *744/482–4564* ⊕ *www.sidek.com.mx* ⬦ *72 rooms, 58 suites* ⟁ *2 restaurants, minibars, some refrigerators, cable TV, 3 pools (1 saltwater), hair salon, sauna, bar, shops, children's programs (ages 3–12), laundry service, meeting room, travel services, free parking* ⊟ *AE,MC, V.*

$ ▦ **Suites Alba.** On a quiet hillside, the Alba is an all-suites hotel with bargain prices, which makes it popular with families. All guest quarters sleep four and have terraces; some have kitchenettes. You can ride a cable car to the hotel's beach club, which is on the bay and next to the Club de Yates and its 330-ft-long toboggan run. From mid-December to mid-April transportation from the hotel to Playa Caleta and downtown is free if you're staying more than one night. ⊠ *Grand Via Tropical 35, Old Acapulco 39390* ☎ *744/483–0073* ☏ *744/483–8378* ⊕ *www.acapulco-cvb.org/suites-alba* ⬦ *244 suites* ⟁ *3 restaurants, some kitchenettes, tennis court, 3 pools, hot tub, beach, bar, shops, laundry service* ⊟ *MC, V.*

$ ▦ **Suites Etel.** On Cerro Pinzona (Pinzona Hill), a five-minute walk from La Quebrada, the Etel has outstanding views of Bahía de Acapulco and spacious rooms with sturdy cedar furniture. All accommodations sleep three, and you can rent a full kitchen and dining room to turn your room into a suite; one studio has a kitchenette. There's a garden on the roof and children's play area by the pool. The owner, gracious Senora Etel Alvarez, is the great-grand-niece of John August Suter, whose gold mine launched the Gold Rush of 1849. ⊠ *Av. Pinzona 92, Old Acapulco 39390* ☎ *744/ 482–2240* ☏ *744/482–2241* ⬦ *12 rooms* ⟁ *Cable TV, fans, some kitchenettes, pool, fishing, car rental* ⊟ *No credit cards.*

¢ ▦ **Misión.** Two minutes from the zócalo, this charming, colonial-style hotel surrounds a greenery-rich courtyard with an outdoor dining area that's only open on Thursday (stop in for the green-and-white pozole). Rooms are small and by no means fancy, with wrought-iron beds, tile floors, painted brick walls, and ceiling fans. Every room has a shower, and there's plenty of hot water. The best rooms are on the second and third floors as you can open the windows and fully appreciate the view; the top-floor room is large but hot in the daytime. ⊠ *Calle Felipe Valle 12, Downtown 39300* ☎ *744/482–3643* ☏ *744/482–2076* ⬦ *20 rooms* ⟁ *Fans; no a/c, no room TVs* ⊟ *No credit cards.*

Pie de la Cuesta

$$$$ ▦ **Parador del Sol.** This all-inclusive's pink villas are scattered throughout gardens along both the lagoon and the Pacific Ocean sides of Carretera Pie de la Cuesta. The spacious rooms have tile floors and fan-cooled terraces with hammocks. In addition to all meals and domestic drinks, rates include shows, dance and aerobics classes, tennis, and nonmotorized water sports. ⊠ *Carretera Pie de la Cuesta–Barra de Coyuca, Km 5, Pie de la Cuesta* ✆ *(A.P. 1070, 39300)* ☎ *744/444–4050; 800/515–4321 in the U.S.* ☏ *744/444–4051* ⬦ *150 rooms* ⟁ *Restaurant, fans, cable TV, miniature golf, 4 tennis courts, 2 pools, fitness classes, gym, fishing, soccer, 2 bars, dance club, shops, children's programs (ages 5 –12), laundry service, meeting rooms, free parking* ⊟ *AE, DC, MC, V* ⦿ *All-inclusive.*

★ **$$** ▦ **Villas Ukae Kim.** You can't miss this colorful, rustic, seaside lodge. The large rooms are painted in bright Mexican hues, and all have terraces and mosquito nets slung over double beds; the honeymoon suite has a private hot tub. Rates includes $21-a-day credit in the restaurant, which is expensive but good and overlooks the beach. ⊠ *Av. Fuerza Aereo Mexicana 356, Pie de la Cuesta 39300* 📠 *744/460–2187* ⏎ *21 rooms, 1 suite* ⚭ *Restaurant, fans, pool, beach, waterskiing, fishing, bar, laundry service, free parking; no a/c in some rooms, no room phones, no room TVs* ▭ *No credit cards.*

$ 🏨 **Hacienda Valma.** Congenial hosts Philippe and Parwin run the Valma with European flair. Twenty white stucco bungalows, named after famous musicians and painters, line the beach. The plain rooms accommodate two, three, or five people and have huge beds protected by mosquito nets; bathrooms are tiny, and there's no hot water. The spa has a hot tub and massages, and the largest pool in Pie de la Cuesta. Rates spike on weekends when the hotel fills with embassy personnel from Mexico City. ⊠ *Av. Fuerza Aereo Mexicana 356, Pie de la Cuesta 39300* 📞 *744/460–2882* 📠 *744/460–0697* ⊕ *www.vayma.com.mx* ⏎ *20 rooms* ⚭ *Restaurant, fans, hot tub, massage, spa, pool, beach, waterskiing, boccie, horseback riding, volleyball, bar, laundry service, free parking; no a/c in some rooms* ▭ *No credit cards.*

NIGHTLIFE

Cultural Shows

The **Acapulco International Center** (⊠ Av. Costera Miguel Alemán, Costera 📞 744/484–3218) has a Mexican Fiesta show with mariachi bands, singers, and the *voladores* (flyers) from Papantla. These Veracruz Indians in traditional dress climb a 52-ft pole, wrap a rope around one foot, and slowly swing down while another performer sits atop the pole playing a flute—it's an ancient ritual honoring the sun. Performances are held on some Wednesday and Friday nights at 8. With an open bar and a buffet the cost is $52; the show alone is $30.

Dance Club

Salon Q (⊠ Av. Costera Miguel Alemán 23, Costera 📞 744/484–3252), the so-called Cathedral of Salsa, is a combination dance hall and disco, where the bands play salsas, merengues, and other Latin rhythms for young and old. Weekends see shows—mostly impersonations of Mexican entertainers—and dance contests.

Discos

Alebrije (⊠ Av. Costera Miguel Alemán 3308, across from Hyatt Regency, Costera 📞 744/484–5902) can accommodate 2,000 people in its love seats and booths. From 10:30 (opening time) to 11:30, the music is slow and romantic; afterward there's dance music and light shows until dawn. The most popular night is Friday, when everyone is bathed in foam.

Andromeda (⊠ Av. Costera Miguel Alemán 15, at Fragata Yucatán, Costera 📞 744/484–8815) is spectacular, even in a city known for its amazing discos. You enter via a torch-lit moat that leads to the Queen of the Sea's castle; inside, you feel as if you're in a submarine surrounded by mermaids. The place is packed with 18- to 25-year-olds dancing to the latest techno sounds. It's open daily from December to April and on weekends only May to November.

Baby O (⊠ Av. Costera Miguel Alemán 22, Costera 📞 744/484–7474) is a private club that's known to open its doors to select nonmembers. Eschewing the glitz and mirrors of Acapulco's older discos, it resembles a jungle cave. The crowd is 25 to 35 and mostly well-dressed, wealthy

Mexicans. As its name suggests **Discobeach** (⊠ Playa Condesa, Costera ☎ 744/484–8230) is right on the sands. It's so informal that the under-30 crowd sometimes even turns up in shorts. The waiters are young and friendly—some people find them overly so, and in fact, this is a legendary pickup spot. Every Wednesday, ladies' night, all the women receive flowers. During the day, you can try the bungee jump on the beach.

★ **Enigma** (⊠ Carretera Escénica, Costera ☎ 744/484–7164) has a lavish Egyptian theme and fantastic sound and light systems. It accommodates 700 at a central bar and in comfortable booths; a glass wall provides an unbelievable view of Bahía de Acapulco and, on weekends, a fireworks show. The music is enough of a mix so that there's something

★ for everyone; it all starts at 10:30. At **Palladium** (⊠ Carretera Escénica, Costera ☎ 744/481–0330), a waterfall cascades down from the dance-floor level. The dance floor itself is nearly surrounded by 50-ft-high windows, giving dancers a wraparound view of Acapulco. **Zucca** (⊠ Carretera

★ Escénica Costera ☎ 744/484–6727) attracts a 25-and-up crowd, mainly couples. People really dress up here, with the men in well-cut pants and shirts and the women in racy outfits and cocktail dresses. Singles gravitate toward the two bars in the back. Zucca is snug, and people come here early to dance to music from the '70s, '80s, and '90s. At 2 AM there's a fireworks display.

SPORTS & THE OUTDOORS

Bullfights

The season runs from about the first week of January to Easter, and *corridas* (bullfights) are held on Sunday at 5:30. Tickets are available through your hotel or at the window in the **Plaza de Toros** (⊠ Av. Circunvalación, across from Playa Caleta, Playa Caleta ☎ 744/482–1181) Monday–Saturday 10–2 and Sunday 10:30–5. Tickets in the shade (*sombra*)—the only way to go—cost about $16. Preceding the fight are performances of Spanish dances and music by the Chili Frito band.

Fishing

You can arrange trips through your hotel or at the Pesca Deportiva near the *muelle* (dock) across from the zócalo (just be sure to ask someone at your hotel about which companies are reliable). For freshwater fishing trips try the companies along Laguna Coyuca. Boats accommodating 4–10 people cost $250–$500 a day, $45–$60 by chair. Excursions leave about 7 AM and return at 1 PM or 2 PM. At the docks, you can hire a boat for $40 a day (two lines). You must get a fishing license ($8–$10, depending on the season) from the Secretaría de Pesca; there's a representative at the dock, but note that the office is closed during siesta, between 2 and 4 in the afternoon.

Golf

There's a public golf course at the **Club de Golf** (☎ 744/484–0781) on the Costera across from the Acapulco Malibú hotel. Greens fees are $37 for nine holes, $55 for 18. Two 18-hole championship golf courses are shared by the **Fairmont Acapulco Princess and Pierre Marqués hotels** (⊠ Playa Revolcadero, Revolcadero ☎ 744/469–1000). Make reservations well in advance. Greens fees are $70 for guests and $93 for nonguests. A round on the 18-hole course at the **Mayan Palace** (⊠ Playa Revolcadero, domicilio conocido, Revolcadero ☎ 744/469–0201) time-share condo complex is $66 for guests, $103 for nonguests. At **Tres Vidas**

(⊠ Carretera al Aeropuerto, domicilio conocido, Tres Vidas ☎ 744/444–5135), greens fees are $180 for 18 holes before 2 PM, $150 afterward.

Jai Alai

The **Jai Alai Acapulco Race & Sports Book** (⊠ Av. Costera Miguel Alemán 498, Costera ☎ 744/484–3195) has two restaurants and a bar, and room for 1,500 spectators. The fast-paced games take place Thursday through Sunday at 9 PM, mid-December through January 6, Easter week, and throughout July and August. Entrance is $7. The slower-paced game of bingo is played year-round, and Sports Book, or betting on major U.S. sporting events, is also a 365-day activity.

Tennis

Court fees range from $9 to $26 an hour during the day and double in the evening. At hotel courts, nonguests pay about $6 more per hour. Lessons with English-speaking instructors start at about $15 an hour; ball boys get a $2 tip.

Costa Club (⊠ Costera ☎ 744/485–9050) has three hard-surface courts, two lighted. In addition to five outdoor courts, the **Fairmont Acapulco Princess** (⊠ Playa Revolcadero, Revolcadero ☎ 744/469–1000) has two air-conditioned indoor courts and a stadium that hosts international tournaments. The **Fairmont Pierre Marqués** (⊠ Playa Revolcadero, Revolcadero ☎ 744/466–1000) has five synthetic-grass courts.

Guests at the **Hyatt Regency Acapulco** (⊠ Av. Costera Miguel Alemán 1, Costera ☎ 744/484–1225) have access to three lighted courts at the Municipal Golf Club. The **Mayan Palace** (⊠ Playa Revolcadero, domicilio conocido, Revolcadero ☎ 744/469–1879) condo complex has 12 lighted clay courts. There are three lighted asphalt courts at the **Park Hotel & Tennis Center** (⊠ Av. Costera Miguel Alemán 127, Costera ☎ 744/485–5992). You'll find five courts at **Tiffany's Racquet Club** (⊠ Av. Villa Vera 120, Costera ☎ 744/484–7949). Some are asphalt and have lights, others are clay and don't. **Villa Vera** (⊠ Lomas del Mar 35, Costera ☎ 744/484–0333) has two lighted clay courts and two lighted hard-surface courts.

Water Sports

You can arrange to water-ski, rent broncos (one-person Jet Skis), parasail, and windsurf at outfitters on the beaches. Parasailing is an Acapulco highlight; a five-minute trip costs $60. Waterskiing is about $40 an hour; broncos cost $40–$95 for a half hour, depending on the size. You can arrange to windsurf at Playa Caleta and most beaches along the Costera, but the best place to actually do it is at Bahía Puerto Marqués. The main surfing beach is Revolcadero.

Arnold Brothers (⊠ Av. Costera Miguel Alemán 205, near El Fuerte de San Diego, Old Acapulco ☎ 744/482–1877) has been running scuba-diving excursions and snorkeling trips for almost 50 years. Scuba trips cost $35; snorkeling costs $20. Lessons are included.

Acapulco's latest attraction, the **Shotover Jet** (⊠ Continental Plaza, Av. Costera Miguel Alemán, Locale 3, Costera ☎ 744/484–1154) is a wild boat ride that's an import from the rivers around Queenstown, New Zealand. An air-conditioned bus takes you to a site near the town of Tierra Colorada, about 35 minutes outside of Acapulco. Twelve-passenger boats provide thrilling 30-minute boat rides on the Río Papagayo, complete with 360-degree turns—one of the Shotover Jet's trademarks—and vistas of local flora and fauna. The cost for the ride and transportation to and from the site is $60. For more thrills, you can shoot the rapids for $60 an hour with a guide. For both rides, you pay $90. You can throw some rock climbing into either package for the same price. Other activities include hiking, caving, and kayaking.

SHOPPING

Most shops are open Monday–Saturday 10–7. The main strip is along Avenida Costera Miguel Alemán from the Costa Club to El Presidente Hotel. Here you can find Guess, Peer, Aca Joe, Amarras, Polo Ralph Lauren, and other fashionable sportswear boutiques. The Costera is also home to branches of Aurrerá, Gigante, Price Club, Sam's, Wal-Mart, and Comercial Mexicana, as well as the upscale Liverpool department store (called Fabricas de Francia). These sell everything from liquor and fresh and frozen food to lightbulbs, clothing, medicines, garden furniture, and sports equipment. Instead of name shops Old Acapulco has inexpensive tailors, patronized by the Mexicans, and lots of souvenir shops.

Sanborns (✉ Av. Costera Miguel Alemán 1226, Costera ☎ 744/484–4413 ✉ Av. Costera Miguel Alemán 3111, Costera ☎ 744/484–2025 ✉ Av. Costera Miguel Alemán 209, Costera ☎ 744/482–6167 ✉ Av. Costera Miguel Alemán, off zócalo Old Acapulco ☎ 744/482–6168) is a very un-Mexican store that is, nevertheless, an institution throughout Mexico. Among its many wares are English-language newspapers, magazines, and books, as well as a line of high-quality souvenirs. All branches are open 7 AM to midnight in high season and 7:30 AM–11 PM the rest of the year.

Malls

Malls in Acapulco range from the delightful air-conditioned shopping arcade at the Princess hotel to rather gloomy collections of shops that sell cheap jewelry and embroidered dresses. **Aca Mall,** which is next door to Marbella Mall, is all white and marble; here you'll find Tommy Hilfiger, Peer, and Aca Joe. The multilevel **Marbella Mall,** at the Diana *glorieta* (traffic circle), is home to Martí, a well-stocked sporting-goods store; a health center (drugstore, clinic, and lab); the Canadian Embassy; and Bing's Ice Cream. There are also several restaurants. **Plaza Bahía,** next to the Costa Club hotel, is an air-conditioned mall with boutiques such as Dockers, Nautica, and Aspasia.

Markets

In an effort to get the itinerant vendors off the beaches and streets, the local government set up a series of flea markets along the Costera, mostly uninviting dark tunnels of stalls that sell inexpensive souvenirs. The selections of archaeological-artifact replicas, bamboo wind chimes, painted wooden birds, shell earrings, and embroidered clothes begin to look identical. Although prices are low, it's good to comparison shop; bargaining is essential.

One large flea market with a convenient location is **La Diana Mercado de Artesanías,** a block from the Emporio hotel, close to the Diana monument in Costera. **El Mercado de Artesanías El Parazal** is a 15-minute walk from Sanborns downtown. You'll find fake ceremonial masks, the ever-present onyx chessboards, $20 hand-embroidered dresses, imitation silver, hammocks, and skin cream made from turtles (don't buy it, because turtles are endangered and you won't get it through U.S. Customs). From Sanborns downtown, head away from Avenida Costera to Vásquez de

León and turn right one block later. The market is open daily 9–9. Don't miss the **Mercado Municipal,** where restaurateurs load up on produce early in the morning, and, later in the day, locals shop for piñatas, serapes, leather goods, baskets, hammocks, amulets to attract lovers or ward off enemies, and velvet paintings of the Virgin of Guadalupe.

Specialty Shops

Art

Edith Matison's Art Gallery (⊠ Av. Costera Miguel Alemán 2010, across from Club de Golf, Costera ☎ 744/484–3084) shows the works of renowned international and Mexican artists—including Calder, Dalí, Siqueiros, and Tamayo—and a large line of Mexican crafts. **Galería Rudic** (⊠ Calle Vicente Yañez Pinzón 9, across from Continental Plaza and adjoining Jardín des Artistes restaurant, Costera ☎ 744/484–1004) has a good collection of top contemporary Mexican artists, including Armando Amaya, Leonardo Nierman, Gastón Cabrera, Trinidad Osorio, and Casiano García.

Pal Kepenyes (⊠ Guitarrón 140, Lomas Guitarrón ☎ 744/484–3738) gets good press for his jewelry and sculpture (some of it rather racy), on display in his workshop. **Sergio Bustamante** (⊠ Av. Costera Miguel Alemán 120–9, across from Fiesta American Condesa hotel, Costera ☎ 744/484–4992 ⊠ Hyatt Regency Acapulco, Av. Costera Miguel Alemán 1, Costera ☎ 744/469–1234) is known for his whimsical, painted papier-mâché and giant ceramic sculptures.

Clothing

Armando's (⊠ Hyatt Regency Acapulco, Av. Costera Miguel Alemán 1, Costera ☎ 744/484–5111 ⊠ Av. Costera Miguel Alemán 1252–7, in La Torre de Acapulco, Costera ☎ 744/469–1234) sells its own line of women's dresses, jackets, and vests with a Mexican flavor. It also has some interesting Luisa Conti accessories. **Esteban's** (⊠ Av. Costera Miguel Alemán 2010, across from Club de Golf, Costera ☎ 744/484–3084) has a clientele of international celebrities and many important local families. Its opulent evening dresses range from $200 to $3,000; daytime dresses average $120. There's a men's clothing section on the second floor. If you scour the sale racks, you can find some items marked down as much as 80%.

Nautica (⊠ Plaza Bahía, Costera ☎ 744/484–1650 ⊠ Las Brisas hotel, Carretera Escénica 5255, Las Brisas ☎ 744/485–7511) is stocked with stylish casual clothing for men. **Men's and Ladies** (⊠ Fairmont Acapulco Princess hotel arcade, Playa Revolcadero, Revolcadero ☎ 744/469–1000) has a smashing line of beach cover-ups and hand-painted straw hats, as well as Israeli bathing suits, Colombian sweaters, Walford body wear, and light dresses. **St. Germaine** (⊠ Av. Costera Miguel Alemán, at entrance to Fiesta Americana Condesa hotel, Costera ☎ 744/485–2515 ⊠ Costa Club, Av. Costera Miguel Alemán 123, Costera ☎ 744/487–3712) sells a sensational line of swimsuits for equally sensational bodies.

Handicrafts

Alebrijes & Caracoles (⊠ Plaza Bahía, Costera ☎ 744/485–0490) consists of two shops designed to look like flea-market stalls. Top-quality merchandise includes papier-mâché fruits and vegetables, Christmas ornaments, wind chimes, and brightly painted wooden animals from Oaxaca. **Arte Para Siempre** (⊠ Av. Costera Miguel Alemán 4834, near Hyatt Regency Acapulco, Costera ☎ 744/484–3624), in the Acapulco Cultural Center, sparkles with handicrafts from the seven regions of Guerrero. Look for hand-loomed shawls, painted gourds, hammocks, baskets, Olinalá boxes, and silver jewelry.

Silver & Jewelry

Buy articles described as being made from semiprecious stones or silver only in reputable establishments, lest you end up with cleverly painted paste or a silver facsimile called *alpaca*. Make sure that 0.925 is stamped on the silver piece; this verifies its authenticity.

Minette (⊠ Fairmont Acapulco Princess hotel arcade, Playa Revolcadero, Revolcadero ☎ 744/469–1000) has diamond jewelry of impeccable design by Charles Garnier and Nouvelle Bague. You'll also find jewelry set with Caledonia stones from Africa, plus Emilia Castillo's exquisite line of brightly colored porcelain ware, inlaid with silver fish, stars, and birds. **Suzett's** (⊠ Hyatt Regency Acapulco, Av. Costera Miguel Alemán 1, Costera ☎ 744/469–1234), a tony shop that's been around for years, has a laudable selection of gold and silver jewelry. **Tane** (⊠ Las Brisas hotel, Carretera Escénica 5255, Las Brisas ☎ 744/469–6900) carries small selections of the exquisite flatware, jewelry, and objets d'art created by one of Mexico's most prestigious (and expensive) silversmiths.

SIDE TRIP

Taxco

275 km (170 mi) north of Acapulco.

In Mexico's premier "silver city," marvelously preserved, white-stucco, red-tile-roof colonial buildings nuzzle cobblestone streets that wind up and down the foothills of the Sierra Madre. Taxco (pronounced *tahss-ko*) is a living work of art. For centuries its silver mines drew foreign mining companies. In 1928 the government made it a national monument. And today its charm, abundant sunshine, flowers, and silversmiths make it a popular getaway.

Hernán Cortés discovered Taxco's mines in 1522 while looking for lead for his armory. The silver rush lasted until the next century. In the 1700s, a Frenchman who Mexicanized his name to José de la Borda, discovered a rich lode that revitalized the silver industry and made him exceedingly wealthy. After Borda, however, Taxco's importance again faded, until the 1930s and the arrival of William G. Spratling, a writer-architect from New Orleans. Enchanted by the city and convinced of its potential as a center for silver jewelry, Spratling set up an apprentice shop. His artistic talent and fascination with pre-Columbian design combined to produce silver jewelry and other artifacts that soon earned Taxco its worldwide reputation as the Silver City once more. Spratling's inspiration lives on in his students and their descendants, many of whom are today's famous silversmiths.

Taxco's biggest cultural event is the Jornadas Alarconianos, which honors one of Mexico's greatest dramatists with plays, dance performances, and concerts in the third week of May. Many other fiestas are an integral part of the town's character, providing chances to honor almost every saint in heaven with music, dancing, and fireworks. Oh, yes. The town is also Mexico's fireworks capital, and its citizens demonstrate their pyrotechnic skills with set pieces—wondrous blazing "castles" made of bamboo.

Because of the byways, alleys, and tiny streets, maneuvering anything bigger than your two feet through Taxco is difficult, so it's good that almost everything of interest is within walking distance of the zócalo. Wear sensible shoes for negotiating the hilly streets. Just be advised that city's altitude is 5,800 ft, so if you've come from sea level, take it easy, particularly on your first day.

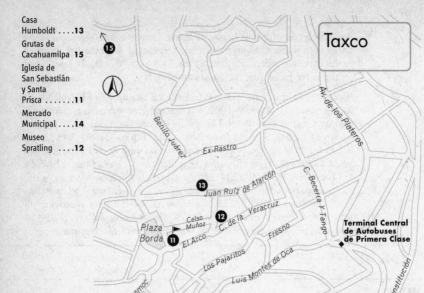

★ ⓫ The **Iglesia de San Sebastián y Santa Prisca** has dominated the busy, colorful Plaza Borda since the 18th century. Usually just called Santa Prisca, it was built by French silver magnate José de la Borda in thanks to the Almighty for Borda's having literally stumbled upon a rich silver vein. According to legend, St. Prisca appeared to workers during a storm and prevented a wall of the church from tumbling. Soon after, the church was named in her honor. The style of the church—a sort of Spanish Baroque—is known as churrigueresque, and its pale pink exterior have made it Taxco's most important landmark. Its facade, naves, and *bovedas* (vaulted ceilings), as well as important paintings by Mexican Juan Cabrera, are slowly being restored. ⊠ *Southwest side of Plaza Borda* ☎ *No phone* ⊙ *Daily 6 AM–9 PM.*

need a break? Around Plaza Borda are several *neverías* (ice cream stands) where you can treat yourself to ice cream in exotic flavors such as tequila, corn, avocado, or coconut. **Bar Paco**, directly across the street from Santa Prisca, is a Taxco institution; its terrace is the perfect vantage point for watching the comings and goings on the zócalo while sipping a margarita or a beer.

⓬ The former home of William G. Spratling houses the **Museo Spratling**. This small gallery explains the working of colonial mines and displays Spratling's collection of pre-Columbian artifacts. ⊠ *Calle Porfirio Delgado 1* ☎ *744/622–1660* ⊠ *$3* ⊙ *Tues.–Sat. 9–6, Sun. 9–3.*

⓭ **Casa Humboldt** was named for German adventurer Alexander von Humboldt, who stayed here in 1803. The Moorish-style, 18th-century house has a finely detailed facade. It now contains a wonderful little museum of colonial art. ⊠ *Calle Juan Ruíz de Alarcón 6* ☎ *7/622–5501* ⊠ *$2.25* ⊙ *Tues.–Sat. 10–5, Sun. 10–3.*

⑭ Saturday and Sunday mornings locals from surrounding towns come to sell and buy produce, crafts, and everything from peanuts to electrical appliances at the **Mercado Municipal.** It's directly down the hill from Santa Prisca. Look for the market's chapel to the Virgin of Guadalupe.

⑮ Mexico's largest caverns, the **Grutas de Cacahuamilpa** (Caves of Cacahuamilpa) are about 15 minutes northeast of Taxco. These 15 large chambers encompass 12 km (7½ mi) of geological formations. All the caves are illuminated, and a tour takes around two hours. 🎟 *$3 (includes tour).*

Where to Stay & Eat

You can find everything from tagliatelle to iguana in Taxco restaurants, and meals are much less expensive than in Acapulco. Dress is casual, but less so than at Acapulco resorts. There are several categories of hotel to choose from within Taxco's two types: the small inns nestled on the hills skirting the zócalo and the larger, more modern hotels on the outskirts of town.

$–$$$ ✕ **Señor Costilla.** The name of this whimsical restaurant translates as "Mr. Ribs." The Taxco outpost of the zany Anderson chain does, indeed, serve barbecued ribs and chops. There's great balcony seating overlooking the main square. ⊠ *Plaza Borda 1* ☎ *7/622–3215* ▤ *MC, V.*

$–$$ ✕ **Cielito Lindo.** This charming restaurant has a Mexican-international menu and a cozy patio. Give the Mexican specialties a try—for example, *pollo en pipian verde* (chicken simmered in a mild, pumpkin seed–based sauce). ⊠ *Plaza Borda 14* ☎ *7/622–0603* ▤ *MC, V.*

★ **$–$$** ✕ **El Mural.** You can eat indoors or out on a poolside terrace, where there's a view not only of a Juan O'Gorman mural but of the stunning Santa Prisca church. The chef prepares classic international surf-and-turf favorites as well as such Mexican specialties as cilantro soup and crepes with *huitlacoche* (corn fungus, a prehispanic delicacy that really is delicious). The daily three-course fixed-price meal is $14. ⊠ *Posada de la Misión, Cerro de la Misión 32* ☎ *762/622–2198* ▤ *AE, DC, MC, V.*

★ **¢–$$** ✕ **Hostería el Adobe.** The lack of a view (there are only two window tables) is more than made up for by the excellent food and such decorations as hanging lamps made of a cluster of masks. Favorite dishes include garlic-and-egg soup and the *queso adobe,* fried cheese on a bed of potato skins, covered with a green tomatillo sauce. ⊠ *Plazuela de San Juan 13* ☎ *7/622–1416* ▤ *MC, V.*

¢–$ ✕ **Santa Fe.** Mexican family-type cooking at its best is served in this simple place. Puebla-style mole, Cornish hen in garlic butter, and enchiladas in green or red chili sauce are among the tasty offerings. There's a daily *comida corrida* (fixed-price) meal for $5. ⊠ *Calle Hidalgo 2* ☎ *762/ 622–1170* ▤ *No credit cards.*

$$ 🏨 **De la Borda.** It may be a bit worn, but De la Borda is still a favorite with bus tours, and the staff couldn't be more hospitable. Ask for a room overlooking town. There's a restaurant and a large marble lobby. ⊠ *Cerro del Pedregal 2* ✉ *(A.P. 6, 40200)* ☎ *762/622–0025* 🖷 *762/ 622–0617* 🛏 *98 rooms, 3 suites* ⌂ *Restaurant, room service, pool, bar, laundry service, free parking* ▤ *AE, MC, V.*

$$ 🏨 **Monte Taxco.** A colonial style predominates at this hotel, which has a knockout view, a funicular, three restaurants, a disco, and nightly entertainment. It's a few miles from town, so plan to take taxis to get back and forth. ⊠ *Lomas de Taxco* ✉ *(A.P. 84, 40210)* ☎ *762/622–1300* 🖷 *762/622–1428* ✉ *montetaxco@silver.net.mx* 🛏 *153 rooms, 6 suites, 32 villas* ⌂ *3 restaurants, cable TV, 9-hole golf course, 3 tennis courts, horseback riding, dance club, laundry service* ▤ *AE, MC, V.*

★ **$$** 🏨 **Posada de la Misión.** Laid out like a colonial-style village, this hotel is within walking distance of town. Rooms range from standard doubles to two-bedroom suites with fireplaces and terraces. The pool area is adorned with a mural by noted Mexican artist Juan O'Gorman. ✉ *Cerro de la Misión 32* ✆ *(A.P. 88, 40230)* ☎ *762/622–0063* 🖷 *762/622–2198* ⌨ *120 rooms, 30 suites* ⚭ *Restaurant, some kitchenettes, cable TV, pool, bar, dance club, free parking* ⊟ *AE, DC, MC, V* ⦿ *MAP.*

$–$$ 🏨 **Rancho Taxco-Victoria.** Under the same management as De la Borda and like that hotel, this one is past its prime but exudes a certain charm. The simple rooms, however, are attractive and always freshly painted. There's also the requisite splendid view. ✉ *CalleCarlos J. Nibbi 5* ✆ *(A. P. 83, 40200)* ☎ *762/622–0210* 🖷 *762/622–0010* ⌨ *60 rooms, 4 suites* ⚭ *Restaurant, some cable TV, pool, bar* ⊟ *AE, MC, V.*

$ 🏨 **Agua Escondida.** Popular with some regular visitors to Taxco, this small hotel has simple rooms with Mexican-style furnishings. ✉ *Calle Guillermo Spratling 4, 40200* ☎ *762/622–1166* 🖷 *762/622–1306* ✉ *aguaesc@taxco.net* ⌨ *50 rooms* ⚭ *Restaurant, café, cable TV, pool, bar, free parking* ⊟ *MC, V.*

¢ 🏨 **Posada de los Castillo.** This in-town inn is straightforward, clean, and good for the price. The Emilia Castillo silver shop is off the lobby. ✉ *Juan Ruíz de Alarcón 7, 40200* ☎ *762/622–1396* ⌨ *14 rooms* ⚭ *No room phones, no TV in some rooms* ⊟ *No credit cards.*

¢ 🏨 **Posada de San Javier.** The secluded San Javier sprawls somewhat haphazardly around a garden with a pool and a wishing well. In addition to the rooms, there are seven one-bedroom apartments with living rooms and kitchenettes that are generally monopolized by wholesale silver buyers. ✉ *Calle Estacas 32 40200* ☎ *762/622-3177* 🖷 *762/622–2351* ⌨ *18 rooms, 7 apartments* ⚭ *Restaurant, some kitchenettes, cable TV, pool, bar* ⊟ *No credit cards.*

Nightlife

The **Bar Paco** (✉ Plaza Borda 12 ☎ 762/622–0064) is a traditional favorite. At **Bertha's** (✉ Plaza Borda 9 ☎ 762/622–0172), Taxco's oldest bar, a tequila, lime, and club soda concoction called a Bertha is the specialty. It's supposedly the forerunner of today's margarita.

La Pachanga (✉ Cerro de la Misión 32 ☎ No phone), a discotheque at Posada de la Misión, is open Tuesday–Sunday and is popular with townsfolk and visitors. **Passagge** (✉ Av. de los Plateros s/n ☎ 762/627–1177) is a popular disco. Much of Taxco's weekend nighttime activity is at Monte Taxco hotel's discotheque, **Windows** (✉ Lomas de Taxco ☎ 762/622–1300). On Saturday night, the hotel has a buffet and a fireworks display.

Shopping

Sidewalk vendors sell lacquered gourds and boxes from the town of Olinalá as well as masks, straw baskets, bark paintings, and many other hand-crafted items native to the state of Guerrero. Sunday is market day, which means that artisans from surrounding villages descend on the town, as do visitors from Mexico City. It can get crowded, but if you find a seat on a bench in Plaza Borda, you're set to watch the show and peruse the merchandise that will inevitably be brought to you by strolling vendors.

Most people come to Taxco with silver in mind. Three types are available: sterling, which is always stamped 0.925 (925 parts in 1,000) and is the most expensive; plated silver; and the inexpensive *alpaca*, which is also known as German or nickel silver. Sterling pieces are usually priced by weight according to world silver prices. Fine workmanship will add to the cost. Bangles start at $4, and bracelets and necklaces range from $10 to $200 and higher.

Many of the more than 2,000 silver shops carry identical merchandise; a few are noted for their creativity. William Spratling, Andrés Mejía, and Emilia Castillo, daughter of renowned silversmith Antonio Castillo, are among the famous names. Designs range from traditional bulky necklaces (often inlaid with turquoise and other semiprecious stones) to streamlined bangles and chunky earrings.

CRAFTS **Arnoldo** (⊠ Calle Palma 2 ☎ 762/622–1272) has ceremonial masks; originals come with a certificate of authenticity as well as a written description of origin and use. For $100 per person, Arnoldo will take you on a tour of the villages where the dances using the masks are performed on February 2, May 15, and December 12. **D'Elsa** (⊠ Plazuela de San Juan 13 ☎ 762/622–1683), owned by Elsa Ruíz de Figueroa, carries a selection of native-inspired clothing for women and a well-chosen selection of crafts.

SILVER **Emilia Castillo** (⊠ Juan Ruíz de Alarcón 7, in the Posada de los Castillo Fodor'sChoice hotel ☎ 762/622–3471) is one of the most exciting silver shops; it's ★ renowned for innovative designs and for combining silver with porcelain (Neiman Marcus sells the wares in its U.S. stores). The stunning pieces at **Galería de Arte en Plata Andrés** (⊠ Av. de los Plateros 113A, near Posada de la Misión ☎ 762/622–3778) are created by the talented Andrés Mejía. He showcases his own designs and those of such promising young designers as Priscilla Canales, Susana Sanborn, and Francisco Diaz.

★ **Spratling Ranch** (⊠ South of town on Carretera Taxco–Iguala, Km 177 ☎ 762/622–6108) is where the heirs of William Spratling turn out designs using his original molds. You can shop only by appointment. **Talleres de los Ballesteros** (⊠ Calle Florida 14 ☎ 762/622–1076 ⊠ Joyería San Agustín ⊠ Calle Cuauhtémoc 4 ☎ 762/622–3416) and their branch, Joyería San Agustín, carry a large collection of well-crafted silver jewelry and serving pieces.

ACAPULCO A TO Z

To research prices, get advice from other travelers, and book travel arrangements, visit www.fodors.com.

AIR TRAVEL

AIRPORT The Aeropuerto Internacional Juan N. Alvarez is 20 minutes east of the city.
🚩 **Aeropuerto Internacional Juan N. Alvarez** ☎ 744/466–9434.

AIRPORT Private taxis aren't permitted to carry passengers from the airport to
TRANSFERS town, so most people rely on Transportes Aeropuerto, a special airport taxi service. The system looks confusing, but there are dozens of helpful English-speaking staff members to help you.

Look for the name of your hotel and its zone number on the overhead sign on the walkway in front of the terminal. Then go to the desk designated with that zone number and buy a ticket for an airport taxi. The ride from the airport to the hotel zone on the strip costs about $8 per person for the *colectivo* (shared minivan) and starts at $31 for a non-shared cab. The drivers are usually helpful and will often take you to hotels that aren't on their list. Tips are optional.
🚩 Taxis & Shuttles **Transportes Aeropuerto** ☎ 744/462–1095.

CARRIERS From the United States, American has nonstop flights from Dallas, with connecting service from Chicago and New York. Continental has nonstop service from Houston and winter and spring service nonstop from Newark. Delta's direct flights are from Los Angeles and Atlanta. Mexicana's flights from Chicago and Los Angeles stop in Mexico City before continuing on to Acapulco. Aeroméxico has nonstop service from Los Angeles; flights from New York stop in Mexico City except December 23–May 5. Aeroméxico also has one-stop or connecting service from Atlanta, Chicago, Houston, Miami, and Orlando. America West has a flight from Phoenix.

Aeroméxico ☎ 744/466–9109. **America West** ☎ 744/466–9257. **American** ☎ 744/466–9227. **Continental** ☎ 744/466–9063. **Delta** ☎ 01800/902–2100 toll-free in Mexico. **Mexicana** ☎ 744/486–7586.

BOAT TRAVEL

Many cruises include Acapulco as part of their itinerary. Most originate from Los Angeles. Celebrity Cruises is popular with tourists. Crystal P&O is a reliable operator. Cunard Line also offers cruises that include Acapulco. Krystal Cruises plies the Riviera Mexicana, which includes Acapulco. Princess Cruises offers trips several times a year. Bookings are generally handled through a travel agent.

BUS TRAVEL

Bus service from Mexico City to Acapulco is excellent. Sistema Estrella Blanca has first-class buses, which leave every hour on the hour from the Tasqueña station; they're comfortable and in good condition. The trip takes 5½ hours, and a one-way ticket costs about $24. Estrella de Oro also has deluxe service, called Servicio Diamante, with airplane-like reclining seats, refreshments, rest rooms, air-conditioning, movies, and hostess service. The deluxe buses leave four times a day, also from the Tasqueña station, and cost about $38. Plus service (regular reclining seats, air-conditioning, and a rest room) on the same bus line costs $25.

First-class Estrella de Oro buses leave Acapulco for Taxco five times a day from 7 AM to 6:40 PM from the Terminal Central de Autobuses de Primera Clase (First-Class Bus Terminal). The cost for the approximately 4½-hour ride is about $14 one-way. Sistema Estrella Blanca buses depart Acapulco several times a day from the Terminal de Autobuses. Purchase your tickets at least one day in advance at the terminal. A first-class, one-way ticket is $12. Buses depart from Taxco just about every hour starting at 6 AM.

Within Acapulco one of the most useful buses runs from Puerto Marqués to Caleta, making stops along the way. Yellow air-conditioned tourist buses, marked ACAPULCO, run about every 15 minutes along this route. If you want to go from the zócalo to the Costera, catch the bus that says LA BASE (the naval base near the Hyatt Regency). It detours through Old Acapulco and returns to the Costera just east of the Ritz Hotel. If you want to follow the Costera for the entire route, take the bus marked HORNOS. Buses to Pie de la Cuesta or Puerto Marqués say so on the front. The Puerto Marqués bus runs about every 10 minutes and is always crowded. The fare is $1.

Estrella de Oro ✉ Av. Cuauhtémoc 158, Old Acapulco, Acapulco ☎ 744/485–8705 or 7/622–0648 ✉ Av. de los Plateros 126, Taxco ☎ 762/485–8705 or 762/622–0648 ✉ Av. Taxqueña 1320, Tlalpan Mexico City ☎ 55/5689–9745. **Sistema Estrella Blanca** ✉ Calle Ejido 47, Old Acapulco, Acapulco ☎ 744/469–2028 ✉ Av. de los Plateros 104, Taxco ☎ 762/622–0131 ✉ Av. Taxqueeña 1320, Tlalpan Mexico, D.F. ☎ 55/5689–9740.

CAR RENTAL

Major Agencies Avis ☎ 744/466–9190. **Budget** ☎ 744/481–2433. **Dollar** ☎ 744/466–9493. **Hertz** ☎ 744/485–8947. **Quick** ☎ 744/486–3420.

CAR TRAVEL

The trip to Acapulco from Mexico City on the old route (Carretera Libre a Acapulco) takes about six hours. A privately built and run four-lane toll road is expensive (about $48 one way) but well maintained, and it cuts driving time between the two cities to 4½ hours. Many people go via Taxco, which can be reached from either road. It takes about three hours to drive to Taxco from Acapulco using the toll road.

If you plan to visit (or stay) in Pie de la Cuesta or Barra Vieja, you might want to rent a car. That said, be prepared for maddening traffic along the Costera from about 8 in the morning until 8 at night. Further it's hard to find a parking spot along the street in town, and there are few lots.

CONSULATES

🖪 **Canadian Consulate** ⊠ Marbella Mall, Suite 23, Costera ☎ 744/484-1305. **U.K. Consuate** ⊠ Acapulco International Center, Av. Costera Miguel Alemán 4455 ☎ 744/484-1735. **U.S. Consulate** ⊠ Continental Plaza Hotel, Av. Costera Miguel Alemán 121-14, Costera ☎ 744/469-0556.

EMERGENCIES

🖪 **Hospital del Pacífico** ⊠ Calle Fraile and Calle Nao 4, Costera ☎ 744/487-7180. **Hospital Privado Magallanes** ⊠ Calle Wilfrido Massieu 2, Costera ☎ 744/485-6194. **Police** ☎ 744/485-0650. **Red Cross** ☎ 744/445-5912.

ENGLISH-LANGUAGE MEDIA

You can find English-language books and periodicals at Sanborns, a reputable department-store chain, and at the newsstands in some of the larger hotels. Many small newsstands carry the Mexico City *News*.

🖪 Bookstores **Sanborns** ⊠ Av. Costera Miguel Alemán 1226, Costera ☎ 744/484-4413 ⊠ Av. Costera Miguel Alemán 3111, Costera ☎ 744/484-2025 ⊠ Av. Costera Miguel Alemán 209, Costera ☎ 744/482-6167 ⊠ Av. Costera Miguel Alemán, off zócalo Old Acapulco ☎ 744/482-6168.

HORSE-DRAWN CARRIAGES

Buggy rides up and down the Costera are available in the evenings. There are two routes: from Parque Papagayo to the zócalo and from Playa Condesa to the naval base. Each costs about $10 (be sure to agree on the price beforehand).

MAIL, INTERNET & SHIPPING

More and more Internet facilities are cropping up in Acapulco to keep you connected while traveling. Smart PCs is in a shopping arcade next to Carlos 'n' Charlie's restaurant. The iNternet Cyber Café is near the Marbella Hotel on the Avenida Costera Miguel Alemán.

🖪 Cybercafés **iNternet Cyber Café** ⊠ Calle Horacio Nelson 40-7A, Costera ☎ 744/484-8254. **Smart PCs** ⊠ Av. Costera Miguel Alemán 112-4, Costera ☎ 744/484-2877. 🖪 Mail & Shipping **Airborne Express** ⊠ Av. Costera Miguel Alemán 178, Costera ☎ 744/484-1076. **Correos** (Post Office) ⊠ Av. Costera Miguel Alemán 215, Old Acapulco ☎ 744/483-1674. ⊠ Acapulco International Center, Av. Costera Miguel Alemán, Costera ☎ 744/484-8029. **DHL** ⊠ Av. Costera Miguel Alemán 810. Fracc. Hornos, Old Acapulco ☎ 744/4859567. **Mail Boxes, Etc.** ⊠ Av. Costera Miguel Alemán 40-3, Costera ☎ 744/481-0565.

MONEY MATTERS

There are many *casas de cambio* (currency exchange offices) around the zócalo and along the Costera. Their hours are generally Monday–Saturday 9–5. Most banks have ATMs and are open weekdays 9–3 and Saturday 9–1.

🖪 Banks **Banamex** ⊠ Av. Costera Miguel Alemán 38-A, Costera ☎ 744/484-3381. **Bancomer** ⊠ Av. Costera Miguel Alemán, at Calle Laurel, Fraccionamiento Club Deportivo, Costera ☎ 744/484-8055. **Bital** ✉ Calle Jesus Carranza 7, Old Acapulco ☎ 744/483-6113.

Exchange Offices **Casa de Cambio Austral** ✉ Av. Costera Vieja 3, Old Acapulco ☎ 744/484-6528. **Casa de Cambio Servicio Auxiliares Monetarios** ✉ Av. Costera Miguel Alemán 88, Old Acapulco ☎ 744/481-0218. **Dollar Money Exchange** ✉ Av. Costera Miguel Alemán 151, Costera ☎ 744/486-9688. **Divisa World Center** ✉ Av. Costera Miguel Alemán 999, Costera ☎ 744/484-5516.

TAXIS & MINIBUSES

Before you go anywhere by cab, find out what the price should be and agree with the driver on a fare. Never let a taxi driver decide where you should eat or shop, since many get kickbacks from small stores and restaurants. Although tipping isn't expected, Mexicans usually leave small change.

Hotel taxis are the most expensive, the roomiest, and in the best condition. A price list that all drivers adhere to is posted in hotel lobbies. Fares in town are $3 to $7; from downtown to the Princess Hotel is about $18; from the hotel zone to Playa Caleta is about $9. Cabs that cruise the streets usually charge by zone, with a minimum charge of $2. A normal fare is about $3 to go from the zócalo to the International Center. Rates are about 30% higher at night. You can also hire a taxi by the hour or the day. Prices vary from about $10 an hour for a hotel taxi to $8 an hour for a street taxi; always negotiate.

Minibuses travel along preset routes through Taxco and charge about 40¢. Volkswagen "bugs" provide inexpensive (average $1.50) taxi transportation.

TOURS

Operators have offices around town and desks in many of the large hotels. Contact Mexico Travel Advisors at La Torre de Acapulco for tours of Acapulco. Viajes Acuario is another reliable tour company. Both companies offer city tours ($20), day tours of Taxco ($65, including lunch), and nightclub tours ($25–$30, including transportation cover charges).

The *Bonanza*'s sunset cruise, with open bar and live and disco music, costs $20–$46 depending if you sign up for just the cruise or cruise, open bar, and buffet. Boats leave from downtown near the zócalo at 4:30 and 10:30. Many hotels and shops sell tickets, as do waterfront ticket sellers.

Bonanza ☎ 744/482-4947. **Mexico Travel Advisors** ✉ Av. Costera Miguel Alemán 1252, Costera ☎ 744/484-7400. **Viajes Acuario** ✉ Av. Costera Miguel Alemán 186-3, Costera ☎ 744/485-6100.

TRAVEL AGENCIES

Local Agent Referrals **American Express** ✉ La Gran Plaza shopping center, Av. Costera Miguel Alemán 1628, Suites 7–9, Costera ☎ 744/469-1166. **Viajes Wagon-Lits** ✉ Carretera Escénica 5255, Las Brisas ☎ 744/484-1650 Ext. 392.

VISITOR INFORMATION

Procuraduría del Turista, the State Attorney General's Tourist Office, is open 9 AM–11 PM daily. Taxco's tourism office is open weekdays 9–2 and 5–8; Saturday 9–3.

Procuraduría del Turista ✉ Acapulco International Center, Av. Costera Miguel Alemán, Costera ☎ 744/484-4416 ⊕ www.visitacapulco.com.mx. **Taxco Tourism Office** ✉ Av. de los Plateros 1 ☎ 762/622-6616.

OAXACA

FODOR'S CHOICE
Hotel Santa Fe, Puerto Escondido
Mujeres Artesanas, Oaxaca City shop
Museo de las Culturas, Oaxaca City
El Naranjo, Oaxaca City restaurant
Playa Zicatela, Puerto Escondido

HIGHLY RECOMMENDED

HOTELS Barceló, Huatulco
Camino Real Zaashila, Huatulco
Hotel Camino Real Oaxaca, Oaxaca City
Misión de los Arcos, Huatulco
Quinta Real, Huatulco
Studios Tabachín, Puerto Escondido

RESTAURANTS Cafecito, Puerto Escondido
Catedral, Oaxaca City
La Escondida, Oaxaca City
La Galería, Puerto Escondido

SHOPPING Artesanías Chimalli, Oaxaca City shop
Central de Abastos, Oaxaca City market
Galería Indigo, Oaxaca City shop
La Mano Mágica, Oaxaca City shop
Mercado de Artesanías, Oaxaca City market

EXPERIENCES Mitla, Maya ruins
Monte Albán, Maya ruins
Museo de Arte Contemporáneo, Oaxaca City
Museo de Arte Prehispánico, Oaxaca City
Playa San Agustanillo, Puerto Ángel

Updated by
Jane Onstott

MEXICO AFICIONADOS HAVE LONG FAVORED the state of Oaxaca (pronounced wah-*hah*-kah) for its geographic, ethnic, and artistic diversity. It and neighboring Chiapas State have the country's largest Indian populations. Two out of three Oaxaqueños descend from Zapotec or Mixtec Indians, whose villages dot the valleys, mountainsides, and coastal lowlands. Within a 40-km (25-mi) radius of the capital, Oaxaca City, the archaeological ruins of Monte Albán, Mitla, and Yagul—and lots of other sites that have barely been excavated—bear witness to the highly advanced cultures of their ancestors. Within the large state's borders there are 17 distinct ethnic groups, and 52 dialects are spoken. In the capital many people are fluent in English as well as Spanish, but in the small hamlets, even Spanish is a second language.

In the 15th century much of the region was conquered by the Aztecs, who gave Oaxaca its name: *Huaxyaca*. In the Nahuatl language it probably means "by the acacia grove," referring to the location of the Aztec military base. The next century witnessed the Spanish conquest of Mexico, for which the monarch Charles V rewarded Hernán Cortés with the title of Marqués del Valle de Oaxaca in 1528. Cortés lived elsewhere, but his descendants kept the property until Mexico's bloody Revolution, which began in 1910.

Two of Oaxaca's sons figured greatly in Mexican politics: Benito Juárez, the first full-blooded Indian to become president, and Porfirio Díaz, a military dictator who declared himself president-for-life. Juárez, often referred to as Mexico's Abraham Lincoln, was a sheepherder from San Pablo Guelatao, a settlement about 64 km (40 mi) north of Oaxaca. As a child he spoke only his native Zapotec tongue. He was later trained for the clergy but ended up studying law and entering politics. Elected governor of the state in 1847, the stocky statesman became chief justice of the Supreme Court of Mexico in 1857, and then president of the republic (1858–72).

In 1864 Napoleon III crowned Austria's Archduke Maximilian emperor of Mexico; Juárez and his supporters resisted the French from a provisional capital city in northern Mexico. When the nascent French empire collapsed in 1867, Juárez returned to Mexico City. He was re-elected shortly thereafter and again in 1871; he died of a heart attack the following year, however. His rival, Porfirio Díaz, rose to power in 1876, maintaining the presidency of the republic until 1911. Dissatisfaction among the country's poor had mounted steadily under Díaz's autocratic, elitist government. The revolutionary movement that finally chased Díaz from power was spearheaded by a wealthy but nonconformist intellectual, Francisco I. Madero, who was elected president that same year.

Oaxaca is in one of three adjacent valleys encircled by the majestic Sierra Madre del Sur. Mexico's fifth-largest state, it's bordered by Chiapas to the east, Veracruz and Puebla to the north, and Guerrero to the west. Southern Oaxaca State is blessed with 509 km (316 mi) of Pacific coast, along which are many magnificent beaches. These sandy stretches include Puerto Escondido—a fishing town that's become a magnet for died-in-the-wool surfers and die-hard sunworshipers—and the even smaller town of Puerto Ángel. The government is also transforming Bahías de Huatulco (Huatulco Bays), 125 km (77 mi) east of Puerto Escondido, into a world-class resort.

If you have only three or five days to spend in the state, you'll have to choose between Oaxaca City and the coast. For a culture-beach combination, plan on at least seven days—Oaxaca City and the coast merit at least three days each.

Numbers in the text correspond to numbers in the margin and on the Oaxaca City and Oaxaca Coast maps.

10

If you have 3 days

If you choose to spend your time in **Oaxaca City** ❶–❾ ⌐, on the first day take in the Catedral Metropolitana de Oaxaca and the adjoining *zócalo,* the Museo de Arte Contemporáneo de Oaxaca, and the Museo de las Culturas. On Day 2, beat the crowds by catching a tour or bus right after breakfast for **Monte Albán,** the ruins of an ancient, mountaintop Zapotec capital. After returning to the city and a late lunch, enjoy coffee at the 16th-century Ex-Convento de Santa Catalina, now the Hotel Camino Real. Visit the Museo de Arte Prehispánico Rufino Tamayo, the Centro Fotográfico Álvarez Bravo, and the city's largest market—the Central de Abastos—on Day 3. Alternatively, you might spend an entire day shopping for fine arts or regional crafts in the historic center. Watch the sun set over Oaxaca from the terrace bar of the Hotel Victoria, just above the city proper.

If you opt to spend your three days on the coast, make ⊠ **Bahías de Huatulco** ❿–❶❺ ⌐ your base. Take a boat tour of the bays on the first day, followed by a sunset cocktail and evening meal at the Camino Real's Chez Binni restaurant. On Day 2, tour the small beaches and hidden bays between Huatulco and **Puerto Escondido** ❿. On Day 3, laze on the beach and, in the late afternoon, taxi to La Crucecita for some strolling, followed by dining at one of the small restaurants on the main square.

If you have 5 days

For an Oaxaca City stay, follow the three-day itinerary above, and on Day 4 add a visit to the Mixtec ruins at **Mitla,** stopping on the way or back to see the 2,000-year-old *ahuehuete* cypress in Tule and to experience a country market day in **Tlacolula** (especially imposing on Sunday). Dine in one of the restaurants on Calle Macedonio Alcalá, or in the zócalo. On Day 5, head to one of the villages outside Oaxaca City for market day or to purchase crafts direct from the artists. Back in the city, visit the Basílica de Nuestra Señora de la Soledad.

If you're staying on the coast, follow the above three-day itinerary, and sign up for bird-watching on Laguna Manialtepec on Day 4. On Day 5, head inland for a special lunch on the coffee plantation tour. If you chose laid-back ⊠ **Puerto Escondido** ❿ as your base, you might spend Day 4 touring Laguna Chacahua, and Day 5 riding horses on the beach in the morning, then relaxing with a soothing *temazcal* steam bath (a pre-Hispanic–style sauna) and massage in the afternoon.

If you have **7 days** or **more**

You can immerse yourself in the cultural treasures of ⊞**Oaxaca City** ❶–❾⟶ and **Monte Albán** before kicking back with some sea and sun. Spend Days 1–4 at the sights outlined in the first four days of the city itinerary. On Day 5, fly to ⊞ **Bahías de Huatulco** ⑫–⑮ and, on arrival, sign up for a boat tour of the bays. On Days 6 and 7, head to the beach, go bird-watching, or explore La Crucecita. If you're staying longer, visit the beautiful beaches of Zipolite and Mazunte.

Exploring Oaxaca

Oaxaca City, the state capital, is in a mountain valley and surrounded by tradition-minded towns and villages and fields of corn, beans, and alfalfa. The city is food for the soul for history and folk-art aficionados, with its magnificent colonial buildings and world-famous crafts. And the ruins of ancient temples are just outside it.

Several rather narrow and potholed highways follow the tortuous curves of the Sierra de Oaxaca south to Pacific surf spots and palm-lined beaches. Puerto Escondido and the even smaller beach towns nearby it are the places to go for a casual, friendly, laid-back vacation. Although relatively unsophisticated by international standards, Huatulco has some incredible scenery and a handful of luxury resorts.

Note: Assaults and highway banditry still occur in Mexico. Among the most obvious targets are first-class buses, especially on the route between Juchitán, on the Oaxaca coast, and San Cristóbal de las Casas in Chiapas. Night buses are most vulnerable; travel by day whenever possible. Although the possibility of an attack is cause for concern, occurrences are infrequent.

About the Restaurants

Traditional Oaxacan dishes are among the finest and most elaborate in all Mexico. Oaxaca is known as "the land of seven moles" (pronounced *mow*-lay) because of its seven distinct kinds of the multispiced sauce. One of the most popular, *mole negro* (black mole), has dozens of ingredients including chocolate, sesame seeds, nuts, chilies, and tortillas. Tamales, either sweet or stuffed with chicken or pork, are another treat. The home- and factory-made *mezcal*, an alcoholic drink derived from the maguey cactus, differs in flavor with each maker and can be as high as 80 proof. The cream variety, thick and sweet, is flavored with nuts, herbs, or citrus fruits.

The open-air cafés surrounding Oaxaca City's *zócalo* (main square) are good for drinks, snacks, and people-watching, with the scene changing from serene early mornings to crowded parades with brass bands, floats, and *monos* (giant papier-mâché dolls) on holiday evenings. Most serve the economical *comida corrida* (midday set menu) after 1:30 PM. But you won't be very much out of pocket wherever you choose to dine.

The dishes that make dining in the capital memorable are less evident along the coast, where seafood reigns. Restaurants in the resort of Huatulco struggle for a consistent client base, and some of the best eateries there are found in the hotels. Puerto Escondido has quite a few interesting restaurants. Cuisine is varied, and competition keeps prices low. In Puerto Ángel and surrounding beach towns, expect the simplest of grilled fish dishes served with white rice and few frills. Dress is casual and reservations are generally unnecessary.

About the Hotels

Oaxaca City has magnificently restored properties, including a 16th-century convent and dozens of smaller, moderately priced accommodations. Hotels and rates vary considerably on the coast. Most Puerto Escondido and Puerto Ángel places fall into the $ or $$ price range. Huatulco several luxury resorts, whose rooms can run as much as $300 a night, as well as a respectable number of moderately priced accommodations. Budget hotels here are scarce; for the cheapest digs try the town of La Crucecita, a short taxi ride from the more posh properties lining the bays.

WHAT IT COSTS				
$$$$	**$$$**	**$$**	**$**	**¢**
RESTAURANTS over $25	$15–$25	$10–$15	$5–$10	under $5
HOTELS over $250	$150–$250	$75–$150	$50–$75	under $50

Restaurant prices are for a main course excluding tax and tip. Hotel prices are for two people in a standard double room in high season, based on the European Plan (EP, with no meals) and excluding service and 17% tax.

Timing

Whether you stay in Oaxaca City or along the coast, book rooms six months to a year in advance for dates around Day of the Dead celebrations (October 31–November 2), Easter week, and Christmas–New Year's vacations. Although July and August fall in the rainy season, they're popular travel months with Mexican and foreign families, as they coincide with school vacations. Expect discounts of 20–50% in low season.

OAXACA CITY

▶ Mexico's diversity and charisma are nowhere more apparent than in Oaxaca City, officially called Oaxaca de Juárez (population 260,000). It's a study in eccentricity, a commingling of sights, smells, and sounds both ancient and new. You'll hear the singsong strains of Zapotec, Mixtec, and other native languages in the streets, and the blare of rock in Spanish and hip-hop in shops and bars. You'll see indigenous faces everywhere you look, as well as the lighter skinned descendants of the conquistadors. Scions of affluent families sip tea or tequila in classy restaurants; out on the streets, men, women, and children of significantly more modest means sell pencils, sweets, and ears of grilled corn.

Exploring Oaxaca City

The Centro Histórico (Historic Center) is a pastel collage of colonial- and republican-era mansions, civic edifices, and churches that delight the eye and lift the spirit. The colonial heart is laid out in a simple grid, with all the attractions within walking distance of one another. Most streets change names once they pass the zócalo.

a good walk

Begin at the shady **zócalo** ❶ ▶. On the south side of this pedestrians-only square step into the **Palacio de Gobierno** ❷ and check out the mural by Arturo García Bustos that stretches from the first to the second floor. Afterward walk to the zócalo's northwest corner and **El Alameda** ❸, a second square that abuts the central plaza. You can't miss the **Catedral Metropolitana de Oaxaca** ❹ on El Alameda's east side. After visiting the cathedral, turn right on Avenida Independencia and left at the next corner. This puts you on Calle Macedonio Alcalá, a pedestrian mall with restored colonial mansions in a palate of pastels as well as galleries, shops, museums, and restaurants. It's also lively and well lighted at night. On your right, 1½ blocks up, is the **Museo de Arte Contemporáneo de Oax-**

aca ⑤. Continue north from here; turn right on Calle Murguía, and left on the first street, Calle 5 de Mayo. Taking up the entire block on the street's east side is the Ex-Convento de Santa Catalina, now the Hotel Camino Real. Continue north until Calle 5 de Mayo ends at Calle Gurrión and the beautiful Iglesia y Ex-Convento de Santo Domingo. Adjacent to the church, the **Museo de las Culturas** ⑥ occupies a former Dominican monastery and contains, among other things, artifacts from Monte Albán.

Walk south, the way you came, on Calle 5 de Mayo. Turn left on Calle Murguía and walk 1½ blocks to the **Centro Fotográfico Álvarez Bravo** ⑦. After seeing the current photo exhibition, retrace your steps along Murguía, passing Calle 5 de Mayo and turning left on Calle Macedonio Alcalá and then right on Avenida Morelos. Just a few blocks down in a tranquil colonial home is the **Museo de Arte Prehispánico Rufino Tamayo** ⑧. After seeing the museum's pre-Hispanic art, continue west on Morelos 2½ blocks. Descend the steps and cross the large plaza to the massive **Basílica de Nuestra Señora de la Soledad** ⑨. On the left side of the church is a small museum with items related to Oaxaca's patron saint. Go east on Avenida Independencia past the post office and you'll be back at El Alameda and the zócalo, where you can watch the daily parade of Oaxaqueños.

What to See

③ **El Alameda.** This shady square is home to the Catedral Metropolitana de Oaxaca and the post office. Locals gossip on wrought-iron benches or read the newspaper while their children chase pigeons or beg for giant balloons,or snacks sold by itinerant vendors.

⑨ **Basílica de Nuestra Señora de la Soledad.** The Baroque basilica houses the statue of the Virgin of Solitude, Oaxaca's patron saint. According to legend, a mule that had mysteriously joined a mule train bound for Guatemala perished at the site of the church; the statue was discovered in its pack, and the event was construed as a miracle—one commemorated by this church, which was built in 1682. Many Oaxaqueños are devoted to the Virgin, who is believed to have more than the usual facility for healing and miracle-working. In the 1980s, robbers removed her jewel-studded crown; she now has a replica of the original and a glass-covered shrine. A small museum at the side of the church displays items left by the faithful over the years. ⊠ *Av. Independencia 107, at Calle Galeana, Centro* ☎ *No phone* ☼ *Daily 7–7.*

④ **Catedral Metropolitana de Oaxaca.** Begun in 1544, the cathedral was destroyed by earthquakes and fire and not finished until 1733. It honors the Virgin of the Assumption, whose statue can be seen on the facade above the door. The chapel at the back of the church and left of the altar houses the revered crucifix of El Señor del Rayo (Our Lord of the Lightning Bolt), the only piece to survive a fire that started when lightning struck the thatch roof of the original structure. ⊠ *Av. Independencia 700, Centro* ☎ *951/516–4401* ☼ *Daily 10 AM–9 PM.*

⑦ **Centro Fotográfico Álvarez Bravo.** The center is named for the self-taught Mexico City photographer, Manuel Álvarez Bravo, who won his first photographic competition in Oaxaca. Bravo's black-and-white photography documents a varied subject matter, from street scenes and country life to nudes. Exhibitions here change every month or two. Inaugurated in the mid-1990s by Oaxaca philanthropist and graphic artist Francisco Toledo, the site also houses a library of music and photography, a darkroom for students who study at the center, and, incongruously, a Braille library. ⊠ *Calle Murguía 302, Centro* ☎ *951/516–4523* ▭ *Free* ☼ *Wed.–Mon. 9:30–8.*

Archaeology

Dramatic Zapotec and Mixtec ruins at Monte Albán, Mitla, and Yagul provide insight into ancient civilizations. Their golden era had already passed when they were conquered by the Aztecs in the 15th century; shortly thereafter, the Spaniards arrived. Despite these conquests, indigenous languages are still extensively spoken in dozens of towns surrounding Oaxaca, where traditional lifestyles are slowly infused with modern trends and mores.

Fiestas

Oaxaca celebrates holidays and festivals with verve. El Día de los Muertos (Day of the Dead) officially begins on October 31, the eve of All Saint's Day, when both city dwellers and country folk decorate altars for deceased family members. Tradition dictates that they also visit the cemetery with candles and flowers, balloons, and the favorite food and drink of the dead. The most frequently visited graveyard is that of Xoxo; Atzompa and Xochimilco also have colorful celebrations.

December is full of fiestas, including those for Mexico's patron saint, the Virgen de Guadalupe (December 12) and Oaxaca state's patron, la Virgen de la Soledad (December 18). December 23 sees the Noche de Rábanos (Night of the Radishes), when the Oaxaca City's zócalo (main square) is packed with growers and artists displaying their hybrid carved radishes, flores inmortales (small, dried "eternal flowers"), and totomoxtl (corn husks, pronounced to-to-mosh-tl)—all arranged in interesting tableaux. December 24 is the Noche de Calendas, in which locals demonstrate their devotion to the Virgin Mary by bearing heavy baskets of flowers from church to church. In related processions circling the zócalo, brass bands accompany floats and marchers carry bright, larger-than-life papier-mâché figures.

Another of Oaxaca's major celebrations is the Guelaguetza (Zapotec for "offering" or "gift"), generally held on the last two Mondays in July. Delegations of traditional dancers from throughout the state converge on Oaxaca City to perform in authentic costumes at the Guelaguetza Auditorium, an open-air amphitheater on a hill just northwest of the city center.

Shopping

Many of the villages surrounding Oaxaca City are known for the skill of artisans who create pottery, woven rugs, and other utilitarian items that often embody generations of craftsmanship and unique family designs. Look also for wood carvings of skeletons and animals as well as the alebrijes (fanciful creatures painted in bright colors and geometric designs). Oaxaca City's galleries exhibit folk and fine art; the city has many painters of international renown. In addition, Oaxaca's marketplaces make for fabulous outings. On market day both mestizos (people of mixed European and Indian descent) and indigenous people head to town to buy and sell, barter, and gossip. As large and lively now as it has been for centuries, Oaxaca City's Abastos Market attracted the attention of D. H. Lawrence, who wrote about it in Mornings in Mexico (1927).

Surfing Puerto Escondido has been a household name for serious surfers the world over since the 1960s. The town's famous surfing spot, Playa Zicatela, ranks up there with Hawaii's North Shore and Australia's Barrier Reef; waves here roll in with impressive force. Many surfers migrate here annually to ride the waves or participate in an international competition.

★ ❺ **Museo de Arte Contemporáneo de Oaxaca (MACO).** Although it's housed in an attractive colonial residence, as its name implies, MACO houses changing exhibitions of contemporary art on its two floors. Inaugurated in 1992 by graphic artist Francisco Toledo, the two-story museum has in its collection quite a few of his etchings and lithos. You'll also find work by fellow Oaxacans Rudolfo Morales and Rufino Tamayo as well as other Mexican painters and sculptors. Be sure to check out the fragments of frescoes that once decorated the walls of this old mansion in the front gallery on the second floor. ⊠ *Calle Macedonio Alcalá 202, Centro* ☎ *951/514–2228* ✑ *$1* ☉ *Wed.–Mon. 10:30–8.*

★ ❽ **Museo de Arte Prehispánico Rufino Tamayo.** You'll find a beautifully displayed collection of pre-Hispanic pottery and sculpture at this carefully restored colonial mansion. Originally it was the private collection of the painter Rufino Tamayo, who presented it to his hometown in 1979. ⊠ *Av. Morelos 503, Centro* ☎ *951/516–4750* ✑ *$3* ☉ *Mon. and Wed.–Sat. 10–2 and 4–7, Sun. 10–3.*

❻ **Museo de las Culturas.** This museum is laid out in a series of galleries around
Fodor'sChoice the cloister of the Ex-Convento de Santo Domingo. The ground floor
★ contains the temporary galleries, a gift shop, the Francisco de Burgoa Library of antique books, and administrative offices. On the second floor you'll find 10 thematic rooms, including those dedicated to Oaxacan music, medicine, indigenous languages, and pottery. More than a dozen other salons have been organized chronologically; here you'll find such Monte Albán treasures as the stunning gold jewelry from Tomb 7—among the greatest archaeological finds of all time. The adjacent **Iglesia de Santo Domingo** is Oaxaca City's most brilliantly decorated church. Its 17th-century facade is framed by two domed bell towers and its interior is an energetic profusion of white and real gold leaf that's typical of the Mexican Baroque style. You can also visit the on-site botanical gardens, where free, one-hour English-language tours are conducted on Tuesday, Thursday, and Saturday at 10 AM and 4 PM. ⊠ *Plaza Santa Domingo, Centro* ☎ *951/516–2991; 951/516–7672 for botanical garden tours* ✑ *Museum: $3.50. Church and gardens: free* ☉ *Museum: Tues.–Sun. 10–7:45. Church and gardens: daily 7 AM–1 PM and 5–8 PM.*

❷ **Palacio de Gobierno.** The 19th-century neoclassical state capitol is on the zócalo's south side. A fresco mural that was completed in 1988 wraps around the stairwell. In it, altars to the dead, painters of codices, fruit sellers, gods, and musicians crowd together to catalog the customs and legends of Oaxaca's indigenous people. The mural also bespeaks the conquest and the Revolution. At the top, on the left side of the mural, note the *apoala* tree, which according to Mixtec legend bore the flowers from which life sprang. ⊠ *Portal del Palacio, Centro* ☎ *951/516–0677* ☉ *Daily 9–8.*

➤ ❶ **Zócalo.** During the day, everyone comes to Oaxaca's shady main plaza, with its green wrought-iron benches and matching bandstand. At night, mariachi and marimba bands play under colonial archways or in the bandstand. It's a historic and truly beloved spot: when McDonald's tried to open a branch on its east side in late 2002, grassroots opposition led by painter and native son Francisco Toledo brought the project to a halt. ☒ *Bounded by Portal de Clavería on the north, Portal del Palacio on the south, Portal de Flores on the west, and Portal de Mercaderes on the east, Centro.*

Where to Stay & Eat

$$$ ✕**El Asador Vasco.** The food at this distinguished restaurant overlooking the town square is a blend of Basque, Mexican, and international flavors. Try the lamb, sumptuous gratiné of oysters in *chipotle* (dried, smoked chili) sauce, or a reasonably priced special such as the chicken breast in rich mole sauce, served with rice, soup, dessert, and coffee. From 8 to 9 PM, serenades by *tunas* (traditionally dressed student minstrels) evoke medieval Spain. Reservations are recommended. ☒ *Portal de Flores 10-A, west side of zócalo, Centro* ☎ *951/514–4755* 🖃 *AE, MC, V.*

★ **$–$$$** ✕**Catedral.** This elegant yet accessible local favorite graces the courtyard and first floor of a colonial house. Popular dishes include mushroom soup flavored with *epazote* (a pungent local herb), chicken in squash-blossom sauce, and *lechón* (suckling pig). Finish your meal with some of Catedral's great strong coffee. There's dancing to live tropical music in the bar Friday and Saturday from 9 PM until 2 or 3 AM. Sunday sees a lavish buffet from 1 to 6. ☒ *Calle García Vigil 105, at Av. Morelos, Centro* ☎ *951/516–3285* 🖃 *AE, MC, V.*

$–$$$ ✕**El Sagrario.** Mexican couples slide into Naugahyde booths during lunch before scurrying over to the salad bar. The cavernous upstairs dining room is a popular spot for pizza, pasta, and Caesar salads, which the waiters prepare table-side. You can do your moves on the tiny dance floor until 2 AM. ☒ *Calle Valdivieso 120, Centro* ☎ *951/514–0303* 🖃 *AE, MC, V.*

$–$$ ✕**El Naranjo.** A sheltered patio welcomes you and soft background music soothes you. Iliana, the bilingual owner, puts a contemporary spin on her Mexican dishes (which earn rave reviews from outsiders), preparing it without the traditional lard. She features each of Oaxaca's seven moles once a week and also has many variations of *chiles rellenos* (stuffed peppers). Try the poblano pepper stuffed with corn, squash blossom, and cheese in puff pastry with almond sauce. Iliana occasionally gives cooking classes. ☒ *Calle Trujano 203, Centro* ☎ *951/514–1878* ⊕ *www.elnaranjo.com.mx* 🖃 *AE, MC, V* ☉ *Closed Sun.*

FodorsChoice ★

★ **$** ✕**La Escondida.** This outdoor lunch buffet (1:30–6:30 PM) just outside the city is a real treat. Waiters bring you a welcome cocktail and a typical appetizer, such as *memelas* (fried discs of corn meal topped with goodies) or tacos. You then select from more than 70 Mexican dishes, including seafood soup, meat fresh from the grill, and a lineup of unusual salads. You can linger here, listening to wandering musicians and letting the kids loose on the small playground. ☒ *Carretera a San Agustín Yatareni, Km 7, San Agustín Yatareni* ☎ *951/517–6655* 🖃 *AE, MC, V.*

$ ✕**El Mesón.** Stop by Mesón's, right off the zócalo, for a snack or a full breakfast, lunch, or dinner buffet. Or choose something à la carte from the paper menu, where you check off your choices. Tortillas are made fresh in the evenings, and there are a variety of tacos, as well as *pozole* (hominy soup) and other Mexican dishes. For a sugar fix, have a cup of rich Oaxacan chocolate and a slice of nut or cheese pie. ☒ *Av. Hidalgo 805, at Calle Valdivieso, Centro* ☎ *951/516–2729* 🖃 *V.*

¢–$$ ✕**El Colibrí.** Upscale Mexican families and beeper-toting businesspeople favor quiet, air-conditioned El Colibrí, perhaps for its romantic background music, free refills of super hot coffee, and extensive menu. In addition to Oaxacan specialties, there are 10 salads, 5

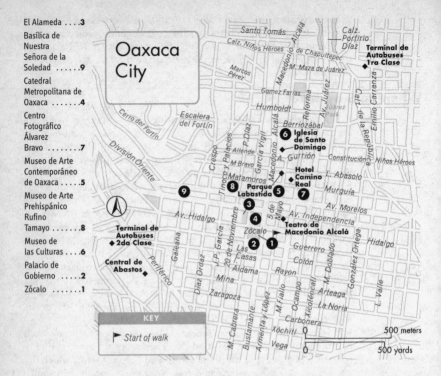

spaghetti dishes, plenty of appetizers, and burgers with fries. It's on the car-choked *periférico* (beltway) ringing Centro, about a 10-minute walk north of Santo Domingo and the Museo de las Culuras. ⊠ *Calz. Niños Héroes de Chapultepec 903, Colonia Reforma* ☎ 951/515–8087 ⊟ *AE, MC, V.*

¢–$ ✕ **La Olla.** The strengths of this restaurant are the large, delicious salads, the health-conscious regional dishes, and the personal supervision of the kitchen by owner Pilar. Service is slow, so you'll have time to admire the works by local artists that adorn the walls. By far the best deal is the fixed-price lunch menu, which includes soup and salad, one of two main dishes, a bread or tortillas, and dessert or espresso coffee. ⊠ *Calle Reforma 402, Centro* ☎ 951/516–6668 ⊟ *AE, MC, V* ☺ *Closed Sun.*

¢–$ ✕ **La Teca.** Deyaneira Aquino runs this charming, truly local eatery out of her home in residential Colonia Reforma, just north of the historic district. Its name is a fond, informal moniker referring to a woman from Deyaneira's native city of Juchitán; all of the recipes are from the Isthmus of Tehuantepec. Sit inside the house or under the pomegranate and orange trees on the back patio, and try her home-style baked chicken, beef ribs, or fish fillet. Or just order beer or wine and an appetizer of *garnachos* (fried cornmeal stuffed with ground beef and minced onions and topped with chipotle chili sauce). ⊠ *Calle Violetas 200, Colonia Reforma* ☎ 951/515–0563 ⊟ *No credit cards* ☺ *Closed Mon. No lunch Tues.–Fri.*

★ $$$–$$$$ ✕⬚ **Hotel Camino Real Oaxaca.** Like many downtown Oaxaca structures, the one that houses this hotel is a National Heritage Site. A monastic air lingers in the patios, courtyards, and enclosed gardens of the Ex-Convento de Santa Catalina, a 16th-century convent. Gregorian chants float on the morning breeze; a rear patio has the font and stone basins where nuns did laundry 400 years ago. Rooms are comfortable and have all the necessary amenities, but as befits a former convent, rather cell-like and small. Enormous buffets with international and regional dishes are the main draws at El Refectorio restaurant. ($–$$$). The Saturday night spread is accompanied by mariachi music; the Sunday brunch is particularly elaborate. ☒ *Calle 5 de Mayo 300, Centro 68000* ☎ *951/ 516–0611* 🖷 *951/516–0732* ⊕ *www.caminoreal.com/oaxaca* ⇥ *84 rooms, 7 suites* ⚸ *Restaurant, room service, in-room safes, minibars, pool, 2 bars, baby-sitting, laundry service, travel services, no-smoking rooms* ▤ *AE, DC, MC, V.*

★ **$$$** ✕⊞ **Casa Oaxaca.** A trio of eccentric Europeans poured their hearts and souls into this unusual bed-and-breakfast. Their 200-year-old house combines colonial scale and traditional materials (adobe, cantera stone, etc.) with minimalist sensibilities. Treat yourself to a dip in the indigo-blue-tile pool or indulge in the shaman-sanctioned *temazcal* (pre-Hispanic-style sweat lodge), a yoga class, or an aromatherapy session. Rooms have fresh flowers, 100% cotton sheets, marble bathrooms, and works by local artists. The restaurant's ($–$$$) gifted young chef prepares imaginative nouvelle Mexican dishes with a light but sure touch. Round-trip airport transportation is included in the rates. ☒ *Calle García Vigil 407, Centro 68000* ☎ *951/514–4173* 🖷 *951/516–4412* ⊕ *www.casaoaxaca.net* ⇥ *6 rooms, 1 suite* ⚸ *Restaurant, room service, pool, massage, bar, laundry service, airport shuttle* ▤ *AE, MC, V* ❘◎❘ *CP.*

$$ ✕⊞ **Hostal de la Noria.** The comfortable rooms in this restored colonial mansion two blocks from the zócalo have unique folkloric touches—in some rooms, it's carved wooden headboards, in others wrought-iron or hammered-tin ones. All quarters have marble baths, coffeemakers, and hair dryers. Chicken mole and foil-wrapped fish fillets steamed in a mezcal sauce top the list of favorites at the elegant Restaurante Asunción ($–$$$). ☒ *Av. Hidalgo 918, Centro, 68000* ☎ *951/514–7844* 🖷 *951/516–3992* ⊕ *www.lanoria.com* ⇥ *17 rooms, 33 suites* ⚸ *Restaurant, room service, bar, baby-sitting, laundry service, free parking* ▤ *AE, MC, V.*

$$–$$$ ⊞ **Hacienda Los Laureles.** This resort hotel is in a quiet, green oasis about a 20-minute drive from Oaxaca's historical center. The pool, hot tub, and spa, which has temazcal steam baths and massage, help you regain your inner balance. If you can't leave your busy world behind, you can stay current via the Internet and business center and read English-language magazines in the library. Staff members will help you arrange horseback excursions, bicycle rides, or ecological tours to the nearby mountains. ☒ *Av. Hidalgo 21, San Felipe del Agua 68000* ☎ *951/501– 5300* 🖷 *951/520–0890* ⊕ *www.hotelhaciendaloslaureles.com* ⇥ *16 rooms, 9 suites* ⚸ *Restaurant, room service, pool, gym, massage, steam room, bar, baby-sitting, laundry service, free parking* ▤ *AE, MC, V.*

$$ ⊞ **Hotel Victoria.** On a hill surrounded by terraced grounds and gardens, this salmon-color complex has rooms, villas, and suites. Be sure to request one with a view, so you can draw back your curtains at dawn and catch your breath at Oaxaca awakening under the Sierra Madre. At night, have a drink and sample crispy grasshoppers, a Zapotec delicacy, at the bar overlooking the city lights. A trio often performs at El Tule restaurant, which is frequently filled with tour groups. A shuttle bus runs on the half hour to the city center, 10 minutes away. ☒ *Calle Lomas del Fortín 1, Lomas del Fortín 68000* ☎ *951/515–2633* 🖷 *951/515–2411* ⊕ *www. hotelvictoriaoax.com.mx* ⇥ *59 rooms, 57 suites, 34 villas* ⚸ *Restaurant, room service, in-room safes, minibars, tennis court, pool, 2 bars, baby-sitting, laundry service, travel services, free parking* ▤ *AE, MC, V.*

¢–$ ⊞ **Posada del Centro.** Simple but clean, with rustic Mexican wardrobes and night tables, comfortable mattresses, and locally made cotton bedspreads, this friendly, family-owned hotel is smack-dab in the center of the old city. Europeans and Aussies converse at several groupings of ta-

CloseUp

IN SEARCH OF THE DEAD

IF YOU ARRIVE IN MEXICO in time for El Día de los Muertos (the Day of the Dead) you might be handed a brochure as you get off the airplane. What at first glance appears to be a guide to holiday observances is really a flyer touting the Día de los Muertos liquor sales at the duty-free shop. Such American-style commercialization has led to this holiday being billed as "Mexican Halloween," but it's much more than that. The festival, which takes place October 31 through November 2, is a hybrid of pre-Hispanic and Christian beliefs that honors the cyclical nature of life and death. Local celebrations are as varied as they are dynamic, often laced with warm tributes and dark humor.

To honor departed loved ones at this time of year, families and friends create ofrendas, altars adorned with photos, flowers, candles, liquor, and other items whose colors, smells, and potent nostalgia are meant to lure their spirits back for a family reunion. The favorite foods of the deceased are also included, prepared extra spicy so that the souls can absorb the essence of these offerings.

Although the ofrendas and the colorful calaveritas (skeletons made from sugar that are a treat for Mexican children) are common everywhere, the holiday is observed in so many ways that a definition of it depends entirely on what part of Mexico you visit. After all, the country's official name is Los Estados Unidos de Mexico (the United States of Mexico), so the differences between Campeche and Chihuahua are as pronounced as they are between, say, Berkeley and Boston.

In Mexico City and smaller towns around Chiapas, people cram the streets Mardi Gras–style and party till dawn. A suburban shopping mall hosts an ofrenda competition in which contestants honor notables from Frida Kahlo to Cervantes. A restaurant owner in rural Yucatán proudly displays his ofrenda, but the handsome folks in its faded black-and-white photo aren't his parents. "I don't know who they are," he admits freely. "I just like the picture."

In Campeche, families make pilgrimages to their loved ones' graves, remove the bones, dust them off, and carefully place them back for another year. In a sandy Isla Mujeres cemetery, Marta, a middle-aged woman wearing a tidy pantsuit and stylish sunglasses, rests on a fanciful tomb in the late-afternoon sun. "She is my sister," Marta says, motioning toward the teal-and-blue tomb. "I painted this today." She exudes no melancholy; rather she's smiling, happy to be spending the day with her sibling.

Nearby, Juan puts the final touches—vases made from shells he's collected—on his father's colorful tomb. A glass box holds a red candle and a statue of the Virgin Mary, her outstretched arms pressing against the glass as if trying to escape the flame. "This is all for him," Juan says, motioning at his masterpiece, "because he is a good man." The intense late-afternoon sun causes even the fake flowers to wilt, perfuming the cemetery with the new-car smell of heated plastic; the palm-leaf shadows creeping across the tomb fail to diminish the intensity of its newest coat of paint. "This is a good day," says Juan, taking in the merrily festooned city of the dead around him. "This is a very good day."

— David Downing

bles and chairs on the front patio, lively with purple bougainvillea, red geraniums, and pink hibiscus. Rooms around this patio share a bath; those off the back patio (where meals are served 8 AM to 6 PM) have private bathrooms. Only the nicer rooms have cable TV, although each room has a color set. ⊠ *Av. Independencia 403, Centro 68000* 🏨 *951/516–1874* ⊕ *www.mexonline.com/posada.htm* 🛏 *23 rooms, some with bath* ♻ *Some cable TV* ⊟ *No credit cards.*

¢ 🏨 **Las Azucenas.** This intimate hotel occupies a charmingly restored old home near La Soledad church downtown. Pluses are the fine bed linens, the helpful staff, and the rooftop patio where coffee, *pan dulce,* cheese, and fresh fruit are served each morning. On the downside, rooms are rather small, with no phones. Ask for a tiny *tele* (TV) at the reception desk if you can't bear to miss the evening news or the nightly Mexican soaps. ⊠ *Calle Martiniano Aranda 203, at Matamoros, Centro 68000* 🕾 *951/514–7918; 877/780–1156 in the U.S.; 877/343–8570 in Canada* 🖶 *951/514–9380* ⊕ *www.hotelazucenas.com* 🛏 *10 rooms* ♻ *No room phones, no room TVs* ⊟ *MC, V.*

¢ 🏨 **Hotel Cazomalli.** Even the baked-earth floor tiles shine at this lovable hostelry in a sleepy, cobblestone district 15 minutes from downtown. Clean, bright, quiet rooms have blond-pine furnishings, handwoven fabrics, and phones. The only TV is in a small, second-floor salon. Friendly owner Marina Flores and her family serve breakfast 8–10 AM. ⊠ *Calle El Salto 104, at Calle Aldama, Jalatlaco, 68080* 🏨 *951/513–3513* ⊕ *www.mexonline. com./cazomalli.htm* 🛏 *15 rooms* ♻ *No room TVs* ⊟ *MC, V.*

¢ 🏨 **Las Mariposas.** María Teresa, the owner of this well-stocked, cozy hotel, proudly shows prospective guests the bathroom amenities, pretty tin mirrors, and other special touches of her restored early 20th-century home. Guests mingle on the open patio gladdened with laurel and lemon trees; those staying in standard rooms may share an outdoor kitchen, with sink, fridge, and cupboards. Studios have kitchenettes with coffeemakers and other essentials. ⊠ *Calle Pino Suárez 517, Centro 68000* 🏨 *951/515–5854* ⊕ *www.mexonline.com/mariposas.htm* 🛏 *7 rooms, 6 studios* ♻ *Some kitchenettes* ⊟ *No credit cards* ⫯◎⫯ *CP.*

Nightlife & the Arts

On Sunday at 12:30 PM the Oaxaca State Band sets up under the Indian laurel trees in the zócalo, whose open-air cafés often have live marimba, Andean music, or nouveau flamenco music at night. Several discotheques play salsa, rock, or techno-pop. See the monthly *Guía Cultural* ($1.20 at the MACO and Sedetur information booth on Avenida Independencia), or the free *Oaxaca Times* for event information.

Dance to live salsa music every night at the longtime leading dance club, **Candela** (⊠ Calle Murguía 413, at Calle Pino Suárez, Centro 🕾 951/514–2010). Push aside the swinging doors of **La Casa del Mezcal** (⊠ Calle Flores Magón 209, Centro 🕾 No phone), near the Juárez market, for a classic cantina experience that's diminished only slightly by the presence of a large TV set (or two). It's a bastion of machismo and strong spirits.

Cinema Pochote (⊠ Calle García Vigil 817, Centro 🕾 951/513–2087) offers art films in various languages, often English, with Spanish subtitles. The metal folding chairs are a bit hard, but, hey—admission is free, the cinema is great, and there are two shows (usually at 6 and 8 PM) every night but Monday. Every Friday night—and more often in busier seasons—the **Hotel Camino Real** (⊠ Calle 5 de Mayo 300, Centro 🕾 951/516–0611) hosts a regional dance show that's considered the town's best. The $30 admission includes a buffet dinner (beginning at 7 PM) and the show (8:30 PM) in the former convent's 16th-century chapel. Drinks aren't included; reservations are recommended.

ON THE MENU IN OAXACA CITY

MODERN OAXACAN FOOD is based on local ingredients and traditional recipes, elements of which predate the Spanish conquest. Oaxaca's markets—and inexpensive eateries near them—are among the most interesting places to sample any of the following regional specialties.

Chapulines: fried grasshoppers seasoned with salt, tangy chili, and lime. Both tiny and large grasshoppers are available, depending on the season; the large ones go down a bit easier if you remove the legs first. According to local lore, one taste will charm you into returning to Oaxaca.

Jicuatote: sweet, white gelatinous dessert made with milk, cloves, cinnamon, and cornmeal. It's served in tubs or cut into cubes and is usually colored red on top.

Tejate: beverage made from the flowers and roasted seeds of the cacao tree, plus corn, coconut milk, sugar, water, and spices. The result—white clumps suspended in brown liquid—is served in a painted gourd bowl. The concoction may look deadly, but it's actually tasty and nutritious.

Tlayudas: huge, flat tortillas spread with refried beans and topped with Oaxacan string cheese, cilantro, fresh vegetables, and, if you like, strips of tasajo (beef) or cecina (pork). They're halfway between soft tortillas and crispy tostadas, and they're hard to eat delicately.

The **Hotel Monte Albán** (✉ Alameda de León 1, Centro ☎ 951/516–2330) presents nightly dance shows at 8:30 PM. Admission is about $7 and dinner and drinks are available. **El Sol y La Luna** (✉ Calle Reforma 502, at Calle Constitución, Centro ☎ 951/514–8069) is the place to listen to live music, most often jazz, but also tango, flamenco, *trova* (ballads), and tropical tunes. You can sit over drinks or dinner on the outside patio or inside at the residence-turned-restaurant, which opens at 1 PM. There's a cover charge of $2 to $4, depending on the band, and the music begins at 9–9:30 PM. Off-season, there's usually music Friday and Saturday only. It's closed on Sunday.

Shopping

If you think you'll be buying more folk art than you can carry home, get receipts showing that you've paid the 15% sales tax on all purchases. This will allow you to send your purchases home through shipping services or shops without having to pay extra for them to provide the paperwork. Ask for referrals to shipping agents when you ask for receipts. Also, check out the high-end shops on Calle Macedonio Alcalá first; then compare prices and quality with the items you find in the *mercados* (markets), smaller shops, or in the pueblos where artisans live and work. Note that some stores are closed Sunday and others close at midday.

Markets

★ Oaxaca's largest and oldest market is held at the **Central de Abastos** (Supply Center) on the southern edge of downtown. Saturday is the traditional market day, but the enormous covered market swarms daily with thousands of buyers and sellers from Oaxaca and the surrounding villages. Along with mounds of multicolored chilies and herbs, piles of tropical fruit, electronics, bootleg tapes, and bright plasticware you'll find straw baskets, fragile green and black pottery, and *rebozos* (shawls) of cotton and silk. Don't burden yourself with lots of camera equipment or purses and bags; and keep an eye out for pickpockets and purse-slashers. Polite bargaining is expected.

★ For textiles, don't miss **Mercado de Artesanías** (✉ Calle J. P. García, near Calle Ignacio Zaragoza, Centro), a great place to shop for hand-woven and embroidered clothing from Oaxaca's seven regions. This is also the place to find the *huipiles* (short, boxy blouses, often made of velveteen) worn in the Isthmus of Tehuantepec.

Close to the zócalo, the daily **Mercado Benito Juárez** (✉ Between Calles 20 de Noviembre and Miguel Cabrera at Las Calas, Centro) has souvenirs, arts and crafts, leather sandals and bags, cheese, mole, chocolate, fruits, and much more. Locals, budget travelers, and other adventurers eat regional food in the lively stalls of the daily **Mercado 20 de Noviembre** (✉ Between Calles 20 de Noviembre and Miguel Cabrera at Calle Aldama, Centro), across the street from the Mercado Benito Juárez.

Specialty Shops

ART GALLERIES **Galería Arte Mexicano** (✉ Plaza Santo Domingo, Calle Macedonio Alcalá 407–16, Centro ☎ 951/516–3255) has local artists' work, and in
★ adjoining rooms, folk art, antiques, and silver jewelry. **Galería Indigo** (✉ Calle Allende 104, Centro ☎ 951/514–3889) is a lovely gallery in an enormous restored mansion. Ceramics, graphics, paintings, and other fine art from talented artists from Oaxaca and beyond are for sale. **Galería Soruco** (✉ Plaza Labastida 104, Centro ☎ 951/514–3938) displays work by up-and-coming artists as well as more established talents such as Sergio Hernández and Shinzaburo Takeda. Media varies, but look for watercolors, oil paintings, and graphic arts.

HANDICRAFTS **ARIPO** (✉ Calle García Vigil 809, Centro ☎ 951/514–4030) is a government-run artists cooperative with competitive prices and exclusively
★ Oaxacan work. **Artesanías Chimalli** (✉ Calle García Vigil 513-A, Centro ☎951/514–2101) has an excellent selection of crafts, including painted copal-wood animals with comical expressions. Chimalli will ship what you buy here, or what you've bought elsewhere.

Fonart (✉ Calle Crespo 114, Centro ☎ 951/516–5764) has a representative selection of quality arts and crafts from elsewhere in Mexico. Doing business since 1961, **Jarciería El Arte Oaxaqueño** (✉ Calle Mina 317, at J. P. García, Centro ☎ 951/516–1581) has a small but good assortment of stamped tin products as well as animals and skeletons carved of feather-
★ light wood; prices are great. **La Mano Mágica** (✉ Calle Macedonio Alcalá 203, Centro ☎ 951/516–4275) is a relatively expensive crafts and fine-arts gallery with a large inventory of interesting pieces.

Milagros Para Ti (✉ Calle 5 de Mayo 412, Centro ☎ 951/501–2009), a shop owned by American transplant Debbie Mounts, sells copper, brass, Talavera pottery, pewter, textiles, and shoes—mainly from Michoacan and Guanajuato—as well as Oaxaca rugs, miniature ceramic figures, woven baskets, art, alebrijes, stained glass, and antique jewelry. You'll support the women artists' co-op (open daily) by shopping
Fodor'sChoice at the huge warren of shops that makes up **Mujeres Artesanas de las**
★ **Regiones de Oaxaca** (✉ Calle 5 de Mayo 204, Centro ☎951/516–0670), often referred to as MARO. The selection and quality are excellent, and prices are reasonable.

EVERYDAY MARKETS

*Almost every neighborhood has its own market day. Check out **Mercado de Conzatti** (⊠ Calle Reforma and Calle Humboldt, Centro) Friday until 4 PM. Sunday is market day for the **Mercado de Merced** (⊠ Calz. de la República and Calle Morelos, Centro).*

Some of the best markets are in villages surrounding Oaxaca. Wednesday is market day in San Pablo Etla, which is famous for its fresh white cheese. In

addition to cooked food, breads, groceries, and clothing, Thursday's market at Zaachila has farmers bartering for spotted piglets, braying goats, and still larger animals—all before noon. Friday's tianguis (open-air market) is held in Ocotlán; where you can also admire the restored Dominican church and monastery of Santo Domingo. Sunday is market day in the Zapotec town of Tlacolula.

JEWELRY The streets west of Mercado 20 de Noviembre between Trujano and Mina are crowded with jewelry shops. Most offer 10- and 12-karat gold and modern and traditional styles.

A family business since 1963, **El Diamante** (⊠ Calle García Vigil 106-H, Centro ☎ 951/516–3983) offers reliable workmanship and courteous service within a few blocks of El Alameda. **Oro de Monte Albán** (⊠ Calle Macedonio Alcalá 403, Centro ☎ 951/514–3813) sells gold and silver reproductions of pre-Columbian jewelry found in the tombs of royalty at Monte Albán (there's also a shop at the archaeological site).

Side Trips

You can easily fill a week with tours to the artisan towns and pre-Hispanic ruins just outside Oaxaca City. A car is helpful, though guided tours provide transportation, and most stop at two or three places. Buses, co-op taxis, and private taxis round out the options. Many of the towns and sites are along or just off Carretera 190 (also known as "the Mitla route") and Carretera 175.

North & West of Oaxaca City

★ ⛰ The onetime holy city of more than 30,000 Zapotecs, **Monte Albán,** on a small road 9 km (5½ mi) west of Oaxaca, is the state's most interesting and extensively excavated ruin. Still, experts estimate that only about 10% of the site has been uncovered. Digs take place whenever the budget permits, unearthing more hints about the fascinating Zapotec people.

Monte Albán overlooks the Oaxaca Valley from a flattened mountaintop 5,085 ft high. Either Zapotecs or their predecessors leveled the site around 600 BC. The Zapotecs then constructed the existing buildings along a north–south axis, with the exception of one structure thought to have been an observatory as it's more closely aligned with the stars than with the Earth's poles. The varying heights of the site follow the contours of distant mountains. The oldest of the four temples is the Dancers' Gallery, so named for the elaborately carved stone figures that once covered the building—most of the originals are now in the site museum. Experts are unsure whether the figures, mostly male nudes, represent captives, medical cases, or warriors; the theory that they were dancers has been discarded.

In the Ball Court one or more games were played. Hips, shoulders, knees, and elbows were probably used to hit a wooden or rubber ball. Although the exact outcome of these games is unknown, there's some speculation that they were a means of solving disputes among factions or villages within the domain or of celebrating the defeat of a rival. Experts generally agree that the losing team was subsequently sacrificed to the gods.

No one knows for sure whether the Zapotecs abandoned the site gradually or suddenly, but by AD 1000 they had vacated it. Years afterward the Mixtecs used Monte Albán as a lofty necropolis of lavish tombs. More than 200 tombs and 300 burial sites have been explored to date. The most fantastic of these, Tomb 7, yielded a treasure unequaled in North America. Inside were more than 500 priceless Mixtec objects, including gold breastplates; jade, pearl, ivory, and gold jewelry; and fans, masks, and belt buckles of precious stones and metals. Many of these items are in the Museo de las Culturas in Oaxaca City. At Monte Albán proper, you'll find a small site museum with a gift shop. The cafeteria isn't half bad and has a great view of the valley of Oaxaca.

Direct buses serve Monte Albán from the Hotel Rivera del Ángel on the half hour from 8:30 to 3:30; the last bus back is at 6 PM. The round-trip fare is about $3; to stay longer than two hours you must pay a small surcharge (you can decide once you're on-site). ☎ 951/516–1215 for museum gift shop ☞ $3.50 ⊙ Daily 8:30–6.

Take some time to wander the few main streets of unimposing **Atzompa**, 8 km (5 mi) northwest of Oaxaca en route to Monte Albán. Its inhabitants produce fanciful clay pots and sculptures as well as the more traditional green-glazed plates, bowls, and cups. You can often visit the potters' simple home workshops. More convenient (although the quality of work can be disappointing) is the *mercado artesanal* (artisans market) open daily from 8 to 7.

off the beaten path

San Pablo Etla and San Agustín Etla. Carretera 190 leads to several unmarked villages worth visiting. About 15 km (9 mm) north of Oaxaca, a narrow road leads to the town of San Pablo Etla, known for its high-quality white cheese. You can purchase it along with fresh buns at the Wednesday market. Just behind the market, La Fonda (open for breakfast and lunch) has no sign, but at its simple indoor and outdoor tables, you're served excellent stuffed chilies and other regional fare. About a mile farther along Carretera 190 is a turnoff for San Agustín Etla, known for its abundance of water. One neighborhood, Vistahermosa, has several sprawling outdoor bathing facilities where you can swim, lie in the sun, lunch in the shade, and sip a cool drink. Balneario Vistahermosa on Calle Hidalgo is one of the nicest facilities; admission is $2.50. Ask locals to direct you to the papermaking co-op in the old hydroelectric plant (closed Sunday) in San Agustín proper.

South & West of Oaxaca City

In prosperous **Arrazola**, 12 km (8 mi) southwest of Oaxaca, off the road leading to Zaachila, artists carve angels, animals, and alebrijes of light, porous copal wood. These statues, from tiny to tremendous, are then painted and decorated with dots, squiggles, and other artful touches. This craft was developed by Arrazola's best-known and highest-paid artisan, Don Manuel Jiménez, and two generations later, most everyone

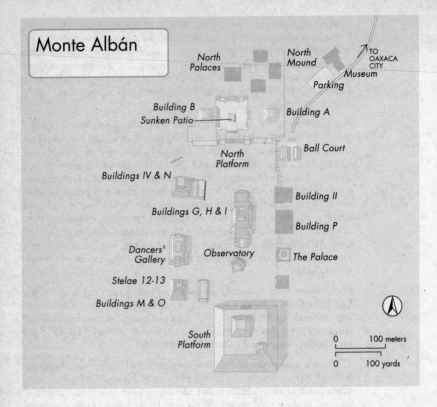

Monte Albán

North Palaces

North Mound

TO OAXACA CITY

Museum

Parking

Building B
Sunken Patio

Building A

North Platform

Ball Court

Buildings IV & N

Buildings G, H & I

Building II

Building P

Dancers' Gallery

Observatory

The Palace

Stelae 12-13

Buildings M & O

South Platform

0   100 meters

0   100 yards

in town has jumped on the bandwagon. Not far beyond Arrazola you'll come to the ruined Dominican church and monastery at **Culiapan.** The long, roofless structure was begun in the 16th century but never finished. The adjoining chapel ($2.50) is often closed.

Zaachila was an important center of Zapotec civic and religious authority at the time of the Spanish invasion. On Thursday, oxcarts loaded with alfalfa or hay head for the area's most authentic livestock market. The town, which is 17 km (11 mi) southwest of Oaxaca, also has a colorful church, a small archaeological zone with two underground tombs, and restaurants that serve regional fare.

The Spanish-Nahuatl name of **San Bartolo Coyotepec** literally translates as "Saint Bartholomew, Place of the Coyotes." The town is 12 km (8 mi) south of Oaxaca on Carretera 175. Across from the stately church is a multistall cooperative where you can buy the fragile, glossy, unglazed black pottery for which the town is deservedly famous. In **Santo Tomás Jalieza,** 20 km (12 mi) south of Oaxaca and along a small road off Carretera 175, women make belts, table runners, and other woven goods on small, back-strap looms. Prices in the co-op in the center of town are uniform and reasonable.

Twenty-nine kilometers (18 miles) south of Oaxaca on Carretera 175 is **San Martín Tilcajete,** a town full of painted wooden animals as well as cute carved devils, stern saints, and multipiece tableaux. **Ocotlán** is known for its handcrafted machetes and knives. The large town, 30 km (18 mi) south of Oaxaca on Carretera 175, has a beautifully restored Dominican church and monastery in an attractive main plaza. At the entrance to town, the Aguilar family makes distinctive figures of clay, which they paint with bright acrylic paints. The traditional Friday market draws buyers and sellers from the surrounding countryside and just a few visitors.

South & East of Oaxaca City

About 14 km (9 mi) east of Oaxaca on Carretera 190, the hamlet of **Santa María del Tule** is known for the huge *ahuehuete* cypress that towers over the pretty colonial-era church behind it. Thought to be more than 2,000 years old, it's one of the world's largest trees, with roots buried more than 60 ft in the ground and a canopy arcing some 140 ft high. It has an estimated weight of nearly 640,000 tons; to embrace the trunk, 35 adults must stretch out their arms around it. The fee to see it is 20¢.

need a break? At informal outdoor eateries in the Tule tree's shadow, local ladies tend large griddles, serving *atole* (a nutritious drink of ground cornmeal or rice), hot chocolate, soups, and snacks.

Giant rug looms sit in the front rooms of many houses in **Teotitlán del Valle,** 30 km (18 mi) southeast of Oaxaca just off Carretera 190. The small Museo Comunitario (closed Monday) on the main square focuses on the anthropology, crafts, and culture of the area. For an expensive (by local standards) but memorable lunch of authentic regional food, head for Tlamanalli at No. 39 Avenida Juárez; the restaurant has been featured in several food magazines. The rug- and *serape*-making town of **Santa Ana del Valle** is less well known than Teotitlán but also worth visiting. It's 35 km (22 mi).

Although most often visited during its bustling weekly market, **Tlacolula,** 31 km (19 mi) east of Oaxaca on Carretera 190, makes an interesting stop midweek, when the market is less important to locals but nearly as impressive to visitors. It's also recommended to visit the Baroque Dominican church. The ruins at **Yagul** aren't as elaborate as those at Monte Albán or Mitla, but they do stand handsomely atop a hill and are certainly worth a visit. This ruin, which is 36 km (22 mi) southeast of Oaxaca off Carretera 190, was predominantly a fortress above a group of palaces and temples; it includes a ball court and more than 30 uncovered underground tombs. ☎ 951/516–0123 ⬚ $3 ☉ *Daily 8–5.*

★ **Mitla,** 46 km (27 mi) southeast of Oaxaca on Carretera 190, expanded and grew in influence as Monte Albán declined. Like its precursor, Mitla is a complex of structures started by the Zapotecs and later taken over by the Mixtecs. Unlike Monte Albán, however, Mitla's charm lies not in the scale and number of buildings but in their unusual ornamentation. The striking architecture is almost without equal within Mexico thanks to the exquisite workmanship on the fine local quarry stone, which ranges in hue from pink to yellow. Unlike other ancient North American buildings, there are no human figures or mythological events represented—only complex, repetitive abstract designs. The name, from the Aztec word *mictlan,* means "place of the dead." Don't expect to see anything resembling a graveyard, however; the Zapotecs and Mixtecs typically buried their dead under the entrance to the structure where the deceased resided. The journey takes about 50 minutes from Oaxaca. Catch a *colectivo* (collective taxi) at the side of Oaxaca City's second-class bus station or a bus from the terminal or along the road to Mitla. ☎ *951/568–0316* ⬚ *$2.70* ☉ *Daily 8–5.*

Oaxaca City A to Z

To research prices, get advice from other travelers, and book travel arrangements, visit www.fodors.com.

AIR TRAVEL

AIRPORT Oaxaca City's Aeropuerto Internacional Benito Juárez is 8 km (5 mi) south of town.

🖪 **Aeropuerto Internacional Benito Juárez** ☎ 951/511-5422.

AIRPORT TRANSFERS At the airport, Transportes Aeropuerto will trundle you into the soonest available van and drop you off at your hotel for $2.50 (more if there are no other passengers). From town, buy a ticket ahead of time (ask to be picked up at your hotel). The company is closed on Sunday; for Monday departures, purchase tickets by the preceding Saturday. Regular cabs cost about $10.

🖪 Shuttles **Transportes Aeropuerto** ⊠ Alameda de León, Centro ☎ 951/514-4350.

CARRIERS Mexicana flies from various U.S. cities (including Chicago, Los Angeles, Miami, New York, and San Francisco) to Oaxaca City with a stop in Mexico City, as does Aeroméxico (from Chicago, Dallas–Fort Worth, Houston, Los Angeles, Miami, New York, and Phoenix). Direct service from Oaxaca to Acapulco and Cancún is available on Aviacsa, which flies to other national destinations via Mexico City. Aero Vega has daily service to Puerto Escondido (sometimes less in low season) and charter service to Huatulco. Aerocaribe has two triangular routes (Oaxaca–Puerto Escondido–Huatulco and in the opposite direction) each day. Aerotucán also has daily flights between Oaxaca City and both Puerto Escondido and Huatulco.

🖪 **Aerocaribe** ☎ 951/511-5247. **Aeroméxico** ☎ 951/516-1066; 800/237-6639 in the U.S. **Aerotucán** ☎ 951/501-0532. **Aero Vega** ☎ 951/516-4982 in Oaxaca; 958/582-0151 in Puerto Escondido. **Aviacsa** ☎ 951/511-5039. **Mexicana** ☎ 951/516-8414; 800/531-7921 in the U.S.

BUS TRAVEL

Deluxe buses make the six-hour nonstop run from Mexico City to Oaxaca for between $28 and $41. Oaxaca City's first-class terminal is called the ADO, from which the ADO and Cristóbal Colón bus lines provide service. The second-class bus station, Central de Autobuses, serves intermediate towns within the state. One of the lines with most destinations of interest to visitors is Fletes y Pasajes.

Avoid night trips whenever possible. Night buses, particularly first-class night buses, are prime targets for highway bandits. Although infrequent, attacks do still occur.

🖪 **ADO/Cristóbal Colón** ⊠ Calz. Niños Héroes de Chapultepec 1036, at Calle Emilio Carranza, ADO ☎ 951/513-0529; 01800/702-8000 toll-free in Mexico. **Fletes y Pasajes** ⊠ Prolongación de Trujano at the Periférico, near Central de Abastos ☎ 951/516-1218.

CAR RENTAL

🖪 Major Agencies **Alamo** ⊠ Calle 5 de Mayo 203, Centro ☎ 951/514-8534. **Budget** ⊠ Calle 5 de Mayo, across from Camino Real Hotel, Centro ☎ 951/515-0330; 951/511-5252 at the airport. **Hertz** ⊠ Plaza Labastida 115-4, Centro ☎ 951/516-2434; 951/511-5478 at the airport.

CAR TRAVEL

From Mexico City, you can take Carretera 190 (Pan American Highway) south and east through Puebla and Izúcar de Matamoros to Oaxaca City—a distance of 546 km (338 mi) along a rather curvy road. This route takes 7 to 12 hours. The toll road (*cuota*) that connects Mexico

City to Oaxaca City via Tehuacán costs about $30 one way. It cuts the driving time to five hours.

You won't need a car in Oaxaca City, which is fairly compact. Even outlying sights are easily accessible by taxi or on a tour. That said, a car is a great way for adventurous souls to see the countryside.

CONSULATES
🖪 Canadian Consulate ✉ Calle Pino Suarez 700, Local 11-B, Centro ☎ 951/513-3777.
U.S. Consulate ✉ Calle Macedonio Alcalá 407, Int. 20, Centro ☎ 951/514-3054.

EMERGENCIES
🖪 General Emergencies ☎ 066. Hospital-Red Cross ✉ Av. Armenta and López 700, Centro ☎ 951/516-4455. Police ☎ 951/516-0400.

ENGLISH-LANGUAGE MEDIA
The small Librería Grañén Porrúa sells books in English as well as Spanish. It also has CDs and high-end gifts.
🖪 Bookstore Librería Grañén Porrúa ✉ Calle M. Alcalá 104, Centro ☎ 951/516-9901.

MAIL, INTERNET & SHIPPING
There are several Internet cafés downtown. Axis, open weekdays 10–8 and Saturday 10–6, charges about $2 an hour. The centrally located *correos* (post office) is open weekdays 8–7 and Saturday 9–1. A good place to ship packages home is Artesanías Chimalli.
🖪 Cyberafé Axis ✉ Calle 5 de Mayo 412, Centro ☎ 951/514-8024.
🖪 Mail Correos ✉ Av. Independencia at El Alameda, Centro ☎ 951/516-2661.
🖪 Shipping Artesanías Chimalli ✉ Calle García Vigil 513-A, Centro ☎ 951/514-2101.

MONEY MATTERS
There are loads of banks in the Centro Histórico, and most have ATMs. *Casas de cambio* (currency exchange offices) have rates comparable to those at banks; in addition, their lines are shorter and they tend to stay open longer. Most hotels and tourist-oriented restaurants and shops accept credit cards and travelers checks; markets and smaller establishments in the city and the villages prefer cash.

The bank Banamex is open weekdays 9–4 and has an ATM. You can exchange currency at the Casa de Cambio Puebla weekdays 9–6 and Saturday 9–2.
🖪 Bank Banamex ✉ Av. Hidalgo 821, 1 block east of the zócalo, Centro ☎ 951/516-5900 is open weekdays 9–4 and has an ATM.
🖪 Exchange House Casa de Cambio Puebla ✉ Calle García Vigil 106, Centro ☎ 951/514-5103.

TAXIS
Taxis are plentiful, clearly marked, and reasonably priced. You can usually find them at any hour of the day cruising on downtown streets. There are also stands on Avenida Independencia at Calle García Vigil, on the north side of El Alameda, and on Calles Abasolo and 5 de Mayo, near the Hotel Camino Real. Cabs aren't metered. Determine the fare ahead of time (in town, usually $2.50–$3), or pay about $15 an hour for destinations within the city. For outlying destinations, ask the driver to show you the tariff card, or agree on a price before embarking on your journey.

TOURS
Many companies offer guided trips to outlying archaeological sites and towns (some of which have weekly market days). Pedro Martínez, of Bicicletas Pedro Martínez, offers both hikes and bike rides of several hours or several days. Viajes Turísticos Mitla and Agencia Marqués del

Valle are among the most established agencies. For expeditions a bit farther afield contact TierrAventura.

You can experience life in the villages for yourself by taking advantage of the Tourist Yu'u project, developed by Sedetur, the state tourism board. You stay in basic, comfortable cabins that have semistocked kitchens or access to simple eateries nearby. Santa Ana del Valle is a Zapotec town with a tradition of making serapes, thick blankets now used as rugs. It's 35 km (22 mi) southeast of Oaxaca. Visit the cold-water springs and fossilized waterfalls at Hierve el Agua or the valley-view village of Benito Juárez, where you can rent bikes or horses for jaunts into the surrounding pine forest. (Note that the cabins are attended by volunteers, villagers who sometimes have commitments to harvest, plant, or otherwise gainfully employ themselves. Don't expect five-star services. It's a good idea to bring reading material, water, and a few provisions.)

🔲 **Agencia Marqués del Valle** ⊠ Portal de Clavería s/n, Centro ☎ 951/514–6970 or 951/514–6962. **Bicicletas Pedro Martínez** ⊠ Av. Hidalgo 100-A, Jalatlaco ☎ 951/518–4452. **TierrAventura** ⊠ Calle Abasolo 217, Centro ☎ 951/501–1363 ⊕ www.tierraventura. com. **Tourist Yu'u Project** ☎ 951/516–4828. **Viajes Turísticos Mitla** ⊠ Hotel Rivera del Ángel, Calle Mina 518, Centro ☎ 951/516–6175.

VISITOR INFORMATION
The Oficina de Turismo is open daily 8–8. The adjoining shop has fairly good quality regional crafts at low prices; money goes directly to the artisans.

🖪 **Oficina de Turismo** ⊠ Av. Independencia 607, at Calle García Vigil, Centro ☎ 951/ 516–0123.

THE OAXACA COAST

Oaxaca's 520-km (322-mi) coastline is one of mainland Mexico's last Pacific frontiers. The town of Puerto Escondido has long been prime territory for international surfers. Its four-block pedestrian walkway—crowded with open-air seafood restaurants, shops, and cafés—is lively. Across the highway, however, the "real" town above, with its busy market and stores, provides a look at local life and a dazzling view of the coast.

Midway between Puerto Escondido and Bahías de Huatulco, tiny Puerto Ángel has a limited selection of hotels and bungalows tucked into the hills. The growing number of accommodations in nearby beach villages such as Zipolite and Mazunte has seduced some of Puerto Ángel's previously faithful sun-lovers.

Bahías de Huatulco (generally called simply Huatulco) covers 51,900 acres, 40,000 of which are dedicated as a nature reserve. The focal point of the development, which was masterminded in the 1980s by Fonatur (the government's tourism developer), is a string of nine sheltered bays that stretches across 35 km (22 mi) of stunning coast. The first in this necklace is Conejos, which has Huatulco's most luxurious private villas and two boutique hotels. The town of La Crucecita, originally built to house the construction crews working on area developments, has the requisite plaza with a Catholic church as well as a thriving market, small shops, budget and moderately priced hotels, and plenty of restaurants.

Bahía Tangolunda is home to Huatulco's most exclusive hotels, whereas Santa Cruz has mid-range hotels as well as a marina and a cruise ship terminal. Development of Bahía Chahué has begun with an 88-slip marina, a luxury spa, and a few small hotels. A parking lot makes the beach

accessible, and a public beach club has changing rooms, a restaurant, and a swimming pool. A Best Western and a few other small hotels, bars, and restaurants are near this bay, but most are across the highway on Boulevard Benito Juárez.

Puerto Escondido

10 *310 km (192 mi) south of Oaxaca City.*

A coffee-shipping port in the 1920s, Puerto Escondido is the first tourist town on the Oaxaca coast along Carretera 200, also known as the *carretera costera* (coast highway). Avenida Oaxaca crosses this highway, becoming Avenida Pérez Gasga. It meanders south into the tourist zone, traveling down a steep hill and passing many hotels. At the bottom of the hill, traffic is prohibited and the street becomes *el adoquín,* a four-block-long pedestrian mall lined with shops, restaurants, and lodgings paralleling the beach. The airport is on the northern edge of town, as are hotels favored by charter groups.

The town market, **Mercado Benito Juárez,** is a long walk (but a short cab or bus ride) from most hotels, and it's worth checking out on market days: Saturday and Wednesday. If you want a bit of pampering, cleanse body and soul according to ancient traditions at **Temazcalli** (⊠ Av. Infraganti 28, at Calle Temazcalli ☎ 958/582–1023), a spa that claims its treatments combine the energy of wood, fire, rock, and medicinal herbs. Choose an individual (for one or two) steam or a ritualistic group cleansing; the latter involves chants and prayers. Or, opt for a good old-fashioned massage with scented oils.

off the
beaten
path

Juquila. This town—just inland from Carretera 131, about halfway between Oaxaca City and the coast—is home to the miracle-working, diminutive Virgen de Juquila. The saint's day, December 8, is preceded by nine days of prayers and festivities, including fireworks, carnival rides, dances, and general gaiety. Any time of year, however, is pleasant to visit the small town in the heart of coffee country. Inexpensive hotels that cater to the constant stream of pilgrims line the hilly streets.

Beaches

Playa Bacocho. South of the airport, this beach has an upscale housing-and-hotel development as well as some inviting bars, discos, and restaurants. The Best Western has a lively beach club, bar, and restaurant here; the swimming pool is a gathering spot for hotel guests and those staying elsewhere. As the rip currents are strong along this stretch of beach backed by high red cliffs, ocean swimming isn't advised.

Playa Principal, Laguna Agua Dulce, Playa Marinero. These stretches run south from *el adoquín* (the tourist strip). The sand is clean but somewhat hard and brown. There are restaurants where you can seek shade and treat yourself to a cool drink. Kids walk up and down hawking seashell key rings and necklaces. Fishing and tour boats leave from Playa Marinero, beyond which, around a jumble of giant rocks creeping out into the surf is the most famous—and dangerous—beach of all, Playa Zicatela.

Fodor'sChoice **Playa Zicatela.** One of the world's top 10 surfing beaches, Zicatela's cream-
★ color sands are battered by the mighty Mexican Pipeline. In November international surfing championships are held here (followed by the even more popular bikini contest), though the town is just about always filled with sun-bleached aficionados of both sexes intent on serious surfing and hard partying. There are often lifeguards on duty, but only the most confident should swim here; even when the waters appear calm, the undertows and rip currents can be deadly. If you have any doubts about your prowess, settle for watching the surfers from the restaurants at the Arco Iris or Santa Fe hotels.

Puerto Angelito and Carrizalillo. Of Puerto Escondido's seven beaches, the safest for swimming and snorkeling are Puerto Angelito and Carrizalillo. You can reach them on foot from paths west of town or by cab ($2–$2.50) or boat ($3 per person) from Playa Marinero. Both beaches have calm, clean water and informal snack shops selling orange juice, sodas, beer, and seafood.

Where to Stay & Eat

★ $-$$ ✕ **La Galería.** This art-filled restaurant on the tourist strip is popular for its homemade pastas and wonderful pizzas. Try the Helena pie with eggplant, garlic, mushrooms, and herbs or the ravioli stuffed with Roquefort, Gouda, Parmesan, provolone, and string cheese. For dessert, order an espresso and a big slice of chocolate cake—dense and not too sweet. ⊠ *Av. Pérez Gasga, west end* ☎ *954/582–2039* ▭ *No credit cards.*

¢-$$ ✕ **La Perla.** Because it's in the "real" town uphill from the tourist zone, this seafood restaurant has some of the best prices around. The cavernous dining room is prepared to serve multitudes; don't feel put off if you're the only one there. The owners have their own fishing fleet and even sell to other local restaurants. The octopus is tender, and the ceviche comes in a spicy cocktail sauce. Breakfast is served daily, too. ⊠ *Calle 3a Poniente s/n, Sector Juárez* ☎ *954/582–0461* ▭ *No credit cards.*

★ ¢-$ ✕ **Cafecito.** Cafecito, known for its whole-grain breads and sinful pastries, serves great breakfasts and respectable lunches. Start your day with good, strong coffee and a bowl of fresh fruit, yogurt, and homemade granola. ⊠ *Calle del Morro s/n, Playa Zicatela* ☎ *No phone* ⊟ *No credit cards* ☉ *No dinner.*

¢–$ ✕ **Perla Flameante.** At the Flaming Pearl, fresh dorado, shark, tuna, and pompano come with teriyaki, Cajun, garlic, or a multitude of other seasonings, and the deep-fried onion rings and zucchini are terrific. The restaurant is open from 5 PM until around 1 AM, and your meal is often accompanied by reggae or jazz. ⊠ *Av. Pérez Gasga, near end of tourist zone* ☎ *954/582–0167* ⊟ *MC, V.*

$$ ✕⊡ **Hotel Aldea del Bazar.** Manicured lawns surround this sparkling white hotel on a bluff overlooking Playa Bacocho. Some rooms have beach views; all are tasteful and have small living rooms. The pre-Hispanic–style eucalyptus sauna will charm you almost as much as the Moorish-style restaurant ($–$$). The food is good, the waiters are attentive, and there's a variety of international dishes and seafood specialties. A ramp leads down to the beach. ⊠ *Av. Benito Juárez 7, 71980* ☎☎ *954/582–0508* ⋑ *47 rooms* ⚭ *Restaurant, cable TV, pool, massage, sauna, spa, beach, bar, travel services, free parking* ⊟ *AE, MC, V.*

$$ ✕⊡ **Hotel Santa Fe.** Exuberant plants frame the Santa Fe, a hotel with
Fodor's Choice colonial-style furnishings, hand-loomed fabrics, and, in keeping with
★ the times, a cybercafé. Some rooms have balconies overlooking the pools and patios or the beach; one-bedroom bungalows have well-stocked kitchenettes, cozy furnishings, and wide verandas. Even nonguests should treat themselves to a meal at the restaurant (¢–$$). Pastas and traditional Mexican dishes are all made with seafood and/or produce. Try the tacos with potato, cheese, and mushrooms—preferably while seated at a table overlooking the surf. ⊠ *Calle del Morro s/n, 71980* ☎ *954/582–0170 or 888/649–6407* 🖷 *954/582–0260* ⊕ *www.hotelsantafe.com.mx* ⋑ *59 rooms, 2 suites, 8 bungalows* ⚭ *Restaurant, some kitchenettes, 3 pools, wading pool, bar, shops, laundry service, Internet, free parking* ⊟ *AE, MC, V.*

$ ✕⊡ **Arco Iris.** This sprawling, three-story hotel resembles an old-fashioned guest house. Simple, clean rooms have firm beds and worn but comfortable furnishings. Some rooms have kitchenettes; most have wide verandas that overlook the surfing beach just beyond. There's a large rectangular pool, a video viewing room, and a second-floor vegetarian restaurant (¢–$) with a wonderful ocean breeze. Menu highlights include a salad of diced prickly pear cactus (without the spines, of course) and the mushroom and spinach salad. The daily lunch specials are economical, and happy hour runs from 5 to 7 PM. ⊠ *Calle del Morro s/n, Playa Zicatela, 71980* ☎☎ *954/582–0432 or 954/582–1494* ⊕ *www.hotel-arcoiris.com* ⋑ *32 rooms, 4 suites* ⚭ *Restaurant, pool, beach, bar, laundry service, free parking* ⊟ *MC, V.*

¢ ✕⊡ **Flor de María.** Hand-painted birds, flowers, and tropical scenes adorn this bright, attractive hotel a half block from Playa Marinero. Crisp sheets cover firm beds in the clean, cheerful rooms. In the restaurant (¢–$), the Canadian chef gives the daily dinner specials Italian and Peruvian touches, and there's always at least one vegetarian choice. Desserts are homemade delights. ⊠ *Entrance to Playa Marinero, 71980* ☎ *954/582–0536* 🖷 *954/582–2617* ⊕ *www.mexonline.com/flordemaria.htm* ⋑ *24 rooms* ⚭ *Restaurant, fans, in-room safes, pool, bar, laundry service; no room phones, no room TVs* ⊟ *MC, V* ☉ *Restaurant closed May–Nov. and on Tues. June–Aug. and Oct.–Nov.*

$$ ⊡ **La Hacienda.** The predominately French country–style suites at this boutique hotel have fresh flowers, a sprinkling of carefully chosen antiques, and such Mexican embellishments as blue-and-white Puebla tiles. The kitchenettes are sizable and well equipped, and the patio restaurant serves French food, preparing one or two items for dinner daily high season (December–March) and with advance notice other times.

⊠ *Calle Atunes 15, 71980* ☎☎ *954/582–0096* ⊕ *www.qan.com/ RealEstate/LaHacienda* ⌁ *7 suites* ⌂ *Restaurant, kitchenettes, pool, beach club, laundry service* ▤ *MC, V.*

$–$$ ▣ **Paraíso Escondido.** Hidden halfway up the steps of Calle Unión, this colonial-style hotel has the charm of a wealthy—and somewhat dotty—relative's house. Each room has its own mix of folksy wooden dressers, tin mirrors, and brightly colored curtains and spreads. Five third-floor suites have kitchenettes and private, ocean-view terraces, one with a Jacuzzi overlooking the sea. The old-fashioned library has some 300 books on Mexican culture and architecture as well as copies of pre-Hispanic codices. ⊠ *Calle Unión 10 71980* ☎ *954/582–0444* ⌁ *20 rooms, 5 suites* ⌂ *Restaurant, pool, bar, library; no room TVs* ▤ *No credit cards.*

¢–$$ ▣ **Villa Belmar.** Maintenance on the Villa Belmar's array of arches, domes, and cupolas—done in Mediterranean white and blue—is zealous, if not always careful. The one-bedroom apartments, comfortable double rooms, and spartan surfer huts attract a mix of people. Many accommodations have balconies from which to admire Playa Zicatela, a short walk away, and the Olympic-size pool. You can rent by the day in high season and by the week or the month at other times. ⊠ *Calle del Morro s/n, Playa Zicatela, 71980* ☎ *954/582–0244* 🖷 *954/582–2520* ⊕ *www.villabelmar.com* ⌁ *18 rooms, 15 suites, 5 apartments* ⌂ *Restaurant, pool, free parking* ▤ *MC, V.*

★ ¢–$ ▣ **Studios Tabachín del Puerto.** Well-stocked kitchenettes, shelves filled with books, and an assortment of clocks, vases, and other items make the studios here homey. Given the location a block from Playa Zicatela and the hearty, complementary breakfasts, the room rates are astonishingly low. Owner Don Pablo also manages a small country inn, the Posada Nopala, about two hours inland. The comfortable yet rustic lodge is in the pine forests of the Oaxaca mountains and is open November through April. ⊠ *Calle de Morro s/n, Playa Zicatela 71980* ☎☎ *954/582–1179* ⊕ *www.tabachin.com.mx* ⌁ *6 apartments* ⌂ *Restaurant, kitchenettes* ▤ *MC, V* ⋈ *BP.*

Nightlife

Beto, the affable host of **Los Flamingos** (⊠ Av. Hidalgo 607, at Calle 6a Oriente, Sector Reforma A ☎954/582–2902), serves up a different *botana* (appetizer) with every drink you order. You can easily make a meal of the delicious little bits. He also concocts amazing French onion soup. The cash-only cantina is open Monday–Saturday 1–8; get the free appetizers from 1 to 5.

For spirited live entertainment, stop by **Son y La Rumba** (☎ no phone), a few steps behind the tourist information booth. Owner Myka sings every night, but you never know who will drop in to jam with her—a classical violinist, a flamenco guitarist, or a European sax player. The bar is open from 10:30 PM until around 2 AM, sometimes later.

Sports & the Outdoors

Some of Puerto Escondido's pretty coves have good swimming beaches. For $45, you and as many as 10 other people can hire a boat at Playa Marinero for 1½-hour bay tours, with time for swimming and a look around for sea turtles. Fishing excursions run about $30 per hour for one to four people.

About 74 km (46 mi) west of Puerto Escondido is a tropical park encompassing the Laguna Chacahua. You can tour the lagoon in a small motor launch, watching the waterbirds that hunt among the mangroves. The bird population is most numerous during the winter months, when migratory species arrive from the frozen north. Most tours include a prosaic visit to a crocodile farm and an hour or two on the beach at Cerro Hermoso, where you eat a simple meal of grilled fish or just play on the sand.

You can rent surfboards or buy surf accessories and beachwear at **Mexpipe** (✉ Calle del Morro s/n ☎ 954/582–0759). Staffers here also give individual classes ($20 the hour) and rent apartments with kitchens by the month.

Puerto Ángel

⑪ *81 km (50 mi) southeast of Puerto Escondido.*

The state's leading seaport 100 years ago, Puerto Ángel today is a tiny hamlet on a beautiful bay. Simply by being overlooked in favor of more accessible sites, it has managed to avoid the commercialization of Huatulco and the growth of Puerto Escondido. The town and the beaches that surround it appeal to those who prefer simple pleasures. Look for the informal tourist information booth across from the main pier (no phone); it's usually staffed weekdays 9–3 and 5–7 and Saturday 9–1.

Beaches

Playa Panteón. The navy has its installations on the central town beach. The most popular swimming-and-sunning territory is past the oceanfront cemetery (*panteón* means "cemetery"). Other good and less-populated swimming and snorkeling beaches are nearby.

Playa Zipolite. Four kilometers (2 miles) west of town this long stretch of creamy sand is known for its nude sunbathers. It's a favorite with surfers, wild young things, and travelers content with a hammock on the beach and little else in the way of creature comforts. The undertow is extremely strong and riptides are unpredictable; swimming here isn't recommended.

★ **Playa San Agustanillo.** This long stretch west of Zipolite is equally pretty and somewhat less dangerous for swimming, although the current is still strong. Vendors roam the sand selling cool drinks and grilled fish on a stick.

Playa Mazunte. About 13 km (8 mi) west of Puerto Ángel, Mazunte is yet another stunning stretch of sand, which, like Zipolite and San Agustanillo, has its share of simple seafood restaurants and low-key wood and thatch accommodations. Mazunte also has the **Centro Mexicano de la Tortuga** (Mexican Sea Turtle Center). Until a 1990 government ban on turtle hunting, the village's economy was based on exploitation of the *golfina* (Olive Ridley) turtle. Since then the slaughterhouse has been closed, and, poachers aside, Mazunte is now devoted to protecting the species. The beach's name derives from the Nahuatl *Maxonteita*, which means "please come and spawn" and indeed four of the world's eight species of marine turtles come to spawn on Oaxaca's shores. A dozen aquariums are filled with turtle specimens that once again flourish in the nearby ocean. ☎ *No phone* ✉ *$2* ◷ *Tues.–Sun. 9–4.*

Where to Stay & Eat

¢ ✕🏠 **La Buena Vista.** Some of the clean, simple accommodations here have balconies, some have terraces with hammocks, but none has hot water. The third-floor restaurant (which serves breakfast and dinner) has one of the most dependable kitchens in town ($), and rooms at the top level of the hotel have a great view as well as the best breezes. There are a lot of steps to negotiate here, and no elevator. ✉ *Calle la Buena Compañía 70902* ⊕ *www.labuenavista.com* ☎☎ *958/584–3104* ➥ *20 rooms* ⚲ *Restaurant* ▭ *No credit cards.*

¢ ✕🏠 **Posada Cañón Devata.** Simple bungalows at this ecological hideaway in a wooded canyon offer private quarters; other rooms and buildings are scattered on the hillsides. Windows have screens; a drawback for some folks is the lack of hot water. The *palapa* (thatched roof) restaurant ($) is a find for vegetarians; it's open to nonguests as well. Reserve ahead for the 7 PM dinner, which runs about $9. The hilltop bar, El Cielo, is a good place to take in the sunset. ⊠ *Past the cemetery, off Blvd. Virgilio Uribe, 70902* 🕾 *958/584–3137* ✐ *janedarshan@yahoo.com* 🖙 *16 rooms, 6 bungalows* ⚲ *Restaurant, bar* 🖃 *No credit cards.*

Bahías de Huatulco

277 km (172 mi) south of Oaxaca City, 111 km (69 mi) east of Puerto Escondido, 48 km (30 mi) east of Puerto Ángel.

⚐ Projects in the Bahías de Huatulco continue to march slowly forward. Because of the fits and starts of its construction, the area has an unfinished look—a lack of polish compared to, say, Cancún. Four of the nine bays have been developed, but only Bahía Tangolunda, with its golf course and luxury hotels, has the look of a resort. Bahía Conejos is the most recently developed, with some posh homes and a few hotels. Cacaluta has been designated a national park, but still has no infrastructure.

If you have a car, you can drive to one of several undeveloped bays and play Robinson Crusoe to your heart's content. Boat tours are also an option. Standard four- to eight-hour trips—depending on how many bays you visit—might include a lunch of freshly caught fish (which costs extra). Fishing, diving, and snorkeling tours visit the beaches or reefs most suitable for those activities.

⑫ **Santa Cruz,** on the bay of the same name, was the center of a 30-family fishing community until development forced everyone inland. Today the bay is the perfect spot for swimming, snorkeling, and boating, and you can arrange boat tours and fishing trips at the marina. Mingle with the locals in the central zócalo—perhaps on the wrought-iron gazebo—or sip a cool drink or cappuccino in the Café Huatulco, a showcase for the region's excellent coffee.

⑬ **La Crucecita,** off Carretera 200, is the only place in Huatulco that resembles—in a prefab way—a real Mexican town. Its central plaza has a Catholic church whose inside walls are covered with naive frescoes. This is also a place where you can dine, hang out at sidewalk cafés, and browse in boutiques. You'll also find a bus station, ice-cream shops, cybercafés, and intimate hotels.

⑭ For a relaxing day on the beach, head to **Bahía Chahué.** The beach parking lot has a lookout point, and the marina has 88 slips, though other services aren't yet in place. You'll find a swimming pool, changing rooms, a restaurant, and shaded lounge chairs at the public beach club; there are also hotels on the main road, Boulevard Benito Juárez. The **Xquenda Huatulco Spa** (🕾 958/583–4448) has tennis courts, a pool, a fitness center, and spa treatments.

⑮ The Huatulco of the future is most evident at **Bahía Tangolunda,** where the poshest hotels are in full swing and the sea is abob with sightseeing *lanchas* (small motorboats), kayaks, and sailboats. The site was chosen by developers because of its five beautiful beaches. Although there's a small complex with shops and restaurants across from the entrance to the Barceló hotel on Boulevard Benito Juárez, most of the shopping and dining take place in the towns of Santa Cruz and La Crucecita, each about 10 minutes from the hotels by taxi or bus. Bahía Tangolunda's challenging 18-hole golf course, the **Campo de Golf Tangolunda** (🕾🕾 958/581–0059), was designed by Mario Schetjnan. The greens fee is $63 for 18 holes; carts rent for $33.

Where to Stay & Eat

$–$$$ ✕ **Don Porfirio.** You can dine inside or out on the covered patio. There's a good variety of seafood and international dishes; try the grasshoppers fried with garlic, or the less exotic combination shish kebab sautéed in tequila, served on a bed of rice with steamed veggies and potato. There's no air-conditioning, and the outdoor patio is loud with street noise, but the food and service are good. ⊠ *Zona Hotelera Tangolunda, across from Hotel Gala, Bahía Tangolunda* ☎ *958/581–0001* 🖃 *AE, MC, V.*

$–$$$ ✕ **Restaurant Ve El Mar.** The owner, Leonarda Liborio, has been here some 25 years and can tell tales about Huatulco's transformation. She converted her snack-by-the-sea place into this friendly restaurant where you can wiggle your toes in soft sand by the water's edge. It's a good spot for a romantic candlelight dinner, a casual lunch, or a "morning after" ceviche. Most dishes come with rice and cooked vegetables; the specialty is *piña rellena,* a hollowed-out pineapple stuffed with baked shrimp au gratin. ⊠ *Bahía Santa Cruz* ☎ *958/587–0364* 🖃 *No credit cards.*

¢–$$ ✕ **Oasis.** An eclectic menu and consistently good food make the Oasis popular. Choose California or Philadelphia rolls or *teppanyaki* (meat or seafood grilled with veggies) from the Japanese menu, or have a burger and fries, a shrimp cocktail, an Oaxacan sampler plate, or a chicken salad. You can sit on the patio overlooking the mostly pedestrian traffic near the square or at the indoor dining room across the street. ⊠ *Calle Flamboyan 211, at Calle Bugambilia, La Crucecita* ☎ *958/ 587–0045* 🖃 *AE, MC, V.*

★ **$$$–$$$$** ✕🏨 **Camino Real Zaashila.** This contemporary stucco resort overlooks a secluded lagoon where there's a beach and a large, free-form pool with built-in lounge chairs around its rim. Gardens, fountains, and waterfalls punctuate the property's 27 acres, and a dreamy nature walk runs from one end of it to the other. All rooms have ocean views; 10 suites and 41 rooms have small private pools. The elegant yet restrained Chez Binni Restaurant ($$–$$$) looks out at the pool and ocean beyond; the creative chef does amazing things with fresh seafood and vegetables: try the bouillabaisse for two or the vegetarian lasagna. ⊠ *Blvd. Benito Juárez 5, 70989 Bahía Tangolunda* ☎ *958/581–0460; 800/722–6466 in the U.S.* 🖷 *958/581–0461* ⊕ *www.caminoreal.com/ zaashila* 🛏 *120 rooms, 10 suites* ♨ *3 restaurants, in-room safes, minibars, tennis court, 2 pools, wading pool, gym, beach, 2 bars, baby-sitting, travel services* 🖃 *AE, DC, MC, V.*

★ **$$** ✕🏨 **Barceló.** There's a bay view from the balcony of any room in this cheerful resort hotel. Hardwood accents lend warmth to the highly polished marble, which is used in the grand public areas and the contemporary rooms. If you choose the all-inclusive rate you'll have free use of most water sports equipment, including kayaks and sailboats; dive masters are on hand with dive equipment, for an extra charge. At night candles flicker in the glamorous Casa Real restaurant (dinner only, $$–$$$); the food is northern Italian, and the pianist is superb. Reservations are essential. ⊠ *Blvd. Benito Juárez, Bahía Tangolunda 70989* ☎ *958/581–0055* 🖷 *958/581–0113* ⊕ *www.barcelo.com* 🛏 *347 rooms, 9 suites* ♨ *3 restaurants, 4 tennis courts, 2 pools, wading pool, gym, massage, sauna, beach, dive shop, boating, 3 bars, shops, children's programs (ages 5–12), travel services, free parking* 🖃 *AE, DC, MC, V* 🍽 *All-inclusive, EP.*

¢ ✕🏨 **Hotel Las Palmas.** Plain but acceptable furnishings and rock-bottom prices are what you'll find at this small, second-story hotel a block from the plaza in La Crucecita. The cramped rooms have TVs, hot water, and both fans and air-conditioning. The informal restaurant, El Sabor de Oaxaca ($), has much more to recommend it, and is almost as popular with locals as it is with visitors. Massive sampler plates introduce neophytes to refried beans, guacamole, tortillas, salsas, stuffed chilies, marinated meats, and more. You can go as exotic as cactus soup or crunchy grasshoppers (in season) or as American as a juicy steak or a burger with fries. ⊠ *Calle Guamuchil 206, 70989 La Crucecita* ☎ *958/587–0060* 🖷 *958/587–0057* 🛏 *8 rooms* ⚒ *Restaurant, fans, bar* ▤ *AE, MC, V.*

$$$$ 🛏 **Las Brisas.** Few of the spacious, minimalist rooms have a balcony, but 90% of them have an ocean view, and all of them are comfortable. For balconies overlooking the ocean, opt for a one- or two-bedroom suite. ⊠ *Blvd. Benito Juárez s/n, 70989 Bahía Tangolunda* ☎ *958/581–0355 or 888/559–4329* 🖷 *958/581–0355* ⊕ *www.brisas.com.mx* 🛏 *280 rooms, 58 suites* ⚒ *4 restaurants, 12 tennis courts, 3 pools, 2 wading pools, gym, spa, beach, dive shop, soccer, squash, volleyball, 3 bars, theater, shops, meeting rooms, travel services, free parking, no-smoking rooms* ▤ *AE, MC, V.*

★ $$$–$$$$ 🛏 **Quinta Real.** This hilltop resort—all Moorish domes and palapas— takes luxury to almost excessive heights. The suites are tranquil, airy, and plush; each has creamy white leather furniture, exquisite Guatemalan tapestries, a Jacuzzi tub, a furnished terrace, and a spectacular ocean view. Eight corner suites have plunge pools, and a few are equipped with telescopes for dolphin- and star-gazing. Vans take you to and from the beach, which is a long walk down from the hotel. ⊠ *Blvd. Benito Juárez 2, 70989 Bahía Tangolunda* ☎ *958/581–0428; 800/457–4000 in the U.S.* 🖷 *958/581–0429* ⊕ *www.quintareal.com* 🛏 *27 suites* ⚒ *2 restaurants, in-room safes, minibars, tennis court, 2 pools, wading pool, shops, bar, baby-sitting, laundry service, free parking, no-smoking rooms* ▤ *AE, MC, V.*

$$$ 🛏 **Gala.** The emphasis here is on fun; there's a kids' club to entertain the tots and plenty of water toys for older children and adults. Rooms are spacious, colorful, and furnished with light-wood pieces and pastel fabrics. Considering that the price per person (double occupancy is required) includes all food, drinks, and most water and gym sports, this isn't a bad deal if you want to do more than just work on your tan. ⊠*Blvd. Benito Juárez 4, 70989 Bahía Tangolunda* ☎ *958/583–0400 or 877/ 888–4252* 🖷 *958/581–0220* ⊕ *www.galaresorts.com* 🛏 *290 rooms, 12 suites* ⚒ *4 restaurants, room service, in-room safes, 3 tennis courts, 3 pools, 2 wading pools, gym, beach, 4 bars, dance club, shops, baby-sitting, children's programs (ages 2–15), meeting rooms, car rental* ▤ *MC, V* ⦿| *All-inclusive.*

$–$$ 🛏 **Hotel Arrecife.** The Arrecife offers lots of special deals and is popular with Mexicans. Rooms have firm beds, ceiling fans, and cable TV, but no phone; a bit more money gets you air-conditioning. The staff is courteous and helpful, and an informal restaurant sits aside the small patio pool. ⊠ *Calle Colorín 510, 70989 La Crucecita* ☎ *958/587– 1707* 🖷 *958/587–1737* 🖉 *hotelarrecife@hotmail.com* 🛏 *28 rooms* ⚒ *Restaurant, fans, cable TV, pool, free parking; no a/c in some rooms, no room phones* ▤ *MC, V.*

★ $–$$ 🛏 **Misión de los Arcos.** Everything about this intimate, classy hotel is luxurious—except for the rates, that is. Each room is different, but all have adobe-style rounded walls, cream and beige appointments, comfortable beds, and either air-conditioning or ceiling fans; most have small balconies. The honeymoon suite has a huge garden patio filled with plants, a wrought-iron table and chairs, and a fountain. ⊠ *Calle Gardenia 902, 70989 La Crucecita* ☎ *958/587–0165* 🖷 *958/587–1904* ⊕ *www. misiondelosarcos.com* 🛏 *15 rooms* ⚒ *Café, fans, gym, Internet; no a/ c in some rooms* ▤ *AE, MC, V.*

Sports & the Outdoors

BICYCLING You can rent bikes or take a guided tour of the mountains, beach, or river through **Aquaterra** (✉ Plaza las Conchas 6, Bahía Tangolunda ☎ 958/581–0012). The company also leads hiking, canyoneering, rock-climbing, snorkel, and bird-watching tours.

FISHING You can arrange sportfishing trips for sailfish, tuna, dorado, marlin, and other fish through your hotel or with the **Sociedad Cooperativa Tangolunda** (☎ 958/587–0081), the boat-owners' cooperative at the marina on Santa Cruz Bay. The cooperative also runs full-day bay tours.

HORSEBACK RIDING Arturo Casillas of **Rancho Caballo de Mar** (☎ 958/587–0530) will collect you from your hotel. Rates are about $30 for a morning or afternoon ride.

RIVER RAFTING The U.S.-base **Agua Azul** (✉ 1770 W. State St., #330, Boise, ID 83702 ☎ 208/863–1100 ⊕ www.aguaazul.com) runs whitewater-kayaking trips year-round. The exciting adventure tours of up to eight days encounter plenty of Class III and IV waters. Runs on either the Ríos Copalita or Zimatán begin in the mountains and end just shy of the Pacific Ocean. **Piraguas**

★ **Aventuras** (☎☎ 958/587–1333 ⊕ www.piraguas.com) conducts rafting and kayaking trips of different levels of difficulty to suit children as well as adults. Most trips run two to seven days and include meals, activities, and hotel or camping at reasonable rates. The company also offers canyoneering excursions: a combination of hiking, swimming, and cliff-jumping.

SCUBA DIVING Most major hotels can arrange dive classes and excursions. The PADI-certified dive masters at **Hurricane Divers** (✉ Bahía Santa Cruz ☎ 958/587–1107 ⊕ www.hurricanedivers.com) are recommended. The outfitter is near the chapel that's in the middle of the beach.

Shopping

María Bonita (✉ Marina Santa Cruz, Bahía Santa Cruz ☎ 958/587–1400), is a gallery-like shop that sells silver, platinum, titanium, and 14- and 18-carat gold jewelry as well as diamonds and other gems (accredited by the Gemology Institute of America). The store also has fine handicrafts from around the state: pewter trays, wooden sculptures, and black pottery. La Crucecita's **Mercado Municipal** (Municipal Market; ✉ Calle Guanacaste at Bugambilias, La Crucecita ☎ No phone) is a fun place to shop for postcards, leather sandals, and souvenirs amid mountains of fresh produce.

The **Museo de Artesanías Oaxaqueñas** (✉ Calle Flamboyan 216, La Crucecita ☎ 958/587–1513) is really a store, not a museum, and the artisans who create the wooden alebrijes, woven tablecloths, typical pottery, painted tinware, and rugs from throughout the state are sometimes on hand for demonstrations. The store is open daily, but you never know whether the artisans will show up. **Paradise** (✉ Calle Gardenia and Calle Guarumbo, La Crucecita ☎ 958/587–0268) has an excellent selection of casual, stylish beach and resort wear, much of which comes from Bali and India. The Mexican crafts include silver jewelry, coconut masks from Guerrero, and black pottery. The shop is open until 9 or 10 PM Monday through Saturday, with reduced hours on Sunday.

Oaxaca Coast A to Z

To research prices, get advice from other travelers, and book travel arrangements, visit www.fodors.com.

AIR TRAVEL

AIRPORTS Aeropuerto Puerto Escondido is a 10-minute taxi ride from town on Carretera 200. Aeropuerto Bahías de Huatulco is about 16 km (10 mi) from Tangolunda on Carretera 200.

📋 **Aeropuerto Bahías de Huatulco** ☎ 958/581-9004. **Aeropuerto Puerto Escondido** ☎ 954/582-0492 or 958/582-0491.

AIRPORT
TRANSFERS

The airport in Puerto Escondido is just about 15 minutes north of city center. Inexpensive taxi service is available through Transportes Turísticos. From Aeropuerto Bahías de Huatulco, Transportes Terrestre and Autotransportes Turísticos have service to and from the airport. The cost to reach Bahía Tangolunda hotels from the airport is $9 for individuals and $42 for up to 8 passengers.

📋 Taxis & Shuttles **Autotransportes Turísticos** ☎ 954/582-0459. **Transportes Terrestre** ☎ 958/581-9024. **Transportes Turísticos** ☎ 954/582-7343 or 954/582-0914.

CARRIERS

Aero Vega has daily service to Puerto Escondido from Oaxaca. Mexicana's subsidiary, Aerocaribe, connects Huatulco and Puerto Escondido to Oaxaca City daily. Mexicana flies to Huatulco from Mexico City; flights from other Mexican cities and U.S. gateways make connections in Mexico City. Aerotucán, based in Oaxaca City, offers regular and charter service to Huatulco and Puerto Escondido.

📋 **Aerocaribe** ☎ 954/582-2023 in Puerto Escondido; 958/587-1220 in Huatulco. **Aerotucán** ☎ 958/582-1725 in Puerto Escondido. **Aero Vega** ☎ 958/582-0151 in Puerto Escondido. **Mexicana** ☎ 958/587-1615 in Huatulco.

BUS TRAVEL

Direct service between Oaxaca City and Puerto Escondido is available on several first-class lines, including Estrella del Valle. Buses leave from Oaxaca City and Puerto Escondido about four or five times a day. Cristóbal Colón has several first-class buses per day leaving from Oaxaca's first-class bus terminal, frequently referred to as the ADO. Most buses travel to both Huatulco and Puerto Escondido via Salina Cruz. There's one daily direct bus between Oaxaca City and Huatulco (eight hours, $18).

Frequent, inexpensive second-class buses connect Puerto Escondido, Puerto Ángel, and Huatulco, making a pit stop at Pochutla, off the highway near Puerto Ángel. These buses roar down the highway every 15 minutes or so, and each leg costs about $2.

Note: Although infrequent, attacks by highway bandits still occur in Mexico, with the most obvious targets being first-class buses. Night buses are most vulnerable; travel by day whenever possible.

📋 **Cristóbal Colón** ✉ Calz. Niños de Chapultepec 1036, Jalatlaco, Oaxaca City ☎ 951/515-1248; 01800/702-8000 toll-free in Mexico. **Estrella del Valle** ✉ Calle Armenta and López 721, Centro, Oaxaca City ☎ 958/581-0588 ✉ Av. Hidalgo 400 at 3a. Oriente Puerto Escondido ☎ 954/582-0050. **Huatulco bus station** ✉ Calle Gardenias and Ocotillo, La Crucecita, Huatulco ☎ 958/587-0261. **Puerto Escondido bus station** ✉ Calle Primera Nte. 201, Puerto Escondido ☎ 954/582-0050.

CAR RENTAL

📋 Major Agencies **Alamo** ✉ Av. Pérez Gasga 113, Puerto Escondido ☎ 954/582-3003. **Budget** ✉ Blvd. Benito Juárez, next to Hotel Aldea del Bazar Puerto Escondido ☎ 954/582-0312; ✉ Calle Ocotillo and Calle Jasmín, La Crucecita, Huatulco ☎ 958/587-0010; 958/581-9000 for Aeropuerto Bahías de Huatulco. **Dollar** ✉ Barceló hotel, Blvd. Benito Juárez, Bahía Tangolunda, Huatulco ☎ 958/581-0055 Ext. 787 or 958/581-0480; 958/581-9004 for Aeropuerto Bahías de Huatulco. **Fast Rentacar** ✉ Plaza las Conchas 6, Bahía Tangolunda, Huatulco ☎ 958/581-0002.

CAR TRAVEL

Although having a car will better enable you to explore secluded beaches, if you don't think you'll use it every day, it may be less expensive to hire a taxi for day outings. The ride on Carretera 175 from Oaxaca City to the coast at Pochutla (eight hours) can be nerve-wracking, with plenty of sheer cliffs and hairpin turns. From Pochutla, you can drive east to

Puerto Ángel or Huatulco or west to Puerto Escondido. Carretera 131, from Oaxaca City to Puerto Escondido via Sola de Vega (seven–eight hours), is theoretically the shorter route but roadwork may add to travel time. Carretera 190 via Salina Cruz is the relatively fast (six–seven hours), not-so-curvaceous route to Huatulco. Leave early; do *not* attempt any of these roads at night.

EMERGENCIES

Red Cross ☎ 958/587-1188 in Bahías de Huatulco; 954/582-0550 in Puerto Escondido. **Police** ☎ 958/587-0020 in Bahías de Huatulco; 954/582-0498 in Puerto Escondido.

INTERNET, MAIL & SHIPPING

In Huatulco, Choco Latté is the most attractive place for a coffee and some time on the Internet. Send letters and packages through MexPost, at the entrance to La Crucecita across from the PEMEX station. Puerto Escondido's correos, north of the coast highway, is open weekdays 9–7 and Saturday 9–noon.

Cybercafé Choco Latté ⊠ Calle Gardenia 902, at Calle Tamarindo, La Crucecita, Huatulco ☎ 958/587-0165.

Mail Correos ⊠ Calle 7 Norte, at Calle Oaxaca, Puerto Escondido ☎ 954/582-0232 ⊠ Blvd. Chahué 100 La Crucecita, Huatulco ☎ 958/587-0551.

MONEY MATTERS

Puerto Escondido has at least one bank on its tourist strip and several more up in town near the market. Huatulco's most convenient bank is in La Crucecita. Hours are generally weekdays 9–4; the banks listed have ATMs.

Banks Banamex ⊠ Av. Pérez Gasga 314, Puerto Escondido ☎ 954/582-0626. **Bital** ⊠ Calle Bugambilia 1504, La Crucecita, Huatulco ☎ 958/587-0884.

TOURS

BIKING Proximity to jungle flora and fauna is one of the appeals of a bicycle tour. Edgar Jiménez offers 10- to 35-km (6- to 21-mi) trips to the mountains on 21-gear aluminum bikes with Aquaterra. Protective helmet, water, and an English-speaking guide are included in the price of $18–$40, depending on length of trip and whether breakfast is included.

BIRD-WATCHING Tour operators often combine a trip to Puerto Ángel's Playa Mazunte, and its sea turtle center, with a visit to Laguna de Ventanilla to see resident and migratory species of waterbirds, as well as crocs. You can also take the 1½-hour, nonmotorized skiff tour. Arrive any day between 8 AM and 4 PM; the lagoon entrance is about five minutes west of the Centro Mexicano de la Tortuga. In Puerto Escondido Canadian ornithologist Michael Malone offers daylong excursions (December–April) into the Laguna Manialtepec. Arrange tours (about $35 per person) through your hotel or through Viajes Ditmar, the most reliable and comprehensive agency in town.

COFFEE PLANTATIONS Visiting the coffee plantations in the mountains is especially alluring when coastal heat and humidity soar. Prices average $40–$50 per day. Contact Azteca Tours for trips to the family coffee plantation of Max Scherenberg. The all-day jaunt includes a typical lunch at the plantation and a visit to the Llano Grande waterfalls with local guides.

SIGHTSEEING Bahías Plus, which has offices in many major hotels, conducts tours to Puerto Ángel and Puerto Escondido, to coffee plantations, and to beaches; prices range from $20 to $50. Paraíso Huatulco has all-day bay cruises for $25 a person, excluding food.

Aquaterra ⊠ Plaza las Conchas 6, Bahía Tangolunda, Huatulco ☎ 958/581-0012. **Azteca Tours** ⊠ Calle Gardenia 1302, La Crucecita, Huatulco ☎ 958/583-4041 **Bahías**

Plus ✉ Calle Carrizal 704, La Crucecita, Huatulco ☎ 958/587-0216 or 958/587-0932.
Paraíso Huatulco ✉ Barceló hotel, Blvd. Benito Juárez, Bahía Tangolunda, Huatulco
☎ 958/581-0218. **Viajes Ditmar** ✉ Av. Pérez Gasga 905, Puerto Escondido ☎ 954/
582-0734.

VISITOR INFORMATION

The Puerto Escondido tourism office is open weekdays 9–3 and 4–7,
Saturday 10–3. The staff at the small information desk on the pedes-
trian walkway's west end is often more helpful than the main tourism
office staff. The booth is open weekdays 10–2 and 4–6, Saturday 10–1.
The Huatulco branch of the state tourism office is open weekdays 8–5,
Saturday 9–1. Sedetur is open Friday 9–5 and Saturday 9–1.

◼ **Convention and Visitors' Bureau Web site** ⊕ www.baysofhuatulco.com.mx. **Puerto
Escondido tourism office** ✉ Blvd. Benito Juárez, about a block from Aldea del Bazar
Hotel, Playa Bacocho, Puerto Escondido ☎ 954/582-0175. **Sedetur** ✉ Blvd. Benito Juárez
s/n, in front of Restaurante Misión Fa-Sol, Bahía Tangolunda, Huatulco ☎ 958/581-
0176 or 958/581-0177.

CHIAPAS AND TABASCO

11

FODOR'S CHOICE

Museo Na Bolom, San Cristóbal de las Casas
Na Bolom, restaurant and hotel, San Cristóbal
Palenque, ruins
Parque Museo La Venta, Villahermosa
Yaxchilán, ruins

HIGHLY RECOMMENDED

HOTELS Camino Real, Tuxtla Gutiérrez
Casa Felipe Flores, San Cristóbal
Chan Kah, Palenque Town
Escudo Jaguar, near Yaxchilán ruins
La Selva, Palenque Town

RESTAURANTS El Asador Castellano, Tuxtla
La Casa del Pan, San Cristóbal
Maya Cañada, Palenque Town
Restaurant L'Eden, San Cristóbal
La Selva, Palenque Town
Los Tulipanes, Villahermosa

SHOPPING Mercado, San Cristóbal

EXPERIENCES Agua Azul, series of cascades
Cañón del Sumidero, Chiapa de Corzo canyon
Misol-Há, waterfall

Updated by
Jane Onstott

KNOWN TO MANY FOR THE RUINS of Palenque, the colonial town of San Cristóbal de las Casas, and the revolutionary Zapatista movement, Chiapas and Tabasco have typically drawn trekkers and travelers rather than tourists. Unlike the country's popular beach resorts, Chiapas and Tabasco require transfers from Mexico City. Substantial bus or car travel is usually part of the itinerary, although San Cristóbal de las Casa, Tuxtla Gutiérrez, and Villahermosa have airports.

World attention was drawn to off-the-beaten-path Chiapas in the mid-1990s, when guerrillas staged a brief but potent rebellion, launching what has turned out to be a long-term struggle for equal rights for Mexico's indigenous groups. A bloody past of exploitation by and fierce confrontation with outsiders remains vividly present, as already impoverished indigenous communities in Chiapas are forced to compete for their lands with developers and new settlers. In fact, Chiapas has been at the margin of the nation's development and is one of the poorest states. Land distribution is skewed as well: 1% of landowners holds 15% of the territory—about 50% of the arable land—keeping the colonial system nearly intact.

It was the indifference of the Mexican government to their plight that helped bring the anger of the indigenous people to a boil in 1994, leading the Zapatista National Liberation Army (EZLN is the Spanish acronym) to an armed uprising. The government of President Vicente Fox held meaningful talks with EZLN, and the national and international interest sparked by the movement bodes well for further development in the region. The pipe-smoking Zapatista spokesperson, Subcomandante Marcos, has become a cult figure in Mexico: his ski-masked image appears on everything from magazine covers to children's toys, and he posts his poetic communiqués on the Internet.

Nominally enriched a half century ago with the discovery of oil in the Gulf of Mexico on its northern border, Tabasco also has a bloody past. During the 1920s and 1930s, Tomás Garrido Canabal, a vehemently anticlerical governor, outlawed priests and had all the churches either torn down or converted to other uses. Riots, deportations, and property confiscations were common. That said, you won't find much evidence of Tabasco's turbulent past today; the spirit that prevails here—at least in modern Villahermosa—is one of commerce.

Travel to Chiapas is getting a boost from a government promotion known as the Mundo Maya Travel Circuit. Although the circuit showcases Maya ruins and colonial cities in the name of regional development and ecotourism, development in the area has done little to help the environment or the indigenous groups. The Lacandon jungle is disappearing at an alarming rate. Massive erosion and deforestation are taking their toll as new settlers, forced off communal farmlands in the highlands, try unsuccessfully to farm the rain forest with highland farming techniques (after a couple of years, the soil loses its nutrients, and the settlers must clear fresh plots). The ecosystem is further compromised by ranchers who move into the abandoned lands to raise their cattle.

When you set out along tortuous mountain roads—full of dramatic hairpin turns along the edges of mist-filled ravines—you'll still find remote clusters of huts and cornfields planted on near-vertical hillsides. You'll pass traditional women wrapped in deep-blue shawls and coarsely woven wool skirts, and Indian children selling fruit and flowers by the road. Chiapas has nine distinct linguistic groups, most notably the highland-dwelling Tzotzils and the Tzeltals, who live in both highland and lowland areas. In more isolated regions, many villagers speak only their native language.

Numbers in the text correspond to numbers in the margin and on the Chiapas and Tabasco and San Cristóbal de las Casas maps.

If you have 3 days

Spend the first day and night at the Maya ruins at ▣ **Palenque** ㉑ ▶, visiting the stunning jungle waterfalls at nearby **Misol-Há** ⑳ and **Agua Azul** ⑲. Tours from Palenque are the best way to pack it all into one day. The next day, drive south to ▣ **San Cristóbal de las Casas** ① – ⑧. Spend at least two hours on a walking tour of this enchanting highland town and spend the night. On Day 3, visit the Maya villages of **San Juan Chamula** ⑭, known for its Catholic church where pre-Hispanic rituals are performed, and **Zinacantán** ⑮, famous for its colorful handwoven tunics and shawls. Return to San Cristóbal to visit the market, shop for folk art, and spend the night.

If you have 5 days

Spend the first day and night in ▣ **Villahermosa** ㉕ ▶, seeing the giant Olmec heads and the anthropology museum. On Day 2, drive or take a bus to ▣ **Palenque** ㉑, visit the ruins, and stay overnight. On Day 3, visit the waterfalls at **Misol-Há** ⑳ and **Agua Azul** ⑲, or the archaeological site of **Toniná** ⑱, near Ocosingo, en route to ▣ **San Cristóbal de las Casas** ① – ⑧. On Day 4, visit **San Juan Chamula** ⑭ and **Zinacantán** ⑮ in the morning and then return to San Cristóbal to shop for native crafts and spend another night. On Day 5, head south on Carretera 190 to see the **Lagos de Montebello** ⑬. On the way back, visit as many of the following as your schedule permits: the small pre-Hispanic sites of **Chinkultik** ⑫ and Tenam Puente; the charming town of **Comitán** ⑪; the pottery-producing village of **Amatenango del Valle** ⑩; and the stalactite- and stalagmite-graced **Grutas de Rancho Nuevo** ⑨. For a less rushed visit, plan to spend the night in Comitán and leave early the next morning for San Cristóbal or **Tuxtla Gutiérrez** ⑰.

If you have 8 days

Spend the first day and night in ▣ **Villahermosa** ㉕ ▶, as in the five-day itinerary, adding a visit to the unusual Maya temples at **Comalcalco** ㉖. Spend the next four days as on Days 2–5 of the five-day itinerary—seeing **Palenque** ㉑, **Misol-Há** ⑳, **Agua Azul** ⑲, and **Toniná** ⑱ on the way to **San Cristóbal de las Casas** ① – ⑧, from which you can take day trips north and southeast. On Day 7, head west, touring colonial **Chiapa de Corzo** ⑯ and the impressive Sumidero Canyon en route to ▣ **Tuxtla Gutiérrez** ⑰. Spend that night and the next in Tuxtla. On Day 8, visit Tuxtla's zoo and stroll in the Parque Jardín de la Marimba in the late afternoon.

If you want to go all out seeing Maya sites, add a day trip to **Bonampak** ㉓ and **Yaxchilán** ㉔ —as a long driving tour or a more leisurely tour aboard a small aircraft. You can arrange to spend the night at the ecotourism site Escudo Jaguar—on the Río Usumacinta and near the boat launch for Yaxchilán—or in Palenque, Ocosingo, or San Cristóbal. From San Cristóbal, you can squeeze in a very full day trip to **Comitán** ⑪, the **Lagos de Montebello** ⑬, and **Chinkultik** ⑫.

Most of those who visit Villahermosa, Tabasco's capital, are traveling for business. But the city has an excellent museum of pre-Columbian anthropology and an unparalleled collection of massive Olmec heads and altars. Both provide a good introduction to the indigenous heritage of Tabasco and Chiapas. Palenque, with its incredible Maya ruins, is culturally and geographically linked with Tabasco's lowlands. Geographically stunning, Tabasco also has lakes, lagoons, caves, and wild rivers that surge through jungle.

Exploring Chiapas & Tabasco

The abode of the ancient Olmecs, Tabasco is lush, green, and pastoral; Chiapas is for the most part mountainous, with archaeological ruins, natural wonders, charming towns, and sinuous roads. The colonial city of San Cristóbal de las Casas dominated both regions when the Spanish conquistadores held sway over the country. Thanks to its petroleum industry, Villahermosa is by far the stronger economic force today.

For most, the highlights of a trip to Chiapas and Tabasco are still the ruins of Palenque and the town of San Cristóbal. These and all other major sights are accessible by road from either Tuxtla Gutiérrez or Villahermosa. The once-isolated ruins of Yaxchilán and Bonampak are now more accessible—by small plane or paved roads (and, in the case of Yaxchilán, an hour's boat ride).

Note: Although travel in the area is reasonably safe, at this writing the U.S. State Department was advising visitors to "exercise caution" in Chiapas because of the presence of armed rebels and armed civilian groups in some areas. Although none of the sporadic confrontations has been near a main tourist destination—and no tourist has ever been harmed—contact the U.S. State Department or any of the Mexican Government Tourist Offices for an update on the situation before you go. Carry your tourist card and passport even on day trips throughout the region, as there are military checkpoints along both main and secondary roads. If you're a first-time visitor, you may be more comfortable taking tours of the region—especially if you don't speak Spanish.

About the Restaurants

Outside a few upscale places in the cities and the high-end hotel restaurants, reservations aren't necessary, there's no dress code to speak of, and prices are reasonable: a filling dinner (helped out by tortillas in one of their myriad forms) usually won't cost more than $10 per person. It's a fairly common practice to eat dinner before 8 PM, and lunch is often the main meal of the day, traditionally served between 1 and 4 PM.

About the Hotels

Most San Cristóbal hotels are within walking distance of the main plaza and are colonial—or if not, at least a century old—in keeping with the rest of the town. Tuxtla Gutiérrez lodgings tend to be more functional than frilly; this town is the no-nonsense business and transportation hub of Chiapas. An exception to the rule is the Camino Real, which resembles a small palace.

Palenque is no longer a jungle outpost, fit only for those who consider rustic amenities colorful. This is a growing town with modern, comfortable hotels. The best and newest are along the Carretera Palenque-Pakalná that goes to the Palenque ruins just outside town. There are quite a few *posadas* (guest houses) and super-budget dive hotels downtown as well as a couple agreeable lodgings and restaurants in the quiet neighborhood of La Cañada, between downtown and the highway.

Archaeological Sites
Ruins of Maya cities in mysterious, overgrown jungles are a big draw in this area. Unparalleled Palenque has the most appeal, and the lesser-known sites of Toniná, Bonampak, and Yaxchilán (pronounced ya-shee-*lan*) are attracting more attention than ever.

Food
The food of Chiapas is influenced by the region's Maya heritage. Try *atole* (a slightly sweetened cornmeal drink); the many local variations of tamales; *cochinito horneado* (smoked pork); candied fruit; and any dishes that contain the tasty herbs, such as *chipilín* and *yerba santa* (or *mumu*, as locals call it). Restaurants are generally not outstanding compared with those in other regions of Mexico.

11

Tabasco saves some of its export beef for the Villahermosa restaurants, which also serve lots of fresh fish from the Gulf and freshwater lakes and rivers. Local specialties include *pejelagarto,* an ugly fish with a head like that of an alligator and a strong, sweet flavor. Also try *puchero,* beef stew with vegetables and plantains; river shrimp; *tostones* (fried plantain chips); baked bananas with cream; banana liqueur; and the region's fresh, white cheese.

Shopping
The weavers of Chiapas produce striking embroidered blouses, *huipiles* (tunics), bedspreads, and tablecloths. Other artisans create leather goods, homemade paper products, and painted wooden crosses. Lacandon bows and arrows and reproductions of the beribboned ceremonial hats worn by Tzotzil indigenous leaders also make interesting souvenirs.

Chiapas is one of the few places in the world that has amber mines, so finely crafted jewelry made from this prehistoric resin is easy to find in San Cristóbal—as are plastic imitations sold by street vendors (stores usually sell amber and street vendors commonly have the fakes, although there's some crossover). San Cristóbal is also known for the wrought-iron crosses that bless its rooftops. Although many of the iron-working shops have closed, you can still find the crosses in a few old-fashioned stores. Tuxtla Gutiérrez and Palenque, although not known for crafts, have a few shops selling quality folk art from throughout the state.

Villahermosa's hotels, which cater to the business interests of the oil industry, are more expensive than those in other towns. These fancier hotels tend to be away from the city center, near the neighborhood called Tabasco 2000 and the Parque Museo La Venta in an area sometimes called the Zona Hotelera (Hotel Zone). But there are comfortable and economic hotels downtown, near the Río Grijalva (Grijalva River) or in the nearby, pedestrian-friendly Zona Luz (Light Zone).

Many, though not all, hotels quote prices that already include the 17% tax. This is especially true of budget and moderately priced lodgings. Be sure to ask about this when you're given a price.

WHAT IT COSTS				
	$$$$	$$$	$$	$	¢
RESTAURANTS	over $25	$15–$25	$10–$15	$5–$10	under $5
HOTELS	over $250	$150–$250	$75–$150	$50–$75	under $50

Restaurant prices are for a main course excluding tax and tip. Hotel prices are for two people in a standard double room in high season, based on the European Plan (EP, with no meals) and excluding service and 17% tax.

Timing

In the highlands, September is the peak of the rainy season, which officially starts in late August and can run till early October. It gets cold at night, and can be chilly during the day as well; pack a warm sweater and a jacket and layer your clothing. The warmest months are April and May. It's very hot and humid in the lowlands most of the year, but especially after February, with temperatures peaking in May and June.

SAN CRISTÓBAL DE LAS CASAS

San Cristóbal is a pretty highland town of about 150,000 people in a valley of pine forests interspersed with maize fields and orchards. Here indigenous women with babies tied tightly in colorful shawls share the plaza with starry-eyed backpackers. The Zapatistas have made international headlines with their sporadic but nevertheless disconcerting harassment of foreigners. But visitors to this town generally aren't put off by articles on government troops and the EZLN. In truth, the rival sides are more likely to snipe at each other via newspaper editorials or the Internet.

For those willing to overlook the political situation, San Cristóbal makes the perfect hub for exploring some of the region's lakes, villages, and archaeological sites. Small enough to see on foot in the course of a day, the town is also captivating enough to invite a stay of three days, a week, or longer. In addition to admiring the town's colorful facades, plan an early morning visit to the *mercado* (market) and spend some time relaxing in a café.

The town's cool climate is a refreshing change from the sweltering heat of the lowlands. On chilly evenings, wood smoke scents the air, curling lazily over the red-tile roofs of small, brightly painted stucco houses and more elegant colonial mansions. The sense of the mystical here is intensified by the fog and low clouds that hover over the surrounding mountains and by the remarkable quality of the early morning and late-afternoon light.

San Cristóbal and the surrounding communities are the ancestral home of the highland Maya, who at the time of the Spanish conquest were centuries past their golden era. In 1526 the Spaniards under Diego de Mazariegos defeated the Chiapan Indians at a battle outside town. Mazariegos founded the city, which was called Villareal de Chiapa de los Españoles, in 1528. For most of the colonial era, Chiapas, with its capital at San Cristóbal, was a province of Guatemala. Lacking the gold and silver of the north, it was of greater strategic than economic importance.

Under Spanish rule the region's resources became entrenched in the *encomienda* system, in which wealthy Spanish landowners forced the locals to work as slaves. "In this life all men suffer," lamented a Spanish friar in 1691, "but the Indians suffer most of all." The situation improved

Chiapas & Tabasco

Bahía de Campeche

Ciudad del Carmen

Laguna de Términos

186

Frontera

Paraíso 27

Comalcalco 26

Villahermosa 25

180

187

195

CAMPECHE

TABASCO

Catazajá

186

199

Palenque Town 22

Palenque 21

Misol-Há 20

Agua Azul 19

199

Tenosique

Río Usumacinta

198

Cañon del Sumidero

San Juan Chamula

Ocosingo

Toniná 18

Oxchuc

Yaxchilán 24

Tuxtla Gutiérrez 17

Zinacantán 14

15

Huixtán

Lacanjá

Bonampak 23

Chiapa de Corzo 16

Las Grutas de Rancho Nuevo 9

Río Colorado

Río Lacanjá

San Cristóbal de las Casas

1 – 8
see detail map

190

SELVA LACANDONA

Amatenango del Valle 10

Comitán 11

La Trinitaria

Lagos de Montebello 13

Chinkultik 12

CHIAPAS

Presa la Angostura

190

SIERRA MADRE DE CHIAPAS

GUATEMALA

200

Motozintla

KEY

Rail Lines

Start of itinerary

Tapachula

Puerto Madero

0   20 miles

0   30 km

only slightly through the efforts of Bartolomé de las Casas, the bishop of San Cristóbal, who in the mid-1500s protested the torture and massacre of the local people; these downtrodden protested in another way, murdering priests and other *ladinos* (Spaniards) in infamous uprisings.

Mexico, Guatemala, and the rest of New Spain declared independence in 1821. Chiapas remained part of Guatemala until electing by plebescite to join Mexico on September 14, 1824—the date is still celebrated throughout Chiapas as the Día de la Mexicanidad (Day of Mexicanization). In 1892, because of San Cristóbal's allegiance to the Royalists during the War of Independence, the capital was moved to Tuxtla Gutiérrez. With that shift went all hope that the town would keep pace with the rest of Mexico. It wasn't until the 1950s that the roads into town were paved and the first automobiles arrived.

Exploring San Cristóbal de las Casas

San Cristóbal is laid out in a grid pattern centered on the zócalo. (Note that street names change on either side of this square: Calle Francisco Madero to the east of the square, for example, becomes Calle Diego de Mazariegos to the west.) The town was originally divided into *barrios* (neighborhoods), which now blend together into a city center that's easy to negotiate.

In colonial times, Indian allies of the triumphant Spaniards were moved onto lands on the outskirts of the nascent city. Each barrio was dedicated to a different occupation. There were Tlaxcala fireworks manufacturers in one part of the town and pig butchers from Cuxtitali in another. Although specific divisions no longer exist, some of the local customs have been kept alive. For example, each Saturday certain houses downtown will put out red lamps to indicate that fresh homemade tamales are for sale.

Surrounding San Cristóbal are many small villages celebrated for the exquisite colors and embroidery work of their inhabitants' costumes. Huixtán (hweesh-*tan*) and Oxchuc (osh-*chuc*) are about 28 km and 43 km (17 mi and 27 mi), respectively, on the road to Ocosingo. The Thursday market in Tenejapa, 27 km (17 mi) northeast of San Cristóbal, is worth seeing.

a good walk

Head for the heart of downtown, the Plaza 31 de Marzo, or **zócalo** ❶ ▶, and take in the surrounding colorful buildings, a few of them built by the conquistadors. Note the 16th-century Casa de Diego de Mazariegos on the southeast corner (it's now the Hotel Santa Clara) and, to the northwest, the neoclassical Palacio Municipal, with its numerous arcades. **La Catedral** ❷ (cathedral), on the north side, has a fascinating facade. Head one block north and one block west to the **Museo del Jade** ❸, with its fabulous reproduction of the sarcophagus lid from Pakal's royal tomb. Walk east two blocks to Avendia General Utrilla and then north (left) 3½ blocks to the 16th-century **Templo de Santo Domingo** ❹ with its Baroque facade. Walk around the complex to its museum and famous textiles cooperative amid the Indian families selling goods in the large exterior courtyard.

Return to Avenida General Utrilla and walk north three blocks to the **mercado** ❺ and its stalls filled with produce, candles, and other necessities. You can catch a cab, or walk nine blocks east on Calle Comitán to the **Museo Na Bolom** ❻, a repository of Indian artifacts. As the museum is shown by tour only, you'll probably want to time your arrival for the 11:30 or 4:30 English- and Spanish-language tours. If you've made prior arrangements, you can end the day at the **Museo Sergio Castro** ❼,

A VOICE OF MANY VOICES

I N THE EARLY HOURS OF JANUARY 1, 1994, while most of Mexico was sleeping off the New Year's festivities, the Zapatista National Liberation Army (EZLN), who took its name from the Mexican revolutionary Emiliano Zapatista, surprised the world when it captured San Cristóbal de las Casas and several surrounding towns, demanding land redistribution and equal rights for Chiapas's indigenous peoples.

The Zapatista triumph was short-lived. The mostly Tzotzil and Tzeltal troops soon departed San Cristóbal, and on January 12, President Carlos Salinas de Gortari called for a unilateral cease-fire. According to government figures, 145 lives were lost during the 12-day struggle. But hundreds have been killed in years of clashes between rebel supporters and paramilitary groups; thousands have been displaced. "We did not go to war on January 1 to kill or to have them kill us," declared Subcomandante Marcos, the EZLN's charismatic leader and spokesperson. "We went to make ourselves heard."

The factors that led to the Zapatista uprising are many. Centuries of land appropriation repeatedly uprooted Chiapas's Maya-descended groups. The North American Free Trade Agreement (NAFTA), which went into effect on January 1, 1994, symbolized Mexico's entry into the First World for its political and business elite. But despite its natural resources (Chiapas provides nearly half of Mexico's electricity and has extensive oil and gas reserves), the state's indigenous residents still suffer appallingly high rates of illiteracy, malnutrition, and infant mortality.

In 1995 President Ernesto Zedillo sent troops into the Lacandon jungle to capture the Zapatista leadership, including Marcos, whom the government identified as former Mexico City communications professor Rafael Sebastián Guillén. The ambush failed. The following year negotiations with the rebels resulted in the so-called San Andrés Accords, which called for a constitutional amendment recognizing indigenous cultural rights and limited autonomy. President Zedillo instead pursued a policy of low-intensity warfare—often in the name of "development" or "reforestation"—for the rest of his administration. The policy led to disastrous results, including the massacre of 45 unarmed Zapatista supporters at the hands of pro-government paramilitary forces in the village of Acteal, Chenalho, in December 1997.

During his presidential campaign, Vicente Fox insisted that he could resolve the Zapatista conflict in 15 minutes, an example of Foxspeak frequently chided by his critics. Nevertheless, during his inaugural address he announced that he was ordering partial troop withdrawals and would submit legislation based on the San Andrés Accords. In turn, Marcos announced three conditions for the restoration of negotiations—further military withdrawals, the release of Zapatista prisoners, and implementation of the accords. The first two have been achieved. Fox, however, continues to be engaged in a media war with Marcos, who began to express doubts about the president's desire to pursue peace. In early 2001, a Zapatista caravan traveled through 12 Mexican states and into the capital to demand negotiations. More than 100,000 gathered in the city's zócalo in a dramatic culmination of the two-week procession.

Fox, who welcomed the Zapatistas to the capital, has come under attack from members of the Institutional Revolutionary Party (PRI) as well as members of his own National Action Party (PAN). Not everyone is convinced of the Zapatistas' noble motives. In February 2003, a group of Zapatistas from the Nuevo Jerusalem community of Ocosingo chased out the American owners of a guest ranch bordering the archaeological ruins of Toniná. The state government declined to intervene. Around the same time, a group of Zapatistas reportedly detained for a few hours tourists on a kayaking trip along the Río Jatate. Whether these are isolated incidents or a matter of Zapatista policy remains to be seen.

where the owner gives nightly slide shows and talks about regional costumes and textiles. Either catch a taxi or walk five blocks south on Avenida Vicente Guerrero and eight blocks west on Calle Real de Guadalupe. If the English-language slide show isn't happening, proceed instead to the **Museo del Ambar** ❽, which as its name implies, has examples of all different types of this semiprecious stone.

What to See

❷ **La Catedral.** Dedicated to San Cristóbal Mártir (St. Christopher the Martyr), the cathedral was built in 1528, then demolished, and rebuilt in 1693, with additions during the 18th and 19th centuries. Note the classic colonial traits on the ornate facade: turreted columns, arched windows and doorways, and beneficent-looking statues of saints in niches. The floral embellishments in rust, black, and white accents on the ocher background are unforgettable. Inside, don't miss the painting *Nuestra Señora de Dolores* (*Our Lady of Sorrows*) to the left of the altar, beside the gold-plated *Retablo de los Reyes* (*Altarpiece of the Three Kings*), the Chapel of Guadalupe in the rear, and the gold-washed pulpit. ⊠ *Calle Guadalupe Victoria at the zócalo* ◷ *Daily 9–2 and 4–8.*

★ ❺ **Mercado.** This municipal market occupies an eight-block area. Best visited early in the morning—especially on the busiest day, Saturday—the market is the social and commercial center for the indigenous groups from surrounding villages. Stalls overflow with produce, turkeys, medicinal herbs, flowers, firewood, and wool, as well as *huaraches* (sandals), grinding stones, candles, and candied fruit. Don't carry anything of value here: robberies are common. If you must bring your camera, be discreet, and, as always, ask permission before photographing people. ⊠ *At Avs. General Utrilla, Nicaragua, Honduras, and Belisario Domínguez* ◷ *Daily 7 AM–dusk.*

❽ **Museo del Ambar de Chiapas.** Staffed by volunteers, this museum has exhibits showing how and where amber is mined as well as its function in Maya and Aztec societies. You'll see samples of everything from fossils to recently quarried pieces to sculptures and jewelry. Labels are in Spanish only; ask for an English-language summary. Staff members can explain and demonstrate how to distinguish between real amber and fake. The store sells souvenirs and jewelry. ⊠ *Plazuela de la Merced, Calle Diego de Mazariegos s/n* ☎ *967/678–9716* ☑ *$1* ◷ *Tues.–Sun. 10–2 and 4–7.*

❸ **Museo del Jade.** Jade was prized as a symbol of wealth and power by Olmec, Teotihuacán, Mixtec, Zapotec, Maya, Toltec, and Aztec nobility, and this museum shows jade pieces from different Mesoamerican cultures. The most impressive piece is a reproduction of the sarcophagus lid from Pakal's tomb, at Palenque. It's said to be one of the most faithful and brilliant Maya reproductions in the world. Reproductions of ancient pieces are for sale in the store. ⊠ *Av. 16 de Septiembre 16* ☎ *967/678–2550* ☑ *$3* ◷ *Daily noon–9.*

❻ **Museo Na Bolom.** It's doubtful that any foreigners have made as much of an impact on San Cristóbal as did the European owners of this home-turned-library-museum-restaurant-hotel. Built as a seminary in 1891, the handsome 22-room house was purchased by Frans and Gertrude (Trudi) Blom in 1950. He was a Danish archaeologist, and she was a Swiss social activist; together they created the Institute for Ethnological and Ecological Advocacy, which carries on today. It got its name, Na Bolom (House of the Jaguar), from the Lacandon Maya with whom Trudi worked: Blom, you see, sounds like the Maya word for jaguar. Both Frans and Trudi were great friends of the small Lacandon tribe,

Fodor'sChoice
★

San Cristóbal
de las Casas

whose traditions and way of life they documented. Their institute is also dedicated to reforestation of the surrounding area. It plants thousands of trees each year, and its own extensive nursery-garden is filled with firs, fruit trees, vegetables, and flowering plants.

Both Bloms are deceased, but Na Bolom showcases their small collection of religious treasures, which was hidden in attics during the anticlerical 1920s and 1930s. Also on display are findings from the Classic Maya site of Moxviquil (pronounced mosh-vee-*keel*), on the outskirts of San Cristóbal, and objects from the daily life of the Lacandon. Trudi's bedroom contains her jewelry, shawls, canes, collection of indigenous crafts, and wardrobe of embroidered dresses. A research library holds more than 10,000 volumes on Chiapas and the Maya. Note that the only way to visit the museum is on one of the tours that are conducted Monday–Saturday in English and Spanish at 11:30 and 4:30 (Sunday-morning tours are in Spanish only; afternoon tours are in English and Spanish.)

Across from the museum, the Jardín del Jaguar (Jaguar Garden) store sells crafts and souvenirs. Look for the thatch hut, a replica of local Chiapan architecture. It consists of a mass of woven palm fronds tied to branches, with walls and windows of wooden slats, and high ceilings that allow the heat to rise. The shop here sells Lacandon crafts such as flutes and bows and arrows, as well as black-and-white photos.

Revenue from Na Bolom's guest house, tours, restaurant, and gift shop supports the work of the institute. You can arrange for a meal at Na Bolom even if you don't stay here. In addition, the staff is well connected within San Cristóbal and can arrange tours to artisans' co-ops, villages, and nature reserves that are off the beaten path. ⊠ *Av. Vicente Guerrero 33, between Calle Comitán and Calle Chiapa de Corzo* ☎ *967/678–1418* ⌨ *Museum and tour $4.50* ⊘ *Tours: Daily 11:30 and 4:30. Library: weekdays 10–4. Store: Mon.–Sat. 9:30–2 and 4–7, Sun. 4–7.*

❼ Museo Sergio Castro. Sergio Castro, an agronomist from northern Mexico who has dedicated himself to building schools in the highlands of Chiapas, has spent a lifetime working with indigenous peoples; many of the ceremonial costumes were given to him as payment for his work in the communities. There are around 1,000 pieces in the collection, including textiles, weavings, wooden saints, musical instruments, and toys. Sergio gives tours and slide shows in English, Spanish, and French, but you must make reservations in advance. Donations toward educational and health projects for indigenous communities are welcomed. ⊠ *Calle Guadalupe Victoria 61* ☎ *967/678–4289* 🖾 *$2.50, including tour and slide show* ⊘ *Daily 5 PM–7 PM.*

❹ Templo de Santo Domingo. This three-block-long complex houses a church, a former monastery, a regional history museum, and the Templo de la Caridad (Temple of the Sisters of Charity). A two-headed eagle—emblem of the Hapsburg dynasty that once ruled Spain and its American dominions—broods over the pediment of the church, which was built between 1547 and 1569. The pink stone facade (which needs a good cleaning) is carved in an intensely ornamental style known as Baroque Solomonic: saints' figures, angels, and grooved columns overlaid with vegetation motifs abound. The interior has lavish altarpieces, an exquisitely fashioned pulpit, a sculpture of the Holy Trinity, and wall panels of gilded, carved cedar—one of the precious woods of Chiapas that centuries later lured Tabasco's woodsmen to the highlands surrounding San Cristóbal. At the complex's southeast corner you'll find the tiny, humble Templo de la Caridad, built in 1715 to honor the Immaculate Conception. Its highlight is the finely carved altarpiece. Indigenous groups from San Juan Chamula often light candles and make offerings here. (Do *not* take photos of the Chamulas.)

The Ex-Convento de Santo Domingo, adjacent to the Santo Domingo church, now houses Sna Jolobil, an Indian cooperative that sells local weavings, embroidered clothing, and colorful postcards. The shop is open Tuesday–Saturday 9–2 and 4–7. The small **Museo de los Altos** (Highlands Museum; ☎ 967/678–1609), also part of the complex, displays a permanent exhibition of historical documents and memorabilia and has two rooms dedicated to changing cultural shows. Hours are Tuesday–Sunday 10–5. Admission is $3. ⊠ *Av. 20 de Noviembre s/n, near Calle Guatemala.*

▶ ❶ Zócalo. The square around which this colonial city was built has in its center a gazebo used by marimba musicians most weekend evenings at 8 PM. You can have a coffee on the ground floor of the gazebo; expect to be approached by children and women selling bracelets and other wares. Surrounding the square are a number of 16th-century buildings, some with plant-filled central patios. On the facade of the Casa de Diego de Mazariegos, now the Hotel Santa Clara, are a stone mermaid and lions that are typical of the plateresque style—as ornate and busy as the work of a silversmith. The yellow-and-white, neoclassical Palacio Municipal (Municipal Palace) on the square's west side was the seat of the state government until 1892, when Tuxtla Gutiérrez became the capital. Today it houses a few government offices, including the municipal tourism office. ⊠ *Between Avs. General Utrilla and 20 de Noviembre and Calles Diego de Mazariegos and Guadalupe Victoria.*

need a break?

Cozy and relaxing, **La Paloma Café** (⊠ Calle Hidalgo 3, ½ block south of the zócalo ☎ 967/678–1547) is the favorite haunt of intellectuals and poets who quaff cappuccino, espresso, and beer until midnight. Appetizers, pizza, and hard liquor are also served. You can enter through the excellent La Galería craft store and art gallery. Live music, often jazz, is played most every evening after 9:30 PM.

Where to Eat

$$ ✕ **Na Bolom.** The kitchen at this famous ethnological-ecological museum
Fodor'sChoice prepares large, home-cooked meals. Overhung with sombrero light fix-
★ tures, the communal oak dining table is shared by international volunteers, Lacandon Indians, resident artists and scholars, and travelers. Continental or a more hearty breakfast is served 7–11, and there's a five-course dinner at 7 (no lunch). Expect such rib-sticking dishes as Mexican goulash (a simple beef stew) or stewed chicken served with soup, up to three different salads, dessert, and coffee or tea. If you're not staying at the institute, call several hours ahead for a reservation. ⊠ *Av. Vicente Guerrero 33* ☎ *967/678–1418* ⊟ *MC, V.*

★ **¢–$** ✕ **La Casa del Pan.** Organically grown fruits, vegetables, and coffee get top billing at this vegetarian bakery and restaurant, which serves a fabulous if leisurely breakfast. The tasty tamales *chiapanecos* with a spicy cheese filling, bean soup, and the best salads in town draw return visits. Other popular dishes include mild chilies stuffed with corn and herbs and Thai stir fry. The bakery sells breads, bagels, coffee, cookies, and fruit preserves. You can also buy Chiapan organic coffee and crafts here. Mellow musical groups, mostly acoustic guitarists, perform Wednesday–Saturday evenings and Sunday at 2:30 PM. ⊠ *Calle Dr. Navarro 10 at Av. Belisario Domínguez* ☎ *967/678–5895* ⊟ *MC, V* ⊘ *Closed Mon.*

¢–$ ✕ **Emiliano's Moustache.** The tortillas here are made fresh by hand throughout the day and go well with the wide variety of meat, chicken, and vegetarian dishes—most served with a small salad and french fries or rice. The upstairs bar overlooks the restaurant, which is named for Mexican revolutionary hero Emiliano Zapata; photos and paintings of him abound. The restaurant is open daily 9 AM–1 AM; there's live music Monday–Saturday 9 PM–11:30 PM. ⊠ *Av. Crescencio Rosas 7, at Calle Diego de Mazariegos* ☎ *967/678–7246* ⊟ *No credit cards.*

¢–$ ✕ **Mayambe.** You can order many different types of Asian food while seated at a table on the large patio—with its overhead skylight, Oriental wall hangings, fireplace, and fountain—or on the floor in the separate Thai dining room. Try the *platillo Vietnamita* (tofu, shrimp, or chicken sautéed with peanuts, cashews, and bits of chili and coconut and served with coconut rice). On weekends there's often live African, Asian, or jazz music. Although Mayambe is open for breakfast, most people come for lunch or dinner. ⊠ *Calle Real de Guadalupe 66* ☎ *967/674–6278* ⊟ *No credit cards* ⊘ *Closed Sun.*

¢–$ ✕ **Restaurante Continental.** The large, enclosed courtyard of a converted neoclassical home is an ideal setting for this family-style restaurant. Every afternoon between 2:30 and 4:30, live marimba music makes it a pleasant place to spend an hour or two. The performances are repeated between 8 and 10 PM. On Sunday, there's a buffet with regional dishes, and folkloric dancers perform from 2 to 4. Try the *trenzado Chamula* (strips of grilled beef and pork) and the guacamole served with tostadas. Craft shops surround the dining area. ⊠ *Calle Real de Guadalupe 24* ☎ *967/678–4861* ⊟ *MC, V.*

★ **¢–$** ✕ **Restaurant L'Eden.** Expats rave about most of the dishes—especially the steaks—at this intimate, chalet-style restaurant in the Hotel El Paraíso. The burnt-orange and cerulean interior has eight cozy candlelit tables, piped-in classical music, a fireplace, Mexican ceramics, and friendly service. Start with margaritas, which are so big you'll laugh out loud when you see them. Swiss delights include classic raclette (melted cheese and potato) and fondue bourguignonne (beef with eight different sauces) for two. These dishes are simple, but perfect. ⊠ *Av. 5 de Febrero 19* ☎ *967/678–0085* ☐ *AE, MC, V.*

¢–$ ✗ **Restaurante el Teatro.** Sunshine streams in the windows here during the day, warming yellow walls hung with European and local artwork. At night, candlelight presides. The French owner keeps things unhurried and makes most everything himself, including the fresh pasta and chocolate mousse. The menu features primarily French and Italian dishes—including chateaubriand and crepes. The wood-fired pizzas and shish kebab are also delicious; a few Mexican dishes are served. ⊠ *Av. 1 de Marzo 8, at Av. 16 de Septiembre* ☎ *967/678–3149* ☐ *MC, V* ☺ *Closed Mon.*

¢ ✗ **La Selva Café.** This coffee shop has more than a dozen organic javas and assorted coffee-flavor concoctions. You can munch on baguette sandwiches, salads and cold plates, codfish pie, chopped-meat pie, and Chiapas tamales. A few tables are in the lush garden out back. A self-styled "culture café," La Selva promotes ecoconsciousness in its eight Mexico City branches. ⊠ *Av. Crescencio Rosas 9, at Calle Cuauhtémoc* ☎ *967/ 678–7244* ☐ *MC, V.*

Where to Stay

★ $ 🏨 **Casa Felipe Flores.** David and Nancy Orr, the friendly owners of this restored 18th-century mansion, are happy to share their knowledge of San Cristóbal and show you around the flower-studded patios and the inviting library, where a fire roars on chilly afternoons. Each guest room has a tile floor with a hand-loomed rug, freestanding wardrobes, and—adjacent to a large fireplace—an old-fashioned bed with carved head and foot boards. Breakfast is served on one of the patios or in the formal dining room, where you'll find loads of Guatemalan folk art and antiques as well as a small honor bar. ⊠ *Calle Dr. Felipe Flores 36, 29230* ☎ *967/678–3996* ➥ *5 rooms* ⚭ *Dining room, bar, library, laundry service, airport shuttle, travel services* ☐ *No credit cards* ❑ *BP.*

$ 🏨 **Casavieja.** Three blocks east of the zócalo, this spectacular hotel maintains the architectural style of the original colonial house, built in 1740. Each comfortable room has Mexican furnishings and large windows looking out onto one of the three interior courtyards. For a mountain view, ask for a room on the second floor of the open courtyard. Suites have whirlpool tubs. The Espinosas, who run and own the hotel, are warm, knowledgeable hosts. ⊠ *Calle Ma. Adelina Flores 27, 29230* ☎ *967/678–0385* ☎ *967/678–6868* ⊕ *www.casavieja.com.mx* ➥ *38 rooms, 2 suites* ⚭ *Restaurant, cable TV, bar, free parking* ☐ *AE, MC, V.*

$ 🏨 **Hotel Arrecife de Coral.** Four blocks from the zócalo, this colonial-style hotel has a large interior lawn presided over by resident peacocks, fruit and cypress trees, and bougainvillea. The charming two-story units are covered with climbing plants. Rooms are plain but clean and pleasant, with bright pastel bedspreads. The owner is an avid diver; hence the name—Coral Reef Hotel. ⊠ *Av. Crescencio Rosas 29, corner of Calle Obregón 29230* ☎ *967/678–2125* 🖨 *967/678–2098* ➥ *60 rooms* ⚭ *Restaurant, cable TV, bar, laundry facilities, laundry service, meeting rooms, free parking* ☐ *MC, V.*

$ 🏨 **Hotel Casa Mexicana.** Good beds, beamed ceilings, and attractive artwork all help make this hostelry in a restored colonial mansion outstanding. A lovely newer wing across the street, also in a colonial home, has a colonnaded courtyard and large, quiet rooms painted light colors and outfitted with wood furniture and tasteful photographs of San Cristóbal. The restaurant, which surrounds a plant-filled courtyard that has a fountain at its center, serves international dishes such as chicken in pistachio sauce and eggplant Parmesan. ⊠ *Calle 28 de Agosto 1, at Av. General Utrilla, 29200* ☏ *967/678–0698, 967/678–0683, or 967/678–1348* 🖷 *967/678–2627* ⊕ *www.hotelcasamexicana.com* ↩ *52 rooms, 3 suites* ⚿ *Restaurant, room service, cable TV, massage, sauna, bar, laundry service, free parking* ▭ *AE, MC, V.*

$ 🏨 **Hotel Santa Clara.** Once the home of city founder Diego de Mazariegos, this rambling 16th-century mansion is now a hotel overlooking the main plaza. It has a tangible air of past grandeur: beamed ceilings, antique oil paintings, saints in niches, and timeworn hardwood floors. Six of the nine roomy units with balconies overlook the zócalo. There's a tiny round pool in the courtyard. Bar Cocodrilos has live Latin rock and pop most nights. Despite the somewhat worn furnishings, the hotel's location and history make it popular. ⊠ *Av. Insurgentes 1, 29200* ☏ *967/678–0871 or 967/678–1140* 🖷 *967/678–0871* ↩ *37 rooms, 2 suites* ⚿ *Restaurant, coffee shop, cable TV, pool, 2 bars, travel services, free parking* ▭ *AE, MC, V.*

$ 🏨 **Posada Diego de Mazariegos.** This quaint hotel—really two perfectly preserved 18th-century colonial homes—has covered interior courtyards, beautiful gardens, and skylights throughout. Rooms have high ceilings and tile bathrooms; some have fireplaces. Ask for one of the rooms that number in the 300s, which are in an older wing and have high wood-beam ceilings as well as working charcoal stoves. Inexpensive suites can sleep up to six people. The bar, Tequilazo, stocks more than 115 brands of tequila. The restaurant serves three meals a day inside its warm wooden confines. ⊠ *Av. 5 de Febrero 1, corner of Av. General Utrilla, 29200* ☏ *967/678–0833* 🖷 *967/678–0827* ⊕ *www.diegodemazariegos. com.mx* ↩ *70 rooms, 4 suites* ⚿ *Restaurant, cafeteria, room service, in-room data ports, cable TV, bar, shop, laundry service, travel services, free parking* ▭ *AE, MC, V.*

$ 🏨 **Rincón del Arco.** The unique details here include a freestanding fireplace in each room. Since each room is different, ask to see several until you find the one you like best. Accommodations in the newer section have a pleasing garden view. Rooms on the top floor share a wide balcony on which you can sit and enjoy a view of red-tile-roof houses clustered around the venerable Church of Guadalupe. The restaurant has a fireplace and wrought-iron wagon-wheel chandeliers. ⊠ *Calle Ejército Nacional 66, 29200* ☏ *967/678–1313* 🖷 *967/678–1568* ↩ *48 rooms, 2 junior suites* ⚿ *Restaurant, cable TV, bar, laundry service, free parking* ▭ *MC, V.*

¢ 🏨 **Hotel El Paraíso.** High, beamed ceilings ennoble the guest rooms in this charming late 19th-century home that was once a hospital. Some rooms have lofts and carpeting; all vary in size. For more solitude, request one of two rooms in the exterior courtyard. Comfortable leather-backed chairs in the lounge overlook a sunny, plant-filled, indoor-outdoor patio where breakfast is served. Owners Daniel and Teresa Suter, who met as students in Switzerland, are attentive. ⊠ *Av. 5 de Febrero 19, 29200* ☏ *967/678–0085* 🖷 *967/678–5168* ⊕ *www.mexonline.com/ hparaiso.htm* ↩ *13 rooms* ⚿ *Restaurant, bar, laundry service* ▭ *AE, MC, V.*

¢ 🏨 **Na Bolom.** Each rustic but cozy room at this center for the study and preservation of the Lacandon Maya and the rain forest has the accoutrements—crafts, photographs, and books—of a specific indigenous community. About half the rooms have bathtubs; all have fireplaces. Na Bolom may be a 10-minute walk from the center, but it has exquisite gardens and an intellectually stimulating environment. Book well in advance, and ask for a garden view. ⊠ *Av. Vicente Guerrero 33, 29200* ☏ *967/678–1418* ⊕ *www.nabolom.org* ↩ *15 rooms* ⚿ *Restaurant, library, shop, free parking* ▭ *MC, V.*

Fodor's Choice ★

¢ 🖻 **Posada San Cristóbal.** The spacious rooms in this grand old building a block from the main plaza have high ceilings, white walls, antique furniture, and heavy French doors; those on the second story have dark plank wood floors. Enjoy the patio, with its cheery walls, blue and white tiles, and white wrought-iron furniture. ⊠ *Av. Insurgentes 3, 29200* 📷📷 *967/678–6881* ↪ *20 rooms* ♦ *Restaurant, room service, cable TV, bar, laundry service, parking (fee); no room phones* ⊟ *MC, V.*

Nightlife & the Arts

Nightlife

Bar Cocodrilos (⊠ Av. Insurgentes 1 ☎ 967/678–0871 or 967/678–1140), in the Hotel Santa Clara, is a laid-back tavern that hosts rock and salsa bands most nights from 9:30 to midnight. The trendy **Café Bar Revolución** (⊠ Av. 20 de Noviembre at Calle Primero de Marzo ☎ no phone) serves great coffee and economical breakfasts and lunches as well as liquor. The café also has computers with Internet access; most nights see live jazz, rock, or ska performances. If that's not enough, videos are screened in a second-floor lounge at noon and 5 PM; the cost is $1 per person.

Latinos (⊠ Calle Francisco Madero 23, corner of Av. Benito Juárez ☎ 967/678–9927) serves up live Latin jazz, salsa, or tropical music after 9:30 every night but Sunday, when it's closed. **Las Velas Danza-Bar** (⊠ Calle Francisco Madero 14 ☎ 967/678–0417) is a disco with live rock and reggae music. It's open nightly 8 PM until 4 AM.

The Arts

Museo Na Bolom (⊠ Av. Vicente Guerrero 33, between Calles Comitán and Chiapa de Corzo ☎ 967/678–1418) occasionally sponsors talks and films. The elegant **Teatro Hermanos Domínguez** (⊠ Diagonal Hermanos Paniagua s/n, just outside the city limits ☎ 967/678–3637) features programs such as folkloric dances from throughout Latin America.

Sports & the Outdoors

A horseback ride into the neighboring indigenous villages is good exercise for mind and body. Most hotels can arrange trips, or you can contact **Chinkultik** (⊠ Posada Margarita, Calle Real de Guadalupe 34 ☎ 967/678–0957 ⊠ Av. Insurgentes 14 ☎ 967/678–7266). Bilingual guides lead five-hour horseback rides to San Juan Chamula and Zinacantán; the cost is $12 per person.

Shopping

Look for the elaborately crafted textiles from communities surrounding San Cristóbal; they incorporate designs that have been around for millennia. San Cristóbal's market, although picturesque, generally sells more produce than arts and crafts. The shops on Avenida General Utrilla, south of the market, have a large selection of Guatemalan goods, the price and quality of which may be lower than Mexican wares. Make sure to bargain and to check merchandise carefully for imperfections. (Note that Guatemalan cloth is often dark-blue cotton with multicolor cotton needlepoint or trim.)

Shops are generally open Monday–Saturday 9–2 and 4–8. Indian women and children will often approach you on the streets with their wares—mostly fake (plastic) amber, woven bracelets, and small dolls. Their selections might not be as varied as those in the shops, but prices will be about the same. On the other hand, you can be assured that these hard-working vendors earn every cent they make.

El Arbol de la Vida (⊠ Calle Real de Guadalupe 27 ☎ 967/678–5050) is a smart shop that specializes in designer amber jewelry mixed with silver and gold. It also has a small museum displaying the different types of amber found around the world. A video explains how the prehistoric resin is extracted and then transformed into precious natural gems. **Artesanías Chiapanecas** (⊠ Calle Real de Guadalupe 46C, at Av. Diego Dugelay ☎ no phone) has an excellent selection of embroidered blouses, huipiles, tablecloths, and bags. The government-run **Instituto de las Artesanías** (⊠ Calle Niños Héroes and Av. Hidalgo ☎ 967/678–1180) sells wooden toys, ceramics, embroidered blouses, bags, and handwoven textiles from throughout the state. You'll also find whole bean coffee, honey, marmalade, candy, and liqueurs.

Among its excellent selection of wares, **Sna Jolobil** (Weaver's House in the Tzotzil language; ⊠ Ex-Convento de Santo Domingo, Calz. Lázaro Cárdenas 42 ☎ 967/678–7178), the regional crafts cooperative, has hand-dyed woolen sweaters and tunics, embroidered pillow covers, and pre-Hispanic-design wall hangings. **Taller Leñateros** (⊠ Calle Flavio A. Paniagua 54 ☎ 967/678–5174), a unique indigenous co-op in an old colonial San Cristóbal home, sells original top-quality crafts and has free informal tours to observe artisans at work. Look for handmade books, boxes, postcards, and writing paper fashioned out of recycled flower petals, plants, and bark. At the Rincón del Arco Hotel, **Textiles Soriano** (⊠ Calle Ejército Nacional 66 ☎ 967/678–1313) specializes in handwoven bedspreads and other cloth, which can be made to order in a few days.

SOUTH & EAST OF SAN CRISTÓBAL

Due east of San Cristóbal is one of the least explored and most exotic regions of Chiapas: the Selva Lacandona, said to be the western hemisphere's second-largest remaining rain forest. Incursions of developers, settlers, and refugees from neighboring Guatemala are transforming Mexico's last frontier, which for centuries has been the homeland of the Lacandon, a small tribe descended from the Maya of Yucatán. Some of the indigenous groups maintain their ancient customs, living in huts and wearing long, plain tunics. Their tradition of not marrying outside the tribe is causing serious problems, however, and their numbers, never large to begin with, have been reduced to about 350.

Las Grutas de Rancho Nuevo

⑨ *13 km (8 mi) south of San Cristóbal off Rte. Carretera 190.*

Spectacular limestone stalactites and stalagmites are illuminated along a 2,475-ft concrete walkway inside the labyrinthine caves known as Las Grutas de Rancho Nuevo (or Las Grutas de San Cristóbal), which were discovered in 1960. Kids from the area are usually available to guide you for a small fee. You can rent horses ($5 per half hour) for a ride around the surrounding pine forest, and there's a small restaurant and picnic area on the site. To get here, catch a Teopisca-bound microbus at Boulevard Juan Sabines Gutiérrez, across from the San Diego church, in San Cristóbal. Make sure to tell the driver to let you off at the "grutas." Get off at the signed entrance, and walk about 1 km (½ mi) along the dirt road. Or, you can catch a taxi from town for about $6. For about twice that price, the driver will wait while you explore the caves. ☎ *No phone* ✉ *$1 per car plus 50¢ per person* ☉ *Daily 9–4:30.*

Amatenango del Valle

⑩ *37 km (23 mi) southeast of San Cristóbal.*

Amatenango del Valle is a Tzeltal village known for the handsome, primitive pottery made by the town's women, whose distinctive red and yellow huipiles are also much remarked upon. Almost every household has wares to sell; look for ocher, black, and natural-clay flowerpots and animal figurines—primarily gray doves. Lining the road to Comitán, at the entrance to town, are some simple shelters where other artisans sell their wares. If you go during the dry season (when rain isn't a threat), you might get to see some of the pots being fired over open flames on the ground outside. Spanish is definitely a second language here, and women negotiate without a lot of chitchat or use younger children as interpreters.

Comitán

⑪ *55 km (34 mi) southeast of Amatenango del Valle.*

This pleasant commercial center and agricultural town of about 120,000 is the base from which many people visit the Lagos de Montebello and the small archaeological sites nearby. Built by the Spaniards, the city flourished early on as a major center linking the lowland temperate plains to the edge of the Maya empire on the Pacific. Even today it serves as a trading hub for the Tzeltal Indians; such Guatemalan goods as sugarcane liquor and orchids come through here. Many of the colonial buildings lining Comitán's pretty plaza and nearby side streets have been preserved. The city also has two notable churches: Santo Domingo de Guzmán, with its Moorish-style architecture, and San Caralampio, whose Spanish Baroque style reveals the influence of Guatemalan artisans.

The **Casa-Museo Dr. Belisario Domínguez,** the lovely former home of a martyr of the revolution, is now a museum with a fascinating collection of medical instruments, pharmaceuticals, and late 19th-century furnishings. It also contains photographs, documents, and letters from the Mexican Revolution, during which the doctor was assassinated for his outspoken criticism of President Victoriano Huerta. ⊠ *Av. Central Sur at Blvd. Dr. Belisario Domínguez 35* ☏ *963/632–1300* ▤ *50¢* ☉ *Tues.–Sat. 10–6:45, Sun. 9–12:45.*

The **Museo de Arte Hermila Castellanos** shows work by modern artists, many of them Mexican. Look for pieces by master painters Rufino Tamayo and Francisco Toledo, both from Oaxaca. The museum also hosts temporary exhibits. ⊠ *Av. Central Sur at Blvd. Dr. Belisario Domínguez 51* ☏ *963/632–2082* ▤ *20¢* ☉ *Tues.–Sat. 10–6, Sun. 9–noon.*

The small but worthwhile **Museo de Arqueología** is dedicated to regional archaeological finds. Most of the exhibits in its four rooms are of ancient Maya carved stone and ceramic vessels. The skeleton and offerings in the reconstructed tomb are original. Placards are in Spanish only. ⊠ *Primera Calle Sur Oriente s/n at Primera Avenida Sur Oriente* ☏ *963/ 632–5760* ▤ *Free* ☉ *Tues.–Sun. 10–5.*

⚠ Some 7 km (4 mi) from Comitán, **Tenam Puente** is on a hill with a spectacular valley view. The Maya ceremonial center was built around the same time as Chinkultik and occupied during the Classic and Postclassic periods. Archaeologists Frans Blom and Oliver LeFarge discovered the site; during restoration in the 1990s a royal tomb was unearthed. There are three ball courts, apparently one each for the lower, middle, and upper classes. Most of the site has yet to be explored. ▤ *Free* ☉ *Daily 9–4.*

Chinkultik

🔺 ⑫ *46 km (29 mi) southeast of Comitán.*

Although this Maya city was occupied into the Postclassic period, most of its buildings date from the Classic (100 BC to AD 900) era. It's a steep hike of about 10 or 15 minutes to the top of a restored pyramid. From here you're rewarded with a fabulous view of the countryside and even a glimpse of the Lagos de Montebello and of the Cenote Agua Azul, the large on-site sinkhole. The ruins, which are only partially restored, also include a ball court and stelae. To get here from Comitán, head south on Carretera 190, and turn left at the sign LAGOS DE MONTEBELLO outside of La Trinitaria. There's a road on the left leading to the ruins, which are 3 km (2 mi) off the highway. A bus runs from Comitán: you have to get off at the road that leads to the ruins and walk to the site. 🔁 *$3* ⊙ *Daily 10–5.*

Where to Stay & Eat

$ ✕🖻 **Museo Parador Santa María.** Built around the remains of a hacienda from the 1830s, this hotel has an excellent restaurant ($), six well-appointed rooms, and a small free museum with religious art from the 16th to the 19th centuries (open daily 10–6). Each room has antiques of a different period or place; some rooms have sunken bathtubs and fireplaces. Top off your visit to the lakes or ruins with the fixed three-course lunch (served 1–4). Memorable dishes include the cream of *chipilín* (a local herb) soup and the pepper-crusted steak. Breakfast and dinner are à la carte. ✉ *Carretera a Lagos de Montebello, Km 22* 🖀 *963/632–5116* 🛏 *6 rooms, 2 suites* ⚒ *Restaurant, bar, laundry service, free parking* ▭ *MC, V.*

Lagos de Montebello

⑬ *64 km (40 mi) southeast of Comitán.*

The 56 lakes and surrounding pine forest of the Lagos de Montebello (Lakes of the Beautiful Mountain) constitute a 2,437-acre park that's shared with Guatemala. Each lake has a different tint—emerald, turquoise, amethyst, azure, steel gray—thanks to various oxides. The setting is serene and majestic, with clusters of oak, pine, and sweet gum. Practically the only denizens of the more accessible part of the forest are the clamorous goldfinches and mockingbirds.

At the park entrance, the paved road forks. The left fork leads to the Lagunas de Colores (Colored Lakes). At Laguna Bosque Azul, the last lake along that road, there's a café; it may be humble, but it's a nice change from all the food stalls set up near every lake with a parking lot. Small boys will approach and offer a 45-minute horse-riding expedition to a cave and two cenotes (sinkholes) within the forest. You can also tour the lake in a rowboat for $5 (up to four people).

The right fork in the road at the park entrance leads past various lakes to Lago Tziscao and, just outside the park boundaries, a village of the same name. A restaurant near the shore has a spectacular view of the lake, where a 30-minute boat ride costs $2.50 per person.

Check with the Comitán tourist office if you'd like to stay in the park; the remodeled yet still basic Albergue Tziscao has several small cabins with private baths and hot water. They cost about $3.50 per person. Although various buses travel to and between the lakes, the tourist office recommends that you take a tour to save time and to be safe. Tourists have been assaulted while walking from one lake to another, although this is not commonplace. There are several police checkpoints in the area, but it's still best to be careful. If you travel on your own, stay on the paved roads. Don't wander off onto the dirt paths. Also, Tziscao and Montebello (which is on the road to Tziscao) are the only lakes that the tourist office recommends for swimming.

NORTH & WEST OF SAN CRISTÓBAL

San Juan Chamula and Zinacantán are traditional villages in the scenic northwestern outskirts of San Cristóbal. The small colonial town of Chiapa de Corzo is the first major community you come to when you drive west from San Cristóbal along Carretera 190. This is the place to catch the motorboat to view the Cañón del Sumidero (Sumidero Canyon). Tuxtla Gutiérrez, the modern state capital, is about 15 km (9 mi) beyond Chiapa de Corzo.

San Juan Chamula

⑭ *12 km (7½ mi) northwest of San Cristóbal de las Casas.*

The spiritual and administrative center of the Chamula Indians is justly celebrated and admired for its cultural traditions. The Chamula are a Tzotzil-speaking Maya group of nearly 52,000 individuals (of a total 300,000 Tzotzils) who live in hamlets throughout the highlands; several thousand of them live in San Juan Chamula.

They're fiercely devout—practicing a religion that's a blend of Catholicism and indigenous beliefs and practices—a trait that has played an important role in their history. The Chamula uprising of 1869 started when some tribesmen were imprisoned for crucifying a boy in the belief that they should have their own Christ. Some 13,000 Chamula then rose up to demand their leaders' release and massacred scores of ladino villagers in the process. Today, there's conflict between those practicing the Catholicism of the area and those who have been converted by evangelical Protestants. In the past 30 years, tens of thousands of converts have been forced to abandon their ancestral lands and ties with Chamula society.

Physically and spiritually, life in San Juan Chamula revolves around the church, a white stucco building whose doorway has a simple yet lovely flower motif. The church is named after Saint John the Baptist, the main god of the universe, according to Chamulan belief; Jesus Christ is revered as his younger brother. To enter, pay a token fee (about 50¢) at the tourist office on the main square. A pamphlet gives guidelines about how to conduct yourself in the church and the village—read it.

Taking photographs and videos inside the church is absolutely prohibited. There are no pews; instead the floor is strewn with fragrant pine needles, on which the Chamula sit praying silently or chanting while facing colorfully attired statues of saints. For the most part, worshipers are oblivious to visitors. They burn candles of various colors, drink soft drinks, and may have a live chicken or eggs with them for healing the sick. (They "pass" the illness to the chicken or egg, which is disposed of later.)

Outside the church there's no ban on photography, but it is illegal to take pictures of Chamulan authorities, who wear black ponchos and carry a baton, and most adults don't appreciate being captured on film. Flocks of children will pester you to buy small trinkets and to photograph them for money (about 50¢ a shot). The most colorful time to visit San Juan Chamula is on Sunday, when the market is in full swing and more formal religious rites are performed.

To get here from San Cristóbal, head west on Calle Guadalupe Victoria, which veers to the right onto Ramón Larrainzar. Continue 4 km (2½ mi) until you reach the entrance to the village. Most of these roads are paved. Because of the threat of robbery, walking between San Cristóbal, San Juan Chamula, and Zinacantán isn't recommended.

Zinacantán

⑮ *4 km (2½ mi) west of San Juan Chamula.*

The village of Zinacantán (Place of the Bats) is even smaller than San Juan Chamula and is reached via a paved road west just outside San Juan Chamula (from San Cristóbal, take the Tuxtla road about 8 km [5 mi] and look for the signed turnoff on your right). Here photography is totally forbidden, except for the row of village weavers on view along the main street. It's the scenery en route to Zinacantán—terraced hillsides with cornfields and orchards—that draws visitors. There isn't much to see in the village except on Sunday, when people gather from the surrounding parishes, or during religious festivals. The men wear bright pink tunics embroidered with flowers; the women cover themselves with bright pink *rebozos* (shawls). If you take a tour you'll visit the homes of back-strap loom weavers and have the opportunity to take some good photos without offending any of the locals.

The **Museo Ik'al Ojov,** on the *calle principal* (main street) behind the church, is in a typical home and displays Zinacantán costumes through the ages. ☎ *No phone* ✉ *Donation suggested* ☉ *Tues.–Sun. 9–5.*

Chiapa de Corzo

⑯ *70 km (43 mi) west of San Cristóbal; 15 km (9 mi) southeast of Tuxtla Gutiérrez.*

The town of Chiapa de Corzo was founded in 1528 by Diego de Mazariegos, who one month later fled the mosquitoes and transported all the settlers to San Cristóbal (then called Chiapa de los Españoles, to distinguish it from Chiapa de los Indios, as Chiapa de Corzo was originally known). The mosquitoes are still here.

Life in this small town on the banks of the Río Grijalva revolves, inevitably, around the zócalo, which is lorded over by *la pila,* a bizarre Mozarabic brick fountain built in 1562 in the shape of the crown of the Spanish monarchs Fernando and Isabella. Several craft shops line the square, selling huaraches, ceramics, lacquerware, carved wooden ceremonial masks, and regional costumes.

The **Centro Cultural Ex-Convento de Santo Domingo de Guzmán,** in front of the public market one block from the zócalo, has a permanent exhibition of Chiapa de Corzo engraver Franco Lázaro Gomez, who died in a tragic accident at 27 in 1949. The center also shows changing exhibits and houses Chiapa's **Museo de la Laca** (lacquerware museum), which has a modest collection of delicately carved and painted *jícaras* (gourds). "The sky is no more than an immense blue jícara, the beloved firmament in the form of a cosmic jícara," according to the *Popul Vuh,* a 16th-century chronicle of the Quiché Maya. The lacquerware here is both local and imported—from Michoacán, Guerrero, Chiapas, Guatemala, and Asia. Free lacquerware workshops are held weekdays 3–7. ✉ *Calle Mexicanidad de Chiapas 10* ☎ *961/616–0055* ✉ *Free* ☉ *Tues.–Sun. 10–5.*

★ The **Cañón del Sumidero,** a canyon 38 km (24 mi) north of Chiapa de Corzo, came into being about 36 million years ago, with the help of the Río Grijalva, which flows north along the canyon's floor. The fissure meanders for some 23 km (14 mi); its near-vertical walls, partly obscured by vegetation, rise 3,500 ft at the highest point. You can admire it from above, as there are five lookout points along the highway; one of them, La Atalaya, has a restaurant.

Boats travel to the canyon from the Chiapa de Corzo dock between 8 AM and 4 PM daily. From the boat you can admire the canyon's steep, striated walls, some odd rock formations, and the animals—including crocodiles, ducks, pelicans, herons, raccoons, iguanas, and butterflies—that live at its base. As you coast along, consider the fate of the Chiapa Indians who reputedly jumped into the canyon rather than face slavery at the hands of the Spaniards during the 16th century.

Where to Eat

¢-$ ✕ **Jardines de Chiapa.** Sample an excellent and inexpensive variety of regional cuisines at this patio restaurant. Try the *tasajo* (sun-dried beef served with pumpkin-seed sauce) and the *chipilín con bolita* soup, made with balls of ground corn paste cooked in a creamy herb sauce and topped with cheese. A marimba band enlivens meals on weekends between 2 and 5 PM. The restaurant is open daily 9–7:30. ☒ *Av. Francisco I. Madero 395* ☎ *961/616–0198* ☎☎ *961/616–0070* ⊟ *AE, MC, V.*

Tuxtla Gutiérrez

❶ *15 km (9 mi) northwest of Chiapa de Corzo, 85 km (53 mi) northwest of San Cristóbal, 289 km (179 mi) southwest of Villahermosa.*

The highway into Tuxtla Gutiérrez (population 550,000), the capital of Chiapas State, is endless. In 1939 Graham Greene characterized it as "not a place for foreigners—the new ugly capital of Chiapas, without attractions." The accuracy of that bleak description is slowly fading, but most people still only pass through Tuxtla, even if it is of vital economic and political importance. It's the state's transportation hub, and it has what is probably Mexico's most innovative zoo. It's also close to Chiapa de Corzo and the Cañón del Sumidero, where there are few accommodations.

Tuxtla's first name derives from the Nahuatl word *tochtlan,* meaning "abundance of rabbits." Its second name, Gutiérrez, honors Joaquín Miguel Gutiérrez, who fought for the state's independence from Spain and incorporation into newly independent Mexico. To get your bearings in the town, stay on the main drag. It runs right into the zócalo, which is known locally as the *parque central* and which is fronted by huge government buildings.

♻ All the animals at the **Miguel Alvarez del Toro Zoo,** also known as ZooMAT, are native to Chiapas, and the more docile creatures roam free. The 100-plus species include jaguars, marsupials, iguanas, quetzal birds, boa constrictors, tapirs, eagles, and monkeys. At this writing, the zoo was closed while exhibits and enclosures were added or enlarged and new paths were created. Call ahead for an update. If work is still in progress, inquire about taking a guided tour of the grounds. ☒ *Calz. Cerro Hueco s/n, southeast of town off Libramiento Sur* ☎ *961/614–4701 or 961/614–4765* ☎ *Free* ◷ *Tues.–Sun. 9–5.*

The **Parque Madero** is home to the Jardín Botánico, which at this writing was closed for renovations. You can still visit the worthwhile Museo Regional de Chiapas, which has excellent history and anthropology displays as well as a salon for revolving cultural exhibits. ⊠ *Between Av. Norte 5a and Calle Oriente 11a, northeast of downtown* ☎ *961/613–4479* 🖵 *Museum $3* ⊗ *Tues.–Sun. 9–4.*

As its name suggests, the **Parque Jardín de la Marimba** (⊠ Av. Central) hosts marimba bands, which play regional music for dancing. You can grab a partner and join in—every evening at 7 and 9.

Where to Stay & Eat

$–$$$$ ✕ **Montebello.** Prime rib and Mexican specialties headline the menu, and every roll, cake, dessert, and tortilla is made on the premises. Montebello's earth-tone elegance is set off by an unusual white mural of the Sumidero cliffs sculpted into a wall. It's particularly romantic here at night, when the city lights shimmer into view. Live, unobtrusive violin and piano music plays after 2 PM. ⊠ *Camino Real hotel, Blvd. Dr. Belisario Domínguez 1195* ☎ *961/617–7777* 🖃 *AE, DC, MC, V* ⊗ *Closed Sun.*

★ **$–$$$** ✕ **El Asador Castellano.** Mouthwatering Spanish dishes are the specialty here; you can also get imported choice U.S. beef cuts. Service is very attentive, and the presentation is flawless. The most popular dish is *lechón a la segoviana,* succulent baby pig that you can order as a straightforward dish for one person or have cut and served with a flourish at your table. The extensive wine list favors Spanish wines hard to find in Mexico City, let alone Chiapas. Reservations are a good idea on weekends. ⊠ *Blvd. Dr. Belisario Domínguez 2320-A* ☎ *961/602–9000* 🖃 *AE, MC, V* ⊗ *No dinner Sun.*

$–$$ ✕ **Restaurant Algarabia.** Choose from a wide array of savory seafood dishes—some prepared at your table—at this spacious *palapa* (thatch-roof restaurant). Try the *camarones en salsa de queso* (shrimp in cheese sauce) or any other of the Mexican-style shrimp dishes. Service is excellent, and a salsa band plays daily 3–5. Monday and Tuesday are buffet days, and on Wednesday all dishes are half price. ⊠ *Av. Central 1440* ☎ *961/614–7148* 🖃 *AE, MC, V.*

¢–$ ✕ **La Carreta.** This handsome, two-story, open-air restaurant has all kinds of grilled meats as well as tacos and salads. Portions are huge, and the mixed grill for two, four, or six people comes with beans, tortillas, and salsa—a super deal. A beautiful wooden staircase leads to the second-floor seating area. Tuesday–Saturday 3–5, marimba musicians play on the patio, striking with its stone arches and iron lanterns. Romantic trios take over after 10 PM. To see the floor show late on Friday and Saturday nights, you must make reservations and prepay in person. ⊠ *Blvd. Dr. Belisario Domínguez 703* ☎ *961/602–5518 or 961/602–5403* 🖃 *MC, V.*

¢–$ ✕ **Las Pichanchas.** An outstanding variety of regional dishes, including tamales and cochinito horneado, is available here, as well as live marimba music in the afternoon (2:30–5:30) and evening (8:30–11:30). There are also folkloric dances 9 PM–10 PM. The restaurant is a favorite among Mexican families. ⊠ *Av. Central Oriente 837* ☎ *961/612–5351* 🖃 *AE, MC, V.*

★ **$$$** ⌸ **Camino Real.** The interior spaces—set around a huge lagoon-pool and bar area with exotic vegetation—are reminiscent of those in superior Caribbean resorts. Yet the list of amenities at this hilltop oasis, a member of the Camino Real chain, is longer than that at many of its more-expensive counterparts. All rooms have mountain views; baths have tubs draped with silky curtains. The 24-hour Los Azulejos restaurant is enclosed in a sky-blue glass dome; its heavenly buffets are well worth the price. The upscale Montebello restaurant is a great place for prime rib. ⊠ *Blvd. Dr. Belisario Domínguez 1195, 29060* ☎ *961/617–7777; 800/722–6466 in the U.S.* 🖷 *961/617–7799* ⊕ *www.caminoreal.com* ⇆ *174 rooms, 36* suites ♿ 3 restaurants, room service, in-room data ports, in-room safes, minibars, cable TV, 2 tennis courts, pool, health club, hair salon, sauna, 2 bars, shop, concierge floor, business services, meeting rooms, car rental, travel services; no-smoking rooms ⊟ AE, DC, MC, V.

$$ ⊞ **Holiday Inn.** Many of the rooms at this hotel on the outskirts of town face the large, main garden; others are off a smaller, more tranquil inner garden. Capacious is the byword here: the pool is huge and the public areas are vast. The bar is a magnet for locals thanks to its dance floor, high-tech lighting system, and DJs and live music on weekends. ⊠ *Blvd. Dr. Belisario Domínguez 1081, 29000* ☏ *961/617–1000* ✆ *117 rooms, 2 suites* ♿ *Restaurant, coffee shop, cable TV, tennis court, pool, gym, bar, business center, meeting rooms, car rental, travel services, free parking; no-smoking rooms* ⊟ *MC, V.*

$ ⊞ **Best Western Hotel Arecas.** The Arecas—about 10 minutes by car from city center—is a haven of quiet gardens with fruit trees, flowering plants, and a secluded swimming pool. Both the rooms and the bungalow-style junior suites have tasteful colonial-style fittings and furnishings. The informal Calabaza restaurant serves a buffet breakfast daily and has an à la carte menu of Mexican specialties for lunch and dinner. ⊠ *Blvd. Dr. Belisario Domínguez, Km 1080, 29020* ☏ *961/615–1122 or 961/615–1128; 800/780–7234 in the U.S.* ☎ *961/615–1121* ⊕ *www.hotelarecas.com.mx* ✆ *44 rooms, 16 suites* ♿ *Restaurant, room service, cable TV, pool, bar, shop, Internet, meeting rooms, free parking* ⊟ *AE, DC, MC, V.*

$ ⊞ **Hotel María Eugenia.** Although a touch sterile, this hotel has clean rooms with floral spreads as well as a floral scent. There's a nice pool surrounded by white wrought-iron furniture. Although there's no definitive "downtown" area in sprawling Tuxtla, many consider this hotel's central location a plus. ⊠ *Av. Central Oriente 507, 29000* ☏ *961/613–3767 or 961/613–3770* ☎ *961/613–2860* ⊕ *www.mariaeugenia.com.mx* ✆ *83 rooms* ♿ *2 restaurants, room service, pool, bar, meeting rooms, travel services, free parking* ⊟ *AE, MC, V.*

THE ROAD TO PALENQUE & BEYOND

The road from San Cristóbal to Palenque veers slightly east on Carretera 190 upon leaving town, then links up to Carretera 199, which heads north to Palenque. You'll pass Ocosingo and the turnoff to Toniná along the first half of the journey, then Agua Azul and Misol-Há before reaching the ruins. It's sierra country most of the way until the mild valleys around Ocosingo; the climate will get progressively hotter and more humid as you descend from the highland and approach Palenque. The vegetation will also change, from mountain pine to thick, green tropical foliage. To get to Villahermosa from Palenque, head north for 56 km (35 mi) on Carretera 199, and then turn left (west) onto Carretera 186 at Catazajá for a fairly straight, leisurely drive. Frequent buses are available for all routes.

Toniná

🔺 ⑱ *98 km (61 mi) northeast of San Cristóbal; 118 km (73 mi) south and east of Palenque.*

Between San Cristóbal and Palenque, on a paved road running along the Río Jataté in the mild Ocosingo Valley, is the archaeological site of Toniná. The name means "house of stone" in Tzeltal. Excavations indicate that the vanquished rulers of Palenque and Yaxchilán were brought here as prisoners for execution. Several ball courts and the main pyramid platform (taller than those of Tikal and Teotihuacán) have been

MAYA ARCHITECTURE

THE MAYA WERE OUTSTANDING ARCHITECTS, *without compare in the Americas. They erected immense palaces and towering pyramids in less-than-hospitable climates without the aid of metal tools, the wheel, or beasts of burden. Their ancient cities still resound with the magnificence of their cultures, even though the civilizations have faded.*

Río Usumacinta. *Builders of pyramids of this style typically gave them additional height by placing them on hillsides or crests—as you'll see at the otherworldly Palenque—and the principal structures were covered with exquisite bas-reliefs carved in stone. The small one-story pyramid-top temples characteristically had vestibules and rooms with vault ceilings. The wide, spacious chambers inside the pyramids had smaller, attached rooms filled with bas-reliefs of important events that occurred during the reign of the ruler who built the pyramid. Río Usumacinta friezes slope inward, rather than standing perpendicular under the large roof combs. Finest examples: Palenque, Yaxchilán.*

Río Bec. *Influenced by Guatemala's Petén style, the pitch of these pyramids is rather steep, and the foundations are elaborately decorated. The stairways on the outside of some pyramids were built for aesthetic rather than practical purposes, and were "false" (unclimbable). The principal structures were long, one-story affairs containing two or sometimes three tall towers. Each was capped by a large roof comb emboldened with a dramatic stucco facade. Río Bec is found only in what is now the state of Campeche. Finest examples: Calakmul, Xpuhil, Río Bec.*

Chenes. *Found mainly in Campeche, this style likewise had long, single-story structures. In this case they were divided into three distinct sections, each with its own doorway charmingly surrounded by a face of the rain god, Chaac, whose mouth is the entrance. Facades were smothered in serpentlike embellishments. Finest examples: Hochob, Chicanná.*

Puuc. *Uxmal is the most striking illustration of the beautifully proportioned Puuc style. Commonly found in the state of Yucatán, it of all styles looks like the "typical" Maya style. The buildings were designed in a low-slung, quadrangle shape and had many rooms. Exterior walls were probably kept plain to show off the friezes above, which were lavishly embellished with stone-mosaic deities surrounded by geometric and serpentine motifs. The corners of buildings were characteristically lined with the curl-nosed Chaac. Pyramids here didn't have roof combs. Finest examples: Uxmal, Labná, Kabah, Sayil.*

Northeast Yucatán. *The fusion of two Maya groups—the early Chichén Maya and later Itzá Maya—produced this Late Classic (AD 600–900) style famously exemplified by Chichén Itzá. Here new forms such as columns and grand colonnades were introduced. Palaces with row upon row of columns carved in the form of serpents looked over private patios, platforms were dedicated to the planet Venus, and pyramids were offered to Kukulcán (the plumed serpent god borrowed from the Toltecs, who called him Quetzalcóatl). Chichén Itzá is also famous for its reclining, carved stone chacmool (a reclining figure with an offering tray carved in its middle)—another Itzá addition. Finest examples: Chichén Itzá, Mayapán.*

Quintana Roo Coast. *Although somewhat influenced by the Itzá Maya, a style entirely different eventually evolved here. The large, squat-looking, one-story buildings have interior columns, wood-beam-supported ceilings, and numerous figures of the descending or Upside Down god that began appearing in the Postclassic era (900–1530). Friezes were distinctively decorated with small niches. Finest example: Tulum.*

— Patricia Alisau

uncovered; an on-site museum (open Tues.–Sun. 9–4) exhibits many relics. Toniná is thought to be the last major Maya ceremonial center to flourish in this area. To get here, follow the road from Ocosingo, off Carretera 199. 🖼 *$3* ⊙ *Daily 9–4.*

Where to Stay & Eat

¢ ✕🏨 **Hospedaje y Restaurant Esmeralda.** A half-block away from Ocosingo's main square you'll find this historic house in its latest incarnation as a hotel. Owners Glen and Ellen will happily dole out lots of tips about area travel. Under a pair of chandeliers in the dining room, visitors and guests tuck into delicious fare like lasagna and homemade bread. Work up an appetite with a two-hour horseback ride ($20). ✉ *Calle Central 14, Ocosingo, 29950* 🖼 *919/673–0014* ⊕ *www.ranchoesmeralda.net* 🛏 *5 rooms* ⌂ *Restaurant, horseback riding, bar, laundry service; no room phones, no room TVs* ▭ *No credit cards.*

Agua Azul

★ ⑲ *68 km (42 mi) northwest of Toniná.*

The series of waterfalls and crystalline blue pools at Agua Azul is breathtaking, especially during the dry season (from about November through March), as wet-season waters are often churned up and brown with mud. You can swim in a series of interconnected pools. The road to the sight is paved and lined with food shacks and camping facilities. Six-hour trips, which include a visit to Misol-Há, cost about $9 per person and include the entrance fees (50¢ per person or $2 per car).

Misol-Há

★ ⑳ *46 km (29 mi) northeast of Agua Azul.*

If the single cascade at Misol-Há is less grandiose than the series of falls and pools at Agua Azul, it's no less breathtaking. You can swim in the pool formed by the 100-ft cascade, or explore behind the falls, where a cave leads to another, subterranean pool. (If there's a guide with flashlight in hand to help you, tip him $1 or so.)

Palenque

⛰ ⚑ ㉑ *18 km (11 mi) northwest of Misol-Há, 191 km (118 mi) northeast of*
FodorśChoice *San Cristóbal de las Casas, 150 km (93 mi) southeast of Villahermosa.*
★

Of all the Maya ruins, none is more sublime than Palenque and only Tikal in Guatemala is its equal. Teotihuacán might be more monumental and Chichén Itzá more expansive, but Palenque is mesmerizing, in part because of the intimacy that the surrounding jungle creates.

Antonio de Solis, a Spanish priest, dug into a buried wall here in 1740 while trying to plant crops. In 1805 a royal Spanish expedition ventured here to follow up on the discovery; 25 years later an eccentric count, Jean-Frédéric Maximilien de Waldeck, set up house with his mistress for a year in the Templo del Conde (Temple of the Count). Explorers John Lloyd Stephens and Frederick Catherwood lived briefly in the palace during their 1840 expedition. Serious excavations began in 1923 under the direction of Frans Blom, cofounder of the Na Bolom foundation in San Cristóbal. Work continued intermittently until 1952, when Alberto Ruz Lhuillier, a Mexican archaeologist, uncovered the tomb of the 7th-century ruler Pakal beneath the Templo de las Inscripciones (Temple of the Inscriptions), a 75-ft pyramid.

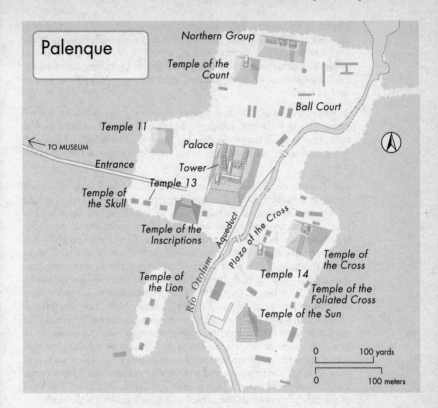

Only around 800 of the thousands of glyphs have been deciphered, but they have already revealed the complex history of the Palenque dynasties. Since late 1994, a huge portion of the ruins around the Templo de las Inscripciones has been reconstructed and is open. Exciting finds by archaeologists from the University of Texas in 1998 introduced a new character, Uc-Pakal-Kinich, into the lineage of Palenque rulers. Other clues unearthed at Templo 19 point to a probable liaison between rulers of Palenque and of Copán, in Honduras. Today less than 40% of the site has been excavated. Explanations are in Spanish, English, and Chol (a type of Maya).

The site's most important buildings date from the Mid- to Late Classic period (AD 300–900), although it was inhabited as early as 1500 BC. At its zenith, the city dominated the greater part of what is today Tabasco and Chiapas. The site was abandoned around AD 800. The reasons for the Mayas' departure are still being debated. A graceful tower—one of the site's signature structures—sets it apart from other Maya cities, as does the Templo de las Inscripciones.

Palenque's elegance makes clear why archaeologist Sylvanus Morley called the Maya the "Greeks of the New World"—not only for their remarkable buildings, but also for the supple naturalism of their art. The masters here shaped stone, stucco, and ceramics into ornate, lyrical designs. Instead of the freestanding stelae of other Maya cities, at Palenque you find highly expressive relief sculpture and elaborate glyphs. In its heyday, Palenque encompassed an astonishing 128-plus square km (49 square mi). Artificial terraces were built to support the temples, which surrounded plazas, a ball court, altars, and burial grounds. The temples had a complex array of corridors, narrow subterranean stairways, and galleries. And they served as fortresses in time of war.

As you enter the site, the first temple on your right is the reconstructed **Templo de la Calavera,** which the Maya had painted red and blue in their time. A skull-shape stucco relief, presumed to be that of a rabbit, was found at the small entrance to the temple. It's now at the top of the stairs.

The **Templo de las Inscripciones** was dedicated to Pakal, who took Palenque to its most glorious heights during his long reign. (He died around AD 692, having become the ruler at age 12 and living into his 40s.) The nine tiers correspond to the nine-level Maya underworld. Atop this temple and the smaller ones around it are vestiges of roof combs—delicate vertical extensions that are among the features of southern Maya cities. You must obtain permission—first thing in the morning at the entrance gate—to descend the steep, damp flight of stairs to view the **tumba de Pakal,** 80 ft below. One of the first crypts found inside a Mexican pyramid, it has a psychoduct—a stone tube in the shape of a snake through which Pakal's soul was thought to have passed to the netherworld. The intricately carved sarcophagus lid weighs some 5 tons and measures 10 by 7 ft. It can be difficult to make out the carvings on the slab, but they depict the ruler, prostrate beneath a sacred ceiba tree. (There's a reproduction in the site museum, and a full-color replica of the lid in its original glory at the Museo del Jade in San Cristóbal de las Casas.) The lords of the nine underworlds are carved into stucco reliefs on the walls.

In 1994, the small and unassuming **Templo 13,** attached to the Temple of the Inscriptions, revealed a royal tomb hidden in its depths. The tomb, which probably belonged to Pakal's mother or grandmother, has been excavated and is open to the public.

The patios, galleries, and other buildings that make up the **palacio** are on a 30-ft-high plinth. Stuccowork adorns the pillars of the galleries and the inner courtyards. Most of the numerous friezes and masks inside depict Pakal and his dynasty. Steam baths in the southwestern patio suggest that priests once dwelled in the adjoining cellars. The palace's iconic tower was built on three levels, representing the three levels of the universe as well as the movement of the stars.

To the east of the palace is the tiny Río Otulum, which in ancient times was roofed over to form a 9-ft-high vaulted aqueduct. Cross the river and climb up 80 easy steps to arrive at the reconstructed **Plaza de la Cruz,** which contains the Templo de la Cruz Foliada (Temple of the Foliated Cross), Templo del Sol (Temple of the Sun), Templo 14, and the Templo de la Cruz (Temple of the Cross), the largest of the group. Inside Templo 14, there's an underworld scene in stucco relief, done 260 days after Pakal died. The most exquisite roof combs are found on these buildings, which are open to the public.

Templo 19 has yielded some exciting finds, including a large sculpted stucco panel, a carved stone platform with hundreds of hieroglyphics, and a limestone table (in pieces but now restored) depicting the ruler K'inich Ahkal Mo' Nahb' III. The latter is on display in the site museum. In **Templo 20,** ground-penetrating radar helped locate a frescoed tomb covered in murals. Both temples are still being excavated and aren't yet open to the public.

To reach the cluster called the **Grupo Norte** (Northern Group) walk north along the river, passing the palace and then the unexcavated ball court on your left. There are five buildings here in various states of disrepair; the largest and best preserved is the **Templo del Conde** (temple of the Count).

A short hike northeast of the Grupo Norte lies **Grupo C**, an area containing remains of the homes of Maya nobles and a few small temples shrouded in jungle. To maintain the natural setting in which the ruins were found, minimal restoration is being done. Human burials, funeral offerings of Jaina figurines, ceramics, and kitchen utensils have been found here as well as in the **Grupo B** area, which lies on the 20-minute "Ecological Path" hike through the jungle. On the way, you'll pass a small waterfall and pool called El Baño de la Reina (The Queen's Bath). The path is poorly marked; be sure to veer left through the Group B ruins when you reach them.

The site museum has a remarkable rendering in stucco of Maya deities in elaborate zoomorphic headdresses, discovered in front of the Temple of the Foliated Cross. The group includes 13 figures of the sun god Kinich Ahau. Also noteworthy are the handsome, naturalistic faces of Maya men. The group includes 13 figures of the sun god Kinich Ahau. Also noteworthy are the handsome, naturalistic stucco faces of Maya men. Displays are labeled in English, Spanish, and Chol. There's also a snack bar and an arts and crafts store with weavings, hand-embroidered fabrics, leather, ceramics, amber jewelry, hand-painted wooden crosses, and toys. You can reach the museum from the main road leading to the ruins. To get more in-depth information about the ruins, hire a multilingual guide at the ticket booth. Guides charge from about $33 for a group of up to 7 people to $50 for a maximum of 25 people. ✉ *Ruins and museum $3.50* ⊘ *Ruins daily 8–5, museum Tues.–Sun. 9–3:45.*

Palenque Town

㉒ *8 km (5 mi) north of the ruins.*

The town of Palenque wraps you in a warm tropical embrace. Its days as a sleepy little cattle town are far behind; the settlement swells with newcomers, and longtime residents rush to turn family homes into rent-paying posadas. In only the past few years, thanks to tourism, such infrastructure upgrades as e-mail servers have arrived; likewise ATMs and reliable long-distance phone service. Highland women and children hawk crafts in front of restaurants and pharmacies along the principal downtown streets.

The dominant landmark is the chalk-white *cabeza Maya,* a giant sculpture of the head of a Maya chieftain that graces the town's one traffic circle. West of downtown, the quiet neighborhood of La Cañada is a mix of residences, restaurants, and inexpensive lodgings.

Where to Stay & Eat

★ $–$$$$ ✕ **La Selva.** Although a stop on the tour-group route, this spacious palapa restaurant is still popular with locals. The setting, surrounded by luxuriant jungle gardens, is superb, and so is the food, including the chips and salsa. There's a scrumptious Sunday brunch buffet after 1:30 PM for about $13. ✉ *Carretera Palenque–Ruinas, Km 0.5* ☎ *916/345–0363* ▭ *MC, V.*

★ $–$$ ✕ **Maya Cañada.** Your Mexican dining experience at this thatch-roof restaurant in La Cañada is enlivened by an attractive blue color scheme and plentiful floral plantings. A romantic tiled terrace upstairs is lighted by iron lanterns and overlooks the back garden, where a few tables are set out for lunch. Mexican wines are served, and there's a full bar. Different types of live music are presented Thursday–Sunday 8 PM–midnight. ⊠ *Calle Merle Green s/n, La Cañada* ☎ *916/345–0216* ⊟ *AE, MC, V.*

¢–$ ✕ **El Arbolito.** On the main road to the ruins, this funky restaurant is full of hacienda memorabilia. There's a wall full of hats, each inscribed with a different Mexican proverb. Other walls have mounted animal heads and pelts. The specialties all come from Puebla, well known for its fine cuisine. Favorites include the spicy *consomé de borrego especial*, a broth with barbecued mutton, onions, and fresh cilantro. Beef tips in smoky chipotle sauce are served with beans, rice, garnish, and piping hot tortillas. There's live marimba music daily between 3 and 7 PM. ⊠ *Carretera Palenque–Pakalná, Km 1.5, across from Casa Inn* ☎ *916/345–0900* ⊟ *MC, V.*

¢–$ ✕ **Maya.** Billed as Palenque's first restaurant, this 1958 original is where locals come for hearty, fresh fare. It may be humble, but the management runs it with pride. Try the $4 set lunch menu or choose something from the extensive appetizer menu, which includes tacos and tostadas. Dishes served à la carte include New York and T-bone steaks and medallion of *robalo* (snook), a local fish that comes fried or breaded. The coffees are the best in town. ⊠ *Av. Independencia at Av. Hidalgo, facing the zócalo* ☎ *916/345–0042* ⊟ *AE, MC, V.*

¢–$ ✕ **Pizzería Palenque.** The thin-crust pizzas (with a Mexican touch) are so good, even Italians rave about them. You can also order pastas, burgers, *tortas* (bread roll sandwiches), or a club sandwich. The restaurant isn't far from the downtown bus station, on the main road. ⊠ *Av. Juárez 168* ☎ *916/345–0332* ⊟ *No credit cards.*

¢–$ ✕ **Las Tinajas.** Simple and unpretentious, Las Tinajas serves well-seasoned, basic food in a modest home. You'll usually strike up a conversation with someone at one of two large tables just outside the front door, or you can choose a table inside, where fans blow the air around. Portions are extremely generous. Try the bean empanadas, the chicken tostadas, or breaded chicken fillet. ⊠ *Av. 20 de Noviembre 414* ☎ *No phone* ⊟ *No credit cards.*

★ $$ ⌑ **Chan Kah.** Don't confuse this Chan Kah, which is in the jungle 4 km (2 mi) from the ruins, with its sister hotel of the same name in downtown Palenque. There's a stone-lined, lagoon-style pool, aromatic jasmine bushes, and a stream flowing around the back. The very comfortable bungalows have wide terraces, mahogany furnishings, and ceiling fans and/or air-conditioning. Bungalows 6–10 have views of the pool and stream. The emphasis here is on tranquility: there are no TVs in the rooms, although the suites have them. ⊠ *Carretera Ruinas, Km 3.5, 29960* ☎ *916/345–1100 or 916/345–1134* 🖷 *916/345–0820* ⇩ *73 rooms, 3 suites* ♿ *Restaurant, fans, pool, billiards, Ping-Pong, bar, recreation room, free parking; no a/c in some rooms, no TVs in some rooms* ⊟ *MC, V.*

$$ ⌑ **Ciudad Real Palenque.** This yellow-and-white, colonial-style hotel is surrounded by thriving gardens. A small waterfall and creek run through the grounds. All rooms have balconies facing the gardens. ⊠ *Carretera Pakal-Na, Km 1.5, 29960* ☎ *916/345–1315 or 916/345–1343* ⊕ *www. ciudadreal.com.mx* ⇩ *69 rooms, 3 suites* ♿ *Restaurant, room service, cable TV, pool, bar, shop, travel services, free parking* ⊟ *AE, MC, V.*

$$ ▣ **Hotel Calinda Nututún Palenque.** A large natural pool forms from a bend in the Río Nututún, which runs through the grounds of this hotel. The plain, ample rooms have tile floors; unlike the rooms, suites have bathtubs, TVs, and terraces. Camping is permitted near the river for about $5.50 per person. ⊠ *Carretera Palenque–Ocosingo, Km 3.5* ⚐ *(Apdo. 74, 29960)* ☏ *916/345–0100 or 916/345–0161; 800/221–2222 in the U.S.* 📠 *916/345–0620* ⇝ *55 suites, 12 rooms* ⌂ *Restaurant, pool, bar, playground, free parking; no TVs in some rooms* ⊟ *AE, MC, V.*

$$ ▣ **Maya Palenque.** This bright-blue, four-story, Best Western affiliate, just behind the cabeza Maya figure that marks the town's main intersection, is simple and reliable. Ask for a room facing the back pool and small garden—the nicest features of an otherwise plain but comfortable hotel. ⊠ *Calle Merle Green at Av. Juárez 29960* ☏ *916/345–0780* 📠 *916/345–0907* ⇝ *48 rooms, 3 junior suites* ⌂ *Restaurant, room service, cable TV, pool, shop, meeting rooms, free parking* ⊟ *AE, DC, MC, V.*

$ ▣ **Casa Inn Tulijá.** You can't beat the location of this cheerful little hotel, which is about a 10-minute walk from downtown. Although its rooms are small, it has the basics for a comfortable stay, and its 25-m pool is great for swimming laps. The tequila bar has more than 35 brands of the distilled agave liquor. ⊠ *Carretera Ruinas, Km 27.5, 29960* ☏ *916/ 345–0104; 800/900–1400 in the U.S.* 📠 *916/345–0163* ⇝ *48 rooms* ⌂ *Restaurant, cable TV, pool, billiards, bar, laundry service, meeting rooms, travel services, free parking* ⊟ *AE, MC, V.*

¢ ▣ **Shivalva.** Named for a Maya deity, this complex of homey, freestanding bungalows is in the leafy La Cañada neighborhood. There's no reception area per se; you pick up keys from the adjacent travel agency. Each unit has screened windows and a ceiling fan. Most look out onto a garden, and four units have square, tiled bathtubs. ⊠ *Calle Merle Green 9, 29960* ☏ *916/345–0411* 📠 *916/345–0392* ⇝ *14 rooms* ⌂ *Restaurant, fans, cable TV, bar, travel services, free parking* ⊟ *AE, MC, V.*

Bonampak

🔺 ㉓ *183 km (113 mi) southeast of Palenque.*

Bonampak, which means "painted walls" in Mayan, is renowned for its courtly murals of Maya life. The settlement was built on the banks of the Río Lacanjá in the 7th and 8th centuries and was uncovered in 1946. Explorer Jacques Soustelle called it "a pictorial encyclopedia of a Maya city." In remarkable tones of ocher, brown, red, green, and yellow, the scenes in the three rooms of the **Templo de las Pinturas** recount subjects such as life at court and the prelude and aftermath of battle.

Segments of the murals are deteriorating because of the humidity. In 1984 Mexican experts devised cleaning and restoration processes, and with the help of the National Geographic Society—and computerized, digital amplification techniques—remarkable details and color have come to light. Still, the reproductions at the archaeological museums in Mexico City and Villahermosa are more legible than these on-site specimens.

Until the 1990s, only the most devoted fans of the Maya attempted the trip here. Now, however, you can drive or take a three-hour bus ride from Palenque on the paved Carretera 198. (If you drive, hook up with tour groups that meet around 6 AM in Palenque and travel together for safety.) Buses or tour vans will take you all the way to the ruins or drop you at Lacanjá so you can hike the last 3 km (2 mi).

Be sure to wear sturdy shoes, and bring insect repellent, good sunglasses, and a hat to protect yourself from mosquitoes, ticks, sand flies, undergrowth, and the jungle sun. The ruins are open daily 8–5; admission is $7, including transportation from the park entrance to the main structures. Note that only four visitors are allowed in each room of the Templo de las Pinturas at a time, and you can't use a flash to take photos.

Yaxchilán

24 *50 km (31 mi) northeast of Bonampak, 190 km (118 mi) southeast of* Fodor'sChoice *Palenque.*

★

Excavations at Yaxchilán (ya-shee-*lan*), on the banks of the Río Usumacinta, have uncovered stunning temples and delicate carvings. Spider monkeys and toucans are, at this point, more prolific than humans, and howler monkeys growl like lions from the towering gum trees and magnificent, 100-year-old ceibas.

Yaxchilán, which means "place of green stones," reached its cultural peak during the Late Classic period, from about AD 600 to 900. It's dominated by two acropolises containing a palace, temples with finely carved lintels, and great staircases. Several generations ago, the Lacandon who live in the vicinity made pilgrimages to this jungle-clad site to leave "god pots" (incense-filled ceramic bowls) in honor of ancient deities. They were awed by the headless sculpture of Yaxachtun (ya-sha-*tun*) at the entrance to the temple (called Structure 33) and believed that the world would end when its head was replaced on its torso.

Yaxchilán was on the trade route between Palenque and Tikal, and the remains of a 600-ft bridge over the Río Usumacinta to connect Yaxchilán to Guatemalan territory has been discovered. The know-how of the people of Yaxchilán is still being deciphered by modern-day engineers.

Getting to Yaxchilán requires a one-hour riverboat ride; you must first drive or take a bus to the small town of Frontera Corozal, off Carretera 198, where boats depart for the ruins and for the Guatemalan border. It's best to arrange trips through travel agencies, tour operators, or tourist offices in Mexico City, Palenque, or San Cristóbal de las Casas; their staffers can also arrange for you to stay at the wonderful Tzeltal Indian cooperative, Escudo Jaguar. Admission to the ruins is $3; they're open daily 8–5.

Where to Stay

★ ¢ 🏠 **Escudo Jaguar.** This ecotourism project is designed to bring people closer to the Maya ruins of Bonampak and Yaxchilán. If you don't mind rustic accommodations, it's the ideal base for exploring the jungle and both archaeological sites. Each of the wooden, thatch-roof cabins has screened windows, mosquito nets, fans, and a wide concrete veranda with two large, colorful hammocks. The restaurant serves full breakfasts, lunches, and dinners. It's best to book trips to Bonampak and Yaxchilán with travel agents or tour operators ahead of time, mentioning that you want to stay at Escudo Jaguar. ⊠ *Frontera Corozal, Ocosingo* ☎ *555/151–1869* 🛏 *13 cabins* ⌂ *Restaurant* ▭ *No credit cards.*

VILLAHERMOSA & TABASCO

Graham Greene's succinct summation of Tabasco in *The Power and the Glory* as a "tropical state of river and swamp and banana grove" captures its essence. Although the state played an important role in Mexico's early history, its past is rarely on view. Instead, it's Tabasco's modern-day status as a supplier of oil that defines it. On a humid coastal plain and crisscrossed by 1,930 km (1,197 mi) of rivers, low hills, and unexplored jungles, the land is still rich in banana and cacao plantations. Shantytowns and refineries are, for the most part invisible; what you're more apt to see are small ranches with pastures of tall, green grass feeding horses and beef cattle.

The capital city of Villahermosa epitomizes the mercurial development of Tabasco, where the airplane arrived before the automobile. Thanks to oil and urban renewal, the cramped and ugly neighborhoods in the mosquito-ridden town of the 1970s have been replaced by spacious boulevards, lush parks, and cultural centers. Sandwiched between the Río Grijalva and the historic downtown, the Zona Luz has been redone as a brick-paved pedestrian zone, with galleries, museums, restaurants, ice cream shops, and a Howard Johnson hotel.

Tabasco contains the route of the Spanish explorations of 1518–19. At that time, the Maya lived along the rivers and waterways, which served as trade routes between the peoples of the north and those of the south. When the Spaniards came, they had to bridge 50 rivers and contend with swarms of mosquitoes, beetles, and ants—as well as the almost unbearable heat. At the same time, the region was so lush that one early chronicler termed it a Garden of Eden.

The Spanish conquest was made easier by the tribal warfare between the Tabascans and their Aztec overlords. Among the 20 slave women turned over to the Spaniards upon their arrival in the Aztec capital was a Chiapan named Malintzín (or Malinche), who was singled out for her ability to speak both the Maya and the Nahuatl languages. Called Doña Marina by the Spaniards, she learned Spanish and became not only Cortés's mistress and the mother of his illegitimate son but also an interpreter. Malinche's cooperation helped the conquistador vanquish both Moctezuma and Cuauhtémoc, the last Aztec rulers. Even today, "La Malinche" is synonymous with "traitor" throughout Mexico.

After the American Civil War, traders from the southern United States began operating in the region and on its rivers, hauling the precious mahogany trees upstream from Chiapas and shipping them north from the small port of Frontera. After this prosperous era, Tabasco slumbered until the oil boom of the 1970s and 1980s. Although the state's infrastructure is still minimal, it has beaches, lagoons, caves, and nature reserves worthy of exploration. The fired-brick Maya ruins of Comalcalco attest to the influence of Palenque, and the region southeast of Villahermosa has interesting rivers and canyons that are home to jaguars, deer, and alligators.

Villahermosa

► **25** *821 km (509 mi) southeast of Mexico City, 632 km (392 mi) southwest of Mérida.*

There are a good many ways to spend your time in Tabasco's capital. The Zona Luz is a grid of pedestrian-only streets with restored colonial buildings, cafés, galleries, and museums.

Most people make a beeline for the **Museo Regional de Antropología Carlos Pellicer** (Carlos Pellicer Regional Museum of Anthropology). This museum on the Grijalva's right bank is named after the man who donated many of its artifacts and who has been called the "poet laureate of Latin America." Pellicer (1897–1978) was deeply influenced by a love of his native Tabasco; his poems record the landscape's rhythms and visual intensity.

The museum is part of the huge CICOM cultural complex dedicated to research on the Olmec and Maya (which is what the Spanish acronym CICOM stands for). Much of the collection is devoted to Tabasco and the Olmec, or "inhabitants of the land of rubber," who flourished as early as 1750 BC and disappeared around 100 BC. The Olmecs have long been honored as inventors of the region's numerical and calendrical systems. The pyramid is also attributed to them. Some of the most interesting artifacts on display here are the remnants of their jaguar cult. The jaguar symbolized the Earth fertilized by rain (i.e., procreation), and many Olmec sculptures portray half-human, half-jaguar figures, and jaguar babies. Other sculptures portray human heads emerging from the mouth of a jaguar, bat gods, bird-headed humans, and female fertility figurines.

Many of Mexico's ancient cultures are represented on the upper two floors, from the red-clay dogs of Colima and the nose rings of the Huichol Indians of Nayarit to the huge burial urns of the Chontal Maya, who built Comalcalco. (Note that all the explanations are in Spanish.) The CICOM complex also houses a theater, restaurant, public library, and arts and crafts shop. ⊠ *Periférico Carlos Pellicer 511, an extension of the malecón (boardwalk)* ☎ *993/312–6344* ✉ *$1* ☉ *Tues.–Sun. 9–7.*

Giant stone heads and other carved Olmec figures were salvaged from the oil fields of La Venta, on Tabasco's western edge near the state of Veracruz. They're on display in the 20-acre **Parque Museo La Venta,** a garden—founded by Carlos Pellicer in 1958—on the beautiful Lago de las Ilusiones (Lake of Illusions). The 6-ft-tall stone heads, which have bold features and wear what look like helmets, weigh up to 20 tons. Scholarly debates about them are endless. It has been theorized that they depict everything from ancient Phoenician slaves to space invaders. The latest and least outlandish theory is that the faces—very similar to today's Tabasco Maya—are portraits of successful Olmec athletes, war heroes, and other public figures. La Venta contains 33 sculptures, including jaguars, priests, monsters, stelae, and stone altars. The park also contains a zoo (closed on Monday)—with river crocodiles, deer, jaguars, monkeys, and parrots—a gift shop, and stands that sell crafts and souvenirs. ⊠ *Blvd. Ruíz Cortines near Paseo Tabasco* ☎ *993/314–1652* ✉ *$2* ☉ *Daily 8–4.*

The small **Museo de la Historia Natural** (Natural History Museum) is just outside the entrance to the Parque Museo La Venta. Of most interest are the displays of Tabasco's native plants and animals, many of which are now under government protection. Other rooms are dedicated to geology, evolution, and the solar system. ⊠ *Blvd. Ruíz Cortines* ☎ *No phone* ✉ *50¢* ☉ *Tues.–Sun. 9–4:30.*

Yumká, which means "the spirit that looks after the forest" in Chontal Maya, is a popular nature reserve with more than 250 acres of jungle, savannah, and wetlands. Half-hour guided walking tours take you over a hanging bridge and past free-roaming endangered species such as spider monkeys, red macaws, toucans, crocodiles, and native *tepezcuintles* (giant rodents). After the walk there's a narrated tram ride past elephants, zebras, and other Asian and African creatures. Optional $1.50 boat tours glide past birds wading or taking flight. ⊠ *16 km (10 mi) from downtown, before the airport at Poblado Dos Montes* ☎ *993/ 356–0115* ✉ *$3* ☉ *Daily 9–5 (ticket window closes at 4).*

Where to Stay & Eat

$$$–$$$$ ✕ **Bougainvillea.** Fresh roses, red carpets, Asian lanterns, and live jazz music by candlelight Wednesday through Saturday make this an intimate fine-dining spot. It's one of the city's more expensive restaurants, but the food and service are well worth the price. Try the carpaccio or breaded Brie for starters and filet mignon or duck à l'orange for the main course. The dessert tray includes such delights as raspberry and peach cobbler with ginger coconut ice cream. ⊠ *Hyatt Regency hotel, Av. Juárez 106* ☎ *993/310–1234* ⊟ *AE, DC, MC, V* ☉ *Closed Sun.*

$–$$$ ✕ **El Mesón del Duende.** Standard meat and fish dishes are prepared with regional accents in the House of the Elf. Try such favorites as *filete en salsa de espinaca y queso* (beef fillet in a spinach and cheese sauce) and *la posta de robalo* (grilled snook). The modest dining room is in keeping with the family-style air. ⊠ *Calle Gregorio Méndez 1703* ☎ *993/315–1324 or 993/314–7060* ⊟ *AE, MC, V.*

★ $–$$$ ✕ **Los Tulipanes.** Delicious seafood and soothing river views are the hallmarks here. Choose a table on the outdoor patio or in the air-conditioned salon. Try the regional appetizers, including stuffed tortillas and empanadas or the *pejelagarto,* a succulent fish. Another regional favorite is *carne salada con chaya,* pieces of beef mixed with plantains and *chaya,* a regional green similar to spinach. The restaurant is open from 8 AM except Monday, when it opens at noon. ⊠ *Periférico Carlos Pellicer 511, in the CICOM complex* ☎ *993/312–9209* ⊟ *AE, MC, V.*

$ ✕ **Don Marisco.** A block from the entrance to Parque Museo La Venta is one of the town's most popular seafood restaurants. The nearly three-story thatch-roof building is an easy landmark: you'll stay cool beneath the high ceiling of this palapa, where breezes and ceiling fans keep things airy. Try the *filete de pescado villahermosa,* fish stuffed with chaya. ⊠ *Paseo Tabasco and Av. Ruíz Cortines* ☎☎ *993/352–0690* ⊟ *MC, V.*

¢–$ ✕ **La Fontana Italiana Trattoria.** If you're tiring of Mexican cuisine, enjoy Italian fare (including pizza) at this air-conditioned restaurant near the Parque Museo La Venta. It's a favorite among locals. The specialty is homemade pasta, and the Caesar salads are also good. ⊠ *Av. Ruíz Cortines 1410* ☎☎ *993/314–3283* ⊟ *AE, MC, V.*

$$$ ▥ **Camino Real.** The rambling lobby, with rattan furniture in attractive niches, leads to the Tabasco 2000 mall, which has the largest number of upscale stores in Villahermosa. Shaded by bamboo curtains, the restaurant's floor-to-ceiling windows overlook a garden; the hotel's pool is one of the state's largest. There's live entertainment in the lobby lounge nightly. Continental breakfast and an appetizer hour are offered to those who stay on the executive floor. ⊠ *Paseo Tabasco 1407, 86030* ☎ *993/316–4400; 800/722–6466 in the U.S.* 🖷 *993/316–4439* ⊕ *www.caminoreal.com/villahermosa* ⊠ *180 rooms, 16 suites* ♤ *Restaurant, coffee shop, room service, in-room data ports, in-room safes, minibars, cable TV, pool, laundry service, concierge floor, Internet, business services, meeting rooms, car rental, travel services, free parking* ⊟ *AE, DC, MC, V.*

$$ ▥ **Calinda Viva & Spa Villahermosa.** The Calinda has a great location across from the Parque Museo La Venta. Its lobby has lots of marble, and its big square pool is surrounded by lounge chairs. Although rooms are simply furnished and decorated, each has many amenities as well as a small balcony. The restaurant serves regional dishes and has daily breakfast and lunch buffets. ⊠ *Av. Ruíz Cortines at Paseo Tabasco, 86050* ☎ *993/315–0000* 🖷 *993/315–3073 or 993/315–1858* ⊠ *239 rooms, 1 suite* ♤ *Restaurant, cable TV, in-room safes, minibar, pool, hot tub, gym, massage, sauna, steam room, 2 bars, dance club, laundry service, Internet, business center, travel services, free parking* ⊟ *AE, MC, V.*

$$ ▦ **Cencali.** This two-story hotel, across from the Parque Museo La Venta, is beside a lagoon and surrounded by coconut-palm, mango, and cacao trees. The big, cheerful rooms have large TVs and small balconies; many overlook the lagoon. Don't miss the fabulous lobby mural of pre-Columbian indigenous life by Tabascan master Daniel Montuy. A daily breakfast buffet for two in the airy La Isla restaurant is included in the rates, as is airport transportation at set times. ⊠ *Av. Juárez at Paseo Tabasco, 86040* 🕾 *993/315–1999* ⊕ *www.cencali.com.mx* 📨 *114 rooms, 8 suites* ⚭ *Restaurant, cable TV, pool, bar, Internet, business services, meeting rooms, airport shuttle, car rental* ▤ *AE, DC, MC, V* ❘⊙❘ *BP.*

$$ ▦ **Hyatt Regency Villahermosa.** Although it's plain on the outside, this American-style luxury hotel has superior service and excellent restaurants. Rooms have marble floors and polished wood furnishings. The pleasingly modern Ceiba Café, which serves a superb daily breakfast buffet, has floor-to-ceiling windows that frame a tropical landscape. The other restaurant, Bougainvillea, is one of the region's finest restaurants for international food. The lobby's Plataforma video bar is decked out like the inside of an offshore oil platform, and there's live music nightly at El Flamboyan, another of the hotel's three bars. ⊠ *Av. Juárez 106, 86050* 🕾 *993/315–1234; 800/228–9000 in the U.S.* 🖷 *993/315–1235* 📨 *198 rooms, 9 suites* ⚭ *2 restaurants, room service, in-room data ports, in-room safes, mini-bars, cable TV, 2 tennis courts, pool, 3 bars, shop, laundry service, concierge floors, Internet, business services, convention center, car rental, travel services, free parking; no-smoking rooms* ▤ *AE, MC, V.*

¢–$ ▦ **Howard Johnson.** This cheery five-story hotel is in the pedestrian-only Zona Luz, not far from the historic downtown and the malecón. It has lots of perks and amenities for the price, including complimentary newspapers, free OJ or coffee with your wake-up call, and a cybercafé. You can ask for a Playstation, VCR, or iron/ironing board to be brought to your room. The coffee shop's attentive waiters serve mugs of hot coffee with real cream; refills aren't a problem. ⊠ *Calle Aldama 404, at Calle 27 de Febrero, 86000* 🕾 *993/314–4645* 🖷 *800/446–4656* ⊕ *www.hojo.com.mx* 📨 *93 rooms, 6 suites* ⚭ *Coffee shop, room service, in-room data ports, in-room safes, cable TV, bar, Internet, meeting rooms, airport shuttle, free parking* ▤ *AE, DC, MC, V.*

¢ ▦ **Plaza Independencia.** The staff is attentive and the location—between the river and the main plaza—is excellent. The lobby and common areas are painted in hot colors: bright pink, sky blue, butter yellow. These colors sneak into guest rooms, sometimes clashing with mint-green or orange furnishings. The large, comfortable beds dominate cramped quarters. Ask for a room with a river view. ⊠ *Av. Independencia 123, 86000* 🕾 *993/312–1299* 🖷 *993/314–4724* 📨 *89 rooms, 1 suite* ⚭ *Restaurant, bar, cable TV, room service, in-room safe, pool, laundry service, meeting rooms, free parking* ▤ *AE, MC, V.*

Comalcalco

🔺 ㉖ *56 km (35 mi) northwest of Villahermosa*

The region's abundant cacao trees provided food and a livelihood for a booming Maya population during the Classic period (100 BC to AD 900). Comalcalco, which was founded in about the 1st century BC, marks the westernmost reach of the Maya; descendants of its builders, the Chontal, still live in the vicinity. Its name, means "place of the clay griddles" (bricks) in Nahuatl, and it's Tabasco's most important Maya site, unique for its use of fired brick (made of sand, seashells, and clay), as the area's swamplands lacked the stone for building. The bricks were often inscribed and painted with figures of reptiles and birds, geometric figures, and drawings of hands and feet before being covered with stucco.

The major pyramid on the Gran Acrópolis del Este (Great Eastern Acropolis) is adorned with carvings as well as large stucco masks of the sun god, Kinich Ahau. The burial sites here also depart radically from Maya custom: the dead were placed in cone-shape clay urns, in a fetal position. Some have been left in situ, others are on display in the site museum along with many of the artifacts that were uncovered here. Admission to the site, which is open daily 10–4:30, is $3.

Paraíso

㉗ *19 km (12 mi) north of Comalcalco.*

As you head toward the Gulf of Mexico coast and Paraíso, stop at one of the cacao plantations and chocolate factories. On the coast you'll get a glimpse of small-town life. Climb the Cerro Teodomiro (Teodomiro Hill) for a spectacular view of Laguna de las Flores (Las Flores Lagoon) and coconut plantations. Small seafood restaurants and several small hotels dot the shore here; others are a few kilometers inland, in town.

The region's small, dark-sand beaches are not among Mexico's prettiest; the best place to spend your time is 5 km (3 mi) southeast of Paraíso, in **Puerto Ceiba,** a fishing community whose inhabitants breed and harvest oysters. You can take a two-hour boat tour aboard the *Puerto Ceiba I* around the mangrove-lined Laguna Mecoacán (Mecoacán Lagoon) and the coastal rivers. Tours, which cost about $5 for adults, leave from the small Puerto Ceiba Restaurant, which also serves some of the freshest seafood you've ever tasted.

If you speak Spanish, call ahead to arrange a short, free tour of **Hacienda Cholula** (☏ 933/334–3815), which is about 2 km (1 mi) from Comalcalco. You'll learn everything about cacao, from the plant to the chocolate stage. There's a small shop that sells products made from cocoa beans, which were used as currency here in pre-Hispanic times.

CHIAPAS & TABASCO A TO Z

To research prices, get advice from other travelers, and book travel arrangements, visit www.fodors.com.

AIR TRAVEL

AIRPORTS You can connect to the region's airports from Guatemala, the United States, Canada, and many places in Mexico—all with a stop in Mexico City. There are daily flights between Mexico City and both the Aeropuerto San Cristóbal, 15 km (9 mi) northwest of downtown on the road to Palenque, and the small airport at Comitán. El Aeropuerto Terán is 8 km (5 mi) southwest of Tuxtla Gutiérrez's airport. Villahermosa's Aeropuerto Capitan Carlos A. Rovirosa is 15 km (9 mi) south of the city in Ranchería dos Montes.

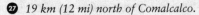 **Aeropuerto Capitan Carlos A. Rovirosa de Villahermosa** ☏ 993/356–0157 or 993/356–0156. **Aeropuerto de Comitán** ☏ 63/636–2143. **Aeropuerto San Cristóbal** ☏ 967/674–3016. **Aeropuerto Terán** ☏ 961/615–0498 or 961/615–1437.

AIRPORT You can catch a *colectivo* (shared minivan) from San Cristóbal's airport
TRANSFERS to downtown for $4 per person. Private taxis cost about $8 for up to three passengers. Taxis from Tuxtla Gutiérrez's airport cost $5 into town. The only transportation from Villahermosa's airport is via taxi. A trip to downtown Villahermosa costs $15. Taxis can also drive you straight to Palenque for $75.

CARRIERS   Aeroméxico has two daily nonstop flights to Villahermosa from Mexico City. Mexicana has five daily nonstop flights to Mexico City from Villahermosa. Aviacsa flies to Villahermosa nonstop to and from Mexico City twice a day and has direct flights to to Tuxtla Gutiérrez from Mexico City, Oaxaca, and Tapachula; from Cancún, Guadalajara, and other cities you have to connect through Mexico City. AeroCalifornia has one nonstop flight five days a week from Villahermosa to Mexico City. Aerocaribe, Mexicana's regional line, connects Villahermosa to Tuxtla Gutiérrez, Cancún, Mérida, and Oaxaca. Aeromar has daily flights between Mexico City and both San Cristóbal and Comitán.

🛪 **AeroCalifornia** ☎ 993/316–8000 for Villahermosa reservations; 800/237–6225 in the U.S. **Aerocaribe** ☎ 993/316–5046 in Villahermosa; 961/602–5651 in Tuxtla Gutiérrez. **Aeromar** ☎ 967/674–3014 in San Cristóbal; 963/636–2143 in Comitán. **Aeroméxico** ☎ 01800/021–4010 toll free in Mexico; 800/237–6639 in the U.S. **Aviacsa** ☎ 01800/711–6733 toll free in Mexico; 888/528–4227 in the U.S. **Mexicana** ☎ 993/356–3132 or 993/356–3135 in Villahermosa; 961/602–5771 in Tuxtla Gutiérrez; 800/531–7921 in the U.S.

BUS TRAVEL

From San Cristóbal, Cristóbal Colón bus station has deluxe and first-class buses to major destinations in Chiapas and beyond. (You can reach Tuxtla and avoid bus station lines by taking one of the Chevy Suburban vans directly across from the station. They leave as soon as they fill up, which is about every 20 minutes, 5 AM–10 PM and cost less than $4 per person.) Ticketbus serves many of the state's primary destinations on first-class buses, and you can buy tickets ahead of time in the center of San Cristóbal. Second-class service on Transportes Tuxtla Express Plus to Tuxtla, Palenque, and Comitán departs from the terminal at Avenida Ignacio Allende.

In Tuxtla, Cristóbal Colón bus line offers deluxe and first-class service to Oaxaca, Palenque, Villahermosa, Tapachula, Mérida, Mexico City, San Cristóbal, Cancún, Puerto Escondido, and Playa del Carmen. First- and second-class transportation within the state is available on Sociedad de Transportes Dr. Rodolfo Figueroa.

From Palenque, first- and luxury-class service is available to Ocosingo, Villahermosa, San Cristóbal, Campeche, Tuxtla Gutiérrez, Mérida, Cancún, and Mexico City on ADO and Cristóbal Colón. They leave from the ADO bus terminal. If you can't get a first-class bus, many of the same destinations can be reached on the second-class buses operated by Transportes Rodolfo Figueroa, a few doors away from the ADO bus terminal.

From Villahermosa, deluxe and first-class service to Campeche, Chetumal, Mérida, Mexico City, Palenque, San Cristóbal, Tapachula, Tuxtla Gutiérrez, Veracruz, and elsewhere is available from the ADO bus terminal, which is served by UNO, G. L., and Cristóbal Colón. There's frequent second-class service to intermediate destinations and small towns from the Central Camionera de 2a Clase.

🚌 **ADO bus terminal** ✉ Av. Juárez near Av. de la Vega, Palenque ☎ 916/345–1344 ✉ Calle F. J. Mina 297, corner of Calle Lino Merino, Villahermosa ☎ 993/312–7692 or 993/312–1446. **Central Camionera de 2a Clase** ✉ Av. Ruíz Cortines s/n at Prolongación de Mina, Villahermosa ☎ 993/312–0863 or 993/312–1091. **Cristóbal Colón** ☎ 993/312–2937 in Villahermosa. **Cristóbal Colón bus station** ✉ Av. Insurgentes and Blvd. Juan Sabines Gutiérrez, San Cristóbal ☎ 967/678–0291 ✉ Av. 2aPoniente Norte 268, Tuxtla Gutiérrez ☎ 961/612–2624. **G. L.** ☎ 993/312–7692 in Villahermosa. **Sociedad de Transportes Dr. Rodolfo Figueroa** ✉ 4a Poniente Sur 1060, Tuxtla Gutiérrez ☎ 916/312–7692. **Ticketbus** ✉ Av. Belisario Domínguez 8, San Cristóbal ☎ 967/678–8503. **Transportes Tuxtla Express Plus** ☎ 967/678–4869 in San Cristóbal. **UNO** ✉ Av. Francisco Javier Mina at Lino Merino s/n, Villahermosa ☎ 993/312–7627.

CAR RENTAL

▪ Agencies **Budget** ✉ Aeropuerto Terán, Tuxtla Gutiérrez ☎ 961/615-0672 ✉ Aeropuerto Capitan Carlos A. Rovirosa de Villahermosa, Villahermosa ☎ 993/356-0118 ✉ Av. 27 de Febrero 712, Villahermosa ☎ 993/314-3790. **Dollar** ✉ Hotel Maya Tabasco, Av. Ruiz Cortines 907, Villahermosa ☎ 993/314-4466 or 993/356-0211. **Excellent** ✉ Calle Real de Guadalupe 5-E, San Cristóbal ☎ 967/678-7656. **Hertz** ✉ Aeropuerto Capitan Carlos A. Rovirosa de Villahermosa, Villahermosa ☎ 993/356-0200 ✉ Hotel Camino Real, Paseo Tabasco 1407, Villahermosa ☎ 993/316-0163 ✉ Aeropuerto Terán, Tuxtla Gutiérrez ☎ 961/615-7070 ✉ Hotel Camino Real, Av. Belisario Domínguez 1195 ☎ 961/615-5348. **National** ✉ Aeropuerto Terán, Tuxtla Gutiérrez ☎ 961/614-6683 ✉ 11a Poniente Sur 1172, Tuxtla Gutiérrez ☎ 961/614-6681.

CAR TRAVEL

From Tuxtla Gutiérrez, Carretera 190 goes east through Chiapa de Corzo to San Cristóbal before continuing southeast to Comitán and the Guatemala border. Carretera 199 to Carretera 186 (the turnoff is at Catazajá) is the preferred route from San Cristóbal to Villahermosa; it takes you via Toniná, Agua Azul, and Palenque. The winding drive from San Cristóbal to Palenque takes about five hours; it's another two hours from Palenque to Villahermosa along a fairly straight stretch.

On the map, Carretera 195 may look like the most direct way to travel between San Cristóbal and Villahermosa, but it entails hours of hairpin curves—it's only for the stalwart and absolutely not to be traveled at night because of seasonal fog as well as a lack of reflectors, illumination, and other cars to help in case of emergency.

A paved road connects Bonampak with the Lagos de Montebello, but if you travel this lonely route get an early start, and be advised that the no emergency services patrol it. To get to Villahermosa from Coatzacoalcos and Veracruz, take Carretera 180. In all cases, exercise caution during the rainy season (June through October), when roads are slick.

As with many other colonial towns, the most enjoyable and thorough way to explore San Cristóbal is on foot. If you do come to town with a car, leave it in the hotel garage until you're ready to take an excursion. The same is true of Palenque Town. Of the three rivers surrounding it, Villahermosa is oriented toward the Río Grijalva to the east, which is bordered by the malecón. The city is huge, and driving can be tricky. The main road through town, Ruíz Cortines, is almost a highway; exit ramps are about 1 km (½ mi) apart, and destinations aren't clearly marked. Drive with caution.

EMERGENCIES

▪ **Cruz Roja** (Red Cross) ✉ Prolongación Ignacio Allende 55, San Cristóbal ☎ 967/678-0772. **Federal Highway Police** ✉ Blvd. Juan Sabines Gutiérrez, s/n, San Cristóbal ☎ 967/678-6466. **Municipal police** ✉ Blvd. Juan Sabines Gutiérrez, s/n, near Unidad Deportiva, San Cristóbal ☎ 967/678-0554.

▪ Hospitals & Clinics **Centro de Salud** ✉ Prolongación Juárez s/n, Palenque ☎ no phone. **Hospital General** ✉ Prolongación Juárez s/n, Palenque ☎ 916/345-0733. **Hospital General** ✉ Av. Insurgentes 24, San Cristóbal ☎ 967/678-0770. **Red Cross Hospital** ✉ Av. Sandino 716 Villahermosa ☎ 993/315-5555 or 993/315-6263.

▪ Late-Night Pharmacies **Farmacia del Ahorro** ✉ Av. Central Poniente 874, Tuxtla ☎ 961/602-6677 ✉ Av. 27 de Febrero 1401, Villahermosa ☎ 933/315-6606. **Farmacia Bios** ✉ Av. Hidalgo at Av. Cuauhtémoc, San Cristóbal ☎ 967/678-1818. **Farmacia Lastra** ✉ Av. Juárez s/n at Abasolo, downtown, Palenque ☎ 916/345-1119.

ENGLISH-LANGUAGE MEDIA

In San Cristóbal, Chilam Balam has travel, archaeology, and art books along with posters, videos, and maps of Mexico. La Pared (closed Monday) has a good selection of English-language books about the Maya and Latin America as well as used fiction titles and travel guides. La Mercantil has the best selection of English-language periodicals.

🛈 Bookstores **Chilam Balam** ⊠ Casa Utrilla at Av. General Utrilla 33 and Calle Dr. Navarro, San Cristóbal ☎ 967/678-0486. **La Mercantil** ⊠ Calle Diego de Mazariegos 21, San Cristóbal. **La Pared** ⊠ Av. Miguel Hidalgo 2 ☎ 967/678-6367.

INTERNET, MAIL & SHIPPING

Correos (post offices) throughout the region have MexPost service, a shipping service that's comparable to DHL or FedEx and slightly cheaper. San Cristóbal has at least one Internet café per block near the center of town. You can check e-mail while you eat and listen to music at the Cafetería del Centro ($1.50/hour), half a block from the zócalo. It's open daily 7 AM–9:30 PM. The CyberCafe is about 10 blocks from the Cristóbal Colón bus station, in Tuxtla Gutiérrez, but the price is right: $1.50 an hour for Internet access. It's open daily 9–2 and 4–8. Palenque's Red Maya, open daily 9 AM–10:30 PM, has a dozen fast computers. An hour costs $1.50. There's a great Internet café in Villahermosa at the coffee shop of the Howard Johnson's hotel, in the popular Zona Luz district. It's open weekdays 8 AM–10 PM, Saturday 8–8, and Sunday noon–8, and charges $2 an hour.

🛈 Cybercafés **Cafetería del Centro** ⊠ Calle Real de Guadalupe 7, San Cristóbal ☎ 967/678-3922. **CyberCafe** ⊠ 3a Norte Poniente 1340, Local 8, Tuxtla Gutiérrez ☎ 961/612-3900. **Howard Johnson's** ⊠ Calle Aldama 404, Villahermosa ☎ 993/314-4645. **Red Maya** ⊠ Av. Juárez 133, Palenque ☎ 916/345-0934.

🛈 Post Offices **Palenque** ⊠ Calle Independencia at Calle Bravo ☎ 916/345-0143.

San Cristóbal ⊠ Calle Ignacio Allende 3, at Calle Diego de Mazariegos ☎ 967/678-0765. **Tuxtla Gutiérrez** ⊠ Primera Av. Norte Poniente, at 2a Calle Oriente Norte ☎ 954/582-0232. **Villahermosa** ⊠ Calle 7 Norte, at Calle Oaxaca ☎ 954/582-0232.

MONEY MATTERS

In Villahermosa and Tuxtla Gutiérrez, most hotels and tourist-oriented restaurants and shops accept credit cards and traveler's checks, while smaller establishments and those in Palenque, Comitán, and San Cristóbal prefer cash. Bank hours are generally weekdays 9–4:30. Most have ATM machines, but you might occasionally be surprised by one (or more) that's broken or out of cash. It's best not to get down to your last pesos before replenishing your funds.

🛈 Banks **Banamex** ⊠ Calle Real de Guadalupe and Av. Insurgentes, San Cristóbal ☎ 967/678-1043 ⊠ Av. Juárez 62, Palenque ☎ 916/345-0490. **Bancomer** ⊠ Av. Juárez 40 Palenque ☎ 916/345-0198. **Banco Inverlat** ⊠ Calle Juárez 415, Villahermosa ☎ 312-5803.

🛈 Currency Exchange **Agencia de Cambio Lacantún** ⊠ Calle Real de Guadalupe 12-A, San Cristóbal ☎ 967/678-2587.

TAXIS

San Cristóbal has private and colectivo taxi service to outlying villages from the *sitio* (taxi stand) at Boulevard Jaime Sabines and Avenida Ignacio Allende, a short distance from the Cristóbal Colón bus station. Within downtown Tuxtla Gutiérrez, taxis cost a minimum of $2. You can take a taxi 10 minutes away to Chiapa de Corzo for $7; to San Cristóbal, about 1½ hours away, the cost is about $30.

In Palenque the sitio is at the town park. A ride to the ruins is $5; it's $6 if you call for a cab from your hotel. Within the city of Villahermosa itself, trips are fixed at $1.50 in yellow colectivo taxis; the minimum fare is $2 in the white *especial* (special or private) taxis.

🛈 **Radio Taxis Uno Tuxtla** ☎ 961/612-5672. **San Cristóbal Taxis Jovel** ☎ 967/678-6899. **Sitio de Taxis Palenque** ☎ 916/345-0379. **Villahermosa radio taxi** ☎ 993/315-8333 or 993/315-8433.

TOURS

SAN CRISTÓBAL   Pepe Santiago, a Lacandon native associated with Museo Na Bolom since childhood, leads tours daily to San Juan Chamula, Zinacantán, and San Nicolás Buenavista. (Pepe's name is a veritable ticket of acceptance in the more remote regions of Chiapas.) The group leaves Museo Na Bolom promptly at 10 AM and returns around 3:30; it's well worth the $11 price. Gabriela Gudiño is a reliable private tour guide who specializes in history and indigenous peoples.

A.T.C., Viajes Pakal, Viajes Chinkultik, Posetur, and Viajes Navarra offer local tours around San Cristóbal and beyond, as well as tours of Bonampak, Yaxchilán, Palenque, Agua Azul, Lagos de Montebello, Amatenango, Chinkultik, and Sumidero Canyon. Chinkultik is especially recommended for its professionalism and its three-day trip to Laguna Miramar: all food, transportation, tents, and even porters (it's a three-hour walk in to the lake) are included in the price of $200 per person.

🚩 **A.T.C.** ✉ Av. 16 de Septiembre 16, San Cristóbal ☎ 967/678-2550 or 967/678-2557. **Gabriela Gudiño** ✉ Calz. México 81, San Cristóbal ☎🖨 967/678-4223. **Museo Na Bolom** ✉ Av. Vicente Guerrero 33, between Calles Comitán and Chiapa de Corzo, San Cristóbal ☎ 967/678-1418 **Posetur** ✉ Posada Diego de Mazariegos, 5 de Febrero 1, San Cristóbal ☎ 967/678-0833. **Viajes Chinkultik** ✉ Calle Real de Guadalupe 34, San Cristóbal ☎ 967/678-0957. **Viajes Navarra** ✉ Calle Real de Guadalupe 15-D, San Cristóbal ☎ 967/678-114. **Viajes Pakal** ✉ Calle Cuauhtémoc 6A, San Cristóbal ☎ 967/678-2818.

TUXTLA   Viajes Miramar offers city tours of Tuxtla Gutiérrez for about $10. It
GUTIÉRREZ   also has a five-hour tour that allows you to see the Sumidero Canyon from the ridge above and from a boat on the river below. The cost is $70 for up to four people.

🚩 **Viajes Miramar** ✉ Hotel Camino Real, Blvd. Dr. Belisario Domínguez 1195, Tuxtla Gutiérrez ☎ 961/617-7777 Ext. 7230 or 961/615-5925.

PALENQUE   Most tour operators offer half-day guided tours of Palenque ruins for about $6, which includes a guide and transportation. Also offered are full-day tours (four hours at Palenque, 30 minutes at the waterfall at Misol-Há, and three hours at Agua Azul for about $14 per person) and longer trips to San Cristóbal, Toniná, and the Sumidero Canyon.

The Sociedad Cooperativo Chambalum has six-hour trips to Agua Azul, which include a visit to Misol-Há; the cost is about $9 per person and includes the entrance fees (50¢ per person or $2 per car). Kukulcán, a reliable, Palenque tour operator, has one- and two-day trips to Bonampak and Yaxchilán. A one-day trip via land and boat costs $30–$40, including transportation, a Spanish-speaking guide, and lunch. Two-day trips, which overnight in tents at the Lacandon village of Lacanjá, cost about $60 and include five meals, transportation, and guide services.

🚩 **Kukulcán** ✉ Av. Juárez s/n at Calle Cinco de Mayo, Palenque ☎ 916/345-1506. **Sociedad Cooperativo Chambalum** ✉ Calle Allende at Av. Juárez s/n, Palenque ☎ no phone.

VILLAHERMOSA   Turismo Creativo specializes in multiday excursions that take in Misol-Ha, Palenque, Cañón de Sumidero, and indigenous villages. The Olmec/Maya Circuit Tour combines visits to Palenque, Comalcalco, and the Parque Museo La Venta in Villahermosa, as well as plane tickets and car rentals. Expedición Ayin specializes in equipped cave tours and trips to the Pantanos de Centla Biosphere Reserve. Rutas del Usumacinta has tours to Chiapas and Guatemala, including Bonampak and Yaxchilán. Agencia de Viajes Tabasco is a big travel agency and a good place to buy air tickets as well as book tours.

🚩 **Agencia de Viajes Tabasco** ✉ Galería Tabasco 2000, Local 173, Zona Hotelera, Villahermosa ☎🖨 993/316-4088 or 993/316-4090.

Expedición Ayin ✉ Av. Pedro Gil Cadena 11, Villahermosa ☎ 993/351-2439. **Rutas del Usumacinta** ✉ Calle Remo 215, Residencial Cuidad Deportiva, Villahermosa ☎ 993/351-0405. **Turismo Creativo** ✉ Av. PaseoTabasco 715, Villahermosa ☎ 993/315-3999.

VISITOR INFORMATION

Chiapas State has a Web site as well as an information hot line that you can dial toll-free from anywhere in Mexico. Sometimes, however, no one answers the hot line, and the Web site is over-engineered and hard to use. San Cristóbal's municipal tourist office is open Monday–Saturday 8–8 and has some information about city. For information about attractions throughout the city and state, try the state tourist office, which is open weekdays 8–8, Saturday 9–8, and Sunday 9–2. The folks at the Tuxtla Gutiérrez state tourist office (open weekdays 9 –9, Saturday 9–7, and Sunday 9–3) are extremely helpful.

In Palenque, the tourism office is open daily 9–9. The staff at the state tourism office can answer questions about Palenque and beyond weekdays 8–4. The people in the Comitán tourist office are very knowledgeable. The office is open Monday–Saturday 8–8; a guard passes out maps and other printed information Sunday 9–2. The Instituto de Turismo de Tabasco, the state tourist office in Villahermosa, is open weekdays 8–4; an auxiliary office at the Parque Museo La Venta is open daily 9–4.

🛈 **Chiapas Tourist Information Hotline** ☎ 01800/280-3500 toll-free in Mexico ⊕ www.turismo.chiapas.gob.mx. **Comitán Tourist Office** ✉ Calle Central Benito Juárez Oriente 6, Comitán ☎ 963/632-4047. **Delegación de Turismo** ✉ Calle Nicolás Bravo at Av. Francisco Javier Mina, Palenque ☎ 916/345-0356. **Instituto de Turismo de Tabasco** ✉ Av. Los Ríos at Calle 13 s/n, Villahermosa ☎ 993/316-3633 or 993/316-2889. **Palenque Tourist Information Office** ✉ Av. Juárez, at Plaza de Artesanías, Palenque ☎ no phone. **San Cristóbal Municipal Tourist Office** ✉ Palacio Municipal, ground floor, on the zócalo, San Cristóbal ☎ 967/678-0665. **San Cristóbal State Tourist Office** ✉ Av. Miguel Hidalgo 1-B, ½ block from zócalo, San Cristóbal ☎ 967/678-6570 or 967/678-1467. **Tabasco web site** ⊕ www.naturalmentetabasco.com.mx **Tuxtla Gutiérrez State Tourist Office** ✉ Edificio Plaza de las Instituciones, ground floor, Blvd. Dr. Belisario Domínguez 950, Tuxtla Gutiérrez ☎ 961/602-5127 or 961/602-5269.

VERACRUZ AND THE NORTHEAST

12

FODOR'S CHOICE

Mariscos Villa Rica Mocambo, open-air restaurant, Veracruz

Gran Café de la Parroquia, Veracruz

Hotel Emporio, Veracruz

Las Monjitas, Monterrey

Museo de Antropología de Jalapa

Museo de Arte Contemporaneo, Monterrey

Posada Coatepec, hotel, Coatepec, near Jalapa

The ruins of El Tajín

HIGHLY RECOMMENDED

RESTAURANTS Gran Café del Portal, Veracruz

La Casa de Mamá, Jalapa

La Estancia de los Tecajetes, Jalapa

Luisiana, Monterrey

Pardiño's, Boca del Río, near Veracruz

Restaurante Sorrento, Papantla de Olarte

Victoria 3020, Nuevo Laredo

Vitrales, Monterrey

HOTELS Hotel Florida, Tuxpán

Hotel Hawaii, Veracruz

Mesón del Alférez, Jalapa

Quinta Real, San Pedro Garza García, near Monterrey

Radisson Plaza Gran Hotel Ancira, Monterrey

EXPERIENCES Acuario de Veracruz, an outstanding aquarium

El Fuerte de San Juan de Ulúa, 16th century fort, Veracruz

A voladores performance, Papantla de Olarte

Updated by
Barbara
Kastelein and
Mark Sullivan

THERE ARE PLENTY of reasons to make your way to the state of Veracruz: its culture, history, cuisine, and a characteristic laid-back friendliness. You can explore El Tajín—its Pyramid of the Niches is one of the most enchanting pre-Columbian buildings in Mexico. Or wander the venerable port of Veracruz, where the Spanish first landed in 1519; witness the fascinating aerial ritual of the *voladores* (fliers) of Papantla; and enjoy an archaeological museum second only to the one in Mexico City. You can also stroll the plazas of quaint mountain villages, laze on sandy beaches, celebrate one of Latin America's biggest *Carnavals*, and dine on some of the best seafood in Mexico.

The three cultural-hybrid border cities of Nuevo Laredo, Reynosa, and Matamoros are industrial areas that lure American day-trippers with moderate-price crafts and authentic Mexican dishes. Improved roads have led more people to take advantage of the opportunity to visit Monterrey, Mexico's third-largest city. With its cultural attractions, five-star hotels and restaurants, modern outlook, and, of course, shops, it's a highlight of the region. In the nearby Sierra Madre, you can explore stunning canyons, cliffs, and caves.

Exploring Veracruz & the Northeast

The lively port city of Veracruz was of vital importance in the history of the Spanish conquest of Mexico. Raucous and sweaty, its Caribbean flavor, energetic music, and multiracial population give it a particular flair. The exuberance of *jarochos,* as the city's residents are known, does not falter even in the broiling midday heat or when faced with the strong *nortes* (brisk north winds).

The lush coastal state of Veracruz also harbors pockets of colonial history, as well as fine native ruins and some of Mexico's most outstanding adventure tourism routes. Jalapa, the state capital, is a pretty university town and cultural hub, studded with parks and stately government buildings and laced with hilly, winding roads.

Northeastern Mexico consists of a string of border towns across from the United States, the city of Monterrey, and some surrounding natural wonders. The border towns' charm is limited, aside from sampling Mexican cuisine and buying crafts. You might prefer to linger in Monterrey, making side trips into the nearby mountains or to the colonial town of Saltillo.

About the Restaurants

There's no need to break out your most dashing suit here; very little in the state of Veracruz or the Northeast is truly formal. In the cities of Veracruz and Monterrey reservations may be needed for popular restaurants; otherwise, you won't need to book in advance. A jacket and tie would look out of place almost anywhere, apart from the business hub of Monterrey.

About the Hotels

The state of Veracruz isn't the place to find cool, ultramodern, world-class hotels—the emphasis is more often on warm service rather than the latest amenities. The port city offers a number of inexpensive hotels with plenty of atmosphere, and both the moderately priced and more expensive places offer good value for your money—especially in comparison with their counterparts in areas of Mexico that see more foreign tourists. Downtown Jalapa has a limited number of upscale choices, but there are plenty of clean, comfortable budget accommodations. The small town of Papantla is improving its lodging options, and even more out-of-the-way places like Los Tuxtlas have an atmospheric hotel or two.

12

The state of Veracruz and northeast Mexico are separate regions, which is how most travelers approach them when planning a trip. Veracruz is closer to Mexico City and is a popular domestic getaway. Northeast Mexico is closer to Texas and is more often frequented by Texans hopping across the border than by people using Mexico City as a gateway. Our approach to the northeast is therefore from Texas. The drive up the coast from Veracruz is possible, but the distances—502 km (311 mi) between Veracruz and Tampico and 1,005 km (623 mi) from Veracruz to Monterrey—may be daunting from behind the wheel.

Numbers in the text correspond to numbers in the margin and on the Veracruz and East Central Mexico, Veracruz, Northeastern Mexico, and Monterrey maps.

If you have 3 days

If you're flying, head straight for the port of ▦ **Veracruz** ❶–❹ ▶, the most Caribbean of the Gulf of Mexico cities. You'll have no problem spending two days here, enjoying the sights and visiting the beaches and seafood restaurants of **Boca del Río,** a small fishing village that has practically turned into a suburb of Veracruz. On Day 3, visit the village of **La Antigua** and the archaeological site of **Cempoala** ❼, a major Totonac city.

If you're driving down from Texas, you could explore the area around ▦ **Monterrey** ⓯–㉔ ▶, the cultural and industrial giant of the northeast. Spend the first day walking around the Macroplaza area, with its outstanding modern-art and history museums. Devote the next two days to some of the region's natural attractions, including the Cañon de la Huasteca, an impressive gorge; the ancient Grutas de García; and the spectacular waterfall in the Parque Nacional Cumbres de Monterrey.

If you have 7 days

Start in ▦ **Veracruz** ❶–❹ ▶. On the third day drive down the coast to the cool hill towns of ▦ **Los Tuxtlas** ❺, where you can consult a *curandero* (healer) for whatever ails you. If you're visiting at the time of a festival, make a foray to **Tlacotalpan** ❻. Another option would be to make your way inland from Veracruz to ▦ **Jalapa** ❽ to visit the anthropology museum. Get your feet wet with either a trip to the magnificent falls at **Xico** or a bit of river rafting. As a third alternative, you could travel farther north to see the ruins of **El Tajín** ❾, staying in ▦ **Papantla de Olarte** ❿ or ▦ **Tuxpán** ⓫. If you're heading south back to Veracruz, stop on the way at La Antigua and the ruins of **Cempoala** ❼.

For six days in the northeast, add excursions to **Saltillo** ㉕ and to ▦ **Tampico** ㉖ to the three-day jaunt.

Catering mostly to business travelers and short-term tourists, accommodations in the border towns increasingly tend to fall into two camps: the chains of more standardized small hotels or the wilting individual establishments whose heyday has passed. Monterrey affords more choices in all price ranges.

	WHAT IT COSTS				
	$$$$	$$$	$$	$	¢
RESTAURANTS	over $25	$15–$25	$10–$15	$5–$10	under $5
HOTELS	over $250	$150–$250	$75–$150	$50–$75	under $50

Restaurant prices are for a main course excluding tax and tip. Hotel prices are for two people in a standard double room in high season, based on the European Plan (EP, with no meals) and excluding service and 17% tax.

Timing

In Veracruz, the weather is balmy between November and April. The notorious *nortes*—gusty winds that blow in off the Golfo de Mexico—usually appear between October and February, and especially in December. Pack a light jacket for evenings and, if you have long hair, hair bands if you plan to travel during these months. In summer, both the temperature and humidity soar, but the frequent rains afford a respite from the heat.

A great time to visit Veracruz is the week before Ash Wednesday for the Mardi Gras *Carnaval,* Mexico's major pre-Lenten bash. It's glitzy, merry, and wild but retains a small-town ambience that keeps it saner and safer than the better-known celebrations in Rio or New Orleans. The biggest problem at such times is finding a room (reserve months in advance). The same is true during Christmas as well as Easter week, when all of Mexico goes on vacation and heads for the beach. An Afro-Caribbean music and dance festival normally takes place for a week in June or July. Dates change, so check ahead with tourist information or the Instituto Veracruzano de la Cultura (IVEC).

The hottest months in the northeast are June through August. The cooling rains arrive in July and last through November. There are never any crowds at the border towns or in Monterrey except during major U.S. holidays, when Americans head south for a day or weekend.

THE STATE OF VERACRUZ

A long, slim crescent of land bordering the Golfo de Mexico, the state of Veracruz is often ignored by foreign travelers. Although Veracruz's beaches don't compare with the white-sand wonders of the Yucatán peninsula, they're cheerful and vibrant, buzzing with Mexican holiday makers slurping coconut milk and kids laughing at the tiny sand crabs that pop up whenever there's a moment's calm. Moreover, the state holds a romantic allure for those drawn to the sensuous joie de vivre of Veracruz city or the mysterious hill towns of the Sierra de Los Tuxtlas.

Descending from the volcanic Sierra, the Veracruz coast consists of flat lowlands that have their share of terrible heat and swamps and are pockmarked by noisome oil refineries. As you head inland—Veracruz is only 140 km (87 mi) across at its widest point—the land rises to meet the Sierra Madre Oriental range, with its stunning 18,400-ft Pico de Orizaba (also called Citlaltépetl), Mexico's highest peak. In the foothills of this range, you'll find the university town and state capital Jalapa, where students share the colonial streets with local farmers marketing their crops. Jalapa is a favored place for foreigners to study Spanish, and the nearby town of Jalcomulco is a base for river-rafting explorations on the Río Pescados.

The state does have some good beaches, but the real reasons to come are the atmosphere, the people, the cuisine, and the history. All these

Fishing

Northeastern Mexico is a popular place for American anglers. You're likely to hook something at La Pesca—as the name would indicate—on the Tamaulipas coast between Matamoros and Tampico east of Ciudad Victoria and Soto La Marina.

Local Specialties

The state of Veracruz is home to some of Mexico's most accessible and delicious regional dishes. Its signature *mole* is the *mole de Xico,* a sauce rich with seasoned fruits and nuts. Many of the traditional specialties show the influence of the Spanish and African communities of nearby Cuba, including the state's signature dish, *huachinango à la veracruzana* (red snapper in the Veracruz style, covered in tomatoes, onions, garlic, green olives, and capers). Leaving without sampling this would be both a shame and a bit of a feat, as every chef has his own version, which he will insist you try. Although this dish recalls Mediterranean cuisine, it also incorporates New World ingredients like jalapeños and tomatoes. Another dish with a similar influence is *salpicón de jaiba,* a spicy crabmeat salad usually prepared with tomatoes, capers, and jalapeños. Other dishes reflect African ties in their use of beans, plantains, yucca, taro, white sweet potatoes, and especially peanuts, which appear in the classic *puerco encacahuatado* (pork in peanut sauce) and the bracing *salsa macha,* made by grinding peanuts with garlic, chilies, and olive oil.

You'll find peanut ice cream all over the state, along with another sweet-tooth tempter, *buñuelos veracruzanos* (Veracruz beignets), golden doughnuts to be dipped in a sugar and cinnamon mixture or served with sticky *piloncillo* (brown loaf-sugar syrup). Look out for the charge of *toritos* (little bulls), a heady alcoholic punch made with cane liquor, milk, and tropical fruit pulp or peanuts.

In Veracruz, as befits a hot, breezy port town, the emphasis is on simple, fresh food, mostly *pescado* (fish) and *mariscos* (shellfish). Night or day, a stop at one of the town's cafés is de rigueur. Jalapa is considered to have the best restaurants in the state, with a creative integration of beans, rice, cheese, and occasionally chilies (this is, after all, the hometown of the jalapeño) into main dishes of meat and river fish such as trout. But some of the best places to eat in the region are the small, family-run seafood *palapas* (thatch-roof huts). Just ask for the *platillo del día* (daily dish).

The Northeast isn't renowned for the subtlety of its cuisine, but its cattle country ensures an abundance of good beef cuts, the most typical being *arrachera.* A prime regional treat is kid (*cabrito*), which, when well prepared, has a delicate lamblike flavor. If you'd like to try it, Monterrey is the place to give it a go; you cannot be in this city for long without seeing goat sizzling on the grill. Plunge ahead and order the back or kidneys, or, if you're a bit apprehensive, the leg or breast.

Volcanoes & Nature Preserves

Veracruz state claims a few national parks—not to mention Mexico's highest peak, the Pico de Orizaba. At over 18,000 ft, this extinct volcano is the third-highest mountain in North

America. Mountaineers attempt the summit during climbing season, between November and March.

Another extinct volcano, the Cofre de Perote, lures climbers to its national park area near the state capital Jalapa. In addition to its *alpinismo* (mountaineering) attractions, the park has plenty of facilities, including a restaurant, cabins, and campsites.

Veracruz's nature preserves give the state enormous potential for ecotourism. Adventure and ecotourism options—from rafting to hiking to bird-watching—are growing every year. State and municipal tourism offices have a list of recommended operators. For most activities, particularly mountaineering, you should be sure to go with a guide. Seasonal weather changes can lead to hazardous conditions.

---

are at their best in the musical, multicultural city of Veracruz, formerly the country's point of entry. Travelers arrived by ship, then boarded a train to Mexico City, often looking back wistfully. Today the fun-loving town lures domestic vacationers with its excellent seafood and lively nightlife. The city remains a working port and navy base with so many marimba bands in the *zócalo* (main square) on weekend evenings that they have to compete to be heard.

Olmec civilization thrived in Veracruz long before the rise of the Maya. The state's best-preserved ruins, at El Tajín near Papantla, are thought to have been the work of yet another (unidentified) civilization, which had its heyday later, between AD 550 and 1100. By the time Hernán Cortés landed in Veracruz in 1519, the Aztecs held sway, but within a very short time the Indian population was decimated by war and European diseases.

The state of Veracruz played a pivotal role in Cortés's march to Tenochtitlán. A government-sponsored circuit called the Ruta de los Dioses (Route of the Gods) traces the Spanish conquistador's footsteps, from his Veracruz landing to his arrival in Mexico City, where he defeated the Aztec rulers. It's a mélange of soft adventure excursions, such as river rafting, combined with visits to colonial cities, old haciendas, and archaeological zones.

Veracruz

502 km (311 mi) south of Tampico, 345 km (214 mi) west of Mexico City.

➤ In 1519 Cortés landed in La Antigua, a slip of a place nested in jungle, but it was Veracruz that became the major gateway for Spanish settlement of Mexico. Its name, which appears throughout Latin America, means "true cross." Pirates frequented the steamy coastal site, and their battles to intercept Spanish goods add a further swashbuckling edge to the history of the oldest port in the Americas. The Spanish brought thousands of African slaves to Veracruz; later, Cuban immigrants flooded the town. Today Veracruz city is still the most important port in Mexico, and you'll immediately sense its extroverted, open-minded character. Huge cargo ships, ocean liners, and fishing vessels crowd its harbor, and the *malecón* (paved boardwalk) is always abuzz with strollers and sailors.

Veracruz's diverse influences can be heard in its contagious music, swayed by African and Caribbean rhythms. The *Son Jarocho* is one of seven different regional variations of Mexican *sones* (musical forms) and can be in 4/6 or 4/4 time. Doubtless the best known is "La Bamba," which originated here and dates back to the 17th century. Traditionally, the *cantadores* (singers) create endless new *coplas* (verses); in addition to their vocal talents, they are talented wordsmiths, ad-libbing messages, jokes, and insults to the dancers or audience.

The music centers on strings and percussion, using *arpas* (harps), *jarana* (a 6–10-string small guitar), violins, *bocona* (a four-string bass), *panderos* (tambourines), and *requinto* (a small rhythm guitar). Musicians, dressed in white, will flock into restaurants to energize the atmosphere with their vigorous strumming. A young woman dancer often accompanies them, performing flamenco-like steps in a frilly frock; the *tarima* (wooden dance platform) where dancers pound out the rhythms becomes another essential instrument. In the evening at the zócalo, the famous Veracruz *marimba* adds to the throng. Bands compete for space and time, their songs often overlapping in a stirring riot of sound.

The *danzón,* a languorous two-person dance with lots of subtle hip movement, was brought to the city by refugees fleeing Cuba in 1879 following its Ten Years' War. Most ended up living outside the city walls (only Veracruz aristocrats were allowed to live inside), but the sons of the Mexican elite sneaked into the poor neighborhoods at night and eventually introduced the danzón to high society. Sensuous compared with the stiff and formal dance that had been the norm until this time, and perfectly designed for hot climates, the danzón was at first considered scandalous, but soon it won over its detractors and became the most popular dance in the city. It still fills dance halls throughout the republic, and inspired a nostalgic 1980s movie, *Danzón,* with Mexican actress and politician María Rojo, largely set in the port of Veracruz. You can see people of all generations dance danzón in the Parque Zamora on Sunday evenings.

What to See

★ ☺ ❹ **Acuario de Veracruz.** Veracruz is home to one of the biggest and best aquariums in Latin America. The main exhibits include a circular *pecera oceánica,* a tank with 2,000 species of marine life native to the Golfo de Mexico, including manta rays, barracudas, sea turtles, and the prehistoric-looking *pejelagartos,* which resemble a combination of crocodile and fish. Other tanks display sharks and a quartet of gentle manatees. Check out the delicate lion fish, the various colorful and comical tropical species, and the 18-ft-long outline of the actual size of a great white shark caught off the coast of Tuxpán. In addition to its accessible public displays, the complex also houses a marine research center. ⊠ *Plaza Acuario, Blvd. Manuel Avila Camacho s/n* ☎ 229/932–7984 *or 229/ 932–8006* ✆ *$5* ⊘ *Mon.–Thurs. 10–7, Fri.–Sun. 10–7:30.*

❸ **Baluarte de Santiago.** The fortress and museum is all that's left of the old city walls; like the El Fuerte de San Juan de Ulúa, the colonial bulwark was built as a defense against pirates. The 1635 structure is impressively solid from the outside and romantically lighted at night. Inside is a tiny museum that has an exquisite permanent exhibition of gold pre-Hispanic jewelry—definitely Spanish plunder—which was discovered by a fisherman in the 1970s. ⊠ *Calle Francisco Canal between Av. Gómez Farías and Av. 16 de Septiembre* ☎ 229/931–1059 ✆ *$3* ⊘ *Tues.–Sun. 10–4:30.*

★ ❷ **El Fuerte de San Juan de Ulúa.** This fabulous, unique coral-stone fort has been witness to some of the most momentous events in Mexican history. During the viceregal era, Veracruz was the only east-coast port permitted to operate in New Spain and so was frequently attacked by pirates. The great island fort, the last territory in Mexico to be held by the Spanish Royalists, is a monument to that buccaneering era. A miniature city in itself, it is a maze of moats, ramparts, drawbridges, prison cells, and torture chambers, smack in the middle of the busy port area. Fortification began in 1535 under the direction of Antonio de Mendoza, the first viceroy of New Spain. A few centuries later, it was used as a prison, housing such prominent figures as Benito Juárez, who was held here by conservative dictator Santa Anna before being exiled to Louisiana in 1853. After independence, it was used in unsuccessful attempts to fight off first the invading French, the Americans, the French again, and, in 1914, the Americans yet again. The fort is under extensive renovation through at least 2005, but remains open to the public. There are no explanatory materials in place yet, but you can explore the former dungeons and store rooms, climb up on the ramparts, and wander across beautiful grassy patios. It's connected to the city center by a causeway; taking a taxi there should cost about $5. You could also catch a bus from the zócalo; look for those marked San Juan de Ulúa. Guides wander around in the site until about 3 PM—an English-speaking guide will cost around $2 per person. ⊠ *Via causeway from downtown Veracruz* ☏ *229/938–5151* ✉ *$3* ⊘ *Tues.–Sun. 9–4:30.*

❶ **Museo de la Ciudad.** This pristine museum is a good place to get oriented (although there are no explanatory materials in English). The region's history is narrated through artifacts and displays, and scale models of the city help you get the lay of the land. Also exhibited are copies of pre-Columbian statues and contemporary art. ⊠ *Av. Zaragoza 397 at Calle Esteban Morales* ☏ *229/989–8873* ✉ *$3* ⊘ *Wed.–Mon. 10–6.*

off the beaten path

La Antigua. This sleepy village, given its name by the Spaniards after they abandoned it, was the site of the first European landing in the New World and the conquistadors' capital for 75 years. The customhouse, which once had 22 rooms surrounding a huge courtyard, is worth seeing if only for its crumbling masonry, taken over by clinging vines and massive tree roots. La Antigua also has the first church of New Spain, Ermita del Rosario, a little white stucco structure that's been restored (and changed) many times over the years. Small seafood restaurants cater for weekend day-trippers when city dwellers come to swim in the river and take boat rides. La Antigua is 25 km (16 mi) northwest of Veracruz, roughly half an hour away, off Highway 180 (toward Poza Rica). The turnoff is just past the toll booth. You can also take the "San Juan De Ulúa" bus from Avenida República; it costs about $1.50.

Beaches

Veracruz City's beaches are not particularly inviting, being on the brownish side of gold, with polluted water. Decent beaches with paler, finer sand begin to the south in **Mocambo,** about 7 km (4½ mi) from downtown, and get better even farther down. The beach in front of the Fiesta Americana hotel is particularly well maintained. (Although it may appear to be claimed by the hotel, it's public.) About 4 km (2½ mi) south of Playa Mocambo is **Boca del Río,** a small fishing village at the mouth of the Río Jamapa, which is quickly getting sucked into Veracruz's orbit. A taxi from the city center costs about $4. **Mandinga** is a farther 8 km (5 mi) south and is less frequented by tourists.

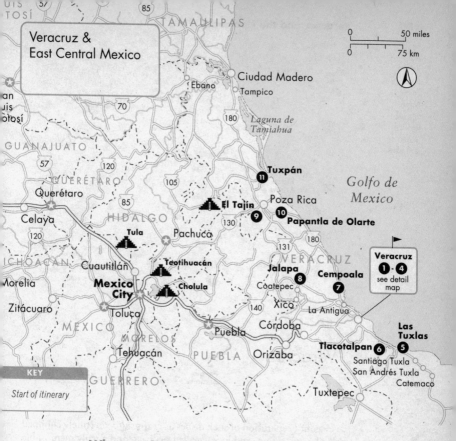

Veracruz & East Central Mexico

Veracruz
1·4
see detail map

KEY

Start of itinerary

Where to Stay & Eat

In addition to the restaurants around the zócalo, you'll want to head to Mocambo and Boca del Río. Boca del Río holds a spot in the *Guinness Book of Records* for the largest fish fillet stuffed with shellfish—408 ft long and weighing almost 2 tons—prepared at Pardiño's restaurant. Many restaurants here are modest but serve some of the finest seafood in the state. If you'd like to eat with the locals, try the Mercado Hidalgo for breakfast or lunch; it's a 10-block walk south from the zócalo.

$$$–$$$$ ✕ **Che Tango.** The smart atmosphere and soft-hued lights at this intimate Argentine steak house near the aquarium encourage guests to linger. If the sun and surf have gone to your head, try the refreshing house cocktail—*Rosita* (a blended anise cocktail)—guaranteed to cool throbbing temples. For starters, order any of the flaky empanadas topped with a secret-recipe *chimichuri* (sauce made with olive oil and parsley). Select your cut of rib eye, tenderloin, top sirloin, or strip steak from the chilled display plate brought to your table; all are charcoal grilled to order. ⊠ *Av. 16 de Septiembre 1938, at Calle Enríquez, Col. Flores Magón* ☎ *229/932–1745 or 229/932–1756* ⊟ *AE, MC, V.*

$$–$$$$ ✕ **El Gaucho Restaurante.** Since 1983, meat-lovers have packed this cavernous family-friendly ranch-style restaurant morning, noon, and night. The epic menu lists nearly 100 dishes—from spicy chorizo and Veracruz-style tongue to chicken fajitas. The house specialty drink, *jarra de clericot* (red wine with chewy bits of watermelon, pineapple, and cantaloupe), is delicious. It opens bright and early for breakfast. ⊠ *Av. Bernal Díaz del Castillo 187, at Calle Colón* ☎ *229/935–0411* ⊟ *AE, MC, V.*

★ $$$ ✕ **Pardiño's.** This modest eatery, a local favorite, is a landmark among Boca del Río's many seafood restaurants and its branches have spread throughout the republic. Plain tables in a nondescript storefront belie

TO LA ANTIGUA

Golfo de
Mexico

TO MOCAMBO
& BOCA DEL RÍO

Veracruz

♦ **Parque
Zamora**

the elegant preparation of such dishes as crabs *salpicón* (finely chopped with cilantro, onion, and lime), grilled sea bass, and a truly memorable huachinango à la veracruzana. ⊠ *Calle Zamora 40, Boca del Río* ☎ *229/986–0135* ⊟ *AE, DC, MC, V.*

$$–$$$
Fodor'sChoice
★

✕ **Mariscos Villa Rica Mocambo.** Tucked away on a small street that runs parallel to Playa Mocambo, this apparently casual open-air palapa eatery is one of the best seafood restaurants in the country. It has a large playground so the cream of jarocho society can bring their children and lunch at leisure within view of the waves. Specialties include mussels, grouper, crab claws, and octopus prepared as you wish. For those who relish spicy food, the *ostiones enchilpayados* (oysters in cream and chipotle chili) are sublime. Popular bands play Thursday–Sunday 3–7, so you may need a reservation on these days. ⊠ *Calz. Mocambo 527, Boca del Río* ☎ *229/922–2113 or 229/922–3743* ⊟ *AE, DC, MC, V.*

★ **$–$$$**
✕ **Gran Café del Portal.** Opened by a Spanish immigrant in 1835 in a former monastery, this now-famous sidewalk café eventually grew to cover an entire city block. Every Mexican president since Benito Juárez has been here. It stays lively from dawn to dusk. The menu has a wide selection of egg dishes, as well as soups, sandwiches, and yet another huachinango à la veracruzana. The weekday lunch set menu is a great deal at about $8 for three courses and coffee. An ongoing rivalry pits the Portal against the Gran Café de la Parroquia as to which place serves the real *tradicional lechero* (coffee with hot milk). ⊠ *Av. Independencia 1185, across from cathedral* ☎ *229/932–9339* ⊟ *No credit cards.*

$–$$
Fodor'sChoice
★

✕ **Gran Café de la Parroquia.** A leisurely stint in the sun here, watching ships unloading their cargo, is what Veracruz is all about. Try for a sidewalk table under the arches, if you can withstand the competing marimbas and the appeals of women selling crafts. Get here before 11 AM to try the classic *picadas y gordas* (puffy, deep-fried tortillas with beans, onion, mole, and cheese). Service may not always be very speedy or coordinated, but when you want more coffee you don't need to say a word, just tinkle your spoon against the side of your cup. Best of all is the tradicional lechero, served flamboyantly with the milk poured from silver jugs at a great height. ☒ *Malecón, between Hotel Hawaii and Hotel Emporio* ☏ *229/932–2626* ☐ *No credit cards.*

$$$ 🏨 **Crowne Plaza.** The lobby in this deluxe yellow high-rise resort on Playa Mocambo is adorned with glass sculptures and pastel oil paintings. Suites have small balconies with fantastic views of the gulf. The cascading poolside fountain and the organized activities in the play area make this a good bet for families traveling with young children. ☒ *Blvd. Adolfo Ruíz Cortines 4300, Playa Mocambo, 94260 Boca del Río* ☏ *229/ 989–2100 800/712–9900 in the U.S.* ☐ *229/989–2121* ⊕ *www. crowneplaza.com* ☜ *212 rooms, 18 suites* ♨ *Restaurant, room service, in-room safes, cable TV, 2 pools, gym, bar, baby-sitting, children's programs (ages 3–11), laundry service, concierge floor, car rental, free parking* ☐ *AE, DC, MC, V.*

$$$ 🏨 **Fiesta Americana.** This splashy, seven-story hotel on Playa Costa de Oro has the best business facilities in the state of Veracruz. Its miles of marble corridors all seem to lead to the giant serpentine pool and lush gardens facing the ocean. Guests have access to a 9-hole golf course 20 minutes away. ☒ *Blvd. Manuel Avila Camacho s/n, at Fracc. Costa de Oro, 94299 Boca del Río* ☏ *229/989–8989 800/343–7821 in the U.S.* ☐ *229/989–8904* ⊕ *www.fiestaamericana.com.mx* ☜ *211 rooms, 22 suites* ♨ *3 restaurants, room service, in-room data ports, in-room safes, cable TV, tennis court, indoor-outdoor pool, 3 hot tubs, massage, dive shop, 2 bars, shops, baby-sitting, children's programs (ages 4 and up), business services, meeting rooms, free parking, no-smoking rooms* ☐ *AE, DC, MC, V.*

$$$ 🏨 **Hotel Emporio.** The lobby of this large, elegant hotel on the malecón

Fodor'sChoice
★ is a dramatic sweep of marble and potted palms. Some of the immaculate, light-filled rooms have superb harbor views and ample balconies; all have marble bathrooms with bathtubs (those in the suites are hot tubs) and satellite TVs. Dine in the popular restaurant, which is decorated in neoclassical French style, or in the shade of an umbrella at any of the hotel's three pools (one is equipped with a waterfall, slides, and a miniature "ship" for kids). ☒ *Paseo del Malecón 244, 91700* ☏ *229/ 932–2222 or 229/932–0020; 800/295–2000 in the U.S.* ☐ *229/932–5752* ⊕ *www.hotelemporio.onmex.com* ☜ *182 rooms, 21 suites* ♨ *Restaurant, coffee shop, 3 pools, gym, sauna, bar, shops, business services, meeting rooms, free parking* ☐ *AE, MC, V.*

$$ 🏨 **Calinda Veracruz.** The rooftop patio (with a pool) at the Calinda has a fantastic view of the zócalo. Immaculate rooms have cool marble floors, bright-peach walls, and cable TVs. Downstairs, Sanborns offers a variety of foreign magazines, candies, and toiletries. ☒ *Av. Independencia s/n, at the corner of Av. Miguel Lerdo, 91700* ☏ *229/931–2233 01800/ 290–0000 toll free in Mexico* ☐ *229/931–5134* ☜ *116 rooms, 14 suites* ♨ *Restaurant, cafeteria, room service, cable TV, in-room safes, pool, laundry service, free parking* ☐ *AE, MC, V.*

★ **$$** 🏨 **Hotel Hawaii.** This sweet hotel with a prime location on the malecón is one of the best deals in town, offering comfort, class, and personalized service at a reasonable price. Rooms are impeccably maintained, the staff is eager to please, and there's always a bowl of flowers at the check-in desk. You can have all the free coffee and ice cream you want at the snug ground-floor coffee shop; maps are available for the asking; and the management also sees to it that each guest receives a bag of Veracruz coffee to take home. ☒ *Paseo del Malecón 458, 91700* ☏ *229/ 931–0427* ☐ *229/932–5524* ☜ *30 rooms* ♨ *Coffee shop, room service, cable TV, pool, laundry service, free parking* ☐ *AE, MC, V.*

$$ 🏨 **Hotel Lois.** For those with a sense of humor, this swanky Boca del Río hotel is an over-the-top mishmash of art deco, '50s kitsch, and riotous neon colors. The coffee shop alone has sparkling ceilings, lavender Naugahyde chairs, etched-glass windows, several random Roman columns, and lots of gleaming chrome. Guest rooms are more conventional, with a subdued pastel palette, rattan furniture, and cable TVs. ⊠ *Blvd. Adolfo Ruíz Cortines 10, 94249 Boca del Río* 🕿🕿 *229/937–7598 or 229/937–8089* ⊕ *www.hotellois.com* ⇆ *112 rooms, 17 suites* ⟆ *Restaurants, coffee shop, room service, in-room safes, minibars, pool, gym, hair salon, sauna, billiards, squash, 2 bars, baby-sitting, children's programs (ages 3–9), meeting room, car rental, free parking* ⊟ *AE, MC, V.*

$$ 🏨 **Hotel Ruíz Millàn.** Although guest rooms in this multistory waterfront hotel are on the small side, they are clean, comfortable, and modern. (Ask for a newly remodeled one.) The invitingly cool marble-floor lobby is usually crowded with Mexican businesspeople, and the hotel itself has the amenities of a more expensive establishment. ⊠ *Paseo del Malecón 432, 91700* 🕿🕿 *229/932–6707* ⇆ *88 rooms* ⟆ *Restaurant, room service, in-room safes, cable TV, indoor pool, meeting room, free parking* ⊟ *AE, MC, V.*

$$ 🏨 **Villa del Mar.** This unassuming hotel, across from one of the nicer sections of the downtown beach, is a good place to bring children. The standard, motel-style rooms are spacious and surround a garden with a tennis court, pool, and small playground. A number of bungalows (accommodating up to five people) are also available: they aren't air-conditioned and are a bit gloomy, but some have kitchenettes. ⊠ *Blvd. Manuel Avila Camacho at Calle Bartolomé de las Casas, 91910* 🕿 *229/989–6500* 🖷 *229/932–7135* ⇆ *91 rooms, 14 bungalows* ⟆ *Restaurant, tennis court, pool, hot tub, bar, playground, laundry service, free parking; no a/c in some rooms* ⊟ *MC, V* ⦿ *BP.*

$ 🏨 **Hotel Concha Dorada.** The basically characterless Concha Dorada has the cheapest accommodations on the zócalo. Rooms are cramped and you should ask for an inside room to avoid the marimba battles that last until the wee hours. The downstairs restaurant–sidewalk café serves simple fare and is especially popular (noisy) at lunchtime and on weekend nights. ⊠ *Av. Miguel Lerdo 77, near Av. Zaragoza, 91700* 🕿 *229/931–2996; 800/712–5342 in the U.S.* 🖷 *229/931–2996* ⇆ *46 rooms, 2 suites* ⟆ *Restaurant, room service, cable TV, bar, laundry service* ⊟ *AE, MC, V.*

Nightlife & the Arts

The **Plaza de Armas** (or *zócalo*) is a pulsing Babel of marimba, norteño music, hustling and dating (to put it politely) every night, with plenty of kids and clowns in attendance, too. Every Tuesday, Friday, and Saturday night after 8, a local troupe, many elderly, dressed in white performs danzón on stage. On Sunday night, there's danzón at **Parque Zamora** from 6 to 9. The **Instituto Veracruzano de la Cultura** (Veracruz Cultural Institute; ⊠ Calle Canal at Av. Zaragoza 🕿 229/931–6967) offers danzón classes for a minimal fee and they don't mind visitors sitting in to watch a class.

For authentic Cuban music, head for the unpretentious **El Rincón de la Trova** (⊠ Callejón de Lagunilla 59 🕿 no phone), where people of all ages gather Thursday through Saturday to dance to famous tropical bands until the wee hours; the floors are cement and the ambience is fun and strictly local. El Rincón de la Trova's six-day Cuban music festival in November draws performers and fans from all over Mexico and the Caribbean.

Discos and video bars are plentiful along the waterfront. Most are packed Friday and Saturday nights with a young, largely local crowd.

Antra (✉ Blvd. Adolfo Ruíz Cortines 15 ☎ 229/922–5142) is a disco popular with the young and groovy. **Carioca** (✉ Blvd. Adolfo Ruíz Cortines 10 ☎ 229/937–8290) has salsa dancing and live music Thursday through Sunday. **Kachimba** (✉ Blvd. Manuel Avila Camacho, Fracc. Sutsem, Boca del Río ☎ 229/927–1980) is a great spot for live Cuban music and dancing, as well as comedy routines. It's open Thursday–Sunday. **Ocean Disco** (✉ Blvd. Adolfo Ruíz Cortines 8 ☎ 229/935–2390) works a tropical theme with rock sculptures, waterfalls, and a light show, but it's only open Friday and Saturday.

Sports & the Outdoors

Deep-sea fishing is popular in Veracruz; you can charter a boat with a guide and gear for a day on the water. Contact the tourism bureau for recommended outfits. An annual **regatta** from the port of Galveston in Texas to the port of Veracruz takes place at the end of May or early June. Check with the Mexican Government Tourist Office (☎ 713/780–3740 in Houston) for details.

Shopping

Stands lining the **malecón** sell a variety of ocean-related items: seashells and beauty creams and powders derived from them, black-coral jewelry, ships-in-a-bottle. You'll also find Coatepec coffee, T-shirts, bloody crucifixes, and tacky stuffed frogs, iguanas, and armadillos. The **Plaza de las Artesanías** market on the malecón purveys high-quality goods, including leather and jewelry—with high prices to match. It's open daily 11–8. For an authentic slice of Mexican daily life, head for the wildly vibrant and chaotic daily **Mercado Hidalgo** (✉ Bounded by Calles Cortés, Soto, Madero, and Hidalgo), where you'll find artful displays of strawberries and chilies beside heaps of mysterious medicinal herbs and platters of cow eyeballs and chicken feet. One of the more unusual shops in town is in the aquarium: **Fiora** (✉ Plaza Acuario, Blvd. Manuel Avila Camacho s/n ☎ 229/932–9950) sells beautiful jewelry designed from miniature flowers grown in Veracruz.

Veracruzanos have adopted the fashion of neighboring Yucatán, and its famous embroidered *guayabera* shirts are as popular here as mariscos. For the best quality guayabera shirts in the area, visit **Guayaberas Fina Cab** (✉ Av. Zaragoza 233, between Calles Arista and Serdán ☎ 229/931–8427). This family-run shop has a great selection of hand-stitched shirts and dresses, with embroidery ranging from basic interlocking cables to elaborate floral designs. **El Mayab** (✉ Calle Zamora 78, at Av. Zaragoza ☎ no phone) has machine-produced guayaberas, which go for less than the hand-embroidered variety.

With its sizable Cuban population, Veracruz does a brisk business in cigars. Around Plaza de Armas, there are plenty of street-side stands that specialize in both Mexican and Caribbean tobacco. For the largest variety of cigars, try the small kiosk on Avenida Independencia, in front of Gran Café del Portal; it sells Cuban Cohibas for less than a buck. Although Cuban smokes are the big draw for cigar-puffing tourists, keep in mind that Veracruz upholds its own proud tradition in the tobacco trade. **Cubahi** (✉ Av. Sarmiento 59 ☎ no phone) offers the finest local-tobacco products.

Los Tuxtlas

⑤ *140 km (87 mi) south of Veracruz.*

Lush and mysterious, Los Tuxtlas is a hilly region where a small volcanic mountain range, the Sierra de Los Tuxtlas, meets the sea. Lakes, waterfalls, rivers, mineral springs, fishing villages, and quiet beaches make it a popular stopover for travelers heading east from Mexico City to the Yucatán. The region's three principal towns—**Santiago Tuxtla, San Andrés Tuxtla,** and **Catemaco**—are carved into the mountainsides some 600 ft above sea level, lending them a freshness even in summer that's the envy of the perspiring masses on the coastal plain. The cool, gray fog that slips over the mountains and lakes provides the perfect setting for Los Tuxtlas' most famous attraction: the *brujos* (witches), also called *curanderos* (healers). Conventional medicine failed to penetrate this jungle area until the 1940s, so the folk traditions have survived, making use of herbal remedies (typically using sweet basil, rosemary, and ingredients of doubtful origin), *limpias* (cleansings), and spells, both for good and for evil. Los Tuxtlas is also known for its cigars; the town of San Andrés Tuxtla makes a famous hand-rolled variety, which comes in several sizes. Tours of the cigar factories can be arranged just by showing up. **Te-Amo** (⊠ Blvd. 5 de Febrero 10) is just outside San Andrés Tuxtla on the highway to Catemaco and Santa Clara, on the bypass road. All the factories have stores open to the public.

Although much of the architecture in Los Tuxtlas is of the 1960s school of looming cement, all three towns are laid out in the colonial style around a main plaza and a church and have a certain amount of charm, especially Santiago Tuxtla. The Olmec civilization, Mexico's oldest, flourished here between 900 and 600 BC and Olmec artifacts and small ruins abound. A huge stone Olmec head dominates the zócalo at Santiago Tuxtla, and 21 km (13 mi) east are the ruins of **Tres Zapotes,** now unspectacular but once an important Olmec ceremonial center. The town's **Museo Regional Tuxteco** holds some valuable stone carvings and is worth a visit to learn about the region's indigenous heritage and contemporary local cultures. ⊠ *Circuito Lic. Angel Carvajal s/n, opposite Parque Juárez,* ☎ *294/947–0196* ⊠ *$2* ☉ *Mon.–Sat. 9–6, Sun. 9–3.*

The largest of the three towns, and the only one with an ATM, is San Andrés, but Catemaco is by far the most picturesque and relaxing place to stay. Many lodgings are on the lake shore; others are grouped around the small square. Catemaco is popular among Mexicans as a summer and Christmas resort and is also the place to go for a *consulta* (consultation) with a brujo for a *limpia* (cleansing). This costs anywhere between $1 and $20 depending on your ailment, which may range from misfortune in love to financial woes to health problems, and the brujo's assessment of how much you are able to pay. Tours of Lake Catemaco, which was formed from the crater of a volcano and harbors a colorful colony of fish-eating baboons, can be arranged through most local hotels. Beyond Catemaco, a paved road continues over the hills and down to a lovely stretch of undeveloped coastline. Twenty kilometers (12½ miles) east from Catemaco is the village of **Sontecomapan,** where you can take a *lancha* (launch) across the lagoon to a desolate beach. A bumpy dirt road follows the coast 19 km (12 mi) north of Sontecomapan to the sleepy fishing village of **Montepío,** which has a wide beach and a couple of inexpensive, basic hotels.

If you've got a yen to see more of the surrounding area, have a taste for ecotourism, and can speak at least a bit of Spanish, look into a guided camping trip. **Campamentos a La Selva de Los Tuxtlas** (☎ 55/5744–7106 or 55/5744–0880 ⊕ www.pormex.com) leads four-day hiking trips. The treks include bird-watching, a swim in the Río Coxcoapan, and a visit to a bat cave. A guide explains the uses of local plants along the way; you might even see spider monkeys.

Where to Stay

$$ 🏨 **Hotel Nanciyaga.** These rustic, four-person cabins surrounded by jungle are among the most secluded and attractive accommodations on the shores of Lake Catemaco. Sheets are clean and, while there is no hot water or electricity, you can enjoy the warm, curative *temascal* steam baths on Saturdays. Lake trips by kayak, jungle tours, and limpias ($10) can be arranged. The restaurant's regional cuisine includes fish from the lake as well as the so-called *carne de chango* (monkey meat), which is actually smoked pork. ⊠ *Carretera Catemaco, Km 7, 70410* ☎ *294/943–0199* ⊕ *www.nanciyaga.com* ⤳ *10 cabins* ⚲ *Restaurant* ▤ *MC, V.*

Tlacotalpan

❻ *90 km (56 mi) south of Veracruz.*

The name Tlacotalpan is of Nahuatl origin and means "in the middle of the earth" or "where the land is divided," referring to the settlement's location on what was then an island, between the banks of the river Paploapan and the lagoon. The old town is very pretty, with lovely streets, attractive churches and squares, and brightly painted houses, but the real attractions are the town's festivals, the most thrilling being that of Tlacotalpan's patron saint, the Virgin de la Candelaria. Before the conquest, native inhabitants worshipped the goddess Chalchiutlicua, better known as *Encamisada de Verde* (gowned in green), who ruled bodies of water. With the arrival of the Spanish and the subsequent Catholic conversion, she was substituted by the Virgin of the Candelaria, patron saint of fishermen, whose saint's day is February 2. Tlacotalpan's fiesta begins January 31 with an equestrian parade involving hundreds of horses, followed by regattas and the famous running of the bulls through the streets. An image of the Virgin floats down the river with a candle, followed by a flotilla of little boats, and there are cockfights, musical competitions, horse races, and more parades. Other lively times to visit are Semana Santa, the week before Easter; *Carnaval*, held in May; and the fiesta of San Miguelito from September 27 to 29. Tlacotalpan is 10 km (6 mi) south of Alvarado on Highway 180 on the dramatic road that heads inland towards Tuctepec.

Cempoala

❼ *42 km (26 mi) northwest of Veracruz.*

Cempoala (often spelled Zempoala) was the capital of the Totonac nation, whose influence spread throughout Veracruz in pre-Hispanic times. The name means "place of 20 waters," after the sophisticated irrigation system the Totonacs used. The site gained its role in history as the place where, in 1519, Cortés formed his first alliance with a native chief. The Totonac leader—dubbed Fat Chief by his own people because of his enormous girth—was an avowed enemy of the powerful Aztecs. At the time, the population of Cempoala was around 25,000; the alliance enlarged Cortés's paltry army of 200 men and encouraged the Spaniard to push on to Mexico City and defeat the Aztecs.

Cempoala was rediscovered by Francisco del Paso y Troncoso in 1891. Ten of the 60 to 90 structures at Cempoala have been excavated and can be visited. All are built of river stones, shells, sand, and "glue" made from the whites of turtle and bird eggs. As the story goes, when Cortés first sighted Cempoala at night, the buildings glowed white under a full moon and the conquistador thought he had discovered a city of silver.

Upon entering the ruins, you see **Circulo de los Gladiadores,** a small circle of waist-high walls to the right of center. This was the site of contests between captured prisoners of war and Totonac warriors: each prisoner was required to fight two armed warriors. One such prisoner, the son of a king from Tlaxcala, won the unfair match and became a national hero. His statue stands in a place of honor in Tlaxcala. Another small structure to the left of the circle marks the spot where an eternal flame was kept lighted during the sacred 52-year cycle of the Totonacs.

The **Templo Mayor**, the main pyramid, is the largest structure on the site. Follow the dirt path that lies straight ahead when you enter. Cortés, after gaining the allegiance of Fat Chief, placed a Christian cross atop this temple—the first gesture of this sort in New Spain—and had mass said by a Spanish priest in his company.

At the smaller **Templo de la Luna** (Temple of the Moon), to the far left of Templo Mayor, outstanding warriors were honored with the title "Eagle Knight" or "Tiger Knight" and awarded an obsidian nose ring to wear as a mark of their status. Just to the left of the Moon Temple is the **Templo del Sol** (Temple of the Sun), where the hearts and blood of sacrificial victims were placed.

Back toward the dirt road and across from it is the **Templo de la Diosa de la Muerte** (Temple of the Goddess of Death), where a statue of the pre-Hispanic deity was found along with 1,700 small idols.

There's a small on-site **museum** housed in a palapa. The voladores of Papantla usually give a performance on weekends. Well-trained guides are available, but tours are mainly in Spanish. ☎ *No phone* ⊕ *www. cnca.gob.mx/cnca/inah/zonarq/zempoala.html or www.xalapa.gob.mx/ zonarq/cempoala.html* ⊠ *$2* ⊙ *Tues.–Sun. 10–5.*

Jalapa

8 *90 km (56 mi) northwest of Veracruz.*

State capital Jalapa, which was a Totonac ceremonial center when Cortés arrived, perches on the side of a mountain between the coastal lowlands of Veracruz and the high central plateau. More than 4,000 ft above sea level, the city has a bizarre climate—sun, rain, and fog are all likely to show themselves in the course of a day. It's also known for its thriving arts scene—its state theater, for instance, attracts big-name performers. The university guarantees a mixed population; wizened campesinos walking to work mix with earnest students and hippies sitting around in cafés.

Much of the city seems to have been built haphazardly, and that's the source of its charm. The hills here pose intriguing engineering problems, and major avenues tend to make 180-degree turns, following level surfaces rather than adhering to a strict grid system. In some places, the twisting cobblestone streets are bordered by 6-ft-high sidewalks to compensate for sudden sharp inclines. Locals refer to the city as a *plato roto* (broken dish) because of this scattered, logic-defying layout. The zócalo, called Parque Juárez, is right in the middle of town, with the neoclassical Palacio de Gobierno on one side and the 18th-century cathedral on the other.

You'll often see the name of the city spelled Xalapa: Jalapa is the Hispanicized version of the original Nahuatl word. Residents of Jalapa call themselves *jalapeños.*

Fodor'sChoice
★

The town's prime cultural attraction is the **Museo de Antropología de Jalapa.** With 3,000 of 29,000 pieces on display, it is second only to Mexico City's archaeological museum. Its treasure trove of artifacts covers the three main pre-Hispanic cultures of Veracruz: Huasteca, Totonac, and most important, Olmec. Its three sections are filled with magnificent stone Olmec heads; carved stelae and offering bowls; terra-cotta jaguars and cross-eyed gods; cremation urns in the forms of bats and monkeys; lovely Totonac murals; and touching life-size sculptures of women who died in childbirth (the ancients elevated them to the status of goddesses). At a burial site, you can see ritually deformed skulls and ceremonial figurines. Tours by English-speaking students are available daily 11–4, but it's best to call in advance and make an appointment, as the tour schedule is unpredictable. ✉ *Av. Jalapa s/n* ☎ *228/815–0920 or 228/815–0708* 💵 *$3* 🕐 *Tues.– Sun. 9–5.*

From downtown Jalapa it's an easy trip to tranquil Coatepec, an important center of coffee production. Coatepec, from the Nahuatl Coatl-Tepetl ("snake hill"), grew during the coffee boom years of the early 20th century; the buildings along its elegant streets are pinned with ornate balconies and grilles. The area's rich soil, temperatures, and high altitude are perfect for growing coffee; "Altura Pluma" (high grown) are the best of Mexico's beans. Coatepec also has one of the best hotels in the state, the Posada Coatepec, making it a good overnight getaway spot. From Jalapa, the 15-km (9-mi) drive takes about 20 minutes; you can get a taxi there if you don't have your own car.

Where to Stay & Eat

★ **$$** ✕ **La Estancia de los Tecajetes.** For fine regional dishes with a dash of creativity, try this rustic, lodgelike restaurant overlooking the lushly tropical Parque Los Tecajetes. (As it's tucked into a small strip mall, the restaurant can be a bit difficult to find.) Inside, it's cozy and relaxing, always buzzing with diners feasting on *cecina* (paper-thin beef fillet) with enchiladas, beans, and avocado and *crepa poblana* (crepes filled with chicken or spinach, with poblano chili sauce and manchego cheese). Corn tortillas are made on the premises, and the tables show charming sepia-tone photos of Jalapa's past. ✉ *Plaza Tecajetes, Av. Avila Camacho 90–12* ☎ *228/818–0732* 🍴 *MC, V* 🕐 *No dinner Sun.*

★ **$–$$** ✕ **La Casa de Mamá.** The dark, antique furnishings and lazy ceiling fan almost succeed in giving this popular restaurant the feel of a northern Mexican hacienda, but the incessant street noise reminds you that you're in a busy capital city. Never mind; you'll be focusing on the generous portions of charcoal-broiled steaks and the succulent shrimp and fish dishes, served with *frijoles charros* (black beans cooked in a spicy sauce) or Mexican rice. The place is known for its desserts, which include flan with caramel and bananas flambéed in brandy. ✉ *Av. Avila Camacho 113* ☎ *228/817–3144* 🍴 *AE, MC, V.*

$ ✕ **La Casona del Beaterio.** In contrast to the cafeteria-style eateries along Avenida Zaragoza, La Casona dishes up fine local fare in a comfortable setting. The restaurant's two spacious rooms, surrounding a courtyard garden with a fountain, are set with sturdy wooden furniture, stained-glass windows, historical photos, and hanging plants. Breakfast specials are a steal, while the generous steak and seafood dinners, including the house specialty—*cazuela de mariscos* (stew of shrimp, octopus, and clams cooked with chipotle chilies)—draw crowds. This is java country, so the menu has a dozen different coffee and espresso concoctions. ✉ *Av. Zaragoza 20* ☎ *228/818–2119* 🍴 *AE, MC, V.*

$ ✕ **La Fonda.** The entrance to this traditional breakfast-and-lunch restaurant is hidden on a small pedestrian walkway off busy Calle Enríquez, a block from Parque Juárez. Brightly colored streamers, baskets, flowers, and paintings of Jalapa churches adorn the walls, and the warm corn tortillas served with every meal are made before your eyes. The food is hearty northern Veracruzan fare: beef or chicken and beans, *nopales* (cactus strips), and/or chili are essential elements of almost every dish. ⊠ *Callejón del Diamante 1, at Calle Enríquez* ☎ *228/818–7282* ▤ *No credit cards* ⊗ *Closed Sun. No dinner.*

$$ 🏨 **Fiesta Inn Xalapa.** This attractive chain hotel is a bit out of the way—in a primarily residential neighborhood 10 minutes by car from the center of town—but a good bet if you're looking for a comfortable, quiet, secure, and well-equipped base. The modern guest rooms in the two-story, colonial-style structure have satellite TVs, phones, air-conditioning, bathtubs, and plenty of morning sunlight. Airport transfers from the port of Veracruz are available for a fee. ⊠ *Carretera Xalapa–Veracruz, Km 2.5, 91000 Fracc. Las Animas* ☎ *228/812–7920; 800/504–5000 in the U.S.* 🖶 *228/812–7946* ➬ *119 rooms, 3 suites* ⟡ *Restaurant, coffee shop, room service, in-room data ports, in-room safes, cable TV, pool, gym, bar, laundry service, meeting room, free parking* ▤ *AE, DC, MC, V.*

$$ 🏨 **Hotel Misión Xalapa.** Though its prices remain reasonable, this hotel is notably well equipped, with many of the amenities of more expensive establishments: facilities for kids; free parking; and a popular disco with a comedy show. The 1960s institutional behemoth sits on a hill above Parque Los Tecajetes; though the building isn't particularly attractive, the rooms are large, sunny, and quiet. ⊠ *Victoria at Bustamante, Zona Centro, 91000* ☎ *228/818–2222 or 228/817–7064* 🖶 *228/818–9424* ➬ *170 rooms, 28 suites, 2 villas* ⟡ *2 restaurants, room service, pool, bar, dance club, baby-sitting, playground, laundry service, meeting rooms, car rental, free parking* ▤ *AE, DC, MC, V.*

$$ 🏨 **Posada Coatepec.** Once the home of a coffee baron, the 19th-century
Fodor'sChoice Posada now specializes in fine food and caters to the elite with an
★ exquisite private villa. It has regal guest rooms, each with original tile floors, satellite TV, and a heater for Coatepec's chilly, rainy winters; ask for one away from the murmur of street noise. The lobby and courtyard are splendidly decorated with a fine collection of antiques; a bar framed by lead-crystal windows is stylishly romantic, and the heated courtyard pool draped in flowering plants is delightful. The hotel is a 15-minute drive from Jalapa. True to its roots, it can arrange tours to nearby coffee plantations. ⊠ *Hidalgo 9, 91500 Coatepec* ☎ *228/816–0544* 🖶 *228/816–0040* ⊕ *www.posadacoatepec.com.mx* ➬ *7 rooms, 16 suites* ⟡ *Restaurant, room service, cable TV, pool, sauna, bar, laundry service, parking (fee)* ▤ *AE, MC, V.*

★ $ 🏨 **Mesón del Alférez.** A royal lieutenant of the Spanish Viceroy lived in this colonial house some 200 years ago. Now it's a gem of a hotel, restored with earthenware tiles, rustic wood, and lime pigment washes on the walls in such luminous hues as lilac, sky blue, and magenta. Rooms surround three small bougainvillea-drenched courtyards and have lovely hand-carved wood headboards, Talavera lamps, and hand-loomed bedspreads, as well as phones and TVs (local channels only). ⊠ *Sebastián Camacho 2, at Av. Zaragoza, 91000* ☎ *228/818–6351 or 228/818–0113* 🖶 *228/812–4703* ➬ *15 rooms, 6 suites* ⟡ *Restaurant, room service, laundry service, free parking* ▤ *AE, MC, V.*

¢ 🏨 **Hotel Posada El Virrey.** This spiffy hotel is a short walk from Parque Juárez. The rooms are quiet, but on the small side, with phones and cable TVs. Bathrooms offer the basics, with showers. Internet service is available for an extra fee. ⊠ *Dr. Lucio 142, Col. Centro 4, north of Parque Juárez, 91000* ☎ *228/818–6100* ➬ *40 rooms* ⟡ *Restaurant, cable TV, bar, laundry service, Internet, free parking* ▤ *AE, MC, V.*

Nightlife & the Arts

The **Agora** (⊠ *Bajos del Parque Juárez s/n* ☎ *228/818–5730*) cultural center has art exhibitions and the occasional folk-music performance and shows classic and avant-garde films in its cinema club. Stop by during the day to see what's planned; it's closed Monday. The **Teatro del Estado** (⊠ Ignacio de la Llave s/n ☎ 228/817–3110) is the big, modern state theater of Veracruz. The Orquesta Sinfónica de Jalapa performs here, often giving free concerts during the off-season (early June–mid-August). Check *Diario Xalapa* (the Jalapa city newspaper in Spanish, available at newsstands) for dates and times of performances, or stop by the Agora. You might find someone who speaks English.

Bar Barova (⊠ Av. Avila Camacho 31 ☎ no phone) is popular with a younger crowd. It's closed Sunday through Tuesday. A good mix of locals, tourists, and expats jams **Bar Boulevard 93** (⊠ Av. Avila Camacho 93 ☎ no phone), a tony, neon-lit all-night club across from Parque Los Tecajetes. The **Bar Lovento** (⊠ 20 de Noviembre Oriente 641 ☎ 228/817–8334) heats up with a salsa beat for dancing Wednesday through Saturday night. **La Corte de los Milagros** (⊠ Calz. del Tejar 3 ☎ 228/812–3511) is a relaxing haunt for trova music (Cuban-influenced ballads); it's open Wednesday through Saturday. **La Quimera** (⊠ Blvd. Adolfo Ruíz Cortines 1 ☎ 228/812–3277) throbs with disco from Wednesday to Saturday nights. **Vertice** (⊠ Av. Murillo Vidal at Zempoala ☎ no phone) is a popular video bar.

Sports & the Outdoors

CLIMBING The 18,400-ft **Pico de Orizaba**, Mexico's highest mountain, will virtually become your traveling companion in Veracruz state—it can feel as though you see it at every turn. The Aztecs called the volcano Citlaltépetl, or Star Mountain, because under the full moon the snowy peak looks like a star. Woodlands spread along its flanks, with a glacier shining above. Tour operators in Orizaba and Jalapa organize climbs to the summit in the dry season, from November to March. (At other times of year, the weather can create dangerous conditions.) Orizaba is 53 km (33 mi) south of Jalapa. **La Cabaña de Manolo** (☎ 273/737–0215) is based in Coscomatepec, a nearby village; ask for Manuel Gutiérrez. Another option is **Operador Veraventuras** (⊠ Santos Degollado 81-8, Jalapa ☎ 228/818–9779); ask for Adolfo Contreras.

RIVER RAFTING With its access to six good rivers for white-water rafting, Veracruz is now an established mecca for the sport in Mexico. The rivers drain the steep slopes rising up to the flanks of Pico de Orizaba and are the usual tropical-storm drains: wide valley floors with shoal-like rapids at every twist and turn. The rafting high season runs from August to November, when the water is high.

The Antigua has five runs, all classed at level IV or under. The nearby Actopan is a beautiful Class III stream. But for pure white-water fun Río Pescados is the best run in the area. In the rainy season, it has some rapids on the high side of Class IV, but mostly the rapids are Class III. Surfing is excellent and tight turns against the towering cliffs make for some great splatting.

Many of the operators who run these trips are trained in Canada and the United States, and are highly professional. Base camps with tents, rafting equipment, and dining facilities are near the river at Jalcomulco, 42 km (26 mi) southeast of Jalapa. **Expediciones Mexico Verde** (⊠ Homero 526, Int. 801, Col. Polanco, 11560 Mexico City ☎ 55/5255–4400; 01800/362–8800 toll free in Mexico ☎☎ 55/5255–4465 ⊠ Av. Murillo Vidal 133, Jalapa ☎ 228/812–0146 or 228/812–0134 ⊕ www.raftingmexicoverde.com) organizes various rafting excursions, from day trips to multiday programs, to the Pescados, Actopan, and Filobobos rivers. Most guides speak English. **Quest Expeditions Inc.** (☎ Box

499, Benton, TN 37307 ☎ 800/277–4537 in the U.S. 🖷 423/338–0283 ⊕ www.questexpeditions.com) leads multiday trips to Actopan and Río Pescados. On trips led by **RioAventura** (⊠ Business Room 20 E, Las Americas Shopping Mall, Boca del Río, Veracruz ☎ 229/922–8640 🖷 229/922–8641 ⊕ www.rioaventura.com.mx), you can combine rafting with other sports.

Shopping

Mexico's finest export coffee is grown in this region, specifically in the highlands around the picturesque colonial towns of Coatepec and Xico, less than 10 km (6 mi) from Jalapa. Shops selling the prized *café de altura* (coffee of the highlands) abound in the main squares of both places. **Cafécali** (⊠ Callejón del Diamante 2, 4, and 6 ☎ 228/818–1339) offers a wide selection of excellent coffee at competitive prices. **Café Colón** (⊠ Calle Primo Verdad 15, between Avs. Zaragoza and Enríquez ☎ 228/817–6097) in Jalapa sells 20 varieties of coffee for about $3 a pound.

Callejón del Diamante, also known as Antonio M. Rivera, is a charming pedestrian street with vendors hawking a variety of wares: cheap jewelry, keepsakes, books, and fleece-lined slippers among them.

The **Mercado Jauregui** (⊠ Av. Revolución and Calle Altamirano), open daily, is a wild indoor bazaar with everything from jewelry, blankets, and fresh vegetables to some rather dubious-looking natural "healing" potions and supposedly aphrodisiacal body pastes.

Side Trip to Xico

★ *19 km (12 mi) south of Jalapa on road to Coatepec.*

If you close your eyes and try to imagine the ideal Mexican small town, it couldn't be any more perfect than Xico. Aside from the occasional passing automobile, this village seems untouched by time; donkeys hauling burlap sacks of fresh beans clip-clop along the quaint cobblestone streets, followed by coffee-picking locals, machetes tied to their waists with red sashes. Lying in coffee country at the base of the mist-filled Perote foothills, Xico is famous for its native cuisine; the tasty mole de Xico includes poblano chili and chocolate sauce. The village is also known for its raucous summer festival that goes on for just over a week at the end of July, celebrating the town's patron saint, Mary Magdalene. Although the tourist infrastructure is still basic, at this writing a new campsite, Campamento Malkiki, was due to open near the Cofre de Perote.

But Xico is perhaps even better known for its natural wonders, notably the **Cascada de Texolo,** a majestic waterfall set in a deep gorge of tropical greenery. The setting for much of the 1984 film *Romancing the Stone,* as well as 2002's controversial *El Crimen del Padre Amaro,* this lush, scenic area is great for exploring; numerous paths lead off from the main falls through forests of banana trees to smaller cascades and crystal-blue pools, perfect for a refreshing swim. There's also a steep staircase that will take you from the observation deck to the base of the falls, a favorite spot for picnicking locals.

The falls are about 3 km (2 mi) from the center of town. To reach them, start from the red-and-white church where Calles Zaragoza and Matamoros meet and follow the cobblestone street downhill, bearing right when you reach the small roadside shrine to the Virgin Mary. Continue through the coffee plantations, following the signs for "La Cascada" until you reach the main observation deck, which includes a small restaurant (and a view of the nearby hydroelectric dam). Entry is free.

Cooperativa Excelsior buses make the trip from Jalapa to Xico several times a day. You could also take a taxi from Jalapa; the drive takes about 40 minutes.

El Tajín

9 *13 km (8 mi) west of Papantla.*

Fodor'sChoice
★

The extensive ruins of El Tajín—the Totonac word means "thunder"—express the highest degree of artistry of any ancient city in the coastal area. The city remained hidden until 1785, when a Spanish engineer came upon it. Early theories attributed the complex—believed to be a religious center—to a settlement of Maya-related Huasteca, one of the most important cultures of the Veracruz area. Because of its immense size and unique architecture, however, scholars now believe it may have been built by a distinct El Tajín tribe related to the Maya. Although much of the site has been restored, many structures are still hidden under thick jungle growth.

El Tajín is thought to have reached its peak between AD 600 and 1200. During this time, hundreds of structures of native sandstone were built here, including temples, double-storied palaces, ball courts, large retaining walls, and hundreds of houses. But El Tajín was already an important religious and administrative center during the first three centuries AD. Its influence is in part attributed to the fact that it had large reserves of cacao beans, used as money in pre-Hispanic times.

Evidence suggests that the southern half of the uncovered ruins—the area around the lower plaza—was reserved for ceremonial purposes. Its centerpiece is the 60-ft-high **Pyramid of the Niches,** surely one of the finest pre-Columbian buildings in Mexico. The finely wrought seven-level structure has 365 coffers—one for each day of the solar year—built in around its seven friezes. The reliefs on the pyramid depict the ruler, 13-Rabbit—all the rulers' names were associated with sacred animals—and allude also to the Tajín tribe's main god, the benign Quetzalcóatl. One panel on the pyramid tells the tale of heroic human sacrifice and of the soul's imminent descent to the underworld, where it is rewarded with the gift from the gods of sacred *pulque,* a milky alcoholic beverage made from cactus.

Just south of the pyramid is a series of ten I-shape **ball courts**—more than at any other site in Mesoamerica—where the sacred pre-Columbian ball game was played. The walls are covered with relief sculpture. The game, played throughout Mesoamerica, is similar in some ways to soccer—players used a hard rubber ball that could not be touched with the hands, and suited up in knee pads and body protectors—but far more deadly. Intricate carvings at this and other complexes indicate that the games ended with human sacrifice. It's still a subject of debate whether the winner or loser of the match was the sacrificial victim. It is surmised that the players may have been high-standing members of the priest or warrior classes.

El Tajín Chico, to the north, is thought to have been the secular part of the city, administrative and residential. It was likely the location of the elite's living quarters. Floors and roofing were made with a pre-Columbian concrete of volcanic rock and limestone. The most important structure here is the Complejo de los Columnos (Complex of the Columns). The columns once held up the concrete ceilings, but early settlers in Papantla removed the ceiling stones to construct houses.

You can leave bags at the visitor center at the entrance, which includes a restaurant and small museum that displays some pottery and sculpture and tells what little is known of the site. But because guided tours of El Tajín aren't available, the rest is left to your imagination. A voladores (Papantla flyers) show normally takes place at midday. The area outside is lined with covered stalls that sell inexpensive meals and tacky souvenirs. Start early to avoid the midday sun, and take water, hat, and sunblock. If you're prepared to work your way through the thick jungle, you can see some more recent finds along the dirt paths that lead over the nearby ridges. ☎ *No phone* 🖃 *$3* 🕙 *Daily 9–5.*

Papantla de Olarte

🔟 *250 km (155 mi) northwest of Veracruz.*

Papantla de Olarte sits amid tropical hills, with Spanish colonial and indigenous influences giving it a distinctive flavor. Totonac men in flowing white pants lead their donkeys through the crowded streets, and palm trees shade the traditional, tile zócalo (here, often called the *parque*). Papantla's in the center of a vanilla-producing region so vanilla products, from liquor to statuettes, are sold in every corner store and restaurant. There's even a vanilla fair in March, which coincides with a relatively new arts and music festival called Cumbre Tajín (⊕ www.cumbretajin.com).

★ Papantla is the home of the **voladores,** who twirl off an 82-ft pole next to the town's ornate cathedral. This ritual was originally performed as a tribute to the god of sun and rain; nowadays you'll have opportunities to see it in various towns in this region. The voladores begin the dance on a platform at the top of the ceremonial pole, each facing one of the cardinal directions. They start their descent from the side of the platform facing east—where the sun rises and the world awakes—twisting left for 13 full rotations each. Between them, the flyers circle the pole 52 times, representing the sacred 52-year cycle of the Totonacs (the Maya calendar had the same 52-year cycle). One man, the prayer giver, sits atop the pole, playing a small flute while keeping rhythm on a drum as the flyers descend. Originally the ceremony was held on the vernal equinox, but now the voladores fly for the crowds every Saturday and Sunday at 12:45 PM and give special shows in late May, around Corpus Christi.

Stop by the **Casa de la Cultura** to peruse a few galleries of regional painting, sculpture, and ceramics. If you're there at 4 PM, you're welcome to take a peek at a traditional dance class—you might see an old regional dance like the *danza de los negritos* or the *danza de los jaguars.* At the **Museo de la Ciudad,** next door, you can see an exhibit on local history, including indigenous clothing. Both collections have information in English. 🖃 *Pino Suárez 216* ☎ *784/842–2427* 🖃 *Free* 🕙 *Weekdays 8–2 and 4–8.*

Where to Stay & Eat

$ ✕ **Plaza Pardo.** From the balcony of this cheerful second-story restaurant you'll have a great view of the goings-on in the zócalo. Brightly colored cloths adorn the tables where house specialties—including *cecina con enchiladas* (salt beef with spicy enchiladas), *bocoles* (chicken- or cheese-stuffed gordita), and *rellenos al gusto* (green chilies stuffed with your choice of chicken, cheese, or beef)—are served. 🖃 *Enríquez 105 Altos A, Col. Centro* ☎ *784/842–0059* 🖃 *No credit cards.*

★ ¢–$ ✕ **Restaurante Sorrento.** With more than 200 items on the menu, this is the most popular restaurant in Papantla, crowded with locals who come to enjoy the cheap regional seafood and to catch a few minutes of the *telenovela* (soap opera) on the corner set. The *platillo mexicano,* a selection of regional appetizers, is big enough for two. Also look for the chicken with red mole, which is tasty but not too spicy. ⊠ *Enríquez 105* ☎ *784/842–0067* ▤ *No credit cards.*

¢–$ ▦ **Hotel Provincia Express.** A renovation in 2002 spruced up this zócalo hotel. The fresh, modern rooms have new wooden furniture, cool tile bathrooms, and little balconies. At this writing, a lobby café was in the works. ⊠ *Enríquez 103, Col. Centro, 93400* ☎ *784/842–1645 or 784/842–4213* 🖷 *784/842–4214* 🖅 *16 rooms, 4 suites* ♻ *Cable TV, laundry service* ▤ *MC, V.*

¢ ▦ **Hotel Tajín.** The trick here is getting the right room; the baker's dozen of junior suites and the five rooms with town views are the best. Otherwise, make sure you'll have air-conditioning rather than just a fan, and check the mattress for firmness before you settle in. All rooms are spick-and-span. Although the staff does not speak English, there's an on-site travel agent. ⊠ *Nuñez and Domínguez 104, Col. Centro, 93400* ☎🖷 *784/842–0121 or 784/842–1623* 🖅 *59 rooms* ♻ *Cable TV, hair salon, laundry service, travel services, free parking; no a/c in some rooms* ▤ *MC, V.*

Shopping

A half block downhill from the zócalo, along Avenida 20 de Noviembre, is a teeming **street market** selling native Totonac costumes, carvings, baskets, handbags, and cassettes. It's a daily market, but much busier on weekends. The quality is not great, but if you poke around, you can find some good deals. The real draw is vanilla, the chief product of this region, which is sold in every conceivable form—beans and extract are common, but for a real souvenir, pick up a box of vanilla-flavor cigars.

Tuxpán

⓫ *193 km (120 mi) south of Tampico, 309 km (192 mi) northwest of Veracruz, 89 km (55 mi) north of Papantla.*

Tuxpán is a peaceful riverside town with graceful winding streets—and the Río Tuxpán is even clean enough to swim in. Juárez, the main street, running parallel to the river, is lined with diners, hotels, and shops. The **Parque Reforma** is the center of social activity in town, with more than 100 tables set around a hub of cafés and fruit stands. It has a memorial to Fausto Vega Santander, a member of the 201st Squadron of the Mexican Air Force and the first Mexican to be killed in combat during World War II. Launches shuttle passengers across the river to the **Casa de Fidel Castro,** where Castro lived for a time while planning the overthrow of Fulgencio Batista. A replica of the *Granma,* the ship that carried Fidel's men from Tuxpán to Cuba, molders outside. Inside, the casa is bare save for some black-and-white photos of Fidel.

Beaches

Tuxpán's main appeal is the untouristed miles of beaches that begin 7 km (4½ mi) east of town. The first, and most accessible beach from Tuxpán, is **Playa Tuxpán.** The surf here isn't huge, but there's enough action to warrant breaking out your surf or boogie board. Of the palapas on Playa Tuxpán, the most established is Restaurant Miramar, which has an extensive menu and also provides umbrella-covered beach chairs for customers.

Where to Stay & Eat

$ ✕**Berra de Mariscos.** Don't be fooled by the white plastic tables and the bare-bones decor: the quality of the seafood dishes here easily rivals fancier places in town. Hunker down with a cold beer and a plate of *pulpos* (octopus cooked with onions, butter, and garlic) or the house specialty, *camarones a la diabla* (a spicy concoction of grilled prawns and chilies). All meals are preceded by a generous serving of freshly made tortilla chips. ⊠ *Av. Juárez 44, at Calle Mina* ☎ *No phone* ☰ *No credit cards.*

¢–$ ✕ **Antonio's.** This quiet, comparatively elegant spot turns out excellent seafood dishes, such as the cazuela de mariscos and the *pez espada bella molineras* (swordfish served with a mushroom and shrimp sauce). On Friday and Saturday nights a trio of musicians swings into action. ⊠ *Av. Juárez 25, at Garizurieta* ☎ *783/834–1602* ☰ *AE, MC, V.*

★ $ 🏨 **Hotel Florida.** Get past the harsh fluorescent light in the lobby and you'll find the best hotel deal in downtown Tuxpán. At this writing, the rooms were being remodeled. Some are on the small side but most have ample light and space as well as immaculate bathrooms. Outer rooms have terraces and views of the cathedral and waterfront. The staff is remarkably friendly and the manager speaks English. ⊠ *Av. Juárez 23, across from cathedral, 92800* ☎ *783/834–0222 or 783/834–0602* ☐ *783/834–0650* ⊕ *www.hotelflorida.com.mx* ⇨ *75 rooms* △ *Restaurant, room service, cable TV, bar, meeting room, free parking* ☰ *DC, MC, V.*

$ 🏨 **Hotel May Palace.** The most luxurious lodgings in Tuxpán are at this hotel in the center of town, a modern five-story property geared to a business clientele. The white-painted rooms have rattan furniture. The small video bar is a good place to hang out, as is the rooftop pool. ⊠ *Av. Juárez 44, facing Parque Reforma, 92800* ☎ *783/834–8882 or 783/834–4461* ⇨ *70 rooms* △ *Restaurant, room service, cable TV, pool, gym, bar, laundry service, meeting room, free parking* ☰ *AE, MC, V.*

$ 🏨 **Hotel Plaza Palmas.** In a sleepy suburban neighborhood five minutes from the city center, this hostelry is a welcome respite from Tuxpán's riverfront bustle. And although the mounted stag heads overseeing the spare lobby give the Palmas a rather incongruous tropical motel–cum–hunting lodge quality, the quirkiness ends there. Two U-shape buildings surround a large palm-lined pool area with tables and a small seafood bar. ⊠ *Galeana and Libramiento Carretera Tuxpán-Tampico s/n, 92820* ☎ *783/834–3529 or 783/834–3574* ☐ *783/834–3535* ⇨ *97 rooms, 4 suites* △ *Restaurant, room service, cable TV, 2 tennis courts, pool, bar, playground, laundry service, 3 meeting rooms, shop, free parking* ☰ *AE, MC, V.*

Sports & the Outdoors

WATER SPORTS For scuba diving, head to **Tamiahua,** a small village just north of Tuxpán, where you can hire a fishing boat for the 45-minute journey to the prime diving around **Isla Lobos** (Wolf Island), a protected ecoreserve that shares its space with a military outpost and a lighthouse. In the shallow water offshore are a few shipwrecks and colorful reefs that host a large variety of sea life, including puffer fish, parrot fish, damselfish, and barracuda. Generally, the best time to dive is between May and August. **Aquasport** (⊠ Carretera la Playa, Km 8.5 ☎ 783/837–0259 or 783/837–0191), just west of Playa Tuxpán, arranges scuba-diving trips to Isla Lobos and also has deep-sea fishing excursions. Other outfits run trips to the island which include permits, scuba gear, lunch, and transportation.

VERACRUZ A TO Z

To research prices, get advice from other travelers, and book travel arrangements, visit www.fodors.com.

AIR TRAVEL

AIRPORTS Heriberto Jara International Airport (VER) is about 8 km (5 mi) south of downtown Veracruz. It's a small airport, but there are some signs in English.

🔲 **Heriberto Jara International Airport** ☎ 22/9934–5372 or 22/9934–9008.

AIRPORT
TRANSFERS
A cab ride between the airport and the city center costs $8.50 and takes roughly half an hour. Taxis are readily available at the airport. No city bus serves the airport. An air-conditioned private car ($10) runs between the airport and the downtown office of Transavion.

🚹 **Transavion** ✉ Av. Díaz Mirón 3008 ☎ 22/9937-8978.

CARRIERS
There are several daily nonstop flights on Mexicana and Aeroméxico from Mexico City to Veracruz. Aerocaribe has three flights a day between Veracruz and Monterrey, plus daily flights to Mérida and Cuernavaca. Continental airlines has one daily flight between Veracruz and Houston, Texas.

🚹 **Aerocaribe** ☎ 229/934-5888 🌐 www.aerocaribe.com. **Aeroméxico** ☎ 22/9935-0833 or 22/9935-0283 🌐 www.aeromexico.com. **Continental** ☎ 229/938-6022; 01800/900-5000 toll-free in Mexico 🌐 www.continental.com. **Mexicana** ☎ 22/9932-2242 or 22/9932-8699 🌐 www.mexicana.com.mx.

BUS TRAVEL TO & FROM VERACRUZ

Of Mexico City's four bus terminals, the one offering the most departures to Veracruz is the Terminal del Oriente (TAPO); buses leave daily about every 20 minutes. The trip costs about $24 and takes about five hours, passing through Puebla and near the magnificent Pico de Orizaba. Veracruz's main bus terminal is about 4 km (2½ mi) south of the zócalo. The main bus company is ADO, with round-the-clock departures. ADO also offers first-class all-day service to Reynosa, on the Texas border. The deluxe bus line UNO links Veracruz, Puebla, and Mexico City daily. A toll-free central reservations service, Ticketbus, covers all lines and will take credit card and Internet bookings; you can pick up your tickets half an hour before departure.

🚹 Bus Depot **Bus Terminal** ✉ Av. Díaz Mirón 1698 ☎ no phone.

🚹 Bus Line **Ticketbus** ☎ 01800/702-8000 toll free in Mexico 🌐 www.ticketbus.com.mx.

BUS TRAVEL WITHIN VERACRUZ

The ADO bus line offers thorough regional coverage. It runs daily buses from Veracruz to Jalapa every 20 minutes between 6 AM and 11:30 PM. The trip takes 2 hours and costs $10. (The deluxe bus line UNO runs daily between Jalapa and Veracruz as well.) ADO buses also shuttle between Veracruz and Tuxpán several times a day; it's a 5-hour trip and costs about $17. There's service half a dozen times a day from Veracruz up to Papantla; the ride lasts about 4 hours and costs roughly $13. (The Tajín ruins have no direct bus service; you'll need the Papantla bus.) Several daily buses make the trip from Veracruz to Catemaco in Los Tuxtlas (3½ hours, about $9) and from Veracruz to Tlacotalpan (just under 2 hours, about $6). All buses run from Veracruz's main bus terminal. As for Jalapa, ADO runs at least six buses a day from its main bus station to Tuxpán (5 hours, $17) and to Papantla (8 hours, $11). ADO and UNO tickets can be purchased through the Ticketbus service. To get to Xico from Jalapa, catch one of the Cooperativa Excelsior buses that make frequent runs from Los Sauces marketplace. The ride costs about $1.50 and lasts 40 minutes.

🚹 **Ticketbus** ☎ 01800/702-8000 toll free in Mexico 🌐 www.ticketbus.com.mx.

CAR RENTAL

Avis is the only service in the Herberto Jara International Airport, but Dollar is close to the center of Veracruz. Hertz has service in Boca del Río.

🚹 **Avis** ✉ Heriberto Jara International Airport ☎ 22/9932-1676 ✉ Calle Collado 241, at 20 de Noviembre, Veracruz ☎ 22/9934-9683. **Dollar** ✉ Víctimas del 5 y 6 de Julio 883 ☎ 22/9935-8807 ✉ Simón Bolívar 501, at García Auly Veracruz ☎ 22/9935-8807.

Hertz ✉ Hotel Costa Verde, Blvd. Manuel Avila Camacho 3797, Boca del Río ☎ 22/9937-4776.

CAR TRAVEL

The city of Veracruz can be reached in about eight hours by traveling south from Tampico via Mexico 180, or in six hours from Mexico City via Mexico 150. The highways throughout the state, paved and kept up with oil money, are generally very good. Pay extra attention when driving in Jalapa, since the streets are so winding; try to use your car as little as possible there. Finding street parking in the cities is generally not a problem.

EMERGENCIES

Dial 060 in Veracruz for medical, fire, and theft emergencies. If you find yourself in a medical emergency situation, call the local Red Cross (Cruz Roja) for ambulance service. The local police can handle small incidents, but if you feel the situation could escalate, contact the Angeles Verdes (Green Angels), a highway patrol service coordinated by the tourism industry.

In Jalapa, Calle Enríquez is lined with pharmacies. For 24-hour service, the Farmacia Plus is your best option. Farmacia Médico, the largest pharmacy in Papantla, is open daily 8 AM–10 PM. In downtown Tuxpán, Farmacia El Fenix is open daily 8 AM–10 PM. In Veracruz, Farmacia del Ahorro is a big, convenient drugstore on the boardwalk with other branches all over town. It offers good prices and does home deliveries; it closes at 10:30 PM daily. For 24-hour home delivery in Veracruz, call Las Torres Pharmacy.

🏥 Hospitals **Centro Médico** ✉ Av. Cuauhtémoc 82, Col. del Valle, Tuxpán ☎ 783/834-7400. **Clínica Santa Cruz** ✉ Calle Rodolfo Curti 122, Zona Centro Papantla ☎ 784/842-0557. **Hospital General de Veracruz** ✉ 20 de Noviembre s/n, Veracruz ☎ 22/9931-7848.

🚨 Emergency Services **Angeles Verdes** ☎ 229/932-8498. **Jalapa Cruz Roja** ☎ 22/8817-8158. **Jalapa Police** ☎ 22/8818-7490 or 22/8818-7199. **Papantla Cruz Roja** ☎ 784/842-0126. **Papantla Police** ☎ 784/842-0075. **Tuxpán Cruz Roja** ☎ 783/834-0158. **Tuxpán Police** ☎ 783/834-0252. **Veracruz Cruz Roja** ☎ 22/9937-5500. **Veracruz Police** ✉ Playa Linda s/n, Veracruz ☎ 22/9938-0664 or 22/9938-0693.

🕐 24-Hour & Late-Night Pharmacies **Farmacia del Ahorro** ✉ Paseo del Malecón 342, at Calle Fariaz, Veracruz ☎ 22/9937-3525. **Farmacia El Fenix** ✉ Calle Morelos 1, at Av. Juárez, Tuxpán ☎ 783/834-0983 or 783/834-3023. **Farmacia El Fenix** ✉ Enrique 103, Zona Centro, Papantla ☎ 784/842-0636. **Farmacia Médico** ✉ Gutiérrez Zamora 103, Papantla ☎ 784/842-0640. **Farmacia Plus** ✉ Av. Revolución 173, Sayago, Jalapa ☎ 22/8817-2797. **Las Torres Farmacia** ✉ Av. Díaz Mirón 165, Veracruz ☎ 22/9932-6363.

INTERNET

You can find Internet cafés in many towns, even in Papantla. All charge roughly $2 an hour. Jalapa's Caseta Telefonica has three computers for e-mail and Internet access and is open weekdays 7 AM–10 PM and weekends 8 AM–9 PM. Compupapel has eight computers; it's open daily 9–8:30.

Several blocks from the Papantla zócalo, PC's Palafox has 10 computers with Internet access; it's open weekdays 8 AM–9 PM, Saturday 8–7, and Sunday 8–5.

Tuxpán's Sesico Internet café has 10 computers and is open Monday–Saturday 9–8:30 and Sunday 10–3.

For Internet access in Veracruz, head to Web Café for the fastest machines; it gives slightly cheaper rates for students. It's open daily 10–10.

Another option is Netcha Boy, open weekdays 9–9 and weekends noon–8.

🖪 Internet Cafés **Caseta Telefonica** ⊠ Calle Enríquez 16, Jalapa ☎ 22/8812–2462. **Compupapel** ⊠ Calle Primo Verdad 23, at Av. Zaragoza, Jalapa ☎ 22/8817–2322. **NetchaBoys** ⊠ Calle Miguel Lerdo 369, Veracruz 🕾 no phone. **PC's Palafox** ⊠ Aquiles Serdán 500, at Calle Galeana, Papantla ☎ 784/842–1357. **Sesico** ⊠ Av. Juárez 52, off Parque Reforma, Tuxpán ☎ 783/834–4505. **Web Café** ⊠ Calle Rayon 579-A, between Avs. Independencia and Zaragoza, Veracruz 🕾 no phone.

MONEY MATTERS

About seven blocks from Jalapa's Parque Juárez, Casa de Cambio Monedas Internacional has good rates; it's open weekdays 9–3 and 5–7:30. You can also change money in the morning at several banks on Parque Juárez. Most have 24-hour ATMs.

There are plenty of banks surrounding the Papantla zócalo, most of which change money weekday mornings. Banamex changes both cash and traveler's checks weekdays 9–noon and has a 24-hour ATM.

The Tuxpán Banamex changes cash and traveler's checks weekdays 9–5; it has a 24-hour ATM. Bancomer has a 24-hour ATM and changes cash and traveler's checks weekdays 8:30–2:30.

The best rates in Veracruz are at Bancomer, but money-changing hours are limited to weekdays 9–noon, so you'll have to arrive early to make it through the lines. The Casa de Cambio Puebla is open weekdays 9–6. Or use the ATMs that are readily available downtown.

🖪 **Banamex** ⊠ Enríquez 102, Papantla ☎ 784/842–0001 or 784/842–1766 ⊠ Av. Juárez at Calle Corregidora, Tuxpán ☎ 783/834–7907. **Bancomer** ⊠ Av. Juárez at Escuela Médico Militar, Tuxpán ☎ 783/834–0009 ⊠ Enríquez 109, Papantla ☎ 784/842–0174 or 784/842–0223 ⊠ Av. Juárez at Av. Independencia, Veracruz ☎ 22/9931–0095 or 22/9989–8000. **Casa de Cambio Monedas Internacional** ⊠ Elustres 48, Jalapa ☎ 22/8817–2060. **Casa de Cambio Puebla** ⊠ Av. Juárez 112, Veracruz ☎ 22/9931–2450.

TOURS

Expediciones Mexico Verde runs 7- or 10-day trips on the Cortés Route, which includes Veracruz City, La Antigua, Cempoala, Jalapa, and Coatepec (in the state of Veracruz) and continues on to conquistador-related sites in the states of Tlaxcala, Puebla, and Mexico. English is spoken.

Boat tours of Veracruz's bay depart from the malecón daily 7–7. Boats leave whenever they're full, and the $2.50 half-hour ride includes a (Spanish-language) talk on Veracruz history. Longer trips to nearby Isla Verde (Green Island) and Isla de Enmedio (Middle Island) leave daily from the shack marked PASEO EN LANCHITA near Plaza Acuario. Boats wait until they're full to set off, so it's best to be in a group. The cost should be about $3–$5 per person, but feel free to bargain.

Centro de Reservaciones Veracruz in Boca del Río runs trips to Cempoala, Jalapa, Catemaco, Tajín, and Papantla. Diving and fishing trips are available, too. BTT Tours, also in Boca del Río, offers trips to La Antigua and Los Tuxtlas, Jalapa, Tajín, and Cempoala. They also offer rafting, airport transfers, and car rental. Guides for these companies speak some English.

VIP Tours offers tours along the Ruta de los Dioses.

🖪 Tour Operator Recommendations **BTT Tours** ⊠ Calz. Costa Verde 85, Fracc. Costa Verde, Boca del Río ☎ 229/921–9827. **Centro de Reservaciones Veracruz** ⊠ Blvd. Adolfo Ruíz Cortines s/n, Fracc. Costa Verde, Boca del Río ☎ 229/935–6423 or 229/935–6422. **Expediciones Mexico Verde** ⊠ Homero 526, Int. 801, Col. Polanco, Mexico D.F. 11560

☎ 55/5255-4400; 01800/362-8800 toll free in Mexico 📠 55/5255-4465 ⊕ www.
raftingmexicoverde.com. **VIP Tours** ☎ 229/922-3315.

VISITOR INFORMATION

The Jalapa tourist office is in the large office building on the way out
of town toward Veracruz (known as Torre Animas) and is open weekdays 9–9. There's also a Jalapa tourist information booth in front of
the Palacio Municipal; it's open daily 9–9.

The Tuxpán tourist office is open daily 8–3 and 4–6. Another good
source in Tuxpán is Aurora Servicios Turísticos; they're in the hotel Río
Paraíso so ask the hotel operator to connect you. They're generally open
9 to 5 weekdays, with an afternoon lunch break. The Papantla office is
open weekdays 8–6 and Saturday 9–noon. Catemaco's tourism office is
open weekdays 9–3 and 7–9, plus Saturday 10–noon. Xico's tourist bureau is open weekdays 9–3 and 6–9; ask for Laura González.

The Veracruz Dirección Municipal de Turismo is open Monday–Saturday 10–6. The Instituto Veracruzano de la Cultura can provide information on exhibitions, festivals, and dance classes.

🖪 **Aurora Servicios Turísticos** ✉ Río Paraíso hotel, Carretera a la Playa, Km 6, Tuxpán ☎783/837–0293. **Catemaco Tourism Office** ✉Ayuntamiento (Town Hall), Av. Venustiano Carraza s/n, Catemaco ☎ 294/943–0258 or 294/943–0016. **Instituto Veracruzano
de la Cultura** ✉ IVEC, Calles Canal and Av. Zaragoza, Veracruz ☎ 229/931–6967.
Jalapa Tourist Information Booth ✉ Calle Enríquez 14, Jalapa 📞 no phone. **Jalapa
Tourist Office** ✉ Blvd. Cristóbal Colón 5, Jardines de las Animas, Jalapa ☎ 22/
8812–8500 Ext. 130 📠 22/8812–5936. **Papantla Tourist Office** ✉ Calle Reforma 100,
Papantla ☎ 784/842–0176 or 784/842–0026. **Tuxpán Tourist Office** ✉ Av. Juárez 26,
Tuxpán ☎ 783/834–0177. **Veracruz Dirección Municipal de Turismo** ✉ Palacio Mu-
nicipal on zócalo, Veracruz ☎ 22/9922–2314 📠 22/9932–7593. **Xico Tourist Office**
✉ Palacio Municipal Hidalgo s/n Xico ☎ 228/813–0327 or 228/813–0334 Ext. 216.

THE NORTHEAST

Northeastern Mexico attracts travelers short on time. Day-trippers
cross the border to soak up the local color at border towns like Nuevo
Laredo, Matamoros, and Reynosa. Those with a couple of days to
spare head south to the fast-paced metropolis of Monterrey or the laid-
back beach town of Tampico. Even those on longer trips through Mexico seldom allot more than a weekend to the entire region.

That's a shame, as there is much here to enjoy. Nature lovers can explore the waterfalls of Parque Nacional Cumbres de Monterrey and the
stalactites and stalagmites of Grutas de García. Culture seekers can immerse themselves in the much-lauded museums in and around Monterrey.

Nuevo Laredo

⑫ *1½ km (1 mi) south of Laredo, Texas.*

Nuevo Laredo was founded in 1848, at the end of the Mexican-American War. When the Río Grande was declared the international borderline,
the residents of the Mexican town of Laredo suddenly found themselves
living in the United States. Many simply moved their homes across the
river.

Of all the towns along the Texas border, Nuevo Laredo bears the biggest
onslaught of Americans. As soon as you cross the International Bridge
you'll be approached by residents eager to guide you to storefronts
where you can buy kitschy keepsakes, cool cocktails, or cheap prescription drugs.

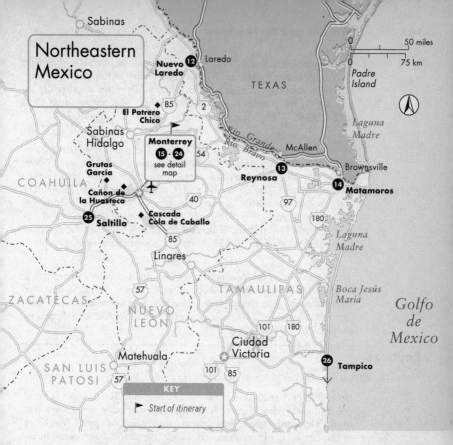

There are a few charming spots in this rough-and-tumble town. The main square, **Plaza Hidalgo,** is a great place to relax after an afternoon of shopping. The lovely ivory-color clock tower, dating from 1915, never seems to tell the correct time. A few blocks north, **Plaza Juárez** is filled with amorous teens after dark.

Where to Stay & Eat

★ **$$$** ✕ **Victoria 3020.** With its walled garden and candlelit courtyard, this is the place for a romantic dinner. The rich entrées could include a broiled New York strip steak topped with a burgundy demi-glace and rainbow trout in a sweet almond sauce. The white-jacketed waiters won't let you get away without trying a dessert called *tunas borrachas* ("drunken" prickly pears soaked in tequila and accompanied by vanilla ice cream). ✉ *Calle Victoria 3020, at Calle Matamoros* ☎ *867/713–3020* ⊟ *AE, MC, V.*

$–$$ ✕ **México Típico.** Mariachis wander in from the street to entertain at this longtime favorite, where the solicitous staff serves up border-town standards like *carne asada* (roasted beef). Murals of various Mexican cities decorate the dining room, and there's a partially covered patio with a fountain. ✉ *Av. Guerrero 934* ☎ *867/712–1525* ⊟ *MC, V.*

$$ ▦ **Hacienda Real.** Carved wooden statues of San Judas and San Miguel guard the tiled lobby here. The decorative touches—wrought-iron balconies, antique lamps along the walkways—make this chain hotel well worth the 15-minute trip from the city center. The bright, immaculate rooms, overlooking a palm-lined pool area, all have hand-carved wooden furniture and embroidered bedspreads. ✉ *Av. Reforma 5530, 88280* ☎ *867/711–4444* 🖷 *867/717–0402* ⊕ *www.posadas.com* ↻ *72 rooms, 2 suites* ⚘ *Restaurant, room service, cable TV, tennis court, pool, hair salon, basketball, bar, meeting room* ⊟ *AE, MC, V.*

¢ ⊡ **La Finca.** A block east of Plaza Hidalgo, this little place is within easy walking distance of all the city's attractions. Simply furnished rooms wrap around a quiet courtyard filled with hibiscus. The rates are virtually an unheard-of bargain for a downtown location. ⊠ *Calle Reynosa 811, 88000* ☎ *867/712–5013* ⤶ *12 rooms* ⟂ *Cable TV* ⊟ *MC, V.*

Nightlife & the Arts

Most of the popular clubs are on Avenida Guerrero, not far from the International Bridge. It won't be hard to locate them, as insistent doormen practically push you inside. Better choices are only a block or two away. **Cadillac** (⊠ Calle Matamoros at Calle Victoria ☎ 867/713–1525) is to the bar scene what its namesake is to the automobile industry: a classic that appeals to a slightly older crowd. Drawing folks across the border since Prohibition, **El Dorado Bar & Grill** (⊠ Calle Ocampo at Calle Belden ☎ 867/712–0015) is still a favorite with Texans.

Shopping

The International Bridge empties into Avenida Guerrero, where you'll find most of Nuevo Laredo's shops. Most stay open until 8 PM. The first stop for many people is the **Nuevo Mercado de la Reforma** (⊠ Av. Guerrero at Calle Belden). Ceramics and other items are found in dozens of shops on two levels.

Reynosa

❿ *16 km (10 mi) south of McAllen, Texas.*

Because of its manageable size and mellow attitude, Reynosa is a favorite point of entry into Mexico. It's a convenient starting point for a trip south. That said, this industrial town has very limited appeal. The heart of the city is tidy **Plaza Principal,** about five blocks beyond the International Bridge. The square's colonial church, bordered on one side by a movie theater and on the other by a Nike outlet, has an incongruous, ultramodern addition.

Where to Stay & Eat

$$ ✕ **La Fogata.** Herculean portions of slow-roasted cabrito, lamb, and beef are all prepared on a smoky open grill at the back of this popular joint. In the classic northern style, each dish comes with side dishes of guacamole, lime, jalapeños, and tortillas. ⊠ *Calle Matamoros Oriente 750, at Calle Chapa* ☎ *899/922–4772* ⊟ *AE, MC, V.*

$ ✕ **Café de Paris.** Cool white-tile floors and strong air-conditioning make this spot an oasis on a hot day. Don't let the name throw you off—you can sample spicy enchiladas as well as a café au lait and a pastry. Walk-in music trios add to the boisterous atmosphere. ⊠ *Blvd. Hidalgo Norte 815* ☎ *899/922–5535* ⊟ *No credit cards.*

$$ ⊡ **Hacienda.** About 16 km (10 mi) south of the U.S. border, this sparkling hotel is a little far from the center of town. But if you are in search of creature comforts, this is your best choice. Both the tiled lobby and the light-filled, cheerful rooms are outfitted with colonial-style furniture. ⊠ *Blvd. Hidalgo 2013, 88650* ☎ *899/924–6100* ⊟ *899/923–5962* ⤶ *20 rooms, 13 suites* ⟂ *Restaurant, room service, cable TV, bar, meeting room* ⊟ *AE, MC, V.*

$$ ⊡ **San Carlos.** This five-story hotel overlooking Plaza Hidalgo wins kudos for its central location. Rooms are decorated with colonial-style furnishings. Business travelers and tourists alike appreciate its friendly staff. ⊠ *Blvd. Hidalgo Norte 970, 88500* ☎ *899/922–1280* ⊟⊟ *899/922–4000* ⤶ *66 rooms, 10 suites* ⟂ *Restaurant, room service, cable TV, laundry service* ⊟ *MC, V.*

$–$$ ⌧ **Astromundo.** As it's close to the market, this downtown hotel gets a lot of traffic from Texans in search of bargains. The efficient air conditioners in the comfortable rooms are a blessing after a day of shopping. You won't lose track of which floor you're on, as each is painted a different bright color. ⊠ *Calle Juárez Norte 675, 88500* ☎ *899/922–5625* 🖷 *899/922–9888* 🖙 *90 rooms, 6 suites* ⌂ *Restaurant, room service, cable TV, bar* ⊟ *AE, MC, V.*

Nightlife & the Arts

The Zona Dorada, the so-called Golden Zone along Emilio Portés Gel, has the most popular nightspots. Your best best is **Frida's** (⊠ Emilio Portés Gel 1410 ☎ 899/922–2233), popular with a younger crowd.

Shopping

Colorful **Calle Hidalgo,** a pedestrian mall lined with vendors, leads off from the plaza. Many Texans save money by having their teeth fixed south of the Río Bravo, hence the many dentists you'll find here.

Treviño's (⊠ Av. Virreyes 1075 ☎ 899/922–1444) has a good selection of Mexican arts and crafts, including some interesting papier-mâché.

Matamoros

⓮ *1 km (about ½ mi) south of Brownsville, Texas.*

With a much longer history than its neighbors to the west, the 18th-century town of Matamoros is a great place to start your journey to Mexico. It's named for one of the many rebellious priests who were executed by the Spanish during the War of Independence. The first major battle of the Mexican-American War was fought here when Mexican troops began lobbing shells to the other side of the Río Bravo. Shortly afterward, General Zachary Taylor and his men occupied the city and began their march south.

Matamoros prides itself on being the hub of a rich agricultural region and a manufacturing center for multinational corporations. Nowhere is this more evident than in the lively **Plaza Hidalgo** (⊠ Calle 6 and Calle Gonzalez). Nearby stands the carefully restored **Teatro de la Reforma** (⊠ Calle 6 and Calle Abasolo ☎ 868/816–6207), which first threw open its doors in 1864. Its stage is once again the place to enjoy music and dance.

The **Museo Casa Mata** is housed in the remains of Fort Mata, built in 1845 to defend the city against American invasion. It never fulfilled its purpose, though; the fortress wasn't completed when Zachary Taylor's troops marched into town. The museum displays photos and artifacts, mostly from the Mexican Revolution. ⊠ *Calle Guatemala and Calle Santos Degollado* ☎ *868/813–5929* ▯ *Free* ⊙ *Mon.–Sat. 9:30–5, Sun. 9:30–3.*

Where to Stay & Eat

$$–$$$$ ✕ **Garcia's.** Talk about tough decisions—there are over a dozen fine tequilas to choose from here, before the debate between lobster and steak. An elevator from the garage whisks you up to the restaurant and bar, where there's dancing until the wee hours. There's even a gift shop with wares from all over Mexico. ⊠ *Av. Alvaro Obregón 82* ☎ *868/812–3929* ⊟ *AE, MC, V.*

$ ✕ **Los Norteños.** A *cabrito al pastor* cooking over hot coals is the not-so-subtle advertisement for the best roasted kid in town. Don't let the decor—an odd mix of stately wooden columns and harsh fluorescent lights—make you pass up a tender T-bone weighing in at 12 ounces. All meals are served with a tasty black-bean soup and a heaping pile of tortillas. ✉ *Calle Matamoros 109, at Calle 8* ☎ *868/813–0037* 🖃 *No credit cards.*

$$ 🏨 **Gran Hotel Residencial.** Although it couldn't be called luxurious, this is by far the best lodging in Matamoros. All rooms have private terraces, and the bathrooms have tubs. The lush garden has a large pool and a children's play area. ✉ *Av. Alvaro Obregón 249, at Calle Amapola, 87330* ☎ *868/813–9811; 800/718–8230 in the U.S.* 🖶 *868/813–2777* ⊕ *www. geocities.com/hotelresidencial* ↩ *109 rooms, 5 suites* ⚫ *Restaurant, room service, cable TV, pool, bar, playground, meeting room, travel services, car rental* 🖃 *AE, MC, V.*

$ 🏨 **Plaza Matamoros.** The superior service and the location near the center of town make this colonial-style hotel a good choice. Decorated with heavy wooden furniture, the clean, comfortable rooms overlook the central courtyard. The terrace restaurant serves up spicy regional fare. ✉ *Calle 9 1421, at Calle Bravo, 87330* ☎ *868/816–1696* 🖶 *868/816–1687* ⊕ *www.hotelplazamatamoros.com* ↩ *40 rooms* ⚫ *Restaurant, room service, cable TV, bar, shops, laundry service, meeting room* 🖃 *AE, MC, V.*

Shopping

The most appealing shops line Avenida Alvaro Obregón, which leads into town from the International Bridge. **Aztlan** (✉ Av. Alvaro Obregón 75 ☎ 868/816–2947) has good-quality jewelry, pewter, and wooden and stone carvings. **Barbara** (✉ Av. Alvaro Obregón 37 ☎ 868/816–5456) sells attractive handicrafts. The shop woos shoppers with free margaritas.

The bustling **Mercado Juárez** (✉ Calle 9 at Calle Matamoros) is the place to haggle over pretty pottery and other souvenirs. The block-long structure is easy to find, as it's three blocks north of Plaza Hidalgo.

Monterrey

235 km (146 mi) southwest of Nuevo Laredo, 225 km (140 mi) west of Reynosa, 325 km (201 mi) west of Matamoros.

➤ A brewer of beer and forger of steel, the industrial powerhouse of Monterrey has nothing in the way of a laid-back lifestyle. Some of the country's most powerful captains of industry hold sway here—a fact that earned the city its nickname, the *Sultana del Norte* (Sultan of the North).

With its focus on the future, Monterrey hasn't preserved as much of its past as other cities. Don't expect colonial splendor here; there's just one building, El Opispado, dating from the colonial period, and the Barrio Antiguo, east of the Macroplaza, is the city's only concentration of century-old structures. The symbol of the city has become a tower of orange concrete called El Faro de Comercio, or the Beacon of Commerce.

Though Monterrey is considered an indispensable stop for those headed south, it's also a destination in itself. Shop-lined pedestrian malls like Avenida J. M. Morelos are perfect for browsing, while the museums, especially the Museo de Arte Contemporaneo, are among the best in the country. The dining is remarkably varied, and the nonstop nightlife might even surpass that of Monterrey's rival to the south, Mexico City. It's easy to get around town, too. There's a modern, efficient metro, which runs along elevated tracks across the city. You enter using magnetic cards purchased in vending machines at the stations. Each ride costs less than 50¢. The metro runs 6 AM–midnight daily.

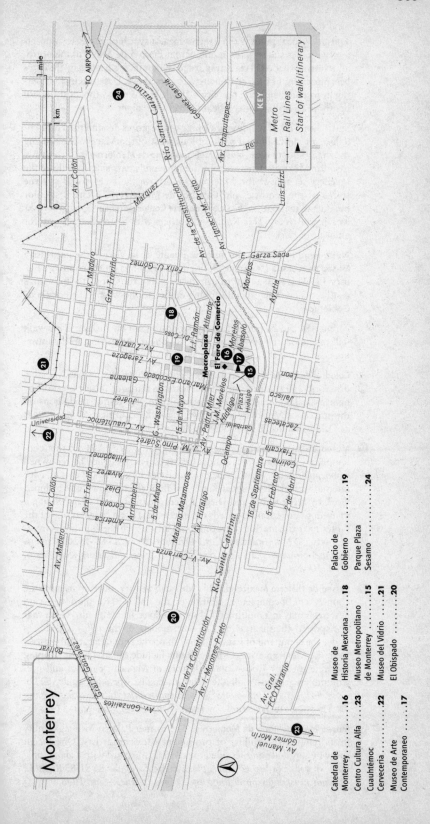

Monterrey

KEY

——— Metro

—•—•— Rail Lines

▲ Start of walk/itinerary

The Macroplaza

The city's focal point is the Macroplaza, a swath of concrete connecting two older squares, the monumental Plaza 5 de Mayo to the north, and the tree-shaded Plaza Zaragoza to the south. It's fringed by the city's best museums; El Faro de Comercio towers above. Designed by Luis Barragán to commemorate the city's 100th anniversary, this postmodern lighthouse's brilliant green beam sweeps the night sky.

A GOOD WALK
Start with a bit of window-shopping at the stores around the Plaza Hidalgo, an old-fashioned park a block west of the Macroplaza. Facing the shady square is the **Museo Metropolitano de Monterrey** ⑮ ☞, a showcase for Mexican artists. From the museum's east side, you'll see the loveliest section of the Macroplaza. Above the trees you'll spy the spires of the centuries-old **Catedral de Monterrey** ⑯. The rust-color building to the south is the **Museo de Arte Contemporaneo** ⑰, where works by Diego Rivera, Frida Kahlo, and others will likely sidetrack you for an hour or two.

Next, head north past the gushing Fuente de la Vida to the impressive **Museo de Historia Mexicana** ⑱, filled with exhibits on the country's history. Cool off with a boat ride in the pool that runs along the museum's southern side. The official-looking edifice to the west is the **Palacio de Gobierno** ⑲.

TIMING
Monterrey can be hot and sticky, so don't plan on rushing. This walk will take at least a few hours, or a full day if you get lost in the museums. Note that the museums are closed Monday.

WHAT TO SEE
Catedral de Monterrey. Construction began in 1600, but the massive cathedral took 250 years to finish. As a result, a Baroque facade is set off by neoclassical columns and two huge ornate plateresque medallions on the main door. Murals by local artists frame the main altar. ⌂ *Macroplaza at Calle Abasolo* ☎ *81/8399–7831.*

⑰ **Museo de Arte Contemporaneo.** Better known as MARCO, this contemporary art museum is a must for art lovers. Designed by renowned Mexican architect Ricardo Legorretta, it has 11 galleries of cutting-edge international art. It mounts rotating exhibits; recent shows have included work by Frida Kahlo and Diego Rivera. Juan Soriano's *La Paloma,* a mammoth dove statue, guards the entrance. Take a break at one of the tables near the marble reflecting pool and watch the fountain's irregular jets. ⌂ *Macroplaza at Calle Ocampo* ☎ *81/8342–4820* ⊕ *www.mtyol.com/marco* ⌁ *$3.50, free Wed.* ☉ *Tues. and Thurs.–Sun. 10–6, Wed. 10–8.*

Fodor's Choice
★

⑱ **Museo de Historia Mexicana.** This Mexican history museum mounts the country's most complete exhibition on the 1910–20 Revolution. Period newsreels play in a multimedia show displayed inside a railroad car that transported the insurgents. Life-size models of the *villistas* (soldiers under the command of Pancho Villa) sit on the roof of a car "liberated" from the Mexican army. Other exhibits include the first bottle-capping machine used by Coca-Cola, a history of Mexican cinema, and pre-Columbian artifacts. Call ahead for an English-speaking guide. ⌂ *Dr. Coss 445* ☎ *81/8345–9898* ⊕ *www.museohistoriamexicana.org.mx* ⌁ *$1, 50¢ Sun., free Tues.* ☉ *Tues.–Thurs. 11–7, Fri.–Sun. 11–8.*

☞ ⑮ **Museo Metropolitano de Monterrey.** The former Palacio Municipal now hosts temporary exhibits of prominent Mexican artists. One recent show by Sergio Rodrígues filled the central courtyard with a giant apple made of soda bottles. ⌂ *Macroplaza at Av. Zaragoza* ☎ *81/8340–2982* ⊕ *www.museometropolitano.org* ⌁ *Free* ☉ *Tues.–Sun. 10–6.*

⑲ Palacio de Gobierno. On the northern tip of the Macroplaza sits one of the city's loveliest buildings. The Government Palace, built in 1908, is especially striking at night, when its slender neoclassical columns are beautifully illuminated. From the statue-studded front terrace you have a splendid view of the entire Macroplaza. ⊠ *Plaza 5 de Mayo.*

Elsewhere in Monterrey

The rest of Monterrey's sights are spread out. Unless you have a car, you will have to take a taxi to the others. While you can take a bus to El Obispado, it lets you off at the bottom of a steep hill. The Museo del Vidrio and Cerveceria Cuauhtémoc are near subway stops, but you'd have to walk through an iffy neighborhood to reach them.

A GOOD TOUR   Start out early to see unobstructed views of the city from **El Obispado** ⑳, on a hill to the west of the city. To the north is **Museo del Vidrio** ㉑, a fascinating look at how a lump of molten glass is turned into a bottle. See what goes into that bottle at **Cerveceria Cuauhtémoc** ㉒, where they brew up most of the country's favorite beers.

If you have teenagers with a working knowledge of Spanish, spend the afternoon at **Centro Cultural Alfa** ㉓, where hands-on scientific exhibits can keep them occupied for hours. Youngsters will probably prefer to play with Cookie Monster and Big Bird at **Parque Plaza Sesamo** ㉔.

TIMING   Factor in plenty of time to get between these sights. It takes 10 to 15 minutes to get to the sights in downtown Monterrey. A ride to the Centro Cultural Alfa or Parque Plaza Sesamo will take 20 to 30 minutes. Note that the Centro Cultural Alfa is closed on Monday, and the brewery is open on Monday only for tours by request.

WHAT TO SEE   **Centro Cultural Alfa.** The country's best science and technology museum, the cylindrical Alfa Cultural Center has an IMAX theater and many hands-on exhibits. There's even a planetarium. Information is in Spanish only. The facility is 7 km (4½ mi) south of the city. ⊠ *Av. Roberto Garza Sada 1000* ☎ *81/8303–0002* ⊕ *www.planetarioalfa.org.mx* ✉ *$3, 2-for-1 admission Wed.* ☉ *Tues.–Fri. 3–8:30, Sat. 2–8:30, Sun. noon–8:30.*

㉒ Cerveceria Cuauhtémoc. The popularity of Mexican beer owes much to this brewery, which opened a century ago. Named after a famous Aztec chief, the brewery is the heart of an industrial empire that produces well-known brands like Carta Blanca and Tecate. The fascinating tour concludes with free beer—obviously the big draw. Call about English tours. ⊠ *Av. Alfonso Reyes Norte 2202* ☎ *81/8328–5355* ✉ *Free* ☉ *Tues.–Fri. 9:30–5:45, weekends 10:30–6. Brewery tours by request, weekdays 9–1 and 3–6.*

㉑ Museo del Vidrio. The Cuauhtémoc brewery spawned a need for many products, including glass bottles. This century-old building is on the property of the glass factory that makes, among other items, the Cuauhtémoc suds bottles. Inside is a museum of the history of glassmaking in Mexico. It also includes a stunning collection of art glass by local artists. All information is in Spanish only. ⊠ *Calle Magallanes 517, at Av. Zaragoza* ☎ *81/8862–1000* ⊕ *museovidrio.vto.com* ✉ *$1* ☉ *Daily 9–5:45.*

⑳ El Obispado. Built in 1788, the hilltop Bishop's Residence is the city's only remaining colonial landmark. Originally intended as a home for retired prelates, the domed structure was used as a fort during the Mexican-American War, the French Intervention, and the Revolution. Today the restored structure houses a wonderful museum focusing on the region's history. (Most info is in Spanish only.) From here you'll have a splendid view of Monterrey. ⊠ *West end of Av. Padre Mier* ☎ *81/ 8346–0404* ⊴ *$3* ⊘ *Tues.–Sun. 10–5.*

☪ ㉔ **Parque Plaza Sesamo.** The cleverly designed Sesame Plaza theme park, built on the grounds of Parque Fundidora, has three main areas. One has 17 water toboggans, pint-size pools, games where splashing is encouraged. A second has a computer center where children can plug into the Internet and play video games. The last has theaters where the park's Sesame Street characters put on musical shows. ⊠ *Calle Agricola Oriente 3700–1, Col. Agricola* ☎ *81/8354–5400* ⊴ *$14* ⊘ *June–Aug., daily 11–9:30; Sept.–May, daily 3–8.*

Where to Stay & Eat

★ $$–$$$ ✕ **Luisiana.** In what might be downtown's most elegant dining room, you can taste a Mexican interpretation of New Orleans cuisine. There are no Cajun specialties on the menu, but the deepwater crawfish are divine. The waiters wear tuxedos, and there's always soft piano music playing at dinnertime. ⊠ *Av. Hidalgo Oriente 530* ☎ *81/8340–3753 or 81/8343–1561* ⊟ *AE, MC, V.*

★ $–$$ ✕ **Vitrales.** A stained-glass ceiling makes this dining room in the Sheraton Ambassador something special. Start with the sizable smoked salmon appetizer, served with fresh herbs, mild onions, and hard-boiled eggs. Entrées aren't too rib-sticking; they could include fresh pasta or broiled fish. ⊠ *Av. Hidalgo Oriente 310* ☎ *81/8380–7000* ⊟ *AE, DC, MC, V.*

$ ✕ **El Rey de Cabrito.** The restaurant's name—The King of Kid—is no lie; it's where locals go to sample slow-roasted baby goat. It's so well known that out-of-towners call in orders. The owner keeps his own herds. The dining room, resembling a hunting lodge, covers half a city block, but you still might have to wait for a table. ⊠ *Av. de la Constitución 817, at Dr. Coss* ☎ *81/8345–3232 or 81/8345–3292* ⊟ *MC, V.*

¢–$ ✕ **La Casa de Maiz.** On a busy street in Barrio Antiguo, the House of Corn has a special flair for turning the local cash crop into delicious *sopas* and *sopes* (the former is soup, the latter an appetizer). The funky decor, with brightly colored walls and quirky art, makes this a popular place with young people, who often stop by for a cold beer before hitting the clubs. ⊠ *Calle Abasolo 870, at Montemayor* ☎ *81/8340–4332* ⊟ *AE, DC, MC, V.*

¢ ✕ **Las Monjitas.** The sight of a white-frocked mother superior in the open-air kitchen may surprise you as you pass this odd little place. Step down into the colonnaded dining room, where waitresses dressed as nuns rush about serving a sinfully delicious comida corrida. You may have to atone for meals like "La Pecadora," thinly sliced grilled chicken topped with mushrooms, fried onions, and melted asadero cheese. ⊠ *Calle Escobedo Sur 903* ☎ *81/8344–6713* ⊟ *AE, MC, V.*

FodorśChoice ★

★ $$$–$$$$ ▨ **Quinta Real.** With its aura of a prosperous hacienda, this hotel just outside the city draws everyone from government officials to business executives. The domed lobby welcomes you with hand-carved furnishings, huge bowls of flowers, and classic Mexican crafts. Suites have hand-carved furnishings and thoughtful extras such as fluffy robes. The excellent restaurant, serving French and Mexican cuisine, has built up quite a following. ⊠ *Av. Diego Rivera 550, Fracc. Valle Oriente, 66260 San Pedro Garza García* ☎ *81/8368–1000 800/713–1966 in the U.S.* 📠 *81/8368–1080* ⊕ *www.quintareal.com* ⇆ *125 suites* ⌂ *Restaurant, room service, minibars, cable TV, gym, sauna, bar, baby-sitting, laundry service, concierge, business services, travel services, car rental, free parking, no-smoking rooms* ⊟ *AE, DC, MC, V.*

$$$ ▨ **Sheraton Ambassador.** You can tell by its no-nonsense facade that this hotel has business on its mind. Its expansive meeting rooms can hold

more than 1,200 people. You can hit the business center or unwind in the comfortable lounge or the piano bar, which has a stained-glass ceiling. ✉ *Hidalgo Oriente 310, 64000* ☎ *81/8380–7000 800/325–3535 in the U.S.* 🖷 *81/8345–1984* ⊕ *www.starwood.com* ⤳ *223 rooms, 16 suites* ⚹ *Restaurant, room service, cable TV, minibars, tennis court, pool, health club, massage, racquetball, bar, laundry service, concierge floor, business services, meeting room, travel services, free parking, no-smoking rooms* ▤ *AE, DC, MC, V.*

★ $$–$$$ 🏨 **Radisson Plaza Gran Hotel Ancira.** Legend has it that Pancho Villa was so taken with this elegant place that he settled in and stabled his horse in the lobby. Reminiscent of the grand hotels of Europe, this neo-classical beauty has been a favorite since 1912. A spiral staircase dominates the expansive art deco lobby; crystal chandeliers shimmer overhead. The guest rooms have hand-carved furniture and large marble baths. ✉ *Ocampo 443, 64000* ☎ *81/8150–7000 800/830–6000 in the U.S.* 🖷 *81/8344–5226* ⊕ *www.hotel-ancira.com* ⤳ *236 rooms, 26 suites* ⚹ *Restaurant, minibars, cable TV, pool, gym, hair salon, outdoor hot tub, sauna, 2 bars, shops, baby-sitting, laundry service, concierge floor, travel services, car rental, free parking, no-smoking rooms* ▤ *AE, DC, MC, V.*

$$ 🏨 **Fiesta Americana Centro Monterrey.** This massive pink sandstone structure is impossible to overlook. The striking atrium lobby is always abuzz with travelers. The suites, each with two generously sized rooms, have fold-out sofas, making a good arrangement for families. Rooms facing the plaza have fabulous views of the surrounding mountains. ✉ *Privada Corregidora Oriente 519, 64000* ☎ *81/8319–0900; 01800/504–5000 toll free in Mexico* 🖷 *81/8319–0980* ⊕ *www. fiestaamericana.com.mx* ⤳ *189 rooms, 18 suites* ⚹ *Restaurant, room service, minibars, cable TV, indoor pool, gym, bar, baby-sitting, business services, laundry service, concierge, parking (fee), no-smoking rooms* ▤ *AE, DC, MC, V.*

¢ 🏨 **Hotel Fundador.** Scalloped awnings mark the facade of the only hotel in the Barrio Antiguo. You'll get a warm greeting as you enter the old-fashioned wood-paneled lobby. Rooms could not be described as luxurious, but they are comfortable and spacious, and those facing the street have pleasant views of the historic neighborhood. ✉ *Calle Montemayor 802, at Calle Mariano Matamoros, 64000* ☎ *81/8342–0121* 🖷 *81/ 8342–1710* ⤳ *40 rooms* ⚹ *Restaurant, bar* ▤ *AE, MC, V.*

Nightlife & the Arts

Charming Barrio Antiguo has a number of live music bars. One local favorite is **Fonda San Miguel** (✉ Av. Morelos Oriente 924 ☎ 81/8342–6659), where you'll find an eclectic mix of people. Kick back on one of the sofas in the mysterious **Kabal Lounge** (✉ Calle Abasolo 870 ☎ 81/8340–4332), which is popular with a young and trendy crowd. It's upstairs in the same building as La Casa de Maiz. **Monasterio** (✉ Calle Escobedo 913 ☎ no phone) presents a wide array of live music—from rock to romantic ballads—Tuesday through Saturday nights.

Shopping

In the wealthy suburb of San Pedro Garza García, **Plaza Fiesta San Agustín** (✉ Av. Real de San Agustín at Calle Lázaro Cárdenas) is an enormous mall where socialites shop for evening gowns, precious gems, and imported perfumes. In the heart of Monterrey is **Galerías Monterrey** (✉ Av. Insurgentes 2500), where you'll find the popular department store Liverpool and dozens of smaller shops.

In a building that was once one of the city's grand hotels, **Plaza Mexico** (✉ Av. Morelos 359) is one of the best places to go for souvenirs. The downtown **Mercado Indio** (⊠ Bolívar Norte 1150) is a sprawling market, but the selection changes little from stall to stall.

Near Plaza Hidalgo you'll find top-quality shops, many specializing in leather goods. Owner Porfirio Sosa handpicks all the items he sells at the upscale **Carápan** (⊠ Av. Hidalgo Oriente 305 ☎ 81/8345–4422). His array of hard-to-find antiques, hand-loomed rugs, and handblown glassware rivals that of stores anywhere in the country.

Side Trips from Monterrey

Monterrey is so densely packed that it's hard to believe a short drive from the city will bring you relative solitude. The Cañon de la Huasteca is nearly deserted during the week; on weekends it's a popular retreat for Monterrey residents. Best of all, it's only a 20-minute drive from the city. The Cascada Cola de Caballo and Grutas de García are slightly more than an hour away. El Potrero Chico is a longer endeavor, but for rock climbers it's worth the trip.

Cañon de la Huasteca

The walls of the 1,000-ft-deep gorge of Huasteca Canyon are spectacularly striated. The trails are various and well maintained, and the stunning peaks—with evocative names like Devil's Tower and Cat's Walk—attract climbing enthusiasts. A children's play area has a miniature train ride and two pools. ⊠ *From Monterrey, 20 km (12 mi) west on Hwy. 40 to Santa Catarina, then 3 km (2 mi) south on a nameless but clearly marked road* ☎ *No phone* ⊠ *$1 per car* ⊙ *Daily 9–6.*

Cascada Cola de Caballo

A highlight of the Parque Nacional Cumbres de Monterrey, tucked into the Sierra Madre, is a view of Horsetail Falls, a dramatic 75-ft-high waterfall that tumbles down from the pine-forested heights. The waterfall is about 1 km (½ mi) from the park's entrance, up a cobblestone road. You can rent a docile horse or burro for about $3 an hour from the local kids who hang out by the ticket booth, or hop on a horse-drawn carriage for $2. ⊠ *From Monterrey, Hwy. 85 northwest 90 km (56 mi) to falls* ☎ *No phone* ⊠ *$1.50* ⊙ *Daily 9–7.*

Grutas de García

The Garcia Caves are an estimated 50–60 million years old and at one time were submerged by an ocean. Petrified sea animals are visible in some of its walls. From the entrance, you can hike the steep 1 km (½ mi) to the caves or hop on a swaying funicular. Guides lead the way through a strenuous mile of underground grottoes and caverns. ⊠ *From Monterrey, Hwy. 40 west for 40 km (25 mi), then 9 km (5½ mi) north on an unnamed but marked road* ☎ *81/8347–1599* ⊠ *$5 with funicular* ⊙ *Daily 9–5.*

El Potrero Chico

This series of rugged limestone cliffs has become popular with climbing enthusiasts over the past several years. The cliffs stretch on for miles, threaded with more than 300 routes ranging from moderate to difficult. There are spectacular views of the surrounding Sierra Madre Oriental. As the area was once under the ocean, the rocks hold plenty of marine fossils. ⊠ *From Monterrey, 100 km (63 mi) north on Hwy. 85* ☎ *No phone* ⊠ *Free.*

Saltillo

25 *85 km (53 mi) southwest of Monterrey.*

While Monterrey shies away from its past, the colonial capital of Saltillo revels in it—it's the only town in the northeastern corner of the country to retain its colonial character. It's hard to imagine a lovelier square than the sedate **Plaza de Armas,** flanked on one side by the Palacio de Gobierno and the other by an ornate cathedral. Chatty older women fill the benches surrounding the gurgling fountain. A few blocks north is noisy **Plaza Manuel Acuña,** the province of men hawking cowboy hats and boys offering to shine your shoes.

A few blocks south of the Plaza de Armas is the **Museo de las Aves,** dedicated to the region's amazing bird population. Hundreds of mounted birds are on display in realistic dioramas. ⊠ *Calle Hidalgo and Calle Bolívar* ☎ *844/439–2745* ⊡ *$1* ☉ *Tues.–Sat. 10–6, Sun. 10–3.*

Where to Stay & Eat

$ ✕ **El Principal.** A kid roasting over a charcoal grill fills the front window of this rustic restaurant. If you're bold, start off with the kidneys, which locals swear are the best part. There are also plenty of steaks on the menu if you aren't in the mood for cabrito. On Friday, entrées are half price. ⊠ *Calle Allende 702* ☎ *844/414–3384* ⊟ *AE, MC, V.*

¢ ⊞ **Hotel Urdiñola.** A gleaming marble staircase stretches up from the lobby of this colonial-era charmer. The rooms are spare, but spacious; ask for one in the back, as those on the street are a bit noisy. The central courtyard overflows with flowers. ⊠ *Calle Victoria 251, 25000* ☎ *844/ 414–0940* ⊜ *844/412–9380* ↩ *55 rooms* ⚭ *Restaurant, bar* ⊟ *AE, DC, MC, V.*

Tampico

26 *504 km (312 mi) south of Matamoros, 583 km (361 mi) southeast of Monterrey.*

Foreigners seem to be drawn to this port on the Gulf of Mexico. In 1828 the Spanish attempted to reconquer their former colony by landing troops here, but were soundly defeated. After later incursions by the Americans and then the French, the port was ignored until oil was discovered in the region in 1901. The Americans returned, this time with the British, to reap the profits.

Although the city focuses on business, Tampico can also be a pleasure. In the center of town, wrought-iron balconies recall New Orleans. **Plaza de la Libertad,** a stone's throw from the harbor, is surrounded by old colonial-era buildings. A block from laid-back Plaza de la Libertad is the regal **Plaza de Armas,** surrounded by towering palms. On its northern edge stands the cathedral. Begun in 1823, the elegant structure was finally completed with funds from U.S. oil magnate Edward L. Doheny, implicated in the Teapot Dome scandal of the 1920s.

The area near the docks, just south of the Plaza de la Libertad, is also a good place to explore by day. Stroll through the daily market, where you can purchase candles that bring bad luck to your enemies. Steer clear of this area at night, though, as it gets pretty rough.

In the neighboring town of Ciudad Madero you'll find the small **Museo de la Cultura Huasteca,** which has an exquisite collection of pre-Hispanic artifacts, some dating back to 1100 BC. ⊠ *Instituto Tecnológico, Av. 1 de Mayo at Calle Sor Juana Inés de la Cruz, Ciudad Madero* ☎ *833/ 210–2217* ⊡ *Free* ☉ *Weekdays 10–6, Sat. 10–3.*

Where to Stay & Eat

$–$$ ✕ **Papa Cuervo Restaurant & Bar.** Ever dreamed of being a buccaneer? Head to this restaurant, equipped with billowing sails, trunks full of treasure, and a monkey hanging off the stern (don't worry, he doesn't bite). Each wall is a three-dimensional mural of the undersea world. Servings tend to be small but satisfying—try the chicken breast stuffed with cheese, spinach, and mushrooms and drizzled with pecan sauce. Save some energy for live music and dancing on the weekends. ☒ *Calle Morelos 779, El Centro* ☎ *833/222–0180* ▱ *No credit cards.*

$–$$ ✕ **La Troya.** For unbeatable views of Plaza de la Libertad, nab one of the tables on the balcony of this longtime favorite. Many of the exceedingly rich meat and seafood dishes, such as the delicious paella, tip their hat to Spain. The signature dish is the tasty *carne asada tampiqueña,* a steak marinated in garlic and spices. ☒ *Calle Madero Oriente 218, at Av. Juárez, El Centro* ☎ *833/214–1155* ▱ *AE, MC, V.*

¢ ✕ **Café y Nevería Elite.** This popular gathering spot not far from the Plaza de Armas serves up delicious coffee and ice-cream treats. For lunch and dinner there is plenty of low-price local fare. Don't be put off by the noise and the rather worn tables; it's all part of the local color. ☒ *Av. Díaz Mirón Oriente 211* ☎ *833/212–0364* ▱ *MC, V.*

$$ ▥ **Camino Real.** This attractive resort about 20 minutes from the city center is the best lodging you'll find in Tampico. Its rooms and bungalows surround a huge garden overflowing with tropical trees and flowers. Fishing excursions can be booked through the on-site travel agency. ☒ *Av. Hidalgo 2000, Col. Smith, 89140* ☎ *833/213–8811; 800/570–0000 in the U.S.* ▤ *833/213–9226* ⊕ *www.caminorealtampico.com* ⇨ *100 rooms, 3 suites* ⚲ *Restaurant, room service, minibars, cable TV, tennis court, pool, bar, laundry service, travel services, car rental* ▱ *AE, DC, MC, V.*

¢ ▥ **Posada del Rey.** Check in to one of the city's oldest buildings, whose art nouveau facade fronts the Plaza de la Libertad. Ask for one of the rooms overlooking the square, as others in the back are a bit shabby. The rooms are dimly lit, but the effect is cozy and quite charming. ☒ *Calle Madero Oriente 218, El Centro 89000* ☎ *833/214–1155* ▤ *833/212–1077* ⇨ *40 rooms* ⚲ *Restaurant, cable TV, bar* ▱ *AE, MC, V.*

Sports & the Outdoors

FISHING Although the Río Pánuco has become too polluted for fishing, those in search of tarpon and snapper can head to **Laguna del Chairel,** in the northern part of the city, where's you'll find boats loaded with all the gear you'll need. The Camino Real and other hotels can arrange for excursions.

GOLF **Lagunas de Miralta** (☒ Carretera Tampico–Altamira, Km 26 ☎ 833/224–0003) offers day passes to its 18-hole course not far from the city. Ask at your hotel about discounts here and at other local clubs.

THE NORTHEAST A TO Z

To research prices, get advice from other travelers, and book travel arrangements, visit www.fodors.com.

AIR TRAVEL

AIRPORTS Monterrey has the region's only international airport, Aeropuerto Internacional Mariano Escobedo (MTY), which is 6 km (4 mi) northeast of downtown. The airport has reasonably priced luggage storage and a currency exchange booth.

Should you need to fly into Tampico's Aeropuerto General Francisco Javier Mina (TAM), there are very expensive domestic flights available. The airport is about 15 km (9 mi) north of town.

🛪 **Aeropuerto General Francisco Javier Mina** ☎ 833/228-0571 **Aeropuerto Internacional Mariano Escobedo** ☎ 81/8369-0753.

AIRPORT TRANSFERS
The only way to get between Monterrey and the airport is by taxi, which will cost about $14.

CARRIERS
From the United States, Continental flies to Monterrey from Chicago, Las Vegas, Los Angeles, Miami, and New York, via Houston. American has six flights a day to Monterrey from Dallas. Aerolitoral has service to Monterrey from McAllen and San Antonio, Texas. Mexicana has flights from Chicago, Denver, Los Angeles, New York, San Antonio, and San Francisco to Monterrey, via Mexico City. Aeroméxico has direct service to Monterrey from Houston and Los Angeles and flights from New York via Mexico City.

From Mexico City, Aeroméxico has service to Matamoros, Tampico, and Reynosa. Mexicana flies to Nuevo Laredo and Tampico, while Aerolitoral has nonstop flights to Tampico.

🛪 **Aerolitoral** ☎ 81/8221-1600 in Monterrey; 833/228-4197 or 833/228-0857 in Tampico ⊕ www.aerolitoral.com. **Aeroméxico** ☎ 868/812-2460 in Matamoros; 81/8343-5560 in Monterrey; 899/922-1115 in Reynosa; 833/213-9600 in Tampico ⊕ www.aeromexico.com. **American** ☎ 81/8340-3031 in Monterrey ⊕ www.aa.com. **Continental** ☎ 81/8348-4282 in Monterrey ⊕ www.continental.com. **Mexicana** ☎ 81/8124-2500 in Monterrey; 867/712-2052 in Nuevo Laredo; 833/213-9600 in Tampico ⊕ www.mexicana.com.mx.

BUS TRAVEL TO & FROM THE NORTHEAST

Northeastern Mexico is easy to reach by bus. Greyhound runs several buses a day to the border from San Antonio, Dallas, and Houston. At the border towns of Laredo, McAllen, and Brownsville, buses operated by Transportes del Norte will whisk you down to Monterrey. The trip from the border takes about three hours.

🚌 **Greyhound** ☎ 402/330-8552; 800/229-9424 in the U.S. ⊕ www.greyhound.com. **Transportes del Norte** ☎ 956/723-4324 in Laredo ☎ 956/686-5479 in McAllen ☎ 956/546-7171 in Brownsville, 81/5587-5400 in Monterrey.

BUS TRAVEL WITHIN THE NORTHEAST

Monterrey's busy terminal, called the Central de Autobuses, is the hub of bus transportation in the northeast. Transportes del Norte buses cover the region quite thoroughly, with frequent service between Monterrey and all the cities in the region. Omnibus de México sends one bus a day between Monterrey and Tampico and Monterrey and Nuevo Laredo; it also offers frequent daily service to Reynosa.

🚌 **Bus Depot Central de Autobuses** ⊠ Av. Colón at Amado Nervo, Monterrey ☎ 81/8374-1648 or 81/8375-3238.

🚌 **Bus Companies Omnibus de México** ☎ 81/8375-7121 in Monterrey. **Transportes del Norte** ☎ 81/8318-3737 in Monterrey.

CAR TRAVEL

Crossing the border in a car is not without its red tape. Many rental companies won't allow you to take their cars across the border, so be sure to inquire in advance. If you plan on taking your own car, remember that your insurance won't cover you south of the border. You must purchase insurance from a Mexican company. Sanborn's Mexican Insurance can help you complete the paperwork before you leave—free if you buy insurance from the company.

If you're making a day trip to a border town, consider leaving your car in the United States. Walking over eliminates the long wait—often a half hour or more—to bring a car back into the country.

When planning your trip, keep in mind that it can take more time than you might expect to drive through this part of Mexico because of the meandering roads through the Sierra Madre Oriente. It generally takes three hours to drive from the border to Monterrey.

Downtown Nuevo Laredo is reached via International Bridge 1, which drops you right into busy Avenida Guerrero. International Bridge 2, just to the east, is favored by those bypassing the city for points south. From Nuevo Laredo, the road splits between the slow Mexico 85 Libre and the speedy Mexico 85 Cuota. Both lead to Monterrey, 242 km (151 mi) south. The latter road is much better maintained, but costs about $15 in tolls.

From Reynosa, a $15 toll gets you onto Mexico 40, which leads south. The highway, although rather monotonous, is the most convenient route to Monterrey. From Matamoros, Mexico 180 runs down the Gulf coast to Tampico, Veracruz, and beyond. If you're headed to Monterrey, Mexico 2 connects with Reynosa.

Tampico is roughly a seven-hour drive from Matamoros on Mexico 180, or eight hours from Monterrey via Mexico 85. Saltillo is an hour and a half from Monterrey on Mexico 40.

🏢 **Bravo Insurance** ⊠ 2212 Santa Ursula St., Laredo, TX 78040 ☎ 956/723-3657 🖨 956/723-0000 ⊕ www.mxins.com. **Sanborn's Mexican Insurance** ⊠ 2009 S. 10th St., McAllen, TX 78503 ☎ 800/222-0158 in the U.S. 🖨 956/686-0732 ⊕ www.sanbornsinsurance.com.

EMBASSIES & CONSULATES

🏢 **Canadian Consulate** ⊠ Calle Mariano Escobedo at Av. Constitución, Monterrey ☎ 81/8344-3200 🖨 81/8344-3048 ⊕ www.canada.org.mx/consular/english/monterrey.asp. **U.S. Consulate** ⊠ Calle 1 232, Matamoros ☎ 868/812-4402 ⊠ Av. Constitución Poniente 411, Monterrey ☎ 81/8343-7124 🖨 8/8343-9399 ⊕ www.usembassy-mexico.gov/Monterrey.html ⊠ Allende 3330, Nuevo Laredo ☎ 867/714-0512 ⊠ Calle Monterrey 390, at Sinaloa, Reynosa ☎ 899/923-9331

EMERGENCIES

Dial 066 for medical, fire, and other emergencies.

Many pharmacies stay open until 9 or 10 PM. Fenix and Benavides are among the better-known chains. If you must reach a hospital, call the local Cruz Roja, or Red Cross, for ambulance service.

🏢 Ambulances **Monterrey Cruz Roja** ⊠ Av. Alfonso Reyes 2503, Monterrey ☎ 81/8375-1212. **Nuevo Laredo Cruz Roja** ⊠ Independencia 1619 at San Antonio, Nuevo Laredo ☎ 867/712-0949 or 867/712-0989. **Reynosa Cruz Roja** ☎ 899/922-1314 or 899/922-6250. **Saltillo Cruz Roja** ☎ 844/414-3333. **Tampico Cruz Roja** ☎ 833/212-1333.

🏢 Hospitals **Hospital Murguerza** ⊠ Av. Hidalgo 2525 Poniente Monterrey ☎ 81/8399-3400. **Hospital Santander** ⊠ Madero at Ortiz Rubyo, Reynosa ☎ 899/922-9622. **Matamoros Cruz Roja Hospital** ⊠ García and L. Caballero, Matamoros ☎ 868/812-0044. **Tampico Cruz Roja Hospital** ⊠ Tamaulipas and Colegio Militar, El Centro, Tampico ☎ 833/212-1333.

🏢 Police **Matamoros Police** ⊠ Pedro Cárdenas at Soledad, Matamoros ☎ 868/817-2205. **Monterrey Police** ⊠ Gonzalitos 2300, at Lincoln, Monterrey ☎ 81/8151-6000. **Nuevo Laredo Police** ⊠ Maclovio Herréra at Ocampo, Nuevo Laredo ☎ 867/712-3930. **Reynosa Police** ⊠ Morelos between Veracruz and Nayarit ☎ 899/922-0008 or 899/22-0790. **Saltillo Police** ⊠ Dr. Coss and Garcia ☎ 844/416-2183. **Tampico Police** ⊠ Calle Sor Juana Inés de la Cruz at Tamaulipas Tampico ☎ 833/214-3249.

▣ Pharmacies **Farmacia Benavides** ⊠ Av. Morelos 499, at Escobedo, Monterrey ☎ 81/8345-0257. **Farmacia Calderón** ⊠ Guerrero 704, Nuevo Laredo ☎ 867/712-5177. **Farmacia Droguería del Pueblo** ⊠ Av. Juárez Sur 308, Tampico ☎ 833/212-1542. **Farmacia El Fenix** ⊠ Calle Abasolo 806, Matamoros ☎ 868/812-2909.

MONEY MATTERS

In the border towns, businesses generally accept U.S. dollars; if you're going beyond the border area you'll need to use pesos. Twenty-four-hour ATMs are plentiful all around northeastern Mexico, so getting cash is no problem. Most machines accept bank cards on both the Cirrus and Plus systems. If you need to exchange currency or cash traveler's checks, banks are generally open weekdays 9–2.

In Monterrey, the banks in the downtown area are generally open weekdays 9–3. If you need cash at other times, Eurodivisas stays open until 8 PM Sunday through Friday and 9 PM Saturday.

There are plenty of banks in downtown Matamoros, mostly around Plaza Hidalgo. Citibank is open weekdays 9–3, Saturdays 9:30–2. Most banks in Reynosa will exchange currency, but Citibank will change traveler's checks weekdays 9–2. In Nuevo Laredo, the Banamex at the corner of Guerrero and Canales is open weekdays 9 to 3.

In Tampico, Citibank changes money and traveler's checks weekdays 9–3, Saturday 9–2. Banamex performs the same services until 5.
▣ **Banamex** ⊠ Guerrero at Canales, Nuevo Laredo ☎ 867/714-7600 ⊠ Calle Madero Oriente 403, Tampico ☎ 833/214-0230. **Citibank** ⊠ Av. Miguel Alemán 100, Reynosa ☎ 899/922-5619 ⊠ Quinta at Morelos, Matamoros ☎ 868/812-0082 ⊠ Aduana Sur 309, Tampico ☎ 833/212-9240. **Eurodivisas** ⊠ Av. Morelos Oriente 359, Monterrey ☎ 81/8340-1683.

TAXIS

Taxis are pretty scarce and expensive in border towns but plentiful and moderately priced in Monterrey. There, it's easy to hail a cab from any corner downtown; this is generally considered safe, but for added security you can call a reliable company such as Metro Taxi. In Saltillo, try Radio Taxi for on-call service.
▣ **Metro Taxi** ☎ 81/8342-2069. **Radio Taxi** ☎ 844/412-6760.

TOURS

Anfitriones Regios Tours organizes tours in and around Monterrey. Other well-regarded agencies include Tours Gray Line and Osetur Tours, which run shopping and sightseeing excursions in the area. The staff of these companies speak English.
▣ **Anfitriones Regios Tours** ⊠ Argentina 2939, Monterrey ☎ 81/8324-1870. **Osetur Tours** ⊠ Calle San Francisco 2700, at Loma Grande, Monterrey ☎ 81/8347-1599 or 81/8347-1614. **Tours Gray Line** ⊠ Av. Eugenio Garza Sada 2256, Monterrey ☎ 81/8369-6472 or 81/8369-6473.

VISITOR INFORMATION

The best sources of information about northeastern Mexico are the Texan border towns' chambers of commerce. You can stop by the offices, open weekdays, or check out their helpful Web sites.

Not every Mexican town has tourism information handy. Monterrey's tourism office is the best of the bunch; it's open Tuesday–Sunday 10–5. The staff bends over backwards to help. The lackluster office in Nuevo Laredo, in the Palacio Municipal, is open daily 8–8. The

Reynosa office, at the International Bridge, is open weekdays 7:30 AM–8 PM. The office in Saltillo is open Monday–Saturday 9–6.

North of the Border **Brownsville Chamber of Commerce** ✉ 1600 E. Elizabeth St., Brownsville, TX 78520 ☎ 956/542-4341 ⊕ www.brownsvillechamber.com. **Laredo Chamber of Commerce** ✉ 2310 San Bernardo, Laredo, TX 78040 ☎ 956/722-9895 ⊕ www.laredochamber.com. **McAllen Chamber of Commerce** ✉ 1200 Ash St., McAllen, TX 78501 ☎ 956/682-2871 ⊕ www.mcallen.org.

South of the Border **Monterrey** ✉ Plaza 5 de Mayo Oriente 525, 3rd floor ☎ 81/8345-0902 ⊕ www.monterrey-mexico.com. **Nuevo Laredo** ✉ González at Galeana ☎ 867/712-7397 ⊕ www.nuevolaredo.gob.mx. **Reynosa** ✉ International Bridge ☎ 899/922-1189 or 899/922-2449. **Saltillo** ✉ Dr. Coss and Acuna ☎ 844/412-5122 ⊕ www.saltillo.gob.mx.

THE YUCATÁN PENINSULA

13

FODOR'S CHOICE

Calesa (carriage) ride in Mérida

Casa San Juan, Mérida hotel

Chichén Itzá, ruins

Ikal del Mar, Playa del Carmen hotel

La Pigua, Campeche City restaurant

Playa Norte, Isla Mujeres beach

Presidente Inter-Continental Paraiso de la Bonita, Puerto Morelos hotel

Scuba diving off the shores of Cozumel

Uxmal, ruins

Tulum, ruins

HIGHLY RECOMMENDED

SHOPPING   Amber Mexicano, Playa del Carmen

Casa de Artesanías, Mérida

EXPERIENCES   Beaches near Tulum ruins

Cobá, ruins

Folkloric Ballet, Mérida

Fuerte de San Miguel, Campeche City

Museo de Arte Popular, Cancún

Palacio Cantón, Mérida

Parque Chankanaab, Cozumel

Parque Natural Río Lagartos

Puerta de Tierra, Campeche City

So many wonderful hotels and restaurants can be found in this area that there's not enough space to list them all on this page. To see what Fodor's editors and contributors highly recommend, please look for the black stars as you leaf through this chapter.

THERE'S A LONG LIST OF REASONS WHY the Yucatán Peninsula is a perennial favorite destination: the high-profile sparkle of Cancún; the laid-back beachcombing of Isla Mujeres; the spectacular seas around Cozumel; the fascinating Spanish-Maya mix of Mérida; the evocative Maya ruins of Tulum, Chichén Itzá, and Uxmal; and the two huge coastal ecozones of the Sian Ka'an Biosphere Reserve and Parque Natural Río Lagartos.

Cancún, Mexico's most popular resort area, owes its success to a location on the east coast, which is washed by exquisitely colored Caribbean waters, lined by unbroken stretches of beach, and blessed with a semitropical climate. The region is also home to the world's second-largest barrier reef, which starts off the coast of the Yucatán Peninsula and runs all the way to South America.

Cancún incarnates the success formula for sun-and-sand travel: luxury hotels, sandy beaches, hot nightclubs, fine restaurants—not to mention proximity to compelling Maya ruins. Cozumel's hotels may not be as showy as those in Cancún, but they're still beloved of scuba divers. On relaxed Isla Mujeres (*ees*-lah moo-*hair*-ayce; Island of the Women), you're likely to stay in a rustic bungalow with ceiling fans and hammocks.

There are also the cities of the Yucatán. Foremost among them is Mérida, whose well-preserved examples of Moorish-inspired colonial architecture make it seem unaltered by time. In this city, café life is still an art, and the Maya still follow the customs of their ancestors. Campeche, one of North America's few walled cities, possesses an eccentric charm; it's slightly out of step with the rest of the country and not the least bothered by the fact.

Wildlife is another of the Yucatán's riches. Iguanas, lizards, tapirs, deer, armadillos, and wild boars thrive on this alternately parched and densely foliated peninsula. Flamingos and herons, manatees and sea turtles—they all find idyllic watery habitats in and above the coastline's mangrove swamps, lagoons, and sandbars, acres of which have been made into national parks.

But perhaps it is the myriad colors that are the peninsula's most remarkable features. From the stark, white, sun-bleached sand, the sea stretches out like some immense canvas painted in bands of celadon greens, pale aquas, and deep blues. At dusk the sea and the horizon meld in the glow of a lavender sunset, the sky just barely tinged with periwinkle and violet.

Inland, the beige, gray, and amber stones of ruined temples are set off by riotous greenery. The colors of newer structures are equally intoxicating: tawny, gray-brown thatched roofs sit atop white oval huts. Colonial mansions favor creamy pastels of bisque, salmon, and coral—highlighted by elegant white arches, white balustrades, and white porticos.

Brilliant colors glimmer in carved hardwood doors, variegated tile floors, brown and green pottery, and rugs affixed to walls. Orchids, bougainvillea, and poinciana are ubiquitous; dazzling reds and pinks and oranges and whites rush down the sides of countless buildings and into countless courtyards. The Yucatán is a treat for all the senses and a place to both relax and re-energize.

Exploring the Yucatán Peninsula

In its entirety, the 113,000-square-km (43,600-square-mi) peninsula encompasses the Mexican states of Yucatán, Campeche, and Quintana Roo, as well as Belize and part of Guatemala. Its north and west sides are lapped by the waters of the Gulf of Mexico; the Caribbean Sea edges it to the east. Within its bounds are tremendous bird-watching, water

Numbers in the text correspond to numbers in the margin and on the Cancún, Isla Mujeres, Cozumel, Riviera Maya, State of Yucatán, Mérida, and Campeche City maps.

13

If you have 3 days

Base yourself on the Caribbean coast, at 🏨 **Playa del Carmen** ⑲ ▸, and relax on the white-sand beach or go diving in nearby reefs. On Day 2, visit the ruins of the Maya city of **Tulum** ㉑ and then climb down to the small beach alongside it for a dip. On Day 3, head for **Akumal** ⑳ for diving, deep-sea fishing, snorkeling, or swimming. Later in the day visit the tiny lagoon of Yalkú.

Alternatively, you could spend two days in 🏨 **Mérida** ㉔–㉟ ▸, savoring the city's unique character as you make your way among its historic structures. You can easily devote a day to exploring the heart of downtown, including the *zócalo* (main square) and its surroundings. Take a second, more leisurely day to visit the Museo de Antropología y Historia in the Palacio Cantón and, perhaps, the Museo de Arte Contemporáneo. On Day 3, drive or take a tour to one of Yucatán's most famous Maya ruins—**Chichén Itzá** ㊱ or **Uxmal** ㊵. Each is within about two hours of Mérida.

If you have 7 days

Base yourself at 🏨 **Playa del Carmen** ⑲ ▸, spending Day 1 on the beach and Day 2 visiting **Tulum** ㉑. On Day 3, tour the Maya ruins of **Cobá** ㉒. Head for **Akumal** ⑳ and its water sports on Day 4. The next day, sign up for a tour of the **Sian Ka'an Biosphere Reserve** ㉓. On Days 6 and 7, head west to the colonial city of 🏨 **Mérida** ㉔–㉟. Spend one day in town and the next out at **Chichén Itzá** ㊱ or **Uxmal** ㊵.

On a weeklong trip in and around Mérida, take in the city's sights first and then take two separate overnight excursions. First, head for **Uxmal** ㊵ and overnight at one of the nearby hotels. The next day explore the Ruta Puuc, the series of lost cities south of Uxmal that includes Kabah, Sayil, and Labná, as well as the fascinating Loltún Caves. On the second excursion, to **Chichén Itzá** ㊱, allow as much as a full day so that you can also explore some of the present-day Maya villages along the way. As an alternate side trip, you could go north of **Valladolid** ㊳ to see the flamingo nesting grounds at **Parque Natural Río Lagartos** ㊴.

If you have 9 days

Spend several days exploring 🏨 **Mérida** ㉔–㉟ ▸ before heading to 🏨 **Campeche City** ㊷–�51. After spending a day seeing the city's sights—almost all those of interest are within the compact historic district—head inland the next morning to **Edzná,** a magnificently restored ceremonial center an hour's drive from the city.

---

sports, archaeology, handicrafts, and savory Yucatecan cuisine. Above all, there are the friendly and open Yucatecos themselves.

International airports at Cancún and Cozumel provide nonstop service from several North American cities. The Mérida airport handles primarily domestic flights. Cruise ships call at Cozumel and Calica, south of Playa del Carmen.

About the Restaurants

In the early days, Yucatecan cuisine was tremendously influenced by French, Cuban, and New Orleans cooking because of continual cultural contact. This multicultural approach resulted in such specialties as *pollo pibíl* (chicken marinated in a sour orange and annatto seed sauce and baked in banana leaves); *poc chuc* (pork marinated in a sour-orange sauce with pickled onions); *tikinchic* (fish marinated in a sour-orange sauce and achiote paste, wrapped in banana leaves, and cooked over an open flame); *panuchos* (fried tortillas filled with black beans and topped with diced turkey, chicken, or pork as well as pickled onions and avocado); *papadzules* (tortillas rolled up with hard-boiled eggs and drenched in a sauce of pumpkin seed and fried tomato); and *codzitos* (rolled tortillas in pumpkin-seed sauce). *Achiote* (annatto seed), cilantro (coriander), and the fiery *chili habañero* are zesty condiments. Along the gulf coast, there's nothing finer than a dish of fresh blue crab, or baby shrimp.

El desayuno can be either a breakfast sweet roll and coffee or milk or a full breakfast of an egg dish such as *huevos a la mexicana* (scrambled eggs with chopped tomato, onion, and chilies) or *huevos rancheros* (fried eggs on a tortilla covered with tomato sauce) plus juice and tortillas. Lunch is called *la comida* or *el almuerzo* and is the biggest meal of the day. Traditional businesses close down between 2 PM and 4 PM for this meal. It usually includes soup, a main dish, and dessert. The lighter evening meal is called *la cena*.

About the Hotels

In Cancún, Cozumel, and Isla Mujeres luxurious international chains have the latest room amenities and lots of restaurants, bars, boutiques, and sports facilities. These beach resort areas also have more-modest accommodations—usually a short walk or a shuttle ride from the water. In the Yucatán's less-populated and -visited areas, accommodations tend to be simpler and more typically Mexican: inexpensive bungalows, campsites, and beachside places to hang a hammock. With the broad range of accommodations comes an equally broad range of travelers: package-tour groups, backpackers, people touring in rental cars.

WHAT IT COSTS					
	$$$$	**$$$**	**$$**	**$**	**¢**
RESTAURANTS	over $25	$15–$25	$10–$15	$5–$10	under $5
HOTELS	over $250	$150–$250	$75–$150	$50–$75	under $50

Restaurant prices are for a main course excluding tax and tip. Hotel prices are for two people in a standard double room in high season, based on the European Plan (EP, with no meals) and excluding service and 17% tax.

Timing

High season in the states of Yucatán and Campeche consists of Christmastime, Easter week, and July and August. Rainfall is heaviest and humidity most uncomfortable from May to October or November. In Cancún, Cozumel, and Isla Mujeres, the peak tourist times are mid-December through late March and again in August. In less visited towns, levels of service differ drastically between the high and low seasons (when staff and activities may be cut back), so be prepared for the trade-off. The rainy season isn't a bad time to visit if you don't mind the afternoon showers and the sometimes reduced attentions. On the coast, hurricane season is usually September to October, though storms can blow through anytime from July to November.

Archaeological Sites

The ancient Maya left an incredible mark in the Yucatán. Pick your period and your preference, whether it's for well-excavated sites or overgrown, out-of-the-way ruins barely touched by a scientist's shovel. The major Maya sites are Cobá, Tulum, Chichén Itzá and Uxmal, but smaller sites scattered throughout the peninsula are often equally fascinating.

13

Beaches

Along the Caribbean coast, the sands are white, the bays are generally curvaceous, and the coves are often rocky. Playa Chacmool and Playa Tortugas are on the bay side of Cancún, which is calmer if less beautiful than the windward side. Playa Norte on Isla Mujeres is known for its great sunsets. Beaches on Cozumel's east coast—once used by buccaneers—are private but rocky, and the waters off them are treacherous; for wide, sandy beaches, head to the relatively sheltered leeward side. There are also long, crowded stretches of white sand at Puerto Morelos, Akumal, and Playa del Carmen. Around Campeche, the gulf waters are deep green, shallow, and tranquil.

Bird-Watching

Habitats range from wildlife and bird sanctuaries to unmarked lagoons, estuaries, and mangrove swamps. Frigates, tanagers, warblers, and herons inhabit Isla Contoy (off Isla Mujeres) and the Laguna Colombia on Cozumel; there's an even greater variety of species in the Sian Ka'an Biosphere Reserve on the Boca Paila Peninsula south of Tulum. Along the north and west coasts—at Río Lagartos, Laguna Rosada, and Celestún—flamingos, herons, ibis, cormorants, pelicans, and peregrine falcons thrive.

Fishing

The waters of both the Caribbean and the Gulf of Mexico support hundreds of species of game fish, making them paradise for deep-sea fishing, fly-fishing, and bonefishing. Between April and July in particular, the waters off Cancún, Cozumel, and Isla Mujeres teem with sailfish, marlin, red snapper, tuna, barracuda, wahoo, and other denizens of the deep. Bill fishing is so rich around Cozumel that it's the site of an annual tournament. Farther south, along the Boca Paila peninsula, bonefishing is a hands-down favorite, as is light-tackle saltwater fishing for shad and sea bass. Oysters, shrimp, and conch lie on the bottom of the Gulf of Mexico near Campeche. On the north coast, sportfishing for grouper, dogfish, and pompano is quite popular.

Scuba Diving

Underwater enthusiasts come to Cozumel, Akumal, and other parts of the Caribbean coast for the clear turquoise waters, the colorful and assorted tropical fish, and the exquisite coral formations along the Palancar Reef system. Currents allow for drift diving, and both reefs and offshore wrecks lend themselves to dives, many of which are safe enough for neophytes. The waters off the peninsula also have cenotes, or natural sinkholes, and underwater caverns.

Thousands of people swarm to Chichén Itzá for the vernal equinox on the first day of spring to see the astronomical phenomenon that makes a shadow resembling a snake—which represented the plumed serpent god Kukulcán—appear on the side of the main pyramid. The phenomenon also occurs on the first day of fall, but autumnal rains tend to discourage visitors. Both the capital and outlying villages of Campeche state celebrate the Day of the Dead (October 31–November 2) with fervor because it corresponds to a similar observance in ancient Maya tradition.

CANCÚN

Updated by
Maribeth
Mellin

Flying into Cancún, you see nothing but green treetops for miles. It's clear from the air that this resort was literally carved out of the jungle. When development began in the early 1970s, the beaches were deserted except for birds and iguanas. Now luxury hotels, malls, and restaurants line the oceanfront. More vacationers come here than to any other part of Mexico, and many come again and again.

Not much was written about Cancún before its birth as a resort. The Maya people settled the area during the Late Preclassic era, around AD 200, and remained until the 14th or 15th century, but little is known about them. Other explorers seem to have overlooked it—it doesn't appear on early navigators' maps. It was never heavily populated, perhaps because its terrain of mangroves and marshes (and resulting swarms of mosquitoes) discouraged settlement. Some minor Maya ruins were discovered in the mid-19th century, but archaeologists didn't get around to studying them until the 1950s.

In 1967, the Mexican government, under the leadership of Luis Echeverría, commissioned a study to pinpoint the ideal place for an international Caribbean resort. The computer chose Cancún, and the Cinderella transformation began. At the time the area's only residents were the three caretakers of a coconut plantation. In 1972 work began on the first hotel, and the island and city grew from there.

Today's Cancún has two different sides. On the mainland is the actual Ciudad Cancún (Cancún City). It's commercial center, known as El Centro, offers an authentic glimpse into the sights and sounds of Mexico. The other half, the Zona Hotelera (Hotel Zone), is the tourist heart. It's actually a 22½-km (14-mi) barrier island off the Yucatán Peninsula. A separate northern strip called Punta Sam, north of Puerto Juárez (where some ferries to Isla Mujeres depart), is sometimes referred to as the Zona Hotelera Norte (Northern Hotel Zone).

During the day you can shop, eat, and lounge in the year-round tropical warmth: the sun shines an average of 240 days a year, and temperatures linger at about 27°C (80°F). The reefs off Cancún and nearby Cozumel, Puerto Morelos, and Isla Mujeres are great places to dive, and Cancún also makes a relaxing base for visiting the ruins of Chichén Itzá, Tulum, and Cobá. At night you can sample Yucatecan food and watch folkloric dance performances, knock back tequila slammers, or listen to great jazz.

Cancún's success hasn't come without a price. Its lagoons and mangrove swamps have been polluted; a number of species, such as conch and lobster, are dwindling; and parts of the coral reef are dead. And although the beaches still appear pristine for the most part, an increased effort will have to be made to preserve the beauty that is the resort's prime appeal.

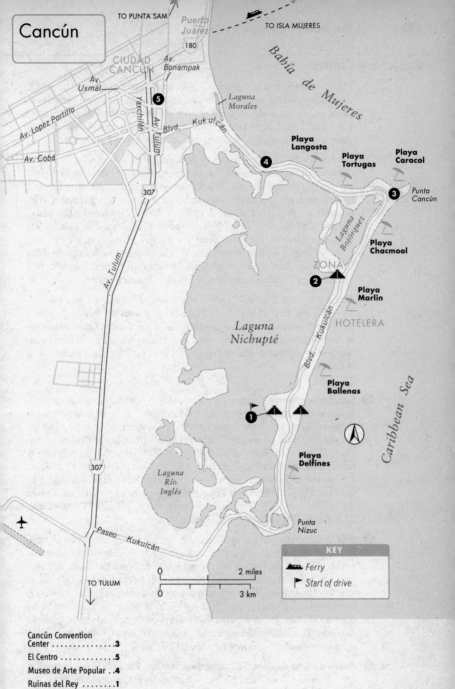

Cancún

TO PUNTA SAM

Puerto
Juárez

TO ISLA MUJERES

Bahía de Mujeres

180

CIUDAD
CANCÚN

Av.
Bonampak

Av.
Uxmal

5

Yaxchilán

Av. Lopez Portillo

Av. Tulum

Blvd. Kukulcán

*Laguna
Morales*

4

**Playa
Langosta**

Av. Cobá

**Playa
Tortugas**

**Playa
Caracol**

3

*Punta
Cancún*

*Laguna
Bojórquez*

**Playa
Chacmool**

ZONA

2

**Playa
Marlin**

307

Av. Tulum

*Laguna
Nichupté*

Blvd. Kukulcán

HOTELERA

Caribbean Sea

**Playa
Ballenas**

1

307

*Laguna
Río
Inglés*

**Playa
Delfines**

*Punta
Nizuc*

Paseo Kukulcán

KEY

TO TULUM

	2 miles
0	
0	3 km

Ferry

Start of drive

Exploring Cancún

The Zona Hotelera is a numeral 7–shape island 4 km (2 mi) east of El Centro. It consists entirely of hotels, restaurants, shopping complexes, marinas, and time-share condominiums, with few residential areas. It's not the sort of place you can get to know by walking or biking, although there is path that starts in Punta Nizuc and ends in El Centro.

a good tour

Cancún's scenery consists mostly of beautiful beaches and crystal-clear waters, but there are also a few intriguing historical sites tucked away among the modern hotels. In addition to the attractions listed below, two modest vestiges of the ancient Maya civilization are worth a visit, but only for dedicated archaeology buffs. Neither is identified by name. On the 12th hole of Pok-Ta-Pok golf course (Boulevard Kukulcán, Km 6.5)—the name means "ball game" in Maya—stands a ruin consisting of two platforms and the remains of other ancient buildings. And the ruin of a tiny Maya shrine is cleverly incorporated into the architecture of the Hotel Camino Real, on the beach at Punta Cancún.

You don't need a car in Cancún, but if you've rented one to make extended trips, start in the Zona Hotelera at **Ruinas del Rey** ❶ ▶. Drive north to **Yamil Lu'um** ❷, and then stop in at the **Cancún Convention Center** ❸, with its small anthropology and history museum, before heading west to the **Museo de Arte Popular** ❹, in El Embarcadero marina, and **El Centro** ❺.

What to See

❸ **Cancún Convention Center.** This strikingly modern venue for cultural events is the jumping-off point for a 1-km (½-mi) string of shopping malls that extends west to the Presidente Inter-Continental Cancún. The **Instituto Nacional de Antropología e Historia** (National Institute of Anthropology and History; ☎ 998/883–0305), a small, ground-floor museum, traces Maya culture with a fascinating collection of 1,000- to 1,500-year-old artifacts from throughout Quintana Roo. Admission to the museum is about $3; it's open Tuesday–Sunday 9–7. Guided tours are available in English, French, German, and Spanish. ✉ *Blvd. Kukulcán, Km 9, Zona Hotelera* ☎ 998/883–0199.

❺ **El Centro.** Downtown has markets, rather than malls, and offers a glimpse into a more provincial Mexico. A huge seashell sculpture in a roundabout is one of the features of the main street, Avenida Tulum. It's also home to many restaurants and shops as well as the Ki Huic—an enormous crafts market. If you're looking for shopping bargains, however, head to places along the parallel Avenida Yaxchilán; the Mercado Veintiocho (Market 28) is a particularly good place to find deals. Just off Avenidas Yaxchilán and Sunyaxchén, the market is El Centro's hub, filled with shops and restaurants frequented by locals.

★ ❹ **Museo de Arte Popular.** The enormous, entrancing Folk Art Museum is on the second floor of El Embarcadero marina. Original works by the country's finest artisans are arranged in fascinating tableaux; plan to spend a couple hours here. It's open daily, and admission is $10. Allow time for the museum's shop. Other marina complex attractions include two restaurants, a rotating scenic tower, the Teatro Cancún, and Xcaret ticket booths. ✉ *Blvd. Kukulcán, Km 4, Zona Hotelera* ☎ 998/849–4848 ✑ *Museum: $10* ◷ *Daily 10 AM–11 PM.*

▶ ❶ **Ruinas del Rey.** Large signs on the Zona Hotelera's lagoon side, roughly opposite El Pueblito hotel, point out the small Ruins of the King. First entered into Western chronicles in a 16th-century travelogue, then sighted in 1842 by American explorer John Lloyd Stephens and his drafts-man, Frederick Catherwood, the ruins were finally explored by ar-chaeologists in 1910, though excavations didn't begin until 1954. In 1975 archaeologists, along with the Mexican government, began restoration work.

Dating from the 3rd to 2nd century BC, del Rey is notable for having two main plazas bounded by two streets—most other Maya cities con-tain only one plaza. The pyramid here is topped by a platform, and in-side its vault are paintings on stucco. Skeletons interred both at the apex and at the base indicate that the site may have been a royal burial ground. Originally named Kin Ich Ahau Bonil, Maya for "king of the solar countenance," the site was linked to astronomical practices in the ancient Maya culture. If you don't have time to visit the major sites, this one will give you an idea of what the ancient cities were like. The ruins are now part of an elaborate dinner show, which you needn't attend to visit the structures. ⊠ *Blvd. Kukulcán, Km 17, Zona Hotelera* ☎ *998/ 883–2080* 🖃 *$4.50* 🕙 *Daily 8–5.*

 ❷ **Yamil Lu'um.** A small sign at the Sheraton directs you to a dirt path lead-ing to this site, which is on Cancún's highest point (the name Yamil Lu'um means "hilly land"). Although it comprises two structures—one prob-ably a temple, the other probably a lighthouse—this is the smallest of Cancún's ruins. Discovered in 1842 by John Lloyd Stephens, the ruins date from the late 13th or early 14th century. ⊠ *Blvd. Kukulcán, Km 12, Zona Hotelera* ☎ *No phone* 🖃 *Free.*

Beaches

Cancún Island is one long, continuous beach. By law the entire coast of Mexico is federal property and open to the public. In reality, security guards discourage locals from using the beaches outside hotels. Some all-inclusives distribute neon wristbands to guests; those without a wristband aren't actually prohibited from being on the beach—just from entering or exiting via the hotel. Everyone is welcome to walk along the beach, as long as you get on or off from one of the public points. Unfortunately, these points are often miles apart. One way around the situation is to find a hotel open to the public, go into the lobby bar for a drink or snack, and afterward go for a swim along the beach.

Most hotel beaches have lifeguards, but, as with all ocean swimming, use common sense—even the calmest-looking waters can have currents and riptides. Overall, the beaches on the windward stretch of the island—those facing the Bahía de Mujeres—are best for swimming; farther out, the undertow can be tricky. *Don't* swim when the red or black danger flags fly; yellow flags indicate that you should proceed with caution, and green or blue flags mean the waters are calm.

Two popular public beaches, Playa Tortugas (Km 7) and Chacmool (Km 10), have restaurants and changing areas, making them especially ap-pealing for vacationers who are staying at the beachless downtown ho-tels. Be careful of strong waves at Chacmool, where it's tempting to walk far out into the shallow water. South of Chacmool are the usually de-serted beaches of Playa Marlin or Playa Ballenas (between Km 15 and Km 16) and Playa Delfines (between Km 20 and Km 21), noted for its expansive views. Swimming can be treacherous in the rough surfs of Bal-lenas and Delfines, but the beaches are breezy, restful places for solitary sunbathing.

CloseUp

A SHORT HISTORY OF THE MAYA

THE MAYA SETTLED in the lowlands of Guatemala, Mexico, and Belize before they moved north onto the Yucatán Peninsula. That puts the height of the Classic period in the north at a time when the southern centers were being abandoned. The following divisions are commonly used by archaeologists who study the Maya.

Preclassic Period (2000BC–AD 200): At this time, farming replaced the nomadic lifestyle as the Maya adopted some of the ways of the Olmec, a more advanced culture. Monumental buildings with corbeled (false) arches and roof combs appeared, as did the first hieroglyphics and a calendar system.

Classic Period (AD 200–AD 900): The Maya eventually developed their own art, language, science, and architecture. Trade routes were established helping the economy to grow. With the cult of the ruler, government became centralized; cities began to resemble small kingdoms or city-states. A distinct class system emerged, with the wealthiest living in elaborate ceremonial sites and the peasants in the rural areas. Regents had temples and pyramids constructed to chronicle their feats in war and to honor the gods. Buildings were placed on superstructures atop stepped platforms and were often decorated with bas-reliefs and ornate frescoes. The population's growing dependence on agriculture inspired the creation of the highly accurate Maya calendar, based on planting cycles. Examples of great Classic architecture are Yaxchilán, Uxmal, and Sayil.

Postclassic Period (900–1521): Every flourishing civilization has its decline. Here, increased military activity and the growth of conquest states were the telltale signs. Powers from other Mexican cultures became part of the ruling bodies of the small sovereign states. This led to an increasingly warlike society, more elaborate temples and palaces, and a greater number of human sacrifices—especially after the Aztecs conquered the Yucatán. At the same time, the quality of Maya craftsmanship fell; for example, carved-stone building facades were replaced by carved stucco. Eventually many of the sites were abandoned. Chichén Itzá and Mayapán are representative of Postclassic architecture.

Where to Eat

Both the Zona Hotelera and El Centro have plenty of great places to eat. There are some pitfalls: restaurants that line Avenida Tulum are often noisy and crowded, gas fumes make it hard to enjoy alfresco meals, and Zona Hotelera chefs often cater to what they assume is a visitor preference for bland food. The key to eating well is to find the local haunts, most of which are in El Centro. The restaurants in the Parque de las Palapas, just off Avenida Tulum, serve expertly prepared Mexican food. Farther into the city center, you can find fresh seafood and traditional fare at dozens of small, reasonably priced restaurants in the Mercado Veintiocho.

Zona Hotelera

$$$$ ✕ **Club Grill.** The dining room is romantic and quietly elegant—with rich wood, fresh flowers, crisp linens, and courtyard views—and the classic dishes have a distinctly Mexican flavor. The sautéed foie gras with caramelized mango is a good starter, followed by the bean and lentil soup with chili habañero. The tasting menu offers a small selection of all the courses paired with wines and followed by wickedly delicious desserts. ☒ *Ritz-Carlton Cancún, Blvd. Kukulcán, Km 14 (Retorno del Rey 36), Zona Hotelera* ☎ *998/881–0808* ▤ *AE, MC, V* ☉ *No lunch.*

★ **$$$–$$$$** ✕ **Aioli.** Dining is relaxed and stylish at this restaurant, with its green-and-taupe plaids, white linens, contemporary table settings, and creative Provençal dishes. Try the duck breast in a potato *galette* (buckwheat pancake) and lavender sauce or Moroccan-style rack of lamb. Fresh fish is grilled to perfection, and the wine list is extensive. The breakfast buffet is superb. ☒ *Le Meridien, Blvd. Kukulcán, Km 14 (Retorno del Rey, Lote 37), Zona Hotelera* ☎ *998/881–2260* ▤ *AE, DC, MC, V.*

$$–$$$$ ✕ **Blue Bayou.** Mexico's first Cajun restaurant is very popular. Five levels of intimate dining areas are done in wood, rattan, and bamboo—all set against a backdrop of waterfalls and greenery. Specialties include Cancún jambalaya, blackened grouper, herb crawfish Louisiana, plantation duckling, and chicken Grand Bayou. There's live jazz nightly and dancing on weekends. ☒ *Hyatt Cancún Caribe, Blvd. Kukulcán, Km 10.5, Zona Hotelera* ☎ *998/848–7800* ⌦ *Reservations essential* ▤ *AE, DC, MC, V* ☉ *No lunch.*

$$–$$$$ ✕ **La Destileria.** Be prepared to have your perceptions of tequila changed forever. In what looks like an old-time distillery, you can sample from a list of 100 varieties—in shots or in superb margaritas. The traditional Mexican menu includes shark panuchos and *El Chiquihuite Maximiliano* (pastry filled with chicken and corn truffle). Afterward, drop by the tequila shop and pick up your favorite brand. ☒ *Blvd. Kukulcán, Km 12.65 (across from Kukulcán Plaza), Zona Hotelera* ☎ *998/885–1087* ▤ *AE, MC, V.*

$$–$$$$ ✕ **Maria Bonita.** This Mexican restaurant looks like a hacienda thanks to its color tile work, ceramics, and paintings. The glass-enclosed patio with a water view is the perfect spot to enjoy such dishes as chicken almond mole (with chocolate, almonds, and chilies). There are also Tex-Mex choices. The menu explains the different chilies used by the kitchen. ☒ *Hotel Camino Real, Punta Cancún, Blvd. Kukulcán, Km 9, Zona Hotelera* ☎ *998/848–7000* ▤ *AE, MC, V* ☉ *No lunch.*

$$–$$$ ✕ **Pacal.** Sophisticated renditions of regional Maya cuisine are served in an equally sophisticated setting of fine linen and silverware and Maya carvings and stelae. Start with the Yucatecan lime soup followed by *ya aax* (duck in a fried peanut and green tomato base). Also on the menu are the classic *cochinita pibíl* (pork baked in banana leaves) and tikinchic. ☒ *Blvd. Kukulcán, Km 8.5, next to Plaza Caracol, Zona Hotelera* ☎ *998/883–2184* ▤ *AE, MC, V.*

$–$$$ ✕ **Cenacolo.** Italian art and stained glass fill the interior of this relaxed restaurant, where musicians serenade you. Outside is a plant-filled patio overlooking Boulevard Kukulcán. The food is consistently good, especially the ricotta ravioli, the lasagna with béchamel, and the filet mignon in balsamic vinegar. The staff spoils you completely. ☒ *Kukulcán Plaza, Blvd. Kukulcán, Km 13.5, Zona Hotelera* ☎ *998/885–3603* ▤ *AE, MC, V.*

$–$$$ ✕ **Gustino Italian Beachside Grill.** You walk up a dramatic staircase to a brick and wood entrance; beyond are the open-air kitchen and the dining room with its leather furniture, sleek table settings, and artistic lighting. The black-shell mussels in a white wine sauce is a good starter followed by the pasta in sweet pepper sauce or the braised veal shank with mushroom polenta. While dining, you'll enjoy views and violin music.

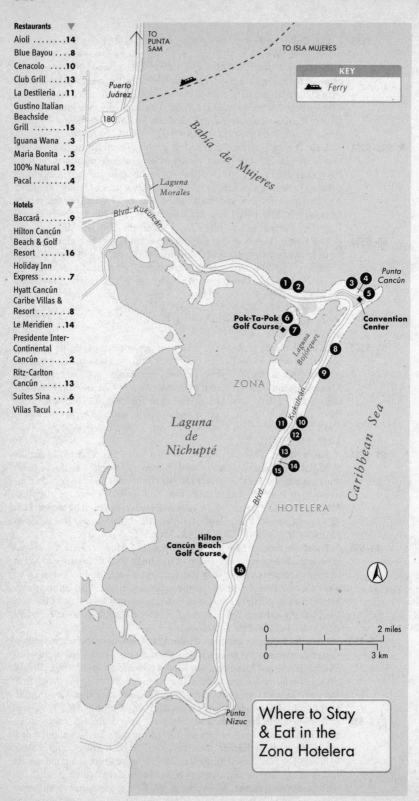

TO
PUNTA
SAM

TO ISLA MUJERES

KEY

Ferry

Puerto
Juárez

180

Bahía de Mujeres

Laguna
Morales

Blvd. Kukulcán

Punta
Cancún

Pok-Ta-Pok
Golf Course

Convention
Center

Laguna
Bojórquez

ZONA

Laguna
de
Nichupté

Kukulcán

Caribbean Sea

HOTELERA

Blvd.

Hilton
Cancún Beach
Golf Course

0   2 miles

0   3 km

Punta
Nizuc

**Where to Stay
& Eat in the
Zona Hotelera**

Reservations are recommended. ☒ *JW Marriott Resort, Blvd. Kukulcán, Km 14.5, Zona Hotelera* ☏ *998/848–9600 Ext. 6649* ▭ *AE, MC, V* ☺ *No lunch.*

$–$$$ ✕ **Iguana Wana.** Art from around Mexico fills this upbeat, contemporary café. There are extensive, inexpensive all-you-can-eat breakfast buffets along with special vegetarian and children's menus. Choose from a number of fajita or grilled dishes. There's also a tempting selection of beers and tequilas. During the day, televised sports provide the entertainment; in the evening, there's live music. ☒ *Plaza Caracol, Blvd. Kukulcán, Km 8.5, Zona Hotelera* ☏ *998/883–0829* ▭ *AE, MC, V.*

¢–$ ✕ **100% Natural.** For light, healthful fare, head to one of these cheery open-air restaurants, done up with plenty of plants and modern Maya sculptures. The menus emphasize soups, salads, fresh fruit drinks, and other nonmeat items, though egg dishes, sandwiches, grilled chicken and fish, and Mexican and Italian specialties are also available. *Zona Hotelera* ☒ *Kukulcán Shopping Plaza, Blvd. Kukulcán, Km 13.5, Zona Hotelera* ☏ *998/885–2903* ☒ *El Centro* ☒ *Av. Sunyaxchén 62, Sm 25* ☏ *998/884–3617* ▭ *MC, V.*

El Centro

★ $$–$$$$ ✕ **La Habichuela.** Elegant yet cozy, the much-loved Green Bean restaurant is full of Maya sculptures and local trees and flowers. Don't miss the famous *crema de habichuela* (a rich, cream-based seafood soup) or the *cocobichuela* (lobster and shrimp in a light curry sauce served inside a coconut). Finish off your meal with Xtabentun, a Maya liqueur made with honey and anise. ☒ *Av. Margaritas 25, Sm 22* ☏ *998/884–3158* ▭ *AE, MC, V.*

$$–$$$$ ✕ **Locanda Paolo.** Flowers and artwork lend warmth to this sophisticated restaurant, and the staff is attentive without being fussy. The cuisine is innovative southern Italian. Don't even think of passing up the black pasta in calamari sauce or the penne with basil and tomato sauce. Also delicious are the steamed lobster in garlic sauce and the lemon fish. ☒ *Av. Uxmal 35, Sm 3* ☏ *998/887–2627* ▭ *AE, DC, MC, V.*

$$–$$$$ ✕ **La Parrilla.** With its palapa-style roof and energetic waiters, this place remains a Cancún classic. Popular dishes are the mixed Mexican grill, which includes chicken, steak, shrimp, and lobster, or the grilled steak Tampiqueña style. Enjoy these and many other Mexican specialties along with a wide selection of tequila. ☒ *Av. Yaxchilán 51, Sm 22* ☏ *998/884–5398* ▭ *AE, MC, V.*

$–$$$ ✕ **El Cejas.** Although the seafood is fresh and the clientele is lively (joining in song with musicians who wander about and who expect to be paid for their tunes), this neighborhood restaurant in the Mercado Veintiocho is somewhat overrated. If you've had a wild night, try the *vuelva la vida*, or "return to life" (conch, oysters, shrimp, octopus, calamari, and fish with a hot tomato sauce). The ceviche and hot, spicy shrimp soup are both good as well, though the quality is inconsistent. ☒ *Mercado Veintiocho, Av. Sunyaxchén, Sm 26* ☏ *998/887–1080* ▭ *No credit cards.*

$–$$$ ✕ **Labná.** Regional cuisine reaches new heights when prepared by chef Carlos Hannan. Even the tortillas are different—loaded with *chaya*, which is similar to spinach. Try the savory *relleno negro* (turkey and ground pork in a dark, smoky sauce), piquant marinated octopus, or pork loin in a Coca-Cola sauce (don't knock it till you've tried it). End with *guayaba* (guava) mousse and Maya coffee made with Xtabentun. In high season, there are folkloric music and dance shows here. ☒ *Av. Margaritas 29, Sm 22* ☏ *998/892–3056* ▭ *AE, MC, V.*

$–$$$ ✕ **Sasha's Bistro.** Owner Alexander (Sasha) Rudin, a Swiss master chef, fuses Asian and European flavors to create some of the most inspired

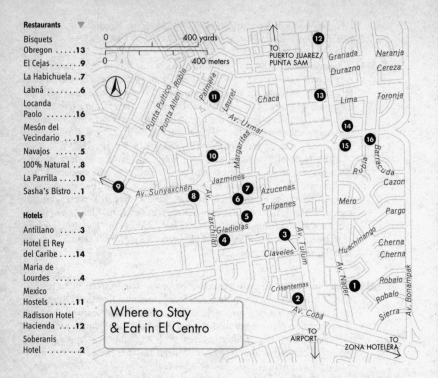

Where to Stay & Eat in El Centro

dishes along this coast—and the presentation is as artful as the food. The menu changes monthly: past masterpieces have included pork chops with a creamy porcini mushroom sauce. ✉ *Av. Nader 118, at Av. Mojarro, Sm 3* ☎ *998/887–4804 or 998/887–9105* ☰ *MC, V* ☺ *Closed Sun.–Mon. No lunch.*

$–$$ ✕ **Mesón del Vecindario.** This sweet little restaurant, tucked away from the street, resembles an A-frame house. The menu has all kinds of cheese and beef fondues along with terrific salads, fresh pasta, and baked goods. Breakfasts are hearty and economical. ✉ *Av. Uxmal 23, Sm 3* ☎ *998/884–8900* ☰ *AE, MC, V* ☺ *Closed Sun.*

$ ✕ **Navajos.** Just behind the Parque de las Palapas, this outdoor restaurant serves simple, light food. Breakfast includes yogurt, sweetbreads, and fruit plates. For lunch and dinner, choose from soups, sandwiches, and salads. There are also daily specials at great prices. As the name suggests, the surroundings are along a Native American theme. It's a great place to watch all the action. ✉ *Av. Alcatraces 18, Sm 25* ☎ *998/887–7269* ☰ *AE, MC, V.*

¢–$ ✕ **Bisquets Obregón.** With its cheery colors, two levels of tables, and sit-down luncheon counter, this cafeteria-style spot is *the* downtown place for breakfast. Begin your day with hearty Mexican classics such as huevos rancheros and *cafe con leche* (coffee with hot milk)—just watching the waiters pour it is impressive. The place opens at 7 AM. ✉ *Av. Nader 9, Sm 2* ☎ *998/887–6876* ☰ *MC, V.*

Where to Stay

For the most part El Centro hotels don't offer the same level of luxury or the same number of amenities as Zona Hotelera properties. El Centro hotels do, however, give you the opportunity to stay in a popular resort without paying resort prices, and many places have free shuttle service to the beach. El Centro hotels are also close to Ki Huic, Cancún's crafts market, and restaurants that are more authentic—and less costly—than those in the Zona.

Zona Hotelera

$$$$ 🏨 **Ritz-Carlton Cancún.** The sumptuous carpets, rich European antiques, and elegant oil paintings may cause you to forget that you're in Mexico. Rooms are done shades of teal, beige, and rose and have wall-to-wall carpeting, large balconies overlooking the Caribbean, and marble bathrooms with separate tubs and showers. In the evening enjoy fine dining at the Club Grill. ✉ *Blvd. Kukulcán, Km 14 (Retorno del Rey 36), Zona Hotelera, 77500* ☎ *998/881–0808; 800/241–3333 in the U.S.* 🖨 *998/881–0815* ⊕ *www.ritzcarlton.com* ⇨ *365 rooms, 40 suites* ♨ *3 restaurants, 3 tennis courts, pro shop, 2 pools, health club, hot tub, spa, beach, 2 bars, shops* ▭ *AE, DC, MC, V.*

$$$ 🏨 **Baccará.** Each suite in this casual boutique hotel has its own mix of Mexican art, furniture, and textiles. All units have kitchens, living and dining areas, and hot tubs that overlook the ocean or the lagoon. The lobby and beach bar are centered on an artfully designed pool area, and the building is stacked on a narrow lot, so there are lots of stairs (and no elevators). The staff is attentive. ✉ *Blvd. Kukulcán, Km 11.5, Zona Hotelera, 77500* ☎ *998/883–2077 or 888/497–4325* 🖨 *998/883–2173* ⊕ *www.avalonvacations.com* ⇨ *28 suites* ♨ *2 restaurants, in-room hot tubs, kitchens, pool, beach, 3 bars, car rental* ▭ *AE, DC, MC, V.*

$$$ 🏨 **Hilton Cancún Beach & Golf Resort.** In the guest rooms, bright yellows and greens complement terra-cotta floors and rattan furniture. All rooms have a balcony or terrace with views of the ocean and/or of the resort's championship 18-hole, par-72 golf course. Lavish, interconnected pools wind through palm-dotted lawns, ending at the magnificent beach. For total luxury consider staying at the Beach Club, with its 80 oceanfront villas. In the evening enjoy incredible Japanese fare at the romantic seaside restaurant, Mitachi. ✉ *Blvd. Kukulcán, Km 17 (Retorno Lacandones), Zona Hotelera, 77500* ☎ *998/881–8000; 800/445–8667 in the U.S.* 🖨 *998/881–8080* ⊕ *www.hilton.com* ⇨ *426 rooms, 4 suites* ♨ *2 restaurants, 18-hole golf course, 2 tennis courts, 7 pools, fitness classes, gym, hair salon, hot tubs, beach, 3 bars, lobby lounge, shops, children's programs (ages 4–12), car rental* ▭ *AE, DC, MC, V* ⧉ *CP.*

$$$ 🏨 **Hyatt Cancún Caribe Villas & Resort.** This intimate, crescent-shape resort has a white marble lobby with rattan furniture in pale colors. Oceanfront rooms are contemporary, with colorful stenciled borders, tile floors, light-wood furniture, and fabrics in dusty pinks and pale greens. Beach-level rooms have gardens. The beachfront villas are private and have kitchens and dining-living areas. Be sure to have at least one meal in the Blue Bayou restaurant. ✉ *Blvd. Kukulcán, Km 10.5, Zona Hotelera, 77500* ☎ *998/848–7800; 800/633–7313 in the U.S.* 🖨 *998/883–1514* ⊕ *www.hyatt.com* ⇨ *226 rooms, 28 villas* ♨ *3 restaurants, some kitchens, 3 tennis courts, 3 pools, hair salon, hot tubs, beach, dock, 2 bars, shop* ▭ *AE, DC, MC, V.*

★ $$$ 🏨 **Le Meridien.** High on a hill, this refined yet relaxed hotel is an artful blend of art deco and Maya styles; there's lots of wood, glass, and mirrors. Rooms have spectacular ocean views. The many thoughtful extras—such as water of a different temperature in each of the swimming pools—make a stay here special. The Spa del Mar is the area's best, with the latest European techniques and treatments and an outdoor hot tub and waterfall. The Aioli restaurant serves fabulous French food. ✉ *Blvd. Kukulcán, Km 14 (Retorno del Rey, Lote 37), Zona Hotelera, 77500* ☎ *998/881–2200; 800/543–4300 in the U.S.* 🖨 *998/881–2201* ⊕ *www.*

meridiencancun.com.mx ⟿ *187 rooms, 26 suites* ♤ *3 restaurants, 2 tennis courts, 3 pools, gym, hot tub, spa, beach, 2 bars, shops, children's programs (ages 4–12)* ⊟ *AE, MC, V.*

$$$ ☷ **Presidente Inter-Continental Cancún.** It's hard to miss the striking yellow entrance. Inside, lavish marble and Talavera pottery fill the public areas, and larger-than-average rooms have royal-blue or beige color schemes with light wicker furniture and area rugs on stone floors. Most don't have balconies; those on the first floor have patios and outdoor hot tubs. Suites have contemporary furnishings, in-room video equipment, and spacious balconies. There's a water feature in the shape of a Maya pyramid by the pool, and the beach is quiet. The Palm Restaurant serves the area's best steaks. ⊠ *Blvd. Kukulcán, Km 7.5, Zona Hotelera, 77500* ☎ *998/848–8700 or 888/567–8725* 🖷 *998/883–2602* ⊕ *www.interconti.com* ⟿ *299 rooms, 6 suites* ♤ *2 restaurants, some in-room VCRs, tennis court, 2 pools, gym, hair salon, hot tubs, beach, bar, shops* ⊟ *AE, MC, V.*

$$$ ☷ **Villas Tacul.** The villas—originally built for visiting dignitaries—are surrounded by well-trimmed lawns and well-tended gardens that lead to the beach. Each villa has a kitchen, two to five bedrooms, red-tile floors, colonial-style furniture, wagon-wheel chandeliers, and tinwork mirrors. Less expensive rooms without kitchens are also available, but they aren't nearly as pleasant. ⊠ *Blvd. Kukulcán, Km 5.5, Zona Hotelera, 77500* ☎ *998/883–0000; 800/842–0193 in the U.S.* 🖷 *998/849–7070* ⊕ *www. villastacul.com.mx* ⟿ *23 villas, 79 rooms* ♤ *Restaurant, kitchens, 2 tennis courts, pool, beach, basketball, bar* ⊟ *AE, MC, V.*

$$ ☷ **Holiday Inn Express.** Within walking distance of the Pok-Ta-Pok golf course, this hotel was built to resemble a Mexican hacienda—but with a pool instead of a courtyard at its center. Rooms have either patios or small balconies that overlook the pool and deck. All rooms are bright in blues and reds; furnishings are modern. Although not luxurious, it's perfect for families in which Dad wants to golf, Mom wants to shop, and the kids want to hit the beach. A free shuttle runs to the shops and beaches, which are five minutes away; taxis are inexpensive alternatives. ⊠ *Paseo Pok-Ta-Pok, Zona Hotelera, 77500* ☎ *998/883–2200* 🖷 *998/883–2532* ⊕ *www.sixcontinentshotels.com/h/d/EX/hd/cnnex* ⟿ *119 rooms* ♤ *Restaurant, pool* ⊟ *AE, MC, V* ⦿ *BP.*

$ ☷ **Suites Sina.** These economical suites are in front of Laguna Nichupté and close to the Pok-Ta-Pok golf course. Each unit has comfortable furniture, a kitchenette, a dining-living room with a sofa bed, a balcony or a terrace, and double beds. Outside is a central pool and garden. ⊠ *Club de Golf, Calle Quetzal 33, Zona Hotelera, 77500* ☎ *998/883–1017 or 877/666–9837* 🖷 *998/883–2459* ⟿ *33 suites* ♤ *Kitchenettes, pool* ⊟ *AE, MC, V.*

El Centro

$$ ☷ **Radisson Hotel Hacienda.** Rooms in this pink, four-story, hacienda-style building have tubs and showers, irons and ironing boards, and small tables. Most rooms overlook a large pool surrounded by tropical plants. The daily breakfast buffet is popular with locals, and there's a shuttle to the beach. At this writing, plans for a gym and in-room e-mail service were on the drawing board. ⊠ *Av. Nader 1, Sm 2, 77500* ☎ *998/ 887–4455 or 888/201–1718* 🖷 *998/884–7954* ⊕ *www.radisson.com* ⟿ *248 rooms* ♤ *2 restaurants, tennis court, pool, hair salon, 2 bars, laundry facilities, car rental, travel services* ⊟ *AE, DC, MC, V.*

$ ☷ **Antillano.** Each room is fitted with wood furnishings, one or two double beds, a sink area separate from the bath, and red-tile floors. The quietest rooms face the interior—avoid the noisier rooms overlooking Avenida Tulum. There's a cozy little lobby bar and a decent-size pool.

✉ *Av. Tulum and Calle Claveles, Sm 21, 77500* ☎ *998/884–1532* 🖨 *998/884–1878* ⊕ *www.hotelantillano.com* 🛏 *48 rooms* ⚲ *Pool, bar, shops* ☰ *AE, MC, V.*

★ $ 🏨 **Hotel El Rey del Caribe.** Thanks to the use of solar energy and to a water-recycling system and composting toilets, this hotel has very little impact on the environment. And its luxuriant garden blocks the heat and noise of downtown. Hammocks hang poolside, and wrought-iron tables and chairs dot the grounds. Rooms are small but pleasant. El Centro's shops and restaurants are within walking distance. ✉ *Av. Uxmal and Av. Nader, Sm 2, 77500* ☎ *998/884–2028* 🖨 *998/884–9857* ⊕ *www. reycaribe.com* 🛏 *25 rooms* ⚲ *Kitchenettes, pool, hot tub* ☰ *MC, V.*

$ 🏨 **Maria de Lourdes.** Although it's looking worn, this hotel has reasonable rates and a convenient location. Basic rooms are furnished with two queen-size beds. Rooms overlooking the street are noisy, but they're brighter and airier than those facing the hallways. A decent-size swimming pool is surrounded by tables, at which guests often play cards. ✉ *Av. Yaxchilán 80, Sm 22, 77500* ☎ *998/884–4744* 🖨 *998/884–1242* 🛏 *57 rooms* ⚲ *Restaurant, pool, bar, parking (fee)* ☰ *No credit cards.*

¢ 🏨 **Mexico Hostels.** Cancún's cheapest accommodation is this clean but cramped hostel four blocks from the main bus terminal. Some rooms are lined with bunk beds and share baths; others are more private. Lockers and access to a full kitchen, a lounge area, laundry facilities, and the Internet add to the value. Those who want to sleep outdoors can share a space with 20 others under a palapa roof. Note that the hostel is open 24 hours. ✉ *Calle Palmera 30 (off Av. Uxmal, beside BMW dealership), Sm 23, 77500* ☎ *998/887–0191 or 212/699–3825 Ext. 7860* 🖨 *425/962–8028* ⊕ *www.mexicohostels.com* 🛏 *64 beds* ☰ *No credit cards* ⑩ *CP.*

¢ 🏨 **Soberanis Hotel.** Rooms here are uncluttered, with modern furniture and white-tile floors. There's also a hostel section, with four bunks to a room and lockers. The neighboring cybercafé has a travel agency and bulletin board with info from other travelers. Downtown banks, shops, and restaurants are within walking distance. ✉ *Av. Cobá, Sm 22, 77500* ☎🖨 *998/884–4564* ⊕ *www.soberanis.com.mx* 🛏 *78 rooms* ⚲ *Restaurant, room service, some cable TV, meeting room, free parking* ☰ *MC, V* ⑩ *CP.*

Nightlife & the Arts

Nightlife

Many restaurants do double duty as party centers; discos have music—sometimes taped, sometimes live—and light shows; and nightclubs have live music. Sometimes the lines between the three types of establishments are blurred. There are several chain clubs, including Hard Rock, Margaritaville, and Carlos 'n Charlie's.

DISCOS Cancún wouldn't be Cancún without its glittering discos, which generally start jumping about 10:30. **La Boom** (✉ Blvd. Kukulcán, Km 3.5, Zona Hotelera ☎ 998/883–1152) is always the last place to close; it has a video bar with a light show and weekly events. The **Bull Dog Night Club** (✉ Krystal Cancún hotel, Blvd. Kukulcán, Km 9, Lote 9, Zona Hotelera ☎ 998/883–1133) has an all-you-can-drink bar, the latest dance music, and an impressive laser-light show.

Dady'O (✉ Blvd. Kukulcán, Km 9.5, Zona Hotelera ☎ 998/883–3333) has been around for a while but is still in with the younger set. Next door to Dady'O, **Dady Rock** (✉ Blvd. Kukulcán, Km 9.5, Zona Hotelera ☎ 998/883–3333) draws a high-energy crowd with live music, a giant TV, contests, and food specials. **Fat Tuesday** (✉ Blvd. Kukulcán, Km 6.5, Zona Hotelera ☎ 998/849–7199), with its large daiquiri bar and live and taped music, is a great place to dance the night away. **Ma'Ax'O** (⊠ Blvd. Kukulcán, Km 1.5, Zona Hotelera ☎ 998/883–5599), in La Isla Shopping Village, is a club-bar with the latest music and a wild dance floor.

MUSIC To mingle with locals and hear great music for free, head to the **Parque de las Palapas** (⊠ Bordered by Avs. Tulum, Yaxchilán, Uxmal, and Cobá, Sm 22) in El Centro. Every Friday night at 7:30 there's live music that ranges from jazz to salsa to Caribbean. There are often shows on Sunday, too, when families gather at the plaza.

Azucar (⊠ Hotel Camino Real, Blvd. Kukulcán, Km 9, Zona Hotelera ☎ 998/883–0100) showcases the very best Latin American bands. Go just to watch the locals dance (the beautiful people tend to turn up here really late). Proper dress is required—no jeans or sneakers. **Batacha** (⊠ Hotel Miramar Misión, Blvd. Kukulcán, Km 9.5, Zona Hotelera ☎ 998/883–1755) is a down-to-earth spot for Latin American and Mexican music. It's also a great place to practice your salsa moves. The **Blue Bayou Jazz Club** (⊠ Blvd. Kukulcán, Km 10.5, Zona Hotelera ☎ 998/883–0044) the lobby bar in the Hyatt Cancún Caribe, has nightly jazz. El Centro's classy **Roots Bar** (⊠ Av. Tulipanes 26, near Parque de las Palapas, Sm 22 ☎ 998/884–2437) is the place for jazz, fusion, flamenco, and blues.

The Arts

El Centro's **Casa de Cultura** (⊠ Av. Yaxchilán, Sm 25 ☎ 998/884–8364) hosts art exhibits, dance performances, plays, and concerts throughout the year. The **Ruinas del Rey** (⊠ Blvd. Kukulcán, Km 17, Zona Hotelera ☎ 998/883–2080) archaeological site is part of an elaborate show that includes a sound-and-light display, a tour of the ruins and a re-created Maya village, and dinner. Tickets are $60.

Every weeknight the **Teatro de Cancún** (⊠ El Embarcadero, Blvd. Kukulcán, Km 4, Zona Hotelera ☎ 998/849–4848) presents two shows: *Voces y Danzas de Mexico* (*Voices and Dances of Mexico*), a colorful showcase of popular songs and dances from different Mexican cities, and *Tradución del Caribe* (*Caribbean Tradition*), which highlights the rhythms, music, and dance of Cuba, Puerto Rico, and other Caribbean destinations. Tickets for each performance are $35. Dinner packages are also available.

Sports & the Outdoors

Boating & Sailing

There are lots of ways to get your adrenaline going on the waters off Cancún. You can arrange to go parasailing (about $35 for eight minutes), waterskiing ($70 per hour), or jet-skiing ($70 per hour, or $60 for Wave Runners). Paddleboats, kayaks, catamarans, and banana boats are readily available, too.

Aqua Fun (⊠ Blvd. Kukulcán, Km 16.5, Zona Hotelera ☎ 998/885–2930) maintains a large fleet of water toys such as Wave Runners, Jet Skis, speedboats, kayaks, and Windsurfers. **AquaWorld** (⊠ Blvd. Kukulcán, Km 15.2, Zona Hotelera ☎ 998/848–8300 ⊕ www.aquaworld.com.mx.) rents boats and water toys and offers parasailing and tours aboard a submarine. **El Embarcadero** (⊠ Blvd. Kukulcán, Km 4, Zona Hotelera ☎ 998/849–4848), the marina complex at Playa Linda, is the departure point for ferries to Isla Mujeres and some tour boats.

Golf

There's an 18-hole, championship golf course at the **Hilton Cancún Beach & Golf Resort** (⊠ Blvd. Kukulcán, Km 17, Zona Hotelera ☎ 998/881–8016).

Greens fees are $130 ($75 for hotel guests), carts included; club rentals run from $20 to $30. The main golf course is at **Pok-Ta-Pok** (✉ Blvd. Kukulcán, Km 7.5, Zona Hotelera ☎ 998/883–1230), a club with fine views of both sea and lagoon; its 18 holes were designed by Robert Trent Jones, Sr. The club also has a practice green, tennis courts, and a restaurant. Greens fees start at $120 ($85 after 3 PM), including an electric cart; and club rental is $26. Playing hours are 6 AM–dusk (last tee-off is at 4).

Fishing

Some 500 species—including sailfish, wahoo, bluefin, marlin, barracuda, and red snapper—live in the waters adjacent to Cancún. You can charter deep-sea fishing boats starting at about $350 for four hours, $450 for six hours, and $550 for eight hours. Rates generally include a captain and first mate, gear, bait, and beverages.

Aqua Tours (✉ Blvd. Kukulcán, Km 6, Zona Hotelera ☎ 998/849–4431) is one of the largest operators, with all sorts of tours and a water taxi. **Marina Punta del Este** (✉ Blvd. Kukulcán, Km 10.3, Zona Hotelera ☎ 998/883–1210) is conveniently located by the convention center. **Marina del Rey** (✉ Blvd. Kukulcán, Km 15.5, Zona Hotelera ☎ 998/885–0273) offers boat tours and has a small market and a souvenir shop. **Mundo Marino** (✉ Blvd. Kukulcán, Km 5.5, Zona Hotelera ☎ 998/883—0554) is the marina closest to downtown.

Snorkeling & Scuba Diving

The snorkeling is best at Punta Nizuc, Punta Cancún, and Playa Tortugas, although you should be careful of the strong currents at Tortugas. You can rent gear for about $10 per day from many of the scuba-diving places as well as at many hotels.

Scuba diving is popular in Cancún, though it's not as spectacular as in Cozumel. A good scuba company will give you a lot of personal attention. Smaller companies are often better at this than larger ones. Regardless, ask to meet the dive master, and check the equipment and certifications thoroughly. A few words of caution about one-hour courses that many resorts offer for free: such courses *do not* prepare you to dive in the ocean, no matter what the high-pressure concession operators tell you. If you've caught the scuba bug, prepare yourself properly by investing in several lessons.

Barracuda Marina (✉ Blvd. Kukulcán, Km 14, Zona Hotelera ☎ 998/885–3444) has a two-hour Wave Runner jungle tour through the mangroves, which ends with snorkeling at the Punta Nizuc coral reef. The fee includes snorkeling equipment, life jackets, and refreshments. **Scuba Cancún** (✉ Blvd. Kukulcán, Km 5, Zona Hotelera ☎ 998/884–2336) specializes in diving trips and offers NAUI, CMAS, and PADI instruction. It's operated by Luis Hurtado, who has more than 35 years of experience. A two-tank dive starts at $64. **Solo Buceo** (✉ Blvd. Kukulcán, Km 9, Zona Hotelera ☎ 998/848–7000) charges $60 for two-tank dives and has NAUI, SSI, and PADI instruction. The outfit goes to Cozumel, Akumal, and Isla Mujeres. Extended trips are available from $130.

Water Parks

To swim with some dolphins or feed some sharks, head over to the **Interactive Aquarium** (✉ Blvd. Kukulcán, Km 12.5, Zona Hotelera ☎ 998/883–5725), at La Isla Shopping Village. Admission is $12; shark feedings and dolphin swims cost considerably more. The $29 entrance fee to **Parque Nizuc** (✉ Blvd. Kukulcán, Km 25, Zona Hotelera ☎ 998/881–3000), a full-service marine park, also buys you admittance to the Wet 'n Wild water park and free snorkeling at the Baxal-Há snorkel area, where you can swim with gentle sharks and manta rays. There's an extra charge to swim or play with the dolphins at the Atlántida Aquarium, which is also on-site.

Shopping

There are many duty-free stores that sell designer goods at reduced prices—sometimes as much as 30% or 40% below retail. Although prices for handicrafts are higher here than in other cities and the selection is limited, you will find handwoven textiles, leather goods, and handcrafted silver jewelry.

A note of caution about tortoiseshell products: the turtles from which they're made are an endangered species, and it's illegal to bring tortoiseshell into the United States and several other countries. Simply refrain from buying anything made from tortoiseshell. Also be aware that there are some restrictions regarding black coral. You must purchase it from a recognized dealer.

Shopping hours are generally weekdays 10–1 and 4–7, although more stores are staying open throughout the day rather than closing for siesta. Many shops keep Saturday-morning hours, and some are now open on Sunday until 1. Malls tend to be open weekdays 9 AM or 10 AM to 8 PM or 9 PM.

Zona Hotelera

At the Zona'a open-air **Coral Negro** market, next to the convention center, about 50 stalls sell crafts. Everything here is overpriced, but you can bargain. The market is open daily until late in the evening.

The **Kukulcán Plaza** (✉ Blvd. Kukulcán, Km 13, Zona Hotelera ☎ 998/885–2200) is a mall that never seems to end, with around 250 shops (including branches of international chains), 12 restaurants, a bar, a liquor store, a bank, bowling lanes, and a video arcade. The plaza is also noted for the many cultural events and shows that take place in its main public area. The **Huichol Collection** (✉ Plaza Kukulcán, Blvd. Kukulcán, Km 13, Zona Hotelera ☎ 998/885–1747 ✉ Plaza Caracol, Blvd. Kukulcán, Km 8.5, Zona Hotelera ☎ 998/883–3379 ✉ La Isla Shopping Village, Blvd. Kukulcán, Km 12.5, Zona Hotelera ☎ 998/883–5540) has several locations. Each store sells beadwork and embroidery made by the Huichol Indians of the west coast. You can also watch a visiting tribe member at work.

Off Plaza Caracol is the Zona's oldest and most varied commercial center: **Mayafair Plaza** (✉ Blvd. Kukulcán, Km 8.5, Zona Hotelera ☎ 998/883–2801). It has a large open-air center lined with shops, bars, and restaurants. An adjacent indoor mall is decorated to resemble a rain forest, complete with replicas of Maya stelae. The **Museo de Arte Popular** (✉ Blvd. Kukulcán, Km 4, Zona Hotelera ☎ 998/849–4848) is by far the best place to shop for high-quality pieces. The selection changes frequently. **Renato Dorfman Gallery** (✉ La Isla Shopping Village, Blvd. Kukulcán, Km 12.5, Zona Hotelera ☎ 998/883–5573) carries Dorfman's original pieces as well as his hand-carved replicas of Maya art.

El Centro

There's a good number of shops along Avenida Tulum, between Avenida Cobá and Avenida Uxmal. **Fama** (✉ Av. Tulum 105, Sm 21 ☎ 998/884–6586) is a department store that sells clothing, English-language books and magazines, sports gear, toiletries, liquor, and *latería* (crafts made of tin). The oldest and largest of Cancún's crafts markets is **Ki Huic** (✉ Av. Tulum 17, between Bancomer and Bital banks, Sm 3 ☎ 998/884–3347). It's open daily 9 AM–10 PM and has about 100 vendors. **Ultrafemme** (✉ Av. Tulum 111, Sm 22 ☎ 998/892–0191) is a popular downtown store that carries duty-free perfume, cosmetics, and jewelry. It also has branches in the Zona Hotelera.

Cancún A to Z

To research prices, get advice from other travelers, and book travel arrangements, visit www.fodors.com.

ADDRESSES
In Cancún addresses, "Sm" stands for Super Manzana, literally a group of houses. Neighborhoods are classified with an Sm number (Sm 23, Sm 25, etc.). Each has its own park or square, with area streets fashioned around it.

AIR TRAVEL
AIRPORT The Aeropuerto Internacional Cancún is 16 km (9 mi) southwest of the heart of Cancún and 10 km (6 mi) from the Zona Hotelera's southernmost point.

🛈 **Aeropuerto Internacional Cancún** ✉ Carretera Cancún–Puerto Morelos/ Carretera Hwy. 307, Km 9.5 ☎ 998/886-0028.

AIRPORT
TRANSFERS The public-transport options are taxis or *colectivos* (vans); buses aren't allowed into the airport due to an agreement with the taxi union. A counter at the airport exit sells colectivo and taxi tickets; prices range from $15 to $40, depending on the destination. Getting back to the airport for your departure is less expensive; taxi fares range from about $15 to $22. Hotels post current rates. Be sure to agree on a price before getting into a cab.

CARRIERS Aeroméxico flies nonstop to Cancún from Los Angeles. American has nonstop service from Chicago, New York, Dallas, and Miami. Continental offers daily direct service from Houston. Mexicana's nonstop flights are from Los Angeles and Miami. From Cancún, Mexicana subsidiaries Aerocaribe and Aerocozumel fly to Cozumel, the ruins at Chichén Itzá, and Mérida and other Mexican cities. Aerocosta flies to mainland cities, ruins, and haciendas.

🛈 **Aerocaribe/Aerocozumel** ☎ 998/884-2000 El Centro; 998/886-0083 airport. **Aerocosta** ☎ 998/884-0383 El Centro. **Aeroméxico** ☎ 998/884-3571 El Centro; 998/886-0161 airport. **American** ☎ 998/883-4460 airport. **Continental** ☎ 998/886-0006 airport. **Mexicana** ☎ 998/881-9093 El Centro; 998/886-0068 airport.

BOAT & FERRY TRAVEL
From El Embarcadero on Cancún, you can take a shuttle boat to the main dock at Isla Mujeres. Ferries carry vehicles and passengers between Cancún's Punta Sam and Isla's dock, and other ferries carry passengers from Puerto Juárez. Aquabus, a Zona Hotelera water-taxi service, travels from the hotels to various restaurants and shops; a one-way fare is $3, a day pass is $15, and a week pass is $35.

🛈 **Aquabus** ☎ 998/883-3155 or 998/883-5649.

BUS TRAVEL
Frequent, reliable public buses run between the Zona Hotelera and El Centro from 6 AM to midnight; the cost is 50¢. There are designated stops—look for blue signs with white buses in the middle—but you can also flag down drivers along Boulevard Kukulcán. Take Ruta 8 (Route 8) to reach Puerto Juárez and Punta Sam for the ferries to Isla Mujeres. Take Ruta 1 (Route 1) to and from the Zona Hotelera. Ruta 1 buses will drop you off anywhere along Avenida Tulum, and you can catch a connecting bus into El Centro. Try to have the correct change and be careful of drivers trying to shortchange you. Also, hold on to the tiny

piece of paper the driver gives you. It's your receipt, and bus company officers sometimes board buses and ask for all receipts.

First- and second-class buses arrive at the downtown bus terminal from all over Mexico. ADO, and Playa Express are the main companies servicing the coast. Buses leave every 20 minutes for Puerto Morelos and Playa del Carmen. Check the schedule for departure times for Tulum, Chetumal, Cobá, Valladolid, Chichén Itzá, and Mérida.

🚍 **ADO** ☎ 998/884-5542. **Bus terminal** ✉ Av. Tulum and Av. Uxmal, Sm 23 ☎ 998/881-1378. **Playa Express** ☎ 998/884-0994.

CAR RENTAL
🚍 Major Agencies **Avis** ☎ 998/886-0221 airport. **Hertz** ☎ 998/886-0045 airport. **National** ☎ 998/886-0153 airport. **Thrifty** ☎ 998/886-0333 airport.
🚍 Local Agencies & Contacts **Car Rental Association** ☎ 998/884-2039. **Econorent** ✉ Av. Bonampak and Av. Cobá, Sm 4 ☎ 998/886-0171. **Executive** ✉ Av. Yaxchilán 160, Sm 20 ☎ 998/884-2899. **Localiza Rent a Car** ✉ Av. La Costa 128, Sm 30 ☎ 998/887-3109. **Zipp Rental Cars** ✉ Baccará Hotel, Blvd. Kukulcán, Km 11.5, Zona Hotelera ☎ 998/883-2077.

CAR TRAVEL
Driving in Cancún isn't for the faint of heart. Traffic moves at a breakneck speed; adding to the danger are the many one-way streets, *glorietas* (traffic circles), sporadically working traffic lights, ill-placed *topes* (speed bumps), numerous pedestrians, and large potholes. Be sure to observe speed limits as traffic police are vigilant and eager. In addition, car travel becomes expensive, as it entails tips for valet parking as well as gasoline and rather costly rental rates.

Although driving in Cancún isn't recommended, exploring the surrounding areas on the peninsula by car is. The roads are excellent within a 100-km (62-mi) radius. Carretera 180 runs from Matamoros at the Texas border through Campeche, Mérida, Valladolid, and into Cancún. The trip from Texas can take up to three days. Carretera 307 runs south from Cancún through Puerto Morelos, Tulum, and Chetumal, then into Belize. Carretera 307 has several Pemex stations between Cancún and Playa del Carmen. For the most part, though, you'll only find gas stations in the major cities and towns, so keep your tank full. When approaching any community, watch out for the speed bumps—hitting them at top speed can ruin your transmission and tires.

CONSULATES
🚍 **Canadian Consulate** ✉ Plaza Caracol 11, 3rd floor, Zona Hotelera ☎ 998/883-3360; 800/706-2900 emergencies **U.S. Consulate** ✉ Plaza Caracol, 3rd floor, Zona Hotelera ☎ 998/883-0272.

EMERGENCIES
🚍 Doctors & Dentists **American Medical Centre** ✉ Blvd. Kukulcán, Km 8, Zona Hotelera ☎ 998/883-1001 or 998/883-0113.
🚍 Emergency Services **Fire Department** ☎ 998/884-6133. **General Emergencies** ☎ 06. **Highway Police** ☎ 998/884-1107. **Immigration Office** ☎ 998/884-1749. **Municipal Police** ☎ 998/884-1913. **Red Cross** ✉ Av. Xcaret and Av. Labná, Sm 21 ☎ 998/884-1616. **Traffic Police** ☎ 998/884-0710.
🚍 Pharmacies **Farmacia Cancún** ✉ Av. Tulum 17, Sm 22 ☎ 998/884-1283. **Paris** ✉ Av. Yaxchilán 32, Sm 3 ☎ 998/884-3005. **Roxsanna's** ✉ Plaza Flamingo, Blvd. Kukulcán, Km 11.5, Zona Hotelera ☎ 998/885-0860.

MAIL, INTERNET & SHIPPING
The *correos* (post office) is open weekdays 8–5 and Saturday 9–1; there's also a Western Union office in the building and a courier service. Postal

service to and from Mexico is extremely slow. Avoid sending or receiving parcels—and never send checks or money through the mail. Invariably they are stolen. Your best bet for packages, money, and important letters is to use a courier service such as DHL or Federal Express.

You can receive mail at the post office if it's marked "Lista de Correos, Cancún, 77500, Quintana Roo, Mexico." If you have an American Express card, you can have mail sent to you at the American Express Cancún office for a small fee. The office is open weekdays 9–6 and Saturday 9–1. To send an e-mail or hop on-line, try Web@internet, which is downtown.

🖪 Cybercafé **Web@internet** ⊠ Av. Tulum 51 El Centro, Sm 26 ☎ 998/887-2833.
🖪 Mail Services **American Express** ⊠ Av. Tulum 208, at Calle Agua, Sm 4 ☎ 998/884-4554 or 998/884-1999. **Correos** ⊠ Av. Sunyaxchén at Av. Xel-há, Sm 26 ☎ 998/884-1418. **DHL** ⊠ Av. Tulum 200, El Centro, Sm 26 ☎ 998/887-1813. **Federal Express** ⊠ Av. Tulum 9, El Centro, Sm 22 ☎ 998/887-3279. **Western Union** ⊠ Av. Sunyaxchén at Av. Xel-há, Sm 26 ☎ 998/884-1529.

MONEY MATTERS

Banks are generally open weekdays 9 to 5; money-exchange desks have hours from 9 to 1:30. Automatic teller machines (ATMs) usually dispense Mexican money; some newer ones also dispense dollars. ATMs at the smaller banks are often out of order, and if your personal identification number has more than four digits, your card may not work. Also, don't delay in taking your card out of the machine. ATMs are quick to eat them up, and it takes a visit to the bank and a number of forms to get them back. If your transactions require a teller, arrive at the bank early to avoid long lines. Banamex and Bital both have El Centro and Zona Hotelera offices and can exchange or wire money.

🖪 Banks **Banamex** Downtown ⊠ Av. Tulum 19, next to City Hall, Sm 1 ☎ 998/884-6403 ⊠ Plaza Terramar, Blvd. Kukulcán, Km 37 Zona Hotelera ☎ 998/883-3100. **Bital** ⊠ Av. Tulum 15, Sm 4 ☎ 998/881-4103 ⊠ Plaza Caracol, Blvd. Kukulcán, Km 8.5 Zona Hotelera ☎ 998/883-4652.

TAXIS

Taxi rides within the Zona Hotelera cost $5–$7; between the Zona Hotelera and El Centro, they run $8 and up; and to the ferries at Punta Sam or Puerto Juárez, fares are $15–$20 or more. Prices depend on distance, your negotiating skills, and whether you pick up the taxi in front of a hotel or save a few dollars by going onto the avenue to hail one yourself (look for green city cabs). Most hotels list rates at the door; confirm the price with your driver *before* you set out. If you lose something in a taxi or have questions or a complaint, call the Sindicato de Taxistas. Some drivers ask for such outrageously high fares it's not worth trying to bargain with them. Just flag down another cab.

🖪 **Sindicato de Taxistas** ☎ 998/888-6985.

TOURS

BOAT TOURS Day cruises to Isla Mujeres generally include snorkeling, shopping, and lunch. Caribbean Carnaval runs a nightly cruise with music and dinner for $60. Capitán Hook runs a nighttime cruise around the bay with lobster or steak dinner and pirate show; it costs $60 or $70, depending on your dinner choice. Dolphin Discovery sails daily from Playas Langosta and Tortugas to the company's dock on Isla Mujeres; its program includes an instruction video, a 30-minute swim session with the dolphins, and time to explore the island. Tickets start at $75.

🖪 **Capitán Hook** ⊠ Playa Langosta, Blvd. Kukulcán, Km 3, Zona Hotelera ☎ 998/849-4452. **Caribbean Carnaval** ⊠ Fat Tuesday, Blvd. Kukulcán, Km 6.5, Zona Hotelera

☎ 998/884-3760. **Dolphin Discovery** ✉ Playa Langosta, Local 16, Blvd. Kukulcán, Km 3, Zona Hotelera ☎ 998/849-4748 or 998/883-0780.

ECOTOURS The 500,000-acre Reserva Ecológica El Edén, 48 km (30 mi) northwest of Cancún, was established by one of Mexico's leading naturalists, Arturo Gómez-Pompa, and his nephew, Marco Lazcano-Barrero, and is dedicated to research and conservation. It offers excursions for people interested in exploring wetlands, mangrove swamps, sand dunes, savannas, and tropical forests. Themes include bird-watching, animal-tracking, stargazing, and archaeology. Rates are based on activities and the number of nights you stay at the station.

Eco Colors runs adventure tours to the wildlife reserves at Isla Holbox and Sian Ka'an, and to remote ruins on the peninsula. It also offers bird-watching, kayaking, camping, and biking excursions around the peninsula.
🧭 **Eco Colors** ✉ Retorno Camarón 32, Sm 27 ☎ 998/884-9580 ⊕ www.ecotravelmexico.com. **Reserva Ecológica El Edén** ⌖ Box 770, 77500 Cancún, Quintana Roo ☎ 998/880-5032 ⊕ www.ucr.edu/pril/peten/images/el_eden/Home.html.

TRAVEL AGENCIES
🧭 Local Agent Referrals **Travel Agency Association** ✉ Plaza México, Av. Tulum 200, Suite 301, Sm 5 ☎ 998/887-1670 🖷 998/884-3738.
🧭 Local Agents **Intermar Caribe** ✉ Av. Tulum at Av. Cobá, Sm 4 ☎ 998/884-4266. **Mayaland Tours** ✉ Av. Robalo 30, Sm 3 ☎ 998/987-2450. **Olympus Tours** ✉ Av. Bonampak 107, Sm 3 ☎ 998/881-9030.

VISITOR INFORMATION
🧭 **Cancún Visitors and Convention Bureau Visitor** ✉ Av. Nader at Av. Cobá, Sm 5 ☎ 998/884-6531 ⊕ www.ovccancun.org. **Quintana Roo State Tourism Office** ✉ Calle Pecari 23, Sm 20 ☎ 998/881-9000.

ISLA MUJERES

Updated by
Maribeth
Mellin

No one is sure who named Isla Mujeres (Island of Women). Many believe it was the ancient Maya, who used the island as a religious center for worshiping Ixchel (ee-*shell*), the Maya goddess of rainbows, the moon, and the sea, and the guardian of fertility and childbirth. Another popular legend has it that the conquistador Hernández de Córdoba named the island when he landed here in 1517 and found hundreds of female-shape clay idols dedicated to Ixchel and her daughters. Others say the name dates from the 17th century, when Isla was a haven for buccaneers and smugglers who stashed their women here before heading out to rob the high seas.

In the 1950s this quiet island became a favorite vacation spot for Mexicans. American hippies and backpackers discovered it in the 1960s. By the late 1970s, day-trippers were streaming off the ferries for quick lunches followed by frenzied shopping. And as Cancún—a mere 8 km (5 mi) away—grew so did Isla.

Although Isla is being developed, it's still a peaceful retreat with its own local history and culture centered on the sea. And it continues to be a favorite of people who prefer such seaside pleasures as scuba diving, snorkeling, and relaxing on the beach to spending time in fast-paced Cancún.

Exploring

Only about 8 km (5 mi) long by 1 km (½ mi) wide, Isla has flat, sandy beaches on its northern end and steep, rocky bluffs to the south. To get your bearings, think of the island as an elongated fish, the head being the southeastern tip, the northwest prong the tail. The minute you step off the boat, you'll see how small Isla is. Directly in front of the ferry piers is the island's only town, known simply as El Pueblo. It extends the full width of Isla's northern "tail" and is sandwiched between sand and sea to the south, west, and northeast, with no high-rises to block the view.

a good tour

You can explore the entire island by taxi, moped, or golf cart. You can walk to Isla's historic **Cementerio** ⑥ ► by going northwest from the ferry piers on Avenida López Mateos. Then head southeast (by car or other vehicle) along Avenida Rueda Medina past the piers to reach the Mexican naval base, where you can see the flag ceremonies at sunrise and sunset. Just don't take any photos—it's illegal to photograph any military sites in Mexico. Continue southeast out of town; 2½ km (1½ mi) farther down the road is **Laguna Makax** ⑦, on the right.

At the lagoon's southeast end, a dirt road to the left leads to the remains of the **Hacienda Mundaca** ⑧. About a block southeast of here, turn right off the main road at the sign that says SAC BAJO to a smaller, unmarked side road, which loops back northwest. Approximately ½ km (¼ mi) farther up on the left is the entrance to the **Tortugranja** ⑨.

Return to Avenida Rueda Medina and continue southeast past Playa Lancheros to **El Garrafón National Park** ⑩. Slightly more than ½ km (¼ mi) farther along the same road, on the windward side of the tip of Isla Mujeres, sit the remains of a small Maya ruin dedicated to Ixchel, the Santuario Maya a la Diosa Ixchel. Follow the paved eastern perimeter road northwest back into town. Known as the Corredor Panorámico (Panoramic Highway), this is a beautiful, scenic drive with a few pull-off areas along the way, perfect for a secluded picnic. Swimming isn't recommended along this coast because of the strong currents and rocky shore.

What to See

► ⑥ **El Cementerio.** Isla's unnamed cemetery, with its century-old headstones, is on Avenida López Mateos, the road that runs parallel to Playa Norte. It's filled with carved angels and flowers; the most beautiful of the decorated graves are those in memory of children. Hidden among them is the tomb of the notorious Fermín Mundaca de Marechaja. This 19th-century slave trader—who's often billed more glamorously as a pirate—carved his own skull-and-crossbones tombstone with the ominous epitaph: AS YOU ARE, I ONCE WAS; AS I AM, SO SHALL YOU BE. Mundaca's grave is empty, however; his remains lie in Mérida, where he died. The monument isn't easy to find—ask a local to point it out.

⑩ **El Garrafón National Park.** Much of the coral reef at this national marine park has died—a result of too many snorkelers—and so the fish have to be bribed with food. The park does have kayaks and a three-floor facility with restaurants and gift shops. Despite these efforts to keep you entertained, bring a book if you intend to spend the day, and try to claim one of the hammocks under the palms on the lawn. Marine-park tickets are available at the park entrance and at kiosks in Cancún and Playa del Carmen. (Note that the Garrafón Beach Club, next door, is a much less expensive alternative, and the snorkeling is equal to if not better than that in the park.)

The sad vestiges of the **Santuario Maya a la Diosa Ixchel** (Sanctuary of the Goddess Ixchel) are part of El Garrafón, on the tip of the island and at the point where the road turns northeast into the Corredor Panorámico. Though Hurricane Gilbert blew most of the temple away in 1988, part of it has been restored, and the walkway to it is lined with sculptures.

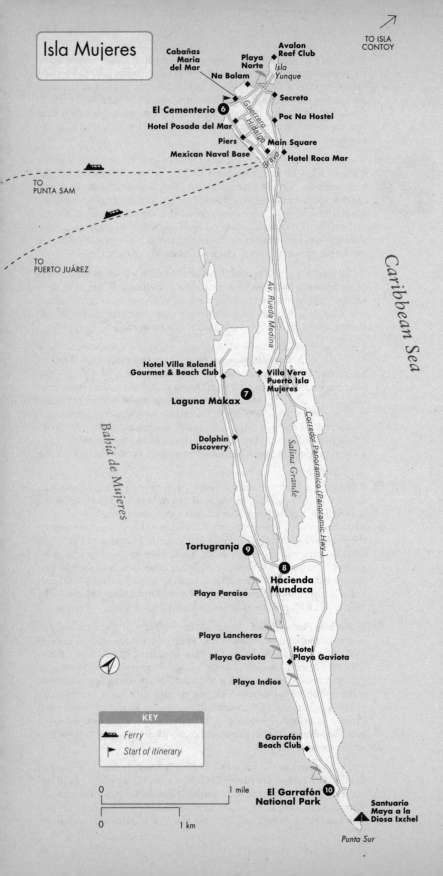

Isla Mujeres

TO ISLA
CONTOY

Cabañas
Maria
del Mar

Playa
Norte

Avalon
Reef Club

Na Balam

*Isla
Yunque*

El Cementerio ⑥

Secreto

Poc Na Hostel

Hotel Posada del Mar

Guerrero Hidalgo

Piers

Main Square

Mexican Naval Base

Bravo

Hotel Roca Mar

TO
PUNTA SAM

TO
PUERTO JUÁREZ

Caribbean Sea

Av. Rueda Medina

Hotel Villa Rolandi
Gourmet & Beach Club

Villa Vera
Puerto Isla
Mujeres

Laguna Makax ⑦

Bahía de Mujeres

Dolphin
Discovery

Salina Grande

Corredor Panorámico (Panoramic Hwy.)

Tortugranja ⑨

⑧
**Hacienda
Mundaca**

Playa Paraíso

Playa Lancheros

Playa Gaviota

Hotel
Playa Gaviota

Playa Indios

Garrafón
Beach Club

KEY

🚢 *Ferry*

▶ *Start of itinerary*

0   1 mile

0   1 km

**El Garrafón
National Park** ⑩

Santuario
Maya a la
Diosa Ixchel

Punta Sur

The fee to enter the site is $5. The view from here, of the open ocean on one side and the Bahía de Mujeres (Bay of Women) on the other, is spectacular. ⊠ *Carretera El Garrafón, 2½ km (1½ mi) southeast of Playa Lancheros* ☎ *998/884–9420 in Cancún; 998/877–1100 at the park* ⊕ *www.garrafon.com* ☒ *$23* ⊙ *Daily 9–5:30.*

❽ Hacienda Mundaca. A dirt drive and a stone arch mark the entrance to what's left of the mansion that 19th-century slave trader–cum–pirate Fermín Mundaca de Marechaja built. When the British navy began cracking down on slavers, Mundaca settled on the island. He fell in love with a local beauty nicknamed La Trigueña (The Brunette). To woo her, Mundaca built a sprawling estate. Unimpressed, La Trigueña married a young islander—and Mundaca went mad waiting for her to change her mind. He died in a Mérida brothel.

There's little to see of the actual hacienda; all that remains are a small crumbling guardhouse, a rusted cannon, an arch, and a well. Note the arch's triangular pediment, in which is carved the following: HUERTA DE LA HACIENDA DE VISTA ALEGRE MDCCCLXXVI (Orchard of the Happy View Hacienda 1876). The gardens are lush and well kept, and there's a small zoo with a jaguar, spider monkeys, and various reptiles. ⊠ *East of Av. Rueda Medina (take main road southeast from town to S-curve at end of Laguna Makax and turn left onto dirt road)* ☎ *No phone* ☒ *$1.50* ⊙ *Daily 9 AM–dusk.*

❼ Laguna Makax. Pirates are said to have anchored their ships in this lagoon as they waited for hapless vessels plying the Spanish Main (the geographical area in which Spanish treasure ships trafficked). These days the lagoon is the site of a shipyard and is considered a safe harbor during hurricane season. It's off of Avenida Rueda Medina about 2½ km (1½ mi) south of town, across the street from a Mexican naval base and some *salinas* (salt marshes).

❾ Tortugranja. Run by an outfit called Eco Caribe, this facility is dedicated to the study and preservation of sea turtles. From May through September upward of 6,000 of them hatch along the coast of Quintana Roo. Some are brought here to be raised until they're large enough to survive at sea. You can view hatchlings and young turtles of various species, go on a biologist-led tour, and watch feedings. A small but well-designed museum explains the various stages of turtle life and different parts of the coral reef. ⊠ *Take Av. Rueda Medina south of town; about a block southeast of Hacienda Mundaca, take the right fork (the smaller road that loops back north); the entrance is about ½ km (¼ mi) farther, on the left* ☎ *998/877–0595* ☒ *$2* ⊙ *Daily 9–5.*

Beaches

The superb Playa Norte, known for its congenial atmosphere, is easy to find: simply head north on any of the north–south streets in town until you hit it. The turquoise sea is as calm as a lake, and you can wade out for 40 yards in waist-deep water. There are several beaches between Laguna Makax and El Garrafón National Park. Playa Paraíso is a good spot for having lunch or for shopping at the small stands that sell local handicrafts, souvenirs, and T-shirts. Pet sea turtles and harmless *tiburones gatos* (nurse sharks) are housed in sea pens at Playa Lancheros. You can have your picture taken with one of the sharks. (These sharks are tamer than the *tintoreras,* or blue sharks, which live in the open seas. They have seven rows of teeth and weigh up to 1,100 pounds.) Playa Gaviota, near the hotel of the same name, is a good place for a swim. You may find that you have the calm Playa Indios all to yourself.

Where to Eat

$$–$$$$ ✕ **Casa Rolandi.** Of the many delicious items on the Swiss–northern Italian menu, the carpaccio *di tonno alla Giorgio* (thin slices of tuna with extra-virgin olive oil and lime juice) is particularly good, as are the pastas—including lasagna and shrimp-filled black ravioli. The restaurant is part of the part of the Rolandi family of restaurants and is in the Hotel Villa Rolandi lobby. It extends out to an open-air deck over the beach; the sunset views are spectacular. ⊠ *Hotel Villa Rolandi Gourmet & Beach Club, Fracc. Laguna Mar Makax, Sm 7* ☎ *998/877–0100* ⊟ *AE, MC, V.*

★ $–$$$ ✕ **Casa O's.** The entrance to this casual yet stylish restaurant crosses a small stream on landscaped grounds. Tables face the sea and the sunset over Cancún. The lobster is excellent, as is all the fresh seafood; the Black Angus steaks cure any beef cravings. A perfect meal might include lobster bisque, shrimp kabobs, and key lime pie. The waiters' names all end in the letter "o." ⊠ *Carretera Garrafón s/n* ☎ *998/888–0170* ⊟ *MC, V.*

$–$$$ ✕ **Velazquez.** This family-owned restaurant on the beach is open until dusk and serves the island's freshest seafood. You haven't eaten Yucatecan until you've tried the regional specialty tikinchic. Feasting on a fantastic fish meal while you sit outside and watch the boats go by is the true Isla experience. ⊠ *Av. Rueda Medina, 2 blocks northwest of ferry docks* ☎ *No phone* ⊟ *No credit cards.*

$–$$ ✕ **Pizza Rolandi.** Nearly everyone stops here for a meal while on the island. The wood-oven-baked pizzas and calzones are legendary, and you can also get roasted chicken. Don't miss the homemade ice cream. ⊠ *Av. Hidalgo 110* ☎ *998/877–0430* ⊟ *MC, V.*

¢–$ ✕ **Café Cito.** The bright blue-and-white Cito has shells decorating its tabletops, simple watercolors on its walls, and wind chimes dangling from its rafters. Breakfast choices include fresh waffles, fruit-filled crepes, and egg dishes, as well as great cappuccino and espresso. For lunch the chef whips up different daily specials. You can join the island's Harley Davidson Club here, or visit Sabrina next door for a tarot reading. ⊠ *Av. Juárez and Av. Matamoros* ☎ *998/877–0438* ⊟ *No credit cards.*

¢–$ ✕ **Taquería.** For an inexpensive and delicious meal of Yucatecan specialties—*sabutes* (fried corn tortillas smothered in chicken and salsa), *tortas* (sandwiches), panuchos, tamales—check out this small hole-in-the-wall, open daily 10–10. The two sisters who do the cooking are a treat. They don't speak English but communicate with you using sign language and their version of Spanglish. ⊠ *Av. Juárez, 1 block south of cemetery* ☎ *No phone* ⊟ *No credit cards.*

Where to Stay

In general the older, more modest hotels are in town, and the newer, more expensive resorts front the beach around Punta Norte or the peninsula near the lagoon. Local travel agents can provide information about self-contained time-share condominiums, which are another option.

$$$$ ▦ **Avalon Reef Club.** This gorgeous all-inclusive is on a tiny island at the northern tip of Isla Mujeres. Regular rooms in the hotel tower are small and don't have balconies, but the suites and seaside villas are spectacular, with terraces and balconies that afford extraordinary views of the water and of town. The hotel has a fast shuttle boat from its dock to Cancún's El Embarcadero marina complex, and you have use of the facilities at the sister property, the Avalon Grand, in Cancún. (Note that the sales pitch to buy a vacation home here can be intense.) ⊠ *Calle Zacil-Ha s/n, Isla Yunque, 77400* ☎ *998/999–2050 or 888/497–4325*

☎ 998/999–2052 ⊕ *www.avaonresorts.net* ⇆ *83 rooms, 6 suites, 55 villas ☼ Restaurant, some in-room hot tubs, some kitchenettes, pool, gym, beach, car rental ▭ AE, MC, V ⍾ All-inclusive.*

★ **$$$$** ⊞ **Hotel Villa Rolandi Gourmet & Beach Club.** A private yacht delivers you to this property and its elegant, brightly colored suites. Each has an ocean view, a king-size bed, and a sitting area that leads to the balcony with a heated whirlpool bath. The shower has *six* adjustable heads and can be converted into a sauna. Both the Casa Rolandi restaurant and the garden pool overlook the Bahía de Mujeres; a path leads down to an intimate beach. ⊠ *Fracc. Laguna Mar Makax, 77400* ☎ *998/877– 0700 or 998/877–0500* ☎ *998/877–0100* ⊕ *www.rolandi.com* ⇆ *20 suites ☼ Restaurant, in-room hot tubs, pool, gym, spa, beach, dock, boating; no kids under 13, no smoking ▭ AE, MC, V ⍾ MAP.*

$$$$ ⊞ **Villa Vera Puerto Isla Mujeres.** When you stay at this small property favored by yachties, you feel as if you've found a secret hideaway. Guest quarters are large and have light woods, rose and blue fabrics, and cozy seating areas. A large lawn separates the rooms from the pool and lagoon, and a shuttle boat ferries you to the hotel's beach club, which faces Cancún. ⊠ *Puerto de Abrigo, Laguna Makax 77400* ☎ *800/508–7923 in the U.S.* ⊕ *www.mexicoboutiquehotels.com/islamujeres* ⇆ *17 suites, 4 villas ☼ Restaurant, in-room hot tubs, some kitchenettes, 3 pools, beach, marina ▭ AE, MC, V ⍾ CP.*

$$$ ⊞ **Na Balam.** Each room in the main building of this intimate Playa Norte hotel has a thatched roof, Mexican folk art or photographs, an eating area, a large bathroom, and either a patio or balcony facing the ocean. Across the street are eight more spacious rooms. There's also a swimming pool, a garden, a meditation room (you can take yoga classes), and a TV lounge. Breakfast at the restaurant is a delightful. ⊠ *Calle Zacil-Ha 118, 77400* ☎ *998/877–0279* ☎ *998/877–0446* ⊕ *www.nabalam.com* ⇆ *31 rooms ☼ Restaurant, pool, beach, bar ▭ AE, MC, V.*

★ **$$$** ⊞ **Secreto.** Chic and sleek, this boutique hotel is on a secluded beach a short walk from town. Rooms are minimalist, with stark white walls, beds draped in white net canopies, and large outdoor living areas with cushioned chairs. ⊠ *Seccion Rocas, Lote 11, Punta Norte, 77400* ☎ *998/877–1039* ☎ *998/877–1048* ⊕ *www.hotelsecreto.com* ⇆ *9 rooms ☼ In-room safes, minibars, refrigerators, pool, beach; no smoking ▭ MC, V ⍾ CP.*

$$ ⊞ **Cabañas Maria del Mar.** One of the first hotels on Playa Norte, this complex has rooms on the sand in the three-story Tower, rooms in thatch-roof cabañas by the pool, and rooms in the three-story Castle facing the street and the restaurant. Each type of accommodation has its merits; ask to see a few or ask a lot of questions about room features and amenities when making reservations. The restaurant-bar, Buho's, is a local favorite for drinks and moderately priced meals. The hotel rents mopeds and golf carts. ⊠ *Av. Arq. Carloso Lazo 1, 77400* ☎ *998/877– 0179* ☎ *998/877–0213* ⊕ *www.cabanasdelmar.com* ⇆ *24 Tower rooms, 31 cabaña rooms, 18 Castle rooms ☼ Restaurant, refrigerators, 2 pools, beach, video game room ▭ MC, V ⍾ CP.*

$–$$ ⊞ **Hotel Roca Mar.** At one of the few downtown hotels overlooking the water, you can see, smell, and hear the ocean from your guest quarters. Each room has a balcony, wooden slats on its windows, and simple furnishings. The courtyard—filled with plants, birds, and benches—overlooks the ocean, too. ⊠ *Calle Nicolas Bravo, Zona Maritima, 77400* ☎ *998/877–0101* ⊕ *www.mjmnet.net/HotelRocaMar/home.htm* ⇆ *31 rooms ☼ Restaurant, fans, pool, beach, snorkeling; no a/c in some rooms, no room phones, no room TVs ▭ AE, MC, V.*

$ ⊡ **Hotel Posada del Mar.** Rooms in this venerable budget hotel are fresh and clean. Stone archways by the pool frame the water and gardens. The restaurant faces Playa Norte, which is across the street, and shops and other restaurants are only a short walk away. ⊠ *Av. Rueda Medina 15-A, 77400* ☎ *998/877–0770* 🖷 *998/877–0266* ⊕ *www. posadadelmar.com* ⤺ *42 rooms* ♢ *Restaurant, pool* ☰ *AE, MC, V.*

$ ⊡ **Playa Gaviota.** The real plus at this hilltop hotel is the beach with its barbecue area, palapas, and gorgeous sunset views. Each of the suites has a blue-and-white color scheme, a kitchenette, two queen-size beds, a small eating area, and a large terrace facing the ocean. There are also smaller, older (but still comfortable) cabins on the beach. The owners, a quiet Mexican family, live on-site. ⊠ *Carretera El Garrafón, Km 4.5, 77400* ☎🖷 *998/877–0216* ⊕ *www.lostoasis.net* ⤺ *10 suites, 3 cabins* ♢ *Fans, kitchenettes, beach; no room phones* ☰ *No credit cards.*

Nightlife

Plaza Isla Mujeres at Avenidas Hidalgo and Guerrero has become the official nightlife spot, with a number of bars and restaurants open until the wee hours. **Buho's** (⊠ Cabañas María del Mar, Av. Arq. Carlos Lazo 1 ☎ 998/877–0179) remains the favorite restaurant on Playa Norte for a relaxing sunset drink. There's a small bar and a large television at **Chiles Loco** (⊠ Plaza Isla Mujeres, Av. Hidalgo 81, Local A-4 ☎ no phone).

Sports & the Outdoors

Boating

Puerto Isla Mujeres (⊠ Puerto de Abrigo, Laguna Makax ☎ 998/877–0330 ⊕ www.puerto-isla.com) is a full-service marina for vessels up to 170 ft. Services include mooring, a fuel station, a 150-ton lift, customs assistance, hookups, 24-hour security, laundry and cleaning services, and boatyard services. If you need to sleep over on land, the Villa Vera resort is steps away from the docks.

Fishing

The **Red Cross Billfish Tournament** (☎🖷 998/877–0443 ⊕ www.mjmnet. net/redcross/fishing.htm) is held in April.

Captain Anthony Mendillo Jr. (⊠ Av. Arq. Carlos Lazo 1 ☎ 998/877–0213) offers specialized fishing trips aboard his 29-ft vessel, the *Keen M.* **Sea Hawk Divers** (⊠ Av. Arq. Carlos Lazo ☎ 998/877–0296) runs fishing trips—for barracuda, snapper, and smaller fish—that start at $200 for a half day. The **Sociedad Cooperativa Turistica** (☎ 998/877–0239) offers four hours of fishing close to shore for $100; eight hours farther out is $240.

Snorkeling & Scuba Diving

DIVE SITES The coral reefs at El Garrafón National Park have suffered tremendously because of human negligence, boats' dropping anchors (now outlawed), and the effects of Hurricane Gilbert in 1988. Some good snorkeling can be had near Playa Norte on the north end.

Isla is a good place to learn how to dive, since the snorkeling is close to shore. Offshore, there's excellent diving and snorkeling at Xlaches (pronounced *ees-lah-chayss*) reef, due north on the way to Isla Contoy. One of Contoy's most alluring dives is the Cave of the Sleeping Sharks, east of the northern tip. The caves were discovered by an island fisherman known as Vulvula and extensively explored by Ramon Bravo, a local diver, cinematographer, and Mexico's foremost expert on sharks. It's a fascinating 150-ft dive for experienced divers only.

SHHH . . . DON'T WAKE THE SHARKS

THE UNDERWATER CAVERNS off Isla Mujeres attract a dangerous species of shark—though nobody knows exactly why. Stranger still, once the sharks swim into the caves they enter a state of relaxed nonaggression seen nowhere else. Naturalists have two explanations, both involving the composition of the water inside the caves—it contains more oxygen, more carbon dioxide, and less salt. According to the first theory, the decreased salinity causes the parasites that plague sharks to loosen their grip, which allows the remora fish (the sharks' personal vacuum cleaner) to eat the parasites more easily. Perhaps the sharks relax in order to facilitate the cleaning, or maybe their deep state of relaxation is a side effect of having been scrubbed clean.

Another theory is that the caves' combination of fresh- and saltwater may produce a euphoric feeling in the sharks, similar to the effect scuba divers experience on extremely deep dives (most divers call the feeling "getting narc'd"). Whatever the sharks experience while "sleeping" in the caves, they pay a heavy price for it: A swimming shark breathes automatically and without effort (water is forced through the gills as the shark swims), but a stationary shark must laboriously pump water to continue breathing. If you dive in the caves of the sleeping sharks, be cautious: Many of the creatures are reef sharks, the species responsible for the largest number of attacks on humans. Dive with a reliable guide and be on your best diving behavior.

At 30 ft–40 ft deep and 3,300 ft off the southwestern coast, the coral reef known as Los Manchones is a good dive site. During the summer of 1994, an ecology group hoping to divert divers and snorkelers from El Garrafón commissioned the creation of a 1-ton, 9¾-ft bronze cross, which was sunk here. Named the Cruz de la Bahía (Cross of the Bay), it's a tribute to all the people who have died at sea. Most area dive spots are also described in detail in Dive Mexico, a colorful magazine readily available in local shops.

DIVE SHOPS The PADI-affiliated **Coral Scuba Dive Center** (⊠ Av. Matamoros 13-A ☎ 998/877–0763) offers two-tank dives ($60), shipwreck dives, and snorkel trips. **Mundaca Divers** (⊠ Av. Francisco Madero 10 ☎ 998/877–0607) has a good reputation with professional divers and a PADI instructor. A two-tank dive costs $60. **Sea Hawk Divers** (⊠ Av. Arq. Carlos Lazo ☎ 998/877–0296) runs dive ($55 for two tanks) and snorkel trips, has a PADI instructor, and will also set up accommodations for divers in pleasant rooms starting at $45 per day during low season, $65 during high.

Water Park
Dolphin Discovery (⊠ Fracc. Laguna Mar Makax, ☎ 998/849–4757) offers humans the chance to play with the delightful sea mammals in a small, supervised group in a pool. There are four dolphin swims daily, at 10, 12, 2, and 3:30. Dolphin encounters (not in the water) are daily at 10, 11:30, 1, 2, and 3:30. The cost of the swim is $119 and the encounter is $64.

Shopping

Shopping on Isla Mujeres is a mixture of stores selling T-shirts, suntan lotion, beer, and groceries and those that sell Mexican silver jewelry, folk art, textiles, and clothes. Most shops accept credit cards. Hours are generally Monday–Saturday 10–1 and 4–7, although many stores stay open during siesta hours (1–4).

Artesanías El Nopal (✉ Av. Guerrero at Av. Matamoros ☎ 998/877–0555) has an excellent selection of fine Mexican handicrafts from across the country—all hand-picked by the owner. Local artists display and sell their works at the public **Mercado de Artesanías** (✉ Av. Matamoros and Av. Arq. Carlos Lazo ☎ No phone); there are plenty of bargains.

Isla Mujeres A to Z

To research prices, get advice from other travelers, and book travel arrangements, visit www.fodors.com.

BIKE, MOPED & GOLF CART TRAVEL

You can rent bicycles on Isla, but keep in mind that it's very hot here and the road conditions aren't great (so many unexpected speed bumps). Don't ride at night; many roads don't have streetlights, so drivers have a hard time seeing you. Most moped rental places carry bicycles starting at about $5.50 an hour.

Mopeds are the most popular mode of transportation. Most rental places charge $22–$27 a day, or $5.50–$11 per hour, depending on the make and year. Many places also rent golf carts, a fun way to get around the island, especially when traveling with children. Ciro's Motorent and P'pe's Rentadora have rates as low as $40 for 24 hours. Although motorists are generally accommodating, be prepared to move to the side of the road to let vehicles pass.

🚩 **Ciro's Motorent** ✉ Av. Guerrero Nte. 11, at Av. Matamoros ☎ 998/877–0578. **El Sol** ✉ Av. Francisco Madero 5 ☎ 998/877–0068. **P'pe's Rentadora** ✉ Av. Hidalgo 19 ☎ 998/877–0019.

BOAT & FERRY TRAVEL

Speedboats and passenger ferries run between the main dock on Isla and Puerto Juárez on the mainland. They leave every 30 or 60 minutes from 6:30 AM to 11 PM. That said, always check the times posted at the dock as schedules are subject to change, depending on the season and weather conditions. A one-way ferry ticket is about $1.80, and the trip takes at least 45 minutes. Delays and crowding aren't unknown, but there's often live music on board, which makes the trips festive. The speedboats *Miss Valentina* and *Caribbean Lady* are air-conditioned cruisers with bar service. A one-way ticket costs $4, and the crossing takes about 30 minutes.

Fast, expensive shuttles to Isla's main dock leave from El Embarcadero marina complex in Cancún's Zona Hotelera. The cost is between $10 and $15 round-trip, and the voyage takes approximately 30 minutes.

Municipal ferries carry vehicles (although you don't really need a car on Isla) and passengers between Isla's dock and Punta Sam, north of Cancún. The ride takes about 45 minutes, and the fare is $1.35 per person and about $12–$17 per vehicle, depending on the size of your car. The ferry runs four times a day.

🚩 **Isla Ferry office** ☎ 998/877–0065. **Isla Shuttle service** ☎ 998/883–3448.

BUS TRAVEL

Municipal buses run at 20- to 30-minute intervals daily between 6 AM and 10 PM, generally following the ferry schedule. The route goes from the Posada del Mar hotel on Avenida Rueda Medina out to Colonia Salinas on the windward side. Service is slow because the buses make frequent stops. Fares are about 55¢.

🚍 **Municipal buses** ☎ 998/877-0307 on Isla; 998/884-5542 in Cancún.

CAR TRAVEL

There aren't any car rental agencies on the island, and there's little reason to bring a car here. Taxis are inexpensive, and the island is small, making bikes, mopeds, and golf carts good ways to get around.

EMERGENCIES

🚑 **Centro de Salud** (Health Center) ✉ Av. Guerrero 5, on the plaza ☎ 998/877-0001. **Police** ☎ 998/877-0082. **Port Captain** ☎ 998/877-0095. **Red Cross Clinic** ✉ Colonia La Gloria, south side of island ☎ 998/877-0280 ⊕ www.mjmnet.net/redcross/home.htm. 🚑 Late-Night Pharmacies **Farmacia Isla Mujeres** ✉ Av. Juárez 8 ☎ 998/877-0178. **Farmacia Lily** ✉ Av. Francisco Madero 17 ☎ 998/877-0116.

MAIL, INTERNET & SHIPPING

The correos is open weekdays 8–7 and Saturday 9–1. You can have mail for you sent to "Lista de Correos, Isla Mujeres, Quintana Roo, Mexico"; the post office will hold it for 10 days, but it will take up to 12 weeks to arrive. There aren't any courier services on the island; for Federal Express or DHL, you have to go to Cancún. To send and E-mail, try Cafe Internet.

🌐 Cybercafé **Cafe Internet** ✉ Av. Hidalgo 15 ☎ 998/877-0461.
📮 Services **Correos** ✉ Av. Guerrero and Av. López Mateos, ½ block from market ☎ 998/877-0085

MONEY MATTERS

Bital, the island's only bank, is open weekdays 8:30–6 and Saturday 9–2. Its ATM often runs out of cash or has a long line, especially on Sunday, so plan accordingly. Bital exchanges currency Monday–Saturday 10–noon. You can also exchange money at Cunex Money Exchange, which is open weekdays 8:30–7 and Saturday 9–2.

🏦 Bank **Bital** ✉ Av. Rueda Medina 3 ☎ 998/877-0005.
💱 Exchange Service **Cunex Money Exchange** ✉ Av. Hidalgo, at Av. Francisco Madero 12-A ☎ 998/877-0474.

TAXIS

Taxis line up by the ferry dock around the clock. Fares run $1.65 to $3 from the ferry or downtown to the hotels on along Playa Norte. You can also hire a taxi for an island tour at about $16.50 an hour.

🚕 **Sitio de Taxis** (Taxi Syndicates) ✉ Av. Rueda Medina ☎ 998/877-0066.

TOURS

Cooperativa Lanchera runs four-hour trips to the lighthouse, the turtles at Playa Lancheros, the coral reefs at Los Manchonesz, and El Garrafón, for about $28 per person including lunch. Cooperativa Isla Mujeres rents boats for a maximum of four hours and six people ($120). An island tour with lunch (minimum six people) costs $20 per person. Sundreamers has full- and half-day tours around the island on its 52-ft catamaran. Prices start at $30 per person and include food and drinks.

Sociedad Cooperativa Isla Mujeres and La Isleña launch boats to Isla Contoy daily at 8:30 AM and return at 4 PM. Groups are a minimum of 6 and a maximum of 12 people. Captain Jaime Avila Canto, a local Isla

Contoy expert, offers an excellent tour for large groups aboard his boat the *Anett.*

The trip to Isla Contoy takes about 45 minutes, depending on the weather and the boat; the cost is $38–$50. Sociedad Cooperativa Isla Mujeres tour operators provide a fruit breakfast on the boat and stop at Xlaches reef on the way to Isla Contoy for snorkeling (gear is included). As you sail, your crew trolls for the lunch it cooks on the beach—you may be in for anything from barracuda to snapper (beer and soda are also included). While the catch is being barbecued, you have time to explore the island, snorkel, check out the small museum and biological station, or just laze under a palapa.

▣ Operators **Captain Jaime Avila Canto** ⊠ Av. Lic Jesús Martínez Ross 38 ☎ 998/877-0478. **Cooperativa Isla Mujeres** ⊠ Av. Rueda Medina ☎ 998/877-0274. **Cooperativa Lanchera** ⊠ Waterfront near dock ☎ No phone. **La Isleña** ⊠ Av. Morelos and Av. Juárez, ½ block from pier ☎ 998/877-0578. **Sociedad Cooperativa Isla Mujeres** ⊠ Pier ☎ 998/877-0500. **Sonadoras del Sol** (Sundreamers) ⊠ Av. Juárez 9 ☎ 998/877-0736 ⊕ www.sundreamers.com.

VISITOR INFORMATION

The Isla Mujeres tourist office is open weekdays 8–8 and weekends 8–noon and has general information the island.

▣ **Isla Mujeres Tourist Office** ⊠ Av. Rueda Medina 130 ☎ 998/877-0307 ⎙ 998/877-0307 ⊕ www.isla-mujeres.net.

COZUMEL

Updated by Maribeth Mellin

The name of this island, 9 km (12 mi) east of the Yucatán peninsula, comes from the Maya word *Ah-Cuzamil-Peten,* which means "land of the swallows." For the Maya, Cozumel was a sacred site of the fertility goddess Ixchel and a trade and navigational center. For the 16th-century Spanish, it made a great naval base. Pirates appreciated its harbors and the catacombs and tunnels left by the Maya. The island went through several periods of settlement and abandonment. It saw an economic boom based on the island's abundant supply of zapote trees, which produce chiclè, a chewing-gum industry staple. But when Jacques Cousteau discovered its incredible reefs in 1961, Cozumel's trajectory was set.

A good deal of the land and the shores has been set aside as national park. About 15% of the island has been developed; San Miguel is its only town. Despite the inevitable effects of cruise ships that dock here, the island remains an earthy, friendly place. A mainstay of Cozumel's mood is the *isleños,* descendants of the Maya who have inhabited the island for centuries.

Exploring Cozumel

Taxis have become so costly that it's worth renting a vehicle for a day or two to explore this 53-km-long (33-mi-long) and 15-km-wide (9-mi-wide) island. It's mostly flat, with an interior covered by parched scrub, dense jungle, and marshy lagoons. Several minor Maya ruins dot the eastern coast. One of them, El Caracol, served as an ancient lighthouse. There are also a couple of minuscule ruins—El Mirador (The Balcony) and El Trono (The Throne)—identified by roadside markers. White, sandy beaches with calm waters and spectacular reefs line the leeward (western) side. The windward (eastern) side, facing the Caribbean Sea, has powerful surf and rocky strands.

Hotels in the town of San Miguel tend to be inexpensive. The Zona Hotelera Norte, north of town, has the best swimming beaches as well as coral reefs and coves that are good for snorkeling. The hotels in this area tend to be large and popular with families. The Zona Hotelera Sur attracts divers, as it's south of town and closer to the best reefs. This area is home to a cluster of large all-inclusives.

a good tour

Head south from **San Miguel** ⑪ ⊢ and in about 15 minutes you come to **Parque Chankanaab** ⑫. Continue past the park to reach the beaches: Playa Corona, Playa San Clemente, Playa San Francisco, and Playa Sol. If you stay on this road you eventually reach, on your left, the turnoff for the ruins of **El Cedral** ⑬. Look for the red arch alongside the road announcing the turnoff.

Back on the main coast road, continue south until you reach the turnoff for Playa del Palancar, where the famous reef lies offshore. At the island's southernmost point, the road swings north, and you come to the entrance of the **Parque Punta Sur** ⑭. The park encompasses Laguna Colombia and Laguna Chunchacaab as well as an ancient Maya lighthouse, El Caracol, and the modern lighthouse, Faro de Celarain. You have to leave your car at the gate and travel by bicycle or the park's bus.

Not far north of the Parque Punta Sur entrance are the minuscule ruins of El Mirador and El Trono. The coast road also passes one beach after another: Playa Paraíso, Punta Chiqueros, Playa de San Martín, and Punta Morena. At Punta Este, the coast road intersects with Avenida Benito Juárez, which runs across the island. You can take this road back into San Miguel or continue toward Punta Molas.

The road to Punta Molas is quite rough, and only half of it is accessible by car—you must walk the rest of the way. The beaches here are marvelously deserted: Ixpal Barco, Los Cocos, Hanan Reef, Ixlapak, and then Playa Bonita, with the small **Castillo Real** ⑮, another Maya site. Farther north are several minor ruins, including a lighthouse, **Punta Molas Faro** ⑯, at the island's northern tip.

If you take Avenida Benito Juárez from Punta Este, you come to the turnoff (just past the army airfield) for the ruins of **San Gervasio** ⑰. Turn right and follow this well-maintained road for 7 km (4½ mi) to get to the ruins. To return to San Miguel, return to Avenida Benito Juárez and continue driving west.

What to See

 ⑮ **Castillo Real.** A Maya site on the near the island's northern tip, the Royal Castle has a lookout tower, the base of a pyramid, and a temple with two chambers capped by a false arch. The waters here harbor several shipwrecks, and it's a fine spot for snorkeling, because there are few visitors to disturb the fish. Note, however, that the surf can get quite strong, so pick a time when the sea is tranquil.

 ⑬ **El Cedral.** The hub of Maya life on Cozumel was discovered by Spanish explorers in 1518. It went on to become the island's first official city, founded in 1847. These days it's a small farming community with modest houses and gardens. Conquistadors tore down much of the Maya structures, and the U.S. Army Corps of Engineers destroyed the rest during World War II to make way for the island's first airport. All that remains of the ruins is a small structure with an arch; be sure to look inside to see the faint traces of paint and stucco. Alongside is a green-and-white cinder-block church, decorated inside with crosses shrouded in embroidered lace where, reportedly, the first Mass in Mexico was celebrated. Every May there's a fair here, with dancing, music, bullfights, and a cat-

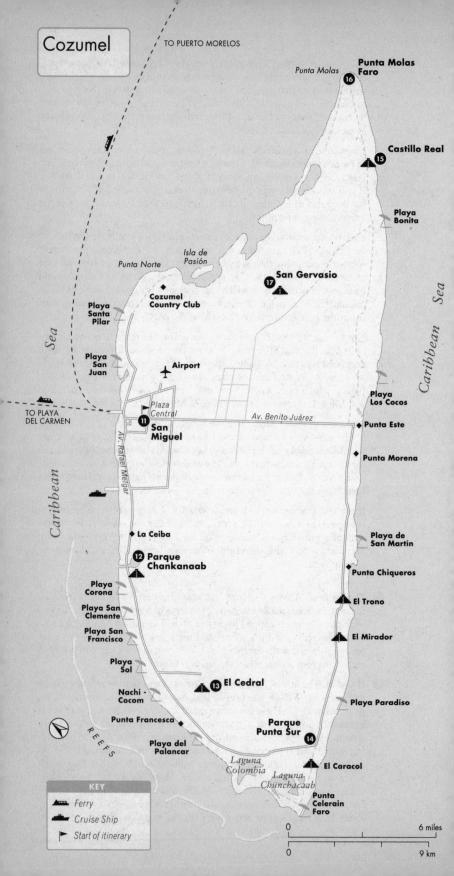

tle show, celebrating the area's agricultural roots. Hidden in the surrounding jungle are other small ruins, but you need a guide to find them. Check with the locals who offer excellent tours on horseback. ☒ *Turn at Km 17.5 off Carretera Sur or Av. Rafael E. Melgar, then drive 3 km (2 mi) inland to the site* ☎ *No phone* ☜ *Free* ☉ *Daily dawn–dusk.*

★ ⑫ **Parque Chankanaab.** A 15-minute drive south of San Miguel, Chankanaab (the name means "small sea") is a national park with a lovely saltwater lagoon, an archaeological park, a botanical garden, a dolphin aquarium, and a wildlife sanctuary. Chankanaab has remained in its natural state for decades; the few developments haven't destroyed its natural beauty.

Scattered throughout the archaeological park are 60 reproductions of Olmec, Toltec, Aztec, and Maya stone carvings from well-known sites in Mexico. Guides lead interesting, informative tours, explaining the history of the most significant pieces. Also on-site is a good example of a typical Maya house. The botanical garden has more than 450 species of regional plants. Enjoy a cool walk to the lagoon, where 60-odd species of marine life, including fish, coral, turtles, and various crustaceans, live.

Swimming isn't allowed in the lagoon; the area's ecosystem has become fragile since the collapse of underwater tunnels linking the lagoon to the sea. But you can swim and rent equipment to go scuba diving or snorkeling at the beach. There's plenty to see under the sea: a sunken ship, crusty old cannons and anchors, a Maya Chacmool (the revered rain god), and a beautiful sculpture of the Virgin del Mar (Virgin of the Sea). In addition, brilliant fish swim around the coral reef. (Note that it's forbidden to feed the fish or touch the coral.)

A small museum near the beach has photographs illustrating the park's history as well as coral and shell exhibits and some sculptures. You can also watch sea lions perform at one of the daily shows (for an additional fee). Come early, as the park fills up fast, particularly on the days when cruise ships dock. ☒ *Carretera Sur, Km 9* ☎ *987/872–2940 for park; 987/872–6606 for dolphin reservations* ☜ *$10* ☉ *Daily 7–6.*

⑭ **Parque Punta Sur.** The 247-acre national preserve is on Cozumel's southernmost tip. Neither cars nor food or drink are allowed on the premises, so you must eat in the park restaurant and use park bicycles or buses. From observation towers you can spot crocodiles and birds in Laguna Colombia or Laguna Chunchacaab. Or visit the ancient Maya lighthouse, El Caracol, constructed to whistle when the wind blows in a certain direction. The Faro de Celarain (Celarain Lighthouse) is now a navigational museum outlining the history of seamanship in the area. You can climb the 134 steps to the top of the lighthouse; it's a steamy effort, but the views are incredible. The beaches here are deserted and wide, and there's great snorkeling offshore. (Equipment is available for rent, as are kayaks.) In addition to a restaurant, which is excellent, the park has an information center, a souvenir shop, and rest rooms. If you don't rent a vehicle to get here, a round-trip taxi ride from San Miguel costs close to $40. ☒ *Southernmost point in Punta Sur Park and the coastal road* ☎ *987/872–2940 or 987/872–0914* ☜ *$15* ☉ *Daily 7–4.*

⑯ **Punta Molas Faro.** At Cozumel's northernmost point, the Molas Point Lighthouse is an excellent spot for sunbathing and birding. The jagged shoreline and the open sea offer magnificent views, making it well worth the time-consuming and somewhat difficult trip. Be prepared to walk some of the way. Area car-rental companies actively discourage visitors from driving here. Access is easier by boat, or you can take a guided tour.

⑰ San Gervasio. These remarkable ruins in a lovely forest make up Cozumel's largest existing Maya and Toltec site. San Gervasio was once the island's capital and ceremonial center, dedicated to the fertility goddess Ixchel. The Classic- and Postclassic-style buildings were continuously occupied from AD 300 to AD 1500. Typical architectural features include limestone plazas and arches atop stepped platforms, as well as stelae and bas-reliefs. Be sure to see the "hands" temple, which has red hand imprints all over its altar. Plaques clearly identify each of the ruins in Maya, Spanish, and English. At the entrance there's a snack bar and some gift shops. If you want a rugged hike, take the 15-km (9-mi) dirt road that travels north to the coast and Castillo Real. ⊠ *From San Miguel, take Av. Benito Juárez east to San Gervasio access road; turn left and follow road for 7 km (4½ mi)* 🖭 *Access to road $1, ruins $3.50* ☉ *Daily 8–5.*

⑪ San Miguel. Although highly commercialized, Cozumel's only town has retained some of the flavor of a Mexican village. Stroll along the malecón and take in the ocean breeze. Locals hang out in the main square, which is particularly busy on Sunday night, when musical groups join the assortment of food and souvenir vendors. Stay out of town if you see lots of cruise ships anchored offshore—the streets will be packed. Wait until the evening when the passengers have returned to the ships and the locals reclaim the town.

Beaches

Cozumel's beaches vary from long, treeless, sandy stretches to isolated coves and rocky shores. Most stretches have concessions that charge a fee for use of facilities such as showers, beach chairs, and umbrellas. The fee may be waived if you have a meal there. Much of the development is on the leeward (western) side, where the coast is relatively sheltered by the proximity of the mainland 19 km (12 mi) to the west.

Several good sand beaches lie along 5 km (3 mi) of the southern half of Cozumel's leeward side. Playa Corona has good snorkeling. At Playa San Clemente you'll find wide, sandy beaches and shallow waters. Playa San Francisco is considered one of Cozumel's longest and finest beaches. Playa del Palancar is near the reef of the same name and is fronted by all-inclusive hotels. Punta Celarain is now part of Parque Sur; you must pay admission to the park to access it.

Reaching beaches on the windward (eastern) side is more difficult and requires transportation, but you'll be rewarded with solitude. Near El Mirador is Playa Paradiso (also known as Playa Bosh), the southernmost of the windward beaches. North of Playa Paradiso, Punta Chiqueros is a moon-shape cove sheltered from the sea by an offshore reef. Where the paved road toward Punta Molas Faro ends lies a long stretch of deserted beaches, including Playa Bonita, which extends to Punta Molas at the island's northern tip. It's unspoiled and quite beautiful—perfect for sunbathing and communing with nature.

Where to Eat

★ $$$–$$$$ ✕ **Arrecife.** Waiters and diners greet each other like old friends at this subtly elegant restaurant. Some locals celebrate every anniversary with dinner in the candelit dining room, where a guitarist croons love songs in English and Spanish. The lobster salad starter is a full meal for light eaters; any beef dish will satisfy a hearty yet discerning appetite. Save room for one of the special flambéed coffees, prepared table-side. Reservations are recommended. ⊠ *Carretera Chankanaab, Km 6.5* ☎ *987/872–0322* ▤ *AE, MC, V* ☺ *No lunch.*

$$–$$$$ ✕ **La Veranda.** Romance oozes from this charming wooden Caribbean house with comfortable rattan furniture, soft lighting, and good music. You can sit and enjoy the evening on the outside terrace or inside. Choices include poblano chilies stuffed with goat cheese, cilantro ravioli with jalapeño pesto, and coconut shrimp; the flambé desserts are sensational. ⊠ *Calle 4 Nte. 140, between Av. 5 and Av. 10 Nte.* ☎ *987/872–4132* ▤ *AE, MC, V* ☺ *No lunch.*

$$–$$$ ✕ **French Quarter.** Owner Mike Slaughter is here nightly making sure that everyone is happy. Options include home-style gumbo, jambalaya, and crawfish étouffée, as well as the more exotic glazed frogs' legs in a Cajun marinade. You can dine outside on the spacious rooftop terrace or inside with the colorful murals. The comfortable bar has a wide variety of imported beers and wines. ⊠ *Av. 5 Sur, between Calle Adolfo Rosada Salas and Calle 3* ☎ *987/872–6321* ▤ *AE, MC, V.*

$–$$$ ✕ **La Cocay.** The name is Maya for "firefly," and like its namesake, this place is a bit magical. The chef creates a new menu every four to five weeks; dishes might include spiced-nut-crusted chicken breast, pumpkin-stuffed *medialunas* (half-moon pasta) with sage and Parmesan butter sauce, or rack of lamb with a red-onion sauce. The sophisticated restaurant has wood tables, wrought-iron chairs, soft lighting, and an open kitchen. Desserts are fantastic, and the wine list has a good selection. ⊠ *Av. 19 1100, at Av. 25* ☎ *987/872–5533* ▤ *No credit cards* ☺ *Closed Sun.–Mon. and Oct. No lunch.*

$–$$ ✕ **Las Tortugas.** The motto at this simple eatery is "delicious seafood at accessible prices," and Las Tortugas lives up to it. The menu consists primarily of fish, lobster, and conch caught by local fishermen, and it changes according to what's available. Fajitas and other traditional Mexican dishes are also options. ⊠ *Av. 30 at Calle 19 Sur* ☎ *987/872–1242* ▤ *MC, V.*

¢–$$ ✕ **Chen Río Restaurant.** Of the several small roadside restaurants on the island's windward side, this is the most popular. That said, note that some of the fish dishes aren't always as good as they could be, and sand flies can be a real pain. Stick with a cold drink and simple grilled fish, and relax under the coconut trees, watch the surf, or go for a swim. ⊠ *East-coast road, Km 28* ☎ *No phone* ▤ *No credit cards.*

¢–$$ ✕ **La Choza.** Purely Mexican in design and cuisine, this family-owned restaurant is a favorite for mole *rojo* (with cinnamon and chilies) and cochinita pibíl. Leave room for the chilled chocolate pie or the intriguing avocado pie. ⊠ *Calle Adolfo Rosado Salas 198, at Av. 10* ☎ *987/872–0958* ▤ *AE, MC, V.*

¢–$ ✕ **Cocos Cozumel.** Start the day with a bountiful breakfast at this cheery café, where the coffee is strong, the muffins enormous, and the egg dishes perfectly prepared. If you've come early enough to beat the heat, sit at a table under the front awning and watch the town come to life. The restaurant is open 7 AM–1 PM. ⊠ *Av. 5 Sur 180* ☎ *987/872–0241* ⌨ *Reservations not accepted* ▤ *No credit cards* ☺ *Closed Mon. and Sept.–Oct. No dinner.*

¢–$ ✕ **Jeanie's Waffle House.** Jeanie's is a wonderful place to start the day. The tables sit on several levels of an outdoor terrace facing the sea. The waffles are fresh, light, and yummy, and they come in more variations than you can imagine. You might have to wait for a table, since lots of locals stop here before heading to work. ⊠ *Av. Rafael E. Melgar 798* ☎ *987/872–6095* ▤ *No credit cards* ☺ *No dinner.*

¢–$ ✕ **Plaza Leza.** You can let the hours slip away while enjoying great Mexican food and watching the action in the square. For more privacy, go indoors to the somewhat secluded, cozy inner patio for everything from poc chuc, enchiladas, and lime soup to chicken sandwiches and coconut ice cream. You can get breakfast here, too. ⊠ *Calle 1 Sur, south side of Plaza Central* ☎ *987/872–1041* ⊟ *AE, MC, V.*

¢–$ ✕ **Rock 'n Java Caribbean Café.** The extensive breakfast menu offers such delights as whole-wheat French toast and cheese blintzes. For lunch or dinner, consider the vegetarian tacos or linguine with clam sauce, or choose from more than a dozen salads. There are also scrumptious pies, cakes, and pastries baked here daily. Enjoy your healthful meal or sinful snack while sitting on the wrought-iron studio chairs. ⊠ *Av. Rafael E. Melgar 602-6* ☎ *987/872–4405* ⊟ *No credit cards* ⊙ *Closed Sun.*

¢–$ ✕ **El Turix.** Off the beaten track, about 10 minutes by cab from downtown, this simple place is worth the trip for a chance to experience true Yucatecan cuisine served by the amiable owners, Rafael and Maruca. Don't miss the pollo pibíl or the poc chuc. There are also daily specials, and paella on request (call 24 hours ahead). ⊠ *Av. 20 Sur, between Calles 17 and 19* ☎ *987/872–5234* ⊟ *No credit cards* ⊙ *No lunch.*

Where to Stay

All of Cozumel's hotels are on the leeward (west) and south sides of the island. Hotels north and south of San Miguel tend to be the larger resorts, and less expensive places are in town. Because of the proximity of the reefs, divers and snorkelers tend to congregate at the southern properties, whereas swimmers prefer the hotels to the north, where the beaches are better.

Zona Hotelera Norte

$$$$ ⬚ **Meliá Cozumel.** A long white-sand beach with clear, shallow water fronts this all-inclusive. The spacious rooms are cool and comfortable and have ocean-view balconies. Families congregate around the kid's club and pool. There's also a gym, a water-sports center, and horseback riding; a golf course is across the street. The meals are very good, and the staff extremely helpful. ⊠ *Carretera Costera Norte, Km 5.8, 77600* ☎ *987/ 872–0411 or 800/336–3542* 🖷 *987/872–1599* ⊕ *www.solmelia.com* 🛏 *147 rooms* ♨ *2 restaurants, snack bar, 2 tennis courts, 2 pools, gym, beach, dive shop, windsurfing, boating, 4 bars, children's programs (ages 5–12), car rental* ⊟ *AE, MC, V* ⦿ *All-inclusive.*

★ $$–$$$ ⬚ **Playa Azul Golf and Beach Resort.** The bright, airy rooms of this romantic boutique hotel face the ocean or gardens and have artistic touches, wicker furnishings, and sun-filled terraces. Master suites have hot tubs. Small palapas shade lounge chairs on the beach, and you can arrange snorkeling and diving trips at the hotel's own dock. The Palma Azul restaurant serves delicious Continental meals. Greens fees at the Cozumel Country Club are included in the room rates. ⊠ *Carretera Costera Norte, Km 4, 77600* ☎ *987/872–0199* 🖷 *987/872–0110* ⊕ *www.playa-azul.com* 🛏 *34 rooms, 16 suites* ♨ *Restaurant, some in-room hot tubs, pool, massage, beach, dive shop, dock, snorkeling, fishing, billiards, 2 bars, car rental* ⊟ *AE, MC, V.*

Zona Hotelera Sur

★ $$$–$$$$ ⬚ **Presidente Inter-Continental Cozumel.** This isn't the place for those seeking swim-up bars, loud music, and lots of action. Rather privacy, comfort, and good service are its hallmarks. Rooms are stylish and contemporary with white cedar furnishings and private terraces; most overlook the ocean. Splurge on an oceanfront suite if you can; terraces lead right to quiet sands. The pool is modest, but the landscaping—including a serene botanical garden—is beautiful, the superb beach has great snorkeling, and the restaurants are highly recommended. ⊠ *Carretera Chankanaab, Km 6.5, 77600* ☎ *987/872–9500 or 800/327–0200*

🕾 987/872–9501 ⊕ *www.interconti.com* ⇌ *253 rooms* ⌂ *2 restaurants, 2 tennis courts, pool, gym, hot tub, beach, dive shop, snorkeling, 3 bars, shops, children's programs (ages 4–12), meeting rooms, car rental* ▤ *AE, DC, MC, V.*

$$$ ▥ **Iberostar.** Jungle greenery surrounds this all-inclusive resort at Cozumel's southernmost point. Rooms are small but pleasant with wrought-iron details, one king-size bed or two queen-size beds, and a terrace or patio with hammocks. There isn't much privacy, though, as paths through the resort wind around the rooms. There are plenty of activities to keep the whole family busy. ⊠ *Carretera Chankanaab, Km 17 (past El Cedral turnoff), 77600* 🕾 *987/872–9900 or 888/923–2722* 🕾 *987/872–9909* ⊕ *www.iberostar.com* ⇌ *300 rooms* ⌂ *3 restaurants, 2 tennis courts, 2 pools, gym, hair salon, beach, dive shop, dock, snorkeling, boating, 3 bars, theater, children's programs (ages 4–12), car rental* ▤ *AE, MC, V* ⍥ *All-inclusive.*

$$ ▥ **Fiesta Americana Cozumel Dive Resort.** A walkway over the road links this hotel to the dive shop, dock, beach, pool, and restaurant. Standard rooms are large, with light-wood furnishings; all have oceanfront balconies. Casitas along jungle paths have balconies with hammocks and outdoor lockers for dive gear. ⊠ *Carretera Chankanaab, Km 7.5, 77600* 🕾 *987/872–2622 or 800/343–7821* 🕾 *987/872–2666* ⊕ *www.fiestaamericana.com* ⇌ *172 rooms, 54 casitas* ⌂ *3 restaurants, 2 tennis courts, 2 pools, dive shop, dock, snorkeling, 3 bars, car rental, travel services* ▤ *AE, MC, V.*

$$ ▥ **Villablanca Garden Beach Hotel.** The architecture is beautiful here— from the white facade to the guest rooms with archways that separate sleeping and living areas. Suites have refrigerators, sunken bathtubs, and private terraces. There's a beach club, a huge garden, and excellent dive packages. The restaurant staff doesn't think twice about preparing special meals for those with dietary restrictions. ⊠ *Carretera Chankanaab, Km 3, 77600* 🕾 *987/872–0730* 🕾 *987/872–0865* ⊕ *www.villablanca. net* ⇌ *50 rooms* ⌂ *Restaurant, some refrigerators, tennis court, pool, beach, dock* ▤ *AE, MC, V* ⍥ *BP, EP.*

San Miguel

$ ▥ **Charrita's.** This charming bed-and-breakfast is in a residential neighborhood 11 blocks from the beach. Each of the five comfortable rooms is individually decorated and has a private bath. Upstairs there's a terrace for sunbathing or taking in sunsets. Guests rave about the huge Mexican breakfast included in the rate. ⊠ *Calle 11 at Av. 55 Bis, 77600* 🕾 *987/ 872–4760* ⊕ *www.cozumelbandb.com* ⇌ *5 rooms* ▤ *No credit cards* ⍥ *BP.*

¢–$ ▥ **Tamarindo Bed & Breakfast.** The owners have blended elements of Mexico with those of France. Many rooms have hammocks; all rooms have unique touches. There are also bungalows and apartments for rent closer to the waterfront. The staff arranges diving expeditions, and there's a rinse tank as well as gear-storage facilities. Breakfast includes delicious French-pressed coffee. ⊠ *Calle 4 Nte. 421, between Avs. 20 and 25, 77600* 🕾🕾 *987/872–3614* ⊕ *www.cozumel.net/bb/tamarind/* ⇌ *5 rooms* ⌂ *Fans, massage, bicycles, baby-sitting, laundry service; no a/c in some rooms* ▤ *MC, V* ⍥ *CP.*

¢ ▥ **Safari Inn.** Above the Aqua Safari dive shop on the waterfront, this small hotel has comfy beds, powerful hot-water showers, air-conditioning, and the camaraderie of fellow scuba fanatics. The owner also operates Condumel, a mall condo complex north of town that has reasonable nightly and weekly rates. ⊠ *Av. Rafael Melgar at Calle 5, 77600* 🕾 *987/872–0101* 🕾 *987/872–0661* ⊕ *www.aquasafari.com* ⇌ *12 rooms* ⌂ *Dive shop* ▤ *MC, V.*

Nightlife

Bars

Cactus (✉ Av. Rafael E. Melgar 145 ☎ 987/872–5799) has a disco, live music, and a bar that stays open until 5 AM. Sports fiends can catch all the news on ESPN at **Sports Page Video Bar and Restaurant** (✉ Av. 5 Nte. and Calle 2 ☎ 987/872–1199).

Discos

The island's oldest disco, **Neptune Dance Club** (✉ Av. Rafael E. Melgar at Av. 11 ☎ 987/872–1537) still lets you boogie into the night. **Viva Mexico** (✉ Av. Rafael E. Melgar ☎ 987/872–0799) has a DJ who spins dance music until the wee hours. There's also an extensive snack menu.

Music

Sunday evenings 8–10, locals head for the zócalo, to hear mariachis and island musicians playing tropical tunes. Every Thursday during high season there's a folkloric performance at the **Fiesta Americana Cozumel Dive Resort** (✉ Carretera Chankanaab, Km 7.5 ☎ 987/872–2622). For sophisticated jazz, smart cocktails, and great cigars, check out the **Havana Club** (✉ Av. Rafael E. Melgar, between Calles 6 and 8, 2nd floor ☎ 987/872–1268). Beware of ordering imported liquors such as vodka and scotch; drink prices are very high.

The food isn't the draw at **Joe's Lobster House** (✉ Av. Rafael E. Melgar, across from the ferry pier ☎ 987/872–3275), but the reggae and salsa bring in the crowds nightly, from 10:30 until dawn. **Señor Frog's and Carlos 'n Charlie's** (✉ Av. Rafael E. Melgar at Punta Langosta ☎ 987/872–0191) attracts lively crowds who want loud rock and a liberated, anything-goes dancing scene.

Sports & the Outdoors

Most people come to Cozumel for the water sports—scuba diving, snorkeling, and fishing are particularly popular. Services and equipment rentals are available throughout the island, especially through major hotels and water-sports centers such as **Scuba Du** (☎ 987/872–9505 ⊕ www.scubadu.com), which has a couple locations.

Because dive shops tend to be competitive, it's well worth your while to shop around. **ANOAAT** (Aquatic Sports Operators Association; ☎ 987/872–5955 ⊕ www.anoaat.com) has listings of affiliated dive operations.

Fishing

Regulations forbid commercial fishing, sportfishing, spear fishing, and collecting any marine life in certain areas around Cozumel. It's illegal to kill certain species within marine reserves, including billfish, so be prepared to return prize catches back to the sea. (Regular participants in the annual billfish tournament have seen some of the same fish caught over and over again.) U.S. Customs allows you to bring up to 30 pounds of fish back into the country.

CHARTERS You can charter high-speed fishing boats for $400 for a half day or $500 for a full day (maximum six people). Your hotel can help you arrange daily charters—some hotels have special deals, with boats leaving from their own dock. **Albatros Deep Sea Fishing** (☎ 987/872–2390 or 888/333–4643) is a local outfit specializing in fishing trips. Full-day rates include the boat and crew, tackle and bait, and lunch with beer and soda. **Marathon Fishing & Leisure Charters** (☎ 987/872–1986) is popular with fishermen. Full-day rates include the boat and crew, tackle and bait, and lunch with beer and soda.

Golf

The **Cozumel Country Club** (⊠ Carretera Costera Norte, Km 5.8 ☎ 987/ 872–9570 ⊕ www.cozumelcountryclub.com.mx) has a championship golf course. The gorgeous fairways amid mangroves and a lagoon are the work of the Nicklaus Design Group. The greens fee is $110, including golf car. Many hotels offer golf packages; the Playa Azul Golf and Beach Resort even includes golf fees in its room rates.

Scuba Diving

Options include deep dives, drift dives, shore dives, wall dives, and night dives, as well as theme dives focusing on ecology, archaeology, and photography. With so many shops to choose from (there are now more than 100), be sure to look for high safety standards, documented credentials, and knowledgable dive masters. The dive shops handle more than 1,000 divers per day; naturally, many of them run what are called "cattle boats," carrying lots of divers and gear. It's worth the extra money to go out with a smaller group with an operator that provides lots of individual attention. Before signing on with a place, ask some experienced divers about it, check credentials, and look over the boats and equipment.

When diving, stay at least 3 ft above the reef, not just because the coral can sting you but also because coral is easily damaged and grows very slowly: it has taken 2,000 years for it to reach its present size.

DIVE SHOPS Equipment rental ranges from $6 for tanks or a lamp to about $8–$10 for a regulator and BC; underwater-camera rentals can cost as much as $35, video-camera rentals run about $75, and professionally shot and edited videos of your own dive are priced at about $160. You can choose from two-tank boat trips and specialty dives ranging from $45 to $60. Most companies also offer one-tank afternoon and night dives for $30–$35.

Aqua Safari (⊠ Av. Rafael E. Melgar 429, between Calles 5 and 7 Sur ☎ 987/872–0301) is one of the oldest and most professional shops and offers PADI certification. **Blue Bubble** (⊠ Av. 5 Sur and Calle 3 Sur ☎ 987/ 872–1865) offers several drive trips at different times of the morning— a blessing for those who hate waking up early. **Del Mar Aquatics** (⊠ Costera Sur, Km 4 ☎ 987/872–5949) offers dive instruction as well as boat and shore dives. **Dive Cozumel** (⊠ Calle Adolfo Rosado Salas 72, at Av. 5 Sur ☎ 987/872–4167) specializes in cave diving for experienced divers.

Snorkeling

Snorkeling equipment is available at nearly all hotels and beach clubs as well as at Chankanaab Bay, Playa San Francisco, and Parque Sur. Gear rents for less than $10 a day. You can also contact dive shops to see if you can tag along when they head to a suitable reef. Official snorkeling tours run from $25 to $50, depending on duration, and take in the shallow reefs off Palancar, Colombia, and Yucab.

Fiesta Holidays (⊠ Calle 11 Sur 598, between Avs. 25 and 30 ☎ 987/ 872–0725) runs snorkeling tours from the 45-ft catamarans *El Zorro* and *Fury*. Rates begin at about $50 per day and include equipment, a guide, soft drinks and beer, and a box lunch. Sunset cruises aboard *El Zorro* are also available; they include unlimited drinks and live entertainment and cost about $35.

Shopping

Cozumel's main shopping area is downtown on the waterfront along Avenida Rafael E. Melgar and on some of the side streets around the plaza; there are more than 150 shops in this area alone. There are also small clusters of shops at Plaza del Sol (east side of the main plaza), Villa Mar (north side of the main plaza), and Plaza Confetti (south side of the main plaza).

The town's **crafts market** (⊠ Calle 1 Sur, behind the plaza) sells a respectable assortment of Mexican wares. The **Puerto Maya** market, by where the cruise ships dock, has some crafts at good prices. Bargains are best after the ships have departed.

Specialty Stores

CLOTHING **Exotica** (⊠ Av. Benito Juárez, at the plaza ☎ 987/872–5880) has high-quality sportswear and shirts with nature-theme designs. **Poco Loco** (⊠ Av. Rafael E. Melgar 18 and Av. Benito Juárez 2-A ☎ 987/872–5499) sells casual wear and beach bags.

JEWELRY **Diamond Creations** (⊠ Av. Rafael E. Melgar Sur 131 ☎ 987/872–5330) lets you custom-design pieces from its collection of loose diamonds, emeralds, rubies, sapphires, or tanzanite. You'll find silver, gold, and coral jewelry—bracelets and earrings especially—at **Joyería Palancar** (⊠ Av. Rafael E. Melgar Nte. 15 ☎ 987/872–1468). Quality gemstones and striking designs are the strong points at **Rachat & Romero** (⊠ Av. Rafael E. Melgar 101 ☎ 987/872–0571).

MEXICAN CRAFTS **Bugambilias** (⊠ Av. 10 Sur, between Calles Adolfo Rosado Salas and 1 Sur ☎ 987/872–6282) sells handmade Mexican linens. **Los Cinco Soles** (⊠ Av. Rafael E. Melgar at Calle 8 Nte. ☎ 987/872–0132) is a good one-stop shop for crafts from around Mexico. The **Hammock House** (⊠ Av. 5 and Calle 4 ☎ no phone) has long been a local curiosity thanks to its bright-blue exterior and the inventory that hangs out front. Manuel Azueta Vivas has been selling hammocks here for more than four decades. His work isn't the finest you can find, but the pleasant, elderly gentleman asks for fair prices. **Talavera** (⊠ Av. 5 Sur 349 ☎ 987/872–0171) carries beautiful tiles from the Yucatán, masks from Guerrero, brightly painted wooden animals from Oaxaca, and carved chests from Guadalajara.

Cozumel A to Z

To research prices, get advice from other travelers, and book travel arrangements, visit www.fodors.com.

AIR TRAVEL

AIRPORT The Aeropuerto Internacional de Cozumel is 3 km (2 mi) north of San Miguel.

🛪 **Aeropuerto Internacional de Cozumel** ☎ 987/872–0928.

AIRPORT TRANSFERS Because of an agreement between the taxi drivers' and bus drivers' unions, there is taxi service *to* the airport but not *from* the airport. The colectivo, a van that seats up to eight, takes arriving passengers to their hotels; the fare is about $7. If you want to avoid waiting for the van to fill or for other passengers to be dropped off, you can hire an *especial*—an individual van. A trip in one of these to hotel zones costs about $15–$25; to the city it's about $10. Taxis to the airport cost between $10 and $25 from the hotel zones and approximately $5 from downtown.

CARRIERS Continental has two nonstop flights from Houston on Saturday and one nonstop flight from Houston the rest of the week. US Airways flies nonstop on weekends from Charlotte, North Carolina, to Cozumel. Mexicana has daily nonstop service from Mexico City. Aerocaribe and

Aerocozumel fly between Cozumel and Cancún and other destinations in Mexico. Charter flights to Chichén Itzá, Chetumal, Mérida, and Playa del Carmen can be arranged.

Aerocaribe ☎ 987/872-0503. **Aerocozumel** ☎ 987/872-3456. **Continental** ☎ 987/872-0487. **Mexicana** ☎ 987/872-2945. **US Airways** ☎ 800/622-1015 in the U.S.

BOAT & FERRY TRAVEL

Passenger-only ferries to Playa del Carmen leave Cozumel's main pier approximately every hour on the hour from 5 AM to 10 PM (no ferries at 11 AM, 1, 7, and 9 PM). They leave Playa del Carmen's dock also about every hour on the hour, from 6 AM to 11 PM (no service at 7 AM, noon, 2, and 8 PM). The trip takes 45 minutes. Call to verify the times. Bad weather often prompts cancellations.

There's also a car ferry from Puerto Morelos. The trip takes three to four hours, the ferry is infrequent, the departure times aren't convenient, and the fare is about $70 for small cars (more for larger vehicles) and $6 per passenger.

Cozumel's main pier ☎ 987/872-1508 or 987/872-1588. **Playa del Carmen dock** ☎ 987/873-0067.

BUS TRAVEL

Because of a union agreement with taxi drivers, public buses cannot operate in the hotel zones; local bus service runs mainly within the town of San Miguel, although there is a route from town to the airport. Service is irregular but inexpensive.

CAR RENTAL

Major Agencies Avis ☎ 987/872-0099 airport. **Hertz** ☎ 987/872-3888 airport. **Local Agencies Aguila Rentals** ✉ Av. Rafael E. Melgar 685 ☎ 987/872-0729. **Rentadora Isleña** ✉ Calle 7 No. 49 ☎ 987/872-0788.

Car Travel

There are several excellent paved roads, but there are also many dirt roads—such as the one to Punta Molas—that aren't maintained very well, if at all; proceed with great caution, especially after rain. Also, be forewarned that most car-rental companies have a policy that voids your insurance when you leave the paved roads and journey to off-road points. If you rent a four-wheel-drive vehicle, check to make sure that it hasn't been disconnected.

EMERGENCIES

General Emergency Numbers Air Ambulance ☎ 987/872-4070. **Police** ✉ Anexo del Palacio Municipal ☎ 987/872-0409.

Hospitals & Clinics Centro Medico de Cozumel (Cozumel Medical Center) ✉ 1A Sur 101, corner of Av. 50 ☎ 987/872-3545 or 987/872-5370. **Centro de Salud** ✉ Av. 20 Sur at Calle 11 ☎ 987/872-0140. **Medical Specialties Center** ✉ Av. 20 Nte. 425 ☎ 987/872-1419 or 987/872-2919. **Red Cross** ✉ Calle Adolfo Rosada Salas at Av. 20 Sur ☎ 987/872-1058.

Late-Night Pharmacies Farmacias Canto ☎ 987/872-5377. **Farmacia Dori** ✉ Calle Adolfo Rosada Salas, between Avs. 15 and 20 Sur ☎ 987/872-0559. **Farmacia Joaquin** ✉ North side of plaza ☎ 987/872-2520.

Recompression Chambers Buceo Medico Mexicano ✉ Calle 9 Sur 21-B ☎ 987/872-2387; 987/872-1430 24-hr hot line. **Cozumel Recompression Chamber** ✉ San Miguel Clinic, Calle 6 between Avs. 5 and 10 ☎ 987/872-3070, 987/872-2387, or 987/872-1848.

MAIL, INTERNET & SHIPPING

The local correos, six blocks south of the plaza, is open weekdays 8–8, Saturday 9–5, and Sunday 9–1. For packages and important letters, you're better off using DHL. You can hop on-line at Coffee Net.

Cybercafé **Coffee Net** ⊠ Av. Rafael Melgar s/n ☎ 987/872-6394.

Mail Services **Correos** ⊠ Calle 7 Sur and Av. Rafael E. Melgar ☎ 987/872-0106. **DHL** ⊠ Av. Rafael Melgar, at Av. 5 Sur ☎ 987/872-3110.

MONEY MATTERS

Most of the banks are in the main square and are open weekdays 9–4 or 5. Many change currency all day. Most have ATMs. The American Express exchange office is open weekdays 9–5. After hours, you can change money at Promotora Cambiaria del Centro, which is open Monday–Saturday 8 AM–9 PM.

Banks **Banamex** ⊠ Av. 5 Nte., at the plaza ☎ 987/872-3411. **Bancomer** ⊠ Av. 5 Nte., at the plaza ☎ 987/872-0550. **Banco Serfín** ⊠ Calle 1 Sur, between Av. 5 and Av. 10 Sur ☎ 987/872-0930. **Bancrecer** ⊠ Calle 1 Sur, between Av. 5 and Av. 10 ☎ 987/872-4750. **Bital** ⊠ Av. Rafael E. Melgar 11 ☎ 987/872-0142.

Exchange Services **American Express** ⊠ Punta Langosta, Av. Rafael Melgar 599 ☎ 987/869-1389. **Promotora Cambiaria del Centro** ⊠ Av. 5 Sur, between Calle 1 Sur and Calle Adolfo Rosada Salas ☎ No phone.

TAXIS

Cabs wait at all the major hotels, and you can hail them on the street. The fixed rates run about $2 within town; $8–$20 between town and either hotel zone; $10–$25 from most hotels to the airport; and about $20–$40 from the northern hotels or town to Parque Chankanaab or Playa San Francisco. The cost from the cruise-ship terminal by La Ceiba to San Miguel is about $10.

Prices quoted by the drivers should be in pesos. Tipping isn't necessary. Despite the established taxi fares, many of the younger and quite aggressive cab drivers have begun charging double or even triple these rates. Be firm on a price before getting into the car. Drivers carry a rather complicated rate sheet with them that lists destinations by zone. Ask to see the sheet if the price seems unreasonably high.

TOURS

BOAT & SUBMARINE TOURS — Atlantis Submarine runs 1½-hour submarine rides that explore the Chankanaab Reef and surrounding area; tickets for the tours are $72 for adults, $36 for children.

Atlantis Submarines ⊠ Carretera Chankanaab, Km 4, across from Hotel Casa del Mar ☎ 987/872-5671 ⊕ www.goatlantis.com.

HORSEBACK TOURS — Aventuras Naturales offers two-hour guided horseback tours. Prices start at $40 and visit Maya ruins and the beach. Rancho Buenavista offers four-hour rides through the jungle starting at $65 per person.

Aventuras Naturales ⊠ Av. 35 No. 1081 ☎ 987/872-1628. **Rancho Buenavista** ⊠ Av. Rafael Melgar and Calle 11 Sur ☎ 987/872-1537.

ORIENTATION — Tours of the island's sights, including the San Gervasio ruins, El Cedral, Parque Chankanaab, and the Museo de la Isla de Cozumel, cost about $45 a person and can be arranged through travel agencies. Fiesta Holidays, which has representatives in most major hotels, sells a variety of tours. Another option is to take a private tour of the island via taxi, which costs about $50 to $70 for the day.

Fiesta Holidays ⊠ Calle 11 Sur 598, between Avs. 25 and 30 ☎ 987/872-0923.

TRAVEL AGENCIES

Local Agents **Fiesta Holidays** ⊠ Calle 11 Sur 598, between Avs. 25 and 30 ☎ 987/872-0923. **IMC** ⊠ Calle 2 Nte. 101-8 ☎ 987/872-1535. **Turismo Aviomar** ⊠ Av. 5 Nte. 8, between Calles 2 and 4 ☎ 987/872-5445.

VISITOR INFORMATION
The state tourism office, Fidecomiso, is open weekdays 9–2:30. The Cozumel Island Hotel Association offers information on affiliated hotels and tour operators.

🅕 **Cozumel Island Hotel Association** ✉ Calle 2 Nte. at Av. 15 ☎ 987/872-3132 🖷 987/872-2809. **Fidecomiso** ✉ Upstairs at Plaza del Sol, at east end of main square ☎☎ 987/872-0972 ⊕ www.islacozumel.com.mx.

THE RIVIERA MAYA

Updated by
Patricia Alisau

South of Cancún, the coast of the Yucatán Peninsula has many tropical possibilities. The beaches are beloved by scuba divers, snorkelers, birders, and beachcombers, and there are accommodations to suit every budget. Puerto Morelos retains the relaxed atmosphere of a Mexican fishing village, while the once laid-back town of Playa del Carmen has resorts as glitzy as those in Cancún. Secluded Boca Paila in the Sian Ka'an Biosphere Reserve has excellent bonefishing and superb diving on virgin reefs. At the same time this coast is one of the most threatened by development; environmentalists are supporting programs that get visitors involved in saving the threatened sea-turtle population.

Against this backdrop is the Maya culture. The modern Maya live in the cities and villages along the coast; the legacies of the ancients inhabit the ruins. The dramatic remains of Tulum are on a bluff overlooking the Caribbean. A short distance inland, at Cobá, towering jungle-shrouded pyramids are testament to the site's importance as a leading center of commerce in the ancient Maya world.

The coast is divided into two areas: from just south of Puerto Morelos to Punta Allen it's called the Riviera Maya; farther south it's referred to as the Costa Maya. Most of the hotels and ancient sites are between Puerto Morelos and Tulum; south of here civilization thins out considerably. This chapter covers the shores as far as the Sian Ka'an Biosphere Reserve, just below Tulum. If you venture farther along, you'll be rewarded by remote beaches, coves, inlets, lagoons, and tropical landscapes.

Puerto Morelos

▶ ⑱ *8 km (5 mi) south of Punta Tanchacté on Carretera 307, 36 km (22 mi) south of Cancún.*

For years, Puerto Morelos was known as the small, relaxed coastal town where the car ferry left for Cozumel. This lack of regard actually helped it avoid the development that engulfed other communities, though now the construction of massive all-inclusive resorts nearby may spoil the fishing-village atmosphere. Still, more and more people are discovering that Morelos, exactly halfway between Cancún and Playa del Carmen, makes a great base for exploring the region.

In ancient times this was one of the points of departure for pregnant Maya women making pilgrimages by canoe to Cozumel, the sacred isle of the fertility goddess, Ixchel. Remnants of Maya ruins exist along the coast here, but nothing has been restored. The town itself is small but colorful, with a central plaza surrounded by shops and restaurants; its trademark is a leaning lighthouse. Puerto Morelos's greatest appeal lies out at sea: a superb coral reef only 1,800 ft offshore is an excellent place to snorkel and scuba dive. Its proximity to shore means that the waters here are calm and safe, though the beach isn't as pretty as others as it isn't regularly cleared of seaweed and turtle grass. Still, you can walk for miles here and see only a few people. In addition, the mangroves in

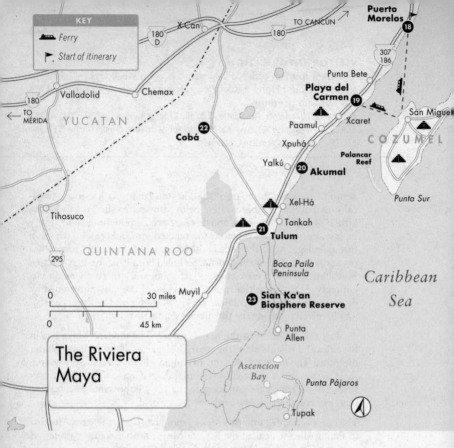

The Riviera Maya

back of town are home to 36 species of birds, making it a great place for birders.

Where to Stay & Eat

★ $ ✕ **Che Carlito's.** Carlito and his family serve some of the town's best food at this lovely restaurant. Choices include delicious empanadas, chicken fajitas, fresh salads, pastas, and incredible steaks that rival anything at the larger steak houses in Cancún (and for half the price). There's an outdoor terrace with a palapa bar that leads down to the beach. ⊠ *Casita del Mar, Calle Heriberto Frias 6* ☎ *998/871–0522* ▤ *MC, V.*

★ $$$$ ▦ **Ceiba del Mar Hotel & Spa.** For peace and quiet, this resort on a secluded beach may be just the ticket. Rooms are in eight buildings, and all have ocean-view terraces. Painted tiles, wrought ironwork, and bamboo details complement the hardwood furnishings from Guadalajara. A first-class spa offers massage and beauty treatments. Your Continental breakfast is discreetly delivered to your room through a hidden closet chamber. ⊠ *Av. Niños Heroes s/n* ☎ *998/872–8060; 877/545–6221 in the U.S.* ▤ *998/872–8061* ⊕ *www.ceibadelmar.com* ⌨ *120 rooms, 6 suites* ♤ *2 restaurants, in-room safes, cable TV with movies, tennis court, pool, spa, beach, dive shop, bar, shop, laundry service, concierge, meeting room, car rental, travel services* ▤ *AE, MC, V* ❘○❘ *CP, FAP, MAP.*

$$$$ ▦ **Presidente Inter-Continental Paraiso de la Bonita Resort and Thalasso.** Eclectic is the byword at this luxury boutique hotel. A pair of stone dragons guards the entrance, and the spacious two-room suites—all with sweeping sea and jungle views—are outfitted with furnishings from Asia, Africa, the Mediterranean, or the Caribbean. The restaurants, which are among the best in the Riviera Maya, adroitly blend Asian and Mexican flavors. The knockout spa has thalassotherapy treatments that take place in specially built outdoor pools and use fresh seaweed. ⊠ *Car-*

FodorsChoice ★

retera Cancún-Chetumal, Km 328 ☎ 998/872–8300; 800/327–7777 in the U.S. 🖷 998/872–8301 ⊕ www.paraisodelabonitaresort.com ➾ 90 suites ⚲ 2 restaurants, cafeteria, in-room data ports, in-room safes, cable TV, golf privileges, tennis court, 2 pools, gym, health club, hot tub, massage, sauna, spa, steam room, beach, snorkeling, fishing, bar, laundry service, Internet, meeting room, airport shuttle, car rental, travel services, free parking; no kids under 13 ▤ AE, MC, V, DC.

★ $ ▦ **Casa Caribe.** This small, pretty hotel sits a few blocks from the town center and five minutes from the beach. The breezy rooms have king-size beds and large tile baths. Terraces have hammocks and views of the ocean or the mangroves. A large kitchen, huge terrace, and lounge area are available for guests' use. The grounds include a walled courtyard and a fragrant tropical garden. ⊠ *Av. Javier Rojo Gómez and Av. Ejercito Mexicano, 3 blocks north of town* ☎ *998/871–0049; 763/ 441–7630 in the U.S.* ⊕ *www.us-webmasters.com/Casa-Caribe* ➾ 6 *rooms* ⚲ *Refrigerators, fans; no a/c, no room phones, no room TVs* ▤ *No credit cards.*

Sports & the Outdoors

Enrique at the PADI-affiliated **Almost Heaven Adventures** (☎ 998/871–0230), in the main square by the currency exchange office, can set up snorkeling and diving trips. Instruction ranges from an $85 beginner course to a $275, four-day, open-water course; dives cost $45 for one tank, $65 for two tanks. **Brecko's** (⊠ Casita del Mar, Calle Heriberto Frias 6 ☎ 998/871–0301) offers snorkeling and deep-sea fishing in a 25-ft boat. Snorkeling trips start at $15–$20 and fishing trips at $200.

Playa del Carmen

🔟 *10 km (6 mi) south of Punta Bete, 68 km (42 mi) south of Cancún.*

⚑ Once upon a time, Playa del Carmen was a village with a ravishing, deserted beach. The citizens fished and raised coconut palms, and the only foreigners who ventured here were beach bums. These days, however, this is Mexico's fastest-growing city, with a population of more than 30,000 and a pace almost as hectic as Cancún's. The beach is still delightful—alabaster-white sand, turquoise-blue waters—it's just not deserted. For the past few years a construction boom has been continually transforming the city every few months. Hotels, restaurants, and shops multiply faster than you can say "Kukulcán."

Where to Stay & Eat

Playa's most luxurious rooms are at the 880-acre Playacar development; the more modest rooms are farther north. Competition among the smaller hotels is fierce, so most ask for a deposit (usually the price of one night) before taking your reservation in the high season. Most restaurants are attractive and the food is decent.

★ $–$$$$ ✕ **Yaxche.** Playa's best restaurant has copies of hand-carved stelae from famous ruins and murals of Maya gods and kings. Such Maya dishes as *halach winic* (chicken in a spicy four-pepper sauce) and tikinchic are accomplished. Finish your meal with a Maya Kiss (Kahlúa and Xtabentun, the local liqueur flavored with anise and honey). ⊠ *Calle 8 at Av. 5 and Av. 10* ☎ *984/873–2502* ▤ *AE, MC, V.*

$–$$$ ✕ **Casa del Agua.** Gunther Spath, the patriarch of the Swiss family that founded this restaurant, learned his trade as manager of Las Palapas hotel north of Playa del Carmen, where he created most of the superb dishes. The German, Italian, and Swiss dishes here are just as praiseworthy. Offerings include sliced chicken Zurich with spaetzle and fresh mushroom gravy and the ever-popular steak Roquefort. Finish up with Mama

Spath's Hot Love, an ice-cream-and-hot-blueberry dessert. ✉ *Av. 5 at Calle 2* ☎ *984/803–0232* 🖃 *MC, V.*

$–$$$ ✕ **Media Luna.** The Canadian couple that runs this stylish restaurant has combined Toronto-style preparations of vegetarian, fish, and chicken dishes (no red meat here) with Mexican flavors. Choices include curried root-vegetable puree with cilantro cream and black-crusted fish with steamed rice. Dine alfresco on the second-floor balcony or people-watch from the street-level dining room. There are fixed-price lunches ($5) and dinners ($10) daily. ✉ *Av. 5 at Calle 12 and Calle 14* ☎ *984/873–0526* 🖃 *No credit cards.*

$ ✕ **Sabor.** The salads, sandwiches, and baked goods are tasty, and the location is great. Seats at breakfast and lunch are hard to find; avoid breakfasting here if you don't like rap music. ✉ *Av. 5 between Calle 2 and Calle 3* ☎ *No phone* 🖃 *No credit cards.*

$$$$ 🏨 **Ikal del Mar.** The name, which means "poetry of the sea" is apt: this romantic jungle lodge vibrates with understated luxury and sophistication. Guests have included European heads of state, who seem to cherish the privacy and serenity. Villas are named after poets and have thatched ceilings with intricate woodwork, sumptuous Egyptian-cotton sheets, Swiss piqué robes, and tony Molton Brown soaps and shampoos. Beside the sea near temple ruins, the spa delicately fuses Maya healing lore and ancient techniques into its treatments. The restaurant serves excellent Mediterranean-Yucatecan cuisine and has an outstanding wine cellar. ✉ *Playa Xcalacoco, 9 km (5 mi) south of Playa del Carmen, Xcalacoco* ☎ *984/877–3000; 888/230–7330 in the U.S.* 🖷 *984/877–3009; 713/528–3697 in the U.S.* ⊕ *www.ikaldelmar.com* ⇄ *29 rooms, 1 suite* ⟁ *Restaurant, in-room data ports, cable TV, pool, fitness classes, gym, spa, beach, dive shop, bar, laundry service, concierge, travel services, car rental, free parking; no kids under 16* 🖃 *AE, MC, V.*

★ $$$$ 🏨 **Royal Hideaway.** On a breathtaking stretch of beach, this 13-acre resort has exceptional amenities and superior service. Art and artifacts from around the world fill the lobby, and streams, waterfalls, and fountains dot the grounds. Rooms are in two- and three-story colonial-style villas, each with its own concierge. Deluxe rooms have two queen-size beds, sitting areas, and ocean-view terraces. The resort is wheelchair accessible. ✉ *Fracc. Playacar, Lote 6, Playacar* ☎ *984/873–4500; 800/858–2258 in the U.S.* 🖷 *984/873–4506* ⊕ *www.allegroresorts.com* ⇄ *192 rooms, 8 suites* ⟁ *5 restaurants, in-room data ports, cable TV, 2 tennis courts, 2 pools, exercise equipment, spa, beach, snorkeling, windsurfing, bicycles, 3 bars, library, recreation room, theater, shops, laundry service, concierge, meeting rooms, travel services, free parking; no kids* 🖃 *AE, MC, V.*

★ $$$ 🏨 **Lunata.** A tall, elegant entrance, Spanish tile floors, and hand-tooled furniture greet you at this classy inn. Guest rooms have dark hardwood furnishings, high-quality crafts, and sitting areas, and terraces—some with hammocks. Service is personal and gracious. Breakfast is laid out in the garden each day. ✉ *Av. 5 between Calle 6 and Calle 8* ☎ *984/873–0884* 🖷 *984/873–1240* ⊕ *www.lunata.com* ⇄ *10 rooms* ⟁ *Cable TV, laundry service* 🖃 *AE, MC, V* ⟟⟆ *CP.*

$$–$$$ 🏨 **Deseo Hotel & Lounge.** The Deseo is eccentric and funky—somewhere between cutting-edge and corny. It starts with a Maya-pyramid stairway that cuts through the stark, modern building. The steps lead you up to the minimalist, white-on-white, open-air lobby, with huge daybeds for sunning, the trendy bar, and the pool, which is lit with purple lights at night. Each of the austere rooms has a bed, a lamp, and clothesline hung with flip-flops, earplugs (the bar has its own DJ), bananas, a beach bag, and some unmentionables. The suites are large and have claw-foot tubs. ✉ *Av. 5 and Calle 12* ☎ *984/879–3620* 🖷 *984/*

FodorśChoice
★

879–3621 ⊕ *www.hoteldeseo.com* ⇨ *15 rooms, 3 suites* ⚇ *Room service, in-room data ports, in-room safes, minibars, pool, bar, travel services, car rental; no room TVs; no kids* ⊟ *AE, MC, V.*

$$ ▦ **Baal Nah Kah.** True to its Maya name, which means "home hidden among the gum trees," this small hotel is quite homey. Guests have the use of a large kitchen, a sitting room, and a barbecue pit. The five bedrooms and one studio are on different levels, affording complete privacy. Two rooms have spacious balconies with ocean views; all have tile baths, double or king-size beds, and Mexican details. There's a small café next door, and the beach is a block away. ⊠ *Calle 12 near Av. 5* ☎ *984/873–2343* 🖷 *984/873–0050* ⊕ *www.playabedandbreakfast. com* ⇨ *5 rooms, 1 studio* ⚇ *Fans; no a/c* ⊟ *No credit cards* ⓞ⎮ *CP.*

$$ ▦ **Itzaes.** Although this modern hotel in a colonial-style building has amenities geared toward business travelers, divers also like to stay here as it's two blocks from the beach. Rooms have tile floors, two double beds, desks, modem hookups, and hair dryers. ⊠ *Av. 10 and Calle 6* ☎ *984/873–2397* 🖷 *984/873–2373* ⊕ *www.itzaes.com* ⇨ *16 rooms* ⚇ *In-room data ports, minibars, cable TV, pool, hot tub, concierge, car rental* ⊟ *MC, V* ⓞ⎮ *CP.*

$$ ▦ **Mosquito Blue.** At once casual, exotic, and elegant, this hotel has a lobby and guest quarters with Indonesian details, mahogany furniture, and soft lighting. King-size beds and great views round out the rooms. The open-air bar and a pool are in a cloistered courtyard. ⊠ *Calle 12 between Avs. 5 and 10* ☎☎ *984/873–1335* ⊕ *www.mosquitoblue.com* ⇨ *46 rooms, 1 suite* ⚇ *Restaurant, cable TV, 2 pools, massage, bar, laundry service, car rental, travel services; no kids under 16* ⊟ *AE, MC, V.*

$–$$ ▦ **Tortuga and Tortugita.** European couples tend to favor this inn on a quiet side street. Mosaic stone pathways cut through winding gardens, and colonial-style hardwood furnishings gleam throughout. Rooms are small but well equipped; junior suites have Jacuzzis. The restaurant specializes in seafood dishes. ⊠ *Calle 14 at Av. 10* ⇨ *36 rooms, 9 suites* ☎ *984/873–1484* 🖷 *984/873–0793* ⊕ *www.hotellatortuga.com* ⇨ *36 rooms, 9 junior suites, 1 suite* ⚇ *Restaurant, cable TV, pool, billiards, travel services, car rental; no kids under 15* ⊟ *AE, MC, V.*

$ ▦ **Delfín.** One of the longer-lived hotels retains the laid-back charm of old Playa. It's the in heart of town, and has bright rooms cooled by sea breezes and decorated with colorful mosaics. Some rooms also have wonderful ocean views. Restaurants and shops are close by. The management is exceptionally helpful. ⊠ *Av. 5 at Calle 6* ☎☎ *984/873–0176* ⊕ *www.hoteldelfin.com* ⇨ *14 rooms* ⚇ *In-room safes, refrigerators; no room phones* ⊟ *MC, V.*

$ ▦ **Posada Mariposa.** Not only is this Italian-style property in the quiet north end of town impeccable and comfortable, but it's also well priced. Rooms center on a garden with a small fountain. All have ocean views, queen-size beds, wall murals, luxurious bathrooms, and shared patios. Suites have full kitchens. Sunset on the rooftop is quite spectacular, and the beach is five minutes away. ⊠ *Av. 5 No. 314, between Calles 24 and 26* ☎ *984/873–3886* 🖷 *984/873–1054* ⊕ *www.posadamariposa. com* ⇨ *18 rooms, 6 apartments* ⚇ *Car rental, free parking; no a/c, no room phones* ⊟ *No credit cards.*

Nightlife

Most of Playa closes down around 11 PM, but a growing number of bars and discos stay open until the wee hours. Note that the drug culture sometimes surfaces in the clubs. Resist the temptation to indulge, not only because it can land you in jail but because you may get robbed during drug transactions.

The **Blue Parrot** (⊠ Calle 12 at Av. 1 ☎ 984/873–0083) has live music every night until midnight; the bar sometimes stays open until 3 AM. **Capitán Tutix** (⊠ Calle 4 Nte. near Av. 5 ☎ 984/803–1595) is a beach bar designed to resemble a ship. Good drink prices and live jazz keep the crowd dancing until dawn. The **Mil y Una Alux** (⊠ Av. Juárez and Calle 55 Sur ☎ 984/803–0713) is a bar/disco/restaurant built into a cavern.

Sports & the Outdoors

The PADI-affiliated **Abyss** (⊠ Calle 12 ☎ 984/873–2164) offers training ($80 for an introductory course) in addition to dive trips ($38 for one tank, $56 for two tanks) and packages. The oldest shop in town, **Tank-Ha Dive Shop** (⊠ Av. 5, between Calle 8 and Calle 10 ☎☎ 984/873–5037) has PADI-certified teachers and runs diving and snorkeling trips to the reefs and caverns. A one-tank dive costs $35; for a two-tank trip it's $55, and for a cenote two-tank trip it's $90. Dive packages are also available. **Yucatek Divers** (⊠ Av. 15 Norte, between Calle 2 and Calle 4 ☎ 984/873–1363), which is affiliated with PADI, specializes in cenote dives and diving packages and works with divers who have disabilities. Introductory courses start at $75 for a one-tank dive and go as high as $350 for a four-day beginner course on open water.

Shopping

Avenida 5 between Calles 4 and 10 is the best place to shop. Unique boutiques sell folk art and textiles from around Mexico, and clothing stores carry original designs created from hand-painted Indonesian batiks. There are also speciality cigar and tequila shops. Hours are usually about 10 AM to 9 or 10 PM.

★ **Amber Mexicano** (⊠ Av. 5 between Calles 4 and 6 ☎☎ 984/873–2357) has amber jewelry elegantly crafted by a local designer who imports the amber from Chiapas. **Telart** (⊠ Av. Juárez 10 ☎ 984/873–0066) carries textiles from all over Mexico.

Akumal

 37 km (23 mi) south of Playa del Carmen, 102 km (63 mi) south of Cancún.

The Maya name means "place of the turtle," and for hundreds of years this beach has been a nesting ground for turtles (the season is June–August and the best place to see them is on Half Moon Bay). The place first attracted international attention in 1926, when explorers discovered the *Mantanceros,* a Spanish galleon that sank in 1741. In 1958, Pablo Bush Romero, a wealthy businessman who loved diving these pristine waters, created the first resort, which became the headquarters for the club he formed—the Mexican Underwater Expeditions Club (CEDAM). Akumal soon attracted wealthy underwater adventurers who flew in on private planes and searched for sunken treasures.

These days Akumal is probably the most Americanized community on the coast. It consists of three areas: Half Moon Bay, with its pretty beaches, terrific snorkeling, and large number of rentals; Akumal Proper, a large resort with a market, grocery stores, laundry facilities, a pharmacy, and the original Maya community; and Akumal Aventuras, to the south, with more condos and homes.

Devoted snorkelers may want to walk the unmarked dirt road to **Yalkú,** a couple of miles north of Akumal in Half Moon Bay. A series of small lagoons that gradually reach the ocean, Yalkú is an eco-park that's home to schools of parrot fish in superbly clear water with visibility to 160 ft. It has rest rooms and an entrance fee of about $6.

Where to Stay & Eat

$–$$ ✕ **Que Onda.** A Swiss Italian couple created this northern Italian restaurant at the end of Half Moon Bay. Dishes are served under a charming palapa and include great homemade pastas, shrimp flambéed in cognac with a touch of saffron, and vegetarian lasagna. Que Onda also has a neighboring six-room hotel that's creatively furnished with Mexican and Guatemalan handicrafts. ⊠ *Caleta Yalkú, lots 97–99; enter through Club Akumal Caribe and turn left, or go north to very end of road at Half Moon Bay* ☎ *984/875–9101* ▭ *MC, V* ☉ *Closed Tues.*

★ **$$** ▦ **Club Akumal Caribe & Villas Maya.** Pablo Bush Romero established this resort in the 1960s to house his diving buddies, and it still has pleasant accommodations and a congenial staff—not to mention some of the best rates along the Riviera Maya. Rooms have rattan furniture, large beds, lovely tile work, and ocean views. The quaint but rustic bungalows are surrounded by gardens and have lots of beautiful Mexican tile. The secluded one-, two-, and three-bedroom units, called Villas Flamingo, are on Half Moon Bay and have kitchenettes as well as a separate beach and pools. Dive and meal-plan packages available. ⊠ *Hwy. 307, Km 104* ☎ *984/875–9012; 800/351–1622 in the U.S. and Canada; 800/343–1440 in Canada* ⊕ *www.hotelakumalcaribe.com* 🛏 *21 rooms, 40 bungalows, 4 villas, 1 condo* ⌂ *Restaurant, grocery, pizzeria, some kitchenettes, pool, beach, 2 dive shops, bar, baby-sitting, children's programs (ages 2–12)* ▭ *AE, MC, V.*

$ ▦ **Vista Del Mar.** Each smallish room has an ocean view, king-size bed, minirefrigerator, and colorful Guatemalan-Mexican accents. Next door are more expensive condos with Spanish-colonial touches. The spacious one-, two-, and three-bedroom units have full kitchens, living and dining rooms, and oceanfront balconies. ⊠ *South end of Half Moon Bay* ☎ *984/875–9060; 800/925–6325 Ext. 15 in the U.S.* ⊕ *www. akumalinfo.com* 🛏 *15 rooms, 8 condos* ⌂ *Restaurant, grocery, some kitchenettes, cable TV with movies, pool, beach, dive shop; no a/c in some rooms* ▭ *AE, MC, V.*

Sports & the Outdoors

Akumal Dive Center (⊠ About 10 mins north of Club Akumal Caribe ☎ 984/875–9025) is the area's oldest and most experienced dive operation, offering reef or cenote diving, fishing, and snorkeling. Dives cost from $33 (one tank) to $110 (four tanks); a two-hour fishing trip for as many as four people runs $99.

Tulum

㉑ *2 km (1 mi) south of Tankah, 130 km (81 mi) south of Cancún.*

FodorsChoice
★

Tulum is the Yucatán Peninsula's most-visited Maya ruin, attracting more than 2 million people annually. This means you have to share the site with roughly half of the tourist population of Quintana Roo on any given day, even if you arrive early. Though most of the architecture is of unremarkable Postclassic (AD 900–AD 1521) style, the amount of attention that Tulum receives is not entirely undeserved. Its location by the blue-green Caribbean is breathtaking.

At the entrance you can hire a guide, but keep in mind that some of their information is more entertaining than historically accurate. (Disregard that stuff about virgin sacrifices atop the altars.) Because you aren't allowed to climb or enter the fragile structures—only three really merit close inspection anyway—you can see the ruins in two hours. You might, however, want to allow extra time for a swim or a stroll on the beach.

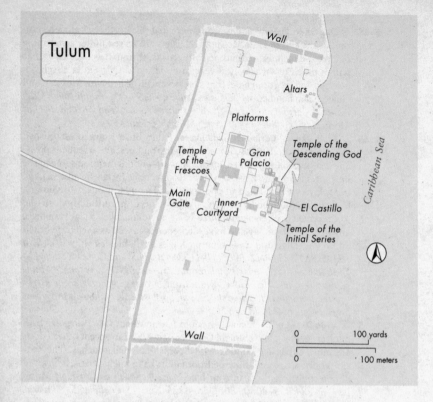

Tulum is one of the few Maya cities known to have been inhabited when the conquistadors arrived in 1518. In the 16th century, it functioned as a safe harbor for trade goods from rival Maya factions; it was considered neutral territory where merchandise could be stored and traded in peace. The city reached its height when traders, made wealthy through the exchange of goods, for the first time outranked Maya priests in authority and power. When the Spaniards arrived, they forbade the Maya traders to sail the seas, and commerce among the Maya died.

Tulum has long held special significance for the Maya. A key city in the League of Mayapán (AD 987–AD 1194), it was never conquered by the Spaniards, although it was abandoned about 75 years after the conquest. For 300 years thereafter, it symbolized the defiance of an otherwise subjugated people; it was one of the last outposts of the Maya during their insurrection against Mexican rule in the War of the Castes, which began in 1846. Uprisings continued intermittently until 1935, when the Maya ceded Tulum to the government.

The first significant structure is the two-story **Temple of the Frescoes**, to the left of the entryway. The temple's vault roof and corbel arch are examples of classic Maya architecture. Faint traces of blue-green frescoes outlined in black on the inner and outer walls refer to ancient Maya beliefs (the clearest frescoes are hidden from sight now that you can't walk into the temple). Reminiscent of the Mixtec style, the frescoes depict the three worlds of the Maya and their major deities and are decorated with stellar and serpentine patterns, rosettes, and ears of maize and other offerings to the gods. One scene portrays the rain god seated on a four-legged animal—probably a reference to the Spaniards on their horses.

CASTE WARS

When Mexico achieved independence from Spain in 1821, the Maya didn't celebrate. The new government didn't return their lost land, and it didn't treat them with respect. In 1846, a Maya rebellion began in Valladolid. A year later, they had killed hundreds and the battle raged on. (The Indians were rising up against centuries of being relegated to the status of "lower caste" people. Hence the conflict was called the Guerra de las Castas or Caste Wars.

Help for the embattled Mexicans arrived with a vengeance from Mexico City, Cuba, and the United States. By 1850, the Maya had been mercilessly slaughtered, their population plummeting from 500,000 to 300,000. Survivors fled to the jungles and held out against the government until its troops withdrew in 1915. The Maya controlled Quintana Roo from Tulum, their headquarters, and finally accepted Mexican rule in 1935.

The largest and most famous building, the **Castillo** (Castle), looms at the edge of a 40-ft limestone cliff just past the Temple of the Frescoes. Atop it, at the end of a broad stairway, is a temple with stucco ornamentation on the outside and traces of fine frescoes inside the two chambers. (The stairway has been roped off, so the top temple is inaccessible.) The front wall of the Castillo has faint carvings of the Descending God and columns depicting the plumed serpent god, Kukulcán, who was introduced to the Maya by the Toltecs. To the left of the Castillo is the **Temple of the Descending God**—so called for the carving of a winged god plummeting to earth over the doorway.

The tiny cove to the left of the Castillo and Temple of the Descending God is a good spot for a cooling swim, but there are no changing rooms. A few small altars sit atop a hill at the north side of the cove and have a good view of the Castillo and the sea. 🎟 $8; use of video camera extra ⊙ Daily 8–5.

Where to Stay & Eat

$–$$$$ ✕ **Restaurante Oscar y Lalo.** A couple of miles outside Tulum, at Bahías de Punta Soliman, is this wonderful restaurant run by a local couple. The seafood is excellent and the pizza divine. If you're inspired to sleep on the beach, campgrounds and RV hookups are available. ⊠ Carretera 307 north of Akumal (look for faded white sign) ☎ 984/804–6973 ▭ No credit cards.

$–$$ ✕ **Vita e Bella.** Italian tourists travel miles out of their way to eat at this utterly rustic eatery set with plastic tables and chairs beside the sea. The menu headlines 15 pasta dishes and pizza prepared in a wood-burning oven with such toppings as squid, lobster, and Italian sausage. Since the place is run by an Italian couple, you know the food is authentic. There's wine, beer, and margaritas to sip with your supper too. ⊠ Carretera Tulum Ruinas, Km 1.5 ☎ 984/877–8145 ▭ No credit cards.

★ $$$ ✕▦ **Las Ranitas.** Both stylish and ecologically correct, Las Ranitas (The Little Frogs) creates its own power through wind-generated electricity, solar energy, and recycled water. Each chic room has gorgeous tile and fabric from Oaxaca. Terraces overlook the gardens and the ocean, and jungle walkways lead to the breathtaking beach. The pièce de résistance is the Russian chef, who creates incredible French and Mexican cuisine that matches the hotel's magic (in the $$–$$$ price range). ⊠ Carretera Tulum–Boca Paila, Km 9 (last hotel before Sian Ka'an Biosphere Reserve) ☎☎ 984/877–8554 ⊕ www.lasranitas.com ⇝ 17 rooms ⚕ Restau-

rant, tennis court, pool, beach, snorkeling 🍴 *No credit cards* 🍴 *CP*
🕐 *Closed mid-Sept.–mid-Nov.*

$$ ✕🏠 **Zamas.** On the wild, isolated Punta de Piedra (Rock Point), with ocean
views as far as the eye can see, this kick-back-and-groove hotel draws a
lot of the U.S. business-suit crowd. The romantically rustic cabanas—
with bare-bulb lighting, mosquito nets over spartan beds, big tile bath-
rooms, and bright Mexican colors—are nicely distanced from one another.
The restaurant ($–$$) has an eclectic Italian-Mexican-Yucatecan menu
and fresh fish. ✉ *Carretera Tulum–Boca Paila, Km 5* 🕿 *984/871–2067;
415/387–9806 in the U.S.* 🌐 *www.zamas.com* ↪ *15 cabanas* ⚒ *Restaurant, beach, bar; no a/c, no room phones* 🍴 *No credit cards.*

Cobá

 ★ ㉒ *49 km (30 mi) northwest of Tulum, 167 km (104 mi) southwest of Cancún.*

Cobá, Maya for "water stirred by the wind," flourished from AD 800
to AD 1100, with a population of as many as 55,000. Now it stands in
solitude, with the jungle having taken many of its buildings. Cobá is often
overlooked by visitors who opt, instead, to visit better–known Tulum.
But this site is much grander and less crowded, giving you a chance to
really immerse yourself in ancient culture. Cobá exudes stillness, the silence broken by the occasional shriek of a spider monkey or the call of
a bird. Processions of huge army ants cross the footpaths as the sun slips
through openings between the tall hardwood trees, ferns, and giant palms.

Near five lakes and between coastal watchtowers and inland cities,
Cobá exercised economic control over the region through a network of
at least 16 *sacbéob* (white stone roads), one of which measures 100 km
(62 mi) and is the longest in the Maya world. The city once covered 70
square km (27 square mi), making it a noteworthy sister state to Tikal
in northern Guatemala, with which it had close cultural and commercial ties. It's noted for its massive temple-pyramids, one of which is 138
ft tall, the largest and highest in northern Yucatán. The main groupings
of ruins are separated by several miles of dense vegetation, so the best
way to get a sense of the immensity of the city is to scale one of the pyramids. It's easy to get lost here, so stay on the main road; *don't* be
tempted by the narrow paths that lead into the jungle unless you have
a qualified guide with you.

The first major cluster of structures, to your right as you enter the
ruins, is the **Cobá Group,** whose pyramids are around a sunken patio.
At the near end of the group, facing a large plaza, is the 79-ft-high Iglesia (Church), which was dedicated to the rain god, Chaac; some Maya
people still place offerings and light candles here in hopes of improving
their harvests. Around the rear to the left is a restored ball court, where
a sacred game was once played to petition the gods for rain, fertility,
and other boons

Farther along the main path to your left is the **Chumuc Mul Group,** little of which has been excavated. The principal pyramid here is covered
with the remains of vibrantly painted stucco motifs (*chumuc mul* means
"stucco pyramid"). A kilometer (½ mile) past this site is the **Nohoch
Mul Group** (Large Hill Group), the highlight of which is the pyramid
of the same name, the tallest at Cobá. It has 120 steps—equivalent to
12 stories—and shares a plaza with Temple 10. The Descending God
(also seen at Tulum) is depicted on a facade of the temple atop Nohoch
Mul, from which the view is excellent.

Beyond the Nohoch Mul Group is the **Castillo,** with nine chambers that are reached by a stairway. To the south are the remains of a ball court, including the stone ring through which the ball was hurled. From the main route follow the sign to **Las Pinturas Group,** named for the still-discernible polychrome friezes on the inner and outer walls of its large, patioed pyramid. An enormous stela here depicts a man standing with his feet on two prone captives. Take the minor path for 1 km (½ mi) to the Macanxoc Group, not far from the lake of the same name. The main pyramid at Macanxoc is accessible by a stairway.

Cobá is a 35-minute drive northwest of Tulum along a pothole-filled road that leads straight through the jungle. You can comfortably make your way around Cobá in a half day, but spending the night in town is highly advised, as doing so will allow you to visit the ruins in solitude when they open at 8 AM. Even on a day trip, consider taking time out for lunch to escape the intense heat and mosquito-heavy humidity of the ruins. Buses depart to and from Cobá for Playa del Carmen and Tulum at least twice daily. Taxis to Tulum are still reasonable (about $16). ☒ *$4; use of video camera $6; $2 fee for parking* ☉ *Daily 8–5.*

Where to Stay & Eat

¢–$ ✕ **El Bocadito.** The restaurant closest to the ruins is owned and run by a gracious Maya family who serve simple but basic Maya cuisine. A three-course, fixed-price lunch costs $4. Look for such such classic dishes like pollo pibíl and cochinita pibíl. ☒ *On road to ruins* ☎ 987/874–2087 ▤ *No credit cards* ☉ *No dinner.*

$ ▦ **Uolis Nah.** This small thatch-roof complex has extra large, quiet rooms with high ceilings, two beds, and tile floors. You're less than a mile from the Tulum highway but away from the noise. An extra person in a double room costs $11 more. ☒ *Km 2 on road to Cobá* ☎ 987/ 879–5013 ➴ *6 rooms* ⚬ *Fans, kitchenettes; no a/c, no room phones* ▤ *No credit cards.*

Sian Ka'an Biosphere Reserve

㉓ *15 km (9 mi) south of Tulum to the Punta Allen turnoff and within Sian Ka'an; 137 km (85 mi) south of Cancún.*

The Sian Ka'an ("where the sky is born") region was first settled by the Maya in the 5th century AD. In 1986 the Mexican government established the 1.3-million-acre Sian Ka'an Biosphere Reserve as an internationally protected area. The next year, it was named a World Heritage Site by the United Nations Educational, Scientific, and Cultural Organization (UNESCO); later, it was extended by 200,000 acres. The Riviera Maya and Costa Maya split the Biosphere Reserve; Punta Allen and north belong to the Riviera Maya, and everything south of Punta Allen is part of the Costa Maya.

The Sian Ka'an reserve constitutes 10% of the land in Quintana Roo and covers 100 km (62 mi) of coast. Hundreds of species of local and migratory birds, fish, other animals and plants, and fewer than 1,000 residents (primarily Maya) share this area of freshwater and coastal lagoons, mangrove swamps, cays, savannas, tropical forests, and a barrier reef. There are approximately 27 ruins (none excavated) linked by a unique canal system—one of the few of its kind in the Maya world in Mexico. This is one of the last undeveloped stretches of North American coast. To see its sites you must take a guided tour offered by one of the private, nonprofit organizations, such as Amigos de Sian Ka'an.

Many species of the once-flourishing wildlife have fallen into the endangered category, but the waters here still teem with rooster fish, bonefish, mojarra, snapper, shad, permit, sea bass, and crocodiles. Fishing the flats for wily bonefish is popular, and the peninsula's few lodges also run deep-sea fishing trips.

Where to Stay

$$$$ 🏨 **Boca Paila Fishing Lodge.** Home of the "grand slam" (fishing lingo for catching three different kinds of fish at once), this charming lodge has nine spacious cottages, each with two double beds, couches, large bathrooms, and screened-in sitting areas. Boats and guides for fly-fishing and bonefishing are provided; you can rent tackle at the lodge. Meals are excellent, ranging from fresh fish to Maya specialties. In high season, a 50% prepayment is required and the minimum stay is one week (three nights the rest of the year). ⊠ *Boca Paila Peninsula* 🕿 *(Reservations: Frontiers, Box 959, Wexford, PA 15090)* ☎ *724/935–1577 or 800/245– 1950* ⊕ *www.frontierstravel.com* ⮐ *9 cottages* ♨ *Restaurant, beach, snorkeling, fishing, bar, laundry service, airport shuttle; no a/c in some rooms, no room phones* ⊟ *No credit cards unless arranged with Frontiers* ⫷⫸ *All-inclusive.*

★ **$$$$** 🏨 **Casa Blanca Lodge.** This American-managed, all-inclusive lodge is on a rocky outcrop on remote Punta Pájaros island—reputed to be one of the best places in the world for light-tackle saltwater fishing. Ten large, modern guest rooms have tile and mahogany bathrooms. An open-air thatch-roof bar welcomes anglers with drinks, fresh fish dishes, fruit, and vegetables at the start and end of the day. Only weeklong packages can be booked March–June. Rates include charter flight from Cancún, all meals, a boat, and a guide; nonfishing packages are cheaper. A 50% prepayment fee is required. ⊠ *Punta Pájaros* 🕿 *(Reservations: Frontiers, Box 959, Wexford, PA 15090* ☎ *724/935–1577; 800/245–1950 to Frontiers* ⊕ *www.frontierstravel.com* ⮐ *10 rooms* ♨ *Restaurant, bar, beach, snorkeling, fishing; no a/c, no room phones* ⊟ *MC, V* ⫷⫸ *All-inclusive.*

The Riviera Maya A to Z

To research prices, get advice from other travelers, and book travel arrangements, visit www.fodors.com.

BOAT & FERRY TRAVEL
Passenger-only ferries and two enormous speedboats depart from the dock at Playa del Carmen for the 45-minute trip to the main pier in Cozumel. They leave approximately every hour on the hour 5 AM–11 PM, with no ferries at noon, 2, 8, or 10. Return service to Playa runs every hour on the hour 4 AM–10 PM, with no ferries at 5, 11 AM, 1, 7, or 9 PM. Call ahead, as the schedule changes often.

🚩 **Playa del Carmen passenger ferry** ☎ 984/872-1508, 984/872-1588, or 984/872-0477.

BUS TRAVEL
Buses traveling between all points except Cancún stop at the terminal at Calle 20 and Calle 12. Buses headed to and from Cancún use the main bus terminal downtown (Avenida Juárez at Avenida 5). Autobuses del Oriente (ADO) runs express, first-class, and second-class buses to major destination points. Service to Cancún is every 10–20 minutes. It's always best to check the times at the terminals as schedules change frequently.

🚩 **ADO** ☎ 984/873-0109.

CAR RENTAL
🚩 Major Agencies **Budget** ⊠ Continental Plaza, Playa del Carmen ☎ 984/873-0100. **Hertz** ⊠ Plaza Marina, Playa del Carmen ☎ 984/873-0702. **Thrifty** ⊠ Calle 8 between Avs. 5 and 10, Playa del Carmen ☎ 984/873-0119.

CAR TRAVEL

The entire coast from Punta Sam near Cancún to the main border crossing to Belize at Chetumal is traversable on Carretera 307. This straight road is entirely paved and has been widened into four lanes south to Tulum. Drive with caution—there are lots of speed demons on this highway. Puerto Morelos, Playa del Carmen, and Tulum have gas stations.

Good roads that run into Carretera 307 from the west are Carretera 180 (from Mérida and Valladolid), Carretera 295 (from Valladolid), Carretera 184 (from central Yucatán), and Carretera 186 (from Villahermosa and, via Carretera 261, from Mérida and Campeche). There's an entrance to the *autopista* toll highway between Cancún and Mérida off Carretera 307 just south of Cancún. Approximate driving times are as follows: Cancún to Felipe Carrillo Puerto, 4 hours; Cancún to Mérida, 4½ hours (3½ hours on the autopista toll road, $27).

If you drive south of Tulum, keep an eye out for military and immigration checkpoints. Have your passport handy, be friendly and cooperative, and don't carry any items, such as firearms or drugs, that might land you in jail.

EMERGENCIES

In Puerto Morelos, there are two drugstores in town on either side of the gas station on Carretera 307. In Playa del Carmen, there's a pharmacy at the Plaza Marina shopping mall; several others are on Avenida 5 between Calles 4 and 12. There are two pharmacies on Avenida Juárez between Avenidas 20 and 25.

🏥 **Centro de Salud** ✉ Av. Juárez at Av. 15, Playa del Carmen ☎ 984/872-1230 Ext. 147. **Police** ✉ Av. Juárez, between Avs. 15 and 20, Playa del Carmen ☎ 984/873-0291. **Red Cross** ✉ Av. Juárez at Av. 25, Playa del Carmen ☎ 984/873-1233.

ENGLISH-LANGUAGE MEDIA

Morgan's Tobacco Shop and Tequila Collection, both in Playa del Carmen, sell English-language magazines and newspapers.

🏪 Stores **Morgan's Tobacco Shop** ✉ Av. 5, at Calle 6, Playa del Carmen ☎ 984/873-2166. **Tequila Collection** ✉ Av. 5, between Calle 4 and Calle 6, Playa del Carmen ☎ 984/803-0876.

MAIL & SHIPPING

The Playa del Carmen correos is open weekdays 8–7. If you need to ship packages or important letters, go through the shipping company Estafeta; there's also a Mail Boxes, Etc. in Playa del Carmen.

📮 Services **Correos** ✉ Av. Juárez, next to the police station, Playa del Carmen ☎ 983/873-0300. **Estafeta** ✉ Calle 20, Playa del Carmen ☎ 984/878-1008. **Mail Boxes, Etc.** ✉ Av. 30, between Calle 12 and Calle 13, Playa del Carmen ☎ 984/873-1541.

MONEY MATTERS

🏦 Banks **Banamex** ✉ Av. Juárez between Avs. 20 and 25, Playa del Carmen ☎ 984/873-0825. **Bancomer** ✉ Av. Juárez between Calles 25 and 30, Playa del Carmen ☎ 984/873-0356 ✉ Av. Alvaro Obregón 222, at Av. Juárez, Chetumal ☎ 984/832-5300. **Bancrecer** ✉ Av. 5 by the bus station, Playa del Carmen ☎ 984/873-1561. **Bital** ✉ Av. Juárez between Avs. 10 and 15, Playa del Carmen ☎ 984/873-0272 ✉ Av. 30 between Avs. 4 and 6, Playa del Carmen ☎ 984/873-0238. **Scotiabank Inverlat** ✉ Av. 5 between Av. Juárez and Av. 2, Playa del Carmen ☎ 984/873-1488.

TAXIS

You can hire taxis in Cancún to go as far as Playa del Carmen, Tulum, or Akumal, but the price is steep unless you have many passengers. Fares run about $65 or more to Playa alone; between Playa and Tulum or Akumal, expect to pay at least another $25–$35. It's much cheaper from

Playa to Cancún, with taxi fare running about $30; negotiate before you hop into the cab. Getting a taxi along Carretera 307 can take a while. Ask your hotel to call one for you.

TOURS

Although some guided tours are available in this area, the roads are quite good for the most part, so renting a car is an efficient and enjoyable alternative. Most of the sights along this stretch are natural, and you can hire a guide at the ruins. If you'd like someone else to do the planning and driving for you, contact Maya Sites Travel Services, which offers inexpensive, personalized tours.

You can visit the ruins of Cobá and the Maya villages of Pac-Chen and Chi Much—deep in the jungle—with Alltournative Expeditions. The group offers a variety of other ecotours as well. ATV Explorer offers two-hour rides through the jungle on all-terrain vehicles; explore caves, see ruins, and snorkel in a cenote. Tours start at $38.50. Based in Playa del Carmen, Tierra Maya Tours runs trips to the ruins of Chichén Itzá, Uxmal, Palenque, and Tikal. It can also help you with transfers, tickets, and hotel reservations.

The nonprofit organization Amigos de Sian Ka'an runs four-hour boat tours of the Sian Ka'an Biosphere Reserve that includes bird-watching, a visit to the Maya ruins of Xlapak (where you can jump into one of the channels and float downstream), and a trip through the mangroves. Tours depart from Cabañas Ana y José in Tulum every Wednesday and Saturday morning; the fee includes a bilingual guide and binoculars.

Alltournative Expeditions ✉ Av. 10 No. 1, Plaza Antigua, Playa del Carmen ☎ 984/873-2036 ⊕ www.alltournative.com. **Amigos de Sian Ka'an** ✉ Crepúsculo 18, at Amanecer, Sm 44, Mz 13, 77506 Cancún ☎ 998/848-1618, 998/848-2136, or 998/880-6024. **ATV Explorer** ✉ Carretera 307, 1 km [½ mi] north of Xcaret ☎ 984/873-1626. **Maya Sites Travel Services** ☎ 719/256-5186; 877/620-8715 in the U.S. ⊕ www.mayasites.com. **Tierra Maya Tours** ✉ Av. 5 at Calle 6, Playa del Carmen ☎ 984/873-1385.

TRAVEL AGENCIES

There are more major travel agencies and tour operators along the coast than ever, and first-class hotels in Playa del Carmen, Puerto Aventuras, and Akumal usually have their own in-house travel services.

Local Agent Referrals Alltournative Expeditions ✉ Av. 10 No. 1, Plaza Antigua, Playa del Carmen ☎ 984/873-2036. **IMC** ✉ Plaza Antigua, Playa del Carmen ☎ 984/873-1439 ⊕ www.imcplay.com.

VISITOR INFORMATION

The Tourist Information Booth in Playa del Carmen is open Monday–Saturday 8 AM–9 PM. Note that Tulum has a Web page where you can find hotels and cabanas, and Mary Lowers of Mayansites can help you arrange house and apartment rentals anywhere along the Riviera Maya.

Mayansites Bookings ☎ 877/620-8715 in the U.S. ⊕ www.mayansites.com. **Playa del Carmen Tourist Information Booth** ✉ Av. Juárez, by the police station, between Calle 15 and Calle 20, Playa del Carmen ☎ 983/873-2804 in Playa del Carmen; 888/955-7155 in the U.S.; 604/990-6506 in Canada; 800/731-6148 in the U.K. **Tulum Hotel Web Site** ⊕ www.hotelstulum.com.

THE STATE OF YUCATÁN

Updated by
Patricia Alisau

This state is the heart of a fascinating juxtaposition of two powerful civilizations—that of the Maya and that of transplanted Europeans. Vestiges of the past are evident in this land of oval thatch-roof huts and stately old mission churches, and in its people—particularly the women who still dress in traditional garb. Mysterious "lost cities" lie hidden in the forests. Fishing villages dot beaches that are so far unjaded by tourism. In the midst of this exotic landscape stands the elegant city of Mérida, for centuries the main stronghold of Spanish colonialism in the land of the Maya.

The celebrated Maya cities—including Chichén Itzá, Uxmal, and a spate of smaller sites—bring most people to the state of Yucatán. Indeed, the Puuc hills south of Mérida have more archaeological sites per square mile than any other place in the hemisphere.

Mérida

24–35 *319 km (200 mi) west of Cancún; 1,510 km (950) mi east of Mexico City.*

⚑ Travelers to Mérida often return again and again. It's the peninsula's cultural and intellectual center, with museums and other attractions that lend great insight, and the state capital. Consider making it one of the first stops in your travels, and make sure your visit includes a Sunday, when traffic is light, diesel fumes and noise are reduced, and the city seems to revert to a more gracious era.

a good walk

Start at the **zócalo 24** ⚑: see the **Casa de Montejo 25** (now a Banamex branch), on the south side; the **Palacio Municipal 26** and the **Centro Cultural de Mérida Olimpo 27**, on the west side; the **Palacio del Gobierno 28**, on the northeast corner, and, catercorner, the **Catedral de San Ildefonso 29**; and the **Museo de Arte Contemporáneo 30** on the east side. Step out on Calle 60 from the cathedral and walk north to Parque Hidalgo and the **Iglesia de la Tercera Orden de Jesús 31**, which is across Calle 59. Continue a block north along Calle 60 to the **Teatro Peón Contreras 32**, on the east side of the street; the entrance to the **Universidad Autónoma de Yucatán 33** is across the way at Calle 57. A block farther north is the Parque Santa Lucía. From here, walk north four blocks and turn right on Calle 47 for two blocks to **Paseo Montejo 34**. Once on this street, continue north for two long blocks to the **Palacio Cantón 35**. From here look either for a *calesa* (horse-drawn carriage) or cabs parked outside the museum to take you back past the zócalo to the Mercado Municipal—or walk if you're up to it.

What to See

25 Casa de Montejo. This stately palace named after the Montejo family sits on the south side of the plaza, on Calle 63. Francisco de Montejo—father and son—conquered the peninsula and founded Mérida in 1542; they built their home 10 years later. The property remained with the family until the late 1970s, when it was restored by banker Agustín Legorreta and converted to a bank. Built in the French style, it represents the city's oldest and finest example of colonial plateresque architecture, which typically has elaborate ornamentation. A bas-relief on the doorway—the facade is all that remains of the original house—depicts Francisco de Montejo the younger, his wife, and daughter as well as Spanish soldiers standing on the heads of the vanquished Maya. Even if you have no banking to do, step into the building weekdays between 9 and 5 to glimpse the leafy inner patio.

29 Catedral de San Ildefonso. Begun in 1561, the St. Ildefonse Cathedral is Mexico's oldest and the North American mainland's second oldest. It took several hundred Maya laborers, working with stones from the pyramids of the ravaged Maya city, 36 years to complete it. Designed in the somber Renaissance style by an architect who had worked on the Escorial in Madrid, its facade is stark and unadorned, with gunnery slits instead of windows and faintly Moorish spires. Inside, the black *Cristo de las Ampollas* (*Christ of the Blisters*) occupies an altar to the left of

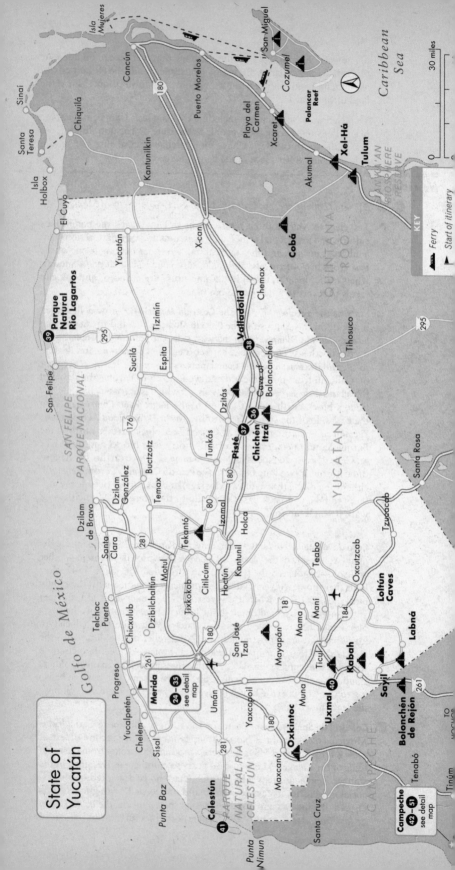

State of Yucatán

Golfo de México

Caribbean Sea

Punta Baz

Punta Nimun

Isla Mujeres

Sinaí

Santa Teresa

Isla Holbox

Chiquilá

San Miguel

Cozumel

Palancar Reef

Cancún

Puerto Morelos

Playa del Carmen

Xcaret

Xel-Há

Tulum

Akumal

Cobá

El Cuyo

Kantunilkin

X-can

Chemax

Tihosuco

QUINTANA ROO

SIAN KA'AN BIOSPHERE RESERVE

39 Parque Natural Río Lagartos

San Felipe

SAN FELIPE PARQUE NACIONAL

Tizimín

Espita

Sucilá

38 Valladolid

Dzitás

Cave of Balancanchén

36

37 Pisté

Chichén Itzá

Santa Rosa

Santa Clara

Buctzotz

Temax

Tunkás

Dzilam González

Dzilam de Bravo

Izamal

Holca

Tekantó

Kantunil

Motul

Citilcúm

Hoctún

YUCATÁN

Santa Rosa

Teabo

Oxkutzcab

Tzucacab

Loltún Caves

Telchac Puerto

Chicxulub

Dzibilchaltún

Tixkokob

San José Tzal

Mayapán

Mama

Maní

Ticul

Labná

Kabah

Sayil

Progreso

Yucalpetén

Chelem

Sisal

Umán

Yaxcopoil

Muna

40 Uxmal

Oxkintoc

Bolonchén de Rejón

Maxcanú

Tenabó

Tinúm

Santa Cruz

PARQUE NATURAL RÍA CELESTÚN

41 Celestún

Merida
24–35
see detail
map

Campeche
42–51
see detail
map

CAMPECHE

TO YUCHS

KEY

Ferry

▲ Start of itinerary

0 ——— 30 miles

180

295

176

281

261

80

18

184

261

180

the main one. The statue is a replica of the original, which was destroyed during the revolution (this was also when most of the gold that typically burnished Mexican cathedrals was carried off). According to one of many legends, the Christ figure burned all night yet appeared the next morning unscathed—except that it was covered with the blisters for which it is named. The crucifix above the side altar is reputedly the world's second largest. ⊠ *Calle 60 at Calle 61, Centro* ☎ *No phone* ☼ *Daily 7–11:30 and 4:30–8.*

㉗ Centro Cultural de Mérida Olimpo. Adjacent to the Palacio Municipal (City Hall), the porticoed Mérida Olimpo Cultural Center—referred to simply as the Olimpo—is the city's best arts venue. Its marble interior hosts international art exhibits, classical-music concerts, conferences, plays, and dance performances. Next door, a beautifully restored 1950s movie house shows art films most nights. The complex also includes a Librería Dante bookstore and a delightful coffee shop. ⊠ *Calle 62 between Calles 61 and 63, Centro* ☎ *999/928–2020* ▣ *Free* ☼ *Tues.–Sun. 10–10.*

㉛ Iglesia de la Tercera Orden de Jesús. To the north of Parque Hidalgo is one of Mérida's oldest buildings and the Yucatán's first Jesuit church. The Church of the Third Order of Jesus was built in 1618 of limestone from a Maya temple that stood on the site, and faint outlines of ancient carvings are still visible on the stonework of the west wall. Although it's a favorite place for society weddings because of its antiquity, its interior isn't very ornate. The former convent rooms in the rear of the building now host the small Pinoteca Juan Gamboa Guzmán (State Repository of Paintings). ⊠ *Calle 59 between Calles 58 and 60, Centro* ☎ *No phone* ▣ *$1* ☼ *Tues.–Sat. 8–8, Sun. 8–2.*

㉚ Museo de Arte Contemporáneo. Designed as an art school but used until 1915 as a seminary, the enormous two-story Museum of Contemporary Art is full of light. It showcases the works of Yucatecan artists such as Gabriel Ramírez Aznar and Fernando García Ponce and has excellent international art exhibits in the second-floor galleries. These make up for the halfhearted reproductions of some of the world's masterpieces in the World History of Art room. There's also a bookstore (closed Sunday). ⊠ *Pasaje de la Revolución 1907, between Calles 58 and 60 (on main square), Centro* ☎ *999/928–3258 or 999/928–3236* ▣ *$2.20* ☼ *Wed.–Mon. 10–6.*

★ ㉟ Palacio Cantón. The most compelling of the mansions on the Paseo Montejo, the pale-peach Palace of the Cantón family was designed by Enrique Deserti, who also did the blueprints for the Teatro Peón Contreras. The building has grandiose airs that seem more characteristic of a mausoleum than a home, but in fact it was built for a general between 1909 and 1911. There's marble everywhere, likewise Doric and Ionic columns and other Italianate beaux arts flourishes. From 1958 to 1967 the mansion served as the residence of the state governor. In 1977 it became the **Museo de Antropología e Historia** (Museum of Anthropology and History). Although not as impressive as similar museums in other Mexican cities, it can serve as an introduction to ancient Maya culture before you visit nearby Maya sites. Exhibits explain the Maya practice of dental mutilation and incrustation. A case of "sick bones" shows how the Maya suffered from osteoarthritis, nutritional maladies, and congenital syphilis. The museum also has conch shells, stones, and quetzal feathers that were used for trading. There's also a bookstore on the premises; it's not open on Sunday. ⊠ *Calle 43, Paseo Montejo* ☎ *999/923–0557* ▣ *$3.50* ☼ *Tues.–Sat. 8–8, Sun. 8–2.*

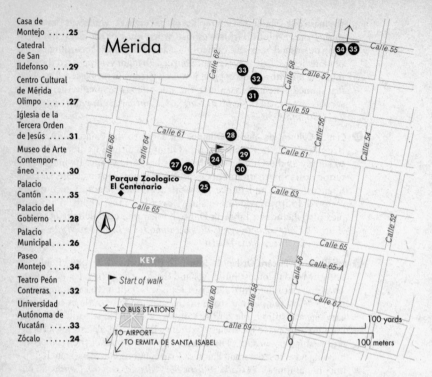

28 **Palacio del Gobierno.** Occupying the northeast corner of the main square is this attractive green structure, built in 1885 on the site of the Casa Real (Royal House). The upper floor of the Statehouse contains Fernando Castro Pacheco's vivid murals of the bloody history of the conquest of the Yucatán, painted in 1978. On the main balcony (visible from outside on the plaza) stands a reproduction of the Bell of Dolores Hidalgo, on which Mexican independence rang out on the night of September 15, 1810, in the town of Dolores Hidalgo in Guanajuato. On the anniversary of the event, the governor tolls the bell to commemorate the occasion. ⊠ *Calle 61 between Calles 60 and 62, Centro* 🆓 *Free* 🕓 *Daily 8 AM or 9 AM–9 PM.*

26 **Palacio Municipal.** The west side of the main square is occupied by the 17th-century City Hall, which is painted pale yellow and trimmed with white arcades, balustrades, and the national coat of arms. Originally erected on the ruins of the last surviving Maya structure, it was rebuilt in 1735 and then completely reconstructed along colonial lines in 1928. It remains the headquarters of the local government. ⊠ *Calle 62 between Calles 61 and 63, Centro* 🕓 *Daily 9–8.*

34 **Paseo Montejo.** North of downtown, this 10-block-long street was *the* place to reside in the late 19th century, when wealthy plantation owners sought to outdo each other in the opulence of their elegant mansions. Inside, the owners typically displayed imported Carrara marble and antiques, opting for the decorative and social standards of New Orleans, Cuba, and Paris over styles that were popular in Mexico City. (At the time there was more traffic by sea via the Gulf of Mexico and the Caribbean than there was overland across the lawless interior.) The broad boulevard is lined with tamarinds and laurels, and many of its mansions have been restored as part of a citywide beautification program.

㉜ Teatro Peón Contreras. This 1908 Italianate theater—named after 19th-century poet and playwright José Contreras—was built along the lines of the grand turn-of-the-20th-century European opera houses. In the early 1980s the marble staircase and the dome and frescoes were restored. Today, in addition to performing arts, the theater also houses the state's main tourist information office to the right of the lobby, as well as the occasional art exhibit. A café at the right of the tourist office spills out onto a patio. ⊠ *Calle 60 between Calles 57 and 59, Centro* ☏ *999/923–7354; 999/924–9290 tourist-information center* ☉ *Theater daily 7 AM–1 AM; tourist-information center daily 8 AM–9 PM.*

㉝ Universidad Autónoma de Yucatán. A Jesuit college built in 1618 previously occupied the site; the present building, which dates from 1711, has crenellated Moorish ramparts and archways. The university plays a major role in the city's cultural and intellectual life. The folkloric ballet performs on the patio of its main building Friday at 9 PM ($4). Bulletin boards just inside the entrance announce upcoming cultural events. ⊠ *Calle 60 between Calles 57 and 59, Centro* ☏ *999/924–8000.*

▶ **㉔ Zócalo.** Meridanos also traditionally call this the Plaza Principal and Plaza de la Independencia, and it's a good spot from which to begin any tour of the city. Ancient, geometrically pruned laurel trees and *confidenciales* (S-shape benches designed for tête-à-têtes) invite lingering. The plaza was laid out in 1542 on the ruins of T'hó, the abandoned Maya city demolished to make way for Mérida. Lampposts keep the park beautifully illuminated at night. ⊠ *Bordered by Calles 60, 62, 61, and 63, Centro.*

Where to Stay & Eat

★ **$–$$$** ✕ **La Habichuela.** Custom-made hardwood furniture, marble floors, and lots of leaded-glass accents lead local businessmen here for power lunches; at night, it's filled with families and couples. For starters, sample seafood crepes or salmon pâté. Meat, fish, and fowl are prepared with flair and served efficiently; try the chicken Veronica stuffed with ham or the shrimp with ginger, tamarind, or fruit sauce. The chocolate-mousse cake is the star of the dessert menu. ⊠ *Calle 21 No. 416, at Calle 8 (about 20 mins by car from main square), Col. México Oriente* ☏ *999/926–3626* ▭ *AE, MC, V.*

$–$$$ ✕ **Alberto's Continental Patio.** This romantic restaurant is in a building that dates from 1727 and was constructed on the site of a Maya temple. It's adorned with the original temple stones and mosaic floors from Cuba. The two dining rooms have handsome antiques, stone sculptures, and candles glowing in glass lanterns. A courtyard surrounded by rubber trees is ideal for starlit dining. There's lots of Lebanese food: shish kebab, fried *kibi* (meatballs of ground beef, wheat germ, and spices), cabbage rolls, hummus, eggplant dip, and tabbouleh; don't forget the almond pie and Turkish coffee. ⊠ *Calle 64 No. 482, at Calle 57, Centro* ☏ *999/928–5367* ▭ *AE, MC, V.*

★ **$** ✕ **Café La Habana.** Old-fashioned ceiling fans and a gleaming wood bar contribute to the Old Havana nostalgia at this overwhelmingly popular café. The aroma of fresh-ground coffee fills the air 24 hours a day. Sixteen javas are offered, and the menu has light snacks as well as some entrées, including spaghetti, fajitas, and breaded shrimp. The waiters are friendly, and service is brisk. ⊠ *Calle 59 and Calle 62, Centro* ☏ *999/928–6502* ▭ *AE, MC, V.*

$$$ ✕▤ **Hacienda Katanchel.** A 17th-century henequen hacienda—one of the Yucatán's most beautiful—was restored and transformed into this hotel by Anibal Gonzalez and his wife, Monica Hernandez. At this writing, the hotel was closed for repairs for storm damage. It is due to reopen in early

2004. ✉ *25 km (15 mi) east of Mérida on Carretera 180 (toward Cancún)* ☎ *999/923–4020; 800/223–6510 in the U.S.* 🖷 *999/923–4000; 888/882–9470 in the U.S.* ⊕ *www.hacienda-katanchel.com* ⇆ *25 rooms, 13 suites* ♨ *Restaurant, pool, massage, bar, car rental, travel services* ☱*AE, MC, V.*

$$ ✕▦ **Hacienda Teya.** The draw at this beautiful henequen hacienda 13 km (8 mi) from the city is the fabulous regional food ($); reservations for Sunday lunch or dinner are essential. After a typical lunch of cochinita pibíl or baked chicken, you can stroll in the orchard, wander through the surrounding botanical gardens, or swim in the huge pool. The 10 guest rooms have handmade rustic furniture and whirlpool baths. ✉ *13 km (8 mi) east of Mérida on Hwy. 180, Kanasín* ☎ *999/924–3800; 999/924–3880 in Mérida* 🖷 *999/924–5853* ⊕ *www.haciendateya.com* ⇆ *10 rooms* ♨ *Restaurant, hot tub, pool, bar, free parking* ☱ *AE, MC, V* ⍟*CP.*

$$–$$$ ▦ **Fiesta Americana Mérida.** The facade of this posh hotel echoes the grandeur of the mansions on Paseo Montejo. The spacious lobby is filled with colonial accents and gleaming marble; there's also a 300-ft-high stained-glass atrium. Floral prints and larger-than-life proportions lend period elegance to the guest rooms, which have all the modern conveniences. Guests on the business floor have access to the Fiesta Club for morning breakfast or afternoon appetizers. ✉ *Av. Colón 451, Paseo Montejo* ☎ *999/942–1111 or 800/343–7821* 🖷 *999/942–1122* ⊕ *www. fiestaamericana.com* ⇆ *323 rooms, 27 suites* ♨ *2 restaurants, in-room data ports, golf privileges, tennis court, pool, health club, massage, 2 bars, shops, baby-sitting, business services, car rental, travel services, free parking, no-smoking rooms* ☱ *AE, MC, V.*

★ $$ ▦ **Casa del Balam.** This pleasant hotel two blocks from the zócalo is still owned by the Barbachanos, pioneers of Yucatán tourism. Colonial touches include rocking chairs in the hallways and carved cedar doors. The rooms are well maintained and have double-pane windows, colorful tile sinks, and hair dryers. Meals are served around the splashing fountain in the courtyard or inside the restaurant. Guests have access to a golf and tennis club about 15 minutes away by car. ✉ *Calle 60 No. 488, Centro* ☎ *999/924–8844; 800/624–8451 in the U.S.* 🖷 *999/924–5011* ⇆ *51 rooms, 3 suites* ♨ *Restaurant, room service, minibars, refrigerators, golf privileges, pool, bars, car rental, travel services, free parking, no-smoking rooms* ☱ *AE, DC, MC, V.*

$–$$ ▦ **Casa Mexilio.** Four blocks from the main square is this eclectic B&B. Middle Eastern wall hangings, French tapestries, and colorful tile floors crowd the public spaces; individually decorated rooms have tile sinks and folk-art furniture. Some find the Casa Mexilio private and romantic, others find it a bit too intimate. A two-night minimum stay is required. ✉ *Calle 68 No. 495, between Calles 57 and 59, Centro, 97000* ☎ *800/538–6802 in the U.S.* 🖷☎ *999/928–2505* ⊕ *www.mexicoholiday. com* ⇆ *8 rooms* ♨ *Restaurant, pool* ☱ *MC, V* ⍟*CP.*

$ ▦ **Medio Mundo.** A Lebanese-Uruguayan couple runs this B&B in the old downtown area. It has Mediterranean accents, custom-made hardwood furniture, and spacious rooms that open off a long wrought-iron passageway. The original thick walls and tile floors are well preserved. A large patio in the back holds the breakfast nook, pool, and an old mango tree. A patio in front harbors fruit and flowering trees. The owners require that you pay for one night in advance. ✉ *Calle 55 between Calles 64 and 66, Centro* ☎ *999/924–5472* 🖷 *999/924–5472* ⊕ *www. hotelmediomundo.com* ⇆ *12 rooms* ♨ *Pool, parking (fee); no a/c in some rooms* ☱ *MC, V* ⍟*CP.*

¢–$ 🏠 **Casa San Juan.** This homey B&B in a restored colonial mansion a few blocks from the zócalo, appeals to Europeans. Original design elements include 10-ft-high wooden doors and tiled floors. Guest rooms vary in size and decoration, but most have double beds and firm mattresses. Affable host Pablo da Costa, a hotelier from Cuba, can give you tips on visiting the city—in five languages. A two-night minimum stay is required. ✉ *Calle 62 No. 545-A, between Calles 69 and 71, Centro* ☎ *999/986-2937* 🖷 *999/986-2937* ⊕ *www.casasanjuan.com* ⤶ *8 rooms* ♿ *Fans, travel services; no a/c in some rooms* ▭ *MC, V (when booked from the U.S, Canada or Europe)* ⊙ *CP.*

¢   🏠 **Dolores Alba.** The newer wing of this comfortable, friendly hotel has spiffy rooms with quiet yet strong air-conditioning, comfortable beds, and many amenities; rooms in the older section cost less and have far fewer amenities. The big, rectangular pool is surrounded by lounge chairs and shaded by giant trees, and there's a comfortable restaurant and bar at the front of the property. ✉ *Calle 63 No. 464, between Calles 52 and 54, Centro* ☎ *999/928–5650* 🖷 *999/928–3163* ⊕ *www.doloresalba.com* ⤶ *95 rooms* ♿ *Restaurant, fans, pool, bar, free parking; no a/c in some rooms* ▭ *No credit cards.*

Nightlife & the Arts

Mérida has an active and diverse cultural life, including free government-sponsored music and dance performances many evenings, as well as sidewalk art shows in local parks. On Saturday check out the Noche Mexicana, a free, outdoor spectacle of music, dance, comedy, and regional handicrafts. It happens from 7 to 11 PM at the foot of Paseo Montejo at Calle 47.

On Sunday, when six blocks around the zócalo are closed off to traffic, you can hear live music at Plaza Santa Lucía and Parque Hidalgo: mariachis, marimbas, folkloric dance, and other treats at the main plaza. For more information on these and other performances, consult the tourist office, the local newspapers, or the billboards and posters around town.

DANCING   **Pancho's** (✉ Calle 59 No. 509, between Calles 60 and 62, Centro ☎ 999/923–0942), open daily 6 PM–2:30 AM, has a lively bar as well as a restaurant and dance floor.

FOLKLORIC SHOWS ★   The **Folkloric Ballet of the University of Yucatán** (✉ Calle 57 at Calle 60, Centro ☎ 999/924–7260) presents a combination of music, dance, and theater every Friday at 9 PM at the university; tickets are $3. (Note that performances are every other Friday in the off-season, and there are no shows from August 1 to September 22 and during the last two weeks of December.)

Sports & the Outdoors

The 18-hole championship golf course at **Club de Golf La Ceiba** (✉ Carretera Mérida–Progreso, Km 14.5 ☎ 999/922–0053) is open to the public. It is about 16 km (10 mi) north of Mérida on the road to Progreso; greens fees are about $60, and it's closed Monday.

Shopping

MARKETS ★   The **Bazar García Rejón** (✉ Calle 65 at Calle 62, Centro) has rather sterile rows of indoor stalls with leather items, palm hats, and handmade guitars, among other things. The government-run **Casa de Artesanías** (✉ Calle 63 No. 503, between Calles 64 and 66, La Mejorada ☎ 999/923–5392) sells folk art from throughout Mexico, including hand-painted wooden mythical animals from Oaxaca; handmade beeswax candles and leather bags from Mérida; and hand-embroidered vests, shawls, blouses, and place mats from Chiapas. The **Mercado Municipal** (✉ Calle 56 at Calle 67, Centro) has crafts, food, flowers, and live birds, among other items.

Pick up a *jipi* (or order one custom made) at **El Becaleño** (✉ Calle 65 No. 483, between Calles 56 and 58, Centro ☎ 999/985–0581); the famous hats are made at Becal in Campeche by the González family. You might not wear a *guayabera* to a business meeting as some men in Mexico do, but these embroidered shirts are cool, comfortable, and attractive; for a good selection, try **Camisería Canul** (✉ Calle 62 No. 484, between Calles 57 and 59, Centro ☎ 999/923–0158). **Mexicanísimo** (✉ Calle 60 No. 496, at Calle 61, Parque Hidalgo ☎ 999/923–8132) sells expensive designer cotton clothing inspired by regional dress.

THE SCENIC ROUTE TO CHICHÉN ITZÁ

Although you can get from Mérida to Chichén Itzá along the shorter Carretera 180, it's far more scenic to follow Route 80 until it ends at Tekantó, then head south to Citilcúm, east to Dzitas, and south again to Pisté. These roads have no signs but are the only paved roads going in these directions.

Chichén Itzá

120 km (74 mi) east of Mérida, 1 km (½ mi) east of Pisté.

One of the four most magnificent Maya ruins—along with Palenque in Chiapas in Mexico, Tikal in Guatemala, and Copán in Honduras— Chichén Itzá was the most important city in Yucatán from the 10th through the 12th centuries. Its architectural mélange covers pre-Hispanic Mesoamerican history and shows the influence of several different Maya groups. Because epigraphers have been able to read 85% of the Chichén inscriptions, the site's history has become clearer to archaeologists.

At one time it was believed that Chichén Itzá was dominated by the Toltecs from present-day central Mexico; now historians believe that the city was indeed influenced by trade with the north, not, however, by conquest. Chichén *was* altered by successive waves of inhabitants, and archaeologists are able to date the arrival of these waves by the changes in the architecture and information contained in inscriptions. That said, they have yet to explain the long gaps of time when the buildings seem to have been uninhabited.

The site is believed to have been first settled in AD 432, abandoned for an unknown period of time, then rediscovered in 868 by the Maya-speaking Itzás, who migrated north from the region of the Petén rain forest around Tikal (in what is now northern Guatemala). The latest data point to the city's having been refounded by not only the Itzás but also by two other groups—one from the Valley of Mexico (near present-day Mexico City) and another from Ek Balam. The trio formed a ruling triumvirate. The Itzás may have also abandoned the site, but they were the dominant group until 1224, when the city appears to have been abandoned for all time.

Chichén Itzá means "the mouth of the well of the Itzás." The enormity and gracefulness of this site are unforgettable. It encompasses approximately 6 square km (2½ square mi), though only 30 to 40 structures and buildings of the several hundred at the site have been fully explored. It's divided into two parts, called old and new, although architectural motifs from the Classic period are found in both sections. A more convenient distinction is topographical, since there are two major complexes of buildings separated by a dirt path.

The martial, imperial architecture of the Itzás and the more cerebral architecture and astronomical expertise of the earlier Maya are married

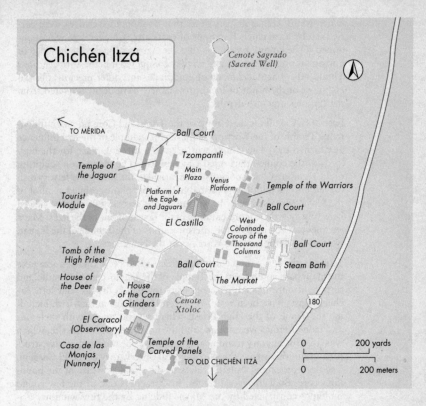

in the 98-ft-tall pyramid called **El Castillo** (the Castle), which dominates the site and rises above all the other buildings. Atop the Castillo is a temple dedicated to Kukulcán/Quetzalcóatl, the legendary Toltec priest-king from Tula in the Valley of Mexico who was held to be an incarnation of the mystical plumed serpent. An open-jawed plumed serpent rests on the balustrade of each stairway, and serpents reappear at the top of the temple as sculptured columns. At the spring and fall equinoxes, the afternoon light strikes one of these balustrades in such a way as to form a shadow representation of Kukulcán undulating out of his temple and down the pyramid to bless the fertile earth. Each evening there's a sound-and-light show that highlights the architectural details in El Castillo and other buildings with a clarity the eye doesn't see in daylight, though its accompanying narration has inaccuracies.

The temple rests on a massive trapezoidal square, on the west side of which is Chichén Itzá's largest **ball court,** one of seven on the site. Its two parallel walls are each 272 ft long, with two stone rings on each side, and 99 ft apart. The game played here was something like soccer (no hands were used), but it had a strictly religious significance. Bas-relief carvings at the court depict a player being decapitated, the blood spurting from his neck fertilizing the earth. Other bas-reliefs show two teams of opposing players pitted against each other during the ball game.

Between the ball court and El Castillo stands a **Tzompantli,** or stone platform, carved with rows of human skulls. In ancient times such walls were made of real skulls: the heads of enemies impaled on stakes. Legend has it that the **Sacred Well,** a cenote 65 yards in diameter that sits 1 km (½ mi) north of El Castillo at the end of a *sacbé* (white road), was used for human sacrifices; another cenote at the site supplied drinking water. Many archaeologists think that nonhuman sacrifices were carried out by local chiefs hundreds of years after Chichén Itzá was abandoned. (The common belief is that the Aztecs brought the practice of human sacrifice to the area when they conquered it in the 15th century.) Thousands of artifacts made of gold, jade, and other precious materials, most of them not of local provenance, have been recovered from the cenote's brackish depths.

East of El Castillo is the Group of the Thousand Columns with the famous **Temple of the Warriors,** a masterful example of the Itzá influence at Chichén Itzá. The temple was used as a meeting place for the high lords of the council that ruled Chichén Itzá. The temple-top sculpture of the reclining Chacmool—its head turned to the side, the offertory dish carved into its middle—is probably the most photographed symbol of the Maya. Murals of everyday village life and scenes of war can be viewed here, and an artistic representation of the defeat of one of the Itzás' Maya enemies can be found on the interior murals of the **Temple of the Jaguar,** west of the Temple of the Warriors at the ball court.

To get to the less visited cluster of structures at New Chichén Itzá take the main path south from the Temple of the Jaguar past El Castillo and turn right onto a small path opposite the ball court on your left. Archaeologists have been restoring several buildings in this area, including the **Tomb of the High Priest,** where several tombs with skeletons and jade offerings were found, and the northern part of the site, which was used for military training and barracks. The most impressive structure within this area is the astronomical observatory called **El Caracol.** The name, meaning "snail," refers to the spiral staircase at the building's core. Built in several stages, El Caracol is one of the few round buildings constructed by the Maya. Judging by the tiny windows oriented toward the four cardinal points, and the structure's alignment with the planet Venus, it was used for observing the heavens. Since astronomy was the province of priests and used to determine rituals and predict the future, the building undoubtedly served a religious function as well. After leaving El Caracol, continue south several hundred yards to the beautiful **La Casa de las Monjas** ("the nunnery") and its annex, which have long carved panels.

At so-called Old Chichén Itzá the architecture shows less outside influence. A combination of Puuc and Chenes Maya styles—with playful latticework, Chaac masks, and gargoylelike serpents on the cornices—dominates. Highlights include the Date Group, so named because of its complete series of hieroglyphic dates; the House of the Phalli; and the Temple of the Three Lintels. Maya guides will lead you down the path by an old narrow-gauge railroad track to even more ruins, barely unearthed, if you ask. A fairly good restaurant and a great ice cream stand are in the entrance building, as is a gift shop. A small museum includes information on the migration patterns of the ancient Maya inhabitants and some small sculptures recovered from the site. ▣ $8.50 (includes museum and sound-and-light show); parking $2; use of video camera $7 ☉ Daily 8–5; sound-and-light show Apr.–Oct., daily at 8 PM, Nov.–Mar., daily at 7 PM.

Where to Stay

★ **$$** ▦ **Hacienda Chichén.** A converted 16th-century hacienda with its own entrance to the ruins, this hotel once served as the headquarters for the Carnegie expedition to Chichén Itzá. Rustic yet chic cottages have handwoven bedspreads, dehumidifiers, and air-conditioning. All rooms, which are simply but beautifully furnished in colonial Yucatecan style, have verandas. There's a satellite TV in the library. An enormous old pool as well as a chapel now used for weddings grace the gardens. Meals are served on the patio overlooking the grounds or in the air-conditioned restaurant. ⊠ *Carretera Mérida–Puerto Juárez, Km 120* ☎ *985/851–0045; 999/924–2150; 800/624–8451 in the U.S.* 🖷 *999/924–5011* ⌁ *24 rooms, 4 suites* ⚐ *Restaurant, pool, bar, free parking; no room phones, no room TVs* 🖃 *AE, DC, MC, V.*

★ **$$** 🏨 **Mayaland.** This charming 1920s lodging is in a large garden and close enough to the ruins to have its own entrance; you can actually see part of Old Chichén from here. Colonial-style guest rooms have decorative tiles, and bungalows have thatched roofs as well as wide verandas with hammocks. Snacks served poolside are a better choice than the expensive meals in the dining room. ⊠ *Carretera Mérida–Puerto Juárez, Km 120* ☎ *999/924–2099; 800/235–4079 in the U.S.* 🖷 *999/924–6290* 🖷🖷 *985/851–0129* ⊕ *www.mayaland.com* ⌁ *24 bungalows, 67 rooms, 10 suites* ⚐ *4 restaurants, room service, minibars, tennis court, 3 pools, volleyball, 2 bars, travel services, free parking* 🖃 *AE, DC, MC, V.*

Pisté

③⑦ *1 km (½ mi) west of Chichén Itzá, 116 km (72 mi) southeast of Mérida.*

The town of Pisté serves mainly as a base camp for travelers to Chichén Itzá. Hotels, campgrounds, restaurants, and handicrafts shops tend to be less expensive here than those at the ruins. At the west end of town is a Pemex gas station, but the town has no bank, so bring all the cash you'll need. On the outskirts of Pisté and a short walk from Chichén Itzá is Pueblo Maya, a pseudo–Maya village with a shopping and dining center for tour groups. The restaurant serves a bountiful buffet at lunch ($12). Across from the Dolores Alba hotel, in town, is the **Parque Ik Kil** ("place of the winds"). The park is built around a lovely cenote where you can swim between 8 AM and 6 PM for $3. The park also has a restaurant, a swimming pool, bungalows inspired by Maya dwellings, and shops where artisans demonstrate their crafts. ⊠ *Carretera Mérida–Puerto Juárez, Km 112* ☎ *985/851–0000.*

Where to Stay

¢ 🏨 **Dolores Alba.** The best low-budget choice near the ruins is this family-run hotel, a longtime favorite south of Pisté. Rooms have colonial-style furniture and air-conditioning. Hammocks hang by one of the two pools, and breakfast and dinner are served family-style in the main building. Free transportation to Chichén Itzá is provided, and there's a covered, guarded parking lot. ⊠ *Carretera Mérida–Cancún, Km 122, 3 km (2 mi) south of Chichén Itzá* ☎ *999/928–5650* 🖷 *999/928–3163* ⊕ *www.doloresalba.com* ⌁ *40 rooms* ⚐ *Restaurant, 2 pools, free parking* 🖃 *No credit cards.*

Valladolid

③⑧ *44½ km (28 mi) east of Chichén Itzá.*

The second-largest city in the state of Yucatán, Valladolid is a picturesque provincial town, much smaller than Mérida. It has been enjoying growing popularity among travelers en route to or from Chichén Itzá or Río Lagartos who want a change from the more touristy places. Montejo founded Valladolid in 1543 on the site of the Maya town of Sisal. The city suffered during the War of the Castes—when the Maya in revolt killed nearly all Spanish residents—and again during the Mexican Revolution.

Today placidity reigns in this agricultural market town. The center is mostly colonial, although it has many 19th-century structures. The main sights are the large Catedral de San Servacio (San Servace Cathedral) on the central square and the 16th-century Convento y Iglesia de San Bernadino (San Bernardino Church and Monastery) three blocks southwest. Both were pillaged during the War of the Castes. A briny but pretty cenote in the center of town draws lots of local boys busily showing off for each other; if you're not up for a dip, visit the adjacent ethnographic museum. Five kilometers (3 miles) west of the main square and on the old highway to Chichén Itzá, you can swim with the catfish in lovely, mysterious Cenote Dzitnup, which is in a cave lit by a small natural skylight; admission is $3.

Valladolid is renowned for its cuisine, particularly its sausages; try one of the restaurants within a block of the central square. You can find good buys on sandals, baskets, and the local liqueur, Xtabentun, flavored with honey and anise.

Where to Stay & Eat

¢–$ ✕⊞ **El Mesón del Marqués.** On the north side of the main square is this well-preserved, very old hacienda, which was built around a lovely courtyard. All rooms are attractively furnished with rustic colonial touches. The 25 junior suites have large bathrooms with bathtubs. The charming restaurant ($), under porticos surrounding the courtyard, serves Yucatecan specialties such as pollo pibíl and local sausage served in different ways. ✉ *Calle 39 No. 203, 97780* ☎ *985/856–2073 or 985/856–3042* 🖷 *985/856–2280* �π *58 rooms, 25 suites* ⌕ *Restaurant, cable TV, pool, bar* ⊟ *MC, V.*

$ ⊞ **Ecotel Quinta Real.** This attractive salmon-color hotel is a mix of colonial Mexican and modern. Near a leafy park five blocks from downtown, the pretty rooms have cool tile floors and spacious balconies. Wander the tree-filled garden; visit the palapa bar or duck pond; or head to the games room. ✉ *Calle 40 No. 160-A, at Calle 27, 97780* ☎ *985/856–3472 or 985/856–3473* 🖷 *985/856–2422* ⊕ *www.ecotelquintareal.com.mx* �π *48 rooms* ⌕ *Restaurant, cable TV, tennis court, pool, billiards, Ping-Pong, bar, car rental, travel services, free parking* ⊟ *MC, V* ⦿ *CP.*

Parque Natural Río Lagartos

★ ㊴ *115 km (72 mi) north Valladolid.*

Actually encompassing a long estuary, the park was developed with ecotourism in mind, though most of the alligators for which it and the village were named have long since been hunted into extinction. The real spectacle is the huge colony of flamingos that quietly feed off small shrimp. The area also has snowy and red egrets, white ibis, great white herons, cormorants, pelicans, and even peregrine falcons flying over its murky waters. Fishing is good, too, and the protected hawksbill and green turtles lay their eggs on the beach at night.

To get here, you can drive or take a bus or a tour out of Mérida or elsewhere. Buses leave Mérida and Valladolid regularly from the second-class bus terminals to either Río Lagartos or, 10 km (6 mi) west of the park, San Felipe. About ½ km (¼ mi) from the entrance to Río Lagartos is an information station. The helpful people who work here can contact a guide with a boat for you. The boat glides up the estuary east of the dock and in 10 minutes is deep into mangrove forests; another hour and the boat is at the flamingo feeding grounds.

THE RUTA PUUC, UXMAL & THE COAST

Passing through the large Maya town of Umán on Mérida's southern outskirts, you enter one of the Yucatán's least populated areas. The highway to Uxmal and Kabah is relatively free of traffic and runs through uncultivated woodlands. The forest seems to become more dense beyond Uxmal, which was connected to a number of smaller ceremonial centers in ancient times by *caminos blancos* (white roads). Several of these satellite sites—including Kabah, with its 250 Chaac masks; Sayil, with its majestic, three-story palace; and Labná, with its iconic, vaulted *puerta* (gateway)—are open to the public along a side road known as the Ruta Puuc, which winds its way eastward and eventually joins busy Carretera 184. Along this route you'll also find the Loltún Caves, the Yucatán's largest known cave system, containing wall paintings and stone artifacts from Maya and pre-Maya times. You can make a loop to all of these sites, ending in the little town of Plaza, which produces much of the pottery you'll see around the peninsula.

Uxmal

78 km (48 mi) south of Mérida on Carretera 261.

If Chichén Itzá is the most impressive Maya ruin in Yucatán, Uxmal is arguably the most beautiful. Where the former has a Maya Itzá grandeur, the latter seems more understated and elegant—pure Maya. The architecture reflects the Late Classical renaissance of the 7th–9th centuries and is contemporary with that of Palenque and Tikal, among other great Maya metropolises of the southern highlands.

The site is considered the finest and largest example of Puuc architecture, which embraces such details as ornate stone mosaics and friezes on the upper walls, intricate cornices with curled noses, rows of columns, and soaring vaulted arches. Lines are clean and uncluttered, with the horizontal—especially the parallelogram—preferred to the vertical. Although most of Uxmal hasn't been restored, three buildings in particular merit attention:

At 125 ft high, the **Pyramid of the Magician** is the tallest and most prominent structure at the site. Unlike most other Maya pyramids, which are stepped and angular, it has a strangely round-corner design. It was built five times at 52-year sequences to coincide with the ceremony of the new fire, each time over the previous structure. The pyramid has a stairway on its western side that leads through a giant open-mouthed mask of Chaac to two temples at the summit. During restoration work in 2002, the grave of a high-ranking Maya official, a ceramic mask, and a jade necklace were discovered at the pyramid's base.

West of the pyramid lies the **Quadrangle of the Nuns,** considered by some to be the finest part of Uxmal. The name was given to it by the Spanish conquistadors because it reminded them of a convent building in Old Spain. According to research, what's called the Nunnery was actually the palace and living quarters of a high lord of Uxmal by the name of Chaan Chak, which means "abundance of rain." You may enter the four buildings; each comprises a series of low, gracefully repetitive chambers that look onto a central patio. Elaborate decoration—masks, geometric patterns, coiling snakes, and some phallic figures—blankets the upper facades.

Continue walking south; you pass the ball court before reaching the **Palace of the Governor,** which archaeologist Victor von Hagen considered the most magnificent building ever erected in the Americas. Interestingly, the palace faces east, whereas the rest of Uxmal faces west. Archaeologists believe this is because the palace was used to sight the planet Venus. Covering 5 acres and rising over an immense acropolis, it lies at the heart of what must have been Uxmal's administrative center.

Today a sound-and-light show recounts Maya legends. The colored light brings out details of carvings and mosaics that are easy to miss when the sun is shining. The show is performed nightly in Spanish; earphones provide an English translation. ⌧ *Site, museum, and sound-and-light show $8.50; free Sun. (English-translation of sound-and-light show, $3); parking $2; use of video camera $8* ⊙ *Daily 8–5; sound-and-light show Apr.–Oct., nightly at 8 PM; Nov.–Mar., nightly at 7 PM.*

Where to Stay

$$$ ▨ **Lodge at Uxmal.** The seemingly rustic, thatch-roof buildings here have glossy red-tile floors, carved and polished hardwood doors and rocking chairs, and local weavings. The effect is comfortable yet luxuriant. All rooms have bathtubs and screened windows; suites have king-size beds and jet baths. ⌧ *Carretera Uxmal, Km 78* ☎ *998/884–4510 in Cancún; 800/235–4079 in the U.S.* ⎙ *998/884–4510 in Cancún* ⊕ *www. mayaland.com* ⇗ *30 rooms, 10 suites* ♨ *2 restaurants, fans, minibars, cable TV, 2 pools, hot tub, bar, free parking* ▭ *AE, MC, V.*

$$ ▨ **Hacienda Uxmal.** Just across the road from the ruins, this pleasant colonial-style building has lovely floor tiles, ceramics, and iron grillwork. The rooms are fronted with wide, furnished verandas; the courtyard has two pools surrounded by gardens. Ask about packages that include free or low-cost car rentals, or comfortable minivans traveling to Mérida, Chichén, or Cancún. ⌧ *Carretera Mérida-Campeche, Km 78* ☎ *997/ 976–2012; 998/884–4510 in Cancún; 800/235–4079 in the U.S.* ⎙ *997/ 976–2011; 998/884–4510 in Cancún* ⊕ *www.mayaland.com* ⇗ *80 rooms, 2 suites* ♨ *2 restaurants, room service, cable TV, 2 pools, billiards, Ping-Pong, bar, free parking* ▭ *AE, MC, V.*

$–$$ ▨ **Villas Arqueológicas Uxmal.** Rooms in this pretty two-story Club Med property are small and functional, with wooden furniture that fits the niches nicely. Half of the rooms have garden views. The French and Continental food served in the restaurant—including niçoise salad, pâté, and filet mignon—can be a delightful change from regional fare. ⌧ *Carretera Uxmal, Km 76* ☎ *997/976–2018 or 800/258–2633* ⎙ *997/976–2020* ⇗ *40 rooms, 3 suites* ♨ *Restaurant, pool, billiards, bar, library, free parking* ▭ *AE, MC, V.*

Celestún

㊶ *90 km (56 mi) west of Mérida.*

This tranquil fishing village, with its air of unpretentiousness, sits at the end of a spit of land separating the Celestún estuary from the gulf on the Yucatán's western hump. Celestún is the only point of entry to the **Parque Natural Ría Celestún,** a 100,000-acre wildlife reserve with extensive mangrove forests and salt flats and one of North America's largest flamingo colonies. The best months for seeing them in abundance—as many as 500 flamingos at a time—are April through June. This is also a very large wintering ground for ducks, with more than 300 other species of birds. There's also a large sea-turtle population.

Where to Stay & Eat

$–$$$$ ✕ **La Palapa.** The town's most popular seafood place has a conch-shell facade and is known for its *camarones a la palapa* (fried shrimp smothered in a garlic and cream sauce). Unless it's windy or rainy, most guests dine on the beachfront terrace. Choose fresh fish (including sea bass and red snapper), plus crab, squid, or the most expensive plate: lobster tail and moro crab. Although La Palapa's hours are 11 AM–7 PM, it sometimes closes early in low season. ☒ *Calle 12 No. 105, between Calles 11 and 13* ☎ *988/916–2063* ☱ *MC, V.*

$$$ ▦ **Hotel Eco Paraíso Xixim.** On an old coconut plantation outside town, this hotel offers classy comfort in thatch-roof bungalows along a shell-strewn beach. Each suite has two comfortable queen beds, tile floors, and attractive wicker, cedar, and pine furniture. The extra-large porch has twin hammocks and comfortable chairs. Biking tours as well as those to old haciendas or archaeological sites can be arranged; kayaks are available for rent. ☒ *Camino Viejo a Sisal, Km 10* ☎ *981/916–2100; 888/ 264–5792 in the U.S.* ☐ *999/916–2111* ⊕ *www.ecoparaiso.com* ⇋ *15 cabanas* ☖ *Restaurant, fans, in-room safes, pool, beach, billiards, bar, library; no a/c, no room phones, no room TVs* ☱ *AE, MC, V* ¶◎¶ *MAP.*

¢ ▦ **Hotel Sol y Mar.** Gerardo Vasquez, the friendly owner of this small hotel across from the town beach, also owns the local paint store next door and chose a tasteful light green for the walls and curtains of these cool, spacious units. The sparsely furnished rooms have two double beds, a table, chairs, and tile bathrooms. The more expensive rooms, downstairs, have air-conditioning, TV, and tiny refrigerators. There's no restaurant, but La Palapa is across the street. ☒ *Calle 12 No. 104, at Calle 10* ☎ *988/916–2166* ⇋ *15 rooms* ☖ *Fans, some refrigerators; no a/c in some rooms, no TV in some rooms* ☱ *No credit cards.*

The State of Yucatán A to Z

To research prices, get advice from other travelers, and book travel arrangements, visit www.fodors.com.

AIR TRAVEL

AIRPORT The Mérida airport, Aeropuerto Manuel Crescencio Rejón, is 7 km (4½ mi) west of the city on Avenida Itzaes, a 20- to 30-minute cab ride. ▯ **Aeropuerto Manuel Crescencio Rejón** ☎ 999/946-1300.

AIRPORT A private taxi from the airport costs $9 or $10. Bus 79 goes from the
TRANSFERS airport to downtown—very inexpensive, but a hassle if you've got more than a day pack or small suitcase. If you're driving into town, take the airport exit road, make a right at the four-lane Avenida Itzaes (the continuation of Carretera 180), and follow it to the one-way Calle 59, just past Parque Zoológico El Centenario. Turn right on Calle 59 and go straight until you reach Calle 62, where you turn right and drive a block to the main square. (Parking is difficult here.)

CARRIERS Aerocaribe, a subsidiary of Mexicana, has flights from Cancún, Chetumal, Cozumel, Oaxaca City, Palenque, Tuxtla Gutiérrez, and Villahermosa, with additional service to Central America. It also flies from Cozumel and Cancún to Chichén Itzá. Aeroméxico flies direct to Mérida from Miami with a stop (but no plane change) in Cancún. Aviacsa flies nonstop from Mérida to Guadalajara, Mexico City, and Tijuana and makes connections to Cancún, Villahermosa, Tuxtla Gutiérrez, Tapachula, Oaxaca, Chetumal, and Mexico City. Mexicana has a connecting flight from Newark via Cancún and a number of other connecting flights from the United States via Mexico City.
▯ **Aerocaribe** ☎ 999/928-6790. **Aeroméxico** ☎ 800/021-4000. **Aviacsa** ☎ 999/ 926-9087 or 999/925-6890. **Mexicana** ☎ 999/946-1332.

BUS TRAVEL

Mérida's municipal buses run daily 5 AM–midnight, but service is somewhat confusing. In the downtown area buses go east on Calle 59 and west on Calle 61, north on Calle 60 and south on Calle 62. You can catch a bus heading north to Progreso on Calle 56. There's no direct bus service from the hotels around the plaza to the long-distance bus station; however, taxis are reasonable.

There are several first-class bus stations offering deluxe buses with air-conditioning and spacious seats. The most frequently used is Camionera Mérida (CAME). From here you can take the major bus lines: ADO, UNO, and Clase Elite to Akumal, Cancún, Chichén Itzá, Playa del Carmen, Tulum, Uxmal, Valladolid, and other major Mexican cities. ADO, UNO, and Super Expresso have direct buses to Cancún from their terminal at the Fiesta Americana hotel, on Paseo Montejo. There are other smaller lines. If you're not sure which line to take, or are heading to a more out-of-the-way destination, look for the free magazine *Yucatán Today,* which often lists all of Mérida's bus stations and their locations and the destinations.

🚌 **ADO/Super Expresso/UNO** ✉ Fiesta Americana, Av. Colón 451 Paseo Montejo Mérida ☎ 999/924-7868, 999/924-8391, or 999/925-0910. **Autotransportes del Sureste** (ATS) ☎ 999/923-2287. **CAME** ✉ Calle 70 No. 555, at Calle 71, Mérida ☎ 999/924-8391 or 999/924-4440. **Clase Elite/Nuevos Horizontes** ☎ 999/923-9913. **Terminal de Autobuses del Noreste** ✉ Calle 50 No. 527-A; between Calles 65 and 67, Mérida ☎ 999/923-4602 or 999/324-6355. **Terminal de Autobuses (2da clase)** ✉ Calle 69 No. 544, between Calles 68 and 70, Mérida ☎ 999/923-2287 or 999/923-4440. **Terminal del Autobuses a Progreso** (Progreso station) ✉ Calle 62 No. 557, between Calles 65 and 67, Mérida ☎ 999/928-3965.

CAR RENTAL

🚗 Major Agencies **Advantage** ✉ Fiesta Americana, Av. Colón 451 Paseo Montejo Mérida ☎ 999/920-1920. **Budget** ✉ Hotel Misión Mérida, Calle 60 No. 491, near Calle 57, Mérida ☎ 999/928-6759 ✉ Holiday Inn, Av. Colón 498 and Calle 60, Mérida ☎ 999/925-6877 Ext. 516 ✉ airport ☎ 999/946-1323. **Hertz** ✉ Fiesta Americana, Av. Colón 451, Paseo Montejo Mérida ☎ 999/925-7595 ✉ Calle 60 between Calles 55 and 57, Mérida ☎ 999/924-2834 or 999/984-0028 ✉ airport ☎ 999/946-1355. **National** ✉ Fiesta Americana, Av. Colón 451, Paseo Montejo Mérida ☎ 999/925-7524 ✉ airport ☎ 999/946-1394.

CAR TRAVEL

Driving in Mérida can be frustrating because of the one-way streets (many of which are in effect one-lane because of the parked cars) and because of dense traffic. But having your own wheels is the best way to take excursions from the city. For more relaxed sightseeing, consider hiring a cab for short excursions. Most charge approximately $12 per hour. Carretera 180, the main road along the gulf coast from the Texas border, passes through Mérida en route to Cancún. Mexico City is 1,550 km (961 mi) west, Cancún 320 km (198 mi) due east.

The autopista is a four-lane toll highway between Mérida and Cancún. Beginning at the town of Kantuníl, 55 km (34 mi) southeast of Mérida, it runs somewhat parallel to Carretera 180. The toll road cuts driving time between Mérida and Cancún—around 4½ hours on Carretera 180—by about an hour and bypasses about four dozen villages. Access to the toll highway is off old Carretera 180 and is clearly marked. The highway has exits for Valladolid and Pisté (Chichén Itzá), as well as rest stops and gas stations. Tolls between Mérida and Cancún total about $25.

CONSULATES

🏢 **Canada** ✉ Av. Colon 309-D, at Calle 62, Mérida ☎ 999/925-6299. **United Kingdom** ✉ Calle 53 No. 498, at Calle 58, Mérida ☎ 999/928-6152. **United States** ✉ Paseo Montejo 453, at Av. Colón, Mérida ☎ 999/925-5011; 999/845-4364 after-hours emergencies.

EMERGENCIES

Doctors & Hospitals Centro Médico de las Américas ⊠ Calle 54 No. 365, between Calle 33-A and Av. Pérez Ponce, Mérida ☎ 999/927-3199. **Red Cross Hospital** ⊠ Calle 68 No. 533, between Calles 65 and 67, Mérida ☎ 999/928-5391.

Emergency Services Fire, police, Red Cross, and general emergency ☎ 060.

Pharmacies Farmacia de Ahorros San Fernando branch ⊠ Calle 60 at Av. Colón, Mérida ☎ 999/925-8126 ⊠ Central branch ⊠ Calle 60 at Calle 63, Mérida ☎ 999/928-5027. **Farmacia Yza** ☎ 999/926-6666 information and delivery.

ENGLISH-LANGUAGE MEDIA

The Plaza Pincheta newsstand carries a few English-language magazines. Librería Dante has a small selection of books in English.

Bookstores Librería Dante ⊠ Calle 62, between Calle 61 and Calle 63, Mérida ☎ 999/928-2020. **Plaza Pincheta** ⊠ Calle 61, between Calle 60 and Calle 62, Mérida ☎ no phone.

MAIL, INTERNET & SHIPPING

Mérida has only one correo, and it's open weekdays 8–3 and Saturday 9–1. You can, however, buy postage stamps at handicrafts shops in town. If you must send mail from Mexico, the Mex Post service can speed delivery, even internationally, though it costs more than regular mail. Cybercafés are popping up all over, though particularly along Mérida's main square and Calle 61 and Calle 63. Express Internet and Vía Olimpico are good bets.

Cybercafés Express Internet ⊠ Café Express, Calle 60 No. 502, at Calle 59, Mérida ☎ 999/928-1691. **Viá Olimpo Café** ⊠ Calle 62, at Calle 61, Mérida ☎ 999/923-5843. **Mail Service Correo** ⊠ Calle 65 at Calle 56, Mérida ☎ 999/928-5404 or 999/924-3590.

MONEY MATTERS

Most banks throughout Mérida are open weekdays 9–5. Banamex has its main offices, open weekdays 9–5 and Saturday 9–1:30, in the handsome Casa de Montejo, on the south side of the main square, with branches at the airport and the Fiesta Americana hotel. All have ATMs. Several other banks can be found on Calle 65, between Calles 62 and 60, and on Paseo Montejo.

CURRENCY EXCHANGE There are several exchange houses in Mérida, including Centro Cambriano Canto, open weekdays 9–1 and 4–7, and two on the ground level of the Fiesta Americana hotel, open weekdays 9–5.

Exchange Services Centro Cambriano Canto ⊠ Calle 61 No. 468, between Calles 52 and 54, Mérida ☎ 999/928-0458.

TAXIS

Taxis charge beach-resort prices, which makes them a little expensive for this region of Mexico. They don't normally cruise the streets for passengers but are available at 13 *sitios* (taxi stands) around the city; you can also get them in front of major hotels. The minimum fare is $3.

Sitio Mejorada ☎ 999/928-5589. **Sitio Parque de la Madre** ☎ 999/928-5322.

TOURS

Mérida has more than 50 tour operators, who generally go to the same places. What differs is the mode of transportation—and whether or not the vehicle is air-conditioned and insured. Beware the *piratas* (street vendors) who stand outside the offices of reputable tour operators and offer to sell you a cheaper trip. They have been known to take your money and not show up; they also do not carry liability insurance.

A two- to three-hour group tour of the city costs $20 to $55 per person. Or you can pick up an open-air sightseeing bus at Parque de Santa

Lucía for $8 (departures are Monday–Saturday at 10, 1, 4, and 7 and Sunday at 10 and 1). A day trip to Chichén Itzá, with guide, entrance fee, and lunch, costs approximately $53. For about the same price you can see the ruins of Uxmal and Kabah in the Puuc region; for a few more dollars you can add the neighboring sites of Sayil, Labná, and the Loltún Caves. Early afternoon departures to Uxmal allow you to take in the sound-and-light show at the ruins and return by 11 PM, for $56 (including dinner). Another option is a tour of Chichén Itzá followed by a drop-off in Cancún, for about $80.

Diego Nuñez is an outstanding guide who conducts boat tours of Río Lagartos. He charges $42 for a 2½-hour tour, which accommodates five or six people. He usually can be found at the restaurant called Isla Contoy, which he runs. German guide Hans Juergen Kramer, who has a degree in anthropology from the University of Bonn, is a savvy guide to Maya ruins around Mérida. He speaks four languages. Ecoturismo Yucatán offers kayaking trips along the northwest coast, as well as birding and biking adventures. Its specialty is arranging custom trips. Celestún Expeditions is a small company run by two natives of Celestún. In addition to the standard flamingo tours, they offer three-hour guided bike tours, jungle walks (day or night), crocodile tours at night, birdwatching excursions, and trips to the Maya ruins and haciendas. Tours range from $20 per person for the bike jaunt to $75 per person for the bird-watching outing.

🛈 **American Express** ⊠ Calle 56 No. 494, between Calles 41 and 43, Mérida ☎ 999/942-8200 or 999/924-4326. **Amigo Travel** ⊠ Av. Colón 508-C, Col. García Ginerés, Mérida ☎ 999/920-0101 or 999/920-0107. **Carmen Travel Service** ⊠ Hotel María del Carmen, Calle 63 No. 550, at Calle 68, Mérida ☎ 999/924-1212. **Celestún Expeditions** ⊠ Calle 10 No. 97, between Calles 9 and 11, Celestún ☎ 988/916-2049. **Diego Nuñez** c/o Restaurant Isla Contoy ⊠ Calle 19 No. 12, Tizimín ☎ 998/862-0000. **Ecoturismo Yucatán** ⊠ Calle 3 No. 235, between Calles 32-A and 34, Col. Pensiones, Mérida ☎ 999/920-2772 or 999/925-2187. **Felgueres Tours** ⊠ Holiday Inn, Av. Colón 498, at Calle 60, Mérida ☎ 999/920-4477 or 999/920-3444. **Hans Juergen Kramer. Yucatán Trails** ⊠ Calle 62 No. 502, between Calles 57 and 59, Mérida ☎ 999/928-2582.

VISITOR INFORMATION

Mérida has an information kiosk at the airport that's open daily 8–8. The city tourist Information center is open daily 8–8. The state tourist center is open daily 8–8.

🛈 **City Tourist Information Center** ⊠ Calle 62, between Calles 61 and 63 on the ground floor of the Palacio Municipal, Mérida ☎ 999/928-2020 Ext. 133. **State Tourist Information Center** ⊠ Teatro Peón Contreras, Calle 60, between Calles 57 and 59, Mérida ☎ 999/924-9290 or 999/924-9389.

CAMPECHE CITY

Updated by
Patricia Alisau

The state of Campeche, the least visited and most underrated corner of the Yucatán, is the perfect place for adventure. Its people are friendly and welcoming; the colonial cities and towns retain an air of innocence; and protected biospheres, farmland, and jungle traverse the remaining expanse. The forts of Campeche City—284 km (180 mi) southwest of Cancún and 1,234 km (725 mi) east of Mexico City—have 300-year-old cannons pointing across the Gulf of Mexico, relics from pirate days that give the city an aura of romance and history.

Beyond Campeche City's walls, the pyramids and ornate temples of ancient Maya kingdoms—some of the most important discoveries in the Maya empire to date—lie waiting in forests. The terrain of Campeche State varies, from the northeastern flatlands to the rolling hills of the south. More than 60% of the territory is covered by jungle, which is filled with precious mahogany and cedar. The Gulf Stream keeps temperatures at about 26°C (78°F) year-round; the humid, tropical climate feels hotter, though the heat is eased by evening breezes.

The city itself has a time-weathered and lovely feel to it—no contrived, ultramodern tourist glitz here, just a friendly city by the sea (population 240,000) that's proud of its heritage and welcomes all to share in it. This good-humored, open-minded attitude is described as *campechano,* an adjective that means "easygoing and cheerful."

Exploring Campeche City

Because Campeche has been walled (though not successfully fortified) since 1686, most of the historic downtown, or Viejo Campeche, is neatly contained in an area measuring just five blocks by nine blocks. The city is easily navigable—on foot, that is. Narrow cobblestone roads and a dearth of parking spaces make driving difficult.

On strategic corners around the old city, or Viejo Campeche, stand the seven remaining *baluartes* (bastions) in various stages of disrepair. These were once connected by a 3-km (2-mi) wall in a hexagonal fortification that was built to safeguard the city against the pirates who continually ransacked it. Only bits of the wall still stand, and two stone archways—one facing the sea, the other the land—are all that remain of the four gates that were once the city's only entrances.

a good walk

Viejo Campeche, the old city center, is the best place to start a walking tour, beginning with the **Baluarte de la Soledad** ㊷ ⚑, which has a small Maya stelae museum. At the nearby Parque Principal, the city's central plaza, view some of the Yucatán Peninsula's most stately Spanish colonial architecture, including the **Catedral** ㊸ and, directly across the park, the **Casa Seis** ㊹. On Calle 10 between Calles 51 and 53 is the Mansión Carvajal; **Baluarte de Santiago** ㊺ is about one block to the north. Head south on Calle 51 several blocks to the small, well-fortified **Baluarte de San Pedro** ㊻, at Circuito Baluartes Norte and Avenida Gobernadores. Walk west along Calle 18 to **Puerta de Tierra** ㊼ and the Baluarte San Francisco; then take **Calle 59** ㊽ past the beautiful **Iglesia de San Francisquito** ㊾. Turn down Calle 10 to reach the **Ex-Templo de San José** ㊿ and then the **Iglesia de San Román** (51). Both are considered masterpieces of colonial religious architecture. Proceed north along Calle 8 for a look at the contrasting, modernistic designs of the Congreso del Estado and the Palacio del Gobierno. Finish the walk along the beachfront malecón.

What to See

⚑ ㊷ **Baluarte de la Soledad.** Built to protect the Puerta de Mar (Sea Door), one of the four city gates through which all seafarers were forced to pass, this bastion dedicated to Our Lady of Soledad is on Parque Principal's west side. Because it stands alone, without any wall to shore it up, it resembles a Roman triumphal arch. The largest of the bastions, this one has comparatively complete parapets and embrasures that offer a sweeping view of the cathedral, municipal buildings, and the 16th- to 19th-century houses along Calle 8. Inside, the **Museo de las Estelas** (Stelae Museum) has artifacts that include a well-preserved sculpture of a man wearing an owl mask, columns from the Edzná and Isla Jaina ruins, and at least a dozen well-proportioned Maya stelae from ruins throughout Campeche. ✉ *Calles 8 and 57, Centro* ☎ *No phone* 💵 *$2* ⏲ *Mon. 8–noon, Tues.–Sun. 8–7:30.*

㊻ **Baluarte de San Pedro.** Built in 1686 to protect the city from land attacks by pirates, St. Peter's Bastion—with its thick walls, flanked by watchtowers—houses a handicrafts and souvenir shop and a satellite office for the Secretary of Tourism, where you can book an English-speaking tour guide. Many of the tours to ruins such as Edzná leave from this point. ⊠ *Av. Gobernadores and Circuito Baluartes, Centro* ☎ *No phone* ☞ *Free* ⊙ *Mon.–Sat. 9–9.*

㊺ Baluarte de Santiago. The St. James Bastion was the last to be built (1704). Although the original structure was demolished at the turn of the last century, and then rebuilt in the 1950s, architecturally the bastion looks much the same as the others in Campeche—a stone fortress with thick walls, watchtowers, and gunnery slits. It has been transformed into the **X'much Haltún Botanical Gardens,** with more than 200 plant species from the region, including the huge, beautiful *ceiba* tree, which, to the Maya, symbolized a link between heaven, earth, and the underworld. There's also a garden containing specimens of medicinal, botanical, and ornamental plants used by the Maya. ⊠ *Calles 8 and 59, Circuito Baluartes, Centro* ☎ *No phone* ☞ *Free* ⊙ *Daily 9–6.*

㊽ Calle 59. On this city street, between Calles 8 and 18, once stood some of Campeche's finest homes, most of them two stories high, with the ground floors serving as warehouses and the upper floors as residences. The richest inhabitants built as close to the sea as possible, in case escape became necessary. (Legend has it that beneath the city a network of tunnels crisscrossed, linking the eight bastions and providing temporary refuge from pirates. The tunnel network has never been found, although rumors of its existence persist.) These days, behind the delicate grillwork and lace curtains, you can glimpse genteel scenes of Campeche life, with faded lithographs on the dun-color walls and plenty of antique furniture and gilded mirrors. To see the oldest houses in Campeche, walk south along Calle 10 past Circuito Baluartes to where it meets the malecón in the San Román neighborhood.

㊹ Casa Seis. One of the first colonial homes built in Campeche, House No. 6 has been beautifully restored and is now a cultural center. The rooms are furnished with original antiques and a few reproductions to create a replica of a typical 19th-century colonial house. Some of the original frescoes that border the tops of the walls date from 1500. The courtyard has Moorish architecture offset by lovely 18th-century stained-glass windows; it's used as an area for exhibits, lectures, and performances. The small restaurant off the original kitchen area serves excellent local specialties daily, from 9 to 2 and 6 to 10. ⊠ *Calle 57, across from main plaza, Centro* ☎ *981/816–1782* ☞ *Free* ⊙ *Daily 9–9.*

㊸ Catedral de la Inmaculada Concepción. It took two centuries (1650–1850) to finish the grand Cathedral of the Immaculate Conception, and as a result, it incorporates both neoclassical and Renaissance elements. The present cathedral occupies the site of a church that was built in 1540 on what is now Calle 55, between Calles 8 and 10. The simple exterior is capped with two bulbous towers rising on each side of the gracefully curved stone entrances; fluted pilasters echo those of the towers. Sculptures of saints in niches recall French Gothic cathedrals. The interior is no less impressive, with a single limestone nave, supported by Doric columns set with Corinthian capitals, arching toward the huge octagonal dome above a black-and-white marble floor. The pièce de résistance, however, is the Holy Sepulchre, carved from ebony and decorated with a multitude of stamped silver angels. ⊠ *East side of the Plaza Principal, Centro* ⊙ *Daily 6–noon and 5:30–7.*

㊿ Ex-Templo de San José. The Jesuits built this fine Baroque structure—formerly the Church of Saint Joseph—in 1756. It has a block-long facade

and a portal that's completely covered with blue-and-yellow tiles and crowned with seven narrow stone finials that resemble both the roof combs on many Maya temples and the combs Spanish women once wore as part of their elaborate hairdos. The former convent school next door is now the Instituto Campechano (Campeche Institute), used for cultural events and art exhibitions. Campeche's first lighthouse, built in 1864, is atop the right tower. Although the church isn't open to the public, evening cultural events are held here sporadically, and the guard at the Instituto Campechano may let you in to look around. ⊠ *Calle 10 at Calle 65, Centro.*

★ ☝ **Fuerte de San Miguel.** Scenic Avenida Ruíz Cortínez, near the city's west end, winds its way to a hilltop, where St. Michael's Fort commands a grand view of Campeche and the Gulf of Mexico. Built between 1686 and 1704, the fort was positioned to bombard enemy ships with its long-range cannons. But as soon as it was completed, pirates stopped attacking the city. Its impressive cannons were fired only once, in 1842, when General Santa Anna used Fuerte de San Miguel as headquarters when he attacked Campeche. The fort houses the outstanding **Museo Arqueológico de San Migual** (San Migual Archaeology Museum), which has some world-class exhibits that include Maya mummies as well as jewelry found at various tombs in the Calakmul ruins. The most famous item is a copy of the mummy of King Yichah Kak or Divine Lord of the Jaguar Paw (the original is in Mexico City undergoing research), who ruled during the period of fierce fighting with Tikal over control of the Petén. You can view his enormous jade breastplate, jade masks, and headdress made of pearls. Also noteworthy are funeral vessels, masks, many wonderfully expressive figurines from Isla Jaina, stelae and stucco masks from the Río Bec ruins, and an excellent pottery collection. The gift shop sells replicas of artifacts but unfortunately almost nothing from Campeche. The tram, *El Guapo* ($2.20 round-trip), makes the trip here daily at 10 AM, 6 PM, and 7 PM, leaving from the east side of the main plaza, across from Los Portales; you're given about 10 minutes to see the fort before the tram returns to the plaza. ✉ *Av. Francisco Morazán s/n, west of town center, Fuerte de San Miguel* ☎ *No phone* 💲 *$2.50* ☉ *Tues.–Sun. 8:30–8.*

㊾ Iglesia de San Francisquito (Iglesia de San Roque). With its elaborately carved altars, Baroque columns adorned with gold leaf, and carved, wooden pews and créches with statues of San Francisco, this long, narrow church—built as a convent in 1565—adds to historic Calle 59's old-fashioned beauty. It was originally called Church of Little St. Francis, but now some know it only as Iglesia de San Roque—a name derived from the neighborhood in which it's set. ✉ *Calle 12 at Calle 59, San Roque* ☉ *Daily 8:30–noon and 5–7.*

㊿ Iglesia de San Román. Just outside the intramural boundary in the barrio of the same name, at Calles 10 and Bravo, the Church of St. Roman, with its bulbous bell tower typical of other Yucatán churches, was built to house the *naboríos* (Indians brought by the Spaniards to aid in the conquest and later used as household servants). The barrio, like other neighborhoods, grew up around the church. Built in the early part of the 16th century, the church became central to the lives of the Indians when an ebony image of Christ, the "Black Christ," was brought from Italy via Veracruz in about 1575. The Indians had been skeptical about Christianity, but this Christ figure came to be associated with miracles. The legend goes that the ship that refused to carry the tradesman and his precious statue was wrecked, whereas the vessel that transported him and his cargo reached Campeche in record time. To this day, the Feast of San Román—when the black-wood Christ mounted on a silver filigree cross is carried through the streets—is the biggest celebration of its kind in Campeche, taking place during the whole month of September. ✉ *Calles 10 and Bravo, San Román* ☉ *Daily 7–1 and 3–7.*

★ ☾ ㊼ Puerta de Tierra. Viejo Campeche ends at the Land Gate, the only one with its basic structure intact. (The walls, arches, and gates were refurbished in 1987.) The stone arch intercepts a stretch of the partially crenulated wall, 26 ft high and 10 ft thick, that once encircled the city. You can walk along the full length of the wall to the Baluarte San Juan, where there are some excellent views of both old and new Campeche. A staircase leads down to an old well, underground storage area, and dungeon. There's a two-hour light show ($2.20) at Puerta de Tierra (in Spanish with French and English subtitles), Tuesday, Friday, and Saturday at 8:30 PM, daily during Christmas vacation periods. Local musicians and dancers add to the spectacle, which gives an excellent historical overview of Campeche. ✉ *Calles 18 and 59, Centro* ☉ *Daily 8–5.*

Where to Stay & Eat

$–$$$ ✕ **La Pigua.** Local professionals enjoy lingering over long lunches here. FodorśChoice The seafood is delicious, and the setting is pleasant: two long glass walls
★ form a terrarium of trees and plants. A truly ambitious lunch would start with a seafood cocktail, plate of cold crab claws, or *camarones al cocado* (coconut-encrusted shrimp), followed by fresh local fish in one of myriad presentations. For dessert, the peaches drenched in sweet liqueurs are a good bet. ✉ *Av. Miguel Alemán 179-A, Col. Lazareto Guadalupe* ☎ *981/811–3365* 🗃 *MC, V* ☉ *No dinner.*

$ ✕ **Casa Vieja.** The food is so-so, but the view overlooking Campeche's main plaza is fabulous. Look for the hidden stairway on the plaza's east side, next to the Modatela store, and climb one floor. The Cuban owner has created an international menu of pastas, salads, and regional food.

Delicious desserts are prepared daily. ⊠ *Calle 10 No. 319 (altos), between Calles 57 and 55, Centro* ☎ *981/811–1311* ⊟ *No credit cards.*

¢–$$ ✕ **Chez Fernando.** This café-style eatery offers Mediterranean, Italian, French, and Mexican food, including fresh pastas, salads, fish, chicken, and steak. The lasagna Florentine and the pollo Dijon are excellent, as is the chocolate mousse. ⊠ *Av. Resurgimiento s/n, Jardín Coca Cola* ☎ *981/816–2125* ⊟ *No credit cards* ✆ *No lunch.*

¢–$$ ✕ **Marganzo.** Traditional Campeche cuisine is served by a traditionally attired waitstaff at this colorful, rustic restaurant a half block south of the plaza. The *pompano en escabèche* (grilled fish with chilies and orange juice) and the fresh shrimp dishes are good. ⊠ *Calle 8 No. 267, between Calles 57 and 59, Centro* ☎ *981/811–3898* ⊟ *AE, MC, V.*

$$ ☷ **Del Mar Hotel.** Rooms are fairly large, with tasteful drapes and floor tiles, rattan furniture, and balconies that overlook the pool or the bay across the street. The lobby coffee shop, El Poquito, serves standard but tasty fare, and Lafitte's pirate-theme bar-restaurant, offers room service until 2 AM. ⊠ *Av. Ruíz Cortínez 51 (on the waterfront), Centro, 24000* ☎ *981/816–2233* 🖷 *981/811–4124* ⊕ *hoteldelmar.com* ⇨ *138 rooms, 11 suites* ⚭ *Restaurant, coffee shop, room service, in-room data ports, cable TV, pool, laundry service, meeting room, travel services, shop, free parking* ⊟ *AE, MC, V.*

★ $ ☷ **Baluartes.** Between the waterfront and the Puerta del Mar (gateway to the old city), the modern Baluartes is much prettier inside than out—thanks primarily to a gleaming marble lobby and an attractive lounge area. Many of the huge light-filled rooms have sea views; all are done in cool blue tones and have white-tile baths. A large pool faces the ocean. ⊠ *Av. 16 de Septiembre 128, Centro, 24000* ☎ *981/816–3911* 🖷 *981/816–2410* ⇨ *100 rooms* ⚭ *Restaurant, coffee shop, room service, cable TV, pool, bar, meeting room, travel services, free parking* ⊟ *AE, MC, V.*

¢ ☷ **Colonial.** This romantic building dates from 1812 but was converted into a hotel in the 1940s, when its colorful tiles were added. All rooms are delightfully different, with cool cotton bedding, good mattresses, tile bathrooms, and window screens. Most rooms still have the original telephones and antique plumbing (which works quite well). Rooms 16, 18, 27, and 28 have wonderful views of the cathedral and city at night. Public areas include two leafy patios, a small sunroof, and a second-floor sitting room. ⊠ *Calle 14 No. 122, between Calles 55 and 57, Centro, 24000* ☎ *981/816–2222* ⇨ *30 rooms* ⚭ *Fans; no a/c in some rooms, no room TVs* ⊟ *No credit cards.*

★ ¢ ☷ **Hostal Campeche.** What a hostel this is: its location in a colonial building facing the main plaza is the envy of the fancy hotels. Guests, most of whom share clean dorm rooms for six to eight people, have access to a library and book exchange, a kitchen, a rooftop sundeck, a washer and dryer, and a large second-floor lobby that's the perfect place to read or people-watch. There are also two air-conditioned doubles that share a bath. ⊠ *Calle 10 and Calle 57, Centro, 24000* ☎ *981/811–6500* ⊕ *www.hostalcampeche.com* ⇨ *40 beds* ⚭ *Bicycles, library, laundry facilities, Internet; no a/c in some rooms, no room TVs, no room phones* ⊟ *No credit cards.*

Nightlife

On Friday and Saturday, laser shows complement the dance music at the high-tech **Jaxx** (⊠ Av. Resurgimiento 112, Carretera a Lerma ☎ 981/818–4555). **KY8** (⊠ Calle 8, between Calles 59 and 61, Centro ☎ No phone), open Friday and Saturday only, plays dance tunes as well as Latin music and is popular with locals.

Sports & the Outdoors

Hunting, fishing, and birding are popular throughout the state of Campeche. Contact **Don José Sansores** (⊠ Snook Inn, Calle 30 No. 1, Centro, Champotón ☎☎ 981/828–0018; 981/816–5538 in Campeche City) to arrange sportfishing or wildlife photo excursions in the Champotón area. **Francisco Javier Hernandez Romero** (⊠ La Pigua restaurant, Av. Miguel Alemán 179–A, Centro ☎ 981/811–3365) can arrange boat or fishing trips to the Peténes Ecological Reserve.

Shopping

In a lovely old mansion, the government-run **Casa de Artesanía Tukulna** (⊠ Calle 10 No. 333, between Calles 59 and 61, Centro ☎ 981/816–9088) sells well-made embroidered dresses, blouses, pillow coverings, regional dress for men and women, hammocks, Campeche's famous Panama hats, posters, books on Campeche ecology in Spanish, jewelry, baskets, and stucco reproductions of Maya motifs. The shop is open Monday–Saturday 9–8 and Sunday 10–2.

Side Trip to Edzná

Carretera 261—the long way from Campeche City to the Yucatán capital of Mérida—passes the Chenes ruins of eastern Campeche. Chenes-style temples are recognized by their elaborate stucco facades decorated with geometric designs, giant masks of jaguars, and birds. Also characteristic of the style are doorways shaped like the open mouth of a monster. It is a scenic route, leading through green hills with tall dark forests and valleys covered by low scrub, cornfields, and citrus orchards.

The Maya ruin of **Edzná**, 55 km (34 mi) southeast of Campeche City, deserves more recognition than it has received. Archaeologists consider it one of the peninsula's most important ruins because of the crucial transitional role it played among several architectural styles. Occupied from around 300 BC to AD 1450, Edzná reached its pinnacle between AD 600 and AD 900. Over the course of several hundred years, Edzná grew from a humble agricultural settlement into a major political-religious center. The city served as a trading center of sorts, situated at a "crossroads" between the cities of the Petén region of Guatemala and the lowlands of northern Yucatán. The region's agricultural products were traded for hand-carved ritual objects and adornments from Guatemala.

Commanding center stage in the Gran Acrópolis (Great Acropolis) is the Pirámide de los Cinco Pisos (Five-Story Pyramid), which rises 102 ft. The structure consists of five levels, each narrower than the one below it, terminating in a tiny temple crowned by a roof comb. Hieroglyphs were carved into the vertical face of the 15 steps between each level, and numerous stelae depict the opulent attire and adornment of the ruling class—quetzal feathers, jade pectorals, and skirts of jaguar skin.

In 1992 Campeche archaeologist Antonio Benavides discovered that the Five-Story Pyramid was so constructed that, during certain dates of the year, the setting sun would illuminate the mask of the creator god, Itzamná, inside one of the pyramid's rooms. This happens annually on May 1, 2, and 3, the beginning of the planting season for the Maya—then and now—when they invoke the god to bring rain. It also occurs on August 7, 8, and 9, the days of harvesting and thanking the god for his help. Near the temple's base, the Templo de la Luna (Temple of the Moon), Templo del Sureste (Southwest Temple), Templo del Norte (North Temple), and Temezcal (steam bath) surround a small plaza.

West of the Great Acropolis, the Puuc-style Plataforma de las Navajas (Platform of the Knives) was so-named by a 1970 archaeological exploration that found a number of flint knives inside. Also in this area is the Edificio de la Vieja Hechicera (Building of the Old Witchcraft), which faces a small plaza. Its name comes from supposed apparitions of witches in modern times here. South of the Great Acropolis lies the Small Acropolis, whose four buildings each face a cardinal point in the compass. Carved into the Temple of the Masks (Building 414), adjacent to the Small Acropolis, are some masks of the sun god with huge protruding eyes, filed teeth, and oversize tongues.

If you're not driving, consider taking one of the inexpensive day trips offered by most travel agencies in Campeche; this is far easier than trying to get to Edzná by municipal buses. ⊠ *Carretera 261 east from Campeche City for 44 km (27 mi) to Cayal, then Carretera 188 southeast for 18 km (11 mi)* ☎ *No phone* ⊠ *$3.30* ☉ *Daily 8–5.*

The State of Campeche A to Z

To research prices, get advice from other travelers, and book travel arrangements, visit www.fodors.com.

AIR TRAVEL

AIRPORT Campeche's Aeropureto Internacional Alberto Acuña Ongay is 16 km (10 mi) north of downtown.

🚹 Airport Information **Aeropureto Internacional Alberto Acuña Ongay** ☎ 981/816-3109.

AIRPORT TRANSFERS Taxis are the only means of transportation to and from the airport. A ride in a private cab to or from the city center will run you around $7. At the airport, you pay your fare ahead of time at the ticket booth outside the terminal; a dispatcher then directs you to your cab.

CARRIER Aeroméxico has two flights daily from Mexico City to Campeche City.
🚹 **Aeroméxico** ☎ 800/021-4000.

BUS TRAVEL

Within Campeche City, buses run along Avenida Ruíz Cortínez and cost the equivalent of about 30¢.

ADO, a first-class line, runs buses from Campeche City to Mérida, Villahermosa, and Ciudad del Carmen almost every hour, with less frequent departures for Cancún, Chetumal, Oaxaca, and other destinations. Adjacent to the ADO station, the second-class bus station has service on Unión de Camioneros to intermediate points throughout the Yucatán Peninsula, as well as less desirable service to Chetumal, Ciudad del Carmen, Escárcega, Mérida, Palenque, Tuxtla Gutiérrez, and Villahermosa.

A half block from the ADO station is the office of the Elite Nuevos Horizontes bus company, which offers first-class service at least once a day to Mérida, Ciudad del Carmen, Mexico City, Veracruz, Cancún, Playa del Carmen, Jalapa, and Villahermosa. Try to avoid an extended stopover in Escárcega, along Carretera 261. Though the government has beefed up security—Escárcega was an unsafe spot for tourists, with bus passengers the targets of robberies and assaults—and things have improved, it's still not a place to linger.

🚹 **ADO** ⊠ Av. Gobernadores 289, at Calle 45, along Carretera 261 to Mérida, Campeche City ☎ 981/816-3445. **Elite Nuevos Horizontes** ⊠ Av. Gobernadores 575, between Calles 15 and 17, Campeche City ☎ 981/811-0261. **Unión de Camioneros** ⊠ Calle Chile at Av. Gobernadores, Campeche City ☎ No phone.

CAR RENTAL
Agencies **AutoRent** ⊠ Hotel del Paseo, Calle 8 No. 215, Campeche City ☎ 981/811-0100. **Maya Rent a Car** ⊠ Del Mar Hotel, Av. Ruíz Cortínez at Calle 59, Campeche City ☎ 981/816-2233 🖶 981/811-1618.

CAR TRAVEL
Campeche City is about two hours from Mérida along the 160-km (99-mi) *via corta* (short way), Carretera 180. The alternative route, the 250-km (155-mi) *via larga* (long way), Carretera 261, takes about three to four hours but passes the major Maya ruins of Uxmal, Kabah, and Sayil.

EMERGENCIES
Doctors & Hospitals **Hospital General de Campeche** ⊠ Av. Central at Circuito Baluarte, Campeche City ☎ 981/816-0920. **Social Security Clinic** ⊠ Av. López Mateos and Av. Talamantes, Campeche City ☎ 981/816-1855 or 981/816-5202.

Emergency Services **General Emergencies** ☎ 060. **Police** ⊠ Av. Resurgimiento 77, Col. Lazareto, Campeche City ☎ 981/816-2309. **Red Cross** ⊠ Av. Las Palmas at Ah-Kim-Pech s/n, Campeche City ☎ 981/815-2411.

24-Hour Pharmacy **Clínica Campeche** ⊠ Av. Central 65, near the Social Security Clinic, Campeche City ☎ 981/816-5612.

MAIL, INTERNET & SHIPPING
The correo in Campeche City is open weekdays 8–8, Saturday 9–1. For important letters or packages, it's best to use DHL. Cybercafés have just started popping up in Campeche City; try Ciber Club downtown.

Cybercafé **Ciber Club** ⊠ Calle 67 No. 1B Altos, Campeche City ☎ 981/811-3577.

Mail Services **Correo** ⊠ Av. 16 de Septiembre, between Calles 53 and 55, Campeche City ☎ 981/816-2134. **DHL** ⊠ Av. Miguel Aleman 169, Campeche City ☎ 981/816-0382.

MONEY MATTERS
Campeche City banks will change traveler's checks and currency weekdays 9–4. Two large chains are Banamex and Bancomer.

Banks **Banamex** ⊠ Calle 53 No. 15, at Calle 10 ☎ 981/816-5251. **Bancomer** ⊠ Av. 16 de Septiembre 120 ☎ 981/816-6622.

TAXIS
You can hail taxis on the street in Campeche City; there are also stands by the bus stations, the cathedral, and the market. Because cabs are scarce, it's quite common to share them with other people headed in the same direction—rarely will you have a cab to yourself, and drivers won't ask your permission to pick up another fare. A shared cab ride costs under $1. If you have one to yourself, it's $2–$3.

Radio Taxis ☎ 981/816-1113 or 981/816-6666.

TOURS
Trolley tours of Campeche City leave from the Plaza Principal several times on the half hour in the morning, and in the evening at 6 and 8 during high season; trips are much more sporadic in the off-season. The one-hour tour costs about $2.20. You can buy tickets on board the trolley, or ahead of time in the municipal tourist office right next to the cathedral, also on the plaza.

Servicios Turísticos Picazh offers transportation only or guided service to Edzná at reasonable prices.

Servicios Turísticos Picazh ⊠ Calle 16 No. 348, between Calles 57 and 59, Campeche City ☎ 981/816-4426.

TRAVEL AGENCIES
Local Agents **American Express/VIPs** ⊠ Prolongación Calle 59, Edificio Belmar, Depto. 5, Campeche City ☎ 981/811-1010 or 981/811-1000. **Intermar Campeche** ⊠ Av.

Miguel Alemán at Av. Guadalupe, Campeche City ☎ 981/816‒9006. **Viajes Programados** ⊠ Calle 59 between Av. 16 de Septiembre and Av. Ruíz Cortínez, Campeche City ☎ 981/811‒1010.

VISITOR INFORMATION

The state tourism office is open daily 9–3 and 6–9. The municipal tourist office is open daily 8–2:30 and 4–8. The staff speaks very little English, but you can pick up a map.

🖪 **Municipal Tourist Office** ⊠ Calle 55, west of the cathedral, Campeche City ☎ 981/811‒3989 or 981/811‒3990. **State Tourist Office** ⊠ Av. Ruíz Cortínez s/n, Plaza Moch Couoh, across from Palacio del Gobierno, Campeche City ☎ 981/811‒9229 🖷 981/816‒6767.

UNDERSTANDING
MEXICO

MEXICO OFFICIALLY ENTERED the 21st century as a new democracy, finally booting out the party that had lorded over Mexican politics for 71 years. The PRI, or Institutional Revolutionary Party, grew out of the 1910 Mexican Revolution, and kept its hold on power through a combination of political maneuvering, co-optation, and outright electoral fraud. In July 2000, however, Mexican voters—armed with new electoral laws and fed up with official corruption and economic hardship—dethroned the PRI. With 43% of the vote (compared with the PRI's 36%), the swashbuckling businessman Vicente Fox, from the center-right National Action Party (PAN), became the first opposition president of modern Mexico. The new president stands tall (six-foot-five) and in striking contrast to those who came before him: he talks colloquially instead of using the stiff speech of traditional *políticos;* he dons cowboy boots and a giant silver belt buckle that reads F-O-X; he entered office a divorced man, then made his presidential campaign adviser the First Lady. He pledged to run the country much like he used to run Coca-Cola de México. The changes President Fox promised during his campaign, however, have been excruciatingly slow in coming, and many Mexicans today question whether or not they're truly any better off than before. Nonetheless, he has taken some important steps toward modernizing the country's economy, battling corruption, and strengthening relations with the United States.

Mexico, for all its ancient history, is a young country. About a third of the population is between 15 and 29 years old. Many of these young people were raised in economic and political turmoil. Mexicans today are tired of seeing themselves as downtrodden. Many prefer to look for inspiration to actress Salma Hayek—a Veracruz native—or to the successful young Harvard Business School entrepreneur Miguel Angel Davila, who started the Cinemex movie chain. Signs of modern Mexico are everywhere: cash machines even in some small towns, *People en Español,* and the proliferation of cell phones. But

as ever, modernity does not come all at once. In much of Mexico, a brand-new VW Beetle may share the road with a burro. Mexico's struggle with progress is like a Latin dance: two steps forward, one step back.

As the country has opened economically over the past two decades, a slow push for political opening followed. Those growing up now are often dubbed the NAFTA generation, after the free-trade agreement: they are more outward-looking, more free-enterprise savvy, and more cynical about traditional (often corrupt) politics. The old one-party system failed them when the bottom fell out of the economy just after the 1994 presidential election, and the memory of what Mexicans simply call *la crisis* is very much alive. Many people are still shy of bank accounts, credit cards, and home loans, which were practically nonexistent for years after the peso crashed but are beginning to resurface. Wages remain below what they were before the crisis, full-time jobs are always in short supply, and the new government has tightened the belt even further, raising sales taxes and cutting government assistance. Much of Mexico, however, appears to be booming. Exports—driven by the free-trade agreement with the United States—are thriving in some sectors. Investors have returned, betting on the perennial comeback. The economy is still vulnerable to global recession, as shown by the layoffs following the recent U.S. economic downturn, but it is much more stable than it was before la crisis.

Emphasizing his experience as a former CEO of Coca-Cola in Mexico, Fox promised to improve Mexico's economy by running the country more like a business. He even announced he'd improve efficiency by placing the government on a "matrix-style management plan." At this writing, however, most of Fox's efforts to create jobs and jump-start the economy had been frustrated by the economic recession on this side of the border and by an oppositional Congress. (The midterm congressional elections of July 2003 determine whether the PRI maintains its narrow majority.) During the first three years of his presidency, Fox met an unprecedented number of times with his newly elected U.S. counterpart, lobbying both George W. Bush and the U.S. Congress for a major liberalization of immigration laws between the two countries. Mexico's 3,141-km (1,952-mi) border with the United States, which serves as a pressure valve during hard times, has always made for tricky politics between the two nations. Although the U.S. Congress at first seemed receptive to the fiery new president's proposals, the September 11, 2001, terrorist attacks effectively ended all talk of loosening immigration laws.

Although change may seem painstakingly slow, it seems clear the 2000 political opening is pervasive. In state and local politics, the PRI has lost considerable ground in recent years. Fox's conservative PAN has won the governorships in 8 of Mexico's 31 states, whereas the liberal Revolution Democratic Party (PRD) controls four states and Mexico City. In the states of Chiapas and Nayarit, the diametrically opposed PAN and PRD formed an alliance to unseat the PRI governors in 1999 and 2000. Opposition parties have also achieved real power in Congress for the first time in modern Mexican history. Congressmen used to be called *levantadedos* (finger lifters) because all they did was vote as the president wished. Today, there is competition—even the occasional fistfight—on the House floor. President Fox, in fact, has been unable to push through many of his major reform measures, including tax reform and labor laws and a proposal to partially privatize the electricity industry, due to Congressional resistance.

Democratic reform has also brought an end to the extreme formality of Mexican politics. No one used to look the Mexican president in the eye, such was his power. Today, some political commentators use the informal *tu* (you) when addressing President Fox, a tradition that began with Fox's PRI predecessor, former President Ernesto Zedillo. Fox is pilloried regularly in political cartoons. The press have angered Fox by poking fun at everything from his cowboy boots, his occasional mispronunciation of words, and the lavish charity benefits thrown by First Lady Martha Sahagun. During the first half of

Fox's presidency, his unruly advisers were dubbed the "Montessori Cabinet."

Much of the credit for Mexico's new democracy is owed to former President Zedillo (1994–2000), who paved the way for his own party's fall from power. Zedillo was often dubbed the "accidental candidate" because he stepped into the presidential race at the last minute after front-runner Luis Donaldo Colosio was assassinated in 1994, a tragedy from which Mexico has never fully recovered. But during his *sexenio* (six-year term), Zedillo proved himself more of an accidental reformer. By not playing the role of ironclad president, he opened the door to the opposition. He expanded political funding for all parties, returned some power and money to the country's 31 states, and relinquished his traditional right to name his successor. This PRI tradition of handpicking the next president, called the *dedazo* (literally "the finger-pointing"), existed from the time the PRI took power in 1929 until 1999, when the party held its first-ever primaries to choose its presidential candidate.

But the PRI's continued power and influence in the new political landscape should not be underestimated. During its seven decades of power, the party showed an uncanny ability to learn from its mistakes and to remake itself to fit the national mood. Many older Mexicans yearn for the security the party once provided. In some states, the PRI seems to be gaining popularity by moving away from its technocrats—the term refers to the cocky young reformers epitomized by former president Carlos Salinas (1988–94). The "Harvard-trained economist," as he was invariably described, brought Mexico free trade, privatization, and all the promises of neoliberalism.

Salinas also brought discredit on his party and his country. Not only did his dream of First World membership die with the peso crisis, but his administration is now considered one of the most corrupt in Mexican history. Salinas lives in self-imposed exile in Dublin, Ireland, but he is still called Mexico's favorite villain. Street vendors sell masks of his face with his inimitable big ears. Bankers who cashed in under Salinas's privatizations have gone on the lam. And Salinas's older brother,

Raúl, has been sentenced to 27 years for allegedly masterminding the murder of a former PRI leader. Meanwhile, Swiss investigators seized $114 million from Raúl's Swiss bank accounts in 1998, arguing that the money came from drug trafficking. In the ongoing legal proceedings, Mexican prosecutors claim that the fortune was built on corrupt political practices.

There has been a kind of don't-ask-don't-tell attitude about drug trafficking in Mexico for years. Since Mexico became the main transportation route for Colombian cocaine growers in the 1980s, drug cartels have insinuated themselves into Mexican life, and Mexican cartels are now every bit as powerful as their Colombian counterparts. Although two top drug lords were arrested in 2002 and 2003, the cartels continue to be formidably strong. Drug use is up, and drug culture, touching everything from clothing to music, is spreading. People wink and nudge each other about the gaudy hotels and new shopping complexes, especially along the U.S. border, that they assume were built with drug money. But they shrug it off. Drug violence hasn't hurt the average citizen enough (except in border cities such as Juárez and Tijuana) for Mexicans to get really angry about it. But increased crime has. Most Mexicans' biggest concern, they'll tell you, is public safety. Although crime is still no worse than in many big U.S. cities, poor policing and weak courts make it seem that way.

As in much of Latin America, hard-liners are making a comeback. Some Mexicans are beginning to clamor for the death penalty, something almost unheard of in Catholic countries. The army has been called in to help fight street crime, drugs, and guerillas. And the human-rights situation, especially in states considered guerilla-friendly, is bleak. In December 1997, paramilitary forces massacred 45 peasants thought sympathetic to the Zapatista rebels in Acteal in the southern state of Chiapas. Digna Ochoa, a leading human-rights attorney who had defended Zapatista sympathizers and environmentalists, was murdered in 2001 in her Mexico City office; her murderers left a note warning her colleagues to stop their work. Peace talks with the Zapatistas, who sprang up in 1995, are stalled even though the cease-fire holds. The Zapatistas, or Ejército Zapatista de Liberación Nacional (EZLN), are only the most publicity-savvy of a few small guerilla groups. They—with their charismatic spokesman Subcomandante Marcos—are still a leftist cause célèbre. At first, Mexicans had a brief romance with the pipe-smoking Marcos because he seemed to speak for the downtrodden. Now, they say they are mostly weary of the violence. President Fox boasted during his campaign that he could solve the Zapatista conflict in 15 minutes. Sadly, this is another promise he has not been able to deliver.

One thing is certain, however. The opening represented by the 2000 presidential elections, along with the growth of nonprofit and civic organizations, has had a tremendous impact on Mexican politics, economics, and culture. There is greater debate from the ballot box to the boardrooms to the kitchen tables every day. From the scathing editorials in the growing free press to the customer-service hot lines at once-indifferent monopolies, Mexico is going through a transition made all the more dramatic in part because it does not always make the nightly news.

— Martha Brandt and Paige Bierma

CHRONOLOGY

Pre-Columbian Mexico

ca. 50,000 bc   Asian nomads cross land bridge over the Bering Strait to North America, gradually migrate south.

ca. 5000–   Archaic period, which marked the beginnings of agriculture and
2000 bc   village life.

ca. 2000–   Formative or Preclassic period: development of pottery, incipient
200 bc   political structures.

ca. 1500–   The powerful and sophisticated Olmec civilization develops along the
900 bc   Gulf of Mexico in the present-day states of Veracruz and Tabasco. Olmec culture, the "mother culture" of Mexico, flourishes along Gulf coast.

ca. 200 bc–   Classic period: height of pre-Columbian culture. Three centers at
AD 900   Teotihuacán (near Mexico City), Monte Albán (Oaxaca), and Maya civilization in the Yucatán. Priest-run city-states produce impressive art and architecture.

650–900   Decline of Classic cultures: fall of Teotihuacán ca. 650 leads to competition among other city-states, exacerbated by migrations of northern tribes.

ca. 900–1150   Toltecs, a northern tribe, establish a flourishing culture at their capital of Tula under the legendary monarch Topiltzin-Quetzalcóatl.

ca. 900–1521   Postclassic period: rule passes to military; war and war gods gain prominence.

ca. 1000–   Maya culture, declining in south, emerges in the Yucatán; under
1450   Toltec rule, Chichén Itzá dominates the peninsula.

1111   Aztecs migrate to mainland from island home off the Nayarit coast. They are not welcomed by the peoples of central Mexico.

ca. 1200   Rise of Mixtec culture at Zapotec sites of Monte Albán and Mitla; notable for production of picture codices, which include historical narratives.

1150–1350   Following the fall of Tula, first the Chichimecs, then the Tepanecs assert hegemony over central Mexico. The Tepanec tyrant Tezozómoc (1320–1426), like his contemporaries in Renaissance Italy, establishes his power with murder and treachery.

1376   Tezozómoc grants autonomy to the Aztec city of Tenochtitlán, built in the middle of Lake Texcoco.

1420–1500   Aztecs extend their rule to much of central and southern Mexico. A warrior society, they build a great city at Tenochtitlán.

1502   Moctezuma II (1466–1520) assumes throne at the height of Aztec culture and political power.

1517   Spanish expedition under Francisco Hernandez de Córdoba (1475–1526) lands on Yucatán coast.

1519   Hernán Cortés (1485–1547) lands in Cozumel, founds Veracruz, and determines to conquer. Steel weapons, horses, and smallpox, combined with a belief that Cortés was the resurrected Topiltzin-

Quetzalcóatl, minimize Aztec resistance. Cortés enters Tenochtitlán and captures Moctezuma.

The Colonial Period

1520–21 Moctezuma is killed; Tenochtitlán falls to Cortés. The last Aztec emperor, Cuauhtémoc, is executed.

1528 Juan de Zumarraga (1468–1548) arrives as bishop of Mexico City, gains title "Protector of the Indians"; conversion to Catholicism begins.

1535 First Spanish viceroy arrives in Mexico.

1537 Pope Paul III issues a bill declaring that native Mexicans are indeed human and not beasts. First printing press arrives in Mexico City.

1546–48 Silver deposits discovered at Zacatecas.

1547 Spanish conquest of Aztec Empire—now known as "New Spain"—completed, at enormous cost to native peoples.

1553 Royal and Pontifical University of Mexico, first university in the New World, opens.

1571 The Spanish Inquisition established in New Spain; it is not abolished until 1820.

1609 Northern capital of New Spain established at Santa Fe (New Mexico).

1651 Birth of Sor (Sister) Juana Inés de la Cruz, greatest poet of colonial Mexico (d. 1695).

1718 Franciscan missionaries settle in Texas, which becomes part of New Spain.

1765 Charles III of Spain (1716–88) sends José de Galvez to tour New Spain and propose reforms.

1769 Franciscan Junípero Serra establishes missions in California, extending Spanish hegemony.

1788 Death of Charles III; his reforms improved administration, but also raised social and political expectations among the colonial population, which were not fulfilled.

1808 Napoléon invades Spain, leaving a power vacuum in New Spain.

The War of Independence

1810 September 16: Father Miguel Hidalgo y Costilla (1753–1811) preaches his *Grito de Dolores*, sparking rebellion.

1811 Hidalgo is captured and executed; leadership of the movement passes to Father José Maria Morelos y Pavón (1765–1815).

1813 Morelos calls a congress at Chilpancingo, which drafts a Declaration of Independence.

1815 Morelos is captured and executed.

The Early National Period

1821 Vicente Guerrero, a rebel leader, and Agustín de Iturbide (1783–1824), a Spanish colonel converted to the rebel cause, rejuvenate the Independence movement. Spain recognizes Mexican independence with the Treaty of Córdoba.

1822   Iturbide is named Emperor of Mexico, which stretches from California through Central America.

1823   After 10 months in office, Emperor Agustín is turned out.

1824   A new constitution creates a federal republic, the Estados Unidos Mexicanos; modeled on the U.S. Constitution, the Mexican version retains the privileges of the Catholic Church and gives the president extraordinary "emergency" powers.

1829   President Vicente Guerrero abolishes slavery. A Spanish attempt at reconquest is halted by General Antonio López de Santa Anna (1794–1876), already a hero for his role in the overthrow of Emperor Agustín.

1833   Santa Anna is elected president by a huge majority; he holds the office for 11 of its 36 changes of hands by 1855.

1836   Although voted in as a liberal, Santa Anna abolishes the 1824 constitution. Already dismayed at the abolition of slavery, Texas—whose population is largely American—declares its independence. Santa Anna successfully besieges the Texans at the Alamo. But a month later he is captured by Sam Houston following the Battle of San Jacinto. Texas gains its independence as the Lone Star Republic.

1846   The U.S. decision to annex Texas leads to war.

1848   The treaty of Guadalupe Hidalgo reduces Mexico's territory by half, ceding present-day Texas, New Mexico, Arizona, California, Nevada, Utah, and part of Colorado to the United States.

1853   Santa Anna agrees to the Gadsden Purchase, ceding a further 48,000 square km (30,000 square mi) to the United States.

The Reform & French Intervention

1855   The Revolution of Ayutla topples Santa Anna and leads to the period of The Reform.

1857   The liberal Constitution of 1857 disestablishes the Catholic Church, among other measures.

1858–61   The Civil War of the Reform ends in liberal victory. Benito Juárez (1806–72) is elected president. France, Spain, and Britain agree jointly to occupy the customhouse at Veracruz to force payment of Mexico's huge foreign debt.

1862   Spain and Britain withdraw their forces; the French, seeking empire, march inland. On May 5, General Porfirio Díaz repulses the French at Puebla.

1863   Strengthened with reinforcements, the French occupy Mexico City. Napoléon III of France appoints Archduke Ferdinand Maximilian of Austria (1832–67) as Emperor of Mexico.

1864   Maximilian and his empress Charlotte, known as Carlotta, land at Veracruz.

1867   With U.S. assistance, Juárez overthrows Mexico's second empire. Maximilian is executed; Carlotta, pleading his case in France, goes mad.

1872   Juárez dies in office. The Mexico City–Veracruz railway is completed, symbol of the new progressivist mood.

The Porfiriato

1876 Porfirio Díaz (1830–1915) comes to power in the revolution of Tuxtepec; he holds office nearly continuously until 1911. With his advisers, the *cientificos,* he forces modernization and balances the budget for the first time in Mexican history. But the social cost is high.

1886 Birth of Diego Rivera (d. 1957).

1890 José Schneider, who is of German ancestry, founds the Cerveceria Cuauhtémoc, brewer of Carta Blanca.

1900 Jesús, Enrique, and Ricardo Flores Magón publish the anti-Díaz newspaper *La Regeneración.* Suppressed, the brothers move their campaign to the United States, first to San Antonio, then to St. Louis.

1906 The Flores Magón group publish their Liberal Plan, a proposal for reform. Industrial unrest spreads.

The Second Revolution

1907 Birth of Frida Kahlo (d. 1954).

1910 On the centennial of the Revolution, Díaz wins yet another rigged election. Revolt breaks out.

1911 Rebels under Pascual Orozco and Francisco (Pancho) Villa (1878–1923) capture Ciudad Juárez; Díaz resigns. Francisco Madero is elected president; calling for land reform, Emiliano Zapata (1879–1919) rejects the new regime. Violence continues.

1913 Military coup: Madero is deposed and murdered. In one day Mexico has three presidents, the last being General Victoriano Huerta (1854–1916). Civil war rages.

1914 American intervention leads to dictator Huerta's overthrow. Villa and Zapata briefly join forces at the Convention of Aguascalientes, but the revolution goes on. Birth of poet-critic Octavio Paz.

1916 Villa's border raids lead to an American punitive expedition under Pershing. Villa eludes capture.

1917 Under a new constitution, Venuziano Carranza, head of the Constitutionalist Army, is elected president. Zapata continues his rebellion, which is brutally suppressed.

1918 CROM, the national labor union, is founded.

1919 On order of Carranza, Zapata is assassinated.

1920 Carranza is assassinated; Alvaro Obregón (1880–1928), who helped overthrow dictator Huerta in 1914, is elected president, beginning a period of reform and reconstruction. Schools are built and land is redistributed. In the next two decades, revolutionary culture finds expression in the art of Diego Rivera and José Clemente Orozco (1883–1949), the novels of Martin Luis Guzmán and Gregorio Lopez y Fuentes, and the music of Carlos Chavez (1899–1978).

1923 Pancho Villa is assassinated. The United States finally recognizes the Obregón regime.

1926–28 Catholics react to government anticlericalism in the Cristero Rebellion.

1934–40 The presidency of Lázaro Cárdenas (1895–1970) leads to the fullest implementation of revolutionary reforms.

1938 Cárdenas nationalizes the oil companies, removing them from foreign control.

1940 On August 20, exiled former Soviet leader Leon Trotsky murdered in his Mexico City home.

Post-Revolutionary Mexico

1951 Mexico's segment of the Pan-American Highway is completed, confirming the industrial growth and prosperity of postwar Mexico. Culture is increasingly Americanized; writers such as Octavio Paz and Carlos Fuentes express disillusionment with the post-revolution world.

1968 The Summer Olympics in Mexico City showcase Mexican prosperity, but massive demonstrations indicate underlying social unrest.

1981–82 Recession and a drop in oil prices severely damage Mexico's economy. The peso is devalued.

1985 Thousands die in the Mexico City earthquake.

1988 American-educated economist Carlos Salinas de Gortari is elected president; for the first time since 1940, support for the PRI, the national political party, seems to be slipping.

1993 North American Free Trade Agreement (NAFTA) is signed with United States and Canada.

1994 Uprising by the indigenous peoples of Chiapas, led by the Zapatistas and their charismatic ski-masked leader, Subcomandante Marcos; election reforms promised as a result.

Popular PRI presidential candidate Luis Donaldo Colosio assassinated while campaigning in Tijuana. Ernesto Zedillo, generally thought to be more of a technocrat and "old boy" PRI politician, replaces him and wins the election.

Zedillo, blaming the economic policies of his predecessor, devalues the peso in December.

1995 Recession sets in as a result of the peso devaluation. The former administration is rocked by scandals surrounding the assassinations of Colosio and another high-ranking government official; ex-President Carlos Salinas de Gortari moves to the United States.

1996 Mexico's economy, bolstered by a $28 billion bailout program led by the United States, turns upward, but the recovery is fragile. The opposition National Action Party (PAN), which is committed to conservative economic policies, gains strength. New details of scandals of the former administration continue to emerge.

1997 Mexico's top antidrug official is arrested on bribery charges. Nonetheless, the United States recertifies Mexico as a partner in the war on drugs. The Zedillo administration faces midterm party elections.

1998 Death of Octavio Paz.

1999 Raúl Salinas, brother of the former president Carlos Salinas de Gortari, sentenced for the alleged murder of a PRI leader.

2000 Spurning long-ruling PRI, Mexicans elect opposition candidate Vicente Fox president.

2001   U.S.-Mexico relations take on increased importance as Fox meets repeatedly with George W. Bush to discuss immigration reform and economic programs.

President Fox frees imprisoned Zapatista rebel sympathizers and signs into law a controversial Indian rights bill in hopes of bringing peace to southern Chiapas state; however, peace talks remain stalled.

Human-rights attorney Digna Ochoa is assassinated, opening the country to accusations of failing to investigate human-rights abuses by the military and police. The case is unsolved.

2002   Under President Fox's orders, the federal Human Rights Commission investigates and confirms that hundreds of people, most suspected leftist rebels, disappeared at the hands of the state after being arrested in the 1960s, '70s, and '80s. Fox also signs into law a freedom of information act and releases nearly 80 million secret intelligence files collected by the government.

To help fight crime in Mexico City, the local government hires former New York City Mayor Rudolph Giuliani as a consultant. City officials also create a special force of English-speaking mounted police officers to patrol the downtown tourist area.

BOOKS & MOVIES

Books

Fiction written in and/or about Mexico is a great place to start learning about the country. The best nonfiction on Mexico blends history, culture, commentary, and travel description. Some of the titles described below may be out of print and available only in libraries.

Pre-Columbian & Colonial Works & Histories.

If the pre-Columbian way of thinking has any appeal to you, Dennis Tedlock's superb translation of the Maya creation myth, *Popol Vuh*, is essential reading.

Good general reference works that can deepen your understanding of Mexico's indigenous peoples (and enrich your trips to the many marvelous archaeological sites in Mexico) include *The Conquest of the Yucatán* by celebrated ethnographer and champion of indigenous cultural survival Frans Blom; *In the Land of the Aztec* and *The Maya and Mexico*, by Michael D. Coe; *The Toltec Heritage*, by Nigel Davies; *The Last Lords of Palenque: The Lacandon Mayas of the Mexican Rain Forest*, by Victor Perera and Robert D. Bruce; *The Blood of Kings: Dynasty & Ritual in Maya Art*, by Linda Schele and Mary Ellen Miller; *Secrets of the Maya* from the editors of *Archaeology* magazine; and the colorful *Ancient Mexico*, by Maria Longhena. Mary Miller has also collaborated with Karl Taube to produce a useful glossary-style handbook called *The Gods and Symbols of Ancient Mexico and the Maya*.

A number of fascinating firsthand accounts of the colonial period by some of its most important figures have been translated and published. Of these, the most compelling may be *Letters from Mexico*, by conquistador Hernán Cortés, and *Tears of the Indians*, an unsparing account of Spanish brutality toward the native population by the outspoken Catholic priest Bartolomé de las Casas. Although no 19th-century history of the conquest of Mexico could be reconciled with our contemporary view of the conquistadors' barbarism, Prescott's *The Conquest of Mexico* is no less intriguing for its dated conceits.

For decades, the standard texts written by scholars for popular audiences have been *A History of Mexico*, by Henry B. Parkes; *Many Mexicos*, by Lesley Byrd Simpson; and *A Compact History of Mexico*, an anthology published by the Colegio de México. Michael C. Meyer and William L. Sherman's *The Course of Mexican History* and Eric Wolf's *Sons of the Shaking Earth* are also good survey works. Alan Knight has contributed works on the Mexican Revolution and a three-volume history text spanning the Spanish Conquest through the 20th century.

Contemporary Histories.

Enrique Krauze's ambitious *Mexico: Biography of Power* begins its romantic sweep with the Insurgent priests of the early 1800s. Jorge Castañeda's 1995 *The Mexican Shock* is an important study of the financial and political crisis in Mexico and its ramifications for United States–Mexico relations. His previous works, *Utopia Unarmed* and, with American political scientist Robert A. Pastor, *Limits to Friendship: The United States and Mexico*, are also excellent resources.

A number of journalists have made important contributions to the literature on historical and contemporary Mexico. Pulitzer Prize–winning *Miami Herald* Latin American correspondent Andres Oppenheimer's *Bordering on Chaos: Mexico's Roller-Coaster Journey to Prosperity* (1996) chronicles two of the most tumultuous years in recent Mexican history. The book investigates the country's descent into turmoil following the 1994 Zapatista uprising, two shocking 1994 political assassinations, the 1994 elections, and the 1995 peso crisis. William Langewiesche's *Cutting for Sign* examines life along the Mexican–U.S. border, and *Los Angeles Times* correspondent Sam Quiñones' *True Tales from Another Mexico: The Lynch Mob, the Popsicle Kings, Chalino, and the Bronx* (2001) recounts engaging stories about everyday Mexican people that manage to reveal the complexities and peculiarities of Mexico's social, economic, and political situations. Alan Riding's *Distant Neighbors: A Portrait of the Mexicans* is a classic description of Mexican politics, society, and finance from the *New York Times* correspondent who lived there during the 1980s. Another former *New York Times* journalist, Jonathan Kandell, penned *La Capital: The Biography of Mexico City* in 1988, a fascinating and detailed history of the city from pre-Colombian times to modern day. Elena Poniatowska, better known in the English-speaking world for her fiction, is one of Mexico's most highly respected journalists. *Massacre in Mexico,* her account of government repression of a demonstration in Mexico City in 1968, is an enlightening and disturbing work. Bill Weinberg writes of oppression and rebellion in one of Mexico's poorest states in *Homage to Chiapas.* Setting Chiapas's indigenous movement of resistance in a broad historical context, it's also an education in Mexican politics, economics, and traditional culture. More academic works on Mexico's modern history include Hector Aguila Camín's *In the Shadow of the Mexican Revolution,* Roderic A. Camp's *Politics in Mexico,* and Merilee Grindle's *Bureaucrats, Politicians and Peasants in Mexico.*

Ethnography. Excellent ethnographies include Oscar Lewis's classic works on the culture of poverty *The Children of Sanchez* and *Five Families; Juan the Chamula,* by Ricardo Pozas, about a small village in Chiapas; *Mexico South: The Isthmus of Tehuantepec,* by Miguel Covarrubias, which discusses Indian life in the early 20th century; Gertrude Blom's *Bearing Witness,* on the Lacandones of Chiapas; and *Maria Sabina: Her Life and Chants,* an autobiography of a shaman in the state of Oaxaca.

Food. Perhaps one of the most unusual and delightful books published on Mexican cookery in recent years is *Recipe of Memory: Five Generations of Mexican Cuisine* (1995). Written by Pulitzer Prize–winning food journalist Victor Valle and his wife, Mary Lau Valle, this book reproduces recipes the couple found in an antique chest passed down through the Valle family and in the process weaves an intriguing family and social history. Two lushly photographed cookbooks capturing the culinary history and culture of Mexico are Patricia Quintana's *The Taste of Mexico* (1993) and *Mexico the Beautiful Cookbook* (1991). Diana Kennedy's culinary works are also wildly popular, including her classic *The Art of Mexican Cooking* (1989) and her most recent compilation work of more than 300 recipes, *The Essential Cuisines of Mexico* (2000). Chef Rick Bayless is another staunch champion of Mexican regional cuisine; his books include *Mexico: One Plate at a Time* (2000) and *Mexican Kitchen* (1996). Marita Adair's *The Hungry Traveler Mexico* (1997), with descriptions of Mexican foods and their origins, goes beyond the typical food list. *Frida's Fiestas: Recipes and Reminiscences of Life with Frida Kahlo* (1994) is a cookbook memoir by the artist's stepdaughter, Guadalupe Rivera Marin. It assembles photos, a personal account of important events in Kahlo's life, and recipes for over 100 dishes Kahlo used to serve to family and friends.

Travelogues. Two of the more straightforward accounts from the early 19th century are the letters of Frances Calderón de la Barca (*Life in Mexico*) and John Lloyd Stephens's *Incidents of Travel in Central America, Chiapas and Yucatán.* Foreign journalists have described life in Mexico during and after the revolution: John Reed (*Insurgent Mexico*); John Kenneth Turner (*Barbarous Mexico*); Aldous Huxley (*Beyond the Mexique Bay*); and Graham Greene (*The Lawless Roads,* a superbly written narrative about Tabasco and Chiapas, which served as the basis for *The Power and the Glory*). In much the same vein, but more contemporary, are works by Patrick Marnham (*So Far from God*), about Central America and Mexico, and Hugh Fleetwood, whose *A Dangerous Place* is informative despite its cantankerousness. Alice Adams's *Mexico: Some Travels and Some Travelers There,* which includes an introduction by Jan Morris, is available in paperback; James A. Michener's novel, *Mexico,* captures the history of the land and the personality of the people. Probably the finest travelogue-cum-guidebook is Kate Simon's *Mexico: Places and Pleasures. Into a Desert Place* chronicles Graham Mackintosh's trek along the Baja coast. So entranced by San Miguel de Allende that he decided to stay, Tony Cohen recounts a gringo's daily life there in *On Mexican Time.* James O'Reilly and Larry Habegger have edited a diverse collection of articles and essays by contemporary authors in *Travelers' Tales Mexico.* Ron Butler's *Dancing Alone in Mexico:*

From the Border to Baja and Beyond recounts the author's capricious, soul-searching travels across the country.

Contemporary Literature. The late poet-philosopher Octavio Paz was the dean of Mexican intellectuals. His best works are *Labyrinth of Solitude,* a thoughtful, far-reaching dissection of Mexican culture, and *Sor Juana,* the biography of Sor Juana Inés de la Cruz, a 17th-century nun and poet. For more on Sor Juana, including her own writings, see Alan Trueblood's *A Sor Juana Anthology.* Other top authors include Carlos Fuentes (*The Death of Artemio Cruz* and *The Old Gringo* are among his most popular novels), Juan Rulfo (his classic is *Pedro Páramo*), Jorge Ibarguengoitia (*Two Crimes, The Dead Girls*), Elena Poniatowska (*Dear Diego, Here's to You Jesusa,* and *Tinisima* among others), Rosario Castellanos (*The Nine Guardians* and *City of Kings*), Elena Garros (*Recollections of Things to Come*), Gregorio López y Fuentes (*El Indio*), Angeles Mastretta (*Mexican Bolero*), and José Emilio Pacheco (*Battles in the Desert and Other Stories*).

Recent biographies of the artist couple Frida Kahlo and Diego Rivera (by Hayden Herrera and Bertram D. Wolfe, respectively) provide glimpses into the Mexican intellectual and political life of the 1920s and '30s. Laura Esquivel's novel-cum-cookbook, *Like Water for Chocolate,* captures the passions and palates of Mexico during the revolution. Edited by Juana Ponce de Léon, *Our Word Is Our Weapon* contains writings by the Subcomandante Insurgente Marcos. They range from communiqués made on behalf of the Zapatista movement to Marcos's own stories and poetry. The Subcomandante has even written a celebrated children's book, *The Story of Colors: A Bilingual Folktale from the Jungles of Chiapas.*

D. H. Lawrence's *The Plumed Serpent* is probably the best-known foreign novel about Mexico, although its noble savage theme is quite offensive. Lawrence recorded his travels in Oaxaca in *Mornings in Mexico.* A far greater piece of literature is Malcolm Lowry's *Under the Volcano.* The mysterious recluse B. Traven, whose fame rests largely on his *Treasure of the Sierra Madre,* wrote brilliantly and passionately about Mexico in *Rebellion of the Hanged*

and *The Bridge in the Jungle.* Also noteworthy is John Steinbeck's *The Log from the Sea of Cortez. The Reader's Companion to Mexico,* edited by Alan Ryan, includes material by Langston Hughes, D. H. Lawrence, and Paul Theroux. The characters of Cormac McCarthy's *Border Trilogy* weave back and forth across the Texas–Mexico border in the 1940s. Harriet Doerr's novels *Stones for Ibarra* and *Consider This, Señora* tell of newcomers's experiences in rural Mexico.

Movies

Mexican cinema cut its teeth during the Mexican Revolution, when both Mexican and U.S. cameramen braved the battlefields to catch the legendary generals in action. Legend has it that American cameramen helped Pancho Villa "choreograph" the Battle of Celaya for on-screen (and military) success. For an early Hollywood portrayal of the Revolution shot partially in Mexico, check out director Elia Kazan's *Viva Zapata!* (1952), written by John Steinbeck and starring Marlon Brando as Emiliano Zapata.

It wasn't long after Kazan's epic that directors of Hollywood westerns hit on Durango state as a cheap, accessible alternative to the usual "Old West" locales north of the border. The quintessential cinema cowboy, John Wayne, made eight movies in the area, including *True Grit* (1969), for which he won an Oscar.

John Huston directed one of the earliest American movies shot in Mexico, the unforgettable prospecting adventure *The Treasure of the Sierra Madre* (1948), filmed in Michoacán state. In 1964, Huston set an adaptation of Tennessee Williams's play *The Night of the Iguana* in Puerto Vallarta. And in 1984, Huston made the beautiful, intense *Under the Volcano,* adapted from Malcolm Lowry's novel. The movie was shot in Morelos, near Cuernavaca, and shows the local Día de los Muertos celebrations.

Hollywood's presence in Mexico continued throughout the 1990s and the early 2000s. After *Titanic* (1997) and parts of *Pearl Harbor* (2001) were filmed in Rosarito, some began referring to the area as "Baja Hollywood." Other recent blockbusters that were shot south of the border include: *Frida* (2002), with Salma Hayek as the Mexican artist, and gorgeous settings in Mexico City's Coyoacán neighborhood; Steven Soderbergh's *Traffic* (2001), which trolls some of the tougher areas of Tijuana and other border towns; and Ted Demme's *Blow* (2001), with Johnny Depp and Penélope Cruz, filmed in glitzy Acapulco. *The Mask of Zorro* (1998), starring Antonio Banderas and Anthony Hopkins, gallops across several locations in central Mexico. Robert Rodriguez made his name with his tales of a mariachi musician dragged into a world of crime. The films *El Mariachi* (1992) and *Desperado* (1995) were capped by *Once Upon a Time in Mexico*, starring Antonio Banderas, Johnny Depp, and Salma Hayek, in 2003.

The predominance of Hollywood films in Mexico has not been without controversy. In 1998, Mexico passed a law requiring movie theaters to reserve 10% of their screen time for domestic films. The government also directed funds to support homegrown Mexican cinema and the effort is already paying off, as recent films gain international attention. Director Carlos Carrera's *El Crimen del Padre Amaro (The Crime of Father Amaro*, 2002) courted scandal with its story of a priest's love affair, becoming Mexico's highest-grossing domestic film in the process. *Y Tu Mamá También (And Your Mother Too*, 2001) swept film festivals across Europe and Latin America. The funny, very sexual coming-of-age tale of two teenage boys was shot in Mexico City and the Oaxaca coast. *Amores Perros (Love's a Bitch*, 2000) is a Mexico City thriller about a car accident and the intertwining stories of loss and regret among the principal characters. For a delicious romance set in early 20th-century Mexico, see *Como Agua Para Chocolate (Like Water for Chocolate)* (1992), based on the novel by Laura Esquivel.

VOCABULARY

English	Spanish	Pronunciation
Basics		
Yes/no	Sí/no	see/no
Please	Por favor	pore fah-*vore*
May I?	¿Me permite?	may pair-*mee*-tay
Thank you (very much)	(Muchas) gracias	(*moo*-chas) *grah*-see-as
You're welcome	De nada	day *nah*-dah
Excuse me	Con permiso	con pair-*mee*-so
Pardon me/what did you say?	¿Como?/Mánde?	ko-mo/mahn-dey
Could you tell me?	¿Podría decirme?	po-*dree*-ah deh-*seer*-meh
I'm sorry	Lo siento	lo see-*en*-toe
Hello	Hola	*oh*-lah
Good morning!	¡Buenos días!	*bway*-nohs *dee*-ahs
Good afternoon!	¡Buenas tardes!	*bway*-nahs *tar*-dess
Good evening!	¡Buenas noches!	*bway*-nahs *no*-chess
Goodbye!	¡Adiós!/¡Hasta luego!	ah-dee-*ohss*/ ah-stah-*lwe*-go
Mr./Mrs.	Señor/Señora	sen-yor/sen-*yore*-ah
Miss	Señorita	sen-yo-*ree*-tah
Pleased to meet you	Mucho gusto	*moo*-cho *goose*-to
How are you?	¿Cómo está usted?	*ko*-mo es-*tah* oo-*sted*
Very well, thank you.	Muy bien, gracias.	*moo*-ee bee-*en*, grah-see-as
And you?	¿Y usted?	ee oos-*ted*
Hello (on the telephone)	Bueno	*bwen*-oh
Numbers		
1	un, uno	oon, *oo*-no
2	dos	dos
3	tres	trace
4	cuatro	*kwah*-tro
5	cinco	*sink*-oh
6	seis	sace
7	siete	see-*et*-ey
8	ocho	o-cho
9	nueve	new-*ev*-ay
10	diez	dee-*es*
11	once	*own*-sey

12	doce	*doe*-sey
13	trece	*tray*-sey
14	catorce	kah-*tor*-sey
15	quince	*keen*-sey
16	dieciséis	dee-es-ee-*sace*
17	diecisiete	dee-*es*-ee-see-*et*-ay
18	dieciocho	dee-*es*-ee-o-cho
19	diecinueve	*dee*-es-ee-new-*ev*-ay
20	veinte	*bain*-tay
21	veinte y uno/ veintiuno	*bain*-te-oo-no
30	treinta	*train*-tah
32	treinta y dos	train-tay-*dose*
40	cuarenta	kwah-*ren*-tah
43	cuarenta y tres	kwah-*ren*-tay-*trace*
50	cincuenta	seen-*kwen*-tah
54	cincuenta y cuatro	seen-*kwen*-tay *kwah*-tro
60	sesenta	sess-*en*-tah
65	sesenta y cinco	sess-*en*-tay *seen*-ko
70	setenta	set-*en*-tah
76	setenta y seis	set-*en*-tay *sace*
80	ochenta	oh-*chen*-tah
87	ochenta y siete	oh-*chen*-tay see-*yet*-ay
90	noventa	no-*ven*-tah
98	noventa y ocho	no-*ven*-tah o-cho
100	cien	see-*en*
101	ciento uno	see-en-toe oo-no
200	doscientos	doe-see-*en*-tohss
500	quinientos	keen-*yen*-tohss
700	setecientos	set-eh-see-*en*-tohss
900	novecientos	no-veh-see-*en*-tohss
1,000	mil	meel
2,000	dos mil	dose meel
1,000,000	un millón	oon meel-*yohn*

Colors

black	negro	*neh*-grow
blue	azul	ah-*sool*
brown	café	kah-*feh*
green	verde	*vair*-day
pink	rosa	*ro*-sah
purple	morado	mo-*rah*-doe
orange	naranja	na-*rahn*-hah

red	rojo	*roe*-hoe
white	blanco	*blahn*-koh
yellow	amarillo	ah-mah-*ree*-yoh

Days of the Week

Sunday	domingo	doe-*meen*-goh
Monday	lunes	*loo*-ness
Tuesday	martes	*mahr*-tess
Wednesday	miércoles	me-*air*-koh-less
Thursday	jueves	who-*ev*-ess
Friday	viernes	vee-*air*-ness
Saturday	sábado	*sah*-bah-doe

Months

January	enero	eh-*neh*-ro
February	febrero	feh-*brair*-oh
March	marzo	*mahr*-so
April	abril	ah-*breel*
May	mayo	*my*-oh
June	junio	*hoo*-nee-oh
July	julio	*who*-lee-yoh
August	agosto	ah-*ghost*-toe
September	septiembre	sep-tee-*em*-breh
October	octubre	oak-*too*-breh
November	noviembre	no-vee-*em*-breh
December	diciembre	dee-see-*em*-breh

Useful Phrases

Do you speak English?	¿Habla usted inglés?	*ah*-blah oos-*ted* in-*glehs*
I don't speak Spanish	No hablo español	no *ah*-blow es-pahn-*yol*
I don't understand (you)	No entiendo	no en-tee-*en*-doe
I understand (you)	Entiendo	en-tee-*en*-doe
I don't know	No sé	no *say*
I am from the United States/ British	Soy de los Estados Unidos/ inglés(a)	soy deh lohs ehs-*tah*-dohs oo-*nee*-dohs/ in-*glace*(ah)
What's your name?	¿Cómo se llama usted?	*koh*-mo say *yah*-mah oos-*ted*
My name is . . .	Me llamo . . .	may *yah*-moh
What time is it?	¿Qué hora es?	keh *o*-rah es
It is one, two, three . . . o'clock.	Es la una; son las dos, tres	es la *oo*-nah/sone lahs dose, trace
How?	¿Cómo?	*koh*-mo

When?	¿Cuándo?	*kwahn*-doe
This/Next week	Esta semana/ la semana que entra	*es*-tah seh-*mah*-nah/ lah say-*mah*-nah keh *en*-trah
This/Next month	Este mes/el próximo mes	*es*-tay mehs/el *proke*-see-mo mehs
This/Next year	Este año/el año que viene	*es*-tay *ahn*-yo/el *ahn*-yo keh vee-*yen*-ay
Yesterday/today/ tomorrow	Ayer/hoy/mañana	ah-*yair*/oy/mahn- *yah*-nah
This morning/ afternoon	Esta mañana/tarde	*es*-tah mahn-*yah*- nah/*tar*-day
Tonight	Esta noche	*es*-tah *no*-cheh
What?	¿Qué?	keh
What is this?	¿Qué es esto?	keh es *es*-toe
Why?	¿Por qué?	pore *keh*
Who?	¿Quién?	kee-*yen*
Where is . . . ?	¿Dónde está . . . ?	*dohn*-day es-*tah*
the train station?	la estación del tren?	la es-tah-see-*on* del *train*
the subway station?	la estación del Metro?	la es-ta-see-*on* del *meh*-tro
the bus stop?	la parada del autobús?	la pah-*rah*-dah del oh-toe-*boos*
the bank?	el banco?	el *bahn*-koh
the ATM?	el cajero automática?	el *kah*-hehr-oh oh-toe-*mah*-tee-kah
the . . . hotel?	el hotel . . . ?	el oh-*tel*
the store?	la tienda . . . ?	la tee-*en*-dah
the cashier?	la caja?	la *kah*-hah
the . . . museum?	el museo . . . ?	el moo-*seh*-oh
the hospital?	el hospital?	el ohss-pea-*tal*
the elevator?	el ascensor?	el ah-*sen*-sore
the bathroom?	el baño?	el *bahn*-yoh
Here/there	Aquí/allá	ah-*key*/ah-*yah*
Open/closed	Abierto/cerrado	ah-be-*er*-toe/ ser-*ah*-doe
Left/right	Izquierda/derecha	iss-key-*er*-dah/ dare-*eh*-chah
Straight ahead	Derecho	der-*eh*-choh
Is it near/far?	¿Está cerca/lejos?	es-*tah* *sair*-kah/ *leh*-hoss
I'd like . . .	Quisiera . . .	kee-see-air-ah
a room	un cuarto/una habitación	oon *kwahr*-toe/ oo-nah ah-bee- tah-see-*on*
the key	la llave	lah *yah*-vay
a newspaper	un periódico	oon pear-ee-*oh*- dee-koh
I'd like to buy . . .	Quisiera comprar . . .	kee-see-*air*-ah kohm-*prahr*
cigarettes	cigarrillo	ce-gar-*reel*-oh

matches	cerillos	ser-*ee*-ohs
a dictionary	un diccionario	oon deek-see-oh-*nah*-ree-oh
soap	jabón	hah-*bone*
a map	un mapa	oon *mah*-pah
a magazine	una revista	*oon*-ah reh-*veess*-tah
paper	papel	pah-*pel*
envelopes	sobres	*so*-brace
a postcard	una tarjeta postal	*oon*-ah tar-*het*-ah post-*ahl*

How much is it?	¿Cuánto cuesta?	*kwahn*-toe *kwes*-tah
Do you accept credit cards?	¿Aceptan tarjetas de crédito?	ah-*sehp*-than tahr-*heh*-tahs deh *creh*-dee-toh?
A little/a lot	Un poquito/mucho . : .	oon poh-*kee*-toe/*moo*-choh
More/less	Más/menos	mahss/*men*-ohss
Enough/too much/too little	Suficiente/demasiado/muy poco	soo-fee-see-*en*-tay/day-mah-see-*ah*-doe/*moo*-ee poh-koh
Telephone	Teléfono	tel-*ef*-oh-no
Telegram	Telegrama	teh-leh-*grah*-mah
I am ill/sick	Estoy enfermo(a)	es-*toy* en-*fair*-moh(ah)
Please call a doctor	Por favor llame un médico	pore fa-*vor* ya-may oon *med*-ee-koh
Help!	¡Auxilio! ¡Ayuda!	owk-*see*-lee-oh/ah-*yoo*-dah
Fire!	¡Encendio!	en-*sen*-dee-oo
Caution!/Look out!	¡Cuidado!	kwee-*dah*-doh

On the Road

Highway	Carretera	car-ray-*ter*-ah
Causeway, paved highway	Calzada	cal-*za*-dah
Speed bump	Tope	*toh*-pay
Toll highway	Carretera de cuota	car-ray-*ter*-ha day dwoh-tah
Toll booth	Caseta	kah-*set*-ah
Route	Ruta	*roo*-tah
Road	Camino	cah-*mee*-no
Street	Calle	*cah*-yeh
Avenue	Avenida	ah-ven-*ee*-dah
Broad, tree-lined boulevard	Paseo	pah-*seh*-oh
Waterfront promenade	Malecón	mal-lay-*cone*
Wharf	Embarcadero	em-bar-cah-*day*-ro

In Town

Church	Templo/Iglesia	*tem*-plo/e-*gles*-se-*ah*
Cathedral	Catedral	cah-tay-*dral*
Neighborhood	Barrio	*bar*-re-o
Foreign exchange shop	Casa de cambio	*cas*-sah day *cam*-be-o
City hall	Ayuntamiento	ah-yoon-tah-mee-*en*-toe
Main square	Zócalo	*zo*-cal-o
Traffic circle	Glorieta	glor-e-*ay*-tah
Market	Mercado (Spanish)/ Tianguis (Indian)	mer-*cah*-doe/ tee-*an*-geese
Inn	Posada	pos-*sah*-dah
Group taxi	Colectivo	co-lec-*tee*-vo
Mini-bus along fixed route	Pesero	pi-*seh*-ro

Dining Out

I'd like to reserve a table	Quisiera reservar una mesa.	kee-*syeh*-rah rreh-sehr-*vahr* oo-nah *meh*-sah
A bottle of . . .	Una botella de . . .	*oo*-nah bo-*tay*-yah deh
A cup of . . .	Una taza de . . .	*oo*-nah *tah*-sah deh
A glass of . . .	Un vaso de . . .	oon *vah*-so deh
Ashtray	Un cenicero	oon sen-ee-*seh*-roh
Bill/check	La cuenta	lah *kwen*-tah
Bread	El pan	el pahn
Breakfast	El desayuno	el day-sigh-*oon*-oh
Butter	La mantequilla	lah mahn-tay-*key*-yah
Cheers!	¡Salud!	sah-*lood*
Cocktail	Un aperitivo	oon ah-pair-ee-*tee*-voh
Mineral water	Agua mineral	*ah*-gwah mee-neh-*rahl*
Beer	Cerveza	sehr-*veh*-sah
Dinner	La cena	lah *seh*-nah
Dish	Un plato	oon *plah*-toe
Dish of the day	El platillo de hoy	el plah-*tee*-yo day oy
Enjoy!	¡Buen provecho!	bwen pro-*veh*-cho
Fixed-price menu	La comida corrida	lah koh-*me*-dah co-*ree*-dah
Is the tip included?	¿Está incluida la propina?	es-*tah* in-clue-*ee*-dah lah pro-*pea*-nah
Fork	El tenedor	el ten-eh-*door*
Knife	El cuchillo	el koo-*chee*-yo

Spoon	Una cuchara	*oo*-nah koo-*chah*-rah
Lunch	La comida	lah koh-*me*-dah
Menu	La carta	lah *cart*-ah
Napkin	La servilleta	lah sair-vee-*yet*-uh
Please give me	Por favor déme	pore fah-*vor* *day*-may
Pepper	La pimienta	lah pea-me-*en*-tah
Salt	La sal	lah sahl
Sugar	El azúcar	el ah-*sue*-car
Waiter!/Waitress!	¡Por favor Señor/Señorita!	pore fah-*vor* sen-*yor*/sen-yor-*ee*-tah

INDEX

NOTES

NOTES

NOTES

NOTES

FODOR'S KEY TO THE GUIDES

America's guidebook leader publishes guides for every kind of traveler.
Check out our many series and find your perfect match.

FODOR'S GOLD GUIDES

America's favorite travel-guide series
offers the most detailed insider reviews
of hotels, restaurants, and attractions
in all price ranges, plus great background information, smart tips, and
useful maps.

COMPASS AMERICAN GUIDES

Stunning guides from top local writers
and photographers, with gorgeous
photos, literary excerpts, and colorful
anecdotes. A must-have for culture
mavens, history buffs, and new
residents.

FODOR'S CITYPACKS

Concise city coverage in a guide plus a
foldout map. The right choice for urban
travelers who want everything under
one cover.

FODOR'S EXPLORING GUIDES

Hundreds of color photos bring your
destination to life. Lively stories lend
insight into the culture, history, and
people.

FODOR'S TRAVEL HISTORIC AMERICA

For travelers who want to experience
history firsthand, this series gives in-
depth coverage of historic sights, plus
nearby restaurants and hotels. Themes
include the Thirteen Colonies, the Old
West, and the Lewis and Clark Trail.

FODOR'S POCKET GUIDES

For travelers who need only the
essentials. The best of Fodor's in
pocket-size packages for just $9.95.

FODOR'S FLASHMAPS

Every resident's map guide, with 60
easy-to-follow maps of public transit,
parks, museums, zip codes, and more.

FODOR'S CITYGUIDES

Sourcebooks for living in the city:
thousands of in-the-know listings for
restaurants, shops, sports, nightlife,
and other city resources.

FODOR'S AROUND THE CITY WITH KIDS

Up to 68 great ideas for family days,
recommended by resident parents.
Perfect for exploring in your own
backyard or on the road.

FODOR'S HOW TO GUIDES

Get tips from the pros on planning the
perfect trip. Learn how to pack, fly
hassle-free, plan a honeymoon or cruise,
stay healthy on the road, and travel
with your baby.

FODOR'S LANGUAGES FOR TRAVELERS

Practice the local language before you
hit the road. Available in phrase books,
cassette sets, and CD sets.

KAREN BROWN'S GUIDES

Engaging guides—many with easy-to-
follow inn-to-inn itineraries—to the
most charming inns and B&Bs in the
U.S.A. and Europe.

BAEDEKER'S GUIDES

Comprehensive guides, trusted since
1829, packed with A–Z reviews and
star ratings.

OTHER GREAT TITLES FROM FODOR'S

Baseball Vacations, The Complete
Guide to the National Parks, Family
Vacations, Golf Digest's Places to Play,
Great American Drives of the East,
Great American Drives of the West,
Great American Vacations, Healthy
Escapes, National Parks of the West,
Skiing USA.

At bookstores everywhere.   www.fodors.com/books